AMERICA

D0112216

DETAIL OF ENGRAVING BASED ON
THE CHASM OF THE COLORADO
BY THOMAS MORAN

AMERICA

A NARRATIVE HISTORY

Brief Ninth Edition

GEORGE BROWN TINDALL

DAVID EMORY SHI

W · W · NORTON & COMPANY · NEW YORK · LONDON

W. W. Norton & Company has been independent since its founding in 1923, when William Warder Norton and Mary D. Herter Norton first published lectures delivered at the People's Institute, the adult education division of New York City's Cooper Union. The firm soon expanded its program beyond the Institute, publishing books by celebrated academics from America and abroad. By mid-century, the two major pillars of Norton's publishing program—trade books and college texts—were firmly established. In the 1950s, the Norton family transferred control of the company to its employees, and today—with a staff of four hundred and a comparable number of trade, college, and professional titles published each year—W. W. Norton & Company stands as the largest and oldest publishing house owned wholly by its employees.

Copyright © 2013, 2010, 2007, 2004, 1999, 1992, 1988, 1984 by W. W. Norton & Company, Inc.

All rights reserved.
Printed in the United States of America.

Editor: Jon Durbin
Project editors: Kate Feighery and Melissa Atkin
Electronic media editor: Steve Hoge
Associate media editor: Lorraine Klimowich
Assistant editor: Justin Cahill
Editorial assistant, media: Stefani Wallace
Marketing manager, History: Heather Arteaga
Production manager: Ashley Horna
Photo editor: Stephanie Romeo
Composition: Jouve International-Brattleboro, VT
Manufacturing: Quad/Graphics-Taunton, MA

Library of Congress Cataloging-in-Publication Data

Tindall, George Brown.
    America : a narrative history / George Brown Tindall,
David Emory Shi.—Brief 9th ed.
        p.   cm.
    Includes bibliographical references and index.
    ISBN 978-0-393-91265-4 (paperback)
    1. United States—History—Textbooks.   I. Shi, David E.   II. Title.
    E178.1.T55 2013   2012034775
    973—dc23

W. W. Norton & Company, Inc., 500 Fifth Avenue, New York, NY 10110-0017
wwnorton.com

W. W. Norton & Company Ltd., Castle House, 75/76 Wells Street, London W1T 3QT

2 3 4 5 6 7 8 9 0

For Bruce and Susan
and for Blair

For
Jason and Jessica

GEORGE B. TINDALL recently of the University of North Carolina, Chapel Hill, was an award-winning historian of the South with a number of major books to his credit, including *The Emergence of the New South, 1913–1945* and *The Disruption of the Solid South*.

DAVID E. SHI is a professor of history and the president emeritus of Furman University. He is the author of several books on American cultural history, including the award-winning *The Simple Life: Plain Living and High Thinking in American Culture* and *Facing Facts: Realism in American Thought and Culture, 1850–1920*.

CONTENTS

Part Two / BUILDING A NATION

Part Four / A HOUSE DIVIDED AND REBUILT

Part Five / G R O W I N G   P A I N S

Part Six / M O D E R N   A M E R I C A

Part Seven / THE AMERICAN AGE

34 | America in a New Millennium   1128

Glossary   A1

Appendix   A59

Further Readings   A123

Credits   A149

Index   A153

MAPS

PREFACE

This edition of *America: A Narrative History* includes the most substantial changes since I partnered with George Tindall in 1984, but I have been diligent to sustain his steadfast commitment to a textbook grounded in a compelling narrative history of the American experience. From the start of our collaboration, we strove to write a book animated by colorful characters, informed by balanced analysis and social texture, and guided by the unfolding of key events. Those classic principles, combined with a handy format and low price, have helped make *America: A Narrative History* one of the most popular and well-respected American history textbooks. This brief edition, which I have crafted by streamlining the narrative by 20 percent, remains the most coherent and lively of its kind.

This Brief Ninth Edition of *America* features a number of important changes designed to make the text more teachable and classroom-friendly. Chief among them are major structural changes, including the joining of several chapters to reduce the overall number from thirty-seven to thirty-four, as well as the re-sequencing of several chapters to make the narrative flow more smoothly for students. Major organizational changes include:

- New Chapter 4, *From Colonies to States*, combines *The Imperial Perspective* and *From Empire to Independence* from previous editions to better integrate the events leading up to the American Revolution.
- New Chapter 9, *The Dynamics of Growth*, now leads off Part III, *An Expansive Nation*, to first introduce the industrial revolution and the growth of the market economy before turning to major political, social, and cultural developments.
- New Chapter 12, *The Old South*, has been moved up, now appearing between the chapters on the Jacksonian era and the American Renaissance, in order to foreground the importance of slavery as a major issue during this period.

- *From Isolation to Global War*, a chapter from previous editions, has been broken up, and its parts redistributed to new Chapter 26, *Republican Resurgence and Decline*, and new Chapter 28, *The Second World War*, in order to better integrate the coverage of domestic politics and international relations during this period.
- New Chapter 30, *The 1950s: Affluence and Anxiety in an Atomic Age*, combines *Through the Picture Window and Conflict and Deadlock: The Eisenhower Years* from the previous editions to better show the relationship between political, social, and cultural developments during the 1950s.

In terms of content changes, the overarching theme of the new edition is the importance of African-American history. While African-American history has always been a central part of the book's narrative, this Brief Ninth Edition features enhanced and fully up-to-date treatment based on the best recent scholarship in African-American history, including African slavery, slavery in America during the colonial era and revolutionary war, the slave trade in the South, slave rebellions, the practical challenges faced by slaves liberated during the Civil War, the Wilmington Riot of 1898, in which an elected city government made up of blacks was ousted by armed violence, President Woodrow Wilson's segregationist views and policies, the Harlem Renaissance, the Double V Campaign during World War II, and the Freedom Summer of 1964.

Of course, as in every new edition, there is new material related to contemporary America—the first term of the Barack Obama administration, the killing of al Qaeda leader Osama bin Laden, and the emergence of the Tea Party and the Occupy Wall Street movements—as well as the stagnant economy in the aftermath of the Great Recession. In addition, I have incorporated fresh insights from important new scholarly works dealing with many significant topics throughout this new edition.

America's **New Student Resources** are designed to make students better readers. New, carefully crafted pedagogical features have been added to the Brief Ninth Edition to further guide students through the narrative.

- **Focus questions, chapter summaries**, and new **bold-face key terms** work together seamlessly to highlight core content. The chapters are enhanced with easy-to-read full-color maps and chapter chronologies.
- New **Author Videos** feature David Shi explaining major developments in American history. Each of the 42 video segments includes addi-

tional media, such as illustrations and maps, to enhance the learning experience.

- New "**Critical Reading Exercises**," tied directly to the Ninth Edition, help students learn how to read the textbook. Students are guided through a series of exercises to identify the most important information from select passages in each chapter.

- New **Cross-Chapter Quizzes** in the Norton Coursepacks are designed to help students prepare for midterm and final examinations by challenging them to think across periods, to trace longer-term developments, and to make connections and comparisons.

- A new edition of *For the Record: A Documentary History of America*, by David E. Shi and Holly A. Mayer (Duquesne University), is the perfect companion reader for *America: A Narrative History*. The new Fifth Edition has been brought into closer alignment with the main text. *For the Record* now has 250 primary-source readings from diaries, journals, newspaper articles, speeches, government documents, and novels, including a number of readings that highlight the substantially updated theme of African-American history in this new edition of *America*. If you haven't looked at *For the Record* in a while, now would be a good time to take a look.

- New **Norton Mix: American History** enables instructors to build their own custom reader from a database of nearly 300 primary and secondary source selections. The custom readings can be packaged as a standalone reader or integrated with chapters from *America* into a custom textbook.

- *America: A Narrative History* **StudySpace** (wwnorton.com/web /america9) provides a proven assignment-driven plan for each chapter. In addition to the new "Critical Reading Exercises" and new "Author Videos," highlights include focus questions, learning objectives, chapter outlines, quizzes, iMaps and new iMap quizzes, map worksheets, flashcards, interactive timelines, and "U.S. History Tours" powered by Google Earth map technology. There are also several hundred multimedia primary-source selections—including documents, images, and audio and video clips—grouped by topic to aid research and writing.

America's **New Instructor Resources** are designed to provide additional resources that will enable more dynamic classroom lectures:

- New **Norton American History Digital Archive** disks on African-American history are the eighth and ninth disks in this extraordinary collection of digital resources for classroom lecture. The 2 new disks come with nearly 400 selections from African-American history, including illustrations, photographs and audio and video clips.

- New **PowerPoint Lectures with dynamic Author Videos**. Replete with every image and map from the textbook, the *America* Ninth Edition **PowerPoints** now also feature the new **Author Videos**. These classroom-ready presentations can be used as lecture launchers or as video summaries of major issues and developments in American history.
- New enhanced **Coursepack** integrates all **StudySpace** content with these handy features and materials: 1) *Forum Questions* designed for online and hybrid courses; 2) *Critical Reading Exercises* that report to your LMS Gradebook; 3) *Cross-Chapter Quizzes* for each half of the survey course.
- The **Instructor's Manual and Test Bank**, by Mark Goldman (Tallahassee Community College), Michael Krysko (Kansas State University), and Brian McKnight (UVA, Wise), includes a test bank of multiple-choice, short-answer, and essay questions, as well as detailed chapter outlines, lecture suggestions, and bibliographies.

It's clear why *America* continues to set the standard when it comes to providing a low-cost book with high-value content. Your students will buy it because it's so affordable, and they'll read it because the narrative is so engaging!

ACKNOWLEDGMENTS

In preparing the Brief Ninth Edition, I have benefited from the insights and suggestions of many people. Some of those insights have come from student readers of the text, and I encourage such feedback. I'd particularly like to thank Eirlys Barker, who has worked on much of the new StudySpace content, Laura Farkas (Wake Technical College), who has created the wonderful new "Critical Reading Exercises," and I'd like to give special thanks to Brandon Franke (Blinn College, Bryan) for his work on the new PowerPoint lectures. Finally, many thanks to Mark Goldman, Michael Krysko, and Brian McKnight for their efforts on the Instructor's Manual and Test Bank.

Numerous scholars and survey instructors advised me on the new edition: Eirlys Barker (Thomas Nelson Community College), Blanche Bricke (Blinn College), Michael Collins (Midwestern State University), Scott Cook (Motlow State Community College), Carl Creasman, Jr. (Valencia College), Stephen Davis (Lone Star College), Susan Dollar (Northwestern State University of Louisiana), Alicia Duffy (University of Central Florida), Laura Farkas (Wake Technical Community College), Jane Flaherty (Texas A&M University), Brandon Franke (Blinn College), Mark Goldman (Tallahassee Community College), James Good (Lone Star College), Barbara Green (Wright State University), D. Harland Hagler (University of North Texas), Michael Harkins (Harper College), Carolyn Hoffman (Prince George's Community College), Marc Horger (Ohio State University), Michael Krivdo (Texas A&M University), Margaret Lambert (Lone Star College), Pat Ledbetter (North Central Texas College), Stephen Lopez (San Jacinto College), Barry Malone (Wake Technical Community College), Dee Mckinney (East Georgia College), Lisa Morales (North Central Texas College), Robert Outland III (Louisiana State University), Catherine Parzynski (Montgomery County Community College), Robert Lynn Rainard (Tidewater Community College), Edward Duke Richey (University of North Texas), Stuart Smith III (Germanna Community

College), Roger Tate (Somerset Community College), Kyle Volk (University of Montana), Vernon Volpe (University of Nebraska), Heidi Weber (SUNY Orange), Cecil Edward Weller, Jr. (San Jacinto College), and Margarita Youngo (Pima Community College).

Once again, I thank my friends at W. W. Norton for their consummate professionalism and good cheer, especially Jon Durbin, Justin Cahill, Steve Hoge, Melissa Atkin, Kate Feighery, Lorraine Klimowich, Stephanie Romeo, Debra Morton-Hoyt, Ashley Horna, Heather Arteaga, Julie Sindel, and Tamara McNeill.

Part One

A NOT-SO-"NEW" WORLD

istory is filled with ironies. Luck and accidents often shape events more than actions. Long before Christopher Columbus happened upon the Caribbean Sea in his effort to find a westward passage to Asia, the native people he mislabeled *Indians* had occupied and transformed the lands of the Western Hemisphere. The first residents in what Europeans came to call the "New World" had migrated from northeastern Asia during the last glacial advance of the Ice Age, nearly 20,000 years ago. By the end of the fifteenth century, when Columbus began his voyage west, there were millions of Native Americans living in the Western Hemisphere. Over the centuries, they had developed diverse and often highly sophisticated societies, some rooted in agriculture, others in trade or imperial conquest. So the New World was "new" only to the Europeans who began exploring, conquering, and exploiting the region at the end of the fifteenth century.

The Indian cultures were, of course, profoundly affected by the arrival of peoples from Europe and Africa. Indians experienced catastrophic cultural change: they were exploited, infected, enslaved, displaced, and exterminated. Millions of acres of tribal lands were taken or bought for a pittance. Yet this conventional tale of tragic conquest oversimplifies the complex process by which Indians, Europeans, and Africans interacted in the Western Hemisphere. The Indians were more than passive victims of European power; they were also trading partners and often allies as well as rivals of the transatlantic newcomers. They became neighbors and advisers, converts and spouses. As such they participated creatively and powerfully in the creation of the new society known as America.

The Europeans who risked their lives to settle in the Western Hemisphere were a diverse lot. Young and old, men and women, they came from Spain, Portugal, France, the British Isles, the Netherlands, Scandinavia, Italy, and the German states (Germany would not become a united nation until the mid–nineteenth century). A variety of motives inspired them to undertake the often-harrowing transatlantic voyage. Some were adventurers and fortune seekers eager to gain glory and find gold, silver, and spices. Others were fervent Christians eager to create kingdoms of God in the "New World." Still others were convicts, debtors, indentured servants, or political or religious exiles. Many were simply seeking a piece of land, higher wages, and greater economic opportunity. A settler in Pennsylvania noted that "poor people (both men and women) of all kinds can here get three times the wages for their labour than they can in England."

Yet such enticements were not sufficient to attract enough workers to keep up with the rapidly expanding colonial economies, so the Europeans forced Indians to work for them. But there were never enough laborers to meet the unceasing demand. Moreover, captive Indians often escaped or were so rebellious that their use as slaves was banned in several colonies. The Massachusetts legislature outlawed forced labor because Indians displayed "a malicious, surly and revengeful spirit; rude and insolent in their behavior, and very ungovernable."

Beginning early in the seventeenth century, colonists turned to Africa for their labor needs. European nations—especially Portugal and Spain—had long been transporting captive Africans to the Western Hemisphere, from Chile to Canada. In 1619 a Dutch warship brought twenty captured Africans to Jamestown, near the coast of Virginia. The Dutch captain exchanged the slaves for food and supplies. This first of many transactions involving enslaved people in British America would transform American society in complex, multilayered ways that no one at the time envisioned. Few Europeans during the colonial era saw the contradiction between the promise of freedom in America for themselves and the expanding institution of race-based slavery. Nor did they reckon with the problems associated with introducing into the colonies people deemed alien and inferior.

The intermingling of people, cultures, and ecosystems from the continents of Africa, Europe, and the Western Hemisphere gave colonial American society its distinctive vitality and variety. In turn, the diversity of the environment and the varying climate spawned quite different economies and patterns of living in the various regions of North America. As the original settlements grew into prosperous and populous colonies, the transplanted Europeans had to fashion social institutions and political systems to manage dynamic growth and control rising tensions.

At the same time, imperial rivalries among the Spanish, French, English, and Dutch triggered costly wars fought in Europe and around the world. The monarchs of Europe struggled to manage often-unruly colonies, which, they discovered, played crucial roles in their frequent European wars. Many of the colonists had brought with them to America a feisty independence, which led them to resent government interference in their affairs. A British official in North Carolina reported that the residents of the Piedmont region were "without any Law or Order. Impudence is so very high, as to be past bearing." As long as the reins of imperial control were loosely held, the colonists and their British rulers maintained an uneasy partnership. But as the royal authorities tightened their control during the mid–eighteenth century, they met resistance from colonists, which became revolt and culminated in revolution.

1

THE COLLISION
OF CULTURES

FOCUS QUESTIONS

 wwnorton.com/studyspace

- What civilizations existed in America before the arrival of Europeans?
- Why were European countries, such as Spain and Portugal, prepared to embark on voyages of discovery by the sixteenth century?
- How did contact between the Western Hemisphere and Europe change through the exchange of plants, animals, and pathogens?
- What were the Europeans' reasons for establishing colonies in America?
- What is the legacy of the Spanish presence in North America?
- What effect did the Protestant Reformation have on the colonization of the "New World"?

The history of the United States of America begins long before 1776. The supposed "New World" discovered by intrepid European explorers was in fact a very "old world" to civilizations thousands of years in the making. Debate continues about when and how the first humans arrived in North America. Until recently, archaeologists had assumed that ancient Siberians some 12,000 to 15,000 years ago had journeyed 600 miles across the frigid Bering Strait near the Arctic Circle on what was then a treeless land connecting northeastern Siberia with Alaska (by about 7000 B.C., the land bridge had been submerged by rising sea levels). These nomadic, spear-wielding hunters and their descendants, called Paleo-Indians ("old Indians") by archaeologists, drifted south in pursuit of large game animals. Over the next 500 years, as the climate warmed and the glaciers receded, a steady stream of small groups fanned out across the entire Western Hemisphere, from the Arctic Circle to the tip of South America.

Recent archaeological discoveries in Pennsylvania, Virginia, and Chile suggest a more complex story of human settlement. The new evidence reveals that prehistoric humans may have arrived much earlier (perhaps 18,000 to 40,000 years ago) from various parts of Asia—and some may even have crossed the Atlantic Ocean from southwestern Europe.

Regardless of when humans first set foot on the North American continent, the region and its native people eventually became a crossroads for immigrants from around the globe: Europeans, Africans, Asians, and others—all of whom brought with them as immigrants distinctive backgrounds, cultures, technologies, and motivations.

Pre-Columbian Indian Civilizations

The first peoples in North America discovered an immense continent with extraordinary climatic and environmental diversity. Coastal plains, broad grasslands, harsh deserts, and soaring mountain ranges generated distinct habitats, social structures, and cultural patterns. By the time Columbus happened upon the Western Hemisphere, the hundreds of tribes living in North America may together have numbered over 10 million people. They had developed a diverse array of communities in which more than 400 languages were spoken. Yet despite the distances and dialects separating them, the Indian societies created extensive trading networks, which helped spread ideas and innovations. Contrary to the romantic myth of early Indian civilizations living in perfect harmony with nature and one another, the native societies often engaged in warfare and exploited the environment by burning vast areas, planting fields, and gathering seeds, berries, and roots while harvesting vast numbers of game animals, fish, and shellfish.

EARLY CULTURES   The ancient Indians adapted to the new environments by developing nature-centered religions, mastering the use of fire, improving technology such as spear points, and domesticating the dog and the turkey. A new cultural stage arrived with the introduction of farming, fishing, and pottery making. Hunters focused on faster, more elusive mammals: deer, antelope, elk, moose, and caribou. Already by about 5000 B.C., Indians in Mexico were generating an "agricultural revolution" by growing the plant foods that would become the primary crops of the hemisphere: chiefly maize (corn), beans, and squash but also chili peppers, avocados, and pumpkins. The annual cultivation of such crops enabled Indian societies to grow larger and more complex, with their own distinctive social, economic, and political institutions.

THE MAYAS, AZTECS, CHIBCHAS, AND INCAS   Between about 2000 and 1500 B.C., permanent farming towns appeared in Mexico. The more settled life in turn provided time for the cultivation of religion, crafts, art, science, administration—and frequent warfare. The Indians in the Western Hemisphere harbored the usual human grievances against their neighbors, and wars were common. From about A.D. 300 to 900, Middle America (Mesoamerica, what is now Mexico and Central America) developed densely populated cities complete with gigantic pyramids, temples, and palaces, all supported by surrounding peasant villages. Moreover, the Mayas used mathematics and astronomy to devise a calendar more accurate than the one the Europeans were using at the time of Columbus.

In about A.D. 900 the complex Mayan culture succumbed to the Toltecs, a warlike people who conquered most of the region in the tenth century. But around A.D. 1200 the Toltecs mysteriously withdrew after a series of droughts, fires, and invasions. During the late thirteenth century the Aztecs—named after the legendary Aztlán from where they were supposed to have come—arrived from the northwest to fill the vacuum in the Basin of Mexico. They founded the city of Tenochtitlán in 1325 and gradually expanded their control over neighboring tribes in central Mexico. The Aztecs developed a thriving commerce in gold, silver, copper, and pearls as well as agricultural products. When the Spanish invaded Mexico in 1519, the sprawling **Aztec Empire**, connected by a network of roads with rest stops every ten miles or so, encompassed perhaps 5 million people.

Farther south, in what is now Colombia, the Chibchas built a similar empire on a smaller scale. Still farther south the Quechuas (better known as the Incas, from the name for their ruler) controlled a huge empire containing as many as 12 million people speaking at least twenty different languages. The Incas had used a shrewd mixture of diplomacy, marriage alliances with rival tribes, and military conquest to create a vast realm that by the fifteenth century stretched 2,500 miles along the Andes Mountains from Ecuador to Chile on the west coast of South America. The Incas were as sophisticated as the Aztecs in transforming their mountainous empire into a flowering civilization with fertile farms, enduring buildings, and an interconnected network of roads.

INDIAN CULTURES OF NORTH AMERICA   The pre-Columbian Indians of the present-day United States created several distinct civilizations, the largest of which were the Pacific Northwest culture; the Hohokam-Anasazi culture of the Southwest; the Adena-Hopewell culture of the Ohio River valley; and, the Mississippian culture east of the Mississippi River. The Native American tribes shared some fundamental myths and beliefs, especially concerning the sacredness of nature, the necessity of communal living, and respect for elders, but they developed in different ways at different times and in different places. In North America alone, there were probably 240 different tribes speaking many different languages when the Europeans arrived.

The Indians of the Pacific Northwest occupied a narrow strip of land and offshore islands along the heavily forested coast, extending 2,000 miles northward from California through what are now Oregon, Washington, and British Columbia, to southern Alaska. They engaged in little farming since the fish, whales, game (mostly deer and mountain sheep), and edible wild plants were so plentiful. The coastal Indians were also talented woodworkers; they built plank houses and large canoes out of cedar trees. Socially, the Indians along the Northwest coast were divided into chiefs, commoners, and slaves; raids to gain slaves were the primary cause of tribal warfare.

The Adena-Hopewell culture in what is today the Midwest left behind enormous earthworks and hundreds of elaborate burial mounds, some of them shaped like great snakes, birds, and other animals. The Adena and, later, the Hopewell peoples were gatherers and hunters who lived in small, isolated communities. They used an intricate kinship network to form social and spiritual alliances. Evidence from the burial mounds suggests that they had a complex social structure featuring a specialized division of labor. Moreover, the Hopewells developed an elaborate trade network that spanned the continent.

The Mississippian culture, centered in the southern Mississippi River valley, flourished between 900 and 1350. The Mississippians forged a complex patchwork of chiefdoms. In river valleys they built substantial towns around central plazas and temples. Like the Hopewells to the north, the Mississippians developed a specialized labor system, an effective governmental structure, and an expansive trading network. They cleared vast tracts of land to grow maize, beans, squash, and sunflowers. The dynamic Mississippian culture peaked in the fourteenth century, but succumbed first to climate change and finally to diseases brought by Europeans.

The Mississippian peoples constructed elaborate regional centers, the largest of which was Cahokia, in southwest Illinois, across the Mississippi River from what is now St. Louis. There the Indians constructed elaborate public structures and imposing shrines. At the height of its influence, between A.D. 1050 and 1250, the Cahokia metropolis hosted thousands of people on some 3,200 acres. Outlying towns and farming settlements ranged up to fifty miles in all directions. For some unknown reason, the residents of Cahokia dispersed after 1400.

The arid Southwest (in what is now Arizona, Nevada, New Mexico, and Utah) spawned irrigation-based cultures, elements of which exist today and heirs to which (the Hopis, Zunis, and others) still live in the adobe cliff dwellings (called **pueblos** by the Spanish) erected by their ancestors. About A.D. 500, the native Hohokam people from present-day Mexico into today's southern Arizona, where they constructed temple mounds similar to those in Mexico. For unknown reasons, the Hohokam society disappeared during the fifteenth century.

The most widespread and best known of the Southwest tribal cultures were the Anasazi ("Enemy's Ancestors" in the Navajo language). In ancient times they developed extensive settlements in the "four corners," where the states of Arizona, New Mexico, Colorado, and Utah meet. In contrast to the Mesoamerican and Mississippian cultures, Anasazi society lacked a rigid class structure. The religious leaders and warriors labored much as the rest of the people did. In fact, the Anasazi engaged in warfare only as a means of self-defense (*Hopi* means "Peaceful People"). Environmental factors shaped Anasazi culture and eventually caused its decline. Toward the end of the thirteenth century, a lengthy drought and the pressure of migrating Indians from the north threatened the survival of Anasazi society.

INDIANS IN 1500　When Europeans arrived in North America in the sixteenth century, as many as 10 million Indians lived on a continent criss-crossed by trails and rivers that formed an extensive trading network. Over thousands of years, the Indians had developed a great diversity of responses to an array of natural environments. The scores of tribes can be clustered according to three major regional groups: the Eastern Woodlands tribes, the Great Plains tribes, and the Western tribes.

The Eastern Woodlands peoples tended to live along the rivers. They included three regional groups distinguished by their languages: the Algonquian, the Iroquoian, and the Muskogean. The dozens of Algonquian-speaking tribes stretched from the New England seaboard to lands along the Great Lakes and into the upper Midwest and south to New Jersey, Virginia, and the Carolinas. The Algonquian tribes along the coast were skilled at fishing; the inland tribes excelled at hunting. All of them practiced agriculture to some extent, and they frequently used canoes hollowed out of trees ("dugouts") to navigate rivers and lakes. Most Algonquians lived in small round shelters called wigwams. Their villages typically ranged from 500 to 2,000 inhabitants.

West and south of the Algonquians were the Iroquoian-speaking tribes (including the Seneca, Onondaga, Mohawk, Oneida, and Cayuga, and the Cherokee and Tuscarora in the South), whose lands spread from upstate New York south through Pennsylvania and into the upland regions of the Carolinas and Georgia. The Iroquois's skill at growing corn led them to create permanent agricultural villages. Around their villages they constructed log walls, and within them they built enormous bark-covered longhouses, which housed several related family clans. Unlike the patriarchal Algonquian culture, Iroquoian society was matriarchal. In part, the matriarchy reflected the frequent absence of Iroquois men. As adept hunters and traders, the men traveled extensively for long periods. Women headed the clans, selected the chiefs, controlled the distribution of property, and planted as well as harvested the crops.

The third major Native American group in the Eastern Woodlands included the tribes who spoke the Muskogean language: the Creeks, Chickasaws, and Choctaws. West of the Mississippi River were the peoples living on the Great Plains and in the Great Basin (present-day Utah and Nevada), many of whom had migrated from the East. The Native Americans of the Great Plains, or Plains Indians, including the Blackfeet, Cheyenne, Arapaho, Comanche, Apache, and Sioux, were nomadic tribes whose culture focused on hunting the vast herds of bison. The Western tribes, living along the Pacific coast, depended upon fishing, sealing, and whaling. Among them were Salish tribes, including the Tillamook, the Chinook, and the Pomo and Chumash.

For at least 15,000 years before the arrival of Europeans, the Indians had occupied the vastness of North America undisturbed by outside invaders. War between tribes, however, was commonplace. Success in warfare was the primary source of a male's prestige among many tribes. As a Cherokee explained in the eighteenth century, "We cannot live without war. Should we make peace with the Tuscororas, we must immediately look out for some other nation with whom we can engage in our beloved occupation."

Over the centuries, the Indians had adapted to the necessity of warfare, changing climate, and varying environments. They would also do so in the face of the unprecedented changes wrought by the arrival of Europeans. In the process of changing and adapting to new realities in accordance with their own traditions, Indians played a significant role in shaping America and the origins of the United States.

THE EXPANSION OF EUROPE

The European exploration of the Western Hemisphere was enabled by several key developments during the fifteenth century. New knowledge and new technologies enabled the construction of full-rigged sailing ships capable of oceanic voyages, more accurate navigation techniques and maps, and more powerful weapons. Driving those improvements was an unrelenting ambition to explore new territories (especially the Indies, a term which then referred to eastern Asia), garner greater wealth and richer commerce, and spread Christianity across the globe. This remarkable age of discovery coincided with the rise of modern science; the growth of global trade, commercial towns, and modern corporations; the decline of feudalism and the formation of nations; the Protestant Reformation and the Catholic Counter-Reformation; and the resurgence of some old sins—greed, conquest, exploitation, oppression, racism, and slavery—that quickly defiled the mythical innocence of the so-called New World.

THE VOYAGES OF COLUMBUS   **Christopher Columbus** learned his trade in the school of Portuguese seamanship. Born in Genoa, Italy, in 1451, Columbus took to the sea at an early age, teaching himself geography, navigation, and Latin. By the 1480s, he was eager to spread Christianity across the globe. Dazzled by the prospect of garnering Asian riches, he developed a bold plan to reach the spice-trade ports of the Indies (India, China, and the East Indies, or Japan) by sailing not south along the African coast but west across the Atlantic. The tall, red-haired Columbus was an audacious visionary whose persistence was as great as his courage. He eventually persuaded the Spanish monarchs Ferdinand and Isabella to award him a tenth share of any riches he gathered abroad: pearls; gold, silver, or other precious metals; and the Asian spices so coveted by Europeans. The legend that the queen had to hock the crown jewels to finance the voyage is as spurious as the fable that Columbus set out to prove the earth was round.

Columbus chartered one seventy-five-foot ship, the *Santa María*, and the Spanish city of Palos supplied two smaller caravels, the *Pinta* and the *Niña*. From Palos on August 3, 1492, this little squadron of tiny ships, with about ninety men, most of them Spaniards, set sail westward for what Columbus thought was Asia. Early on October 12 a lookout yelled, "Tierra! Tierra!" ("Land! Land!"). He had sighted an island in the Bahamas east of Florida that Columbus named San Salvador (Blessed Savior). Columbus decided, incorrectly, that they must be near the Indies, so he called the island people *los Indios*. At every encounter with these native people, known as Tainos or Arawaks, his first question was whether they had any gold. If they had gold the Spaniards seized it; if they did not, the Europeans forced them to search for it.

After leaving San Salvador, Columbus continued to search for a passage to the fabled Indies through the Bahamas, down to Cuba, and then eastward to the island he named Hispaniola (now Haiti and the Dominican Republic), where he first found significant amounts of gold jewelry and was introduced to tobacco.

At the end of 1492, Columbus, still believing he had reached Asia, decided to return to Europe. He left about forty men on Hispaniola and captured a dozen Indians to present as gifts to the Spanish king and queen. When Columbus reached Spain, he received a hero's welcome. Thanks to the newly invented printing press, news of his westward voyage spread rapidly across Europe. The Spanish monarchs Ferdinand and Isabella told Columbus to prepare for a second voyage, instructing him to "treat the Indians very well and lovingly and abstain from doing them any injury." Columbus and his men would repeatedly defy this order.

The Spanish monarchs also sought to solidify their legal claim against Portugal's possible pretensions to the newly discovered lands. With the help of the pope (a Spaniard), rivals Spain and Portugal reached a compromise, called the Treaty of Tordesillas (1494), which drew an imaginary line west of the Cape Verde Islands (off the west coast of Africa) and stipulated that the area to its west—which included most of the Americas—would be a Spanish sphere of exploration and settlement. Africa and what was to become Brazil were granted to Portugal. In practice, this meant that while Spain developed its American empire in the sixteenth century, Portugal provided it with enslaved African laborers.

Flush with success and convinced that he was an agent of God's divine plan, Columbus returned across the Atlantic in 1493 with seventeen ships and 1,400 men. Also on board were Catholic priests charged with converting the Indians. Columbus discovered that the camp he had left behind was in chaos. The unsupervised soldiers had run amok, raping women, robbing villages, and, as Columbus's son later added, "committing a thousand excesses for which they were mortally hated by the Indians."

Columbus returned to Spain in 1496. Two years later he sailed west again, discovering the island of Trinidad and exploring the northern coast of South

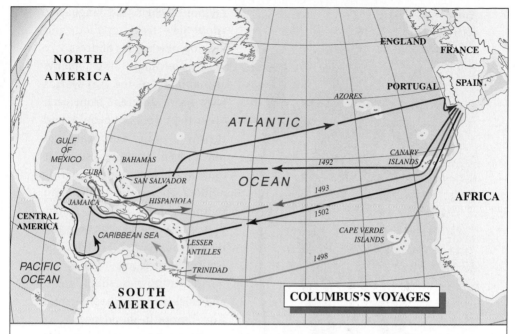

How many voyages did Columbus make to the Americas? What is the origin of the name for the Caribbean Sea? What happened to the colony that Columbus left on Hispaniola in 1493?

America. He led a fourth and final voyage in 1502, during which he sailed along the coast of Central America, still looking in vain for a passage to the Indies. To the end of his life, Columbus insisted that he had discovered the outlying parts of Asia, not a new continent. By one of history's greatest ironies, this lag led Europeans to name the "New World" not for Columbus but for another Italian explorer, **Amerigo Vespucci**, who sailed across the Atlantic in 1499. Vespucci landed on the coast of South America and reported that it was so large it must be a "new" continent. European mapmakers thereafter began to label the "New World" using a variant of Vespucci's first name: America.

THE GREAT BIOLOGICAL EXCHANGE

The first European contacts with the Western Hemisphere began an unprecedented worldwide biological and social exchange that ultimately worked in favor of the Europeans at the expense of the indigenous peoples. The Indians, Europeans, and eventually Africans intersected to create new

painting them felues when they goe to their generall huntings, or at theire Solemne feasts.

Algonquian chief in warpaint

From the notebook of English settler John White, this sketch depicts an Indian chief.

religious beliefs and languages, adopt new tastes in food, and develop new modes of dress.

If anything, the plants and animals of the two worlds were more different from each other than were the peoples and their ways of life. Europeans had never seen creatures such as iguanas, bison, cougars, armadillos, opossums, sloths, and hummingbirds. Turkeys, guinea pigs, llamas, and alpacas were also new to Europeans. Nor did the Native Americans know of horses, cattle, pigs, sheep, goats, and chickens, which soon arrived from Europe in abundance.

The exchange of plant life between Old and New Worlds worked a revolution in the diets of both hemispheres. Before Columbus's voyage, three foods were unknown in Europe: maize (corn), potatoes (sweet and white), and many kinds of beans (snap, kidney, lima, and others). The white potato, although commonly called Irish, is actually native to South America. Explorers brought it back to Europe, where it thrived. The "Irish potato" was eventually transported to North America by Scots-Irish immigrants during the early eighteenth century. Other Western Hemisphere food plants included peanuts, squash, peppers, tomatoes, pumpkins, pineapples, sassafras, papayas, guavas, avocados, cacao (the source of chocolate), and chicle (for chewing gum). Europeans in turn introduced rice, wheat, barley, oats, wine grapes, melons, coffee, olives, bananas, "Kentucky" bluegrass, daisies, and dandelions to the Americas.

The beauty of the biological exchange was that the food plants were more complementary than competitive. Corn, it turned out, could flourish almost anywhere in the world. The nutritious food crops exported from the

Americas thus helped nourish a worldwide population explosion probably greater than any since the invention of agriculture. The dramatic increase in the European populations fueled by the new foods in turn helped provide the surplus of people who colonized the "New World."

By far the most significant aspect of the biological exchange, however, was the transmission of infectious diseases. During the three centuries after Columbus's first voyage, European colonists and enslaved Africans brought with them deadly pathogens that Native Americans had never experienced: smallpox, typhus, diphtheria, bubonic plague, malaria, yellow fever, and cholera. The results were catastrophic. Far more native people—tens of millions—died from contagions than from combat. Deadly diseases such as typhus and smallpox produced pandemics on an unprecedented scale. Unable to explain or cure the diseases, Native American chiefs and religious leaders often lost their stature. As a consequence, tribal cohesion and cultural life disintegrated, and efforts to resist European assaults collapsed.

THE SPANISH EMPIRE

During the sixteenth century, Spain created the world's most powerful empire. At its height, it encompassed much of Europe, most of the Americas, parts of Africa, and various trading outposts in Asia. But it was the gold and especially the silver looted from the Americas that fueled the engine of Spain's "Golden Empire." And the benefits of global empire came at the expense of Indians. Heroic Spanish adventurers were also ruthless exploiters. By plundering, conquering, and colonizing the Americas and converting and enslaving its inhabitants, the Spanish planted Christianity in the Western Hemisphere and gained the resources to rule the world.

The Caribbean Sea served as the funnel through which Spanish power entered the Americas. After establishing colonies on Hispaniola, including Santo Domingo, which became the capital of the West Indies, the Spanish proceeded eastward to Puerto Rico (1508) and westward to Cuba (1511–1514). Their motives were explicit, as one soldier explained: "We came here to serve God and the king, and also to get rich."

Many of the Europeans in the first wave of settlement died of malnutrition or disease. But the Indians suffered far more casualties, for they were ill equipped to resist the European invaders. Disunity everywhere—civil disorder, rebellion, and tribal warfare—left them vulnerable to division and foreign conquest. Attacks by well-armed soldiers and deadly germs from

Europe perplexed and overwhelmed the Indians. Europeans took for granted the superiority of their civilization and ways of life. Such arrogance undergirded the conquest and enslavement of Indians, the destruction of their way of life, and the seizure of their land and treasures.

A CLASH OF CULTURES   The often-violent encounter between Spaniards and Indians involved more than a clash between different peoples. It also involved contrasting forms of technological development. The Indians of Mexico had copper and bronze but no iron. They used wooden canoes for transportation, while the Europeans sailed in heavily armed oceangoing vessels. The Spanish ships not only carried human cargo, but also steel swords, firearms, explosives, and armor. Arrows and tomahawks were seldom a match for guns, cannons, and smallpox.

The Europeans enjoyed other cultural advantages. For example, before the arrival of Europeans the only domesticated four-legged animals in North America were dogs and llamas. The Spanish, on the other hand, brought with them horses, pigs, and cattle. Horses provided greater speed in battle and introduced a decided psychological advantage. "The most essential thing in new lands is horses," reported one Spanish soldier. "They instill the greatest fear in the enemy and make the Indians respect the leaders of the army." Even more feared among the Indians were the greyhound fighting dogs that the Spanish used to guard their camps.

CORTES'S CONQUEST   The most dramatic European conquest of a major Indian civilization on the North American mainland occurred in Mexico. On February 18, 1519, **Hernán Cortés**, driven by dreams of gold and glory in Mexico, set sail from Cuba. His fleet of eleven ships carried nearly 600 soldiers and sailors. Also on board were 200 Cubans, sixteen horses, and cannons. After the invaders landed at what is now Veracruz, on the coast of the Gulf of Mexico, they assaulted a confederation of four small Native American kingdoms opposed to the domineering Aztecs. Cortés shrewdly persuaded the vanquished warriors to join his advance on the hated Aztecs.

Cortés's soldier-adventurers, called *conquistadores*, received no pay; they were military entrepreneurs willing to risk their lives for a share in the expected plunder and slaves. To prevent any men from deserting, Cortés had the ships burned, sparing one vessel to carry the expected gold back to Spain. The nearly 200-mile march of Cortés's army from Veracruz through difficult mountain passes to the magnificent Aztec capital of **Tenochtitlán** took nearly three months.

Cortés in Mexico

Page from the Lienzo de Tlaxcala, a historical narrative from the sixteenth century. The scene, in which Cortés is shown seated on a throne, depicts the arrival of the Spanish in Tlaxcala.

THE AZTECS Cortés was one of the most audacious figures in world history. With his small army, the thirty-four-year-old adventurer brashly set out to conquer the opulent Aztec Empire, which extended from central Mexico to what is today Guatemala. The Aztecs—their most accurate name is Mexica—were a once-nomadic people who had wandered south from northern Mexico and settled in the central highlands in the fourteenth century. On marshy islands on the west side of Lake Tetzcoco, the site of present-day Mexico City, they built Tenochtitlán, a dazzling capital city dominated by towering stone temples, broad paved avenues, thriving markets, and some 70,000 adobe huts. By 1519, when the Spanish landed on the Mexican coast, the Aztecs were one of the most powerful civilizations in the world. Their arts were flourishing; their architecture was magnificent.

AZTEC RELIGION Like most agricultural peoples, the Aztecs centered their spiritual beliefs on the cosmic forces of nature. Many of the Aztec gods were aligned with natural forces—the sun, the sky, water, wind, fire—and the gods perpetually struggled with one another for supremacy. Like most Mesoamericans, the Aztecs regularly offered human sacrifices—captives, slaves, women, and children—to please the gods and to promote rain, enable good harvests, and ensure victory in battle. The Aztecs also used the religious obligation to offer sacrifices as a means of justifying their relentless imperial assaults against other tribes. Prisoners of war in vast numbers were needed as sacrificial offerings. In elaborate weekly rituals at temples and in the streets, Aztec priests used stone knives to cut out the beating hearts of live victims. By the early sixteenth century as many as 10,000 people a year were sacrificed at numerous locations across Mesoamerica. The Spanish were aghast at this "most horrid and abominable custom," but it is important to remember that sixteenth-century Europeans also conducted public torture and executions of the most ghastly sort—beheadings, burnings, hangings. Between 1530 and 1630, England alone executed 75,000 people.

SPANISH INVADERS   As Cortés and his army marched across Mexico, they heard fabulous accounts of Tenochtitlán. With some 200,000 inhabitants, it was the largest city in the Americas and much larger than most European cities. Graced by wide canals, stunning gardens, and formidable stone pyramids, the lake-encircled capital seemed impregnable. But Cortés made the most of his assets. By a combination of threats and deceptions, Cortés and his indigenous allies entered Tenochtitlán peacefully and captured the emperor, Montezuma II. Cortés explained to Montezuma why the invasion was necessary: "We Spaniards have a disease of the heart that only gold can cure." Montezuma acquiesced in part because he mistook Cortés for a god.

After taking the Aztecs' gold and silver, the Spanish forced Montezuma to provide laborers to mine more of the precious metals. This state of affairs lasted until the spring of 1520, when disgruntled Aztecs, regarding Montezuma as a traitor, rebelled, stoned him to death, and attacked the Spaniards. The Spaniards lost about a third of their men as they retreated. Their 20,000 Indian allies remained loyal, however, and Cortés gradually regrouped his forces. In 1521, having been reinforced with troops from Cuba and thousands of Indians eager to defeat the Aztecs, he besieged the imperial city for eighty-five days, cutting off its access to water and food and allowing a smallpox epidemic to decimate the inhabitants. The ravages of smallpox and the support of thousands of anti-Aztec allies help explain how such a small force of determined Spaniards lusting for gold and silver was able to vanquish a proud nation of nearly 1 million people. After the Aztecs surrendered, a merciless Cortés ordered the leaders hanged and the priests devoured by dogs. In two years, Cortés and his disciplined army had conquered a fabled empire that had taken centuries to develop.

Cortés set the style for waves of plundering conquistadores to follow. Within twenty years Spain had established a sprawling empire in the "New

World." In 1531, **Francisco Pizarro** led a band of soldiers down the Pacific coast from Panama toward Peru, where they brutally subdued the Inca Empire. The Spanish invaders seized the Inca palaces and country estates, took royal women as mistresses and wives, and looted the empire of its gold and silver. From Peru, Spain extended its control southward through Chile by about 1553 and north, to present-day Colombia, by 1538.

SPANISH AMERICA   As the sixteenth century unfolded, Spain expanded its settlements in the "New World" and established far-flung governmental and economic centers in Mexico, the Caribbean, Central America, and South America. The crusading conquistadores transferred to America a socioeconomic system known as the ***encomienda***, whereby favored officers became privileged landowners who controlled indigenous villages. As *encomenderos*, they were called upon to protect and care for the villages and support missionary priests. In turn, they could require Indians to provide them with goods and labor. Spanish America therefore developed from the start a society of extremes: wealthy conquistadores and *encomenderos* at one end of the spectrum and Indians held in poverty at the other end.

Missionaries in the "New World"

A Spanish mission in New Mexico, established to spread the Catholic faith among the indigenous peoples.

By the mid-1500s, Native Americans were nearly extinct in the West Indies, reduced more by European diseases than by Spanish brutality. To take their place, as early as 1503 the Spanish colonizers began to transport enslaved Africans, the first in a wretched traffic that eventually would carry millions of captive people across the Atlantic into bondage. In all of Spain's "New World" empire, by one estimate, the indigenous population plummeted from about 50 million at the outset to 4 million in the seventeenth century.

SPANISH EXPLORATION IN NORTH AMERICA   During the sixteenth century, Spanish America gradually developed into a settled society. The conquistadores were succeeded by a second generation of bureaucrats, and the *encomienda* gave way to the *hacienda* (a great farm or ranch) as the claim to land became a more important source of wealth than the Spanish claim to labor. From the outset, in sharp contrast to the later English experience, the Spanish government regulated every detail of colonial administration.

Throughout the sixteenth century no European power other than Spain held more than a brief foothold in the "New World." Spain had the advantage not only of having arrived first but also of having stumbled onto those regions that would produce the quickest profits. While France and England were struggling with domestic quarrels and religious conflict, Spain had forged an intense national unity. Spain dominated Europe as well as the "New World" during the first half of the sixteenth century. The treasures of the Aztecs and the Incas added to its power, but the single-minded focus on gold and silver also tempted the Spanish government to live beyond its means. The influx of gold and silver from the "New World" financed the growth of the Spanish Empire (and army) while causing inflation throughout Europe.

For most of the colonial period, much of what is now the United States belonged to Spain, and Spanish culture etched a lasting imprint upon American ways of life. Spain's colonial presence lasted more than three centuries, much longer than either England's or France's. New Spain was centered in Mexico, but its frontiers extended from the Florida Keys to Alaska. Hispanic place-names—San Francisco, Santa Barbara, Los Angeles, San Diego, Tucson, Santa Fe, San Antonio, Pensacola, and St. Augustine—survive to this day, as do Hispanic influences in art, architecture, literature, music, law, and cuisine.

Juan Ponce de León, then governor of Puerto Rico, made the earliest known exploration of Florida in 1513. Meanwhile, Spanish explorers skirted the Gulf of Mexico coast from Florida to Veracruz, scouted the Atlantic coast from Key West to Newfoundland, and established a short-lived colony on the Carolina coast.

In 1539, **Hernando de Soto** and 600 men landed on Florida's west coast, hiked up as far as western North Carolina, and then moved westward beyond the Mississippi River and up the Arkansas River, looting and destroying indigenous villages along the way. In the spring of 1542, de Soto died near Natchez, Mississippi; the next year the survivors among his party floated down the Mississippi River, and 311 of the original adventurers found their way to Mexico. In 1540, Francisco Vásquez de Coronado, inspired by rumors of gold, traveled northward into New Mexico and northeast across Texas and Oklahoma as far as Kansas. He returned in 1542 without gold but with a more realistic view of what lay in those arid lands.

The Spanish established provinces in North America not so much as commercial enterprises but as defensive buffers protecting their more lucrative empire in Mexico and South America. They were concerned about French traders infiltrating from Louisiana, English settlers crossing into Florida, and Russian seal hunters wandering down the California coast.

The first Spanish outpost in what is today the United States emerged in response to French encroachments on Spanish claims. In the 1560s, spirited French Protestants (called Huguenots) established France's first American colonies on the coast of what became South Carolina and Florida. In 1565 a Spanish outpost on the Florida coast, St. Augustine, became the first European town in the present-day United States. Spain's colony at St. Augustine included a fort, church, hospital, fish market, and over one hundred shops and houses—all built decades before the first English settlements at Jamestown and Plymouth. While other early American outposts failed, St. Augustine survived as a defensive base perched on the edge of a continent.

THE SPANISH SOUTHWEST The Spanish eventually established other permanent settlements in what are now New Mexico, Texas, and California. Eager to pacify rather than fight the far more numerous Indians of the region, the Spanish used religion as an instrument of colonial control. Missionaries, particularly Franciscans and Jesuits, established isolated Catholic missions, where they imposed Christianity on the indigenous people. After about ten years a mission would be secularized: its lands would be divided among the converted Indians, the mission chapel would become a parish church, and the inhabitants would be given full Spanish citizenship—including the privilege of paying taxes. The soldiers who were sent to protect the missions were housed in presidios, or forts; their families and the merchants accompanying them lived in adjacent villages.

The land that would later be called New Mexico was the first center of mission activity in the American Southwest. In 1598, Juan de Oñate, a wealthy,

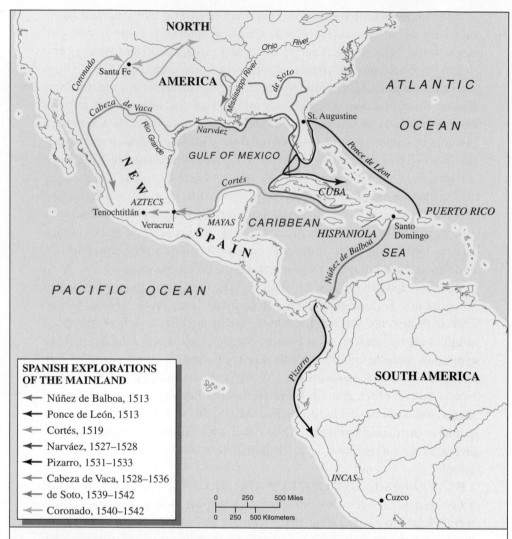

SPANISH EXPLORATIONS OF THE MAINLAND

← Núñez de Balboa, 1513
← Ponce de León, 1513
← Cortés, 1519
← Narváez, 1527–1528
← Pizarro, 1531–1533
← Cabeza de Vaca, 1528–1536
← de Soto, 1539–1542
← Coronado, 1540–1542

What were the Spanish conquistadores' goals for exploring the Americas? How did Cortés conquer the Aztecs? Why did the Spanish first explore North America, and why did they establish St. Augustine, the first European settlement in what would become the United States?

imperious son of a Spanish mining family in Mexico, received a land grant for the territory north of Mexico above the Rio Grande. With an expeditionary military force made up mostly of Mexican Indians and *mestizos* (the offspring of Spanish fathers and indigenous mothers), he took possession of New Mexico, established a capital north of present-day Santa Fe, and sent out expeditions to search for gold and silver deposits. He promised the local Indians, called Pueblos, that Spanish dominion would bring them peace, justice, prosperity, and protection. Conversion to Catholicism offered even greater benefits: "an eternal life of great bliss" instead of "cruel and everlasting torment."

Some Indians welcomed the missionaries as "powerful witches" capable of easing their burdens. Others tried to use the Spanish invaders as allies against rival tribes. Still others saw no alternative but to submit. The Indians living in Spanish New Mexico were required to pay tribute to their *encomenderos* and perform personal tasks for them, including sexual favors. Soldiers and priests flogged disobedient Indians.

Before the end of the province's first year, in December 1598, the Pueblos revolted, killing several soldiers and incurring Oñate's wrath. During three days of relentless fighting, Spanish soldiers killed 500 Pueblo men and 300 women and children. Survivors were enslaved. Pueblo males over the age of twenty-five had one foot severed in a public ritual intended to frighten the Pueblos and keep them from escaping or resisting. Children were taken from their parents and placed under the care of a Franciscan mission, where, Oñate remarked, "they may attain the knowledge of God and the salvation of their souls."

During the first three quarters of the seventeenth century, Spanish New Mexico expanded very slowly. The hoped-for deposits of gold and silver were never found, and a sparse food supply blunted the interest of potential colonists. In 1608 the government decided to turn New Mexico into a royal province. The following year it dispatched a royal governor, and in 1610, as English settlers were struggling to survive at Jamestown, in Virginia, the Spanish moved the province's capital to Santa Fe, the first permanent seat of government in the present-day United States. By 1630 there were fifty Catholic churches and friaries in New Mexico and some 3,000 Spaniards.

Franciscan missionaries claimed that 86,000 Pueblos had been converted to Christianity. In fact, however, resentment among the Indians increased with time. In 1680 a charismatic indigenous leader named Popé organized a massive rebellion among twenty Indian towns. The Native Americans burned Catholic churches; tortured, mutilated, and executed priests; and destroyed all relics of Christianity. Popé then established Santa Fe as the capital of his confederacy. The Pueblo Revolt of 1680 constituted the greatest defeat that Indians ever inflicted on European efforts to conquer and colonize the "New World." It took fourteen years and four military assaults for the Spanish to reestablish control over New Mexico.

HORSES AND THE GREAT PLAINS   Another major consequence of the Pueblo Revolt was the opportunity it afforded Indian rebels to acquire hundreds of coveted Spanish horses (Spanish authorities had made it illegal for Indians to own horses). The Pueblos in turn established a thriving horse trade with Navajos, Apaches, and other tribes. By 1690, horses were evident in Texas, and they soon spread across the Great Plains, the vast rolling grasslands extending from the Missouri River valley in the east to the base of the Rocky Mountains in the west.

Horses were a disruptive ecological force in North America. Prior to the arrival of horses, Indians hunted on foot and used dogs as their beasts of burden. But dogs are carnivores, and it was difficult to find enough meat to feed them. Horses thus changed everything, providing the Plains Indians with a transforming source of mobility and power. Horses are grazing animals, and the vast grasslands of the Great Plains offered plenty of forage. Horses could also haul up to seven times as much weight as dogs, and their speed and endurance made the indigenous people much more effective hunters and warriors. In addition, horses enabled Indians to travel farther to trade and fight.

In the short run the horse brought prosperity and mobility to the Plains Indians. Horses became the center and symbol of Indian life on the plains. Yet the Indians began to kill more bison than the herds could replace. In addition, horses competed with the bison for food, often depleting the

Plains Indians

The horse-stealing raid depicted in this hide painting demonstrates the essential role horses played in Plains life.

prairie grass and compacting the soil in the river valleys during the winter. And as tribes traveled greater distances and encountered more people, infectious diseases spread more widely.

THE PROTESTANT REFORMATION

The zealous efforts of the Spanish to convert Indians to Catholicism illustrated the murderous intensity with which Europeans engaged in religious life in the sixteenth century. Spiritual concerns were paramount. Religion inspired, consoled, and united people. In matters of faith, the Roman Catholic Church and the Bible were the pervasive sources of authority. Social life centered on worship services, prayer rituals, and religious festivals and ceremonies. People believed fervently in heaven and hell, devils and witches, demons and angels, magic and miracles, astrology and the occult. Europeans also took for granted the collaboration of church and state; monarchs required religious uniformity. Heresy and blasphemy were not tolerated. Christians were willing to kill and die for their beliefs. During the **Reformation**, when "protestant" dissidents challenged the supremacy of the Roman Catholic Church, Catholics and Protestants persecuted, imprisoned, tortured, and killed each other—in large numbers.

The Protestant Reformation intensified national rivalries, and, by challenging Catholic Spain's power, profoundly affected the course of early American history. When Columbus sailed west in 1492, all of western Europe acknowledged the supremacy of the Catholic Church and its pope in Rome. The unity of Christendom began to crack in 1517, however, when **Martin Luther** (1483–1546), a German monk, priest, and professor, posted on the door of his Wittenberg church his *Ninety-five Theses* in protest against the corruption of Catholic officials. Sinners, Luther argued, could win salvation neither by doing good works nor by purchasing indulgences (whereby monks and priests would forgive the sins of the living or the dead in exchange for money or goods), but only by receiving the gift of God's grace through the redemptive power of Christ and through a direct personal relationship with God—the "priesthood of all believers."

Lutheranism spread rapidly among the German-speaking people and their rulers—some of them with an eye to seizing property owned by the Catholic Church. Church officials lashed out at Luther, calling him "a leper with a brain of brass and a nose of iron." When the pope expelled Luther from the church in 1521, reconciliation became impossible. The German states erupted in religious conflicts; a settlement did not come until 1555, when each prince was allowed to determine the religion of his subjects. Most of northern Germany, along with Scandinavia, became Lutheran.

The Protestant Reformation spread rapidly across Europe during the sixteenth century. It was in part a theological dispute, in part a political movement, and in part a catalyst for social change, civil strife, colonial expansion, and imperial warfare. Martin Luther's bold ideas shattered the unity of Catholic Europe and ignited civil wars and societal upheavals. Once unleashed, the flood of Protestant rebellion flowed in directions unexpected and unwanted by Luther and his allies. Militant Protestants pursued Luther's rebellious doctrine to its logical end by preaching religious liberty for all.

CHALLENGES TO THE SPANISH EMPIRE

The success of Catholic Spain in conquering and exploiting much of the Western Hemisphere spurred Portugal, France, England, and the Netherlands to develop their own imperial claims. The French were the first to pose a serious threat. Spanish treasure ships sailing home from New Spain offered tempting targets for French privateers. In 1524 the French king sent the Italian Giovanni da Verrazano west across the Atlantic in search of a passage to Asia. Sighting land (probably at Cape Fear, North Carolina), Verrazano ranged along the coast as far north as Maine. On a second voyage, in 1528, his life met an abrupt end in the West Indies at the hands of the Caribs.

Unlike the Verrazano voyages, those of **Jacques Cartier**, beginning in the next decade, led to the first French effort at colonization in North America. During three voyages, Cartier explored the Gulf of St. Lawrence and ventured up the St. Lawrence River, between what would become Canada and New York. Twice he got as far as present-day Montreal, and twice he wintered at or near the site of Quebec, near which a short-lived French colony appeared in 1541–1542. From that time forward, however, French kings lost interest in Canada for over half a century. From the mid-1500s, greater threats to Spanish power arose from the growing strength of the Dutch and the English. The United Provinces of the Netherlands (Holland), which had passed by inheritance to the Spanish king and become largely Protestant, rebelled against Spanish rule in 1567. A long, bloody struggle for independence ensued. Spain did not accept the independence of the Dutch republic until 1648.

Almost from the beginning of the Protestant Dutch revolt against Catholic Spain, the Dutch plundered Spanish ships in the Atlantic and carried on illegal trade with Spain's colonies. While Queen Elizabeth steered a tortuous

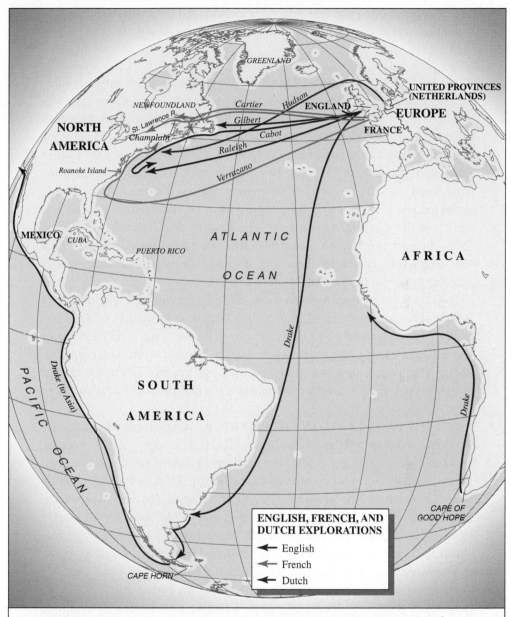

Who were the first European explorers to rival Spanish dominance in the "New World," and why did they cross the Atlantic? Why was the defeat of the Spanish Armada important to the history of English exploration? What was the significance of the voyages of Gilbert and Raleigh?

course to avoid open war with Spain, she encouraged both Dutch and English sea captains to engage in smuggling and piracy at the expense of the Spanish.

THE DEFEAT OF THE ARMADA   The plundering of Spanish shipping by English privateers continued for some twenty years before open war erupted. In 1588, Philip II, the king of Catholic Spain, assembled the fabled Spanish Armada: 130 ships, 8,000 sailors, and at least 18,000 soldiers—the greatest invasion fleet in history. On May 28, 1588, the Armada left Lisbon headed for the English Channel. The English navy, whose almost one hundred warships were smaller but faster, was waiting for them. As the battle unfolded, the heavy Spanish galleons could not compete with the speed and agility of the smaller English ships. The English fleet harried the Spanish ships through the English Channel before the storm-tossed Spanish fleet was swept into the North Sea. The stunning defeat of Catholic Spain's Armada bolstered the Protestant cause across Europe.

Defeat of the Spanish Armada marked the beginning of England's global naval supremacy and cleared the way for English colonization of America. English colonists could now make their way to North America without fear of Spanish interference. The naval victory was the climactic event of Queen Elizabeth's reign. England at the end of the sixteenth century was in the springtime of its power, filled with a youthful zest for new worlds and new wonders.

ENGLISH EXPLORATION OF AMERICA   English efforts to colonize America began when Sir Humphrey Gilbert, a favorite of the queen's, secured royal permission to establish a colony in America. Gilbert, after two false starts, set out with a colonial expedition in 1583, intending to settle near Narragansett Bay (in present-day Rhode Island). He instead landed in Newfoundland (Canada) and took possession of the land for Elizabeth. With winter approaching and his largest vessels lost, Gilbert returned home. While in transit, however, his ship vanished, and he was never seen again.

The next year, Sir Walter Raleigh, Gilbert's half brother, persuaded the queen to renew Gilbert's colonizing mission in his own name. The flotilla discovered the Outer Banks of North Carolina and landed at **Roanoke Island**, where the soil seemed fruitful and the Native Americans friendly. Raleigh decided to name the area Virginia, in honor of childless Queen Elizabeth, the "Virgin Queen." After several false starts, Raleigh in 1587 sponsored another expedition of about one hundred colonists, including women and children, under Governor John White. White spent a month on Roanoke Island and then returned to England for supplies, leaving behind his daughter Elinor and his granddaughter Virginia Dare, the first English

The Arrival of the English in Virginia

The arrival of English explorers on the Outer Banks, with Roanoke Island at left.

child born in the "New World." White's return was delayed because of the war with Spain. When he finally landed, in 1590, he discovered that Roanoke had been abandoned and pillaged.

No trace of the "lost colonists" was ever found. Indians may have killed them, or hostile Spaniards—who had certainly planned to attack—may have done the job. The most recent evidence indicates that the "Lost Colony" fell prey to a horrible drought. Tree-ring samples reveal that the colonists arrived during the driest seven-year period in 770 years. While some may have gone south, the main body of colonists appears to have gone north, to the southern shores of Chesapeake Bay, as they had talked of doing, and lived there for some years until they were killed by local Indians.

There was not a single English colonist in North America when Queen Elizabeth died, in 1603. The Spanish controlled the only colonial outposts on the continent. But that was about to change. Inspired by the success of the Spanish in exploiting the "New World," and emboldened by their defeat of the Spanish Armada in 1588, the English—as well as the French and the Dutch—would soon develop their own versions of American colonialism.

CHAPTER SUMMARY

- **Pre-Columbian America** At the time of contact, Indian tribes, such as the Aztecs and Mayas of Central America, had developed empires sustained by large-scale agriculture and long-distance trade. Native North Americans, however, were less well organized. The Anasazi and the indigenous peoples in the Ohio and Mississippi Valleys did establish important trading centers sustained by intensive agriculture.

- **Age of Exploration** By the 1490s, Europe was experiencing a renewed curiosity about the world. New technologies led to the creation of better maps and navigation techniques. Nation-states searching for gold and glory emerged; and Europeans desired silks and spices from Asia.

- **Great Biological Exchange** Contact resulted in a great biological exchange. Crops such as maize, beans, and potatoes became staples in the Old World. Indigenous peoples incorporated into their culture such Eurasian animals as the horse and pig. The invaders carried pathogens that set off pandemics of smallpox, plague, and other illnesses to which Indians had no immunity.

- **Colonizing the Americas** When the Spanish began to colonize the "New World," the conversion of Indians to Catholicism was important, but the search for gold and silver was primary. In that search, the Spanish demanded goods and labor from their new subjects. As the Indian population declined, the Spanish began to "import" enslaved Africans.

- **Spanish Legacy** Spain left a lasting legacy in the borderlands from California to Florida. Catholic missionaries contributed to the destruction of the old ways of life by actively exterminating "heathen" beliefs in the Southwest, a practice that led to open rebellion in 1598 and 1680.

- **Protestant Reformation** The Protestant Reformation shattered the unity of Catholic Europe. By the time of Elizabeth I of England, religious differences had led to state-supported plunder of Spanish treasure ships, then to open hostility with Spain. England's defeat of the Spanish Armada cleared the path for English dominance in North America.

CHRONOLOGY

by 12,000 B.C.	Humans have migrated to the Americas, most of them from Siberia
A.D. 1492	Columbus, sailing for Spain, makes first voyage of discovery
1497	John Cabot explores Newfoundland
1503	First Africans are brought to the Americas
1513	Juan Ponce de León explores Florida
1517–1648	Protestant Reformation spurs religious conflict between Catholics and Protestants
1519	Hernán Cortés begins the Spanish conquest of the Aztec Empire
1531	Francisco Pizarro subdues the Incas of Peru
1541	Jacques Cartier, sailing for France, explores the St. Lawrence River
1561	St. Augustine, the first European colony in present day America, is founded
1584–1587	Raleigh's Roanoke Island venture
1588	The English defeat the Spanish Armada
1680	Popé leads rebellion in New Mexico

KEY TERMS & NAMES

Aztec Empire p. 7

pueblos p. 9

Christopher Columbus p. 11

Amerigo Vespucci p. 13

Hernán Cortés p. 16

conquistadores p. 16

Tenochtitlán p. 16

Francisco Pizarro p. 19

encomienda p. 19

Hernando de Soto p. 21

Reformation p. 25

Martin Luther p. 25

Jacques Cartier p. 26

Raleigh's Roanoke Island Colony p. 28

2 BRITAIN AND ITS COLONIES

FOCUS QUESTIONS

  wwnorton.com/studyspace

- What were Britain's reasons for establishing colonies in North America?
- Why did the first English colony, at Jamestown, experience hardships in its first decades?
- How important was religion as a motivation for colonization?
- How did British colonists and Indians adapt to each other's presence?
- Why was it possible for England to establish successful colonies by 1700?

The England that Queen Elizabeth governed at the beginning of the seventeenth century was a unique blend of elements. The Anglican Church mixed Protestant theology and Catholic rituals. And the growth of royal power had paradoxically been linked to the rise of civil liberties for the English people, in which even Tudor monarchs took pride. In the course of their history, the English people have displayed a genius for "muddling through," a gift for the pragmatic compromise that at times defies logic but in the light of experience somehow works.

THE ENGLISH BACKGROUND

Dominated by England, the British Isles also included the kingdoms of Wales, Ireland, and Scotland. The United Kingdom, set off from continental Europe by the English Channel, had safe frontiers after the union of the English and Scottish crowns in 1603. Such comparative isolation enabled the nation to develop institutions quite different from those on the Continent. Unlike the absolute monarchs of France and Spain, the British rulers shared power with the nobility and a lesser aristocracy, known as the gentry, whose representatives formed the bicameral legislature known as Parliament, made up of the House of Lords and the House of Commons.

ENGLISH LIBERTIES   That England was a parliamentary monarchy made it distinctive among the European nations in the sixteenth century. The Magna Carta (Great Charter) of 1215, a statement of rights and liberties wrested by feudal nobles from the king, had established the principle that the people had basic rights, the most important of which was that everyone was equal before the law and no person was above the law, including those in power. The most important power allocated to the Parliament was the authority to enact or modify taxes. By controlling government tax revenue, the legislative body exercised important leverage over the monarchy.

ENGLISH ENTERPRISE   The cherished tradition of English liberties inspired a sense of personal initiative and entrepreneurial enterprise that spawned prosperity and empire. Unlike the Spanish, the English formed for-profit joint-stock companies as their mode of global expansion. These entrepreneurial ventures were the ancestors of the modern corporation. Private investors, not the government, shared the risks and profits associated with maritime exploration and colonial settlement. In the late sixteenth century, some of the larger companies managed to get royal charters that entitled them to monopolies in certain territories and even government powers in their outposts. Such joint-stock companies were the most important organizational innovation of the era, and they provided the first instruments of British colonization in America.

PARLIAMENT AND THE STUARTS   With the demise of Queen Elizabeth in 1603, the Tudor family line ran out, and the throne fell to the first of the Stuarts, whose dynasty would span most of the seventeenth century, a turbulent time during which the British planted their overseas empire. In 1603, James VI of Scotland became King James I of England. While the Tudors had wielded power through constitutional authority, James promoted the theory of divine right, by which monarchs answered only to God. James I inherited from his cousin Queen Elizabeth a divided Church of England, with the reform-minded Puritans in one camp and the conservative Anglican establishment in the other. The Puritans had hoped the new king would support their opposition to the Catholic trappings of Anglicanism; they found instead a testy autocrat who promised to banish them from the British Isles. He offended even Anglicans by deciding to end Queen Elizabeth's war with Catholic Spain.

Charles I, who succeeded his father, James, in 1625, proved to be an even more stubborn defender of absolute royal power. Like the French and Spanish monarchs, King Charles I preferred a highly centralized kingdom specializing in oppression and hierarchy. He disbanded Parliament from 1629 to 1640, levied taxes by decree, and allowed the systematic persecution of Puritans. The monarchy went too far when it tried to impose Anglican forms of worship on Presbyterian Scots. In 1638, Scotland rose in revolt, and in 1640 King Charles, desperate for money, told Parliament to raise taxes for the defense of his kingdom. The "Long Parliament" refused, going so far as to condemn to death the king's chief minister. In 1642, when the king tried to arrest five members of Parliament, a prolonged civil war erupted. In 1646 parliamentary forces captured King Charles and eventually tried him on charges of high treason. The judges found the king guilty, labeling him a "tyrant, traitor, murderer, and public enemy." Charles was beheaded in 1649.

Oliver Cromwell, the commander of the parliamentary army, filled the vacuum created by the execution of the king. He operated like a military dictator, ruling first through a council chosen by Parliament (the Commonwealth) and, after he dissolved the Parliament, as "lord protector" (the Protectorate). Cromwell extended religious toleration to all Britons except Catholics and Anglicans, but his arbitrary governance and his stern moralistic codes provoked growing resentment. When, after his death, in 1658, his son proved too weak to rule, the army once again took control, permitted new elections for Parliament, and in 1660 supported the Restoration of the Stuart monarchy under young Charles II, son of the executed king.

Charles II accepted as terms of the Restoration settlement the principle that he must rule jointly with Parliament. His younger brother, the Duke of York (who became James II upon succeeding to the throne in 1685), was less flexible. He openly avowed Catholicism and adopted an unyielding authoritarian stance. He had opponents murdered or imprisoned, and he defied parliamentary statutes. The people could bear the king's efforts to mimic France's Sun King, Louis XIV, so long as they expected one of his Protestant daughters, Mary or Anne, to succeed him. In 1688, however, the birth of a royal son who would be reared a Catholic brought matters to a crisis. Determined to avoid a Catholic monarch, political, religious, and military leaders invited the king's Protestant daughter Mary Stuart and her Protestant husband, William III of Orange, the ruling Dutch prince, to assume the British throne as joint monarchs. When William landed in England with a Dutch army, King James II fled to France, his adopted home. The Parliament then reasserted its right to counterbalance the authority of the monarchy.

By ending a long era of internal conflict, royal absolutism, and chronic instability, the "Glorious Revolution" greatly enhanced Britain's world power. Moreover, Parliament finally established its freedom from monarchical control. The monarchy would henceforth derive its power not from God but from the people. Under the Bill of Rights, drafted in 1689, William and Mary gave up the royal right to suspend laws, appoint special courts, keep a standing army, or levy taxes except by Parliament's consent. They further agreed to hold frequent legislative sessions and allow freedom of speech. The Glorious Revolution helped to change the Church of England from an intolerant, persecuting church to one that acknowledged the right of dissenters.

SETTLING THE CHESAPEAKE

During these eventful years all but one of Britain's North American colonies were founded. The Stuart kings were eager to weaken the power of France and Spain and gain Britain's share of overseas colonies, trade, and plunder. The British colonies in America began not as initiatives undertaken by the monarchy but as profit-seeking corporations. In 1606, King James I chartered a joint-stock enterprise called the **Virginia Company**, with two divisions, the First Colony of London and the Second Colony of Plymouth. King James assigned to the Virginia Company an explicit religious mission. He decreed that the settlers would bring the "Christian religion" to the Indians who "live in darkness and miserable ignorance of the true knowledge and worship of God." But as was true of most colonial ventures, such pious intentions were mixed with the lure of profits. The stockholders viewed the colony as a source of gold and other minerals; products—such as wine, citrus fruits, and olive oil—that would free England from dependence upon Spain; and pitch, tar, potash, and other forest products needed by the navy. Investors promoted colonization as an opportunity to trade with the Indians; some also saw it as a way to transplant the growing number of jobless vagrants from Britain to the Americas. Few if any foresaw what the first English colony would actually become: a place to grow tobacco.

VIRGINIA The Virginia Company planted the first permanent colony in Virginia. On May 6, 1607, three tiny ships carrying 105 men and boys (39 of the original voyagers had died at sea) reached Chesapeake Bay after four

"Ould Virginia"

A 1624 map of Virginia by John Smith, showing Chief Powhatan in the upper left.

storm-tossed months at sea. They chose a river with a northwest bend—in the hope of finding a passage to Asia—and settled about forty miles inland, to hide from marauding Spaniards. The river they called the James and the colony, Jamestown, in what would become the province of Virginia, named after Queen Elizabeth, the "Virgin Queen."

On a low-lying peninsula fed by brackish water and swarming with malarial mosquitoes, the sea-weary colonists built a fort, thatched huts, a storehouse, and a church. They needed to grow their own food, but most were either townsmen unfamiliar with farming or "gentleman" adventurers who scorned manual labor. They had come expecting to find gold, friendly Indians, and easy living. Instead they found disease, drought, starvation, dissension, and death. Supplies from England were undependable, and only some effective leadership and trade with the Indians, who taught the ill-prepared colonists to grow maize, enabled them to survive.

The indigenous peoples of the region were loosely organized. Powhatan was the powerful chief of numerous Algonquian-speaking villages in eastern Virginia, representing over 10,000 Indians. The two dozen tribes making up the so-called Powhatan Confederacy were largely an agricultural people focused on raising corn. They lived in some 200 villages along rivers in fortified settlements and resided in wood houses sheathed with bark. **Chief Powhatan** collected tribute from the tribes he had conquered—fully 80 percent of the corn that they grew was handed over. Powhatan also developed a lucrative trade with the English colonists, exchanging corn and hides for hatchets, swords, and muskets; he realized too late that the newcomers wanted more than corn; they intended to seize his lands and subjugate his people.

The colonists, as it happened, had more than a match for Powhatan in **Captain John Smith**, a short, stocky, twenty-seven-year-old soldier of fortune with rare powers of leadership and self-promotion. The Virginia Company, impressed by Smith's exploits in foreign wars, had appointed him a member of the council to manage the new colony in America. It was a wise decision. Of the original 105 settlers, only 38 survived the first nine months. With the colonists on the verge of starvation, Smith imposed strict discipline and forced all to labor, declaring that "he that will not work shall not eat."

In 1609 the Virginia Company sent more colonists to Jamestown, including several women. A new charter replaced the largely ineffective council with an all-powerful governor. The company then lured new investors and attracted new settlers with the promise of free land after seven years of labor. With no gold or silver in Virginia, the company in effect had given up hope of prospering except through the sale of land, which would rise in value as the colony grew. Hundreds of new settlers overwhelmed the infant colony. During the "starving time" of the winter of 1609–1610, most of the colonists died of disease or starvation. Desperate colonists consumed their horses, cats, and dogs, then survived on rats and mice. A few even ate the leather from their shoes and boots. Some fled to nearby indigenous villages, only to be welcomed with arrows. One desperate man killed, salted, and ate his pregnant wife. His fellow colonists tortured and executed him.

Over the next seven years the Jamestown colony limped along until it gradually found a lucrative source of revenue: tobacco. The plant had been grown on Caribbean islands for years, and smoking had become a popular—and addictive—habit in Europe. In 1612, having been introduced to growing tobacco by the Indians, colonist John Rolfe began growing Chesapeake tobacco for export to Britain. Virginia's tobacco production soared during the seventeenth century, leading the Virginia Company in 1616 to change its land policy. Instead of colonists being treated as laborers, whereby they worked the land for the company, colonists were thereafter allowed to own their own land. But still there was a chronic shortage of labor. Tobacco became such a profitable, labor-intensive crop that planters purchased more and more indentured servants (colonists who exchanged several years of labor for the cost of passage to America and the grant of land), thus increasing the flow of immigrants to the colony. Indentured servitude became a primary source of labor in English America during the seventeenth century. Over half of the white immigrants to the British colonies arrived under indenture.

In 1618, Sir Edwin Sandys, a prominent member of Parliament, became head of the Virginia Company and instituted a series of reforms. First of all he inaugurated a new "headright" policy: any Englishman who bought a share in the company and could get to Virginia could have fifty acres on arrival, and fifty more for any servants he brought along. The following year the company relaxed the colony's military regime and promised that the settlers would have the "rights of Englishmen," including a legislature. This was a crucial development, for the English had long enjoyed the greatest civil liberties and the least intrusive government in Europe. Now, the English colonists in Virginia were to enjoy the same rights. On July 30, 1619, the first General Assembly of Virginia met in the Jamestown church, "sweating & stewing, and battling flies and mosquitoes," as they assumed responsibility for representative government.

The year 1619 was eventful in other respects. In that year, a ship with ninety young women aboard arrived in the overwhelmingly male colony. Men rushed to claim them as wives by providing 125 pounds of tobacco for the cost of their transatlantic passage. And a Dutch ship stopped by and dropped off "20 Negars," the first Africans known to have reached English America. By this time, Europeans had been selling enslaved Africans for over a century. The increasingly profitable tobacco trade intensified the settlers' lust for land, slaves, and women. English planters especially coveted the fields cultivated by Indians because they had already been cleared and were ready to be planted. In 1622 the Indians tried to repel the land-grabbing English. They killed a fourth of the settlers, some 350 colonists, including John Rolfe (who had returned from England). The vengeful English thereafter decimated Indians in Virginia. The 24,000 Algonquians who inhabited the colony in 1607 were reduced to 2,000 by 1669.

Some 14,000 English men, women, and children had migrated to Jamestown since 1607, but most of them had died; the population in 1624 stood at a precarious 1,132. In 1624 an English court dissolved the struggling Virginia Company, and Virginia became a royal colony. No longer were the settlers mere laborers toiling for a company; they were now free to own private property and start business enterprises.

Sir William Berkeley, who arrived as Virginia's royal governor in 1642, presided over the colony's growth for most of the next thirty-five years. The turmoil of Virginia's early days gave way to a more stable period. Tobacco prices surged, and the large planters began to consolidate their economic gains through political action. The relentless stream of new settlers and indentured servants into Virginia exerted constant pressure on indigenous lands and produced unwanted economic effects and social unrest. The largest planters bought up the most fertile land along the coast, thereby forcing freed servants to become tenants or claim less fertile land inland. In either case the tenants found themselves at a disadvantage. They grew dependent upon planters for land and credit, and small farmers along the western frontier became more vulnerable to Indian attacks. By 1676 a fourth of the free white men in Virginia were landless. Vagabonds roamed the countryside, squatting on private property, working at odd jobs, or poaching game or engaging in other petty crimes in order to survive. Alarmed by the growing social unrest, the large planters who controlled the assembly lengthened terms of indenture, passed more stringent vagrancy laws, stiffened punishments, and stripped the landless of their political rights. Such efforts only increased social friction.

BACON'S REBELLION   In the mid-1670s a variety of simmering tensions—caused by depressed tobacco prices, rising taxes, roaming livestock, and crowds of freed servants greedily eyeing indigenous lands—contributed to the tangled events that have come to be labeled **Bacon's Rebellion**.

In 1676, Nathaniel Bacon defied Governor Berkeley's authority by assuming command of a group of frontier vigilantes. The tall, slender twenty-nine-year-old Bacon, a graduate of Cambridge University, had been in Virginia only two years. Later historians would praise Bacon as the leader of the first struggle of common folk versus aristocrats. In part that was true. The rebellion he led was largely a battle of servants, small farmers, and even

STRANGE NEWS

FROM

VIRGINIA;

Being a full and true

ACCOUNT

OF THE

LIFE and DEATH

OF

Nathanael Bacon Esquire,

Who was the only Cause and Original of all the late Troubles in that COUNTRY.

With a full Relation of all the Accidents which have happened in the late War there between the Christians and Indians.

LONDON,
Printed for *William Harris,* next door to the Turn-Stile without *Moor-gate.* 1677.

News of the Rebellion

A pamphlet printed in London provided details about Bacon's Rebellion.

slaves against Virginia's wealthiest planters and political leaders. But Bacon was also a rich squire's spoiled son with a talent for trouble. It was his ruthless assaults against peaceful Indians and his greed for power and land rather than any commitment to democratic principles that sparked his conflict with the governing authorities.

Bacon despised indigenous people and resolved to kill them all. Berkeley opposed Bacon's genocidal plan not because he liked Indians but because he wanted to protect his lucrative monopoly over the deerskin trade. Bacon ordered the governor arrested. Berkeley's forces resisted—but only feebly—and Bacon's men burned Jamestown. Bacon, however, could not savor the victory long; he fell ill and died a month later.

Governor Berkeley quickly regained control, hanged twenty-three rebels, and confiscated several estates. For such severity the king denounced Berkeley as a "fool" and recalled him to England, where he died within a year. A royal commission made peace treaties with the remaining Indians, about 1,500 of whose descendants still live in Virginia on tiny reservations guaranteed them by the king in 1677. The result of Bacon's Rebellion was that new lands were opened to the colonists, and the wealthy planters became more cooperative with the small farmers. But the rebellion by landless whites also convinced many large planters that they would be better served by bringing in more enslaved Africans to work their fields.

MARYLAND   In 1634, ten years after Virginia became a royal colony, a neighboring settlement appeared on the northern shores of Chesapeake Bay. Named Maryland in honor of English queen Henrietta Maria, it was granted to Lord Baltimore by King Charles I and became the first **proprietary colony**—that is, it was owned by an individual, not by a joint-stock company. Sir George Calvert, the first Lord Baltimore, converted to Catholicism in 1625 and sought the American colony as a refuge for persecuted English Catholics. His son, Cecilius Calvert, the second Lord Baltimore, actually founded the colony.

In 1634, Calvert planted the first settlement in Maryland at St. Marys, near the mouth of the Potomac River. Calvert recruited Catholic gentlemen as landholders, but a majority of the indentured servants were Protestants. The charter gave Calvert power to make laws with the consent of the freemen (all property holders). The first legislative assembly met in 1635 and divided into two houses in 1650, with governor and council sitting separately, an action instigated by the predominantly Protestant freemen—largely immigrants from Virginia and former servants who had become landholders. The charter also empowered the proprietor to grant huge

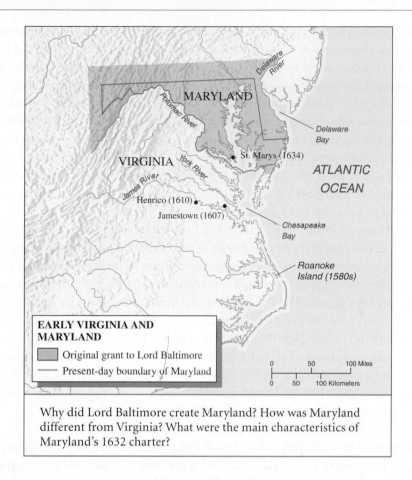

EARLY VIRGINIA AND MARYLAND

Why did Lord Baltimore create Maryland? How was Maryland different from Virginia? What were the main characteristics of Maryland's 1632 charter?

manorial estates, and Maryland had some sixty before 1676, but the Lords Baltimore soon found that to recruit settlers they had to offer them small farms, most of which grew tobacco. Unlike Virginia, which struggled for years to reach economic viability, Maryland prospered quickly because of its ability to grow tobacco. And its long coastline along the Chesapeake Bay gave planters easy access to shipping.

SETTLING NEW ENGLAND

Far to the north of the Chesapeake Bay colonies, quite different English settlements were emerging. The New England colonists were generally made up of middle-class families that could pay their own way across the Atlantic. In the Northeast there were relatively few indentured servants, and there was no planter elite. Most male settlers were small farmers, merchants, seamen, or fishermen. New England also attracted more women than did the southern colonies. Although its soil was not as fertile as that of the Chesapeake and its growing season much shorter, New England was a much healthier place to settle. Because of its colder climate, it avoided the infectious diseases that ravaged the southern colonies. Life expectancy was much longer. During the seventeenth century only 21,000 colonists arrived in New England, compared with the 120,000 who went to the Chesapeake Bay colonies. But by 1700, New England's white population exceeded that of Maryland and Virginia.

Unlike the early Jamestown colonists who arrived in America seeking adventure and profit, most early New Englanders were motivated by religious ideals. They were devout **Puritans** who embraced a much more rigorous Protestant faith than did the Anglican colonists who settled Virginia and Maryland. In 1650, for example, Massachusetts had eight times as many ministers as Virginia. The Puritans who arrived in America were on a divine mission to create a model Christian society living according to God's commandments. In the New World these self-described "saints" intended to purify their churches of all Catholic and Anglican rituals and enact a code of laws and a government structure based upon biblical principles. Such a holy settlement, they hoped, would provide a beacon of righteousness for a wicked England to emulate.

PLYMOUTH   In 1620 a band of Puritan refugees heading for Virginia strayed off course and made landfall at Cape Cod, off the southern coast of what became Massachusetts. These "Pilgrims" belonged to the most radical sect of Puritans, the Separatists (also called Nonconformists). The Church of England, according to the Puritans, had retained too many vestiges of Catholicism. Viewing themselves as the "godly," they demanded that the Anglican Church rid itself of "papist" rituals. No use of holy water. No elegant robes (vestments). No jeweled gold crosses. No worship of saints and relics. No kneeling for communion. No "viperous" bishops and archbishops. No organ music.

The Separatists went further. Having decided that the Church of England could not be fixed, they resolved to create their own godly congregations. Such rebelliousness infuriated the leaders of the Church of England. During the late sixteenth century, Separatists were "hunted & persecuted on every side." English authorities imprisoned Separatist leaders, three of whom were hanged, drawn, and quartered. King James I resolved to eliminate the Puritan Separatists. "I shall make them conform," he vowed in 1604, "or I will hurry them out of the land or do worse." Many Separatists fled to Holland to escape persecution. After ten years in the Dutch city of Leiden, they decided to move to America.

In 1620, about a hundred men, women, and children, led by William Bradford, crammed aboard the tiny *Mayflower*. Their ranks included both "saints" (people recognized as having been selected by God for salvation) and "strangers" (those yet to receive the gift of grace). The stormy voyage led them to Cape Cod. "Being thus arrived at safe harbor, and brought safe to land," William Bradford wrote, "they fell upon their knees and blessed the God of Heaven who had brought them over the vast and furious ocean." Since they were outside the jurisdiction of any organized government, forty-one of the Pilgrim leaders entered into the Mayflower Compact, a formal agreement to abide by the laws made by leaders of their own choosing.

On December 26 the *Mayflower* reached harbor at the place the Pilgrims named Plymouth, after the English port from which they had embarked, and they built dwellings on the site of an abandoned indigenous village. Nearly half of them died of disease over the winter, but in the spring of 1621 the colonists met Squanto, a Indian who showed them how to grow corn and catch fish. By autumn the Pilgrims had a bumper crop of corn and a flourishing fur trade. To celebrate, they held a harvest feast with the Indians. That event provided the inspiration for what has become the annual Thanksgiving holiday in the United States.

Throughout its existence, until it was absorbed into Massachusetts in 1691, the Plymouth colony held a land grant but no charter of government from any English authority. Their government grew instead out of the Mayflower Compact, which was a covenant (or agreement) to form a church. Thus the civil government grew naturally out of the church government, and the members of each were identical at the start. The signers of the compact at first met as the General Court, which chose the governor and his assistants (or council). Others were later admitted as members, or "freemen," but only church members were eligible. Eventually, as the colony grew, the General Court became a body of representatives from the various towns.

MASSACHUSETTS BAY The Plymouth colony's population never rose above 7,000, and after ten years it was overshadowed by its larger neighbor, the Massachusetts Bay Colony. That colony, too, was intended to be a holy commonwealth bound together in the harmonious worship of God. Like the Pilgrims, most of the Puritans who colonized Massachusetts Bay were Congregationalists, who formed self-governing churches with

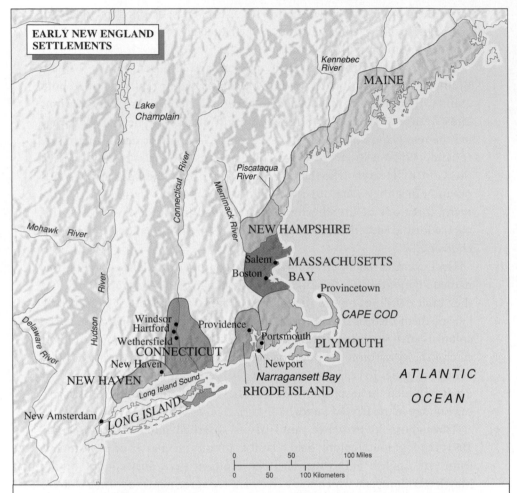

EARLY NEW ENGLAND SETTLEMENTS

Kennebec River

MAINE

Lake Champlain

Connecticut River

Merrimack River

Piscataqua River

Mohawk River

NEW HAMPSHIRE

Salem

MASSACHUSETTS BAY

Boston

Provincetown

River

CAPE COD

Delaware River

Hudson River

Windsor
Hartford
Wethersfield
CONNECTICUT
New Haven

Providence

Portsmouth

PLYMOUTH

NEW HAVEN

Newport

Narragansett Bay

RHODE ISLAND

ATLANTIC

OCEAN

New Amsterdam

Long Island Sound

LONG ISLAND

| 0 | 50 | 100 Miles |
| 0 | 50 | 100 Kilometers |

Why did European settlers first populate the Plymouth colony? How were the settlers of the Massachusetts Bay Colony different from those of Plymouth? What was the origin of the Rhode Island colony?

membership limited to "visible saints"—those who could demonstrate receipt of the gift of God's grace. But unlike the Plymouth Separatists, the Puritans still hoped to reform ("purify") the Church of England from within, and therefore they were called Nonseparating Congregationalists.

In 1629, King Charles I had chartered a joint-stock company called the Massachusetts Bay Company. It consisted of a group of English Puritans led by **John Winthrop**, a lawyer animated by profound religious convictions. Winthrop resolved to use the colony as a refuge for persecuted Puritans. To do so, he shrewdly took advantage of a fateful omission in the royal charter for the Massachusetts Bay Company: the usual proviso that the joint-stock company maintain its home office in England. Winthrop's group took its charter with them, thereby transferring government authority to Massachusetts Bay, where they hoped to ensure local control. So unlike the Virginia Company, which ruled Jamestown from London, the Massachusetts Bay Company was self-governing.

John Winthrop

The first governor of Massachusetts Bay Colony, in whose vision the colony would be as "a city upon a hill."

In 1630 the *Arbella*, with John Winthrop and the charter aboard, embarked with ten other ships for Massachusetts. There were 700 Puritans on board. Some 200 of the exiles died in the crossing. In "A Modell of Christian Charity," a lay sermon delivered on board, Winthrop told his fellow Puritans that they were a chosen people on a divine mission: "We must consider that we shall be a city upon a hill"—a shining example to England of what a godly community could be. They landed in Massachusetts, and by the end of the year seventeen ships bearing 1,000 more colonists had arrived. As settlers—both Puritan and non-Puritan—poured into the region, Boston became the new colony's chief city and capital.

It is hard to exaggerate the crucial role played by John Winthrop in establishing the Massachusetts Bay Colony. He displayed extraordinary leadership abilities. A devout pragmatist who often governed as an enlightened despot, Winthrop prized stability and order and hated democracy, which he called the "worst of all forms of government." Like many Puritan leaders, Winthrop believed that enforcing religious orthodoxy (the "true religion") and ensuring civil order justified the persecution of dissenters and heretics. Dissenters, whether they were Catholics, Anglicans, Quakers, or Baptists, would be punished, imprisoned, banished, or executed.

The *Arbella* migrants were the vanguard of a massive movement, the Great Migration, which carried some 80,000 Britons to new settlements around the world over the next decade. Most of them traveled to the Americas. They went not only to New England and the Chesapeake Bay colonies but also to the islands in the West Indies: St. Christopher (first settled in

1624), Barbados (1625), Nevis (1632), Montserrat (1632), Antigua (1632), and Jamaica (1655). During the first half of the seventeenth century, more English emigrants lived on the "sugar islands" in the Caribbean than in New England and the Chesapeake colonies. The West Indian islands started out to grow tobacco but ended up in the more profitable business of producing sugar cane. By the late eighteenth century, the value of commerce from Jamaica alone—sugar, slaves, and molasses—was greater than all of the trade generated by the North American colonies.

The transfer of the Massachusetts charter, whereby an English trading company evolved into a provincial government, was a unique venture in colonization. Under the royal charter, power rested with the Massachusetts General Court, which elected the governor and the assistants. The General Court consisted of shareholders, called freemen. At first the freemen had no power except to choose "assistants," who in turn chose the governor and deputy governor. In 1634, however, the freemen turned themselves into a representative body called the General Court, with two or three deputies to represent each town. A final stage in the evolution of the government came in 1644, when the General Court divided itself into a bicameral assembly, with all decisions requiring a majority in each house.

Thus, over a period of fourteen years, the Massachusetts Bay Company, a trading corporation, evolved into the governing body of a holy commonwealth. Membership in a Puritan church replaced the purchase of stock as the means of becoming a freeman, which was to say a voter. The General Court, like Parliament, had two houses: the House of Assistants, corresponding roughly to the House of Lords, and the House of Deputies, corresponding to the House of Commons. Although the charter remained unchanged, government was quite different from the original expectation.

RHODE ISLAND   More by accident than design, Massachusetts became the staging area for the rest of New England as new colonies grew out of religious quarrels that prompted some to leave the original colony. Young **Roger Williams** (1603–1683), who had arrived from England in 1631, was among the first to cause problems, precisely because he was the purest of Puritans. He criticized the failure of his Massachusetts brethren to repudiate all elements of the "whorish" Church of England. Whereas John Winthrop cherished authority, Williams championed liberty and promoted mercy. Williams was one of a small but growing number of Puritans who posed a provocative question: If one's salvation depends solely upon God's grace, why bother to have churches at all? Why not endow individuals with the authority to exercise their free will in worshipping God?

In Williams's view the purity of the church required complete separation of church and state and freedom from all coercion in matters of faith. "Forced worship," he declared, "stinks in God's nostrils." Governments should be impartial regarding religions: all faiths should be treated equally; the individual conscience (a "most precious and invaluable Jewel") should be sacrosanct. He resisted the attempts by governmental authorities to force the Indians to abandon their "own religions."

Such radical views prompted the church to expel Williams. The General Court then banished him to England. Williams, however, slipped away with his family and a few followers and found shelter among the Narragansetts. In 1636, he established the town of Providence at the head of Narragansett Bay, the first permanent settlement in Rhode Island and the first in America to allow freedom of religion and to prohibit residents from "invading or molesting" the Indians. In Rhode Island, Williams welcomed all who fled religious persecution in Massachusetts Bay, including Baptists, Quakers, and Jews. For their part, Boston officials came to view Rhode Island as a refuge for rogues. Thus the colony of Rhode Island and Providence Plantations, the smallest in America, began in Narragansett Bay as a refuge for dissenters who agreed that the state had no right to coerce religious belief. In 1652 Rhode Island passed the first law in North America outlawing slavery.

ANNE HUTCHINSON Roger Williams was only one of several prominent Puritan dissenters. Another, **Anne Hutchinson**, quarreled with the Puritan leaders for different reasons. She was the articulate, strong-willed, intelligent wife of a prominent merchant. Hutchinson raised thirteen children, served as a healer and midwife, and hosted meetings in her Boston home to discuss sermons. Soon, however, the discussions turned into well-attended forums for Hutchinson's own commentaries on religious matters. Blessed with vast biblical knowledge and a quick wit, she claimed to have experienced direct revelations from the

The Trial of Anne Hutchinson

In this nineteenth-century wood engraving, Anne Hutchinson stands her ground against charges of heresy from the leaders of Puritan Boston.

Holy Spirit that revealed which of her neighbors had been saved and which were damned, including ministers.

A pregnant Hutchinson was hauled before the General Court in 1637, and for two days she sparred on equal terms with the magistrates and ministers. Her ability to cite chapter-and-verse biblical defenses of her actions led an exasperated Governor Winthrop at one point to explode, "We do not mean to discourse with those of your sex." He found Hutchinson to be "a woman of haughty and fierce carriage, of a nimble wit and active spirit, and a very voluble tongue." As the trial continued, an overwrought Hutchinson was eventually lured into convicting herself by claiming direct revelations from God—blasphemy in the eyes of orthodox Puritans.

Banished in 1638 as a leper not fit for "our society," Hutchinson settled with her family and about sixty followers on an island south of Providence, near what is now Portsmouth, Rhode Island. But the arduous journey had taken its toll. Hutchinson grew sick, and her baby was stillborn, leading her critics in Massachusetts to assert that the "monstrous birth" was God's way of punishing her sins. Hutchinson's spirits never recovered. After her husband's death, in 1642, she moved near New York City, then under Dutch jurisdiction, and the following year she and six of her children were massacred during an attack by Indians. Her fate, wrote a vindictive Winthrop, was "a special manifestation of divine justice."

NEW ENGLAND EXPANDS Connecticut had a more conventional beginning than Rhode Island. In 1633 a group from Plymouth settled in the Connecticut River valley. Three years later Thomas Hooker led three entire church congregations from Massachusetts Bay to the Connecticut River towns of Wethersfield, Windsor, and Hartford. In 1637 the inhabitants organized the self-governing colony of Connecticut. Two years later the Connecticut General Court adopted the Fundamental Orders, a series of laws that provided for a "Christian Commonwealth" like that of Massachusetts, except that voting was not limited to church members. The Connecticut constitution specified that the Congregational churches would be the colony's official religion, supported by governmental tax revenues and protected by the civil authorities. The governor was commanded to rule according to "the word of God."

To the north of Massachusetts, most of what are now the states of New Hampshire and Maine was granted in 1622 by the Council for New England to Sir Ferdinando Gorges and Captain John Mason and their associates. In 1629, Mason and Gorges divided their territory, with Mason taking the southern part, which he named New Hampshire, and Gorges taking the northern part, which became the province of Maine. During the English civil strife in the early 1640s, Massachusetts took over New Hampshire and in the 1650s extended its authority to the scattered settlements in Maine. This led to lawsuits, and in 1678 English judges decided against Massachusetts in both cases. In 1679, New Hampshire became a royal colony, but Massachusetts continued to control Maine as its proprietor. A new Massachusetts charter in 1691 finally incorporated Maine into Massachusetts.

INDIANS IN NEW ENGLAND

The English settlers who poured into New England found not a "virgin land" of uninhabited wilderness but a developed region populated by over 100,000 Indians, who coped with the newcomers in different ways. Many resisted, others sought accommodation, and still others grew dependent upon European culture. In some areas, indigenous peoples survived

Algonquian ceremony celebrating harvest

As with most Indians, the Algonquians' dependence on nature for survival shaped their religious beliefs.

and even flourished in concert with settlers. In other areas, land-hungry whites quickly displaced or decimated the Indians. In general, the English colonists adopted a strategy for dealing with the Indians quite different from that of the French and the Dutch. Merchants from France and the Netherlands were not seeking gold or sugar; they were preoccupied with exploiting the profitable fur trade. The thriving commerce in animal skins—especially beaver, otter, and deer—helped to spur exploration of the vast American continent. It also alternately enriched and devastated the lives of Indians. To facilitate their acquisition of fur pelts from the Indians, the French and Dutch built permanent trading outposts along the western frontier and established amicable relations with the indigenous peoples in the region, who greatly outnumbered them. In contrast, the English colonists were more interested in pursuing their "God-given" right to fish and farm. They sought to exploit Indians rather than deal with them on an equal footing. And they ensured that the Indians, for the most part, lived separately in their own villages and towns. Their goal was subordination rather than collaboration.

THE INDIANS OF NEW ENGLAND   In Maine the Abenakis were primarily hunters and gatherers dependent upon the natural offerings of the land and waters. The men did the hunting and fishing; the women retrieved the dead game and prepared it for eating. Women were also responsible for setting up and breaking camp, gathering fruits and berries, and raising the children. The Algonquian tribes of southern New England—the Massachusetts, Nausets, Narragansetts, Pequots, and Wampanoags—were more horticultural. Their highly developed agricultural system centered on three primary crops: corn, beans, and pumpkins.

Initially the coastal Indians helped the white settlers develop a subsistence economy. They also developed a flourishing trade with the newcomers, exchanging furs for manufactured goods and "trinkets." The various Indian tribes of New England often fought among themselves, usually over disputed land. Had they been able to forge a solid alliance, they would have been better able to resist the encroachments of white settlers. As it was, they were not only fragmented but also vulnerable to the infectious diseases carried on board the ships transporting British settlers to the New World. Smallpox epidemics devastated the Indian population, leaving the coastal areas "a widowed land." Governor William Bradford of Plymouth reported that the Indians "fell sick of the smallpox, and died most miserably." By the hundreds they died "like rotten sheep."

THE PEQUOT WAR   Indians who survived the epidemics and refused to yield their lands were forced out. In 1636, settlers in Massachusetts accused a Pequot of murdering a colonist; they took revenge by setting fire to a Pequot village on the Mystic River. As Indians fled their burning huts, the Puritans shot and killed them—men, women, and children. The militia commander who ordered the massacre declared that God had guided his actions: "Thus the Lord was pleased to smite our Enemies . . . and give us their land for an Inheritance." Sassacus, the Pequot chief, organized the survivors and attacked the English. During the **Pequot War** of 1637, the colonists and their Narragansett allies killed hundreds of Pequots in their village near West Mystic, in the Connecticut River valley. The Puritan minister Cotton Mather later described the slaughter as a "sweet sacrifice" and "gave the praise thereof to God." Under the terms of the Treaty of Hartford (1638), the Pequot Nation was dissolved. Only a few colonists regretted the massacre. Roger Williams warned that the lust for land would become "as great a God with us English as God Gold was with the Spanish."

KING PHILIP'S WAR   After the Pequot War the prosperous fur trade contributed to peaceful relations between Europeans and the remaining Indians, but the relentless growth of white population and the decline of the beaver population began to reduce the eastern tribes to relative poverty. The colonial government repeatedly encroached upon indigenous settlements, forcing them to embrace English laws and customs. By 1675 the Indians and English settlers had come to know each other well—and fear each other deeply.

The era of peaceful coexistence that had begun with the Treaty of Hartford in 1638 came to a bloody end during the last quarter of the seventeenth century. Tribal leaders, especially the chief of the Wampanoags, **Metacomet** (known to the colonists as **King Philip**), resented English efforts to convert Indians to Christianity. In the fall of 1674, John Sassamon, a Christian Indian who had graduated from Harvard College, warned the English that Metacomet and the Wampanoags were preparing for war. A few months later Sassamon was found dead in a frozen pond. Colonial authorities convicted three Wampanoags of murder and hanged them. Enraged Wampanoag warriors then attacked and burned Puritan farms on June 20, 1675. Three days later an Englishman shot a Wampanoag, and the Wampanoags retaliated by ambushing and beheading a group of Puritans.

Both sides suffered incredible losses in what came to be called King Philip's War, or Metacomet's War. The fighting killed more people and caused more destruction in New England in proportion to the population than any American conflict since. Bands of warriors assaulted fifty towns. Within a year the Indians were threatening Boston itself. The situation was so desperate that the colonies instituted America's first conscription laws, drafting into the militia all males between the ages of sixteen and sixty. Finally, however, shortages of food and ammunition and staggering casualties wore down indigenous resistance. Some of the tribes surrendered, a few succumbed to disease, while others fled to the west. Those who remained were forced to resettle in villages supervised by white settlers. Metacomet initially escaped, only to be hunted down and killed in 1676. The victorious colonists marched his severed head to Plymouth, where it sat atop a pole for twenty years, a gruesome reminder of the British determination to control the Indians. King Philip's War devastated the indigenous Indian culture in New England.

SETTLING THE CAROLINAS

The Restoration of Charles II to the English throne in 1660 revived interest in colonial expansion. Within twelve years the English would conquer New Netherland, settle Carolina, and nearly fill out the shape of the colonies. In the middle region, formerly claimed by the Dutch, four new colonies emerged: New York, New Jersey, Pennsylvania, and Delaware. The new colonies were proprietary, awarded by the king to men ("proprietors") who had remained loyal to the monarchy during the civil war, who had brought about his restoration, or in one case, to whom he was indebted. In 1663, for example, King Charles II granted Carolina to eight prominent allies, who became lords proprietors (owners) of the region.

THE CAROLINAS   From the start Carolina comprised two widely separated areas of settlement, which eventually became two distinct colonies. The northernmost part, long called Albemarle, had been settled in the 1650s by colonists who had drifted southward from Virginia. For half a century, Albemarle remained a remote scattering of farmers along the shores of Albemarle Sound. The eight lords proprietors to whom the king had given Carolina neglected Albemarle and instead focused on more promising sites to the south. They recruited seasoned British planters from the Caribbean island of Barbados to replicate in South Carolina the profitable West Indian sugar-plantation system based on the labor of enslaved Africans. The first British colonists arrived in South Carolina in 1669 at Charles Town (later

EARLY SETTLEMENTS IN THE SOUTH

VIRGINIA

James River

APPALACHIAN MOUNTAINS

Roanoke River

PIEDMONT

Albemarle Sound

Occaneechi Trading Path

Bath

Roanoke Island

Cape Fear River

NORTH CAROLINA

SOUTH CAROLINA

Savannah River

Ocoñee R.

Ashley River

Cooper River

Charles Town

GEORGIA

Altamaha River

Savannah

ATLANTIC OCEAN

Added to Georgia, 1763

St. Marys River

FLORIDA (Spanish)

St. Augustine (Spanish)

GULF OF MEXICO

| 0 | 100 | 200 Miles |
| 0 | 100 | 200 Kilometers |

How were the Carolina colonies created? What were the impediments to settling North Carolina? How did the lords proprietors settle South Carolina? What were the major items traded by settlers in South Carolina?

named Charleston). Over the next twenty years, half the South Carolina colonists came from Barbados.

The government of South Carolina rested upon one of the most curious documents of colonial history, the Fundamental Constitutions of Carolina, drawn up by one of the eight proprietors, Lord Anthony Ashley Cooper, with the help of his secretary, the philosopher John Locke. Its cumbersome frame of government and its provisions for an elaborate nobility had little effect in the colony except to encourage a practice of large land grants. From the beginning, however, smaller headrights (land grants) were given to every immigrant who could afford the cost of transit. The most enticing constitutional provision was a grant of religious toleration, designed to encourage immigration, which gave South Carolina a greater degree of religious freedom (extending even to Jews and "heathens") than England or any other colony except Rhode Island and, once it was established, Pennsylvania.

South Carolina became a separate royal colony in 1719. North Carolina remained under the proprietors' rule for ten more years, until they transferred their governing rights to the British Crown.

ENSLAVING INDIANS   The eight English proprietors of South Carolina wanted the colony to focus on producing commercial crops (staples). Such production took time to develop, however. Land had to be cleared and then crops planted, harvested, transported, and sold. These activities required laborers. Some Carolina planters brought enslaved Africans and white indentured servants with them from British-controlled islands in the West Indies. Yet slaves and servants were expensive to purchase and support. The quickest way to raise capital in the early years of South Carolina's development was through trade with Indians.

In the late seventeenth century, English merchants began traveling southward from Virginia into the Piedmont region of Carolina, where they developed a prosperous trade with the Catawbas. By 1690, traders from Charles Town, South Carolina, had made their way up the Savannah River to arrange deals with the Cherokees, Creeks, and Chickasaws. Between 1699 and 1715, Carolina exported to England an average of 54,000 deerskins per

The Broiling of Their Fish over the Flame

In this drawing by John White, Algonquian men in North Carolina broil fish, a dietary staple of coastal societies.

year. Europeans, in turn, transformed the valuable hides into bookbindings, gloves, belts, hats, and work aprons. The voracious demand for the soft skins almost exterminated the deer population.

The growing trade with the English exposed indigenous peoples to contagious diseases that decimated the population. Commercial activity also entwined Indians in a dependent relationship with Europeans that would prove disastrous to their traditional way of life. Beyond capturing and enslaving Indians, the English traders began providing the Indians with goods, firearms, and rum as incentives to persuade them to capture members of rival tribes to be sold as slaves. Because indigenous captives often ran away, the traders preferred to ship them to New York, Boston, and the West Indies and import enslaved Africans to work in the Carolinas.

The profitability of indigenous captives prompted a frenzy of slaving activity among white settlers. Slave traders turned tribes against one another in order to ensure a continuous supply of captives. As many as 50,000 Indians, most of them women and children, were sold as slaves in Charles Town between 1670 and 1715. More enslaved Indians were exported during that period than Africans were imported. Thousands more captured Indians circulated through New England ports. The burgeoning trade in enslaved Indians triggered bitter struggles between tribes, gave rise to unprecedented colonial warfare, and spawned massive internal migrations across the southern colonies.

THE MIDDLE COLONIES AND GEORGIA

NEW NETHERLAND BECOMES NEW YORK   During the early seventeenth century, having gained its independence from Spain, the tiny, densely populated nation of the Netherlands (Holland) emerged as a maritime and financial giant. By 1670 the mostly Protestant Dutch had the largest merchant fleet in the world and the highest standard of living. They controlled northern European commerce and became one of the most diverse societies in Europe. The extraordinary success of the Netherlands also proved to be its downfall, however. Like imperial Spain, the Dutch Empire expanded too rapidly; they could not efficiently manage their far-flung global possessions. It did not take long for European rivals to exploit the weak points in the lucrative Dutch Empire. By the mid–seventeenth century, England and the Netherlands were locked in ferocious commercial warfare.

In London, King Charles II resolved to pluck out that old thorn in the side of the English colonies in America: **New Netherland**. The Dutch colony was older than New England. The Dutch East India Company (organized in 1602) had hired an English captain, Henry Hudson, to explore America in hopes of finding a northwest passage to the spice-rich Indies. Sailing along the upper coast of North America in 1609, Hudson had discovered Delaware Bay. He also explored the river named for him. Like Virginia and Massachusetts, New Netherland was created as a profit-making enterprise. In 1610 the Dutch established lucrative fur-trading posts on Manhattan Island and upriver at Fort Orange (later Albany). In 1626, Governor Peter Minuit purchased Manhattan from the Indians for 60 gilders, or about $1000 in current values. The Dutch then built a fort at the lower end of the island. The village of New Amsterdam (later New York City), which grew up around the fort, became the capital of New Netherland. Unlike their Puritan counterparts in Massachusetts Bay, the Dutch in New Amsterdam were preoccupied more with profits and freedoms than with piety and restrictions. They embraced free enterprise and ethnic and religious pluralism.

Dutch settlements gradually dispersed in every direction in which furs might be found. In 1638 a Swedish trading company established Fort Christina at the site of present-day Wilmington, Delaware, and scattered a few hundred settlers up and down the Delaware River. The Dutch in 1655 took control of New Sweden. The chief contribution of the short-lived New Sweden to American culture was the idea of the log cabin, which the Swedes and a few Finnish settlers had brought from the woods of Scandinavia to Delaware.

Like the French, the Dutch focused on the fur trade. The European demand for beaver hats created huge profits. In 1629, however, the Dutch West India Company decided that it needed a mass of settlers to help protect the colony's "front door" at the mouth of the Hudson River. It provided that any stockholder might obtain a large estate (a patroonship) in exchange for peopling it with fifty adults within four years. The "patroon" was obligated to supply cattle, tools, and buildings. His tenants, in turn, paid him rent. The experiment amounted to transplanting the feudal manor to the New World, and it met with as little luck as similar efforts in Maryland and South Carolina. Volunteers for serfdom were hard to find when there was land to be had elsewhere; most settlers took advantage of the company's provision that one could have as farms (*bouweries*) all the lands one could improve.

The New Netherland government was under the almost absolute control of a governor sent out by the Dutch West India Company. The governors were mostly stubborn autocrats, either corrupt or inept, and especially clumsy at Indian relations. They depended upon a small army garrison for defense, and the inhabitants were hardly devoted to the Dutch government.

New Amsterdam was one of the most ethnically diverse colonial cities. Its residents included Swedes, Norwegians, Spaniards, Sephardic Jews, free blacks, English, Germans, and Finns—as well as Dutch. The ethnically diverse colonists prized their liberties and lived in a smoldering state of near mutiny against the colony's governors. In fact, in 1664 they showed almost total indifference when Governor Peter Stuyvesant called them to arms against a threatening British fleet. Almost defenseless, the old soldier Stuyvesant blustered and stomped about on his wooden leg but finally surrendered without firing a shot.

The English plan to conquer New Netherland had been hatched by the Duke of York, later King James II. When he predicted that New Netherland could easily be conquered, his brother King Charles II granted the region to him. The English thus transformed New Amsterdam into New York City and Fort Orange into Albany. The Dutch, however, left a permanent imprint on the land and the language: place-names such as Wall Street (the original wall being for protection against Indians), and Broadway (Breede Wegh) remained, along with family names like Rensselaer, Roosevelt, and Van Buren. The Dutch presence lingered, too, in the Dutch Reformed (Calvinist) Church; in words like *boss, cookie, crib, snoop, stoop, spook,* and *kill* (for "creek"); and in the legendary Santa Claus and in Washington Irving's Rip van Winkle.

JUDAISM IN NORTH AMERICA   In September 1654, ten years before the English took control of the Dutch colony of New Netherland, a French ship arrived in New Amsterdam (New York) Harbor. On board were twenty-three Sephardi, Jews of Spanish-Portuguese descent. Penniless and weary, they had come seeking refuge from Brazil, where they had earlier fled from Spain and Portugal after being exiled by the Catholic Inquisition. They were the first Jewish settlers to arrive in North America, and they were not readily embraced. Leading merchants as well as members of the Dutch Reformed Church asked Peter Stuyvesant, the dictatorial Dutch director general of New Netherland, to expel them. Stuyvesant despised Jews, Lutherans, Catholics, and Quakers. He characterized Jews as "deceitful," "very repugnant," and "blasphemous." Stuyvesant's employers at the Dutch West India Company disagreed, however. Early in 1655 they ordered him to accommodate the homeless Jews, explaining that he should "allow every one to have his own belief, as long as he behaves quietly and legally, gives no offense to his neighbor and does not oppose the government." But it would not be until the late seventeenth century that Jews could worship in public. Such restrictions help explain why the American Jewish community grew so slowly. In 1773, over 100 years after the first Jewish refugees arrived in New Amsterdam, Jews represented only one tenth of 1 percent of the entire colonial population. Not until the nineteenth century would the American Jewish community experience dramatic growth.

THE IROQUOIS LEAGUE   One of the most significant effects of European settlement in North America during the seventeenth century was the intensification of warfare among Indians. The same combination of forces that decimated the indigenous populations of New England and the Carolinas affected the tribes around New York City and the lower Hudson River valley. Dissension among the Indians and their susceptibility to infectious disease left them vulnerable to exploitation by whites and other Indians.

In the interior of New York, however, a different situation arose. There the tribes of the Iroquois (an Algonquian term signifying "Snake" or "Terrifying Man") forged an alliance so strong that the outnumbered Dutch and, later, English traders were forced to work with Indians in exploiting the lucrative beaver trade. By the early 1600s some fifty sachems (chiefs) governed the 12,000 members of the **Iroquois League**, or Iroquois Confederacy. When the Iroquois began to deplete the local game during the 1640s, they used firearms supplied by their Dutch trading partners to seize the Canadian hunting grounds of the neighboring Hurons and Eries. The relentless search for furs and captives led Iroquois war parties to range far across what is today eastern North America. They gained control over a huge area from the St. Lawrence River to Tennessee and from Maine to Michigan. For over twenty years, warfare raged across the Great Lakes region. In the 1690s the French and their Indian allies destroyed Iroquois crops and villages, infected them with smallpox, and reduced the male population by more than a third. Facing extermination, the Iroquois made peace with the French in 1701. During the first half of the eighteenth century, they maintained a shrewd neutrality in the struggle between the two rival European powers, which enabled them to play the British off against the French while creating a thriving fur trade for themselves.

NEW JERSEY   Shortly after the conquest of New Netherland, the Duke of York granted his lands between the Hudson and Delaware Rivers to Sir George Carteret and Lord John Berkeley (brother of Virginia's governor) and named the territory for Carteret's native Jersey, an island in the English Channel. In 1676, by mutual agreement, New Jersey was divided by a diagonal line into East and West Jersey, with Carteret taking the east. Finally, in 1682, Carteret sold out to a group of twelve, including William Penn, who in turn brought into the partnership twelve more proprietors, for a total of twenty-four. In East Jersey, peopled at first by perhaps 200 Dutch who had crossed the Hudson River, new settlements gradually arose. In the west, facing the Delaware River, a scattering of Swedes, Finns, and Dutch remained, soon to be overwhelmed by swarms of English and Welsh Quakers, as well as German and Scots-Irish settlers. In 1702, East and West Jersey were united as the single royal colony of New Jersey.

PENNSYLVANIA AND DELAWARE   The **Quaker** sect, as the Society of Friends was called in ridicule (because they were supposed to "tremble at the word of the Lord"), became the most influential of many radical religious groups that emerged from the turbulence of the English Civil War. Founded by George Fox in about 1647, the Quakers discarded all formal sacraments and even a formal ministry, refused deference to persons of rank, used the familiar *thee* and *thou* in addressing everyone, and embraced pacifism. Quakers were subjected to intense persecution—often their zeal seemed to invite it—but never inflicted it upon others. Their tolerance extended to complete religious freedom for everyone, whatever one's belief or disbelief, and to equality of the sexes, including the full participation of women in religious affairs.

The settling of English Quakers in West Jersey encouraged other Friends to migrate, especially to the Delaware River side of the colony. And soon across the river arose William Penn's Quaker commonwealth, the colony of Pennsylvania. Penn was the son of Admiral Sir William Penn. As a student at Oxford University he had become a Quaker. Upon his father's death, Penn inherited a substantial estate, including proprietary rights to a huge tract in America. The land was named, at the king's insistence, for Penn's father: Pennsylvania (literally, "Penn's Woods").

When William Penn assumed control of the area, there was already a scattering of Dutch, Swedish, and English settlers on the west bank of the Delaware River. But Penn soon made vigorous efforts to bring more settlers. Unlike John Winthrop in Massachusetts, Penn encouraged people of different religious affiliations (as long as they believed in God) to settle in his new colony. By the end of 1681, about 1,000 settlers were living in his province. By that time a town was growing up at the junction of the Schuylkill and Delaware Rivers. Penn called it Philadelphia ("City of Brotherly Love").

The relations between the Indians and the Quakers were cordial from the beginning, because of the Quakers' friendliness and Penn's careful policy of purchasing land titles from the Indians. Penn even took the trouble to learn an indigenous language, something few colonists ever tried. For some fifty years the settlers and the Indians lived side by side in peace.

Quaker meeting

The presence of women at this meeting is evidence of Quaker views on gender equality.

The colony's government, which rested on three Frames of Government drafted by Penn, resembled that of other proprietary colonies except that the freemen (taxpayers and property owners) elected the council members as well as the assembly. The governor had no veto—although Penn, as proprietor, did. Penn hoped to show that a government could operate in accordance with Quaker principles, that it could maintain peace and order without oaths or wars, and that religion could flourish without government support and with absolute freedom of conscience.

In 1682 the Duke of York also granted Penn the area of Delaware, another part of the former Dutch territory. At first, Delaware became part of Pennsylvania, but after 1704 it was granted the right to choose its own assembly. From then until the American Revolution, it had a separate assembly but shared Pennsylvania's governor.

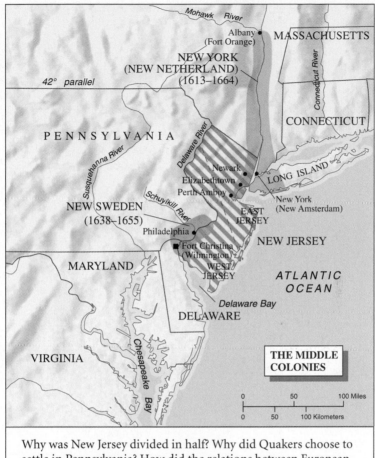

Why was New Jersey divided in half? Why did Quakers choose to settle in Pennsylvania? How did the relations between European settlers and Indians in Pennsylvania differ from such relations in the other colonies?

GEORGIA   Georgia was the last of the British continental colonies to be established—half a century after Pennsylvania. During the seventeenth century, settlers pushed southward into the borderlands between the Carolinas and Florida. They brought with them enslaved Africans and a desire to win the Indian trade from the Spanish. Each side used guns, goods, and rum to influence the Indians, and the Indians in turn played off the English against the Spanish.

In 1732, King George II gave the land between the Savannah and Altamaha Rivers to the twenty-one trustees of Georgia. In two respects, Georgia was

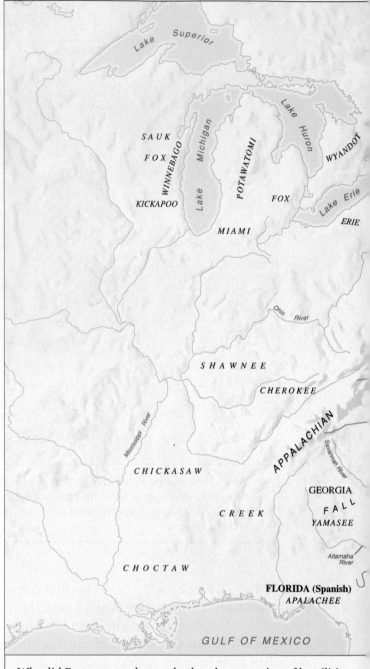

Why did European settlement lead to the expansion of hostilities among the Indians? What were the consequences of the trade and commerce between the English settlers and the southern indigenous peoples? How were the relationships between the settlers and the members of the Iroquois League different from those between settlers and tribes in other regions?

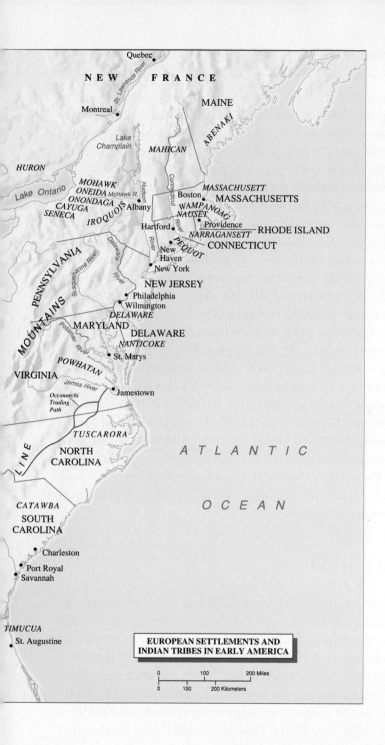

QUEBEC

NEW FRANCE

Montreal

MAINE

Lake Champlain

ABENAKI

HURON

MAHICAN

Lake Ontario

MOHAWK
ONEIDA Mohawk R.
ONONDAGA
CAYUGA Albany
SENECA

IROQUOIS

MASSACHUSETT
Boston MASSACHUSETTS
WAMPANOAG
NAUSET
Providence
NARRAGANSETT RHODE ISLAND
Hartford
PEQUOT CONNECTICUT
New Haven
New York

PENNSYLVANIA

MOUNTAINS

NEW JERSEY

Philadelphia
Wilmington
DELAWARE

MARYLAND DELAWARE
NANTICOKE
St. Marys

POWHATAN

VIRGINIA

James River
Occaneechi Trading Path
Jamestown

LINE

TUSCARORA

NORTH CAROLINA

ATLANTIC

OCEAN

CATAWBA

SOUTH CAROLINA

Charleston
Port Royal
Savannah

TIMUCUA
St. Augustine

**EUROPEAN SETTLEMENTS AND
INDIAN TRIBES IN EARLY AMERICA**

0   100   200 Miles

0   100   200 Kilometers

unique among the colonies: it was set up as a philanthropic experiment and as a military buffer against Spanish Florida. General James E. Oglethorpe was appointed to head the province. In 1733 a band of about 120 colonists founded Savannah on the coast near the mouth of the Savannah River. Carefully laid out by Oglethorpe, the old town, with its geometric pattern and numerous little parks, remains a wonderful example of city planning. Protestant refugees from Austria began to arrive in 1734, followed by Germans and German-speaking Moravians and Swiss, who made the colony for a time more German than English. The addition of Welsh, Highland Scots, Sephardic Jews, and others gave the early colony a cosmopolitan character much like that of Charleston.

As a buffer against Florida, the colony succeeded, but as a philanthropic experiment it failed. Efforts to develop silk and wine production foundered. Landholdings were limited to 500 acres, rum was prohibited, and the importation of slaves was forbidden, partly to leave room for servants brought on charity, partly to ensure security. But the utopian rules soon collapsed. The regulations against rum and slavery were widely disregarded and finally abandoned. By 1759 all restrictions on landholding had been removed.

In 1754 the trustees' charter expired, and the province reverted to the Crown. As a royal colony, Georgia acquired an effective government for the first time. The colony developed slowly over the next decade but grew rapidly in population and wealth after 1763. Instead of wine and silk, as was Oglethorpe's plan, Georgians exported rice, indigo, lumber, beef, and pork and carried on a lively trade with the West Indies. The colony had inadvertently become a commercial success.

THRIVING COLONIES

By the early eighteenth century the English had outstripped both the French and the Spanish in the New World. British America had become the most populous, prosperous, and powerful region on the continent. By the mid–seventeenth century, American colonists on average were better fed, clothed, and housed than their counterparts in Europe, where a majority of the people lived in destitution. But the English colonization of North America included failures as well as successes. Many settlers found only hard labor and an early death in the New World. Others flourished only because they exploited Indians, indentured servants, or Africans.

The English succeeded in creating a lasting American empire because of crucial advantages they had over their European rivals. The centralized control imposed by the monarchs of Spain and France eventually hobbled innovation.

By contrast, the enterprising English acted by private investment and with a minimum of royal control. Not a single colony was begun at the direct initiative of the Crown. In the English colonies poor immigrants had a much greater chance of getting at least a small parcel of land. The English and Dutch, unlike their rivals, welcomed people from a variety of nationalities and dissenting religious sects who came in search of a new life or a safe harbor. And a greater degree of self-government made the English colonies more responsive to new circumstances—though they were sometimes stymied by controversy.

The compact pattern of English settlement, whereby colonies were settled contiguous to one another, contrasted sharply with Spain's far-flung conquests and France's far-reaching trade routes to the interior by way of the St. Lawrence and Mississippi Rivers. Geography reinforced England's bent for the concentrated settlement of its colonies. The rivers and bays that indent the Atlantic seaboard served as communication arteries along which colonies first sprang up, but no great river offered a highway to the far interior. For 150 years the farthest outreach of British settlement stopped at the slopes of the Appalachian Mountains. To the east lay the wide expanse of ocean, which served not only as a highway for the transport of people, ideas, commerce, and ways of life from Europe to America but also as a barrier that separated old ideas from new, allowing the new to evolve in a "new world."

End of Chapter Review

CHAPTER SUMMARY

- **British Colonization** Profit from minerals and exotic products was the over-riding objective of the joint-stock Virginia Company, organized to finance the 1607 Jamestown venture. Proprietary colonies, such as Maryland and the Carolinas, were given to individuals who desired wealth but did not usually become colonists themselves. The colonies were also an outlet for Britain's poor.

- **Jamestown Hardships** The early years of Jamestown were grim because food was in short supply except when the Powhatans provided corn. Relations with the Indians deteriorated, however, culminating in an Indian uprising in 1622. English investors searched for profits from minerals and trade with Indians, not from agriculture. A high mortality rate caused a scarcity of labor.

- **Religion and Colonization** Religion was the primary motivation for the founding of several colonies. The Plymouth colony was founded by separatists on a mission to build a Christian commonwealth outside the structure of the Anglican Church. The Massachusetts Bay Colony was created by Puritans who wished to purify the established church. Rhode Island was established by Roger Williams, a religious dissenter from Massachusetts. Maryland was founded as a refuge for English Catholics. William Penn, a Quaker, founded Pennsylvania and invited Europe's persecuted religious sects to his colony. The Dutch, with their policy of toleration, allowed members of all faiths to settle in New Netherland.

- **Indian Relations** Settler-Indian relations were complex. Trade with the Powhatans in Virginia enabled Jamestown to survive its early years, but brutal armed conflicts occurred as settlers invaded indigenous lands. Puritans retaliated harshly against indigenous resistance in the Pequot War of 1637 and in King Philip's War from 1675–1676. Only Roger Williams and William Penn treated Indians as equals. Conflicts in the Carolinas—the Tuscarora and Yamasee Wars—occurred because of trade of enslaved Indians and other abuses by traders. France and Spain used indigenous peoples to further their imperial ambitions, which allowed the Indians to play the European powers against each another.

- **British America** By 1700, England was a great trading empire. British America was the most populous and prosperous area of North America. Commercial rivalry between the Dutch and the English led to war, during which the Dutch colony of New Netherland surrendered to the English in 1664. Indigenous allies, such as the Iroquois, traded pelts for English goods. By relying increasingly on slave labor, the southern colonies provided England with tobacco and other plantation crops.

CHRONOLOGY

1607	Jamestown, Virginia, the first permanent English colony, is established
1616	Pocahontas marries John Rolfe
1619	First Africans arrive in English America
1620	Plymouth colony is founded; Pilgrims agree to the Mayflower Compact
1622	Indian uprising in Virginia
1630	Massachusetts Bay Colony is founded
1634	Settlement of Maryland begins
1637	Pequot War
1642–1651	English Civil War
1660	Restoration of the English monarchy
1675–1676	King Philip's War
1676	Bacon's Rebellion in Virginia
1681	Pennsylvania is established
1733	Georgia is founded

KEY TERMS & NAMES

3

COLONIAL WAYS
OF LIFE

FOCUS QUESTIONS wwnorton.com/studyspace

- What were the social, ethnic, and economic differences among the southern, middle, and New England colonies?

- What were the prevailing attitudes of English colonists toward women?

- How important was indentured servitude to the development of the colonies, and why had the system been replaced by slavery in the South by 1700?

- How did the colonies participate in international and imperial trade?

- What were the effects of the Enlightenment in America?

- How did the Great Awakening affect the colonies?

The process of carving a new civilization out of an abundant "New World" involved often violent encounters among European, African, and Native American cultures. War, duplicity, displacement, and enslavement were the tragic results. Yet on another level the process of transforming the American continent was not simply a story of conflict but also of accommodation, a story of diverse peoples and cultures engaged in the everyday tasks of building homes, planting crops, trading goods, raising families, enforcing laws, and worshipping their gods. Those who colonized America during the seventeenth and eighteenth centuries were part of a massive social migration occurring throughout Europe and Africa. Everywhere, it seemed, people were moving from farms to villages, from villages to cities, and from homelands to colonies. They moved for different reasons. Most Britons and Europeans were responding to powerful social and economic forces as rapid population growth and the rise of commercial agriculture squeezed people off the land. Many migrants traveled in search of political security or religious freedom. A tragic exception was the Africans, who were captured and transported to new lands against their will.

Those who settled in colonial America were mostly young (over half were under twenty-five), male, and poor. Almost half were indentured servants or slaves, and during the eighteenth century England would transport some 50,000 convicts to the North American colonies. Only about a third of the settlers came with their families. Once in America, many of the newcomers kept moving, trying to take advantage of inexpensive western land or new business opportunities. Whatever their status or ambition, this extraordinary mosaic of adventurous people created America's enduring institutions and values, as well as its distinctive spirit and energy.

THE SHAPE OF EARLY AMERICA

POPULATION GROWTH England's first footholds in America were bought at a fearsome price: many settlers died in the first years. But once the brutal seasoning phase was past and the colonies were on their feet, Virginia and its successors grew rapidly. By 1750 the number of colonists had passed 1 million; by 1775 it stood at about 2.5 million. The prodigious increase of the colonial population did not go unnoticed. Benjamin Franklin, a keen observer of many things, published in 1751 his *Observations Concerning the Increase of Mankind*, in which he pointed out two facts of life that distinguished the colonies from Europe: land was plentiful and cheap, and laborers were scarce and expensive. The opposite conditions prevailed in the Old World. From this reversal of conditions flowed many of the changes that European culture underwent in America— not the least being that more land and good fortune beckoned enterprising immigrants and induced settlers to replenish the earth with large families. Where labor was

Colonial farm

This plan of a newly cleared American farm shows how trees were cut down and the stumps left to rot.

scarce, children could lend a hand and, once grown, find new land for themselves if need be. Colonists tended, as a result, to marry and start families at an earlier age than did their Old World counterparts.

BIRTHRATES AND DEATH RATES Given the better economic prospects in the colonies, a greater proportion of white women married, and the birthrate remained much higher than it did in Europe. In England the average age at marriage for women was twenty-five or twenty-six; in America it dropped to twenty. Men also married younger in the colonies than in the Old World. The birthrate rose accordingly, since women who married earlier had time for about two additional pregnancies during their childbearing years.

Equally responsible for the burgeoning colonial population was a much lower death rate than that in Europe. After the difficult first years of settlement, infants generally had a better chance of reaching maturity in the New World, and adults had a better chance of reaching old age. In seventeenth-century New England, apart from childhood mortality, men could expect to reach seventy, and women nearly that age.

This longevity resulted from several factors. Since the land was bountiful, famine seldom occurred after the first year, and although the winters were more severe than those in England, firewood was plentiful. Being younger on the whole—the average age in the new nation in 1790 was sixteen—Americans were less susceptible to disease than were Europeans. That they were more scattered than in the Old World meant they were also less exposed to infectious diseases. That began to change, of course, as cities grew and trade and travel increased. By the mid–eighteenth century the colonies were beginning to have levels of contagion much like those in Europe.

WOMEN IN THE COLONIES In contrast to New Spain and New France, British America had far more women, and this different sex ratio largely explains the difference in population growth rates among the European empires competing in the New World. Most colonists brought to America deeply rooted convictions about the inferiority of women. As one minister stressed, "the woman is a weak creature not endowed with like strength and constancy of mind." The prescribed role of women was clear: to obey and serve their husbands, nurture their children, and endure the taxing labor required to maintain their households. Governor John Winthrop insisted that a "true wife" would find contentment only "in subjection to her husband's authority." Both social custom and legal codes ensured that most women in most colonies could not vote, preach, hold office, attend public schools or colleges, bring lawsuits, make contracts, or own property.

During the colonial era, women played a crucial, if restricted, role in religious life. No denomination allowed women to be ordained as ministers. Only the Quakers let women hold church offices and preach ("exhort") in public. Puritans cited biblical passages claiming that God required "virtuous" women to submit to male authority and remain "silent" in congregational matters. Governor John Winthrop demanded that women "not meddle in such things as are proper for men" to manage.

In colonial America the religious roles of black women were quite different from those of their white counterparts. In most West African tribes, women were not subordinate to men, and women frequently served as priests and cult leaders. Furthermore, some enslaved Africans had been exposed to Christianity or Islam in Africa, through slave traders and missionaries. Most of them, however, tried to sustain their traditional African religion once they arrived in the colonies. In America, black women (and men) were often excluded from church membership for fear that Christianized slaves might seek to gain their freedom. To clarify the situation, Virginia in 1667 passed a law specifying that children of slaves would be slaves even if they had been baptized as Christians.

"WOMEN'S WORK"   In the eighteenth century, "women's work" typically involved activities in the house, garden, and yard. Farm women usually rose at four in the morning and prepared breakfast by five-thirty. They then fed and watered the livestock, woke the children, churned butter, tended the garden, prepared lunch, played with the children, worked the garden again, cooked dinner, milked the cows, got the children ready for bed, and cleaned the kitchen before retiring, at about nine. Women also combed, spun, spooled, wove, and bleached wool for clothing, knit linen and cotton, hemmed sheets, pieced quilts, made candles and soap, chopped wood, hauled water, mopped floors, and washed clothes. Female indentured servants in the southern colonies commonly worked as field hands, weeding, hoeing, and harvesting.

Despite the laws and traditions that limited the sphere of women, the scarcity of labor in the colonies created opportunities. In the towns, women commonly served as tavern hostesses and shopkeepers and occasionally also worked as doctors, printers, upholsterers, painters, silversmiths, tanners, and shipwrights—often, but not always, they were widows carrying on their husbands' trade.

Over time, the colonial environment did generate slight improvements in the status of women. The acute shortage of women in the early years made

The First, Second, and Last Scene of Mortality

Prudence Punderson's needlework (ca. 1776) shows the domestic path, from cradle to coffin, followed by most colonial women.

them more highly valued than they were in Europe, and the Puritan emphasis on a well-ordered family life led to laws protecting wives from physical abuse and allowing for divorce. In addition, colonial laws allowed wives greater control over property that they had contributed to a marriage or that was left after a husband's death. But the age-old notions of female subordination and domesticity remained firmly entrenched in colonial America. As a Massachusetts boy maintained in 1662, the superior aspect of life was "masculine and eternal; the feminine inferior and mortal."

SOCIETY AND ECONOMY IN THE SOUTHERN COLONIES

As the southern colonies matured, inequalities became more pronounced and social life grew more stratified. The wealthy ("gentry") increasingly became a class apart, distinguished by their sumptuous living and their disdain for their social "inferiors," both white and black.

RELIGION   It has often been said that Americans during the seventeenth century took religion more seriously than they have at any time since. That may have been true, but many early Americans—especially in the southern colonies—were not active communicants. One estimate holds that fewer than one in fifteen residents of the southern colonies was a church member. After 1642, Virginia governor William Berkeley decided that his colony was to be officially Anglican, and he sponsored laws requiring "all noncon-formists . . . to depart the colony." Puritans and Quakers were hounded out. By the end of the seventeenth century, Anglicanism predominated in the Chesapeake region, and it proved especially popular among the large land-holders. In the early eighteenth century it became the established (official) church throughout the South. The tone of religious belief and practice in the eighteenth-century South was less demanding than that in Puritan New England or Quaker Pennsylvania. As in England, colonial Anglicans tended to be more conservative, rational, and formal in their modes of worship than their Puritan, Quaker, or Baptist counterparts. Anglicans stressed collective rituals over personal religious experience. They did not require members to give a personal, public, and often emotional account of their conversion. Nor did they expect members to practice self-denial. Anglicans preferred ministers who stressed the reasonableness of Christianity, the goodness of God, and the capacity of humankind to practice benevolence.

CROPS   The southern colonies had one unique economic advantage: the climate. The warm weather and plentiful rainfall enabled the colonies to grow exotic staples (profitable market crops such as tobacco and rice) prized by the mother country. Virginia, as King Charles I put it, was "founded upon smoke." Tobacco production soared during the seventeenth century. "In Virginia and Maryland," wrote Governor Leonard Calvert in 1629, "Tobacco as our Staple is our All, and indeed leaves no room for anything else." After 1690, rice was as much the profitable staple crop in South Carolina as tobacco was in Virginia. Rice loves water; it flourishes in warm, moist soils, and it thrives when visited by frequent rains or watered by regular irrigation. The daily rise and fall of tidewater rivers perfectly suited a crop that required the alternate flooding and draining of fields. In addition, southern pine trees provided lumber and key items for the maritime industry. The resin from pine trees could be boiled to make tar, which was in great demand for waterproofing ropes and caulking the seams of wooden ships. From their early leadership in the production of pine tar, North Carolinians would earn the nickname of Tar Heels. In the Carolinas a cattle industry presaged life on the Great Plains—with cowboys, roundups, brandings, and long drives to the market.

Virginia plantation wharf

Southern colonial plantations were constructed with easy access to oceangoing vessels, as shown on this 1730 tobacco label.

LABOR   Voluntary indentured servitude accounted for probably half the white settlers (mostly from England, Ireland, or Germany) in all the colonies outside New England. The name derived from the indenture, or contract, by which a person promised to work for a fixed number of years in return for transportation to America. Not all the servants went voluntarily. The London underworld developed a flourishing trade in "kids" and "spirits," who were "kidnapped" or "spirited" into servitude in America. After 1717, by act of Parliament, convicts guilty of certain major crimes could escape the hangman by relocating to the colonies.

Once in the colonies, servants contracted with masters. Their rights were limited. As a Pennsylvania judge explained in 1793, **indentured servants** occupied "a middle rank between slaves and free men." They could own property but could not engage in trade. Marriage required the master's permission. Runaway servants were hunted down and punished just as runaway slaves were. Masters could whip servants and extend their indentures for bad behavior. Many servants died from disease or the exhaustion of cultivating tobacco in the broiling sun and intense humidity. In due course, however, usually after four to seven years, the indenture ended, and the servant claimed the "freedom dues" set by custom and law: money, tools, clothing, food, and occasionally small tracts of land. Some former servants did very well for themselves. In 1629 seven members of the Virginia legislature were former indentured servants. Others, including Benjamin Franklin's grandmother, married the men who had originally bought their services. Many servants died before completing their indenture, however, and most of those who served their term remained relatively poor thereafter.

COLONIAL SLAVERY   Colonial America increasingly became a land of white opportunity and black slavery. Africans were the largest ethnic group to come to British America during the colonial era. Some of the first Africans in America were treated as indentured servants, with a limited term of servitude. Those few African servants who worked out their term of indenture gained freedom, and some of them, as "free blacks," acquired slaves and white indentured servants. Gradually, however, with racist rationalizations based on color difference, lifelong servitude for black slaves became the custom—and law—of the land. Slaves cost more to buy than servants, but they served for life. By the 1660s colonial legislative assemblies had legalized lifelong slavery.

During the seventeenth and eighteenth centuries, the incredibly profitable sugar islands of the French and British West Indies and the cane fields of Portuguese Brazil had the most voracious appetite for enslaved Africans. By 1675 the British West Indies had over 100,000 slaves while the colonies in North America had only about 5,000. But as staple crops became established on the American continent and as economic growth in England slowed the number of white laborers traveling to the Americas, the demand for mostly male Indian or African slaves grew. Though British North America took less than 5 percent of the total slaves imported to the Western Hemisphere during more than three centuries of that squalid traffic, it offered better chances for survival, if few for human fulfillment.

As overall living conditions improved in the colonies, slave mortality improved. By 1730 the black slave population in Virginia and Maryland had become the first in the Western Hemisphere to achieve a self-sustaining rate of population growth. By 1750 about 80 percent of the slaves in the Chesapeake region had been born there. The natural increase of blacks in America approximated that of whites by the end of the colonial period. During the colonial era, slavery was recognized in all the colonies but was most prevalent in the southern colonies.

AFRICAN ROOTS The transport of Africans across the Atlantic to the Americas was the largest forced migration in world history. Over 10 million people made the journey, so many that it changed the trajectory of Africa's development. The vast majority of Africans were taken to Brazil or the West Indian islands. Only 5 percent of them—including twice as many men as women—were taken to British North America, often in ships built in New England and owned by merchants in Boston and Newport. Most of the enslaved were young—between the ages of fifteen and thirty.

Such aggregate statistics can be misleading, however. Enslaved Africans are so often lumped together as a social group that their great ethnic diversity is overlooked. They came from lands as remote from each other as Angola is from Senegal. They spoke as many as fifty different languages and worshipped many different gods. Some lived in large kingdoms and others in dispersed villages. All of them prized their kinship ties.

Africans preyed upon Africans, however, for centuries, rival tribes had conquered, kidnapped, enslaved, and sold one another. Slavery in Africa, how-

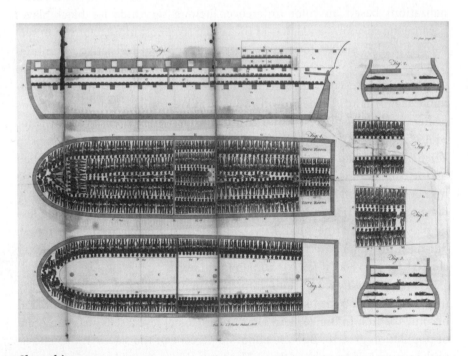

Slave ships

One in six African died while crossing the Atlantic in ships like this one, from an American diagram ca. 1808.

ever, was more benign than the culture of slavery that developed in North America. In Africa, slaves were not isolated as a distinct caste; they also lived with their captors, and their children were not automatically enslaved. The involvement of Europeans in commercial slavery changed that.

During the seventeenth and eighteenth centuries, African middlemen brought captives (debtors, thieves, war prisoners, and those who refused to convert to Islam) to dozens of "slave forts" along the Atlantic coast where they were subjected to humiliating physical inspections before being sold to European slave traders. To reduce the threat of rebellion, traders split up family and tribal members. Once purchased, the millions of people destined

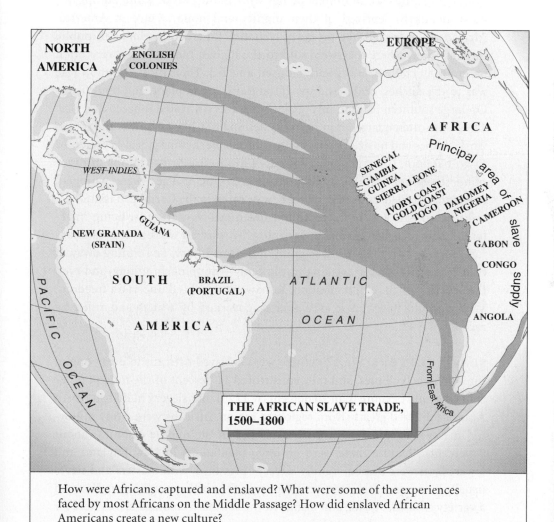

How were Africans captured and enslaved? What were some of the experiences faced by most Africans on the Middle Passage? How did enslaved African Americans create a new culture?

for slavery in the Americas were branded on the back or buttocks with a company mark, shackled, and loaded onto horrific slave ships, where they were packed tightly like animals below deck. The Africans then endured a four-week to six-month Atlantic voyage, known as the Middle Passage. It was so brutal that one in six captives died en route. Almost one in every ten slave ships experienced a revolt during the crossing. On average, twenty-five Africans were killed in such uprisings. Far more died of disease. Some committed suicide by jumping off the ships.

Slavery in the Western Hemisphere was driven by high profits and rationalized by a pervasive racism. Race-based slavery entailed the dehumanization of an entire class of human beings who, in the eyes of white Europeans, were justifiably deprived of their dignity and honor. Once in America, Africans were treated like property ("chattel"), herded in chains to public slave auctions where they were sold to the highest bidder. They were often barefoot, ill clothed, and poorly housed and fed. Their most common role was to dig ditches, drain swamps, build dams, clear, plant, and tend fields. On large southern plantations, "gangs" of slaves cultivated tobacco and rice. They were often quartered in barracks, fed in bulk, like livestock, and issued work clothes and unsized shoes so uncomfortable that many slaves preferred to go barefoot. Colonial laws allowed whites to use brutal means to discipline slaves and enforce their control over them. They were whipped, branded, shackled, castrated, or sold away, often to the Caribbean islands.

Enslaved Africans, however, found ingenious ways to resist being "mastered." Some rebelled against their captors by resisting work orders, sabotaging crops and stealing tools, feigning illness or injury, or running away. If caught, runaways faced certain punishment—whipping, branding, and even the severing of an Achilles tendon. Runaways also faced uncertain freedom. Where would they run *to* in a society governed by whites and ruled by racism?

SLAVE CULTURE   In 1700 there were enslaved Africans in every one of the American colonies, and they constituted 11 percent of the total population (it would be more than 20 percent by 1770). But slavery in British North America differed greatly from region to region. Africans were a tiny minority in New England (about 2 percent) and in the middle colonies (about 8 percent). Because there were no large plantations in New England and fewer slaves were owned, "family slavery" prevailed, with masters and slaves usually living under the same roof. Slaves in the northern colonies performed a variety of tasks, outside and inside. In the southern colonies, slaves were far more numerous, and most of them worked on farms and plantations.

African cultural heritage in the south

The survival of African culture among enslaved Americans is evident in this late-eighteenth-century painting of a South Carolina plantation. The musical instruments and pottery are of African (probably Yoruban) origin.

In the process of being forced into lives of bondage in a new world, diverse blacks from diverse homelands forged a new identity as African Americans while leaving entwined in the fabric of American culture more strands of African heritage than historians and anthropologists can ever disentangle, including new words that entered the language, such as *tabby, tote, cooter, goober, yam*, and *banana* and the names of the Coosaw, Pee Dee, and Wando Rivers.

Most significant are African influences in American music, folklore, and religious practices. On one level, slaves used such cultural activities to distract themselves from their servitude; on another level they used songs, stories, and religious preachings to circulate coded messages expressing their distaste for masters or overseers. Slave religion, a unique blend of African and Christian beliefs, was frequently practiced in secret. Its fundamental theme was deliverance: God would eventually free African Americans from slavery and open the gates to heaven's promised land. The planters, however, sought to strip slave religion of its liberationist hopes. They insisted that being "born again" as Christians had no effect upon their workers' status as slaves.

Africans brought with them to America powerful kinship ties. Even though most colonies outlawed slave marriages, many owners believed that slaves would work harder and be more stable if allowed to form families. Though many families were broken up when members were sold to different owners, slave culture retained its powerful domestic ties. It also developed gender roles distinct from those of white society. Most enslaved women were by necessity field workers as well as wives and mothers responsible for child-rearing and household affairs. Since they worked in proximity to enslaved men, they were treated more equally (for better or worse) than were most of their white counterparts.

SOCIETY AND ECONOMY IN NEW ENGLAND

There was remarkable diversity among the American colonies during the seventeenth century and after. The prevalence of slavery, for example, was much less outside the southern colonies. Other environmental, social, and economic factors also contributed to striking differences between New England and the middle Atlantic and southern regions.

TOWNSHIPS   Unlike the settlers in the southern colonies or in Dutch New Netherland, few New England colonists received huge tracts of land. Township grants were usually awarded to organized groups. A group of settlers, often already gathered into a church, would petition the general court for a town (what elsewhere was commonly called a township) and then divide its acres according to a rough principle of equity—those who invested more or had larger families or greater status might receive more land—retaining some pasture and woodland in common and holding some for later arrivals. In some early cases the towns arranged each settler's land in separate strips after the medieval practice, but over time the land was commonly divided into separate farms distant from the close-knit village.

ENTERPRISE   Early New England farmers and their families led hard lives. Simply clearing rocks from the glacier-scoured soil might require sixty days of hard labor per acre. The growing season was short, and no staple (profitable) crops grew in the harsh climate. The crops and livestock were

Profitable fisheries

Fishing for, curing, and drying codfish in Newfoundland in the early 1700s. For centuries the rich fishing grounds of the North Atlantic provided New Englanders with a prosperous industry.

those familiar to the English countryside: wheat, barley, oats, some cattle, pigs, and sheep. Many New Englanders turned to the sea for their livelihood. Cod, a commercial fish that can weigh hundreds of pounds, had been a regular element of the European diet for centuries, and the waters off the New England coast had the heaviest concentrations of cod in the world. Whales, too, abounded in New England waters and supplied oil for lighting and lubrication, as well as ambergris, a waxy substance used in the manufacture of perfumes. The New England fisheries, unlike the farms, supplied a product that could be profitably exported to Europe, with lesser grades of fish going to the West Indies as food for slaves. Fisheries encouraged the development of shipbuilding, and experience at seafaring spurred transatlantic commerce.

TRADE By the end of the seventeenth century, the American colonies had become part of a complex North Atlantic commercial network, trading not only with the British Isles and the British West Indies but also—and often illegally—with Spain, France, Portugal, Holland, and their colonies. Out of necessity the colonists imported manufactured goods from Europe. The colonies were blessed with abundant natural resources—land, furs, deerskins, timber, fish, tobacco, indigo, rice, and sugar, to mention a few—but they lacked capital (money to invest in new enterprises) and laborers.

The mechanism of trade in New England and the middle colonies differed from that in the South in two respects: the lack of **staple crops** to exchange for English goods was a relative disadvantage, but the success of the region's own shipping and commercial enterprises worked in their favor. After 1660, in order to protect England's agriculture and fisheries, the government placed prohibitive duties (taxes) on certain colonial exports—fish, flour, wheat, and meat—while leaving the door open to timber, furs, and whale oil, products in great demand in the home country. New York and New England between 1698 and 1717 bought more from England than they sold to England, incurring an unfavorable trade balance.

The northern colonies addressed the import/export imbalance partly by using their own ships and merchants, thus avoiding the "invisible" charges by British middlemen, and by finding other markets for the staples excluded from England, thus acquiring goods or coins to pay for imports from the mother country. American lumber and fish therefore went to southern Europe for money or in exchange for wine; lumber, rum, and provisions went to Newfoundland; and all of these and more went to the sugar-producing island colonies in the West Indies, which became the most important trading outlet of all. American merchants could sell fish, bread, flour, corn, pork, bacon, beef, and horses to West Indian planters. In return, they got gold, sugar, molasses, rum, indigo, dyewoods, and other products, many of which went eventually to England.

These circumstances gave rise to the famous "**triangular trade**" (more a descriptive convenience than a uniform pattern), in which New Englanders shipped rum to the west coast of Africa, where they bartered for slaves; took the enslaved Africans to the West Indies; and returned home with various commodities, including molasses, from which they manufactured rum. In another version they shipped provisions to the West Indies, carried sugar and molasses to England, and returned with goods manufactured in Europe.

The colonies suffered from a chronic shortage of hard currency (coins), which drifted away to pay for imports and shipping charges. Merchants tried various ways to get around the shortage of gold or silver coins. Some engaged in barter, using commodities such as tobacco or rice as currency. In addition, most of the colonies at one time or another issued bills of credit, on promise of payment later (hence the dollar "bill"), and most set up "land banks" that issued paper money for loans to farmers who used their land for collateral. Colonial farmers knew that printing paper money inflated crop prices, and they therefore asked for more and more paper money. Thus

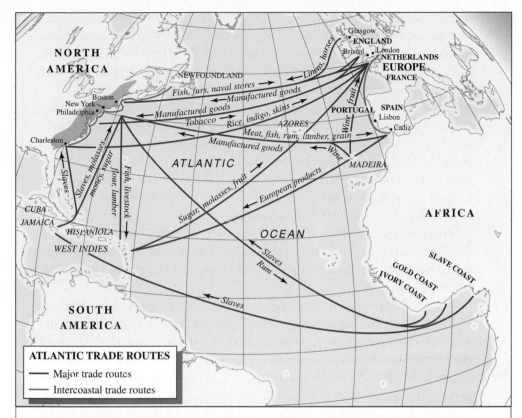

NORTH AMERICA

Glasgow
ENGLAND
Bristol · London
NETHERLANDS
EUROPE
FRANCE

NEWFOUNDLAND
Fish, furs, naval stores →
←*Manufactured goods*
Linens, horses

Boston
New York
Philadelphia
←*Manufactured goods*
Tobacco
Rice, indigo, skins →
Manufactured goods

PORTUGAL **SPAIN**
Lisbon
Wine, fruit
· Cadiz

Charleston
Meat, fish, rum, lumber, grain →
Manufactured goods ←
AZORES

Slaves, molasses
money, sugar
flour, lumber
Fish, livestock
ATLANTIC
←*Wine*
MADEIRA

Slaves
← *European products*
Sugar, molasses, fruit

CUBA
JAMAICA
HISPANIOLA
WEST INDIES
OCEAN
Slaves
Rum →
AFRICA

SLAVE COAST
GOLD COAST
IVORY COAST

← *Slaves*

SOUTH AMERICA

ATLANTIC TRADE ROUTES
—— Major trade routes
—— Intercoastal trade routes

How was overseas trade in the South different from that in New England and the middle colonies? What was the "triangular trade"? What were North America's most important exports?

began in colonial politics what was to become a recurrent issue in later times, the complex question of currency inflation. Whenever the issue arose, debtors (often farmers) commonly favored growth in the money supply, which would make it easier for them to pay long-term debts, whereas creditors favored a limited money supply, which would increase the value of their capital. British merchants wanted gold or silver, and they convinced Parliament to outlaw paper money in New England in 1751 and throughout the colonies in 1764.

CHURCH AND STATE   The Puritans who settled Massachusetts, unlike the Separatists of Plymouth, proposed only to form a purified version of the Anglican Church. They were called Nonseparating Congregationalists. That is, they remained loyal to the Church of England, the unity of church and state, and the principle of compulsory religious uniformity. But their remoteness from England led them to adopt a congregational form of church government identical with that of the Pilgrim Separatists and for that matter little different from the practice of Anglicans in the southern colonies.

In the Puritan version of John Calvin's theology, God had voluntarily entered into a *covenant*, or contract, with worshippers through which they could secure salvation. By analogy, therefore, an assembly of true Christians could enter into a congregational covenant, a voluntary union for the common worship of God. From this idea it was a fairly short step to the idea of people joining together to form a government. The early history of New England included several examples of such limited steps toward constitutional government: the Mayflower Compact, the charter of the Massachusetts Bay Colony, the Fundamental Orders of Connecticut, and the informal arrangements whereby the Rhode Island settlers governed themselves until they secured a charter in 1663.

The covenant theory contained certain kernels of democracy in both church and state, but democracy was no part of Puritan political thought, which like so much else in Puritan belief began with an emphasis on original sin. Humanity's innate depravity made government necessary. The Puritan was more of a biblical fundamentalist than a political democrat, dedicated to seeking the will of God, not the will of the people. The ultimate source of authority was not majority rule but the Bible. Biblical passages often had to be interpreted, however. So Puritans looked to ministers to explain God's will. By law, every town had to collect taxes to support a church. And every community member was required to attend midweek and Sunday religious services. The average New Englander heard 7,000 sermons in a lifetime.

Although Puritan New England has often been called a theocracy, individual congregations were entirely separate from the state—except that the residents were taxed to support the churches. And if not all inhabitants were official church members, all were nonetheless required to attend church services.

DIVERSITY AND SOCIAL STRAINS   Despite long-enduring myths, New England towns were not always pious, harmonious, and self-sufficient utopias populated by praying Puritans. Several communities were founded not as religious refuges but as secular centers of fishing, trade, or commercial agriculture. The animating concerns of residents in such commercial towns tended to be more entrepreneurial than spiritual. After a Puritan minister delivered his first sermon to a congregation in the Massachusetts port of Marblehead, a crusty fisherman admonished him: "You think you are preaching to the people of the Bay. Our main end was to catch fish."

In many of the godly inland communities, social strains increased as time passed, a consequence primarily of population pressure on the land and increasing disparities of wealth. "Love your neighbor," said Benjamin Franklin, "but don't pull down your fence." With the growing pressure on land in the settled regions, poverty and social tension increased in what had once seemed a country of unlimited opportunity.

More damaging to the Puritan utopia was the gradual erosion of religious fervor. More and more children of the "visible saints" found themselves unable to give the required testimony of spiritual regeneration. In 1662 an assembly of Boston ministers created the "**Half-Way Covenant**," whereby baptized children of church members could be admitted to a "halfway" membership and secure baptism for their own children in turn. Such partial members, however, could neither vote in church nor take communion. A further blow to Puritan control came with the Massachusetts royal charter of 1691, which required toleration of religious dissenters and based the right to vote in public elections on property rather than church membership.

THE DEVIL IN NEW ENGLAND   The strains accompanying Massachusetts's transition from Puritan utopia to royal colony reached a tragic climax in the witchcraft hysteria at Salem Village (now the town of Danvers) in 1692. Belief in witchcraft was widespread throughout Europe and New England in the seventeenth century. Prior to the dramatic episode in Salem, almost 300 New Englanders (mostly middle-aged women) had been accused of practicing witchcraft, and more than 30 had been hanged.

The Salem episode was unique in its scope and intensity, however. During the winter of 1691–1692, several adolescent girls became fascinated with the fortunetelling and voodoo practiced by Tituba, a West Indian slave owned by a minister. The entranced girls began to behave oddly—shouting, barking, groveling, and twitching for no apparent reason. When asked who was tormenting them, the girls replied that three women—Tituba, Sarah Good, and Sarah Osborne—were Satan's servants. Authorities thereupon arrested the three accused women. At a special hearing, the "afflicted" girls rolled on the floor in convulsive fits as the accused women were questioned. Tituba not only confessed to the charge of witchcraft but also listed others in the community who she claimed were performing the devil's work. Within a few months the Salem Village jail was filled with townspeople—men, women, and children—all accused of practicing witchcraft.

As the accusations and executions spread, leaders of the Massachusetts Bay Colony began to worry that the witch hunts were out of control. The governor intervened when his own wife was accused of serving the devil. He disbanded the special court in Salem and ordered the remaining suspects released. A year after it had begun, the frenzy was finally over. Nineteen people (including some men married to women who had been convicted) had been hanged, one man—the courageous Giles Corey—was pressed to death with heavy stones for refusing to sacrifice family and friends to the demands of the court, and more than one hundred others were jailed. Nearly everybody responsible for the Salem executions later recanted, and nothing quite like it happened in the colonies again.

What explains Salem's witchcraft hysteria? It may have represented nothing more than theatrical adolescents trying to enliven the dreary routine of everyday life. Others have highlighted the fact that most of the accused witches were women, many of whom had in some way defied the traditional roles assigned to females. Some had engaged in business transactions outside the home; others did not attend church; some were curmudgeons. Most were middle-aged or older and without sons or brothers. They thus stood to inherit property and live independently. The notion of autonomous spinsters flew in the face of prevailing social conventions.

Still another interpretation stresses the hysteria caused by frequent Native American attacks occurring just north of Salem, along New England's northern frontier. Some of the participants in the witch trials were girls from Maine who had been orphaned by Indian violence. The terrifying threat of Indian attacks created a climate of fear that helped fuel the witchcraft hysteria. "Are you guilty or not?" the Salem magistrate John Hathorne demanded of fourteen-year-old Abigail Hobbs in 1692. "I have seen sights and been scared," she answered. Whatever the precise cause, the witchcraft controversy reflected the peculiar social dynamics of the Salem community.

SOCIETY AND ECONOMY IN THE MIDDLE COLONIES

Both geographically and culturally, the middle colonies stood between New England and the South, blending their own influences with elements derived from the older regions on either side. In so doing, they more completely reflected the diversity of colonial life and more fully foreshadowed the pluralism of the American nation than the other regions did.

AN ECONOMIC MIX   The primary crops in the middle colonies were those of New England but more bountiful, owing to more fertile soil and a longer growing season. They developed surpluses of foodstuffs for export to the plantations of the South and the West Indies: wheat, barley, oats, and other cereals, flour, and livestock. Three great rivers—the Hudson, the Delaware, and the Susquehanna—and their tributaries gave the middle colonies ready access to the backcountry and the extremely profitable fur trade with Native Americans. As a consequence, the region's bustling commerce rivaled that of New England, and indeed Philadelphia in time supplanted Boston as the largest city in the colonies.

Land policies in the middle colonies followed the headright system of the South. In New York the early royal governors carried forward, in practice if not in name, the Dutch device of the patroonship, granting influential men (called patroons) vast estates on Long Island and throughout the Hudson and Mohawk River valleys. The patroons lorded over self-contained domains farmed by tenants who paid fees to use the landlords' mills, warehouses, smokehouses, and wharves. But with free land available elsewhere, New York's population languished, and the new waves of immigrants sought the promised land of Pennsylvania.

AN UNRULY ETHNIC MIX   In the makeup of their population, the middle colonies of British North America stood apart from both the mostly English Puritan settlements and the biracial plantation colonies to the south. In New York and New Jersey, for instance, Dutch culture and language lingered. Along the Delaware River the few Swedes and Finns, the first settlers, were overwhelmed by the influx of English and Welsh Quakers, followed in turn by Germans, Irish, and Scots-Irish. By the mid-eighteenth century, the middle colonies were the fastest growing area in North America.

The Germans came to America (primarily Pennsylvania) mainly from the war-torn Rhineland region of Europe. (Until German unification, in 1871, ethnic Germans—those Europeans speaking German as their native language—lived in a variety of areas and principalities in central Europe.) William Penn's recruiting brochures encouraging settlement in Pennsylvania circulated throughout central Europe in German translation, and his promise of religious freedom appealed to persecuted sects, especially the Mennonites, German Baptists whose beliefs resembled those of the Quakers.

In 1683 a group of Mennonites founded Germantown, near Philadelphia. They were the vanguard of a swelling migration in the eighteenth century that included Lutherans, Reformed Calvinists, Moravians, and members of other evangelical German sects, a large proportion of whom paid their way as indentured servants, or "redemptioners," as they were commonly called. The relentless waves of German immigrants during the eighteenth century alarmed many English colonists. Benjamin Franklin expressed the fear of many that the Germans "will soon . . . outnumber us."

The feisty Scots-Irish began to arrive later and moved still farther out into the backcountry throughout the eighteenth century. (Scotch-Irish is an enduring misnomer for Ulster Scots or Scots-Irish, mostly Presbyterians transplanted from Scotland to northern Ireland to give that Catholic country a more Protestant tone.) During the eighteenth century these people were more often called "Irish" than "Scots-Irish," a term later preferred by their descendants. Most arrived in Philadelphia, then gravitated to the backwoods of Pennsylvania before streaming southward into the fertile valleys stretching southwestward into Virginia and western Carolina. Land was the great magnet attracting the waves of Scots-Irish settlers. They were, said a recruiting agent, "full of expectation to have land for nothing" and were "unwilling to be disappointed." In most cases, the lands they "squatted on" were owned and occupied by Native Americans. In 1741 a group of Delaware Indians protested to Pennsylvania authorities that the Scotch-Irish intruders were taking "our land" without giving "us anything for it." If the government did not intervene, the Native Americans threatened, then they would "drive them off."

The Scots-Irish and Germans became the largest non-English elements in the colonies. Other minority ethnic groups enriched the population in New York and the Quaker colonies: Huguenots (Protestants whose religious freedom had been revoked in Catholic France in 1685), Irish, Welsh, Swiss, and Jews. New York had inherited from the Dutch a tradition of ethnic and religious tolerance, which had given the colony a diverse population before the English conquest: French-speaking Walloons (a Celtic people of southern Belgium), French, Germans, Danes, Portuguese, Spaniards, Italians, Bohemians, Poles, and others, including some New England Puritans. The Sephardic Jews who landed in New Amsterdam in 1654 quickly founded a synagogue there.

COLONIAL CITIES

The eighteenth century was a period of rapid expansion and soaring population growth in British North America, during which the colonies grew much more diverse. A rough estimate of the national origins of the white population as of 1790 found it to be 61 percent English; 14 percent

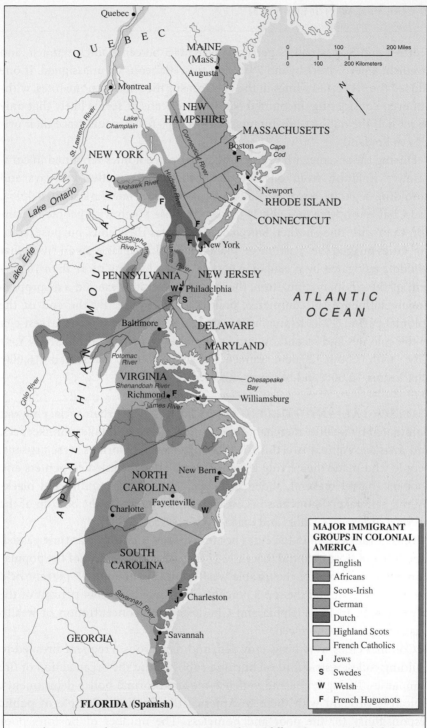

Quebec

QUEBEC

MAINE
(Mass.)
Augusta

Montreal

NEW
HAMPSHIRE

Lake
Champlain

MASSACHUSETTS

Boston
F

Cape
Cod

NEW YORK

Mohawk River

F

J

Newport

RHODE ISLAND

CONNECTICUT

Lake Ontario

Susquehanna
River

F

F

New York

Lake Erie

PENNSYLVANIA

NEW JERSEY

W

J

Philadelphia

S

S

Baltimore

DELAWARE

MARYLAND

Potomac
River

Ohio River

VIRGINIA

Shenandoah River

Richmond

F

Chesapeake
Bay

Williamsburg

James River

NORTH
CAROLINA

New Bern

F

Fayetteville

Charlotte

W

SOUTH
CAROLINA

Savannah River

F

J

Charleston

GEORGIA

Savannah

J

FLORIDA (Spanish)

ATLANTIC
OCEAN

0   100   200 Miles
0   100   200 Kilometers

N

**MAJOR IMMIGRANT
GROUPS IN COLONIAL
AMERICA**

English

Africans

Scots-Irish

German

Dutch

Highland Scots

French Catholics

J   Jews

S   Swedes

W   Welsh

F   French Huguenots

What attracted German immigrants to the middle colonies? Why did the
Scots-Irish spread across the Appalachian backcountry? What major population changes were reflected in the 1790 census?

Scottish and Scots-Irish; 9 percent German; 5 percent Dutch, French, and Swedish; 4 percent Irish; and 7 percent miscellaneous or unassigned. If one adds to the 3,172,444 whites in the 1790 census the 756,770 nonwhites, without even considering uncounted Native Americans, it seems likely that only about half the nation's inhabitants, and perhaps fewer, could trace their origins to England.

During the seventeenth century the American colonies remained in comparative isolation from one another, evolving distinctive folkways and unfolding separate histories. Residents of Boston, New York, Philadelphia, and Charleston were more likely to keep in close touch with people in London than with one another. Since commerce was their chief purpose, colonial cities hugged the coastline or, like Philadelphia, sprang up on rivers that could be navigated by oceangoing vessels. Never holding more than 10 percent of the colonial population, the large coastal cities exerted a disproportionate influence on commerce, politics, and culture. By the end of the colonial period, Philadelphia, with some 30,000 people, was the largest city in the colonies and second only to London in the British Empire. New York City, with about 25,000, ranked second; Boston numbered 16,000; Charleston, 12,000; and Newport, Rhode Island, 11,000.

THE SOCIAL AND POLITICAL ORDER   The urban social elite was dominated by wealthy merchants and a middle class of retailers, innkeepers, and artisans. Almost two thirds of the urban male workers were artisans, people who made their living at handicrafts. They included carpenters and coopers (barrel makers), shoemakers and tailors, silversmiths and blacksmiths, sailmakers, stonemasons, weavers, and potters. At the bottom of the pecking order were sailors and unskilled workers.

Class stratification in the cities became more pronounced as time passed. One study of Boston found that in 1687 the richest 15 percent of the population held 52 percent of the taxable wealth; by 1771 the top 15 percent held about 67 percent and the top 5 percent contributed some 44 percent of the city's wealth. In Philadelphia and Charleston the concentration of wealth was even more pronounced.

Colonial cities were busy, crowded, and dangerous. Frequent fires led to building codes, restrictions on burning rubbish, and the organization of fire companies. Rising crime and violence required formal police departments. Colonists brought with them to America the English principle of public responsibility for the poor and homeless. The number of Boston's poor receiving public assistance rose from 500 in 1700 to 4,000 in 1736; in New York the number rose from 250 in 1698 to 5,000 in the 1770s. Most of the public assistance went to "outdoor" relief in the form of money, food, clothing, and fuel. Almshouses were built to house the destitute.

THE URBAN WEB   Transit within and between colonial cities was initially difficult. The first roads were Native American trails, which were widened with travel, then made into roads. Land travel was initially by horse or by foot. The first public stagecoach line opened in 1732. Taverns were an important aspect of colonial travel, as movement at night was treacherous. (During the colonial era it was said that when the Spanish settled an area, they would first build a church; the Dutch, in their settlements, would first construct a fort; and the English, in theirs, would first erect a tavern.) By the end of the seventeenth century, there were more taverns in America than any other business. There were fifty-four taverns in Boston alone, half of them operated by women. Colonial taverns and inns were places to drink, relax, read a newspaper, play cards or billiards, gossip about people or politics, learn news from travelers, or conduct business. Local ordinances regulated them, setting prices and usually prohibiting them from serving liquor to African Americans, Native Americans, servants, or apprentices.

Taverns served as a collective form of communication; long-distance communication, however, was more complicated. Postal service in the seventeenth

Taverns

A tobacconist's business card from 1770 captures the atmosphere of late-eighteenth-century taverns. Here men in a Philadelphia tavern converse while they drink ale and smoke pipes.

century was almost nonexistent—people entrusted letters to travelers or sea captains. Under a parliamentary law of 1710, the postmaster of London named a deputy in charge of the colonies, and a postal system eventually extended the length of the Atlantic seaboard. Benjamin Franklin, who served as deputy postmaster for the colonies from 1753 to 1774, sped up the service with shorter routes and night-traveling post riders.

More reliable mail delivery gave rise to newspapers in the eighteenth century. Before 1745 twenty-two newspapers had been started: seven in New England, ten in the middle colonies, and five in the South. An important landmark in the progress of freedom of the press was John Peter Zenger's trial for publishing criticisms of New York's governor in his newspaper, the *New York Weekly Journal*. Zenger was imprisoned for ten months and brought to trial in 1735. English common law held that one might be punished for "libel," or criticism that fostered "an ill opinion of the government." Zenger's lawyer startled the court with his claim that the editor had published the truth—which the judge ruled an unacceptable defense. The jury, however, held the editor not guilty. The libel law remained standing as before, but editors thereafter were emboldened to criticize officials more freely.

THE ENLIGHTENMENT IN AMERICA

By the middle of the eighteenth century, the thirteen colonies were rapidly growing and maturing. Schools and colleges were springing up, and the standard of living was rising as well. More and more colonists had easier access to the latest consumer goods—and the latest ideas percolating in Europe. Through their commercial contacts, newspapers, and other channels, colonial cities became centers for the dissemination of new ideas. Most significant was a burst of intellectual activity known as the **Enlightenment** that originated in Europe and soon spread to the colonies. Like the Renaissance, the Enlightenment celebrated rational inquiry, scientific research, and individual freedom. Curious people wanted to dissect the workings of nature by close observation, scientific experimentation, and precise calculation. Unlike their Renaissance predecessors, however, many enlightened thinkers during the eighteenth century were willing to discard orthodox religious beliefs in favor of more "rational" ideas and ideals.

DISCOVERING THE LAWS OF NATURE   One manifestation of the Enlightenment was a scientific revolution in which the ancient view of an earth-centered universe, which reinforced Christian mythology, was overthrown in the early sixteenth century by the controversial heliocentric (sun-centered) solar system proposed by the Polish cleric Nicolaus Copernicus. His discovery that the earth orbits the sun was more than controversial; in an age governed by religious orthodoxy, it was heretical.

The climax to the scientific revolution came with Sir Isaac Newton's theory of gravitation, which he announced in 1687. Newton challenged biblical notions of the cosmos by depicting a mechanistic universe moving in accordance with natural laws that could be grasped by human reason and explained by mathematics. He implied that natural laws govern all things—the orbits of the planets and the orbits of human relations: politics, economics, and society. Reason could make people aware, for instance, that the natural law of supply and demand governs economics or that the natural rights to life, liberty, and property determine the limits and functions of government.

When people carried Newton's scientific outlook to its ultimate logic, as the Deists did, the idea of natural law reduced God from a daily presence to a remote Creator who planned the universe and set it in motion but no longer interacted with the earth and its people. Evil in the world, in this view, results not from original sin and innate depravity so much as from ignorance, an imperfect understanding of the laws of nature. The best way, therefore, to improve both society and human nature was by the application and improvement of Reason, which was the highest Virtue (Enlightenment thinkers often capitalized both words).

THE AGE OF REASON IN AMERICA   Such illuminating ideas profoundly affected the climate of thought in the eighteenth century. The premises of Newtonian science and the Enlightenment, moreover, fitted the American experience, which placed a premium on observation, experiment, reason, and the need to think anew. America was therefore especially receptive to the new science. **Benjamin Franklin** epitomized the Enlightenment in the eyes of both Americans and Europeans. Born in Boston in 1706, a descendant of Puritans, Franklin left home at the age of seventeen, bound for Philadelphia. There, before he was twenty-four, he owned a print shop, where he edited and published the *Pennsylvania Gazette*. When he was twenty-six, he published *Poor Richard's Almanack*, a collection of homely maxims on success and happiness. Before he retired from business, at the age of forty-two, Franklin, among other achievements, had founded a library, organized a fire company, helped start the academy that became the University of Pennsylvania, and organized a debating club that grew into the American Philosophical Society.

Franklin was devoted to science and the scientific method. Skeptical and curious, pragmatic and irreverent, he was a voracious reader and an inventive genius. His wide-ranging experiments traversed the fields of medicine, meteorology, geology, astronomy, and physics, among others. He developed the Franklin stove, the lightning rod, and a glass harmonica.

Franklin's love of commonsensical reason and his pragmatic skepticism clashed with prevailing religious beliefs. Although raised as a Presbyterian, he became a freethinker who had no patience with religious orthodoxy and sectarian squabbles. Franklin prized reason over revelation. He was not burdened with anxieties regarding the state of his soul. Early on, he abandoned the Calvinist assumption that God had predestined salvation for a select few. He grew skeptical of the divinity of Jesus and the authenticity of the Bible as God's word. Like the

Benjamin Franklin

A champion of reason, Franklin was an inventor, philosopher, entrepreneur, and statesman.

European Deists, Franklin came to believe in a God that had created a universe animated by natural laws, laws that inquisitive people could discern through the use of reason.

Benjamin Franklin and other like-minded thinkers, such as Thomas Jefferson and James Madison, derived an outlook of hope and optimism from modern science and Enlightenment rationalism. Such enlightened thinking, founded on freedom of thought and expression, clashed with the religious assumptions that had shaped Puritan New England in the seventeenth century. The eighteenth-century Enlightenment thus set in motion intellectual forces in the colonies that challenged the "truthfulness" of revealed religion and the logic of Christian faith. Those modern forces, however, would inspire stern resistance among the defenders of religious orthodoxy.

THE GREAT AWAKENING

Religion was put on the defensive by the rational emphases of the Enlightenment and the growing materialism of eighteenth century life. But religious fervor has always shown remarkable resilience in the face of new ideas and secular forces. During the early eighteenth century, the colonies experienced a widespread revival of religious zeal. Hundreds of new congregations were founded between 1700 and 1750. Most Americans (85 percent) lived in colonies with an "established" church, meaning that the government officially sanctioned—and collected taxes to support—a single official denomination. Anglicanism was the established church in Virginia, Maryland, Delaware, and the Carolinas. Congregationalism was the official faith in New England. In New York, Anglicanism vied with the Dutch Reformed Church for control. Pennsylvania had no single state-supported church, but Quakers dominated the legislative assembly. New Jersey and Rhode Island had no official denomination and hosted numerous sects.

Most colonies with an established church organized religious life on the basis of well-regulated local parishes, which defined their borders and defended them against dissenters and heretics. No outside preacher could enter the parish and speak in public without permission. Then, in the 1740s, the parish system was thrown into turmoil by the arrival of outspoken traveling (itinerant) evangelists, who claimed that the parish ministers were incompetent. The evangelists also insisted that Christians must be "reborn" in their convictions and behavior; traditional creeds or articles of faith were unnecessary for rebirth. By emphasizing the individualistic strand embedded in Protestantism, the so-called **Great Awakening** ended up invigorating—and fragmenting—American religious life. Unlike the Enlightenment, which affected primarily the intellectual elite, the Great Awakening appealed to the masses and spawned Protestant evangelicalism. It was the first popular movement before the American Revolution that spanned all thirteen colonies. As Benjamin Franklin observed of the Awakening, "Never did the people show so great a willingness to attend sermons. Religion is become the subject of most conversation."

FIRST STIRRINGS   During the early eighteenth century the currents of rationalism stimulated by the Enlightenment aroused concerns among orthodox believers in Calvinism. Many people seemed to be drifting away from the moorings of piety. And out along the fringes of settlement, many of the colonists were unchurched. On the frontier, people had no minister to preach to them or administer sacraments or perform marriages. According to some ministers, these pioneers had lapsed into a primitive and sinful life, little different from that of the "heathen" Native Americans. By the 1730s the sense of religious decline had provoked the Great Awakening.

In 1734–1735 a remarkable spiritual revival occurred in the congregation of **Jonathan Edwards**, a Congregationalist minister in Northampton, in western Massachusetts. One of America's most brilliant philosophers and theologians, Edwards had entered Yale College in 1716, at age thirteen, and graduated as valedictorian four years later. In 1727, Edwards was called to serve the Congregational church in Northampton. He was shocked at the town's tepid spirituality. Edwards claimed that the young people of Northampton were addicted to sinful pleasures, such as "night walking and frequenting the tavern"; they indulged in "lewd practices" that "exceedingly corrupted others." Christians, he believed, had become preoccupied with making and spending money. Religion had lost its emotional force. Edwards lambasted Deists for believing that "God has given mankind no other light to walk by but their own

Jonathan Edwards

One of the foremost preachers of the Great Awakening, Edwards dramatically described the torments that awaited sinners in the afterlife.

reason." Edwards resolved to restore deeply felt spirituality. "Our people," he said, "do not so much need to have their heads stored [with new knowledge] as to have their hearts touched." His own vivid descriptions of the torments of hell and the delights of heaven helped rekindle spiritual fervor among his congregants. By 1735, Edwards could report that "the town seemed to be full of the presence of God; it never was so full of love, nor of joy." To judge the power of the religious awakening, he thought, one need only observe that "it was no longer the Tavern" that drew local crowds, "but the Minister's House."

The Great Awakening saved souls but split churches. At about the same time that Jonathan Edwards was promoting revivals in New England, William Tennent, an Irish-born Presbyterian revivalist, was stirring souls in Pennsylvania. He and his sons charged that many of the local ministers were "cold and sapless"; they showed no evidence of themselves having experienced a convincing conversion experience, nor were they willing to "thrust the nail of terror into sleeping souls." Tennent's oldest son, Gilbert, defended their aggressive (and often illegal) tactics by explaining that he and other traveling evangelists invaded parishes only when the "settled ministry" showed no interest in the "Getting of Grace and Growing in it." The

Tennents caused great consternation because they and other unauthorized ministers offered a compelling fire-and-brimstone alternative to the settled parish preachers. They promoted a passionate piety, and they refused to accept the prevailing structure of denominations and clerical authority. Competition was emerging in colonial religious life.

The great catalyst of the Great Awakening was a young English minister, **George Whitefield**, whose reputation as a spellbinding evangelist preceded him to the colonies. Congregations were lifeless, he claimed, "because dead men preach to them." Too many ministers were "slothful shepherds and dumb dogs." His objective was to restore the fires of religious fervor to American congregations. In the autumn of 1739, Whitefield, then twenty-five, arrived in Philadelphia and began preaching to huge crowds. After visiting Georgia, he made a triumphal procession northward to New England, drawing thousands and releasing "Gales of Heavenly Wind" that blew gusts throughout the colonies.

The cross-eyed Whitefield enthralled audiences with his golden voice, flamboyant style, and unparalleled eloquence. Even the skeptical Benjamin Franklin, who went to see Whitefield preach in Philadelphia, was so carried away that he emptied his pockets into the collection plate. Whitefield urged his listeners to experience a "new birth"—a sudden, emotional moment of conversion and salvation. By the end of his sermon, one listener reported, the entire congregation was "in utmost Confusion, some crying out, some laughing, and Bliss still roaring to them to come to Christ, as they answered, I will, I will, I'm coming, I'm coming."

Jonathan Edwards took advantage of the commotion stirred up by Whitefield to spread his own revival gospel throughout New England. The Awakening reached its peak in 1741 when Edwards delivered his most famous sermon at Enfield, Massachusetts (in present-day Connecticut). Titled "Sinners in the Hands of an Angry God," it represented a devout appeal to repentance. Edwards reminded his congregation that hell is real and that God's vision is

George Whitefield

The English minister's dramatic eloquence roused American congregants, inspiring many to experience a religious rebirth.

omnipotent, his judgment certain. He noted that God "holds you over the pit of hell, much as one holds a spider, or some loathsome insect, over the fire, abhors you, and is dreadfully provoked . . . he looks upon you as worthy of nothing else, but to be cast into the fire." When Edwards finished, he had to wait several minutes for the congregants to quiet down before leading them in a closing hymn.

The Great Awakening encompassed a worldwide resurgence of evangelical Protestantism and "enthusiastic" expressions of faith. Women, both white and black, were believed to be more susceptible to fits of spiritual emotion than men. The Tennents, Whitefield, and other traveling evangelists thus targeted women because of their spiritual virtuosity. Whitefield and the other ecstatic evangelists believed that conversion required a visceral, emotional experience. Convulsions, shrieks, and spasms were the physical manifestation of the Holy Spirit at work, and women seemed more willing to let the Spirit move them. Some of the revivalists, especially Baptists, initially loosened traditional restrictions on female participation in worship.

Edwards and Whitefield were selfless promoters of Christian revivalism who insisted on the central role of the emotions in spiritual life. Critics of the Awakening decried the emotionalism generated by the revivalists. They were especially concerned that evangelicals were encouraging "women, yea, girls to speak" at revivals. One critic of "female exhorters" reminded congregations of the scriptural commandment "let your women keep silence in the churches."

PIETY AND REASON   The Great Awakening undermined many of the established churches by emphasizing that individuals could receive God's grace without the assistance of traditional clergy. It also gave people more religious choices, splitting the Calvinistic churches. Presbyterians divided into the "Old Side" and the "New Side," Congregationalists into "Old Light" and "New Light." New England religious life would never be the same. Jonathan Edwards lamented the warring factions. We are "like two armies," he said, "separated and drawn up in battle array, ready to fight one another." Church members chose sides and either dismissed their ministers or deserted them. Many of the New Lights went over to the Baptists, and others flocked to Presbyterian or, later, Methodist groups, which in turn divided and subdivided into new sects.

The Great Awakening subsided by 1750, although revivalism in Virginia continued unabated for another twenty years. The Awakening, like its counterpart, the Enlightenment, influenced the American Revolution and set in motion powerful currents that still flow in American life. It implanted in American culture the evangelical impulse and the emotional appeal of revivalism. The movement weakened the status of the old-fashioned clergy and state-supported churches, encouraged believers to exercise their own judgment, and thereby weakened habits of deference generally. By encouraging the proliferation of denominations, it heightened the need for toleration of dissent. But in some respects the counterpoint between the Awakening and the Enlightenment, between the urgings of the spirit and the logic of reason, led by different roads to similar ends. Both movements emphasized the power and right of individual decision making, and both aroused millennial hopes that America would become the promised land in which people might attain the perfection of piety or reason, if not both.

CHAPTER SUMMARY

- **Colonial Differences** Agriculture diversified: tobacco was the staple crop in Virginia, and rice and naval stores were the staples in the Carolinas. Family farms and a mixed economy characterized the middle and New England colonies, while plantation agriculture based on slavery became entrenched in the South. By 1790, German, Scots-Irish, Welsh, and Irish immigrants had settled in the middle colonies, along with members of religious groups such as Quakers, Jews, Huguenots, and Mennonites.

- **Women in the Colonies** English colonists brought their belief systems with them, including convictions about the inferiority of women. The initial shortage of women gave way to a more equal gender ratio as women immigrated—alone and in family groups—thereby enabling a dramatic population growth in the colonies.

- **Indentured Servants** In response to the labor shortage in the early years, Virginia relied on indentured servants. By the end of the seventeenth century, enslaved Africans had replaced indentured servants in the South. With the supply of slaves seeming inexhaustible, the Carolinas adopted slavery as its primary labor source.

- **Triangular Trade** British America sent raw materials, such as fish and furs, to England in return for manufactured goods. The colonies participated in the triangular trade with Africa and the Caribbean, building ships and exporting manufactured goods, especially rum, while "importing" slaves from Africa.

- **The Enlightenment** The attitudes of the Enlightenment were transported along the trade routes. Isaac Newton's scientific discoveries culminated in the belief that Reason could improve society. Benjamin Franklin, who believed that people could shape their own destinies, became the face of the Enlightenment in America.

- **The Great Awakening** Religious diversity in the colonies increased. By the 1730s a revival of faith, the Great Awakening, swept through the colonies. New congregations formed, as evangelists, who insisted that Christians be "reborn," challenged older sects. Individualism, not orthodoxy, was stressed in this first popular movement in America's history.

CHRONOLOGY

1619	First Africans arrive at Jamestown
1636	Harvard College is established
1662	Puritans initiate the "Half-Way Covenant"
1662	Virginia enacts law declaring that children of slave women are slaves
1691	Royal charter for Massachusetts is established
1692	Salem witchcraft trials
1730s–1740s	Great Awakening
1735	John Peter Zenger is tried for seditious libel
1739	Stono Uprising
1739	George Whitefield preaches his first sermon in America, in Philadelphia
1741	Jonathan Edward preaches "Sinners in the Hands of an Angry God"

KEY TERMS & NAMES

4

FROM COLONIES TO STATES

FOCUS QUESTIONS wwnorton.com/studyspace

- How did the British Empire administer the economy of its colonies?
- How were colonial governments structured, and how independent were they of the mother country?
- What were the causes of the French and Indian War?
- How did victory in the French and Indian War affect the British colonies in North America?
- How and why did British colonial policy change after 1763?
- What were the main motivations and events that led to a break with the mother country?

Three great European powers—Spain, France, and England, took the lead in conquering and colonizing North America during the sixteenth and seventeenth centuries. The English differed from the Spanish and French in the degree of freedom they initially allowed their colonies. Unlike New France and New Spain, New England was in effect a self-governing community. There was much less control by the mother country in part because England was a less authoritarian, less militaristic, and less centralized nation-state than Spain or France. The monarchy shared power with Parliament, and citizens enjoyed specified rights and privileges. In 1606, for example, the Virginia Company took care in drawing up its charter to ensure that the colonists who settled in America would enjoy all the "liberties, franchises, and immunities" of English citizens.

But colonists did not have all the rights of English citizens. The English government insisted that the Americans contribute to the expense of maintaining the colonies but did not give them a voice in shaping administrative policies. Such inconsistencies spawned growing grievances and tensions. By the mid–eighteenth century, when Britain tried to tighten its control of the colonies, it was too late. Americans had developed a far more powerful sense of their rights than any other colonial people, and in the 1770s they resolved to assert and defend those rights against the English government's efforts to limit them.

ENGLISH ADMINISTRATION OF THE COLONIES

Throughout the colonial period, the British monarchy was the source of legal authority in America. For much of the seventeenth century, however, England remained too distracted by the constant struggle between Parliament and the Stuart kings to perfect either a systematic colonial policy or effective agencies of imperial control. The English Civil War (1642–1646) had profound effects in the colonies, primarily in that it sharply reduced the inflow of money and people from England to America, created great confusion about the colonial relationship to the mother country, and kept the English government from effectively overseeing colonial affairs. The victory of Oliver Cromwell's army over royalist forces in the civil war led to the creation during the 1650s of the Puritan Commonwealth and Protectorate. As England's ruler, Cromwell showed little interest in regulating the American colonies, but he had a lively concern for colonial trade. In 1651, therefore, Parliament adopted the first in a series of Navigation Acts designed to increase the nation's commercial revenues by restricting the economic freedom of its colonies in ways that would also take commerce away from their Dutch enemies. The act of 1651 required that all goods imported to England or the colonies from Asia and Africa be carried only in ships built in England and owned by Englishmen, ships that also would be captained and crewed by a majority of English sailors. Colonial merchants resented such new regulations because they had benefited from Dutch shippers that charged only two thirds as much as English ships to transport American products across the Atlantic. English colonists in sugar-rich Barbados and tobacco-rich Virginia and Maryland initially defied the new law, only to relent when the English government dispatched warships to enforce the new requirements. By 1652 England and the Netherlands were at war, the first of three maritime conflicts that erupted between 1652 and 1674.

THE MERCANTILE SYSTEM   The Navigation Act of 1651 reflected the prevailing emphasis of the English and European governments on an economic and political policy known as the **mercantile system**. Mercantilism grew out of the prolonged warfare among the major European nations, and it centered on the belief that international power and influence depended upon a nation's wealth and its ability to become economically self-sufficient. A nation, the theory went, could gain wealth only at the expense of another nation—by seizing its gold and silver and dominating its trade. Under mercantilism, the government controlled all economic activities, limiting foreign imports so as to preserve a favorable balance of trade whereby exports exceeded imports. This required that the government promote domestic manufacturers, through subsidies and monopolies if need be. Mercantilism also required a nation to acquire colonies that would enrich the mother country by providing the raw materials for goods manufactured in the mother country, goods that would be sold at home as well as to its colonists.

It was such mercantilist assumptions that prompted England to create more **Navigation Acts** to tighten its control over commerce with its colonies. After the English monarchy was restored in 1660, the new royalist Parliament passed the Navigation Act of 1660, which ordered that all trade between the colonies be carried in English ships, three quarters of whose crews now must be English. The act also specified that certain products from the colonies were to be shipped only to England or to other English colonies. The list of "enumerated" products initially included tobacco, cotton, indigo, ginger, and sugar. Rice, hemp, masts, copper, and furs, among other items, were added later. Not only did England (and its colonies) become the sole outlet for those "enumerated" colonial exports, but the Navigation Act of 1663 required that *all* colonial imports from Europe to America stop first in England, be offloaded, and have a tax paid on them before their reshipment to the colonies. The Navigation Acts, also called the British Acts of Trade, gave England a monopoly over the incredibly profitable tobacco and sugar produced in Maryland, Virginia, and the British-controlled islands of the West Indies. The acts also increased customs revenues collected in England, channeled all colonial commerce through English merchants (rather than Europeans), enriched English shipbuilders, and required that only English-owned ships could conduct trade with Great Britain.

Over time these Navigation Acts ensured that the commercial activities of the American colonies became ever more important to the economic strength of the British Empire. In one respect the new regulations worked as planned: the English by 1700 had supplanted the Dutch as the world's lead-

Boston from the southeast

This view of eighteenth-century Boston shows the importance of shipping and its regulation in the colonies, especially in Massachusetts Bay.

ing maritime power. Virtually all of the colonial trade by then was carried in British ships and passed through British ports on its way to Europe. And by 1700 British North America was prospering at a rate unsurpassed around the world. What the English government did not predict or fully understand was that the Navigation Acts would arouse growing resentment, resistance, and rebellion in the colonies. Colonial merchants and shippers loudly complained that the Navigation Acts were burdensome and costly. But the British paid no heed. Slowly and erratically, the English government was developing a more coherent imperial policy exercising greater control over its wayward transatlantic colonies, and for a while, this policy worked.

The actual enforcement of the Navigation Acts was spotty, however. Americans found ingenious ways to avoid the regulations. Smuggling was rampant. During the 1670s, the government appointed collectors of customs duties (fees levied on imports/exports) in all the colonies. In 1678 a defiant Massachusetts legislature declared that the Navigation Acts had no legal standing in the colony. Six years later, in 1684, the Lords of Trade tried to teach the rebellious colonists a lesson by annulling the charter of Massachusetts.

THE DOMINION OF NEW ENGLAND In 1685, King Charles II died and was succeeded by his brother, the Duke of York, as James II. To impress upon the colonies their subordinate status and institute tighter regulatory controls, the new king approved a proposal to consolidate the New England colonies into a single royal colony called the Dominion of New England that would undermine the authority of Puritanism and abolish elected assemblies. In 1686 the newly appointed royal governor, the authoritarian Sir Edmund Andros, arrived in Boston to take control of the new Dominion of New England. Andros levied taxes, suppressed town governments, enforced the Navigation Act, and punished smugglers. Most ominous of all, Andros and his lieutenants took control of a Puritan church in Boston and began using it for Anglican services.

THE GLORIOUS REVOLUTION IN AMERICA The Dominion of New England was scarcely established before the **Glorious Revolution** erupted in England in 1688. When news reached Boston that James II had fled to France and that William was the new king of England, the city staged its own bloodless revolution. Merchants, ministers, and militias (citizen-soldiers) mobilized to arrest the hated Governor Andros and his aides, seize a royal ship in Boston harbor, and remove Massachusetts from the hated Dominion. The other colonies that had been absorbed into the Dominion followed suit. All were permitted to revert to their former status except Massachusetts Bay and Plymouth, which after some delay were united under a new charter in 1691 as the royal colony of Massachusetts Bay. The new British monarchs, William and Mary, were determined to reassert royal control in America. To that end, they appointed new royal governors in Massachusetts, New York, and Maryland. In Massachusetts the new governor was given authority to veto acts of the assembly, and he removed the Puritans' religious qualification for voting.

The Glorious Revolution had significant long-term effects on American history in that the Bill of Rights and the Act of Toleration, passed in England in 1689, influenced attitudes and events in the colonies. Even more significant, the overthrow of King James II set a precedent for the removal of a hated monarch. The justification for revolution appeared in 1690 when the English philosopher John Locke published his *Two Treatises on Government*, which had an enormous impact on political thought in the colonies. Locke refuted the prevailing theories of the "divine" right of kings to govern with absolute power. He also insisted that people are endowed with "natural rights" to life, liberty, and property. The need to protect those "natural" rights led people to establish governments. When rulers failed to protect the property and lives of their subjects, Locke argued, the people had the right— in extreme cases—to overthrow the monarch and change the government.

THE HABIT OF SELF-GOVERNMENT

Government within the diverse American colonies evolved without plan. In broad outline, the governor, council, and assembly in each colony corresponded to the king, lords, and commons in England. Over the years certain anomalies appeared as colonial governments diverged from that of England. On the one hand, the governors retained powers and prerogatives that the king had lost in the course of the seventeenth century. On the other hand, the assemblies acquired powers, particularly with respect to government appointments, that Parliament had yet to gain for itself.

POWERS OF THE ROYAL GOVERNORS English monarchs never vetoed acts of Parliament after 1707, but the colonial royal governors, most of whom were mediocre or incompetent, still held an absolute veto over the assemblies. As chief executives, the governors could appoint and remove officials, command the militia, and grant pardons. In these respects their authority resembled the Crown's, for the king still exercised executive authority and had the power to name administrative officials. For the king, those powers often strengthened an effective royal influence in Parliament, since the king could appoint members or their friends to lucrative offices. While this arrangement might seem a breeding ground for corruption or tyranny, it was often viewed in the eighteenth century as a stabilizing influence, especially by the king's friends. But it was an influence less and less available to the governors as the authorities in England more and more drew the control of colonial patronage into their own hands.

POWERS OF THE COLONIAL ASSEMBLIES The English colonies in America, unlike their counterparts under Spanish rule, benefited from elected legislative assemblies. Whether called the House of Burgesses (Virginia), Delegates (Maryland), or Representatives (Massachusetts) or simply the assembly, the "lower" houses were chosen by popular vote. Not all colonists could vote, however. Only male property owners could vote, based upon the notion that only men who held a tangible "stake in society" could vote responsibly. Because property holding was widespread in America, a greater proportion of the population could vote in the colonies than anywhere else in the world. Women, Indians, and African Americans were excluded from the political process—as a matter of course—and continued to be excluded for the most part into the twentieth century.

The most profound political trend during the early eighteenth century was the growing power exercised by the colonial assemblies. Like Parliament, the assemblies controlled the budget by their right to vote on taxes and expenditures, and they held the power to initiate legislation. Most of the colonial assemblies also exerted leverage on the royal governors by controlling their salaries. Throughout the eighteenth century the assemblies expanded their power and influence, sometimes in conflict with the governors, sometimes in harmony with them. Self-government in America became first a habit, then a "right." By the mid–eighteenth century, the colonies had become largely self-governing.

TROUBLED NEIGHBORS

SPANISH AMERICA IN DECLINE   By the start of the eighteenth century, the Spanish controlled a huge colonial empire spanning much of North America. Yet their sparsely populated settlements in the borderlands north of Mexico were small and weak when compared with the North American colonies of the other European powers. The Spanish failed to create thriving colonies in what is now the American Southwest for several reasons. The region lacked the gold and silver that attracted the Spanish to Mexico and Peru. In addition, the Spanish were distracted by their need to control the perennial unrest among the Indians and the mestizos (people of mixed Indian and European ancestry). Moreover, the Spaniards who led the colonization effort in the Southwest failed to produce settlements with self-sustaining economies. Instead, the Spanish concentrated on building Catholic missions and forts and looking—in vain—for gold. Whereas the French and the English based their Native American policies on trade (which included supplying Indians with firearms), Spain emphasized the conversion of indigenous peoples to Catholicism, forbade manufacturing within its colonies, and strictly limited trade with the Native Americans.

NEW FRANCE   French settlements in the New World differed considerably from both the Spanish and the English models. The French settlers were predominantly male but much smaller in number than the English and Spanish colonists. Although the population of France was three times that of Spain, only about 40,000 French came to the New World during the seventeenth and eighteenth centuries. This forced the French to develop cooperative relationships with the Indians. Unlike the English colonists, the French typically established fur-trading outposts rather than farms, mostly along the St. Lawrence River, on land not claimed by Indians. They thus did not have to confront initial hostility from Indians; they lived among them.

French traders sometimes served as mediators among rival Great Lakes tribes. This diplomatic role gave them much more influence among the Indians than their English counterparts had.

The heavily outnumbered and disproportionately male French settlers sought to integrate themselves with Indian culture rather than eliminate it. Many French traders married Indians, exchanging languages and customs in the process of raising families. This more fraternal bond between the French and the Indians proved to be a source of strength in the wars with the English, enabling New France to survive until 1760 despite the lopsided disparity in numbers between the two colonial powers.

French settlement of North America began when the enterprising Samuel de Champlain landed on the shores of the St. Lawrence River in 1603 and, two years later, at Acadia (later Nova Scotia). In 1608, a year after the English landed at Jamestown, Champlain led another expedition, during which he founded Quebec. While Acadia remained a remote outpost, New France expanded well beyond Quebec, from which Champlain pushed his explorations up the great river and into the Great Lakes as far as Lake Huron, and southward to the lake that still bears his name. There, in 1609, he joined a band of Huron and Algonquian allies in a fateful encounter. When an Iroquois war party attacked Champlain's group, the French explorer shot and killed two chiefs, and the Indians fled. The episode ignited in the Iroquois a hatred for the French that the English would capitalize upon. The vengeful Iroquois stood as a buffer against French plans to move southward from Canada toward the English colonies and as a constant menace on the flank of the French waterways to the interior. For over a century, in fact, Indians determined the military balance of power within North America. In 1711 the governor general of New France declared that "the Iroquois are more to be feared than the English colonies."

Until his death, in 1635, Champlain governed New France under a trading company that won a profitable monopoly of the huge fur trade. But a provision that limited the population to French Catholics stunted the growth of New France. Neither the enterprising, seafaring Huguenots (Protestants) of coastal France nor foreigners of any faith were allowed in New France, which therefore remained a scattered patchwork of dependent peasants, Jesuit missionaries, priests, soldiers, officials, and *coureurs de bois* (literally, "runners of the woods"), who roamed the interior in quest of furs. In 1663, King Louis XIV changed New France into a royal colony and dispatched new settlers, including shiploads of young women. The government provided tools and livestock for farmers and nets for fishermen. The population grew from about 4,000 in 1665 to about 15,000 in 1690.

Champlain in New France

Samuel de Champlain firing at a group of Iroquois, killing two chiefs (1609).

FRENCH LOUISIANA From the Great Lakes, French explorers in the early 1670s moved southward down the the Mississippi River all the way to the Gulf of Mexico. They named the vast area Louisiana, after King Louis XIV. Settlement of the Louisiana country finally began in 1699, when Pierre Le Moyne, sieur d'Iberville, established a colony near Biloxi, Mississippi. The main settlement then moved to Mobile Bay and, in 1710, to the present site of Mobile, Alabama. For nearly half a century the driving force in Louisiana was Jean-Baptiste Le Moyne, sieur de Bienville, a younger brother of Iberville. Bienville arrived with settlers in 1699, when he was only nineteen, and left the colony for the last time in 1743, when he was sixty-three. Sometimes called the Father of Louisiana, he served periodically as governor, and in 1718 he founded New Orleans, which shortly thereafter became the capital.

"France in America had two heads," the historian Francis Parkman wrote, "one amid the snows of Canada, the other amid the canebrakes of Louisiana." The French thus had one enormous advantage over their English rivals: access to the great inland rivers that led to the heartland of the continent. In the Illinois region, scattered French settlers began farming the fertile soil, and **Jesuits** established missions at places such as Terre Haute (High Land) and Des Moines (Some Monks). Because of geography as well as deliberate policy, however, French America remained largely a vast wilderness traversed by a mobile population of traders, trappers, missionaries—and, mainly, Indians. In 1750, when the English colonials numbered about 1.5 million, the total French population was no more than 80,000. Yet in some ways the French had the edge on the British. They offered European goods to Indians in return for furs and encroached far less upon indigenous lands. They thereby won Native American allies against the English. French governors could mobilize for action without any worry about rebellious colonial assemblies or ethnic and religious diversity. The British may have had the greater population, but their separate colonies often worked at cross-purposes.

THE COLONIAL WARS

For most of the seventeenth century, the Spanish, French, Dutch, and British colonies in North America developed in relative isolation from each other. By the end of the century, however, the rivalries among the European nations began to spill over into the Americas. The Glorious Revolution of 1688 worked an abrupt reversal in English diplomacy, as the new King William III, a Protestant, was an ardent foe of Catholic France's Louis XIV. William's ties to the Netherlands and England helped to form a Grand Alliance of European nations against the French in a transatlantic war known in the American colonies as King William's War (1689–1697).

King William's War was the first of four great wars fought in Europe and the colonies over the next seventy-four years. In each case, England and its European allies were aligned against Catholic France or Spain and their allies. By far the most significant of the four conflicts was the last one, the Seven Years' War (called in North America the French and Indian War, which in fact lasted nine years in America, from 1754 to 1763). In all four of the wars except the Seven Years' War, the battles in America were but a sideshow accompanying massive warfare in Europe. Although the wars involved many nations, including Indian tribes on both sides, they centered on the implacable struggle for global supremacy between the British and the French, a struggle that ended up profoundly shifting the international balance of power among the great powers of Europe. By the end of the eighteenth century, Spain would be in decline, while France and Great Britain fought for supremacy.

The prolonged international warfare during the eighteenth century had a devastating effect on New England, especially Massachusetts, for it was closest to the battlefields of French Canada. The wars also would reshape the contours of Britain's relationship with America. Great Britain emerged from the wars as the most powerful nation in the world, solidifying its control over Ireland and Scotland in the process. International commerce became even more essential to the expanding British Empire, thus making the American colonies even more strategically significant. The wars with France led the English government to build a huge navy and massive army, which created an enormous government debt that led to new efforts to wring more government revenue from the British people. During the early eighteenth century, the changes in English financial policy and political culture led critics in Parliament to charge that traditional liberties were being usurped by a tyrannical central government. After the French and Indian War, American colonists began making the same point.

THE FRENCH AND INDIAN WAR   The climactic conflict between Britain and France in North America was the French and Indian War. It was sparked by competing claims over the ancestral Indian lands in the sprawling Ohio River valley, the "most fertile country of America." Indians, Virginians, Pennsylvanians, and the French in Canada had long squabbled over who owned the region. To defend their interests in the Ohio River valley, the French built forts in what is now western Pennsylvania. When the Virginia governor learned of the French fortifications, he sent an ambitious twenty-one-year-old Virginia militia officer, Major George Washington, to warn the French to leave the area. With an experienced guide and a few others, Washington made his way by horseback, foot, canoe, and raft the 450 miles to Fort Le Boeuf (just south of Lake Erie, in northwest Pennsylvania) in late 1753. He gave the French commander a note from the Virginia governor demanding that they withdraw from the Ohio Country. After the French captain rejected the request, Washington trudged home through deepening snow, having accomplished nothing in "as fatiguing a journey as it is possible to conceive."

In the spring of 1754, Washington led 150 inexperienced volunteers and Iroquois allies back across the Alleghenies. Their mission was to build a fort at the convergence of the Allegheny, Monongahela, and Ohio Rivers (where the city of Pittsburgh later developed). After two months of difficult travel, Washington learned that French soldiers had beaten him to the strategic site and erected Fort Duquesne, named for the French governor of Canada. Washington decided to make camp about forty miles from the fort and await reinforcements. The next day, the Virginians ambushed a French scouting party. Ten French soldiers were killed, including the commander, and twenty-one were captured. The Indians tomahawked and scalped several of the wounded soldiers as a stunned Washington looked on. The mutilated soldiers were the first fatalities in what would become the French and Indian War.

George Washington and his troops, reinforced by more Virginians and British soldiers dispatched from South Carolina, hastily constructed a stockade at Great Meadows, dubbed Fort Necessity, which a large force of vengeful French soldiers attacked during a rainstorm a month later, on July 3, 1754. After a daylong battle, Washington surrendered, having seen a third of his 300 men killed or wounded. France was now in undisputed control of the Ohio Country. George Washington's blundering expedition triggered a series of events that would ignite a protracted world war. As a British politician exclaimed, "the volley fired by a young Virginian in the backwoods of America set the world on fire."

In London the government decided to force a showdown with the "presumptuous" French in North America. In June 1755 a British fleet captured the French forts on Nova Scotia along the Atlantic coast of Canada and expelled thousands of Roman Catholic residents, called Acadians. The Acadians were put on ships and scattered throughout the colonies, from Maine to Georgia. Hundreds of them eventually found their way to French Louisiana, where they became the Cajuns (a corruption of *Acadians*), many of whose descendants still speak French.

BRADDOCK'S DEFEAT   In 1755 the British government also dispatched over a thousand troops to Virginia to dislodge the French from the Ohio Country. The arrival of unprecedented numbers of "redcoat" soldiers on American soil would change the dynamics of British North America. Although the colonists endorsed the use of force against the French, they later would oppose the use of British soldiers to enforce colonial regulations.

The British commander in chief of North American operations, Major General Edward Braddock, was a seasoned, stubborn, overconfident officer. Neither he nor his troops had any experience fighting in the American wilderness. The imperious Braddock viewed Indians with contempt, and his cocksure ignorance would prove fatal. With the addition of some colonial troops, including George Washington as a volunteer, Braddock's force hacked a 125-mile road through the rugged mountains to the vicinity of Fort Duquesne. Braddock's army was on the verge of success when, on July 9, 1755, six miles from Fort Duquesne, their failure to recruit Indian scouts led them into an ambush. The surrounding woods suddenly came alive with Ojibwas and French militiamen. Beset on three sides by concealed enemies,

The first American political cartoon

Benjamin Franklin's exhortation to the colonies to unite against the French in 1754 would become popular again twenty years later, when the colonies faced a different threat.

the British troops—dressed in bright-red woolen uniforms in the summer heat—stood their ground for most of the afternoon before retreating in disarray. General Braddock was mortally wounded. George Washington, his own coat riddled by four bullets, helped other officers contain the rout and lead a hasty retreat.

Though they lost 23 of their own, the French and their Native American allies killed 63 of 86 British officers (including Braddock), 914 out of 1,373 soldiers, and captured the British cannons, supplies, and secret papers. It was one of the worst British defeats of the eighteenth century. Twelve of the wounded British soldiers left behind on the battlefield were stripped, bound, and burned at the stake by Indians. A devastated George Washington wrote his brother that the British army had "been scandalously beaten by a trifling body of men." The vaunted redcoats "broke & run as sheep before Hounds," but the Virginians "behaved like Men and died like Soldiers."

A WORLD WAR   Braddock's stunning defeat sent shock waves through the colonies. Emboldened by the news, Indians allied with the French launched widespread assaults on frontier farms throughout western Pennsylvania, Maryland, and Virginia. Newly arrived French troops assaulted British garrisons along the Great Lakes. It was not until May 1756, however, that England and France formally declared war on each other, and the French and Indian War in America bled into what would become the Seven Years'

War in Europe. A truly world war, it would eventually be fought on four continents and three oceans around the globe.

British military planners decided that North America should be the primary battleground in the world war with France. Some 45,000 British troops were mobilized in Canada and America, half of whom were American colonists. In 1759 the French and Indian War reached its climax with a series of resounding British triumphs on land and at sea around the world. The most decisive British victory was at Quebec, the gateway to Canada. Thereafter the war in North America

George III

At age thirty-three, the young king of a victorious empire.

dragged on until 1763, but the rest was a process of mopping up. In the South, where little significant action had occurred, belated fighting flared up between the Carolina settlers and the Cherokee Nation. A force of British regulars and colonial militia broke Cherokee resistance in 1761.

On October 25, 1760, King George II, as was his habit, arose at 6 A.M., drank his morning chocolate, and then died on his toilet as the result of a ruptured artery. The twenty-two-year-old, inexperienced grandson he despised thereupon ascended the throne as George III. Initially timid and insecure, the boyish king soon proved himself to be a strong leader. He quickly dismissed the inner circle of politicians who had dominated his grandfather's reign and replaced them with a compliant group called the "king's friends." He then oversaw the military defeat of France and Spain and the signing of a magisterial peace treaty that made Great Britain the ruler of an enormous world empire and a united kingdom brimming with confidence and pride. No nation in 1763 was larger or richer or militarily as strong.

THE TREATY OF PARIS   The Treaty of Paris, signed in February 1763, brought an end both to the world war and to the French empire in North America. In winning the long war against France and Spain, Great Britain had gained a vast global empire. Victorious Britain took all of France's North American possessions east of the Mississippi River: all of Canada and all of what was then called Spanish Florida (including much of present-day Alabama and Mississippi).

In compensation for its loss of Florida in the Treaty of Paris, Spain received the vast Louisiana Territory (including New Orleans and all French land west of the Mississippi River) from France. Unlike the Spanish in Florida, however, few of the French settlers left Louisiana after 1763. The French government encouraged the settlers to work with their new Spanish governors to create a Catholic bulwark against further English expansion.

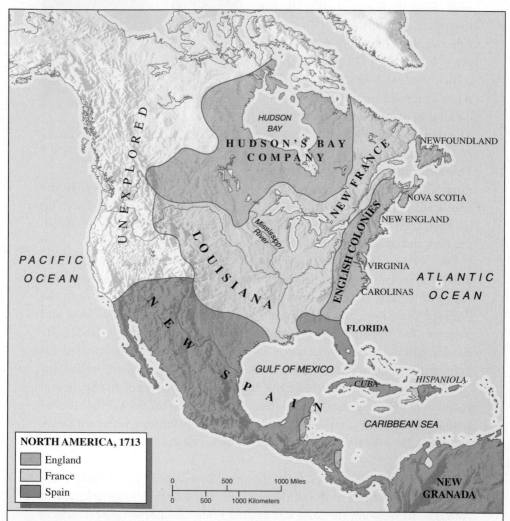

NORTH AMERICA, 1713

- England
- France
- Spain

What events led to the first clashes between the French and the British in the late seventeenth century? Why did New England suffer more than other regions of North America during the wars of the eighteenth century? What were the long-term financial, military, and political consequences of the wars between France and Britain?

Spain would hold title to Louisiana for nearly four decades but would never succeed in erasing the territory's French roots. The French-born settlers always outnumbered the Spanish. The loss of Louisiana left France with no territory on the continent. British power reigned supreme over North America east of the Mississippi River.

But Britain's spectacular military success also created future problems. Humiliated France thirsted for revenge against an "arrogant" Britain. Victory

How did the map of North America change between 1713 and 1763? How did Spain win Louisiana? What were the consequences of the British winning all the land east of the Mississippi?

was also costly. Britain's national debt doubled during the war. The cost of maintaining the North American empire, including the permanent station-ing of British soldiers in the colonies, was staggering. Simply taking over the string of French forts along the Great Lakes and in the Ohio and Mississippi river valleys would require 10,000 additional British soldiers. Even more sol-diers would be needed to manage the rising tensions generated by continuing white encroachment into Indian lands in the trans-Appalachian West. And the victory required that Britain devise ways to administer (and finance the supervision of) half a *billion* acres of new colonial territory. How were the vast, fertile lands (taken from Indians) in the Ohio Country to be "pacified," exploited, settled, and governed? The British may have won a global empire as a result of the Seven Years' War, but their grip on the American colonies would grow ever weaker as the years passed.

MANAGING A NEW EMPIRE No sooner was the Treaty of Paris signed than King George III set about reducing the huge national debt caused by the prolonged world war. In 1763 the average Briton paid 26 shillings a year in taxes; the average American colonist paid only one shilling. The British government's efforts to force colonists to pay their share of the finan-cial burden set in motion a chain of events that would lead to revolution and independence. That Americans bristled at efforts to get them to pay their "fair share" of the military expenses led British officials to view them as selfish and self-centered. At the same time, the colonists who fought in the French and Indian War and celebrated the British victory soon grew perplexed at why the empire they served, loved, and helped to secure seemed determined to treat them as "slaves" rather than citizens. "It is truly a miserable thing," said a Connecticut minister in December 1763, "that we no sooner leave fighting our neighbors, the French, but we must fall to quarreling among ourselves."

PONTIAC'S REBELLION American colonists were rabid expansion-ists. With the French out of the way and vast new western lands to exploit, they looked to the future with confidence. Already the population of America in 1763 was a third the size of Great Britain's—and was growing more rapidly. No sooner had the Seven Years' War ended than land speculators began squabbling over disputed claims to sprawling tracts of Indian–owned land west of the Appalachian Mountains.

The Peace of Paris did not in fact bring peace to North America. News of the treaty settlement devastated those Indians who had been allied with the French. Their lands were being given over to the British without consultation. The Shawnees, for instance, demanded to know "by what right the French could pretend" to transfer their ancestral lands to the British. In a desperate effort to recover their lands, Indians struck back in the spring of 1763, capturing most of the British forts around the Great Lakes and in the Ohio River valley—and killing hundreds of British soldiers in the process. They also raided colonial settlements in Pennsylvania, Maryland, and Virginia, destroying hundreds of homesteads and killing several thousand people.

The widespread Indian attacks in the spring and summer of 1763 came to be called **Pontiac's Rebellion** because of the prominent role played by the charismatic Ottawa chieftain. The attacks convinced most colonists that all Indians must be killed or removed. The British government took a different stance, negotiating an agreement with the Indians that allowed redcoats to reoccupy the frontier forts in exchange for a renewal of the generous trading and gift giving long practiced by the French. Still, as Chief Pontiac stressed, the Indians denied the legitimacy of the British claim to their territory under the terms of the Treaty of Paris. He told a British official that the "French never conquered us, neither did they purchase a foot of our Country, nor have they a right to give it to you."

To keep peace with the Indians, King George III issued the Proclamation of 1763, which drew an imaginary line along the crest of the Appalachian Mountains from Canada in the north to Georgia in the south, beyond which white settlers ("our loving subjects") were forbidden to go. For the first time, American territorial expansion was to be controlled by royal officials—and 10,000 British soldiers were dispatched to the frontier to enforce the new rule. Yet the proclamation line was ineffective. Land-hungry settlers defied the prohibitions and pushed across the Appalachian ridges into Indian country.

REGULATING THE COLONIES

The Proclamation of 1763 was the first of a series of efforts by the British government to more effectively regulate the American colonies. Little did the king and his ministers know that their efforts at efficiency would spawn a revolution.

GRENVILLE'S COLONIAL POLICY   Just as the Proclamation of 1763 was being drafted, a new British ministry had begun to grapple with the complex problems of imperial finances. The new chief minister, George Grenville, was a strong-willed accountant whose humorless self-assurance verged on pomposity. In developing new policies regulating the American colonies, Grenville took for granted the need for British soldiers to defend the western frontier. Because the average Briton paid twenty-six times the average annual taxes paid by Americans (the "least taxed people in the world"), Grenville—and most other Britons—reasoned that the "spoiled" Americans should share more of the cost of the British troops providing their defense. He also resented the large number of Americans who defied British trade regulations by engaging in rampant smuggling. So Grenville ordered colonial officials to tighten the enforcement of the Navigation Acts, and he dispatched warships to capture American smugglers. He also set up a new court in the Canadian port of Halifax, granting its single judge jurisdiction over all the American colonies and ensuring that there would be no juries of colonists sympathetic to smugglers. Under Grenville, the period of "salutary neglect" in the enforcement of the Navigation Acts was abruptly coming to an end, causing American merchants (and smugglers) great annoyance.

Strict enforcement of the Molasses Act of 1733 posed a serious threat to New England's prosperity. Making rum from molasses, a syrup derived from sugarcane, was quite profitable. Grenville recognized that the long-neglected molasses tax, if enforced, would devastate a major colonial industry. So he put through the American Revenue Act of 1764, commonly known as the Sugar Act, which cut the duty on molasses in half. Doing so, he believed, would reduce the temptation to smuggle or to bribe customs officers. But the Sugar Act also levied new duties on imports into America of textiles, wine, coffee, indigo, and sugar. The new revenues generated by the Sugar Act, Grenville estimated, would help defray "the necessary expenses of defending, protecting, and securing, the said colonies and plantations."

The Sugar Act was momentous. For the first time, Parliament had adopted so-called external duties designed to raise *revenues* in the colonies and not merely intended to *regulate* trade. As such, it was an example of Parliament trying to "tax" the colonists without their consent. Critics of the Sugar Act pointed out that British subjects could only be taxed by Parliament. Because the colonists had no elected representatives in Parliament, the argument went, Parliament had no right to impose taxes on them.

Another of Grenville's regulatory measures, the Currency Act of 1764, originated in the complaints of London merchants about doing business with Americans, especially Virginians. The colonies had long faced a chronic shortage of "hard" money (gold and silver coins, called *specie*), which kept flowing overseas to pay debts in England. To meet the shortage of specie, they issued their own paper money or, as in the case of Virginia planters, used tobacco as a form of currency. British creditors feared payment in a currency of such fluctuating value, however. To alleviate their fears,

Grenville prohibited the colonies from printing more paper money. This caused the value of existing paper money to plummet. As a Philadelphia newspaper lamented, "The Times are Dreadful, Dismal, Doleful, Dolorous, and DOLLAR-LESS."

THE STAMP ACT   As prime minister, George Grenville excelled at doing the wrong thing—repeatedly. The Sugar Act, for example, did not produce net revenue for Great Britain. Its administrative costs were four times greater than the additional revenue it generated. Yet Grenville compounded the problem by pushing through an even more provocative measure to raise money in America: a stamp tax. On February 13, 1765, Parliament passed the Stamp Act, which created revenue stamps to be purchased and affixed to every form of printed matter used in the colonies: newspapers, pamphlets, bonds, leases, deeds, licenses, insurance policies, college diplomas, even playing cards. The requirement was to go into effect November 1, nine months later. The Stamp Act affected all the colonists, not just New England merchants, and it was the first outright effort by Parliament to place a direct—or "internal"—tax specifically on American goods and services rather than an "external" tax on imports and exports.

That same year, Grenville completed his new system of colonial regulations when he persuaded Parliament to pass the Quartering Act. In effect it was yet another tax. The Quartering Act required the colonies to feed and house British troops. The new requirement raised troubling questions in the colonies. Why was it necessary for British soldiers to be stationed in colonial cities in peacetime? Was not the Quartering Act another example of taxation without representation because the colonies had neither requested the troops nor been asked their opinion? Some colonists decided that the Quartering Act was an effort to use British soldiers to tyrannize the Americans.

THE IDEOLOGICAL RESPONSE   Grenville's colonial policies outraged Americans. Unwittingly, he had stirred up a storm of protest and set in motion a profound exploration of colonial rights and imperial relations. From the start of English settlement in America, free colonists had come to take for granted certain essential principles and practices: self-government, religious freedom, economic opportunity, and territorial expansion. All of those deeply embedded values seemed threatened by Britain's efforts to tighten its control over the colonies after 1763. The tensions between the colonies and mother country began to take on moral and spiritual overtones associated with the old Whig principle that no Englishman could be taxed without his consent through representative government. Americans opposed to English policies began to call themselves true **Whigs** and label the king and his "corrupt" ministers as "Tories."

In 1764 and 1765, American Whigs decided that Grenville was imprisoning them in the very chains of tyranny from which Parliament had rescued England in the seventeenth century. A standing army—rather than a militia—was the historic ally of despots, yet now with the French defeated and Canada under English control, thousands of British soldiers remained in the colonies. For what purpose—to protect the colonists or to subdue them? Other factors heightened colonial anxiety. Among the fundamental rights of English people were trial by jury and the presumption of innocence, but the new admiralty court in Halifax excluded juries and put the burden of proof on the defendant. Most important, English citizens had the right to be taxed only by their elected representatives. Now, however, Parliament was usurping the colonial assemblies' power of the purse strings. This could lead only to tyranny and enslavement, critics argued. Sir Francis Bernard, the royal governor of Massachusetts, correctly predicted that the new stamp tax "would cause a great Alarm & meet much Opposition" in the colonies. Indeed, the seed of American independence was planted by the fiery debates over the stamp tax.

PROTEST IN THE COLONIES   The Stamp Act aroused a ferocious response among the colonists. In a flood of pamphlets, speeches, and resolutions, critics repeated a slogan familiar to all Americans: "no taxation without representation." Through the spring and summer of 1765, resentment boiled over at meetings, parades, bonfires, and other demonstrations. The protesters, calling themselves **Sons of Liberty**, met underneath "liberty trees"—in Boston a great elm, in Charleston, South Carolina, a live oak.

In mid-August 1765, nearly three months before the Stamp Act was to take effect, a Boston mob sacked the homes of the lieutenant governor and the local customs officer in charge of enforcing the stamp tax. Thoroughly shaken, the Boston stamp agent resigned, and stamp agents throughout the colonies were hounded out of office. By November 1, its effective date, the Stamp Act was a dead letter. Colonists by the thousands signed nonimportation agreements, promising not to buy imported British goods as a means of exerting leverage in London.

The widespread protests involved courageous women as well as men, and the boycotts of British goods encouraged colonial unity as Americans discovered that they had more in common with each other than with London. The Virginia House of Burgesses struck the first blow against the Stamp Act with the Virginia Resolves, a series of resolutions inspired by the ardent young Patrick Henry. Virginians, the burgesses declared, were entitled to all the rights of Englishmen, and Englishmen could be taxed only by their own elected representatives. Newspapers spread the Virginia Resolves throughout the colonies, and other assemblies hastened to copy Virginia's example.

In 1765 the Massachusetts House of Representatives invited the other colonial assemblies to send delegates to confer in New York about their opposition to the Stamp Act. Nine responded, and from October 7 to 25, 1765, the **Stamp Act Congress** formulated a Declaration of the Rights and Grievances of the Colonies. The delegates insisted "that no taxes should be imposed on them, but with their own consent, given personally, or by their representatives." Parliament, in other words, had no right to levy taxes on people who were unrepresented in that body. Grenville responded by denouncing colonial critics as "ungrateful."

REPEAL OF THE STAMP ACT The storm had scarcely broken before Grenville's ministry was out of office and the Stamp Act was repealed. For reasons unrelated to his colonial policies, Grenville had lost the confidence

The Repeal, or the Funeral Procession of Miss America-Stamp

This 1766 cartoon shows Grenville carrying the dead Stamp Act in its coffin. In the background, trade with America starts up again.

of the king, who replaced Grenville with Lord Rockingham, a leader of a Whig faction critical of Grenville's colonial policies. Pressure from British merchants who feared the economic consequences of the colonial non-importation movement convinced the Rockingham-led government that the Stamp Act was a mistake. The prime minister asked Parliament to rescind the Stamp Act. In 1766, Parliament did so but at the same time passed the Declaratory Act, which asserted the power of Parliament to make laws binding the colonies "in all cases whatsoever." It was a cunning evasion that made no concession with regard to taxes but made no mention of them either. For the moment, however, the Declaratory Act was a face-saving gesture. News of the repeal of the Stamp Act set off excited demonstrations throughout the colonies. Amid the rejoicing and relief on both sides of the Atlantic, few expected that the quarrel between Britain and its American colonies would be reopened within a year.

FANNING THE FLAMES

Meanwhile, King George III continued to play musical chairs with his prime ministers. In July 1766 the king replaced Rockingham with William Pitt, the former prime minister who had exercised heroic leadership during the French and Indian War. Alas, by the time he returned as prime minister, Pitt was so mentally unstable that he deferred policy decisions to the other cabinet members. For a time in 1767, the guiding force in the ministry was the witty but reckless Charles Townshend, chancellor of the exchequer (treasury), whose "abilities were superior to those of all men," said a colleague, "and his judgment below that of any man."

THE TOWNSHEND ACTS In 1767, Townshend put his ill-fated revenue plan through the House of Commons, and a few months later he died at age forty-two, leaving behind a bitter legacy: the Townshend Acts. With this legislation, Townshend had sought first to bring New York's colonial assembly to its senses. That body had defied the Quartering Act by refusing to provide beds or supplies for British troops. Parliament, at Townshend's behest, had suspended all acts of New York's assembly until it would yield. New Yorkers protested but finally caved in, inadvertently confirming the British suspicion that too much indulgence had encouraged colonial bad manners. Townshend had followed up with the Revenue Act of 1767, which levied duties on colonial imports of glass, lead, paint, paper, and tea. The Townshend duties increased government revenues, but the intangible costs were greater. The duties taxed goods exported from England, indirectly hurting British manufacturers. But the highest cost came in the form of added conflict with the colonists. The Revenue Act of 1767 posed a more severe threat to colonial assemblies than Grenville's taxes had, for Townshend proposed to use these revenues to pay colonial governors and other officers and thereby release them from financial dependence upon the assemblies.

The Townshend Acts surprised and angered the colonists, but this time the storm gathered more slowly than it had two years before. Once again, colonial activists, including a growing number of women calling themselves Daughters of Liberty, resolved to resist. They boycotted the purchase of imported British goods, made their own clothes ("homespun"), and developed their own manufactures.

SAMUEL ADAMS AND THE SONS OF LIBERTY As American anger bubbled over, loyalty to the mother country waned. British officials could not cope with firebrands like **Samuel Adams** of Boston, who was emerging as the supreme genius of revolutionary agitation. Adams became a tireless agitator, whipping up the Sons of Liberty and organizing protests at the Boston town meeting and in the provincial assembly. Early in 1768 he and the Boston attorney James Otis formulated a letter that the Massachusetts assembly dispatched to the other colonies. The letter's tone was polite and logical: it restated the illegality of taxation without colonial representation in Parliament and invited the support of other colonies. British officials ordered the Massachusetts assembly to withdraw the Adams-Otis letter. The assembly refused and was dissolved by royal decree. In response to an appeal by the royal governor, 4,000 British troops were dispatched to Boston in October 1768 to maintain order. Loyalists, as the Americans who supported the king and Parliament were called, welcomed the soldiers; Patriots, those rebelling against British authority, viewed the troops as an occupation force intended to quash dissent.

Meanwhile, in London the king's long effort to reorder British politics to his liking was coming to fulfillment. In 1769 new elections for Parliament finally produced a majority of the "king's friends." And George III found a new chief minister to his taste in Frederick, **Lord North**. In 1770 the king installed a cabinet of the "king's friends," with the stout Lord North as first minister.

THE BOSTON MASSACRE By 1770 the American nonimportation agreements were strangling British trade and causing unemployment in England. The impact of colonial boycotts had persuaded Lord North to modify the Townshend Acts—just in time to halt a perilous escalation of tensions. The presence of 4,000 British soldiers ("lobster backs") in Boston had become a constant provocation. Crowds heckled and ridiculed the red-coated soldiers, many of whom earned the abuse by harassing and intimidating colonists.

On March 5, 1770, in the square outside the Boston customhouse, a group of rowdies began taunting and hurling icicles at the British sentry. His call for help brought reinforcements. Then someone rang the town fire bell, drawing a larger crowd to the scene. At their head, or so the story goes, was Crispus Attucks, a runaway Indian–African American slave. Attucks and others continued to bait the British troops. Finally, a soldier was knocked down; he rose to his feet and fired into the crowd, as did others. When the smoke cleared, five people lay dead or dying, and eight more were wounded. The cause of colonial resistance now had its first martyrs, and the first to die was Attucks. The British soldiers were indicted for murder. John Adams,

The Bloody Massacre

Paul Revere's partisan engraving of the Boston Massacre.

Sam's cousin, was one of the defense attorneys. He insisted that the accused soldiers were the victims of circumstance, provoked, he said, by a "motley rabble of saucy boys, negroes and mulattoes." All of the British soldiers were acquitted except two, who were convicted of manslaughter and branded on their thumbs.

The so-called Boston Massacre sent shock waves throughout the colonies—and to London. Late in April 1770, Parliament repealed all the Townshend duties except for the tea tax. Angry colonists insisted that pressure be kept on British merchants until Parliament gave in altogether, but the nonimportation movement soon faded. Parliament, after all, had given up the substance of the taxes, with one exception, and much of the colonists' tea was smuggled in from the Netherlands (Holland) anyway.

For two years thereafter, colonial discontent remained at a simmer. The Stamp Act was gone, as were all the Townshend duties except that on tea. But most of the Grenville-Townshend innovations remained in effect: the Sugar Act, the Currency Act, the Quartering Act, the vice-admiralty courts. The redcoats had left Boston, but they remained nearby, and the British navy still patrolled the coast. Each remained a source of irritation and the cause of occasional incidents.

A WORSENING CRISIS

In 1772 a maritime incident further eroded the colonies' fragile relationship with the mother country. Near Providence, Rhode Island, the *Gaspee*, a British warship, ran aground while chasing smugglers, and its hungry crew proceeded to commandeer local sheep, hogs, and poultry. An angry crowd from the town boarded the ship, shot the captain, removed the crew, and set fire to the vessel. The *Gaspee* incident reignited tensions between the colonies and the mother country. Ever the agitator, Sam Adams convinced the Boston town meeting to form the Committee of Correspondence, which issued a statement of rights and grievances and invited other towns to do the same. Similar committees sprang up across Massachusetts and in other colonies. A Massachusetts Loyalist called the committees "the foulest, subtlest, and most venomous serpent ever issued from the egg of sedition." The crisis was escalating. "The flame is kindled and like lightning it catches from soul to soul," reported Abigail Adams, the wife of future president John Adams.

THE BOSTON TEA PARTY   Lord North soon provided the colonists with the occasion to bring resentment from a simmer to a boil. In 1773, he tried to help some friends bail out the East India Company, which had in its British warehouses some 17 million pounds of tea it desperately needed to sell. Under the Tea Act of 1773, the government would allow the grossly mismanaged company to send its south Asian tea directly to America without paying any duties. British tea merchants could thereby undercut the prices charged by their colonial competitors, most of whom were smugglers who bought tea from the Dutch. At the same time, King George III told Lord North that his job was to "compel obedience" in the colonies; North ordered British authorities in New England to clamp down on American smuggling.

The Committees of Correspondence, backed by Boston merchants, alerted colonists to the new danger. The British government, they said, was trying to purchase colonial acquiescence with cheap tea. They saw the reduction in the price of tea as a clever ruse to make them accept taxation without consent. Before the end of the year, large shipments of tea left Britain for the major colonial ports. In Boston irate colonists decided that their passion for liberty outweighed their love for tea. On December 16, 1773, scores of Patriots disguised as Mohawks boarded three British ships and threw the 342 chests of East India Company tea overboard—cheered on by a crowd along the shore. John Adams applauded the vigilante action. The destruction of the disputed tea, he said, was "so bold, so daring, so firm, intrepid and inflexible" that it would have "important consequences." Indeed it did.

The Boston Tea Party pushed British officials to the breaking point. They had tolerated abuse, evasion, and occasional violence, but the destruction of so much valuable tea convinced the furious king and his advisers that a firm response was required. "The colonists must either submit or triumph," George III wrote to Lord North, who decided to make an example of Boston to the rest of the colonies. In the end, however, he helped make a revolution that would cost England far more than three shiploads of tea.

THE COERCIVE ACTS In 1774 Parliament enacted a cluster of harsh measures, called the Coercive Acts in the colonies, intended to punish rebellious Boston. The Boston Port Act closed the harbor from June 1, 1774, until the city paid for the lost tea. A new Quartering Act directed local authorities to provide lodging in the city for British soldiers. Finally, the Massachusetts Government Act made all of the colony's civic officers appointive rather than elective, declared that sheriffs would select jurors, and stipulated that no town meeting could be held without the royal governor's consent. In May, Lieutenant-General Thomas Gage, commander in chief of British forces in North America, became governor of Massachusetts and assumed command of the 4,000 British soldiers in Boston.

Elsewhere, colonists rallied to the cause of besieged Boston, raising money, sending provisions, and boycotting, as well as burning, British tea. In Williamsburg, when the Virginia assembly met in May, a young member of the Committee of Correspondence, **Thomas Jefferson**, proposed to set aside June 1, the effective date of the Boston Port Act, as a day of fasting and prayer in Virginia. The royal governor immediately dissolved the assembly, whose members then retired to the Raleigh Tavern and resolved to form a Continental Congress to represent all the colonies. As George Washington prepared to leave Virginia to attend the gathering of the First Continental Congress in Philadelphia, he declared that Boston's fight against British tyranny "now is and ever will be considered as the cause of America (not that we approve their conduct in destroying the Tea)." The alternative, Washington added in a comment that betrayed his moral blind spot, was to become "tame and abject slaves, as the blacks we rule over with such arbitrary sway."

THE CONTINENTAL CONGRESS On September 5, 1774, the fifty-five delegates making up the First Continental Congress assembled in Philadelphia. Their mission was to assert the rights of the colonies and create collective measures to defend them. During seven weeks of meetings, the Congress endorsed the Suffolk Resolves, which declared the Intolerable Acts null and void and urged Massachusetts to resist British tyranny with force. The Congress then adopted a Declaration of American Rights, which proclaimed once again the rights of Americans as English citizens, denied Parliament's authority to regulate internal colonial affairs, and proclaimed the right of each colonial assembly to determine the need for British troops within its own province.

Finally, the Continental Congress adopted the Continental Association of 1774, which recommended that every community form committees to enforce an absolute boycott of all imported British goods. These elected committees became the organizational and communications network for the Revolutionary movement. Seven thousand men across the colonies served on the committees of the Continental Association. The committees often required colonists to sign an oath to join the boycotts against British goods. Those who refused to sign were ostracized and intimidated; some were tarred and feathered. The nonimportation movement of the 1760s and 1770s provided women with a significant public role. The Daughters of Liberty again resolved to quit buying imported British apparel and to make their own clothing.

Such efforts to gain economic self-sufficiency helped bind the diverse colonies by ropes of shared resistance. Thousands of ordinary men and women participated in the boycott of British goods, and their sacrifices on behalf of colonial liberties provided the momentum leading to revolution. For all of the attention given to colonial leaders such as Sam Adams and Thomas Jefferson, it was common people who enforced the boycott, volunteered in "Rebel" militia units, attended town meetings, and increasingly exerted pressure on royal officials in the colonies. The "Founding Fathers" (a phrase coined in 1916) could not have led the Revolutionary movement without such widespread popular support. As the people of Pittsfield, Massachusetts, declared in a petition, "We have always believed that the people are the fountain of power."

In London the king fumed. He wrote Lord North that "blows must decide" whether the Americans "are to be subject to this country or independent." In early 1775, Parliament declared that Massachusetts was "in rebellion" and prohibited the New England colonies from trading with any nation outside the empire. There would be no negotiation with the rebellious Continental Congress; force was the only option. British military leaders assured the king that the colonies could not mount a significant armed resistance. On February 27, 1775, Lord North issued a Conciliatory Proposition, sent to the individual colonies rather than the unrecognized Continental Congress. It offered to resolve the festering dispute by eliminating all revenue-generating taxes on any colony that voluntarily paid both its share for military defense and the salaries of the royal governors.

But the colonial militants were in no mood for reconciliation. In March 1775, Virginia's leading rebels met to discuss their options. While most of the Patriots believed that Britain would relent in the face of united colonial resistance, the theatrical **Patrick Henry** decided that war was imminent. He urged Patriots to prepare for combat. The twenty-nine-year-old Henry, a former farmer and storekeeper turned lawyer who fathered eighteen children, claimed that the colonies "have done everything that could be done to avert the storm which is now coming on," but their efforts had been met only by "violence and insult." Freedom, the defiant Henry shouted, could be bought only with blood. If forced to choose, he shouted, "give me liberty"— he paused dramatically, clenched his fist as if it held a dagger, then plunged it into his chest—"or give me death."

SHIFTING AUTHORITY

As Patrick Henry had predicted, events during 1775 quickly moved beyond conciliation toward conflict. The king and Parliament had lost control of their colonies; they could neither persuade nor coerce them to accept new regulations and revenue measures. In Boston General Gage warned his British superiors that armed conflict with the Americans would unleash the "horrors of civil war." But British politicians scoffed at the idea of any serious armed resistance. Lord Sandwich, the head of the navy, dismissed the colonists as "raw, undisciplined, cowardly men." Major John Pitcairn agreed, writing home from Boston in 1775, "that one active campaign, a smart action, and burning two or three of their towns, will set everything to rights."

LEXINGTON AND CONCORD   Major Pitcairn soon had his chance to suppress the resistance. On April 14, 1775, the British army in Boston received secret orders to stop the "open rebellion" in Massachusetts. General Gage decided to arrest rebel leaders and seize the militia's gunpowder stored at Concord, about twenty miles northwest of Boston. After dark on April 18, some seven hundred redcoats crossed the Charles River after midnight, and set out west to Lexington, accompanied by American Loyalists who volunteered to guide the troops and "spy" for them. When Patriots got wind of the plan, Boston's Committee of Safety sent **Paul Revere** and William Dawes by separate routes on their famous ride to warn the rebels. Revere reached Lexington about midnight and alerted rebel leaders John Hancock and Sam Adams, who were hiding there. Joined by Dawes and Samuel Prescott, Revere rode on toward Concord. A British patrol intercepted the trio, but Prescott slipped through and delivered the warning.

At dawn on April 19, the British advance guard of 238 redcoats found Captain John Parker, a veteran of the French and Indian War, and about seventy "**Minutemen**" lined up on the Lexington town square. Parker apparently intended only a silent protest, but Major Pitcairn rode onto the green, swung his sword, and yelled, "Disperse, you damned rebels! You dogs, run!" The greatly outnumbered militiamen had already begun backing away when someone, perhaps an onlooker, fired a shot, whereupon the British soldiers, without orders, loosed a volley into the Minutemen, then charged them with bayonets, leaving eight dead and ten wounded.

The British officers hastily brought their men under control and led them along the road to Concord. There the Americans resolved to stop the British advance. The Americans inflicted fourteen casualties, and by noon the British had begun a ragged retreat back to Lexington, where they were joined by reinforcements. By then, however, the narrow road back to Boston had turned into a gauntlet of death as hundreds of rebels fired from behind stone walls, trees, barns, and houses. Among the Americans were Captain Parker and the reassembled Lexington militia, some of them with bandaged

The Battle of Lexington

Amos Doolittle's impression of the Battle of Lexington as combat begins.

wounds from their morning skirmish. By nightfall the redcoat survivors were safely back in Boston, having suffered three times as many casualties as the Americans. A British general reported to London that the Americans had earned his respect: "Whoever looks upon them as an irregular mob will find himself much mistaken."

THE SPREADING CONFLICT The Revolutionary War had begun. When the Second Continental Congress convened at Philadelphia on May 10, 1775, the British army in Boston was under siege by Massachusetts militia units. On the very day that Congress met, Britain's Fort Ticonderoga, on Lake Champlain near the Canadian border, fell to a Patriot force of "Green Mountain Boys" led by Ethan Allen of Vermont and Massachusetts volunteers under Benedict Arnold. Two days later the Patriots captured a smaller British fort at Crown Point, north of Ticonderoga.

The Continental Congress, with no legal authority and no resources, met amid reports of spreading warfare. On June 15 it unanimously named forty-three-year-old George Washington commander in chief of a Continental army. Washington accepted but refused to be paid. The Congress selected Washington because his service in the French and Indian War had made him one of the most experienced officers in America. That he was from influential Virginia, the wealthiest and most populous province, added to his attractiveness. And, as many people commented then and later, Washington looked like a leader. He was tall and strong, a superb horseman, and a fearless fighter.

On June 17, the very day that Washington was commissioned, Patriots engaged British forces in their first major clash, the inaccurately named Battle of Bunker Hill. On the day before the battle, colonial forces fortified the high ground overlooking Boston. Breed's Hill was the battle location, nearer to Boston than Bunker Hill, the site first chosen (and the source of the battle's erroneous name). The British reinforced their army with troops commanded by three senior generals: William Howe, Sir Henry Clinton, and John Burgoyne.

The Patriots were spoiling for a fight. As Joseph Warren, a dapper Boston physician, put it, "The British say we won't fight; by heavens, I hope I shall die up to my knees in blood!" He soon got his wish. With civilians looking on from rooftops and church steeples, the British attacked in the blistering heat, with 2,400 troops moving in tight formation through tall grass. The Americans watched from behind their earthworks as the waves of British troops in their beautiful but impractical uniforms, including bearskin hats, advanced up the hill. The militiamen, mostly farmers, waited until the attackers had come within fifteen to twenty paces, then loosed a shattering volley that devastated the British ranks.

The British re-formed their lines and attacked again. Another sheet of flames and lead greeted them, and the redcoats retreated a second time. Still, despite the appalling slaughter, the proud British generals were determined not to let the ragtag rustics humiliate them. On the third attempt, when the colonials began to run out of gunpowder and were forced to throw stones, a bayonet charge ousted them. The British took the high ground, but at the cost of 1,054 casualties. American losses were about 450 killed or wounded out of a total of 1,500 defenders. "A dear bought victory," recorded a British general; "another such would have ruined us."

The Battle of Bunker Hill had two profound effects. First, the high number of British casualties made the English generals more cautious in subsequent encounters with the Continental army. Second, the Continental Congress recommended that all able-bodied men enlist in a militia. After the Battle of Bunker Hill, the two armies, American and British, settled in for a nine-month stalemate.

In July 1775, the Continental Congress authorized an ill-fated offensive against Quebec, in the vain hope of rallying support among the French inhabitants in Canada, Britain's fourteenth American colony, and also winning the allegiance of the Indian tribes in the region. One Patriot force, under General Richard Montgomery, headed toward Quebec by way of Lake Champlain along the New York–Canadian border; another, under General Benedict Arnold, struggled west through the dense Maine woods. The American units arrived outside Quebec in September, tired, exhausted, and hungry. A silent killer then ambushed them: smallpox. As the deadly virus raced through the American camp, General Montgomery faced a brutal dilemma. Most of his soldiers had signed up for short tours of duty, many of which were scheduled to expire at the end of the year. He could not afford to wait until spring for the smallpox to subside. Seeing little choice but to fight, Montgomery ordered a desperate attack on the British forces at Quebec during a blizzard, on December 31, 1775. The assault was a disaster. Montgomery was killed early in the battle and Benedict Arnold wounded. Over 400 Americans were taken prisoner. The rest of the Patriot force retreated to its camp outside the walled city and appealed to the Continental Congress for reinforcements.

As the fighting spread north into Canada and south into Virginia and the Carolinas, the Continental Congress negotiated treaties of peace with Indian tribes, organized a network of post offices headed by Benjamin Franklin, and authorized the formation of a navy and Marine Corps. But the delegates continued to hold back from declaring independence.

Meanwhile, in Boston, the prolonged standoff between Patriot and British forces ended in dramatic fashion when a hardy group of American troops led by Colonel Henry Knox captured the strategic British Fort Ticonderoga in upstate New York. Then, through a herculean effort across hundreds of miles of snow-covered, mountainous terrain, they brought back with them to Boston sleds loaded with captured British cannons and ammunition. The added artillery finally gave General Washington the firepower needed to make an audacious move. In early March 1776, Patriot forces, including Indian allies, occupied Dorchester Heights, to the south of the Boston peninsula, and aimed their newly acquired cannons at the besieged British troops and their "Tory" supporters in the city.

In March 1776 the British army in Boston decided to abandon the city. The last British forces, along with 2,000 panicked Loyalists ("Tories"), boarded a fleet of 120 ships and sailed for Canada on March 17, 1776. By the time the British forces fled Boston, they were facing not the suppression of a rebellion but the reconquest of a continent.

On July 6 and 8, 1775, the Continental Congress issued an appeal to the king known as the Olive Branch Petition, written by Pennsylvanian John Dickinson. It professed continued loyalty to George III and urged the king to seek reconciliation with his aggrieved colonies. When the Olive Branch Petition reached London, George III refused even to look at it. On August 22, he declared the American rebels "open and avowed enemies."

COMMON SENSE The Revolutionary War was well underway in January 1776 when Thomas Paine, a recent English emigrant to America, provided the Patriot cause with a stirring pamphlet titled ***Common Sense***. Until his fifty-page pamphlet appeared, colonial grievances had been mainly directed at the British Parliament; few colonists considered independence an option. Paine, however, directly attacked allegiance to the monarchy, which had remained the last frayed connection to Britain. The "common sense" of the matter, he stressed, was that King George III bore the responsibility for the rebellion. Americans, Paine urged, should consult their own interests, abandon George III, and assert their independence: "The blood of the slain, the weeping voice of nature cries, 'TIS TIME TO PART." Only by declaring independence, Paine predicted, could the colonists enlist the support of France and Spain and thereby engender a holy war of monarchy against monarchy.

INDEPENDENCE

Within three months more than 150,000 copies of Paine's pamphlet were circulating throughout the provinces, an enormous number for the time. "*Common Sense* is working a powerful change in the minds of men," George Washington reported. In May 1776 the Second Continental Congress

The coming revolution

The Continental Congress votes for independence, July 2, 1776.

authorized all thirteen colonies to form themselves into new state govern-ments. Thereafter, one by one, the colonies authorized their delegates in the Continental Congress to take the final step. On June 7, Richard Henry Lee of Virginia moved "that these United Colonies are, and of right ought to be, free and independent states." Lee's resolution passed on July 2, a date that "will be the most memorable epoch in the history of America," John Adams wrote to his wife, Abigail. In the meantime, as he looked at his troops, George Washington declared that the "fate of unborn millions will now depend, under God, on the courage and conduct of this army." The more memorable date, however, became July 4, 1776, when the Congress formally adopted the Declaration of Independence as the official statement of the American position.

JEFFERSON'S DECLARATION   In June 1776 the Continental Congress appointed a committee of five men—Jefferson, Benjamin Franklin, John Adams, Robert Livingston of New York, and Roger Sherman of Connecticut—to write a public rationale for independence. The group asked Adams and Jef-ferson to produce a first draft, whereupon Adams deferred to Jefferson because of the thirty-three-year-old Virginian's reputation as an eloquent writer.

Jefferson shared his draft with the committee members, and they made several minor revisions before submitting the document to the Congress. The legislators made eighty-six changes in Jefferson's declaration, including the insertion of two references to God and the deletion of a section blaming the English monarch for imposing African slavery on the colonies (delegates from Georgia and South Carolina had protested that the language smacked of abolitionism).

The resulting Declaration of Independence introduced the radical con-cept that "all men are created equal" in terms of their God-given right to maintain governments of their own choosing. This represented a compelling restatement of John Locke's contract theory of government—the theory, in Jefferson's words, that governments derive "their just Powers from the con-sent of the people," who are entitled to "alter or abolish" those governments that deny people (white people, in Jefferson's eyes) their "unalienable rights" to "life, Liberty, and the pursuit of Happiness." Parliament, which had no proper authority over the colonies, was never mentioned by name. The stated enemy was a king trying to impose "an absolute Tyranny over these States." The "Representatives of the United States of America," therefore, declared the thirteen "United Colonies" to be "Free and Independent States."

General George Washington ordered the Declaration read to every unit in the Continental army. Benjamin Franklin acknowledged how high the stakes

The Declaration of Independence

The Declaration in its most frequently reproduced form,
an 1823 engraving by William J. Stone.

were: "Well, Gentlemen," he told the Congress, "we must now hang together,
or we shall most assuredly hang separately." The Declaration of Independence converted what had been an armed rebellion—a civil war between
British subjects—into a war between Britain and a new nation.

"WE ALWAYS HAD GOVERNED OURSELVES" So it had come to
this, thirteen years after Britain had defeated France and gained control of
North America with the Treaty of Paris in 1763. In explaining the causes of
the Revolution, historians have highlighted many factors: the excessive
British regulation of colonial trade, the restrictions on settling western
lands, the growing tax burden, the mounting debts to British merchants, the
lack of American representation in Parliament, the abrupt shift from a mercantile to an "imperial" policy after 1763, class conflict, and revolutionary
agitators.

I am very affectionately your Friend
Phillis Wheatley
Boston March 21. 1774.

Phillis Wheatley

An autographed portrait of Phillis Wheatley, America's first African American poet.

Each of those factors (and others) contributed to the collective grievances that rose to a climax in a gigantic failure of British statesmanship. A conflict between British sovereignty and American rights had come to a point of confrontation that adroit diplomacy might have avoided, sidestepped, or outflanked. The rebellious colonists saw the tightening of British regulations as the conspiracy of a despotic king—to impose an "absolute Tyranny."

Yet colonists sought liberty from British tyranny for many reasons, not all of which were selfless or noble. The Boston merchant John Hancock embraced the Patriot cause in part because he was the region's foremost smuggler. Paying British taxes would have cost him a fortune. Likewise, South Carolina's Henry Laurens and Virginia's Landon Carter, wealthy planters, were concerned about the future of slavery under British control. The seeming contradiction between American slaveholders demanding liberty from British oppression was not lost on observers at the time. The talented writer Phillis Wheatley, the first African American to see her poetry published in America, highlighted the hypocritical "absurdity" of white colonists' demanding their freedom from British tyranny while continuing to exercise "oppressive power" over enslaved Africans. Wealthy slave owner George Washington was not devoid of self-interest in his opposition to British policies. An active land speculator, he owned 60,000 acres in the Ohio Country west of the Appalachians and very much resented British efforts to restrict white settlement on the frontier.

Perhaps the last word on the complex causes of the Revolution should belong to an obscure participant, Levi Preston, a Minuteman from Danvers, Massachusetts. Asked sixty-seven years after Lexington and Concord about British oppressions, the ninety-one-year-old veteran responded by asking his young interviewer, "What were they? Oppressions? I didn't feel them." He was then asked, "What, were you not oppressed by the Stamp Act?" Preston replied that he "never saw one of those stamps . . . I am certain I never paid a penny for one of them." What about the tax on tea? "Tea-tax! I never drank a drop of the stuff; the boys threw it all overboard." His interviewer finally asked why he decided to fight for independence. "Young man," Preston explained, "what we meant in going for those redcoats was this: we always had governed ourselves, and we always meant to. They didn't mean we should."

CHAPTER SUMMARY

- **Mercantilism** The Navigation Acts decreed that enumerated goods had to go directly to England and discouraged manufacturing in the colonies. Raw materials were shipped to the mother country to be processed into manufactured goods. These mercantilist laws were designed to curb direct trade with other countries, such as the Netherlands, and keep the wealth of the empire in British hands.

- **"Salutary Neglect"** Lax administration by the mother country allowed the colonies a measure of self-government. The dynastic problems of the Stuart kings aided the New England colonists in their efforts to undermine the Dominion of New England. The Glorious Revolution of 1688 resulted in a period of "salutary neglect." The American colonies pursued their interests with minimal intervention from the British government, which was preoccupied with European wars.

- **The French and Indian War** Four European wars affected America between 1689 and 1763 as the British and French confronted each other throughout the world. The Seven Years' War (1754–1763), known as the French and Indian War in the American colonies, was the first world war and was eventually won by the British. A plan to unify all of Britain's American colonies, including those in Canada, proposed by Benjamin Franklin at the Albany Congress, failed to gain colonial support.

- **The Effects of the Seven Years' War** At the Peace of Paris in 1763, France lost all its North American possessions. Britain gained Canada and Florida, while Spain acquired Louisiana. With the war's end, Indians were no longer regarded as essential allies and so had no recourse when settlers squatted on their lands. The Treaty of Paris set the stage for conflict between the mother country and the American colonies as Britain tightened control to pay for the colonies' defense.

- **British Colonial Policy** After the French and Indian War, the British government was saddled with an enormous national debt. To reduce that imperial burden, the British government concluded that the colonies ought to help pay for their own defense. Thus, the ministers of King George III began to implement various acts and impose new taxes.

- **Road to the American Revolution** Colonists based their resistance to the Crown on the idea that taxation without direct colonial representation in Parliament violated their rights. Colonial reaction to the Stamp Act of 1765 was the first intimation of real trouble for imperial authorities. Conflict intensified when the British government imposed additional taxes. Spontaneous resistance led to the Boston Massacre; organized protesters staged the Boston Tea Party. The British response, called the Coercive Acts, sparked further violence. Compromise became less likely, if not impossible.

CHRONOLOGY

1608	Samuel de Champlain founds Quebec
1660	Restoration of the Stuart monarchy—King Charles II
1673	The French explore the Mississippi River valley from Canada to the Gulf of Mexico
1684	Dominion of New England is established
1688	Glorious Revolution
1754	Albany Congress adopts Plan of Union
1754–1763	French and Indian War
1763	Pontiac's Rebellion
1764	Parliament passes the Revenue (Sugar) Act
1766	Parliament repeals the Stamp Act and passes the Declaratory Act
1767	Parliament levies the Townshend duties
1770	Boston Massacre
1773	Colonists stage the Boston Tea Party
1774	Parliament passes the Coercive Acts; colonists hold First Continental Congress
1775	Battles of Lexington and Concord
1775	Colonists hold Second Continental Congress
1776	Thomas Paine's *Common Sense* is published; Declaration of Independence is signed

KEY TERMS & NAMES

Part Two

BUILDING

A

NATION

The signing of the Declaration of Independence in early July 1776 exhilarated the rebellious colonists and ended the ambivalence about the purpose of the revolt. Americans now had a sober choice: to remain subjects of King George III and thus traitors to the new United States of America, or to embrace the rebellion and become a traitor to Great Britain. Yet it was one thing for Patriot leaders to declare American independence from British authority and quite another to win it on the battlefield. The odds greatly favored the British: barely a third of the colonists actively supported the Revolution, and almost as many ("Loyalists") fought tenaciously against it. The political stability of the fledgling nation was uncertain, and George Washington found himself in command of a poorly supplied, inexperienced army facing the world's greatest military power.

Yet the Revolutionary movement would persevere and prevail. The skill and fortitude of General Washington and his lieutenants enabled the American forces to exploit their geographic advantages. Even more important was the intervention of the French on behalf of the Revolutionary cause. The Franco-American military alliance, negotiated in 1778, proved to be the decisive event in the war. In 1783, after eight years of sporadic fighting and heavy human and financial losses, the British gave up the fight and their American colonies.

Amid the Revolutionary turmoil the Patriots faced the daunting task of forming new governments for themselves. Their deeply ingrained resentment of British imperial rule led them to decentralize political power and grant substantial sovereignty to the individual states. As Thomas Jefferson declared, "Virginia, Sir, is my country." Such powerful local ties help explain why the colonists focused their attention on creating new state constitutions rather than a powerful national government. The Articles of Confederation, ratified in 1781, provided only the semblance of national authority. Final power to make and execute laws remained with the states.

After the Revolutionary War, the flimsy political bonds authorized by the Articles of Confederation could not meet the needs of the new—and rapidly expanding—nation. This realization led to the calling of the Constitutional Convention in 1787. The process of drafting and ratifying the new constitution prompted a heated debate on the relative significance of national power, local control, and individual freedom that has provided the central theme of American political thought ever since.

The Revolution involved much more than the apportionment of political power, however. It also unleashed social forces that would help reshape the very fabric of American culture. What would be the role of women, African Americans, and Native Americans in the new republic? How would the quite different economies of the various regions of the new United States be developed? Who would control access to the vast territories to the west of the original thirteen states? How would the new republic relate to the other nations of the world?

These controversial questions helped spawn the first national political parties in the United States. During the 1790s, Federalists, led by Alexander Hamilton, and Republicans, led by Thomas Jefferson and James Madison, furiously debated the political and economic future of the new nation. With Jefferson's election as president in 1800, the Republicans gained the upper hand in national politics for the next quarter century. In the process they presided over a maturing republic that aggressively expanded westward at the expense of the Native Americans, ambivalently embraced industrial development, fitfully engaged in a second war with Great Britain, and ominously witnessed a growing sectional controversy over slavery.

5

THE AMERICAN
REVOLUTION

FOCUS QUESTIONS   wwnorton.com/studyspace

- What were the military strategies and challenges for both the American and the British forces?
- What were the war's major turning points?
- Who were the Loyalists and what became of them?
- Why was it possible for the new United States to gain European allies in its war for independence?
- To what extent was the American Revolution a social revolution in matters of gender equality, race relations, and religious freedom?

Few foreign observers thought that the upstart American revolutionaries could win a war against the world's greatest empire—and the Americans ended up losing most of the battles in the Revolutionary War. But they eventually forced the British to sue for peace and grant their independence, a stunning result reflecting the tenacity of the Patriots as well as the peculiar difficulties facing the British as they tried to conduct a far-flung campaign thousands of miles from home. The British Empire dispatched two thirds of its entire army and one half of its formidable navy to suppress the American rebellion. The costly military commitments that the British maintained elsewhere around the globe further complicated their war effort, and the intervention of the French on behalf of the struggling Americans in 1778 proved to be the war's key turning point. The Patriots also had the advantage of fighting on their home ground; the American commanders knew the terrain and the people. Perhaps most important of all, the Americans led by George Washington did not have to win the war; they simply had to avoid losing the war. Over time, as they discovered, the British government and the British people would tire of the human and financial expense of a prolonged war.

Fighting in the New World was not an easy task for either side, however. The Americans had to create and sustain an army and navy from scratch. Recruiting, supplying, equipping, training, and paying soldiers and sailors were monumental challenges, especially for a new nation in the midst of forming its first governments. The Patriot army encircling British-controlled Boston in 1775 was little more than a rustic militia made up of volunteers who had enlisted for six months. The citizen-soldiers lacked training and discipline. They came and went as they pleased, gambled frequently, and drank liquor freely. **General George Washington** recognized immediately that the foremost needs of the new army were capable officers, intensive training, strict discipline, and longer enlistment contracts. Washington was pleased to see that the soldiers from the different colonies were as one in their "continental" viewpoint; hence, he called it the **Continental army**. He soon began whipping his army into shape. Recruits who violated army rules were placed in the stockade, flogged, or sent packing. Some deserters were hanged. The tenacity of Washington and the Revolutionaries bore fruit as war-weariness and political dissension in London hampered British efforts to suppress the rebel forces.

Like all major wars, the Revolution had unexpected consequences affecting political, economic, and social life. It not only secured American independence, generated a sense of nationalism, and created a unique system of self-governance, but it also began a process of societal change that has yet to run its course. The turmoil of revolution upset traditional social relationships and helped transform the lives of people who had long been relegated to the periphery of social status—African Americans, women, and Indians. In important ways, then, the Revolution was much more than simply a war for independence. It was an engine for political experimentation and social change.

1776: WASHINGTON'S NARROW ESCAPE

On July 2, 1776, the day that Congress voted for independence, British redcoats landed on undefended Staten Island, across New York Harbor from Manhattan. They were the vanguard of a gigantic effort to suppress the American revolution and the first elements of an enormous force that gathered around the harbor over the next month. By mid-August, British general **William Howe** had some thirty-two thousand men at his disposal, the largest single force mustered by the British in the eighteenth century. The British recruited mercenaries (hired foreign soldiers) in Europe to assist them in putting down the American revolt. Eventually almost thirty thousand Germans served in America, about seventeen thousand of them from the principality of Hesse-Cassel—thus *Hessian* became the name applied to all of them.

After the British withdrew their forces from Boston, George Washington transferred most of his troops to New York, but he could gather only about nineteen thousand poorly trained local militiamen and members of the new Continental army. It was much too small a force to defend New York, but Congress wanted it held. This meant that Washington had to expose his outnumbered men to entrapments from which they escaped more by luck than by any strategic genius on the part of the American commander. Although a veteran of frontier fighting, Washington had never commanded a large unit or supervised artillery. As he confessed to the Continental Congress, he had no "experience to move [armies] on a large scale" and had only "limited . . . knowledge . . . in Military Matters." In 1776 he was still learning the art of generalship, and the British invasion of New York taught him some costly lessons.

FIGHTING IN NEW YORK AND NEW JERSEY In late August 1776 the massive British armada began landing troops on Long Island. It was the largest seaborne military expedition in world history. Short of munitions and greatly outnumbered, the new American army suffered a humiliating defeat at the Battle of Long Island. Had the British moved more quickly, they could have trapped Washington's army in lower Manhattan. The main American force, however, withdrew northward, crossed the Hudson River, and retreated across New Jersey and over the Delaware River into Pennsylvania. As Washington's army fled New York City, so, too, did Patriot civilians. Local Loyalists (**Tories**) welcomed the British occupation of New York City, which came to be called Torytown.

By December 1776, General Washington had only three thousand men

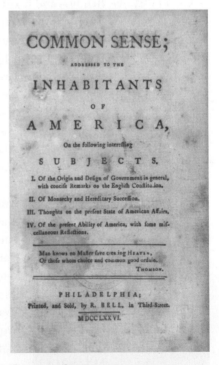

Common Sense

Thomas Paine's inspiring pamphlet was originally published anonymously because of its treasonous content.

left under his command. Thousands of militiamen had simply gone home. Unless a new army could be raised quickly, Washington warned, "I think the game is pretty near up." But it wasn't. In the retreating American army marched Englishman Thomas Paine. Having opened the eventful year of 1776 with his inspiring pamphlet *Common Sense,* Paine now composed *The American Crisis,* in which he penned these uplifting lines:

> These are the times that try men's souls: The summer soldier and the sunshine patriot will, in this crisis, shrink from the service of his country; but he that stands it NOW deserves the love and thanks of man and woman. Tyranny, like Hell, is not easily conquered. Yet we have this consolation with us, that the harder the conflict, the more glorious the triumph.

Paine's stirring pamphlet bolstered the shaken morale of the Patriots—as events would soon do more decisively. Congress's decision to offer recruits cash, land, clothing, and blankets proved more important than Thomas Paine's inspiring words in lifting the spirits of the revolutionaries.

General Howe, firmly—and luxuriously—based in New York City (which the British held throughout the war), settled down with his Loyalist mistress to wait out the winter. George Washington, however, was not ready to hibernate. He knew that the morale of his men and the hopes of a new nation required "some stroke" of good news in the face of the devastating losses around New York City. So he seized the initiative with a desperate gamble to achieve a much-needed first victory before more of his soldiers returned home once their initial enlistment contracts expired.

George Washington at Princeton
By Charles Willson Peale.

On Christmas night 1776, General Washington led some 2,400 men across the icy Delaware River. Near dawn at Trenton, New Jersey, the Americans surprised a garrison of 1,500 sleeping Hessians. It was a total rout, from which only 500 Hessians escaped death or capture. Just two of Washington's men were killed and four wounded, one of whom was Lieutenant James Monroe, the future president. A week later, at nearby Princeton, the Americans improbably won another battle, outmaneuvering the British before taking refuge in winter quarters at Morristown,

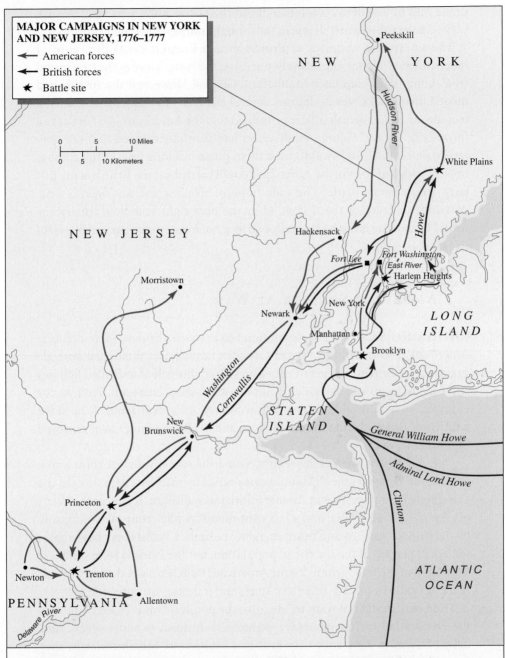

MAJOR CAMPAIGNS IN NEW YORK AND NEW JERSEY, 1776–1777

← American forces
← British forces
★ Battle site

0   5   10 Miles
0   5   10 Kilometers

N E W   Y O R K

Peekskill

Hudson River

White Plains

Howe

NEW JERSEY

Hackensack

Fort Lee

Fort Washington
East River
Harlem Heights

Morristown

Newark

New York

Manhattan

LONG ISLAND

Brooklyn

Washington

Cornwallis

STATEN ISLAND

General William Howe

Admiral Lord Howe

Clinton

New Brunswick

Princeton

Newton

Trenton

Allentown

PENNSYLVANIA

Delaware River

ATLANTIC OCEAN

Why did Washington lead his army from Brooklyn to Manhattan and from there to New Jersey? How could General Howe have ended the rebellion in New York? What is the significance of the Battle of Trenton?

in the hills of northern New Jersey about thirty-five miles west of New York City (eighteenth-century armies rarely fought during the winter months).

The unexpected victories at Princeton and Trenton saved the cause of independence. By not aggressively pursuing the Americans as they retreated from Long Island and later Manhattan, General Howe and the British had missed their great chance—indeed, several chances—to bring the Revolution to a speedy end. A British officer grumbled that the Americans had "become a formidable enemy." George Washington had painfully realized that the only way to defeat the British was to wear them down in a long war. As the combat in New York had shown, the Americans could rarely beat the British army in a large conventional battle. The only hope of winning the war was to wear down the patience of the British. Over the next eight years, the Americans would outlast the invaders through a strategy of evasion punctuated by selective confrontations.

AMERICAN SOCIETY AT WAR

CHOOSING SIDES   The Revolution was as much a brutal civil war among Americans (and their Native American allies) as it was a prolonged struggle against Great Britain. The act of choosing sides in the colonies divided families and friends, towns and cities. Benjamin Franklin's illegitimate son, William, for example, was the royal governor of New Jersey. An ardent Loyalist, he sided with Great Britain during the Revolution, and his Patriot father later removed him from his will.

Opinion among the colonists concerning the war divided in three ways: Patriots, or Whigs (as the Revolutionaries called themselves), who formed the Continental army and fought in state militias; Loyalists, or Tories, as the Patriots derisively called them; and a less committed middle group swayed mostly by the better organized and more energetic radicals. Loyalists may have represented 20 percent of the American population, but the Patriots were probably the largest of the three groups. Some Americans switched sides during the war; there were also numerous deserters, spies, and traitors—on both sides.

The Loyalists did not want to "dissolve the political bands" with Britain, as the Declaration of Independence demanded. Instead, as some seven hundred of them in New York City said in a petition to British officials, they "steadily and uniformly opposed" this "most unnatural, unprovoked Rebellion." Where the Patriots rejected the monarchy, the Loyalists staunchly upheld royal authority. They viewed the Revolution as an act of treason. Loyalists were concentrated in the seaport cities, especially New York City and Philadelphia, but they came from all walks of life. Governors, judges, and other royal officials were almost all Loyalists; most Anglican ministers also preferred the mother country, as did many Anglican parishioners. In the backcountry of New York and the Carolinas, many small farmers rallied to the Crown. More New York men during the Revolution joined Loyalist regiments than opted for the Continental army. In few places, however, were there enough Loyalists to assume control without the presence of British troops, and nowhere for very long.

MILITIA AND ARMY   American militiamen served two purposes: they constituted a home guard, defending their local communities, and they helped augment the Continental army. To repel an attack, the militia somehow materialized; the danger past, it evaporated, for there were chores to do at home. They "come in, you cannot tell how," Washington said in exasperation, "go, you cannot tell when, and act you cannot tell where, consume your provisions, exhaust your stores [supplies], and leave you at last at a critical moment."

The national Continental army, by contrast, was on the whole better trained and more reliable. Unlike the professional soldiers in the British army, Washington's troops were citizen soldiers, mostly poor native-born Americans or immigrants who had been indentured servants or convicts. Many of the Patriots found camp life debilitating and combat horrifying.

American militia

This sketch of militiamen by a French soldier at Yorktown, Virginia, shows an American frontiersman turned soldier (second from right), and it is also one of the earliest depictions of an African American soldier.

Desertions grew as the war dragged on. At times, General Washington could put only two to three thousand men in the field.

PROBLEMS OF FINANCE AND SUPPLY   Congress found it difficult to finance the war and supply the army. The states rarely provided their designated share of the war's expenses, and Congress reluctantly let army agents take supplies directly from farmers in return for promises of future payment. At the start of the fighting there were no uniforms, and the weapons they carried were "as various as their costumes." Congress did better at providing munitions than at providing other supplies. In 1777 it established a government arsenal at Springfield, Massachusetts, and during the war, states offered bounties for the manufacture of guns and powder. Still, most munitions were supplied either by wartime captures or by importation from France, whose government was all too glad to help the rebels fight its archenemy.

During the harsh New Jersey winter at Morristown (1776–1777), George Washington's army nearly disintegrated as enlistments expired and deserters fled the hardships of brutally cold weather, inadequate food, and widespread disease. One soldier recalled that "we were absolutely, literally starved . . . . I saw several of the men roast their old shoes and eat them." Smallpox continued to wreak havoc among the American armies. By 1777, Washington had come to view the virus with greater dread than "the Sword of the Enemy." The threat of smallpox to the war effort was so great that in early 1777 Washington ordered a mass inoculation, which he managed to keep secret from the British. Inoculating an entire army was an enormous, risky undertaking. Washington's daring gamble paid off. The successful inoculation of the American army marks one of his greatest strategic accomplishments of the war.

Only about a thousand Continental soldiers and a few militiamen stuck out the Morristown winter. With the spring thaw, however, recruits began arriving to claim the bounty of $20 and 100 acres of land offered by Congress to those who would enlist for three years or for the duration of the conflict, if less. With some nine thousand regular troops, Washington began sparring and feinting with Howe's British forces in northern New Jersey. Howe had been making plans, however, and so had other British officers.

1777: SETBACKS FOR THE BRITISH

The British plan to defeat the "American rebellion" involved a three-pronged assault on New York. By gaining control of that important state, they would cut off New England from the rest of the colonies. The plan called for a

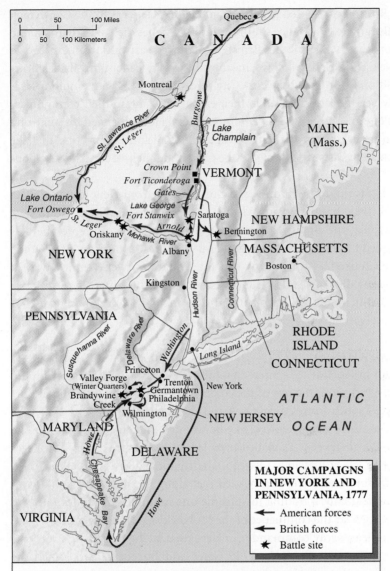

**MAJOR CAMPAIGNS
IN NEW YORK AND
PENNSYLVANIA, 1777**

← American forces

← British forces

★ Battle site

What were the consequences of Burgoyne's strategy of dividing
the colonies with two British forces? How did life in Washington's
camp at Valley Forge transform the American army? Why was
Saratoga a turning point in the American Revolution?

northern British army based in Canada and led by **General John "Gentleman Johnny" Burgoyne** to advance southward from Quebec via Lake Champlain to the Hudson River, while another British force moved eastward from Oswego, in western New York. General Howe, meanwhile, would lead a third British army up the Hudson River from New York City. As often happens with ambitious war plans, however, the British failed in their execution—and in their communications with one another. At the last minute, General Howe changed his mind and decided to move against the Patriot capital, Philadelphia, expecting that the Pennsylvania Loyalists would rally to the Crown and help secure the rebellious colony.

General Washington withdrew most of his men from New Jersey to meet the new British threat in Pennsylvania. At Brandywine Creek, southwest of Philadelphia, the British army routed the Americans on September 11, then occupied Philadelphia, the largest and wealthiest American city. George Washington retired with his army to winter quarters twenty miles away at Valley Forge, while Howe and his men remained for the winter in the relative comfort of Philadelphia. The displaced Continental Congress relocated to York, Pennsylvania.

THE CAMPAIGN OF 1777 The British plan to defeat the Americans in their war for independence centered on the northern theater. In an attempt to cut off New York from the rest of the colonies, an overconfident General Burgoyne moved south from Canada toward Lake Champlain in June 1777. The heavily laden army struggled to cross the wooded, marshy terrain in upstate New York. Burgoyne sent a smaller army led by Barrimore "Barry" St. Leger southward on Lake Ontario to Oswego, where a force of Iroquois allies joined them. The combined force then headed east along the fertile Mohawk River valley toward Albany, a trading town some one hundred fifty miles north of New York City near the confluence of the Mohawk and Hudson rivers.

The American army commander in New York facing Burgoyne's redcoats was General Horatio Gates. In 1745 Gates and Burgoyne had joined the same British regiment. Now they were commanding opposing armies. At Oriskany, New York, on August 6, 1777, a band of Patriot militiamen, mostly local German farmers and their Indian allies, withstood an ambush by Loyalists and Indians and gained time for Patriot reinforcements to arrive at nearby Fort Stanwix, which had been besieged by British soldiers. When the British demanded that the fort's commander surrender, Gates rejected the offer "with disdain," saying that the fort would be defended to the "last extremity." As the days passed, the Iroquois deserted the British army, leading the British commander to order a withdrawal, after which the strategic

General John Burgoyne

Commander of Britain's northern forces. Burgoyne and most of his troops surrendered to the Americans at Saratoga on October 17, 1777.

Mohawk River valley was secured for the Patriot forces.

To the east, at Bennington, Vermont, on August 16, New England militiamen, led by grizzled veteran Colonel John Stark, decimated a detachment of Hessians and Loyalists foraging for supplies. Stark had pledged that morning, "We'll beat them before night, or Molly Stark will be a widow." As Patriot militiamen converged from across central New York, Burgoyne pulled his dispirited forces back to the village of **Saratoga**, where General Gates's reinforced American army surrounded the outnumbered, stranded, and nearly starving British army. Desperate to retreat to Canada, the British twice tried to break through the encircling Americans, but to no avail. On October 17, 1777, Burgoyne, resplendent in his scarlet, gold, and white uniform, signed an agreement with the plain, blue-coated Horatio Gates to leave North America. The shocking British defeat at Saratoga prompted the British political leader William Pitt, the Earl of Chatham, who as prime minister had engineered the British triumph over France in 1763, to tell Parliament upon hearing the news about Burgoyne's surrender: "You CANNOT conquer America."

ALLIANCE WITH FRANCE The surprising American victory at Saratoga was strategically important because it convinced the French to sign two crucial treaties in early 1778. Under the Treaty of Amity and Commerce, France recognized the new United States and offered trade concessions, including important privileges to American shipping. Under the Treaty of Alliance, both parties agreed, first, that if France entered the war, both countries would fight until American independence was won; second, that neither would conclude a "truce or peace" without "the formal consent of the other first obtained"; and third, that each guaranteed the other's possessions in America "from the present time and forever against all other powers." France further bound itself to seek neither Canada nor other British possessions on the mainland of North America.

By June 1778, British vessels had fired on French ships, and the two nations were at war again. The French decision to join the infant United States in its fight for independence was the most important factor in America's winning the Revolutionary War. Even more important than French supplies and financial assistance was the role of the French navy in allowing the Americans to hold out against the British. In 1779, Spain entered the war as an ally of France but not of the United States. In 1780, Britain declared war on the Dutch, who persisted in a profitable trade with the French and the Americans. The rebellious farmers at Lexington and Concord had indeed fired a shot "heard round the world." A civil war between Britain's colonies and the mother country had mushroomed into another world war, as the fighting now spread to the Mediterranean, Africa, India, the West Indies, and the high seas.

1778: BOTH SIDES REGROUP

After the British defeat at Saratoga and the news of the French alliance with the United States, Lord North decided that the war was unwinnable, but the king refused to let him either resign or make peace. On March 16, 1778, the House of Commons in effect granted all the demands that the American rebels had made prior to independence. Parliament repealed the Townshend tea duty, the Massachusetts Government Act, and the Prohibitory Act, which had closed the colonies to commerce, and sent peace commissioners to Philadelphia to negotiate an end to hostilities. But Congress refused to begin any negotiations until Britain recognized American independence or withdrew its forces.

VALLEY FORGE   For Washington's army at Valley Forge, the winter of 1777–1778 was a season of intense suffering. The American force, encamped near Philadelphia, endured unrelenting cold, hunger, and disease. Some troops lacked shoes and blankets. Their makeshift log-and-mud huts offered little protection from the howling winds and bitter cold. Most of the army's horses died of exposure or starvation. By February, seven thousand troops were too ill for duty. More than two thousand five hundred soldiers died at Valley Forge; another thousand deserted. Fifty officers resigned on one December day. Several hundred more left before winter's end.

Desperate for relief, Washington sent troops on foraging expeditions into New Jersey, Delaware, and the Eastern Shore of Maryland, confiscating horses, cattle, and hogs in exchange for "receipts" to be honored by the Continental Congress. By March 1778 the once-gaunt troops at Valley Forge saw their strength restored. By the end of the winter, the ragtag soldiers at Valley Forge were beginning to resemble a professional army. The army's morale rose when Congress promised extra pay and bonuses after the war. The good news from France about the formal military alliance also helped raise their spirits. In the spring of 1778, British forces withdrew from Pennsylvania to New York City, with the American army in hot pursuit. Once the British were back in Manhattan, Washington's army encamped at White Plains, north of the city. From that time on, the northern theater, scene of the major campaigns and battles early in the war, settled into a long stalemate.

ACTIONS ON THE FRONTIER The one major American success of 1778 occurred far from the New Jersey battlefields. The Revolution had spawned two wars. In addition to the main conflict between British and American armies, a frontier guerrilla war of terror and vengeance pitted Indians and Loyalists against isolated Patriot settlers along the northern and western frontiers. The British incited frontier Loyalists and Indians to raid farm settlements and offered to pay bounties for American scalps. To end the English-led attacks, young George Rogers Clark took 175 Patriot frontiersmen on flatboats down the Ohio River early in 1778, marched through the woods, and on the evening of July 4 captured English-controlled Kaskaskia (in present-day Illinois). The French inhabitants, terrified at first, "fell into transports of joy" at news of the French alliance with the Americans. Then, without bloodshed, Clark took Cahokia (in present-day Illinois across the Mississippi River from St. Louis) and Vincennes (in present-day Indiana). After the British retook Vincennes, Clark marched his men (almost half of them French volunteers) through icy rivers and flooded prairies, sometimes in water neck deep, and laid siege to the astonished British garrison. Clark's men, all hardened woodsmen, captured five Indians carrying American scalps. Clark ordered his men to tomahawk the Indians in sight of the fort. The British thereupon surrendered the fort.

While Clark's Rangers were in Indiana, a much larger American expedition moved through western Pennsylvania to attack Iroquois strongholds in western New York. There the Loyalists and Indians had terrorized frontier settlements throughout the summer of 1778. Led by the charismatic Mohawk **Joseph Brant**, the Iroquois had killed hundreds of militiamen along the Pennsylvania frontier. In response, Washington dispatched an expedition of four thousand men under General John Sullivan to suppress

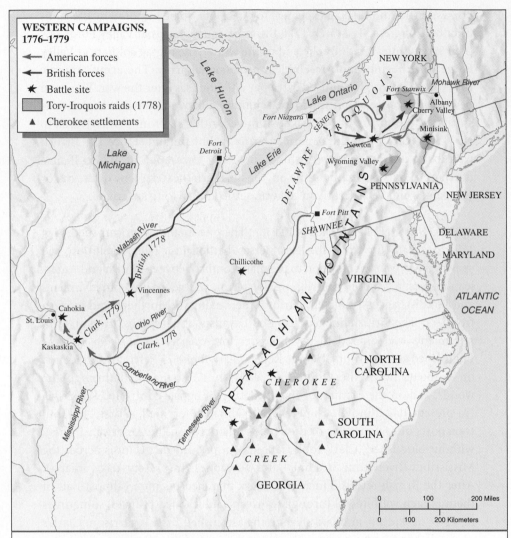

WESTERN CAMPAIGNS, 1776–1779

⟵ American forces

⟵ British forces

✳ Battle site

▨ Tory-Iroquois raids (1778)

▲ Cherokee settlements

How did George Rogers Clark secure Cahokia and Vincennes? Why did the American army destroy Iroquois villages in 1779? Why were the skirmishes between settlers and Indian tribes significant for the future of the trans-Appalachian frontier?

"the hostile tribes" and "the most mischievous of the Tories." At Newton, New York (near Elmira), on August 29, 1779, Sullivan carried out Washington's instruction that the Iroquois country be not "merely overrun but destroyed." The American force burned about forty Seneca and Cayuga villages, together with their orchards and food supplies, leaving many of the Indians homeless and without enough provisions to survive. The campaign against the Loyalists and Indians broke the power of the Iroquois Confederacy for all time, but it did not completely pacify the frontier. Sporadic encounters with various tribes continued to the end of the war.

THE WAR IN THE SOUTH

At the end of 1778, the focus of the British military efforts shifted to the southern theater. The whole region from Virginia southward had been free of major military action since 1776. Now the British would test King George's belief that a dormant Loyalist sentiment in the South needed only the presence of redcoats to be awakened. The new commander of British forces in America, General Sir Henry Clinton, dispatched three thousand redcoats, Hessians, and Loyalists to take Savannah, on the southeast Georgia coast, and roll northeast, gathering momentum by enlisting support from local Loyalists and the Cherokee Indians. Initially, Clinton's southern strategy worked. Within twenty months, the British and their allies had defeated three American armies, retaken the strategic port cities of Savannah and Charleston, occupied Georgia and much of South Carolina, and killed, wounded, or captured some seven thousand American soldiers, nearly equaling the British losses at Saratoga. The success of the "southern campaign" led one British official to declare that there soon would be a "speedy and happy termination of the American war." But his optimistic prediction ran afoul of three developments: first, the Loyalist strength in the South was—again—less than estimated; second, the British effort to unleash Indian attacks convinced many undecided backcountry settlers to join the Patriot side; and, third, some of the British and Loyalist soldiers behaved so harshly that they drove even some Loyalists to switch to the rebel side.

SAVANNAH AND CHARLESTON In November 1778 a British force attacked Savannah, the capital and largest city of Georgia, the least populous American colony. The invaders quickly overwhelmed the Patriots, took the town, and hurried northeast toward Charleston, the capital of South Carolina, plundering plantation houses along the way. The Carolina campaign took a major turn when British forces, led brilliantly by generals Clinton and **Charles Cornwallis**, bottled up an American force on the Charleston Peninsula. On May 12, 1780, the American general surrendered Charleston and its 5,500 defenders, the greatest single Patriot loss of the war. American resistance to the British onslaught in the South seemed to have been crushed. At that point, Congress, against George Washington's advice, turned to the victor at Saratoga, Horatio Gates, to take command and sent him south to form a new army. General Cornwallis, in charge of the British troops in the South, engaged Gates's much larger force at Camden, South Carolina, routing his new army, which retreated all the way to Hillsborough, North Carolina, 160 miles away. General Gates, the hero of Saratoga, fled to safety on a fast horse.

THE CAROLINAS   From the point of view of British imperial goals, the southern colonies were ultimately more important than the northern ones because they produced valuable staple crops such as tobacco, rice, and indigo. Eventually the war in the Carolinas aroused the ruthless passions and violence of a frontier civil war among neighbors that degenerated into savage guerrilla-style raids and reprisals between "partisan" Patriots and local Loyalists along with Cherokees allied with the British. Each side at times tortured, scalped, and executed prisoners.

General Cornwallis had Georgia and most of South Carolina under British control by 1780, but his two most ruthless cavalry officers, Sir Banastre Tarleton and Patrick Ferguson, who were in charge of mobilizing, training, and leading Loyalist militiamen, overreached themselves. The British officers often let their men burn Patriot farms, liberate slaves, and destroy livestock. Ferguson sealed his doom when he threatened to march over the Blue Ridge Mountains, hang the mostly Scots-Irish backcountry Patriot leaders ("barbarians"), and destroy their farms. Instead, the feisty "overmountain men" from southwestern Virginia and western North and South Carolina (including "Tennesseans"), mostly hunters rather than soldiers, went after Ferguson and his army of Loyalists. They clashed on partially wooded ground near King's Mountain, just across the North Carolina border, about fifty miles west of Charlotte. There, on October 7, 1780, in a ferocious hour-long battle, the frontier sharpshooters decimated the Loyalists and Major Ferguson, their British commander, whose dead body was found riddled with seven bullet holes.

The Battle of King's Mountain was the turning point of the war in the South. The British forces under General Cornwallis retreated into South Carolina and found it virtually impossible to recruit more Loyalists. By proving that the British were not invincible, the Battle of King's Mountain emboldened farmers to join guerrilla bands under such colorful leaders as Francis Marion, "the Swamp Fox," and Thomas Sumter, "the Carolina Gamecock."

In late 1780 Congress chose a new commander for the southern theater, **General Nathanael Greene**, "the fighting Quaker" of Rhode Island. A former blacksmith blessed with infinite patience, skilled at managing men and

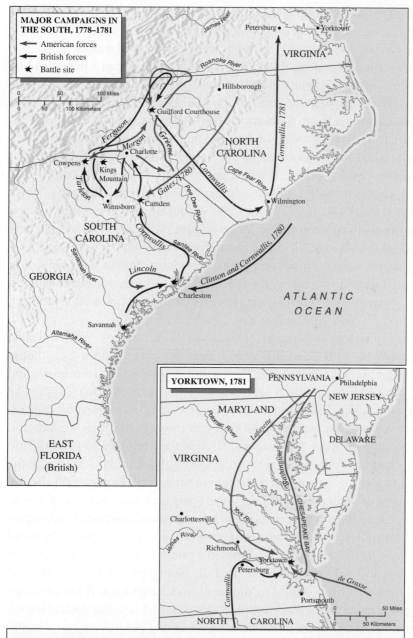

MAJOR CAMPAIGNS IN THE SOUTH, 1778–1781

YORKTOWN, 1781

Why did the British suddenly shift their campaign to the South? Why were the battles at Savannah and Charleston major victories for the British? How did Nathanael Greene undermine British control of the Deep South? Why did Cornwallis march to Virginia and camp at Yorktown? How was the French navy crucial to the American victory? Why was Cornwallis forced to surrender?

saving supplies, careful to avoid needless risks, he was Washington's ablest general—and well suited to a prolonged, patient war against the British forces. Greene was surprised by the brutality of the civil war in the Carolinas. "The division among the people is much greater than I imagined," he wrote to Colonel Alexander Hamilton, one of Washington's top aides. "The Whigs and Tories persecute each other with little less than savage fury."

From Charlotte, North Carolina, where Greene arrived in December 1780, he moved his army eastward and sent General Daniel Morgan with about seven hundred men on a sweep to the west of Cornwallis's headquarters at Winnsboro, South Carolina. Taking a position near Cowpens, a cow-grazing area in northern South Carolina, Morgan's force engaged Tarleton's British army on January 17, 1781. Once the battle was joined, Tarleton rushed his men forward, only to be ambushed by Morgan's cavalry. Tarleton escaped, but over a hundred British were killed, and more than seven hundred were taken prisoner. Cowpens was the most complete tactical victory for the American side in the Revolution. It was one of the few times that Americans won a battle in which the two sides were evenly matched. When General Cornwallis learned of the American victory, he said the news "broke my heart."

After the victory at Cowpens, Morgan's army moved into North Carolina and linked up with General Greene's main force at Guilford Courthouse (near what became Greensboro). Greene lured Cornwallis's army north, and then attacked the redcoats at Guilford Courthouse on March 15, 1781. The Americans inflicted such heavy losses that Cornwallis marched his men off toward Wilmington, on the North Carolina coast, to lick their wounds and take on supplies from British ships. Greene then resolved to go back into South Carolina in the hope of drawing Cornwallis after him or forcing the British to give up the state. There he joined forces with local guerrilla bands. In a series of brilliant actions, the Americans kept narrowly losing battles while winning the war by prolonging it. It had become a contest of endurance, and the Americans held the advantage in time, men, and supplies; they could outlast the British as long as they avoided a catastrophic defeat. "We fight, get beat, rise, and fight again," Greene said. By September 1781, the Americans had narrowed British control in the South to Charleston and Savannah, although for more than a year longer local Patriots and Loyalists slashed at each other in the backcountry, where there was "nothing but murder and devastation in every quarter," Greene said.

Meanwhile, Cornwallis had pushed his British army north, away from Greene, reasoning that Virginia must be eliminated as a source of reinforcement and supplies before the Carolinas could be subdued. In May 1781 the British force marched into Virginia. There, since December 1780, the traitorous **Benedict Arnold**, now a *British* general, had been engaged in a war of maneuver against the American forces. Arnold, until September 1780, had been the American commander at West Point, New York. But like many soldiers during the Revolution, Arnold had switched sides. Traitors have a price, and Arnold had found his: he had crassly plotted to sell out the American garrison at West Point to the British, and he even suggested how they might seize George Washington himself. Only the fortuitous capture of the British go-between, Major John André, had ended Arnold's plot. Warned that his plan had been discovered, Arnold had joined the British in New York City, while the Americans hanged André as a spy.

YORKTOWN When Cornwallis linked up his army with Arnold's at Petersburg, Virginia, their combined forces totaled 7,200 men. As the Americans approached, Cornwallis picked **Yorktown**, Virginia, on Chesapeake Bay, as a defensible site on which to establish a base of operations. There appeared to be little reason to worry about a siege, since General Washington's main land force seemed preoccupied with attacking New York, and the British navy controlled American waters.

To be sure, there was a small American navy, but it was no match for the British fleet. Yet American privateers distracted and wounded the massive British ships. Most celebrated were the exploits of Captain John Paul Jones. Off the English coast on September 23, 1779, Jones and his crew won a desperate battle with a British frigate, which the Americans captured and occupied before their own ship sank. This was the occasion for Jones's stirring and oft-repeated response to a British demand for surrender: "I have not yet begun to fight."

Still, such heroics were little more than nuisances to the British. But at a critical point, thanks to the French navy, the British navy lost control of Chesapeake Bay. Indeed, it is impossible to imagine an American victory in the Revolution without the assistance of the French. As long as the British navy maintained supremacy at sea, the Americans could not hope to win the war. For three years, George Washington had waited to get some strategic military benefit from the French alliance. In July 1780 the French had finally landed six thousand soldiers at Newport, Rhode Island, which the British had given up to concentrate on the South, but the French army had sat there for a year, blockaded by the British fleet.

Then, in 1781, the elements for a combined Franco-American action suddenly fell into place. In May, as Cornwallis's army moved into Virginia, George Washington persuaded the commander of the French army in Rhode Island to join forces for an attack on the British army in New York. The two armies linked up in July, but before they could strike at the British in New York, word came from the West Indies that Admiral François-Joseph-Paul de

Grasse was bound for the Chesapeake Bay with his large French fleet and some three thousand soldiers. The news led Washington to change his strategy. He immediately began moving his army south toward Yorktown. Meanwhile, French ships slipped out of the British blockade at Newport, Rhode Island and also headed south toward Chesapeake Bay.

On August 30, Admiral de Grasse's fleet reached Yorktown, and French troops landed to join the Americans confronting Cornwallis's army. On September 6, the day after a British fleet appeared, de Grasse attacked and forced the British navy to give up the effort to relieve Cornwallis, whose fate was quickly sealed. De Grasse then sent ships up the Chesapeake to ferry down the allied armies that were marching south, bringing the total American and French armies to more than sixteen thousand men, or better than double the size of Cornwallis's besieged British army.

The siege of Yorktown began on September 28. On October 17, 1781, an abject Cornwallis sued for peace, and on October 19, the surrendering British force of more than seven thousand marched out as its band played a somber tune titled "The World Turned Upside Down." Cornwallis himself claimed to be too ill to participate. His dispatch to London was telling: "I have the mortification to inform your Excellency that I have been forced to . . . surrender the troops under my command."

THE TREATY OF PARIS

Any lingering hopes of victory the British had vanished at Yorktown. In London, Lord North reacted to the news of the surrender as if he had "taken a ball in the breast," said the messenger who delivered the report. "O God," the prime minister exclaimed, "it is all over." In December King George III and his ministers decided to send no more troops to America. Although British forces still controlled New York City, Wilmington, North Carolina, Charleston, and Savannah, the House of Commons voted against continuing the war on February 27, 1782, and on March 20 Lord North resigned. The British leaders decided to end the war in America so that they could concentrate their efforts on the global conflict with France and Spain. The Continental Congress named commissioners to negotiate a peace treaty in Paris; the commissioners included John Adams, who was representing the United States in the Netherlands; John Jay, minister (ambassador) to Spain; and Benjamin Franklin, already in France. The cranky **John Adams** was an odd choice since, as Thomas Jefferson said, he seemed to hate everyone: "He hates [Benjamin] Franklin, he hates John Jay, he hates the French, he hates the English." In the end, Franklin and Jay did most of the work leading to a peace treaty, and they did it very well.

The negotiations dragged on for months until finally, on September 3, 1783, the Treaty of Paris was signed. Its provisions were surprisingly favorable to the United States. Great Britain recognized the independence of the thirteen former colonies making up the United States, but it surprisingly agreed to view the Mississippi River as America's western boundary, thereby more than doubling the territory of the new nation. The boundaries of the United States created by the treaty encompassed some nine hundred thousand square miles, nearly 70 percent of which was *west* of the Proclamation Line of 1763, a vast region long inhabited by Indians and often referred to as Transappalachia. The Indian tribes were by far the biggest losers as a result of the treaty negotiations, which they were not allowed to participate in.

The treaty's ambiguous references to America's northern and southern borders would be disputed for years. Florida, as it turned out, passed back to Spain from Britain. On the matter of the prewar debts owed by Americans to British merchants, the U.S. negotiators promised that British merchants should "meet with no legal impediment" in seeking to collect money owed them. And on the tender point of the thousands of Loyalists whose homes, lands, and possessions had been confiscated (and sold) by state governments, the negotiators agreed that Congress would "earnestly recommend" to the states that the confiscated property be restored.

THE POLITICAL REVOLUTION

The Americans had won their War of Independence. Had they undergone a political revolution as well? Years later, John Adams insisted that the Revolution began before the shooting started: "The Revolution was in the minds and hearts of the people . . . . This radical change in the principles, opinions, sentiments, and affections of the people, was the real American Revolution." Yet Adams's observation ignores the fact that the Revolutionary War itself ignited a prolonged debate about what new forms of government would best serve the new American republic.

REPUBLICAN IDEOLOGY   Americans promoted a "republican" ideology instead of the aristocratic or monarchical governments that had long dominated Europe. In its simplest sense, the new republic was a nation whose citizens (property-holding white men) were deemed equal before the law and governed themselves through elected and appointed representatives.

NORTH AMERICA, 1783

England
United States
Spain
Russia

How did France's treaties with Spain complicate the peace-treaty negotiations with the British? What were the terms of the Treaty of Paris? Why might the ambiguities in the treaty have led to conflicts among the Americans, the Spanish, and the British?

To preserve the delicate balance between liberty and power, the revolutionary leaders believed that their new governments must be designed to protect individual and states' rights from being trammeled by the national government. The conventional British model of mixed government sought to balance monarchy, aristocracy, and the common people and thereby protect individual liberty. The new United States of America, however, professed new political assumptions and required new governmental institutions.

America had no monarchy or formal aristocracy. Yet how could sovereignty reside in the people? How could Americans ensure the survival of their new republic, long assumed to be the most fragile form of government? The war for independence thus sparked a spate of state constitution making that remains unique in history.

STATE CONSTITUTIONS   Most of the political experimentation between 1776 and 1787 occurred at the state level in the form of written constitutions in which the people delegated limited authority to the government. These state-level political innovations created a reservoir of ideas and experience that formed the basis for the creation of the federal constitution in 1787.

The first state constitutions varied mainly in detail. They formed governments much like the colonial governments, but with elected governors and senates instead of appointed governors and councils. Generally they embodied a separation of powers (legislative, executive, and judicial) as a safeguard against abuses. Most also included a bill of rights that protected the time-honored rights of petition, freedom of speech, trial by jury, freedom from self-incrimination, and the like. They tended to limit the powers of governors and increase the powers of the legislatures.

THE ARTICLES OF CONFEDERATION   No sooner had the American colonies declared their independence in 1776 than the rebels faced the challenge of forming a national government as well as state governments. Before March 1781, the Continental Congress had exercised emergency powers without any constitutional authority. Plans for a permanent frame of government emerged very quickly, however. As early as July 1776, a committee appointed by the Continental Congress had produced a draft constitution called the Articles of Confederation and Perpetual Union. When the Articles of Confederation became effective during the war, in March 1781, they essentially legalized what had become the prevailing practice. What came to be called the Confederation Congress had a multitude of responsibilities but little authority to carry them out. Congress was intended not as a legislature, nor as a sovereign entity unto itself, but as a collective substitute for the monarch. In essence it was to be a legislative body serving as the nation's executive rather than a parliament. It had full power over foreign affairs; it could decide disputes between the states; it had authority over coinage, the postal service, and Indian affairs as well as the western territories. But it had no courts and no power to enforce its resolutions and ordinances. It also had no power to levy taxes and had to rely on requisitions from the states, which state legislatures could ignore.

The states, after their colonial battles with Parliament, were in no mood for a strong central government. Congress in fact had less power than the colonists had once accepted in Parliament, since it could not regulate interstate and foreign commerce. For certain important acts, moreover, a "special majority" was required. Nine states had to approve measures dealing with war, treaties, coinage, finances, and the army and navy. Unanimous approval of the states was needed to levy tariffs (often called "duties" or taxes) on imports. Amendments to the Articles also required unanimous ratification by all the states. The Confederation had neither an executive nor a judicial branch; there was no administrative head of government (only the president of Congress, chosen annually), and there were no federal courts.

For all its weaknesses, however, the Confederation government represented the most practical structure for the new nation fighting for its very survival. After all, the Revolution on the battlefields had yet to be won, and America's statesmen could not risk the prolonged, divisive debates over the distribution of power that other forms of government would have entailed.

THE SOCIAL REVOLUTION

Political revolutions and the chaos of war often spawn social revolutions. What did the Revolution mean to those workers, servants, farmers, and freed slaves who participated in the Stamp Act demonstrations, supported the boycotts, and fought in the army, navy, and militias? Many working-class Americans hoped that the Revolution would remove, not reinforce, the elite's traditional political and social advantages. Many wealthy Patriots, on the other hand, would have been content to replace royal officials with the rich, the wellborn, and the able and let it go at that. But other revolutionaries raised the question not only of gaining independence but also of who should rule at home. The energy embedded in the concepts of liberty, equality, and democracy changed the dynamics of American social and political life in ways that people did not imagine in 1776.

THE EXODUS OF LOYALISTS   The Loyalists were the biggest losers in the brutal civil war that was embedded within the Revolutionary war. They suffered greatly for their stubborn loyalty to King George III and for their refusal to pledge allegiance to the new United States. During and after the Revolution, their property was confiscated, and many Loyalists were assaulted, brutalized, and executed by Patriots (and vice versa). After the American victory at Yorktown, tens of thousands of panicked Loyalists made their way to coastal seaports to board British ships to flee the new United States. Thousands of African Americans, mostly runaway slaves, also flocked to New York City, Charleston, and Savannah, with many of their angry owners in hot pursuit. Boston King, a runaway, said he saw white slave owners seizing upon "their slaves in the streets of New York, or even dragging them out of their beds."

Some eighty thousand desperate refugees—white Loyalists, free blacks, freed slaves, and Indians who had allied with the British—dispersed throughout the British Empire, changing it in the process. Some twelve thousand Georgia and South Carolina Loyalists, including thousands of their slaves (the British granted freedom only to the slaves of Patriots), went to British-controlled East Florida, only to see their new home handed over to Spain in 1783. Spanish authorities gave them a hard choice: swear allegiance to the Spanish king and convert to Catholicism or leave. Most of them left. Some of the doubly displaced Loyalists sneaked back into the United States while most of them went to British islands in the Caribbean. The largest number of Loyalist exiles landed in Canada, where royal officials wanted them to displace the earlier French presence. Among the emigrants landing in Canada were 3,500 former slaves who had been given their freedom in exchange for their joining the British cause. The departure of so many Loyalists from America was one of the most important social consequences of the Revolution. Their confiscated homes, vast tracts of land, and vacated jobs created new social, economic, and political opportunities for Patriots.

EQUALITY AND ITS LIMITS Participation in the Revolutionary army or militia excited men who had taken little interest in politics before. The new political opportunities afforded by the creation of state governments led more ordinary citizens to participate than ever before. The property qualifications for voting, which already admitted an overwhelming majority of white men, were lowered after 1776. In Pennsylvania, Delaware, North Carolina, and Georgia, any male taxpayer could vote. In addition, farmers, tradesmen, and shopkeepers began to be elected to state legislatures. New developments in land tenure that grew out of the Revolution extended the democratic trends of suffrage requirements. All state legislatures seized Tory estates. These properties were of small consequence, however, in contrast to the unsettled areas formerly at the disposal of the Crown and proprietors but now in the hands of popular assemblies. Much of that land was now used for bonuses to reward veterans of the war. Moreover, western lands across the Appalachian Mountains, formerly closed by the

Royal Proclamation of 1763 and the Quebec Act of 1774, were soon thrown open to settlers hungry for their own land.

THE PARADOX OF SLAVERY Ironies abounded amid a revolutionary war fought in the name of liberty. Freedom, for example, was intended for whites only in most of the newly created states. African Americans made up 20 percent of the population in the thirteen colonies at the time of the Revolution, but their role in the conflict was long ignored until recent years. During 1773 and 1774, as white colonists increasingly protested the curtailment of their "freedoms" by the British government, few of them acknowledged the hypocrisy of Patriots maintaining the widespread practice of race-based slavery in the colonies. The rhetoric of liberty circulated widely in slave communities. In 1773 slaves in Boston pleaded with the British governor to address their "intolerable condition." They complained of having "no Property! We have no Wives! No Children! We have no City! No Country!" Such pleas were largely ignored, however. In 1775 the prominent South Carolinian William Henry Drayton expressed his horror that "impertinent" slaves were claiming "that the present contest [with Great Britain] was for obliging us to give them liberty."

The sharpest irony of the Revolution is that the British offered more enticing opportunities for freedom to enslaved blacks than did the new United States. When the war began, the British promised freedom to slaves, as well as indentured servants, who would bear arms for the Loyalist cause. In December 1775, John Murray, Lord Dunmore, the last royal governor of Virginia, issued such an offer; within a month the British had attracted three hundred former servants and slaves to what came to be called the "Ethiopian Regiment." Within a year the number had grown to almost a thousand males and twice as many women and children.

Dunmore's proclamation promising freedom for slaves who fought on the British side had profound effects. The British recruitment of slaves stunned whites in Virginia, where forty percent of the population was black. People in the South had long been terrified at the prospect of armed slave insurrections; now the threat was real. Members of the all-black British regiment wore uniforms embroidered with the motto "Liberty to Slaves." Dunmore's effort to recruit the slaves owned by Patriots into the "Ethiopian Regiment" infuriated George Washington and other Virginia planters. Washington predicted that if Dunmore's efforts were "not crushed" soon, the number of slaves joining him would "increase as a Snow ball by Rolling."

In the end, the British strategy of encouraging a great black exodus from slavery backfired. The "terrifying" news that British troops would liberate and arm their enslaved African Americans persuaded many southerners to join the Patriot cause. For many whites, especially in Virginia, the Revolution became primarily a war to defend slavery. Edward Rutledge of South Carolina said that the British decision to arm and liberate slaves did more to create "an eternal separation between Great Britain and the colonies than any other expedient."

In response to the British recruitment of enslaved African Americans, General Washington at the end of 1775 authorized the enlistment of free blacks into the army but not slaves. Southerners, however, convinced the Continental Congress to instruct General Washington in February 1776 to enlist no more African Americans, free or enslaved. But as the American war effort struggled, the exclusionary policy was at times ignored in order to put men in uniform. Massachusetts organized two all-black companies, and Rhode Island organized one, which also included Indians. However, two states, South Carolina and Georgia, refused to allow any blacks to serve in the Patriot forces. No more than about five thousand African Americans fought on the Patriot side, and most of them were free blacks from northern states.

Slaves who supported the cause of independence won their freedom and, in some cases, received parcels of land as well. But the British army, which liberated twenty thousand enslaved blacks during the war, including many of those owned by Thomas Jefferson, Patrick Henry, and George Washington, was a far greater instrument of emancipation than the American forces. Most of the newly freed blacks found their way to Canada or to British colonies on Caribbean islands. American Patriots had shown no mercy to blacks caught aiding or abetting the British cause. In Virginia a captured fifteen-year-old runaway was greeted by her owner with a whipping of eighty lashes, after which he rubbed burning coals into her wounds. A Charleston mob hanged and then burned Thomas Jeremiah, a free African American who was convicted of telling slaves that the British "were come to help the poor Negroes."

While thousands of free blacks and runaway slaves fought in the war, the vast majority of African Americans did not choose sides so much as they chose freedom. Several hundred thousand enslaved blacks, mostly in the southern states, took advantage of the chaos of war to seize their freedom. In the northern states, which had far fewer slaves than the southern states, the doctrines of liberty undergirding the dispute with Great Britain led most states to end slavery, either during the fighting or shortly afterward.

THE STATUS OF WOMEN The logic of liberty spawned by the Revolution applied to the status of women as much as to that of African Americans. The legal status of women in the colonies was governed by British common law, which essentially treated them like children, limiting their roles to the domestic sphere. They could not vote or hold office. Nor could they preach. Few had access to formal education. A married woman had no right to buy, sell, or manage property. Technically, any wages earned belonged to the husband. Women could not sign contracts or sue others or testify in court. Divorces were extremely difficult to obtain. A wife was obliged to obey her husband.

Yet the Revolution offered women new opportunities outside the domestic sphere. Women supported the armies in various roles: by handling supplies, serving as couriers or spies, and working as camp followers—cooking, cleaning, and nursing the soldiers. Wives often followed their husbands to camp and on occasion took their place in the line, as Margaret Corbin did when her husband fell at his artillery post and as Mary Ludwig Hays (better known as Molly Pitcher) did when her husband collapsed of heat exhaustion. An exceptional case was Deborah Sampson, who joined a Massachusetts regiment as "Robert Shurtleff" and served from 1781 to 1783 by the "artful concealment" of her gender.

Early in the Revolutionary struggle, **Abigail Adams**, one of the most learned, spirited, and independent women of the time, wrote to her husband, John: "In the new Code of Laws which I suppose it will be necessary for you to make I desire you would remember the Ladies . . . . Do not put such unlimited power into the hands of the Husbands." Since men were "Naturally Tyrannical," she wrote, "why then, not put it out of the power of the vicious and the Lawless to use us with cruelty and indignity with impunity." Otherwise, "if particular care and attention is not paid to the Ladies we are determined to foment a Rebellion, and will not hold ourselves bound by any Laws in which we have no voice, or Representation." Husband John expressed surprise that women might be discontented, but he clearly knew the privileges enjoyed by males and was determined to retain them: "Depend upon it, we know better than to repeal our Masculine systems." Thomas Jefferson was of one mind with Adams on the matter. When asked about women's voting rights, he replied that "the tender breasts of ladies were not formed for political convulsion."

The legal status of women did not improve dramatically as a result of the Revolutionary ferment. Married women in most states still forfeited control of their own property to their husbands, and women gained no permanent political rights. Under the 1776 New Jersey Constitution, which neglected to specify an exclusively male franchise because the delegates apparently took the distinction for granted, women who met the property qualifications for voting exercised the right until they were denied access early in the nineteenth century.

INDIANS AND THE REVOLUTION   The war for American independence had profound effects on the Indians in the southern backcountry and in the Old Northwest region west of New York and Pennsylvania. Most tribes sought to remain neutral in the conflict, but both British and American agents lobbied the chiefs to fight on their side. The result was the disintegration of the alliance among the six tribes making up the Iroquois League. The Mohawks, for example, succumbed to British promises to protect them from encroachments by American settlers on their lands. The Oneidas, on the other hand, fought on the side of the American Patriots. The result of such alliances was chaos on the frontier. Indians on both sides attacked villages, burned crops, and killed civilians.

The new American government assured its Indian allies that it would respect their lands and their rights. But the American people adopted a very different goal: they sought to use the turmoil of war to displace and destroy all Native Americans. Once the war ended and independence was secured, the U.S. government turned its back on most of the pledges made to Native Americans. By the end of the eighteenth century, land-hungry American whites were again pushing into Indian territories on the western frontier.

FREEDOM OF RELIGION   The Revolution also tested traditional religious loyalties and set in motion a transition from the toleration of religious dissent to a complete freedom of religion as embodied in the principle of separation of church and state. The Anglican Church, established as the official religion in five colonies and parts of two others, was especially vulnerable. Anglicans tended to be pro-British. And non-Anglican dissenters, most notably Baptists and Methodists, outnumbered Anglicans in all states except Virginia. All but Virginia eliminated tax support for the church before the fighting was over, and Virginia did so soon afterward. Although Anglicanism survived in the form of the new Episcopal Church, it never regained its pre-Revolutionary size or stature. Newer denominations, such as Methodists and Baptists, as well as Presbyterians, filled the vacuum created by the shrinking Anglican Church.

In 1776 the Virginia Declaration of Rights guaranteed the free exercise of religion, and in 1786 the Virginia Statute of Religious Freedom (written by Thomas Jefferson) declared that "no man shall be compelled to frequent or support any religious worship, place or ministry whatsoever" and "that all men shall be free to profess, and by argument to maintain, their opinions in matters of religion." These statutes and the Revolutionary ideology that justified them helped shape the course that religion would take in the new United States: pluralistic and voluntary rather than state supported and monolithic.

Religious development

The Congregational Church developed a national presence in the early nineteenth century, and Lemuel Haynes, depicted here, was its first African American preacher.

THE EMERGENCE OF AN AMERICAN CULTURE

The Revolution helped excite a sense of common nationality. One of the first ways in which a national consciousness was forged was through the annual celebration of the new nation's independence from Great Britain. On July 2, 1776, when the Second Continental Congress had resolved "that these United Colonies are, and of right ought to be, free and independent states," John Adams had written Abigail that future generations would remember that date as their "day of deliverance." People, he predicted, would celebrate the occasion with "solemn acts of devotion to God Almighty" and with "pomp and parade, with shows, games, sports, guns, bells, bonfires and illuminations [fireworks] from one end of this continent to the other, from this time forward, forever more."

Adams got everything right but the date. As luck would have it, July 4 became Independence Day by accident. In 1777, Congress forgot to make any acknowledgment of the first anniversary of independence until July 3, when it was too late to honor July 2. As a consequence, the Fourth won by default.

The celebration of Independence Day quickly became the most important public ritual in the United States. Huge numbers of people from all walks of life suspended their normal routine in order to devote a day to parades, formal orations, and fireworks displays. In the process the infant republic began to create its own myth of national identity that transcended local or regional concerns. "What a day!" exclaimed the editor of the *Southern Patriot* in 1815. "What happiness, what emotion, what virtuous triumph must fill the bosoms of Americans!"

AMERICA'S "DESTINY" American nationalism embodied a stirring idea. This new nation, unlike the Old World nations of Europe, was not rooted in antiquity. Its people, except for the Native Americans, had not inhabited it over many centuries, nor was there any notion of a common ethnic descent. "The American national consciousness," one observer wrote, "is not a voice crying out of the depth of the dark past, but is proudly a product of the enlightened present, setting its face resolutely toward the future."

Many people, at least since the time of the Pilgrims, had thought of the "New World" as singled out for a special identity, a special mission assigned by God. John Adams proclaimed the opening of America "a grand scheme and design in Providence for the illumination and the emancipation of the slavish part of mankind all over the earth." This sense of providential mission was neither limited to New England nor rooted solely in Calvinism. From the democratic rhetoric of Thomas Jefferson to the pragmatism of George Washington to heady toasts bellowed in South Carolina taverns, patriots everywhere articulated a special role for American leadership in history. The mission was now a call to lead the world toward greater liberty and equality. Meanwhile, however, Americans had to address more immediate problems created by their new nationhood. The Philadelphia doctor and scientist Benjamin Rush issued a prophetic statement in 1787: "The American war is over: but this is far from being the case with the American Revolution. On the contrary, but the first act of the great drama is closed."

CHAPTER SUMMARY

- **Military Strategies** The Americans had to create an army—the Continental army—from scratch and sustain it. To defeat the British, Washington realized that the Americans had to wage a war of attrition, given that the British army was fighting a war thousands of miles from its home base. To defeat the Americans, Britain's initial strategy was to take New York and sever the troublesome New England colonies from the rest.

- **Turning Points** The American victory at Saratoga in 1777 was the first major turning point of the war. George Washington's ability to hold his forces together despite daily desertions and two especially difficult winters was a second major turning point. The British lost support from the southern colonies when they executed the rebels they captured in backcountry skirmishing.

- **Loyalists, "Tories"** The American Revolution was a civil war, dividing families and communities. There were at least one hundred thousand Tories, or Loyalists, in the colonies. They included royal officials, Anglican ministers, wealthy southern planters, and the elite in large seaport cities; they also included many humble people, especially recent immigrants. After the hostilities ended, most Loyalists, including slaves who had fled their plantations to support the British cause, left for Canada, the West Indies, or England.

- **Worldwide Conflict** The French were prospective allies from the beginning of the conflict, because they resented their losses to Britain in the Seven Years' War. After the British defeat at Saratoga, France and the colonies agreed to fight together until independence was won. Further agreements with Spain and the Netherlands helped to make the Revolution a worldwide conflict. French supplies and the presence of the French fleet ensured the Americans' victory at Yorktown.

- **A Social Revolution** The American Revolution disrupted and transformed traditional class and social relationships. More white men gained the vote as property requirements were removed. Northern states began to free slaves, but southerner states were reluctant. Although many women had undertaken nontraditional roles during the war, they remained largely confined to the domestic sphere afterward, with no changes to their legal or political status. The Revolution had catastrophic effects on the Native Americans, regardless of which side they had embraced. American settlers seized Native American land, often in violation of existing treaties.

CHRONOLOGY

1776	General Washington's troops cross the Delaware River; Battle of Trenton
1776–1777	Washington's troops winter at Morristown, New Jersey
1777	Battle of Saratoga; General Burgoyne surrenders
1777–1778	Washington's troops winter at Valley Forge, Pennsylvania
1778	Americans and French form an alliance
1781	Battles of Cowpens and Guilford Courthouse
1781	General Cornwallis surrenders at Yorktown, Virginia
1781	Articles of Confederation are ratified
1783	Treaty of Paris is signed
1786	Virginia adopts the Statute of Religious Freedom

KEY TERMS & NAMES

General George Washington p. 148

Continental army p. 148

General William Howe p. 148

Tories p. 149

General John Burgoyne p. 156

Battle of Saratoga p. 157

Joseph Brant p. 159

General Charles Cornwallis p. 161

General Nathanael Greene p. 162

Benedict Arnold p. 164

surrender at Yorktown p. 165

John Adams p. 166

Abigail Adams p. 174

6

SHAPING
A FEDERAL UNION

FOCUS QUESTIONS wwnorton.com/studyspace

- What were the achievements of the Confederation government?
- What were the shortcomings of the Articles of Confederation?
- Why did the delegates to the Constitutional Convention draft a completely new constitution?
- How important was the issue of slavery in the Constitution?
- What were the main issues in the debate over ratification of the Constitution?

The new United States of America was distinctive among the nations of the world in that it was born out of ideas and ideals rather than from centuries-old shared racial or ancestral bonds. Those ideals were captured in phrases that still resonate in American culture: All men are created equal. Liberty and justice for all. *E pluribus unum* ("Out of many, one"—the phrase on the official seal of the United States). The development of the new nation after 1783 reflected the varied and at times conflicting ways that Americans understood, applied, and violated these ideals over time. The ideals that led Revolutionaries to declare their independence from Great Britain and then win an unlikely victory on the battlefields shaped an upstart nation that had neither the luxury of time nor the adequacy of resources to guarantee its survival.

The American Revolution created not only an independent new republic but also a different conception of politics than prevailed in Europe. Americans rejected the notion that nations should necessarily be divided into a hierarchy of classes—monarchs, nobles or aristocrats, and commoners. Instead, the United States was created to protect individual interests ("life, liberty, and the pursuit of happiness") and to defend individual rights against arbitrary government power. To do so, the Revolutionaries developed radically new forms of representative government and new models for dividing power among the various branches of government—and the people.

THE CONFEDERATION GOVERNMENT

THE CRITICAL PERIOD   In an address to his fellow graduates at the Harvard commencement ceremony in 1787, young John Quincy Adams, a future American president, bemoaned "this critical period" when the country was "groaning under the intolerable burden of . . . accumulated evils." The same phrase, "critical period," has often been used to label the period during which the United States was governed under the Articles of Confederation, between 1781 and 1787. Fear of a powerful national government dominated the period, and the result was fragmentation and stagnation. Yet while the Confederation government had its weaknesses, it also generated major achievements. Moreover, lessons learned during the "critical period" would prompt the formulation of a new national constitution that better balanced federal and state authority.

The Articles of Confederation established a unicameral Congress dominated by the state legislatures that appointed its members (there was no national executive or judiciary). The Congress had little authority. It could ask the states for money, but could not levy taxes; it could neither regulate foreign or interstate commerce nor pay off the nation's debts; it could approve treaties with other nations but had no power to enforce their provisions; it could call for the raising of an army but could not fill the ranks.

After the war ended, the Confederation Congress was virtually helpless to cope with foreign relations and a postwar economic depression that would have challenged the resources of a much stronger government. It was not easy to find men of stature to serve in such a weak congress, and it was often hard to gather a quorum of those who did. Yet in spite of its handicaps, the Confederation Congress somehow managed to survive the war years and to lay important foundations for the new national government. It concluded the Treaty of Paris in 1783, ending the Revolutionary War. It created the first executive departments. And it formulated principles of land distribution and territorial government that would guide westward expansion all the way to the Pacific coast.

FINANCE   The closest thing to an executive leader of the Confederation was **Robert Morris**, who as superintendent of finance in the final years of the war became the most influential figure in the government. To make both himself and the Confederation government more powerful, Morris developed a program of taxation and debt management to make the national government financially stable. As he confided to a friend, "a public debt supported by public revenue will prove the strongest cement to keep our confederacy together." The powerful financiers who had lent the new government funds to buy supplies and pay its bills would, Morris believed, give stronger support to a government committed to paying its debts. Morris therefore welcomed the chance to issue new government bonds that would help pay off wartime debts. With a sounder federal Treasury—certainly one with the power to raise taxes—the bonds could be expected to rise in value, creating new capital with which to finance banks and economic development.

To anchor his financial plan in the midst of the ongoing Revolutionary War, Morris secured a congressional charter in 1781 for the Bank of North America, which would hold government funds, lend money to the government, and issue currency. Though a national bank, it was in part privately owned and was expected to turn a profit for Morris and other shareholders, in addition to performing a crucial public service. But Morris's program depended ultimately upon the government's having a secure income, and it foundered on the requirement of unanimous state approval for amendments to the Articles of Confederation. Local interests and the fear of a central authority—a fear strengthened by the recent quarrels with king and Parliament—hobbled action.

THE NEWBURGH CONSPIRACY   To carry their point, Morris and his nationalist friends in 1783 risked a dangerous gamble. After the British surrendered at Yorktown but before the peace treaty with Great Britain was completed, George Washington's army, encamped at Newburgh, New York, on the Hudson River, had grown restless in the final winter of the war. The soldiers' pay was late as usual, and the officers feared that the land grants promised them by the government as a reward for their service might never be honored once the war officially ended. A delegation of concerned army officers traveled to Philadelphia, where they soon found themselves drawn into a scheme to line up army officers and public creditors with nationalists in Congress and confront the states with the threat of a coup d'état unless they yielded more power to Congress. **Alexander Hamilton**, congressman from New York and former aide to General Washington, sought to bring his beloved commander into the plan.

General Washington sympathized with the basic purpose of Hamilton's scheme. If congressional powers were not enlarged, he had told a friend, "anarchy and confusion must ensue." But Washington was just as deeply convinced that a military coup would be both dishonorable and dangerous. In March 1783, when he learned that some of the plotting officers had planned an unauthorized meeting, he confronted the conspirators. He told them that any effort to intimidate the government by threatening a mutinous coup violated the very purposes for which the war was being fought and directly challenged his own integrity. While agreeing that the officers had been poorly treated by the government and deserved their long-overdue back pay and future pensions, Washington expressed his "horror and detestation" of any effort by the officers to assume dictatorial powers. A military revolt would open "the flood-gates of civil discord" and "deluge our rising empire in blood." It was a virtuoso performance. When Washington finished, his officers, many of them fighting back tears, unanimously adopted resolutions denouncing the recent "infamous propositions," and the so-called Newburgh Conspiracy came to a sudden end.

In the end the Confederation government never did put its finances in order. The currency issued by the Continental Congress had become worthless. It was never redeemed. The national debt, domestic and foreign, grew from $11 million to $28 million as Congress paid off citizens' and soldiers' claims. Each year, Congress ran a deficit in its operating expenses.

LAND POLICY The Confederation Congress might ultimately have drawn a rich source of income from the sale of western lands. Thinly populated by Indians, French settlers, and a growing number of American squatters, the region north of the Ohio River and west of the Appalachian Mountains had long been the site of overlapping claims by Indians, colonies, and speculators. Under the Articles of Confederation, land not included within the boundaries of the thirteen original states became public domain, owned and administered by the national government.

Between 1784 and 1787 the Confederation Congress set forth three major ordinances for the orderly development of the West. These documents, which rank among the Confederation's greatest achievements—and among the most important in American history—set precedents that the United States would follow in its expansion all the way to the Pacific. Thomas Jefferson in fact was prepared to grant self-government to western states at an early stage, allowing settlers to meet and choose their own officials. Under the land ordinance that Jefferson wrote in 1784, when a territory's population equaled that of the smallest existing state, the territory would be eligible for full statehood.

A year later, in the Land Ordinance of 1785, the delegates outlined a plan of land surveys and sales that would eventually stamp a rectangular pattern

on much of the nation's surface. Wherever Indian titles had been extinguished, the Northwest was to be surveyed and six-square-mile townships
established along east-west and north-south lines. Each township was in
turn divided into thirty-six lots (or sections) one square mile (or 640 acres).
The 640-acre sections were to be sold at auction for no less than $1 per acre,
or $640 total. Such terms favored land speculators, of course, since few com-
mon folk had that much money or were able to work that much land. In later
years new land laws would make smaller plots available at lower prices; but
in 1785, Congress was faced with an empty Treasury, and delegates believed
that this system would raise the needed funds most effectively. In each township, however, Congress did reserve the income from the sale of the sixteenth
section of land for the support of schools—a significant departure at a time
when public schools were rare.

THE NORTHWEST ORDINANCE   Spurred by the plans for land sales
and settlement, Congress drafted a more specific frame of territorial government to replace Jefferson's ordinance of 1784. The new plan backed off from
Jefferson's recommendation of early self-government. Because of the trouble
that might be expected from squatters who were clamoring for free land, the
Northwest Ordinance of 1787 required a period of preparation for statehood. At first the territory fell subject to a governor, a secretary, and three
judges, all chosen by Congress. Eventually there would be three to five territories in the region, and when any one of them had a population of five
thousand free male adults, it could choose an assembly. Congress then
would name a council of five from ten names proposed by the assembly. The
governor would have a veto over actions by the territorial assembly, and so
would Congress.

The resemblance of these territorial governments to the old royal colonies
is clear, but there were three significant differences. First, the ordinance
anticipated statehood when any territory's population reached a population
of sixty thousand "free inhabitants." At that point a convention could be
called to draft a state constitution and apply to Congress for statehood. Ohio
was the first territory to receive statehood in this way. Second, the ordinance
included a bill of rights that guaranteed religious freedom, legislative representation in proportion to the population, trial by jury, and the application
of common law. Finally, the ordinance excluded slavery permanently from
the Northwest—a proviso that Thomas Jefferson had failed to get accepted
in his ordinance of 1784. This proved a fateful decision. As the progress of
emancipation in the existing states gradually freed all slaves above the
Mason-Dixon line, the Ohio River boundary of the Old Northwest extended

the line between freedom and slavery all the way to the Mississippi River, encompassing what would become the states of Ohio, Indiana, Illinois, Michigan, and Wisconsin.

The Northwest Ordinance of 1787 had a larger importance, beyond establishing a formal procedure for transforming territories into states. It represented a sharp break with the imperialistic assumption behind European expansion into the Western Hemisphere: the new states were to be admitted to the American republic as equals rather than treated as subordinate colonies.

The lands south of the Ohio River followed a different line of development. Title to the western lands remained with Georgia, North Carolina, and Virginia for the time being, but settlement proceeded at a far more rapid pace during and after the Revolution, despite the Indians' fierce resentment of encroachments upon their hunting grounds. The Iroquois and Cherokees, badly battered during the Revolution, were in no position to resist encroachments by American settlers. By the Treaty of Fort Stanwix (1784), the Iroquois were forced to cede land in western New York and Pennsylvania. With the Treaty of Hopewell (1785), the Cherokees gave up all claims in South Carolina, much of western North Carolina, and large portions of present-day Kentucky and Tennessee. Also in 1785 the major Ohio tribes dropped their claim to most of Ohio, except for a chunk bordering the western part of Lake Erie. The Creeks, pressed by the state of Georgia to cede portions of their lands in 1784–1785, went to war in the summer of 1786 with covert aid from Spanish-controlled Florida. When Spanish aid diminished, however, the Creek chief traveled to New York and in 1791 finally struck a bargain that gave the Creeks favorable trade arrangements with the United States but did not restore the lost land.

TRADE AND THE ECONOMY   The American economy after the Revolution went through an acute contraction between 1770 and 1790, the result primarily of the war and separation from the British Empire. Although farmers enmeshed in local markets maintained their livelihood during the Revolutionary era, commercial agriculture dependent upon trade with foreign markets collapsed during the war. Virginia planters saw many of their enslaved workers liberated by the British. Chesapeake planters also lost their lucrative foreign markets. The tobacco trade was especially hard hit. The British decision to close its West Indian colonies to American commerce devastated what had been a thriving market for timber, wheat, and other foodstuffs.

British trade with America resumed after 1783. American ships were allowed to deliver American products to Britain and return to the United

States with British goods. American ships could not carry British goods anywhere else, however. The pent-up demand for goods imported from London created a vigorous market in exports to America. The result was a quick cycle of postwar boom and bust, a buying spree followed by a money shortage and economic troubles that lasted several years.

By 1787 American seaports were flourishing as never before. Trade treaties opened new markets with the Dutch (1782), the Swedes (1783), the Prussians (1785), and the Moroccans (1787), and American shippers found new outlets on their own in Europe, Africa, and Asia. The most spectacular new development, if not the largest, was trade with China. It began in 1784–1785, when the *Empress of China* sailed from New York to Canton (Kuang-Chou)* and back, around the tip of South America. Profits from its cargo of silks and tea encouraged the outfitting of other ships, which carried American goods to exchange for the luxury goods of east Asia.

By 1790 the dollar value of American commerce and exports had far exceeded the amount of trade generated by the colonies before the Revolution. Merchants owned more ships than they had had before the war. Farm exports were twice what they had been. Although most of the exports were the products of forests, fields, and fisheries, during and after the war more Americans had turned to small-scale manufacturing, mainly for domestic markets.

DIPLOMACY   Yet while postwar trade flourished, the shortcomings of the Articles of Confederation prompted a growing chorus of complaints. In the diplomatic arena, there remained the nagging problems of relations with Great Britain and Spain, both of which still kept military posts on American soil and conspired with Indians to foment unrest. The British, despite pledges made in the peace treaty of 1783, held on to a string of forts along the Canadian border. They argued that their continued occupation was justified by the failure of Americans to pay their prewar debts to British creditors. According to one Virginian, a common question in his state was, "If we are now to pay the debts due to British merchants, what have we been fighting for all this while?"

Another major irritant in U.S.-British relations was the American confiscation of Loyalist property. The Treaty of Paris had encouraged Congress to

---

*The traditional (Wade-Giles) spelling is used here. Nearly two centuries after these events, the Chinese government adopted pinyin transliterations, which became more widely used after 1976, so that, for example, Peking became Beijing and, in this case, Kuang-Chou became Guanzhou.

end confiscations of Tory property, to guarantee immunity to Loyalists for twelve months, during which they could return from Canada or Great Britain and wind up their affairs, and to recommend that the states give back confiscated property. Persecutions, even lynchings, of Loyalists occurred after the end of the war. Some Loyalists who had fled returned unmolested, however, and resumed their lives in their former homes. By the end of 1787, moreover, at the request of Congress, all the states had rescinded any laws that were in conflict with the peace treaty.

With Spain the chief issues were the disputed southern boundary of the United States and the right of Americans to navigate the Mississippi River. According to the preliminary treaty with Britain, the United States claimed a southern boundary line as far south as the 31st parallel; Spain held out for the line running eastward from the mouth of the Yazoo River (at 32°28'N), which it claimed as the traditional boundary. The Treaty of Paris had also given the Americans the right to ship goods by barge and boat down the Mississippi River to its mouth. Still, the international boundary ran down the middle of the river for most of its length, and the Mississippi was entirely within Spanish Louisiana in its lower reaches. The right to send boats or barges down the Mississippi was crucial to the growing American settlements in Kentucky and Tennessee, but in 1784 Louisiana's Spanish governor closed the river to American commerce and began to conspire with Indians against the American settlers and with settlers against the United States.

THE CONFEDERATION'S PROBLEMS The tensions between land-hungry trans-Appalachian settlers and the British and the Spanish seemed remote from the everyday concerns of most Americans, however. Most people were more affected by economic troubles and the acute currency shortage after the war. Merchants who found themselves prevented from reviving old trade relationships with the island economies

Domestic industry

American craftsmen, such as this cabinetmaker, favored tariffs on foreign goods that competed with their own products.

in the British West Indies called for trade reprisals against the British. State governments, in response, imposed special taxes on British vessels and special tariffs on the goods they brought to the United States. State action alone, however, failed to work because of a lack of uniformity among the states. British ships simply diverted their ports of call to states whose import duties were less restrictive. The other states tried to meet this problem by taxing British goods that flowed across state lines, creating the impression that states were involved in commercial war with each other. Chaos ensued. By 1787 there was a clear need for the national government to regulate interstate trade.

After the Revolution, mechanics (skilled workers who made, used, or repaired tools and machines) and artisans (skilled workers who made products) developed an array of new industries. Their products ranged from crude iron nails to fine silver bowls and flatware. These skilled workers wanted reprisals against British goods as well as British ships. They sought, and to various degrees obtained from the states, tariffs (taxes) on imported foreign goods that competed with theirs. Nearly all the states gave some preference to American goods, but again the lack of uniformity in their laws put them at cross-purposes, and so urban artisans along with merchants were drawn into the movement calling for a stronger central government in the interest of uniform trade regulations.

The shortage of cash and other postwar economic difficulties gave rise to more immediate demands for paper currency, for postponement of tax and debt payments, and for laws to "stay" (delay) the foreclosure of mortgages. Farmers who had profited during the war found themselves squeezed afterward by depressed crop prices and mounting debts. Creditors demanded that borrowers pay back their loans in gold or silver coins, but such "hard money" was in short supply—and paper money was almost nonexistent after the depreciation of the wartime currency. By 1785 the demand for new paper money became the most divisive issue in state politics. In a drama that would be replayed many times over the next century, debtors promoted the use of paper money as a means of easing repayment, and farmers saw paper money as an inflationary means of raising commodity prices.

In 1785–1786 seven states (Pennsylvania, New York, New Jersey, South Carolina, Rhode Island, Georgia, and North Carolina) began issuing paper money to help hard-pressed farmers and to pay the bonuses earned by war veterans. In spite of the cries of calamity at the time, the money never seriously depreciated in Pennsylvania, New York, and South Carolina. In Rhode Island, however, the debtor party ran wild. In 1786 the Rhode Island legislature issued more paper money than any other state in proportion to its population. Creditors fled the state to avoid being paid in worthless paper.

SHAYS'S REBELLION   Newspapers throughout the nation followed the chaotic developments in Rhode Island. The little commonwealth, stubbornly independent since its founding, became the prime example of democracy run riot—until its riotous neighbor, Massachusetts, provided the final proof (some said) that the new nation was poised on the brink of anarchy: **Shays's Rebellion**. There the trouble was not too much paper money but too little, as well as high taxation.

After 1780, Massachusetts had remained in the grip of a rigidly conservative state government, which levied ever-higher taxes to pay off a massive war debt held mainly by wealthy creditors in Boston. The taxes fell most heavily upon beleaguered farmers and the poor in general. When the Massachusetts legislature adjourned in 1786 without providing paper money or any other relief from taxes and debts, three western agricultural counties erupted in revolt.

Armed bands of angry farmers closed the courts and prevented farm foreclosures. A ragtag "army" of some one thousand two hundred unruly farmers led by Daniel Shays, a destitute war veteran, advanced upon the federal arsenal

Shays's Rebellion

Shays and his followers demanded a more flexible monetary policy and the right to postpone paying taxes until the postwar agricultural depression lifted.

at Springfield in 1787. Shays and his followers sought a more flexible monetary policy, laws allowing them to use corn and wheat as money, and the right to postpone paying taxes until the postwar agricultural depression lifted.

The state government responded to the uprising by sending 4,400 militiamen armed with cannons. The soldiers scattered the debtor army with a single volley that left four farmers dead. The rebels nevertheless had a victory of sorts. The new state legislature decided to relieve the agricultural crisis by eliminating some of the taxes on farmers. But a more important consequence was the impetus that Shays's Rebellion gave to conservatism and nationalism across the new United States.

CALLS FOR A STRONGER GOVERNMENT   Well before the Shaysite turmoil in New England, concerned Americans had been calling for a special convention of the states to strengthen the national government by revising the Articles of Confederation. Many bankers, merchants, and mechanics promoted a stronger central government as the only alternative to anarchy. Americans were gradually losing the fear of a strong central government as they saw evidence that tyranny might come from other quarters, including the common people themselves. During the 1780s the newspapers as well as public speeches were filled with dire warnings that the fragile new nation's situation "is critical and dangerous"; the nation's "vices" were threatening "national ruin."

Such concerns led many of the Founding Fathers to revise their assessment of the American character. "We have, probably," concluded George Washington in 1786, "had too good an opinion of human nature in forming our confederation." Washington and other so-called Federalists concluded that the new republic must now depend for its success upon the constant virtue of the few rather than the public-spiritedness of the many.

CREATING THE CONSTITUTION

THE CONSTITUTIONAL CONVENTION   After stalling for several months, Congress in 1787 called for a convention of the states in Philadelphia "for the sole and express purpose of revising the Articles of Confederation." By then five states had already named delegates; before the meeting, called to begin on May 14, 1787, six more states had acted. New Hampshire delayed until June, its delegates arriving in July. Fearful of consolidated power, tiny Rhode Island kept aloof throughout. (Critics labeled the fractious little state "Rogue Island.") Virginia's Patrick Henry, an implacable foe of centralized government, claimed to "smell a rat" and refused to represent his state. Twenty-nine delegates from nine states began work on May 25. Fifty-five men attended at one time or another, and after four months of deliberations in stifling summer heat, thirty-nine signed the new federal constitution they had drafted. Only three of the delegates refused to sign.

The durability and flexibility of that document testify to the remarkable men who made it. The delegates were surprisingly young: forty-two was the average age. They were farmers, merchants, lawyers, and bankers, many of them widely read in history, law, and political philosophy. Yet they were also practical men of experience, tested in the fires of the Revolution. Twenty-one had served in the military during the conflict, seven had been state governors, most had been members of the Continental Congress, and eight had signed the Declaration of Independence.

The magisterial George Washington served as presiding officer but participated little in the debates. Eighty-one-year-old Benjamin Franklin, the oldest delegate, also said little from the floor but provided a wealth of experience, wit, and common sense behind the scenes. More active in the debates were **James Madison,** the ablest political philosopher in the group; Massachusetts's dapper Elbridge Gerry, a Harvard graduate who earned the nickname Old Grumbletonian because, as John Adams once said, he "opposed everything he did not propose"; George Mason, the author of the Virginia Declaration of Rights and a slaveholding planter with a deep-rooted suspicion of all government; the witty, eloquent, arrogant New York aristocrat Gouverneur Morris, who harbored a venomous contempt for the common people; Scottish-born James Wilson of Pennsylvania, one of the ablest lawyers in the new nation and next in importance at the convention only to Washington and Madison; and Roger Sherman of Connecticut, a self-trained lawyer adept at negotiating compromises. John Adams, like Thomas Jefferson, was serving abroad on a diplomatic mission. Also conspicuously absent during most of the convention was Alexander Hamilton, the staunch nationalist who regretfully went home

James Madison

Madison was only thirty-six when he assumed a major role in the drafting of the Constitution. This miniature (1783) is by Charles Willson Peale.

when the other two New York delegates walked out to protest what they saw as the loss of states' rights.

James Madison emerged as the central figure at the convention. Small of stature—barely over five feet tall and weighing only one hundred thirty pounds—and frail in health, the thirty-six-year-old bookish bachelor was descended from wealthy slaveholding Virginia planters. He suffered from chronic headaches and was painfully shy. Crowds made him nervous, and he hated to use his high-pitched voice in public, much less in open debate. But the Princeton graduate possessed an agile mind and had a voracious appetite for learning. The convincing eloquence of his arguments—and his repeated willingness to embrace compromises—proved decisive. "Every person seems to acknowledge his greatness," wrote one delegate. Madison had arrived in Philadelphia with trunks full of books and a head full of ideas. He had been preparing for the convention for months and probably knew more about historical forms of government than any other delegate.

For the most part, the delegates' differences on political philosophy fell within a narrow range. On certain fundamentals they generally agreed: that government derives its just powers from the consent of the people but that society must be protected from the tyranny of the majority; that the people at large must have a voice in their government but that any one group must be kept from abusing power; that a stronger central authority was essential but that all power is subject to abuse. Most of the delegates assumed, with Madison, that even the best people are naturally selfish. Government, therefore, could not be founded altogether upon a trust in the citizenry's goodwill and virtue. By a careful arrangement of checks and balances within and among three and only three branches of government—executive, legislative, and judicial—the Founding Fathers hoped to devise institutions that could constrain individual sinfulness and channel self-interest to benefit the public good.

THE VIRGINIA AND NEW JERSEY PLANS   At the outset of the Constitutional Convention, James Madison drafted the framework of the discussions. His proposals, which came to be called the **Virginia Plan**, embodied a revolutionary idea: that the delegates scrap their instructions to *revise* the Articles of Confederation and instead submit an entirely new document to the states. Madison's plan proposed separate legislative, executive, and judicial branches and a truly national government to make laws binding upon individual citizens as well as states. The new Congress would be divided into two houses: a lower house chosen by the citizenry and an upper house of senators elected by the state legislatures. Congress could disallow state laws under the plan and would itself define the extent of its and the states' authority.

On June 15, delegates critical of some aspects of Madison's proposals submitted an alternative: the **New Jersey Plan**, which sought to keep the existing structure of equal representation of the states in a unicameral Congress but give Congress the power to levy taxes and regulate commerce and the authority to name an executive (with no veto) and a supreme court.

The two competing plans presented the convention with two major issues: (1) whether simply to amend the Articles of Confederation or to draft a new document; and, (2) whether to determine congressional representation by state or by population. On the first point the convention voted to work toward establishing a new national government as envisioned by Madison and the other Virginians. Regarding the powers of this government, there was little disagreement except in the details. Experience with the Articles of Confederation had persuaded the delegates that an effective central government, as distinguished from a confederation of equal states, needed the power to levy taxes, regulate commerce, fund an army and navy, and make laws binding upon individual citizens. The painful lessons of the 1780s suggested to them, moreover, that in the interest of order and uniformity the states must be denied certain powers: to issue money, make treaties, wage war, and levy tariffs.

These issues sparked furious disagreements. The first clash in the convention involved congressional representation, and it was resolved by the Great Compromise (sometimes called the Connecticut Compromise, as it was proposed by Roger Sherman), which gave both groups their way: the more populous states won apportionment by population in the proposed House of Representatives, whereas the states that sought to protect states' power won equality of representation in the Senate, with the vote by individuals, not by state legislatures.

An equally contentious struggle ensued between northern and southern delegates over race-based slavery and the regulation of trade, an omen of sectional controversies to come. Of all the issues that emerged during the Constitutional Convention of 1787, none was more volatile than the question of slavery and its future. During the eighteenth century the agricultural economies of Virginia, the Carolinas, and Georgia had become dependent upon enslaved workers, and delegates from those states were determined to protect the future of slavery as they drafted the new federal constitution. A third of the people living in the southern states were enslaved blacks. A South Carolinian stressed that his delegation and the Georgians would oppose any new constitution that failed to protect slavery. The threat worked. James Madison of Virginia reported that "the real difference of interests" at the Constitutional Convention "lies not between the large and small [states] but between the Northern and Southern states. The institution of slavery and its consequences form the [dividing] line." The framers of the Constitution did not even consider the possibility of abolishing slavery, nor did they view the enslaved peoples as human beings whose rights should be protected by the constitution. In this they reflected the prevailing attitudes among white Americans. Most agreed with South Carolina's John Rutledge when he asserted, "Religion and humanity [have] nothing to do with this [slavery] question. Interest alone is the governing principle of nations."

The "interest" of southern delegates, with enslaved African Americans so numerous in their states and so crucial to the plantation economy, dictated that slaves be counted as part of the population in determining the number of a state's congressional representatives. Northerners were willing to count slaves when deciding each state's share of taxes but not for purposes of representation. The delegates finally compromised on this issue by adding the number of "free persons" to three fifths of "all other persons" [the enslaved] as a basis for apportioning both representatives and direct taxes to those states with slaves.

A more sensitive issue for the delegates involved an effort to prevent the federal government from stopping the slave trade with Africa. Virginia's George Mason, himself a slaveholder, condemned the "infernal traffic," which his state had already outlawed. He argued that the issue concerned "not the importing states alone but the whole union." People in the western territories were "already calling out for slaves for their new lands." He feared that they would "fill the country" with enslaved Africans if the transatlantic traffic in slaves were not prohibited. Such a development would bring forth "the judgment of Heaven" on the country. Southern delegates rejected Mason's reasoning. They argued that the continued importation of African slaves was vital to their states' economies.

To resolve the question, the delegates established a time limit: Congress could not prohibit the transatlantic slave trade before 1808, but it could levy a tax of $10 a head on all imported Africans. In both provisions a sense of delicacy—and hypocrisy—dictated the use of euphemisms. The Constitution never explicitly mentions the word *slavery*. Instead it speaks of "free persons" and "all other persons," of "such persons as any of the states now existing shall think proper to admit," and of persons "held to service of labor." The odious word *slavery* did not appear in the Constitution until the Thirteenth Amendment (1865) abolished the "peculiar institution."

If the delegates found the slavery issue fraught with peril, they considered irrelevant any discussion of the legal or political role of women under the new constitution. The Revolutionary rhetoric of liberty had excited some women to demand political equality for themselves. "The men say we have no business [with politics]," Eliza Wilkinson of South Carolina observed as the Constitution was being framed, "but I won't have it thought that because we are the weaker sex as to bodily strength we are capable of nothing more than domestic concerns." Her complaint, however, fell on deaf ears. There was never any formal discussion of women's rights at the constitutional convention. The framers of the constitution still defined politics and government as realms for men only.

The Constitution also said little about the processes of immigration and naturalization, and most of what it said was negative. In Article II, Section 1, the Constitution prohibits any future immigrant from becoming president, limiting that office to a "natural born Citizen." In Article I, Sections 2 and 3, respectively, it stipulates that no person can serve in the House of Representatives who has not "been seven Years a Citizen of the United States" or in the Senate who has not "been nine Years a Citizen." On the matter of defining citizenship, the Constitution gives Congress the authority "to establish a uniform Rule of Naturalization" but offers no further guidance on the matter. As a result, naturalization policy (citizenship for immigrants) has changed significantly over the years in response to fluctuating social attitudes and political moods. In 1790 the first Congress passed a naturalization law that allowed "free white persons" who had been in the United States for as few as two years to be made naturalized citizens in any court. This meant that persons of African descent were denied citizenship by the federal government; it was left to individual states to determine whether free blacks were citizens. And because Indians were not "free white persons," they were also treated as aliens rather than citizens. Not until 1924 would Native Americans be granted citizenship—by an act of Congress rather than a constitutional amendment.

THE SEPARATION OF POWERS The details of the government structure embedded in the Constitution aroused less debate than the basic issues pitting the large states against the small and the northern states against the southern. Existing state constitutions, several of which already separated powers among legislative, executive, and judicial branches, set an example that reinforced the convention's resolve to counter centralized power with checks and balances. Although the Founding Fathers hated royal tyranny, most of them also feared rule by the people and favored various mechanisms to check the possible tyrannies of majority rule. Most of them feared what James Madison called the "passions" of the people; they worried that majorities might tyrannize minorities. Some delegates displayed a thumping disdain for any democratizing of the political system. Elbridge Gerry asserted that most of the nation's problems "flow from an excess of democracy." Alexander Hamilton once called the people "a great beast."

Those elitist views were accommodated by the Constitution's mixed legislative system. The United States was to be a *representative,* not a literal, democracy. "Pure democracies," Madison explained, "have ever been spectacles of turbulence and contention." He and others designed the lower house of Congress to be closer to the voters, who elected its delegates every two years. It would be, according to Virginia's George Mason, "the grand repository of the democratic principle of the Government." The upper house, or Senate, its members elected by the state legislatures, was intended to be more detached from the voters. Staggered six-year terms for senators prevent the choice of a majority in any given year and thereby further isolate senators from acting on the passions of moment.

The delegates to the Constitutional Convention struggled over issues related to the new executive branch. The decision that a single person be made the chief executive caused the delegates "considerable pause," according to James Madison. George Mason protested that this would create a "fetus of monarchy." Indeed, several of the chief executive's powers actually exceeded those of the British monarch. This was the sharpest departure from the recent experience in state government, where the office of governor had commonly been diluted because of the recent memory of struggles with royal governors during the colonial period. The new president would have a veto over acts of Congress, subject to being overridden by a two-thirds vote in each house, whereas in England the royal veto had long since fallen into complete disuse. The president was named commander in chief of the armed forces and responsible for the execution of the laws. The chief executive could make treaties with the advice and consent of two thirds of the Senate and had the power to appoint diplomats, judges, and other officers with the consent of a majority of the Senate. The president was instructed to report annually on the state of the nation and was authorized to recommend legislation, a provision that presidents eventually would take as a mandate to present extensive legislative programs to the Congress for approval.

But the president's powers were limited in certain key areas. The chief executive could neither declare war nor make peace; those powers were reserved for Congress. Unlike the British monarch, moreover, the president could be removed from office. The House could impeach (indict) the chief executive—and other civil officers—on charges of treason, bribery, or "other high crimes and misdemeanors." Upon the conviction of an impeached president, the Senate could remove the president by a two-thirds vote. The presiding officer at the trial of a president would be the chief justice, since the usual presiding officer of the Senate (the vice president) would have a personal stake in the outcome.

The leading nationalists at the constitutional convention—men such as James Madison, James Wilson, and Alexander Hamilton—wanted to strengthen the independence of the president by entrusting the choice to popular election. But an elected executive was still too far beyond the American experience. Besides, a national election would have created enormous problems of organization and voter qualification. Wilson suggested instead that the people of each state choose presidential electors equal to the number of their senators and representatives. Others proposed that the legislators make the choice. Finally, the convention voted to let the legislature decide the method in each state. Before long nearly all the states were choosing the presidential electors by popular vote, and the electors were casting their votes as they had pledged them before the election. This method diverged from the original expectation that the electors would deliberate and make their own choices.

The third branch of government, the judiciary, provoked surprisingly little debate. Both the Virginia and the New Jersey Plans had called for a supreme

Signing the Constitution, September 17, 1787

Thomas Pritchard Rossiter's painting shows George Washington presiding over what Thomas Jefferson called "an assembly of demi-gods" in Philadelphia.

court, which the Constitution established, providing specifically for a chief justice of the United States and leaving up to Congress the number of other justices. Although the Constitution nowhere authorizes the courts to declare laws void when they conflict with the Constitution, the power of the Supreme Court to review congressional actions is implied. The new court soon exercised such "judicial review" in cases involving both state and federal laws. Article VI declares the federal Constitution, federal laws, and treaties to be "the supreme Law of the Land," state laws or constitutions "to the Contrary notwithstanding." The advocates of states' rights thought this a victory, since it eliminated the proviso in the Virginia Plan for Congress to settle all conflicts between the federal government and individual states. As it turned out, however, the clause became the basis for an important expansion of judicial review of legislative actions.

Although the Constitution extended vast new powers to the national government, the delegates' mistrust of unchecked power is apparent in repeated examples of countervailing forces: the separation of the three branches of government, the president's veto, the congressional power of impeachment and removal, the Senate's power to approve or reject treaties and appointments, and the courts' implied right of judicial review. In addition, the new form of government specifically forbade Congress to pass bills of attainder (criminal condemnation by a legislative act) or ex post facto laws (laws adopted after an event to criminalize deeds that have already been committed). It also reserved to the states large areas of sovereignty—a reservation soon made explicit by the Tenth Amendment. By dividing sovereignty between the people and the government, the framers of the Constitution provided a distinctive contribution to political theory. That is, by vesting ultimate authority in the people, they divided sovereignty *within* the government. This constituted a dramatic break with the colonial tradition. The British had always insisted that the sovereignty of the king in Parliament was indivisible.

The most glaring defect of the Articles of Confederation was the rule requiring that any amendments must gain the unanimous approval of the states before being adopted. The delegates in Philadelphia therefore sought to provide a less forbidding, though still difficult, method of amending the Constitution. Amendments can be proposed either by a two-thirds vote of each house in the national Congress or by a convention specially called, upon application of two thirds of the state legislatures. Amendments can be ratified by approval of three fourths of the states acting through their legislatures or in special conventions. The national convention has never been used, however, and state conventions have been called only once—in 1933 to ratify the repeal of the Eighteenth Amendment, which had prohibited "the manufacture, sale, or transportation of" alcoholic beverages.

THE FIGHT FOR RATIFICATION   The final article of the Constitution provided that it would become effective upon ratification not by the unanimous consent of the thirteen state legislatures but by at least nine state-ratifying conventions specially elected for that purpose. The Confederation Congress submitted the draft of the Constitution to the states on September 28, 1787. For the first time in world history the diverse peoples making up a large nation were able to discuss, debate, and decide by a peaceful vote how they would be governed.

In the fierce political debate that ensued, advocates of the new Constitution assumed the name *Federalists*. Opponents, who favored a more decentralized federal system, became *anti-Federalists*. The debate over ratification of the constitution was heated; at times it boiled over into violence. New Yorker Gilbert Livingstone spoke for many when he called the debate the "greatest transaction" of their lives. Newspapers aggressively took sides in the dispute, and readership soared, leading one New Englander to argue that the newspapers were being "read more than the Bible." Mobs in Philadelphia, Albany, and New York City rioted as a result of disputes over the new constitution. In the prolonged debate, the Federalists had several advantages. Their leaders had been members of the constitutional convention and were already familiar with the disputed issues in the document. They were not only better prepared but also better organized and, on the whole, made up of the more able leaders in the political community.

The anti-Federalist leaders—Patrick Henry, George Mason, Richard Henry Lee, and future president James Monroe of Virginia, George Clinton of New York, Samuel Adams and Elbridge Gerry of Massachusetts, Luther Martin and Samuel Chase of Maryland—were often men whose careers and reputations had been established well before the Revolution. The Federalist leaders were more likely to be younger men whose public careers had begun during the Revolution—men such as Hamilton, Madison, and Jay.

The two groups fiercely disagreed more over means than ends, however. Both sides, for the most part, acknowledged that a stronger national authority was needed and that such an authority required an independent source of revenue to function properly. Both sides were convinced that the people must erect safeguards against tyranny, even the tyranny of the majority. Few of the Constitution's supporters liked it in its entirety, but most believed that it was the best document obtainable; few of its opponents found it unacceptable in its entirety. Once the new government had become an accomplished fact, few wanted to undo the work of the Philadelphia convention. The losers in the debate—the anti-Federalists—graciously accepted defeat; they did not resort to violence, and many of them went on to become prominent leaders in the federal government: James Monroe became the fifth president; George Clinton and Elbridge Gerry became vice presidents; and Samuel Chase served on the Supreme Court. For their part, the winners in the debate over the new constitution acknowledged that the document could be improved by the addition of amendments that came to be called the "**Bill of Rights**."

THE FEDERALIST Among the supreme legacies of the debate over the Constitution is *The Federalist,* a collection of essays originally published in New York newspapers between 1787 and 1788. Instigated by Alexander Hamilton, the eighty-five articles published under the name Publius include about fifty by Hamilton, thirty by James Madison, and five by New Yorker John Jay. Written in support of ratification, the essays defended the principle of a supreme national authority while reassuring doubters that the people and the states had little reason to fear tyranny in the new federal government.

In perhaps the most famous *Federalist* essay, Number 10, Madison argued that the very size and diversity of the expanding United States would make it impossible for any single faction to form a majority that could dominate the government. This contradicted the conventional wisdom of the time, which insisted that republics could survive only in small, homogeneous countries like Switzerland and the Netherlands. Large republics, on the other hand, would fragment, dissolving into anarchy and tyranny through the influence of factions. Quite the contrary, Madison insisted. Given a balanced federal government, a republic could work in large, diverse nations probably better than in smaller nations. "Extend the sphere," he wrote, "and you take in a greater variety of parties and interests; you make it less probable that a majority of the whole will have a common motive to invade the rights of other citizens."

Madison and the other Federalists also insisted that the new constitution would promote prosperity by reducing taxes, paying off the war bonds, and expanding the money supply. The anti-Federalists, however, highlighted the dangers of placing more power in the hands of the central government. Mercy Otis Warren of Massachusetts, the most prominent woman in the new nation to write regular political commentary, compared the constitution to "shackles on our own necks." She and other anti-Federalists highlighted the absence of a bill of rights to protect the rights of individuals and states. They also found the process of ratification highly irregular, as it was—indeed, it was illegal under the Articles of Confederation.

THE DECISION OF THE STATES Ratification of the new constitution gained momentum before the end of 1787, and several of the smaller states were among the first to act, apparently satisfied that they had gained all the safeguards they could hope for in equality of representation in the Senate. Delaware, New Jersey, and Georgia voted unanimously in favor. Massachusetts, still sharply divided in the aftermath of Shays's Rebellion, was the first state in which the outcome was close. Massachusetts barely approved the Constitution by 187 to 168 on February 6, 1788.

New Hampshire was the ninth state to ratify the Constitution, allowing it to be put into effect, but the Union could hardly succeed without the approval of Virginia, the most populous state, or New York, which had the third highest population and occupied a key position geographically. Both states harbored strong opposition groups. In Virginia, Patrick Henry became the chief spokesman for backcountry farmers who feared the powers of the new government, but wavering delegates were won over by the same stratagem as in Massachusetts. When it was proposed that the convention should recommend a bill of rights, Edmund Randolph, who had refused to sign the finished document, announced his conversion to the cause.

Upon notification that New Hampshire had become the ninth state to ratify the Constitution, the Confederation Congress began to draft plans for

RATIFICATION OF THE CONSTITUTION

Order of Ratification	State	Date of Ratification
1	Delaware	December 7, 1787
2	Pennsylvania	December 12, 1787
3	New Jersey	December 18, 1787
4	Georgia	January 2, 1788
5	Connecticut	January 9, 1788
6	Massachusetts	February 6, 1788
7	Maryland	April 28, 1788
8	South Carolina	May 23, 1788
9	New Hampshire	June 21, 1788
10	Virginia	June 25, 1788
11	New York	July 26, 1788
12	North Carolina	November 21, 1789
13	Rhode Island	May 29, 1790

the transfer of power to the new federal government created by the Constitution. On September 13, 1788, it selected New York City as the initial capital of the new government and fixed the date for the first elections. On October 10, 1788, the Confederation Congress transacted its last business and passed into history. Both sides in the ratification debate could claim victory. The Constitution was adopted, but the spirited resistance to it convinced the first new Congress under the constitution to propose the first amendments now known as the Bill of Rights.

"Our constitution is in actual operation," the elderly Benjamin Franklin wrote to a friend; "everything appears to promise that it will last; but in this world nothing is certain but death and taxes." George Washington was even more uncertain about the future under the new plan of government. He had told a fellow delegate as the convention adjourned, "I do not expect the Constitution to last for more than twenty years."

The Constitution has lasted much longer, of course, and in the process it has provided a model of resilient republican government whose features have been repeatedly borrowed by other nations through the years. Yet what makes the U.S. Constitution so distinctive is not its specific provisions or many compromises but its remarkable harmony with the particular "genius of the people" it governs. The Constitution has provided a flexible system of government that presidents, legislators, judges, and the people have adjusted to changing social, economic, and political circumstances.

The tension between preserving states' rights and expanding federal authority embedded in the debate over ratification of the Constitution did not end in 1787; it became the defining drama of American history thereafter. In this sense the Founding Fathers not only created "a more perfect

The Constitution

Many local newspapers published the Constitution in 1787, allowing Americans across the country to read and discuss it.

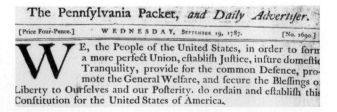

Union" in 1787; they also engineered a frame of government whose resilience (and ambiguities) enabled later generations to continue to perfect their republican experiment. But the framers of the Constitution failed in one significant respect: in skirting the issue of slavery so as to cement the Union, they unknowingly allowed tensions over the "peculiar institution" to reach the point where there would be no political solution—only civil war.

CHAPTER SUMMARY

- **Confederation Government** Despite the weak form of government deliberately crafted under the Articles of Confederation, the Confederation government managed to construct alliances, wage the Revolutionary War to a successful conclusion, and negotiate the Treaty of Paris. It created executive departments and established the way in which western lands would be organized and governments would be formed in the territories.

- **Articles of Confederation** Postwar economic conditions were difficult because British markets were closed to the new nation and the Articles had not provided for a means to raise taxes or stimulate economic recovery. Shays's Rebellion made many Americans fear that anarchy would destroy the new republic and led them to clamor for a stronger national government.

- **Constitutional Convention** Delegates gathered at the convention in Philadelphia to revise the existing government, but almost immediately they proposed scrapping the Articles of Confederation. An entirely new document emerged, delineating separate executive, legislative, and judicial branches. Argument about representation was resolved by establishing a two-house Congress, with equal representation by state in the Senate and by population in the House of Representatives.

- **Slavery and the Constitution** Southern delegates would not support a constitution that failed to protect the institution of slavery and provide for the international slave trade. In determining how enslaved people would be counted for the sake of apportioning direct taxes and representation in the lower house, the framers decided that three fifths of the enslaved population would be counted. It was also agreed that Congress would not forbid participation in the transatlantic slave trade before 1808. Nevertheless, the framers of the Constitution avoided using the word *slavery* in the Constitution.

- **Ratification of the Constitution** Ratification of the Constitution was difficult, especially in the key states of Virginia and New York. Anti-Federalists such as Virginia's Patrick Henry favored a decentralized federal system and feared that the absence of a bill of rights would lead to a loss of individual and states' rights. To sway New York State toward ratification, Alexander Hamilton, James Madison, and John Jay wrote *The Federalist,* a series of articles defending a strong national authority. Ratification became possible only with the promise of a bill of rights.

CHRONOLOGY

1781	Articles of Confederation take effect
1783	General Washington puts an end to the Newburgh Conspiracy
1784	Treaty of Fort Stanwix forces the Iroquois to give up land in New York and Pennsylvania
1785	Land Ordinance outlines a plan for surveying and selling government lands
1786	Delegates call for a constitutional convention
1786–1787	Shays's Rebellion
1787	Northwest Ordinance outlines a detailed plan for organizing western territories
1787	The Constitutional Convention is held in Philadelphia
1787–1788	*The Federalist Papers* are published
1788	Confederation government is phased out
1790	Rhode Island becomes the last state to ratify the Constitution

KEY TERMS & NAMES

7

THE FEDERALIST ERA

FOCUS QUESTIONS wwnorton.com/studyspace

- What were the main challenges facing Washington's administration?
- What was Hamilton's vision of the new republic?
- How did religious freedom become a reality for the new country?
- How did European affairs complicate the internal political and diplomatic problems of the new country?
- Why did Madison and Jefferson lead the opposition to Hamilton's policies?

The Constitution was ratified in 1788 because it promised to create a more powerful central government better capable of managing a sprawling—and rapidly growing—new republic. Although the U.S. Constitution has become the world's most enduring national charter, skeptics in the late eighteenth century doubted that it would survive more than a few years. A Massachusetts anti-Federalist said that governing such an "extensive empire . . . upon republican principles" was impossible. It was one thing to draft a new constitution but quite another to exercise the expanded powers it allowed. Creating a "more perfect union" would prove to be a long, complicated, and painful process. With each passing year the new United States witnessed growing political factionalism. During the 1790s, the new federal government would confront civil rebellions, threats of secession, international intrigues, and foreign wars. In 1789, Americans wildly celebrated the inauguration of George Washington as the nation's first president just as chaos was erupting in France because of a violent revolution against the monarchy. But amid the excitement was a turbulent undercurrent of uncertainty, suspicion, and anxiety. The new Constitution provided a framework for nationhood but not a blueprint; it left unanswered many questions about the actual structure and conduct of the new government. As James Madison had acknowledged, "We are in a wilderness without a single footstep to guide us."

A NEW NATION

In 1789 the United States and its western territories reached from the Atlantic Ocean to the Mississippi River and hosted almost 4 million people. Overall, the United States in 1790 was predominantly a rural society. Eighty percent of households were involved in agricultural production. Only a few cities had more than 5,000 residents. The first national census, taken in 1790, counted 750,000 African Americans, almost a fifth of the population. Most of them lived in the five southernmost states; less than ten percent lived outside the South. Most African Americans, of course, were enslaved, but there

New beginnings

An engraving from the title page of *The Universal Asylum and Columbian Magazine* (published in Philadelphia in 1790). America is represented as a woman laying down her shield to engage in education, art, commerce, and agriculture.

were many more free blacks as a result of the social turmoil during the Revolutionary War. In fact, the proportion of free to enslaved blacks was never higher before the Civil War than it was in 1790. The 1790 census did not even count the many Indians still living east of the Mississippi River. Most Americans viewed the Native Americans as those people whom the Declaration of Independence had dismissed as "merciless Indian Savages."

A NEW GOVERNMENT   On March 4, 1789, the new Congress of the United States convened its first meeting in New York City. Only eight senators and thirteen representatives attended. It would be another month before both chambers could gather a quorum. Only then could the presiding officer of the Senate certify the foregone conclusion that George Washington, with 69 votes, was the unanimous choice of the Electoral College for president. John Adams, with 34 votes, the second-highest number, became vice president.

Washington was a reluctant first president. He told a friend as he prepared to assume office in New York City that he felt like a "culprit who is going to the place of his execution." Yet Washington agreed to serve because he had been "summoned by my country." A self-made man who lost his father at age eleven and had little formal education, he had never visited Europe. The acidic John Adams once declared that Washington was "too illiterate, unlearned, unread for his station and reputation." But Washington had virtues that Adams lacked. He was a military hero and prosperous planter who brought to his new office a remarkable capacity for moderation and mediation that helped keep the infant republic from disintegrating. As a military strategist, statesman, and inspirational leader, Washington had influenced every phase of the Revolutionary War. While learning how to defeat the British army, he also displayed great political skills in convincing the Continental Congress (and the states) to keep his army supplied. Although at times stern and hot tempered, Washington was remarkably self-disciplined; he possessed extraordinary stamina and patience, integrity and resolve, courage and resilience. Few doubted that he was the best person to lead the new nation.

In his inaugural address, Washington appealed for national unity, pleading with the new Congress to abandon "local prejudices" and "party animosities" in order to create the "national" outlook necessary for the fledgling republic to thrive. Within a few months the new president would see his hopes dashed. Personal rivalries, sectional tensions, and partisan conflict dominated political life in the 1790s.

THE GOVERNMENT'S STRUCTURE   President Washington had a larger staff at his plantation in northern Virginia than he did as the first president of the United States. During the summer of 1789, Congress created executive departments corresponding to those formed under the Confederation. To head the Department of State, Washington named Thomas Jefferson, recently back from his diplomatic duties in France. To head the Department of the Treasury, Washington picked his brilliant thirty-four-year-old wartime aide, Alexander Hamilton, now a prominent New York lawyer. Edmund Randolph, former governor of Virginia, filled the new position of attorney general.

The structure of the federal court system, like that of the executive departments, was left to Congress, except for a chief justice and the Supreme Court. Congress set the membership of the highest court at six (now nine)—the chief justice and five associates—and created thirteen federal district courts. Washington named New Yorker John Jay as the first chief justice of the Supreme Court, a post Jay held until 1795. His reputation as the state's finest lawyer had led New York to send him as its representative to the First and Second Continental Congresses. After serving as president of the Continental Congress in 1778–1779, Jay became the American minister (ambassador) in Spain. While in Europe, he helped John Adams and Benjamin Franklin negotiate the Treaty of Paris in 1783. After the Revolution, Jay served as secretary of foreign affairs. He joined James Madison and Alexander Hamilton as co-author of the *The Federalist* and became one of the most effective champions of the Constitution.

THE BILL OF RIGHTS   The ratification of the Constitution did not end the concern about the centralization of power in the federal government. Amid the debates over ratification of the Constitution, four states—Massachusetts, New York, Virginia, and North Carolina—requested that a "bill of rights" be added to protect individual freedoms, states' rights, and civil liberties. To address such concerns, Congressman James Madison presented to Congress in May 1789 a cluster of constitutional amendments that have since become known as the Bill of Rights. Congress approved the amendments in September 1789, and by the end of 1791, the necessary three fourths of the states had approved ten of the twelve proposed amendments.

The first eight Amendments to the Constitution provide safeguards for specified rights of individuals: freedom of religion, press, speech, and assembly; the right to own firearms; the right to refuse to house soldiers in a private home; protection against unreasonable searches and seizures; the right to refuse to testify against oneself; the right to a speedy public trial, with legal counsel present, before an impartial jury; and protection against "cruel and unusual" punishment.

The Ninth and Tenth Amendments address the demand for specific statements that the enumeration of rights in the Constitution "shall not be construed to deny or disparage others retained by the people" and that "powers not delegated to the United States by the Constitution, nor prohibited by it to the States, are reserved to the States respectively, or to the people." The ten amendments constituting the Bill of Rights became effective on December 15, 1791.

RELIGIOUS FREEDOM   The debates over the Constitution and the Bill of Rights generated a religious revolution as well as a political revolution. Unlike the New England Puritans who sought to ensure that colonial governments explicitly supported their particular religious beliefs, the men who drafted and amended the Constitution made no direct mention of God. They were determined to protect freedom of religion from government interference and coercion. The First Amendment declares that "Congress shall make no law respecting an establishment of religion or prohibiting the free exercise thereof." This statement has since become one of the most important—and most disputed—principles of American government. In 1789 many people feared that the new national government might impose a particular religious faith on the people. The First Amendment was intended to create a pluralistic framework within which people of all religious persuasions could flourish. It prohibits the federal government from endorsing or supporting any particular religion or interfering with the religious choices that people make. As Thomas Jefferson later explained, the First Amendment was intended to erect a "wall of separation between church and State."

HAMILTON'S FINANCIAL VISION

RAISING REVENUE   Raising money to operate its affairs was the new federal government's most critical task. Governments have three basic ways to raise money to pay their bills: they can impose taxes, they can borrow money by selling interest-paying government bonds, and they can print money. When George Washington was elected president, the federal treasury was virtually empty. To raise necessary funds, James Madison and Alexander Hamilton in the summer of 1789 proposed a modest federal tariff (a tax on imports) to generate revenue.

The levying of tariffs marked but the beginning of the effort to get the new country on sound fiscal footing. In 1789 Alexander Hamilton seized the initiative. Shrewd, energetic, charismatic, and combative, the red-haired, blue-eyed attorney was consumed with social and political ambition and blessed with powerful analytical skills. During the Revolutionary War, Hamilton had witnessed the near-fatal weaknesses of the Confederation Congress. Its lack of authority and money almost lost the war. Now, as the nation's first secretary of the Treasury, he was determined to transform an economically weak cluster of states into a powerful nation and global power comparable to Great Britain. To do so, Hamilton believed, the United States needed to unleash the energy and ambition of its citizens so as to create a vibrant economy driven by the engines of capitalism.

Alexander Hamilton

Secretary of the treasury from 1789 to 1795.

ESTABLISHING THE PUBLIC CREDIT In a series of brilliant reports submitted to Congress between January 1790 and December 1791, Hamilton outlined his visionary program for government finances and the economic development of the United States. The first of two "Reports on Public Credit" dealt with the $79 million debt that state and federal governments had incurred during the War for Independence. The Constitution required the new federal government to assume the debts of the Confederation government. How that should be done was a source of heated debate.

Some argued that many of the debts should not be repaid. Hamilton disagreed, insisting that the state debts from the Revolution were a *national* responsibility because all Americans had benefited from the war for independence. Hamilton also believed that a government commitment to repay its debts would give wealthy investors a direct stake in the success of the new national government. A federal debt, he claimed, would serve as a "mechanism for national unity" and prosperity.

Hamilton's controversial first report on public credit made two key recommendations: first, it called for funding the federal debt at face value, which meant that citizens holding deflated war bonds could exchange them for new interest-bearing bonds; and, second, it declared that the federal government should assume state debts from the Revolution. The debt-funding scheme was controversial because many farmers and former soldiers in immediate need of money had recently sold their government bonds for a fraction of their value to speculators. The original bondholders argued that they should be reimbursed for their losses; otherwise, the speculators would gain a windfall from the new government's decision to fund bonds at face value. Hamilton sternly resisted their pleas. The speculators, he argued, had "paid what the commodity was worth in the market, and took the risks." Therefore, they should reap the profits. In fact, Hamilton insisted, the government should favor the speculative investors because they represented the bedrock of a successful capitalist economy.

THE EMERGENCE OF SECTIONAL DIFFERENCES Hamilton's sophisticated financial proposals created a political firestorm. The Virginian James Madison, who had been Hamilton's close ally in promoting ratification of the Constitution, broke with him over the merits of a national debt. Madison did not question whether the war-related debt should be paid; he was troubled, however, that speculative investors would become the chief beneficiaries. That far more debt was owed to northerners than to southerners further troubled him. Madison's opposition to Hamilton's plan ignited a vigorous debate, but Hamilton carried his point by a margin of 3 to 1 when the House brought it to a vote.

Madison's opposition to Hamilton's plan to have the federal government assume responsibility for state debts got more support, however, and clearly signaled a growing political division along geographic lines. The southern states, with the exception of South Carolina, had whittled down their war debts. New England, with the largest unpaid debts, stood to be the greatest beneficiary of Hamilton's plan for the federal government to pay off the state debts. Rather than see Virginia victimized, Madison held out yet another alternative. Why not, he suggested, have the government assume state debts as they stood in 1783, at the conclusion of the peace treaty? Debates on this point deadlocked the whole question of debt funding, and Hamilton grew so frustrated with the legislative stalemate that he considered resigning.

The gridlock ended in the summer of 1790, when Jefferson, Hamilton, and Madison agreed to a famous compromise. In return for northern votes in favor of locating the permanent national capital on the Potomac River, Madison pledged to seek enough southern votes to pass the debt assumption plan. This Compromise of 1790 secured enough votes to carry Hamilton's funding and assumption proposals. The national capital would be moved from New York City to Philadelphia for ten years, after which it would be settled at a new federal city (called Washington) on the Potomac River.

Hamilton's debt-financing scheme was an immediate success. The new bonds issued by the federal government were snatched up by eager investors within a few weeks. By 1794 the young United States had the highest financial credit rating among all the nations of Europe. A leading French official explained why: the American government bonds were "safe and free from reverses. They have been funded in such a sound manner and the prosperity of this country is growing so rapidly that there can be no doubt of their solvency." Of course, the fact that war had erupted in Europe as a result of the French Revolution also played a role in the success of Hamilton's plans, because American exports to the warring nations soared.

A NATIONAL BANK After securing Congressional approval of his debt funding scheme, Hamilton authored three more crucial economic reports: the second of the "Reports on Public Credit," which included a proposal for a liquor tax to raise revenue to help repay the nation's debts; a report recommending the establishment of a national bank and a national mint (to provide coins and currency), both of which were set up in 1791–1792; and the "**Report on Manufactures**," which proposed an extensive program of government aid and other encouragement to stimulate the development of manufacturing enterprises so as to reduce America's dependence on imported goods.

Hamilton's proposed **Bank of the United States** would have three primary responsibilities: (1) to serve as a secure repository for government funds and facilitate the transfer of monies to other nations; (2) to provide loans to the federal government and to other banks to facilitate economic development; and (3) to manage the nation's money supply by regulating the money-issuing activities of state-chartered banks. By holding government bonds and using them for collateral, the national bank could issue banknotes (paper money), thereby providing a national currency that would address the chronic shortage of gold and silver coins. Government bonds held by the national bank would back up the value of its new banknotes. The national bank, chartered by Congress, would remain under government control, but private investors would supply four fifths of the $10 million capital and name twenty of the twenty-five directors; the government would provide the other fifth of the capital and name five directors.

Once again Congressman James Madison rose to lead the opposition to Hamilton, arguing that he could find no basis in the Constitution for a national bank. Nevertheless, Congress approved the bank bill. The vote revealed the growing sectional division in the young United States. Representatives from the northern states voted 33 to 1 in favor of the national bank; southern congressmen opposed the bank 19 to 6.

Before signing the controversial bill, President Washington sought the advice of his cabinet, where he found an equal division of opinion. The result was the first great debate on constitutional interpretation. Should there be a strict or a broad construction of the Constitution? Were the powers of Congress only those explicitly stated, or were others implied? The argument turned chiefly on Article I, Section 8, which authorizes Congress to "make all Laws which shall be necessary and proper for carrying into Execution the foregoing Powers."

Such language left room for disagreement and led to a confrontation between Jefferson and Hamilton. Hamilton convinced Washington to sign the bank bill. In doing so, the president had, in Jefferson's words, opened up "a boundless field of power," which in the coming years would lead to a further broadening of the president's implied powers under the Constitution. On July 4, 1791, stock in the new Bank of the United States was put up for sale, and it sold out within an hour.

ENCOURAGING MANUFACTURES Hamilton's audacious economic vision for the new republic was not yet complete. In the last of his celebrated reports, the "Report on Manufactures," he set in place the capstone of his design for a modern national economy: the active governmental encouragement of manufacturing enterprises. Hamilton believed that several advantages would flow from the aggressive development of an industrial sector. It would bring diversification to an economy dominated by agriculture; improve productivity through greater use of machinery; provide paid work for those not ordinarily employed outside the home, such as women and children; encourage immigration to provide industrial workers; create more opportunities for entrepreneurial activity; and expand the domestic market for agricultural products.

To nurture industrial development, Hamilton endorsed the imposition of federal tariffs (taxes) on foreign imports to make American products more competitive with European manufactures. He also recommended that the federal government provide financial incentives to encourage capitalists to launch new industries and to encourage inventions and new technologies. Finally, Hamilton urged the federal government to fund improvements in transportation, including the development of roads, canals, and rivers for commercial traffic. Some of Hamilton's tariff proposals were enacted in 1792. Otherwise the program was filed away—but not forgotten. It provided an arsenal of arguments for the advocates of manufactures in years to come.

Largely owing to the skillful Hamilton, the Treasury Department during the early 1790s began to pay down the Revolutionary War debt, and foreign capital began to flow into the American economy. Economic growth, so elusive in the 1780s, flourished by the end of the century. But Hamilton's policies had done much more than revive the economy. They had established the foundations for what would become the world's most powerful capitalist republic.

THE REPUBLICAN ALTERNATIVE

Hamilton's controversial financial ideas provided the economic foundation of the political party known as the Federalists; in opposition, Madison and Jefferson led those who took the name **Republicans** (also called the Democratic Republicans or Jeffersonian Republicans), thereby implying that the Federalists aimed at a monarchy. The Federalists agreed with Hamilton about the need for a stronger national government with sound credit and currency managed by a national bank in order to ensure prosperity and security. Republicans worried about the threats to individual freedoms and states' rights posed by a strong central government. Republicans also questioned the legitimacy of a national bank, arguing that the Constitution did not empower the government to create such a bank. On the whole, Jeffersonian Republicans promoted a strict interpretation of the Constitution, while the Federalists believed that the Constitution should be interpreted broadly whenever the national interest dictated such flexibility.

Neither side in the disagreement over national policy deliberately set out to create organized political parties. But there were growing differences of both philosophy and self-interest that would not subside. At the outset, James Madison assumed leadership of Hamilton's opponents in Congress. Madison, like Thomas Jefferson, was rooted in Virginia, where opposition to Hamilton's economic policies predominated. Patrick Henry, for example, proclaimed that Hamilton's policies were "dangerous to the rights and subversive of the interests of the people."

After the Compromise of 1790, which enabled the nationalizing of state debts, Madison and Jefferson ever more resolutely opposed Hamilton's policies: his effort to place a tax on whiskey, which laid a burden especially on the trans-Appalachian farmers, whose livelihood depended upon the production and sale of the beverage; his proposal for the national bank; and his "Report on Manufactures." Hostility between Jefferson and Hamilton festered within the cabinet, much to the distress of President Washington.

Thomas Jefferson

A portrait by Charles Willson Peale (1791).

Like Hamilton, Jefferson was brilliant. He developed a breadth of cultivated interests that ranged widely in science, the arts, and the humanities. He read or spoke seven languages. He was an architect of distinction (his home at Monticello, the Virginia state capitol, and the University of Virginia are monuments to his talent), an intellectually curious gentleman who understood mathematics and engineering, an inventor, and an agronomist. He knew music and practiced the violin, although one wit remarked that only Patrick Henry played it worse.

Hamilton and Jefferson represented contrasting visions of the character of the Union. Their differing philosophical and political issues still echo more than two centuries later. Thomas Jefferson, twelve years Hamilton's senior, was in most respects his opposite. Jefferson was an aristocrat and at times a radical utopian. He was by nature an optimist and a visionary. Hamilton was a hardheaded urban realist. Jefferson was an agrarian idealist who feared that the growth of crowded cities would divide society into a capitalist aristocracy on the one hand and a deprived proletariat on the other. Hamilton feared anarchy and loved stability; Jefferson feared tyranny and loved liberty.

Hamilton was a pro-British champion of a strong central government that would encourage urban-industrial growth. Jefferson was a devout admirer of French culture who wanted to preserve a decentralized agrarian republic made up primarily of small farmers. "Those who labor in the earth," he wrote, "are the chosen people of God, if ever he had a chosen people, whose breasts He has made His peculiar deposit for genuine and substantial virtue." Jefferson did not oppose all forms of manufacturing; he simply feared that the unlimited expansion of commerce and industry would produce a growing class of wage laborers who were dependent upon others for their livelihood and therefore subject to political manipulation and economic exploitation.

By mid-1792, Hamilton and Jefferson could no longer disguise their disdain for each other. Hamilton was convinced that Jefferson was "bent upon my subversion." And he was. Jefferson told a friend that the two rivals "daily pitted in the cabinet like two cocks." The Virginian believed that Hamilton's British-inspired policies would "undermine and abolish the republic." President Washington grew so frustrated by the political infighting within his cabinet that he begged his chief officers to put an end to the "wounding suspicions and irritating charges."

Still, amid the rising political tensions, there was little opposition in either party to George Washington, who longed to retire from politics to his beloved plantation at Mount Vernon and had even begun drafting a farewell address but was urged by both Hamilton and Jefferson to continue in public life. Secretary of State Jefferson told Washington that the unstable new nation needed him: "North and South will hang together if they have you to hang on." In the fragile infancy of the new nation, Washington was the only man able to transcend party differences and hold things together with his unmatched prestige. In 1792, Washington was unanimously reelected to serve a second term.

CRISES FOREIGN AND DOMESTIC

During George Washington's second term, the problems of foreign relations surged to center stage as the result of the cascading consequences of the French Revolution, which had begun in 1789, during the first months of his first presidential term. Americans followed the tumultuous events in France with almost universal sympathy, for in the early months the French idealists seemed to be emulating the American Revolution. In July 1789 French rebels stormed the Bastille, the Parisian prison that had long been a symbol of monarchical tyranny; in August revolutionary leaders penned the Declaration of the Rights of Man and Citizen; and, the following year, the French republicans drafted their own constitution.

By early 1793, however, the most radical of the French revolutionaries, having abolished the monarchy and declared a republic, executed the king and queen as well as hundreds of aristocrats and priests. Then the revolutionary government declared war on Great Britain on February 1, 1793. The much-celebrated French experiment in liberty, equality, and fraternity began to transform itself into a monster.

As the new French government plunged into war with Austria and Prussia, the Revolution began devouring its own children, along with its enemies, during the Terror of 1793–1794. The revolutionary rulers used guillotines to execute thousands of political prisoners, and barbarism ruled the streets of Paris and other major cities. Secretary of State Thomas Jefferson, who had served as U.S. minister to France during the 1780s, wholeheartedly endorsed the efforts of French Revolutionaries to replace the monarchy with a republican form of government. By contrast, Vice President John Adams decided that the French Revolution had run amok; it had become barbarous and godless. Such conflicting attitudes toward the French Revolution transformed the first decade of American politics into one of the most fractious periods in the nation's history.

The French Revolution also transformed international relations and set in motion a series of complex European alliances and prolonged wars that would frustrate the desire of the young United States to remain neutral in world affairs. After the execution of King Louis XVI, early in 1793, Great Britain and Spain entered into the coalition of European monarchies at war with the chaotic French republic. For the next twenty-two years, Britain and France were at war, with only a brief respite, until the final defeat of the French forces under Napoléon Bonaparte in 1815. The European war presented George Washington, just beginning his second term in 1793, with an awkward decision. By the 1778 Treaty of Alliance, the United States was a perpetual ally of France, obligated to defend the European nation's possessions in the West Indies.

But Americans wanted no part of the European war. They were determined to maintain their lucrative trade with both sides. And besides, the Americans had no navy with which to wage a war. Neutrality was the only sensible policy. For their part, Hamilton and Jefferson found in the neutrality policy one issue on which they could agree. Where they differed was in how best to implement it. Hamilton had a simple answer: declare the French alliance formed during the American Revolution invalid because it had been made with a French government that no longer existed. Jefferson preferred to delay and use the alliance as a bargaining point with the British. In the end, however, Washington followed the advice of neither. Taking a middle course, the president issued a neutrality proclamation on April 22, 1793, that declared the United States "friendly and impartial toward the belligerent powers" and warned U.S. citizens that they might be prosecuted for "aiding or abetting hostilities" or taking part in other un-neutral acts. Instead of settling matters in his cabinet, however, Washington's proclamation brought to a boil the feud between Hamilton and Jefferson. Jefferson dashed off an angry letter to James Madison, urging his ally to "take up your pen" and cut Hamilton "to pieces" in the newspapers.

CITIZEN GENET   At the same time, President Washington accepted Jefferson's argument that the United States should recognize the new French revolutionary government (becoming the first nation to do so) and welcome its new ambassador to the United States, the headstrong, indiscreet twenty-nine-year-old Edmond-Charles-Édouard Genet. Early in 1793, **Citizen Genet** landed at Charleston, South Carolina to a hero's welcome. Along the route to Philadelphia, the enthusiasm of his American sympathizers gave the swaggering Genet an inflated notion of his influence. In Charleston he had recruited privateers to capture British ships, and he also conspired with frontiersmen and land speculators to organize an attack on Spanish Florida and Louisiana.

Genet quickly became an embarrassment even to his Republican friends. In August 1793, President Washington demanded that he return to France. But a new party of radicals had gained power in France, and they sent agents to America to arrest Genet. Instead of returning to Paris and risk the guillotine, Genet sought asylum in the United States.

The war between France and Great Britain deeply divided public opinion in the United States. The division gave rise to curious loyalties: slaveholding planters like Thomas Jefferson joined the cheers for radical Revolutionaries who confiscated the lands of aristocrats in France, and they supported the protest against British seizures of New England ships; Massachusetts shippers still profited from the British trade and kept quiet. Boston, once a hotbed of revolution itself, became a bastion of Federalism. Jefferson was so disgusted by President Washington's refusal to support the French Revolution and by his own ideological warfare with Hamilton that he resigned as secretary of state at the end of 1793. Vice President Adams greeted the news by saying "good riddance."

JAY'S TREATY   By 1794 a prolonged foreign-policy crisis between the United States and Great Britain threatened to renew warfare between the old enemies. The 1783 Peace of Paris that ended the Revolutionary War had left the western and southern boundaries of the new United States in dispute. In addition, in late 1793 British warships violated international law by seizing any American ship that carried French goods or was sailing for a French port. By early 1794 several hundred American ships in the West Indies had been confiscated. Their crews were given the terrible choice of joining the British navy or being imprisoned. At the same time, British troops in the Ohio River valley were arming Indians who in turn attacked American settlers. Early in 1794 the Republican leaders in Congress were gaining support for commercial retaliation to end British trade abuses when the British gave President Washington a timely opening for a settlement. They stopped seizing American ships, and on April 16, 1794, Washington asked Chief Justice

John Jay to go to London to settle the major issues between the two nations: to get British troops out of their forts along the Great Lakes and to secure reparations for the losses of American shippers, compensation for southern slaves carried away by British ships in 1783, and a new commercial treaty that would legalize American trade with the British West Indies.

To win his objectives, Jay accepted the British definition of neutral rights—that exports of tar, pitch, and other products needed for warships were contraband (war supplies) and that such military products could not go in neutral ships to enemy ports. Through Jay's negotiations, Britain also gained advantages in its trade with the United States and a promise that French privateers would not be outfitted in American ports. Finally, Jay conceded that the British need not compensate U.S. citizens for the enslaved African Americans who had escaped during the Revolutionary War and that the pre-Revolutionary American debts to British merchants would be paid by the U.S. government. In return for these concessions, the chief justice won three important promises from the British: they would evacuate their six northwestern forts by 1796; reimburse Americans for the seizures of ships and cargo in 1793–1794; and grant American merchants the right to trade with the British West Indies. But the last of these (Article XII) was hedged with restrictions.

Public outrage greeted the announcement of **Jay's Treaty** (also known as the Treaty of London of 1794). The debate was so intense that some Americans feared civil war might erupt. Thomas Jefferson and the Democratic Republicans who favored France in its war with Britain were furious; they wanted no concessions to the hated British. Jefferson dismissed Jay's Treaty as an "infamous act." Opponents of the treaty took to the streets, hanged John Jay in effigy, and claimed that the treaty was unconstitutional. The heated dispute helped to crystallize the differences between the nation's first competing political parties, the Jeffersonian Republicans and the Federalists.

The uproar over the treaty created the gravest crisis of Washington's presidency. He worried that his opponents were prepared to separate "the Union into Northern & Southern." After he officially endorsed Jay's Treaty, there were even calls for his impeachment. Yet the president, while acknowledging that the proposed agreement was imperfect, concluded that adopting it was the only way to avoid a war with Britain that America was bound to lose. In the end, Jay's Treaty barely won the necessary two-thirds majority in the Senate on June 24, 1795. Some 80 percent of the votes for the treaty came from New England or the middle Atlantic states; 74 percent of those voting against the treaty were southerners.

FRONTIER TENSIONS Other events also had an important bearing on Jay's Treaty, adding force to the importance of its settlement of the Canadian frontier and strengthening Spain's conviction that it needed to settle long-festering problems along America's southwestern frontier. While Jay was haggling in London, frontier conflict with Indians escalated, with U.S. troops twice crushed by northwestern tribes. At last, President Washington named General Anthony Wayne to head a military expedition into the Northwest Territory. In the fall of 1793, Wayne marched into Indian country with some two thousand six hundred men, built Fort Greenville, and went on the offensive in 1794.

In August some two thousand Shawnee, Ottawa, Chippewa, and Potawatomi warriors, reinforced by Canadian militias, engaged Wayne's troops in the Battle of Fallen Timbers, south of Detroit. The Americans repulsed them and then destroyed their fields and villages. The Indians, frustrated by their inability to stop the relentless waves of white settlers encroaching upon their tribal lands, finally agreed to the Treaty of Greenville, signed in August 1795. According to the terms of the treaty, the United States bought from twelve tribes the rights to the southeastern quarter of the Northwest Territory (now Ohio and Indiana) and enclaves at the sites of Detroit, Chicago, and Vincennes, Indiana.

THE WHISKEY REBELLION Soon after the Battle of Fallen Timbers, the Washington administration resolved on another show of strength in the backcountry, this time against the so-called **Whiskey Rebellion**. Alexander Hamilton's federal tax on liquor, levied in 1791, had outraged frontier farmers because it taxed their most profitable commodity. During the eighteenth and early nineteenth centuries nearly all Americans drank alcoholic beverages: beer, hard cider, ale, wine, rum, brandy, or whiskey. In the areas west of the Appalachian Mountains, the primary cash commodity was liquor distilled from grain or fruit. Backcountry farmers were also suspicious of the new federal government in Philadelphia. The frontiersmen considered the whiskey tax another part of Hamilton's scheme to pick the pockets of the poor to enrich the urban rich. Throughout the backcountry, from Georgia to Pennsylvania and beyond, the whiskey tax provoked resistance and evasion.

In the summer of 1794, discontent exploded into open rebellion in western Pennsylvania. A mob of five hundred armed men burned the house of the federal tax collector. Other rebels destroyed the stills of those who paid the whiskey tax, robbed the mails, stopped court proceedings, and threatened an

Whiskey Rebellion

George Washington as commander in chief reviews the troops mobilized to quell the Whiskey Rebellion in 1794.

assault on Pittsburgh. On August 7, 1794, President Washington issued a proclamation ordering the insurgents home and calling out twelve thousand nine hundred militiamen from Virginia, Maryland, Pennsylvania, and New Jersey. Getting no response from the "Whiskey boys," he ordered the army to suppress the rebellion.

Under the command of General Henry Lee, thirteen thousand soldiers marched out from Harrisburg across the Alleghenies. George Washington himself accompanied the troops during the first few days, the only American president to lead troops in the field while in office. The massive show of federal force worked. The whiskey rebels vanished into the hills, and the troops met with little opposition. They finally rounded up twenty barefoot, ragged prisoners, whom they paraded down Market Street in Philadelphia and clapped into prison. The government had made its point and gained "reputation and strength," claimed Alexander Hamilton, by suppressing the elusive rebellion—one that, according to Jefferson, "could never be found." The use of such excessive force, however, led many who sympathized with the frontiersmen to become Republicans, and Jefferson's party scored heavily in the next Pennsylvania elections. Nor was it the end of whiskey rebellions, which continued in an unending war of wits between moonshiners and federal tax officers, known as *revenuers*.

PINCKNEY'S TREATY   While these turbulent events were unfolding in Pennsylvania, the Spanish began discussing ways to reduce tensions between the two countries by resolving the disputed boundary between the United States and Spanish territory in the South and West. U.S. negotiator Thomas Pinckney pulled off a diplomatic triumph in 1795 when he won acceptance of a boundary at the 31st parallel, open access for Americans to ship goods on the Mississippi River, the right to transport goods to Spanish-controlled New Orleans, and a promise by each side to refrain from inciting Indian attacks on the other side. Senate ratification of Pinckney's Treaty came quickly. In fact, it was immensely popular, especially among westerners eager to use the Mississippi River to transport their crops to market.

SETTLEMENT OF NEW LAND

The treaties signed by John Jay and Thomas Pinckney triggered a renewed surge of settlers headed into the western territories. Their lust for land ignited a fierce debate in Congress over the issue of federal land policy. There were two basic viewpoints on the matter: some held that federal land should serve mainly as a source of revenue, whereas others thought it was more important to get the new country settled quickly, an endeavor that required low land prices. In the long run, the evolution of policy would be from the first to the second viewpoint, but for the time being the federal government's need for revenue took priority.

LAND POLICY   Opinions on land policy, like opinions on other issues, separated Federalists from Republicans. Influential Federalists, like Hamilton and Jay, preferred to build the population of the eastern states first, lest the East lose both political influence and a labor force important to the growth of manufactures. Men of their persuasion favored high prices for federal land to enrich the Treasury, and they preferred that federal lands be sold in large parcels to speculators rather than small plots to settlers. Jefferson and Madison were reluctantly prepared to go along for the sake of reducing the national debt, but Jefferson expressed the hope for a plan by which the lands could be more readily settled by the masses. In any case, he suggested, frontiersmen would do as they had done before: "They will settle the lands in spite of everybody."

For the time being, however, Federalist policy prevailed. With the Land Act of 1796, Congress extended the rectangular surveys ordained in 1785 but doubled the price to $2 per acre, with only one year in which to complete payment. Half the townships would be sold in 640-acre sections, making the minimum cost $1,280, and alternate townships would be sold in blocks of eight sections, or 5,120 acres, making the minimum cost $10,240. Either price was well beyond the means of ordinary settlers and a bit much even for speculators, who could still pick up state-owned lands at lower prices. By 1800 federal land offices had sold fewer than 50,000 acres under the act. Continuing criticism in the West led to the Land Act of 1800, which reduced the minimum unit to 320 acres and spread payments over four years. Thus, with a down payment of $160, one could buy a farm. Under the Land Act of 1804, the minimum unit was reduced to 160 acres, which became the traditional homestead, and the price per acre went down to $1.64.

TRANSFER OF POWER

By 1796, President Washington had decided that two terms in office were enough. Weary of the increasingly bitter political quarrels and the venom of the partisan newspapers, he was ready to retire at last to his beloved plantation in northern Virginia, Mount Vernon. He would leave behind a formidable record of achievement: the organization of a new national government, a secure national treasury, the recovery of territory from Britain and Spain, a stable northwestern frontier, and the admission of three new states: Vermont (1791), Kentucky (1792), and Tennessee (1796).

WASHINGTON'S FAREWELL   With the considerable help of Alexander Hamilton, Washington drafted a valedictory speech to the nation. His farewell address, dated September 17, 1796, called for unity among the people in backing their new government. Washington regretted the rising spirit of partisanship and sectionalism; he feared the emergence of regional political parties promoting local interests. In foreign relations, Washington said, the United States should avoid getting involved in the quarrels of warring nations. It was, moreover, "our true policy to steer clear of permanent alliances with any portion of the foreign world." A key word here is *perma-*

nent. Washington opposed permanent alliances like the one with France, still technically in effect, but he endorsed "temporary alliances for extraordinary emergencies." Washington's warning against permanent foreign entanglements served as a fundamental principle in U.S. foreign policy until the early twentieth century.

THE ELECTION OF 1796   With George Washington out of the race, the United States had its first partisan election for president. In Philadelphia a caucus of Federalist congressmen chose John Adams of Massachusetts as their heir apparent, with Thomas Pinckney of South Carolina, fresh from his diplomatic triumph in Spain, as the nominee for vice president. As expected, the Republicans drafted Thomas Jefferson and added geographic balance to the ticket with Senator Aaron Burr of New York.

The campaign of 1796 was intensely partisan. Republicans caricatured John Adams as "His Rotundity" because of his short, paunchy body. They also labeled him a pro-British monarchist. The Federalists countered that Jefferson was a French-loving atheist eager to incite another war with Great Britain. They also charged that the philosophical Jefferson was unsuited to executive leadership; he was not decisive enough. The increasing strength of the Republicans, fueled by the smoldering resentment of Jay's Treaty, very nearly swept Jefferson into office and perhaps would have but for the French ambassador's public appeals for his election—an action that backfired. Then, despite a Federalist majority among the electors, Hamilton hatched an impulsive scheme that very nearly threw the election away after all. Hamilton decided that Pinckney would be more subject to his influence than would the strong-minded Adams. He therefore sought to have the South Carolina Federalists withhold a few votes for Adams and bring Pinckney in first. The Carolinians more than cooperated—they divided their vote between Pinckney and Jefferson—but the New Englanders got wind of the scheme and dropped Pinckney. The upshot of Hamilton's scheme was to cut Pinckney out of both the presidency and the vice presidency and elect Jefferson as vice president with 68 electoral votes to Adams's 71.

THE ADAMS ADMINISTRATION

Vain and cantankerous, John Adams had crafted a distinguished career as a Massachusetts lawyer, as a leader in the Revolutionary movement, as the hardest working member of the Continental Congress, as a diplomat in France, Holland, and Britain, and as George Washington's vice president. Adams

John Adams

Political philosopher and politician, Adams was the first president to take up residence in the White House, in early 1801.

was always haunted by a feeling that he was never properly appreciated—and he may have been right. Yet on the overriding issue of his administration, war and peace, he kept his head when others about him were losing theirs—probably at the cost of his reelection.

THE WAR WITH FRANCE As America's second president, Adams faced the daunting task of succeeding the most popular man in the nation. He also inherited an undeclared naval war with France, a by-product of Jay's Treaty. By the time of Adams's inauguration, in 1797, the French had plundered some three hundred American ships presumed to be trading with the British. As ambassador to Paris, Monroe had become so pro-French and so hostile to Jay's Treaty that George Washington had removed him for his indiscretions. France, grown haughty and contemptuous with Napoléon's military conquests, had then refused to accept Monroe's replacement, Charles Cotesworth Pinckney (brother of Thomas), and ordered him out of the country.

John Adams immediately acted to restore relations with France in the face of an outcry for war from the "high Federalists," including Secretary of State Timothy Pickering. In 1797, Adams sent Pinckney back to Paris with John Marshall, a Virginia Federalist, and Elbridge Gerry, a Massachusetts Republican, for further negotiations. After nagging delays the three commissioners were accosted by three French officials (whom Adams labeled X, Y, and Z in his report to Congress). The French diplomats confided to the Americans that negotiations could begin only if the United States paid a bribe of $250,000.

Such bribes were common eighteenth-century diplomatic practice, but the answer from the American side, according to the commissioners' report, was "no, no, not a sixpence." When the so-called **XYZ affair** was reported in Congress and the public press, the response was translated into the more stirring slogan "Millions for defense but not one cent for tribute." There-

Conflict with France

A cartoon indicating the anti-French sentiment generated by the XYZ affair. The three American negotiators (at left) reject the Paris Monster's demand for money.

after, the expressions of hostility toward France rose in a crescendo and even the most partisan Republicans—with the exception of Thomas Jefferson—quit making excuses for the French, and many of them joined the cry for war. Yet President Adams resisted a formal declaration of war; the French would have to bear the onus for that. Congress, however, authorized the capture of armed French ships, suspended commerce with France, and renounced the 1778 Treaty of Alliance, which was already a dead letter.

Amid a nation churning with patriotism and war fever, Adams strengthened American defenses. Militias marched and mobilized, and a navy began to emerge. An American navy had ceased to exist at the end of the Revolution. No armed ships were available when Algerian brigands began to prey on American commerce in the Mediterranean in 1794. As a result, Congress had authorized the arming of six ships. The job was still incomplete in 1796, however, when President Washington bought peace with the Algerians, but Congress allowed work on three of the ships to continue: the *Constitution,* the *United States,* and the *Constellation,* all completed in 1797. In 1798, Congress authorized a Department of the Navy, and by the end of the year, an undeclared naval war had begun in the West Indies with the French capture of an American schooner.

While the naval war was being fought, Congress, in 1798, authorized an army of ten thousand men to serve three years. Adams called George Washington from retirement to be its commander, and Washington agreed only on condition that Alexander Hamilton be named his second in command. Adams relented but expressed his disgust at naming Hamilton a general, for he was "the most restless, indefatigable and unprincipled Intriguer in the United States, if not in the world." The rift among the Federalists thus widened further.

Peace overtures began to come from the French by the autumn of 1798, before the naval war was fully under way. In 1799, Adams dispatched a team of three Americans to negotiate with a new French government under First Consul Napoléon Bonaparte. By the Convention of 1800, they won the best terms they could from the triumphant Napoléon. In return for giving up all claims of indemnity for American losses, they got official suspension of the 1778 perpetual alliance with France and an end to the naval conflict with France. The Senate ratified the agreement, contingent upon outright abrogation of the alliance, and it became effective on December 21, 1801.

THE WAR AT HOME The simmering naval conflict with France mirrored a ferocious ideological war at home between Federalists and Republicans. Already-heated partisan politics had begun boiling over during the latter years of Washington's administration. The rhetoric grew so personal and tempers grew so short that opponents commonly resorted to duels. Federalists and Republicans saw each other as traitors to the principles of the American Revolution. Jefferson, for example, decided that Hamilton, Washington, Adams, and other Federalists were suppressing individual liberty in order to promote selfish interests. He adamantly opposed Jay's Treaty because it was pro-British and anti-French, and he was disgusted by the army's forceful suppression of the Whiskey Rebellion. Federalists and Jeffersonians during the 1790s displayed fundamental disagreements over the role of the federal government, states' rights, foreign policy, and slavery.

Such combustible issues forced Americans to take sides, and the Revolutionary generation of leaders, a group that John Adams had earlier called the "band of brothers," began to fragment into die-hard factions. Long-standing political friendships disintegrated amid the partisan attacks, and sectional divisions between North and South grew more fractious. Jefferson observed that a "wall of separation" had come to divide the nation's political leaders.

"Politics and party hatreds," he told his daughter, "destroy the happiness of every being here."

The real purpose of the French crisis all along, the more ardent Republicans suspected, was to provide Federalists with an excuse to suppress their American critics. The infamous **Alien and Sedition Acts** of 1798 lent credence to the Republicans' suspicions. These and two other acts, passed in the wave of patriotic war fever, limited freedom of speech and the press and the liberty of aliens. Proposed by extreme Federalists in Congress, the acts did not originate with Adams but had his blessing. Goaded by his wife, Abigail, his primary counselor, Adams signed the controversial statutes and in doing so made the greatest mistake of his presidency. Timothy Pickering, his secretary of state, claimed that Adams had acted without consulting "any member of the government and for a reason truly remarkable— because he knew we should all be opposed to the measure." By succumbing to the partisan hysteria and enacting the vindictive acts, Adams seemed to bear out what Benjamin Franklin had said about him years before: he "means well for his country, is always an honest man, often a wise one, but sometimes and in some things, absolutely out of his senses."

Three of the four repressive acts engineered by the Federalists reflected hostility to foreigners, especially the French and the Irish, a large number of whom had become active Republicans and were suspected of revolutionary intent. The Naturalization Act lengthened from five to fourteen years the residency requirement for citizenship. The Alien Act empowered the president to deport "dangerous" aliens. The Alien Enemies Act authorized the president in time of declared war to expel or imprison enemy aliens at will. Finally, the Sedition Act defined as a high misdemeanor any conspiracy against legal measures of the government, including interference with federal officers and insurrection or rioting. What is more, the law forbade writing, publishing, or speaking anything of "a false, scandalous and malicious" nature against the government or any of its officers.

The Sedition Act was designed to punish Republicans, whom Federalists lumped together with French revolutionary radicals and American traitors. To be sure, partisan Republican journalists published scandalous lies and misrepresentations, but so did Federalists; it was a time when both sides seemed afflicted with paranoia. But the fifteen indictments brought under the Sedition Act, with ten convictions, were all directed at Republicans.

Accused Republicans based their defense on the unconstitutionality of the Sedition Act, but Federalist judges dismissed the notion. It ran against the Republican grain, anyway, to have federal courts assume the authority to declare laws unconstitutional. To offset the "reign of witches" unleashed by the Alien and Sedition Acts, therefore, Jefferson and Madison drafted what came to be known as the **Kentucky and Virginia Resolutions**, passed by the legislatures of their respective states in 1798. The Kentucky and Virginia Resolutions, much alike in their arguments, denounced the Alien and Sedition Acts as "alarming infractions" of constitutional rights. Since the Constitution arose as a compact among the states, the resolutions argued, the states should decide when Congress had exceeded its powers. The Virginia Resolutions, drafted by James Madison, declared that states "have the right and are in duty bound to interpose for arresting the progress of the evil." The second set of Kentucky Resolutions, in restating the states' right to judge violations of the Constitution, added, "That a nullification of those sovereignties, of all unauthorized acts done under color of that instrument, is the rightful remedy."

These doctrines of interposition and nullification, reworked and edited by later theorists, were destined to be used for causes unforeseen by their authors. (Years later, Madison would disclaim the doctrine of nullification as developed by John C. Calhoun, but his own doctrine of interposition would resurface as late as the 1950s as a device to oppose racial integration.) At the time, it seems, both men intended the resolutions to serve chiefly as propaganda, the opening guns in the political campaign of 1800. Neither Kentucky nor Virginia took steps to nullify or interpose its authority in the enforcement of the Alien and Sedition Acts. Instead, both called upon the other states to help them win a repeal. In Virginia, citizens talked of armed resistance to the federal government. Jefferson counseled against any thought of violence: it was "not the kind of opposition the American people will permit." He assured a fellow Virginian that the Federalist "reign of witches" would soon end, that it would be discredited by the arrival of the tax collector more than anything else.

REPUBLICAN VICTORY As the presidential election of 1800 approached, civil unrest boiled over. Grievances mounted against Federalist policies: taxation to support an unneeded army; the Alien and Sedition Acts, which cast the Federalists as anti-liberty; the lingering fears of "monarchism"; the hostilities aroused by Alexander Hamilton's economic programs; the suppression of the Whiskey Rebellion; and Jay's Treaty. When Adams opted for peace with France in 1800, he probably doomed his one chance for reelection—a wave of patriotic war fever with a united party behind him. His decision gained him much goodwill among Americans at large but left the Hamiltonians angry and his party divided. In 1800 the Federalists summoned enough unity to name as their candidates Adams and Charles Cotesworth Pinckney; they agreed to cast all their electoral votes for both. But the Hamiltonian Federalists continued to snipe at Adams and his policies, and soon after his renomination Adams removed two of them from his cabinet. A furious Hamilton struck back with a pamphlet questioning Adams's fitness to be president, citing his "disgusting egotism." Intended for private distribution among Federalist leaders, the pamphlet reached the hands of New York Republican Aaron Burr, who put it in general circulation.

Jefferson and Burr, as the Republican presidential candidates, once again represented the alliance of Virginia and New York. Jefferson, perhaps even more than Adams, was attacked by Federalists as a supporter of the radical French revolutionaries and an atheist. His election would supposedly bring civil war—"dwellings in flames, hoary hairs bathed in blood, female chastity violated . . . children writhing on the pike and halberd." Jefferson kept quiet, refused to answer the attacks, and directed the campaign by mail from his home at Monticello. His supporters portrayed him as the farmers' friend, the champion of states' rights, frugal government, liberty, and peace.

Adams proved more popular than his party, whose candidates generally fared worse than the president, but the Republicans edged him out by 73 electoral votes to 65. The decisive states were New York and South Carolina, either of which might have given the victory to Adams. But in New York former senator Aaron Burr's organization won control of the legislature, which cast the electoral votes. In South Carolina, Charles Pinckney (cousin of the Federalist Pinckneys) won over the legislature by well-placed promises of Republican patronage. Still, the result was not final, for Jefferson and Burr had tied with 73 votes each, and the choice of the president was thrown into the House of Representatives (a constitutional defect corrected by the Twelfth Amendment), where Federalist diehards tried vainly to give the election to Burr. This was too much for Hamilton, who opposed Jefferson but held a much lower opinion of Burr. Jefferson, Hamilton wrote to a fellow Federalist, at least had "pretensions to character," but Burr had "nothing in his favor." The stalemate in the House continued for thirty-five ballots. The deadlock was broken only when a confidant of Jefferson's assured a Delaware congressman that Jefferson, if elected, would refrain from the wholesale removal of Federalists appointed to federal offices and would uphold Hamilton's financial policies. The representative resolved to vote for Jefferson, and several other Federalists agreed simply to cast blank ballots, permitting Jefferson to win without any of them having to vote for him.

Before the Federalists relinquished power to the Jeffersonian Republicans on March 4, 1801, their lame-duck Congress passed the Judiciary Act of 1801.

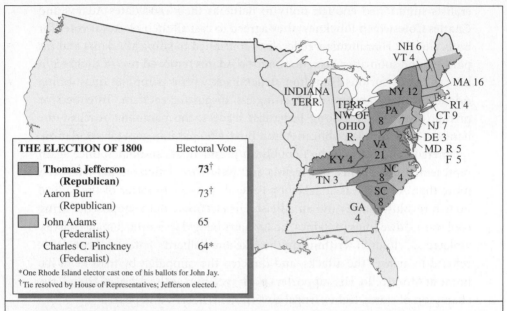

THE ELECTION OF 1800   Electoral Vote

Thomas Jefferson   73[†]
(Republican)

Aaron Burr   73[†]
(Republican)

John Adams   65
(Federalist)

Charles C. Pinckney   64*
(Federalist)

*One Rhode Island elector cast one of his ballots for John Jay.
[†]Tie resolved by House of Representatives; Jefferson elected.

Why was the election of 1800 a key moment in American history? How did the Republicans win New York and South Carolina? How did Congress break the tie between Jefferson and Burr?

Intended to ensure Federalist control of the judicial system, this act provided that the next vacancy on the Supreme Court would not be filled, created sixteen federal circuit courts with a new judge for each, and increased the number of federal attorneys, clerks, and marshals. Before he left office, Adams named John Marshall to the vacant office of chief justice and appointed Federalists to all the new positions, including forty-two justices of the peace for the new District of Columbia. The Federalists, defeated and destined never to regain national power, had in the words of Jefferson "retired into the judiciary as a stronghold."

The election of 1800 harshly divided the young republic and marked a major turning point in American political history. It was the first time that one political party, however ungracefully, relinquished power to the opposition party. Jefferson's hard-fought victory signaled the emergence of a new, more democratic political system, dominated by parties, partisanship, and wider public participation—at least by white men. Before and immediately after independence, politics was popular but not democratic: people took a keen interest in public affairs, but socially prominent families, the "rich, the able, and the wellborn," dominated political life. However, the fierce political battles of the late 1790s, culminating in 1800 with Jefferson's election as the nation's third president, wrested control of politics from the governing elite and established the right of more people to play an active role in governing the young republic. The differences between John Adams and Thomas Jefferson signaled a deepening ideological split that divided Americans into political factions. With the gradual elimination of property qualifications for voting and the proliferation of newspapers, pamphlets, and other publications, the "public sphere" in which political issues were debated and decided expanded enormously in the early nineteenth century.

The Republican victory in 1800 also marked the political triumph of the slaveholding South. The population of the southern states was growing rapidly at the end of the eighteenth century, and the burgeoning presence of enslaved Africans increasingly distinguished the region from the rest of the nation. Three Virginia slaveholders—Thomas Jefferson, James Madison, and James Monroe—would control the White House for the next twenty-four years. While Republicans celebrated democracy, many of them also prospered because of slavery. The tensions between republican ideals and plantation slavery would eventually lead to civil war.

John Adams regretted the democratization of politics and the rise of fractious partisanship. "Jefferson had a party, Hamilton had a party, but the commonwealth had none," he sighed. The defeated president was so distraught at the turn of events that he decided not to participate in Jefferson's inauguration in the new capital, Washington, D.C. Instead, he boarded a stagecoach for the five-hundred-mile trip to his home in Quincy, Massachusetts. He and Jefferson would not communicate for the next twelve years. As Adams returned to work on his Massachusetts farm, he reported that he had exchanged "honors and virtue for manure." He told his son John Quincy, who would become president himself, that the American president "has a hard, laborious, and unhappy life."

CHAPTER SUMMARY

- **Formation of the Government** The Constitution left many questions unanswered about the structure and conduct of the government. Congress had to create executive departments and organize the federal judiciary. The ratification of the first ten amendments, the Bill of Rights, was a leading issue; however, strengthening the economy was the highest priority.

- **Hamiltonian Vision** Alexander Hamilton wanted to create a vibrant economy. He succeeded in establishing a sound foundation for American capitalism by crafting a budget with a funded national debt, a federal tax system, a national bank, and a customs service.

- **Religious Freedom** In terms of religion, the Constitution does not mention a deity and the First Amendment guarantees people the right to worship freely, regardless of their religious persuasion.

- **Neutrality** With the outbreak of European-wide war during the French Revolution, George Washington's policy of neutrality violated the terms of the 1778 treaty with France, which had established a perpetual alliance. The French began seizing British and American ships and an undeclared war was under way. The resulting unrest contributed to the creation of the first two political parties: Hamiltonian Federalists and Jeffersonian Republicans.

- **Jeffersonian Vision** James Madison and Thomas Jefferson became increasingly critical of Hamilton's policies, which favored a strong federal government and weaker state governments. Jefferson, on the other hand, championed an agrarian vision, in which independent small farmers were the backbone of American society. He feared that the growth of cities would enrich the aristocracy and widen divisions between the rich and the poor.

CHRONOLOGY

1789	President George Washington is inaugurated
1789	French Revolution begins
1791	Bill of Rights is ratified
1791	Bank of the United States is created
1793	Washington issues a proclamation of neutrality
1794	Jay's Treaty is negotiated with England
1794	Whiskey Rebellion
1795	By the Treaty of Greenville, the United States purchases western lands from Native Americans
1795	Pinckney's Treaty is negotiated with Spain
1796	President Washington delivers his farewell address
1797	XYZ affair
1798	Alien and Sedition Acts are passed
1800	Thomas Jefferson is elected president

KEY TERMS & NAMES

8

THE EARLY REPUBLIC

FOCUS QUESTIONS wwnorton.com/studyspace

- What were the main achievements of Jefferson's administration?
- What was the impact of the Marshall court on the U.S. government?
- How did the Louisiana Purchase change the United States?
- What were the causes and effects of the War of 1812?

The decades after the Revolution were years of dynamic change as Americans laid the foundation for the nation's development as the first society in the world organized by the principle of democratic capitalism and its promise of equal opportunity for all—except African Americans, Native Americans, and women. As Thomas Jefferson said, America was becoming an "empire of liberty" in which all facets of society—politics, education, science, religion, and livelihoods—were experiencing dynamic change.

THE NEW AMERICAN NATION

In 1800 there were 5,300,000 people living in the United States, a fifth of whom were enslaved blacks. Americans in the fifty years after independence were in perpetual motion: they were on the move and on the make. Many Americans believed that they were a nation of destiny. Their prospects seemed unlimited, their optimism unrestrained. The opportunity to pursue one's dreams animated the drama of American life. As John Adams observed, "There is no people on earth so ambitious as the people of America . . . because the lowest can aspire as freely as the highest."

Land sales west of the Appalachian Mountains soared in the early nineteenth century as aspiring farmers shoved Indians aside in order to establish homesteads of their own. Enterprising, mobile, and increasingly diverse in religion and national origin, tens of thousands of people uprooted themselves from settled communities and went west in search of personal advancement, occupying more territory in a single generation than had been settled in the 150 years of colonial history. Between 1800 and 1820 the trans-Appalachian population soared from 300,000 to 2 million. By 1840, over 40 percent of Americans lived west of the Appalachians in eight new states.

The spirit of opportunistic independence affected free African Americans as well as whites, Indians as well as immigrants. Free blacks were the fastest-growing segment of the population during the early nineteenth century. Many enslaved Americans had gained their freedom during the Revolutionary War by escaping, joining the British forces, or serving in American military units. Every state except South Carolina and Georgia promised freedom to slaves who fought the British. Afterward, state after state in the North outlawed slavery, and anti-slavery societies blossomed, exerting increasing pressure on the South to end the degrading practice. Pressure of another sort affected the besieged Indian tribes. The westward migration of Americans brought incessant conflict with Native Americans. Indians fiercely resisted the invasion of their ancestral lands but ultimately succumbed to a federal government and a federal army determined to displace them.

Most whites, however, were less concerned about Indians and slavery than they were about seizing their own opportunities. Politicians north and south suppressed the volatile issue of slavery; their priorities were elsewhere. Westward expansion, economic growth, urban-industrial development, and the democratization of politics preoccupied a generation of Americans born after 1776—especially outside the South. In 1790 nine out of ten Americans lived on the land and engaged in household rather than commercial production; their sphere of activity was local. But with each passing year, more and more farmers focused on producing surplus crops and livestock to sell in regional markets. Such commercial agriculture was especially evident in the South, where European demand for cotton caused prices to soar. The burgeoning market economy produced boom-and-bust cycles, but overall the years from 1790 to 1830 were quite prosperous, with young Americans experiencing unprecedented opportunities for economic gain and geographic mobility.

ECONOMIC GROWTH With independence, Americans were freed from British restrictions on their economic life; they could now create new industries and exploit new markets. It was not simply Alexander Hamilton's financial initiatives and the capitalistic energies of wealthy investors and speculators that sparked America's dramatic commercial growth in these years. It was also the strenuous efforts of ordinary men and women who were willing to take risks, uproot families, use unstable paper money issued by unregulated local banks, purchase factory-made goods, and tinker with new machines and tools. Free enterprise was the keynote of the era.

While most Americans continued to work as farmers, a growing number found employment in new or greatly expanded enterprises: textiles, banking, transportation, publishing, retailing, teaching, preaching, medicine, law, construction, and engineering. Technological innovations (steam power, power tools, and new modes of transportation) and their social applications (mass communication, turnpikes, the postal service, banks, and corporations) fostered an array of new industries and businesses. The emergence of a factory system transformed the nature of work for many Americans. In short, the decentralized agrarian republic of 1776, nestled along the Atlantic seaboard, had by 1830 become a sprawling commercial nation connected by networks of roads and canals and cemented by economic relationships—all animated by a restless spirit of enterprise, experimentation, and expansion.

JEFFERSONIAN SIMPLICITY

Political life in the new republic was also transformed during the early nineteenth century, as an increasing proportion of white males gained the right to vote when property qualifications were reduced. The first president of the nineteenth century promoted such democratization. On March 4, 1801, the fifty-seven-year-old Thomas Jefferson, tall and thin, with red hair and a ruddy complexion, became the first president to be inaugurated in the new national capital named Washington, District of Columbia. The new city was still a motley array of buildings clustered around two centers, Capitol Hill and the executive mansion. Congress, having met in eight towns and cities since 1774, had at last found a permanent home but enjoyed few amenities. There were only two places of amusement—one a racetrack, the other a theater thick with "tobacco smoke, whiskey breaths, and other stenches."

Jefferson's informal inauguration befitted the primitive surroundings. The new president left his lodgings and walked down a stump-strewn Pennsylvania Avenue to the unfinished Capitol. He entered the Senate chamber, took the oath administered by Chief Justice John Marshall, read his inaugural address in a barely audible voice, and returned to his boardinghouse for dinner. A tone of simplicity and conciliation ran through his inaugural speech. The campaign between Federalists and Jeffersonian Republicans had been so fierce that some had predicted civil war. Jefferson now appealed for unity. "We are all Republicans—we are all Federalists," he said. "If there be any among us who would wish to dissolve this Union or to change its republican form, let them stand undisturbed as monuments of the safety with which error of opinion may be tolerated where reason is left free to combat it."

JEFFERSON IN OFFICE   The deliberate display of republican simplicity at Jefferson's inauguration set the style of his administration. Although a cosmopolitan man with expensive personal tastes, especially in land, wine, and books, he took pains to avoid the "monarchical" occasions of pomp and circumstance that had characterized the Federalist administrations. Jefferson's political platform called for shrinking the infant federal government by slashing its budget and strictly interpreting the Constitution so as not to infringe upon states' rights.

Jefferson called his election the "revolution of 1800," but the electoral margin had been razor thin, and the policies that he followed were more conciliatory than revolutionary. His overwhelming reelection in 1804 attested to the popularity of his first term. Jefferson placed in policy-making positions men of his own party, and he was the first president to pursue the role of party leader, cultivating congressional support at his dinner parties and elsewhere. In the cabinet the leading figures were Secretary of State James Madison, a longtime neighbor and political ally, and Secretary of the Treasury Albert Gallatin, a Swiss-born Pennsylvania Republican whose financial skills had won him the respect of the Federalists. In an effort to cultivate Federalist-controlled New England, Jefferson chose men from that region for the positions of attorney general, secretary of war, and postmaster general.

In lesser offices, however, Jefferson often succumbed to pressure from the Republicans to remove Federalists. In one area he removed the offices altogether. In 1802, the Republican-controlled Congress repealed the Judiciary Act of 1801 and so abolished the circuit judgeships and other offices to which John Adams had made his "midnight appointments."

MARBURY V. MADISON   The midnight judicial appointments that John Adams made just before leaving office sparked the pathbreaking case of **Marbury v. Madison** (1803), the first in which the Supreme Court declared a federal law unconstitutional. The case involved the appointment of the Maryland Federalist William Marbury, a prominent land speculator, as justice of the peace in the District of Columbia. Marbury's letter of appointment, or

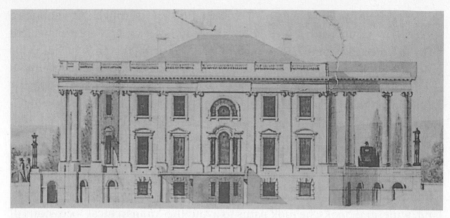

The executive mansion

A watercolor of the president's house during Jefferson's term in office. Jefferson described it as "big enough for two emperors, one pope, and the grand lama in the bargain."

commission, signed by President Adams two days before he left office, was still undelivered when Madison took office as secretary of state, and Jefferson directed him to withhold it. Marbury then sued for a court order directing Madison to deliver his commission.

The Supreme Court's unanimous opinion, written by **Chief Justice John Marshall**, a brilliant Virginia Federalist and ardent critic of Jefferson, his distant relative, held that Marbury deserved his commission but denied that the Court had jurisdiction in the case. Section 13 of the Federal Judiciary Act of 1789, which gave the Court original jurisdiction in such proceedings, was unconstitutional, the Court ruled, because the Constitution specified that the Court should have original jurisdiction only in cases involving foreign ambassadors or states. The Court, therefore, could issue no order in the case. With one bold stroke the Federalist Marshall had chastised the Jeffersonian Republicans while subtly avoiding an awkward confrontation with an administration that might have defied his order. At the same time, he established a stunning precedent: the Court declared a federal law invalid on the grounds that it violated provisions of the Constitution. Marshall stressed that it "is emphatically the province and duty of the judicial department to say what the law is." In other words, the Supreme Court was assuming the right of *judicial review*, meaning that it would decide whether acts of Congress were constitutional. So even though Marbury never gained his judgeship, Marshall established the Supreme Court as the final judge of constitutional interpretation. Since the Marbury decision, the Court has struck down over 150 acts of Congress and over 1,100 acts of state legislatures.

DOMESTIC REFORMS   Although Marshall got the better of Jefferson in court, the president's first term produced a succession of triumphs in both domestic and foreign affairs. Jefferson did not set out to dismantle Alexander Hamilton's economic program, despite his harsh criticism of it. Under the tutelage of Treasury Secretary Gallatin, he learned to accept the national bank as an essential convenience. Jefferson detested Hamilton's belief that a federal debt was a national "blessing" because it gave the bankers and investors who lent money to the U.S. government a direct financial stake in the success of the new republic. Jefferson believed that a large federal debt would bring only high taxes and government corruption, so he set about reducing government expenses and paying down the debt. At the same time, he won the repeal of the whiskey tax, much to the relief of backwoods distillers, drinkers, and grain farmers.

Without the income from such taxes, frugality was all the more necessary to a federal government dependent for its revenues chiefly upon tariffs on imports and the sale of government-owned western lands. Fortunately, however, both sources of income flourished during Jefferson's presidency. The continuing wars in Europe increased American shipping traffic and thus padded the federal Treasury. Commercial prosperity was directly linked to the ability of Americans to trade with both sides in the European wars. At the same time, settlers flocked to land in the western territories they purchased from the government. Ohio's admission to the Union in 1803 increased to seventeen the number of states.

Jefferson's commitment to "wise and frugal government" enabled the United States to live within its income. The basic formula was simple: cut back on military expenses. National defense should be left to state militias. The navy, which the Federalists had already reduced, ought to be reduced further.

While reducing the expense of the federal government, Jefferson in 1807 signed a landmark bill—long overdue—that outlawed the importation of enslaved Africans into the United States. The new law took effect on January 1, 1808, the earliest date possible under the Constitution. At the time, South Carolina was the only state that still permitted the foreign slave trade, having reopened it in 1803.

THE BARBARY PIRATES   Issues of foreign relations emerged early in Jefferson's first term, when events in the distant Mediterranean Sea gave him second thoughts about the need for a navy. On the Barbary Coast of North Africa, the Islamic rulers of Morocco, Algiers, Tunis, and Tripoli had for years promoted piracy and extortion, preying upon European and American merchant ships in the Mediterranean Sea. After the Revolution, Mediterranean pirates in small, fast ships called *corsairs* captured American vessels and enslaved the crews. The U.S. government made blackmail payments, first to Morocco in 1786, then to the others in the 1790s. In 1801, however, the pasha (ruler) of Tripoli upped his demands and declared war on the United States. Jefferson sent warships to blockade Tripoli. A wearisome naval war dragged on until 1805, punctuated in 1804 by the notable exploit of Lieutenant Stephen Decatur, who slipped into Tripoli Harbor by night and set fire to the frigate *Philadelphia*, which had been captured (along with its crew) after it ran aground. The pasha finally settled for a $60,000 ransom and released the *Philadelphia*'s crew, whom he had held hostage for more than a year. It was still blackmail (called "tribute" in the nineteenth century), but less than the $300,000 the pasha had demanded at first and much less than the cost of war.

THE LOUISIANA PURCHASE   While the conflict with the Barbary pirates continued, events elsewhere led to the greatest single achievement of the Jefferson administration. The vast Louisiana Purchase of 1803 was a brilliant diplomatic coup that more than doubled the territory of the United States. The purchase included territory extending far beyond the boundaries of present-day Louisiana. Its estimated 875,000 square miles, from which would be formed six states in their entirety and most or part of nine more, comprised the entire Mississippi River valley west of the river. The Louisiana territory had been ceded to Spain in 1763, following the Seven Years' War, with Great Britain receiving Florida from Spain in an exchange of sorts. Since that time the dream of retaking Louisiana had stirred the French, and the audacious general Napoléon Bonaparte had retrieved it for France from his Spanish allies in 1800. Spain had decided, under French pressure, that the region was too costly to administer—and defend.

When word of the deal transferring the Louisiana Territory from Spain to France reached Washington in 1801, an alarmed President Jefferson sent Robert R. Livingston to Paris as the new U.S. minister to France. Spain in control of the Mississippi River outlet was bad enough, but the power-hungry Napoléon in control could only mean serious trouble. "The day that France takes possession of New Orleans," Jefferson wrote Livingston, "we must marry ourselves to the British fleet and nation," an unhappy prospect for the French-loving Jefferson.

Burning of the Frigate *Philadelphia*

Lieutenant William Decatur set fire to the captured *Philadelphia* during the United States' standoff with Tripoli over the enslavement of American sailors.

Early in 1803, Jefferson sent his trusted Virginia friend James Monroe to assist Livingston in Paris. Their goal was to purchase New Orleans from France. No sooner had Monroe arrived than the French surprised Livingston by asking if the United States would like to buy the whole of the Louisiana Territory. Livingston snapped up the offer. Napoléon was willing to sell the Louisiana Territory because his French army in Saint-Domingue (Haiti) had been decimated not only by a massive slave revolt but also by yellow fever. Some 350,000 Haitians and 24,000 French soldiers had died in Haiti. Concerned about financing another round of warfare in Europe, Napoléon decided to cut French losses in the Americas by selling the entire Louisiana Territory and thereby gaining cash for his ongoing war with Great Britain.

By the Treaty of Cession, dated April 30, 1803, the United States obtained the Louisiana Territory for about $15 million. The surprising turn of events presented President Jefferson with a "noble bargain," but also with a constitutional dilemma. Nowhere did the Constitution mention the purchase of territory. Jefferson acknowledged that the purchase was "beyond the Constitution." Like a velvet hypocrite, Jefferson, the champion of states' rights and "strict construction" of the Constitution, allowed his desire for empire to trump his legal scruples. He lamely expressed the hope "that the good sense of our country will correct the evil of loose construction [of the Constitution] when it shall produce ill effects."

Jefferson and other Republicans supported the Louisiana Purchase for several reasons. Acquiring the immense territory, the president explained, would be "favorable to the immediate interests of our Western citizens" and would promote "the peace and security of the nation in general" by removing French power from the region and by creating a protective buffer separating the United States from the rest of the world. Jefferson also hoped that the new territory might become a haven for free blacks and thereby diminish racial tensions along the Atlantic seaboard. New England Federalists, however, were not convinced by such arguments. Many of them worried that the growing westward exodus was driving up wages on the Atlantic coast by reducing the workforce and lowering the value of real estate in their region. They also boggled at the prospect of new western states that would likely be settled by southern slaveholders who were Jeffersonian Republicans. In a reversal that anticipated many more reversals on constitutional issues, Federalists found themselves arguing for strict construction of the Constitution in opposing the Louisiana Purchase, while Jefferson and the Republicans brushed aside Federalist reservations. The opportunity to double the size of the United States trumped any legal reservations.

The Senate ratified the treaty by an overwhelming vote of 26 to 6, and on December 20, 1803, U.S. officials took formal possession of the sprawling Louisiana Territory. For the time being the Spanish kept West Florida, but within a decade that area would be ripe for the plucking. In 1810 American settlers staged a rebellion in Baton Rouge against Spanish rule and proclaimed the republic of West Florida, which was quickly annexed and occupied by the United States as far east as the Pearl River. In 1812, upon becoming the Union's eighteenth state, Louisiana absorbed the Florida parishes. In 1813, with Spain itself a battlefield for French and British forces, Americans took over the rest of West Florida, the Gulf coast of the future states of Mississippi and Alabama. Legally, as the U.S. government has claimed ever since, all these areas were included in the Louisiana Purchase.

Jefferson's decision to swallow his constitutional reservations and acquire the vast Louisiana territory proved to be one of the most important factors shaping America's development. It was by far the most popular and significant event of his presidency. His decision was also embedded with irony. By adding the Louisiana Territory, Jefferson, the lover of liberty and owner of slaves, helped expand the sphere of slavery, an institution that anguished him all the while he reinforced it. As a newspaper editor asked in 1803, "Will Republicans, who glory in their sacred regard to the rights of human nature, purchase an immense wilderness for the purpose of cultivating it with the labor of slaves?" The answer was a resounding yes.

LEWIS AND CLARK Thomas Jefferson was fascinated by the mysterious region he had purchased west of the Mississippi River. To learn more about its geography, its flora and fauna, and its prospects for trade and agriculture, he asked Congress in 1803 to fund a mapping and scientific expedition to the far Northwest, beyond the Mississippi River, in what was still foreign territory. Congress approved, and Jefferson assigned as the commanders of the expedition two former army officers: Meriwether Lewis and William Clark.

In 1804 the "**Corps of Discovery**," numbering nearly fifty, set out from a small village near St. Louis to ascend the muddy Missouri River. Six months after leaving St. Louis, near the Mandan Sioux villages in what would become North Dakota, they built Fort Mandan and wintered in relative comfort, sending downriver a barge loaded with maps, soil samples, and live specimens, such as the prairie dog and the magpie, previously unknown in America.

One of Lewis and Clark's maps

In their journals, Lewis and Clark sketched detailed maps of unexplored regions.

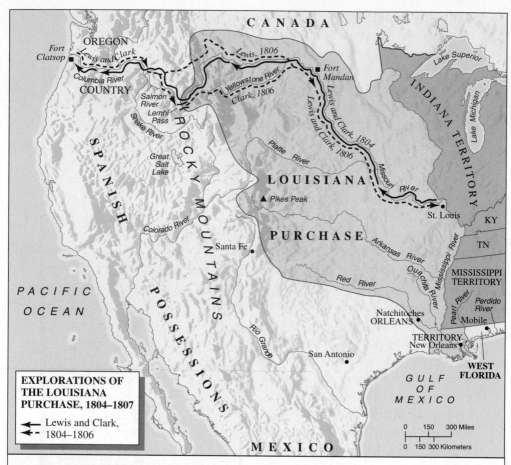

EXPLORATIONS OF THE LOUISIANA PURCHASE, 1804–1807

← Lewis and Clark, 1804–1806

How did the United States acquire the Louisiana Purchase? What was the mission of Lewis and Clark's expedition? What were the consequences of Lewis and Clark's reports about the western territory?

In the spring, Lewis and Clark added to their main party a remarkable young Shoshone woman named Sacagawea, who proved an enormous help as a guide, translator, and negotiator as the group headed westward into uncharted territory. They crossed the Rocky Mountains and used canoes to descend the Snake and Columbia Rivers to the Pacific ocean. Near the future site of Astoria, Oregon, at the mouth of the Columbia River, they built Fort Clatsop, where they spent the winter, struggling to find enough to eat. The following spring they split into two parties, with Lewis's group backtracking by almost the same route and Clark's band going by way of the Yellowstone River. Remarkably, they reunited at the juncture of the Missouri and Yellowstone Rivers, returning together to St. Louis in 1806, having been gone nearly two and a half years. No longer was the Far West unknown country. The explorers' reports of friendly Indians and abundant beaver pelts quickly attracted traders and trappers to the region and gave the United States a claim to the Oregon Country by right of discovery and exploration.

POLITICAL SCHEMES Thomas Jefferson's policies, including the Louisiana Purchase, brought him solid support in the South and the West. In New England, however, Federalists panicked at the implications of the Louisana Purchase. The acquisition of a vast new empire in the West would reduce New England and the Federalist party to insignificance in political affairs. Federalists hatched a scheme to link New York to New England. To that end, they contacted Vice President **Aaron Burr**, a prominent New Yorker who had been on the outs with the Jeffersonians. Their plan, which depended upon Burr's election as governor of New York, could not win the support of even the extreme Federalists: Alexander Hamilton bitterly opposed it on the grounds that Burr was "a dangerous man, and one who ought not to be trusted with the reins of government."

Those remarks led to Hamilton's famous duel with Burr, in July 1804 at Weehawken, New Jersey, across the Hudson River from New York City. Hamilton's sense of honor compelled him to meet the vice president's challenge and demonstrate his courage—yet he was determined not to fire at his opponent. Burr had no such scruples; he shot and killed Hamilton. The killing of Hamilton ended Burr's political career. Burr would lose the gubernatorial election, but his defeat did not end his secret schemes to garner wealth and stature for himself.

In the meantime, the presidential campaign of 1804 began when a congressional caucus of Republicans renominated Jefferson and chose the New Yorker George Clinton for vice president. (By then, to avoid the problems associated with parties running multiple candidates for the presidency, Congress had passed, and the states would soon ratify, the Twelfth Amendment, stipulating that electors use separate ballots to vote for the president and vice president.) Opposed by the Federalists Charles C. Pinckney and Rufus King, Jefferson and Clinton won 162 of the 176 electoral votes. It was the first landslide election in American history.

DIVISIONS IN THE REPUBLICAN PARTY

Freed from a strong opposition—Federalists made up only a quarter of the new Congress—the dominant Republican majority began to fragment into warring factions during the first decade of the nineteenth century. The

Virginian John Randolph—known also as John Randolph of Roanoke—was initially a loyal Jeffersonian, but over time he emerged as the most conspicuous of the Republican dissidents. Randolph became the feisty spokesman for a shifting group of "Old Republicans," whose adherence to party principles had rendered them more Jeffersonian than Jefferson himself. The Old Republicans were mostly southerners who defended states' rights and strict construction of the Constitution. They opposed any compromise with the Federalists and promoted an agrarian way of life. The Jeffersonian Republicans tended to be more moderate, pragmatic, and nationalistic in their orientation. As Thomas Jefferson himself demonstrated, they were willing to go along with tariffs on imports and a national bank, and to stretch the "implied powers" of the Constitution to accommodate the Louisiana Purchase.

THE BURR CONSPIRACY   For all of his popularity, Jefferson in some quarters aroused intense opposition. Aaron Burr, for example, despised the president. Sheer brilliance and opportunism had carried Burr to the vice presidency in 1800. He might easily have become Jefferson's heir apparent, but a taste for backroom deal making was his tragic flaw. After the controversy over his mortal duel with Alexander Hamilton subsided, Burr focused his attention on a cockeyed scheme to carve out a personal empire for himself in the West. What came to be known as the Burr Conspiracy was hatched when Burr met with General James Wilkinson. Just what Wilkinson and Burr were up to may never be known. The most likely explanation is that they conspired to get the Louisiana Territory to secede from the Union and set up an independent republic. Earlier Burr had solicited British support for his scheme to separate "the western part of the United States in its whole extent."

Whatever the goal, Burr learned in early 1807 that Jefferson had ordered his arrest for treason. He tried to flee to Florida but was caught and brought for trial before Chief Justice John Marshall. Since the prosecution failed to produce two witnesses to an overt act of treason by Burr, the jury found him not guilty. Treason under the Constitution, Marshall wrote, consists of "levying war against the United States or adhering to their enemies" and requires "two witnesses to the same overt act" for conviction. As for Burr, with further charges pending, he skipped bail and took refuge in France, but he returned unmolested in 1812 to practice law in New York. He survived to a virile old age. At seventy-eight, shortly before his death in 1836, he was divorced on the grounds of adultery.

WAR IN EUROPE

Thomas Jefferson learned a hard lesson that would affect most presidents of the United States: rarely did their second terms garner as much success as their first terms. During Jefferson's second term he ran afoul of intractable problems created by the renewal of the European war pitting Napoleonic France against Great Britain—and most of Europe—in 1803, which tested Jefferson's desire to avoid "entangling alliances" with European nations.

HARASSMENT BY BRITAIN AND FRANCE   For two years after the renewal of European warfare, American shippers reaped the financial benefits, taking over trade with the French and Spanish West Indies. But the warring powers soon started limiting the freedom of neutral nations to trade with their enemies. In 1807 the commercial provisions of Jay's Treaty expired, and the British interference with American shipping increased, not just in a desperate effort to keep supplies from Napoléon's continent but also to hobble U.S. competition with British merchant ships. The situation presented American shippers with a dilemma: if they complied with the demands of the British to stop trading with the French, they were subject to seizure by the French, and vice versa. In the meantime, British warships stopped, searched, and seized a growing number of American merchant ships crossing the Atlantic.

The prospects for profits were so great, however, that American shippers ran the risk. For seamen the danger was heightened by the British renewal of the practice of **impressment**. Great Britain needed twelve thousand new sailors each year to man its warships. The use of armed "press-gangs" to kidnap men in British (and colonial) ports was a

Preparation for war to defend commerce

In 1806 and 1807, American shipping was caught in the crossfire of the war between Britain and France.

long-standing method of recruitment used by the British navy. The seizure of British subjects from American vessels provided a new source of recruits, justified on the principle that British citizens remained British subjects for life: "Once an Englishman, always an Englishman." To Americans, the British practice of impressment assaulted the honor and dignity of the new nation.

On June 22, 1807, the British warship *Leopard* accosted a U.S. naval vessel, the *Chesapeake,* on its maiden voyage, about eight miles off the Virginia coast. After the *Chesapeake*'s captain refused to be searched for British deserters, the *Leopard* opened fire, killing three Americans and wounding eighteen. The *Chesapeake,* unready for battle, was forced to strike its colors (to lower the flag as a sign of surrendering). A British search party seized four men, one of whom was later hanged for desertion from the British navy. Soon after the *Chesapeake* limped back into Norfolk, the *Washington Federalist* editorialized: "We have never, on any occasion, witnessed . . . such a thirst for revenge." Public wrath was so aroused by the *Chesapeake* incident that Jefferson could have declared war on the spot. Had Congress been in session, he might have been forced into one. But Jefferson, like John Adams before him, resisted war fever—and suffered politically as a result. Jefferson ordered all British warships out of U.S. ports on July 12, 1807. But such a timid response angered many Americans. One Federalist called Jefferson a "dish of skim milk curdling at the head of our nation."

THE EMBARGO   Congress decided to go beyond Jefferson's effort at "peaceable coercion." In 1807 legislators passed the unprecedented Embargo Act, which stopped all exports of American goods and prohibited American ships from leaving for foreign ports. The U.S. Navy was deployed to enforce the embargo. In effect, the United States blockaded its own shipping. Congress was empowered to declare an embargo by its constitutional authority to regulate commerce, which in this case Republicans interpreted broadly as the power to *prohibit* commerce altogether.

Jefferson's embargo failed from the beginning because few Americans were willing to make the necessary sacrifices required by the shutting off of foreign trade. Merchants in New England howled at the loss of their greatest industry: oceangoing commerce. The value of American exports plummeted from $48 million in 1807 to $9 million a year later. Meanwhile, smuggling grew rampant, especially along the border with Canada. While American ships sat idle in ports, their crews laid off and unpaid, the British enjoyed a near monopoly on legitimate trade with Canada and the West Indies. As it turned out, France was little hurt by the embargo, which led some Americans to argue that Jefferson intended the embargo to aid the French in the war against Britain.

American resistance to the embargo revived the Federalist party in New England, which charged that Jefferson was in league with the French. At the same time, commercial farmers and planters in the South and West suffered for want of foreign outlets for their grain, cotton, and tobacco. After fifteen months, Jefferson accepted failure and repealed the ineffective embargo in 1809, shortly before he relinquished the "splendid misery" of the presidency.

In the election of 1808 the presidential succession passed to another Virginian, Secretary of State James Madison. The Federalists, backing Charles C. Pinckney of South Carolina and Rufus King of New York, revived enough as a result of the public backlash against the embargo to win 47 electoral votes to Madison's 122.

THE DRIFT TO WAR   The brilliant Madison may have been the "Father of the Constitution," but he proved a mediocre chief executive. From the beginning his presidency was entangled in foreign affairs and crippled by naïveté. Madison and his advisers repeatedly overestimated the young republic's diplomatic leverage and military strength. The result was humiliation. Like Jefferson, Madison insisted on upholding the principle of freedom of the seas for neutral nations, but he was unwilling to create a navy strong enough to support it. He continued Jefferson's policy of "peaceable coercion" by different but no more effective means. In place of the embargo, Congress reopened trade with all countries except France and Great Britain and authorized the president to reopen trade with whichever of these gave up its restrictions on American trade. The British minister in Washington, David Erskine, assured Madison's secretary of state that Britain would revoke its restrictions in 1809. With that assurance, Madison reopened trade with Britain, but Erskine had acted on his own, and his superiors repudiated his action and recalled him. Madison's trade restrictions proved as ineffective as the embargo. The president's policies sparked an economic recession and brought no change in British behavior. In the vain search for an alternative, Congress in 1810 reversed itself and adopted a measure introduced by Nathaniel Macon of North Carolina. Called Macon's Bill number 2, it reopened trade with the warring powers but provided that if either Great Britain or France dropped its restrictions on American trade, the United States would embargo trade with the other.

This time, Napoléon took a turn at trying to bamboozle Madison. The French foreign minister, the Duke de Cadore, informed the U.S. minister in Paris that Napoléon had withdrawn the Berlin and Milan Decrees, but the carefully worded Cadore letter had strings attached: revocation of the decrees depended upon the British doing likewise. The strings were plain to see, but Madison either misunderstood or, more likely, foolishly went along in the hope of putting pressure on the British. The British initially refused to give in, and on June 1, 1812, Madison reluctantly asked Congress to declare war.

On June 5, the House of Representatives voted for war by 79 to 49. Two weeks later, the Senate concurred by a narrower vote, 19 to 13. The southern and western states wanted war; the Northeast, fearful of losing its maritime trade across the Atlantic, opposed war. Every Federalist in Congress opposed the war; 80 percent of Republicans supported it. On June 16, however, the British foreign minister, facing an economic crisis, ended restraints on U.S. trade. Britain preferred not to risk war with the United States on top of its war with Napoléon. But on June 18, not having heard of the British action, Madison signed the declaration of war. He did so for three reasons: (1) to protest the British Orders in Council, which allowed the Royal Navy to interfere with American shipping; (2) to stop the British impressments of sailors from American ships; and (3) to end British encouragement of Indian attacks on Americans living along the western and northern frontiers. With more time or more patience, Madison's policy would have been vindicated without resort to war. By declaring war, Republicans hoped to unite the nation and discredit the Federalists. To generate popular support for the war, Jefferson advised Madison that he needed, above all, "to stop Indian barbarities. The conquest of Canada will do this."

THE WAR OF 1812

In 1812 the United States found itself embroiled in another war against Great Britain, barely thirty years after the Revolutionary War had ended. How that happened remains contested terrain among historians.

CAUSES The main cause of the war—the violation of American shipping rights—dominated President Madison's war message and provided the most evident reason for a mounting American hostility toward the British. Yet the geographic distribution of the congressional vote for war raises a troubling question. The preponderance of the vote came from members of Congress representing the farm regions from Pennsylvania southward and westward. The maritime states of New York and New England, the region that bore the brunt of British attacks on U.S. shipping, voted *against* the declaration of war. One explanation for this seeming anomaly is simple enough: the farming regions suffered damage to their markets for grain, cotton, and tobacco while New England shippers made profits from smuggling in spite of the British restrictions.

Other plausible explanations for the sectional vote, however, include frontier Indian attacks in the Old Northwest (Ohio, Indiana, Michigan, Kentucky) that were blamed on British agents, competition with the British over the profitable fur trade in the Great Lakes region, and the desire among Americans for new land in Canada and the Floridas (West and East). Conflicts with Indians were endemic to a rapidly expanding West. Land-hungry settlers and speculators kept moving out ahead of government surveys and sales in search of fertile acres. The constant pressure to sell tribal lands repeatedly forced or persuaded Indians to sign treaties they did not always understand. It was an old story, dating from the Jamestown settlement, but one that took a new turn with the rise of two Shawnee leaders, **Tecumseh** and his twin brother, Tenskwatawa, "the Prophet."

THE BATTLE OF TIPPECANOE Tecumseh saw with blazing clarity the consequences of Indian disunity. From his base on the Tippecanoe River in northern Indiana, he traveled from Canada to the Gulf of Mexico to form a confederation of tribes to defend Indian hunting grounds, insisting that no land cession to whites was valid without the consent of all tribes, since they held the land in common. In October 1811 the charismatic Tecumseh called on a council meeting of Creeks and other southern tribes to "let the white race perish!" He told them that nothing good would come of continued treaty negotiations with whites.

William Henry Harrison, the governor of the Indiana Territory, learned of Tecumseh's plans, met with him twice, and pronounced him "one of those uncommon geniuses who spring up occasionally to produce revolutions and overturn the established order of things." In the fall of 1811, Harrison decided that Tecumseh's effort to organize a massive anti-American tribal confederacy must be stopped. He gathered a thousand troops and advanced on

Tecumseh

The Shawnee leader who tried to unite Indian tribes in defense of their lands. Tecumseh was killed in 1813 at the Battle of the Thames.

Tecumseh's capital, Prophetstown, on the Tippecanoe River, while the leader was away. Tecumseh's followers attacked Harrison's encampment on the river, but the Shawnees lost a bloody engagement that left about a quarter of Harrison's men dead or wounded. Harrison's troops burned the town and destroyed its supplies. Tecumseh's dreams of an Indian confederacy went up in smoke, and Tecumseh himself fled to British protection in Canada.

THE ASSAULT ON CANADA   The Battle of Tippecanoe reinforced suspicions that British agents in the Great Lakes region were inciting the Indians. Actually the incident was mainly Harrison's doing. With little hope of help from war-torn Europe, British officials in Canada had steered a careful course, discouraging warfare but seeking to keep the Indians' friendship and fur trade. The British treated the Indians as independent peoples living between British Canada and the United States. By contrast, most Americans on the northern border loathed and feared Indians, deeming them murderous, heathen savages deserving of extinction. To eliminate the Indian menace, Americans reasoned, they needed to remove its foreign support, and they saw the British Canadian province of Ontario as a pistol pointing at the United States.

Conquest of Canada would accomplish a twofold purpose: it would eliminate British influence among the Indians and open a new empire for land-hungry Americans. It was also one place where the British, in case of war, were vulnerable to an American attack. Madison and others acted on the mistaken assumption that many Canadians were eager to be liberated from British control. That there were nearly 8 million Americans in 1812 and only 300,000 Canadians led many bellicose Americans to believe the conquest of Canada would be quick and easy. New York alone had a million in habitants compared to just 75,000 in neighboring Upper Canada. Thomas Jefferson had told President Madison that the American "acquisition of Canada" was simply a "matter of marching" north with a military force. To the far south, the British were also vulnerable. East Florida, still under Spanish control, posed a similar threat to the Americans. Spain was too weak or simply unwilling to prevent sporadic Indian attacks across the border with Georgia. In addition, the British were suspected of smuggling goods through Florida and conspiring with Indians along the coast of the Gulf of Mexico.

Such concerns helped generate war fever. In the Congress that assembled in late 1811, new members from southern and western districts clamored for war in defense of "national honor" and to rid the Northwest of the "Indian problem." Among them were Henry Clay and Richard Mentor Johnson of Kentucky, Felix Grundy of Tennessee, and John C. Calhoun of South Carolina. John Randolph of Roanoke christened these "new boys" the "**war hawks**."

After they entered the House, Randolph said, "We have heard but one word—like the whip-poor-will, but one eternal monotonous tone—Canada! Canada! Canada!" The new speaker of the house, young Henry Clay, a tall, rawboned westerner who, like **Andrew Jackson**, was known for his combative temperament and propensity for dueling, yearned for war. "I am for resistance by the *sword*," he vowed. He promised that the Kentucky militia stood ready to march on Canada to acquire its lucrative fur trade and to suppress the British effort to incite Indian attacks along the American frontier. "I don't like Henry Clay," Calhoun said. "He is a bad man, an imposter, a creator of wicked schemes. I wouldn't speak to him, but, by God, I love him." When then Congressman Calhoun heard the news of the outbreak of war, he threw his arms around House Speaker Henry Clay's neck and led his warhawk colleagues in an Indian war dance.

WAR PREPARATIONS   As it turned out, the war hawks would get neither Canada nor Florida, for James Madison had carried into war a nation that was ill prepared both financially and militarily. The Jeffersonian Republican emphasis on small federal budgets and military cutbacks was not an effective way to win a war. And Madison, a studious, soft-spoken man, lacked the martial qualities needed to inspire national confidence and resolve. He was no George Washington.

Moreover, the national economy was not prepared for war. In 1811, despite earnest pleas from Treasury Secretary Gallatin, Congress had let the twenty-year charter of the Bank of the United States expire. In addition, once war began, the British navy blockaded American ports, thereby cutting off imports, a major source of national revenue. By March 1813, Gallatin warned President Madison that: "We have hardly enough money to last till the end of the month." Furthermore, the extinction of the Bank of the United States brought chaos to the nation's financial system. Loans were now needed to cover about two thirds of the war costs, and northeastern opponents of the war were reluctant to lend money to the federal government.

The military situation was almost as bad. War had become more and more likely for nearly a decade, but Jefferson's defense cutbacks had prevented preparations. When the War of 1812 began, the army numbered only 3,287 men, ill trained, poorly equipped, and miserably led by aging officers past their prime and with little combat experience. In January 1812 Congress authorized an army of 35,000 men, but a year later, only 18,500 had been recruited—only by enticing them with promises of land and cash bounties. The British, on the other hand, had nearly 250,000 men in uniform worldwide.

The U.S. Navy was in comparatively good shape, with able officers and trained men whose seamanship had been tested in the fighting against

France and Tripoli. Its ships were well outfitted and seaworthy—all sixteen of them (the British had six hundred warships). In the first year of the war, it was the navy that produced the only U.S. victories, in isolated duels with British vessels, but their effect was mainly an occasional boost to morale. Within a year the British had blockaded the U.S. coast, except for New England, where they hoped to cultivate anti-war feeling, and most of the little American fleet was bottled up in port.

A CONTINENTAL WAR   The War of 1812 ended up involving three wars fought on three separate fronts. One conflict occurred on the waters of the Atlantic and the Chesapeake Bay and along the middle Atlantic coast. The second war occurred in the south, in Alabama, Mississippi, and West and East Florida, culminating in the Battle of New Orleans in 1815. In that theater, American forces led by General Andrew Jackson invaded lands owned by the Creeks and other Indians as well as the Spanish. The third war might be more accurately called the Canadian-American War. It began in what was then called the Old Northwest, in what is now northern Indiana and Ohio, southeastern Michigan, and regions around Lakes Huron and Michigan. There the fighting raged back and forth along the ill-defined border between the United States and British Canada.

THE WAR IN THE NORTH   The only place where the United States could effectively strike at the British was Canada. There the war essentially became a civil war, very much like the American Revolution, in which one side (Canadians—many of whom were former American Loyalists who had fled north in 1783) remained loyal to the British Empire while the other side (Americans) sought to continue the continental revolution against the empire. On both sides of the border the destruction and bloodshed embittered the combatants as well as civilians. Indians dominated the heavily wooded area around the Great Lakes, using British-supplied weapons and ammunition to resist the steady advance of American settlers into the contested region. At the same time, the British authorities had grown dependent on the Indians to help them defend Canada from attack. Michigan's governor recognized the reciprocal relationship: "The British cannot hold Upper Canada without the assistance of the Indians," but the "Indians cannot conduct a war without the assistance of a civilized nation [Great Britain]."

The Madison administration opted for a three-pronged assault on British Canada: along the Lake Champlain route toward Montreal, with General Henry Dearborn in command; along the Niagara River, with forces

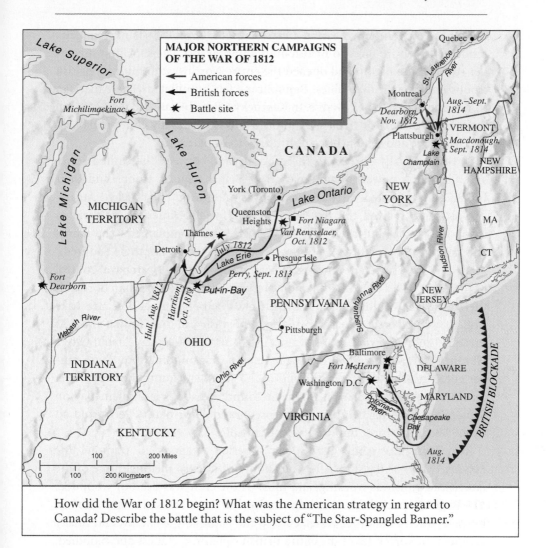

MAJOR NORTHERN CAMPAIGNS OF THE WAR OF 1812

← American forces
← British forces
★ Battle site

How did the War of 1812 begin? What was the American strategy in regard to Canada? Describe the battle that is the subject of "The Star-Spangled Banner."

under General Stephen Van Rensselaer; and into Upper Canada (today called Ontario) from Detroit, with General William Hull and some two thousand men.

In 1812, Hull marched his troops across the Detroit River but was pushed back by the British. Sickly and senile, the indecisive Hull procrastinated in cramped, dirty Detroit while his position worsened. The British commander cleverly played upon Hull's worst fears. Gathering what redcoats he could to parade in view of Detroit's defenders, he announced that thousands of Indian allies were at the rear and that once fighting began, he would be unable to control them. Fearing a massacre of Detroit's civilians, Hull surrendered his entire force to British bluff and bravado. The shocking surrender stunned the nation and opened the entire Northwest to raids by British troops and their Indian allies. Republicans felt humiliated. The American soldiers appeared to be cowards. In Kentucky a Republican said General Hull must be a "traitor" or "nearly an idiot." He was eventually court-martialed for cowardice and sentenced to death, only to be pardoned.

In the especially porous northern borderland between the United States and Canada, a powerful combination of British regular troops and their Indian allies repeatedly defeated U.S. invasion efforts. The botched American attempts revived the British contempt for the American soldiers as inept, unreliable, and cowardly. As one American complained, "the taunts and sarcasms of the Tories on both sides of the river are not to be endured." Madison's navy secretary now pushed vigorously for American naval control of the Great Lakes and other inland waterways along the Canadian border. If the Americans could break the British naval supply line and secure Lake Erie, they could erect a barrier between the British and their Indian allies. At Presque Isle (near Erie), Pennsylvania, in 1813, twenty-eight-year-old Oliver Hazard Perry, already a fourteen-year veteran, was building ships from timber cut in nearby forests. By the end of the summer, Commodore Perry set out in search of the British, whom he found at Lake Erie's Put-in-Bay on September 10. After completing the preparations for battle, Perry told an aide, "This is the most important day of my life."

Two British warships used their superior weapons to pummel the *Lawrence,* Perry's flagship. After four hours of intense shelling, none of the *Lawrence*'s guns was working, and most of the crew was dead or wounded. The British expected the Americans to flee, but Perry refused to quit. He had himself rowed to another vessel, carried the battle to the enemy, and finally accepted the surrender of the entire British squadron. Hatless and bloodied, Perry sent to General William Henry Harrison the long-awaited message: "We have met the enemy and they are ours."

American naval control of Lake Erie forced the British to evacuate Upper Canada. They gave up Detroit, and an American army defeated them at the Battle of the Thames on October 5. British power in Upper Canada was eliminated. In the course of the battle, Tecumseh fell, his dream of Indian unity dying with him. Perry's victory on Lake Erie and Harrison's defeat of Tecumseh enabled the Americans to recover control of Michigan and seize the Western District of Upper Canada.

THE WAR IN THE SOUTH   In the South, too, the war flared up in 1813. On August 30, so-called "Red Stick" Creeks allied with the British

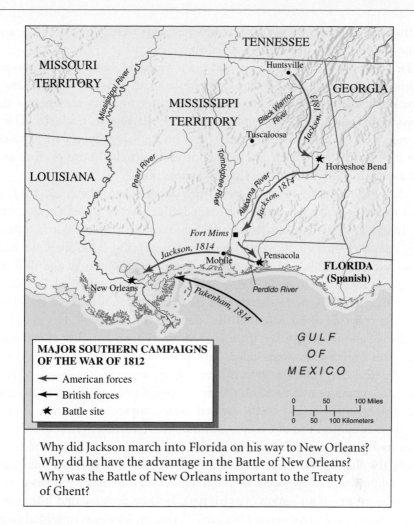

TENNESSEE

MISSOURI
TERRITORY

Huntsville

GEORGIA

MISSISSIPPI
TERRITORY

Mississippi River

Black Warrior River

Jackson, 1813

Tuscaloosa

Pearl River

Tombigbee River

Alabama River

Jackson, 1814

LOUISIANA

Horseshoe Bend

Fort Mims

Jackson, 1814

Mobile

Pensacola

FLORIDA
(Spanish)

New Orleans

Pakenham, 1814

Perdido River

GULF
OF
MEXICO

**MAJOR SOUTHERN CAMPAIGNS
OF THE WAR OF 1812**

← American forces

← British forces

✶ Battle site

| 0 | 50 | 100 Miles |
| 0 | 50 | 100 Kilometers |

Why did Jackson march into Florida on his way to New Orleans?
Why did he have the advantage in the Battle of New Orleans?
Why was the Battle of New Orleans important to the Treaty
of Ghent?

attacked Fort Mims, on the Alabama River thirty miles above the Gulf coast
town of Mobile, killing 553 men, women, and children, butchering and
scalping half of them. The news of the massacre outraged Americans, especially those eager to remove the Creeks from the Mississippi Territory
(which then included Alabama). When word of the Fort Mims slaughter
reached Andrew Jackson at his home in Tennessee, he was in bed recovering
from a Nashville street brawl with Thomas Hart Benton, later a senator from
Missouri. As the commanding general of the Army of West Tennessee, the
flinty Jackson, his injured arm still in a sling, summoned about 2,500 volunteer state militiamen (including Private David Crockett). Jackson told all
"brave Tennesseans" that their "frontier [was] threatened with invasion by
the savage foe" and that the Indians were advancing "towards your frontier

with scalping knives unsheathed, to butcher your wives, your children, and your helpless babes. Time is not to be lost."

Jackson's volunteers then set out on a vengeful campaign southward across Alabama that crushed the Creek resistance, village by village. David Crockett remembered that the Americans, eager to exact revenge for the massacre at Fort Mims, surrounded one Creek village and attacked at dawn. Dozens of "Red Sticks" sought safety in a house, whereupon Crockett and the Americans "shot them like dogs; and then set the house on fire, and burned it up with the forty-six Creek warriors in it."

The decisive battle in the "Creek War" occurred on March 27, 1814, at Horseshoe Bend, on the Tallapoosa River, in the heart of Upper Creek country in east-central Alabama. Jackson's Cherokee allies played a crucial role in the assault against an elaborate Creek fort harboring 1,100 men, women, and children. Jackson's forces surrounded the fort, set fire to it, and shot the Creeks as they tried to escape. Nine hundred of them were killed, including three hundred who were slaughtered as they struggled to cross the river. Jackson reported to his wife that the "carnage was dreadful." His men had "regained all the scalps taken from Fort Mims." Fewer than fifty of Jackson's men and Indian allies were killed. The Battle of Horseshoe Bend was the worst defeat ever inflicted upon Native Americans. With the Treaty of Fort Jackson, signed in August 1814, the devastated Creeks were forced to cede two thirds of their land to the United States, some twenty-three million acres, including a third of Georgia and most of Alabama. Even those Creeks who had fought on Jackson's side were forced to give up their lands. Red Eagle, the chief of the Creeks defeated by the Americans, told Jackson: "I am in your power. . . . My people are all gone. I can do no more but weep over the misfortunes of my nation." For his part, Jackson declared that "the power of the Creeks is I think forever broken." President Madison rewarded Jackson by naming him a major general in the regular army of the United States.

Four days after the Battle of Horseshoe Bend, Napoléon's European empire collapsed with the defeat of his French army by British and Prussian forces at the Battle of Waterloo in Belgium. Now free to deal solely with the United States, the British in 1814 invaded America from Canada. They also implemented a naval blockade of the New England ports and launched raids on coastal towns from Delaware south to Florida. The final piece of the British war plan was to seize New Orleans in order to sever American access to the Mississippi River, lifeline of the West.

THOMAS MACDONOUGH'S NAVAL VICTORY The main British military effort focused on launching from Canada a massive invasion of the

United States. The outnumbered American defenders were saved only by the superb ability of Commodore Thomas Macdonough, commander of the U.S. naval squadron on Lake Champlain. The British army bogged down while its warships engaged Macdonough's ships in a battle that ended with the entire British fleet either destroyed or captured. The Battle of Lake Champlain (also called the Battle of Plattsburgh) forced the British to abandon the northern campaign. The British forces retreated to Canada.

FIGHTING IN THE CHESAPEAKE   Meanwhile, however, U.S. forces suffered the most humiliating experience of the war as British troops captured and burned Washington, D.C. In August 1814, four thousand British troops landed at Benedict, Maryland, and headed for undefended Washington, thirty-five miles away. Thousands of frightened Americans fled the city. All President Madison could do was frantically call out the poorly led ragtag militia. The president then left the White House to join the militiamen marching to confront the British in Maryland, but their feeble defense disintegrated as the British invaders attacked.

On August 24 the redcoats marched unopposed into the American capital, where British officers ate a meal in the White House that had been prepared for President Madison and his wife, Dolley, who had fled the grounds just in time, after first saving a copy of the Declaration of Independence and George Washington's portrait. The vengeful British, aware that American troops had earlier burned and sacked the Canadian capital at York (Toronto), then burned the White House, the Capitol, the Library of Congress, and most other government buildings. A tornado the next day compounded the damage, but a violent thunderstorm dampened both the fires and the enthusiasm of the British forces, who headed north to assault Baltimore.

The British destruction of Washington, D.C., infuriated Americans. A Baltimore newspaper reported that the "spirit of the nation is roused." That vengeful spirit showed itself when fifty British warships sailed into Baltimore harbor on September 13. About a thousand Americans held Fort McHenry on an island in the harbor. The British fleet unleashed a ferocious, nightlong bombardment of the fort. Yet the Americans refused to surrender. **Francis Scott Key**, a Washington, D.C., lawyer and occasional poet, watched the siege on a British ship in the harbor, having been dispatched to negotiate the release of a captured American. The sight of the American flag (the "star-spangled banner") still in place at dawn meant that the fort and the city had survived the British onslaught. The scene inspired him to scribble the verses of what came to be called "The Star-Spangled Banner," which began, "Oh, say can you see by the dawn's early light?" Later revised and set to the tune of an English drinking song, it eventually became America's national anthem. The inability of the British to conquer Fort McHenry led them to abandon the attack on Baltimore.

While the fighting raged in the United States, American representatives, including Albert Gallatin, Henry Clay, and John Quincy Adams, had begun meetings in Ghent, near Brussels in present day Belgium, to discuss ending the war. The prolonged, contentious negotiations began just after British victories in the war, and the British diplomats responded by making outrageous demands about transferring American territory to Canada. The American delegation refused. Then, after the Battle of Lake Champlain and the failure of the British invasion of Baltimore, the British grew more flexible. Still, the negotiations dragged on throughout the fall of 1814. Finally, on Christmas Eve, 1814, the diplomats reached an agreement.

The willingness of the British to continue fighting in North America was eroded by the eagerness of British merchants to renew trade with America, and by the war-weariness of a tax-burdened public. The British finally decided that the American war was not worth the cost. One by one, demands were dropped on both sides, until the envoys agreed to end the war, return the prisoners, restore the previous boundaries, and settle nothing else. What had begun as an American effort to invade and conquer Canada had turned into a second war of independence against the world's greatest empire. Although the Americans lost the northern war for Canada, they had won the western and southern wars to subdue the Indians.

THE BATTLE OF NEW ORLEANS   The signing of the peace treaty in Belgium did not end the fighting, however. It took weeks for news of the **Treaty of Ghent** to arrive in the United States, so the fighting continued in America even after the treaty was signed in Europe. Along the Gulf coast, forty-seven-year-old Major General Andrew Jackson had been busy shoring up the defenses of Mobile and New Orleans. Without authorization he had invaded the Panhandle region of Spanish Florida and took Pensacola, putting an end to British efforts to organize Indian attacks on American settlements. In mid-December he was back in Louisiana, where he began to erect defensive barriers on the approaches to New Orleans as a British fleet, with some eight thousand soldiers under General Sir Edward Pakenham fresh from their victory over Napoléon in Europe, took up positions just south of New Orleans, the second busiest port in the United States (after New York). The British hoped to capture New Orleans and thereby control the entire Mississippi River Valley. Federalists fed up with "Mr. Madison's War" predicted that New Orleans would be lost; some called for Madison's impeachment.

General Pakenham's painfully careful approach—he waited weeks until all his artillery was available—gave Jackson time to build defensive earthworks bolstered by barrels and casks of sugar. It was an almost invulnerable position, but Pakenham, contemptuous of Jackson's much smaller multiethnic and multiracial force of four thousand frontier militiamen, Creole aristocrats, free blacks, a few slaves, and several notorious pirates rashly ordered a frontal assault at dawn on January 8, 1815. His brave but blundering redcoats ran into a murderous hail of artillery shells and rifle fire. Before the British withdrew, about two thousand had been wounded or killed, including Pakenham himself. There were only a handful of American casualties. A British officer, after watching his battered and retreating troops, wrote that there "never was a more complete failure."

Although the Battle of New Orleans occurred after the peace treaty had already been signed in Europe, the battle was still strategically important, as the treaty had yet to be officially ratified by either the United States or Great Britain. Had the British won at New Orleans, they might have tried to revise the treaty in their favor. Jackson's lopsided victory ensured that both governments acted quickly to ratify the treaty. The unexpected American triumph at New Orleans also generated a wave of patriotic nationalism that would later help transform a victorious general, Andrew Jackson, into a dynamic president.

THE HARTFORD CONVENTION　While the diplomats converged on a peace settlement in Europe, an entirely different kind of meeting was taking place in Hartford, Connecticut. The **Hartford Convention** represented the climax of New England's disaffection with "Mr. Madison's war." New England had managed to keep aloof from the war while extracting a profit from illegal trading and privateering. Both Massachusetts and Connecticut had refused to contribute militias to the war effort; merchants had continued to sell supplies to British troops in Canada. After the fall of Napoléon in 1815, however, the British extended their blockade to New England, occupied Maine, and conducted several raids along the coast. Even Boston seemed threatened. Instead of rallying to the American flag, however, Federalists in the Massachusetts legislature voted in October 1814 to hold a convention of New England states to plan independent action.

On December 15 the Hartford Convention assembled with delegates chosen by the legislatures of Massachusetts, Rhode Island, and Connecticut as well as two delegates from Vermont and one from New Hampshire—twenty-two in all. The convention proposed seven constitutional amendments designed to limit Republican (and southern) influence: abolishing the counting of slaves in apportioning state representation in Congress, requiring a two-thirds vote to declare war or admit new states, prohibiting embargoes lasting more than sixty days, excluding foreign-born individuals from holding federal office, limiting the president to one term, and forbidding successive presidents from the same state.

Their call for a later convention in Boston carried the unmistakable threat of secession if the demands were ignored. Yet the threat quickly evaporated. In February 1815, when messengers from Hartford reached Washington, D.C., they found the battered capital celebrating the good news from Ghent and New Orleans. "Their position," according to a French diplomat, was "awkward, embarrassing, and lent itself to cruel ridicule," and they swiftly withdrew their recommendations. The consequence was a fatal blow to the Federalist party, which never recovered from the stigma of disloyalty stamped on it by the Hartford Convention. News of the victory at New Orleans and the arrival of the peace treaty from Europe transformed the national mood. Almost overnight, President Madison had gone from being impeached to being a national hero.

THE AFTERMATH   For all the fumbling ineptitude with which the strange War of 1812 was fought, it generated an intense patriotism. Despite the standoff with which it ended at Ghent, Americans nourished a sense of victory, courtesy of Andrew Jackson and his men at New Orleans as well as

We Owe Allegiance to No Crown

The War of 1812 generated a renewed spirit of nationalism.

the heroic exploits of American frigates in their duels with British ships. Under Republican leadership, the nation had survived a "second war of independence" against the greatest power on earth and emerged with new symbols of nationhood and a new gallery of heroes. The people, observed Albert Gallatin in 1815, "are more American; they feel and act more as a nation; and I hope that the permanency of the Union is thereby better secured." The war also launched the United States toward economic independence as the interruption of trade with Europe had encouraged the growth of American manufactures. After forty years of independence, it dawned on the world that the new American republic was rapidly emerging as a world power. "Never did a country occupy more lofty ground," said U.S. Supreme Court Justice Joseph Story in 1815. "We have stood the contest, single-handed, against the conqueror of Europe; and we are at peace, with all our blushing victories thick crowding on us."

As if to underline the point, Congress authorized a quick, decisive blow at the pirates of the Barbary Coast. During the War of 1812, North Africans had again set about plundering American ships in the Mediterranean. On March 3, 1815, little more than two weeks after the Senate ratified the Treaty of Ghent, Congress sent Captain Stephen Decatur with ten vessels to the Mediterranean. Decatur seized two Algerian ships and then sailed boldly into the harbor of Algiers. On June 30, 1815, the Algerian ruler agreed to cease molesting American ships and to give up all U.S. prisoners. Decatur's show of force induced similar treaties from other North African countries. This time the United States would not pay blackmail; this time, for a change, the Barbary pirates paid for the damage they had done. This time, victory put an end to the region's tradition of piracy and extortion.

One of the strangest results of the War of 1812 and its aftermath was a reversal of roles by the Republicans and the Federalists. Out of the wartime experience the Republicans had learned some lessons in nationalism. Certain needs and inadequacies revealed by the war had "Federalized" Madison or "re-Federalized" this Father of the Constitution. Perhaps, he reasoned, a peacetime army and navy were necessary. The lack of a national bank had added to the problems of financing the war; half of the state banks opened between 1810 and 1820 went bankrupt. In 1816 Madison chartered the Second Bank of the United States for twenty years. The rise of new industries during the war prompted calls for increased tariffs on imports to protect the infant American companies from foreign competition. Madison went along. The problems of overland transportation in the West experienced by American armies had revealed the need for better roads and bridges. Madison agreed, but on that point kept his constitutional scruples. He wanted a constitutional amendment that would authorize the federal government to construct such "internal improvements." So while Madison embraced nationalism and broad construction of the Constitution, the Federalists took up the Jeffersonians' position of states' rights and strict construction in an effort to oppose Madison's policies. It was the first great reversal of partisan political roles in constitutional interpretation. It would not be the last.

CHAPTER SUMMARY

- **Jefferson's Administration** Thomas Jefferson did not dismantle much of Hamilton's economic program, but he did promptly repeal the whiskey tax and cut back on government expenditures. He involved the navy in subduing the Barbary pirates and negotiated with the Spanish and then with the French to ensure that the Mississippi River remained open to American commerce. The purchase of the Louisiana Territory through negotiations with French Emperor Napoléon Bonaparte dramatically expanded the boundaries of the United States.

- **Marshall Court** John Marshall, a Federalist, played influential roles in many crucial decisions during his long tenure as chief justice of the Supreme Court. In *Marbury v. Madison,* the Court declared a federal act unconstitutional for the first time. With that decision, the Court assumed the right of judicial review over acts of Congress. As chief justice, Marshall established the constitutional supremacy of the federal government over state governments.

- **Louisiana Purchase** The Louisiana Purchase led to a debate on the nature of the Constitution, in which Federalists feared the addition of new territories would strengthen the Republicans. Jefferson's "Corps of Discovery," led by Meriwether Lewis and William Clark, explored the new region's resources, captured the public imagination, and gave the United States a claim to the Oregon Country.

- **War of 1812** Renewal of the European war in 1803 created conflicts with Britain and France. Neither country wanted its enemy to purchase U.S. goods, so both declared blockades. In retaliation, Jefferson had Congress pass the Embargo Act, which prohibited *all* foreign trade. James Madison ultimately declared war over the issue of neutral shipping rights and the fear that the British were inciting Native Americans to attack frontier settlements.

- **Aftermath of the War of 1812** The Treaty of Ghent, signed in 1814, ended the War of 1812 without settling any of the disputes. One effect of the conflict over neutral shipping rights was to launch the economic independence of the United States, as goods previously purchased from Britain were now manufactured at home. Federalists and Republicans seemed to exchange roles: delegates from the waning Federalist party met at the Hartford Convention to defend states' rights and threaten secession, whereas Republicans promoted nationalism and a broad interpretation of the Constitution.

CHRONOLOGY

1803	*Marbury v. Madison*
1803	Louisiana Purchase
1804–1806	Lewis and Clark expedition
1807	*Chesapeake* affair
1807	Embargo Act is passed
1808	International slave trade is outlawed
1811	Battle of Tippecanoe
1814	Battle of Horseshoe Bend
1814	Treaty of Ghent
1814	Hartford Convention
1815	Battle of New Orleans

KEY TERMS & NAMES

Part Three

AN
EXPANSIVE
NATION

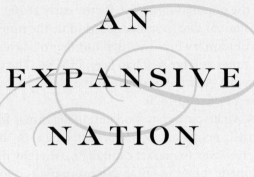

During the nineteenth century, the United States experienced a wrenching transformation from an agrarian to an urban industrial society. Between 1790 and 1820 the nation grew rapidly: its boundaries expanded and the population soared. By the early 1820s, there were ten states with substantial slave populations, double the number of states during the Revolutionary Era. The total number of slaves was more than two and a half times as large as it had been in 1790. The white population grew as rapidly. And the number of free blacks in the United States doubled between 1790 and 1820.

In 1800 most Americans grew food and made things for themselves or to barter with their neighbors. By 1900, such a local or "household" economy had given way to market capitalism, whereby most people grew food and made things to sell to distant markets. Most Americans welcomed such changes, for their standard of living rose. But the transition from an agrarian to a capitalist society was neither easy nor simple; it involved massive changes in the way people lived, worked, and voted.

During the early nineteenth century, most Americans continued to earn their living from the soil, but textile mills and manufacturing plants began to dot the landscape and transform the nature of work and the pace of life. By mid-century, the United States was emerging as one of the world's major commercial and manufacturing nations. In addition, the lure of cheap land and plentiful jobs, as well as the promise of political and religious freedom, attracted hundreds of thousands of immigrants from Europe. The newcomers, mostly from Germany and Ireland, benefited from the civil liberties and higher standard of living in America, but they also encountered ethnic prejudices, religious persecution, and language barriers that made assimilation into American culture a difficult process.

What historians have called a "market revolution" transformed the young American economy during the first half of the nineteenth century. With each passing year, farmers, merchants, and manufacturers devoted themselves more and more to producing commodities and goods for commercial markets, which often lay far from the sources of production. American capitalism was maturing—rapidly. Accompanying and accelerating the "market revolution" during the first half of the nineteenth century was the expansion of the United States across the continent. Thousands of Americans spilled over the Appalachian Mountains, crossed the Mississippi River, and, in the 1840s, reached the Pacific Ocean. Wagons, canals, flatboats, steamboats, and eventually railroads helped transport them. The feverish expansion of the United States into new Western territories brought more conflict with Native Americans, Mexicans, the British, and the Spanish. Only a few people, however, expressed moral reservations about displacing others. Most Americans believed it was the "manifest destiny" of the United States to spread throughout the continent—at whatever cost and at whomever's expense. Americans generally assumed that they enjoyed the blessing of Providence in their efforts to consolidate and exploit the continent.

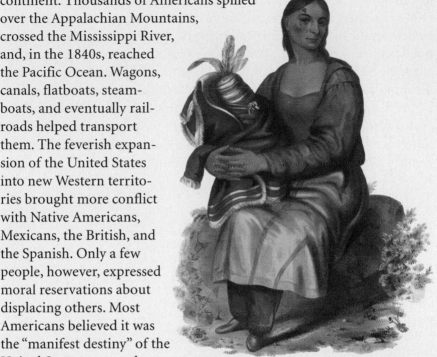

These developments gave life in the second quarter of the nineteenth century a dynamic quality. The United States, said the philosopher-poet Ralph Waldo Emerson, was "a country of beginnings, of projects, of designs, of expectations." A restless optimism characterized the period. People of a lowly social status now strove to climb the social ladder and to enter the political arena. The republic governed by Jefferson and Madison gave way to the frontier democracy promoted by Andrew Jackson. Americans were no longer content to be governed by a small, benevolent aristocracy of talent and wealth. They began to demand—and obtain—government of, by, and for the people.

The exuberant individualism displayed by Americans embodied in such mythic expressions of economic equality and political democracy spilled over into the cultural arena. The so-called Romantic movement applied democratic ideals to philosophy, religion, literature, and the fine arts. In New England, Ralph Waldo Emerson and Henry David Thoreau joined other "transcendentalists" in espousing a radical individualism. Other reformers were motivated more by a sense of spiritual calling than by democratic individualism. Reformers of all stripes sought to promote public-supported schools, abolish slavery, reduce the consumption of alcoholic beverages, and improve the lot of the disabled, the insane, and the imprisoned. Their efforts ameliorated some of the problems created by the frenetic economic growth and territorial expansion. But reformers made little headway against slavery, which only intensified sectional differences and political conflicts. Ultimately, only a brutal civil war would dislodge America's "peculiar institution."

9

THE DYNAMICS OF GROWTH

FOCUS QUESTIONS

 wwnorton.com/studyspace

- How did the explosive growth of industry, agriculture, and transportation change America?
- What were some of the inventions that economically and socially improved the country?
- How had immigration changed by the mid–nineteenth century?
- Why did early labor unions emerge?

Amid the jubilation that followed the War of 1812, Americans were transforming their young nation. Hundreds of thousands of people streamed westward to the Mississippi River and beyond. The largely local economy was being transformed into a national marketplace enabled by dramatic improvements in communication and transportation. The spread of plantation slavery and the cotton culture into the Old Southwest—Alabama, Mississippi, Arkansas, Louisiana, and Texas as well as the frontier areas of Tennessee, Kentucky, and Florida—disrupted family ties and transformed social life. In the North and the West, meanwhile, an urban middle class began to flourish in towns and cities. Such changes prompted vigorous political debates over economic policies, transportation improvements, and the extension of slavery into the new territories. In the process the nation began to divide into three powerful regional political blocs—North, South, and West—whose shifting alliances would shape public policy until the Civil War.

Between 1815 and 1850, the United States became a transcontinental power, expanding all the way to the Pacific coast. An industrial revolution in the Northeast began to reshape the region's economy and propel an unrelenting process of urbanization. In the West, commercial agriculture began to emerge, in which surplus corn, wheat, and cattle were sold to distant markets. In the South, cotton became king, and its reign fed upon the expanding institution of slavery. At the same time, innovations in transportation and communications—larger horse-drawn wagons, called **Conestogas**; canals; steamboats; railroads; and the new telegraph system—knit together an expanding national market for goods and services. In sum, the eighteenth-century economy based primarily upon small-scale farming and local commerce was maturing rapidly into a far-flung capitalist marketplace entwined with world markets. These economic developments in turn helped expand prosperity and freedom. The dynamic economy generated changes in every other area of life, from politics to the legal system, from the family to social values, from work to recreation.

TRANSPORTATION AND THE MARKET REVOLUTION

NEW ROADS   Transportation improvements helped spur the development of a national economy. As settlers moved west, people demanded better roads. In 1795 the Wilderness Road, along the trail blazed by Daniel Boone twenty years before, was opened to wagon and stagecoach traffic, thereby easing the route through the Cumberland Gap into Kentucky and along the Walton Road, completed the same year, into Tennessee. To the northeast a movement for graded and paved roads (using packed-down crushed stones) gathered momentum after completion of the Philadelphia-Lancaster Turnpike in 1794 (the term *turnpike* derives from a pole, or pike, at the tollgate, which was turned to admit the traffic in exchange for a small fee). By 1821 some four thousand miles of turnpikes had been completed.

WATER TRANSPORTATION   By the early 1820s, the turnpike boom was giving way to dramatic advances in water transportation: river steamboats, flatboats, and canal barges carried people and commodities far more cheaply than did wagons. The first commercially successful steamboat appeared when Robert Fulton and Robert R. Livingston sent the *Clermont* up New York's Hudson River in 1807. Thereafter the use of steamboats spread rapidly to other eastern rivers and to the Ohio and Mississippi, opening nearly half a continent to water traffic. Steamboats transformed inland water transportation.

By 1836, 361 steamboats were navigating the western waters, reaching ever farther up the tributaries that fed into the Mississippi River. By bringing two-way traffic to the Mississippi River valley, steamboats created a transcontinental market and an agricultural empire that became the nation's new breadbasket.

The **Erie Canal** in New York was one of the most important catalysts for the creation of a national economy. After it opened in 1825, having taken eight years to build, it drew eastward much of the midwestern trade that earlier had been forced to make the long journey down the Ohio and Mississippi Rivers to the Gulf of Mexico. This development would have major economic and political consequences, tying together the economies of the West and the East while further isolating the Deep South. The majestic Erie Canal, forty feet wide and four feet deep, extended 363 miles from Albany to Buffalo; additional branches soon put most of the state within its reach. The canal, built by tens of thousands of laborers, mostly Irish immigrants, brought a "river of gold" to burgeoning New York City and caused small towns such as Syracuse, Rochester, and Buffalo in New York, as well as Cleveland, Ohio, and Chicago, Illinois, to blossom into major commercial cities.

The Erie Canal reduced travel time from New York City to Buffalo from twenty days to six, and the cost of moving a ton of freight plummeted from

The Erie Canal

Junction of the Northern and Western Canals (1825), an aquatint by John Hill.

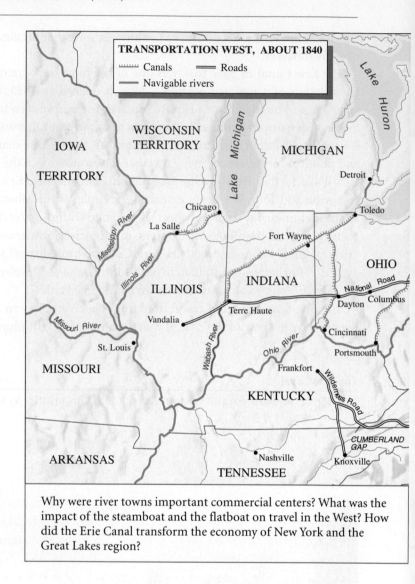

TRANSPORTATION WEST, ABOUT 1840

⌐⌐⌐ Canals   ═══ Roads
──── Navigable rivers

Why were river towns important commercial centers? What was the impact of the steamboat and the flatboat on travel in the West? How did the Erie Canal transform the economy of New York and the Great Lakes region?

$100 to $5. The speedy success of the New York canal system inspired a mania for canals in other states that lasted more than a decade and spawned about three thousand miles of waterways by 1837. But no canal ever matched the spectacular success of the Erie, which rendered the entire Great Lakes region an economic tributary to the port of New York City.

RAILROADS   The financial panic of 1837 and the subsequent depression cooled the canal fever. Meanwhile, a more versatile form of transportation rapidly overtook the canal: the railroad. In 1825, the year the Erie Canal was

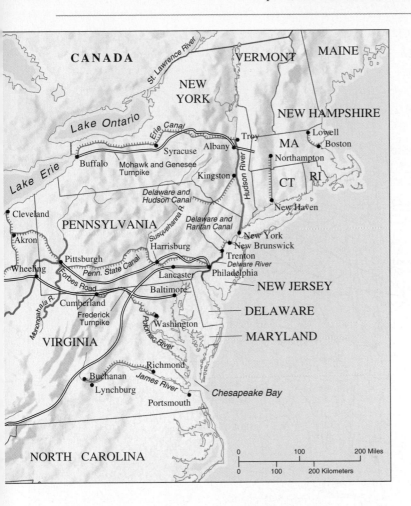

completed, the world's first commercial steam railway began operation in England. By the 1820s, the American port cities of Baltimore, Charleston, and Boston were alive with schemes to connect the port cities to the hinterlands by rail. In 1830 there were only 23 miles of railroad track in the United States. Thereafter, an "epidemic" of railroad building swept across the nation. Over the next twenty years, railroads grew nearly tenfold, covering 30,626 miles; more than two thirds of that total was built in the 1850s.

The railroad gained supremacy over other forms of transportation because of its speed, carrying capacity, and reliability. Railroads made it possible to transport people and freight faster, farther, and cheaper than ever before. The early trains averaged ten miles per hour, more than twice the speed of stagecoaches and four times that of boats. The ability of railroads to operate year-round in most kinds of weather gave them a huge advantage. By 1859,

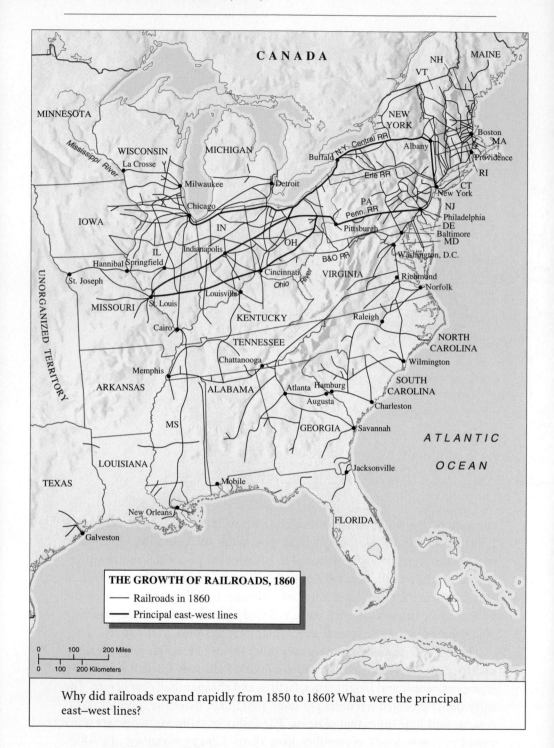

THE GROWTH OF RAILROADS, 1860

— Railroads in 1860

━ Principal east-west lines

0   100   200 Miles

0   100   200 Kilometers

Why did railroads expand rapidly from 1850 to 1860? What were the principal east–west lines?

railroads had greatly reduced the cost of freight and passenger transportation. Perhaps most important, the railroads connected what in the eighteenth century had been a chaos of local markets into an interconnected national market. Railroads thereby expanded the geography of American capitalism, making possible larger industrial and commercial enterprises. They also provided indirect benefits by encouraging new western settlement and the expansion of farming. The railroads' demand for iron, cross ties, spikes, bridges, locomotives, freight cars, and equipment of various kinds created an enormous market for the industries that made these capital goods.

But the railroad mania had negative effects as well. By opening up possibilities for quick and shady profits, it helped corrupt political life. Railroad titans often bribed legislators to provide government financing. By facilitating access to the trans-Appalachian West, the railroad helped accelerate the decline of Native American culture.

OCEAN TRANSPORTATION   The year 1845 witnessed a great innovation in ocean transport with the launching of the first clipper ship, the *Rainbow*. Built for speed, the sleek clippers were the nineteenth-century equivalent of the supersonic jetliner. They doubled the speed of the older merchant ships. Long and lean, with taller masts and more sails, they cut dashing figures during their brief but colorful career, which lasted less than two decades. The lure of Chinese tea, a drink long coveted in America but in scarce supply, prompted the clipper boom. Asian tea leaves were a perishable commodity that had to reach the market quickly after harvest, and the new clipper ships made this possible. Even more important, the discovery of California gold in 1848 lured thousands of prospectors and entrepreneurs from the Atlantic seaboard. The massive wave of miners generated an urgent demand for goods, and the clippers met it. In 1854 the *Flying Cloud* took eighty-nine days and eight hours to travel from New York to San Francisco. But clippers, while fast, lacked ample cargo space, and after the Civil War they would give way to the steamship.

THE ROLE OF GOVERNMENT The dramatic transportation improvements during the nineteenth century were financed by both state governments and private investors. The federal government helped too, despite ferocious debates over whether direct involvement in internal improvements was constitutional. The national government bought stock in turnpike and canal companies and, after the success of the Erie Canal, extended land grants to several western states for the support of canal projects. Congress provided for railroad surveys by government engineers and reduced the tariff rates on imported iron used in railroad construction. In 1850, Senator Stephen A. Douglas of Illinois and others prevailed upon Congress to extend a major land grant to support a north–south rail line connecting Chicago and Mobile, Alabama. Regarded at the time as a special case, the 1850 grant set a precedent for other bounties that totaled about 20 million acres by 1860—a small amount compared with the land grants that Congress awarded transcontinental railroads during the 1860s.

A COMMUNICATIONS REVOLUTION

The transportation revolution helped Americans overcome the challenge of distance and thereby helped expand markets for goods and services, which in turn led to fundamental changes in the production, sale, and consumption of agricultural products and manufactured goods. Innovations in transportation also helped spark dramatic improvements in communications. At the beginning of the century, it took days—often weeks—for news to travel along the Atlantic seaboard. For example, after George Washington died in 1799 in Virginia, the news of his death did not appear in New York City newspapers until a week later. Naturally, news took even longer to travel to and from Europe. It took forty-nine days for news of the peace treaty ending the War of 1812 to reach New York from Belgium.

The speed of communications accelerated greatly as the nineteenth century unfolded. By 1830 it was possible to "convey" Andrew Jackson's inaugural address from Washington, D.C., to New York City in sixteen hours. It took six days to reach New Orleans. Mail began to be delivered by "express," a system in which riders could mount fresh horses at a series of relay stations. Still, even with such advances, the states and territories west of the Appalachian Mountains struggled to get timely deliveries and news.

AMERICAN TECHNOLOGY   During the nineteenth century, Americans became famous for their "practical" inventiveness. Technological advances helped improve living conditions: houses could be larger, better heated, and better illuminated. The first sewer systems helped cities begin to rid their streets of human and animal waste, while underground water lines enabled firemen to use hydrants rather than bucket brigades. Machine-made clothes usually fit better and were cheaper than those sewed by hand from homespun cloth; newspapers and magazines were more abundant and affordable, as were clocks and watches.

A spate of inventions in the 1840s generated dramatic changes. In 1844, Charles Goodyear patented a process for "vulcanizing" rubber, which made the product stronger and more elastic. In 1846, Elias Howe patented his design of the sewing machine, soon improved upon by Isaac Merritt Singer. In 1844 the first intercity telegraph message was transmitted, from Baltimore to Washington, D.C., on the device **Samuel F. B. Morse** had invented back in 1832. The telegraph may have triggered more social changes than any other invention. By the end of the 1840s, telegraph lines connected all major cities. It was during the 1840s that modern marketing emerged as a national enterprise. That decade saw the emergence of the first national brands, the first department stores, and the first advertising agencies.

AGRICULTURE AND THE NATIONAL ECONOMY

Economic opportunities were abundant during the early nineteenth century, especially in the Deep South. Cotton, the profitable new cash crop, transformed the region's economic and political life. The "cotton belt" spread rapidly from South Carolina and Georgia into the fertile lands of Mississippi, Alabama, Louisiana, and Arkansas.

COTTON Manufacturing cotton cloth, first in Europe and then the United States, emerged as the first great industry generated by the Industrial Revolution. Cotton had been used from ancient times, but the spread of water- and steam-powered textile mills during the late eighteenth century created a rapidly growing global market for the fluffy fiber. Until the start of the nineteenth century, cotton clothing had been expensive because of the need for intensive hand labor to separate the lint fibers from the tenaciously sticky seeds. While a person could pick as much as fifty pounds of cotton bolls in a day, that same person working all day could separate barely one pound of fiber from seeds. The profitability of cotton depended upon finding a better way.

At Mulberry Grove plantation in coastal Georgia, discussion often focused on the problem of separating cotton seeds from the cotton fiber. In 1792 young **Eli Whitney**, a recent Yale graduate from New England, visited Mulberry Grove. There he wrote his father that he had "heard much said of the difficulty of ginning cotton" and that the person who invented a "machine" to gin cotton would become wealthy overnight. A few days later, Whitney devised a simple mechanism using nails attached to a roller to remove the seeds from cotton. In the spring of 1793, Whitney's prototype cotton "gin" (short for *engine*) enabled the operator to gin fifty times as much cotton as a worker could by hand.

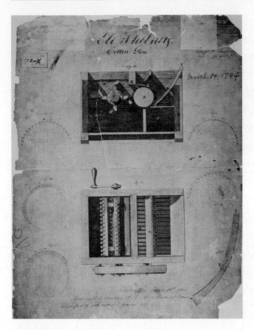

Whitney's cotton gin

Eli Whitney's drawing, which accompanied his 1794 federal patent application, shows the side and top of the machine as well as the sawteeth that separated the seeds from the fiber.

Whitney's invention launched an economic revolution. The cotton gin made cotton America's most profitable cash crop and in the process transformed southern agriculture. When British textile manufacturers declared their preference for "upland" southern cotton over the different varieties grown in the Caribbean, Brazil, and the East Indies, the demand for American cotton skyrocketed, as did prices. The commercial growing of cotton for world markets revitalized the emphasis on plantation slavery. Cotton first engulfed the "piedmont" region of the Carolinas and Georgia. Then, after the War of 1812, it migrated into the contested Indian lands to the west—Tennessee, Alabama, Florida, Mississippi, Louisiana, Arkansas, and Texas. Soon New Orleans became a bustling port—and active slave market—because of the many bales of cotton being grown in the region and shipped down the Mississippi River. From the mid-1830s to 1860, cotton accounted for more than half the value of all exports in the nation. The South supplied the North with both raw materials and markets for manufactures. Income from the North's role in handling the cotton trade then provided surpluses for capital investment in new factories and businesses. Cotton thereby became a crucial element of the national economy—and the driving force behind efforts to expand slavery into the western territories.

Cotton is a labor-intensive crop, requiring 70 percent more labor than corn. Southerners solved the labor problem by using slaves—lots of them. The price of slaves soared with the price of cotton. As farmland in Virginia diminished in fertility after years of relentless tobacco planting, many whites sold their surplus slaves to the rapidly growing number of whites establishing farms and plantations in the new cotton-growing areas of the Old Southwest. Between 1790 and 1860, some 835,000 slaves were "sold south." In 1790 planters in Virginia and Maryland had owned 56 percent of all the slaves in the United States; by 1860 they owned only 15 percent. A new cotton farmer in Mississippi urged a friend back in Kentucky to sell his farm and join him: "If you could reconcile it to yourself to bring your negroes to the Miss. Terr., they would certainly make you a handsome fortune in ten years by the cultivation of Cotton." Slaves became so valuable that stealing slaves became a common problem in the states of the Old Southwest.

FARMING THE WEST The westward flow of planters and slaves to Alabama and Mississippi during these flush times mirrored another migration through the Ohio Valley and the Great Lakes region, where the Indians had been forcibly pushed westward. By 1860 more than half the nation's population resided in trans-Appalachia, and the restless migrants had long since spilled across the Mississippi River and touched the shores of the Pacific.

North of the expanding cotton belt, the fertile woodland soil, riverside bottomlands, and black loam of the prairies drew farmers from the rocky lands of New England and the exhausted soils of the Southeast. A new national land law of 1820, passed after the panic of 1819, reduced the price of federal land. Even that was not enough for westerners, however, who began a long—and eventually victorious—agitation for further relaxation of the federal land laws. They favored "preemption," the right of squatters to purchase land at the minimum price, and "graduation," the progressive reduction of the price of land that did not sell immediately. Congress eventually responded to the land mania with two bills. Under the Preemption Act of 1830, squatters could get 160 acres at the minimum price of $1.25 per acre. Under the Graduation Act of 1854, prices of unsold lands were to be lowered in stages over thirty years.

The process of settling new lands followed the old pattern of clearing trees, grubbing out the stumps and underbrush, and settling down at first to a crude subsistence. The development of effective iron plows greatly eased the back-breaking job of tilling the soil. In 1819, Jethro Wood of New York developed an improved iron plow with separate replaceable parts. Further improvements would follow, including Vermonter John Deere's steel plow (1837).

Other technological improvements quickened the growth of commercial agriculture. By the 1840s new mechanical seeders had replaced the process of sowing seed by hand. Even more important, in 1831 twenty-two-year-old **Cyrus Hall McCormick** of Virginia invented a mechanical reaper to harvest wheat, a development as significant to the agricultural economy of the

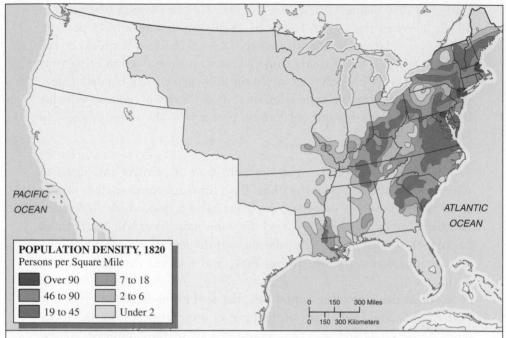

POPULATION DENSITY, 1820
Persons per Square Mile

- Over 90
- 46 to 90
- 19 to 45
- 7 to 18
- 2 to 6
- Under 2

In 1820, which regions had the greatest population density? Why? How did changes in the 1820 land law encourage western expansion? What events caused the price of land to decrease between 1800 and 1841?

Midwest, Old Northwest, and the Great Plains as the cotton gin was to the South. After tinkering with his strange-looking horse-drawn machine for almost a decade, in 1847 McCormick began selling his reapers so fast that he moved to Chicago and built a manufacturing plant for his reapers and mowers. Within a few years he had sold thousands of machines, transforming the scale of commercial agriculture. Using a handheld sickle, a farmer could harvest a half acre of wheat a day; with a McCormick reaper two people could work twelve acres a day. By reducing the number of farm workers, such new agricultural technologies helped send displaced rural laborers to work in textile mills, iron foundries, and other new industries.

THE INDUSTRIAL REVOLUTION

While the South and the West developed the agricultural basis for a national economy, the North was initiating an industrial revolution. Technological breakthroughs such as the cotton gin, mechanical harvester, and

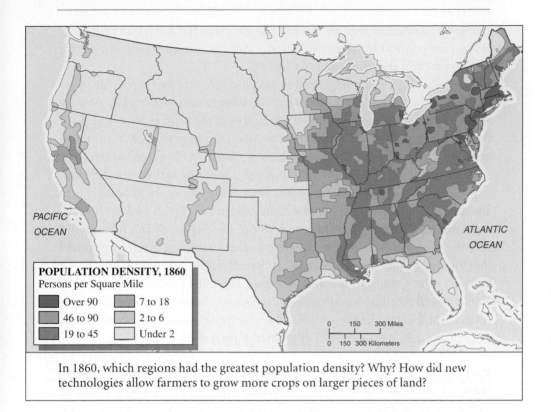

POPULATION DENSITY, 1860
Persons per Square Mile

- Over 90
- 46 to 90
- 19 to 45
- 7 to 18
- 2 to 6
- Under 2

In 1860, which regions had the greatest population density? Why? How did new technologies allow farmers to grow more crops on larger pieces of land?

railroad had quickened agricultural development and to some extent decided its direction. But technology altered the economic landscape even more profoundly, by giving rise to the factory system.

EARLY TEXTILE MANUFACTURES   In 1789 Samuel Slater arrived in America from England with a detailed plan of a water-powered spinning machine in his head. He contracted with an enterprising merchant-manufacturer in Rhode Island to build a mill in Pawtucket, and in that little mill, completed in 1790, nine children began making cotton yarn. The growth of American textile production was slow and faltering until Thomas Jefferson's embargo in 1807 stimulated the production of cloth. By 1815, textile mills numbered in the hundreds.

After the War of 1812, a flood of cheap imported British cloth nearly killed the infant American textile industry. A delegation of desperate New England mill owners traveled to Washington, D.C., to demand a federal tariff on imported cloth to deter British producers whose comparative advantages enabled them to sell cloth in the United States for less than the prices charged by American manufacturers. The efforts of the American mill owners to gain political assistance initiated a culture of industrial lobbying for tariff protection that continues to this day.

What the mill owners neglected to acknowledge was that tariff duties are rarely paid by foreign manufacturers; the import taxes are usually paid by American consumers, to whom the added cost of the tariff is passed along in the form of higher prices. Over time, as Adam Smith explained in his path-breaking treatise on capitalism, *Wealth of Nations* (1776), consumers not only pay higher prices for foreign goods as a result of tariffs, but they also pay higher prices for domestic goods, since local producers invariably take advantage of opportunities to raise their own prices. Tariffs end up insulating American industries from competition, the engine of innovation and efficiency in a capitalist economy. New England shipping interests opposed the idea of higher tariffs because it would reduce shipping across the Atlantic. Many southerners also opposed the bill because they feared it would provoke Britain and France to impose retaliatory tariffs on southern cotton and tobacco. In the end the, the mill owners won. The Tariff Bill of 1816 placed a 25-cent-per-yard duty on imported cloth.

THE LOWELL SYSTEM The factory system sprang full-blown upon the American scene at Waltham, Massachusetts, in 1813, when a group of capitalists known as the Boston Associates constructed the first textile mill in which the processes of spinning and weaving by power machinery were brought together under one roof. In 1822, the Boston Associates developed a new water-powered mill at a village along the Merrimack River, which they renamed Lowell.

The founders of the Lowell mills were idealistic capitalists; they sought to design model factory communities. To avoid the drab, crowded, and wretched life of the English mill villages, they located their mills in the countryside and established an ambitious program of paternal supervision of the workers. The factory workers at Waltham and Lowell were mostly young women from New England farm families. Employers preferred to hire women because of their dexterity in operating machines and their willingness to work for wages lower than those paid to men. Moreover, by the 1820s there was a surplus of women in the region because so many men had migrated westward in search of cheap land and new economic opportunities. In the early 1820s, a steady stream of single women began flocking toward Lowell. To reassure worried parents, the mill owners promised to provide the "**Lowell girls**" with tolerable work, prepared meals, comfortable boardinghouses, moral discipline, and educational and cultural opportunities.

The Union Manufactories of Maryland in Patapsco Falls, Baltimore County (ca. 1815)

A textile mill established during the embargo of 1807. The Union Manufactories would eventually employ more than 600 people.

Initially the "Lowell idea" worked pretty much according to plan. The "Lowell girls" lived in dormitories staffed by matronly supervisors who enforced mandatory church attendance and curfews. Despite thirteen-hour work days and six-day workweeks, some of the women found the time and energy to form study groups, publish a literary magazine, and attend lectures. But Lowell soon lost its innocence as it experienced mushrooming growth. By 1840, there were thirty-two mills and factories in operation, and the once rural town had become an industrial city—bustling, grimy, and bleak.

Other factory centers sprouted up across New England, displacing forests and farms and engulfing villages, filling the air with smoke, noise, and stench. Between 1820 and 1840, the number of Americans engaged in manufacturing increased eightfold, and the number of city dwellers more than doubled. The United States was rapidly becoming a global industrial power second only to Great Britain. Booming growth transformed the Lowell experiment, however. By 1846 a concerned worker told young farm women thinking about taking a mill job that "it will be better for you to stay at home on your fathers' farms than to run the risk of being ruined in a manufacturing village."

During the 1830s, as textile prices and mill wages dropped, relations between workers and managers deteriorated. A new generation of owners and foremen began stressing efficiency and profit margins over community values. They worked employees and machines at a faster pace. In response,

Mill girls

Massachusetts mill workers of the mid–nineteenth century, photographed holding shuttles. Although mill work initially provided women with an opportunity for independence and education, conditions soon deteriorated as profits took precedence.

the women organized strikes to protest deteriorating conditions. In 1834, for instance, they unsuccessfully "turned out" (went on strike) against the mills after learning of a proposed sharp cut in their wages.

INDUSTRIALIZATION AND CITIES The rapid growth of commerce and industry spurred the growth of cities. The creation of cities is perhaps humanity's greatest social innovation. As people gather into ever-larger groups, they share knowledge, mobilize capital and other resources, and forge interdependent networks. The larger a city's population, the greater the likelihood it will foster innovation and wealth. Density fosters growth, and cities attract skilled people and spawn new businesses. American economic development in the first half of the nineteenth century was propelled by the rise of cities.

The census defines *urban* as a place with 8,000 inhabitants or more. Between 1790 and 1860, the proportion of urban to rural populations grew from 3 percent to 16 percent. Because of their strategic locations along rivers flowing into the ocean, the four great Atlantic seaports of New York City, Philadelphia, Baltimore, and Boston remained the largest cities. New Orleans became the nation's fifth-largest city because of its role as a major port shipping goods to the East coast and Europe. New York outpaced all its competitors and the nation as a whole in its population growth. By 1860, it was the first city to reach a population of more than 1 million, largely because of its superior harbor and its unique access to commerce.

Pittsburgh, at the head of the Ohio River, was already a center of iron production by 1800, and Cincinnati, at the mouth of the Little Miami River, soon surpassed all other meatpacking centers. Louisville, because it stood at the falls of the Ohio River, became an important trading center. On the

Milling and the environment

A milldam on the Appomattox River near Petersburg, Virginia, in 1865. Milldams were used to produce a head of water for operating a mill.

Great Lakes the leading cities—Buffalo, Cleveland, Detroit, Chicago, and Milwaukee—also stood at important breaking points in water transportation. Chicago was well located to become a hub of both water and rail transportation, connecting the Northeast, the South, and the trans-Mississippi West. During the 1830s, St. Louis tripled in size mainly because most of the western fur trade was funneled down the Missouri River. By 1860, St. Louis and Chicago were positioned to challenge Baltimore and Boston for third and fourth places.

THE POPULAR CULTURE

During the colonial era, Americans had little time for play or amusement. Most adults worked from dawn to dusk six days a week. By the early nineteenth century, however, a more urban society enjoyed more diverse

Bare Knuckles

Blood sports emerged as popular urban entertainment for men of all social classes.

forms of recreation. Laborers and shopkeepers sought new forms of leisure and entertainment as pleasant diversions from their long workdays.

URBAN RECREATION   Social drinking was pervasive during the first half of the nineteenth century. In 1829 the secretary of war estimated that three quarters of the nation's laborers drank at least four ounces of "hard liquor" daily. This drinking culture cut across all regions, races, and classes. Taverns and social or sporting clubs in the burgeoning cities served as the nexus of recreation and leisure. So-called blood sports were also a popular form of amusement. Cockfighting and dogfighting at saloons attracted excited crowds and frenzied betting. Prizefighting, also known as boxing, eventually displaced the animal contests.

THE PERFORMING ARTS   Theaters were the most popular form of indoor entertainment during the first half of the nineteenth century. People of all classes flocked to opera houses, playhouses, and music halls to watch a wide spectrum of performances: Shakespeare's tragedies, "blood and thunder" melodramas, comedies, minstrel shows, operas, performances by acrobatic troupes, and local pageants. Audiences were predominantly young and middle aged men. "Respectable" women rarely attended; the prevailing "cult of domesticity" kept women in the home.

The 1830s witnessed the emergence of the first uniquely American form of mass entertainment: blackface minstrel shows, featuring white performers made up as blacks. "Minstrelsy" drew upon African American subjects and reinforced prevailing racial stereotypes. It featured banjo and fiddle music, "shuffle" dances, and lowbrow humor. Between the 1830s and the 1870s, minstrel shows were immensely popular, especially among northern working-class ethnic groups and southern whites.

The most popular minstrel songs were written by a young white composer named Stephen Foster. He composed many famous songs like "Oh! Susanna," "Old Folks at Home" (popularly known as "Way Down upon the Swanee River"), "Massa's in de Cold, Cold Ground," "My Old Kentucky Home," and "Old Black Joe," all of which perpetuated the sentimental myth of contented slaves, and none of which used actual African American melodies.

The Crow Quadrilles

This sheet music cover, printed in 1837, shows eight vignettes caricaturing African Americans. Minstrel shows enjoyed nationwide popularity while reinforcing racial stereotypes.

IMMIGRATION

Throughout the nineteenth century, the United States remained a strong magnet for immigrants, offering them chances to take up farming or urban employment. In 1834 an English immigrant reported that America is ideal "for a poor man that is industrious, for he has to want for nothing." After 1837, a worldwide economic slump accelerated the tempo of immigration to the United States. The years from 1845 to 1854 saw the greatest proportional influx of immigrants in U.S. history, 2.4 million, or about 14.5 percent of the total population in 1845. In 1860, America's population was 31 million, with more than one of every eight residents foreign-born. The three largest groups were the Irish (1.6 million), the Germans (1.2 million), and the British (588,000).

THE IRISH What caused so many Irish to flee their homeland in the nineteenth century was the onset of a prolonged depression that brought immense social hardship. After an epidemic of potato rot in 1845, called the Irish potato famine, killed more than 1 million peasants, the flow of Irish immigrants to Canada and the United States became a flood. By 1850 the Irish constituted 43 percent of the foreign-born population of the United States. Unlike the German immigrants, who were predominantly male, a slight majority of the Irish newcomers were women. Most of the Irish arrivals had been tenant farmers, but their rural sufferings left them with little taste for farmwork and little money with which to buy land in America. Great numbers of the men hired on with the construction crews building canals and railways. Others worked in iron foundries, steel mills, warehouses, mines, and shipyards. Many Irish women found jobs as servants, laundresses, or workers in textile mills in New England. In 1845 the Irish constituted only 8 percent of the workforce in the Lowell mills; by 1860, they made up 50 percent. Relatively few immigrants found their way to the South, where land was expensive and industries scarce. The widespread use of slavery also left few opportunities in the region for immigrant laborers.

By the 1850s the Irish made up over half the population of Boston and New York City and were almost as prominent in Philadelphia. They typically crowded into filthy, poorly ventilated tenements, plagued by high rates of crime, infectious disease, prostitution, alcoholism, and infant mortality. The archbishop of New York at mid-century described the Irish as "the poorest and most wretched population that can be found in the world."

But many enterprising Irish immigrants forged remarkable careers. Twenty years after arriving in New York, Alexander T. Stewart became the owner of the nation's largest department store and thereafter accumulated vast real estate holdings in Manhattan. Michael Cudahy, who began work in a Milwaukee meatpacking business at age fourteen, became head of the Cudahy Packing Company and developed a process for the curing of meats under refrigeration. Dublin-born Victor Herbert emerged as one of America's most revered composers, and Irish dancers and playwrights came to dominate the stage. Irishmen were equally successful in the boxing arena and on the baseball diamond.

These accomplishments, however, did little to quell the anti-Irish sentiments prevalent in nineteenth-century America. Irish immigrants confronted demeaning stereotypes and intense anti-Catholic prejudices. Many employers posted "No Irish Need Apply" signs. Irish Americans, however, could be equally contemptuous of other groups, such as free African Americans, who competed with them for low-status jobs. In 1850 the *New York Tribune* expressed concern that the Irish, having themselves escaped from "a galling, degrading bondage" in their homeland, voted against proposals for equal rights for blacks and frequently arrived at the polls shouting, "Down with the Nagurs! Let them go back to Africa, where they belong." For their part, many African Americans viewed the Irish with equal disdain. In 1850 a slave expressed a common sentiment: "My Master is a great tyrant, he treats me badly as if I were a common Irishman."

After becoming citizens, the Irish formed powerful voting blocs. They along with other ethnic groups were drawn mainly to the Democrats, the party of Andrew Jackson. In Jackson the Irish immigrants found a hero. Himself the son of Scots-Irish colonists, he was also popular for having defeated the hated English at New Orleans. In addition, the Irish immigrants' loathing of aristocracy, which they associated with English rule, attracted them to a politician and a party claiming to represent "the common man." In the 1828 election, masses of Irish voters made the difference in the presidential race between Jackson and John Quincy Adams. One newspaper expressed alarm at this new force in politics: "It was emphatically an Irish triumph. The foreigners have carried the day."

Perhaps the greatest collective achievement of the Irish immigrants was stimulating the growth of the Catholic Church in the United States. Years of persecution had instilled in Irish Catholics a fierce loyalty to the doctrines of the church as "the supreme authority over all the affairs of the world." Such passionate attachment to Catholicism generated both community cohesion among Irish Americans and fears of Roman Catholicism among American Protestants. By 1860, Catholicism had become the largest denomination in the United States.

THE GERMANS   A new wave of German immigration peaked in 1854, just a few years after the crest of Irish arrivals, when 215,000 Germans disembarked in U.S. ports. These immigrants included a large number of learned, cultured professional people—doctors, lawyers, teachers, engineers—some of them refugees from the failed German revolution of 1848. In addition to an array of political opinions, the Germans brought with them a variety of religious preferences: most of the new arrivals were Protestants (usually Lutherans), a third were Catholics, and a significant number were Jews or freethinking atheists or agnostics. By the end of the century, some 250,000 German Jews had emigrated to the United States.

Unlike the Irish, more Germans settled in rural areas than in cities, and the influx included many independent farmers, skilled workers, or shop-keepers who arrived with the means to get themselves established on the land or in skilled jobs. More so than the Irish, they migrated in families and groups rather than individually, and this clannish quality helped them better sustain elements of their language and culture in the New World. More of them also tended to return to their native country. About 14 percent of the Germans eventually went back to their homeland, compared with 9 percent of the Irish.

Among the German immigrants who prospered in the New World were Ferdinand Schumacher, who began peddling flaked oatmeal in Ohio and whose business eventually became part of the Quaker Oats Company; Heinrich Steinweg, a piano maker who in America changed his name to Steinway and became famous for the quality of his instruments; and Levi Strauss, a Jewish tailor who followed the gold rushers to California and began making durable work pants that were later dubbed blue jeans, or Levi's. Major centers of German settlement developed in southwestern Illinois and Missouri (around St. Louis), Texas (near San Antonio), Ohio, and Wisconsin (especially around Milwaukee). The larger German communities developed traditions of bounteous food, beer, and music, along with German turnvereins (gymnastic societies), sharpshooter clubs, fire-engine companies, and kindergartens.

THE BRITISH, SCANDINAVIANS, AND CHINESE   British immigrants continued to arrive in the United States in large numbers during the first half of the nineteenth century. They included professionals, independent farmers, and skilled workers. Two other groups that began to arrive in noticeable numbers during the 1840s and 1850s served as the vanguard for greater numbers of their compatriots. Annual arrivals from Scandinavia did not exceed 1,000 until 1843, but by 1860, 72,600 Scandinavians were living in the United States. The Norwegians and Swedes gravitated to Wisconsin and Minnesota, where the climate and woodlands reminded them of home. By the 1850s the rapid development of California was attracting Chinese, who, like the Irish in the East, did the heavy work of construction. Infinitesimal in number until 1854, the Chinese in America numbered 35,500 by 1860.

NATIVISM   Not all Americans welcomed the flood of immigrants. Many "natives" resented the newcomers, with their alien languages and mysterious customs. The flood of Irish and German Catholics aroused Protestant hos-

A Know-Nothing cartoon

This cartoon shows the Catholic Church supposedly attempting to control American religious and political life through Irish immigration.

tility to "popery." A militant Protestantism growing out of the evangelical revivals of the early nineteenth century fueled the anti-Catholic hysteria. There were also fears that German communities were fomenting political radicalism and that the Irish were forming ethnic voting blocs. In 1834 a series of anti-Catholic sermons by Lyman Beecher, a popular Congregationalist minister, incited a mob to attack and burn a Catholic convent in Massachusetts. In 1844 armed clashes between Protestants and Catholics in Philadelphia caused widespread injuries and deaths.

Nativists organized themselves into formal groups to try to thwart the tide of foreign immigrants. The Order of the Star-Spangled Banner, founded in New York City in 1849, grew into a formidable third party known as the American Party. Members pledged never to vote for any foreign-born or Catholic candidate. When asked about the organization, they were to say, "I know nothing." In popular parlance the American Party became the **Know-Nothing party**. For a season, the party appeared to be on the brink of achieving major-party status. In state and local campaigns during 1854, the Know-Nothings carried one election after another. They swept the Massachusetts legislature, winning all but two seats in the lower house. That fall they elected more than forty congressmen. The Know-Nothings demanded the exclusion of immigrants and Catholics from public office and the extension of the period for naturalization (citizenship) from five to twenty-one years, but the American party never gathered the political strength to enact such legislation. Nor did Congress restrict immigration in any way during that period. For a while, the Know-Nothings threatened to control New England, New York, and Maryland and showed strength elsewhere, but the anti-Catholic movement subsided when slavery became the focal issue of the 1850s.

ORGANIZED LABOR

Skilled workers in American cities before and after the Revolution were called artisans, craftsmen, or mechanics. They made or repaired shoes, hats, saddles, ironware, silverware, jewelry, glass, ropes, furniture, tools, weapons, and an array of wooden products, and printers published books, pamphlets, and newspapers. As in medieval guilds, skilled workers in the United States organized themselves by individual trades. These trade associations pressured politicians for tariffs to protect their industries from foreign imports, provided insurance benefits, and drafted regulations to improve working conditions, ensure quality control, and provide equitable treatment of apprentices and journeymen. In addition, they sought to control the total number of tradesmen in their profession so as to maintain wage levels.

The use of slaves as skilled workers also caused controversy among tradesmen. White journeymen in the South objected to competing with enslaved laborers. Other artisans refused to take advantage of slave labor. The Baltimore Carpenters' Society, for example, admitted as members only those employers who refused to use forced labor. During the 1820s and 1830s, artisans who emphasized quality and craftsmanship for a custom trade found it hard to meet the low prices made possible by the new factories and massproduction workshops. At the time few workers belonged to unions, but a growing fear that they were losing status led artisans in the major cities to form unions.

EARLY UNIONS Early labor unions faced serious legal obstacles—they were prosecuted as unlawful conspiracies. In 1806, for instance, Philadelphia shoemakers were found guilty of a "combination to raise their wages." The court's decision broke the union. Such precedents were used for many years to impede labor organizations, until the Massachusetts Supreme Judicial

Court made a landmark ruling in *Commonwealth v. Hunt* (1842). In this case, the court declared that forming a trade union was not in itself illegal, nor was a demand that employers hire only members of the union. The court also declared that workers could strike if an employer hired nonunion laborers.

Until the 1820s labor organizations took the form of local trade unions, confined to one city and one craft. From 1827 to 1837, however, organization on a larger scale began to take hold. In 1834 the National Trades' Union was formed to federate the city societies into a national organization. At the same time, shoemakers, printers, combmakers, carpenters, and handloom weavers established national craft unions, but all the national groups and most of the local ones vanished in the economic collapse of 1837.

LABOR POLITICS   With the widespread removal of property qualifications for voting, working-class politics flourished during the Jacksonian Era, especially in Philadelphia. A Workingmen's party, formed there in 1828, gained the balance of power in the city council that fall. This success inspired other Workingmen's parties in about fifteen states. The Workingmen's parties were broad reformist groups devoted to the interests of labor, but they faded quickly. The inexperience of labor politicians left the parties prey to manipulation by political professionals. In addition, major national parties co-opted some of their issues. Labor parties also proved vulnerable to charges of social radicalism, and the courts typically sided with management.

While the working-class parties elected few candidates, they did succeed in drawing notice to their demands, many of which attracted the support of middle-class reformers. Above all they promoted free public education for all children and the abolition of imprisonment for debt, causes that won widespread popular support. The labor parties and unions also called for a ten-hour workday to prevent employers from abusing workers. In 1836 President Andrew Jackson established the ten-hour workday at the Naval Shipyard in Philadelphia in response to a strike, and in 1840 President Martin Van Buren extended the limit to all government offices and projects. In private jobs the ten-hour workday became increasingly common, although by no means universal, before 1860.

THE REVIVAL OF UNIONS   After the financial panic of 1837, the infant labor movement declined, and unions did not begin to revive until business conditions improved in the early 1840s. Even then unions remained

Symbols of organized labor

A pocket watch with an International Typographical Union insignia.

local and weak. Often they came and went with a single strike. The greatest labor dispute before the Civil War occurred on February 22, 1860, when shoemakers at Lynn and Natick, Massachusetts, walked out after their requests for higher wages were denied. Before the strike ended, it had spread through New England, involving perhaps twenty-five towns and twenty thousand workers. The strike stood out not just for its size but also because the workers won. Most of the employers agreed to wage increases, and some also agreed to recognize the union as a bargaining agent.

By the mid–nineteenth century, the labor union movement was maturing. Workers began to emphasize the importance of union recognition and regular collective-bargaining agreements. They also shared a growing sense of solidarity. In 1852 the National Typographical Union revived the effort to organize skilled crafts on a national scale. Others followed, and by 1860 about twenty such organizations had appeared, although none was yet strong enough to do much more than hold national conventions and pass resolutions.

The Rise of the Professions

The dramatic social changes of the first half of the nineteenth century opened up an array of new professions. Bustling new towns required new services—retail stores, printing shops, post offices, newspapers, schools, banks, law firms, medical practices, and others—that created more high-status jobs than had ever existed before. By definition, professional workers are those who have specialized knowledge and skills that ordinary people lack. To be a professional in Jacksonian America, to be a self-governing individual exercising trained judgment in an open society, was the epitome of the democratic ideal, an ideal that rewarded hard work, ambition, and merit.

The rise of various professions resulted from the rapid expansion of new communities, public schools, and institutions of higher learning; the emergence of a national market economy; and the growing sophistication of American life and society, which was fostered by new technologies. In the process, expertise garnered special prestige. In 1849, Henry Day delivered a lecture titled "The Professions" at the Western Reserve School of Medicine. He declared that the most important social functions in modern life were the professional skills. In fact, Day claimed, American society had become utterly dependent upon "professional services."

TEACHING Teaching was one of the fastest-growing vocations in the antebellum period. Public schools initially preferred men as teachers, usually hiring them at age seventeen or eighteen. The pay was so low that few stayed in the profession their entire career, but for many educated, restless young adults, teaching was a convenient first job that offered independence and stature, as well as an alternative to the rural isolation of farming. Church groups and civic leaders started private academies, or seminaries, for girls. Initially viewed as finishing schools for young women, these institutions soon added courses in the liberal arts: philosophy, music, literature, Latin, and Greek.

LAW, MEDICINE, AND ENGINEERING Teaching was a common stepping-stone for men who became lawyers. In the decades after the Revolution, young men, often hastily or superficially trained, swelled the ranks of the legal profession. They typically would teach for a year or two before clerking for a veteran attorney, who would train them in the law in exchange for their labors. The absence of formal standards for legal training helps explain why there were so many attorneys in the antebellum period. In 1820 eleven of the twenty-three states required no specific length or type of study for aspiring lawyers.

Like attorneys, physicians in the early nineteenth century often had little formal academic training. Healers of every stripe and motivation assumed the title of *doctor* and established a medical practice without regulation. Most of them were self-taught or had learned their profession by assisting a doctor for several years, occasionally supplementing such internships with a few classes at the handful of new medical schools, which in 1817 graduated only 225 students. That same year there were almost ten thousand physicians in the nation. By 1860 there were sixty thousand self-styled physicians, and quackery was abundant. As a result, the medical profession lost its social stature and the public's confidence.

The industrial expansion of the United States during the first half of the nineteenth century spurred the profession of engineering, a field that has since become the single largest professional occupation for men in the United States. Specialized expertise was required for the building of canals and railroads, the development of machine tools and steam engines, and the construction of roads and bridges. Beginning in the 1820s, Americans gained access to technical knowledge in mechanics' institutes, scientific libraries, and special schools that sprouted up across the young nation. By the outbreak of the Civil War, engineering had become one of the largest professions in the nation.

WOMEN'S WORK   Women during the first half of the nineteenth century still worked primarily in the home. The only professions readily available to women were nursing (often midwifery, the delivery of babies) and teaching, both of which were extensions of the domestic roles of health care and child care. Teaching and nursing commanded relatively lower status and pay than did the male-dominated professions.

Many middle-class women spent their time outside the home engaged in religious and benevolent work; they were unstinting volunteers in churches and reform societies. A very few women, however, courageously pursued careers in male-dominated professions. Harriet Hunt of Boston was a teacher who, after nursing her sister through a serious illness, set up shop in 1835 as a self-taught physician and persisted in medical practice although the Harvard Medical School twice rejected her for admission. Elizabeth Blackwell of Ohio managed to gain admission to the Geneva Medical College of Western New York despite the disapproval of the faculty. When she arrived at her first class, "a hush fell upon the class as if each member had been struck with paralysis." Blackwell had the last laugh when she finished first in her class in 1849, but thereafter the medical school refused to admit any more women. Blackwell went on to found the New York Infirmary for Women and Children and later had a long career as a professor of gynecology at the London School of Medicine for Women.

EQUAL OPPORTUNITIES   The dynamic economic environment during the first half of the nineteenth century helped foster the egalitarian idea that individuals should have an equal opportunity to better themselves in the workplace through their own abilities and hard work. In America, observed a journalist in 1844, "one has as good a chance as another according to his talents, prudence, and personal exertions." Egalitarianism, however, is hard to control once it is unleashed and embraced.

The same ideals that excited so many white immigrants to risk all in order to come to the United States began to be equally appealing to those groups that still did not enjoy equal opportunities: African Americans and women. They too began to demand their right to "life, liberty, and the pursuit of happiness."

CHAPTER SUMMARY

- **Transportation and Communication Revolutions** While the cotton culture boomed in the South, with a resultant increase in slavery, commercial agriculture emerged in the West, aided by a demand for corn, wheat, and cattle and by many inventions. The first stages of the Industrial Revolution in the Northeast reshaped the region's economy and led to the explosive growth of cities and factories. The Erie Canal contributed to New York City's status as the nation's economic center and spurred the growth of Chicago and other midwestern cities. The revolution in transportation and communication linked rural communities to a worldwide marketplace.

- **Inventions and the Economy** Inventions in agriculture included the cotton gin, which increased cotton production in the South. Other inventions, such as John Deere's steel plow and Cyrus McCormick's mechanized reaper, helped Americans, especially westerners, farm their land more efficiently and more profitably. Canals and other improvements in transportation allowed goods to reach markets quicker and more cheaply than ever before. The railroads, which expanded rapidly during the 1850s, and the telegraph diminished the isolation of the West and united the country economically and socially.

- **Immigration** The promise of cheap land and good wages drew millions of immigrants to America. Those who arrived in the 1840s came not just from the Protestant regions of Britain and Europe that had supplied most of America's previous immigrants. The devastating potato famine led to an influx of destitute Irish Catholic families. Also, Chinese laborers were drawn to California's goldfields, where nativists objected to their presence because of their poverty and their religion.

- **Workers Organize** The first unions, formed by artisans who feared a loss of status in the face of mechanization, were local and based on individual crafts. An early attempt at a national union collapsed with the panic of 1837. Unions faced serious legal obstacles even after a Massachusetts court ruled in 1842 that the formation of unions was legal. Weak national unions had reappeared by 1860.

CHRONOLOGY

1793	Eli Whitney invents the cotton gin
1794	Philadelphia-Lancaster Turnpike is completed
1795	Wilderness Road opens
1807	*Clermont,* the first successful steamboat, sails to Albany
1825	Erie Canal opens
1831	Cyrus McCormick invents a mechanical reaper
1834	National Trades' Union is organized
1837	John Deere invents the steel plow
1842	Massachusetts Supreme Judicial Court issues *Commonwealth v. Hunt* decision
1845	*Rainbow,* the first clipper ship, is launched
1846	Elias Howe invents the sewing machine
1848	California gold rush begins

KEY TERMS & NAMES

10

NATIONALISM AND SECTIONALISM

FOCUS QUESTIONS

 wwnorton.com/studyspace

- How did economic policies after the War of 1812 reflect the nationalism of the period?
- What characterized the Era of Good Feelings?
- What were the various issues that promoted sectionalism?
- How did the Supreme Court under John Marshall strengthen the federal government and the national economy?
- What were the main diplomatic achievements of these years?

ECONOMIC NATIONALISM

During the early nineteenth century, the United States was a fragile confederation of diverse states wrestling with a fundamental challenge: how to develop a shared sense of nationhood in the face of conflicting regional economic interests and social concerns. After the surprising outcome of the War of 1812, Americans experienced a new surge of patriotic nationalism. Prolonged prosperity after the war fed a widespread sense of well-being and enhanced the prestige of the national government. Ironically, Thomas Jefferson's embargo had spawned the factories and cities that he abhorred, since Americans had to produce for themselves the products they had normally imported from Europe. During the War of 1812 the idea spread that the young agricultural nation needed a more balanced economy of farming, commerce, and manufacturing. Shortages of farm products in war-torn Europe benefited American farmers by raising prices of American exports and stimulating agricultural expansion. Higher prices for farm products generated a wild speculation in farmland. Cotton, tobacco, and rice grown in the southern states came to represent about two thirds of U.S. exports. The South, with its slave-based plantation system, was becoming an agricultural dynamo while New England continued to dominate the commercial and manufacturing sectors. After the War of 1812, however, the American economy was flooded with inexpensive British goods that threatened to undercut the infant manufacturing sector in the United States.

President James Madison, in his first annual message to Congress after the war, promoted a new emphasis on economic nationalism reminiscent of the programs instituted by Alexander Hamilton and George Washington. The president recommended several steps to strengthen the government and the national economy: improved fortifications, a permanent national army and a strong navy, a new national bank, protection of new industries from unfair foreign competition, a federally funded system of roads, bridges, canals, and ports for commercial and military use, and, to top it off, a great national university. Madison's expansive proposals stretched the traditional meaning of Jeffersonian Republicanism. "The Republicans have out-Federalized Federalism," one New Englander remarked. Congress responded by authorizing a standing army of ten thousand and strengthening the navy as well.

THE BANK OF THE UNITED STATES The trinity of ideas promoting postwar economic nationalism—proposals for a second national bank; for tariffs to protect American manufacturers from cheap British imports; and for government-financed roads, canals, and eventually railroads (called internal improvements) inspired the greatest controversies. Issues related to money—the reliability and availability of a uniform currency, the relative value of paper money and "specie" (silver and gold coins), and the structure and regulation of the banking system—often dominated political debates throughout the nineteenth century. After the first national bank expired, in 1811, the country fell into a financial muddle. States began chartering new local banks with little or no regulation, and their banknotes (paper money) flooded the economy with diverse currencies of uncertain value. State banks often issued paper money for loans far in excess of the "hard money" they stored in their vaults. Such loose lending practices led initially to an economic boom but were followed by a dramatic inflation fed by the excess of paper money circulating in the economy. Eventually the value of the excess banknotes plummeted and the bubble would burst, causing first a sharp recession and then a prolonged depression during the late 1830s and 1840s. In sum, the absence of a central national bank had created chronic instability and occasional chaos in the banking sector.

In the face of this growing financial turmoil, President Madison and most of the younger generation of Republicans swallowed their longstanding constitutional reservations about a powerful national bank. In 1816, Congress adopted, over the protest of Old Republicans, a provision for a **second Bank of the United States** (B.U.S.), which would be located in Philadelphia. The B.U.S. could establish branches throughout the states, and its banknotes were accepted in payments to the government. In return for its privileges, the bank had to handle the government's funds without charge, lend the government up to $5 million upon demand, and pay the government a cash bonus of $1.5 million.

The bitter debate over the B.U.S., then and later, helped set the pattern of sectional debates on most other economic issues. Missouri senator Thomas Hart Benton predicted that the currency-short western towns would be at the mercy of a centralized eastern bank in Philadelphia. "They may be devoured by it any moment! They are in the jaws of the monster! A lump of butter in the mouth of a dog! One gulp, one swallow, and all is gone!"

The debate over the B.U.S. was also noteworthy because of the leading roles played by the era's greatest statesmen: **John C. Calhoun** of South Carolina, **Henry Clay** of Kentucky, and **Daniel Webster** of New Hampshire. Calhoun, still in his youthful phase as a war-hawk nationalist, introduced the national bank bill and pushed it through, justifying its constitutionality by citing the congressional power to regulate the currency. Clay, who had long opposed a national bank, reversed himself; he now admitted that circumstances had made one indispensable to the growing American economy. Webster, on the other hand, led the opposition of the New England Federalists, who did not want the nation's banking center moved from Boston to Philadelphia. Later, after he had moved from New Hampshire to Massachusetts, Webster would return to Congress as the champion of a much stronger national government, whereas events would steer Calhoun in the opposite direction, toward a defiant embrace of states' rights.

A PROTECTIVE TARIFF   The shift of investment capital from commerce to manufactures, begun during the embargo of 1807, had accelerated during the war. But new manufacturers needed "protection" from foreign competitors (especially the British) who enjoyed longstanding advantages in productive efficiency and trading networks. American owners of new factories and mills could not offer prices for their products as low as their foreign competitors, who had a generation's head start. After the War of 1812 ended, British manufacturers flooded the American market with low-priced goods, leading American manufacturers and their political representatives to promote federal tariffs (taxes on imports) to "protect" infant American industries from "unfair" foreign competition. New England shippers and southern farmers generally opposed tariffs because they reduced overseas trade and forced consumers to pay higher prices, but in both regions sizable minorities believed that the promotion of new industry by means of tariffs enhanced both local economic interests and the national welfare.

The **Tariff of 1816**, intended more to protect industries against foreign competition than to raise federal revenue, passed easily in Congress. Overall, New England supported the tariff and the South opposed it; the middle Atlantic states and the Old Northwest cast only five negative votes altogether. The minority of southerners who voted for the tariff, led by John C. Calhoun, did so because they hoped that the South itself might become a manufacturing center. South Carolina, for example, was then developing a few textile mills. According to the census of 1810, the southern states had about as many manufacturers as New England. Within a few years, however, New England would move well ahead of the South in manufacturing, and Calhoun would do an about-face and thereafter aggressively opposed tariffs. The tariff would then become a sectional issue, with manufacturers favoring higher tariffs while southern cotton planters and northern shipping interests would favor lower duties—or none at all.

INTERNAL IMPROVEMENTS   The third major economic issue in the first half of the nineteenth century involved federal government support for "internal improvements," which meant the building of roads and canals. In 1803, when Ohio became a state, Congress decreed that 5 percent of the proceeds from land sales in the state would go toward building a National Road from the Atlantic coast into Ohio and beyond as the territory developed. Construction of the National Road began in 1815. Originally called the Cumberland Road, it was the first federally financed interstate roadway. By 1818 it was open from Cumberland, Maryland, to Wheeling, Virginia (now West Virginia), on the Ohio River. By 1838 the road extended all the way to Vandalia, Illinois. By reducing transportation costs and opening up new markets, the National Road and other privately financed turnpikes helped accelerate the commercialization of agriculture.

In 1817, John C. Calhoun put through the House a bill to fund more internal improvements. He believed that western development would help his native South by opening up trading relationships between the two regions. Opposition to federal spending on transportation projects centered in New England and the South, which expected to gain the least from federal projects intended to spur western development. Support for federal spending on internal improvements came largely from the West, which badly needed good roads. On his last day in office, President Madison vetoed the bill. While sympathetic to its purpose, he could not find a provision in the Constitution authorizing such federal expenditures. As a result, internal improvements remained for another hundred years, with few exceptions, the responsibility of states and private enterprise. The federal government did not enter the field on a large scale until passage of the Federal Highways Act of 1916.

THE AMERICAN SYSTEM   The national banking system, protective tariffs, and transportation improvements were all intended to spur the development of what historians have called a "market revolution" that was transforming the young American economy. With each passing year, farmers, merchants, and manufacturers devoted themselves more and more to producing commodities and goods for commercial markets, which often lay far from the sources of production. American capitalism was maturing—rapidly. While many Old Republicans lamented the transition to an increasingly urban-industrial-commercial society, others decided that such democratic capitalism was the wave of the future.

Henry Clay emerged during the first half of the nineteenth century as the foremost spokesman for a cluster of economic initiatives that he came to call the "**American System**." Born and raised in Virginia, Clay became a successful frontier lawyer in Lexington, Kentucky, before launching a political career. Like his foe Andrew Jackson, he was fond of gambling and liquor, and he had a brawling temper that led to several duels. During the 1820s, as Speaker of the House, Clay became the chief proponent of economic nationalism. Prosperity, he insisted, depended upon the federal government's assuming an active role in shaping the economy. He scoffed at the old Jeffersonian fear that an urban-industrial society would necessarily grow corrupt. Clay instead promoted the "market revolution" and the rapid development of the new western states and territories. The American System he championed included several measures: (1) high tariffs to impede the import of European products and thereby "protect" fledgling American industries, (2) higher prices for federal lands, the proceeds of which would be distributed to the states to finance internal improvements that would facilitate the movement of goods to markets, and (3) a strong national bank to regulate the nation's money supply and thereby ensure sustained economic growth.

Clay's American System aroused intense support—and opposition. Some critics argued that higher prices for federal lands would discourage western migration. Others believed that tariffs benefited industrialists at the expense of farmers and the "common" people, who paid higher prices for the goods produced by tariff-protected manufacturers. And many feared that the B.U.S. was potentially a tyrannical force, a central bank so powerful that it could dictate the nation's economic future at the expense of states' rights and individual freedoms. The debates grew in scope and intensity during the first half of the nineteenth century. In the process, they would help aggravate sectional tensions to the breaking point.

"An Era of Good Feelings"

JAMES MONROE   As James Madison approached the end of a turbulent two-term presidency, he, like Thomas Jefferson, turned to a fellow Virginian, another secretary of state, to be his successor. For Madison that man would be **James Monroe**, who went on to win the Republican nomination. In the 1816 election, he overwhelmed his Federalist opponent, Rufus King of New York, with 183 to 34 votes in the Electoral College. The "Virginia dynasty" of presidents continued. Like three of the four presidents before him, Monroe was a Virginia planter, but with a difference: his plantation holdings were much smaller. At the outbreak of the Revolution, he was just beginning his studies at the College of William and Mary. He joined the army at the age of sixteen, fought with Washington during the Revolution, and later studied law with Jefferson.

Monroe had served as a representative in the Virginia assembly, as governor of the state, as a representative in the Confederation Congress, as a U.S. senator, and as U.S. minister (ambassador) in Paris, London, and Madrid. Under Madison he was secretary of state and doubled as secretary of war. Monroe, with his powdered wig, cocked hat, and knee breeches, was the last of the Revolutionary generation to serve in the White House and the last president to dress in the old style.

Firmly grounded in traditional Republican principles, James Monroe failed to keep up with the onrush of the "new nationalism." He accepted as an accomplished fact the B.U.S. and the protective tariff, but during his tenure there was no further extension

James Monroe

Portrayed as he entered the presidency in 1817.

of economic nationalism. Indeed, there was a minor setback: he permitted the National Road to be extended, but in his veto of the 1822 Cumberland Road bill, he denied the authority of Congress to collect tolls to pay for its repair and maintenance. Like Jefferson and Madison, Monroe urged a constitutional amendment to remove all doubt about federal authority in the field of internal improvements.

Monroe surrounded himself with some of the ablest young Republican leaders. John Quincy Adams became secretary of state. William H. Crawford of Georgia continued as secretary of the Treasury. John C. Calhoun headed the War Department after Henry Clay refused the job in order to stay on as Speaker of the House. The new administration found the country in a state of well-being: America was at peace, and the economy was flourishing. Soon after his inauguration, in 1817, Monroe embarked on a goodwill tour of New England. In Boston, a Federalist newspaper commented upon the president's visit under the heading "Era of Good Feelings." The label became a popular catchphrase for Monroe's administration.

In 1820 the president was reelected without opposition. The Federalists were too weak to put up a candidate. The Republican party was dominant— for the moment. In fact, it was about to follow the Federalists into oblivion. Amid the general political contentment of the era, the first political party system was fading away, but rivals for the succession soon began forming new parties.

RELATIONS WITH BRITAIN   Fueling the contentment after the War of 1812 was a growing trade with Britain and its far-flung global empire. The Treaty of Ghent had ended the war but left unsettled a number of minor disputes between the two nations. Subsequently two important treaties, the Rush-Bagot Agreement of 1817 and the Convention of 1818, removed several potential causes of irritation. In the first, resulting from an exchange of letters between Acting Secretary of State Richard Rush and the British minister to the United States, Charles Bagot, the threat of naval competition on the Great Lakes vanished with an arrangement to limit forces there to several U.S. ships collecting customs duties. Although the exchange made no reference to the land boundary between the United States and Canada, its cooperative spirit gave rise to the tradition of an unfortified border between the two North American countries, the longest in the world.

The Convention of 1818 covered three major points. It finally settled the disputed northern limit of the Louisiana Purchase by extending the national boundary along the 49th parallel west from what would become Minnesota to the crest of the Rocky Mountains. West of that point the **Oregon Country** would be open to joint occupation by the British and the Americans, but the boundary remained unsettled.

The chief remaining problem was Britain's exclusion of American ships from the British West Indies in order to reserve that lucrative trade for the British. This remained a chronic irritant, and the United States retaliated with several measures. Under the Navigation Act of 1817, importation of West Indian products was restricted to American vessels or vessels belonging to West Indian merchants. In 1818, U.S. ports were closed to all British vessels arriving from a colony that was legally closed to vessels of the United States. In 1820, Monroe approved an act of Congress that specified total "nonintercourse"—with British vessels, with all British colonies in the Americas, and even with goods taken to England and reexported. The rapprochement with Britain therefore fell short of perfection.

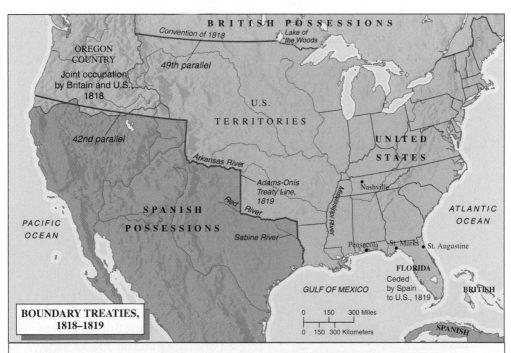

What territorial terms did the Convention of 1818 settle? How did Andrew Jackson's actions in Florida help John Quincy Adams claim the territory from Spain? What were the terms of the treaty with Spain?

THE EXTENSION OF BOUNDARIES The year 1819 was one of the more fateful years in American history. Controversial efforts to expand U.S. territory, an intense financial panic, a tense debate over the extension of slavery, and several landmark Supreme Court cases combined to bring an unsettling end to the Era of Good Feelings. The new spirit of nationalism reached a climax with the acquisition of Florida and the extension of America's southwestern boundary to the Pacific, but nationalism quickly began to run afoul of domestic crosscurrents that would enmesh the nation in sectional squabbles.

Spanish sovereignty over Florida during the early nineteenth century was more a technicality than an actuality. Spain, once dominant in the Americas and the world, was now a declining power, unable to enforce its obligations, under Pinckney's Treaty of 1795, to pacify the Florida frontier. In 1816, U.S. soldiers clashed with a group of escaped slaves who had taken over a British fort on the Apalachicola River in West Florida. Seminole Indians were soon fighting white settlers in the area, and in 1817, Americans burned a Seminole border settlement, killed five of its inhabitants, and dispersed the rest across the border into Florida.

At that point, Secretary of War Calhoun authorized the use of federal troops against the Seminoles, and he summoned General Andrew Jackson from Nashville, Tennessee, to take command. Jackson's orders allowed him to pursue Indians into Spanish territory but not to attack any Spanish posts. A frustrated Jackson pledged to President Monroe that if the United States wanted Florida, he could wind up the whole controversy in sixty days.

When it came to Spaniards or Indians, few white Tennesseans—and certainly not Andrew Jackson—bothered with legal technicalities. In early 1818, without presidential approval, Jackson ordered his force of two thousand federal soldiers, Tennessee volunteers, and Creek allies to cross the border into Spanish Florida from their encampment in south Georgia. In April the Americans assaulted a Spanish fort at St. Marks and destroyed Seminole villages. They also captured and court-martialed two Indian chiefs and two British traders accused of inciting Indian attacks. Jackson ordered their immediate execution, an act that outraged the British government and caused great consternation among President Monroe's cabinet. But

Unrest in Florida

Portrait of an escaped slave who lived with the Seminoles in Florida.

the Tennessee general kept moving. In May he captured Pensacola, the Spanish capital of West Florida, established a provisional American government, and then returned to Tennessee.

Jackson's exploits excited American expansionists and aroused anger in Spain and concern in Washington, D.C. Spain demanded the return of its territory and the punishment of Jackson, but Spain's impotence was plain for all to see. Monroe's cabinet was at first prepared to disavow Jackson's actions, especially his direct attack on Spanish posts. Secretary of War Calhoun was inclined, at least officially, to discipline Jackson for disregard of orders—a stand that would later cause bad blood between the two men—but privately confessed a certain pleasure at Jackson's expedition. In any case a man as popular as General Jackson was almost invulnerable. And he had one important friend, Secretary of State John Quincy Adams, who realized that Jackson's conquest of West Florida had strengthened his own hand in negotiations under way with the Spanish minister to purchase the territory. U.S. forces withdrew from Florida, but negotiations resumed with the knowledge that the United States could retake Florida at any time.

With the fate of Florida a foregone conclusion, John Quincy Adams turned his eye to a larger goal, a precise definition of the ambiguous western boundary of the Louisiana Purchase and—his boldest stroke—extension of its boundary to the Pacific coast. In lengthy negotiations with Spain, Adams gradually gave ground on claims to Texas but stuck to his demand for a transcontinental line for the Louisiana Territory, extending that boundary to the Pacific Ocean. In 1819 he convinced the Spanish to sign the Transcontinental Treaty (also called the Adams-Onís Treaty), which gave all of Florida to the United States in return for a cash settlement. In addition, the treaty specified that the western boundary of the Louisiana Purchase would run along the Sabine River and then, in stair-step fashion, up to the Red River, along the Red, and up to the Arkansas River. From the source of the Arkansas, it would go north to the 42nd parallel and thence west to the Pacific coast. Florida became a U.S. territory, and its first governor, albeit briefly, was Andrew Jackson. In 1845, Florida would achieve statehood.

CRISES AND COMPROMISES

The so-called Era of Good Feelings did not last long. At the end of the nineteenth century's second decade, the young American republic began to experience turbulence at home and abroad that would transform political life by creating two new national parties.

THE PANIC OF 1819   John Quincy Adams's Transcontinental Treaty of 1819 was a diplomatic triumph and the climactic event of the postwar nationalism. Even before it was signed, however, two thunderclaps signaled the end of the brief Era of Good Feelings and gave warning of stormy weather ahead: the financial **panic of 1819** and the controversy over Missouri statehood. The occasion for the panic was the sudden collapse of cotton prices after British textile mills spurned high-priced American cotton in favor of cheaper cotton from other parts of the world. The collapse of cotton prices reduced the demand for other American goods.

New American factory owners struggled to find markets for their goods and to fend off more experienced foreign competitors. Even the Tariff of 1816 had not been high enough to eliminate British competition. Moreover, businessmen, farmers, and land speculators had recklessly borrowed money to fuel their entrepreneurial schemes. In many cases, land speculators had purchased large tracts, paying only a fourth down, and then sold the parcels to settlers with the understanding that they would pay the remaining installments. With the collapse of crop prices and the decline of land values during and after 1819, both speculators and settlers saw their income plummet.

The reckless practices of the mushrooming state banks compounded the economic turbulence. To generate more loans, the state banks issued more paper money. Even the second Bank of the United States, which was supposed to bring stability to the chaotic financial arena, got caught up in the easy-credit mania. Its first president yielded to the contagion of the get-rich-quick fever that was sweeping the country. The proliferation of branches, combined with little supervision by the central bank, carried the national bank into the same reckless extension of loans that state banks had pursued. In 1819, just as alert businessmen began to take alarm, newspapers revealed a case of extensive fraud and embezzlement in the Baltimore branch of the Bank of the United States. The disclosure prompted the appointment of Langdon Cheves, a former congressman from South Carolina, as the new president of the B.U.S.

Cheves reduced salaries and other costs, postponed the payment of dividends, cut back on the volume of loans, and presented for redemption the state banknotes that came in, thereby forcing the state-chartered banks to keep specie reserves. Cheves rescued the bank from near ruin, but only by putting pressure on the state banks. State banks in turn put pressure on their debtors, who found it harder to renew old loans or get new ones. Hard times lasted about three years, and many people blamed the B.U.S. for the slowdown. After the panic passed, resentment of the national bank lingered in the South and the West.

THE MISSOURI COMPROMISE Just as the financial panic spread over the country, another cloud appeared on the horizon: the onset of a fierce sectional controversy over efforts to expand slavery into the new western territories. By 1819 the country had an equal number of slave and free states—eleven of each. The line between them was defined by the southern and western boundaries of Pennsylvania and the Ohio River. Although slavery lingered in some places north of the line, it was on its way to extinction there. In the vast region west of the Mississippi River, however, no move had been made to extend the dividing line across the Louisiana Territory, where slavery had existed since the days when France and Spain had colonized the area. At the time, the Missouri Territory encompassed all of the Louisiana Purchase except the state of Louisiana and the Arkansas Territory. The old French town of St. Louis became the funnel through which settlers, largely southerners who brought their slaves with them, rushed westward beyond the Mississippi River.

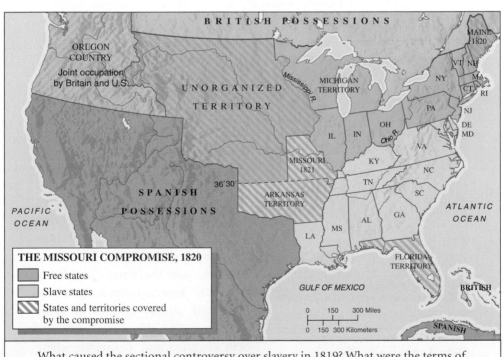

THE MISSOURI COMPROMISE, 1820

- Free states
- Slave states
- States and territories covered by the compromise

What caused the sectional controversy over slavery in 1819? What were the terms of the Missouri Compromise? What was Henry Clay's solution to the Missouri constitution's ban on free blacks in that state?

In 1819 the House of Representatives was asked to approve legislation enabling the Missouri Territory to draft a state constitution and apply for statehood, its population having passed the minimum of sixty thousand white settlers. At that point, Representative James Tallmadge Jr., a New York congressman, electrified the proceedings by proposing a controversial resolution prohibiting the transport of more slaves into Missouri. Tallmadge's resolution infuriated southern slaveowners, many of whom had developed a profitable trade selling slaves to be taken out west. Any effort to restrict slavery in the western territories, southern congressmen threatened, could lead to civil war. After fiery debates, the House passed the Tallmadge Amendment on an almost strictly sectional vote. The Senate rejected it by a similar tally.

The coincidental application for statehood by Maine, which had been part of Massachusetts since colonial times, made it easier to arrive at a compromise agreement. The Senate decided to link Maine's request for separate statehood with Missouri's and voted to admit Maine as a free state and Missouri as a slave state, thus maintaining the balance between free and slave states in the Senate. A senator from Illinois, Jesse Thomas, further extended the so-called **Missouri Compromise** by an amendment to exclude slavery in all of the rest of the Louisiana Purchase north of latitude **36°30'**, Missouri's southern border. Slavery thus would continue in the Arkansas Territory and in the new state of Missouri but would be excluded from the remainder of the vast area west of the Mississippi River. By a very close vote the Thomas Amendment passed the House on March 2, 1820.

Henry Clay

Clay entered the Senate at twenty-eight, despite the requirement that senators be at least thirty years old.

Then another problem arose. The pro-slavery faction that dominated Missouri's constitutional convention inserted in the proposed state constitution a proviso excluding free blacks and mulattoes from the state. This clearly violated the federal Constitution. Free blacks were already citizens of many states, including the slave states of North Carolina and Tennessee, where until the mid-1830s they also enjoyed voting privileges.

The renewed controversy threatened to unravel the deal to admit Missouri as a state until Henry Clay formulated a "second" Missouri Compromise whereby Missouri's admission as a state would depend upon assurance from the Missouri legislature that it would never deny free blacks their constitutional rights. It was one of the more artless dodges in American history, for it required the legislature to affirm that the state constitution did not mean what it clearly said, yet the compromise worked. The Missouri legislature duly adopted the pledge while denying that the legislature had any power to bind the people of the state to it. On August 10, 1821, President Monroe proclaimed the admission of Missouri as the twenty-fourth state. For the moment the sectional controversy had subsided. "But this momentous question," Thomas Jefferson wrote to a friend after the first compromise, "like a firebell in the night awakened and filled me with terror. I considered it at once as the knell of the Union."

JUDICIAL NATIONALISM

JOHN MARSHALL, CHIEF JUSTICE Meanwhile, the spirit of nationalism still flourished in the Supreme Court, where Chief Justice John Marshall preserved Hamiltonian Federalism for yet another generation, establishing the power of the Supreme Court by his force of mind and crystalline logic. During Marshall's early years on the Court (he served thirty-four years altogether), he affirmed that the Supreme Court had the authority (and responsibility) to assess the constitutionality of state and federal legislative actions (called judicial review). In *Marbury v. Madison* (1803) and *Fletcher v. Peck* (1810), the Court struck down first a federal law and then a state law as unconstitutional. In the cases of *Martin v. Hunter's Lessee* (1816) and *Cohens v. Virginia* (1821), the Court assumed the right to consider appeals from state courts on the grounds that the Constitution, the laws, and the treaties of the United States could remain the supreme law of the land only if the Court could review the decisions of state courts. Justice Marshall was a consistent nationalist. He viewed Thomas Jefferson and his Republican followers in Virginia as a dangerous threat to the new nation because they preferred states' rights over federal authority. During the Madison and Monroe administrations, Marshall sustained his judicial offensive against the "powerful and violent party in Virginia" whose goal was to "convert our government into a mere league of states."

John Marshall

Chief justice and pillar of judicial nationalism.

PROTECTING CONTRACT RIGHTS

In the fateful year of 1819, John Marshall and the Supreme Court made two more major decisions that limited the powers of states and strengthened the power of the federal government. One of them, *Dartmouth College v. Woodward,* involved an attempt by the New Hampshire legislature to alter a provision in Dartmouth College's charter, under which the college's trustees became a self-perpetuating board. In 1816 the state's Republican legislature, offended by this relic of monarchy and even more by the Federalist majority on the board, placed Dartmouth College under a new board of trustees named by the governor. The college's original group of trustees sued to block the move. Their effort lost in the state courts but, with Daniel Webster as counsel, won on appeal to the Supreme Court. The college's original charter, John Marshall said in drafting the Court's opinion, was a valid contract that the state legislature had impaired, an act forbidden by the Constitution. This decision implied a new and enlarged definition of *contract* that seemed to put private corporations beyond the reach of the states that had chartered them. Thereafter states commonly wrote into the charters incorporating businesses and other organizations provisions making them subject to modification. Such provisions were then part of the "contract."

STRENGTHENING THE FEDERAL GOVERNMENT

The second major Supreme Court case of 1819 was John Marshall's single most important interpretation of the constitutional system: *McCulloch v. Maryland.* James McCulloch, a clerk in the Baltimore branch of the Bank of the United States, had failed to affix state revenue stamps to banknotes (paper money) as required by a Maryland law taxing the notes. Indicted by the state, McCulloch, acting for the bank, appealed to the Supreme Court, which handed down a unanimous judgment upholding the power of Congress to charter the B.U.S. and denying the state's right to tax it. In a lengthy opinion, Marshall said that Maryland's effort to tax the national bank conflicted with the supreme law of the land. One great principle that "entirely pervades the Constitution," Marshall wrote, is "that the Constitution and the laws made in pursuance thereof are supreme: . . . they control the Constitution and laws of the respective states, and cannot be controlled by them." The effort by a state to tax a federal bank therefore was unconstitutional, for the "power to tax involves the power to destroy"—which was precisely what the legislatures of Maryland and several other states had in mind with respect to the national bank.

REGULATING INTERSTATE COMMERCE John Marshall's last great judicial decision, *Gibbons v. Ogden* (1824), established the federal government's supremacy in regulating interstate commerce. In 1808, Robert Fulton and Robert R. Livingston, who pioneered commercial use of the steamboat, won from the New York legislature the exclusive right to operate steamboats on the state's rivers and lakes. Fulton and Livingston then gave Aaron Ogden the exclusive right to navigate the Hudson River between New York and New Jersey. Thomas Gibbons, however, operated ships under a federal license that competed with Ogden. On behalf of a unanimous Court, Marshall ruled that the monopoly granted by the state to Ogden conflicted with the constitutional authority of the federal government to regulate *interstate* commerce. An elderly Thomas Jefferson cringed at the judicial nationalism practiced by John Marshall. The Court's ruling in the *Gibbons* case, the eighty-two-year-old former president said, culminated the "rapid strides with which the Federal branch of our Government is advancing towards the usurpation of all the rights reserved to the States, and the consolidation in itself of all powers, foreign and domestic."

Nationalist Diplomacy

THE DISPUTED NORTHWEST In foreign affairs, too, nationalism prevailed during the early nineteenth century. A few years after Secretary of State John Quincy Adams negotiated the Transcontinental Treaty with Spain, he settled another important transcontinental boundary dispute. In 1821 the Russian czar tried to claim control of territory along the northwest Pacific coast, which in the American view lay within the Oregon Country. In 1823, Adams contested "the right of Russia to any territorial establishment on this continent." The U.S. government, he informed the Russians, assumed "that the American continents are no longer subjects for any new European colonial establishments." His protest resulted in a treaty signed in 1824, whereby Russia, which had more pressing concerns in Europe, accepted the line of 54°40′ as the southern boundary of its claim. In 1825 a similar agreement between Russia and Britain gave the Oregon Country clearly defined boundaries, although it was still subject to joint occupation by the United States and Great Britain under their agreement of 1818. In 1827 both countries agreed to extend indefinitely the provision for joint occupation of the Oregon region, subject to termination by either power.

THE MONROE DOCTRINE   Perhaps the most important diplomatic policy crafted by President Monroe and Secretary of State Adams involved their effort to end European involvement in the Western Hemisphere. One consequence of the Napoleonic Wars raging across Europe and the French occupation of Spain and Portugal was a series of wars of liberation in colonial Latin America. Within little more than a decade after the flag of rebellion was first raised in 1811, Spain had lost almost its entire empire in the Americas. All that was left were the islands of Cuba and Puerto Rico and the colony of Santo Domingo on the island of Hispaniola.

In 1823, rumors emerged that France wanted to take control of the remnants of Spain's empire in the Americas. The British foreign minister, George Canning, told the U.S. that the two countries should jointly oppose any new incursions by France or Spain in the Western Hemisphere. Monroe initially agreed with the British proposal. Secretary of State Adams, however, urged the president to go it alone and proclaim a unilateral policy prohibiting European involvement in the hemisphere. Adams knew that, as a practical matter, the British navy would stop any aggressive action by European powers in Latin America. The British, moreover, wanted the United States to agree not to acquire any more Spanish territory, including Cuba, Texas, and California, but Adams preferred to avoid such a commitment.

President Monroe incorporated the substance of Adams's views into his annual message to Congress in 1823. The **Monroe Doctrine**, as it was later called, comprised four major points: (1) that "the American continents . . . are henceforth not to be considered as subjects for future colonization by any European powers"; (2) that the political system of European powers was different from that of the United States, which would "consider any attempt on their part to extend their system to any portion of this hemisphere as dangerous to our peace and safety"; (3) that the United States would not interfere with existing European-controlled colonies; and (4) that the United States would keep out of the internal affairs of European nations and their wars.

The Monroe Doctrine became one of the cherished principles of American foreign policy, but for the time being it slipped into obscurity for want of any occasion to invoke it. The doctrine had no standing in international law. It was merely a statement of intent sent by an American president to Congress and did not even draw enough interest at the time for European powers to acknowledge it. Symbolically, however, the Monroe Doctrine was an important statement of American intentions and an important example of the young nation's determination to join the world's great powers.

ONE-PARTY POLITICS

Almost from the start of James Monroe's second term, in 1821, the jockeying for the presidential succession began. Three members of Monroe's cabinet were active candidates: Secretary of War John C. Calhoun, Secretary of the Treasury William H. Crawford, and Secretary of State John Quincy Adams. Speaker of the House Henry Clay also hungered for the office. And on the fringes of the Washington scene, a new force appeared in the person of former general Andrew Jackson, the scourge of the British, Spanish, Creeks, and Seminoles. Although a celebrated military hero, Jackson had only recently entered the national political scene, having been chosen a U.S. Senator from Tennessee in 1823. All of the presidential candidates in 1824 were Republicans, for no Federalist stood a chance. But the Republican presidential contenders were competing in a new political world, one complicated by the crosscurrents of nationalism and sectionalism. With only one viable national party there was in effect no party, for there existed no generally accepted method for choosing a presidential candidate.

PRESIDENTIAL NOMINATIONS The tradition of selecting presidential candidates by congressional caucus, already under attack in 1816, had disappeared in the wave of unanimity that reelected James Monroe in 1820 without the formality of a nomination. In 1822 there was a rash of presidential endorsements by state legislatures and public meetings. In 1822, for instance, the Tennessee legislature named Andrew Jackson as their choice to succeed Monroe. In 1824 a mass meeting of Pennsylvanians also endorsed Jackson for president and John C. Calhoun for vice president. Meanwhile, the Kentucky legislature had nominated its favorite son, Henry Clay, in 1822. The Massachusetts legislature nominated John Quincy Adams in 1824. That same year, a group of states' rights Republican Congressmen nominated William Crawford of Georgia.

Of the four candidates, only two had clearly defined platforms, and the outcome was an early lesson in the danger of committing oneself on the issues too soon. Crawford's friends emphasized his devotion to states' rights and strict construction of the Constitution. Clay, on the other hand, championed his vision of the "American System" of economic nationalism: a national bank, a protective federal tariff designed to make imported European goods so expensive so that Americans would buy relatively cheap American-made goods, high prices for federal land sales, and a program of federally funded internal improvements to bind the country together and strengthen its economy. Adams was close to Clay, openly dedicated to the national government providing internal improvements to stimulate economic development but less strongly committed to the tariff. Jackson, where issues were concerned, carefully avoided commitment so as to capitalize on his popularity as the hero of the Battle of New Orleans at the end of the War of 1812. Thomas Jefferson viewed Jackson's candidacy with horror: "He is one of the most unfit men I know."

THE "CORRUPT BARGAIN" The result of the 1824 election was inconclusive. In the Electoral College, Jackson had 99 votes, Adams 84, Crawford 41, Clay 37. In the popular vote the trend ran about the same: Jackson, 154,000; Adams, 109,000; Crawford, 47,000; and Clay, 47,000. Whatever else might have been said about the outcome, one thing seemed apparent—it was a defeat for Clay's American System promoting national economic development: New England and New York opposed his call for the federal funding of internal improvements; the South and the Southwest rejected his promotion of the protective tariff. Sectionalism had defeated nationalism.

Yet Clay, the dynamic advocate of economic nationalism and Speaker of the House, now assumed the role of president maker, as the deadlocked election was thrown into the House of Representatives, where the Speaker's influence was decisive. Clay disdained all three of the other candidates, but he had little trouble choosing, since he regarded Jackson as a "military chieftain" unfit for the office. Clay disliked Adams, and vice versa, but Adams supported the high tariffs, internal transportation improvements, and strong national bank that comprised Clay's American System. Clay also expected Adams to name him secretary of state. What many thereafter called the "corrupt bargain" between Clay and Adams broke the impasse. Clay endorsed Adams, and the House of Representatives elected Adams with 13 state delegation votes to Jackson's 7 and Crawford's 4.

It was a costly victory, for the result united Adams's foes and crippled his administration before it got under way. Andrew Jackson dismissed Henry Clay as a "scoundrel," the "Judas of the West," who had entered into a selfishly **"corrupt bargain"** whereby Adams gained the presidency and then named Clay his secretary of state. Adams's Puritan conscience could never quite overcome a sense of guilt at the maneuverings that were necessary to gain his election. Likewise, Clay would never live down Jackson's claim that he had sold his vote to make Adams president. Jackson supporters launched a campaign to elect him president in 1828 almost immediately after the 1824 decision. Crawford's supporters, including Martin Van Buren, "the Little Magician" of New York politics, soon moved into the Jackson camp. So, too, did the new vice president, John C. Calhoun, of South Carolina, who had run on the ticket with both Adams and Jackson but favored the general from Tennessee.

JOHN QUINCY ADAMS Short, plump, peppery **John Quincy Adams** was one of the ablest men, hardest workers, and finest intellects ever to enter the White House. Yet he also was one of the most ineffective presidents. Like his father, the aristocratic Adams lacked the common touch and the politician's gift for compromise. A stubborn, snobbish man who saw two brothers and two sons die from alcoholism, he suffered from chronic bouts of depression that reinforced his grim self-righteousness and self-pity, qualities that did not endear him to fellow politicians. He acknowledged the "defects" in his character, but admitted that he could not change his ways. His idealism also irritated the party faithful. He refused to play the game of partisan political patronage. In four years he removed only twelve officeholders.

Adams's first message to Congress included a grandiose blueprint for national development, set forth in such a blunt way that it became a disaster of political ineptitude. In the boldness and magnitude of its conception, his vision of an expanded federal government outdid the plans of Alexander Hamilton, James Monroe, and Henry Clay. The federal government, the new president stressed, should promote internal improvements (roads, canals, harbors, and bridges), create a national university, finance scientific explorations, build astronomical observatories, and create a department of the interior to manage the vast federal lands. To refrain from using broad federal powers, Adams insisted, "would be treachery to the most sacred of trusts."

The merits of Adams's bold message to Congress were obscured by an unhappy choice of language. For the son of John Adams to praise the example "of the nations of Europe and of their rulers" was downright suicidal. With one fell swoop, he had revived all the Republican suspicions of the Adamses as closet monarchists and

John Quincy Adams

Adams was a brilliant man but an ineffective leader.

provoked the emergence of a new party system. The minority who cast their lot with the economic nationalism of Adams and Clay were turning into National Republicans; the opposition, the growing party of those supporting Andrew Jackson, now called themselves the Democratic Republicans; they would eventually drop the name Republican and become Democrats.

Adams's headstrong plunge into nationalism and his refusal to play the game of backroom politics condemned his administration to utter frustration. Congress ignored his ambitious domestic proposals, and in foreign affairs the triumphs that he had scored as secretary of state had no sequels. The climactic effort of Adams's opponents to discredit him centered on the tariff issue. The panic of 1819 had elicited calls in 1820 for a higher tariff, but the effort failed by one vote in the Senate. In 1824 the tariff advocates renewed the effort, with greater success. The Tariff of 1824 favored the middle Atlantic and New England manufacturers by raising duties on imported woolens, cotton, iron, and other finished goods. Clay's Kentucky won a tariff on hemp (a fibrous plant used to make rope and twine).

When the tariff bill passed, in May 1828, John C. Calhoun's reversed his position from twelve years before and spoke out in strident opposition to the new tariff. To express his disgust, he wrote the *South Carolina Exposition and Protest* (1828), which was published anonymously along with a series of resolutions by the South Carolina legislature. In that document, Calhoun declared that a state could nullify an act of Congress—in this case the new tariff bill—that it found unconstitutional.

THE ELECTION OF ANDREW JACKSON   Thus the stage was set for the ferocious election of 1828, which might more truly than that of 1800 be called a political revolution. Both sides in the campaign reached depths of partisan viciousness that had not been plumbed since 1800. Those campaigning for a second term for Adams denounced Jackson as a hot-tempered, ignorant barbarian, an eager participant in numerous duels and frontier brawls, a man whose fame rested upon his reputation as a killer. In addition, his enemies dredged up the story that Jackson had lived in adultery with his wife, Rachel, before they were legally married. In fact, they had lived together for two years in the mistaken belief that the divorce from her former husband was final. As soon as the divorce was official, Andrew and Rachel had remarried. A furious Jackson blamed Henry Clay for the campaign slurs against his wife. He bitterly dismissed his longtime enemy as "the basest, meanest scoundrel that ever disgraced the image of his god."

The Jacksonians, however, got in their licks against Adams, condemning him as a man who had lived his adult life on the public treasury, who had been corrupted by foreigners in the courts of Europe, and who had allegedly delivered up an American girl to serve the lust of Czar Alexander I while serving as minister to Russia. They stressed that Adams despised the common people and that he had gained the presidency in 1824 by a "corrupt bargain" with Henry Clay.

In the 1828 presidential campaign, Jackson held most of the advantages. As a military hero and a fabled Indian fighter, he was beloved in the frontier states. As a planter, lawyer, and slaveholder, he had the trust of the southern elite. Debtors and local bankers who hated the national bank also embraced Jackson. He also benefited from a growing spirit of democracy in which many voters were no longer satisfied to look to their betters for leadership, as they had done in the eighteenth century. It had become politically fatal to be labeled an aristocrat, and John Quincy Adams had struck many voters as an elitist.

After the Revolution and especially after 1800, more and more white men were gaining the right to vote. The traditional story is that a surge of "Jacksonian Democracy" came out of the West like a great wave, supported mainly by small farmers, leading the way for the East. But in the older seaboard states there were other forces enabling more men to vote: the Revolutionary doctrine of social and political equality spawned during the Revolutionary War and the feeling on the part of the urban workers, artisans, and small merchants, as well as small farmers and landed gentry, that broader voting rights provided a means to combat the traditional power exercised by the economic and social elites. From the beginning, Pennsylvania in 1776 had opened the ballot box to all adult males (black or white) who paid taxes. Vermont, in 1791, became the first state with universal manhood suffrage, having first adopted it in 1777. Kentucky, admitted to the Union in 1792, became the second. Tennessee, admitted in 1796, had only a modest taxpaying qualification for voting. New Jersey in 1807 and Maryland and South Carolina in 1810 abolished property and taxpaying requirements for voting, and after 1815 the new states of the West came into the Union with either white manhood suffrage or a low taxpaying requirement. Connecticut in 1818, Massachusetts in 1821, and New York in 1821 abolished their property requirements for voting.

The democratization of voting also affected many free black males in northern states, half of which provided voting rights for blacks. Rufus King, a member of the New York delegation to the Constitutional Convention in 1787, declared that in New York, "a citizen of color was entitled to all the privileges of a citizen. . . . [and] entitled to vote."

Along with the broadening of male suffrage during the late eighteenth and early nineteenth centuries went a liberalization of other features of

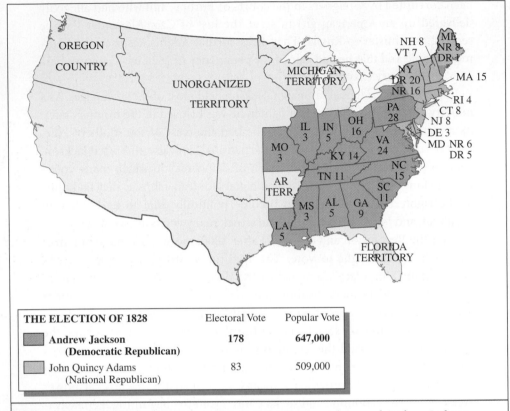

THE ELECTION OF 1828	Electoral Vote	Popular Vote
Andrew Jackson (Democratic Republican)	178	647,000
John Quincy Adams (National Republican)	83	509,000

How did the two presidential candidates, John Quincy Adams and Andrew Jackson, portray each other? Why did Jackson seem to have the advantage in the election of 1828? How did the broadening of suffrage affect the presidential campaign?

government. Representation at local, state, and federal levels was reapportioned more nearly in line with the population. An increasing number of officials, even judges, were chosen by popular vote rather than appointment. By 1828 the popular vote prevailed in all but South Carolina and Delaware and by 1832 in all but South Carolina.

The extension of voting rights to people with little or no wealth helped bring a new type of politician to the fore: the man who had special appeal to the masses or knew how to organize the people for political purposes and who became a vocal advocate of the people's right to rule. Andrew Jackson fit perfectly the ideal of this more democratic political world, a rustic leader sprung from the people rather than a member of the social elite, a frontiersman of humble origin who had scrambled up the political ladder by will and tenacity. "Adams can write," went one of the campaign slogans, "but Jackson can fight." He could write, too, but he once said that he had no respect for a man who could think of only one way to spell a word.

When the 1828 election returns came in, Jackson had won by a comfortable margin. The electoral vote was 178 to 83, and the popular vote was about 647,000 to 509,000 (the figures vary). Adams had won New Jersey, Delaware, all of New England (except 1 of Maine's 9 electoral votes), 16 of the 36 from New York, and 6 of the 11 from Maryland. All the rest belonged to Jackson. The new president, the first to come from the west, was still seething with resentment at the way his opponents had besmirched the reputation of his deceased wife. He relished the chance to launch a new era in American political development.

CHAPTER SUMMARY

- **Economic Policies** The Tariff of 1816 protected American manufacturing, and the second Bank of the United States provided a stronger currency, thus strengthening the national economy. Henry Clay's American System anticipated an active economic role for the federal government with its vision of a national bank, a protective tariff, and federally funded internal improvements, such as roads and canals.

- **Era of Good Feelings** James Monroe's term in office was initially dubbed the Era of Good Feelings because it began with peace and prosperity. The demise of the Federalists ended the first party system in America, leaving the Republicans as the only political party in the nation. The seeming unity of the Republicans was shattered by the election of 1824, which Andrew Jackson lost as a result of what he believed was a "corrupt bargain" between John Quincy Adams and Henry Clay.

- **Sectionalism** The growth of the cotton culture transformed life in the South, in part by encouraging the expansion of slavery. As settlers streamed west, the extension of slavery into the new territories became the predominant concern of southern politicians. The Missouri Compromise, a short-term solution, exposed the emotions and turmoil that the problem generated. During this time, the North changed as well, as an urban middle class emerged.

- **Strengthening the Federal Government** Led by John Marshall, the Supreme Court used the "necessary and proper" clause to endorse the exercise of implied constitutional powers of the federal government. In striking down a federal law and a state law, the Court confirmed the primacy of the national judiciary. Further decisions of the Marshall court protected contract rights against state action and established the federal government's supremacy over interstate commerce.

- **The Monroe Doctrine** The main diplomatic achievements of the period between the end of the War of 1812 and the coming civil war concerned America's boundaries and the resumption of trade with its old enemy, Great Britain. The Monroe Doctrine expressed the idea that the Americas were no longer open to colonization and proclaimed American neutrality in European affairs.

CHRONOLOGY

1810	Supreme Court issues *Fletcher v. Peck* decision
1815	Construction of the National Road begins
1816	Second Bank of the United States is established
	First protective tariff goes into effect
1819	Supreme Court issues *McCulloch v. Maryland* decision
	United States and Spain agree to the Transcontinental (Adams-Onís) Treaty
	Tallmadge Amendment
1821	Florida becomes a territory
	Missouri becomes a state
1823	President Monroe enunciates the principles of the Monroe Doctrine
1824	Supreme Court issues *Gibbons v. Ogden* decision
	John Quincy Adams wins the presidential election by what some critics claim is a "corrupt bargain" with Henry Clay
1828	John C. Calhoun publishes the *South Carolina Exposition and Protest*
	Andrew Jackson wins presidential election

KEY TERMS & NAMES

second Bank of the United States p. 306

John C. Calhoun p. 306

Henry Clay p. 306

Daniel Webster p. 306

Tariff of 1816 p. 307

American System p. 308

James Monroe p. 309

Oregon Country p. 311

panic of 1819 p. 314

Missouri Compromise p. 316

36°30' p. 316

Monroe Doctrine p. 320

"corrupt bargain" p. 322

John Quincy Adams p. 323

11

THE JACKSONIAN ERA

FOCUS QUESTIONS

 wwnorton.com/studyspace

- To what extent did Andrew Jackson's election in 1828 initiate a new era in American politics?
- What was Jackson's attitude toward federal involvement in the economy?
- How did Jackson respond to the nullification controversy?
- What happened to the Indians living east of the Mississippi River by 1840?
- Why did a new party system of Democrats and Whigs emerge?

In his extraordinary novel *Moby-Dick* (1851), Herman Melville celebrated the "democratic dignity" of ordinary men. After all, he wrote, it was the "great democratic God" who picked "up Andrew Jackson from the pebbles; who didst hurl him upon a warhorse; who didst thunder him higher than a throne!" Jackson did indeed take the nation by storm. His distinctive personality and invincible popularity initiated a new era in American politics and social development. No political figure was so widely loved nor more deeply hated.

As a self-made soldier, politician, and slave-owning land speculator from the backcountry, he symbolized the changing social scene and the emergence of the "common man" in political life. The nation he prepared to govern was vastly different from that led by George Washington and Thomas Jefferson. In 1828 the United States boasted twenty-four states and nearly 13 million people, many of them recent arrivals from Germany and Ireland. The national population was growing at a phenomenal rate, doubling every twenty-three years. A surge in foreign demand for southern cotton and other American goods, along with substantial British investment in an array of new American enterprises, helped fuel an economic boom and a transportation revolution. That President-elect Jackson rode to his inauguration in a horse-drawn carriage and left Washington eight years later on a train symbolized the dramatic changes occurring in the pace and tone of American life.

The Jacksonians sought to expand economic opportunity and political participation. Yet to call the Jacksonian era the "age of the common man," as many historians have done over the years, is misleading. While political participation increased, most of the common people remained *common* people. The period never produced true economic and social equality. Power and privilege, for the most part, remained in the hands of an "uncommon" elite of powerful men. Jacksonians in power often proved to be as opportunistic and manipulative as the patricians they displaced. And they never embraced the principle of economic equality. "Distinctions in society will always exist under every just government," Andrew Jackson observed. "Equality of talents, or education, or of wealth cannot be produced by human institutions." He and other Jacksonians wanted every American to have an equal chance to compete in the marketplace and in the political arena, but they never sanctioned equality of results. In the afterglow of Jackson's electoral victory in 1828, few observers troubled with such distinctions. It was time to celebrate the "commoner's" ascension to the presidency.

SETTING THE STAGE

Born in 1767 along the border between the two Carolinas, Andrew Jackson was the first president not to come from a prominent colonial family. His parents were typical of the poor, land-hungry Scots-Irish immigrants who streamed into the Carolinas in the second half of the eighteenth century. Jackson's father was killed in a farm accident just before Andrew was born. His widowed mother scratched out a meager living as a housekeeper. The extended Jackson clan engaged in guerrilla warfare against the British during the Revolution. One of Andrew's brothers was killed in the fighting, and Andrew, along with his other brother were captured and abused. Andrew was gashed and scarred by a British officer's saber. Thereafter, Jackson carried with him an enduring rage against the British and a hair-trigger temper and brawling personality. After the Revolution Jackson learned enough about the law to become an attorney in backwoods Tennessee. He dabbled enough in farming and land speculation to grow wealthy while fighting Indians as a militia officer.

Jackson could not have been more different from the aloof aristocrat and former Harvard professor John Quincy Adams. "I was born for a storm," the fearless Jackson boasted; "a calm does not suit me." Tall and lean, the rough-hewn Jackson looked gaunt and domineering. His ashen skin, chiseled features, penetrating eyes, jutting chin, and iron-gray hair accentuated his steely personality. A British visitor said he had a "gamecock look." The pugnacious Jackson engaged in numerous personal quarrels, several of which culminated in duels. During a duel with a man reputed to be the best shot in Tennessee, Jackson nevertheless let his opponent fire first. For his gallantry the future president received a bullet wedged next to his heart. He nevertheless straightened himself, patiently took aim, and killed his foe. "I should have hit him," Jackson claimed, "if he had shot me through the brain." He assaulted another opponent with a cane, another with his fists. Two bullets remained lodged in his body most of his life.

Now, as the nation's seventh president, Jackson was determined to change the structure and tone of the federal government. He appealed to the hard-pressed farming and working people who were ripe for political rebellion. Senator Daniel Webster scoffed at the huge, unruly crowd attending Jackson's inauguration: "Persons have come 500 miles to see Genl. Jackson; & they really seem to think that the Country is rescued from some dreadful danger." At the post-inaugural party at the White House, Supreme Court Justice Joseph Story noted he had never seen such "a mixture" of people. "The reign of KING MOB seemed triumphant." The partying crowd was finally lured out of the White House when the liquor was carried out onto the lawn. "His passions are terrible," said Thomas Jefferson, who deemed the volatile Jackson "dangerous" and "unfit" for the presidency.

Jackson did view himself as a savior of sorts, as a crusading president determined to protect "the poor and humble" people from the "tyranny of wealth and power" exercised by the "monied aristocracy." He was willing to assault the "rich and the powerful" in an effort to create the egalitarian republic envisioned by Thomas Jefferson. National politics, he had decided, had fallen under the sway of wealthy bankers and corrupt public officials preoccupied with promoting their self-interest at the expense of the public good. Jackson vowed to eliminate such corrupting elitism. Yet ironies abounded as the brash new president assumed leadership of a self-consciously democratic revival. An ardent Jeffersonian whom Jefferson himself distrusted, the slave-owning Jackson wanted to lower taxes, reduce government spending, shrink the federal bureaucracy, pay off the federal debt (a "national curse"), and destroy the Second Bank of the United States. His first

All Creation Going to the White House

In this depiction of Jackson's inauguration as president, satirist Robert Cruikshank draws a visual parallel to Noah's Ark, suggesting that people of all walks of life were now welcome in the White House.

presidential priority was to remove the "ill-fated race" of Indians from all of the states so that white Americans could exploit their lands. Yet he wanted to do all of those things while bolstering states' rights and diminishing federal power. In pursuing these conflicting goals, Jackson acted quickly—and decisively.

APPOINTMENTS AND RIVALRIES   Andrew Jackson believed that politicians should serve a term in government, then return to the status of private citizen, for officials who stayed in office too long grew corrupt. So he vowed to replace federal officials with his own supporters. Opponents called the wholesale removal of federal employees the "**spoils system**." During his first year in office, however, Jackson replaced only about 9 percent of the appointed officials in the federal government and during his entire term replaced fewer than 20 percent.

Jackson's administration was from the outset divided between the partisans of Secretary of State **Martin Van Buren** and those of Vice President John C. Calhoun. Much of the political history of the next few years would turn upon the rivalry of these two statesmen as each jockeyed to become successor. Jackson, new to political administration, leaned heavily upon Van Buren for advice. Van Buren had perhaps more skill at backroom politics than Calhoun and certainly more freedom to maneuver because his home base of New York was more secure politically than Calhoun's base in South Carolina. But Calhoun, a Yale graduate of towering intellect and fiery determination, could not be taken lightly. As vice president, Calhoun was determined to defend southern interests, especially the preservation of slavery, against the worrisome advance of northern industrialism and abolitionism.

THE EATON AFFAIR   In his battle with Calhoun over political power, Van Buren had luck on his side. Fate handed him a trump card: the succulent scandal known as the **Peggy Eaton affair**. John Eaton was a close friend of Jackson who had managed his 1824 presidential campaign. Three months before he became Jackson's secretary of war, Eaton married his mistress, who was scarcely a virtuous woman in the eyes of the proper ladies of Washington. The daughter of an Irish tavern owner, Margaret (Peggy) O'Neale was a vivacious widow whose husband had supposedly committed suicide upon learning of her affair with the then-senator Eaton of Tennessee. Floride Calhoun, the vice president's wife, especially objected to Peggy Eaton's lowly origins and unsavory past. She pointedly snubbed her, and the cabinet wives followed suit.

Peggy's plight reminded Jackson of the mean-spirited gossip that had pursued his own wife, Rachel, and he pronounced Peggy Eaton "chaste as a virgin." His cabinet members, however, were unable to cure their wives of what Van Buren dubbed "the Eaton Malaria." Mrs. Eaton finally gave in to the chill and in 1831 withdrew from the social scene in Washington. Her husband resigned from the cabinet. The outraged Jackson linked his nemesis, John C. Calhoun, to what he called the "wicked machinations" by Floride Calhoun against Peggy Eaton. The president concluded that Calhoun was one of the "basest and most dangerous men living—a man, devoid of principle, and would sacrifice his friend, his country, and forsake his god, for selfish personal ambition."

Jackson decided that the only way to restore harmony in his cabinet was to disband it and start over. Critics claimed that Jackson did not have the skill to lead the nation. One newspaper announced that the ship of state "is sinking and the rats are flying! The hull is too leaky to mend, and the hero of two wars and a half has not the skill to keep it afloat."

INTERNAL IMPROVEMENTS
While Washington social life weathered the gossip-filled winter of 1829–1830, Van Buren delivered some additional blows to Calhoun. It was easy to persuade Jackson to oppose congressional efforts to use federal monies to fund transportation improvements, programs with which Calhoun had long been identified. In 1830 the Maysville Road bill, passed by Congress, offered Jackson a chance for a dual thrust at rivals Calhoun and Henry Clay. The bill authorized the government to buy stock in a sixty-mile-long road to be built from Maysville, Kentucky, to Clay's hometown of Lexington. Because the proposed road would be entirely within the state of Kentucky, Jackson vetoed the bill, calling it unconstitutional, and his decisive action garnered widespread acclaim. That the veto allowed him to take a swipe at Clay, his likely oppo-

King Andrew the First

Opponents considered Jackson's veto of the Maysville Road bill an abuse of power. This cartoon shows "King Andrew" trampling on the Constitution, internal improvements, and the Bank of the United States.

nent in the 1832 presidential race, made it especially satisfying for the president. Clay was stunned. "We are all shocked and mortified by the rejection of the Maysville road," he wrote a friend. But Clay had no luck convincing Congress to override the veto.

NULLIFICATION

The veto of the Maysville Road bill illustrated Jackson's forceful personality. He eventually would veto twelve congressional bills, more than all of the previous presidents combined. Congress would censure him and critics would condemn him as a tyrant, but Jackson was determined to strengthen the executive branch to and to stick to his principles. His commitment to

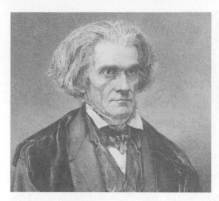

John C. Calhoun

During the Civil War, the Confederate government printed, but never issued, a one-cent postage stamp bearing this likeness of Calhoun.

assertive nationalism was nowhere more evident than in the nullification crisis centered in South Carolina.

CALHOUN'S THEORY There is a fine irony to Vice President John C. Calhoun's plight in the Jackson administration, for the South Carolinian was now midway between his early phase as a war-hawk nationalist and his later phase as a states' rights sectionalist. Conditions in his home state caused the change in his stance. Throughout the 1820s, South Carolina suffered from prolonged agricultural depression. The state lost almost seventy thousand residents to emigration during the 1820s; it would lose nearly twice that number in the 1830s, with many of them moving to Texas. Most South Carolinians blamed the protective tariff for raising the price of manufactured goods imported from Europe. Not only were tariff rates increasing, but so too was the number of products subject to tariffs. Insofar as tariffs discouraged the sale of foreign goods in the United States, they reduced the ability of the British and French to buy southern cotton because of the loss of export income. This situation worsened already existing problems of low cotton prices and thousands of acres of farmland exhausted from perennial overplanting.

The unexpected passage of the Tariff of 1828, called the "tariff of abominations" by its critics because it pushed rates up to almost 50 percent of the value of imported goods, left Calhoun no choice but to join those in opposition or give up his base of political support in his home state. Calhoun's *South Carolina Exposition and Protest,* written in opposition to the new tariff, proposed the concept of nullification as a means of avoiding secession. Calhoun asserted that an aggrieved state could convene a special state convention that could declare a federal law null and void within the state's borders because it violated the Constitution. One of two outcomes would then be possible: the federal government would have to abandon the law, or it would have to propose a constitutional amendment removing all doubt as to its validity. The immediate issue was the constitutionality of a tariff designed mainly to protect northern manufacturers from foreign competition.

THE WEBSTER-HAYNE DEBATE After Jackson assumed the presidency in early 1829, neither he nor Congress saw fit to reduce the tariff duties. There the issue stood until 1830, when the great **Webster-Hayne debate** in Congress sharpened the lines between states' rights and the Union and provoked a national crisis. During a debate over the status of government-owned western land, Senator Robert Y. Hayne of South Carolina argued that the government endangered the Union by imposing any policy that would cause a hardship on one section of the nation to the benefit of another. Senator Daniel Webster of Massachusetts then rose to defend the East. Blessed with a thunderous voice and a theatrical flair, Webster was the nation's foremost orator and lawyer. He denied that the East had ever shown a restrictive policy toward the West. Webster then lured Hayne into defending states' rights and upholding the doctrine of nullification instead of pursuing a coalition with the West.

Hayne took the bait. The Union constituted a compact of the states, he argued, and the federal government, which was their "agent," could not be the judge of its own powers, else its powers would be unlimited. Rather, the states must judge when their agent—the federal government—had overstepped the bounds of its constitutional authority. The right of state

Daniel Webster

The eloquent Massachusetts senator stands to rebut the argument for nullification in the Webster-Hayne debate.

interposition was "as full and complete as it was before the Constitution was formed."

In rebutting the idea that a state could thwart a federal law, Webster professed a nationalistic view of the Constitution. From the beginning, he asserted, the American Revolution had been fought by a united nation rather than by separate colonies. True sovereignty resided in the people as a whole, for whom both federal and state governments acted as agents in their respective spheres. If a single state could nullify a law of the national government, Webster insisted, then the Union would be a "rope of sand," a practical absurdity. A state could neither nullify a federal law nor secede from the Union. South Carolina's defiance of federal sovereignty, he charged, "is nothing more than resistance by *force*—it is disunion by *force*—it is secession by *force*—it is Civil War."

The impassioned speech made Webster a hero among National Republicans and a household name throughout the United States. Webster's closing statement became an American classic, committed to memory by young orators: "Liberty and Union, now and forever, one and inseparable." In the practical world of coalition politics, Webster had the better argument, for the Union and majority rule meant more to westerners, including President Jackson, than the abstractions of state sovereignty and nullification. Whatever one might argue about the origins of the Union, its evolution would validate Webster's position: the states could not act separately from the national government.

THE RIFT WITH CALHOUN   The nation now awaited President Jackson's reaction to the debate over nullification. Like Vice President John C. Calhoun, he was a slaveholder, and he might have been expected to sympathize with South Carolina, his native state. But he did not. On April 13, 1830, the Democratic party hosted the annual Jefferson Day dinner to honor the birthday of the former president. When his turn came to propose a toast, Jackson raised his glass, glared at Calhoun, and announced: "Our Union—It must be preserved!" Calhoun tried to parry Jackson's criticism with a toast to "the Union, next to our liberty most dear! May we all remember that it can only be preserved by respecting the rights of the States and distributing equally the benefit and the burden of the Union!" But Jackson had set off a bombshell that exploded the plans of the states' righters.

A month later, Jackson drove the final nail into the coffin of Calhoun's presidential ambitions. On May 12, 1830, the president saw for the first time documents detailing how in 1818 Calhoun, serving as secretary of war in the Monroe administration, had urged that General Jackson be disciplined for his unauthorized invasion of Spanish-held Florida. A tense correspondence between Jackson and Calhoun followed, ending with a curt note from Jackson cutting it off. "Understanding you now," Jackson wrote two weeks later, "no further communication with you on this subject is necessary."

The acidic rift between the two proud men prompted Jackson to take a dramatic step: he removed all Calhoun partisans from the cabinet. Before the end of the summer of 1831, the president had for the second time a new cabinet, one entirely loyal to him. He named Martin Van Buren, who had resigned from his post as secretary of state, minister (ambassador) to England, and Van Buren departed for London. Van Buren's friends now urged Jackson to repudiate his previous intention of serving only one term. They believed it

The Rats Leaving a Falling House

During his first term, Jackson was beset by dissension within his administration. Here "public confidence in the stability of this administration" is toppling.

might be hard to win the 1832 nomination for the New Yorker, who had been charged with intrigues against Calhoun, and the still-popular Carolinian might yet gain the presidency.

Jackson relented and in the fall of 1831 announced his readiness for one more term, with the idea of bringing Van Buren back from London in time to win the presidency in 1836. But in 1832, when the Senate reconvened, Van Buren's enemies opposed his London appointment and gave Calhoun, as vice president, a vengeful chance to reject the nomination with a tie-breaking vote. "It will kill him, sir, kill him dead," Calhoun told Senator Thomas Hart Benton. Benton disagreed: "You have broken a minister, and elected a Vice-President." So, it turned out, he had. Calhoun's peevish vote against Van Buren evoked popular sympathy for the New Yorker, who returned from London and would soon be nominated to succeed Calhoun as vice president.

Now that his presidential hopes were blasted, Calhoun openly opposed Jackson by assuming public leadership of the South Carolina nullificationists. Jackson sought to defuse the crisis by asking Congress in 1829 to reduce tariffs on goods "which cannot come in competition with our own products." Late in the spring of 1830, Congress lowered tariff duties on consumer products—tea, coffee, salt, and molasses. The lower tariff and the Maysville veto, coming at about the same time, mollified a few South Carolinians, but nullifiers dismissed Jackson's actions as "nothing but sugar plums to pacify children." By the end of 1831, Jackson was calling for further tariff reductions to take the wind out of the nullificationists' sails. The **Tariff of 1832**, pushed through by former president John Quincy Adams (now serving in Congress), reduced duties on many items, but tariffs on cloth and iron remained high.

THE SOUTH CAROLINA ORDINANCE South Carolina, a state dominated by slaveholding planters and consumed by "Carolina fever," as an observer called the mania for nullification, seethed with resentment toward Jackson—and the federal government. One hotheaded South Carolina Congressman called the Union a "foul monster." He and other white South Carolinians, living in the only state where slaves were a majority of the population, feared that the federal authority to impose tariffs might eventually be used to end slavery. John C. Calhoun declared that the "peculiar domestic institutions of the southern states [slavery]" were at stake. In November 1832 a South Carolina state convention overwhelmingly adopted an ordinance of nullification that repudiated the federal tariff acts of 1828 and 1832 (declaring them "null, void, and no law") and forbade federal agents in Charleston to collect the federal tariff revenue after February 1, 1833. The reassembled state legislature then provided that any citizen whose property was seized by federal authorities for failure to pay the duty could get a state court order to recover twice its value. The legislature chose Robert Hayne as governor and elected Calhoun to succeed him as senator. Calhoun promptly resigned as vice president in order to defend nullification on the Senate floor. New South Carolina governor Hayne called for a volunteer state militia force of ten thousand men to protect the state from federal intervention.

JACKSON'S FIRM RESPONSE In the nullification crisis, South Carolina found itself standing alone: other southern states expressed sympathy, but none endorsed nullification. President Jackson's response to South Carolina was measured but not rash—at least not in public. He promised to confront the crisis with "firmness and forbearance" but angrily promised "woe to those nullifiers who shed the first blood." Like James Madison, he viewed nullification as an act of treason. In private he was furious about South Carolina's defiance. He threatened to hang Calhoun and all other traitors. In his annual message, on December 4, 1832, Jackson appealed to the people of South Carolina not to follow false leaders: "The laws of the United States must be executed. . . . Those who told you that you might peaceably prevent their execution, deceived you. . . . Their object is disunion. . . . Disunion by armed force is treason."

CLAY'S COMPROMISE   Jackson then sent federal soldiers and a warship to Charleston, South Carolina to uphold national authority. The South Carolina nullifiers mobilized the state militia. In 1833 the president requested from Congress a "**force bill**" authorizing him to use the army to compel compliance with federal law in South Carolina. The nullifiers postponed enforcement of their ordinances in anticipation of a compromise. Passage of the compromise bill depended upon the support of the shrewd Kentucky senator Henry Clay, who finally yielded to those urging him to save the day. On February 12, 1833, he circulated a plan to reduce the tariff gradually until 1842. It was less than South Carolina preferred, but it got the nullifiers out of the dilemma they had created.

On March 1, 1833, Congress passed the compromise tariff and the force bill, and the next day Jackson signed both. The South Carolina convention then met and rescinded its nullification of the tariff acts. In a face-saving gesture, the delegates nullified the force bill, for which Jackson no longer had any need. Both sides were able to claim victory. Jackson had upheld the supremacy of the Union and South Carolina had secured a reduction of the federal tariff. A sulking Calhoun, worn out by the controversy, returned to his plantation. "The struggle, so far from being over," he ominously wrote, "is not more than fairly commenced."

JACKSON'S INDIAN POLICY

If Jackson's firm stance against nullification constituted his finest hour, his forcible removal of Indians from their ancestral lands in the South was one of his lowest moments. Andrew Jackson hated Indians. He viewed them as barbarians who were better off out of the way. Jackson believed that a "just, humane, liberal policy toward Indians" dictated moving all of them onto territory west of the Mississippi River, to the Great American Desert, which white settlers would never covet since it was believed to be fit mainly for lizards and rattlesnakes. State laws in Alabama, Georgia, and Mississippi had already abolished tribal units and stripped them of their powers, rejected ancestral Indian land claims, and denied Indians the right to vote or bring suit or testify in court.

INDIAN REMOVAL   In response to a request by Jackson, Congress in 1830 narrowly approved the Indian Removal Act. It authorized the president to give Indians federal land west of the Mississippi River in exchange for the land they occupied in the East and the South. By 1835 some forty-six thousand Indians were relocated at government expense. The policy was enacted with remarkable speed, but even that was too slow for state authorities in the South and Southwest. Unlike in the Ohio Valley and the Great Lakes region, where the flow of white settlement had constantly pushed Indians westward before it, settlement in the Old Southwest moved across Kentucky and Tennessee and down the Mississippi, surrounding the Creeks, Choctaws, Chickasaws, Seminoles, and Cherokees. These "civilized tribes" had over the years taken on many of the features of white society. The Cherokees, for example, had developed a constitution and a written language and owned African American slaves.

Most of the northern tribes were too weak to resist the offers of federal commissioners who, if necessary, used bribery and alcohol to woo the chiefs. On the whole, there was remarkably little resistance. But in Illinois and the Wisconsin Territory, an armed clash erupted in 1832, which came to be known as the Black Hawk War. The Illinois militia mobilized to expel the Sauk and Fox tribes, chased them into the Wisconsin Territory, and massacred women and children as they tried to escape across the Mississippi.

In the South, two Indian nations, the Seminoles and the Cherokees, put up a stubborn resistance to the federal removal policy. The Seminoles of Florida fought a protracted guerrilla war in the Everglades from 1835 to 1842. But their resistance waned after 1837, when their leader, **Osceola**, was seized by treachery under a flag of truce, imprisoned, and left to die at Fort Moultrie near Charleston Harbor. After 1842 only a few hundred Seminoles remained, hiding out in the swamps. Most of the rest had been banished to the West.

THE TRAIL OF TEARS   Some 21,500 Cherokees had, by the end of the eighteenth century, fallen back into the mountains of northern Georgia and western North Carolina, settling on land guaranteed to them in 1791 by a treaty with the U.S. government. But when Georgia ceded its western lands to the federal government in 1802, it did so on the ambiguous condition that

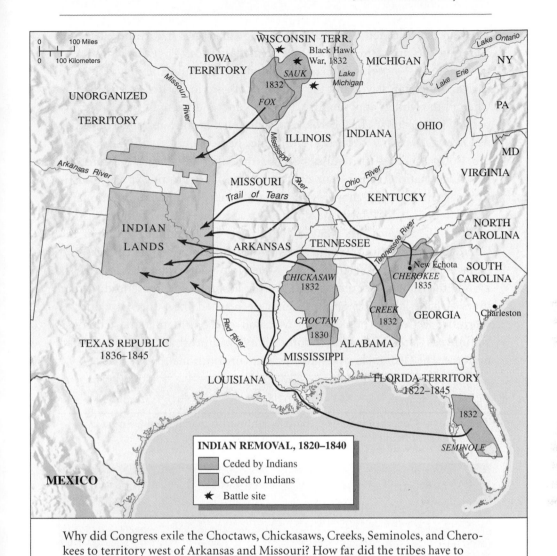

Why did Congress exile the Choctaws, Chickasaws, Creeks, Seminoles, and Cherokees to territory west of Arkansas and Missouri? How far did the tribes have to travel, and what were the conditions on the journey? Why were the Indians not forced to move before the 1830s?

the United States extinguish all Indian titles within the state "as early as the same can be obtained on reasonable terms." In 1827 the Cherokees, relying upon their established treaty rights, adopted a constitution in which they declared that they were not subject to the laws or control of any other state or nation. In 1828, shortly after Jackson's election, Georgia announced that after June 1, 1830, the authority of state law would extend to the Cherokees living within the boundaries of the state.

Of all the so-called Civilized Tribes, the Cherokees had come closest to adopting the prevailing customs of white America. They had developed farms, schools, stores, newspapers, and churches—and they owned 2,100 African American slaves. But the discovery of gold in north Georgia in 1829 whetted the whites' appetite for Cherokee land and brought bands of trespassing prospectors. The Cherokees sought relief in the Supreme Court, but in *Cherokee Nation v. Georgia* (1831) Chief Justice John Marshall ruled that the Court lacked jurisdiction because the Cherokees were a "domestic dependent nation" rather than a foreign state in the meaning of the Constitution. Marshall added, however, that the Cherokees had "an unquestionable right" to their lands "until title should be extinguished by voluntary cession to the United States." In 1830 a Georgia law had required whites in the Cherokee territory to obtain licenses authorizing their residence there and to take an oath of allegiance to the state. Two New England missionaries among the Indians refused to abide by the law and were sentenced to four years at hard labor. On appeal their case reached the Supreme Court as *Worcester v. Georgia* (1832). The Marshall court held that the Cherokee Nation was "a distinct political community" within which Georgia law had no force. The Georgia law was therefore unconstitutional.

The Trail of Tears

Thousands of Cherokee Indians died on a nightmarish march from Georgia to Oklahoma after being forced from their native lands.

President Andrew Jackson refused to enforce the Court's decision, claiming that he had no authority to intervene in Georgia. In fact, Jackson regarded any treaties with Indians as an "unenforceable" absurdity. Under the circumstances there was nothing for the Cherokees to do but give in and sign a treaty, which they did in 1835. They gave up their land in the Southeast (about 100 million acres) in exchange for tracts in the "Indian Territory," some 32 million acres west of Arkansas. By 1838, seventeen thousand Cherokees had departed westward on the "**Trail of Tears**," following other tribes on an eight-hundred-mile journey. Four thousand of the refugees died on the Trail of Tears. A few held out in the mountains and acquired title to federal land in North Carolina; thenceforth they were the "Eastern Band" of Cherokees.

THE BANK CONTROVERSY

The overriding national issue in the presidential campaign of 1832 was neither Jackson's Indian policy nor South Carolina's obsession with the tariff. It was the question of renewing the charter of the Bank of the United States, which Congress had first established in 1791.

THE BANK'S OPPONENTS Andrew Jackson's stance against the national bank was as unrelenting as his prejudice against Indians. The national bank, based in Philadelphia and with branches in major cities across the country, also served as the depository for all federal funds but also issued currency and made loans. From the start this combination of private and public functions caused problems for the Bank of the United States (B.U.S.) As the government's revenues soared, the bank became the most powerful lending institution in the country, a central bank, in effect, whose huge size enabled it to determine the amount of credit available for the nation. The charter of the first B.U.S. expired in 1811 and was renewed in 1816 as the Second Bank of the United States.

While providing the infant American economy with a stable currency, the national bank was controversial from the start. Local banks and state governments—especially in the South and West—feared the scope and power of the "monopolistic" national bank. Southerners and westerners claimed that the small group of national bank directors manipulated the nation's financial system to the advantage of the North and themselves.

Andrew Jackson had absorbed the western hostility toward the B.U.S. after the panic of 1819. "Every one that knows me," he told a friend, knows "that I have always been opposed to the U. States Bank, nay all banks." He believed that "hard" money—gold and silver coins—was the only legitimate medium of exchange. He remained skeptical of all forms of paper currency (hence the irony of his picture now being on twenty-dollar bills), and he was convinced that the central bank was unconstitutional—no matter what Chief Justice John Marshall had said in *McCulloch v. Maryland* (1819).

Under the astute management of the brilliant but haughty **Nicholas Biddle**, the Second Bank of the United States had prospered and grown. With twenty-nine branches and a third of the nation's bank deposits, it had facilitated business expansion and supplied a stable currency by forcing the 464 state banks to keep enough gold or silver in their vaults to back their paper currency. Arrayed against the bank were powerful enemies with conflicting interests: some of the state and local banks that had been forced to reduce their volume of paper money, groups of debtors who suffered from the reduction (deflation) in the money supply, and businessmen and speculators on the make, who wanted more money in circulation to facilitate their entrepreneurial ventures.

Like Jackson, many westerners and workingmen believed that the bank was a "Monster," a financial monopoly controlled by a wealthy few. "I think it right to be perfectly frank with you," Jackson told Biddle in 1829. "I do not dislike your Bank any more than [I dislike] all banks." Jackson characterized bankers as "vipers and thieves." He was perhaps right in his instinct that the national bank lodged too much power in private hands, but he was mistaken in his understanding of the bank's policies. By issuing paper money of its own, the bank provided a stable, uniform currency for the expanding economy as well as a mechanism to control the pace of economic growth.

THE RECHARTER EFFORT In 1829, in his first annual message, President Jackson questioned the national bank's constitutionality and asserted (whatever the evidence to the contrary) that it had failed to maintain a sound currency. The Second Bank of the United States' twenty-year charter would run through 1836, but Nicholas Biddle could not afford the uncertainty of waiting until then for a renewal. Leaders of the National Republicans, especially Henry Clay and Daniel Webster (who was legal counsel to the B.U.S. as well as a senator), told Biddle that he needed to act quickly, before the presidential election of 1836. Friends of the bank held a majority in Congress, and Jackson would risk loss of support in the election if he vetoed its renewal. But Biddle and his allies failed to grasp both Jackson's tenacity and the depth of public suspicion of the bank. In the end, Biddle, Clay, and the National Republicans handed Jackson a popular issue on the

Rechartering the Bank

President Andrew Jackson battling the "Hydra-headed" Bank of the United States.

eve of the election. "The Bank," Jackson told Martin Van Buren in May 1832, "is trying to kill me. But I will kill it."

Early in the summer of 1832, both houses of Congress passed the bank recharter bill by a comfortable margin. On July 10, 1832, Jackson vetoed the bill, sending it back to Congress with a blistering denunciation of the bank's monopoly powers that benefited the rich and powerful at the expense of the people. Jackson called the B.U.S. a "hydra-headed monster of corruption" that was "dangerous to our liberties." An effort to overrule Jackson's veto failed in the Senate, thus setting the stage for a nationwide financial crisis and a dramatic presidential campaign.

CONTENTIOUS POLITICS

CAMPAIGN INNOVATIONS   In 1832, for the first time in a presidential election, a third party entered the field. The **Anti-Masonic party** grew out of popular hostility toward the Masonic fraternal order, a private social organization that originated in Great Britain early in the eighteenth century. By the start of the American Revolution, there were a hundred Masonic "lodges" scattered across the United States with about a thousand members, including George Washington and Benjamin Franklin. By 1830 the number had grown to two thousand lodges and one hundred thousand Masons, including Andrew Jackson and Henry Clay.

The Masonic movement generated little opposition until one of its members from western New York, fifty-two-year-old William Morgan, disappeared in 1826. Morgan had threatened to reveal the secret rituals of the Masonic order. Masons, some of them local officials, had burned down Morgan's shop and arrested him. Soon thereafter, someone paid for his release and spirited Morgan away. His body was never found. Between 1826 and 1831, the state of New York launched over twenty investigations into Morgan's disappearance (and presumed murder) and conducted a dozen trials but never gained a conviction. Each legal effort aroused more public indignation because most of the judges, lawyers, and jurors were Masons.

Fears and suspicions of the Masonic order as a tyrannical secret organization intent on subverting democracy gave rise to the grassroots political movement known as the Anti-Masonic party. More than a hundred Anti-Masonic newspapers emerged across the nation. Their common purpose was to stamp out an organization that was contaminating the "heart of the republic." Former president John Quincy Adams said that disbanding the "Masonic institution" was the most important issue facing "us and our posterity." Opposition to a fraternal organization was hardly the foundation upon which to build a lasting political party, but the Anti-Masonic party had three important firsts to its credit: in addition to being the first third party, it was the first party to hold a national nominating convention and the first to announce a platform, both of which it accomplished in 1831 when 116 delegates from thirteen states gathered in Baltimore to nominate William Wirt of Maryland for president. The former attorney general in President Monroe's administration, he was one of the nation's leading lawyers. Wirt had decided that Masonry was undermining the "fundamental principles" of American democracy.

The Democrats and the National Republicans followed the example of the Anti-Masonic Party by holding national conventions of their own. In December 1831 the delegates of the National Republican party assembled in Baltimore to nominate Henry Clay, the charming, yet imperious legislative genius from Kentucky whose arrogance was matched only by his burning ambition to be president. Jackson endorsed the idea of a nominating convention for the Democratic party to demonstrate popular support for its candidates. To that purpose the convention, also meeting at Baltimore, first adopted the two-thirds rule for nomination (which prevailed until 1936, when it became a simple majority) and then named Martin Van Buren as Jackson's running mate. The Democrats, unlike the other two parties, adopted no formal platform at their first convention and relied to a substantial degree upon hoopla and the popularity of the president to carry their cause.

The outcome was an overwhelming endorsement of Jackson in the Electoral College, with 219 votes to 49 for Clay, and a less overwhelming but solid victory in the popular vote, 688,000 to 530,000. William Wirt carried only Vermont, winning seven electoral votes. Wayward South Carolina, preparing for nullification and unable to stomach either Jackson or Clay, delivered its 11 votes to Governor John Floyd of Virginia.

THE REMOVAL OF GOVERNMENT DEPOSITS Andrew Jackson interpreted his lopsided reelection as a mandate to close the B.U.S. He asked Congress to investigate the safety of government deposits in the bank. After a committee had checked on the bank's operations, the Calhoun and Clay forces in the House of Representatives passed a resolution affirming that government deposits were safe and could be continued. The resolution passed on March 2, 1833, by chance the same day that Jackson signed the compromise tariff and the force bill. With the nullification issue out of the way, Jackson was free to wage war on the bank. He now resolved to remove all government deposits from the national bank.

When Secretary of the Treasury Louis McLane balked, Jackson fired him. In the reshuffling, Attorney General Roger B. Taney moved to the Treasury Department, where he complied with the presidential wishes, which corresponded to his own views. Taney continued to draw on government accounts with Biddle's bank but deposited all new federal receipts in state banks. By the end of 1833, twenty-three state banks—"**pet banks**," as they came to be called—had the benefit of federal deposits. Transferring the government's deposits was a highly questionable action under the law, and the Senate voted to censure Jackson for it. Biddle refused to surrender. He ordered the B.U.S. to curtail loans throughout the nation and demand the redemption of state banknotes in gold or silver as quickly as possible. He sought to bring the economy to a halt, create a sharp depression, and reveal to the nation the importance of maintaining the bank.

Biddle's contraction policy, however, unwittingly unleashed a speculative binge encouraged by the deposit of government funds in the pet banks. With the restraint of Biddle's bank removed, the state banks unleashed their wild-cat tendencies. Hundreds of new state banks emerged, printing banknotes with abandon for the purpose of lending money to speculators. Sales of public lands rose from 4 million acres in 1834 to 15 million in 1835 and 20 million in 1836. At the same time, the states plunged heavily into debt to finance the building of roads and canals, inspired by the success of New York's Erie Canal. By 1837 total state indebtedness had soared to $170 million. The supreme irony of Jackson's war on the bank was that it sparked the speculative mania that he most feared.

FISCAL MEASURES The surge of unstable paper money reached its peak in 1836, when events combined suddenly to deflate it. Most important among these were the Distribution Act and the Specie Circular. Distribution of the government's surplus funds to the states had long been a pet project of Henry Clay's. One of its purposes was to eliminate the federal surplus, thus removing one argument for cutting the tariff. Much of the federal surplus, however, resulted from the "land-office business" in western property sales and was therefore in the form of banknotes that had been issued to speculators. Many westerners thought that the solution to the surplus was simply to lower the price of land; southerners preferred to lower the tariff—but such action would now upset the delicate compromise achieved with the Tariff of 1833. For a time the annual surpluses could be applied to paying off the government debt, but the debt, reduced to $7 million by 1832, was entirely paid off by 1835.

Still, the federal surplus continued to mount. Clay again proposed distributing the funds to the states, but Jackson had constitutional scruples about the process. Finally a compromise was worked out whereby the government would distribute most of the surplus as loans to the states. To satisfy Jackson's concerns, the funds were technically loans, but in reality the government never asked to be repaid. Distribution of the surplus was to be in proportion to each state's representation in the two houses of Congress and was to be paid out in quarterly installments beginning in 1837.

The Specie Circular, issued by the secretary of the Treasury at Jackson's order, applied the president's hard-money conviction to the sale of public lands. According to his order, the government would accept only gold or silver coins in payment for land. Since few settlers had gold or silver coins, however, they were now left all the more at the mercy of speculators when they tried to purchase land. Both the Distribution Act and the Specie Circular put many state banks in a plight. The distribution of the surplus to the state governments resulted in federal funds' being withdrawn from the state banks. In turn, the state banks had to require many borrowers to pay back their loans immediately in order to be able to transfer the federal funds to the state governments. This situation caused greater disarray in the already chaotic state banking community. At the same time the new requirement that only hard money be accepted for federal land purchases put an added strain on the supplies of gold and silver.

BOOM AND BUST   But the boom-and-bust cycle of the 1830s had causes larger even than Andrew Jackson, causes that were beyond his control. The soaring inflation of the mid-1830s was rooted not so much in a feverish expansion of banknotes, as it seemed at the time, but in an increase of gold and silver payments from England, France, and especially Mexico for investment and for the purchase of American cotton and other products. At the same time, British credits enabled Americans to buy British goods without having to export gold or silver. Meanwhile, the flow of hard coins to China, where silver had been much prized, decreased. Now the Chinese took in payment for their goods British credits, which they could in turn use to cover rapidly increasing imports of opium from British India.

VAN BUREN AND THE NEW PARTY SYSTEM

THE WHIG COALITION   As the economy showed signs of strain, the Jacksonian Democrats reaped a political bonanza. Jackson had slain the dual monsters of nullification and the bank, and the people loved him for it. The hard times following the contraction of the economy turned Americans against Biddle and the B.U.S. but not against Jackson, the professed friend of "the people" and foe of the "selfish" interests of financiers and speculators. But in 1834, Jackson's opponents began to pull together a new coalition of diverse elements, united chiefly by their hostility to his authoritarian style. The imperious demeanor of the feisty champion of democracy had given rise to the nickname "King Andrew I." Jackson's followers therefore were deemed Tories, supporters of the "tyrannical" king, and his opponents became **Whigs**, a name that linked them to the Patriots of the American Revolution.

The diverse coalition making up the Whigs clustered around the National Republican party of John Quincy Adams, Henry Clay, and Daniel Webster. Into the combination came remnants of the Anti-Masonic and Democratic parties, who for one reason or another were alienated by Jackson's stand on the national bank or states' rights. Of the forty-one Democrats in Congress who had voted to recharter the bank, twenty-eight had joined the Whigs by

1836, including Congressman David Crockett from Tennessee, the mythical hunter and gregarious storyteller. Crockett was a national folk hero who during an 1835 speech in Philadelphia lamented the terrible economic calamity resulting from the policies of Jackson, his former commander during the War of 1812. Crockett called Jackson an "old man . . . whose popularity, like the lightning from heaven, blasts and withers all that comes within its influence." For the next twenty years the Whigs and the Democrats would be the two major political parties.

The core Whigs were the supporters of Henry Clay and his economic nationalism. They favored federal support for constructing internal improvements—roads, bridges, canals—to foster economic growth. And they supported a national bank and high tariffs. In the South the Whigs enjoyed the support of the urban banking and commercial interests. In the West, farmers who valued government-funded internal improvements joined the Whig ranks. Unlike the Democrats, who attracted Catholics from Germany and Ireland, Whigs tended to be native-born or British-American evangelical Protestants—Congregationalists, Presbyterians, and Baptists—who were active in promoting social reforms such as abolition and temperance.

THE ELECTION OF 1836   In 1835, eighteen months before the election, the Democrats held their second national convention, nominating Jackson's handpicked successor, Vice President Martin Van Buren. The Whig coalition, united chiefly in its opposition to Jackson, held no convention but adopted a strategy of multiple candidacies, hoping to throw the election into the House of Representatives.

Martin Van Buren

Van Buren earned the nickname the "Little Magician."

The result was a free-for-all reminiscent of 1824, except that this time one candidate stood apart from the rest: it was Martin Van Buren against the field. The Whigs put up three favorite sons: Daniel Webster, named by the Massachusetts legislature; Hugh Lawson White, chosen by anti-Jackson Democrats in the Tennessee legislature; and William Henry Harrison of Indiana, nominated by a predominantly Anti-Masonic convention in Harrisburg, Pennsylvania. In the South the Whigs made heavy inroads on the Democratic vote by arguing that Van

Buren would be soft on anti-slavery advocates and that the South could trust only a southerner—that is, Hugh White—as president. In the popular vote, Van Buren outdistanced the entire Whig field, with 765,000 votes to 740,000 for the Whigs, most of which were cast for Harrison. Van Buren won 170 electoral votes; Harrison, 73; White, 26; and Webster, 14.

Martin Van Buren, the eighth president, was the first of Dutch ancestry. Although trained as an attorney, he had been for most of his adult life a professional politician, so skilled in the arts of organization and manipulation that he came to be known as the Little Magician. Elected governor of New York in 1828, he quickly resigned to join Jackson's cabinet and became vice president in 1833.

THE PANIC OF 1837 Van Buren inherited a terrifying financial panic. An already precarious economy was tipped over by a depression in England, which resulted in a drop in the price of American cotton and caused English banks and investors to cut back their American commitments and refuse extensions of loans. This was a particularly hard blow because much of America's economic expansion depended upon European—and mainly English—investment capital. On top of everything else, in 1836 there had been a failure of the wheat crop, the export of which in good years helped offset the drain of payments abroad. States curtailed ambitious plans for roads and canals and in many cases felt impelled to repudiate their debts. In the crunch forty percent of the wildcat state banks succumbed. In April 1837, some 250 businesses failed in New York City alone.

The working class, as always, was particularly hard hit during the economic slump and largely had to fend for itself. By the fall of 1837, a third of the workforce was jobless, and those still fortunate enough to have jobs saw their wages cut by 30 to 50 percent within two years. At the same time, prices for food and clothing soared. As the winter of 1837 approached, a journalist reported that in New York City two hundred thousand people were "in utter and hopeless distress with no means of surviving the winter but those provided by charity." There was no government aid; churches and charitable societies were the major sources of support for the indigent.

Van Buren did not believe that he or the government had any responsibility to rescue hard-pressed farmers or businessmen or to provide relief for the jobless and homeless. He did feel obliged to keep the government itself in a healthy financial situation, however. To that end he called a special session of Congress in 1837, which quickly voted to postpone indefinitely the distribution of the surplus because of a probable upcoming deficit and approved an issue of Treasury notes (currency) to cover immediate expenses.

AN INDEPENDENT TREASURY   Van Buren believed that the government should cease risking its deposits in shaky state banks and set up an independent Treasury. Under this plan, the government would keep its funds in its own vaults and do business entirely in hard money. The Independent Treasury Act elicited opposition from a combination of Whigs and conservative Democrats who feared deflation, and it took Van Buren several years of maneuvering to get what he wanted. Calhoun signaled a return to the Democratic fold, after several years of flirting with the Whigs, when he endorsed the Treasury act. Van Buren gained western support by backing a more liberal policy regarding federal land sales. Congress finally passed the Independent Treasury Act on July 4, 1840. Although it lasted little more than a year (the Whigs repealed it in 1841), it would be restored in 1846.

The drawn-out struggle over the Treasury was only one of several squabbles that preoccupied politicians during the Van Buren years. A flood of petitions for Congress to abolish slavery and the slave trade in the District of Columbia ignited a fiery debate, especially in the House of Representatives. Fairly or not, the administration became the target of growing discontent. The president won renomination easily enough but could not get the Democratic convention to agree on his vice-presidential choice, which was left up to the Democratic electors.

THE "LOG CABIN AND HARD CIDER" CAMPAIGN   Because of the scope and depth of the economic depression, the Whigs fully expected to win the 1840 presidential election. They got an early start on their campaign when they met at Harrisburg, Pennsylvania, on December 4, 1839, to choose a candidate. Henry Clay, the Kentucky legislator who had been the presidential nominee in 1832 and then the most consistent foe of Andrew Jackson during the 1830s, expected 1840 to be his year. But several party leaders thought otherwise. Although Clay led on the first ballot, the convention sought a Whiggish Jackson, as it were, a military hero who could enter the race with few known political convictions or enemies. The delegates finally turned to William Henry Harrison, an Ohio soldier and politician from a prominent Virginia family. Harrison's credentials were impressive: victor at the Battle of Tippecanoe against the Shawnees in 1811, former governor of the Indiana Territory, briefly congressman and senator from Ohio, more briefly minister to Colombia. Another advantage of Harrison's was that the Anti-Masons liked him. To rally their states' rights wing, the Whigs chose for vice president John Tyler of Virginia.

The Whigs had no platform, but they fastened on a catchy campaign slogan, "Tippecanoe and Tyler Too." And they soon had a rousing campaign

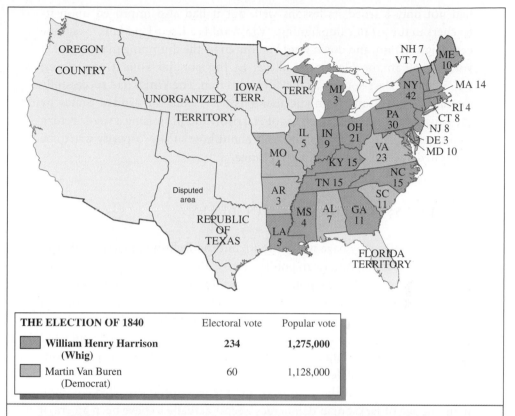

THE ELECTION OF 1840	Electoral vote	Popular vote
William Henry Harrison (Whig)	**234**	**1,275,000**
Martin Van Buren (Democrat)	60	1,128,000

Why did Van Buren carry several western states but few others? How did the Whigs achieve a decisive electoral victory over the Democrats? How was their strategy in 1840 different from their campaign in 1836?

theme, which a Democratic newspaper unwittingly supplied when the *Baltimore Republican* declared that General Harrison, at sixty-seven the oldest man yet to seek the presidency, was the kind of man who would spend his retirement "days in a log cabin [sipping apple cider] on the banks of the Ohio [River]." The Whigs seized upon the cider and log cabin symbols to depict Harrison as a simple man sprung from the people in contrast to Martin Van Buren's wealthy, aristocratic lifestyle. Actually, Harrison sprang from one of the first families of Virginia and lived in a large farmhouse.

The Whig "Log Cabin and Hard Cider" campaign featured portable log cabins rolling through the streets along with barrels of cider. All the devices of hoopla were mobilized: placards, emblems, campaign buttons, floats, effigies, great rallies, and a campaign newspaper, the *Log Cabin*. The Whig party had not only learned its lessons well, but it had also improved upon its teachers in the art of campaigning. "Van! Van! Is a Used-Up Man!" went one campaign refrain, and down went Van Buren by the thumping margin of 234 votes to 60 in the Electoral College. In the popular vote it was closer: 1,275,000 for Harrison; 1,128,000 for Van Buren. The Whigs had successfully distracted Americans from the major issues facing the United States by focusing on the personal qualities of Harrison and promising a vague return to prosperity. There was no consensus about how such prosperity was to be generated. It was simply time for a change.

Assessing the Jackson Years

The Whigs may have won in 1840, but the Jacksonian Democrats had permanently altered American politics during the 1830s. People had become much more involved in the political process. By 1840 both national political parties were organized down to the precinct level, and the proportion of white men who voted in the presidential election had tripled, from 27 percent in 1824 to nearly 80 percent in 1840. That much is beyond dispute, but the phenomenon of Andrew Jackson, the heroic symbol for an age, continues to spark historical debate.

A supreme irony of the times was that the age of the so-called common man, the age of Jacksonian democracy, seems actually to have been an era of growing economic and social inequality. During the years before the Civil War, the American legend of young men rising from rags to riches was a durable and consoling myth. Speaking to the Senate in 1832, Kentucky's Henry Clay claimed that almost all the successful factory owners he knew were "enterprising self-made men, who have whatever wealth they possess by patient and diligent labor." While men of moderate means could sometimes turn an inheritance into a fortune by good management and prudent speculation, those who started out poor and uneducated seldom made it to the top. In 1828 the top 1 percent of New York's families (worth $34,000 or more) held 40 percent of the wealth, and the top 4 percent held 76 percent. Similar circumstances prevailed in Philadelphia, Boston, and other cities.

But despite growing social distinctions, it seems likely that the white population of America, at least, was better off than the general run of Europeans. New frontiers, both geographic and technological, raised the level of material well-being for all. And religious as well as political freedoms continued to attract people eager for liberty in a new land. For all of the exaggerated rhetoric about the second quarter of the nineteenth century witnessing the triumph of the "common man," there seems little question that Andrew Jackson and his supporters promoted an ideal of republican virtue, of returning America to Thomas Jefferson's ideal that the federal government would play as limited a role as possible. In the Jacksonian view, the alliance of government and business was always an invitation to special favors and an eternal source of corruption. The national bank was the epitome of such evil. The right policy for government, at the national level in particular, was to refrain from granting special privileges and to let free competition in the marketplace regulate the economy.

In the bustling world of nineteenth-century enterprise, however, the idea of a return to agrarian simplicity was a futile exercise in nostalgia. Instead, free-enterprise policies opened the way for a host of aspiring entrepreneurs eager to replace the established economic elite with a new order of free-enterprise capitalism. And in fact there was no great conflict in the Jacksonian mentality between the farmer or planter who delved into the soil and the independent speculator and entrepreneur who grew wealthy by other means. Jackson himself was both. What the Jacksonians did not foresee was the degree to which, in a growing country, unrestrained entrepreneurial activities could lead to new centers of economic power largely independent of government regulation. But history is forever marked by unintended consequences. Here the ultimate irony would be that the laissez-faire rationale for republican simplicity eventually became the justification for the growth of unregulated corporate powers far greater than any ever wielded by Biddle's bank.

CHAPTER SUMMARY

- **Jacksonian Democracy** Andrew Jackson's America was very different from the America of 1776. Most white men had gained the vote when states removed property qualifications for voting. The Jacksonians sought to democratize economic opportunity; thus politics changed with the advent of national conventions, at which party leaders chose their party's candidates and platforms. Powerful elites remained in charge of society and politics, however.

- **Jacksonian Policies** Jackson wanted to lower taxes and reduce government spending. He vetoed bills to use federal funds for internal improvements, and his belief that banks were run by corrupt businessmen for their own ends led him to veto a bill for the rechartering of the Second Bank of the United States.

- **Nullification Controversy** When a South Carolina convention nullified the Tariffs of 1828 and 1832, Jackson requested that Congress pass a "force bill" authorizing the army to compel compliance with the tariffs. After South Carolina accepted a compromise tariff put forth by Henry Clay, the state convention nullified the force bill. Nullification, an extreme states' rights ideology, had been put into action. The crisis was over, but both sides claimed victory.

- **Indian Removal Act of 1830** The Indian Removal Act of 1830 authorized the relocation of eastern Indians to federal lands west of the Mississippi River. The Cherokees used the federal court system to try to block this relocation, but despite the Supreme Court's decision in their favor, federal troops forced them to move; the event and the route they took came to be known as in the Trail of Tears. By 1840 only a few Seminoles and Cherokees remained, hiding in remote areas of the Southeast.

- **Democrats and Whigs** Jackson's arrogant behavior, especially his use of the veto, led many to regard him as "King Andrew." Groups who opposed him coalesced into a new party, known as the Whigs, thus forming the country's second party system. The panic of 1837, during Martin Van Buren's administration, ensured Whig victory in the election of 1840 despite the party's lack of a coherent political program.

CHRONOLOGY

1828	"Tariff of Abominations" goes into effect
1830	Congress passes the Indian Removal Act
	Andrew Jackson vetoes the Maysville Road Bill
1831	Supreme Court issues *Cherokee Nation v. Georgia* decision
1832	Supreme Court issues *Worcester v. Georgia* decision
	South Carolina issues ordinance of nullification
	Andrew Jackson vetoes the Bank Recharter Bill
1833	Congress passes Henry Clay's compromise tariff
1836	Martin Van Buren is elected president
1837	Financial panic follows a drop in the price of cotton
1837–1838	Eastern Indians are forced west on the Trail of Tears
1840	William Henry Harrison, a Whig, is elected president

KEY TERMS & NAMES

12

THE OLD SOUTH

FOCUS QUESTIONS

 wwnorton.com/studyspace

- How diverse was the Old South's economy, and what was its unifying feature?

- How did dependence on agriculture and slavery shape the distinctive culture of the Old South? Why did southern whites who did not hold slaves defend the "peculiar institution"?

- How did enslaved people respond to their bondage during the antebellum period? How did free persons of color fit into southern society?

- How did expansion into the Southwest influence slavery and its defense?

Of all the regions of the United States during the first half of the nineteenth century, the South was the most distinctive. Southern society remained rural and agricultural long after the rest of the nation had embraced urban-industrial development. Likewise, the southern elite's tenacious efforts to expand and preserve slavery stifled reform impulses in the South and ignited a prolonged political controversy that would end in civil war. The rapid settlement of the western territories set in motion a ferocious competition between North and South for political influence in the burgeoning West. Would the new western states be "slave" or "free"? The volatile issue of allowing slavery into the new territories involved more than humanitarian concern for the plight of enslaved blacks. By the 1840s, the North and South had developed quite different economic interests and political tactics. The North wanted high tariffs on imported manufactures to "protect" its new industries from foreign competition. Southerners, on the other hand, favored free trade because they wanted to import British goods in exchange for the profitable cotton they provided British textile mills.

The South's increasing defensiveness about slavery during the first half of the nineteenth century reflected the region's proud sense of its own distinctiveness. Southerners, a North Carolina editor once wrote, are "a mythological people, created half out of dream and half out of slander, who live in a still legendary land." Most Americans, including southerners themselves, have long harbored a cluster of myths and stereotypes about the South. Perhaps the most enduring myths come from the classic movie *Gone with the Wind* (1939). The Old South portrayed in such romanticized Hollywood productions is a stable agrarian society led by paternalistic white planters and their families, who live in white-columned mansions and represent a "natural" aristocracy of virtue and talent within their communities. In *Gone with the Wind* and similar accounts, southerners are kind to their slaves and devoted to the rural values of independence and chivalric honor, values celebrated by Thomas Jefferson.

By contrast, a much darker myth about the Old South emerged from pamphlets promoting the abolition of slavery and from Harriet Beecher Stowe's best-selling novel, *Uncle Tom's Cabin* (1852). Those exposés of the dark side of southern culture portrayed the planters as arrogant aristocrats who raped enslaved women, brutalized slaves, and lorded over their local communities with haughty disdain. They treated slaves like cattle, broke up slave families, and sold slaves "down the river" to incessant toil in the Louisiana sugar mills and rice plantations. "I'd rather be dead," said one white overseer, "than a nigger in one of those big plantations."

Such contrasting myths are both rooted in reality. Nonetheless, efforts to pinpoint what set the Old South apart from the rest of the nation generally pivot on two lines of thought: the impact of the environment (climate and geography) and the effects of human decisions and actions. The South's warm, humid climate was ideal for the cultivation of profitable crops such as tobacco, cotton, rice, indigo, and sugarcane. The growth of those lucrative cash crops helped foster the plantation system and its dependence upon enslaved labor. The lust for profits led southerners to ignore concerns over the morality of slavery. By the 1850s, most southern leaders could not imagine a future for their region without slavery. In the end, the profitability of slavery and the racist attitudes it engendered brought about the sectional conflict over the extension of slavery that ignited the Civil War.

THE DISTINCTIVENESS OF THE OLD SOUTH

While geography was and is a key determinant of the South's economy and culture, what made the South most distinctive was the expanding institution of slavery. Most southern whites did not own slaves, but they nevertheless supported the continuation of the "**peculiar institution**." The profitability and convenience of owning slaves—as well as the psychological appeal of theories of racial superiority—created a sense of racial unity that bridged class divisions among most whites. Yet the biracial character of the region's population exercised an even greater influence over southern culture. In shaping patterns of speech and folklore, music, religion, literature, and recreation, black southerners immeasurably influenced and enriched the region's development.

The South differed from other sections of the country, too, in the high proportion of native-born Americans in its population, both whites and blacks. Despite the considerable ethnic diversity in the colonial population, the South drew few overseas immigrants after the Revolution. One reason was that the main shipping lines went from Europe to northern ports such as Boston, New York City, and Philadelphia; another, that the prospect of competing with slave labor deterred immigrants. The South's determination to expand slavery in the face of growing criticism in the North and around the world further isolated and defined the region. A prickly defensiveness increasingly shaped southern attitudes and actions.

The South also differed from the rest of the nation in its architecture; its penchant for fighting, guns, horsemanship, and the military; and its attachment to an agrarian ideal and a cult of masculine "honor." The preponderance of farming remained a distinctive regional characteristic, whether pictured as the Jeffersonian yeoman living by the sweat of his brow or the lordly planter overseeing his slave gangs. But in the end what made the South distinctive was its people's belief—and other people's belief—that the region *was* so distinctive.

DIVERGENT SOUTHS For all of the common threads tying the Old South together, it in fact included three distinct subregions with quite different economic interests and diverging degrees of commitment to slavery. The seven states making up the Lower South (South Carolina, Georgia, Florida, Alabama, Mississippi, Louisiana, and Texas) grew increasingly dependent upon labor-intensive cotton production and slave labor. By 1860, slaves represented nearly half the population of the Lower South. The states of the Middle South (Virginia, North Carolina, Tennessee, and Arkansas) had more diversified agricultural economies and included large areas without slavery. In the Upper or Border South (Delaware, Maryland, Kentucky, and Missouri), slavery was beginning to decline by 1860.

The shifting differences among the economic and social life of these three southern subregions help explain the varied intensity of feelings about both the fate of slavery and ultimately the decision to secede. About all that the three subregions shared in common was an opposition to the immediate abolition of slavery. Many white slave owners in the upper South, who held far fewer slaves than their counterparts in the lower South, were so morally ambivalent about slavery that they adopted an attitude of **paternalism** toward slaves by incorporating them into their households. A few actually worked to end slavery by prohibiting the importation of more slaves. Others supported "**colonization**" efforts to ship slaves and freed blacks to Africa or encouraged owners upon their deaths to free their slaves, as did George Washington.

Slave family in a Georgia cotton field

The invention of the cotton gin sent cotton production soaring, deepening the South's dependence on slavery.

Slave owners in the lower South scoffed at such efforts to end slavery, however. With a disproportionately large investment in slavery, planters in the states of the lower South viewed the forced labor system as an asset and a blessing rather than a moral burden. Whites in the Lower South were also much more concerned about the possibility of an organized slave revolt as had occurred in French-controlled Haiti. Whites increasingly believed that only constant vigilance, supervision, terror, intimidation, and punishment would keep enslaved workers under control. At the same time, as the dollar value of a slave soared, white planters from the lower southern states led efforts to transplant slavery into the new western territories, voted for secession, and, in 1861, formed the Confederate States of America.

STAPLE CROPS During the first half of the nineteenth century, cotton became the most profitable cash crop in the South—by far. But other crops remained viable. Tobacco, the region's first staple crop, had been the mainstay of Virginia and Maryland during the colonial era and was also common in North Carolina. After the Revolution, the tobacco economy spread into Kentucky and as far west as Missouri. Since rice production required substantial capital for floodgates, irrigation ditches, and machinery, it was limited to the relatively few large plantations that could afford it, and those were in the low-country of North and South Carolina and Georgia, where fields could easily be flooded and drained by tidal rivers flowing into the ocean. Sugar, like rice, required a heavy capital investment to purchase machinery to grind the cane. Since sugar needed the prop of a protective tariff to enable its farmers to compete with foreign suppliers, it produced the anomaly in southern politics of pro-tariff congressmen from Louisiana, where sugar was king.

Cotton, however, eventually outpaced all the others put together. At the end of the War of 1812, annual cotton production was less than 150,000 bales (a bale is a compressed bundle of cotton weighing between 400 and 500 pounds); in 1860 production was 4 million bales. Three factors accounted for the dramatic growth: (1) the invention of cotton gins exponentially increased the amount of cotton that could be cultivated; (2) the demand for southern cotton among British and French textile manufacturers soared as the industry grew in size and technological sophistication; and (3) the aggressive cultivation of farmlands in the newer states of Alabama, Mississippi, Arkansas, Louisiana, and Texas (a region then called the Old Southwest).

The Old South witnessed a mass movement from Virginia and the Carolinas to more fertile, inexpensive cotton lands farther west and south. The Old Southwest's low land prices and suitability for cotton cultivation (as well as sugarcane in Louisiana) served as a powerful magnet, luring hundreds of thousands of settlers from Virginia, and the Carolinas when the seaboard economy faltered during the 1820s and 1830s. Between 1810 and 1840, the cumulative population of Georgia, Alabama, and Mississippi increased from about 300,000 (252,000 of whom were in Georgia) to 1,657,799. Over 40 percent of the residents were enslaved blacks, many of whom had been moved in chained gangs (called "coffles") from plantations and slave markets in the Carolinas, Virginia, and New Orleans. The migrating southerners carved out farms, built churches, established towns, and eventually brought culture and order to a raw frontier.

By 1860 the center of the cotton belt stretched from eastern North Carolina, South Carolina, and Georgia through the fertile Alabama-Mississippi black belt (so called for the color of the soil), through Louisiana, on to Texas, and up the Mississippi River valley as far as southern Illinois. As cotton production soared, vast acreages shifted from other crops, in part because cotton could be cultivated on small farms, unlike sugar and rice. The rapid expansion of the cotton belt throughout the South ensured that the region became more, rather than less, dependent on enslaved black workers. More than half of the slaves worked in cotton production.

During the antebellum era, slavery became such a powerful, profitable engine of economic development that its mushrooming significance defied domestic and international criticism. By 1860, after the addition of Texas and the rise of plantation slavery there, the dollar value of enslaved blacks outstripped the value of all banks, railroads, and factories combined. The southern economy led the nation in exports. The result was staggering wealth among the large planters and their brokers. The twelve richest counties in the United States by 1860 were all in the South.

MANUFACTURING AND TRADE   By 1840 some southerners decided that the farm-centered region desperately needed to develop its own manufacturing and trade because of its dependence upon northern industry and commerce: cotton and tobacco were exported mainly in northern vessels. Southerners also relied upon northern merchants for imported goods—economically the South had become a kind of colonial dependency of the North.

Southerners offered two major explanations for the region's lag in industrial development. First, blacks were presumed unsuited to factory work. Second, the ruling planter-commercial elite of the Old South had developed a lordly disdain for industrial production. As Thomas Jefferson had demonstrated, a certain aristocratic prestige derived from owning land and holding slaves. But any argument that African American labor was incompatible with industrial work simply flew in the face of the evidence, since southern factory owners bought or hired enslaved blacks to operate just about every kind of mechanical equipment. In the 1850s, between 150,000 and 200,000 slaves—about 5 percent of the total number—worked at industrial jobs in the South.

The notion that aristocratic planters were not sufficiently motivated by profits to promote industrial development is also a myth. Large planters were very entrepreneurial; they were capitalists preoccupied with profits. By a strictly economic calculation, slaves and land on which cotton could be grown were the most profitable investments available in the antebellum South. The largest slaveholders, particularly in the newer cotton lands of the Old Southwest, were so incredibly rich that they saw little need for promoting industrial development.

WHITE SOCIETY IN THE SOUTH

If an understanding of the Old South requires understanding the power of social myths, it involves acknowledging the tragic dimension of the region's history. Since colonial days, white southerners had won short-term economic gains that over time ravaged the soil and aroused the moral indignation of much of the world. The concentration on agriculture and the growing dependence on slaves at the expense of urban development and immigration deprived the South of the most dynamic sources of innovation. The slaveholding South hitched its wagon not to a star but to the (largely British and French) demand for cotton. By 1860, Britain was importing more than 80 percent of its cotton from the South. And the growing of cotton was directly linked to the use of enslaved labor. As the economist Karl Marx, co-author of *The Communist Manifesto*, noted from Britain in 1846, "Without cotton you have no modern industry.... without slavery, you have no cotton."

During the late 1850s, cotton production became so profitable that it fostered some tragic misperceptions. The South, "safely entrenched behind her cotton bags . . . can defy the world—for the civilized world depends on the cotton of the South," said a Mississippi newspaper in 1860. The soaring profitability of cotton made some southerners cocky and even belligerent. In a famous speech to the Senate in 1858, South Carolina's James H. Hammond warned the North: "You dare not make war on cotton. No power on earth dares make war upon it. Cotton is King." What such aggressive southern boosters could not perceive was what they could least afford: the imminent slackening of the world demand for cotton. The heyday of expansion in

King Cotton Captured

This engraving shows cotton being trafficked in Louisiana.

British textiles had ended by 1860, but by then the Deep South was locked into large-scale cotton production for generations to come.

WHITE PLANTERS   Although there were only a few giant plantations in each southern state, their owners exercised disproportionately powerful influence in economic, political, and social life. As a western Virginian observed in the mid-1830s, "the old slaveholding families exerted a great deal of control . . . and they affected the manner and prejudices of the slaveholding part of the state." What distinguished a plantation from a neighboring farm, in addition to its size, was the use of a large enslaved labor force, under separate control and supervision, to grow primarily staple crops (cotton, rice, tobacco, and sugarcane). A clear-cut distinction between management and labor set the planter apart from the small slaveholder, who often worked side by side with slaves at the same tasks.

If, to be called a **planter**, one had to own twenty slaves, only one out of every thirty whites in the South in 1860 was a planter. The 1860 census listed eleven planters with five hundred slaves and one with as many as a thousand. Yet this privileged elite exercised disproportionate social and political influence. The planter group, making up less than 4 percent of the white men in

MRS. CHESTNUT
of South Carolina

Mary Chestnut

Mary Chestnut's diary describing the Civil War was republished in 1981 and won the Pulitzer Prize.

the South, held more than half the slaves. The number of slaveholders was only 383,637 out of a total white population in the southern states of 8 million. But assuming that each family numbered five people, then whites with some proprietary interest in slavery constituted 1.9 million, or roughly a fourth of the South's white population.

THE PLANTATION MISTRESS
The mistress of the plantation, like the master, seldom led a life of idle leisure. She supervised the domestic household in the same way the planter took care of the business, overseeing the supply and preparation of food and linens, the housecleaning and care of the sick, and a hundred other details. Mary Boykin Chesnut of South Carolina complained that "there is no slave like a wife." The wives of all but the most wealthy planters supervised daily the domestic activities of the household and managed the slaves. The son of a Tennessee slaveholder remembered that his mother and grandmother were "the busiest women I ever saw."

White women living in a slaveholding culture confronted a double standard in terms of moral and sexual behavior. While they were expected to behave as exemplars of Christian piety and sexual purity, their husbands, brothers, and sons often followed an unwritten rule of self-indulgent hedonism. "God forgive us," Mary Chesnut wrote in her diary,

> but ours is a monstrous system. Like the patriarchs of old, our men live all in one house with their wives and their [enslaved] concubines; and the mulattoes one sees in every family partly resemble the white children. Any lady is ready to tell you who is the father of all the mulatto children in everybody's household but her own. Those, she seems to think, drop from the clouds.

Such a double standard both illustrated and reinforced the arrogant authoritarianism displayed by many male planters. Yet for all their private complaints and daily burdens, few plantation mistresses engaged in public criticism of the prevailing social order and racist climate.

THE WHITE MIDDLE CLASS   Overseers on the largest plantations generally came from the middle class of small farmers or skilled workers or were younger sons of planters. Most aspired to become slaveholders themselves. They moved often, seeking better wages. A Mississippi planter described white overseers as "a worthless set of vagabonds." There were few black overseers; the highest management position to which a slave could aspire was usually that of "driver," placed in charge of a small group ("gang") of slaves with the duty of getting them to work without creating dissension.

The most numerous white southerners were the small farmers (**yeomen**), those who lived with their families in simple two-room cabins rather than columned mansions. They raised a few hogs and chickens, grew some corn and cotton, and traded with neighbors more than they bought from stores. Women on such small farms worked in the fields during harvest time but spent most of their days attending to domestic chores. Many of these "middling" farmers owned a handful of slaves, but most had none. In the backcountry and mountainous regions of the South, yeoman farmers dominated the social structure; there were few plantations in western North Carolina and Virginia, upcountry South Carolina, eastern Tennessee, and northern Georgia and Alabama.

Southern farmers were typically mobile folk, ever willing to pull up stakes and move west or southwest in pursuit of better land. They tended to be fiercely independent and suspicious of government authority, and they overwhelmingly identified with the Democratic party of Andrew Jackson and the spiritual fervor of evangelical Protestantism. Though only a minority of the middle-class farmers held slaves, most of them supported the slave system. They feared that the slaves, if freed, would compete with them for land, and they enjoyed the privileged status that racially based slavery afforded them. As a white farmer told a northern traveler, "Now suppose they was free. You see they'd all think themselves as good as we." Such racist sentiments pervaded the Deep South—and much of the rest of the nation.

BLACK SOCIETY IN THE SOUTH

Although degrading, dangerous, and unstable, slavery was one of the fastest growing elements of national life during the first half of the nineteenth century. In 1790 there were fewer than 700,000 enslaved blacks in the United

States. By 1830 there were more than 2 million, and by 1860 there were almost 4 million. In rural areas, the lives of whites and blacks were interwoven in innumerable and often intimate ways. As the enslaved population grew, slave owners felt the need to develop much more explicit rules, regulations, and restrictions governing slaves and limiting their rights. Throughout the seventeenth and well into the eighteenth century, slavery had largely been an uncodified system of forced labor practiced in most of the European colonies in the Western Hemisphere. Enslaved workers were initially treated like indentured servants. After the American Revolution, however, slavery became a highly regulated institution centered in the South. Enslaved people were subject to the arbitrary authority—and everyday whims—of their masters and owners. They could be moved or sold as their master saw fit. They could not legally marry. They suffered tight restrictions on their movements and were subjected to harsh, violent punishments. Yet despite such restrictions, slaves found ways to forge networks of community that enabled them to sustain their folk heritage. Amid the horrors of the slave system the enslaved managed to create a degree of cultural autonomy for themselves.

"FREE PERSONS OF COLOR" In the Old South, free persons of color occupied an uncertain status between slavery and freedom, subject to racist restrictions not imposed upon whites. Free blacks attained their status in a number of ways. Over the years some slaves were able to purchase their freedom, and others were freed ("manumitted") by their owners. By 1860 there were some 260,000 free blacks in the slave states, most of them very poor. Some of the men were tailors or shoemakers or carpenters; others worked as painters, bricklayers, butchers, or barbers. Still others worked on the docks or on board boats and ships. Women worked as seamstresses or vendors, washerwomen or house servants.

Free blacks

This badge, issued in Charleston, South Carolina, was worn by a free black so that he would not be mistaken for someone's "property."

Among them were a large number of **mulattoes**, people of mixed racial ancestry. The census of 1860 reported 412,000 people of mixed parentage in the United States, or about 10 percent of the black population, probably a drastic undercount. In cities such as Charleston and especially New Orleans, "colored" society became virtually a third caste, a new people who occupied a status somewhere between that of blacks and that of whites. Some mulattoes built substantial fortunes and even became slaveholders. They often operated inns serving a white clientele. Jehu Jones, for instance, was the "colored" proprietor of one of Charleston's best hotels. In Louisiana a mulatto, Cyprien Ricard, paid $250,000 for an estate that had ninety-one slaves. In Natchez, Mississippi, William Johnson, son of a white father and a mulatto mother, operated three barbershops, owned 1,500 acres of land, and held several slaves.

Black slaveholders were few in number, however. The 1830 census revealed that 3,775 free blacks, about 2 percent of the total free black population, owned 12,760 slaves. Some blacks held slaves for humanitarian purposes. One minister, for instance, bought slaves and then enabled them to purchase their freedom from him on easy terms. Most often, black slaveholders were free blacks who bought their own family members with the express purpose of freeing them.

THE TRADE IN SLAVES   The rise in the slave population mainly occurred naturally, especially after Congress outlawed American involvement with the African slave trade in 1808. But banning the import of slaves from Africa had the effect of increasing the cash value of slaves in the United States. This in turn convinced some owners to treat their slaves better. As one planter remarked in 1849, "The time has been that the farmer would kill up and wear out one Negro to buy another, but it is not so now." The dramatic rise in the monetary value of enslaved workers brought better treatment for many. "Massa was purty good," one ex-slave recalled. "He treated us jus' 'bout like you would a good mule." Another said his master "fed us reg'lar on good, 'stantial food, jus' like you'd tend to you hoss, if you had a real good one." Some slaveholders hired wage laborers, often Irish immigrants, for ditching and other dangerous work rather than risk the lives of the more valuable slaves. And with the rising cash value of slaves, more and more owners sought to ensure that enslaved women bore children—as many as possible. A South Carolina planter named William Johnson explained in 1815 that the "interest of the owner is to obtain from his slaves labor *and increase.*"

The end of the African slave trade increased the importance of the domestic slave-trading network, with slaves moving mainly from the worn-out lands of the Southeast into the booming new country of the Old Southwest. Many slaves were taken south and west with the planters who owned them,

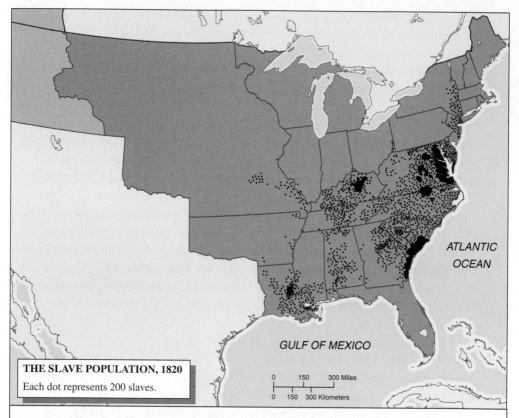

THE SLAVE POPULATION, 1820

Each dot represents 200 slaves.

ATLANTIC OCEAN

GULF OF MEXICO

0   150   300 Miles

0   150   300 Kilometers

Consider where the largest populations of slaves were clustered in the South in 1820. Why were most slaves clustered in these regions and not in others? How was the experience of plantation slavery different for men and women?

but selling slaves became big business. Slave markets and auction houses sprang up like mushrooms to meet the demand, and communities constructed slave "jails" to house the shackled men, women, and children who were waiting to be sold to the highest bidder. The worst aspect of the domestic slave trade was the separation of children from parents and husbands from wives. Only Louisiana and Alabama (from 1852) forbade separating a child younger than ten from his or her mother, and no state forbade the separation of husband from wife.

Almost a million captive blacks were "sold south" and taken to the Old Southwest during the antebellum era, most of them in the 1830s. A third of the transplanted slaves were transported with their owners. The other two

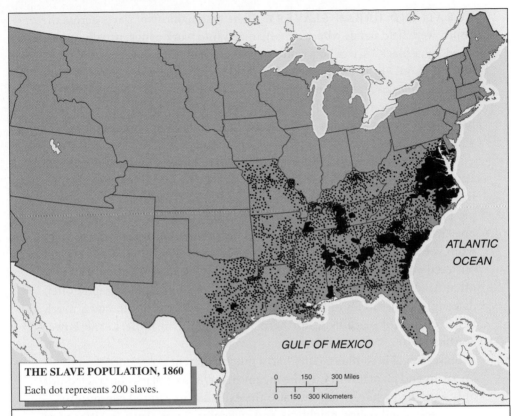

THE SLAVE POPULATION, 1860

Each dot represents 200 slaves.

ATLANTIC OCEAN

GULF OF MEXICO

0   150   300 Miles

0   150   300 Kilometers

Why did slavery spread west? What patterns do you see? Why would slaves have resisted migrating west?

thirds were sold at slave auctions in New Orleans, Virginia and the Carolinas and moved west by slave traders. White owners—as well as Indians who purchased enslaved blacks—worked the slaves especially hard in the Old Southwest, clearing land and planting cotton. Slaves came to fear the harsh working conditions and torpid heat and humidity of the new territory. But they were especially despondent at the breakup of their family ties. A white Virginian noted in 1807 that "there is a great aversion amongst our Negroes to be carried to distant parts, & particularly to our new countries." Because the first task in the new region involved the clearing of land, enslaved males were most in demand. Relatively few black women were taken to the Old Southwest, thus making it difficult to reestablish kinship ties.

RURAL AND URBAN SLAVERY   The vast majority of slaves across the South were field hands who were organized into work gangs, usually supervised by a black "driver" or white overseer. Plantation slaves were usually housed in one- or two-room wooden shacks with dirt floors. The wealthiest planters built slave cabins out of brick. A set of clothes was distributed twice a year, but shoes were generally provided only in winter. About half of all slave babies died in the first year of life, a mortality rate more than twice that of whites.

Field hands worked long hours, from dawn to dusk. Although owners and slaves often developed close and even affectionate relationships, the "peculiar institution" was enforced by a system rooted in brutal force that defined people primarily as property. The difference between a good owner and a bad one, according to one ex-slave, was the difference between one "who did not whip you too much" and one who "whipped you till he'd bloodied you and blistered you." Over fifty thousand slaves a year escaped. Those not caught often headed for Mexico, the northern states, or Canada. Geography often determined the success of runaways. Those in the Upper South had a much better chance of reaching a northern "free" state than those in the Lower South.

Slaves living in southern cities had a much different experience than those on farms and plantations. City life meant that enslaved blacks interacted not only with their white owners but also the extended interracial community— shopkeepers and police, neighbors and strangers. Some slaves in cities were "hired out" on the condition that that they paid a percentage of their earned wages to their owners. Generally speaking, slaves in cities enjoyed greater mobility and freedom than their counterparts in rural areas.

SLAVE WOMEN   Although enslaved men and women often performed similar labors, they did not experience slavery in the same way. Once slaveholders realized how profitable a fertile female slave could be over time, giving birth every two and a half years to a child who eventually could be sold, they encouraged reproduction through a variety of incentives. Pregnant slaves were given less work to do and more food. Some plantation owners rewarded new mothers with dresses and silver dollars.

But if motherhood endowed enslaved women with stature and benefits, it also entailed exhausting demands. Within days after childbirth, the mother was put to work spinning, weaving, or sewing. A few weeks thereafter, mothers were sent back to the fields; breast-feeding mothers were often forced to take their babies to the fields with them. Enslaved women were expected to do "man's work" outside: cut trees, haul logs, plow fields with mules, dig ditches, spread fertilizer, slaughter animals, hoe corn, and pick cotton. As an escaped slave reported, "Women who do outdoor work are used as bad as men."

Once women passed their childbearing years, around the age of forty, their workload was increased. Slaveholders put middle-aged women to work full-time in the fields or performing other outdoor labor. On larger plantations elderly women, called grannies, kept the children during the day while their mothers worked outside. Women worked as cooks and seamstresses, midwives and nurses, healers and folk doctors. Enslaved women of all ages usually worked in sex-segregated gangs, which enabled them to form close bonds with one another. To enslaved African Americans, developing a sense of community and camaraderie meant emotional and psychological survival. Older women assumed primary responsibility for nurturing family and kinship networks and anchoring slave communities.

Unlike enslaved men, enslaved girls and women faced the threat of sexual abuse. Sometimes a white master or overseer would rape a woman in the fields or cabins. Sometimes he would lock a woman in a cabin with a male slave whose task was to impregnate her. Female slaves responded to the sexual abuse in different ways. Some seduced their master away from his wife. Others fiercely resisted the sexual advances—and were usually whipped or even killed for their disobedience. Some women killed their babies rather than see them grow up in slavery.

CELIA   A single historical narrative helps illustrate the exploitation, deprivation, and vulnerability of enslaved people operating within an inequitable web of laws and customs. Such is the case of an enslaved teen named Celia. Her tragic story reveals complexity of slavery and the limited options available to the enslaved. As Celia discovered, slaves often could improve their circumstances only by making extraordinarily difficult choices that carried no guarantee of success.

In 1850 fourteen-year-old Celia was purchased by Robert Newsom, a prosperous, respected Missouri farmer who told his daughters that he had bought Celia to work as their domestic servant. In fact, however, the recently widowed Newsom wanted a sexual slave. After purchasing Celia, he raped the girl while taking her back to his farm. For the next five years, Newsom treated Celia as his mistress, even building her a brick cabin fifty yards from his house. During that time she gave birth to two children, presumably his offspring. By 1855, Celia had fallen in love with another slave, George, who demanded that she "quit the old man." Desperate for relief from her tormentor, Celia appealed to Newsom's two grown daughters, but they either could not or would not intervene.

Soon thereafter, on June 23, 1855, the sixty-five-year-old Newsom entered Celia's cabin, ignored her frantic appeals, and kept advancing until she struck and killed him with a large stick. Celia was not allowed to testify at her murder trial because she was a slave. Her attorneys, all of them slaveholders, argued that the right of white women to defend themselves against sexual assault should be extended to enslaved women. The prevailing public opinion in the slave states, however, stressed that the rape of a slave by an owner was not a crime. The judge and jury, all white men, pronounced Celia guilty. On December 21, 1855, after two months of trials and futile appeals, Celia was hanged.

The grim story of Celia's brief life and abused condition highlights the skewed power structure in southern society before the Civil War. Celia bore a double burden, that of a slave and that of a woman living in a male-dominated society rife with racism and sexism.

FORGING A SLAVE COMMUNITY   To generalize about slavery is to miss its various incarnations from place to place and time to time. The experience was as varied as people are. Enslaved African Americans were victims of terrible injustice, abuse, and constraints, but to stop at so obvious a reality would be to miss important evidence of endurance, resilience, and achievement. If ever there was an effective melting pot in American history, it may have been that in which Africans with a variety of ethnic, linguistic, and tribal origins formed new communities and new cultures as African Americans. Wherever they could, African Americans forged their own coherent sense of community, asserted their individuality, and devised ingenious ways to resist their confinement. For example, although most slaves were prohibited from marrying, the law did not prevent slaves from choosing partners and forging a family life for themselves within the constraints of the slave system. Slaves also gathered secretly for religious worship and to engage in folk rituals. They also used encoded songs ("**spirituals**") to express their frustration at being kept in bondage. Slave culture incorporated many African elements, especially in areas with few whites. Elements of African culture have thus survived, adapted, and interacted with those of the other cultures with which slaves came in contact.

AFRICAN AMERICAN RELIGION AND FOLKLORE   Among the most important elements of African American culture was its dynamic religion, a unique mixture of African, Caribbean, and Christian elements often practiced in secret because many slaveholders feared the effects of shared religion on enslaved workers. Slaves found in religion both balm for the soul

Plantation of J. J. Smith, Beaufort, South Carolina, 1862

Several generations of a family raised in slavery.

and release for their emotions. Most Africans brought with them to the Americas a concept of a Creator, or Supreme God, whom they could recognize in the Christian Jehovah, and lesser gods, whom they might identify with Christ, the Holy Ghost, and the saints, thereby reconciling their African beliefs with Christianity. Alongside the church they maintained beliefs in spirits (many of them benign), magic, and conjuring. Enslaved Africans and their African American descendants took for granted the existence of root doctors and sorcerers, witches and wizards. Belief in magic is in fact a common human response to conditions of danger or helplessness.

By 1860, about 20 percent of adult slaves had joined Christian denominations. Many others displayed aspects of the Christian faith in their forms of worship but were not deemed Christians. As a white minister observed of slave worshippers, "Their notions of the Supreme Being; of the character and offices of Christ and of the Holy Ghost; of a future state; and of what constitutes the holiness of life are indefinite and confused." Some slaves had "heard of Jesus Christ, but who he is and what he has done for a ruined world, they cannot tell."

Slaves found the Bible inspiring in its tributes to the poor and oppressed, and they embraced its promise of salvation through the sacrifice of Jesus. Likewise, the lyrics of religious "spirituals" helped slaves endure the strain of field labor and provided them with a musical code with which to express their own desire for freedom on earth. The former slave Frederick Douglass stressed that "slaves sing most when they are most unhappy," and spirituals offered them deliverance from their worldly woes. A slave preacher explained that the "way in which we worshiped is almost indescribable. The singing helped provoke a certain ecstasy of emotion, clapping of hands, tossing of heads, which would continue without cessation about half an hour. The old house partook of the ecstasy; it rang with their jubilant shouts, and shook in all its joints."

SLAVE REBELLIONS   Southern whites were paranoid about the possibility of slave uprisings. Nothing worried them more. Any sign of resistance or rebellion by slaves risked a brutal response. In 1811, for example, two of Thomas Jefferson's nephews, Lilburn and Isham Lewis, tied a seventeen-year-old slave named George to the floor of their Kentucky cabin and killed him with an axe in front of seven other slaves. They then handed the axe to one of the slaves and forced him to dismember the body and put the pieces in the fireplace. The ostensible reason for the murder was that George had broken a valuable pitcher, but in fact the brothers murdered him because he had frequently spoken out against slavery and had run away several times. The Lewises, who had been drinking heavily, wanted "to set an example for any other uppity slaves."

The overwhelming authority and firepower of southern whites made organized resistance by slaves very risky. The nineteenth-century South witnessed only four major slave insurrections, two of which were betrayed before they got under way. In 1800 a slave blacksmith named Gabriel on a plantation near Richmond, Virginia, hatched a revolt involving perhaps a thousand other slaves. They planned to seize key points in the city, capture the governor, James Monroe, and overthrow the economic elite. Gabriel expected that the "poor white people" would join their effort to overthrow the merchant elite. But it rained on the day Gabriel launched his rebellion. Most of the insurgent slaves could not reach the meeting point. Amid the confusion someone alerted whites to the gathering. They captured Gabriel and his fellow conspirators. Gabriel and twenty-six of his fellow "soldiers" were hanged, and ten others were deported to the West Indies. A white Virginian who observed the public executions noted that the rebels on the gallows displayed a "sense of their [natural] rights, [and] a contempt for danger."

In early 1811 the largest slave revolt in American history occurred just north of New Orleans in the Louisiana Territory. Wealthy planters cultivating sugarcane in the region had acquired one of the densest populations of slaves in North America; they greatly outnumbered the local whites. Late in the evening on January 8, a group of slaves armed with axes, knives, and machetes broke into their master's sugar plantation house along the Mississippi River. The planter was able to escape, but his son was hacked to death. The leader of the assault was Charles Deslondes, a trusted mixed-race slave overseer responsible for supervising the field hands. Deslondes and his fellow rebels seized weapons, horses, and militia uniforms from the plantation and, bolstered by liquor and reinforced by more slaves, they headed toward New Orleans, burning houses and killing whites along the way. Over the next two days their ranks swelled to over two hundred. But their success was short-lived. Angry whites—as well as several free blacks who were later praised for their "tireless zeal & dauntless courage"—mobilized to suppress the insurrection. U.S. Army units and militia joined the effort. They surrounded and then assaulted the rebel slaves holed up at a plantation. Dozens of slaves were killed or wounded; most of those who fled were captured over the next week. "We made considerable slaughter," reported one planter. Many of the imprisoned slaves were tortured and then executed. Deslondes had his hands severed and thighs broken before he was shot and his body burned. As many as a hundred slaves were killed and beheaded. Their severed heads were placed on poles along the Mississippi River to strike fear into enslaved workers. A month after the rebellion was put down, a white resident noted, "all the negro difficulties have subsided and gentle peace prevails."

The Denmark Vesey plot in Charleston, discovered in 1822, involved a similar effort to assault the white population. The rebels planned to seize ships in the harbor, burn the city, and head for Santo Domingo (Haiti), where slaves in the former French sugar colony had staged a successful revolt in 1792. The Vesey plot never got off the ground, however. Instead, thirty-five supposed slave rebels were executed, and thirty-four were deported. The city also responded by curtailing the liberties of free blacks.

The **Nat Turner** insurrection of August 1831, in a rural area of Virginia where the enslaved blacks greatly outnumbered free whites, panicked whites throughout the South. Turner, a trusted black overseer, was also a self-anointed preacher who believed he had a divine mission in leading a slave rebellion. A solar eclipse in February 1831 convinced him that he was called to lead a slave revolt. The revolt began when a small group of slaves joined

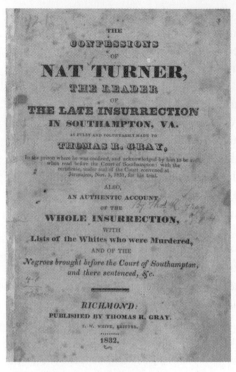

The Confessions of Nat Turner

Published account of Turner's rebellion, written by Turner's lawyer, Thomas Gray.

Turner in killing the adults, children, and infant in his owner's household. They then set off down the road, repeating the process at other farmhouses, where other slaves joined in. Before it ended, fifty-seven whites had been killed, most of them women and children. Federal troops, Virginia militiamen, and volunteers, driven by raging anger and fear, indiscriminately killed many slaves in the process of putting down the rebels. A Virginia journalist said the behavior of the white vigilantes was comparable in "barbarity to the atrocities of the insurgents." Seventeen slaves were hanged; several were decapitated and their severed heads placed on poles along the highway. Turner, called the "blood-stained monster," eluded capture for six weeks. He then was tried, found guilty, and hanged. More than any other event, Nat Turner's Rebellion terrified white southerners by making real the lurking fear that enslaved blacks might revolt. The Virginia legislature responded by restricting the ability of slaves to learn to read and write and to gather for religious meetings. In addition, throughout the South, states tightened their policing of slaves.

Slaves were willing to risk much for freedom—being hunted down, brutally punished, or even killed. Most slaves, however, did not rebel or run away. Instead, they more often retaliated against oppression by malingering, feigning illness, engaging in sabotage, stealing or breaking tools, or destroying crops or livestock. Yet there were constraints on such behavior, for laborers would likely eat better on a prosperous plantation than on a struggling one. And the shrewdest slaveholders knew that offering rewards was more profitable than inflicting pain.

THE SOUTH—A REGION APART Although the Old South included distinct sub-regions with striking differences from one another, what increasingly set the southern tier of states apart from the rest of the nation was a cash-crop agricultural economy (tobacco, cotton, sugar cane, and rice) dependent on race-based slavery. The recurring theme of southern politics and culture from the 1830s to the outbreak of civil war in 1861 was the region's determination to remain a society dominated by whites who in turn exercised domination over people of color. Slavery was the paramount issue controlling all else. A South Carolinian asserted that "slavery with us is no abstraction—but a great and vital fact. Without it, our every comfort would be taken from us."

Protecting the right of southerners to own, transport, and sell slaves became the overriding focus of southern political leaders during the 1830s and after. As a Mississippi governor insisted in 1850, slavery "is entwined with our political system and cannot be separated from it." To southerners, said a Georgian, slavery shaped everything about southern culture: "life and property, safety and security." It was race-based slavery that generated the South's prosperity as well as its growing sense of separateness from the rest of the nation. As an Arkansas senator insisted, slavery "affects the personal interest of every white man." Throughout the 1830s, southern state legislatures stood "one and indivisible" on the preservation of race-based slavery. They shouted defiance against northern abolitionists who called for an end to the immorality of slavery. Virginia's General Assembly, for example, declared that only the southern states had the right to control slavery and that such control must be "maintained at all hazards." The Georgia legislature agreed, announcing that "upon this point there can be no discussion— no compromise—no doubt." A U.S. Senator from Tennessee told Congress that slavery had become "sacred" to the South's future, and no interference would be tolerated. The increasingly militant efforts of northerners to abolish slavery helped reinforce the sense of southern unity while provoking an emotional defensiveness that would culminate in secession and war.

CHAPTER SUMMARY

- **The Southern Economy** Cotton was not the only profitable crop in the South. The Border South and Middle South became increasingly diversified, producing tobacco and grains. Sugar and other crops were grown along with cotton in the Lower South. Despite the belief that slaves were unsuited for factory work, some manufacturing ventures in the South employed slaves. Slavery was the unifying element in most southern enterprises.

- **Southern Culture** Throughout the antebellum era the South became increasingly committed to a cotton economy, which in turn was dependent upon slave labor. Despite efforts to diversify the economy, the wealth and status associated with cotton prompted the westward expansion of the plantation culture.

- **Southern Black Culture** The enslaved responded to their oppression in a variety of ways. Although many slaves attempted to run away, only a few openly rebelled because the consequences were so harsh. Some survived by relying on their own communities, family ties, and Christian faith. Most free blacks in the South were mulattoes and some even owned slaves, often purchasing members of their own family.

- **Expansion into the Southwest** Westward expansion resulted from soil exhaustion and falling prices from Virginia to Georgia. Sons of Southern planters wanted to take advantage of cheap land on the frontier to make their own fortunes and way of life. Slaves were worked harshly preparing the terrain for cotton cultivation and experienced the breakup of family ties.

CHRONOLOGY

1792	Slave revolt in Santo Domingo (Haiti)
1800	Gabriel conspiracy in Richmond, VA
1808	Participation in the international slave trade is outlawed
1811	Charles Deslondes revolt in Louisiana
1816	American Colonization Society is founded
1822	Denmark Vesey conspiracy is discovered in Charleston, South Carolina
1831	Nat Turner leads slave insurrection in Virginia
1852	Harriet Beecher Stowe's *Uncle Tom's Cabin* is published

KEY TERMS & NAMES

13

RELIGION, ROMANTICISM, AND REFORM

FOCUS QUESTIONS

wwnorton.com/studyspace

- What were the main changes in the practice of religion in America during the early nineteenth century?
- What were the distinguishing characteristics of American literature during the antebellum period?
- What were the goals of the social-reform movement?
- What was the status of women during this period?
- How and where did opposition to slavery emerge?

During the first half of the nineteenth century, the world's largest—and youngest—republic was a festival of contrasts. Europeans traveling in America marveled at the nation's restless energy and buoyant optimism, its democratic idealism and entrepreneurial spirit. At the same time, however, visitors noticed that the dynamic young republic was experiencing growing pains, sectional tensions, and increasingly heated debates over the morality and future of slavery in a nation dedicated to freedom and equality. Such tensions made for an increasingly partisan political environment whose conflicts were mirrored in the evolution of American social and cultural life. Unlike nations of the Old World, which had long been steeped in history and romance, the United States in the early nineteenth century was an infant republic founded by religious seekers and economic adventurers but weaned on the rational ideas of the Enlightenment. Those "reasonable" ideas, most vividly set forth in Thomas Jefferson's Declaration of Independence, influenced religion, literature and the arts, and various social reform movements during the first half of the nineteenth century. Politics was not the only contested battleground during the first half of the nineteenth century; religious and cultural life also wrenching strains and new outlooks.

RATIONAL RELIGION

After the Revolution many Americans were more interested in religious salvation than political engagement. Christian activists assumed that the United States had a God-mandated mission to provide the world with a shining example of republican virtue, much as Puritan New England had once stood before sinful humanity as an example of an ideal Christian community. The concept of America's having a special mission still carried strong spiritual overtones, for the religious fervor that quickened in the Great Awakening had reinforced the idea of the nation's fulfilling a providential purpose. This idea contained an element of perfectionism—and an element of impatience when reality fell short of expectations. The combination of widespread religious energy and fervent social idealism brought major reforms and advances in human rights during the first half of the nineteenth century. It also brought disappointments that at times triggered cynicism and alienation.

DEISM The currents of the rational Enlightenment and the spiritual Great Awakening, now mingling, now parting, flowed on into the nineteenth century and in different ways eroded the remnants of Calvinist orthodoxy. As time passed, the puritanical image of a stern God promising predestined hellfire and damnation gave way to a more optimistic religious outlook. Enlightenment rationalism stressed humankind's inherent goodness rather than its depravity and encouraged a belief in social progress and the promise of individual perfectibility.

Many leaders of the Revolutionary War era, such as Thomas Jefferson and Benjamin Franklin, were Deists. After the American Revolution, and especially during the 1790s, when the French Revolution generated excited attention in the United States, interest in Deism increased. In every major city "deistical societies" emerged, and college students especially took delight in criticizing conventional religion. By the use of reason, Deists believed, people might grasp the natural laws governing the universe. Deists rejected the belief that every statement in the Bible was literally true. They were skeptical of miracles and questioned the divinity of Jesus. Deists also defended free speech and opposed religious coercion of all sorts.

UNITARIANISM AND UNIVERSALISM Orthodox Christians, who remained the preponderant majority in the United States, could hardly distinguish Deism from atheism, but Enlightenment rationalism soon began to make deep inroads into American Protestantism. The old Puritan churches around Boston proved most vulnerable to the appeal of religious liberalism. Boston's progress—or, some would say, its degeneration—from Puritanism to prosperity had persuaded many affluent families that they were anything but sinners in the hands of an angry God. By the end of the eighteenth century, many well-educated New Englanders were embracing Unitarianism, a belief that emphasizes the oneness and benevolence of a loving God, the inherent goodness of humankind, and the primacy of reason and conscience over religious creeds and organized churches. Unitarians believe that Jesus was a saintly man but he was not divine. People are not inherently depraved, Unitarians stressed; people are capable of doing tremendous good, and *all* are eligible for salvation. Boston was the center of the Unitarian movement, and it flourished chiefly within Congregational churches. During the early nineteenth century, "liberal" churches adopted the name *Unitarian.*

A parallel anti-Calvinist movement, Universalism, attracted a different—and much larger—social group: working-class people. In 1779, John Murray, a British ex-Methodist clergyman, founded the first Universalist church, in Gloucester, Massachusetts. Universalism stresses the salvation of all people, not just a predestined few. God, it teaches, is too merciful to condemn anyone to eternal punishment. "Thus, the Unitarians and Universalists were in fundamental agreement," wrote one historian of religion, "the Universalists holding that God was too good to damn man; the Unitarians insisting that man was too good to be damned." Although both sects remained relatively small, they exercised a powerful influence over intellectual life, especially in New England.

THE SECOND GREAT AWAKENING

By the end of the eighteenth century, Enlightenment secularism had made deep inroads among the best-educated Americans, but most people remained profoundly religious, as they have been ever since. There was, the perceptive French visitor Alexis de Tocqueville observed, "no country in the world where the Christian religion retains a greater influence over the souls of men than in America."

After the American Revolution, religious life witnessed a profound transformation. The established denominations gave way to newer, more democratic sects. Anglicanism was affected the most. It suffered the stigma of being aligned with the Church of England, and it lost its status as the official religion in most states. To diminish their pro-British image, Virginia Anglicans renamed themselves Episcopalians. But even the new name did not prevent the denomination from losing its traditional leadership position in the South, as the insurgent Methodist and Baptist faiths attracted masses of congregants.

Around 1800, fears that secularism was taking root among well-educated Americans sparked a counterattack in the form of an intense series of revivals that grew into the **Second Great Awakening**. An early revivalist leader, Timothy Dwight, became president of Yale College in 1795 and resolved to purify a campus that had turned into "a hotbed of infidelity." Like his grandfather Jonathan Edwards, Dwight helped launch a series of revivals that captivated Yale

John Wesley

Wesley's gravestone reads, "Lord let me not live to be useless."

students and spread to all of New England. Over the next forty years the flames of revivalism crisscrossed the United States. By the time those flames died down, the landscape of American religious life had been turned topsy-turvy. The once-dominant Congregational and Anglican churches were displaced by newer sects, such as the Baptists and the Methodists. By the mid–nineteenth century, there would be more Methodist churches by far than those of any other denomination. The percentage of Americans who joined Protestant churches increased sixfold between 1800 and 1860.

The Second Great Awakening involved two very different centers of activity. One emerged among the elite New England colleges, especially Yale, and then spread west across New York into Pennsylvania and Ohio, Indiana, and Illinois. The other center of revivalism coalesced in the backwoods of Tennessee and Kentucky and spread across rural America. What both forms of Protestant revivalism shared was a simple message: salvation is available not just to a select few but to anyone who repents and embraces Christ.

FRONTIER REVIVALS   In its frontier phase, the Second Great Awakening, like the first, generated great excitement and dramatic behavior. It gave birth, moreover, to two religious phenomena—the backwoods circuit-riding preacher and the camp meeting—that helped keep the fires of revivalism burning in the backwoods. Evangelists found ready audiences among lonely frontier folk hungry for spiritual intensity and a sense of community. Revivals were often unifying events; they bridged many social, economic, political, and even racial divisions. Women especially flocked to the rural revivals and sustained religious life on the frontier. In small rural hamlets, the traveling revival was as welcome an event as the traveling circus—and as entertaining.

Among the established sects, Presbyterianism was entrenched among the Scots-Irish, from Pennsylvania to Georgia. Presbyterians gained further from the Plan of Union, worked out in 1801 with the Congregationalists of Connecticut and later with Congregationalists of other states. Since the Presbyterians and the Congregationalists agreed on doctrine and differed mainly on the form of church government they adopted, they were able to form unified congregations and call a minister from either church. The result through much of the Old Northwest was that New Englanders became Presbyterians by way of the "Presbygational" churches.

The Baptists, often unschooled, embraced a simplicity of doctrine and organization that appealed especially to rural people. Their theology was grounded in the infallibility of the Bible and the recognition of innate human depravity. But they replaced the Calvinist notion of predestination and selective salvation with the concepts of free will and universal redemption, while highlighting the ritual of adult baptism. They also stressed the equality of all before God, regardless of wealth, social standing, or education. Each congregation was its own highest authority, so a frontier church had no denominational hierarchy to report to.

The Methodists, who shared with Baptists the belief that everyone could gain salvation by an act of free will, established a much more centralized church structure. They also developed the most effective evangelical method of all: the traveling minister on horseback, who sought out rural converts in the most remote areas with the message of salvation as a gift free for the taking. The "circuit rider" system began with Francis Asbury, a tireless British-born revivalist who scoured the trans-Appalachian frontier for lost souls, traversing fifteen states and preaching thousands of sermons. Asbury established a mobile evangelism perfectly suited to the frontier environment and the new democratic age. After Asbury, Peter Cartwright emerged as the most successful circuit rider and grew justly famous for his highly charged sermons. Cartwright roamed across Kentucky, Tennessee, Ohio, and Indiana, preaching a sermon a day for over twenty years. His message was simple: salvation is free for all to embrace. By the 1840s, the Methodists had grown into the largest Protestant church in the nation.

African Americans were especially attracted to the new Methodist and Baptist churches. Richard Allen, who would later help found the African Methodist Episcopal (AME) Church, said in 1787 that "there was no religious

Religious revival

An aquatint of a backwoods Methodist camp meeting in 1819.

sect or denomination that would suit the capacity of the colored people as well as the Methodist." He decided that the "plain and simple gospel suits best for any people; for the unlearned can understand [it]." But even more important, the Methodists actively recruited blacks. They were "the first people," Allen noted, "that brought glad tidings to the colored people." The Baptists did as well. Like the Methodists, they offered a gospel of salvation open to all, regardless of wealth, social standing, gender, or race. As free as well as enslaved African Americans joined white Baptist or Methodist churches, they infused the congregations with exuberant energy and emotional songs called spirituals.

During the early nineteenth century, the energies of the Great Revival, as the Second Great Awakening was called, spread through the western states and into more settled regions back East. Camp meetings were typically held in late summer or fall, when farm work slackened. People came from far and wide, camping in wagons, tents, or crude shacks. African Americans, whether enslaved or free, were allowed to set up their own adjacent camp revivals. The largest camp meetings tended to be ecumenical affairs, with Baptist, Methodist, and Presbyterian ministers working as a team. The crowds often numbered in the thousands, and the unrestrained atmosphere at times made for chaos. If a particular hymn or sermon excited participants, they would shout, dance, or repeat the phrase. Mass excitement swept up even the most skeptical onlookers, and infusions of the spirit sparked strange behavior. Some went into trances; others contracted the "jerks," laughed "the holy laugh," babbled in unknown tongues, or got down on all fours and barked like dogs to "tree the devil," as a hound might tree a raccoon.

But dwelling on the bizarre aspects of the camp meetings distorts an activity that offered a redemptive social outlet to isolated rural folk. This was especially true for women, for whom the camp meetings provided an alternative to the rigors and loneliness of farm life. Women, in fact, played the predominant role at camp meetings, as they had in earlier revivals. Evangelical ministers repeatedly applauded the spiritual energies of women and affirmed their right to give public witness to their faith. Camp meetings provided opportunities for women to participate as equals in large public rituals. In addition, the various organizational needs of large revivals offered numerous opportunities for women to exercise leadership roles outside the home, including service as traveling evangelists themselves. Phoebe Worrall Palmer, for example, hosted revival meetings in her New York City home, then traveled across the United States as a camp meeting evangelist. Such opportunities to assume traditional male roles bolstered women's self-confidence and expanded their horizons beyond the domestic sphere. Their religious enthusiasm often inspired them to work on behalf of various social-reform efforts, including expanded educational opportunities for women and the right to vote. So in many ways and on many levels, the energies of the revivals helped spread a more democratic faith among people living on the frontier. The evangelical impulse also led to an array of inter-denominational initiatives intended to ensure that new converts sustained their faith. Various denominations, for example, joined forces to create the American Bible Society and the American Sunday School Union. The Bible Society gave free Bibles to new converts, and the Sunday School Union provided weekly educational instruction, including basic literacy, even in backwoods communities.

CHARLES FINNEY AND THE BURNED-OVER DISTRICT   Regions swept by revival fevers were compared to forests devastated by fire. Western New York, in fact, experienced such intense levels of evangelical activity that it was labeled the **burned-over district**. The most successful evangelist in the burned-over district was an energetic former lawyer named Charles Grandison Finney (1792–1875). In the winter of 1830–1831, he preached with "a clear, shrill voice" for six months in upstate New York, three evenings a week and three times on Sunday, and generated one hundred thousand conversions. Finney claimed that it was "the greatest revival of religion . . . since the world began." Where rural camp meeting revivals attracted farm families and other working-class groups, Finney's audiences attracted more affluent seekers. "The Lord," Finney declared, "was aiming at the conversion of the highest classes of society."

Finney wrestled with a question that had plagued Protestantism for centuries: what role can the individual play in earning salvation? Orthodox Calvinists had long argued that people could neither earn nor choose salvation of their own accord. Grace was a gift of God to a select few, a predetermined decision by God incapable of human understanding or control. In contrast, Finney insisted that the only thing preventing conversion was the individual. The sinner must simply choose salvation by embracing the promise of Jesus. Finney and other "free will" evangelists wanted to democratize the process of salvation, just as Jacksonians sought to democratize the political process. Finney transformed revivals into well-organized popular spectacles: collective conversion experiences in which spectacular public events displaced the private worship experience.

Finney compared his theatrical methods with those of campaigning politicians who used advertising and showmanship to attract attention. He carried the methods of the frontier revival to the cities and factories of the East and as far as Great Britain. His gospel combined faith and good works: revival led to efforts at social reform. By embracing Christ, a convert could thereafter be free of sin, but Christians also had an obligation to improve the larger society. Finney therefore helped found an array of groups designed to reform various social ills: alcoholism, prostitution, war, and slavery. The revivals thus provided one of the most powerful motives for the sweeping reform impulse that characterized the age. Lyman Beecher, one of the towering champions of revivalism, stressed that the Second Great Awakening was not focused simply on promoting individual conversions; it was also intended to "reform human society."

Finney and other evangelists stirring the Second Great Awakening had a profound impact upon the contours of religious and social life. By 1830 the percentage of Americans who were church members had doubled over that of 1800. Moreover, more people engaged in religious activities than political activities. Among the most intensely committed religious believers were those embracing a new denomination, the **Church of Jesus Christ of Latter-day Saints**, or the **Mormons.**

THE MORMONS The Second Great Awakening not only generated a "revival" of spiritual intensity among traditional denominations; it also helped to spawn new religious groups. The burned-over district in western New York crackled with spiritual fervor and gave rise to several religious movements, the most important of which was Mormonism. Its founder,

Joseph Smith, was the barely literate child of wandering Vermont farmers who finally settled in the village of Palmyra in western New York. In 1820 young Smith reported to his vision-prone parents that he had seen God and Christ, both of whom had forgiven his sins and told him that all religious denominations were false. Three and a half years later, in 1823, Smith, who had become an avid seeker of buried treasure and an ardent believer in folk magic and the occult, reported that an angel named Moroni had visited him and led him to a hillside near his father's farm, where he unearthed golden tablets on which was etched the Book of Mormon, supposedly a lost "gospel" of the Bible buried some 1,400 years earlier.

With the remarkable Book of Mormon as his gospel, the charismatic Smith set about forming his own church. He dismissed all Christian denominations as frauds, denied that there was a hell, opposed slavery, and promised that the Second Coming was imminent. Within a few years, Smith, whom the Mormons simply called Joseph, had gathered thousands of devout converts, most of them poor New England farmers who, like Smith's family, had migrated to western New York. These religious seekers, many of them cut off from organized communities and traditional social relationships, found in Mormonism the promise of a pure kingdom of Christ in America. Mormons rejected the notion of original sin staining the human race in favor of an optimistic creed stressing human goodness.

From the outset the Mormon "saints" upset their "gentile" neighbors as well as the political authorities. Mormons stood out with their close-knit sense of community, their secret rituals, their assurance of righteousness, and their refusal to abide by local laws and conventions. Joseph Smith denied the legitimacy of civil governments and the federal Constitution. As a result, no community wanted to host him and his "peculiar people." In their search for a refuge from persecution and for the "promised land," the ever-growing contingent of Mormons moved from western New York to Ohio, then to Missouri, and finally, in 1839, to the half-built town of Commerce, Illinois, on the west bank of the Mississippi River, which they renamed Nauvoo (a Hebrew word meaning "beautiful land"). Within a few years, Nauvoo had become a bustling, well-planned community of twelve thousand centered on an impressive neo-classical temple overlooking the river. In the process of developing Nauvoo, Joseph Smith, "the Prophet," became the community's leading planner, entrepreneur, and political czar: he owned the hotel and general store, served as mayor and commander of the city's militia (the Nauvoo Legion), and was the trustee of the church. Smith's lust for power grew as well. He began excommunicating dissidents and in 1844 announced his intention to become president of the United States, proclaiming that the

United States should peacefully acquire not only Texas and Oregon but all of Mexico and Canada.

Smith also excited outrage by practicing "plural marriage," whereby he accumulated two dozen wives and encouraged other Mormon leaders to do the same. In 1844, a crisis arose when Mormon dissidents, including Smith's first wife, Emma, denounced his polygamy. The upshot was not only a schism in the church but also an attack on Nauvoo by non-Mormons from the neighboring counties. When Smith ordered Mormons to destroy an opposition newspaper, he and his brother Hyrum were arrested and charged with treason. On June 27, 1844, an anti-Mormon lynch mob of masked men stormed the feebly defended jail in the nearby town of Carthage and killed Joseph and Hyrum Smith.

Brigham Young

Young was the president of the Mormons for thirty years.

In **Brigham Young** (1801–1877), the remarkable successor to Joseph Smith, the Mormons found a stern new leader who was strong-minded, intelligent, and authoritarian (as well as husband eventually to twenty-seven wives who bore fifty-six children). A Vermont carpenter and an early convert to Mormonism, Young succeeded Smith and promised Illinois officials that the Mormons would leave the state. Their new destination was 1,300 miles away, in the isolated, barren valley near the Great Salt Lake in Utah, a vast, sparsely populated area owned by Mexico. In early 1846, in wagons and on foot, twelve thousand Mormon migrants started their grueling trek to the "promised land" of Utah. On a good day they traversed only about ten miles. The first to arrive at Salt Lake, in July 1847, found only "a broad and barren plain hemmed in by the mountains . . . the paradise of the lizard, the cricket and the rattlesnake." But Brigham Young declared that "this is the place" for the Mormons to settle.

By the end of 1848, the Mormons had developed an efficient irrigation system, and over the next decade they brought about a spectacular greening of the desert. At first they organized their own state, named Deseret (meaning "Land of the Honeybee," according to Young), but their independence was short-lived. In 1848, Mexico, having been defeated by U.S. armies, signed the Treaty of Guadalupe Hidalgo, ceding to the United States what is now

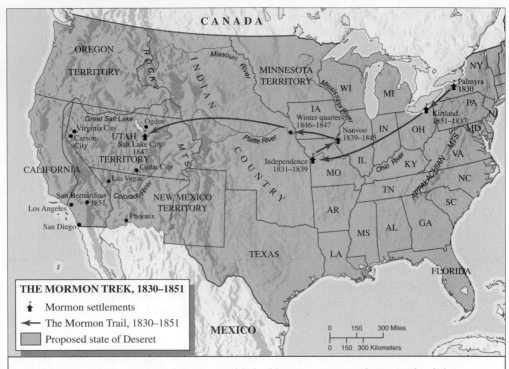

THE MORMON TREK, 1830–1851

🔺 Mormon settlements

◀— The Mormon Trail, 1830–1851

▨ Proposed state of Deseret

Where were Mormon settlements established between 1830 and 1851? Why did Joseph Smith initially lead his congregation west? Why was the Utah Territory an ideal place for the Mormons to settle, at least initially?

California, Nevada, Utah, Texas, and parts of Arizona, New Mexico, Colorado, and Wyoming. Two years later, Congress incorporated the Utah Territory, including the Mormons' Salt Lake settlement, into the United States. Nevertheless, when Brigham Young was named the territorial governor, the new arrangement afforded the Mormons virtual independence. For over twenty years, Young successfully defied federal authority. By 1869 some eighty thousand Mormons had settled in Utah, and they had developed an aggressive program to convert the twenty thousand Indians in the territory.

ROMANTICISM IN AMERICA

The democratization of religious life and revivalism during the early 1800s represented a widespread tendency throughout the United States and Europe to accentuate the stirrings of the spirit and the heart rather than succumb to the dry logic of reason. Another great victory of heart over head was the Romantic movement in thought, literature, and the arts. By the 1780s a revolt was brewing in Europe against the well-ordered world of scientific rationalism. Were there not, after all, more things in this world than reason and logic could box up and explain: moods, impressions, and feelings; mysterious, unknown, and half-seen things? Americans also took readily to the Romantics' emphasis on individualism, idealizing the virtues of common people, now the idea of original or creative genius in the artist, the author, or the great personality.

The German philosopher Immanuel Kant gave the transatlantic Romantic movement a summary definition in the title of his *Critique of Pure Reason* (1781), an influential book that emphasized the limits of science and reason in explaining the universe. People have innate conceptions of conscience and beauty, the Romantics believed, and religious impulses too strong to be dismissed as illusions. In areas in which science could neither prove nor disprove concepts, the Romantics believed that people were justified in having faith. The impact of such ideas elevated intuitive feelings at the expense of rational knowledge.

TRANSCENDENTALISM The most intense proponents of such Romantic ideals were the transcendentalists of New England, America's first cohesive group of public intellectuals. The transcendental movement was another form of religious awakening stirring American thought during the early nineteenth century. It drew its name from its emphasis on those things that transcend (or rise above) the limits of reason. **Transcendentalism**, said one of its apostles, meant an interest in areas "a little beyond" the scope of reason. If transcendentalism drew much of its inspiration from Immanuel Kant and the Romantic movement he inspired, it was also a reaction against Calvinist orthodoxy and the "corpse-cold" rationalism of Unitarianism. The transcendentalists sought to embody the "truest" piety—a pure form of personal spirituality, which in their view had been corrupted and smothered by the bureaucratic priorities and creedal requirements of organized religion. Transcendentalists wanted to "awaken" a new outlook for a new democratic age. Their goal was to foster spirituality in harmony with the perfectionism of both the divine and of divinity's creation: nature. All people, they believed, had the capacity to realize the divine potential ("spark") present in all of God's creatures. Transcendentalism during the 1830s became the most influential intellectual and spiritual force in American culture.

In 1836 an informal discussion group known as the Transcendental Club began to meet in Boston and nearby Concord, Massachusetts, to discuss philosophy, literature, and religion. It was a loosely knit group of diverse individualists who rejected traditional norms and nurtured a relentless intellectual curiosity. Some were focused on individual freedom while others stressed collective efforts to reform society. They were united by their differences. The transcendentalists called themselves the "club of the like-minded," quipped a Boston preacher, "because no two . . . thought alike." A woman who participated in the discussions more tartly noted that the transcendentalists "dove into the infinite, soared into the illimitable, and never paid cash." They asserted the right of individuals to interpret life in their own way. The club included liberal clergymen and militant reformers such as Theodore Parker, George Ripley, and James Freeman Clarke; writers such as Henry David Thoreau, Bronson Alcott, Nathaniel Hawthorne, and Orestes Brownson; and learned women such as Elizabeth Peabody and her sister Sophia (who married Hawthorne in 1842) and Margaret Fuller. Fuller edited the group's quarterly review, the *Dial* (1840–1844), for two years before the duty fell to Ralph Waldo Emerson, soon to become the acknowledged high priest of transcendentalism.

RALPH WALDO EMERSON More than any other person, **Ralph Waldo Emerson** embodied the transcendentalist gospel. Sprung from a line of New England ministers, he set out to be a Unitarian parson but quit the "cold and cheerless" denomination before he was thirty. Emerson thereafter dismissed all religious denominations. "In the Bible," he explained, "you are not directed to be a Unitarian or a Calvinist or an Episcopalian." After traveling in Europe, where he met England's greatest Romantic writers, Emerson settled in Concord to take up the life of an essayist, poet, and popular speaker on the lecture circuit, preaching the sacredness of Nature and celebrating the virtues of optimism, self-reliance, and the individual's unlimited potential. Having found pure reason "cold as a cucumber," he was determined to *transcend*

Ralph Waldo Emerson

Emerson is most remembered for leading the transcendentalist movement.

the limitations of inherited conventions and rationalism in order to penetrate the inner recesses of the self.

The spirit of freedom in Emerson's lectures and writings, often stated in maddeningly vague language, expressed the core of the transcendentalist worldview. His notable speech titled "The American Scholar," delivered at Harvard in 1837, urged young Americans to put aside their awe of European culture and explore their own new world. It was "our intellectual Declaration of Independence," said one observer.

Emerson's essay on "Self-Reliance" (1841) has a timeless appeal to youth, with its message of individualism and independence. Like most of Emerson's writings, it is crammed with pungent quotations that express the distinctive transcendentalist outlook:

> Whoso would be a man, must be a nonconformist. . . . Nothing is at last sacred but the integrity of your own mind. . . . It is easy in the world to live after the world's opinion; it is easy in solitude to live after our own; but the great man is he who in the midst of a crowd keeps with perfect sweetness the independence of solitude. . . . A foolish consistency is the hobgoblin of little minds, adored by little statesmen and philosophers and divines. . . . Speak what you think now in hard words and tomorrow speak what tomorrow thinks in hard words again, though it contradict everything you said today. . . . To be great is to be misunderstood.

HENRY DAVID THOREAU Emerson's young friend and Concord neighbor Henry David Thoreau practiced the reflective self-reliance that Emerson preached. "I like people who can do things," Emerson stressed, and Thoreau, fourteen years his junior, could do many things well: carpentry, masonry, painting, surveying, sailing, gardening. The philosophical son of a man who was a pencil maker and a woman who was a domineering reformer, steadfastly opposed to slavery, Thoreau displayed a sense of uncompromising integrity, outdoor

Henry David Thoreau

Thoreau was a lifelong abolitionist.

vigor, and prickly individuality that Emerson found captivating. "If a man does not keep pace with his companions," Thoreau wrote, "perhaps it is because he hears a different drummer."

Thoreau himself marched to a different drummer all his life. After Harvard, where he exhausted the resources of the library in gargantuan bouts of reading, and after a brief stint as a teacher, during which he got in trouble for refusing to cane his students, Thoreau settled down to eke out a living by making pencils with his father. But he made frequent escapes to drink in the beauties of nature. Thoreau revered Nature as a living Bible. He showed no interest in the contemporary scramble for wealth, for it too often corrupted the pursuit of happiness. "The mass of men," he wrote, "lead lives of quiet desperation."

Thoreau was committed to lead what Emerson called a life of "plain living and high thinking." Thoreau rented a room at the Emersons' home for a time and then embarked upon an unusual experiment in self-reliance. On July 4, 1845, he took to the woods to live in a tiny, one-room cabin he had built on Emerson's land near Walden Pond outside of Concord. Thoreau wanted to free himself from the complexities and hypocrisies of conventional life so as to devote his time to observation, reflection, and writing. His purpose was not to lead a hermit's life. He frequently walked the mile or so to Concord to dine with his friends and often welcomed guests at his cabin. "I went to the woods because I wished to live deliberately," he wrote in *Walden, or Life in the Woods* (1854), ". . . and not, when I came to die, discover that I had not lived."

While Thoreau was at Walden Pond, the Mexican War erupted. He quickly concluded that it was an unjust war to advance the cause of slavery. He refused to pay his poll tax as an anti-war gesture, for which he was put in jail (for only one night; an aunt paid the tax). The incident was so trivial as to be almost comic, but out of it grew Thoreau's classic essay "Civil Disobedience" (1849), which would later influence the passive-resistance movements of Mahatma Gandhi in India and Martin Luther King, Jr. in the American South. "If the law is of such a nature that it requires you to be an agent of injustice to another," Thoreau wrote, "then, I say, break the law."

The broadening ripples of influence more than a century after Thoreau's death show the impact that a contemplative person can have on the world of action. Thoreau and the other transcendentalists taught a powerful lesson: people must follow their conscience. Transcendentalists portrayed the movement as a profound expression of moral idealism; critics dismissed it as an outrageous expression of egotism. Though the transcendentalists attracted only a small following in their own time, they inspired many reform movements, including a revived emphasis on the importance of education.

EDUCATION

A well-informed citizenry equipped with knowledge not only for obtaining a vocation but also for promoting civic virtue was one of the animating ideals of the Founding Fathers. Literacy in Jacksonian America was surprisingly widespread. In 1840, according to census data, some 78 percent of the total population and 91 percent of the white population could read and write. Ever since the colonial period, in fact, Americans had had the highest literacy rate in the Western world. Most children were taught to read in church or in private "dame" schools, by formal tutors, or by their families. By 1830

Politics in an Oyster House (1848) **by Richard Caton Woodville**

Newspapers often fueled public discussions and debates.

no state had a public school system in the modern sense, although for nearly two centuries Massachusetts had required towns to maintain schools.

EARLY PUBLIC SCHOOLS In the 1830s, the demand for public schools peaked. Workers wanted free schools to give their children an equal chance to pursue the American dream. In 1830 the Workingmen's party of Philadelphia called for "a system of education that shall embrace equally all the children of the state, of every rank and condition." Education, it was argued, would improve manners and at the same time reduce crime and poverty.

Horace Mann of Massachusetts led the early drive for statewide school systems. Trained as a lawyer, he sponsored the creation of a state board of education, and then served as its leader. Mann went on to sponsor many reforms in Massachusetts, including the first state-supported "normal school" for the training of teachers, a state association of teachers, and a minimum school year of six months. He repeatedly promoted the public-school system as the way to achieve social stability and equal opportunity.

In the South, North Carolina led the way in state-supported education. By 1860, North Carolina had enrolled more than two thirds of its white school-age population for an average term of four months, kept so low because of

The George Barrell Emerson School, Boston, ca. 1850

Although higher education for women initially met with some resistance, seminaries like this one, started in the 1820s and 1830s, taught women mathematics, physics, and history, as well as music, art, and the social graces.

the rural state's need for children to do farm work. But the educational pattern in the South continued to reflect the aristocratic pretensions of the region: the South had a higher percentage of college students than any other region but a lower percentage of public-school students. And the South had some five hundred thousand white illiterates, more than half the total number in the young nation.

For all the effort to establish state-supported schools, conditions for public education were seldom ideal. Funds were insufficient for buildings, books, and equipment; teachers were poorly paid and often poorly prepared. Most students going beyond the elementary grades attended private academies, often subsidized by church and public funds. Such schools, begun in colonial days, multiplied until in 1850 there were more than six thousand of them. In 1821 the Boston English High School opened as the nation's first free public secondary school, set up mainly for students not going on to college. By a law of 1827, Massachusetts required a high school in every town of five hundred; in towns of four thousand or more, the school had to offer

Latin, Greek, rhetoric, and other college-preparatory courses. Public high schools became well established only after the Civil War. In 1860 there were barely three hundred in the whole country.

THE REFORM IMPULSE

The United States in the first half of the nineteenth century was awash in reform movements led by prophets, dreamers, and activists who saw injustice and fought to correct it despite the blindness and outright hostility of the larger society. The urge to eradicate evil had its roots in the widespread sense of spiritual zeal and moral mission, which in turn drew upon the growing faith in human perfectibility promoted by both revivalists and Romantic idealists such as the transcendentalists. Reformers tackled varied issues such as observance of the Sabbath, dueling, crime and punishment, the hours and conditions of work, poverty, vice, care of the disabled, pacifism, foreign missions, temperance, women's rights, and the abolition of slavery.

While an impulse to "perfect" people and society helped excite the reform movements during the first half of the nineteenth century, social and economic changes helped supply many of the reformers themselves, most of whom were women. The rise of an urban middle class offered affluent women greater time to devote to societal concerns. Prosperity enabled them to hire cooks and maids, often Irish immigrants, who in turn freed them from the performance of household chores. Many women joined churches and charitable organizations, most of which were led by men. Some reformers proposed legislative remedies for social ills; others stressed personal conversion or private philanthropy. Whatever the method or approach, earnest social reformers mobilized in great numbers during the second quarter of the nineteenth century.

TEMPERANCE The temperance crusade was perhaps the most widespread of all the reform movements. The census of 1810 reported some 14,000 distilleries producing 25 million gallons of alcoholic spirits each year. William Cobbett, an English reformer who traveled in the United States, noted in 1819 that one could "go into hardly any man's house without being asked to drink wine or spirits, even *in the morning*." In 1826, a group of ministers in Boston organized the American Society for the Promotion of Temperance, which organized lectures, press campaigns, an essay contest, and the formation of local and state societies. A favorite device was to ask each person who took the pledge to put by his or her signature a T for "total abstinence." With that a new word entered the language: *teetotaler*. In 1833, the society organized a national convention in Philadelphia, where the American Temperance Union was formed. Like nearly every reform movement of the day, temperance had a wing of absolutists. They would brook no compromise with Demon Rum and carried the day with a resolution that liquor was evil and ought to be prohibited by law. The Temperance Union, at its spring convention in 1836, called for abstinence from all alcoholic beverages, a costly victory in that it caused moderates to abstain from the temperance movement instead.

PRISONS AND ASYLUMS The Romantic impulse often included the liberal belief that people are innately good and capable of improvement. Such an optimistic view of human nature brought about major changes in the treatment of prisoners, the disabled, and dependent children. Public institutions (often called asylums) arose that were dedicated to the treatment and cure of social ills. If removed from society, the theory went, the needy and the deviant could be made whole again. Unhappily, however, the asylums had a way over time of turning into breeding grounds for brutality and neglect.

Gradually the idea of the penitentiary developed as a new approach to reforming criminals. It would be a place where the guilty experienced penitence and underwent rehabilitation, not just punishment. An early model of the new system, widely copied, was the Auburn Penitentiary, which opened in New York in 1816. The prisoners at Auburn had separate cells and gathered only for meals and group labor. Discipline was severe. The men were marched out in lockstep and never put face-to-face or allowed to talk. But prisoners were at least reasonably secure from abuse by their fellow prisoners. The system, its advocates argued, had a beneficial effect on the prisoners and saved money, since the workshops supplied prison needs and produced goods for sale at a profit. By 1840, there were twelve penitentiaries of the Auburn type scattered across the nation.

The Romantic reform impulse also found outlet in the care of the insane. Before 1800 few hospitals provided care for the mentally ill. The insane were usually confined at home with hired keepers or in jails or almshouses. In the years after 1815, however, asylums that separated the disturbed from the criminal began to appear.

The most important figure in heightening the public's awareness of the plight of the mentally ill was **Dorothea Lynde Dix**. A pious Boston schoolteacher, she was called upon to instruct a Sunday-school class at the East Cambridge House of Correction in 1841. There she found a roomful of insane people completely neglected, without even heat on a cold March day. Dix was so disturbed by the scene that she commenced a two-year investigation of jails and almshouses in Massachusetts. In a report to the state legislature in 1843, she revealed that insane people were confined "in *cages, closets, cellars, stalls, pens! Chained, naked, beaten with rods,* and *lashed* into obedience." Those managing asylums dismissed her charges as "slanderous lies," but she won the support of leading reformers. From Massachusetts she carried her campaign throughout the country and abroad. By 1860 she had persuaded twenty states to heed her advice, thereby helping to transform social attitudes toward mental illness.

WOMEN'S RIGHTS　Dorothea Dix was but one sterling example of many middle-class women who devoted themselves to improving the quality of life in American society. Others argued that women should first focus on improving domestic life. Catharine Beecher, a leader in the education movement and founder of women's schools in Connecticut and Ohio, published a best-selling guide prescribing the domestic sphere for women. *A Treatise on Domestic Economy* (1841) became the leading handbook of what historians have labeled the cult of domesticity. While Beecher upheld high standards in women's education, she also accepted the prevailing view that the "woman's sphere" was the home and argued that young women should be trained in the domestic arts.

The social custom of assigning the sexes different roles was not new, of course. In earlier agrarian societies gender-based functions were closely tied to the household and often overlapped. As the more complex industrial economy of the nineteenth century matured, economic production came to be increasingly separated from the home, and the home in turn became a refuge from the outside world, with separate and distinct functions for men and women. Some have argued that the home became a trap for women, a suffocating prison that hindered individual fulfillment. But others noted that the middle-class home often gave women a sphere of independence in which they might exercise a degree of initiative and leadership. The so-called cult of domesticity idealized a woman's moral role in civilizing husband and family.

The official status of women during the first half of the nineteenth century remained much as it had been in the colonial era. Women were barred from the ministry and most other professions. Higher education was hardly an option. Women could not serve on juries, nor could they vote. A wife often had no control over her property or even over her children. A wife could not make a will, sign a contract, or bring suit in court without her husband's permission. Her legal status was like that of a minor, a slave, or a free black.

Gradually, however, women began to protest their status, and men began to listen. The organized movement for women's rights emerged in 1840, when the anti-slavery movement split over the question of women's right to participate. Women decided then that they needed to organize on behalf of their own emancipation, too.

In 1848, two prominent moral reformers and advocates of women's rights, Lucretia Mott, a Philadelphia Quaker, and **Elizabeth Cady Stanton**, a graduate of New York's Troy Female Seminary who refused to be merely "a household drudge," called a convention to discuss "the social, civil, and religious condition and rights of women." The hastily organized Seneca Falls Convention, the first of its kind, issued on July 19, 1848, a clever paraphrase of Thomas Jefferson's Declaration of Independence. Called the Declaration of Sentiments, it proclaimed the self-evident truth that "all men and women are created equal." All laws that placed women "in a position inferior to that of men, are contrary to the great precept of nature, and therefore of no force or authority." Such language was too strong for most of the one thousand delegates, and only about a third of them signed the radical document. Yet the Seneca Falls gathering represented an important first step in the evolving campaign for women's rights.

Elizabeth Cady Stanton and Susan B. Anthony

Stanton (left) "forged the thunderbolts and Miss Anthony hurled them."

From 1850 until the Civil War, the leaders of the women's rights movement held annual conventions, delivered lectures, and circulated petitions. The movement struggled in the face of meager funds and anti-feminist women and men. Its success resulted from the work of a few undaunted women who refused to be cowed by the odds against them. Susan B. Anthony, already active in temperance and anti-slavery groups, joined the crusade in the 1850s. Unlike Stanton and Mott, she was unmarried and therefore able to devote most of her attention to the women's crusade. As one observer put it, Stanton "forged the thunderbolts and Miss Anthony hurled them." Both were young when the movement started, and both lived into the twentieth century, focusing after the Civil War on demands for women's suffrage. Many of the feminists, like Elizabeth Stanton and Lucretia Mott, had supportive husbands, and the movement recruited prominent male champions, such as Ralph Waldo Emerson, Walt Whitman, William Ellery Channing, and William Lloyd Garrison.

The fruits of the women's rights movement ripened slowly. Women did not gain the vote but did make some legal gains. In 1839, Mississippi became the first state to grant married women control over their property; by the 1860s, eleven more states had such laws. Still, the only jobs open to educated women in any number were nursing and teaching, both of which extended the domestic roles of health care and nurture to the outside world. Both professions brought relatively lower status and pay than "man's work" despite the skills, training, and responsibility involved.

UTOPIAN COMMUNITIES Amid the pervasive climate of reform during the early nineteenth century, the quest for utopia flourished. Plans for ideal communities had long been an American passion, at least since the Puritans set out to build a wilderness Zion in New England. More than a hundred utopian communities sprang up between 1800 and 1900. Those founded by the Shakers, officially the United Society of Believers in Christ's Second Appearing, proved to be long lasting. Ann Lee (Mother Ann Lee) arrived in New York from England with eight followers in 1774. Believing religious fervor to be a sign of inspiration from the Holy Ghost, Mother Ann and her followers had strange fits in which they saw visions and prophesied. These manifestations later evolved into a ritual dance—hence the name Shakers. Shaker doctrine held God to be a dual personality: in Christ the masculine side was manifested; in Mother Ann, the feminine element. Mother Ann preached celibacy to prepare Shakers for the perfection that was promised them in heaven.

Mother Ann died in 1784, but the group found new leaders. From the first community, at New Lebanon, New York, the movement spread into New England, Ohio, and Kentucky. By 1830 about twenty groups were flourishing. In these Shaker communities all property was held in common. The Shakers' farms were among the nation's leading sources of garden seed and medicinal herbs, and many of their manufactures, including clothing, household items, and especially furniture, were prized for their simple beauty.

John Humphrey Noyes, founder of the Oneida Community, had a quite different model of the ideal community. The son of a Vermont congressman, educated at Dartmouth College and Yale Divinity School, Noyes was converted at one of Charles Grandison Finney's revivals and entered the ministry. He was forced out, however, when he declared that with true conversion came perfection and a complete release from sin. In 1836 he gathered a group of "Perfectionists" around his home in Putney, Vermont. Ten years later, Noyes announced a new doctrine, "complex marriage," which meant that every man in the community was married to every woman and vice versa. "In a holy community," he claimed, "there is no more reason why sexual intercourse should be restrained by law, than why eating and drinking should be." Authorities thought otherwise, and Noyes was arrested for practicing his "free love" theology. He fled to New York State and in 1848 established the Oneida Community, which numbered more than two hundred by 1851.

Brook Farm in Massachusetts was the most celebrated of all the utopian communities because it grew out of the Transcendental movement. George Ripley, a Unitarian minister and Transcendentalist, conceived of Brook Farm as a kind of early-day think tank, combining high thinking and plain living. In 1841 he and several dozen other like-minded utopians moved to the 175-acre farm eight miles southwest of Boston. Brook Farm became America's first secular utopian community. One of its members, the novelist Nathaniel Hawthorne, called Brook Farm "our beautiful scheme of a noble and unselfish life." The social experiment attracted excited attention and hundreds of visitors. Its residents shared the tasks of maintaining the buildings, tending the fields, and preparing the meals. They also organized picnics, dances, lectures, and discussions. The place survived, however, mainly because of an excellent community school that drew tuition-paying students from outside. In 1846, Brook Farm's main building burned down, and the community spirit expired in the embers.

Utopian communities, with few exceptions, quickly ran out of steam. The communal social experiments, performed in relative isolation, had little effect on the outside world, where reformers wrestled with the sins of the multitudes. Among all the targets of the reformers' wrath, one great evil would finally take precedence over the others: human bondage. The Transcendentalist reformer Theodore Parker declared that slavery was "the blight of this nation, the curse of the North and the curse of the South." The paradox of American slavery coupled with American freedom, of "the world's fairest hope linked with man's foulest crime," in the novelist Herman Melville's words, would inspire the climactic crusade of the age, abolitionism, one that would ultimately move to the center of the political stage and sweep the nation into an epic civil war.

ANTI-SLAVERY MOVEMENTS

The men who drafted the federal constitution in 1787 were pragmatists. They realized that many of the southern states would tolerate no effort to weaken, much less abolish, the "peculiar institution" of slavery. So they worked out compromises that avoided dealing with the moral stain of slavery on a young nation dedicated to liberty. But most of them knew that there eventually would be a day of reckoning. That day of reckoning approached as the nineteenth century unfolded.

EARLY OPPOSITION TO SLAVERY Efforts to weaken or abolish slavery gathered momentum with each passing year after 1800. The first organized emancipation movement appeared in 1817 with the formation of the American Colonization Society, which proposed to return freed slaves to Africa. Its supporters included such prominent figures as James Madison, James Monroe, Henry Clay, John Marshall, and Daniel Webster. Some supported the colonization movement because of their opposition to slavery; others saw it as a way to bolster slavery by getting rid of potentially troublesome free blacks. Leaders of the free black community denounced it from the start. The United States of America, they stressed, was their native land. Nevertheless, in 1821, agents of the American Colonization Society acquired from local chieftains in West Africa a parcel of land that became the nucleus of a new nation. In 1822 the first freed slaves were transported there, and twenty-five years later the society relinquished control to the Free and Independent Republic of Liberia. But given its uncertain purpose, the African colonization movement received only meager support from either anti-slavery or pro-slavery elements. In all only about fifteen thousand blacks migrated to Africa up to 1860, approximately twelve thousand with the help of the Colonization Society. The number was infinitesimal compared with the number of slave births each year in the United States.

FROM GRADUALISM TO ABOLITIONISM Meanwhile, in the early 1830s the anti-slavery movement adopted an aggressive new strategy. Its initial efforts to promote a *gradual* end to slavery by prohibiting it in the new western territories and encouraging owners to free their slaves by the act of *manumission* gave way to demands for *immediate* **abolition** everywhere. A zealous white Massachusetts activist named **William Lloyd Garrison** best exemplified the change in outlook.

In 1831, Garrison launched in Boston a new anti-slavery newspaper, *The Liberator.* Garrison had edited several anti-slavery papers but had grown

Portrait of William Lloyd Garrison

Garrison was a vocal abolitionist: an advocate of immediate emancipation.

impatient with the strategy of moderation. In the first issue of *The Liberator,* he renounced "the popular but pernicious doctrine of gradual emancipation." In calling for immediate abolition, he vowed, "I will be as harsh as truth, and as uncompromising as justice. . . . I am in earnest—I will not equivocate—I will not excuse—I will not retreat a single inch—AND I WILL BE HEARD."

Garrison's militancy outraged slave owners as well as some whites in the North. In 1835 a mob of angry whites dragged Garrison through the streets of Boston at the end of a rope. A southern slaveholder warned Garrison "to desist your infamous endeavors to instill into the minds of the negroes the idea that 'men must be free.'" Garrison reminded critics that, however violent his language, he was a pacifist opposed to the use of force. "We do not preach rebellion," he stressed. The prospect "of a bloody insurrection in the South fills us with dismay," but "if any people were ever justified in throwing off the yoke of their tyrants, the slaves are the people."

During the 1830s, Garrison became the nation's most fervent, principled, and unyielding foe of slavery. He and others making up the vanguard of the abolitionist crusade were evangelical Christians. Most of the northerners involved in the anti-slavery movement were white churchgoers and their ministers. In 1831, two prominent New York City evangelical merchants, Arthur and Lewis Tappan, provided Garrison with the funds to launch his abolitionist newspaper, *The Liberator.* Two years later, the Tappans, Garrison, and a group of Quaker reformers, black activists, and evangelicals organized the American Anti-Slavery Society. That same year, Parliament ended slavery throughout the British Empire by passing the Emancipation Act of 1833, whereby slaveholders were paid to give up their "human property." In 1835 the Tappans hired Charles Grandison Finney to head the anti-slavery faculty at Oberlin, the new college established by the Tappans in northern Ohio.

The American Anti-Slavery Society, financed by the Tappans, created a national network of newspapers, offices, chapters, and activists. Virtually every chapter was affiliated with a local Christian church. By 1840, some 160,000 people belonged to the American Anti-Slavery Society and its affiliate organizations. The Society stressed that "slaveholding is a heinous crime in the sight of God, and that the duty, safety, and best interests of all concerned, require its *immediate abandonment.*" The society went beyond the issue of emancipation to argue that blacks should "share an equality with the whites, of civil and religious privileges." The group organized a barrage of propaganda for its cause, including periodicals, tracts, agents, lecturers, organizers, and fund-raisers. In 1835, the American Anti-Slavery Society flooded the South with anti-slavery pamphlets and newspapers. Infuriated southern slaveholders called for state and federal laws to prevent the distribution of anti-slavery literature.

The most radical figure among the mostly white Garrisonians was a free black named David Walker. In 1829, he published *Walker's Appeal,* in which he denounced the hypocrisy of Christians in the slaveholding South endorsing the practice of race-based human bondage. "Are we men?" he asked. "I ask you, O my brethren, are we MEN? Did our Creator make us to be slaves to dust and ashes like ourselves?"

A SPLIT IN THE MOVEMENT   As the abolitionist movement spread, debates over tactics intensified. The Garrisonians felt that American society had been corrupted from top to bottom and needed universal reform. Garrison embraced every important reform movement of the day: abolition, temperance, pacifism, and women's rights. He also championed equal social and legal rights for African Americans. His unconventional religious ideas led him to break with the organized church, which to his mind was in league with slavery. The federal government was all the more so. The Constitution, he said, was "a covenant with death and an agreement with hell." Garrison therefore refused to vote.

Other reformers were less dogmatic and sweeping. They saw American society as fundamentally sound and concentrated on purging it of slavery. Garrison struck them as an impractical fanatic. A showdown came in 1840 on the issue of women's rights. Women had joined the abolition movement from the start, but largely in groups without men. At that time, it was common practice to allow women speakers to address audiences comprised only of women. Then the activities of the Grimké sisters brought the issue of women's rights to center stage.

Sarah and Angelina Grimké, daughters of a prominent South Carolina slaveholding family, had broken with their parents and moved north to embrace Quakerism, abolitionism, feminism, and other reforms. As anti-slavery activists, they set out speaking first to audiences of women and eventually to both men and women. Their unconventional behavior provoked

Sarah (left) and Angelina (right) Grimké

After moving away from their slaveholding family, the Grimké sisters devoted themselves to abolitionism and feminism.

the Congregational clergy of Massachusetts to chastise them for engaging in unfeminine activity. The chairman of the Connecticut Anti-Slavery Society declared, "No woman shall speak or vote where I am a moderator." Catharine Beecher reminded the activist sisters that women occupy "a subordinate relation in society to the other sex" and that they should therefore limit their activities to the "domestic and social circle." Angelina Grimké stoutly rejected such conventional arguments. "It is a woman's right," she insisted, "to have a voice in all laws and regulations by which she is to be governed, whether in church or in state."

The debate over the role of women in the anti-slavery movement crackled and simmered until it finally exploded in 1840. At the Anti-Slavery Society's annual meeting that year, the Garrisonians convinced a majority of delegates that women should participate equally in the organization. They did not commit the group to women's rights in any other way, however. Contrary opinion, mainly from the Tappans' New York group, ranged from outright anti-feminism to the fear of scattering shots over too many reforms. The Tappans and their supporters walked out of the convention and formed the American and Foreign Anti-Slavery Society.

A third faction of the American Anti-Slavery Society also broke with Garrison. They had grown skeptical that the "moral suasion" promoted by Garrison would ever lead to abolition. In 1840, they formed the Liberty party in an effort to elect an American president who would abolish slavery. Their nominee, James Gillespie Birney, was a former slaveholder turned abolitionist from Alabama. Birney had converted to abolitionism and moved to Ohio. In 1837, he had become executive secretary of the American Anti-Slavery Society. In the 1840, election he polled only seven thousand votes, but in 1844 he won sixty thousand, and from that time forth an anti-slavery party contested every national election until Abraham Lincoln won the presidency in 1860.

BLACK ANTI-SLAVERY ACTIVITY Many white abolitionists also balked at granting full recognition to black abolitionists of either sex. White abolitionists expected free blacks to take a backseat in the movement. Despite the invitation to form separate groups, African American leaders were active in the white societies from the beginning. Three attended the organizational meeting of the American Anti-Slavery Society in 1833, and some—notably former slaves, who could speak from firsthand experience—became outstanding agents for the movement. Garrison pronounced men such as Henry Bibb and William Wells Brown, both escapees from Kentucky, and **Frederick Douglass**, who had fled enslavement in Maryland, "the best qualified to address the public on the subject of slavery."

Douglass, blessed with an imposing frame and a simple eloquence, became the best-known black man in America. "I appear before the immense assembly this evening as a thief and a robber," he told a Massachusetts group in 1842. "I stole this head, these limbs, this body from my master, and ran off with them." Fearful of capture after publishing his *Narrative of the Life of Frederick Douglass* (1845), he left for an extended lecture tour of the British Isles, returning two years later with enough money to purchase his freedom. He then started an abolitionist newspaper for blacks, the *North Star*, in Rochester, New York.

Douglass's *Narrative* was but the best known among hundreds of such accounts. Escapees often made it out of slavery on their own—Douglass borrowed a pass (required in the slave states for blacks to circulate in society) from a free black seaman—but many were aided by the **Underground Railroad**, which grew into a vast system of secret routes and safe stopping places that concealed runaways and spirited them to freedom, often over the Canadian border. Between 1810 and 1850, tens of thousands of southern slaves ran away and fled north. A few intrepid refugees returned to the slave

Portraits of Frederick Douglass (left) and Sojourner Truth (right)

Both Douglass and Truth were leading abolitionists and captivating orators.

states to organize more escapes. Fearless **Harriet Tubman**, the most cele-brated runaway, risked everything to venture back to the South nineteen times and helped three hundred slaves escape.

Equally courageous was the black abolitionist **Sojourner Truth**. Born to slaves in the Dutch farming culture of upstate New York in 1797, she was given the name Isabella "Bell" Hardenbergh but renamed herself in 1843 after experiencing a conversation with God, who told her "to travel up and down the land" preaching against the sins of slavery. She did just that, criss-crossing the country during the 1840s and 1850s, exhorting audiences to support women's rights and the immediate abolition of slavery. Having been a slave until freed by a New York law in 1827, Sojourner Truth was able to speak with conviction and knowledge about the evils of the "peculiar insti-tution" and the inequality of women. As she told a gathering of the Ohio Women's Rights Convention in 1851, "I have plowed, and planted, and gath-ered into barns, and no man could head me—and ar'n't I a woman? I have borne thirteen children, and seen 'em mos' all sold off into slavery, and when I cried out with a mother's grief, none but Jesus heard—and ar'n't I a woman?"

Through such compelling testimony, Sojourner Truth demonstrated the powerful intersection of abolitionism and feminism, and in the process she tapped the distinctive energies that women brought to reformist causes. "If the first woman God ever made was strong enough to turn the world upside down all alone," she concluded in her address to the Ohio gathering, "these women together ought to be able to turn it back, and get it right side up again!"

REACTIONS TO ABOLITIONISM   Racism was a pervasive national problem in the nineteenth century. Even in the North, abolitionists confronted hostile white crowds who disliked blacks or found anti-slavery agitation bad for business. In 1837 a mob in Illinois killed the anti-slavery newspaper editor Elijah P. Lovejoy, giving the movement a martyr to the causes of both abolition and freedom of the press.

Lovejoy had begun his career as a Presbyterian minister in New England. He moved to St. Louis, in slaveholding Missouri, where he published a newspaper that repeatedly denounced alcohol, Catholicism, and slavery. When a pro-slavery mob destroyed his printing office, he moved across the Mississippi River to Alton, Illinois. There mobs twice more destroyed his printing press. When a new press arrived, Lovejoy and several of his supporters armed themselves and took up defensive positions. On November 7, 1837, thugs gathered outside, hurling stones and firing shots into the building. One of Lovejoy's allies fired back, killing one of the rioters. The mob then set fire to the warehouse, shouting, "Kill every damned abolitionist as he leaves." A shotgun blast killed Lovejoy. His murder aroused a frenzy of indignation. John Quincy Adams said that Lovejoy's death sent "a shock as of an earthquake throughout the continent." At one of the hundreds of memorial services across the North a grizzled, lean John Brown rose, raised his right hand, and declared, "Here, before God, in the presence of these witnesses, from this time, I consecrate my life to the destruction of slavery!" Brown and other militants decided that only violence would dislodge the sin of slavery.

In the 1830s, abolitionism (also called *immediatism*) took a political turn, focusing at first on Congress. One shrewd strategy was to deluge Congress with petitions calling for the abolition of slavery in the District of Columbia. Most such petitions were presented by former president John Quincy Adams, elected to the House from Massachusetts in 1830. In 1836, however, the House adopted a rule to lay abolition petitions automatically on the table, in effect ignoring them. Adams, "Old Man Eloquent," stubbornly fought this "gag rule" as a violation of the First Amendment and hounded its supporters until the rule was repealed in 1844.

THE DEFENSE OF SLAVERY The growing strength and visibility of the abolitionist movement prompted southerners to launch an equally aggressive defense of slavery. During the 1830s and after, pro-slavery leaders worked out an elaborate rationale for the supposed benefits of slavery. The evangelical Christian churches in the South, which had widely condemned slavery at one time, gradually turned pro-slavery. Biblical passages were cited to buttress slaveholding. Had not the patriarchs of the Hebrew Bible held people in bondage? Had not Saint Paul advised servants to obey their masters and told a fugitive servant to return to his master? And had not Jesus remained silent on the subject, at least so far as the Gospels reported his words? In 1844–1845, disputes over slavery split two great denominations along sectional lines and led to the formation of the Southern Baptist Convention and the Methodist Episcopal Church, South. Presbyterians, the only other major denomination to divide by regions, did not do so until the Civil War.

Biblical defenses of slavery were soon joined by more audacious arguments in favor of the "peculiar institution." In February 1837, South Carolina's John C. Calhoun, the most prominent southern political leader, told the Senate that slavery was not evil. Instead, it was "good—a great good." He brazenly asserted that the Africans brought to America "had never existed in so comfortable, so respectable, or so civilized a condition, as that which is now enjoyed in the Southern states." If slavery were abolished, Calhoun warned, the principle of white racial supremacy would be compromised: "the next step would be to raise the negroes [sic] to a social and political equality with the whites." What is more, Calhoun and other defenders of slavery claimed, blacks could not be expected to work under conditions of freedom. They were too shiftless and improvident, the argument went, and if freed, they would be a danger to themselves as well as to others. White workers, on the other hand, feared the competition for jobs if slaves were freed. Calhoun's strident defense of slavery as a "positive good" led Henry Clay of Kentucky, himself a slave owner, to describe the South Carolina leader as "a rigid, fanatic, ambitious, selfishly partisan and sectional turncoat with too much genius and too little common sense, who will either die a traitor or a madman."

The increasingly heated debate over slavery drove a widening wedge between North and South. Of the many reform movements that swept across the nation during the first half of the nineteenth century, abolitionism would send tremors throughout the Union. In 1831, William Lloyd Garrison noted that the "bond of our Union is becoming more and more brittle." He predicted—correctly—that an eventual "separation between the free and slave States" was "unavoidable." Although few northerners in the 1830s viewed slavery as the nation's foremost issue, that would change by the 1850s. By mid-century, a large number of Americans, mostly Whigs, had come to see southern slavery as a national abomination that should not be allowed to expand into the new western territories. The militant reformers who were determined to prevent slavery from expanding came to be called "free soilers," and their crusade to improve American life would reach a fiery climax in the Civil War.

End of Chapter Review

- **Second Great Awakening** The Second Great Awakening, an evangelical movement, generated widespread revivals. The Calvinist doctrine of predestination was often replaced by the concept of salvation by free will. The more democratic sects, such as Baptists and Methodists, gained huge numbers of converts. Evangelists preached to enslaved people that everyone is equal in the eyes of God.

- **Religious Movements** The burned-over district in western New york was the birthplace of several religious movements, including the Church of Jesus Christ of Latter-day Saints, whose followers call themselves Mormons. Largely because they allowed multiple marriages, Mormons were persecuted, and their "prophet," Joseph Smith, lost his life. Smith's successor, Brigham Young, led the Mormons on a trek to then-isolated Utah in the hope that they could worship freely there. Another sect of this period, the Shakers, established celibate communities and believed that the Second Coming of Christ was imminent.

- **Romanticism** The transcendentalists embraced the Romantic movement in reaction to scientific rationalism and Calvinist orthodoxy, producing works that transcended reason and the material world. At the same time, improved technology and communication allowed the works of novelists, essayists, and poets to reach a mass market.

- **Social Reform Movements** America had an astonishingly high literacy rate, and reformers sought to establish statewide school systems. New colleges, most with religious affiliations, also sprang into existence. A few institutions, such as Vassar College, aimed to provide women with an education equal to that available to men at the best colleges. Social reformers sought to eradicate such evils as excessive drinking. They were active in the Sunday-school movement and in reforming prisons and asylums. With the Seneca Falls Convention of 1848, social reformers also launched the women's rights movement.

- **Anti-Slavery Movement** Northern opponents of slavery promoted several solutions, including deportation of African Americans to colonies in Africa, gradual emancipation, and immediate abolition. Radical abolitionist efforts in the North provoked a strong reaction among southern whites, stirring fears for their safety and resentment of interference. Yet many northerners shared the belief in the racial inferiority of Africans.

- **Defense of Slavery** In defense of slavery, evangelical churches declared that it was sanctioned by the Bible; southerners proclaimed it a "positive good" for African Americans. Whereas only a quarter of white southerners held slaves, the planter elite set the standard for southern white culture.

CHRONOLOGY

1826	Ministers organize the American Society for the Promotion of Temperance
1830–1831	Charles G. Finney begins preaching in upstate New York
1830	Joseph Smith reveals the Book of Mormon
1831	William Lloyd Garrison begins publication of *The Liberator*
1833	American Anti-Slavery Society is founded
1836	Transcendental Club holds its first meeting
1837	Abolitionist editor Elijah P. Lovejoy is murdered
1840	Abolitionists form the Liberty party
1845	*Narrative of the Life of Frederick Douglass* is published
1846	Mormons, led by Brigham Young, undertake trek to Utah
1848	At the Seneca Falls Convention, women issue the Declaration of Sentiments
	John Humphrey Noyes establishes the Oneida Community
1851	Sojourner Truth delivers her famous speech *Ain't I a Woman?*
1852	Harriet Beecher Stowe's *Uncle Tom's Cabin* is published
1854	Henry David Thoreau's *Walden, or Life in the Woods* is published
1855	Walt Whitman's *Leaves of Grass* is published

KEY TERMS & NAMES

Part Four

A HOUSE DIVIDED AND REBUILT

In 1840, most Americans were optimistic about the future as their young nation matured. The United States was already the world's largest republic. Its population continued to grow rapidly, economic conditions were improving, and war with Great Britain seemed a part of the distant past. Above all, Americans continued to move westward, where vast expanses of land beckoned farmers, ranchers, miners, and shopkeepers. By the end of the 1840s, the United States—yet again—had dramatically expanded all the territory, claiming from Texas to California and the Pacific Northwest. In the process it developed a continental empire from the Atlantic to the Pacific.

This extraordinary expansion, gained at the expense of Indians and Mexicans, was not an unmixed blessing, however. How to deal with the new western territories emerged as the nation's flashpoint issue at mid-century as the differences between America's three distinctive regions—North, South, and West—grew more divisive. A series of political compromises had glossed over the fundamental issue of slavery during the first half of the nineteenth century, but abolitionists refused to give up their crusade against extending slavery into the new territories. Moreover, a new generation of politicians emerged in the 1850s, leaders who were less willing to seek political compromises. The continuing debate over allowing slavery into the new western territories kept sectional tensions at a fever pitch. By the time Abraham Lincoln was elected president in 1860, many Americans had decided that the nation could not survive half-slave and half-free; something had to give.

In a last-ditch effort to preserve the institution of slavery from federal restrictions, eleven southern states seceded from the Union and created a separate Confederate nation. That, in turn, prompted northerners such as Lincoln to support a civil war to restore the Union. No one realized in 1861 how prolonged and costly the War between the States would become. Over 620,000 soldiers and sailors would die of wounds or disease. The colossal carnage caused even the most seasoned observers to blanch in disbelief. As President Lincoln confessed in his second inaugural address, in 1865, no one expected the war to become so "fundamental and astonishing."

Nor did anyone envision how sweeping the war's effects would be upon the future of the nation. The northern victory in 1865 restored the Union and in the process helped accelerate America's transformation into a modern nation-state. National power and a national conscious- ness began to displace the sectional emphases of the antebellum era. A Republican-led Congress enacted federal legislation to foster indus- trial and commercial development and western expansion. In the pro- cess the United States began to leave behind the Jeffersonian dream of a decentralized agrarian republic.

The Civil War also ended slavery, yet the status of the freed African Americans remained precarious. Former slaves found themselves legally free, but few of them had property, a home, education, or training. Although the Fourteenth Amendment (1868) set forth guarantees for the civil rights of African Americans and the Fifteenth Amendment (1870) provided that black men could vote, southern officials found ingenious—and often violent—ways to avoid the spirit and the letter of the new laws.

The restoration of the former Confederate states to the Union did not come easily. Bitterness and resistance festered among the van- quished. Although Confederate leaders were initially disenfranchised, they continued to exercise considerable authority in political and eco- nomic matters. In 1877, when the last federal troops were removed from the occupied South, former Confederates declared themselves "redeemed" from the stain of federal military occupation. By the end of the nineteenth century, most states of the former Confederacy had devised a system of legal discrimination against blacks that re-created many aspects of slavery.

14

AN EMPIRE IN THE WEST

FOCUS QUESTIONS wwnorton.com/studyspace

- What were the dominant issues in national politics in the 1840s?
- Why did settlers migrate west, and what conditions did they face?
- Why did Texas declare independence from Mexico in 1836, and why were many Americans reluctant to accept it as a new state in the Union?
- What were the causes of the Mexican War?
- What territories did the United States gain from the Mexican War, and what controversial issue consequently arose?

Geography is said to be destiny. In the American experience, the West's bounty and boundlessness have always exercised a magical allure. Moving westward was one of the primary sources of energy and hope in the development of the United States. The West—whether defined as the enticing lands over the Allegheny Mountains that became Ohio and Kentucky or, later, the fertile prairies watered by the Mississippi River or, finally, the spectacular lands along the Pacific coast that became the states of California, Oregon, and Washington—served as a powerful magnet for adventurous people dreaming of freedom, self-fulfillment, and economic gain. During the 1840s and after, Americans moved west in droves, seeking a better chance and more space. "If hell lay to the west," one pioneer declared, "Americans would cross heaven to get there." Millions of Americans crossed the Mississippi River and endured unrelenting hardships in order to fulfill their "providential destiny" to displace the Indians and subdue the entire continent. By 1860, some 4.3 million people had settled in the trans-Mississippi West.

Most of these settlers and adventurers sought to exploit the many economic opportunities afforded by the new land. Trappers and farmers, miners and merchants, hunters, ranchers, teachers, household servants, and prostitutes, among others, headed west seeking their fortune. Others sought religious freedom or new converts to Christianity. Whatever the reason, the pioneers formed an unceasing migratory stream flowing across the Great Plains and the Rocky Mountains. Of course, the West was not empty land waiting to be developed by hardy pioneers, trappers, and miners. Others had been there long before the American migration. The Indian and Hispanic inhabitants of the region soon found themselves swept aside by successive waves of American settlement, all facilitated by presidents who encouraged the nation's continental expansion.

THE TYLER PRESIDENCY

When the amiable President William Henry Harrison took office in 1841, he was the oldest man (sixty-eight) and the first Whig to be inaugurated as president. Like Andrew Jackson, he was elected mainly on the strength of his military record and because of his evasiveness on volatile issues. Whig leaders expected him to be a pliant figurehead, a tool in the hands of the era's most prominent—and most cunning—statesmen, Daniel Webster and Henry Clay. Nicholas Biddle, the outspoken former president of the Second Bank of the United States, told Webster that "the coming administration will in fact be your administration." Webster, as it turned out, became secretary of state, the cabinet position that had regularly produced future presidents. Clay, still lusting to become president himself, opted to stay in the Senate, but he sought to fill Harrison's cabinet with friends he could manipulate. Within a few days of the inauguration, signs of strain appeared between Harrison and Clay, whose disappointment at missing the nomination had made him peevish on top of his natural tendencies to be arrogant and dictatorial. At one point an exasperated Harrison exploded: "Mr. Clay, you forget that I am the President." But the quarrel never had a chance to fester, for Harrison served the shortest term of any president. At his inauguration, held on a chilly, rainy day, he caught a stubborn cold after delivering a two-hour speech. On April 4, 1841, exactly one month after the inauguration, the new president died of pneumonia. He was the first president to die in office.

Thus, John Tyler of Virginia, the first vice president to succeed upon the death of a president, served practically all of Harrison's term. And if there was ambiguity about where Harrison stood on the issues, there was none about Tyler's convictions. At age fifty-one, the tall, thin, slave-owning Virginian was the youngest president to date, but he had already served a long career as state legislator, governor, congressman, and senator, and his opinions on all the important issues had been forcefully stated and were widely known. Although officially a Whig, at an earlier time he might have been called an Old Republican: he was stubbornly opposed to everything associated with the Whig party's "American System," Henry Clay's program of economic nationalism—protective tariffs, a national bank, and internal improvements at national expense—and, like Thomas Jefferson, Tyler endorsed states' rights, strict construction of the Constitution, and territorial expansion.

John Tyler was a southerner first and foremost. When asked about the concept of nationalism, he said there was "no such word in my political vocabulary." (When he died in 1862, he was serving as a member of the Confederate Congress.) Originally a Democrat, Tyler had broken with the party over Andrew Jackson's "condemnation" of South Carolina's attempt to nullify federal laws. Tyler believed that South Carolina had a constitutional right to secede from the nation. In 1840, although Tyler was a renegade Democrat with no allegiance to Whig principles, he had been chosen as the party's vice-presidential nominee to "balance" the Whig ticket with a southerner. No one expected that Harrison would die only thirty days after taking office. Acid-tongued John Quincy Adams said that Tyler was "a political sectarian of the slave-driving, Virginian, Jeffersonian school, principled against all improvement, with all the interests and passions and vices of slavery rooted in his moral and political constitution."

DOMESTIC AFFAIRS With more finesse, Henry Clay might have bridged the nasty dispute between him and President Tyler over financial issues. But for once, driven by an unrelenting quest to be president, the Great Compromiser lost his instinct for compromise. When Congress met in a special session in 1841, Clay introduced a series of resolutions designed to supply the platform that the Whig party had evaded in the election. Clay proposed repealing the Independent Treasury Act, establishing another Bank of the United States, distributing to the states the money raised from federal land sales, and raising tariffs on imports. The "haughty and imperious" Clay then set about pushing his program through Congress without presidential support. "Tyler dares not resist. I will drive him before me," he said.

Tyler, it turned out, was not easily driven. Although he agreed to the repeal of the Independent Treasury Act and signed a higher tariff bill in 1842, Tyler on August 16, 1841, vetoed Clay's pet project: a new national bank. Clay was furious. The domineering leader of the Senate belittled the president in Congress, calling him a traitor who had abandoned his party and accusing him of "pride, vanity, and egotism," qualities that applied equally well to Clay himself. Clay convinced Tyler's entire cabinet to resign in September, with the exception of Secretary of State Daniel Webster. Tyler replaced the defectors with anti-Jackson Democrats who, like him, had become Whigs. The political climate grew incendiary; fistfights erupted in the Congress. Clay and other irate Whigs expelled Tyler from the party, and Democrats viewed him as an untrustworthy renegade. By 1842, Clay's vaunted legislative program was in ruins. Yet by opposing Clay and the Whigs, Tyler had become a president without a party, shunned by both Whigs and Democrats. Such political turmoil was occurring amid the worst economic depression in the history of the young nation. Bank failures mounted. Unemployment soared. But the self-assured Tyler remained both obstinate and unfazed.

FOREIGN AFFAIRS In foreign relations, tensions with Great Britain captured President Tyler's attention. In 1841, British ships patrolling off the coast of Africa threatened to board and search vessels flying the American flag to see if they carried slaves. Relations were further strained late in 1841 when 135 slaves on the American ship *Creole* mutinied and sailed into Nassau, in the Bahamas, where the British authorities set them free. Secretary of State Daniel Webster demanded that the slaves be returned as American property, but the British refused (the dispute was not settled until 1853, when England paid $110,000 to the owners of the freed slaves).

At this point, a new British government decided to meet with Webster to resolve various disputes between the two nations. They sent Lord Ashburton to Washington, D.C., where the meetings were fruitful. The **Webster-Ashburton Treaty** (1842) provided for joint naval patrols off Africa to suppress the outlawed slave trade. The treaty also resolved a long-standing dispute between the United States and Great Britain over the northern boundary of the United States with Canada. In the end, Webster settled for about seven twelfths of the contested land along the Maine boundary, and except for Oregon, which remained under joint Anglo-American occupation, he settled the other border disputes with Great Britain by accepting the existing line between the Connecticut and St. Lawrence Rivers and compromising on the line between Lake Superior and Lake of the Woods in what is now Minnesota.

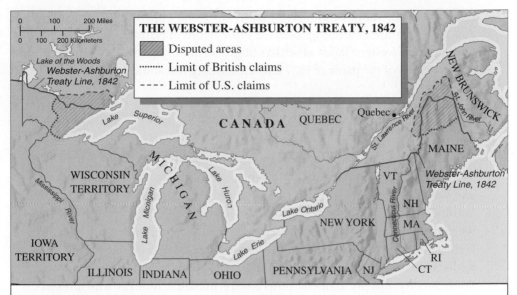

THE WEBSTER-ASHBURTON TREATY, 1842

- ░ Disputed areas
- ⋯⋯⋯ Limit of British claims
- ---- Limit of U.S. claims

What led to negotiations between Webster and Ashburton? Which territorial conflicts with Britain were settled, and which ones remained after the 1842 treaty? In addition to settling the dispute over land, what other issues did the Webster-Ashburton Treaty settle?

THE WESTERN FRONTIER

In the early 1840s, most Americans were no more stirred by the quarrels of John Tyler and Henry Clay over such issues as the banking system and the tariff policy than students of history are today. What did arouse public interest were the ongoing economic slump and the mounting evidence that the United States was hurdling the barriers of the Great American Desert and the Rocky Mountains, reaching out toward the Pacific coast. In 1845, a New York newspaper editor and Democratic-party propagandist named John L. O'Sullivan gave a name to this aggressive spirit of territorial expansion. "Our **manifest destiny**," he wrote, "is to overspread the continent allotted by Providence for the free development of our yearly multiplying millions." God, in other words, deemed that the United States should extend itself from the Atlantic to the Pacific—and beyond. At best, this much-trumpeted notion of manifest destiny offered a moral justification for territorial expansion, a prescription for what an enlarged United States could and should be. At worst, it was a cluster of flimsy rationalizations for naked greed and imperial ambition. The concept of manifest destiny ignored the prior claims of Native Americans and Hispanics on western lands as settlers began streaming into the Far West in the aftermath of the panic of 1837 and the ensuing economic depression.

WESTERN INDIANS   In the sprawling territory across the Mississippi River, white settlers encountered a new environment as well as Native American tribes heretofore unknown to most Americans. The Great Plains and the Far West were already occupied by Indians and Hispanics, who had lived in the region for centuries and had established their own distinctive customs and ways of life. Historians estimate that over 325,000 Indians inhabited the Southwest, the Great Plains, California, and the Pacific Northwest in 1840, when the great migration of white settlers began to pour into the region. The Native Americans were divided into more than two hundred tribes, each with its own language, religion, kinship practices, and system of governance. Some were primarily farmers; others were nomadic hunters who preyed upon game animals, as well as other Indians.

Many tribes resided on the Great Plains, a vast grassland stretching from the Mississippi River west to the Rocky Mountains and from Canada south to Mexico. Plains Indians such as the Arapaho, Blackfoot, Cheyenne, Kiowa, and Sioux were horse-borne nomads; they migrated across the grasslands, carrying their tepees with them. Quite different Indian tribes lived to the south and west of them. In the arid region including what is today Arizona, New Mexico, and southern Utah were the peaceful Pueblo tribes: Acoma, Hopi, Laguna, Taos, Zia, Zuni. They were sophisticated farmers who lived in adobe villages along rivers that irrigated their crops of corn, beans, and squash. Their rivals were the Apache and the Navajo, warlike hunters who roamed the countryside in small bands and preyed upon the Pueblos. They, in turn, were periodically harassed by their powerful enemies, the Comanches.

To the north, in the Great Basin between the Rocky Mountains and the Sierra Nevadas, Paiutes and Gosiutes struggled to survive in the harsh, arid region of what is today Nevada, Utah, and eastern California. They traveled in family groups and subsisted on berries, pine nuts, insects, and rodents. West of the mountains, along the California coast, Indians lived in small villages. They gathered wild plants and acorns and were adept at fishing in the rivers and bays.

The Indian tribes living in the Pacific Northwest—the Nisqually, Spokane, Yakama, Chinook, Klamath, and Nez Perce (Pierced Nose)—enjoyed the most abundant natural resources and the most temperate climate. The ocean and rivers provided bountiful supplies of food: whales, seals, salmon, and crabs. The lush inland forests harbored game, berries, and nuts. And the majestic forests of fir, redwood, and cedar offered wood for cooking and shelter.

Buffalo Hunt, Chasing Back (1860s)

This painting by George Catlin shows a hunter outrunning a buffalo.

All these Indian tribes eventually felt the unrelenting pressure of white expansion and conquest. Because Native American life on the plains depended upon the buffalo, the influx of white settlers and hunters posed a direct threat to the Indians' cultural survival. When federal officials could not coerce, cajole, or confuse Indian leaders into selling the title to their tribal lands, fighting ensued. And after the discovery of gold in California in early 1848, the tidal wave of white expansion flowed all the way to the west coast, violently engulfing Native Americans and Mexicans in its wake.

THE SPANISH WEST AND MEXICAN INDEPENDENCE As American settlers trespassed across Indian lands, they also encountered Spanish-speaking peoples. Many whites were as contemptuous of Hispanics as they were of Indians. Senator Lewis Cass, an expansionist from Michigan who would be the Democratic candidate for president in 1848, expressed the sentiment of many Americans during a debate over the annexation of New Mexico. "We do not want the people of Mexico," he declared, "either as citizens or as subjects. All we want is their . . . territory."

In 1821, Mexico had gained its independence from Spain. The infant Mexican republic struggled to develop a stable government and an effective economy, however. Localism and corruption flourished, and Americans were eager to take advantage of Mexico's instability.

Mexican independence from Spain unleashed tremors throughout the Southwest. American fur traders streamed into New Mexico and Arizona and developed a lucrative commerce in beaver pelts. American entrepreneurs also flooded into the western Mexican province of California and soon became a powerful force for change; by 1848, Americans made up half the non-Indian population. In Texas, American adventurers decided to seize their own independence from a chaotic Mexican government. Suddenly, it seemed, the Southwest was ripe for a new phase of exploitation and settlement.

THE ROCKY MOUNTAINS AND OREGON COUNTRY   During the early nineteenth century, the Far Northwest consisted of the Nebraska, Washington, and Oregon Territories. Fur traders were especially drawn to the vast watershed of the Missouri River. By the mid-1820s, the "rendezvous system" had developed, in which trappers, traders, and Indians from the Rocky Mountain territories gathered annually at some designated place, usually in or near the Grand Tetons, to trade pelts and hides. But by 1840 the great days of the western fur trade were over, as the streams no longer teemed with beavers; they had been hunted nearly to extinction by Indians and French trappers.

During the 1820s and 1830s, the fur trade had inspired "**mountain men**" to abandon civilization in pursuit of beaver pelts and revert to a primitive existence in the wilderness. The rugged trappers lived sometimes in splendid isolation, sometimes in the shelter of primitive forts, and sometimes among Indians. They were the first whites to find their way around the Rocky Mountains, and they pioneered the trails that settlers by the 1840s were beginning to travel as they flooded the Oregon Country and trickled across the border into California.

Beyond the mountains the Oregon Country stretched from the 42nd parallel north to 54°40′, a region in which Spain and Russia had given up their rights, leaving Great Britain and the United States as the only claimants. By the Convention of 1818, the two countries had agreed to "joint occupation" of the Oregon Country, which then included land that has become the states of Washington, Oregon and Idaho, parts of Montana and Wyoming, and the Canadian province of British Columbia.

Word of Oregon's fertile soil, plentiful rainfall, and magnificent forests gradually spread eastward. By the late 1830s, during the economic hard times after the panic of 1837, a trickle of emigrants—farmers, missionaries, fur traders, and shopkeepers—was flowing along the Oregon Trail, a 2,000-mile trail connecting the Missouri River near St. Louis with Oregon. Soon, however, "**Oregon fever**" swept the nation. In 1841 and 1842, the first sizable wagon trains made the trip, and in 1843 the movement became a mass migration. "The Oregon fever has broke out," wrote a settler in 1843, "and is now raging like any other contagion." By 1845 there were about five thousand settlers in Oregon's Willamette Valley.

Fur Traders Descending the Missouri (1845)

One of George Caleb Bingham's paintings from his winter in central Missouri. A bear cub is depicted at the bow.

THE SETTLEMENT OF CALIFORNIA   California was also an alluring attraction for new settlers and entrepreneurs. Spanish Catholic missionaries, aided by Spanish soldiers, had by the nineteenth century gathered most of the coastal Indian population in California under their control. The Franciscan friars enticed the local Indians into the adobe-walled, tile-roofed missions by offering gifts or impressing them with their "magical" religious rituals. Once inside the missions, the Indians were baptized as Catholics, taught the Spanish language, and stripped of their native heritage. Soldiers living in the missions enforced the will of the friars. Rebellious Indians were whipped or imprisoned. Mission Indians died at an alarming rate. One Franciscan friar reported that "of every four Indian children born, three die in their first or second year, while those who survive do not reach the age of twenty-five." Infectious disease was the primary threat, but the grueling labor regimen took a high toll as well. The Native American population along the California coast declined from 72,000 in 1769 to 18,000 by 1821. Saving souls cost many lives.

EARLY DEVELOPMENT OF CALIFORNIA   For all of its rich natural resources, California remained thinly populated by Indians and mission friars well into the nineteenth century. In 1821, when Mexico wrested its independence from Spain, Californians took comfort in the fact that Mexico City was so far away it that it would exercise little effective control over its farthermost state. During the next two decades, Californians, including many recent American arrivals, staged ten revolts against the Mexican governors dispatched to lord over them.

Yet the shift from Spanish to Mexican rule did produce a dramatic change in California history. In 1824, Mexico passed a colonization act that granted hundreds of huge *rancho* estates to Mexican settlers. With free labor extracted from Indians, who were treated like slaves, the rancheros cast covetous eyes on the vast estates controlled by the **Franciscan missions**. In 1833–1834 they persuaded the Mexican government to confiscate the missions, exile the Franciscan friars, release the Indians from church control, and make the mission lands available for economic development. Within a few years some 700 new rancho grants of 4,500 to 50,000 acres were issued along the California coast. Organized like feudal estates, these sprawling ranches resembled southern plantations—but the death rate among Indian workers was twice as high as that of enslaved blacks in the Deep South.

Among the immigrants into California in the mid-nineteenth century was John A. Sutter, a native of Switzerland who had abandoned his family in Europe in order to avoid arrest for bankruptcy. He found his way to California and persuaded the Mexican governor to give him land on which to plant a colony of Swiss émigrés. At the juncture of the Sacramento and American Rivers (later the site of the city of Sacramento), Sutter built an enormous enclosure that guarded an entire village of settlers and shops. At New Helvetia (Americans called it Sutter's Fort), completed in 1843, no Swiss colony materialized, but the baronial estate, worked by local Indians, became a magnet for Americans bent on settling the Sacramento country. It stood at the end of what became the most traveled route through the Sierra Nevada mountains, the California Trail, which forked off the Oregon Trail and led through the mountains near Lake Tahoe. By the start of 1846, there were perhaps eight hundred Americans in California, along with eight thousand to twelve thousand Californios (settlers of Hispanic descent).

Moving West

Most of the western pioneers during the second quarter of the nineteenth century were American-born whites from the Upper South and the Midwest. Only a few African Americans joined in the migration. What precipitated the massive migration westward across the Mississippi River was the continuing population explosion in the United States. (America's rate of population growth remained much higher than that of Europe.) Although some emigrants traveled by sea to California, most went overland. Between 1841 and 1867, some 350,000 men, women, and children made the arduous trek to California or Oregon, while hundreds of thousands of others settled along the way, in Colorado, Texas, Arkansas, and other areas.

THE SANTA FE TRAIL   After gaining its independence from Spain in 1821, the new Mexican government was much more interested in trade with the United States than Spain had been. In Spanish-controlled Santa Fe, in fact, all commerce with the United States had been banned. After 1821, however, trade flourished. Hundreds of American traders made the thousand-mile trek from St. Louis to Santa Fe, forging a route that became known as the Santa Fe Trail. Soon Mexican traders began leading caravans east to Missouri. By the 1830s, there was so much commercial activity between Mexico and St. Louis that the Mexican silver peso had become the primary medium of exchange in Missouri.

THE OVERLAND TRAILS   Like those on the Santa Fe Trail, travelers bound for Oregon and California rode in wagon caravans. But on the **Overland Trails** to the West Coast, most of the pioneers were settlers rather than traders, and they traveled mostly in family groups and came from all over the United States. The Oregon-bound wagon trains followed the trail west from Independence, Missouri, along the North Platte River into what is now Wyoming, through South Pass down to Fort Bridger (abode of the celebrated mountain man Jim Bridger), then down the Snake River to the Columbia River and along the Columbia to their goal in Oregon's fertile Willamette River valley. They usually left Missouri in late spring, completing the grueling two-thousand-mile trek in six months. Traveling in ox-drawn canvas-covered wagons nicknamed "prairie schooners," they jostled their way across the dusty or muddy trails and rugged mountains. By 1845, some 5,000 people were making the arduous journey annually. The discovery of gold in California in 1848 brought some 30,000 pioneers along the Oregon Trail in 1849. By 1850, the peak year of travel along the trail, the annual count had risen to 55,000.

The journey to the west coast was extraordinarily difficult. The diary of Amelia Knight, who set out for Oregon in 1853 with her husband and seven children, reveals the mortal threats along the trail: "Chatfield quite sick with scarlet fever. A calf took sick and died before breakfast. Lost one of our oxen; he dropped dead in the yoke. I could hardly help shedding tears. Yesterday my eighth child was born." Cholera claimed many lives. On average there was one grave every eighty yards along the trail.

The hard labor of the trails understandably provoked tensions within families and powerful yearnings for home. Many a tired pioneer could identify with the following comment in a girl's journal: "Poor Ma said only this morning, 'Oh, I wish we had never started.' She looks so sorrowful and dejected." Another woman wondered "what had possessed my husband, anyway, that he should have thought of bringing us away out through this

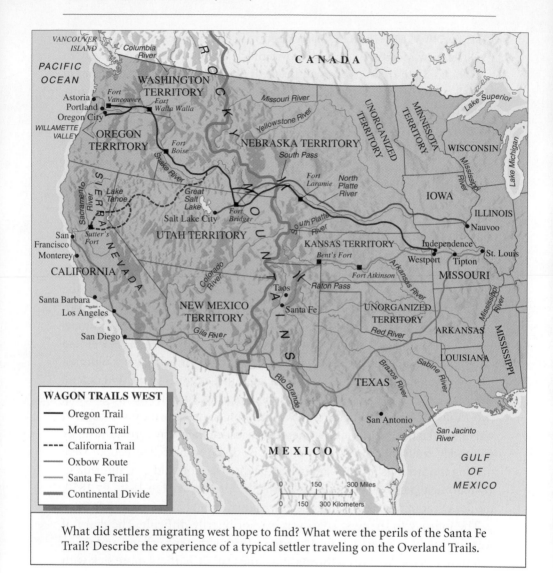

WAGON TRAILS WEST
— Oregon Trail
— Mormon Trail
---- California Trail
— Oxbow Route
— Santa Fe Trail
— Continental Divide

What did settlers migrating west hope to find? What were the perils of the Santa Fe Trail? Describe the experience of a typical settler traveling on the Overland Trails.

God forsaken country." Some turned back, but most continued on. And once in Oregon or California they set about establishing stable communities. Noted one settler: "Friday, October 27.—Arrived at Oregon City at the falls of the Willamette. Saturday, October 28.—Went to work."

THE INDIANS AND GREAT PLAINS ECOLOGY The massive migrations along the Overland Trails wreaked havoc on the environment of the Great Plains. Hundreds of thousands of settlers and traders brought with them millions of animals—horses, cattle, oxen, and sheep—all of which consumed huge amounts of prairie grass. The wagons and herds trampled vegetation and gouged ruts in the landscape that survive to this day. With the onset of the California gold rush in 1848, Plains Indians, led by Cheyennes, began supplying buffalo meat and skins to the white pioneers. Tracking and killing buffalo required many horses, and the four-legged creatures added to the strain on the prairie grasslands and river bottoms.

In 1851, U.S. officials invited the Native Americans tribes from the northern plains to a conference in the grassy valley along the North Platte River, near Fort Laramie in what is now southeastern Wyoming. Almost 10,000 Indians—men, women, and children—attended the treaty council. What made the huge gathering even more remarkable is that so many of the tribes were at war with one another. After nearly three weeks of heated discussions, during which the chiefs were presented with a mountain of gifts, federal negotiators and tribal leaders agreed to what became known as the Fort Laramie Treaty. The government promised to provide an annual cash payment to the Indians as compensation for the damage caused by wagon trains traversing their hunting grounds. In exchange the Indians agreed to stop harassing white caravans, allow federal forts to be built, and confine themselves to a specified area "of limited extent and well-defined boundaries." The Fort Laramie Treaty was significant. As the first comprehensive treaty with the Plains Indians, it foreshadowed

Indian rendering of the Fort Laramie Treaty

This buffalo-hide robe commemorates the 150th anniversary of the signing of the Fort Laramie Treaty.

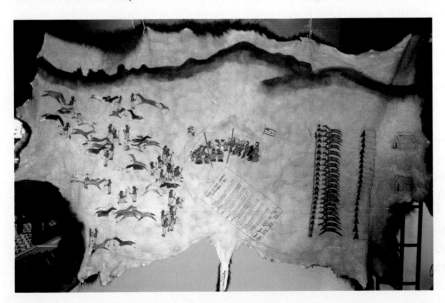

Wagon-wheel ruts near Guernsey, Wyoming

The wheels of thousands of wagons traveling to Oregon cut into solid rock as oxen strained up hillsides, leaving indentations that are still visible today.

the "reservation" concept that would come to define Indian life by the end of the nineteenth century.

THE DONNER PARTY The most tragic story of the Overland Trails involved the party led by George Donner, a prosperous sixty-two-year-old farmer from Illinois, who led his family and a train of other settlers along the Oregon Trail in 1846. They made every mistake possible: starting too late in the year, overloading their wagons, and taking a foolish shortcut to California across the Wasatch Mountains in the Utah Territory. In the Wasatch, they were joined by a group of thirteen other pioneers, bringing the total to eighty-seven. Finding themselves lost on their "shortcut," they backtracked before finding their way across the mountains and into the desert leading to the Great Salt Lake. Crossing the desert exacted a terrible toll. They lost over 100 oxen and were forced to abandon several wagons and their precious supplies.

When the Donner party reached Truckee Pass, the last mountain barrier before reaching the Sacramento River valley in California, a two-week-long snowfall trapped them in two separate camps. By December, eighty-one settlers, half of them children, were marooned with only enough food to last through the end of the month. At the main camps, at Alder Creek and Truckee Lake, the survivors had slaughtered and eaten the last of the livestock, then proceeded to boil hides and bones. When the rescue party finally reached them, they discovered a grisly scene. Thirteen people had died, and cannibalism had become commonplace; one pioneer had noted casually in his diary, "Mrs. Murphy said here yesterday that she thought she would commence on Milt and eat him." As the rescuers led the forty-seven survivors over the pass, George Donner, so weakened that he was unable to walk, stayed behind to die. His wife chose to remain with him.

THE PATHFINDER: JOHN FRÉMONT Despite the hardships and dangers of the overland crossing, the Far West proved an irresistible attraction. The most enthusiastic champion of American settlement in Mexican California and the Far West was an impetuous junior Army officer John

Charles Frémont, "the Pathfinder"—who mainly "found" paths that mountain men showed him. In 1842, Frémont and two dozen soldiers mapped the eastern half of the Oregon Trail—and met Christopher "Kit" Carson, one of the most knowledgeable of the mountain men, who became his frequent associate. In 1843–1844, Frémont, typically clad in a deerskin shirt, blue army trousers, and moccasins, went on to Oregon, then surprised his superior officers when he impetuously launched a "military" expedition. Frémont swept down the eastern slopes of the Sierra Nevadas, headed southward through the central valley of Mexican California, and returned via the Great Salt Lake in Utah. His excited reports on both expeditions, published together in 1845, gained a wide circulation and played a crucial role in prompting the mass migration of American settlers to Oregon and California.

ANNEXING TEXAS

AMERICAN SETTLEMENTS   The lust for new western land focused on the most accessible of all the Mexican borderlands, Texas. By the 1830s, the sparsely populated Mexican state of Texas was rapidly turning into a province of the United States, for Mexico initially recruited white American settlers, known as Anglos or Texians, on the condition that they would become loyal Mexican citizens. Foremost among the promoters of American settlement in Texas was **Stephen F. Austin**, a Missouri resident who won from Mexico a huge land grant originally given to his father by Spanish authorities. Austin promised to create a "buffer" on the northern frontier of Texas between the marauding Comanches and the settlements to the south. By 1824 more than two thousand hardy souls had settled on his land, and many others followed, settling across Texas. Most of the newcomers were southern or western farmers drawn to rich new cotton land selling for only a few cents an acre. A few were wealthy planters who brought large numbers of slaves with them to Texas at a time when Mexico was prohibiting the importation of slaves (1829). By 1830 the coastal region of Texas had about twenty thousand white settlers and one thousand enslaved black brought in to work the cotton.

The Mexican government, increasingly opposed to slavery, grew alarmed that the effort to recruit Americans had become too successful. The Anglos engulfed Mexico's Texas province, prompting President Andrew Jackson in 1829 to offer to buy Texas from Mexico. The Mexican government spurned the request, and in the Law of April 6, 1830, it outlawed further American immigration into Texas or, Tejas, as the Mexicans called it. The new law also encouraged Mexicans to migrate north into Texas to counterbalance the rapidly growing American presence. But illegal immigrants from the United States moved across the long border as easily as illegal Mexican immigrants would later cross in the opposite direction. And the Texians increasingly ignored Mexican laws. A Mexican congressman warned in 1830 that the Americans in Texas were not loyal to Mexico. They instead displayed a "greed for territory. . . . They have made their homes with us, but their hearts are with their native land." By 1835, the some thirty thousand Anglos (and three thousand black slaves) outnumbered the **Tejanos** (Spanish-speaking Texans of Mexican or Spanish descent clustered around San Antonio) ten to one.

The changing political landscape in Mexico exacerbated the growing tensions between Texians and Mexican authorities. **General Antonio López de Santa Anna**, ardently opposed to slavery, was elected president of Mexico in 1833. The following year, he dissolved the national congress and became a self-promoting dictator, calling himself the "Napoleon of the West." Anglo Texans feared that the new Mexican leader intended to free "our slaves and to make slaves of us." In the fall of 1835, wary Texans rebelled against Santa Anna's "despotism." A furious Santa Anna ordered all Americans expelled, all Texans disarmed, and all rebels arrested. As fighting erupted, volunteers from southern states rushed to assist the 30,000 Texan Anglos in their revolution against a Mexican nation of 7 million people. One reason the Texan war for independence relied so heavily on white volunteers (called *filibusterers*) streaming in from the southern states was that the widespread fear of slave uprisings prevented many Texians from joining the fight against the Mexican army.

TEXAS INDEPENDENCE   At San Antonio, in southern Texas, the Mexican army assaulted a small garrison of Texians, Hispanics, and American volunteers recently arrived from southern states holed up behind the adobe walls of an abandoned mission called the Alamo. Nearly two hundred rebels in the Alamo were led by the twenty-six-year-old colonel William B. Travis, a hot-tempered young lawyer from Alabama. Among the other American settlers and volunteers who defended the Alamo, the most celebrated was David Crockett, the Tennessee frontiersman, bear hunter, and sharpshooter who had fought Indians under Andrew Jackson and served as an anti-Jackson Whig congressman. He told his fellow defenders in the Alamo that he had come "to aid you all that I can in your noble cause."

In February 1836, General Santa Anna arrived with six thousand Mexican troops and demanded that the vastly outnumbered defenders of the Alamo surrender. They answered with a cannon shot. The Mexicans then launched a series of assaults and bombardments against the outnumbered defenders. For twelve days the Mexicans were repulsed, suffering heavy losses. Then, on the chilly morning of March 6, the defenders of the Alamo were awakened by the sound of Mexican bugles playing the dreaded "Degüello" (No Mercy to the Defenders). Soon thereafter, wave after wave of Santa Anna's men attacked from every side. They were twice forced back, but on the third try the Mexicans broke through the battered north wall. Most of the Alamo defenders were killed or wounded. The only survivors of the Alamo were a handful of women, children, and slaves. It was a complete victory for the Mexicans, but a costly one, for the **Battle of the Alamo** became a heroic legend and provided a rallying cry for Texians. While General Santa Anna proclaimed a "glorious victory," his aide wrote in his own diary, "One more such 'glorious victory' and we are finished."

On March 2, 1836, while the siege of the Alamo continued, delegates from all fifty-nine Texas towns met at the village of Washington-on-the-Brazos and signed a declaration of independence. Over the next seventeen days, the delegates drafted a constitution for the Republic of Texas and established an interim government. The delegates then hastily adjourned as Santa Anna's troops, fresh from their victory at the Alamo, bore down upon them.

The commander in chief of the Texas forces was **Sam Houston**, a Tennessee frontiersman who had learned war under the tutelage of General Andrew Jackson. After living among the Cherokee Indians and serving in Congress as well as governor of Tennessee, Houston had moved to Texas in 1832. After learning of the Anglo defeat at the Alamo, Houston and his Texian army surprised a Mexican army encampment on April 21, 1836. The Texians charged, yelling "Remember the Alamo," and overwhelmed the panic-stricken Mexicans. Virtually the entire Mexican army was killed; many of them were slain while trying to surrender by vengeful Texians. General Santa Anna was captured the next day. The Mexican dictator then bought his freedom by signing a treaty recognizing the independence of the Republic

Sam Houston

Houston was commander in chief of the Texas forces.

of Texas, with the Rio Grande as its southern boundary with Mexico. The Mexican Congress, however, deposed Santa Anna and repudiated the treaty and never officially recognized the loss of its northern province, but the war was at an end.

NEGOTIATIONS FOR ANNEXATION In 1836, the **Lone Star Republic** drafted a constitution that legalized slavery and banned free blacks, elected Sam Houston its first president, voted overwhelmingly for annexation to the United States, and began systematically suppressing and displacing the Indians living in Texas. The American president at the time was Houston's old friend Andrew Jackson, who personally wanted Texas to join the Union, but even Old Hickory could be discreet when political delicacy demanded it. The addition of Texas as a new slave state in 1836 threatened a serious sectional quarrel that might endanger the election of Martin Van Buren, Jackson's handpicked successor. Worse than that, it raised the specter of war with Mexico. Jackson delayed official recognition of the Republic of Texas until his last day in office, early in 1837, and Van Buren shied away from the issue of annexation during his single term as president.

Texan leaders, rebuffed by Van Buren, began to talk of expanding their new nation to the Pacific, thus rivaling the United States as a continental power. Sam Houston, serving again as president of the Republic of Texas, confronted enormous challenges: there was little money in the Texas treasury, a mounting government debt, and continuing friction with Mexico. He grew convinced that there were only two choices for the struggling republic: annexation to the United States or closer economic ties to Great Britain. France and Britain extended formal diplomatic recognition to the republic and began to develop trade relations with Texas merchants. Meanwhile, thousands more Americans poured into Texas. The population more than tripled between 1836 and 1845, from 40,000 to 150,000. Many white settlers were attracted by the low land prices and the pro-slavery policies. In fact, the enslaved population of the Republic of Texas grew even faster than the free population.

Soon after John Tyler became president, in 1841, he vigorously promoted the idea of annexing Texas as well as other western territories. Secret negotiations with Texas began in 1843, and in April, South Carolinian John C. Calhoun, then secretary of state, completed an annexation treaty that went to the Senate for ratification. Calhoun had long been the most outspoken champion of slavery within the Senate, and now, as the nation's chief diplomat, he sent the British government a letter trumpeting the blessings of slavery. The letter was made public, and many people were outraged that Calhoun was so openly supporting annexation as a means of promoting the expansion of slavery. It was so worded, one observer wrote to Andrew Jackson, as to "drive off every northern man from the support" of Texas annexation. Sectional division, plus fear of a war with Mexico, contributed to the Senate's overwhelming rejection of the Texas annexation treaty in 1843. Solid Whig opposition, led by abolitionists, including former president John Quincy Adams, was the most important factor behind its defeat.

THE ELECTION OF 1844   Although adding Texas to the Union was an enormously popular idea among many Americans, prudent leaders in both political parties had hoped to keep the divisive issue out of the 1844 presidential campaign. Whig Henry Clay and Democrat Martin Van Buren, the leading candidates for their party's nomination, had reached the same conclusion about pro-slavery Texas: when the annexation treaty was submitted to the Senate, both opposed it for fear the debate might spark civil war. Van Buren's southern supporters, including Andrew Jackson, abandoned him because of his principled opposition to Texas annexation. Jackson wrote his former vice president a brutally frank letter, expressing his intense disappointment with Van Buren's anti-Texas stance. He told the New Yorker that his chances of being elected were now about as great as an effort to reverse the flow of the Mississippi River. A future president, James Buchanan, the head of the Pennsylvania Democrats, declared that Van Buren's stance against annexing pro-slavery Texas would cost him the party's nomination. Van Buren, he said, was like a "dead cock in the pit."

With the Democratic Convention deadlocked, annexationists, including Andrew Jackson, rallied to nominate **James Knox Polk**, former Speaker of the House and former governor of Tennessee (he had been defeated for reelection in 1841), an ardent expansionist who was determined to make the United States a transcontinental global power. On the ninth ballot Polk became the first "dark horse" candidate to win a major-party nomination. The party platform embraced the annexation of Oregon and Texas. Pro-slavery southerners gloated at Polk's nomination. "We have triumphed," declared Francis Pickens of South Carolina. "Polk is nearer to us than any public man who was named. He is a large Slave holder & plants cotton."

The 1844 presidential election proved to be one of the most significant in American history. The Democratic combination of southern and western expansionism offered a winning strategy, one so popular it forced the Whig candidate Henry Clay to alter his position on Texas at the last minute; now he claimed that he had "no personal objection to the annexation" if it could be achieved "without dishonor, without war, with the common consent of the Union, and upon just and fair terms." The net result of Clay's stand on Texas was to turn more anti-slavery votes to the new Liberty party, which increased its count from about 7,000 in 1840 (the year it was founded) to more than 62,000 in 1844. In the western counties of New York, the Liberty party drew enough votes from the Clay and the Whigs to give the state to Polk and the Democrats. Had he carried New York, the overconfident Clay would have won the national election by 7 electoral votes. Instead, Polk won a narrow national plurality of 38,000 popular votes (the first president since John Quincy Adams to win without a majority) but a clear majority of the Electoral College, 170 to 105. A devastated Henry Clay had lost his third and last effort to win the presidency. His rival, Daniel Webster, blamed the savagely ambitious Clay for the Whig defeat, declaring that he had behaved as if he were willing to say or do anything to gain the White House, and "his temper was bad—resentful, violent & unforgiving."

The humiliated but still haughty Clay could not understand how a statesman of his stature could have lost to James K. Polk, a "third-rate" politician lacking natural leadership abilities. Yet Polk had been surprising people his whole career. Born near Charlotte, North Carolina, he graduated first in his class at the University of North Carolina, then moved to Tennessee where he became a successful lawyer and planter, entered politics early, and served fourteen years in Congress (four as Speaker of the House) and two as governor of Tennessee. "Young Hickory," as his partisans liked to call him, was a short, slender man with a shock of grizzled hair and a seemingly permanent grimace. Humorless, drab, and dogmatic, he had none of Old Hickory's charisma, but he was adept at continuing Jackson's opposition to a national bank and other Whig economic policies. Although at forty-nine Polk was America's youngest president up to that time, he worked so hard during his four years in the White House that his health deteriorated, and he died in 1849, at age fifty-three, just three months after leaving office. He died knowing that his strenuous presidential efforts had paid off. Polk was one of the few presidents to accomplish all of his major objectives—and one of the few to pledge that he would serve only one term.

POLK'S PROGRAM "Young Hickory" Polk reflected the growing influence of the slaveholding South on the Democratic party. Abolitionism, Polk warned, could destroy the Union. Anti-slavery northerners had already begun to abandon the Democratic party, which they complained was coming to represent southern slaveholding interests. Polk himself had slaves on his

Tennessee and Mississippi plantations. Like Andrew Jackson and most Americans of the time, Polk was a racist about both African Americans and Native Americans, and he sought to avoid any public discussion of slavery. Polk's major presidential objectives were reducing tariffs on imports, reestablishing Van Buren's independent Treasury ("We need no national banks!"), resolving the Oregon boundary dispute with Britain, and acquiring California from Mexico. He gained them all. The Walker Tariff of 1846, in keeping with longstanding Democratic beliefs, slashed tariff rates. In the same year, Polk persuaded Congress to restore the independent Treasury, which the Whigs had eliminated. Twice Polk vetoed bills for federally funded construction projects. In each case, his blows to the economic policies promoted by Henry Clay's Whigs satisfied the slaveholding South, but at the cost of annoying northerners who wanted higher tariffs and westerners who longed for internal improvements in the form of federally financed roads and harbors.

THE STATE OF TEXAS   Polk's top priority was geographic expansion. He wanted to complete the annexation of Texas and also acquire California and New Mexico, preferably by purchase. The acquisition of slaveholding Texas was already under way when Polk entered the White House. In his final months in office, President John Tyler had asked Congress to annex Texas by joint resolution, which required only a simple majority in each house and avoided the two-thirds Senate vote needed to ratify a treaty. The resolution narrowly passed by votes of 27 to 25 in the Senate and 120 to 98 in the House. The Whig leader Daniel Webster was aghast. He felt "sick at heart" to see Congress aggravate sectional tensions by endorsing the "greediness for more slave Territory and for the greater increase of Slavery!"

On March 1, 1845, in his final presidential action, President Tyler signed the resolution admitting Texas to the Union. Texas, which had remained an independent republic for ten years, formally joined the United States as the twenty-eighth state on December 29, 1845. An outraged Mexico denounced the annexation of Texas as "an act of aggression" and dispatched troops to the Rio Grande border as enterprising Americans rushed to settle in the newest state. Texas then had 100,000 whites living in it and 38,000 blacks, nearly all of them enslaved. By 1850, the Texas population—both white and black—had soared by almost fifty percent (the census then did not include Native Americans).

OREGON   Meanwhile, the dispute with Great Britain over the Oregon territory boundary heated up as expansionists insisted that President Polk abandon previous offers to settle with Britain and fulfill the

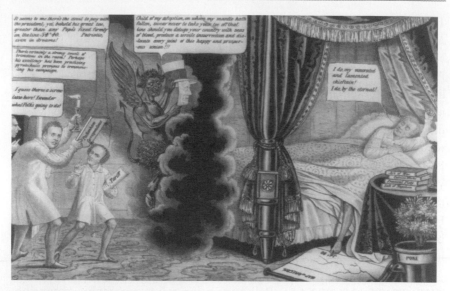

Polk's Dream (1846)

The devil advises Polk to pursue 54°40′ even if "you deluge your country with seas of blood, produce a servile insurrection and dislocate every joint of this happy and prosperous union!!!"

Democrats' platform pledge to take all of the Oregon Country ("54°40′ or Fight"). The expansionists were prepared to risk war with Britain over the Oregon issue. "All of Oregon or none," they cried. The British sent a warship to the disputed area. Polk was not to be bullied, however. In his inaugural address, the president had claimed that the American title to Oregon was "clear and unquestionable," and he was willing to go to the brink of war to achieve his goals. "If we do have war," Polk said, "it will not be our fault."

Fortunately for Polk, the British government was unwilling to risk war over a remote wilderness territory at the cost of profitable trade relations with the United States. So in 1846, the British submitted a draft treaty that extended the border between the United States and Canada along the 49th parallel. On June 15, James Buchanan, now Polk's secretary of state, signed it, and three days later the Buchanan-Pakenham Treaty was ratified in the Senate. The only opposition came from a group of expansionists who wanted more, but most Americans were satisfied. Southerners cared less about Oregon than about Texas, and northern business interests valued British trade more than they valued trying to gain all of the Oregon Territory. Besides, the country by then was at war with Mexico.

THE MEXICAN WAR

THE OUTBREAK OF WAR   While tensions with the British were rising over the Oregon boundary dispute, Texas was officially—and eagerly—joining the Union. On March 6, 1845, two days after James Polk took office, the Mexican government broke off relations with the United States to protest the U.S. annexation of Texas. When an effort at negotiation failed, the hard-driving Polk focused his efforts on subverting Mexican authority in California.

Meanwhile, Polk ordered several thousand U.S. troops under General Zachary Taylor to advance some 150 miles south of the Texas frontier and take up positions around Corpus Christi, near the Rio Grande. The U.S. troops were in territory that was doubly disputed: Mexico recognized neither the American annexation of Texas nor the Rio Grande boundary. Polk's aggressive actions in Texas gained widespread support from rabid expansionists. The Democratic newspaper editor John L. O'Sullivan exclaimed that God wanted Americans to take over the lands owned by the "imbecile and distracted" Mexico because of their racial superiority. "The Anglo-Saxon foot is already on its borders. Already the irresistible army of Anglo-Saxon emigration has begun to pour down upon it, armed with the plow and the rifle." O'Sullivan spoke for many Americans who believed it their duty (their "manifest destiny") to redeem the Mexican people from their "backward" civilization and their chaotic government.

Polk decided that he could achieve his expansionist purposes only by force. On May 9, he won cabinet approval of a war message to Congress. That evening, the news arrived that Mexican troops had attacked U.S. soldiers north of the Rio Grande. Eleven Americans were killed, five wounded, and the remainder taken prisoner. Polk's scheme to provoke an attack had worked. As a U.S. Army officer in Texas wrote in his diary, "We have not one particle of right to be here. It looks as if the government sent a small force on purpose to bring on a war, so as to have a pretext for taking California and as much of this country [Mexico] as it chooses."

In his war message to Congress, Polk claimed that war was the only response to Mexican aggression. Mexico, he reported, "has invaded our territory, and shed American blood upon the American soil." Congress quickly passed the war resolution, and Polk signed the declaration of war on May 13, 1846. Congress then authorized the recruitment of fifty thousand soldiers, but sixty-seven Whigs voted against the measure, a sign of a rising anti-war opposition, especially in the North, where people assumed that the southerner Polk wanted a war with Mexico in order to acquire more territory for the expansion of slavery.

OPPOSITION TO THE WAR   In the Mississippi River Valley, where expansion fever ran high, the war with Mexico was immensely popular. Bonfires were lit, parades held, stirring poems and songs composed, and patriotic speeches delivered. So many men rushed to volunteer that tens of thousands had to be turned back. In Illinois, efforts to form four regiments produced fourteen.

In New England, however, there was much less enthusiasm for "Mr. Polk's War." Congressman John Quincy Adams, who voted against the war resolution, called it "a most unrighteous war" designed to extend slavery. An obscure new congressman from Illinois named Abraham Lincoln, upon taking his seat in 1847, began introducing "spot resolutions," calling on President Polk to identify the spot where American blood had been shed on American soil, implying that U.S. troops may, in fact, have been in Mexico when fired upon. The Whig leader Daniel Webster was convinced that the outbreak of war with Mexico was driven by a Democratic party scheme to add more slave states to the Union. The Massachusetts senator worried that an "expensive and bloody war" would end up fragmenting the Union. He was "quite alarmed for the state of the Country." Many other New Englanders denounced the war as the work of pro-slavery southerners seeking new territories. The fiery abolitionist William Lloyd Garrison charged that the unjust war was one "of aggression, of invasion, of conquest, and rapine—marked by ruffianism, perfidy, and every other feature of national depravity."

PREPARING FOR BATTLE   The United States was ill prepared for the Mexican War. At the outset of the fighting, the regular army numbered barely over 7,000, in contrast to the Mexican force of 32,000. Before the war ended, the U.S. military had grown to 78,718 troops, of whom about 31,000 were regular army troops and marines; the others were state militiamen. The state militiamen were often frontier toughs who lacked uniforms, standard equipment, and discipline. Repeatedly, these undisciplined soldiers engaged in plunder, rape, and murder.

Yet the motley American troops outmatched larger Mexican forces, which had their own problems with training, discipline, morale, supplies, and munitions. Many of the Mexican soldiers had been forced into service or recruited from prisons, and they made less than enthusiastic fighters. Mexican artillery pieces were generally obsolete, and the gunpowder was so faulty that American soldiers could often dodge cannonballs that fell short and bounced ineffectively along the ground.

The Mexican War would last two years, from March 1846 to April 1848, and would be fought on four fronts: southern Texas, central Mexico,

New Mexico, and California. The United States entered the war without even a tentative military strategy, and politics complicated matters. **Winfield Scott**, general in chief of the army, was a politically ambitious Whig. Nevertheless, Polk at first named him to take charge of the southern Texas front. When Scott quarreled with Polk's secretary of war, however, the exasperated president withdrew the appointment.

There now seemed a better choice for commander. General Zachary Taylor's men had scored two victories over Mexican forces north of the Rio Grande, at Palo Alto (May 8) and Resaca de la Palma (May 9). On May 18, Taylor crossed the Rio Grande and occupied Matamoros, which a demoralized and bloodied Mexican army had abandoned. These quick victories brought Taylor instant popularity, and the president responded willingly to the public demand that he be made overall commander for the conquest of Mexico. Old "Rough-and-Ready" Taylor impressed Polk as less of a political threat than Scott.

THE ANNEXATION OF CALIFORNIA   Along the Pacific coast, the conquest of Mexican territory was under way before news of the Mexican War erupting had arrived. Near the end of 1845, **John C. Frémont**, overflowing with self-importance, recruited a band of sixty frontiersmen and headed into California's Sacramento Valley, where they encouraged Americans in the area to mimic their Texas counterparts and declare their independence from Mexico. They captured Sonoma on June 14, proclaimed the Republic of California, and hoisted a hastily designed flag featuring a grizzly bear and star, a version of which would later become the state flag. But the **Bear Flag Republic** lasted only a month. In July, the commodore of the U.S. Pacific Fleet, having heard of the outbreak of hostilities with Mexico, sent troops ashore to raise the American flag and proclaim California part of the United States. Most Californians of whatever origin welcomed a change that promised order in preference to the confusion of the infant Bear Flag Republic.

Before the end of July, a new navy commodore, Robert F. Stockton, led the American occupation of Santa Barbara and Los Angeles, on the California coast. By mid-August, Mexican resistance had evaporated. On August 17, Stockton declared himself governor, with John C. Frémont as military governor in the north. At the same time, another American military expedition headed for New Mexico. On August 18, General Stephen Kearny and 1,600 U.S. soldiers entered Santa Fe. After naming a civilian governor, Kearny divided his force, leading 300 men west toward California.

In southern California, Kearny's troops met up with Stockton's forces at San Diego and joined them in the conquest of southern California. They entered Los Angeles on January 10, 1847. Mexican forces capitulated three days later. As for Lieutenant Colonel Frémont, Kearny had him arrested when he refused to transfer his title of military governor. Frémont was eventually convicted of mutiny. President Polk, however, commuted his sentence of a dishonorable discharge, but Frémont elected to resign anyway.

TAYLOR'S BATTLES Both California and New Mexico had been taken from Mexican control before General **Zachary Taylor** fought his first major battle in northern Mexico. Having waited for more men and munitions, he assaulted the fortified city of Monterrey in September 1846, which surrendered after a five-day siege. The old dictator General Antonio López de Santa Anna, forced out of power in 1845, got word to Polk from his exile in Cuba that in return for the right considerations he would bring about a settlement of the Mexican War. Polk in turn assured the exiled Mexican leader that the U.S. government would pay well for any territory taken from Mexico. In August 1846, on Polk's orders, Santa Anna was permitted to pass through the American blockade into Veracruz. Soon he was again in command of the Mexican army and was named president once more. Polk's scheme had unintentionally put the feisty Mexican general back in command, where he busily organized his forces to strike at Taylor. As it turned out, General Santa Anna was much more remarkable at raising armies than leading them in battle.

By then another American front had been opened, and Taylor was ordered to wait in place, outside Matamoros. In October 1846, Polk and his cabinet ordered U.S. troops to assault Mexico City by way of Veracruz, a port city on the Gulf of Mexico southeast of Mexico City. Polk named General Winfield Scott to the field command. Taylor, miffed at his reduction to a minor role, disobeyed orders and moved west to attack Mexican forces near the hacienda of Buena Vista. Santa Anna met Taylor's untested volunteers with a large but ill-trained and tired army. The Mexican general invited the outnumbered Americans to surrender. "Tell him to go to hell," Taylor replied. In the hard-fought Battle of Buena Vista (February 22–23, 1847), Taylor's son-in-law, Colonel Jefferson Davis, the future president of the Confederacy, led a regiment that broke up a Mexican cavalry charge. Neither side could claim victory. It was the last major action on the central Mexican front, and Taylor was granted leave to return home. The general's growing popularity forced Polk to promote him, despite the president's concerns about his political aspirations. In a self-serving moment, Polk recorded in his diary that Taylor

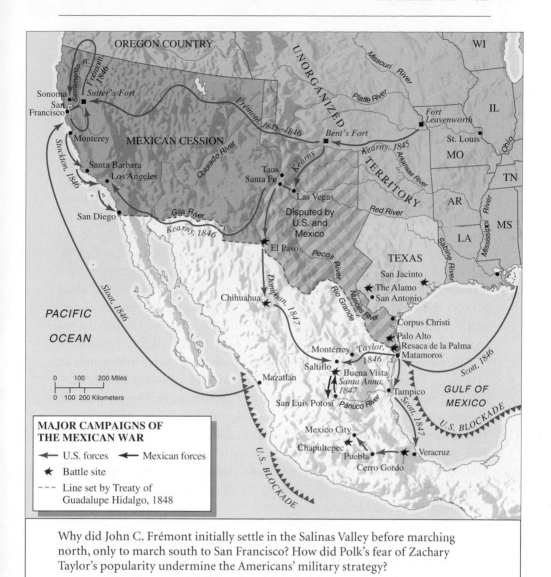

Why did John C. Frémont initially settle in the Salinas Valley before marching north, only to march south to San Francisco? How did Polk's fear of Zachary Taylor's popularity undermine the Americans' military strategy?

was a "hard fighter" but had "none of the other qualities of a great general." For his part, Taylor came to view Polk with contempt.

SCOTT'S TRIUMPH   Meanwhile, the long-planned assault on Mexico City had begun on March 9, 1847, when Winfield Scott's army landed on the beaches south of Veracruz. Scott then set out on the route taken by Cortés and his Spanish troops more than three hundred years before. After a series of battles in which they overwhelmed Mexican defenses,

U.S. forces entered Mexico City on September 13, 1847. At the national palace a battalion of marines raised the American flag and occupied "the halls of Montezuma." News of the victory led some expansionists to new heights of land lust. The editor John O'Sullivan, who had coined the term *manifest destiny*, shouted, "More, More, More! Why not take all of Mexico?"

THE TREATY OF GUADALUPE HIDALGO   After the fall of the capital, General Santa Anna resigned and a month later left the country. Meanwhile, talks leading to a peace treaty began on January 2, 1848, at the village of Guadalupe Hidalgo, just outside the capital, and dragged on through the month. By the Treaty of Guadalupe Hidalgo, signed on February 2, 1848, Mexico gave up all claims to Texas above the Rio Grande and ceded California and New Mexico to the United States. In return for the transfer of half a million square miles of territory, more than half of all of Mexico, the United States agreed to pay $15 million and assume the claims of U.S. citizens against Mexico up to $3.25 million. Like the Louisiana Purchase, what came to be called the Mexican Cession was a remarkable bargain.

Polk submitted the treaty to the Senate. A growing movement to annex all of Mexico briefly excited the president, but as Polk confided in his diary, rejecting the treaty would be too risky. If he should spurn a treaty made in accord with his own original terms in order to gain more territory, "the probability is that Congress would not grant either men or money to prosecute the war." In that case he might eventually have to withdraw the army and lose everything. So the Treaty of Guadalupe Hidalgo went to the Senate, which ratified it on March 10, 1848. By the end of July, the last remaining U.S. soldiers had left Mexico.

THE WAR'S LEGACIES   The Mexican War cost the United States 1,733 killed in battle, 4,152 wounded, and, as usual, far more—11,550—dead of disease, mostly dysentery and chronic diarrhea ("Montezuma's revenge"). It remains the deadliest war in American history in terms of the percentage of combatants killed. Out of every 1,000 soldiers in Mexico, some 110 died. The next highest death rate would be in the Civil War, with 65 dead out of every 1,000 participants.

The Mexican War was a crushing defeat for Mexico and a defining event for the United States. As a result of the conflict, the United States expanded its national domain by over a third. It acquired more than 500,000 square miles of territory (almost 1 million, counting Texas), including the future states of California, Nevada, and Utah and parts of New Mexico, Arizona, Colorado, and Wyoming. Except for a small addition made by the Gadsden Purchase of 1853, these annexations rounded out the continental United States and doubled its size. The area taken from Mexico was larger than the Louisiana Purchase.

Several important firsts are associated with the Mexican War: the first successful imperial American war, the first occupation of an enemy capital, the first in which West Point graduates played a major role, and the first reported by war correspondents. It was also the first significant combat experience for a group of junior officers who would later serve as leading generals during the Civil War: Robert E. Lee, Ulysses S. Grant, Thomas "Stonewall" Jackson, George B. McClellan, George Meade, and others.

Initially the victory in Mexico unleashed a surge of national pride in the United States, but as the years passed, the Mexican War also proved to be a catalyst in deepening sectional tensions over slavery. It was increasingly seen as a shameful war of conquest and imperialistic plunder directed by a president bent on territorial expansion for the sake of slavery. Ulysses S. Grant later called it "one of the most unjust wars ever waged by a stronger against a weaker nation." America's terrible Civil War fifteen years later, he added, was "our punishment" for the unholy Mexican War. For a brief season the glory of conquest added political luster to the names of Generals Zachary Taylor and Winfield Scott, who both had presidential aspirations. Polk's presidency proved to be as tragic as it was triumphant. Despite his best efforts, he had manufactured the next, and last, two Whig candidates for president. One of them, Taylor, would replace him in the White House, with the storm of sectional conflict already on the horizon.

The acquisition of Oregon, Texas, California, and the New Southwest made the United States a transcontinental nation. Extending authority over this vast new land greatly expanded the scope of the federal government. In 1849, for example, Congress created the Department of the Interior to supervise the distribution of land, the creation of new territories and states, and the "protection" of the Indians and their land. President Polk naively assumed that the dramatic expansion of American territory to the Pacific would strengthen "the bonds of Union." He was wrong. No sooner was Texas annexed and gold discovered in California than a violent debate erupted over the extension of slavery into the new territories. That debate would culminate in a war that would nearly destroy the Union.

CHAPTER SUMMARY

- **Nationalism** Nationalism and westward expansion were the dominant issues in the 1840s, although President John Tyler, a former Democrat turned Whig, vetoed traditional Whig policies, such as a new national bank and higher tariffs. Boundaries with Canada were finally settled. The desire for westward expansion culminated in the Mexican War.

- **Westward Migration** Many Americans believed that the West was divinely ordained to be part of the United States. Although populated by Indians and Latinos, the West was portrayed as an empty land. The lure of cheap, fertile land led to Oregon fever, and settlers moved along the Overland Trails, enduring great physical hardships.

- **Texas Republic** Many southerners had moved to the Mexican province of Texas to grow cotton, taking their slaves with them. The Mexican government opposed slavery and in 1830 forbade further immigration. American settlers declared Texas independent in 1836, and the slaughter at the Alamo made the independence of Texas a popular cause in the United States. As soon as Mexico recognized the Texas Republic, many Texans clamored for annexation. The notion was unpopular among the growing anti-slavery faction, however, because it meant adding another slave state to the Union; thus, Texas remained independent for nearly a decade.

- **Mexican War** Annexation of Texas, declared by a joint resolution of Congress in 1845, infuriated Mexico. The newly elected president, James K. Polk, sought to acquire California and New Mexico as well as Texas, but negotiations soon failed. When Mexican troops crossed the Rio Grande, Polk urged Congress to declare war.

- **Results of the Mexican War** In 1848, in the Treaty of Guadalupe Hidalgo, Mexico ceded California and New Mexico to the United States and gave up claims to land north of the Rio Grande. The vast acquisition did not strengthen the Union, however, because a fierce debate immediately erupted about allowing slavery in the new territories.

CHRONOLOGY

1821	Mexico gains independence from Spain
1836	Americans are defeated at the Alamo
1841	John Tyler becomes president
1842	Americans and British agree to the Webster-Ashburton Treaty
1845	United States annexes Texas
	Mexican War begins
1846	Most members of the Donner party die en route to California
1848	Treaty of Guadalupe Hidalgo ends the Mexican War
1849	California gold rush begins
1851	Plains Indians agree to the Fort Laramie Treaty

KEY TERMS & NAMES

15

THE GATHERING STORM

FOCUS QUESTIONS wwnorton.com/studyspace

- Who were the members of the free-soil coalition, and what arguments did they use to demand that slavery not spread to the territories?
- Why did the issue of statehood for California precipitate a crisis for the Union?
- What were the major elements of the Compromise of 1850?
- How did the Kansas-Nebraska Act initiate the collapse of the second party system?
- Why did the southern states secede?

John C. Calhoun of South Carolina and Ralph Waldo Emerson of Massachusetts had little in common, but both men saw in the Mexican War the omens of a national disaster. Mexico, Calhoun warned, was "the forbidden fruit; the penalty of eating it would be to subject our institutions to political death." Calhoun knew that the addition of new territory acquired from Mexico would ignite a political firestorm over the expansion of slavery. Emerson agreed. "The United States will conquer Mexico," Emerson conceded, "but it will be as the man swallows the arsenic. . . . Mexico will poison us." Wars, as both men knew, have a way of corrupting ideals and breeding new wars, often in unforeseen ways. America's victory in the war with Mexico spawned heated quarrels over newly acquired lands, quarrels that set in motion a series of fractious disputes that would fracture the union.

SLAVERY IN THE TERRITORIES

The dispute over the motives behind the Mexican War carried over into American political life during the 1850s. During the mid–nineteenth century, the United States remained a largely rural nation. Its 23 million people were increasingly diverse in ethnic background and religious beliefs, but they shared a passion for politics and political issues. Participation in civic life was high. Nearly three fourths of the electorate participated in the two presidential elections during the 1850s. People flocked to hear political speeches and avidly read the partisan daily newspapers. A European tourist reported that in America "you meet newspaper readers everywhere." At mid-century, newspapers spread the word that political storm clouds over the fate of slavery were forming. In 1833, Andrew Jackson had predicted that south-erners "intend to blow up a storm on the slave question." He added that the pro-slavery firebrands "would do any act to destroy this union and form a southern confederacy bounded, north, by the Potomac River." In 1848, the storm over the expansion of slavery swept across the nation.

THE WILMOT PROVISO   The Mexican War was less than three months old when the seeds of a new political conflict began to sprout. On August 8, 1846, a Democratic congressman from Pennsylvania, David Wilmot, delivered a provocative speech to the House in which he endorsed the annexation of Texas as a slave state. But slavery had come to an end in the rest of Mexico, he noted, and if new Mexican territory should be acquired, Wilmot declared, "God forbid that we should be the means of planting this institution [slavery] upon it." If any additional land should be acquired from Mexico, Wilmot proposed, then "neither slavery nor involuntary servitude shall ever exist" there.

The proposed **Wilmot Proviso** ignited the festering debate over the exten-sion of slavery. For a generation, since the Missouri controversy of 1819–1821, the issue had been lurking in the wings. The Missouri Compromise had provided a temporary solution by protecting slavery in states where it already existed but not allowing it in any newly acquired territories. Now, with the addition of new territories taken from Mexico, the stage was set for an even more volatile national debate. In 1846, the House of Representatives adopted the Wilmot Proviso, but the Senate balked. When Congress reconvened in December 1846, President James K. Polk, who believed a debate over slavery had no place in the conduct of the war in Mexico, dismissed the proviso as "mischievous and foolish." He convinced David Wilmot to withhold his amendment from any bill dealing with the annexation of Mexican territory.

By then, however, others were ready to take up the cause. In one form or another, Wilmot's idea kept cropping up in Congress for years thereafter. Abraham Lincoln later recalled that during his one term as a congressman, in 1847–1849, he voted for it "as good as forty times."

Senator John C. Calhoun of South Carolina, meanwhile, devised a thesis to counter Wilmot's proviso, which he set before the Senate on February 19, 1847. Calhoun began by reasserting his pride in being a slaveholding cotton planter. He made no apologies for holding slaves and insisted that slaveholders had an unassailable right to take their slaves into any territories. Wilmot's effort to exclude slaves from territories acquired from Mexico, Calhoun declared, would violate the Fifth Amendment, which forbids Congress to deprive any person of life, liberty, or property without due process of law, and slaves *were* property. By this clever stroke of logic, Calhoun took that basic guarantee of liberty, the Bill of Rights, and turned it into a basic guarantee of slavery. The irony was not lost on his critics, but the point became established southern dogma—echoed by his colleagues and formally endorsed by the Virginia legislature.

The burly senator Thomas Hart Benton of Missouri, himself a slaveholder but also a nationalist eager to calm sectional tensions, found in Calhoun's stance a set of abstractions "leading to no result." Wilmot and Calhoun between them, he said, had fashioned a pair of shears. Neither blade alone would cut very well, but joined together they could sever the nation in two. One factor increasing the political tensions over slavery was the sharp rise in the price paid for slaves during the 1850s. The expansion of slavery into the new southwestern states created a spike in demand that meant that only the wealthy could afford to purchase slaves. Owning slaves and controlling the fruits of their labors became the foremost determinants of wealth in the South during the 1850s. And with wealth came political power. Large slaveholders and their supporters grew increasingly fierce in their insistence that owners be allowed to take their slaves into the new territories. To them, there was too much at stake to be denied access to new lands. Slavery thus played the crucial role in the series of events dividing the nation and prompting **secession** and civil war.

POPULAR SOVEREIGNTY Senator Benton and others sought to bypass the brewing conflict over slavery in the new territories. President Polk was among the first to suggest extending the Missouri Compromise, dividing free and slave territory at the latitude of 36°30′, all the way to the Pacific Ocean. Senator Lewis Cass of Michigan suggested that the citizens of a territory "regulate their own internal concerns in their own way," like the citizens of a state. Such an approach would take the contentious issue of allowing slavery in new territories out of the national arena and put it in the hands of those directly affected.

Popular sovereignty, or "squatter sovereignty," as the idea was also called, appealed to many Americans. Without directly challenging the slaveholders' access to the new lands, it promised to open the lands quickly to non-slaveholding farmers, who would almost surely dominate the territories. With this tacit understanding the idea prospered in the Midwest, where Senator Stephen A. Douglas of Illinois and other prominent Democrats soon endorsed it.

In 1848, when the Mexican War ended, the issue of introducing slavery into the new territories was no longer hypothetical. Nobody doubted that Oregon would become a free-soil (non-slave) territory, but it, too, was drawn into the growing controversy. Territorial status for Oregon, pending since 1846, was delayed because its provisional government had excluded slavery. To concede that provision would imply an authority drawn from the powers of Congress, since a territory was created by Congress. After much wrangling, an exhausted Congress let Oregon organize without slavery but postponed a decision on the Southwest territories. President Polk signed the bill on the principle that Oregon was north of 36°30′, the latitude that had formed the basis of the Missouri Compromise in 1820.

President Polk had promised to serve only one term; exhausted and having accomplished his major goals, he refused to run again. At the 1848 Democratic Convention, Michigan senator Lewis Cass won the presidential nomination, but the party refused to endorse Cass's "squatter sovereignty" plan. Instead, it simply denied the power of Congress to interfere with slavery in the states and criticized all efforts by anti-slavery activists to bring the question before Congress. The Whigs devised an even more artful shift. Once again, as in 1840, they passed over their party leader, Henry Clay, in favor of General Zachary Taylor, whose fame had grown since the Battle of Buena Vista. Taylor, born in Virginia and raised in Kentucky, was a Louisiana resident who owned more than a hundred slaves. He was an apolitical figure who had never voted in a national election, but he was also unusual among slaveholders in that he vigorously opposed the extension of slavery into new western territories and denounced the idea of secession.

THE FREE-SOIL COALITION As it had done in the 1840 election, the Whig party adopted no platform in an effort to avoid the divisive issue of slavery. But the anti-slavery impulse was not easily squelched. Congressman David Wilmot had raised a standard for resisting the expansion of slavery, to which a broad coalition could rally. Those Americans who had qualms about slavery but shied away from calling for abolition where it already existed could readily endorse the exclusion of slavery from the western territories. The Northwest Ordinance and the Missouri Compromise supplied honored precedents for doing so. Free soil in the new territories, therefore, rather than abolition in the slave states, became the rallying point for those opposed to slavery—and also the name of a new political party.

Three major groups combined to form the free-soil coalition: rebellious northern Democrats, anti-slavery Whigs, and members of the Liberty party, which was formed in 1840. Disaffection among the Democrats centered in New York, where the Van Burenite "Barnburners" seized upon the free-soil issue as a moral imperative. The Whigs who promoted Free-soil principles were centered in Massachusetts, where a group of "Conscience" Whigs battled the "Cotton" Whigs, a coalition of northern businessmen and southern planters. Conscience Whigs rejected the slaveholding nominee of their party, Zachary Taylor.

In 1848 these groups—Van Burenite Democrats, Conscience Whigs, and followers of the Liberty party—combined to create the **Free-Soil party** at a convention at Buffalo, New York, and nominated Martin Van Buren for president. The party's platform stressed that slavery would not be allowed in the new territories acquired from Mexico. The new party infuriated John C. Calhoun and other southern Democrats committed to the expansion of slavery. Calhoun called Van Buren a "bold, unscrupulous and vindictive demagogue." Other Democrats, both northern and southern, denounced Van Buren as a traitor and a hypocrite, while the New Yorker's supporters praised his service as a "champion of freedom."

The impact of the new Free-Soil party on the election was mixed. The Free-Soilers split the Democratic vote enough to throw New York to the Whig Zachary Taylor, and they split the Whig vote enough to give Ohio to the Democrat Lewis Cass, but Van Buren's 291,000 votes lagged well behind the totals of 1,361,000 for Taylor and 1,222,000 for Cass. Taylor won with 163 to 127 electoral votes, and both major parties retained a national following. Taylor took eight slave states and seven free; Cass, just the opposite: seven slave and eight free.

THE CALIFORNIA GOLD RUSH   Meanwhile, a new dimension had been introduced into the vexing question of the western territories: on January 24, 1848, on the property of John A. Sutter along the south fork of the American River, gold was discovered in the Mexican province of California, which nine days later would be ceded to the United States as a result of the treaty ending the Mexican War. Word of the gold strike spread quickly.

THE BUFFALO HUNT.

Martin Van Buren

Martin Van Buren was nominated as the presidential candidate for the Free-Soil party, at the party's convention in Buffalo, New York. In this cartoon, he is shown riding a buffalo past the Democratic and Whig party candidates.

In 1849 nearly one hundred thousand Americans, mostly men, set off for California, determined to find riches; by 1854 the number would top three hundred thousand. The California gold rush constituted the greatest mass migration in American history—and one of the most significant events in the first half of the nineteenth century. The infusion of California gold into the U.S. economy triggered a surge of prosperity and dramatic growth that eventually helped finance the Union military effort in the Civil War. The gold rush transformed the sleepy coastal village of San Francisco into the nation's largest city west of Chicago.

The gold rush also shifted the nation's center of gravity westward, spurred the construction of railroads and telegraph lines, and excited dreams of an eventual American empire based in the Pacific. The massive migration to California had profound effects nationwide. So many men left New England, for instance, that it would be years before the region's gender ratio evened out again. The "forty-niners" included people from every social class and every state and territory, as well as slaves brought by their owners. Most forty-niners went overland; the rest sailed around South America or to Panama, where steamship passengers would have to disembark and make

Gold miners, ca. 1850

Miners panning for gold at their claim.

their way across the isthmus to the Pacific coast, where they would board another steamship for the trip to San Francisco. Getting to California by sea could take as long as six months.

Unlike the land-hungry pioneers who traversed the overland trails, the miners were mostly unmarried young men with varied ethnic and cultural backgrounds. Few were interested in establishing a permanent settlement. They wanted to strike it rich and return home. The mining camps in California's valleys and canyons and along its creek beds thus sprang up like mushrooms and disappeared almost as rapidly. As soon as rumors of a new strike made the rounds, miners converged on the area, joined soon thereafter by a hodgepodge of merchants and camp followers. When no more gold could be found, they picked up and moved on.

Women were as rare in the mining camps as liquor and guns were abundant. In 1850 less than 8 percent of California's population was female, and even fewer women dared to live in the camps. Those who did could demand a premium for their work, as cooks, laundresses, entertainers, and prostitutes. In the polyglot mining camps, white Americans often looked with disdain upon the Hispanics and Chinese, who were most often employed as wage laborers to help in the panning process, separating gold from sand and gravel. But the whites focused their contempt on the Indians in particular. In the mining culture, it was not a crime to kill Indians or work them to death.

American miners tried several times to outlaw foreigners in the mining country but had to settle for a tax on foreign miners, which was applied to Mexicans in express violation of the treaty ending the Mexican War.

CALIFORNIA STATEHOOD   In 1849 the new president, Zachary Taylor, turned out to be a southern man who championed Union principles. He decided to use California's request for statehood as a lever to end the stalemate in Congress brought about by the slavery issue. Inexperienced in politics, Taylor had a soldier's practical mind. Slavery should be upheld where it existed, he believed, but he had little patience with abstract theories about slavery in territories where it probably could not exist. Why not make California and New Mexico free states immediately, he reasoned, and bypass the vexing issue of slavery?

But the Californians, in desperate need of organized government, were ahead of him. By December 1849, without consulting Congress, Americans in Hispanic California had put a free-state (no-slavery) government into operation. New Mexico responded more slowly, but by 1850 Americans there had adopted a free-state constitution. The Mormons around Salt Lake, meanwhile, drafted a basic law for the state of Deseret, which embraced most of the Mexican cession, including a slice of the coast from Los Angeles to San Diego.

In his annual message on December 4, 1849, President Taylor endorsed immediate statehood for California and urged Congress to avoid injecting slavery into the issue. The new Congress, however, was in no mood for simple solutions. By 1850, tensions over the morality and the future of slavery were boiling over. At the same time that tempers were flaring over the issue of allowing slavery into the new western territories, anti-slavery members of the House of Representatives were proposing legislation to ban slavery in the District of Columbia. Further complicating the political debate was the claim by Texas, a slave state, to half of the New Mexico Territory. These were only a few of the complex dilemmas confronting the nation's statesmen as they assembled in Washington, D.C., for the 1850 legislative session.

THE COMPROMISE OF 1850

At the end of 1849, southerners fumed over President Taylor's efforts to bring California and New Mexico into the union as free states. After all, some of them reasoned, mostly southerners had fought in the Mexican War, and therefore their desire for the expansion of slavery should be given more weight. Other southerners demanded a federal fugitive slave law that would require northern authorities to arrest and return runaways. Irate southern-ers threatened to leave the Union. "I avow before this House and country, and in the presence of the living God," shouted Robert Toombs, a Georgia congressman, "that if by your legislation you seek to drive us [slaveholders] from the territories of California and New Mexico . . . and to abolish slavery in this District [of Columbia] . . . *I am for disunion.*"

As the new legislative session opened, the spotlight fell on the Senate, where a stellar cast—the triumvirate of Henry Clay, John C. Calhoun, and Daniel Webster, with William H. Seward, Stephen A. Douglas, and Jefferson Davis in supporting roles—enacted one of the great dramas of American politics: the **Compromise of 1850**. With southerners threatening secession, leaders again turned to seventy-two-year-old Henry Clay, who, as Abraham Lincoln later said, was "regarded by all, as *the* man for the crisis." Clay had earlier fashioned the Missouri Compromise, and those seeking peace between the regions looked to him again. Unless some compromise could be found, the senator warned, a war "so furious, so bloody, so implacable and so exterminating" would fracture the Union.

THE GREAT DEBATE   On January 29, 1850, having gained the support of Daniel Webster, Clay presented to Congress a package of eight resolutions meant to settle the "controversy between the free and slave states, growing out of the subject of slavery." His proposals represented what he called a "great national scheme of compromise and harmony." He proposed (1) to admit California as a free state; (2) to organize the territories of New Mexico and Utah without restrictions on slavery, allowing the residents to decide the issue for themselves; (3) to deny Texas its extreme claim to much of New Mexico; (4) to compensate Texas by having the federal government pay the pre-annexation Texas debts; (5) to retain slavery in the District of Columbia; but (6) to abolish the slave trade in the nation's capital; (7) to adopt a more effective federal fugitive slave law; and (8) to deny congressional authority to interfere with the interstate slave trade. His complex cluster of proposals became in substance the Compromise of 1850, but only after the most cele-brated debate in Congressional history.

On February 5–6, Clay summoned all his eloquence in promoting his proposed settlement to the Senate. In the interest of "peace, concord and harmony," he called for an end to "passion, passion—party, party—and intemperance." Otherwise, he warned, continued sectional bickering would lead to a "furious, bloody" civil war.

On March 4, John C. Calhoun, the uncompromising defender of slavery, left his sickbed to sit in the Senate chamber, a gaunt, pallid figure draped in a black cloak, as a colleague read his defiant speech in which he blamed the North for inciting civil war. "I have, Senators, believed from the first that the agitation of the subject of slavery would, if not prevented by some timely and effective measure, end in disunion," said James M. Mason on Calhoun's behalf. Neither Clay's compromise nor Taylor's efforts would serve the Union, he added. The South simply needed Congress to accept its rights: equality of treatment in the territories, the return of fugitive slaves, and some guarantee of "an equilibrium between the sections." Otherwise, Calhoun warned, the "cords which bind" the Union would be severed. The South would leave the Union and form its own government.

Three days later, Calhoun, who would die in three weeks, returned to the Senate on March 7 to hear Daniel Webster speak. He chose as the central theme of his much-anticipated three-hour speech the preservation of the Union: "I wish to speak today, not as a Massachusetts man, not as a Northern man, but as an American. . . . I speak today for the preservation of the Union." The geographic extent of slavery had already been determined, Webster insisted, by the Northwest Ordinance, by the Missouri Compromise, and in the new territories by the law of nature. He criticized extremists on both sides.

Clay's compromise

Warning against an impending sectional conflict, Henry Clay outlines his plan for "compromise and harmony" on the Senate floor.

Webster's conciliatory speech brought down a storm upon his head. New England anti-slavery leaders lambasted him for betraying the ideals of his region. On March 11, William Seward, the Whig senator from New York, gave the anti-slavery reply to Webster. He declared that *any* compromise with slavery was "radically wrong and essentially vicious." There was, he said, "a *higher law* than the Constitution," and it demanded the abolition of slavery. Abolitionists loved Seward's address, but southerners as well as northern conservatives despised it. "Senator Seward is against all compromise," the *New York Herald* reported. His "views are those of the extreme fanatics of the North, looking forward to the utter destruction of the institutions of the South."

TOWARD A COMPROMISE   On July 4, 1850, supporters of the Union staged a grand rally at the base of the unfinished Washington Monument in Washington, D.C. President Zachary Taylor went to hear the speeches, lingering in the hot sun and humid heat. Five days later he died of cholera, likely caused by tainted food or water.

President Taylor's sudden death strengthened the chances of a congressional compromise over the slavery issue. Taylor, a soldier, was replaced by Vice President Millard Fillmore. The son of a poor upstate New York farmer, Fillmore supported Henry Clay's compromise. It was a strange switch: Taylor, the Louisiana slaveholder, had been ready to make war on his native region; Fillmore, who southerners thought opposed slavery, was ready to make peace.

Millard Fillmore

Fillmore's support of the Compromise of 1850 helped sustain the Union through the crisis.

At this point, the young senator **Stephen A. Douglas** of Illinois, a rising star in the Democratic party, rescued Henry Clay's faltering compromise. Brash and brilliant, short and stocky, and famous for his large head, Douglas argued that given nearly everybody's objections to one or another provision of Clay's "comprehensive scheme," perhaps the solution was to break it up into separate measures. Few members were prepared to vote for all of them, but Douglas hoped to mobilize a majority for each.

The plan worked. By September 20, President Fillmore had signed the last of the measures into law. The Union had muddled through another crisis, and the settlement went down in history as the Compromise of 1850. For a time it defused an explosive situation, settled each of the major points at issue, and postponed secession and civil war for ten years.

In its final version, the Compromise of 1850 included the following elements: (1) California entered the Union as a free state, ending forever the old balance of free and slave states; (2) the Texas–New Mexico Act made New Mexico a territory and set the Texas boundary at its present location. In return for giving up its claims, Texas was paid $10 million, which secured payment of the state's debt; (3) the Utah Act set up the Utah Territory. The territorial act in each case omitted reference to slavery except to give the territorial legislature authority over "all rightful subjects of legislation" with provision for appeal to the federal courts. For the sake of agreement, the deliberate ambiguity of the statement was its merit. Northern congressmen could assume that the territorial legislatures might act to exclude slavery; southern congressmen assumed that they could not; (4) a new Fugitive Slave Act put the matter of apprehending runaway slaves wholly under federal jurisdiction and stacked the cards in favor of slave catchers; and, (5) as a gesture to anti-slavery forces, the public sale of slaves, but not slavery itself, was abolished in the District of Columbia. The awful spectacle of chained-together slaves passing through the streets of the nation's capital, to be sold at public auctions, was brought to an end.

President Millard Fillmore pronounced the five measures making up the Compromise of 1850 "a final settlement." Still, doubts lingered that both North and South could be reconciled to the measures permanently. In the South the disputes of 1846–1850 had transformed the abstract doctrine of secession into a growing reality fed by "fire-eaters" such as Robert Barnwell Rhett of South Carolina, William Lowndes Yancey of Alabama, and Edmund Ruffin of Virginia.

But once the furies aroused by the Wilmot Proviso had been spent, the compromise left little on which to focus pro-slavery agitation. Ironically, after its formation, California tended to elect pro-slavery men to Congress. New Mexico and Utah were far away, and in any case at least hypothetically open to slavery. In fact, both states adopted slave codes, but the census of 1860 reported no slaves in New Mexico and only twenty-nine in Utah.

THE FUGITIVE SLAVE ACT   The **Fugitive Slave Act** was the most controversial element of the compromise. It was the one clear-cut victory for the cause of slavery, but would the North enforce it? Southern insistence on the Fugitive Slave Act as part of the Compromise of 1850 outraged abolitionists. The act did more than strengthen the hand of slave catchers; it offered a strong temptation to kidnap free blacks in northern "free" states. The law denied alleged fugitives a jury trial. In addition, federal marshals could require citizens to help locate and capture runaways. Abolitionists fumed. "This filthy enactment was made in the nineteenth century, by people who could read and write," Ralph Waldo Emerson marveled in his diary. He advised neighbors to break the new law "on the earliest occasion." The occasion soon arose in Detroit, Michigan, where only military force stopped the rescue of an alleged fugitive slave by an outraged mob in October 1850. There were relatively few such incidents, however. In the first six years of the Fugitive Slave Act, only three runaways were forcibly rescued from slave catchers. On the other hand, probably fewer than two hundred were returned to bondage during those years. The Fugitive Slave Act was a powerful emotional and symbolic force arousing the anti-slavery impulse in the North.

UNCLE TOM'S CABIN During the 1850s, anti-slavery forces found their most persuasive appeal not in the Fugitive Slave Act but in the fictional drama of Harriet Beecher Stowe's best-selling novel, *Uncle Tom's Cabin* (1852). The pious daughter, sister, and wife of Congregationalist ministers, Stowe epitomized the powerful religious underpinnings of the abolitionist movement. She had decided to write the novel because of her disgust with the Fugitive Slave Act of 1850. *Uncle Tom's Cabin* was a smashing commercial success; by 1855 it was called "the most popular novel of our day." The novel depicts a combination of unlikely saints and sinners, stereotypes, fugitive slaves, and melodramatic escapades, and made the brutal realities of slavery real to readers. The abolitionist leader Frederick Douglass, a former slave himself, said that Stowe's powerful novel was like "a flash" that lit "a million camp fires in front of the embattled hosts of slavery." Slaveholders were incensed by Stowe's best-selling book. One of them mailed Stowe an anonymous parcel containing the severed ear of a disobedient slave. Yet it took time for

"The Greatest Book of the Age"

Uncle Tom's Cabin, as this advertisement indicates, was a best seller.

the novel to work its effect on public opinion. At the time of its publication, the country was enjoying a surge of prosperity fueled by California gold, and the course of the presidential campaign in 1852 reflected a common desire to lay sectional quarrels to rest.

THE ELECTION OF 1852 In 1852, the Democrats chose Franklin Pierce of New Hampshire as their presidential candidate; their platform endorsed the Compromise of 1850. For their part, the Whigs repudiated the lackluster Millard Fillmore, who had faithfully supported the Compromise of 1850, and once again tried to exploit martial glory. It took fifty-three ballots, but the convention finally chose General Winfield Scott, the hero of the Mexican War and a Virginia native backed mainly by northern Whigs. The Whig Convention dutifully endorsed the compromise, but with some opposition from the North. Scott, an able army commander but an inept politician, had gained a reputation for anti-slavery and nativist sentiments, alienating German- and Irish-American voters. In the end, Scott carried only Tennessee, Kentucky, Massachusetts, and Vermont. Pierce overwhelmed him in the Electoral College, 254 to 42, although the popular vote was close: 1.6 million to 1.4 million. The third-party Free-Soilers mustered only 156,000 votes, for John P. Hale, in contrast to the 291,000 they had tallied for Van Buren in 1848.

Forty-eight-year-old Franklin Pierce, an undistinguished but handsome former congressman and senator who had fought in the Mexican War, was, like James Polk, touted as another Andrew Jackson. He eagerly promoted western expansion, even if it meant adding more slave states to the Union. But the youngest president to date was unable to unite the warring factions of his party. He was neither a statesman nor a leader. After the election, Pierce wrote a poignant letter to his wife in which he expressed his frustration at the prospect of keeping North and South together. "I can do no right," he sighed. "What am I to do, wife? Stand by me." By the end of Pierce's first year in office, the leaders of his own party had decided he was a failure. By trying to be all things to all people, Pierce was labeled a "doughface": a "Northern man with Southern principles."

THE KANSAS-NEBRASKA CRISIS

America's growing commercial interests in Asia during the mid-nineteenth century helped spark a growing desire for a transcontinental railroad line connecting the eastern seaboard with the Pacific coast. During the

1850s the only land added to the United States was a barren stretch of some thirty thousand square miles south of the Gila River in present-day New Mexico and Arizona. By the Gadsden Purchase of 1853, the United States paid Mexico $10 million for land offering a likely route for a transcontinental railroad. The idea of building a railroad linking the far-flung regions of the new continental domain of the United States reignited sectional rivalries and reopened the slavery issue.

DOUGLAS'S NEBRASKA PROPOSAL   In 1852 and 1853, Congress debated several proposals for a transcontinental rail line. Secretary of War Jefferson Davis favored the southern route and promoted the Gadsden Purchase. Any other route, he explained, would go through the territories granted to Indians, which stretched from Texas to the Canadian border. Senator Stephen A. Douglas of Illinois offered an alternative: Chicago should be the transcontinental railroad's eastern terminus. Since 1845, Douglas and other supporters of a northern transcontinental route had offered bills for a new territory west of Missouri and Iowa bearing the Indian name Nebraska.

In 1854, settlers in Kansas and Nebraska asked Congress to grant them official status as U.S. territories eligible for statehood. New territories, however, raised the vexing question of slavery. As chairman of the Committee on Territories, Senator Douglas introduced a bill, later called the **Kansas-Nebraska Act**, that included the entire unorganized portion of the Louisiana Purchase, extending to the Canadian border. To win the support of southern legislators, Douglas championed the principle of "popular sovereignty," whereby voters in each territory could decide whether to allow slavery.

It was a clever dodge, since the 1820 Missouri Compromise would exclude slaves until a territorial government had made a decision. Southerners quickly spotted the barrier, and Douglas just as quickly made two more concessions. He supported an amendment for repeal of the Missouri Compromise insofar as it excluded slavery north of latitude 36°30′, and he agreed to the creation of two new territorial governments, Kansas, west of Missouri, and Nebraska, west of Iowa and Minnesota.

Stephen A. Douglas, ca. 1852
Author of the Kansas-Nebraska Act.

Douglas's motives remain unclear. Railroads were foremost in his mind, but he was also influenced by the desire to win support for his bill in the South, by the hope that his promotion of "popular sovereignty" would quiet the slavery issue and open the Great Plains to development, or by a chance to split the Whigs over the issue. Whatever his reasoning, he had blundered, damaging his presidential chances and setting the country on the road to civil war. In abandoning the long-standing Missouri Compromise boundary line and allowing territorial residents to decide the issue of slavery for themselves, Douglas renewed sectional tensions and forced moderate political leaders to align with the extremes. In the end the Kansas-Nebraska Act would destroy the Whig party, fragment the Democratic party, and spark a territorial civil war in Kansas.

The tragic flaw in Douglas's reasoning was his failure to appreciate the growing intensity of anti-slavery sentiment spreading across the country. His proposal to repeal the Missouri Compromise was less than a week old when six anti-slavery congressmen published a protest, the "Appeal of the Independent Democrats." It denounced the proposed Kansas-Nebraska Act as a "gross violation of a sacred pledge [the Missouri Compromise]." The manifesto urged Americans to use all means to defeat Douglas's bill and thereby "rescue" the nation "from the domination of slavery, . . . for the cause of human freedom is the cause of God." Across the North, editorials, sermons, speeches, and petitions echoed this indignation. What had been the opinion of a radical minority was fast becoming the common view of northerners.

In Congress, however, Douglas had masterfully assembled the votes for his Kansas-Nebraska Act, and he forced the issue with tireless energy. The inept President Pierce impulsively added his support. Southerners lined up behind Douglas, with notable exceptions, such as Texas senator Sam Houston, who denounced the act's violation of two solemn compacts: the Missouri Compromise and the confirmation of the territory deeded to the Indians "as long as grass shall grow and water run." He was not the only one concerned about the Indians; federal agents were already busy hoodwinking or bullying Indians into relinquishing their lands or rights. Douglas and Pierce whipped reluctant Democrats into line (though about half the northern Democrats refused to yield), pushing the passage of the Kansas-Nebraska bill by a vote of 37 to 14 in the Senate and 113 to 100 in the House. The anti-slavery faction in the Congress had been crushed.

Many in the North reasoned that if the Missouri Compromise was not a sacred pledge, then neither was the Fugitive Slave Act. On June 2, 1854, Boston witnessed the most dramatic demonstration against the act. Free

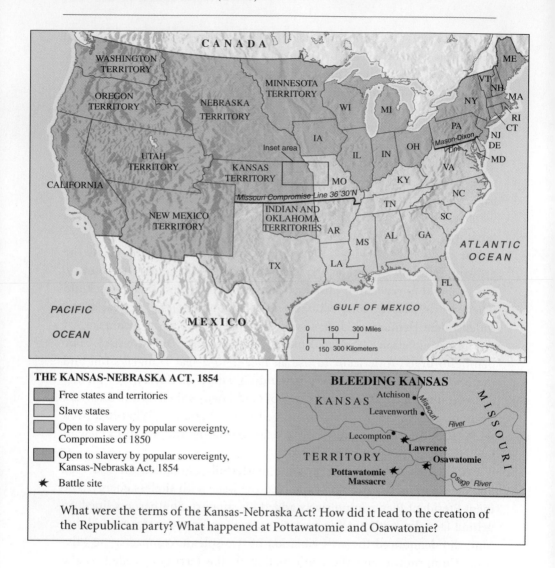

THE KANSAS-NEBRASKA ACT, 1854

- Free states and territories
- Slave states
- Open to slavery by popular sovereignty, Compromise of 1850
- Open to slavery by popular sovereignty, Kansas-Nebraska Act, 1854
- ✱ Battle site

BLEEDING KANSAS

What were the terms of the Kansas-Nebraska Act? How did it lead to the creation of the Republican party? What happened at Pottawatomie and Osawatomie?

blacks in Boston had taken in a runaway Virginia slave named Anthony Burns; federal marshals then arrived to arrest and return him. Incensed by what had happened, a crowd of two thousand abolitionists led by a minister stormed the jail in an effort to free Burns. In the melee a federal marshal was killed. At Burns's trial, held to determine whether he indeed was a fugitive, a compromise was proposed that would have allowed Bostonians to buy Burns his freedom, but the plan was scuttled by President Pierce, who was determined to enforce the Fugitive Slave Act. On June 2, the day that state militia and federal troops marched Burns through Boston to a ship waiting to return him to Virginia, some fifty thousand people lined the streets. Many of them shouted insults at the federal officials. As it happened, Anthony Burns was the last fugitive slave to be returned from Boston and was soon freed through purchase by the African American community of Boston.

THE EMERGENCE OF THE REPUBLICAN PARTY   By the mid-1850s, the sharp tensions over slavery were fracturing the nation. The national organizations of Baptists and Methodists, for instance, had split over slavery by 1845 and formed new northern and southern organizations supported the two denominations. The national parties were also beginning to buckle under the strain of slavery. The Democrats managed to postpone disruption for a while, but their congressional delegation lost heavily in the North, enhancing the influence of their southern wing.

The strain of the Kansas-Nebraska Act soon destroyed the Whig party. Southern Whigs now tended to abstain from voting, while northern Whigs gravitated toward two new parties. One was the American ("Know-Nothing") party, which had emerged in response to the surge of mostly Catholic immigrants from Ireland and Germany. The anti-Catholic "Know-Nothings" embraced nativism (opposition to foreign immigrants) by promoting the denial of citizenship to newcomers. In the early 1850s, Know-Nothings won several local elections in Massachusetts and New York.

The other new party, which attracted even more northern Whigs, was formed in 1854 when the so-called conscience Whigs, those opposed to slavery, split from the "cotton Whigs" and joined with independent Democrats and Free-Soilers to form the Republican party. A young Illinois Congressman named Abraham Lincoln illustrated the transition of many northern Whigs to the new Republican party. He said that the passage of Douglas's Kansas-Nebraska Act angered him "as he had never been before." It transformed his views on slavery. Unless the North mobilized to stop the efforts of pro-slavery southerners, the future of the Union was imperiled. From that moment on, Lincoln focused his energies on reversing the Kansas-Nebraska Act and promoting the anti-slavery movement.

"BLEEDING KANSAS"   After the controversial passage of the Kansas-Nebraska Act in 1854, attention swung to the plains of Kansas, where opposing elements gathered to stage a rehearsal for civil war. While Nebraska would become a free state, Kansas soon exposed the potential for mischief in Senator Douglas's idea of popular sovereignty. The ambiguity of the law, useful to Douglas in getting it passed, only added to the chaos. The people living in the Kansas Territory were "perfectly free to form and regulate their domestic institutions in their own way, subject only to the Constitution." That in itself invited conflicting interpretations, but the law said nothing about the timing of any decision, adding to each side's sense of urgency in getting political control of the fifty-million-acre territory.

The settlement of Kansas therefore differed from the typical pioneering efforts. Groups sprang up in North and South to hurry right-minded migrants westward. When Kansas's first federal governor arrived, in 1854, he ordered a census taken and scheduled an election for a territorial legislature in 1855. On election day, several thousand "border ruffians" crossed the river from Missouri, illegally swept the polls for pro-slavery forces, and vowed to kill every "God-damned abolitionist in the Territory." The governor denounced the vote as a fraud but did nothing to alter the results, for fear of being killed himself. The territorial legislature expelled its few anti-slavery members, adopted a drastic slave code, and made it a capital offense to aid a fugitive slave and a felony even to question the legality of slavery in the territory.

Outraged free-state advocates rejected this "bogus" government and moved directly toward application to Congress for statehood. In 1855, a constitutional convention, the product of an extralegal election, met in Topeka, drafted a state constitution excluding both slavery and free blacks from Kansas, and applied for admission to the Union. By 1856 a free-state "governor" and "legislature" were functioning in Topeka; thus there were two illegal governments in the Kansas Territory. The prospect of getting any government to command authority seemed dim, and both sides began to arm.

Finally, the tense confrontation began to slip into violent conflict. In May 1856 a pro-slavery mob entered the free-state town of Lawrence, Kansas, destroyed newspaper presses, set fire to the free-state governor's home, stole property, and demolished the Free-State Hotel.

The "sack of Lawrence" resulted in just one casualty, but the excitement aroused a zealous abolitionist named **John Brown**, who had a history of mental instability. The child of fervent Ohio Calvinists who taught their children that life was a crusade against sin, Brown believed that slavery was the most wicked of sins. Two days after Lawrence was sacked, Brown set out with four of his sons and three other men for Pottawatomie, Kansas, the site of a pro-slavery settlement near the Missouri border, where they dragged five men from their houses and hacked them to death with swords in front of their screaming families. "God is my judge," Brown told his son upon their return. "We were justified under the circumstances."

The **Pottawatomie Massacre** (May 24–25, 1856) set off a guerrilla war in the Kansas Territory that lasted through the fall. On August 30, Missouri ruffians raided the free-state settlement at Osawatomie, Kansas. They looted and burned the houses and shot John Brown's son Frederick through the heart. The elder Brown, who barely escaped, looked back at the town being devastated by "Satan's legions" and swore to his surviving sons and followers, "I have only a short time to live—only one death to die, and I will die fighting for this cause." Altogether, by the end of 1856, about 200 settlers had been killed in Kansas and $2 million in property destroyed during the territorial civil war over slavery. Approximately 1,500 federal troops were dispatched to restore order.

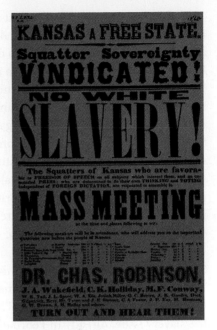

Kansas a Free State

This broadside advertises a series of mass meetings in Kansas in support of the free-state cause, based on the principle of "squatter" or popular sovereignty.

VIOLENCE IN THE SENATE

The violence in Kansas over slavery spilled over into Congress. On May 22, 1856, the day after the burning of Lawrence and two days before the Pottawatomie Massacre, a sudden flash of violence on the Senate floor electrified the whole country. Just two days earlier, Senator Charles Sumner of Massachusetts, an unyielding foe of slavery, had delivered an inflammatory speech on "The Crime against Kansas." His incendiary two-day speech insulted slaveowners. Sumner singled out the elderly senator Andrew Pickens Butler of South Carolina for censure. Butler, Sumner charged, had "chosen a mistress . . . who . . . though polluted in the sight of the world, is chaste in his sight—I mean the harlot, Slavery."

Sumner's indignant rudeness might well have backfired had it not been for Butler's cousin Preston S. Brooks, a fiery-tempered South Carolina congressman. For two days, Brooks brooded over the insult to his relative, knowing that Sumner would refuse a challenge to a duel. On May 22 he confronted Sumner at his Senate desk, accused him of slander against South Carolina and Butler, and began beating him about the head with a cane while stunned colleagues looked on. Sumner, struggling to rise, wrenched the desk from the floor and collapsed. Brooks kept beating him until his cane broke.

Brooks had satisfied his rage, but in doing so had created a martyr for the anti-slavery cause. For two and a half years, Sumner's empty Senate seat was a solemn reminder of the violence done to him. When the House censured Brooks, he resigned, only to return after being triumphantly reelected. The South Carolina governor held a banquet in Brooks's honor, and hundreds of southern admirers sent him new canes. The editor of the *Richmond Enquirer* urged Brooks to cane Sumner again: "These vulgar abolitionists in the Senate . . . must be lashed into submission." Northerners hastened to Sumner's defense. The news of the beating drove John Brown "crazy," his eldest son remembered, "*crazy*." The brutal beating of Senator Sumner had a direct political effect by driving more northerners into the new Republican party. By the late spring of 1856 there were Republican party offices in twenty-two states and the District of Columbia.

SECTIONAL POLITICS Within the span of five days in May of 1856, "Bleeding Kansas," "Bleeding Sumner," and "Bully Brooks" had set the tone for another presidential election. The major parties could no longer evade the slavery issue. Already in February it had split the infant American Party wide open. Southern delegates, with help from New York, killed a resolution to restore the Missouri Compromise and nominated Millard Fillmore for president. Later what was left of the Whig party endorsed him as well.

At its first national convention, the Republican party passed over its leading figure, New York senator William H. Seward, who was awaiting a better chance in 1860. The party instead fastened on a military hero, John C. Frémont, "the Pathfinder," who had led the conquest of Mexican California. The Republican platform also owed much to the Whigs. It favored federal funding for a transcontinental railroad and, in general, more government-financed internal improvements. It condemned the repeal of the Missouri Compromise, the Democratic policy of territorial expansion, and "those twin relics of barbarism—Polygamy and Slavery." It was the first time a major-party platform had taken a stand against slavery.

The Democrats, meeting two weeks earlier in June, had rejected Franklin Pierce, the hapless victim of so much turmoil. Pierce, who struggled most of his life with alcoholism and self-doubt, may have been the most hated person in the nation by 1856. The Pierce presidency, a Philadelphia newspaper charged, was one of "weakness, indecision, rashness, ignorance, and an entire and utter absence of dignity." Pierce remains the only elected president to be denied renomination by his party. The Democrats also turned their back on Stephen A. Douglas because of the damage done by his Kansas-Nebraska Act. The party therefore turned to

James Buchanan of Pennsylvania, a former senator and secretary of state who had long sought the nomination. The party and its candidate nevertheless supported Pierce's policies. The Democratic platform endorsed the Kansas-Nebraska Act, called for vigorous enforcement of the fugitive slave law, and stressed that Congress should not interfere with slavery in either states or territories. The party reached out to its newly acquired Irish and German voters by condemning nativism and endorsing religious liberty.

The campaign of 1856 resolved itself as a sectional contest in which parties vied for northern or southern votes. The Republicans had few southern supporters and only a handful in the border states, where fear of disunion held many Whigs in line. Buchanan thus went into the campaign as the

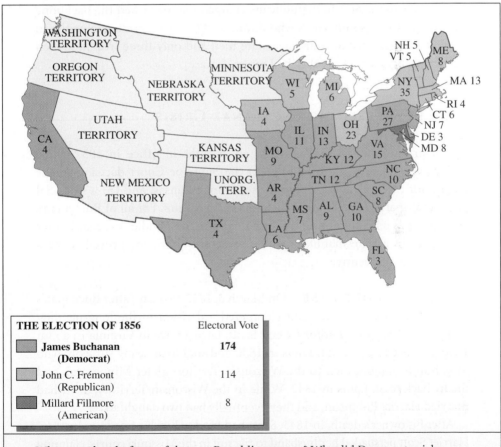

THE ELECTION OF 1856	Electoral Vote
James Buchanan (Democrat)	174
John C. Frémont (Republican)	114
Millard Fillmore (American)	8

What was the platform of the new Republican party? Why did Democrats pick James Buchanan? What were the key factors that decided the election?

candidate of the only remaining national party. Frémont swept the north-ernmost states with 114 electoral votes, but Buchanan added five free states—Pennsylvania, New Jersey, Illinois, Indiana, and California—to his southern majority for a total of 174.

The sixty-five-year-old Buchanan, America's first unmarried president, brought to the White House a portfolio of impressive achievements in poli-tics and diplomacy. His political career went back to 1815, when he served as a Federalist legislator in Pennsylvania before switching to Andrew Jackson's party in the 1820s. He had served in Congress for over twenty years and had been ambassador to Russia and Britain as well as James K. Polk's secretary of state. His long quest for the presidency had been built on his commitment to states' rights and his aggressive promotion of territorial expansion. His political debts reinforced his belief that saving the Union depended upon concessions to the South. Republicans charged that he lacked the backbone to stand up to the southerners who dominated the Democratic majorities in Congress. His choice of four slave-state men and only three free-state men for his cabinet seemed another bad omen. It was.

THE DEEPENING SECTIONAL CRISIS

During James Buchanan's first six months in office in 1857, three major events caused his undoing: (1) the Supreme Court decision in the *Dred Scott* case, (2) new troubles in strife-torn Kansas, and (3) a financial panic that sparked a widespread economic depression. For all of Buchanan's experience as a legislator and diplomat, he failed to handle those and other key issues in a statesmanlike manner. The new president proved to be a mediocre chief executive.

THE *DRED SCOTT* CASE   On March 6, 1857, two days after Buchanan's inauguration, the Supreme Court rendered a decision in the long-pending case of **Dred Scott v. Sandford**. Dred Scott, born a slave in Virginia in about 1800, had been taken to St. Louis in 1830 and sold to an army surgeon, who took him to Illinois, then to the Wisconsin Territory (later Minnesota), and finally back to St. Louis in 1842. While in the Wisconsin Territory, Scott had married Harriet Robinson, and they eventually had two daughters.

After his owner's death, in 1843, Scott had tried to buy his freedom. In 1846, Harriet Scott persuaded her husband to file suit in the Missouri courts, claiming that residence in Illinois and the Wisconsin Territory had made him free. A jury decided in his favor, but the state supreme court ruled against him. When the case rose on appeal to the Supreme Court, the nation anxiously awaited its opinion on whether freedom once granted could be lost by returning to a slave state.

Seventy-nine-year-old Chief Justice Roger B. Taney, an ardent supporter of the South and slavery, wrote the Court's majority opinion. He ruled that Scott lacked legal standing because he lacked citizenship, as did all former slaves. At the time the Constitution was adopted, Taney claimed, blacks "had for more than a century been regarded as . . . so far inferior, that they had no rights which the white man was bound to respect." On the issue of Scott's residency, Taney argued that the Missouri Compromise of 1820 had deprived citizens of property by prohibiting slavery in selected states, an action "not warranted by the Constitution."

The upshot was that Chief Justice Taney and the rest of the Supreme Court had declared an act of Congress unconstitutional for the first time since *Marbury v. Madison* (1803). Congress had repealed the Missouri Compromise in the Kansas-Nebraska Act three years earlier, but the *Dred Scott* decision now challenged the concept of popular sovereignty. If Congress itself could not exclude slavery from a territory, then presumably neither could a territorial government created by an act of Congress.

Far from settling the issue of slavery in the territories, Taney's ruling fanned the flames of dissension. Republicans protested the *Dred Scott* decision because it nullified their anti-slavery program. It had also reinforced the suspicion that the pro-slavery faction was hatching a conspiracy. Were not all but one of the justices who had voted with Taney in the Dred Scott case southerners? And President Buchanan had sought to influence the Court's decision both before and during his inaugural ceremony. Besides, if Dred Scott were not a citizen and had no standing in court, there was no case before the Court. The majority ruling about slavery in the territories was an obiter dictum—a statement not essential to deciding the case and therefore not binding.

Pro-slavery elements greeted the Court's opinion as binding. Now the most militant among them were emboldened to make yet another demand. It was not enough to deny Congress the right to interfere with slavery in the territories; Congress had an obligation to protect the property of slaveholders, making a federal slave code the next step in the militant effort to defend slavery.

THE LECOMPTON CONSTITUTION Meanwhile, out west, in the Kansas Territory, the struggle over slavery in the future state continued. Just before President Buchanan's inauguration, in early 1857, the pro-slavery territorial legislature called for a constitutional convention. Since no provision was made for a referendum on the constitution, however, the governor vetoed the measure, and then the legislature overrode his veto. The Kansas governor resigned on the day Buchanan took office, and the new president replaced him with Robert J. Walker. A native Pennsylvanian who had made a political career first in Mississippi and later as a member of Polk's cabinet, Walker had greater prestige than his predecessors, and he put the fate of the Union above the expansion of slavery. In Kansas he sensed a chance to advance the cause of both the Union and his party. Under Stephen A. Douglas's principle of "popular sovereignty," fair elections would produce a state that would be both free and Democratic.

Walker arrived in Kansas in 1857, and with Buchanan's approval the new governor pledged to the free-state Kansans (who made up an overwhelming majority of the residents) that the new constitution would be submitted to a fair vote. In spite of his pleas, however, he arrived too late to persuade free-state men to vote for convention delegates in elections they were sure had been rigged against them. Later, however, Walker did persuade the free-state leaders to vote in the election of a new territorial legislature.

As a result a polarity arose between an anti-slavery legislature and a pro-slavery constitutional convention. The convention, meeting at Lecompton, Kansas, drafted a constitution under which Kansas would become a slave state. Free-state men boycotted the vote on the new constitution because in their view it was rigged. At that point, President Buchanan took a fateful step. Influenced by southern advisers and politically dependent upon powerful southern congressmen, he decided to renege on his pledge to Governor Walker and endorse the pro-slavery Lecompton convention. A new wave of outrage swept across the northern states. Democratic senator Stephen A. Douglas dramatically broke with the president over the issue, siding with Republicans because the people of Kansas had been denied the right to decide the issue. Governor Walker resigned in protest, and the election went according to form: 6,226 for the constitution with slavery, 569 for the constitution without slavery. Meanwhile, the acting governor had convened the anti-slavery legislature, which called for another election to vote the Lecompton Constitution up or down. Most of the pro-slavery settlers boycotted this election, and the result, on January 4, 1858, was overwhelming: 10,226 against the constitution, 138 for the constitution with slavery, 24 for the constitution without slavery.

The combined results suggested a clear majority against slavery, but the pro-southern Buchanan stuck to his support of the unpopular Lecompton Constitution, driving another wedge into the Democratic party. In the Senate, administration forces convinced enough northern Democrats to follow his lead, and in 1858 the Lecompton Constitution was passed. In the House enough anti-Lecompton Democrats combined to put through an amendment for a new, carefully supervised popular vote in Kansas. On August 2, 1858, Kansas voters rejected the Lecompton constitution, 11,300 to 1,788. With that vote, Kansas, now firmly in the hands of its new anti-slavery legislature, largely ended its provocative role in the sectional controversy.

THE PANIC OF 1857   The third emergency of Buchanan's first half year in office, a national financial crisis, occurred in August 1857. It was brought on by a reduction in foreign demand for American grain, overly aggressive railroad construction, a surge in manufacturing production that outran the growth of market demand, and the continued confusion caused by the state banknote system. The failure of the Ohio Life Insurance and Trust Company on August 24, 1857, precipitated the panic, which was followed by an economic slump from which the country did not emerge until 1859.

Every major event in the late 1850s seemed to get drawn into the vortex of the festering sectional conflict, and business troubles were no exception. Northern businessmen tended to blame the depression on the Democratic Tariff of 1857, which had cut rates on imports to their lowest level since 1816. The agricultural South weathered the crisis better than the North. Cotton prices fell, but slowly, and world markets for cotton quickly recovered. The result was an exalted notion of King Cotton's importance to the world economy and an apparent confirmation of the growing argument that the southern system of slave-based agriculture was superior to the free-labor system of the North.

DOUGLAS VERSUS LINCOLN   Amid the recriminations over the *Dred Scott* decision, "Bleeding Kansas," and the floundering economy, the center could not hold. The controversy over slavery in Kansas put severe strains on the most substantial cord of union that was left, the Democratic party. To many, Senator Stephen A. Douglas seemed the best hope for unity and union, one of the few remaining Democratic leaders with support in both the North and the South. In 1858 he faced reelection to the Senate against the opposition of both Buchanan Democrats and Republicans. The year 1860 would give him a chance for the presidency, but first he had to secure his home base in Illinois.

To oppose him, Illinois Republicans named a small-town lawyer from Springfield, **Abraham Lincoln**, the lanky, rawboned former Whig state legislator and one-term congressman. Lincoln had served in the Illinois legislature until 1842 and in 1846 had won a seat in Congress. After a single term, he had retired from active politics to cultivate his law practice in Springfield. In 1854, however, the Kansas-Nebraska Act drew Lincoln back into the political arena. When Douglas appeared in Springfield to defend his idea of popular sovereignty, Lincoln countered from the same platform. Lincoln abhorred slavery but was no abolitionist. He did not believe the two races could coexist as equals, but he did oppose any further extension of slavery into new territories. Like many others at the time, Lincoln assumed that over time slavery would die a "natural death." Slavery, he said in the 1840s, was a vexing but "minor question on its way to extinction."

At first Lincoln had held back from the rapidly growing Republican party, but in 1856 he had joined it and had given some fifty speeches promoting the Frémont presidential ticket in Illinois and nearby states. By 1858, as the obvious choice to oppose Douglas for the Senate seat, he was resorting to the classic ploy of the underdog: he challenged the favorite to debate him. Douglas agreed to meet him in seven locations around the state.

Thus the titanic **Lincoln-Douglas debates** took place, from August 21 to October 15, 1858. They attracted thousands of spectators and were read in the newspapers by many more. The debates transformed an Illinois contest for a Senate seat into a battle for the very future of the Republic. At the time and since, much attention focused on the second debate, at Freeport, where Lincoln asked Douglas how he could reconcile his concept of popular sovereignty with the *Dred Scott* ruling that citizens had the right to carry slaves into *any* territory. Douglas's answer, thenceforth known as the **Freeport Doctrine**, was to state the obvious: whatever the Supreme Court might say about slavery, it could not exist anywhere unless supported by local police regulations.

The basic difference between the two men, Lincoln insisted, lay in Douglas's professed indifference to the moral question of slavery. He said he cared "more for the great principle of self-government, the right of the people to rule, than I do for all of the negroes in Christendom." Douglas was preoccupied with process ("popular sovereignty"); Lincoln was focused on principle. He

𐂷𐂷𐂷𐂷𐂷𐂷𐂷𐂷𐂷

Last Great Discussion.

Let all take notice, that on Friday next, HON. S. A. DOUGLAS and HON. A. LINCOLN, will hold the seventh and closing joint debate of the canvass at this place. We hope the country will turn out, to a man, to hear these gentlemen.

The following programme for the discussion has been decided upon by the Joint Committee appointed by the People's Party Club and the Democratic Club for that purpose.

Debate announcement

An announcement for the seventh and final Lincoln-Douglas debate.

insisted that the American government could not "endure, permanently half *slave* and half *free*. . . . It will become *all* one thing, or *all* the other."

If Lincoln had the better of the argument in the long view, Douglas had the better of a close election in traditionally Democratic Illinois. Douglas retained his Senate seat (senators were then selected by legislatures, not by a popular vote), but Lincoln's energetic campaign had made him a national figure well positioned to become the Republican presidential candidate in 1860. Across the nation, however, Democrats did not fare as well as Douglas in 1858. As the balance of power in the Democratic party shifted more and more to the southern wing, as northern Democrats switched to the new Republican party, party loyalties no longer served to promote a national outlook. The political parties grew increasingly sectional in their composition and outlook: Democrats in the South and Republicans in the North. Most Democratic congressional candidates who aligned themselves with President Buchanan lost their elections in 1858, thus signaling in the North and the West the political shift toward the new Republican party and its antislavery principles.

At the same time that the political balance in the North was beginning to shift from the Democrats to the Republicans, political tensions over slavery were becoming more intractable—and violent. In 1858, members of Congress engaged in the largest brawl ever staged on the floor of the House of Representatives. Harsh words about slavery incited the melee, which involved more than fifty legislators shoving, punching, and wrestling one another. The fracas culminated when John "Bowie Knife" Potter of Wisconsin yanked off the wig of a Mississippi congressman and claimed, "I've scalped him." Like the scuffling congressmen, more and more Americans began to feel that slavery could be ended or defended only with violence. The editor of a Kansas newspaper exclaimed that he yearned to kill an abolitionist: "If I can't kill a man, I'll kill a woman; and if I can't kill a woman, I'll kill a child."

JOHN BROWN'S RAID The gradual return of prosperity in 1859 offered hope that the sectional storms of the 1850s might yet pass. But the slavery issue remained tornadic. In October 1859, the militant abolitionist John Brown once again surfaced, this time in the East. Since the Pottawatomie Massacre in 1856, he had led a furtive existence, acquiring money and weapons from prominent New England sympathizers. His heartfelt commitment to abolish the "wicked curse of slavery" and promote complete racial equality had intensified to a fever pitch because he saw the institution of slavery becoming more deeply entrenched in American society, cemented by law, economics, and religious sanction. Brown

John Brown

Although his anti-slavery efforts were based in Kansas, Brown was a native of Connecticut.

was driven by a sense of vengeful righteousness. His penetrating gray eyes and flowing beard, as well as his conviction that he was an instrument of God, struck fear into supporters and opponents alike. Brown was one of the few whites willing to live among black people and to die for them. He viewed himself as carrying out a divine mission on behalf of a vengeful God.

On October 16, 1859, the crusading Brown launched his supreme gesture. From a Maryland farm he clambered down mist-shrouded bluffs and crossed the Potomac River with about twenty heavily armed men, including five African Americans. Under cover of darkness, they occupied the federal arsenal in Harpers Ferry, Virginia (now West Virginia), at the confluence of the Potomac and Shenandoah rivers, some sixty miles northwest of Washington, D.C. "I want to free all the negroes in this state," Brown told one of his first hostages, a night watchman. "If the citizens interfere with me, I must only burn the town and have blood." Brown's ludicrous plan was to seize the arsenal and then arm thousands of the slaves in the area, who he assumed would flock to his cause; then he would set up a black stronghold in the mountains of western Virginia, thus providing a nucleus of support to inspire slave insurrections across the South.

What Brown and his soldiers of a vengeful God actually did was take the town by surprise, cut the telegraph lines, and take control of the railroad station, musket factory, rifle works, and arsenal. Brown then sent a handful of his men to kidnap several prominent slave owners in the area and spread the word for local slaves to rise up and join the rebellion. But only a few slaves heeded Brown's call to arms. By dawn local white militias and enraged townsmen had surrounded Brown's raiders. Brown and a dozen of his men, along with eleven white hostages (including George Washington's grandson) and two of their slaves, holed up for thirty-two hours. In the morning Brown sent his son Watson and another man out under a white flag, hoping to trade his hostages for his freedom, but the angry crowd shot them both. Intermittent shooting continued, and another Brown son was wounded. He begged his father to kill him to end his suffering, but Brown refused, screaming, "If you must die, die like a man." A few minutes later the son was dead.

Throughout the day hundreds of men poured into Harper's Ferry to dislodge Brown and his raiders. Late that night Lieutenant Colonel Robert E. Lee, one of the army's most promising officers, arrived with his aide, Lieutenant J.E.B. Stuart, and a force of U.S. marines, having been dispatched from Washington, D.C., by President Buchanan. The following morning, October 18, Stuart and his troops, with thousands of spectators cheering, broke down the barricaded doors and rushed in. A young lieutenant found Brown kneeling with his rifle cocked. Before Brown could fire, however, the marine used the hilt of his sword to beat Brown unconscious. The siege was over. Altogether, Brown's men had killed four townspeople and wounded another dozen. Of their own force, ten were killed (including two of Brown's sons) and five were captured; another five escaped.

Brown and his accomplices were quickly tried for treason, murder, and "conspiring with Negroes to produce insurrection." He was convicted on October 31 and hanged on December 2, 1859. (Among the crowd watching the execution was a popular young actor named John Wilkes Booth, who would later assassinate Abraham Lincoln.) On his way to the gallows Brown predicted that slavery would end only "after much bloodshed." If Brown had failed in his primary purpose to ignite a massive slave rebellion, he had achieved two things: he had become a martyr for the anti-slavery cause, and he had set off a panic throughout the slaveholding South. At his sentencing he delivered one of America's classic speeches: "Now, if it is deemed necessary that I should forfeit my life for the furtherance of the ends of justice, and mingle my blood further with the blood of my children and with the blood of millions in this slave country whose rights are disregarded by wicked, cruel, and unjust enactments, I say, let it be done."

When John Brown, still unflinching, embraced martyrdom for the abolitionist cause and was hanged, there were solemn observances in the North. "That new saint," Ralph Waldo Emerson said, " . . . will make the gallows glorious like the cross." Brown wielded more power and influence dead than alive. "Living, he made life beautiful," the writer Louisa May Alcott wrote on the day Brown died. "Dying, [he] made death divine." The nation's leading white abolitionist, the pacifist William Lloyd Garrison, was not as impressed by Brown's effort to wreak justice by the shedding of blood. He dismissed the raid on Harper's Ferry as "misguided, wild, and apparently insane."

John Brown's quixotic raid marked the point of no return: it set in motion a series of events that would lead to rebellion and war. Brown's martyrdom embodied the South's greatest fear: that armed slaves would revolt. Another effect of Brown's raid was to encourage pro-slavery southerners to equate the militant abolitionism of John Brown with the Republican party. All through the fall and winter of 1859–1860, overheated rumors of abolitionist conspiracies and slave insurrections swept through the slave states. Dozens of new militia companies were organized and began training to thwart an uprising. Every northern visitor, commercial traveler, or schoolteacher came under suspicion, and many were driven out. "We regard every man in our midst an enemy to the institutions of the South," said the *Atlanta Confederacy*, "who does not boldly declare that he believes African slavery to be a social, moral, and political blessing."

THE CENTER COMES APART

THE DEMOCRATS DIVIDE   Amid such emotional hysteria the nation ushered in another presidential election, destined to be the most fateful in its history. In April 1860 the Democrats gathered for their presidential convention in Charleston, South Carolina, a pro-slavery hotbed. Illinois senator Stephen A. Douglas's supporters tried to straddle the slavery issue by promising southerners to defend the institution in their region while assuring northerners that slavery would not spread to new states. Southern firebrands, however, demanded federal protection for slavery in the territories. The platform debate reached a heady climax when the Alabama hothead William Yancey informed the northern Democrats that their error had been the failure to defend slavery as a positive good. An Ohio senator offered a blunt reply. "Gentlemen of the South," he said, "you mistake us—you mistake us. We will not do it."

When the pro-slavery planks lost, Alabama's delegates walked out of the convention, followed by those representing most of the other southern states. "We say, go your way," exclaimed a Mississippi delegate to Douglas's supporters, "and we will go ours." The convention then decided to leave the overwrought atmosphere of Charleston and reassemble in Baltimore on June 18. The Baltimore convention finally nominated Stephen A. Douglas and reaffirmed the 1856 platform. The Charleston seceders met first in Richmond and then in Baltimore, where they adopted the pro-slavery platform defeated in Charleston and named Vice President John C. Breckinridge of Kentucky as their candidate for president. Thus another cord of union had snapped: the last remaining national party had fragmented.

"Prospect of a Smash Up" (1860)

This cartoon shows the Democratic party—the last remaining national party—about to be split by sectional differences and the onrush of Republicans, led by Abraham Lincoln.

LINCOLN'S ELECTION   The Republicans, having become the dominant force in northern politics by combining alienated Democrats, former Whigs, and members of the nativist American Party ("Know-Nothings"), gathered in May in Chicago for their presidential convention. There everything suddenly came together for Abraham Lincoln, the uncommon common man who remained an obscure figure in terms of the national political landscape. He had emerged on the national scene during his unsuccessful Illinois senatorial campaign two years before and had since taken a stance designed to make him available for the nomination. He was strong enough on the containment of slavery to satisfy the abolitionists yet moderate enough to seem less threatening than they were. In 1860, he had gone east to address an audience of influential Republicans at Cooper Union, a newly established art and engineering college in New York City, where he emphasized his view of slavery "as an evil, not to be extended, but to be tolerated and protected only because of and so far as its actual presence among us makes that toleration and protection a necessity."

At the Chicago Republican Convention, an overconfident New York senator, William H. Seward, was the early leader among the presidential nominees, but he had been tagged as an extremist for his earlier statements about a looming "irrepressible conflict" over slavery. On the first ballot, Lincoln finished in second place. On the next ballot he drew almost even with

Seward. Pandemonium erupted among the ten thousand delegates as they saw the momentum shifting toward the dark horse Lincoln. When a third ballot pushed Lincoln within one and a half votes of a majority, the Ohio delegation dramatically switched four votes to put him over the top. The resulting cheer, wrote one journalist, was "like the rush of a great wind." Inside the convention building, the "wildest excitement and enthusiasm" swelled to a "perfect roar."

The Republican party platform denounced both the Supreme Court's *Dred Scott* decision allowing slavery in all federal territories and John Brown's raid as "among the gravest of crimes." It also promised "the right of each state to order and control its own domestic institutions." The party reaffirmed its resistance to the extension of slavery and, in an effort to gain broader support, endorsed a series of measures promoting national economic expansion: a higher protective tariff for manufacturers, free homesteads on federal lands, a more liberal naturalization law for immigrants, and federally-financed internal improvements, including a transcontinental railroad. With this platform, Republicans made a strong appeal to eastern businessmen, western farmers, and the large immigrant population. The Republican platform also frightened southern cotton planters, who presumed that their slave-based agriculture was doomed if the Republicans won the presidential election.

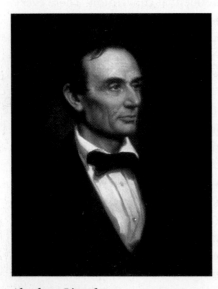

Abraham Lincoln

Republican candidate for president, June 1860.

Both major presidential nominating conventions revealed that opinions tended to become more radical in the Upper North and the Deep South. Attitude followed latitude. In the border states a sense of moderation aroused the die-hard former Whigs to make one more try at reconciliation. Meeting in Baltimore a week before the Republicans met in Chicago, they reorganized as the Constitutional Union party and nominated John Bell of Tennessee for president. Their platform centered on a vague statement promoting "the Constitution of the Country, the Union of the States, and the Enforcement of the Laws."

None of the four candidates generated a national following, and the bitterly contested six-month-long campaign devolved into a choice between Lincoln and Douglas in the North (Lincoln was not even on the ballot in the South), and Breckinridge and Bell in the South. One consequence of the separate campaigns was that each section gained a false impression of the other. The South never learned to distinguish Lincoln from the militant abolitionists; the North, and especially Lincoln, failed to gauge the force of southern intransigence. A few days before the election the *Charleston Mercury* spoke for most South Carolinians when it declared that "the existence of slavery is at stake" in the balloting. The editor called for secession in "each and all of the southern states" should the "abolitionist white man" capture the White House. For his part, Lincoln stubbornly refused to offer the South assurances or to clarify his position on slavery, which he said was a matter of public record.

The one man who attempted to penetrate the veil that was falling between the North and the South was Douglas, who tried to mount the first nationwide campaign tour. Only forty-seven but weakened by excessive drink, ill health, and disappointments, he wore himself out in one final, glorious campaign. Early in October 1860, at Cedar Rapids, Iowa, he learned of Republican victories in the Pennsylvania and Indiana state legislatures. "Mr. Lincoln is the next President," he said. "We must try to save the Union. I will go South." Down through the hostile states of Tennessee, Georgia, and Alabama, Douglas carried appeals on behalf of the Union. "I do not believe that every Breckinridge man is a disunionist," he said, "but I do believe that every disunionist is a Breckinridge man." Douglas promised voters that he would "make war boldly against Northern abolitionists and Southern disunionists."

By midnight on November 6, Lincoln's victory was clear. In the final count he had 39 percent of the total popular vote, the smallest plurality ever, but he won a clear majority (180 votes) in the Electoral College. He carried every one of the eighteen free states, and by a margin wide enough to elect him even if the votes for the other candidates had been combined. But hidden in the balloting was an ominous development: for the first time a president had been elected by a clear sectional vote. Among the four candidates, only Douglas had won electoral votes from both slave and free states, but his total of 12 was but a pitiful remnant of Democratic unionism. Bell took Virginia, Kentucky, and Tennessee for 39 votes, and Breckinridge swept the other slave states to come in second with 72.

THE RESPONSE IN THE SOUTH   Lincoln's election convinced many white southerners that their only choice was secession, which would likely lead to war. In their view, the "Black Republican," as they called Lincoln, was determined to end slavery. Many slaves believed the same thing. News of the election circulated "like a whirlwind" throughout the African American community. Some interpreted the election results as ensuring their freedom. On a plantation near Petersburg, Virginia, south of Richmond, seventeen slaves responded to the news of Lincoln's election by declaring their independence and walking to freedom. A slave in Louisiana who did the same told his captors in late May 1861 that "the North was fighting for the Negroes now and that he was as free as his master." Some slave owners viewed such efforts by slaves to seize their freedom as pathetic evidence of their misreading of the political process. A Louisiana planter reported that "the Negroes have gotten a confused idea of Lincoln's Congress meeting and of the war; they think it is all to help them and they expected for 'something to turn up.'"

SECESSION OF THE DEEP SOUTH STATES   Between November 8, 1860, when Lincoln was elected, and March 4, 1861, when he was inaugurated, the United States of America disintegrated. Soon after Lincoln's election, the South Carolina legislature called for a state secession convention to meet in December to remove the slave state from the Union. The coastal state had a higher percentage of slaves in its population (60 percent) than any other state, and its political leadership was dominated by firebrands. It had been a one-party state for decades, and it was the only state of the then thirty-three states that did not allow its citizens to vote in presidential elections; the state legislature did the balloting. Meeting in Charleston on December 20, 1860, the special state convention, most of whose 169 delegates were slave owners, unanimously endorsed an Ordinance of Secession, explaining that a purely sectional (Republican) party had elected to the presidency a man "whose opinions and purposes are hostile to slavery," who had declared "government cannot endure permanently half slave, half free" and that slavery "is in the course of ultimate extinction." Two days after South Carolina seceded, President Lincoln told Georgian Alexander Stephens, soon to become the vice president of the Confederacy, that southerners had no need to worry that he would interfere with slavery in the South: he was opposed to slavery, but he was not an abolitionist. But many southerners were not convinced by such presidential promises.

By February 1, 1861, Mississippi, Florida, Alabama, Georgia, Louisiana, and Texas had also seceded. Three days later, representatives of the seven seceding states met in Montgomery, Alabama, where they adopted a provisional constitution for the Confederate States of America, and two days later they elected Mississippi's Jefferson Davis as president. He was inaugurated on February 18, with Alexander H. Stephens of Georgia as vice president. Stephens left no doubt about why the Confederacy was formed. "Our new government," he declared, "is founded upon . . . the great truth that the negro is not equal to the white man; that slavery, subordination to the superior [white] race, is his natural and normal condition."

In all seven Deep South states a solid majority had voted for secessionist delegates, but their combined vote would not have been a majority of the presidential vote in November. What happened, it seemed, was what often

THE ELECTION OF 1860	Electoral Vote	Popular Vote
Abraham Lincoln (Republican)	180	1,866,000
Stephen A. Douglas (Democrat—northern)	12	1,383,000
John C. Breckinridge (Democrat—southern)	72	848,000
John Bell (Constitutional Union)	39	593,000

What caused the division in the Democratic party? How did Abraham Lincoln position himself to win the Republican nomination? What were the major factors that led to Lincoln's electoral victory?

happens in revolutionary situations: a determined group of secessionists acted quickly in an emotionally charged climate and carried out its program over the weak objections of a confused, indecisive opposition.

BUCHANAN'S WAITING GAME   History is full of might-have-beens. A bold stroke, even a bold statement, by the lame-duck president at this point might have changed the course of events by slowing the momentum of secession. But James Buchanan lacked boldness. He was weary and irresolute. Besides, he feared that a bold stroke might have hastened the conflict. No bold stroke came from Lincoln either, nor would he consult with the Buchanan administration during the months before his inauguration on March 4. He inclined all too strongly to the belief that the secessionists were bluffing. In public he maintained a stately silence about the secession crisis.

In his annual message on December 3, President Buchanan criticized northern agitators for trying to interfere with "slavery in the southern states." He then declared that secession was illegal but that he lacked the constitutional authority to coerce a state to rejoin the Union. The president reaffirmed his duty to "take care that the laws be faithfully executed" insofar as he was able. If the president could enforce the law upon all citizens, he would have no need to "coerce" a state. Indeed, his position became the policy of the Lincoln administration, which ended up fighting a civil war on the theory that individuals, but not states, were in rebellion.

The feckless Buchanan held firm to his timidity as 1860 came to a close. Meanwhile, the secessionists seized federal property, arsenals, and forts. And many southerners holding federal posts in the South resigned. Fort Sumter, guarding the harbor at Charleston, South Carolina, was commanded by Major Robert Anderson, a Kentucky Unionist, when South Carolina secessionists demanded withdrawal of all federal forces. President Buchanan rejected South Carolina's ultimatum. He dispatched a steamer, *Star of the West*, to Fort Sumter with reinforcements and provisions. As the ship approached Charleston Harbor, Confederate cannons opened fire on January 9, 1861, and drove it away. It was in fact an act of war, but Buchanan chose to ignore the challenge. He decided instead to hunker down and ride out the remaining weeks of his term, hoping against hope that one of several compromise efforts would prevail.

FINAL EFFORTS AT COMPROMISE   Amid the confusion and turmoil of the secession fever, members of Congress made desperate efforts at a compromise that would avoid a civil war. On December 18, 1860, Senator John J. Crittenden of Kentucky had proposed a series of amendments and resolutions that allowed for slavery in the territories south of the 36°30' parallel and guaranteed the maintenance of slavery where it already existed. Meanwhile, a peace conference met at Willard's Hotel in Washington, D.C., in February 1861. Twenty-one states sent delegates. Former president John Tyler presided, but the convention's proposal, substantially the same as the Crittenden Compromise, failed to win the support of either house of Congress. The only proposal that met with any success was a constitutional amendment guaranteeing slavery where it existed. Many Republicans, including Lincoln, were prepared to go that far to save the Union, but they were unwilling to repudiate their principled stand against extending slavery into the western territories. As it happened, after passing the House, the slavery amendment passed the Senate without a vote to spare, by 24 to 12, on the dawn of Lincoln's inauguration day. It would have become the Thirteenth Amendment, with the first use of the word *slavery* in the Constitution, but the states never ratified it. When a Thirteenth Amendment was ratified, in 1865, it did not guarantee slavery—it abolished it.

CHAPTER SUMMARY

- **Free-Soil Coalition** David Wilmot's declaration that the Mexican territories had been free and therefore should remain so attracted a broad coalition of Americans, including many northern Democrats and anti-slavery Whigs, as well as members of the new Liberty party. Like the Wilmot Proviso, the Free-Soil party demanded that slavery not be expanded to the territories.

- **California Statehood** Californians wanted their territory to enter the Union as a free state. Southerners feared that they would lose federal protection of their "peculiar institution" if more free states than slave states emerged. Whereas Senator John C. Calhoun maintained that slavery could not constitutionally be banned in any of the territories, anti-slavery forces demanded that all the territories remain free.

- **Compromise of 1850** It had been agreed that popular sovereignty would settle the status of the territories, but when the territories applied for statehood, the debate over slavery was renewed. The Compromise of 1850 was the result of the impassioned debate over whether to allow slavery in the territories gained from Mexico, which had banned slavery. By the Compromise of 1850, California entered the Union as a free state, the territories of Texas, New Mexico, and Utah were established without direct reference to slavery, the slave trade (but not slavery itself) was banned in Washington, D.C., and a new, stronger Fugitive Slave Act was passed.

- **Kansas-Nebraska Act** The proposal to overturn the Missouri Compromise by opening to slavery the territories north of 36°30′ outraged the nation's growing anti-slavery faction. The Kansas-Nebraska Act destroyed the Whig party, limited the influence of the Democrats, and led to the creation of the Republican party, which absorbed many Free-Soilers and Know-Nothings.

- **Southern Secession** The Democrats' split into northern and southern factions contributed to the success of Abraham Lincoln and the new Republican party in the election of 1860. The Republicans' victory was the immediate cause of secession. Southerners, reeling from John Brown's raid at Harpers Ferry, equated anti-slavery violence with the Republican party. More important, the Republican victory showed that the South no longer had enough votes in Congress to protect its "peculiar institution."

CHRONOLOGY

1848	Free-Soil party is organized
	California gold rush begins
1853	With the Gadsden Purchase, the United States acquires thirty thousand square miles from Mexico
1854	Congress passes the Kansas-Nebraska Act
	The Republican party is founded
1856	A pro-slavery mob sacks Lawrence, Kansas; John Brown stages the Pottawatomie Massacre in retaliation
	Charles Sumner of Massachusetts is caned and seriously injured by a pro-slavery congressman in the U.S. Senate
1857	U.S. Supreme Court issues the *Dred Scott* decision
	Lecompton Constitution declares that slavery will be allowed in Kansas
1858	Abraham Lincoln debates Stephen A. Douglas during the 1858 Illinois Senate race
October 1859	John Brown and his followers stage raid at Harpers Ferry, Virginia, in an attempt to incite a massive slave insurrection
December 1860	South Carolina secedes from the Union
	Crittenden Compromise is proposed

KEY TERMS & NAMES

16

THE WAR OF THE UNION

FOCUS QUESTIONS wwnorton.com/studyspace

- What events led to the firing of the first shots of the Civil War?
- What were the major strategies of the Civil War?
- How did the war affect the home front in both the North and the South?
- What were the reasons for the Emancipation Proclamation?
- How did most enslaved people become free in the United States?

In mid-February 1861, Abraham Lincoln boarded a train in Springfield, Illinois, for a long, roundabout trip to Washington, D.C., for his presidential inauguration. Along the way, he told the New Jersey legislature that he was "devoted to peace" but warned that "it may be necessary to put the foot down." At the end of the weeklong journey, Lincoln reluctantly yielded to threats against his life. Accompanied by his bodyguards, he passed unnoticed on a night train through Baltimore and slipped into Washington, D.C. before daybreak on February 23, 1861.

THE END OF THE WAITING GAME

In early 1861, as the possibility of civil war captured the attention of a divided nation, no one imagined that a prolonged conflict of horrendous scope and intensity lay ahead. On both sides, people mistakenly assumed that if fighting erupted it would be over quickly and that their daily lives would go on as usual. The new president of the United States still sought peace.

LINCOLN'S INAUGURATION   In his March 4 inaugural address, the fifty-two-year-old Lincoln repeated his pledge not "to interfere with the institution of slavery in the states where it exists." But the immediate question facing the nation and the new president had shifted from slavery to secession. Most of the speech emphasized Lincoln's view that "the Union of these States is perpetual." No state, Lincoln insisted, "can lawfully get out of the Union." He pledged to defend federal forts in the South, collect taxes, and deliver the mail unless repelled, but beyond that "there will be no invasion, no using of force against or among the people anywhere." In the final paragraph of the speech, Lincoln appealed for regional harmony:

> I am loath to close. We are not enemies, but friends. We must not be enemies. Though passion may have strained, it must not break our bonds of affection. The mystic chords of memory, stretching from every battlefield and patriot grave to every living heart and hearthstone all over this broad land, will yet swell the chorus of the Union, when again touched, as surely they will be, by the better angels of our nature.

Southerners were not impressed with Lincoln's eloquence. The next day a North Carolina newspaper warned that Lincoln's inauguration made civil war "inevitable."

Lincoln not only entered the White House amid the gravest crisis yet faced by a president, but he also confronted unusual problems of transition. The new president displayed his remarkable magnanimity in making his cabinet appointments. Four of the seven cabinet members had been his rivals for the presidency: William H. Seward at the State Department, Salmon P. Chase at the Treasury Department, Simon Cameron at the War Department, and Edward Bates as attorney general. Four were former Democrats, and three were former Whigs. They formed a group of better-than-average ability, though most were so strong-minded they thought themselves better qualified to lead than Lincoln. Only later did they acknowledge with Seward that Lincoln "is the best man among us." Throughout the Civil War the leaders of the young Republican party remained a fragile coalition of former Whigs, Democrats, immigrants, conservatives, moderates, and radicals. One of Lincoln's greatest challenges was to hold such a diverse coalition together amid the pressures of a ghastly civil war.

THE FALL OF FORT SUMTER   On March 5, 1861, President Lincoln began his first day in office by reading a letter from South Carolina revealing that time was running out for the federal troops at **Fort Sumter** in

War begins

An interior view of the ruins of Fort Sumter.

Charleston Harbor. Major Robert Anderson, the commander, reported that they had enough supplies for only a month to six weeks, and Confederates were encircling the fort with a "ring of fire." On April 4, 1861, Lincoln faced his first major crisis as president. Most of his cabinet members and senior military officers urged him to withdraw the troops from Fort Sumter to preserve peace. Lincoln, however, believed that giving up Fort Sumter would mean giving up the Union. So he ordered that ships be sent to Charleston to resupply the sixty-nine federal soldiers at Fort Sumter. On April 9, President **Jefferson Davis** and his Confederate cabinet in Montgomery, Alabama, decided to oppose Lincoln's effort to resupply the fort. Only Robert Toombs, the Confederate secretary of state, opposed the decision. He told Davis that attacking Fort Sumter "will lose us every friend at the North. You will only strike a hornet's nest. . . . Legions now quiet will swarm out and sting us to death. It is unnecessary. It puts us in the wrong. It is fatal."

On April 11 the Confederate general Pierre G. T. Beauregard, a dapper Louisiana native who had studied the use of artillery under Robert Anderson at West Point repeated the demand that Fort Sumter surrender. Anderson, his former professor, refused. At four-thirty on the morning of April 12 the Confederate shelling of Fort Sumter began. After some thirty-four hours, his ammunition exhausted, the outgunned Anderson lowered the flag on April 13. The fall of Fort Sumter started the Civil War and ignited a wave of bravado across the Confederate states. A southern woman prayed that God would "give us strength to conquer them, to exterminate *them*, to lay waste every Northern city, town and village, to destroy them utterly."

The guns of Charleston signaled the end of the waiting game. The New York poet Walt Whitman wrote that the Confederate "firing on the flag" at Fort Sumter generated a "volcanic upheaval" in the North. On April 15, Lincoln called upon the loyal states to supply seventy-five thousand militiamen to subdue the rebellious states. Volunteers flocked to military recruiting stations on both sides. On April 19, Lincoln ordered a naval blockade of southern ports, which, as the Supreme Court later ruled, confirmed the existence of war. Federal ships closed the Mississippi River to commerce while naval squadrons cordoned off the southern ports along the Atlantic coast and Gulf of Mexico. The massive naval operation quickly choked off southern commercial activity. Shortages of basic commodities generated a dramatic inflation in the prices of foodstuffs in the Confederacy. By the spring of 1863, prices for food were rising 10 percent a month.

THE CAUSES OF WAR   Many southerners, then and since, argued that the Civil War was fought on behalf of states' rights rather than because of slavery. In this view, South Carolina and the other states had a constitutional right to secede from the Union to protect their sovereign rights, including the right to own slaves and to transport them into the western territories. To be sure, southerners had many grievances against the North. Southerners had long claimed that federal tariffs and taxes discriminated against their region. With the election of the Republican Lincoln, they were convinced that the federal government would continue to "oppress" them and abridge their "states' rights." One of those "rights" was the right to secede from the Union. Southern leaders argued that the 1787 federal constitution created a "compact" among the original thirteen states, all of which thereafter retained their sovereign rights, including the right to leave the Union.

To argue that the Civil War was primarily a defense of liberty and the right of self-government, however, ignores the actual reasons that southern leaders used in 1860–1861 to justify secession and war. In 1860, for example, William Preston, a prominent South Carolina leader, declared: "Cotton is not our king—slavery is our king. Slavery is our truth. Slavery is our divine right." The South Carolina Declaration on the Immediate Causes of Secession highlighted "an increasing hostility on the part of the non-slaveholding states to the institution of slavery." Yes, southerners asserted their constitutional right to secede from the Union, but it was the passionate desire to preserve slavery that led southern leaders to make such constitutional arguments. It is inconceivable that the South would have seceded from the Union in 1860-1861 had there been no institution of slavery. As Abraham Lincoln noted in his second inaugural address, everyone knew that slavery "was somehow the cause of the war."

TAKING SIDES   The fall of Fort Sumter prompted four more southern states to join the Confederacy. Virginia acted first. Its convention passed an Ordinance of Secession on April 17. The following month, the Confederate Congress in Montgomery voted to move the new nation's capital from Montgomery, Alabama to much larger Richmond, Virginia (Alabama, Mississippi, and South Carolina voted against the move). Three other states quickly followed Virginia in seceding: Arkansas on May 6, Tennessee on May 7, and North Carolina on May 20. All four of the holdout states, especially Tennessee and Virginia, had areas (mainly in the mountains) where slaves were scarce and Union support ran strong. In east Tennessee the mountain counties would supply more volunteers to the Union than to the Confederate cause. Unionists in western Virginia, bolstered by a Union army from Ohio under General George B. McClellan, organized a loyal government of

Why did South Carolina and six other states secede from the Union before the siege at Fort Sumter? Why did secession not win unanimous approval in Tennessee and Virginia? How did Lincoln keep Missouri and Kentucky in the Union?

Virginia that formed a new state. In 1863, Congress admitted West Virginia to the Union with a constitution that provided for gradual emancipation of the few slaves there.

Of the other "border" slave states, Delaware remained firmly in the Union, but Maryland, Kentucky, and Missouri went through bitter struggles to decide which side to support. All of these border states eventually stayed in the Union, but not without fierce debates and even civil wars within them.

CHOOSING SIDES   The Civil War affected everyone—men and women, white and black, immigrants and Native Americans, free and enslaved. Those already serving in the U.S. Army faced an agonizing choice: which side to support. On the eve of the Civil War, the U.S. Army was small, comprising only 16,400 men, about 1,000 of whom were officers. Of these, about 25 percent, like Robert E. Lee, resigned to join the Confederate army. On the other hand, many southerners made great sacrifices to remain loyal to the Union. Some left their native region once the fighting began; others remained in the South but found ways to support the Union. In every Confederate state except South Carolina, whole regiments were organized to fight for the Union. Some 100,000 men from the southern states fought against the Confederacy. One out of every five soldiers from Arkansas killed in the war fought on the Union side.

THE BALANCE OF FORCE

Shrouded in an ever-thickening mist of larger-than-life mythology, the Union triumph in the Civil War has acquired an aura of inevitability. The Confederacy's fight for independence, on the other hand, has taken on the aura of a romantic lost cause, doomed from the start by the region's sparse industrial development, smaller pool of able-bodied men, paucity of gold and warships, and spotty transportation network. But in 1861 the military situation did not seem so clear-cut by any means. For all of the South's obvious disadvantages, it initially enjoyed a huge captive labor force (slaves) and the benefits of fighting a defensive campaign on familiar territory. Jefferson Davis and other Confederate leaders were confident that their cause would prevail. The outcome of the Civil War was not inevitable: it was determined as much by human decisions and human willpower as by physical resources.

REGIONAL ADVANTAGES   The South seceded in part out of a growing awareness of its minority status in the nation; a balance sheet of the regions in 1861 shows the accuracy of that perception. The Union held twenty-three states, including four border slave states, while the Confederacy included eleven states. The population count was about 22 million in the Union to 9 million in the Confederacy, and about 4 million of the latter were enslaved African Americans. The Union therefore had an edge of about four to one in human resources. To help redress the imbalance, the Confederacy mobilized 80 percent of its military-age white men, a third of whom would die during the prolonged war.

An even greater advantage for the North was its industrial development. The southern states that formed the Confederacy produced just 7 percent of the nation's manufactured goods on the eve of the war. The Union states produced 97 percent of the firearms and 96 percent of the railroad equipment. The North's advantage in transportation weighed heavily as the war went on. The Union had more wagons, horses, and ships than the Confederacy and an impressive edge in the number of railroad locomotives.

As the Civil War began, the Confederacy enjoyed a major geographic advantage: it could fight a defensive war on its own territory. In addition, the South had more experienced military leaders. Some of those advantages were soon countered, however, by the Union navy's blockade of the major southern ports. On the inland waters Federal gunboats and transports played an even more direct role in securing the Union's control of the Mississippi River and its larger tributaries, which provided easy invasion routes into the center of the Confederacy.

The War's Early Course

After the fall of Fort Sumter, partisans on both sides hoped that the war might end with one sudden bold stroke, the capture of Washington or the fall of Richmond. Nowhere was this naive optimism more clearly displayed than at the **First Battle of Bull Run** (or Manassas).* General Beauregard hurried the main Confederate army to the railroad center at Manassas Junction, Virginia, about twenty-five miles southwest of Washington. Lincoln decided that General Irvin McDowell's hastily assembled Union army of some thirty-seven thousand might overrun the outnumbered Confederates and quickly march on to Richmond, the Confederate capital.

---

*The Federals most often named battles for natural features; the Confederates, for nearby towns—thus Bull Run (Manassas), Antietam (Sharpsburg), Stones River (Murfreesboro), and the like.

It was a hot, dry day on July 21, 1861, when McDowell's raw Union recruits encountered Beauregard's army dug in behind a meandering stream called Bull Run. The two generals, former classmates at West Point, adopted markedly similar battle plans: each would try to turn the other's left flank. The Federals almost achieved their purpose early in the afternoon, but Confederate reinforcements, led by General Joseph E. Johnston, poured in to check the Union offensive. Amid the fury a South Carolina officer rallied his men by pointing to Thomas Jackson's brigade: "Look! there is Jackson with his Virginians, standing like a stone wall!" The reference thereafter served as "Stonewall" Jackson's nickname.

After McDowell's last assault faltered, the Union army's frantic retreat turned into a panic as fleeing soldiers and terrified civilians clogged the road to Washington, D.C. But the Confederates were about as disorganized and exhausted by the battle as the Yankees were, and they failed to give chase. The Battle of Bull Run was a sobering experience for both sides, each of which had underrated the other's strength and tenacity. Much of the romance—the splendid uniforms, bright flags, rousing songs—gave way to the agonizing realization that this would be a long, costly struggle. *Harper's Weekly* bluntly warned: "From the fearful day at Bull Run dates war. Not polite war, not incredulous war, but war that breaks hearts and blights homes."

THE WAR'S EARLY PHASE   General Winfield Scott, the seasoned seventy-five-year-old commander of the Union armies, devised a three-pronged plan that called first for the Union Army of the Potomac to defend Washington, D.C., and exert constant pressure on the Confederate capital at Richmond. At the same time the Federal navy would blockade southern ports and cut off the Confederacy's access to foreign goods and weapons. The final component of the plan would divide the Confederacy by invading the South along the main water routes running from north to south: the Mississippi, Tennessee, and Cumberland Rivers. This so-called **"anaconda" strategy** would slowly entwine and crush the southern resistance, like an anaconda snake strangling its prey.

The Confederate strategy was simpler. Jefferson Davis was better prepared than Lincoln at the start of the war to guide military strategy. A graduate of the U.S. Military Academy at West Point, he had commanded a regiment during the Mexican War and had served as secretary of war in the Franklin Pierce administration from 1853 to 1857. If the Union forces could be stalemated, Davis and others hoped, then the cotton-hungry British or French might be persuaded to join their cause, or perhaps public sentiment in the North would force Lincoln to seek a negotiated settlement. So while armies were forming in the South, Confederate diplomats were seeking assistance in London and Paris, and Confederate sympathizers in the North were urging an end to the Union's war effort.

CONFEDERATE DIPLOMACY   Both the Union and the Confederacy sent agents to influence opinion in Britain and Europe. The first Confederate emissaries to England and France were pleased when the British foreign minister met with them after their arrival in London in 1861; they even won a promise from France to recognize the Confederacy if Britain would lead the way. But the British foreign minister refused to meet the Confederates again, partly in response to Union pressure and partly out of British self-interest.

One incident early in the war threatened to upset British neutrality. In November 1861 a Union warship near Cuba stopped a British steamship, the *Trent*, and took into custody two Confederate agents, James M. Mason and John Slidell, who were on their way to London and Paris to seek foreign assistance. Celebrated as a heroic deed by a northern public still starved for victories, the *Trent* affair roused a storm of protest in Britain. The British government condemned the violation of neutral rights and threatened war with the United States if Mason and Slidell were not released. Lincoln reluctantly decided to release the two agents. Mason and Slidell were more useful as martyrs to their own cause than they could ever have been as diplomats in London and Paris.

FORMING ARMIES   Once the fighting began, the Federal Congress recruited five hundred thousand more men and after the Battle of Bull Run added another five hundred thousand. The nineteenth-century U.S. army often organized its units along community and ethnic lines. The Union army, for example, included a Scandinavian regiment (the 15th Wisconsin Infantry), a Highland Scots unit (the 79th New York Infantry), a French regiment (the 55th New York Infantry), a Polish Legion (the 58th New York Infantry), and a mixed unit of Poles, Hungarians, Germans, Spaniards, and Italians (the 39th New York Infantry).

In the Confederacy, Jefferson Davis initially called up one hundred thousand twelve-month volunteers. Once the fighting started, he was authorized to enlist up to four hundred thousand three-year volunteers. Thus, by early 1862 most of the veteran Confederate soldiers were nearing the end of their enlistment without having encountered much significant action. They were also resisting bonuses and furloughs offered as incentives for reenlistment. The Confederate government thus turned to conscription. By an act passed

The U.S. Army recruiting office in City Hall Park, New York City

The sign advertises the money offered to those willing to serve: $677 to new recruits, $777 to veteran soldiers, and $15 to anyone who brought in a recruit.

on April 16, 1862, all white male citizens aged eighteen to thirty-five were declared members of the army for three years, and those already in service were required to serve out three years. In 1862 the upper age was raised to forty-five, and in 1864 the age range was further extended from seventeen to fifty.

The Confederate conscription law included two loopholes, however. First, a draftee might escape service either by providing an able-bodied substitute who was not of draft age or by paying $500 in cash. Second, exemptions, designed to protect key civilian work, were subject to abuse by men seeking "bombproof" jobs. The exemption from the draft of planters with twenty or more slaves led to bitter complaints about "a rich man's war and a poor man's fight." Equally galling to many Confederate soldiers was the behavior of wealthy officers who brought their enslaved servants with them to army camps.

The Union took nearly another year to force men into service. In 1863 the government began to draft men aged twenty to forty-five. Exemptions were granted to specified federal and state officeholders and to others on medical or compassionate grounds. For $300 one could avoid service. Widespread public opposition to the draft impeded its enforcement in both the North and the South.

New York Sprouts Violence

picked out, shot, and fell dead in the midst of his imprecations and threats. Some four or five hundred rioters were killed by the military. Victims of the mob numbered eight-

ATTENTION!

By Resolution of a large Meeting of the Merchants and Bankers of New York, held at two o'clock, at the Merchants' Exchange. Merchants are requested to close their Stores, and meet with their Employees on South side of Wall St., for immediate organization.

July 14, 2 P. M.

Call for merchants and clerks to defend their shops during the Draft Riots, 1863.

een, eleven of whom were colored men who were strung up to lamp posts and either shot or strangled to death. About fifty buildings were burned and destroyed, and the property

Draft riots

This broadside called upon store owners to defend their shops during the New York draft riots of 1863.

BLACKS IN THE SOUTH The outbreak of the Civil War disrupted everyday life, especially in the South. The white planter-merchant elite struggled to maintain the traditional social system that sustained the power of whites over blacks, free people over the enslaved, rich over poor, and men over women. Initially, most slaves bided their time. Before long, however, enslaved African Americans took advantage of the turmoil created by the war to run away, engage in sabotage, join the Union war effort, or pursue their own interests. A white owner of three plantations in war-ravaged Tennessee was disgusted by the war's effect on his slaves, as he confessed in his diary: "My Negroes all at home, but working only as they see fit, doing little." Some of them had reported that they had "rather serve the federals rather than work on the farm." Later, he revealed that with the arrival of Union armies in the vicinity, his slaves had "stampeded" to join the Union armies. "Many of my servants have run away and most of those left had [just] as well be gone, they being totally demoralized and ungovernable." Some enslaved blacks served as spies or guides for Union forces; others escaped to join the Union army or navy. Union generals whose armies took control of Confederate areas enlisted escaped slaves to serve as laborers in the camps. In Corinth, Mississippi, General Grenville Dodge armed a thousand escaped male slaves to form the 1st Alabama Infantry Regiment of African Descent. The rebellion of southern whites against the Union's efforts to constrain slavery had spawned a rebellion of slaves against their white masters.

THE WEST AND THE CIVIL WAR During the Civil War western settlement continued. New discoveries of gold and silver in eastern California and in Montana and Colorado lured thousands of prospectors and their suppliers. New transportation and communication networks emerged to serve the growing population in the West. Telegraph lines sprouted above the plains, and stagecoach lines fanned out to serve the new communities. Dakota, Colorado, and Nevada gained territorial status in 1861, Idaho and Arizona in 1863, and Montana in 1864. Silver-rich Nevada gained statehood in 1864.

The most intense fighting in the West occurred along the Kansas-Missouri border. There the disputes between the pro-slavery and anti-slavery settlers of the 1850s turned into brutal guerrilla warfare. The most prominent pro-Confederate leader in the area was William Quantrill. He and his pro-slavery followers, mostly teenagers, fought under a black flag, meaning that they would kill anyone who surrendered. In destroying Lawrence, Kansas, in 1863, Quantrill ordered his forces to "kill every male and burn every house." By the end of the day, 182 boys and men had been killed. Their opponents, the Jayhawkers, responded in kind. They tortured and hanged pro-Confederate prisoners, burned houses, and destroyed livestock.

Many Indian tribes found themselves caught up in the Civil War. Indian regiments fought on both sides, and in Oklahoma they fought against each other. Indians among the "Five Civilized Tribes" held African American slaves and felt a natural bond with southern whites. Oklahoma's proximity to Texas influenced the Choctaws and Chickasaws to support the Confederacy. The Cherokees, Creeks, and Seminoles were more divided in their loyalties. For those tribes the Civil War served as a wedge that fractured their unity. The Cherokees, for example, split in two, some supporting the Union and others supporting the South.

FIGHTING IN THE WESTERN THEATER   Little happened of military significance in the eastern theater (east of the Appalachians) before May 1862. On the other hand, the western theater (from the Appalachians to the Mississippi River) flared up with several encounters and an important penetration of the Confederate states. In western Kentucky, the Confederate general Albert Sidney Johnston had perhaps forty thousand men stretched over some 150 miles. Early in 1862, General Ulysses S. Grant made the first Union thrust against the weak center of Johnston's overextended lines. Moving on boats out of Cairo, Illinois, and Paducah, Kentucky, the Union army swung southward up the Tennessee River and captured Fort Henry in northern Tennessee on February 6. Grant then moved quickly overland to attack nearby Fort Donelson, where on February 16 a force of twelve thousand Confederates surrendered. It was the first major Union victory of the war, and it touched off wild celebrations throughout the North. President Lincoln's elation was tempered by the death of his eleven-year-old son Willie, who succumbed to typhoid fever. The tragedy in the White House "overwhelmed" the president. It "showed me my weakness as I had never felt it before," a grieving Lincoln confessed to a friend.

SHILOH   After suffering defeats in Kentucky and Tennessee, the Confederate forces in the western theater regrouped at Corinth, in northern Mississippi, near the Tennessee border. Ulysses Grant, meanwhile, moved his Union army southward along the Tennessee River during the early spring of 1862. Grant then made a costly mistake. While planning his attack on Corinth, he exposed his forty-two thousand troops on a rolling plateau

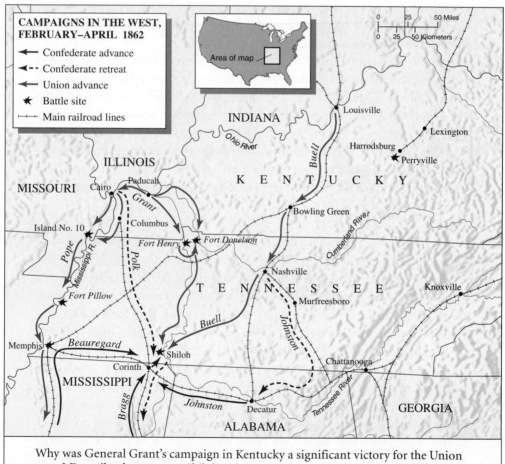

Why was General Grant's campaign in Kentucky a significant victory for the Union army? Describe the events at Shiloh. What were the costs to the Union as a result of the Battle of Shiloh?

between two creeks flowing into the Tennessee River and failed to dig defensive trenches. General Albert Sidney Johnston shrewdly recognized Grant's oversight, and on the morning of April 6 the Kentuckian ordered an attack on the vulnerable Federals, urging his men to be "worthy of your race and lineage; worthy of the women of the South."

The forty-four thousand Confederates struck suddenly at Shiloh, the site of a log church in the center of the Union camp in southwestern Tennessee. They found most of Grant's troops still sleeping or eating breakfast; many died in their bedrolls. After a day of carnage and confusion, the Union soldiers were pinned against the river. The Union army might well have been defeated had General Johnston not been mortally wounded at the peak of the battle; his second in command called off the attack. Bolstered by reinforcements, Grant took the offensive the next day, and the Confederates glumly withdrew to Corinth, leaving the Union army too battered to pursue. Casualties on both sides totaled over twenty thousand.

Shiloh, a Hebrew word meaning "Place of Peace," was the costliest battle in which Americans had ever engaged, although worse was yet to come. Like so many battles thereafter, Shiloh was a story of missed opportunities and debated turning points punctuated by lucky incidents and accidents. Throughout the Civil War, winning armies would fail to pursue their retreating foes, thus allowing the wounded opponent to slip away and fight again.

After the battle at Shiloh, General Henry Halleck, already jealous of Grant's success, spread the false rumor that Grant had been drinking during the battle. Some called upon Lincoln to fire Grant, but the president refused: "I can't spare this man; he fights." Halleck, however, took Grant's place as field commander, and as a result the Union thrust southward ground to a halt. For the remainder of 1862, the chief action in the western theater was a series of inconclusive maneuvers.

MCCLELLAN'S PENINSULAR CAMPAIGN The eastern theater remained fairly quiet for nine months after the Battle of Bull Run. In the wake of the Union defeat, Lincoln had replaced McDowell with General **George B. McClellan**, Stonewall Jackson's classmate at West Point. As head of the Army of the Potomac, the thirty-four-year-old McClellan, handsome and imperious, set about building a powerful, well-trained army that would be ready for its next battle. Yet for all of McClellan's organizational ability, his innate caution would prove crippling. Months passed while McClellan remained in a state of perpetual preparation, building and training his massive army to meet the superior numbers he claimed the Confederates were deploying. Worried that the Union was running out of money, Lincoln finally lost his vaunted patience and ordered McClellan to attack. "[You] must strike a blow," he told his reluctant commander.

In mid-March 1862, McClellan finally moved his army down the Potomac River and the Chesapeake Bay to the Virginia peninsula southeast of Richmond. This bold move put the Union forces within sixty miles of the Confederate capital. Thousands of Richmond residents fled the city in panic, but McClellan waited to strike, failing to capitalize on his advantages. As Lincoln told McClellan, the war could be won only by *engaging* the rebel army, not by endless maneuvers and efforts to occupy Confederate territory. "Once more,"

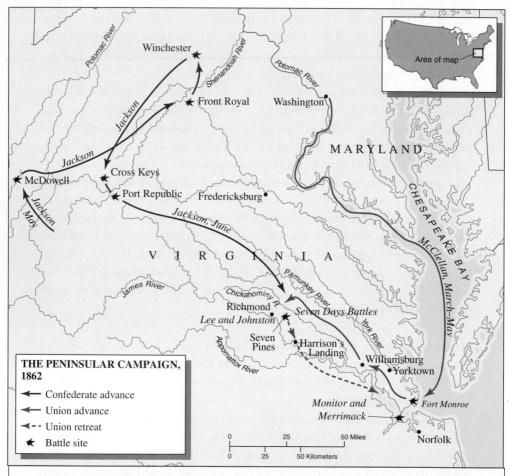

THE PENINSULAR CAMPAIGN, 1862

- Confederate advance
- Union advance
- Union retreat
- ✳ Battle site

What was General McClellan's strategy for attacking Richmond? How did General Jackson divert the attention of the Union army? Why did President Lincoln demote McClellan after the Peninsular campaign?

Lincoln told his commanding general, "let me tell you, it is indispensable to *you* that you strike a blow."

On May 31 the Confederate general Joseph E. Johnston struck at McClellan's forces along the Chickahominy River. In the Battle of Seven Pines (Fair Oaks), only the arrival of Federal reinforcements, who somehow crossed the swollen river, prevented a disastrous Union defeat. Both sides took heavy casualties, and General Johnston was severely wounded.

At this point, **Robert E. Lee** assumed command of the Army of Northern Virginia, a development that changed the course of the war. Dignified yet fiery, Lee was an audacious commander. He led by example, and his men loved him. Unlike Joseph E. Johnston, Lee enjoyed Jefferson Davis's trust. More important, he knew how to use the talents of his superb field commanders such as **Thomas "Stonewall" Jackson**, the pious, fearless mathematics professor from the Virginia Military Institute.

On July 9, when Lincoln visited McClellan's headquarters, the general complained that the administration had failed to support him and instructed the president at length on military strategy. Such insubordination was ample reason to remove McClellan. After returning to Washington, Lincoln called Henry Halleck from the West to take charge as general in chief. Miffed at his demotion, McClellan angrily dismissed Halleck as an officer "whom I know to be my inferior."

SECOND BULL RUN Lincoln and Halleck ordered McClellan to leave the Virginia peninsula and join the Washington defense force, now under the command of the bombastic John Pope, who had been called back from the West for a new overland assault on Richmond. In a letter to his wife, McClellan predicted—accurately—that "Pope will be thrashed and disposed of" by Lee. As McClellan's Army of the Potomac began to pull out, Lee moved northward to strike Pope's army before McClellan's troops arrived. Dividing his forces, Lee sent Jackson's "foot cavalry" around Pope's right flank to attack his supply lines in the rear. At the Second Battle of Bull Run (or Manassas), fought on almost the same site as the earlier battle, Pope assumed that he faced only Jackson, but Lee's main army by that time had joined in. On August 30, a crushing Confederate attack on Pope's flank drove the Federals from the field.

SLAVES IN THE WAR The Confederate victories in 1862 devastated Northern morale and convinced Lincoln that bolder steps would be required to win the war over an enemy fighting for and aided by enslaved labor. Now the North had to assault slavery itself. Once fighting began in 1861, the Union's need to hold the border slave states dictated caution on the volatile issue of emancipation. Beyond that, several other considerations deterred action. For one, Lincoln had to contend with a deep-seated racial prejudice in the North. While most abolitionists promoted both complete emancipation and the social integration of the races, many anti-slavery activists wanted slavery prohibited only in the new western territories and states. They were willing to allow slavery to continue in the South and were

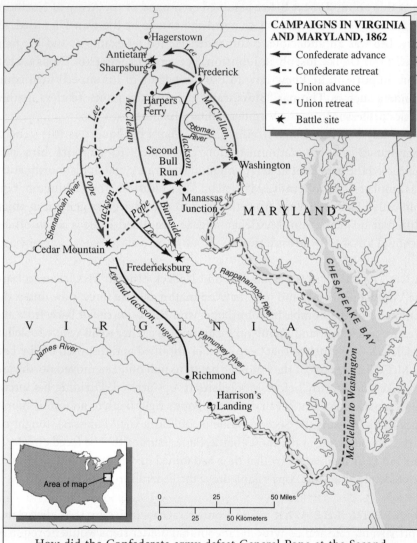

CAMPAIGNS IN VIRGINIA AND MARYLAND, 1862

◄— Confederate advance

◄-- Confederate retreat

◄— Union advance

◄-- Union retreat

★ Battle site

How did the Confederate army defeat General Pope at the Second Battle of Bull Run? Why was General Burnside's decision to attack at Fredericksburg a mistake?

opposed to racial integration. Though committed to the view that the rebellious states remained legally in the Union, Lincoln himself harbored doubts about his constitutional authority to emancipate slaves. The only way around the problem would be to justify emancipation as a military necessity.

The expanding war forced the issue. As Federal forces pushed into the Confederacy, fugitive slaves began to turn up in Union army camps, and the army commanders did not know whether to declare them free. One Union general designated the fugitive slaves "contraband of war," and thereafter the slaves who sought protection and freedom with Union forces were known as "contrabands." Some Union officers put the contrabands to work digging trenches and building fortifications; others set them free. Lincoln, meanwhile, began to edge toward emancipation. On April 16, 1862, he signed an act that abolished slavery in the District of Columbia; on June 19 another act excluded slavery from the western territories, without offering owners compensation. A Second Confiscation Act, passed on July 17, liberated slaves held by anyone aiding the rebellion. Still another act forbade the army to help return runaways to their border-state owners.

In 1862, Lincoln decided that emancipation of slaves in the Confederate states was necessary to win the war. Millions of enslaved laborers were being used to bolster the Rebel war effort. Moreover, sagging morale in the North needed the boost of a moral cause, and public opinion was swinging toward emancipation as the war dragged on. Proclaiming a war on slavery, moreover, would end forever any chance that France or Britain would support the Confederacy. In July 1862, Lincoln confided to his cabinet that he had decided to issue a proclamation freeing the slaves in Confederate-controlled areas. "Decisive and extreme measures must be adopted," he explained. Emancipation was "a military necessity, absolutely necessary to the preservation of the Union. We must free the slaves or be ourselves subdued." Secretary of State William H. Seward concurred, but he advised Lincoln to delay the announcement until after a Union victory on the battlefield in order to avoid any semblance of desperation.

ANTIETAM   Robert E. Lee made a momentous decision in the summer of 1862: he would invade the North and perhaps thereby gain foreign recognition and military supplies for the Confederacy. In September 1862, he and his battle-tested troops pushed north into western Maryland headed for Pennsylvania. The Rebel army encountered Union forces at Antietam Creek near Sharpsburg, Maryland. On September 17, 1862, the Union and Confederate armies commenced the furious Battle of Antietam (Sharpsburg). Outnumbered more than two to one, the Confederates forced a standoff in the most costly day of the Civil War. The next day the battered Confederates slipped south across the Potomac River to the safety of Virginia. General Lee's northern invasion had failed. McClellan called the Battle of Antietam "the most terrible battle of the age." It was the bloodiest single day in American history. Some 6,400 soldiers on both sides were killed, and another 17,000 were wounded. A Union officer counted "hundreds of dead bodies lying in rows and in piles." The scene was "sickening, harrowing, horrible. O what a terrible sight!"

President Lincoln was pleased that Lee's army had been forced to retreat, but he was disgusted by General McClellan's failure to gain a truly decisive victory by staying engaged with the retreating Confederates. The president sent a curt message to the general: "I have just read your dispatch about sore-tongued and fatigued horses. Will you pardon me for asking what the horses of your army have done . . . that fatigues anything?" Failing to receive a satisfactory answer, Lincoln relieved McClellan of his command of the Army of the Potomac and assigned him to recruiting duty in New Jersey. Never again would he command troops.

FREDERICKSBURG   The Battle of Antietam was significant on many levels. It revived sagging northern morale, emboldened Abraham Lincoln to issue the **Emancipation Proclamation**, which freed all slaves in the Confederate states, and dashed the Confederacy's hopes of foreign recognition. Yet the war was far from over. In his search for a fighting general, Lincoln now made the worst choice of all. He turned to Ambrose E. Burnside, who had twice before turned down the job on the grounds that he felt unfit for so large a command. But if the White House wanted him to fight, he would attack, even in the face of the oncoming winter. Burnside was an eager fighter and a poor strategist. He was said to possess "ten times as much heart as he has head."

On December 13, 1862, Burnside foolishly sent the 122,000 men in the Army of the Potomac west across the icy Rappahannock River to assault Lee's forces, who were well entrenched on ridges and behind stone walls west of Fredericksburg, Virginia, between Richmond and Washington, D.C. Confederate artillery and muskets chewed up the advancing blue columns as they crossed a mile of open land outside the town. It was, a Federal general sighed, "a great slaughter-pen." The scene was both awful and awesome, prompting Lee to remark, "It is well that war is so terrible—we should grow too fond of it." After taking more than twelve thousand casualties, compared with fewer than six thousand for the Confederates, General Burnside wept as he gave the order to withdraw.

The year 1862 ended with forces in the East deadlocked and the Union advance in the West stalled since midyear. Union morale plummeted: northern Democrats were calling for a negotiated peace. Republicans—even Lincoln's own cabinet members—grew increasingly fierce in their criticism of the president. Lincoln referred to the mounting dissension as being a "fire in the rear." General Burnside, too, was under fire, with some of his own officers ready to testify publicly to his shortcomings.

But amid the dissension the deeper currents of the war were turning in favor of the Union: in the lengthening war, the North's superior resources turned the tide. In both the eastern and the western theaters the Confederate counterattack had been repulsed. And while the armies clashed, Lincoln, by the stroke of a pen, changed the conflict from a war to restore the Union to a struggle to end slavery. On January 1, 1863, he signed the Emancipation Proclamation.

EMANCIPATION

On September 22, 1862, five days after Lee's Confederate army had been forced to retreat from Maryland, Lincoln issued a proclamation in which he repeated that his goal was mainly to restore the Union and that he favored proposals for paying slaveholders for their losses. He promised that if the southern states abandoned secession and returned to the Union they could retain their slaves (none accepted the offer). But the essential message of the document was his warning that on January 1, 1863, all slaves in the Rebel states would be "forever free." On January 1, 1863, Lincoln urged blacks to abstain from violence except in self-defense, and he added that free blacks would now be received into the armed services of the United States. As he wrote his name on the Emancipation Proclamation, Lincoln said, "I never, in my life, felt more certain that I was doing the right thing than I do in signing this paper."

REACTIONS TO EMANCIPATION Among the Confederate states, Tennessee and the Union-controlled parts of Virginia and Louisiana were exempted from the Emancipation Proclamation. Thus no slaves who were within Union lines at the time were freed. But many enslaved African Americans living in those areas claimed their freedom anyway. The African American abolitionist leader Frederick Douglass was overjoyed at Lincoln's "righteous decree." By contrast, Democratic newspapers in the North savagely attacked the proclamation, calling it dictatorial, unconstitutional, and catastrophic.

Two views of the Emancipation Proclamation

The Union view (top) shows a thoughtful Lincoln composing the proclamation, the Constitution and the Holy Bible in his lap. The Confederate view (bottom) shows a demented Lincoln, his foot on the Constitution and his inkwell held by the devil.

BLACKS IN THE MILITARY   Lincoln's Emancipation Proclamation sparked new efforts to organize all-black Union military units. Frederick Douglass stressed that military service was the best route for African Americans to gain the rights of citizenship. Once a black man enlisted in the Union army, he predicted, "there is no power on earth . . . which can deny that he has earned the right to citizenship in the United States." More than 180,000 blacks responded to the government's efforts to recruit African Americans into the United States Colored Troops. Some 80 percent of the "colored troops" were former slaves or free blacks from the South. Some 38,000 gave their lives. In the navy, African Americans accounted for about a fourth of all enlistments; of these, more than 2,800 died. Their courage under fire was quite evident; once in battle, they fought tenaciously. A white Union army private reported in the late spring of 1863 that the black troops "fight like the Devil."

To be sure, racism influenced the status of African Americans in the Union military. Blacks were not allowed to be commissioned officers. They were also paid less than whites (seven dollars per month for black privates versus sixteen dollars for white privates), and black recruits were ineligible for the enlistment bounty paid to white recruits. Still, as Frederick Douglass declared, "this is no time for hesitation. . . . this is our chance, and woe betide us if we fail to embrace it." Service in the Union army provided former slaves with a unique educational opportunity to grow in confidence, awareness, and maturity. As soldiers they were able to mingle former slaves and free blacks from North and South. Many of them also learned to read and write while in the army camps. A northern social worker in the South Carolina Sea Islands was "astonished" at the positive effects of "soldiering" on ex-slaves. "Some who left here a month ago to join [the army were] cringing, dumpish, slow," but now they "are ready to look you in the eye— are wide awake and active."

By mid-1863, African American units were involved in significant action. Commenting on Union victories at Port Hudson and Milliken's Bend, Louisiana, Lincoln reported that "some of our commanders . . . believe that . . . the use of colored troops constitutes the heaviest blow yet dealt to the rebels." As the war entered its final months, freedom for enslaved blacks emerged more fully as a legal reality. Three major steps occurred in January 1865, when both Missouri and Tennessee abolished slavery by state action and the U.S. House of Representatives passed an abolition amendment. Upon ratification by three fourths of the reunited states, the **Thirteenth Amendment** became part of the Constitution on December 18, 1865, and removed any lingering doubts about the legality of emancipation. By then, in fact, slavery remained only in the border states of Kentucky and Delaware.

THE WAR BEHIND THE LINES

The scale and scope of the Civil War affected everyone—not simply the combatants. Feeding, clothing, and supplying the vast armies required tremendous sacrifices on the home fronts. The fighting knew no boundaries, as farms and villages were transformed into battlefields and churches became makeshift hospitals.

WOMEN AND THE WAR   While breaking the bonds of slavery, the Civil War also loosened traditional restraints on female activity. "No conflict in history," a journalist wrote at the time, "was such a woman's war as the Civil War." Women on both sides played prominent roles in the conflict. They worked in factories, sewed uniforms, composed patriotic poems and songs, and raised money and supplies. In Greenville, South Carolina, when T. G. Gower went off to fight in the Confederate army, his wife Elizabeth took over the family business, converting their carriage factory to produce military wagons, caissons for carrying artillery shells, and ambulances. Thousands of northern women worked with the U.S. Sanitary Commission, a civilian agency that collected enormous sums of donations to provide organized medical relief and other services for soldiers. Other women, black and white, supported the freedmen's aid movement to help impoverished freed slaves.

In the North alone, some twenty thousand women served as nurses or other health-related volunteers. The most famous nurses were Dorothea Lynde Dix and Clara Barton, both untiring volunteers in service to the wounded and the dying. Dix, the earnest reformer of the nation's insane asylums, became the Union army's first superintendent of women nurses. She soon found herself flooded with applications from around the country. Dix explained that nurses should be "sober, earnest, self-sacrificing, and self-sustained" women between the ages of thirty-five and fifty who could "bear the presence of suffering and exercise entire self control" and who could be "calm, gentle, quiet, active, and steadfast in duty."

In many southern towns and counties the home front became a world of white women and children and African American slaves. A resident of Lexington, Virginia, reported in 1862 that there were "no men left" in town by mid-1862. Women suddenly found themselves farmers or plantation managers, clerks, munitions-plant workers, and schoolteachers. Hundreds of women disguised themselves as men and fought in the war; dozens served as spies; others traveled with the armies, cooking meals, writing letters, and assisting with amputations.

RELIGION AND THE CIVIL WAR Wars intensify religious convictions (and vice versa), and this was certainly true of the Civil War. Religious concerns pervaded the conflict. Both sides believed they were fighting a holy war with God's divine favor. The Confederate constitution, unlike the U.S. Constitution, explicitly invoked the guidance of Almighty God. Southern leaders thus asserted that the Confederacy was the only truly Christian nation. Clergymen in the North and the South—Protestant,

Nursing and the war

Clara Barton oversaw the distribution of medicines to Union troops. She later helped found the American Red Cross of which she remained president until the age of eighty-three.

Catholic, and Jewish—saw the war as a righteous crusade. They were among the most partisan advocates of the war, in part because they were so certain that God was on their side and would ensure victory. During the war both President Lincoln and President Davis proclaimed numerous official days of fasting and prayer in the aftermath of important battles. Such national rituals were a means of mourning the "martyrs" who had given their lives for the righteous cause. Salmon P. Chase, the U.S. secretary of the Treasury, added the motto "In God We Trust" to American coins as a means of expressing the nation's religious zeal. Many soldiers were armed with piety as well as muskets.

Every regiment on both sides had an ordained chaplain, and devotional services in military camps were regularly held and widely attended. More than 1,300 clergymen served in the military camps, with the Methodists providing the largest number. By late 1862, Christian religious revivals were sweeping through both northern and southern armies. To facilitate such battlefield conversions, religious organizations distributed millions of Bibles and religious tracts to soldiers and sailors. During the winter of 1863–1864, the widespread conversions among the Union army camped in northern Virginia led one reporter to claim that the soldiers' martial piety might "win the whole nation to Christ." The revivals in the Confederate camps were even larger. Mary Jones, the wife of a Confederate minister in Georgia whose son was a soldier, reported the good news that "revivals in our army are certainly the highest proofs we can possible desire or receive of the divine favor" shrouding the Confederacy. Abraham Lincoln took keen interest in the religious fervor among Confederate soldiers. He expressed concern that "rebel soldiers are praying with a great deal more earnestness" than Union soldiers.

With so many ministers away at the front, lay people, especially women, assumed even greater responsibility for religious activities in churches and synagogues. The war also transformed the religious life of African Americans, who saw the war as a recapitulation of the biblical Exodus: God's miraculous intervention in history on behalf of a chosen people. In those areas of the South taken over by Union armies, freed slaves were able to create their own churches for the first time.

In the end the war revealed how important religion was in American life. It also showed how problematic it is to claim that God is on any particular side. Yes, he observed, both sides claimed providential sanction. In this regard, he said, "Both *may* be, and one *must* be wrong. God can not be *for* and *against* the same thing at the same time." After all, Lincoln noted, God could give victory to either side at any moment. "Yet the contest proceeds." Thus Lincoln was one of the few Americans to suggest that God's divine purpose might be something other than simple victory or defeat.

GOVERNMENT DURING THE WAR

Freeing 4 million slaves and loosening the restraints on female activity constituted a momentous social and economic revolution. But an even broader revolution began as power in Congress shifted from South to North during the Civil War. Before the war, southern congressmen exercised disproportionate influence, but once the secessionists had abandoned Congress to the Republicans, a dramatic change occurred. Several projects that had been stalled by sectional controversy were adopted before the end of 1862. Congress passed a higher tariff bill to deter imports and thereby "protect" American manufacturers. A transcontinental railroad was approved, to run through Omaha, Nebraska, to Sacramento, California. A Homestead Act granted 160 acres to settlers who agreed to work the land for five years. The National Banking Act followed in 1863. Two other key pieces of legislation were the Morrill Land Grant Act (1862), which provided federal aid to state colleges teaching "agriculture and mechanic arts," and the Contract Labor Act (1864), which encouraged the importation of immigrant labor. All of these had long-term significance for the expansion of the national economy—and the federal government.

UNION FINANCES   In December 1860, as southern states announced their plan to secede from the Union, the federal treasury was virtually empty. There was not enough cash on hand to pay the salaries of Congress, much let fund a massive war. To meet the war's escalating expenses, Congress focused on three options: raising taxes, printing paper money, and borrowing. The taxes came chiefly in the form of the Morrill Tariff on imports and taxes on manufactures and nearly every profession. A butcher, for example, had to pay thirty cents for every head of beef he slaughtered, ten cents for every hog, and five cents for every sheep. In 1862, Congress passed the Internal Revenue Act, which created an Internal Revenue Service to implement a new income tax.

But federal tax revenues trickled in so slowly—in the end they would meet only 21 percent of wartime expenditures—that Congress in 1862 resorted to printing paper money. Beginning with the Legal Tender Act of 1862, Congress ultimately authorized $450 million in paper currency, which soon became known as greenbacks because of the color of the ink used to print the bills. The congressional decision to allow the Treasury to print paper money was a profoundly important development for the U.S. economy, then and since. Unlike previous paper currencies issued by local banks, the federal greenbacks could not be exchanged for gold or silver. Instead, their value relied upon public trust in the government. Many bankers were outraged by the advent of the greenbacks, but the desperate need to finance the expanding war demanded such a solution. As the months passed, the greenbacks helped ease the Union's financial crisis without causing the ruinous inflation that the unlimited issue of paper money caused in the Confederacy.

The federal government also relied upon the sale of bonds to help finance the war effort. A Philadelphia banker named Jay Cooke (sometimes tagged the Financier of the Civil War) mobilized a nationwide campaign to sell $2 billion in government bonds to private investors.

State currency

Banknotes were promissory notes. Generally, the better the art on the note, the more it was trusted.

CONFEDERATE FINANCES Confederate finances were a disaster from the start. The new Confederate government had to create a treasury and a revenue-collecting bureaucracy from scratch. Moreover, the South's agrarian economy was land-rich but cash-poor when compared to the North. While the Confederacy owned 30 percent of America's assets in 1861, it contained only 12 percent of the currency. In the first year of its existence, the Confederacy enacted a tax of one half of 1 percent on most forms of property, which should have yielded a hefty income, but the Confederacy farmed out its collection of the taxes to the states. The result was chaos. In 1863 the desperate Confederate Congress began taxing nearly everything, but enforcement of the taxes was poor and evasion easy. Altogether, taxes covered no more than 5 percent of Confederate costs; bond issues accounted for less than 33 percent; and treasury notes (paper money), for more than 66 percent. Over the course of the Civil War, the Confederacy issued more than $1 billion in paper money which exacerbated the inflationary effect on consumer prices caused by the Union naval blockade. By 1864 a turkey sold in the Richmond market for $100, flour brought $425 a barrel, and bacon was $10 a pound. Such rampant inflation caused great distress. Poverty drove some southerners to take desperate measures. Dissent over the price of war increasingly erupted into mass demonstrations, rioting, looting, burning of houses, and desertions from the military.

UNION POLITICS AND CIVIL LIBERTIES On the home front, the crisis of war brought no moratorium on partisan politics, northern or southern. Within his own party, Lincoln faced a radical wing in Congress composed mainly of militant abolitionists. Led by House members such as Thaddeus Stevens and George Washington Julian and senators such as Charles Sumner, Benjamin Franklin Wade, and Zachariah Chandler, the **Radical Republicans** pushed for confiscation of southern plantations, immediate emancipation of slaves, and a more vigorous prosecution of the war. The majority of Republicans, however, continued to back Lincoln's more cautious approach. The party was generally united on economic policy.

The Democratic party suffered the loss of its southern wing and the death of its leader, Stephen A. Douglas, in June 1861. By and large, northern Democrats supported a war for the Union "as it was" before 1860, giving reluctant support to Lincoln's policies but opposing restraints on civil liberties and the new economic legislation. "War Democrats," such as Tennessee senator Andrew Johnson and Secretary of War Edwin M. Stanton, supported Lincoln's policies, while a peace wing of the party preferred an end to the fighting, even if that meant risking the Union. An extreme fringe of the peace wing even flirted with outright disloyalty. The Copperhead Democrats, as they were called, were strongest in states such as Ohio, Indiana, and Illinois. They sympathized with the Confederacy and called for an end to the war.

"Abraham's Dream!"

This cartoon depicts President Lincoln having a nightmare about the election of 1864. Lady Liberty brandishes the severed head of a black man at the door of the White House as General McClellan mounts the steps and Lincoln runs away.

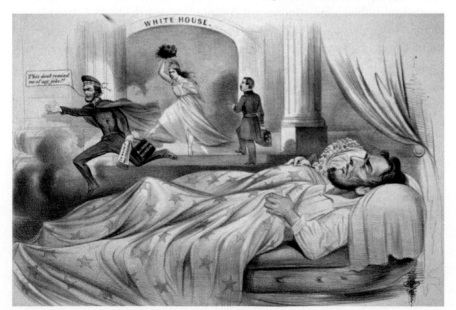

Such open sympathy for the enemy led Lincoln to crack down hard. Like all wartime leaders, he faced the challenge of balancing the needs of winning a war with the protection of civil liberties. Early in the war, Lincoln had assumed emergency powers, including the power to suspend the writ of habeas corpus, which guarantees arrested citizens a speedy hearing. The Constitution states that habeas corpus may be suspended only in cases of rebellion or invasion, but congressional leaders argued that Congress alone had the authority to take such action. By the Habeas Corpus Act of 1863, Congress authorized the president to suspend the writ.

At their 1864 national convention in Chicago, the Democrats called for an immediate end to the war, to be followed by a national convention that would restore the Union. They named General George B. McClellan as their candidate, but McClellan distanced himself from the peace platform by declaring that agreement on Union would have to precede peace.

Radical Republicans, who still regarded Lincoln as soft on treason, tried to thwart his nomination for a second term, but he outmaneuvered them at every turn. Lincoln promoted the vice-presidential nomination of Andrew Johnson, a "war Democrat" from Tennessee, on the "National Union" ticket, so named to promote bipartisanship. As the war dragged on through 1864, however, with General Grant's Union army taking heavy losses in Virginia, Lincoln expected to lose the 1864 election. Then Admiral David Farragut's capture of Mobile, Alabama, in August and General William Tecumseh Sherman's timely capture of Atlanta on September 2, 1864, turned the tide. As a Republican U.S. senator said, the Union conquest of Atlanta "created the most extraordinary change in public opinion here [in the North] that ever was known." The South's hope that northern discontent would lead to a negotiated peace vanished. McClellan carried only New Jersey, Delaware, and Kentucky, with 21 electoral votes to Lincoln's 212, and he won only 1.8 million popular votes (45 percent) to Lincoln's 2.2 million (55 percent).

CONFEDERATE POLITICS Unlike Lincoln, Jefferson Davis never had to face a presidential contest. He and his vice president, Alexander Stephens, were elected without opposition in 1861 for a six-year term. But discontent flourished as the war dragged on. The growing cost of the war aroused class tensions. More than ever before, poor white southerners expressed resentment of the planter elite. Food grew scarce, and prices skyrocketed. A bread riot in Richmond on April 2, 1863, ended only when Davis himself threatened to shoot the protesters (mostly women). After the Confederate congressional elections of 1863, about a third of the legislators were ardent critics of Davis.

Davis's greatest challenge came from the southern politicians who had embraced secession and then guarded states' rights against the authority of the central government of the Confederacy as zealously as they had against that of the Union. Georgia and, to a lesser degree, North Carolina were strongholds of such sentiments. The states' rights advocates challenged, among other things, the legality of the military draft, taxes on farm produce, and above all the suspension of habeas corpus. Vice President Stephens carried on a running battle against Davis's effort to establish "military despotism," and he eventually left Richmond to sulk at his Georgia home. Robert Toombs, the former Confederate secretary of state,

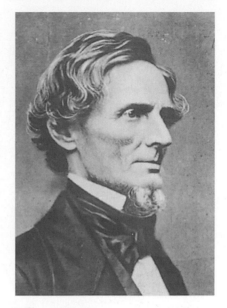

Jefferson Davis

President of the Confederacy.

also turned against "that scoundrel Jeff Davis." He accused Davis of pursuing "an illegal and unconstitutional course" of actions that "outraged justice" and brought a "tide of despotism" across the South.

Among other fatal flaws, the Confederacy suffered from an excess of dogma. Where Lincoln was the consummate pragmatist, Davis was a brittle ideologue with a waspish temper. Once he made a decision, nothing could change his mind. One southern politician said that Davis was "as stubborn as a mule." Davis could never admit a mistake. Such a personality was ill suited to the chief executive of an infant—and fractious—nation.

THE FALTERING CONFEDERACY

CHANCELLORSVILLE   After the Union disaster at Fredericksburg at the end of 1862, Lincoln's search for a capable general turned to General Joseph Hooker, whose pugnacity had earned him the nickname "Fighting Joe." With a force of 130,000 men, the largest Union army yet gathered, and a brilliant plan, Hooker failed his leadership test at Chancellorsville, Virginia, on May 1–5, 1863. Robert E. Lee, with perhaps half as many troops, staged what became a textbook example of daring and maneuver. On May 2, the Confederates

Thomas "Stonewall" Jackson

Jackson was mortally wounded by his own men.

surprised the Federals at the edge of a densely wooded area called the Wilderness, but the fighting died out in confusion as darkness fell. General Thomas "Stonewall" Jackson rode out beyond the skirmish line to locate the Union forces. Shooting erupted in the darkness, and nervous Confederates mistakenly opened fire on Jackson, who was struck by three bullets that shattered his left arm and right hand. The next day, a surgeon amputated his arm. The indispensable Jackson seemed to be recovering well but he then contracted pneumonia and died. Jackson had been a fearless general famous for leading rapid marches, bold flanking movements, and furious assaults. "I have lost my right arm," Lee lamented, and "I do not know how to replace him." The next day, Lee forced Hooker's Union army to retreat. It was the peak of Lee's career, but Chancellorsville was his last significant victory.

VICKSBURG   While Lee's army held the Federals at bay in the East, **Ulysses S. Grant**, his appointment as a field commander reinstated, had been inching his army down the Mississippi River toward the Confederate stronghold of Vicksburg, in western Mississippi. If Union forces could gain control of the Mississippi River, they could split the Confederacy in two. While the Union navy ran gunboats and transports past the Confederate cannons commanding the river at Vicksburg, Grant moved his army eastward on a campaign that Lincoln later called "one of the most brilliant in the world." Grant captured Jackson, Mississippi, before pinning the thirty thousand Confederates inside Vicksburg, a strategic city perched on bluffs two hundred feet above the Mississippi River and its commercial traffic. Grant decided to wear down the Confederates through constant bombardment and gradual starvation. The Rebel soldiers and the city's inhabitants were hopelessly trapped; they could neither escape nor be reinforced or supplied. As the weeks passed, the besieged Confederates ate their horses and mules, then dogs and cats, and, finally, rats.

GETTYSBURG   The plight of besieged Vicksburg put the Confederate high command in a quandary. General Joseph E. Johnston, now in charge of the western Confederate forces, wanted to lure Grant's army into Tennessee and thereby relieve the siege of Vicksburg. Lee had another idea for a diversion. Once more he sought to win a major battle on northern soil, this time in the hope of not just saving Vicksburg but also persuading northern public opinion to end the war. In June he again moved his army northward across Maryland.

Neither side chose **Gettysburg**, Pennsylvania, as the site for a major battle, but Confederate troops entered the town in search of shoes and encountered units of Union cavalry on June 30, 1863. The main forces quickly converged on that point. On July 1, the Confederates pushed the Federals out of the town, but into stronger positions on high ground to the south. The new Union commander, General George Meade, hastened reinforcements to his

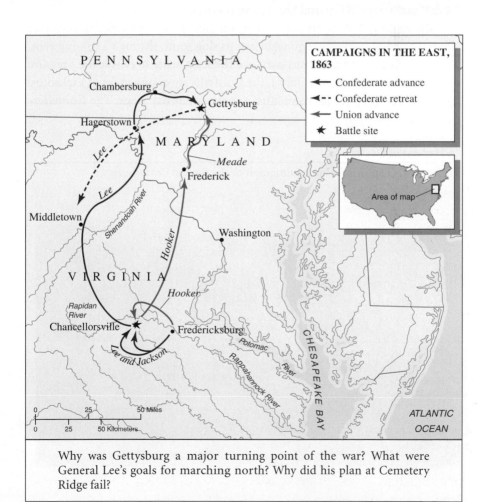

Why was Gettysburg a major turning point of the war? What were General Lee's goals for marching north? Why did his plan at Cemetery Ridge fail?

new lines along the heights. On July 2, Confederate units assaulted Meade's army, but in vain.

The next day, July 3, Lee staked everything on one final assault on the Union center at Cemetery Ridge. At about two in the afternoon, General George Pickett's thirteen thousand Confederate troops emerged from the woods into the brilliant sunlight, formed neat ranks, and began their suicidal advance uphill across open ground commanded by Union artillery. The few Confederates who got within range of hand-to-hand combat made a final desperate lunge at the center of the Union line, but they were quickly overwhelmed. What Robert E. Lee had called the "grand charge" was a grand failure. As he watched the few survivors returning from the bloody field, General Lee muttered, "All this has been my fault." He then ordered Pickett to regroup his division to repulse a possible counterattack, only to have Pickett tartly reply, "General Lee, I have no division now."

With nothing left to do but retreat, on July 4 Lee's mangled army, with about a third of its number gone, began to slog south through a driving rain. They had failed in all their purposes, not the least being to relieve the pressure on Vicksburg. On that same July 4, the Confederate commander at Vicksburg surrendered his entire garrison after a forty-seven-day siege. The Confeder-

"A Harvest of Death"

Timothy H. O'Sullivan's grim photograph of the dead at Gettysburg.

acy was now split in two. Had Meade pursued Lee, he might have ended the war, but yet again the winning army failed to capitalize on its victory.

After the fighting at Gettysburg had ended, a group of northern states funded a military cemetery for the six thousand soldiers killed in the battle. On November 19, 1863, the new cemetery was officially dedicated. In his brief remarks, since known as the Gettysburg Address, President Lincoln eloquently expressed the pain and sorrow of the brutal civil war. The prolonged conflict was testing whether a nation "dedicated to the proposition that all men are created equal . . . can long endure." Lincoln declared that all living Americans must ensure that the "honored dead" had not "died in vain." In stirring words that continue to inspire, Lincoln predicted that "this nation, under God, shall have a new birth of freedom—and that government of the people, by the people, and for the people, shall not perish from the earth."

CHATTANOOGA   The third great Union victory of 1863 occurred in fighting around Chattanooga, the railhead of eastern Tennessee and gateway to northern Georgia. In the late summer, a Union army led by General William Rosecrans took Chattanooga and then rashly pursued General Braxton Bragg's Rebel forces into Georgia, where they met at Chickamauga. The intense battle (September 19–20) had the makings of a Union disaster, since it was one of the few times in the war that the Confederates had a numerical advantage (about seventy thousand to fifty-six thousand). Only the stubborn stand of Union troops under George H. Thomas (thenceforth dubbed the "Rock of Chickamauga") prevented a rout. The battered Union forces fell back into Chattanooga while Bragg held the city virtually under siege from the heights to the south and the east. Rosecrans reported that "we have met a serious disaster. Enemy overwhelmed us, drove our right, pierced our center, and scattered troops there."

Rosecrans seemed stunned and apathetic, but Lincoln urged him to hang on: "If we can hold Chattanooga, and East Tennessee, I think rebellion must dwindle and die." The Union command rushed reinforcements to Tennessee from Virginia. General Grant, given overall command of the western theater of operations, replaced Rosecrans with Thomas. On November 24, the Federal troops took Lookout Mountain in what was mainly a feat of mountaineering aided by a dense fog that concealed their movements. The next day Union forces dislodged the Rebels atop Missionary Ridge. The Union victory at Missionary Ridge confirmed that Grant was a formidable commander. Lincoln had at last found his fighting general. In early 1864, Grant arrived in Washington to assume the role of general in chief.

The Confederacy's Defeat

The dramatic Union victories at Vicksburg, Gettysburg, and Chattanooga turned the tide against the Confederacy. Yet Jefferson Davis and other Confederate leaders still hoped for a "political victory" whereby simply prolonging the war might convince war-weary northerners to defeat Lincoln in the 1864 election and negotiate a peace settlement. Union leaders, sensing the momentum swinging their way, stepped up their pressure on Confederate forces. The Union command's main targets now were Robert E. Lee's army in Virginia and General Joseph E. Johnston's forces in Georgia. Grant personally would accompany George Meade, who retained direct command over the Army of the Potomac; operations in Georgia were entrusted to Grant's longtime lieutenant, William Tecumseh Sherman. As Sherman put it later, Grant "was to go for Lee, and I was to go for Joe Johnston."

Grant hoped to force Lee's army in Virginia into a climactic single battle, but Lee's evasive skills forced the Union commander to adopt a policy of aggressive attrition. Only "complete conquest" would bring an end to the long war. Grant's unyielding faith that the Union armies were destined for victory enabled him to impose his tenacious will upon his troops; his unflappable calmness in the face of adversity and danger inspired armies. With the benefit of far more soldiers and supplies than Lee, Grant relentlessly attacked, keeping the pressure on the Confederates, grinding down their numbers and their will to fight. Grant would now wage total war, confiscating or destroying civilian property of use to the military. It was a brutal and costly—but effective—plan.

Ulysses S. Grant

At his headquarters in City Point (now Hopewell), Virginia.

GRANT'S PURSUIT OF LEE

In May 1864, the Union's Army of the Potomac, numbering about 115,000 to Lee's 65,000, moved south across the Rappahannock and Rapidan Rivers into the wilderness of eastern Virginia. In the nightmarish Battle of the Wilderness (May 5–6), the armies fought blindly through the woods, the horror and suffering of the scene heightened by crackling brushfires. Grant's men suffered heavier casualties than the Confederates, but the Rebels were running out of replacements. Always before when bloodied by Lee's troops, Union forces had pulled back to nurse their wounds, but Grant slid off to his left and continued to push southward, engaging Lee's men near Spotsylvania Court House. "Whatever happens," he assured Lincoln, "we will not retreat."

Again Grant's forces slid off to the left of Lee's army and kept moving. Along the banks of the Chickahominy River, the two sides clashed again at Cold Harbor (June 1–3), ten miles east of Richmond. Grant ordered his troops to assault the heavily entrenched Confederate lines. As the Confederates had discovered at Gettysburg, such a frontal assault was murder. The Union army was massacred at Cold Harbor: in twenty minutes almost seven thousand attacking Federals were killed or wounded. Grant later admitted that the attack was his greatest mistake. Critics called him "the Butcher" after Cold Harbor. Yet the relentless Grant brilliantly maneuvered his battered forces around Lee and headed for Petersburg, south of Richmond, where the major railroads converged.

The two armies then dug in for a long siege along lines that extended for twenty-five miles above and below Petersburg. Grant telegraphed Lincoln that he intended "to fight it out on this line if it takes all summer." For nine months, the two armies faced each other down while Grant's troops tried to cut the railroad arteries that were Lee's lifeline. During that time, Grant's troops, twice as numerous as the Confederate army, were generously supplied by Union vessels moving up the James River, while Lee's forces, beset by hunger, cold, and desertion, wasted away. Petersburg had become Lee's prison while disasters piled up for the Confederacy elsewhere.

SHERMAN'S MARCH   When Grant's army headed south from northern Virginia, General William Tecumseh Sherman moved south from Tennessee toward the railroad hub of Atlanta, with ninety thousand Union men against sixty thousand Confederates. He sent a worrisome threat to Atlantans: "prepare for my coming." Three times in eight days, the Confederate army lashed out at the Union lines, each time meeting a bloody rebuff. Sherman at first resorted to a siege of Atlanta, then slid off to the right again, cutting the rail lines below the city. The Confederates evacuated Atlanta on September 1. Now in control of Atlanta, Sherman ordered its twenty thousand residents to leave. When city officials protested the order, Sherman replied: "War is cruelty; you cannot refine it." His men thereupon set fire to the city's infrastructure: railroads, iron foundries, shops, mills, schools, hotels, and businesses.

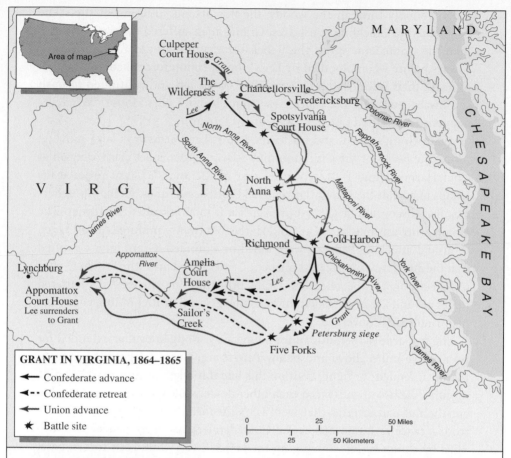

GRANT IN VIRGINIA, 1864–1865

◄— Confederate advance
◄- - Confederate retreat
◄— Union advance
★ Battle site

How were General Grant's tactics in the Battle of the Wilderness different from the Union's previous encounters with General Lee's army? Why did Grant have the advantage at Petersburg?

Sherman now laid plans for a rapid march south through central Georgia, where no organized Confederate armies remained. His intention was to "whip the rebels, to humble their pride, to follow them into their inmost recesses, and make them fear and dread us." The Confederate army, meanwhile, pushed northward into Tennessee. So unfolded the curious spectacle of the main armies' moving off in opposite directions. But it was a measure of the Confederates' plight that Sherman could cut a swath of destruction across Georgia (the "**March to the Sea**") with impunity, while the Confederate army marched into disaster in Tennessee.

In the Battle of Franklin (November 30), near Nashville, Confederate commander John B. Hood sent his army across two miles of open ground defended by entrenched Union troops backed by massed artillery. It was mass suicide. Six waves broke against the Union lines, leaving the ground strewn with Confederate dead. Six Confederate generals were killed at Franklin. A Confederate captain from Texas, scarred by the battle's senseless butchery, wrote that the "wails and cries of the widows and orphans made at Franklin, Tennessee will heat up the fires of the bottomless pit to burn the soul of General J. B. Hood for murdering their husbands and fathers." Finally, in the Battle of Nashville (December 15–16), the Federals scattered what was left of the Confederate Army of Tennessee.

William Tecumseh Sherman

Sherman's campaign developed into a war of maneuver, but without the pitched battles of Grant's campaign.

Meanwhile, Sherman's Union army was marching southward through Georgia. He abandoned the conventional practice of long supply lines supporting his advancing army and instead plundered his way across the state, waging war against the people's resources and their will to resist. In his effort to demoralize the civilian populace, Sherman sought to "make Georgia howl." One of his aides explained that modern warfare must "make the innocent suffer as well as the guilty; it must involve plundering, burning, killing." The Union army moved southeast from Atlanta, living off the land and destroying any provisions that might serve Confederate forces.

More than any other Civil War general, Sherman recognized the connections among the South's economy, its morale, and its ability to wage war. He explained that "we are not only fighting hostile armies, but a hostile people" who must be made to "feel the hard hand of war." He wanted the Rebels to "fear and dread us." When, after a month of ravaging the Georgia countryside, Sherman's army arrived in Savannah, on the coast, his troops had freed over forty thousand slaves and burned scores of plantations. After the war a Confederate officer acknowledged that Sherman's march through Georgia was in fact well conceived and well managed. "I don't think there was ever an army in the world that would have behaved better, in a similar expedition, in an enemy country. Our army certainly wouldn't."

After occupying Savannah, Sherman's army crossed the Savannah River into South Carolina, the "hell-hole of secession." There the Union soldiers

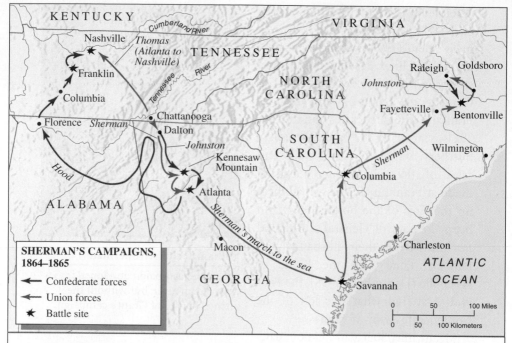

SHERMAN'S CAMPAIGNS, 1864–1865
← Confederate forces
← Union forces
✶ Battle site

What was General Sherman's goal as he marched across Georgia? How much damage did Sherman do in Georgia and South Carolina? How did it affect the Confederate war effort?

wrought even greater destruction. As Sherman reported, his "whole army is burning with an insatiable desire to wreak vengeance upon South Carolina. I almost tremble at her fate, but feel she deserves all that seems in store for her." More than a dozen towns were burned in whole or part, including the state capital of Columbia, which was captured on February 17, 1865 (recent scholarship suggests that the fires were started by fleeing Confederates, however). Meanwhile, Charleston's defenders abandoned the city and headed north to join a ragtag Rebel army that Joseph E. Johnston was desperately pulling together in North Carolina. Johnston mounted an attack on Sherman's army at Bentonville (March 19–20), but that would be his last major battle.

During the late winter and early spring of 1865, the Confederacy found itself besieged on all sides. Defeat was in the air. But Jefferson Davis dismissed any talk of surrender. If the Confederate armies should be defeated, he wanted the soldiers to disperse and fight a guerrilla war. "The war came and now it must go on," he stubbornly insisted, "till the last man of this generation falls in his tracks, and his children seize his musket and fight our battle."

While Confederate forces made their last stands, Abraham Lincoln prepared for his second term as president. He was the first president since

Andrew Jackson to have been reelected. The weary commander in chief had weathered constant criticism during his first term, but with the war nearing its end, Lincoln now garnered deserved praise. The *Chicago Tribune* observed that the president "has slowly and steadily risen in the respect, confidence, and admiration of the people."

APPOMATTOX During the spring of 1865, General Grant's army kept pushing, probing, and battering the Rebels defending Petersburg, Virginia, twenty miles south of Richmond. The badly outnumbered Confederates were slowly starving. On April 2, 1865, Lee's army, its supply lines having been cut, abandoned Richmond and Petersburg in a desperate flight south. President Jefferson Davis, exhausted but still defiant, too stubborn and vain to concede, fled by train ahead of the advancing Federals, only to be captured in Georgia by Union cavalry on May 10. He was imprisoned at Fortress Monroe, near Hampton Roads, Virginia.

By then the Confederacy was all but dead. On April 7, Grant sent a note to Lee urging him to surrender. With his army virtually surrounded, Lee

Lincoln's second inauguration

As Lincoln delivered his second inaugural address on the Capitol portico, John Wilkes Booth was likely among those standing on the porch, overhead.

Robert E. Lee

Mathew Brady took this photograph in Richmond eleven days after Lee's surrender at Appomattox.

recognized that "there is nothing left for me to do but go and see General Grant," he told a Confederate general, "and I would rather die a thousand deaths." On April 9 (Palm Sunday) the tall, stately Lee, in his dress uniform replete with a red silk sash, met the short, mud-spattered Grant in the parlor of Wilmer McLean's home at Appomattox Court House to tender his surrender. Grant displayed extraordinary generosity in keeping with Lincoln's desire for a gracious rather than vengeful peace. At Lee's request, he let the Confederates keep their pistols, horses, and mules. After signing the surrender documents, a distraught Lee mounted his horse.

The next day, as the gaunt, hungry Confederate troops formed ranks for the last time, Joshua Chamberlain, the Union general in charge of the surrender ceremony, ordered his troops to salute their foes as they paraded past. His Confederate counterpart signaled his men to do likewise. General Chamberlain remembered that there was not a sound—no trumpets or drums, no cheers or jeers, simply an "awed stillness . . . as if it were the passing of the dead."

The remaining Confederate forces scattered across the South surrendered during May. The brutal war was at last over. Upon learning of the surrender, John Wilkes Booth, a popular young actor in Washington, D.C., wrote in his diary that "something decisive and great must be done" to avenge the Confederate defeat.

A MODERN WAR

The Civil War was the most traumatic event in American history. It shattered lives and destroyed property while preserving the Union, reshaping institutions, expanding the power and scope of the federal government, and giving freedom to four million slaves. In many respects it was the world's first modern war. Its scope and scale were unprecedented, fought on battlefields across the continent, from Pennsylvania to New Mexico and from Florida to Kansas. Troops were moved by ships and railroads and commanded by telegraph messages. One out of every twelve men served in the war, and few families were unaffected by the struggle. Over 620,000 soldiers and sailors (37,000 of whom were blacks fighting for the Union side) died in the conflict from wounds or disease, 50 percent more than the number who died fighting in World War II. The equivalent death toll today would be 6 million. Of the surviving combatants, 50,000 returned home with one or more limbs amputated. Disease, however, was the greatest threat to soldiers, killing twice as many as were lost in battle. Some 50,000 civilians were also killed during the war.

The Civil War was also modern in that much of the warfare was distant, impersonal, and mechanical. Men were killed at long distance, without knowing who had fired the shot that felled them. The opposing forces used an array of new weapons and instruments of war: cannons with "rifled," or grooved, barrels for greater accuracy, repeating rifles, ironclad ships, observation balloons, wire entanglements, and the widespread destruction of civilian property. The Civil War was also modern in the sense that civilians could monitor its activities by reading the large-circulation newspapers that sent reporters to the front lines, and people could also visit exhibitions of photographs taken at the battlefields and camps.

In some respects, the Civil War has not yet been resolved. Historians have provided conflicting assessments of the reasons for the Union victory. Some have focused on the inherent weaknesses of the Confederacy: its lack of industry, the fractious relations between the states and the central government in Richmond, poor political leadership, faulty coordination and communication, the burden of maintaining the institution of slavery, and the disparities in population and resources compared with those of the North. Still others have highlighted the erosion of Confederate morale in the face of chronic food shortages and unimaginable human losses. The debate over why the North won and the South lost the Civil War will probably never end, but as in other modern wars, firepower and manpower were essential factors. Robert E. Lee's own explanation of the Confederate defeat retains an enduring legitimacy: "After four years of arduous service marked by unsurpassed courage and fortitude, the Army of Northern Virginia has been compelled to yield to overwhelming numbers and resources."

CHAPTER SUMMARY

- **Civil War Begins** In his inaugural address, Abraham Lincoln made it clear that secession was unconstitutional but that the North would not invade the South. War came when the federal government attempted to resupply forts in the South. When South Carolinians shelled Fort Sumter, in Charleston Harbor, Lincoln issued his call to arms. Other southern states seceded at that point, and the Civil War was under way.

- **Civil War Strategies** The Confederates had a geographic advantage in that they were fighting to defend their own soil. They expected support from Britain and France because of those nations' dependence on southern cotton for their textile industries. The Union quickly launched a campaign to seize the Confederate capital, Richmond, Virginia. Initial hopes for a rapid victory died at the First Battle of Bull Run. The Union then adopted the "anaconda plan," which involved imposing a naval blockade on southern ports and slowly crushing resistance on all fronts. The Union's industrial might was a deciding factor in a long war of attrition.

- **Wartime Home Fronts** Both sides passed conscription laws drafting men into military service. Most of the fighting took place in the South; thus, although the North had more casualties, the impact on the South was greater. Its population was smaller, and its civilians experienced local violence and food shortages. The landscape, food supply, and wildlife were destroyed in many areas. In both the North and the South, women played nontraditional roles on farms and even at the battlefront.

- **Emancipation Proclamation** Initially, President Lincoln declared that the war's aim was to restore the Union and that slavery would be maintained where it existed. Gradually, he came to see that the Emancipation Proclamation was justified as a military necessity because it would deprive the South of its labor force. He hoped that southern states would return to the Union before his January 1863 deadline, when all slaves under Confederate control were declared free.

- **Freedom from Slavery** Many slaves freed themselves by escaping to Union army camps. Although the Emancipation Proclamation announced the war aim of abolishing slavery, it freed only those people enslaved in areas still under Confederate control. The Thirteenth Amendment freed all enslaved people throughout the United States.

CHRONOLOGY

March 4, 1861	Abraham Lincoln is inaugurated president
April 1861	Fort Sumter falls to Confederate forces; Lincoln issues call to arms
July 1861	First Battle of Bull Run (Manassas)
November 1861	The *Trent* affair commences when a Union warship stops a British ship on the high seas and takes two Confederate agents into custody
March–July 1862	Peninsular campaign
April, August, September 1862	Battles of Shiloh, Second Bull Run, and Antietam
January 1, 1863	Lincoln signs the Emancipation Proclamation
May–July, November 1863	Siege of Vicksburg, Battles of Gettysburg and Chattanooga
April 9, 1865	Robert E. Lee surrenders at Appomattox Court House
1865	Thirteenth Amendment is ratified

KEY TERMS & NAMES

Fort Sumter p. 495

Jefferson Davis p. 496

Battles of Bull Run (First and Second Manassas) p. 500

anaconda strategy p. 501

George B. McClellan p. 507

Robert E. Lee p. 509

Thomas "Stonewall" Jackson p. 509

Emancipation Proclamation p. 512

Thirteenth Amendment p. 515

Radical Republicans p. 521

Ulysses S. Grant p. 524

Battle of Gettysburg p. 525

William T. Sherman's "March to the Sea" p. 530

17

RECONSTRUCTION: NORTH AND SOUTH

FOCUS QUESTIONS

 wwnorton.com/studyspace

- What were the different approaches to the Reconstruction of the Confederate states?

- How did white southerners respond to the end of the old order in the South?

- To what extent did blacks function as citizens in the reconstructed South?

- What were the main issues in national politics in the 1870s?

- Why did Reconstruction end in 1877?

In the spring of 1865, the Civil War was finally over. At a frightful cost of 620,000 lives and the destruction of the southern economy and much of its landscape, the Union had emerged triumphant, and some 4 million enslaved Americans had seized their freedom. The ratification of the Thirteenth Amendment in December 1865 abolished slavery everywhere. Now the nation faced the daunting task of reuniting. A civil war fought by the North to save the Union had become a transforming social force. The abolition of slavery, the war-related disruptions to the economy, and the horrifying human losses suffered during the war had destroyed the plantation system and upended racial relations in the South. The defeated Confederacy now had to come to terms with a new order as the United States set about "reconstructing" a ravaged and often resentful South. The era of Reconstruction, from 1865 to 1877, was a period of political complexity and social turbulence that generated far-reaching implications for American life. It witnessed a prolonged debate about issues of enduring significance, questions about the nature of freedom, equality, and opportunity.

By far the most important of those questions was the fate of African Americans. The Union could not have been saved without the help of the blacks, but what would be their status in the postwar era?

THE WAR'S AFTERMATH

In the war's aftermath the victors confronted difficult questions: How should the United States be reunited? What was the status of the states that had seceded? Should the Confederate leaders be tried for treason? Should former Confederates automatically have their U.S. citizenship restored? How should new governments be formed in the South? How and at whose expense was the South's economy to be rebuilt? Should debts incurred by the Confederate state governments be honored? Who should pay to rebuild the South's railroads and public buildings, dredge the clogged southern harbors, and restore damaged levees? What was to be done for the freed slaves? Were they to be given land? social equality? education? voting rights?

Such complex questions required sober reflection and careful planning, but policy makers did not have the luxury of time or the benefit of consensus. Some northerners wanted the former Confederate states returned to the Union with little or no changes in the region's social, political, and economic life. Others wanted southern society punished and transformed. The editors of the nation's foremost magazine, *Harper's Weekly*, expressed this vengeful attitude when they declared at the end of 1865 that "the forgive-and-forget policy . . . is mere political insanity and suicide."

DEVELOPMENT IN THE NORTH   To some Americans the Civil War had been more truly a social revolution than the War of Independence, for it reduced the once-dominant influence of the South's planter elite in national politics and elevated the power of the northern "captains of industry." During and after the Civil War, the U.S. government grew increasingly aligned with the interests of corporate leaders. The wartime Republican Congress had delivered on the party's major platform promises of 1860. In the absence of southern members, the Congress had centralized national power and enacted the Republican economic agenda. It passed the Morrill Tariff, which doubled the average level of import duties. The National Banking Act created a uniform system of banking and bank-note currency and helped finance the war. Congress also decided that the first transcontinental railroad would run along a north-central route, from Omaha, Nebraska, to

Sacramento, California, and it donated public land and sold bonds to ensure its financing. In the Homestead Act of 1862, moreover, Congress provided free federal homesteads of 160 acres to settlers, who had only to occupy the land for five years to gain title. No cash was needed. The Morrill Land Grant Act of the same year conveyed to each state 30,000 acres of federal land per member of Congress from the state. The sale of some of the land provided funds to create colleges of "agriculture and mechanic arts." Such measures helped stimulate the North's economy in the years after the Civil War.

DEVASTATION IN THE SOUTH   The postwar South offered a sharp contrast to the victorious North. Throughout the South, property values had collapsed. Confederate bonds and paper money were worthless; most railroads were damaged or destroyed. Cotton that had escaped destruction was seized by federal troops. Emancipation wiped out $4 billion invested in human flesh and left the labor system in disarray. The great age of expansion in the cotton market was over. Not until 1879 would the cotton crop again equal the record harvest of 1860; tobacco production did not regain its prewar level until 1880; the sugar crop of Louisiana did not recover until 1893; and the old rice industry along the coast of South Carolina and Georgia never regained its prewar levels of production or profit.

A street in the "burned district"

Ruins of Richmond, Virginia, in the spring of 1865.

For many southerners, the emotional devastation caused by the war was worse than the physical destruction. Many families had lost sons and husbands; other war veterans returned with one or more limbs missing. Few families were untouched by the war, and most Confederates resented the humiliation of military occupation. The scars felt by a war-damaged, land-proud South would take time to heal, a very long time.

A TRANSFORMED SOUTH   The defeat of the Confederacy transformed much of southern society. The freeing of slaves, the destruction of property, and the collapse of land values left many planters destitute and homeless. Amanda Worthington, a planter's wife from Mississippi, saw her whole world destroyed. In the fall of 1865, she assessed the damage: "None of us can realize that we are no longer wealthy—yet thanks to the Yankees, the cause of all unhappiness, such is the case." Union soldiers who fanned out across the defeated South to impose order were cursed and spat upon. Fervent southern nationalists, both men and women, implanted in their children a hatred of Yankees and a defiance of northern rule.

LEGALLY FREE, SOCIALLY BOUND   In the former Confederate states, the newly freed slaves often suffered most of all. They were no longer slaves, but were they citizens? After all, the U.S. Supreme Court in the *Dred Scott* decision (1858) had declared that enslaved Africans and their descendants were not eligible for citizenship. Abraham Lincoln's Emancipation Proclamation of 1863 implied that former slaves would become U.S. citizens, but citizenship was then defined and protected by *state* law, and the southern states in 1865 did not have state governments. The process of forming new state governments required first deciding the official status of the seceded states: Were they now conquered territories? If so, then the Congress had the authority to recreate their state governments. But what if it were decided, as Lincoln argued, that the former Confederate states had never officially left the Union because the act of secession was itself illegal? In that circumstance, the process of re-forming state governments would fall within the jurisdiction of the executive branch and the citizens of the states.

Adding to the political confusion was the need to help the former slaves, most of whom had no land, no home, and no food. A few northerners argued that what the ex-slaves needed most was their own land. In coastal South Carolina and in Mississippi, former slaves had been "given" land by Union armies after they had taken control of Confederate areas during the war. But such transfers of white-owned property to former slaves were reversed during 1865. Even northern abolitionists balked at proposals to confiscate white-owned land and distribute it to the freed slaves. Citizenship and legal rights were one thing, wholesale confiscation of property and land redistribution quite another. Instead of land or material help, the freed slaves more often got advice about proper behavior.

THE FREEDMEN'S BUREAU It fell to the federal government to address the desperate plight of the former slaves. On March 3, 1865, while the war was still raging, Congress created within the War Department the Bureau of Refugees, Freedmen, and Abandoned Lands to provide "such issues of provisions, clothing, and fuel" as might be needed to relieve "destitute and suffering refugees and freedmen and their wives and children." It was the first federal experiment in social welfare, albeit temporary. In May 1865, General Oliver O. Howard, commissioner of what came to be called the **Freedmen's Bureau,** declared that freed slaves "must be free to choose their own employers, and be paid for their labor." He sent Freedmen's Bureau agents to the South to negotiate labor contracts (something new for both blacks and white planters), provide medical care, distribute food, and set up schools. The bureau organized its own courts to deal with labor disputes and land titles, and its agents were authorized to supervise trials involving blacks in other courts.

The intensity of racial prejudice in the South often thwarted the efforts of Freedmen's Bureau agents—as well as federal troops—to protect and assist the former slaves. In late June 1865, for example, a white planter in the low country of South Carolina, near Charleston, signed a contract with sixty-five of his former slaves calling for them to "attend & cultivate" his fields "according to the usual system of planting rice & provision lands, and to conform to all reasonable rules & regulations as may be prescribed" by the white owner. In exchange, the workers would receive "half of the crop raised after having deducted the seed of rice, corn, peas & potatoes." Any workers who violated the terms of the contract could be evicted from the plantation, leaving them jobless and homeless. A federal army officer who witnessed the contract reported that he expected "more trouble on this place than any other on the river." Another officer objected to the contract's provision that the owner could require workers to cut wood or dig ditches without compensation. But most worrisome was that the contract essentially enslaved the workers because no matter "how much they are abused, they cannot leave without permission of the owner." If they chose to leave, they would forfeit any right to a portion of the crop. Across the former Confederacy at the end of the war, it was evident that the former white economic elite was determined to continue to control and constrain African Americans.

THE BATTLE OVER POLITICAL RECONSTRUCTION

The question of how to reconstruct the South's political structure centered on deciding which governments would constitute authority in the defeated states. As Union forces advanced into the Confederacy during the Civil War, President Lincoln in 1862 had named military governors for conquered Tennessee, Arkansas, and Louisiana. By the end of the following year, he had formulated a plan for regular governments in those states and any others that might be liberated from Confederate rule.

LINCOLN'S PLAN AND CONGRESS'S RESPONSE   In late 1863, President Lincoln had issued a Proclamation of Amnesty and Reconstruction, under which any former Rebel state could form a Union government whenever a number equal to 10 percent of those who had voted in 1860 took an oath of allegiance to the Constitution and the Union and had received a presidential pardon. Participants also had to swear support for laws and proclamations dealing with emancipation. Certain groups, however, were excluded from the pardon: Confederate officials; senior officers of the Confederate army and navy; judges, congressmen, and military officers of the United States who had left their federal posts to aid the rebellion; and those accused of failure to treat captured African American soldiers and their officers as prisoners of war.

Under this plan, governments loyal to the Union appeared in Tennessee, Arkansas, and Louisiana during the war, but Congress recognized neither their representatives nor their electoral votes in the 1864 presidential election. In the absence of specific provisions for Reconstruction in the Constitution, politicians disagreed as to where authority to restore Rebel states properly rested. Lincoln claimed the right to direct Reconstruction under the clause that set forth the presidential power to grant pardons and under the constitutional obligation of the United States to guarantee each state a republican form of government. Many Republican congressmen, however, argued that this obligation implied that Congress, not the president, should supervise Reconstruction.

A few conservative and most moderate Republicans supported Lincoln's program of immediate restoration. The Radical Republicans, however, favored a sweeping transformation of southern society based upon granting freed slaves full-fledged citizenship. The Radicals hoped to reconstruct southern society so as to dismantle the planter elite and the Democratic party.

The Radical Republicans were talented, earnest legislators who insisted that Congress control the Reconstruction program. In 1864 they helped pass the Wade-Davis Bill, sponsored by Senator Benjamin Franklin Wade of Ohio and Representative Henry Winter Davis of Maryland. In contrast to Lincoln's 10 percent plan, the Wade-Davis Bill would have required that a majority of white male citizens declare their allegiance and that only those who could take an "ironclad" oath (required of federal officials since 1862) attesting to their *past* loyalty could vote or serve in the state constitutional conventions. The conventions, moreover, would have to abolish slavery, exclude from political rights high-ranking civil and military officers of the Confederacy, and repudiate debts incurred during the conflict.

But the Wade-Davis Bill never became law: Lincoln vetoed it. In retaliation furious Republicans penned the Wade-Davis Manifesto, which accused the president of exceeding his constitutional authority. Lincoln offered his last view of Reconstruction in his final public address, on April 11, 1865. Speaking from the White House balcony, he pronounced that the Confederate states had never left the Union. Those states were simply "out of their proper practical relation with the Union," and the object was to get them back "into their proper practical relation." At a cabinet meeting, Lincoln proposed the creation of new southern state governments before Congress met in December. He shunned the vindictiveness of the Radicals. He wanted "no persecution, no bloody work," no radical restructuring of southern social and economic life.

THE ASSASSINATION OF LINCOLN　On the evening of April 14, 1865, Abraham Lincoln and his wife Mary went to see a play at Ford's Theatre. With his trusted bodyguard called away to Richmond and the policeman assigned to his theater box away from his post, Lincoln was defenseless as **John Wilkes Booth** slipped into the unguarded presidential box. Booth, a crazed actor and Confederate sympathizer, fired his pistol point-blank at the back of the president's head. As the president slumped forward, Booth pulled out a knife, stabbed Lincoln's aide, and jumped from the box to the stage, breaking his leg in the process. He then mounted a waiting horse and fled the city. The president died nine hours later. Accomplices of Booth had simultaneously targeted Vice President **Andrew Johnson** and Secretary of State William H. Seward. Seward and four others, including his son, were victims of severe knife wounds. Johnson escaped injury, however, because his would-be assassin got cold feet and wound up tipsy in the barroom of the vice president's hotel.

Booth was pursued into Virginia and killed in a burning barn. Three of his collaborators were convicted by a military court and hanged, along with the woman at whose boardinghouse they had plotted the attacks.

JOHNSON'S PLAN Lincoln's death elevated to the White House Andrew Johnson of Tennessee, a combative man who lacked most presidential virtues. Johnson was provincial and bigoted—he harbored fierce prejudices. He was also short-tempered and impetuous. At the inaugural ceremonies in early 1865, he had delivered his vice-presidential address in a state of slurring drunkenness that embarrassed Lincoln and the nation. Johnson was a war (pro-Union) Democrat who had been put on the National Union ticket in 1864 as a gesture of unity. As a southerner, he had long been an advocate of the small farmers in opposition to the privileges of the large planters—"a bloated, corrupted aristocracy." He also shared the racist attitudes of most white yeomen. "Damn the negroes," he exclaimed to a friend during the war, "I am fighting those traitorous aristocrats, their masters."

Johnson's loyalty to the Union sprang from a strict adherence to the Constitution and a fervent belief in limited government. When discussing what to do with the former Confederate states, Johnson preferred the term *restoration* to *reconstruction*. In 1865, he declared that "there is no such thing as reconstruction. Those States have not gone out of the Union. Therefore reconstruction is unnecessary." Like many other whites he also opposed the growing Radical sentiment to grant the vote to African Americans.

Johnson's plan to restore the Union thus closely resembled Lincoln's. A new Proclamation of Amnesty, issued in May 1865, excluded not only those Lincoln had barred from pardon but also everybody with taxable property worth more than $20,000. They were allowed to make special applications for pardon directly to the president, and before the year was out Johnson had issued some thirteen thousand pardons.

Johnson followed up his amnesty proclamation with his own plan for readmitting the former Confederate states. In each state a native Unionist became provisional governor, with authority to call a convention of men elected by loyal voters. Johnson called upon the state conventions to invalidate the secession ordinances, abolish slavery, and repudiate all debts incurred to aid the Confederacy. Each state, moreover, had to ratify the Thirteenth Amendment ending slavery. In his final public address, Lincoln had endorsed a limited black suffrage. Johnson

Andrew Johnson
A pro-Union Democrat from Tennessee.

repeated Lincoln's advice. He reminded the provisional governor of Mississippi, for example, that the state conventions might "with perfect safety" extend suffrage to African Americans with education or with military service so as to "disarm the adversary," the adversary being "radicals who are wild upon" giving all African Americans the right to vote.

The state conventions for the most part met Johnson's requirements. But southern whites had accepted the situation because they thought so little had changed after all. Emboldened by Johnson's indulgence, they ignored his pleas for moderation and conciliation. Suggestions of black suffrage were scarcely raised in the state conventions and promptly squelched when they were.

SOUTHERN INTRANSIGENCE   When Congress met in December 1865, for the first time since the end of the war it faced the fact that the new state governments in the postwar South were remarkably like the Confederate ones. Southern voters had acted with extreme disregard for northern feelings. Among the new members presenting themselves to Congress were Georgia's Alexander Stephens, former vice president of the Confederacy, now claiming a seat in the Senate, four Confederate generals, eight colonels, and six cabinet members. Congress forthwith denied seats to all such officials. It was too much to expect, after four bloody years, that the Unionists in Congress would welcome back ex-Confederate leaders.

Furthermore, the new all-white southern state legislatures, in passing repressive "**black codes**" designed to restrict the freedom of African Americans, demonstrated that they intended to preserve slavery as nearly as possible. As one white southerner stressed, "The ex-slave was not a free man; he was a free Negro," and the black codes were intended to highlight the distinction.

The black codes varied from state to state, but some provisions were common in many of them. Existing marriages, including common-law marriages, were recognized (although interracial marriages were prohibited), and testimony of blacks was accepted in legal cases involving blacks—and in six states in all cases. Blacks could own property. They could sue and be sued in the courts. On the other hand, they could not own farmland in Mississippi or city lots in South Carolina; they were required to buy special licenses to practice certain trades in Mississippi. Only a few states allowed blacks to serve on juries. Blacks who worked for whites were required to enter into labor contracts with their employers, to be renewed annually. Unemployed ("vagrant") blacks were often arrested and punished with severe fines, and if unable to pay they were forced to labor in the fields of those who paid the courts for this source of cheap labor. In other words, aspects of slavery were simply being restored in another guise. When a freedman in South Carolina

(?) "Slavery Is Dead" (?)

Thomas Nast's cartoon suggests that slavery was not dead in the postwar south.

told a white employer that he wanted to get a federal army officer to review his labor contract, the employer killed him.

Faced with such blatant evidence of southern intransigence, moderate Republicans in Congress drifted toward the Radicals' views. In early 1866 the new Congress set up a Joint Committee on Reconstruction, with nine members from the House and six from the Senate, to gather evidence of southern efforts to thwart Reconstruction. Initiative fell to determined Radical Republicans who knew what they wanted: Benjamin Franklin Wade of Ohio, George Washington Julian of Indiana, and—most conspicuously of all—**Thaddeus Stevens** of Pennsylvania and Charles Sumner of Massachusetts.

THE RADICAL REPUBLICANS Most Radical Republicans had been connected with the anti-slavery cause for decades. In addition, few could escape the bitterness bred by the long war or remain unaware of the partisan advantage that would come to the Republican party from black suffrage. The Republicans needed African American votes to maintain their control of Congress and the White House. They also needed to disenfranchise former Confederates to keep them from helping to elect Democrats eager to restore the old southern ruling class to power. In public, however, the Radical Republicans rarely disclosed such partisan self-interest. Instead, they asserted that the Republicans, the party of Union and freedom, could best guarantee the fruits of victory and that extending voting rights to African Americans would be the best way to promote their welfare.

The growing conflict of opinion over Reconstruction policy brought about an inversion in constitutional reasoning. Secessionists—and Andrew Johnson—were now arguing that the Rebel states had in fact remained in the Union, and some Radical Republicans were contriving arguments that they had left the Union after all. Thaddeus Stevens argued that the Confederate states should be viewed as conquered provinces, subject to the absolute will of the victors, and that the "whole fabric of southern society must be changed." Most Republicans, however, held that the Confederate states continued to exist as entities, but by the acts of secession and war they had forfeited "all civil and political rights under the Constitution." And Congress, not the president, was the proper authority to determine how and when such rights might be restored.

JOHNSON'S BATTLE WITH CONGRESS A long year of political battling remained, however, before this idea triumphed. By the end of 1865, the Radical Republicans' views had gained a majority in Congress, if one not yet large enough to override presidential vetoes. But the critical year of 1866 saw the gradual waning of Andrew Johnson's power and influence, much of which was self-induced. Johnson first challenged Congress in 1866, when he vetoed a bill to extend the life of the Freedmen's Bureau. For the time being, Johnson's prestige remained sufficiently intact that the Senate upheld his veto.

Three days after the veto, however, during an impromptu speech, Johnson undermined his already weakening authority with a fiery assault upon the Radical Republican leaders. From that point forward, moderate Republicans deserted a president who had opened himself to counterattack. The Radical Republicans took the offensive. Johnson was "an alien enemy of a foreign state," Stevens declared. Sumner called him "an insolent drunken brute," a charge Johnson was open to because of his behavior at the 1865 inauguration.

In mid-March 1866 the Radical-led Congress passed the Civil Rights Act, written by Illinois senator Lyman Trumbull (who also drafted the Thirteenth Amendment). A response to the black codes and the neo-slavery system created by unrepentant southern state legislatures, it declared that "all persons born in the United States and not subject to any foreign power, excluding Indians not taxed," were citizens entitled to "full and equal benefit of all laws." The granting of citizenship to native-born blacks, Johnson fumed, exceeded the scope of federal power. It would, moreover, "foment discord among the races." Johnson vetoed the bill, but this time, on April 9, Congress overrode the presidential veto. On July 16, it enacted a revised Freedmen's Bureau Bill, again overriding a presidential veto. From that point on, Johnson steadily lost both public and political support.

THE FOURTEENTH AMENDMENT To remove all doubt about the legality of the new Civil Rights Act, the joint committee recommended a new constitutional amendment, which passed Congress on June 16, 1866, and was ratified by the states two years later, on July 28, 1868. The **Fourteenth Amendment** went far beyond the Civil Rights Act by establishing a constitutional guarantee of basic citizenship for all Americans, including African Americans. The amendment reaffirms the state and federal citizenship of persons born or naturalized in the United States, and it forbids any state (the word *state* would be important in later litigation) to "abridge the privileges or immunities of citizens," to deprive any *person* (again an important term) "of life, liberty, or property, without due process of law," or to "deny any person . . . the equal protection of the laws." These three clauses have been the subject of many lawsuits, resulting in applications not widely, if at all, foreseen at the time. The "due-process clause" has come to mean that state as well as federal power is subject to the Bill of Rights, and it has been used to protect corporations, as legal "persons," from "unreasonable" regulation by the states. The Fourteenth Amendment also prohibited the president from granting pardons to former Confederate leaders.

President Andrew Johnson's home state was among the first to ratify the Fourteenth Amendment. In Tennessee, which had more Unionists than any other Confederate state, the government had fallen under Radical Republican control. The state's governor, in reporting the results to the secretary of the Senate, added, "Give my respects to the dead dog of the White House." His words illustrate the growing acrimony on both sides of the Reconstruction debates. In May and July, race riots in Memphis and New Orleans added fuel to the flames. Both incidents involved indiscriminate massacres of blacks by local police and white mobs. The carnage, Radical Republicans argued, was the natural fruit of Andrew Johnson's lenient policy toward white supremacists. "Witness Memphis, witness New Orleans," Massachusetts senator Charles Sumner cried. "Who can doubt that the President is the author of these tragedies?"

RECONSTRUCTING THE SOUTH

THE TRIUMPH OF CONGRESSIONAL RECONSTRUCTION As 1866 drew to an end, the congressional elections promised to be a referendum on the growing split between President Andrew Johnson and the Radical Republicans. To win votes, Johnson went on a speaking tour of the

Midwest. But his efforts backfired when several of his speeches turned into undignified shouting contests between him and his critics. In Cleveland, Johnson described the Radical Republicans as "factious, domineering, tyrannical" men, and he foolishly exchanged hot-tempered insults with a heckler. At another stop, while Johnson was speaking from the back of a railway car, the engineer mistakenly pulled the train out of the station, making the president appear quite the fool. Such incidents tended to confirm Johnson's image as a "ludicrous boor" and a "drunken imbecile," an image that Radical Republicans promoted. The 1866 congressional elections were a devastating defeat for Johnson; Republicans won more than a two-thirds majority in each house, a comfortable margin with which to override presidential vetoes.

The Republican-controlled Congress in fact enacted several important provisions even before the new members took office. Two acts passed in 1867 extended voting rights to African Americans in the District of Columbia and the territories. Another law provided that the new Congress would convene on March 4 instead of the following December, depriving Johnson of a breathing spell. On March 2, 1867, two days before the old Congress expired, it passed, over Johnson's vetoes, three crucial laws promoting what came to be called "Congressional Reconstruction": the Military Reconstruction Act, the Command of the Army Act (an amendment to an army appropriation), and the Tenure of Office Act.

Congressional Reconstruction was designed to prevent white southerners from manipulating the reconstruction process. The Command of the Army Act required that all orders from the commander in chief go through the headquarters of the general of the army, a post then held by Ulysses S. Grant. The Radical Republicans distrusted President Johnson and trusted General Grant, who was already leaning their way. The Tenure of Office Act required Senate permission for the president to remove any federal officeholder whose appointment the Senate had confirmed. The purpose of at least some congressmen was to retain Secretary of War Edwin Stanton, the one Radical Republican sympathizer in Johnson's cabinet.

The Military Reconstruction Act was hailed—or denounced—as the triumphant victory of Radical Reconstruction, for it set a precedent among former slave societies in providing voting rights to freed slaves almost immediately after emancipation. It also represented the nation's first effort in military-enforced nation building. The North's effort to "reconstruct" the South by force after the Civil War set a precedent for future American military occupations and attempted social transformations. The act declared that "no legal state governments or adequate protection for life and property now exists in the rebel States." One state, Tennessee, was exempted from the application of the new act because it had already ratified the Fourteenth Amendment. The other ten southern states were divided into five military districts, and the commanding officer of each was authorized to keep order and protect the "rights of persons and property." The Military Reconstruction Act then stipulated that new constitutions in each of the former Confederate states were to be framed by conventions elected by male citizens aged twenty-one and older "of whatever race, color, or previous condition." Each state constitution had to guarantee the right of African American males to vote. Once the constitution was ratified by a majority of voters and accepted by Congress, other criteria had to be met. The new state legislature had to ratify the Fourteenth Amendment, and once the amendment became part of the Constitution, any given state would be entitled to representation in Congress.

Several hundred African American delegates participated in the statewide political conventions. Most had been selected by local political meetings or churches, fraternal societies, Union Leagues, or black army units from the North, although a few simply appointed themselves. The African American delegates "ranged [across] all colors and apparently all conditions," but free mulattoes from the cities played the most prominent roles. At Louisiana's Republican state convention, for instance, nineteen of the twenty black delegates had been born free. President Johnson reluctantly appointed military commanders under the new Military Reconstruction Act. Before the end of 1867, new elections had been held in all the states but Texas, and blacks participated in high numbers, giving virtually all of their votes to Republican candidates.

Some people expected the Supreme Court to strike down the act, and no process existed for the new elections. Congress quickly remedied that on March 23, 1867, with the Second Reconstruction Act, which directed the army commanders to register all adult men who swore they were qualified. A Third Reconstruction Act, passed on July 19, directed registrars to go beyond the loyalty oath and determine each person's eligibility to take it and authorized district army commanders to remove and replace officeholders of any existing "so-called state" or division thereof. Before the end of 1867, new elections had been held in all the states but Texas.

Having clipped the president's wings, the Republican Congress moved a year later to safeguard its Reconstruction program from possible interference by the Supreme Court. On March 27, 1868, Congress simply removed the power of the Supreme Court to review cases arising under the Military Reconstruction Act, which Congress clearly had the right to do under its power to define the Court's appellate jurisdiction. The Court accepted this curtailment of its authority on the same day it affirmed the principle of an "indestructible Union" in *Texas v. White* (1869). In that case the Court also asserted the right of Congress to reframe state governments, thus endorsing the Radical Republican point of view.

THE IMPEACHMENT AND TRIAL OF JOHNSON By 1868, Radical Republicans had decided that Andrew Johnson must be removed from office. The Republicans had unsuccessfully tried to impeach Johnson early in 1867, alleging a variety of flimsy charges, none of which represented an indictable crime. Then Johnson himself provided the occasion for impeachment when he deliberately violated the Tenure of Office Act in order to test its constitutionality. Secretary of War Edwin Stanton had become a thorn in Johnson's side, refusing to resign despite his disagreements with the president's Reconstruction policy. On August 12, 1867, during a congressional recess, Johnson suspended Stanton and named General Ulysses S. Grant in his place. When the Senate refused to confirm Johnson's action, however, Grant returned the office to Stanton.

The Radical Republicans now saw their chance to remove the president. On February 24, 1868, the Republican-dominated House passed eleven articles of impeachment by a party-line vote of 126 to 47. Most of the articles focused on the charge that Johnson had unlawfully removed Secretary of War Stanton.

The Senate trial began on March 5, 1868, and continued until May 26, with Chief Justice Salmon P. Chase presiding. It was a great spectacle before a packed gallery. The five-week trial ended in May 1868, and the Senate voted 35 to 19 for conviction, only one vote short of the two thirds needed for removal from office. Although the Senate failed to remove Johnson, the trial crippled his already weakened presidency. In 1868, Johnson sought the Democratic presidential nomination but lost to New York governor Horatio Seymour, who then lost to the Republican, Ulysses S. Grant, in the general election. The impeachment of Johnson was in the end a great political mistake, for the failure to remove the president damaged Radical Republican morale and support. Nevertheless, the Radical cause did gain something: to stave off impeachment, Johnson agreed not to obstruct the process of Congressional-led Reconstruction.

REPUBLICAN RULE IN THE SOUTH In June 1868, Congress agreed that eight southern states—all but Virginia, Mississippi, and Texas—had met the more stringent conditions for readmission. Congress rescinded Georgia's admission, however, when the state legislature expelled twenty-eight African American members and seated former Confederate leaders. The federal military commander in Georgia then forced the legislature to reseat the black members and remove the Confederates, and the state was compelled to ratify the **Fifteenth Amendment** before being admitted in July 1870. Mississippi, Texas, and Virginia had returned earlier in 1870, under the added requirement that they, too, ratify the Fifteenth Amendment. That amendment, submitted to the states in 1869 and ratified in 1870, forbids the states to deny any person the vote on grounds of "race, color, or previous condition of servitude." Kentucky, the birthplace of Abraham Lincoln, was the only state in the nation that failed to ratify all three of the constitutional amendments related to ending slavery—the Thirteenth, Fourteenth, and Fifteenth.

Long before the new governments were established, groups promoting the Republican party had begun to spring up in the South, chiefly sponsored by the Union League, founded in Philadelphia in 1862 to support the Union. League recruiters in the South enrolled African Americans and loyal whites, initiated them into the secrets and rituals of the order, and instructed them "in their rights and duties." Their recruiting efforts were so successful that in 1867, on the eve of South Carolina's choice of convention delegates, the league reported eighty-eight chapters, which claimed to have enrolled almost every adult black male in the state.

THE RECONSTRUCTED SOUTH

THE FREED SLAVES   African Americans in the postwar South were active agents in affecting the course of Reconstruction, though it was not an easy process. During the era of Reconstruction, whites, both northern and southern, harbored racist views of blacks. A northern journalist traveling in the South after the war reported that the "whites seem wholly unable to comprehend that freedom for the negro means the same thing as freedom for them." Whites used terror, intimidation, and violence to suppress black efforts to gain social and economic equality. In Texas a white farmer told a former slave that his freedom would do him "damned little good . . . as I intend to shoot you"—and he did. The Civil War had brought freedom to enslaved African Americans, but it did not bring them protection against exploitation or abuse.

Participation in the Union army or navy had provided many freedmen with training in leadership. Black military veterans would form the core of the first generation of African American political leaders in the postwar South. Military service gave many former slaves their first opportunities to learn to read and write. Army life also alerted them to new opportunities for economic advancement, social respectability, and civic leadership. Fighting for the Union cause also instilled a fervent sense of nationalism. A Virginia freedman explained that the United States was "now *our* country—made emphatically so by the blood of our brethren."

Former slaves established churches after the war, which quickly formed the foundation of African American community life. Many blacks preferred the Baptist denomination, in part because its decentralized structure allowed each congregation to worship in its own way. By 1890 over 1.3 million African Americans in the South had become Baptists, nearly three times as many as had joined any other black denomination. In addition to forming viable new congregations, freed African Americans organized thousands of fraternal, benevolent, and mutual-aid societies, as well as clubs, lodges, and associations. Memphis, for example, had over two hundred such organizations; Richmond boasted twice that number.

Freed blacks also hastened to reestablish their families. Marriages that had been prohibited during slavery were now legitimized through the assistance of the Freedmen's Bureau. By 1870 a preponderant majority of former slaves were living in two-parent households. With little money or technical training, freed blacks faced the prospect of becoming wage laborers. Because there were so few banks left in the South, it was virtually impossible for former slaves to get loans to buy farm land. For many freed blacks (and poor whites) the primary vocational option after the war was sharecropping, in which the crop produced was divided between the tenant farmer and the landowner. Sharecropping enabled mothers and wives to contribute directly to the family's income.

African American communities in the postwar South also sought to establish schools. Planters had denied education to blacks in part because they feared that literate slaves would read abolitionist literature and organize uprisings. After the war the white elite worried that formal education would encourage poor whites and poor blacks to leave the South in search of better social and economic opportunities. Economic leaders wanted to protect the competitive advantage afforded by the region's low-wage labor market. "They didn't want us to learn nothin," one former slave recalled. "The only thing we had to learn was how to work."

White opposition to education for blacks made education all the more important to African Americans. South Carolina's Mary McLeod Bethune, the fifteenth child of former slaves, reveled in the opportunity to gain an education: "The whole world opened to me when I learned to read." She walked five miles to school as a child, earned a scholarship to college, and went on to become the first black woman to found a school that became a four-year college, Bethune-Cookman, in Daytona Beach, Florida.

AFRICAN AMERICANS IN SOUTHERN POLITICS   In the post-war South the new role of African Americans in politics caused the most controversy. If largely uneducated and inexperienced in the rudiments of politics, southern blacks were little different from the millions of newly enfranchised propertyless whites in the age of Andrew Jackson's political reforms or immigrants in postwar cities. Some freedmen frankly confessed their disadvantages. Beverly Nash, an African American delegate to the South Carolina convention of 1868, told his colleagues: "I believe, my friends and fellow-citizens, we are not prepared for this suffrage. But we can learn. Give a man tools and let him commence to use them, and in time he will learn a trade. So it is with voting."

By 1867, however, former slaves had begun to gain political influence and vote in large numbers, and this development revealed emerging tensions within the African American community. Some southern blacks resented the presence of northern brethren who moved south after the war, while others complained that few ex-slaves were represented in leadership positions. There developed real tensions in the black community between the few who owned

Freedmen voting in New Orleans

The Fifteenth Amendment, ratified in 1870, guaranteed at the federal level the right of citizens to vote regardless of "race, color, or previous condition of servitude." But former slaves had been registering to vote—and voting in large numbers—in state elections since 1867, as in this scene.

property and the many who did not. In North Carolina by 1870, for example, less than 7 percent of blacks owned land, and most of them owned only a few acres; half of black property owners had less than twenty acres. Northern blacks and the southern free black elite, most of whom were urban dwellers and many of whom were mulattoes, often opposed efforts to redistribute land to the freedmen, and many insisted that political equality did not mean social equality. As a black Alabama leader stressed, "We do not ask that the ignorant and degraded shall be put on a social equality with the refined and intelligent." In general, however, unity rather than dissension prevailed, and African Americans focused on common concerns such as full equality under the law.

Brought suddenly into politics in times that tried the most skilled of statesmen, many African Americans served with distinction. Nonetheless, the derisive label "black Reconstruction," used by later critics, exaggerates African American political influence, which was limited mainly to voting. Such criticism also overlooks the political clout of the large number of white Republicans, especially in the mountain areas of the Upper South, who also favored the Radical plan for Reconstruction. Only one of the new state conventions, South Carolina's, had a black majority, seventy-six to forty-one. Louisiana's was evenly divided racially, and in only two other conventions were more than 20 percent of the members black: Florida's, with 40 percent, and Virginia's, with 24 percent. The Texas convention was only 10 percent black, and North Carolina's was 11 percent—but that did not stop a white newspaper from calling it a body consisting of "baboons, monkeys, mules . . . and other jackasses."

In the new state governments any African American participation was a novelty. Although some six hundred blacks—most of them former slaves—served as state legislators, no black man was ever elected governor, and only a few served as judges. In Louisiana, however, Pinckney Pinchback, a northern black and former Union soldier, won the office of lieutenant governor and served as acting governor when the white governor was indicted for corruption. Several African Americans were elected lieutenant governor, state treasurer, or secretary of state. There were two black senators in Congress, Hiram Revels and Blanche K. Bruce, both Mississippi natives who had been educated in the North, and fourteen black members of the House of Representatives during Reconstruction.

"CARPETBAGGERS" AND "SCALAWAGS" The top positions in postwar southern state governments went for the most part to white Republicans, whom the opposition whites labeled "**carpetbaggers**" and "**scalawags**," depending upon their place of birth. Northerners who allegedly rushed

South with all their belongings in carpetbags to grab the political spoils were more often than not Union veterans who had arrived as early as 1865 or 1866, drawn South by the hope of economic opportunity and other attractions that many of them had seen in their Union service. Many other so-called carpetbaggers were teachers, social workers, or preachers animated by a sincere missionary impulse.

The scalawags, or native white Republicans, were even more reviled and misrepresented. A Nashville newspaper editor called them the "merest trash." Most scalawags had opposed secession, forming a Unionist majority in many mountain counties as far south as Georgia and Alabama and especially in the hills of eastern Tennessee. Among the so-called scalawags were several distinguished figures, including the former Confederate general James Longstreet, who decided after Appomattox that the Old South must change its ways. He became a successful cotton broker in New Orleans, joined the Republican party, and supported the Radical Reconstruction program. Other scalawags were former Whigs attracted by the Republican party's economic program of industrial and commercial expansion.

THE RADICAL REPUBLICAN RECORD Former Confederates resented the new state constitutions because of their provisions allowing for black voting and civil rights. Yet most of those constitutions remained in effect for some years after the end of Radical Republican control, and later constitutions incorporated many of their features. Conspicuous among the Radical innovations were such steps toward greater democracy as requiring universal manhood suffrage, reapportioning legislatures more nearly according to population, and making more state offices elective. In South Carolina, former Confederate leaders opposed the Radical state legislature not simply because of its black members but also because lower-class whites were enjoying unprecedented political power too.

Given the hostile circumstances under which the Radical governments operated, their achievements were remarkable. They constructed an extensive railroad network and established state-supported public school systems. Some six hundred thousand black pupils were enrolled in southern schools by 1877. State governments under the Radicals also gave more attention to the poor and to orphanages, asylums, and institutions for the deaf and the blind of both races. Public roads, bridges, and buildings were repaired or rebuilt. African Americans achieved rights and opportunities that would never again be taken away, at least in principle: equality before the law and the rights to own property, carry on business, enter professions, attend schools, and learn to read and write.

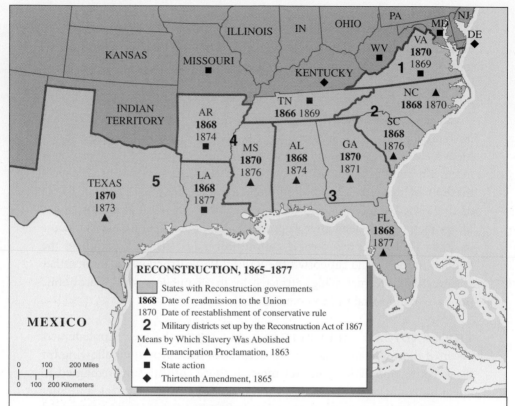

RECONSTRUCTION, 1865–1877

☐	States with Reconstruction governments
1868	Date of readmission to the Union
1870	Date of reestablishment of conservative rule
2	Military districts set up by the Reconstruction Act of 1867

Means by Which Slavery Was Abolished

▲	Emancipation Proclamation, 1863
■	State action
◆	Thirteenth Amendment, 1865

How did the Military Reconstruction Act reorganize governments in the South in the late 1860s and 1870s? What did the former Confederate states have to do to be readmitted to the Union? Why did "Conservative" parties gradually regain control of the South from the Republicans in the 1870s?

Yet several of these Republican state regimes also engaged in corrupt practices. Bids for state government contracts were accepted at absurdly high prices, and public officials took their cut. Public money and public credit were often awarded to privately owned corporations, notably railroads, under conditions that invited influence peddling. Corruption was not invented by the Radical Republican regimes, nor did it die with them. Louisiana's "carpetbag" governor recognized as much. "Why," he said, "down here everybody is demoralized. Corruption is the fashion."

RELIGION AND RECONSTRUCTION The religious community played a critical role in the implementation and ultimate failure of Radical Reconstruction, and religious commentators offered quite different interpretations of what should be done with the defeated South. Thaddeus Stevens and many other Radical Republican leaders who had spent their careers promoting the abolition of slavery and racial equality were motivated primarily by religious ideals and moral fervor. They wanted no compromise with racism. Likewise, most of the Christian missionaries who headed south after the Civil War brought with them a progressive vision of a biracial "beloved community" emerging in the reconstructed South, and they strove to promote social and political equality for freed slaves. For these crusaders, civil rights was a sacred cause. They used Christian principles to challenge the prevailing theological and "scientific" justifications for racial inferiority. They also promoted Christian solidarity across racial and regional lines.

At the same time, the Protestant denominations, all of which had split into northern and southern branches over the issues of slavery and secession, struggled to reunite after the war. A growing number of northern ministers promoted reconciliation between the warring regions after the Civil War. These "apostles of forgiveness" prized white unity over racial equality. For example, the Reverend Henry Ward Beecher, the powerful New York minister whose sister Harriet Beecher Stowe wrote *Uncle Tom's Cabin*, wanted white southern planters—rather than federal officials or African Americans themselves—to oversee Reconstruction. Not surprisingly, Beecher's views gained widespread support among evangelical ministers in the South.

The collapse of the Confederacy did not prompt southern whites to abandon their belief that God was on their side. In the wake of defeat and emancipation, white southern ministers reassured their congregations that they had no reason to question the moral foundations of their region or their defense of white racial superiority. For African Americans, however, the Civil War and emancipation demonstrated that God was on *their* side. Emancipation was in their view a redemptive act through which God wrought national regeneration. African American ministers were convinced that the United States was

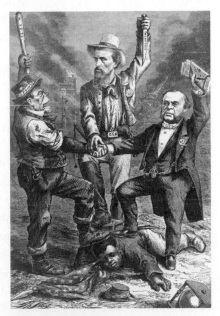

The "white republic"

This cartoon illustrates white unity against racial equality.

indeed a divinely inspired nation and that blacks had a providential role to play in its future. Yet neither black nor idealistic white northern ministers could stem the growing chorus of whites who were willing to abandon goals of racial equality in exchange for national religious reconciliation. By the end of the nineteenth century, mainstream American Protestantism promoted the image of a "white republic" that conflated whiteness, godliness, and nationalism.

THE GRANT YEARS

Ulysses S. Grant, who served as president during the collapse of Republican rule in the South, brought to the White House little political experience. But in 1868 northern voters supported the "Lion of Vicksburg" because of his record as the Union army commander. He was the most popular man in the nation. Both parties wooed him, but his falling-out with President Andrew Johnson had pushed him toward the Republicans. They were, as Thaddeus Stevens said, ready to "let him into the church."

THE ELECTION OF 1868 The Republican party platform of 1868 endorsed congressional Reconstruction. One plank cautiously defended black suffrage as a necessity in the South but a matter each northern state should settle for itself. Another urged payment of the national debt "in the utmost good faith to all creditors," which meant in gold. More important than the platform were the great expectations of a heroic soldier-president and his slogan, "Let us have peace."

The Democrats took opposite positions on both Reconstruction and the debt. The Republican Congress, the Democratic party platform charged, instead of restoring the Union had "so far as in its power, dissolved it, and subjected ten states, in the time of profound peace, to military despotism and Negro supremacy." As for the federal debt, the party endorsed Representative George H. Pendleton's "Ohio idea" that, since most war bonds had been bought with depreciated **greenbacks**, they should be paid off in greenbacks rather than in gold. The Democratic Convention nominated Horatio Seymour, wartime governor of New York, who made it a closer race than the electoral vote revealed. While Grant swept the Electoral College by 214 to 80, his popular majority was only 307,000 out of a total of over 5.7 million votes. More than 500,000 African American voters accounted for Grant's margin of victory.

Grant had proved himself a great military leader, but as the youngest president ever (forty-six years old at the time of his inauguration), he was often blind to the political forces and influence peddlers around him. He was awestruck by men of wealth and unaccountably loyal to some who betrayed his trust, and he passively followed the lead of Congress.

Grant betrayed a fatal gift for losing men of talent and integrity from his cabinet. Secretary of State Hamilton Fish of New York turned out to be a happy exception; he guided foreign policy throughout the Grant presidency. Other than Fish, however, the Grant cabinet overflowed with incompetents.

THE GOVERNMENT DEBT   Financial issues dominated Grant's presidency. After the war the Treasury had assumed that the $432 million worth of greenbacks issued during the conflict would be retired from circulation and that the nation would revert to a "hard-money" currency—gold coins. But many agrarian and debtor groups resisted any contraction of the money supply resulting from the elimination of greenbacks, believing that it would mean lower prices for their crops and more difficulty repaying long-term debts. They were joined by a large number of Radical Republicans who thought that a combination of high tariffs and inflation would generate more rapid economic growth. In 1868 congressional supporters of such a "soft-money" policy halted the withdrawal of greenbacks from circulation. There matters stood when Grant took office.

The "sound-money" (or hard-money) advocates, mostly bankers and merchants, claimed that Grant's election was a mandate to save the country from the Democrats' "Ohio idea" of using greenbacks to repay government bonds. The influential hard-money advocates also reflected the deeply ingrained popular assumption that gold coins were morally preferable to paper currency. Grant agreed as well. On March 18, 1869, the Public Credit Act, which said that the federal debt must be paid in gold, became the first act of Congress that Grant signed.

SCANDALS   The complexities of the "money question" exasperated Grant, but that was the least of his worries, for his administration soon fell into a cesspool of scandal. In the summer of 1869, two unscrupulous financial buccaneers, Jay Gould and James Fisk, connived with the president's brother-in-law to corner the nation's gold market. That is, they would create a public craze for gold by purchasing massive quantities of the precious yellow metal. As more buyers joined the frenzy, the value of gold would soar. The only danger to the scheme lay in the possibility that the federal Treasury would burst the bubble by selling large amounts of gold, which would deflate its value.

Grant apparently smelled a rat from the start, but he was seen in public with the speculators, leading people to think that he supported the run on gold. As the rumor spread on Wall Street that the president was pro-gold, the value of gold rose from $132 to $163 an ounce. Finally, on Black Friday, September 24, 1869, Grant ordered the Treasury to sell a large quantity of gold, and the bubble burst. Fisk got out by repudiating his agreements and hiring thugs to intimidate his creditors. "Nothing is lost save honor," he said.

The plot to corner the gold market was only the first of several scandals that rocked the Grant administration. During the presidential campaign of 1872, the public learned about the corruption of the **Crédit Mobilier** of America, a sham construction company run by directors of the Union Pacific Railroad who had milked the Union Pacific for exorbitant fees in order to line the pockets of the insiders who controlled both firms. Union Pacific shareholders were left holding the bag. The schemers bought political support by giving congressmen shares of stock in the enterprise. This chicanery had transpired before Grant's election in 1868, but it now touched a number of prominent Republicans. The beneficiaries of the scheme included Speaker of the House Schuyler Colfax, later vice president, and Representative James A. Garfield, later president. Of the thirteen members of Congress involved, only two were censured.

Even more odious disclosures soon followed, some involving the president's cabinet. The secretary of war, it turned out, had accepted bribes from merchants who traded with Indians at army posts in the West. At the same time, post-office contracts, it was revealed, went to carriers who offered the highest kickbacks. The secretary of the Treasury had awarded a political friend a commission of 50 percent for the collection of overdue taxes. In St. Louis a "whiskey ring" bribed tax collectors to bilk the government out of millions of dollars in revenue. Grant's private secretary was enmeshed in that scheme, taking large sums of money and other valuables in return for inside information. There is no evidence that Grant himself was ever involved in, or personally profited from, any of the fraud, but his poor choice of associates and his gullibility earned him widespread criticism. Democrats castigated Republicans for their "monstrous corruption and extravagance."

WHITE TERROR   President Grant initially fought hard to enforce the federal efforts to reconstruct the postwar South. But southern resistance to "Radical rule" increased and turned violent. In Grayson County, Texas, three whites murdered three former slaves because they felt the need to "thin the niggers out and drive them to their holes."

The prototype of all the terrorist groups was the Ku Klux Klan (KKK), organized in 1866 by some young men of Pulaski, Tennessee, as a social club, with the costumes and secret rituals common to fraternal groups. At first a group of pranksters, its members soon turned to intimidation of blacks and white Republicans. The KKK spread rapidly across the South. Klansmen rode about at night, hiding behind masks and under robes, spreading horrendous rumors, issuing threats,

"Worse Than Slavery"

This Thomas Nast cartoon chides the Ku Klux Klan and the White League for promoting conditions "worse than slavery" for southern blacks after the Civil War.

harassing African Americans, and wreaking violence and destruction. "We are going to kill all the Negroes," a white supremacist declared during one massacre.

Klansmen focused their terror on prominent Republicans, black and white. In Mississippi they killed a black Republican leader in front of his family. Three white "scalawag" Republicans were murdered in Georgia in 1870. That same year an armed mob of whites assaulted a Republican political rally in Alabama, killing four blacks and wounding fifty-four. In South Carolina white supremacists were especially active—and violent. Virtually the entire white male population of York County joined the KKK, and they were responsible for eleven murders and hundreds of whippings. In 1871, some five hundred masked men laid siege to the Union County jail and eventually lynched eight black prisoners.

At the urging of President Grant, who showed true moral courage in trying to protect southern blacks, the Republican-dominated Congress struck back with three Enforcement Acts (1870–1871). The first of these measures levied penalties on anyone who interfered with any citizen's right to vote. A second placed the election of congressmen under surveillance by federal election supervisors and marshals. The third (the Ku Klux Klan Act) outlawed the characteristic activities of the KKK—forming conspiracies, wearing disguises, resisting officers, and intimidating officials—and authorized the president to suspend habeas corpus where necessary to suppress "armed combinations." In 1871, the federal government singled out nine counties in upcountry South Carolina as an example and pursued mass prosecutions. In general, however, the Enforcement Acts suffered from weak and inconsistent execution. As time passed, President Grant vacillated between clamping down on the Klan and capitulating to racial intimidation. The unrelenting efforts of whites to use violence to thwart Reconstruction continued into the 1870s.

REFORM AND THE ELECTION OF 1872 Long before President Grant's first term ended, a reaction against Radical Reconstruction and incompetence and corruption in the administration had incited mutiny within the Republican ranks. A new faction, called Liberal Republicans, favored free trade rather than tariffs, the redemption of greenbacks with gold, a stable currency, an end to federal Reconstruction efforts in the South, the restoration of the rights of former Confederates, and civil service reform. In 1872 the Liberal Republicans held their own national convention, in which they produced a compromise platform condemning the Republicans' Radical Reconstruction policy, as well as government corruption, but they remained silent on the protective tariff. The delegates embraced a quixotic presidential candidate: **Horace Greeley**, the prominent editor of the *New York Tribune* and a longtime champion of just about every reform available. Greeley had promoted vegetarianism, socialism, and spiritualism. His image as an eccentric was complemented by his record of hostility to the Democrats, whose support the Liberals needed. The Democrats nevertheless swallowed the pill and gave their nomination to Greeley as the only hope of beating Grant.

The result was a foregone conclusion. Republican regulars duly endorsed Grant, Radical Reconstruction, and the protective tariff. Greeley carried only six southern and border states and none in the North. Grant won by 3,598,235 votes to Greeley's 2,834,761.

CONSERVATIVE RESURGENCE The KKK's impact on southern politics varied from state to state. In the Upper South it played only a modest role in facilitating a Democratic resurgence in local elections. But in the Deep South, Klan violence and intimidation had more substantial effects. In overwhelmingly black Yazoo County, Mississippi, vengeful whites used terrorism to reverse the political balance of power. In the 1873 elections the Republicans cast 2,449 votes and the Democrats 638; two years later the Democrats polled 4,049 votes, the Republicans 7. Throughout the

"What I Know about Raising the Devil"

With the tail and cloven hoof of the devil, Horace Greeley (center) leads a small band of Liberal Republicans in pursuit of incumbent president Ulysses S. Grant and his supporters in this 1872 cartoon.

South the activities of the Klan and other white supremacists weakened black and Republican morale, and in the North they encouraged a growing weariness with efforts to reconstruct the South and protect civil rights. "The plain truth is," noted *The New York Herald*, "the North has got tired of the Negro."

The erosion of northern interest in civil rights resulted from more than weariness, however. Western expansion, Indian wars, new economic opportunities, and political controversy over the tariff and the currency distracted attention from southern outrages against Republican rule and black rights. Given the violent efforts of reactionary whites to resist Reconstruction, it would have required far more patience and conviction to protect the civil rights of blacks than the North possessed, and far more resources than the pro-Reconstruction southerners could employ. In addition, after a devastating business panic that occurred in 1873 followed by a prolonged depression, desperate economic circumstances in the North and the South created new racial tensions that helped undermine federal efforts to promote racial justice in the former Confederacy. Republican control in the South gradually loosened as "Conservative" parties mobilized the white vote. Prewar political leaders reemerged to promote the antebellum Democratic goals of limited government, states' rights, and free trade. They politicized the race issue to excite the white electorate and intimidate black voters. Where persuasion failed to work, Democrats were willing to use chicanery. As one enthusiastic Democrat boasted, "The white and black Republicans may outvote us, but we can outcount them."

Republican political control collapsed in Virginia and Tennessee as early as 1869; in Georgia and North Carolina it collapsed in 1870, although North Carolina had a Republican governor until 1876. Reconstruction lasted longest in the Deep South states with the largest black population, where whites abandoned Klan masks for barefaced intimidation in paramilitary groups such as the Mississippi Rifle Club and the South Carolina Red Shirts. By 1876, Radical Republican regimes survived only in Louisiana, South Carolina, and Florida, and those collapsed after the elections of that year.

PANIC AND REDEMPTION   Economic distress followed close upon the public scandals besetting the Grant administration. Such developments help explain why northerners lost interest in Reconstruction. A contraction of the nation's money supply resulting from the withdrawal of greenbacks and investments in new railroads helped precipitate a financial crisis. During 1873 the market for railroad bonds turned sour as some twenty-five railroads defaulted on their interest payments. The prestigious investment bank of Jay Cooke and Company went bankrupt on September 18, 1873, and the ensuing stampede of investors eager to exchange securities for cash forced the stock market to close for ten days. The panic of 1873 set off a depression that lasted six years, the longest and most severe that Americans had yet suffered. Thousands of businesses went bankrupt, millions of people lost their jobs, and as usually occurs, voters blamed the party in power for their economic woes.

Hard times and political scandals hurt Republicans in the midterm elections of 1874. The Democrats won control of the House of Representatives and gained seats in the Senate. The new Democratic House launched inquiries into the scandals and unearthed further evidence of corruption in high places. The financial panic, meanwhile, focused attention once more on greenback currency.

Since the value of greenbacks was lower than that of gold, greenbacks had become the chief circulating medium. Most people spent greenbacks first and held their gold or used it to settle foreign accounts, thereby draining much gold out of the country. The postwar reduction of greenbacks in circulation, from $432 million to $356 million, had made for tight money. To relieve the currency shortage and stimulate business expansion, the Treasury issued more greenbacks. As usually happened during economic hard times in the nineteenth century, debtors, the people hurt most by depression, called upon the federal government to inflate the money supply so as to make it easier for them to pay their obligations.

For a time the advocates of paper money were riding high. But in 1874, Grant vetoed a bill to issue more greenbacks. Then, in his annual message, he called for the redemption of greenbacks in gold, making greenbacks "good as gold" and raising their value to a par with that of the gold dollar. Congress obliged by passing the Specie Resumption Act of 1875. The payment in gold to people who turned in their paper money began on January 1, 1879, after the Treasury had built a gold reserve for that purpose and reduced the value of the greenbacks in circulation. This act infuriated those promoting an inflationary monetary policy and prompted the formation of the Greenback party, which elected fourteen congressmen in 1878. The much-debated and very complex "money question" was destined to remain one of the most divisive issues in American politics.

THE COMPROMISE OF 1877   President Grant, despite the controversies swirling around him, wanted to run again in 1876, but many Republicans balked at the prospect of the nation's first three-term president. After all, the Democrats had devastated the Republicans in the 1874 congressional elections: the decisive Republican majority in the House had evaporated, and the Democrats had taken control. In the summer of 1875, Grant acknowledged the growing opposition to his renomination and announced his retirement. James Gillespie Blaine of Maine, former Speaker of the House and one of the nation's favorite orators, emerged as the Republican front-runner, but he, too, bore the taint of scandal. Letters in the possession of James Mulligan of Boston linked Blaine to dubious railroad dealings, and the "Mulligan letters" found their way into print.

The Republican Convention therefore eliminated Blaine and several other hopefuls in favor of Ohio's favorite son, Rutherford B. Hayes. Elected governor of Ohio three times, most recently as an advocate of gold rather than greenbacks, Hayes had also made a name for himself as a civil service reformer. But his chief virtue was that he offended neither Radicals nor reformers. As a journalist put it, he was "a third rate nonentity, whose only recommendation is that he is obnoxious to no one."

The Democratic Convention was abnormally harmonious from the start. The nomination went on the second ballot to Samuel J. Tilden, a wealthy corporation lawyer and reform governor of New York who had directed a campaign to overthrow the notorious Tweed ring controlling New York City politics.

The Compromise of 1877

This illustration represents the compromise between Republicans and southern Democrats that ended Radical Reconstruction.

The 1876 campaign raised no burning issues. Both candidates favored the trend toward relaxing federal authority and restoring white conservative rule in the South. In the absence of strong differences, Democrats aired the Republicans' dirty linen. In response, Republicans waved "the bloody shirt," which is to say that they linked the Democratic party to secession, civil war, and the outrages committed against Republicans in the South. As one Republican speaker insisted, "The man that assassinated Abraham Lincoln was a Democrat. . . . Soldiers, every scar you have on your heroic bodies was given you by a Democrat!"

Despite the lack of major issues, the 1876 election generated the most votes in American history up to that point. Early election returns pointed to a Tilden victory. Tilden enjoyed a 254,000-vote edge in the balloting and had won 184 electoral votes, just one short of a majority. Hayes had only 165 electoral votes, but the Republicans also claimed 19 doubtful votes from Florida, Louisiana, and South Carolina. The Democrats laid a counterclaim to 1 of Oregon's 3 electoral votes, but the Republicans had clearly carried that state. In the South the outcome was less certain, and given the fraud and intimidation perpetrated on both sides, nobody will ever know what might have happened if, to use a slogan of the day, "a free ballot and a fair count" had prevailed.

In all three of the disputed southern states, rival election boards sent in different returns. The Constitution offered no guidance in this unprecedented situation. Finally, on January 29, 1877, the Congress decided to set up a special Electoral Commission with fifteen members, five each from the House, the Senate, and the Supreme Court. The commission's decision went by a vote of 8 to 7 along party lines, in favor of Hayes. After much bluster and the threat of a filibuster by the Democrats, the House voted on March 2 to accept the report and declared Hayes elected by an electoral vote of 185 to 184.

Critical to this outcome was the defection of southern Democrats, who had made several informal agreements with the Republicans. On February 26, 1877, prominent Ohio Republicans (including future president James A. Garfield) and powerful southern Democrats struck a secret bargain at Wormley's Hotel in Washington, D.C. The Republicans promised that if Hayes were elected, he would withdraw the last federal troops from Louisiana and South Carolina, letting the Republican governments there collapse. In return, the Democrats promised to withdraw their opposition to Hayes, accept in good faith the Reconstruction amendments (including civil rights for blacks), and refrain from partisan reprisals against Republicans in the South.

THE END OF RECONSTRUCTION In 1877, new president Hayes withdrew federal troops from Louisiana and South Carolina, and those states' Republican governments collapsed soon thereafter. Over the next three decades the protection of black civil rights crumbled under the pressure of restored white rule in the South and the force of Supreme Court decisions narrowing the scope of the Reconstruction amendments to the Constitution. As a former slave observed in 1877, "The whole South—every state in the South—has got [back] into the hands of the very men that held us as slaves."

Radical Reconstruction never offered more than an uncertain commitment to black civil rights and social equality. Yet it left an enduring legacy— the Thirteenth, Fourteenth, and Fifteenth Amendments—not dead but dormant, waiting to be reawakened. If Reconstruction did not provide social equality or substantial economic opportunities for African Americans, it did create the foundation for future advances. It was a revolution, sighed former governor of North Carolina Jonathan Worth, and "nobody can anticipate the action of revolutions."

CHAPTER SUMMARY

- **Reconstruction** Abraham Lincoln and his successor, southerner Andrew Johnson, wanted a lenient and quick plan for Reconstruction. Lincoln's assassination made many northerners favor the Radical Republicans, who wanted to end the grasp of the old planter class on the South's society and economy. Congressional Reconstruction included the stipulation that to reenter the Union, former Confederate states had to ratify the Fourteenth and Fifteenth Amendments. Congress also passed the Military Reconstruction Act, which attempted to protect the voting rights and civil rights of African Americans.

- **Southern Violence** Many white southerners blamed their poverty on freed slaves and Yankees. White mobs attacked blacks in 1866 in Memphis and New Orleans. That year, the Ku Klux Klan was formed as a social club; its members soon began to intimidate freedmen and white Republicans. Despite government action, violence continued and even escalated in the South.

- **Freed Slaves** Newly freed slaves suffered economically. Most did not have the resources to succeed in the aftermath of the war's devastation. There was no redistribution of land; former slaves were given their freedom but nothing else. The Freedmen's Bureau attempted to educate and aid freed slaves and reunite families. Many former slaves found comfort in their families and the independent churches they established. Some took part in state and local government under the last, radical phase of Reconstruction.

- **Grant Administration** During Ulysses S. Grant's administration fiscal issues dominated politics. Paper money (greenbacks) was regarded as inflationary; and agrarian and debtor groups opposed its withdrawal from circulation. Many members of Grant's administration were corrupt; scandals involved an attempt to corner the gold market, construction of the intercontinental railroad, and the whiskey ring's plan to steal millions of dollars in tax revenue.

- **End of Reconstruction** Most southern states had completed the requirements of Reconstruction by 1876. The presidential election returns of that year were so close that a special commission was established to count contested electoral votes. A decision hammered out at a secret meeting gave the presidency to the Republican, Rutherford B. Hayes; in return, the Democrats were promised that the last federal troops would be withdrawn from Louisiana and South Carolina, putting an end to the Radical Republican administrations in the southern states.

CHRONOLOGY

1862	Congress passes the Morrill Land Grant Act
	Congress guarantees the construction of a transcontinental railroad
	Congress passes the Homestead Act
1864	Lincoln refuses to sign the Wade-Davis Bill
1865	Congress sets up the Freedmen's Bureau
April 14, 1865	Lincoln is assassinated
1866	Ku Klux Klan is organized
	Congress passes the Civil Rights Act
1867	Congress passes the Military Reconstruction Act
	Congress passes the Tenure of Office Act
1868	Fourteenth Amendment is ratified
	Congress impeaches President Andrew Johnson; the Senate fails to convict him
1877	Compromise of 1877 ends Reconstruction

KEY TERMS & NAMES

Part Five

GROWING PAINS

The Federal victory in 1865 restored the Union and in the process helped accelerate America's stunning transformation into an agricultural empire and an urban-industrial nation-state. A distinctly national consciousness began to displace the regional emphases of the antebellum era. During and after the Civil War, the Republican-led Congress pushed through legislation to foster industrial and commercial development and western expansion. In the process of ruthlessly exploiting the resources of the continent, the United States abandoned the Jeffersonian dream of a decentralized agrarian republic and began to forge a dynamic new industrial economy nurtured by an increasingly national and even international market for American goods.

After 1865, many Americans turned their attention to the unfinished business of settling a continent and completing an urban-industrial revolution begun before the war. Fueled by innovations in mass production and mass marketing, huge corporations began to dominate the economy. As the prominent social theorist William Graham Sumner remarked, the process of industrial development "controls us all because we are all in it. It creates the conditions of our own existence, sets the limits of our social activity, and regulates the bonds of our social relations."

The Industrial Revolution was not only an urban phenomenon; it transformed rural life as well. Those who got in the way of the new emphasis on large-scale, highly mechanized commercial agriculture and ranching were brusquely pushed aside. Farm folk, as one New Englander stressed, "must understand farming as a business; if they do not it will go hard with them." The friction between new market forces and traditional folkways generated political revolts and social unrest during the last quarter of the nineteenth century. Fault lines appeared throughout the social order, and they unleashed tremors that exerted what one writer called "a seismic shock, a cyclonic violence" upon the political culture.

The clash between tradition and modernity peaked during the 1890s, one of the most strife-ridden decades in American history. A deep depression, agrarian unrest, and labor violence unleashed fears of class warfare. This turbulent situation transformed the presidential-election campaign of 1896 into a clash between rival visions of America's future. The Republican candidate, William McKinley, campaigned on behalf of modern urban-industrial values. By contrast, William Jennings Bryan, the nominee of the Democratic and Populist parties, was an eloquent defender of America's rural past. McKinley's victory proved to be a watershed in American political and social history. By 1900 the United States would emerge as one of the world's greatest industrial powers, and it would thereafter assume a new leadership role in world affairs—for good and for ill.

18

BIG BUSINESS AND ORGANIZED LABOR

FOCUS QUESTIONS

 wwnorton.com/studyspace

- What fueled the growth of the post–Civil War economy?
- What roles were played by leading entrepreneurs like John D. Rockefeller, Andrew Carnegie, and J. Pierpont Morgan?
- Who composed the labor force of the period, and what were labor's main grievances?
- What led to the rise of labor unions?

America emerged as an industrial and agricultural giant in the late nineteenth century. Blessed with vast natural resources, impressive technological advances, relentless population growth and entrepreneurial energy, and little government regulation, the economy grew more rapidly and changed more dramatically than ever before. Within three generations after the Civil War, the predominantly rural nation burst forth as the world's preeminent commercial, agricultural, and industrial power. By 1900, the United States dominated global markets in steel and oil, wheat and cotton. Corporations grew in size and power, and social tensions and political corruption worsened with the rising scale of business enterprise.

THE RISE OF BIG BUSINESS

In the decades after the Civil War, huge corporations came to dominate the economy—as well as political and social life. As businesses grew, their owners sought to integrate all the processes of production and distribution of goods into single companies, thus creating even larger firms. Others grew by mergers, joining forces with their competitors in an effort to dominate entire industries. This process of industrial development transformed the nation's economy and social life. It also sparked widespread dissent and the emergence of an organized labor movement representing wage workers.

Many factors converged to help accelerate economic growth after the Civil War. The nation's unparalleled natural resources—forests, mineral wealth, rivers—along with a rapidly expanding population, were crucial ingredients. At the same time, inventors and business owners developed more efficient, labor-saving machinery and mass-production techniques that spurred dramatic advances in productivity and efficiency. Innovative, bold leadership was another crucial factor spurring economic transformation. A group of shrewd, determined, and energetic entrepreneurs took advantage of fertile business opportunities to create huge new enterprises. Federal and state politicians after the Civil War actively encouraged the growth of business by imposing high tariffs on foreign imports as a means of blunting competition and by providing land and cash to finance railroads and other transportation improvements. At the same time that the federal government was issuing massive land grants to railroads and land speculators, it was also distributing 160-acre homesteads to citizens, including single women and freed slaves, through the important Homestead Act of 1862.

Equally important in propelling the post–Civil War economic boom was what government did not do in the decades after the Civil War: it did not regulate the activities of big businesses, nor did it provide any oversight of business operations or working conditions. Business leaders spent a lot of time—and money—ensuring that government stayed out of their businesses. In fact, political corruption was so rampant that it was routine. Business leaders usually got what they wanted from Congress and state legislators—even if they had to pay for it. The collaboration between elected officials and business executives was so commonplace that in 1868 the New York state legislature legalized the bribery of politicians.

At the same time that the industrial sector was witnessing an ever-increasing concentration of large companies, the agricultural sector by 1870 was also experiencing such rapid growth that it had become the world's leader, fueling the rest of the economy by providing wheat and corn to be milled into flour and meal. With the advent of the commercial cattle industry, the processes of slaughtering and packing meat themselves became major industries. So the farm sector directly stimulated the industrial sector of the economy. A national government-subsidized network of railroads connecting the East and West Coasts played a crucial role in the development of related industries and in the evolution of an interconnected national market for goods and services. The industrial transformation also benefited from an abundance of power sources—water, wood, coal, oil, and electricity—that were inexpensive compared with those of the other nations of the world.

THE SECOND INDUSTRIAL REVOLUTION The Second Industrial Revolution began in the mid–nineteenth century and was centered in the United States and Germany. It was spurred by three related developments. The first was the creation of interconnected transportation and communication networks, which facilitated the emergence of a national and even an international market for American goods and services. Contributing to this development were the completion of the national telegraph and railroad networks; the emergence of steamships, which were much larger and faster than sailing ships; and the laying of the undersea telegraph cable, which spanned the Atlantic Ocean and connected the United States with Europe.

During the 1880s a second major breakthrough—the widespread application of electrical power—accelerated the pace of industrial change. Electricity created dramatic advances in the power and efficiency of industrial machinery. It also spurred urban growth through the addition of electric trolleys and subways, and it greatly enhanced the production of steel and chemicals.

The third major catalyst for the Second Industrial Revolution was the systematic application of scientific research to industrial processes. Laboratories staffed by graduates of new research universities sprouted up across the country, and scientists and engineers discovered dramatic new ways to improve industrial processes. Researchers figured out, for example, how to refine kerosene and gasoline from crude oil and how to improve steel production. Inventors developed new products—telephones, typewriters, adding machines, sewing machines, cameras, elevators, and farm machinery—that resulted in lower prices for an array of consumer items. These advances in turn expanded the scope and scale of industrial organizations. Capital-intensive industries such as steel and oil, as well as processed food and tobacco, took advantage of new technologies to gain economies of scale that emphasized maximum production and national as well as international marketing and distribution.

RAILROADS More than any other technological innovation, the railroads symbolized the urban-industrial revolution. No other form of transportation exercised as much influence in the development of post–Civil War America. Railroads shrunk time and distance. They moved masses of people and goods faster and farther than any other form of transportation. It was the advent of the nation's railroad network that prompted the creation of uniform national and international time zones and spurred the use of wrist-watches, for the trains were scheduled to run on time. A British traveler in America in the 1860s said that a town's connection to a railroad was "the first necessity of life, and gives the only hope of wealth." Although the first great wave of railroad building occurred in the 1850s, the most spectacular growth took place during the quarter century after the Civil War. From about thirty-five thousand miles of track in 1865, the national rail network grew to nearly two hundred thousand miles by 1897. The transcontinental rail lines led the way, and they helped populate the Great Plains and the Far West. Such a sprawling railroad system was expensive, and the long-term debt required to finance it would become a major cause of the financial panic of 1893 and the ensuing depression.

But the railroads created problems as well as blessings. Too many of them were built, often in the wrong places, at a time when they were not needed. In their race to build new rail lines, companies allowed for dangerous working conditions that caused thousands of laborers to be killed or injured. Shoddy construction caused tragic accidents and required rickety bridges and trestles to be rebuilt. Numerous railroads were poorly or even criminally managed and went bankrupt. The lure of enormous profits helped to corrupt the political system as the votes of politicians were "bought" with cash or shares of stock in the railroad companies. Railroad executives essentially created the modern practice of political "lobbying," and they came to exercise a dangerous degree of influence over both the economy and the political system. As Charles Francis Adams Jr., the head of the Union Pacific Railroad, acknowledged, "Our method of doing business is founded upon lying, cheating, and stealing—all bad things."

BUILDING THE TRANSCONTINENTALS The renewal of railroad building after the Civil War filled out the rail network east of the Mississippi River. Gradually, tracks in the South that had been destroyed during the war were rebuilt, and a web of new trunk lines was added throughout the country. But the most spectacular achievements were the monumental transcontinental lines built west of the Mississippi River across desolate plains, over roaring rivers and deep canyons, and around as well as through the nation's tallest mountains.

Before the Civil War, differences between the North and South over the choice of routes had held up the start of a transcontinental line. Secession and the departure of southern congressmen for the Confederacy in 1861 finally permitted Republicans in Congress to pass the Pacific Railway Act in 1862, which authorized the construction of a rail line along a north-central

Transcontinental railroads

Using picks, shovels, wheelbarrows, and horse-drawn carts, Chinese laborers largely helped to construct the Central Pacific track.

route, to be built by the Union Pacific Railroad westward from Omaha, Nebraska, and by the Central Pacific Railroad eastward from Sacramento, California. Both companies began construction during the war, but most of the work was done after 1865. The first transcontinental railroads were utterly dependent on government support. They received huge loans, massive grants of "public" land taken from the Indians, and lavish cash subsidies from the federal government.

The executives and financiers directing the transcontinental railroads often cut corners, bribed legislators, and manipulated accounts to line their own pockets. They also ruthlessly used federal troops to suppress the Plains Indians. But the shenanigans of the railroad barons do not diminish the fact that the transcontinental railroads were, in the words, of General William Tecumseh Sherman, the "work of giants." Building rail lines across the West involved heroic feats of daring by workers and engineers who laid the rails, erected the bridges and trestles, and gouged out the tunnels under dangerous working conditions and harsh weather. The transcontinental railroads tied the nation together, changed the economic and political landscape, and enabled the United States to emerge as a world power.

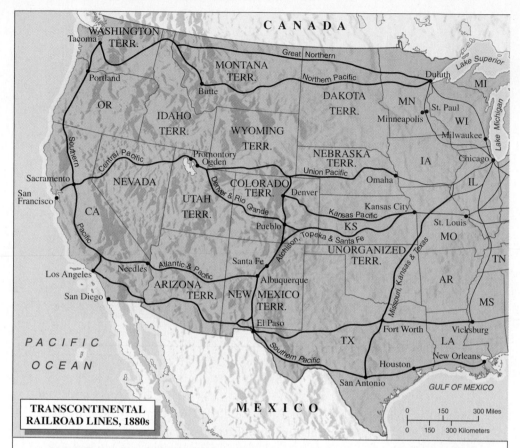

TRANSCONTINENTAL RAILROAD LINES, 1880s

What was the route of the first transcontinental railroad, and why was it not in the South? Who built the railroads? How were they financed?

It took armies of laborers to build the railroads. Some ten thousand men worked on the two railroads as they raced to connect with one another. The Union Pacific work crews, composed of former Union and Confederate soldiers, former slaves, and Irish and German immigrants, coped with bad roads, water shortages, extreme weather conditions, Indian attacks, and frequent accidents and injuries. The Central Pacific crews were mainly Chinese workers lured to America first by the California gold rush and then by railroad jobs. Most of these "coolie" laborers were single men intent upon accumulating money and returning to their homeland, where they could then afford to marry and buy a parcel of land. Their temporary status and dream of a good life back in China apparently made them more willing than American laborers to endure the low pay of railroad work and the dangerous working conditions. Many railroad construction workers died on the job.

All sorts of issues delayed the effort to finish the transcontinental line. Iron prices spiked. Broken treaties prompted Indian raids. Blizzards shut down work for weeks. Fifty-seven miles east of Sacramento, construction crews encountered the towering Sierra Nevada Mountains, which they had to cross before reaching more level terrain in Nevada. The Union Pacific had built 1,086 miles compared with the Central Pacific's 689 when the race ended on the salt flats at Promontory, Utah. There, on May 10, 1869, former California governor Leland Stanford drove a gold spike symbolizing the railroad's completion. Before the end of the century, five major trunk lines existed, supplemented by connections that enabled the construction of other transcontinental routes.

INVENTIONS SPUR MANUFACTURING The story of manufacturing after the Civil War shows much the same pattern of expansion and merger in old and new industries. Technological innovations spurred phenomenal

The Union Pacific meets the Central Pacific

The celebration of the completion of the first transcontinental railroad, Promontory, Utah, May 10, 1869.

increases in industrial productivity. The U.S. Patent Office, which had recorded only 276 inventions during its first decade of existence, the 1790s, registered almost 235,000 new patents a century later, in the 1890s. The list of commercial innovations after the Civil War was lengthy: barbed wire, farm implements, the air brake for trains (1868), steam turbines, electrical devices, typewriters (1867), vacuum cleaners (1869), and countless others. Before the end of the century, the internal-combustion engine and the motion picture were stimulating new industries that would emerge in the twentieth century.

These technological advances transformed daily life. Few if any inventions of the time could rival the importance of the telephone, which twenty-nine-year-old inventor Alexander Graham Bell patented in 1876. To promote the new device transmitting voices over wires, the inventor and his supporters formed the Bell Telephone Company, which was eventually surpassed by the American Telephone and Telegraph Company.

In the development of electrical industries, the name Thomas Alva Edison stands above those of other inventors. In his laboratory in Menlo Park, New Jersey, Edison invented the phonograph in 1877 and the first light bulb in 1879. Altogether he created or perfected hundreds of new devices and processes, including the storage battery, Dictaphone, mimeograph, electric motor, electric transmission, and the motion picture camera and projector.

Until 1880 or so the world was lit by flickering oil and gas lamps. In 1882 the Edison Electric Illuminating Company supplied electrical current to eighty-five customers in New York City, beginning the great electric utility industry. The invention of electric motors enabled factories to locate wherever they wished; they no longer had to cluster around waterfalls and coal deposits for a ready supply of energy. The electric motor also led to the development of elevators and streetcars. Buildings could go higher with electric elevators, and cities could spawn suburbs because of electric streetcars providing transportation.

Entrepreneurs

Thomas Alva Edison and George Westinghouse were rare examples of inventors with the luck and foresight to get rich from the industries they created. The great captains of commerce during the Gilded Age were more often pure entrepreneurs rather than inventors, outsized men who were ruthless competitors adept at increasing production, lowering prices, and garnering efficiencies. Several post–Civil War entrepreneurs stand out for both their achievements and their special contributions: John D. Rockefeller, Andrew Carnegie, and J. Pierpont Morgan.

ROCKEFELLER AND THE OIL TRUST   Born in New York, **John D. Rockefeller** moved as a youth to Cleveland, Ohio. Soon thereafter his father abandoned the family. Raised by his mother, a devout Baptist, Rockefeller developed a passion for systematic organization and self-discipline. Scrupulously honest but fiercely ambitious, he was obsessed with precision, order, and tidiness. And early on he decided to bring order and rationality to the chaotic oil industry.

John D. Rockefeller

His Standard Oil Company dominated the oil industry.

The railroad and shipping connections around Cleveland made it a strategic location for servicing the booming oil fields of western Pennsylvania. The first oil well in the United States began producing in 1859 in Titusville, Pennsylvania, and led to the Pennsylvania oil rush of the 1860s. Because oil could be refined into kerosene, which was widely used in lighting, heating, and cooking, the economic importance of the oil rush soon outstripped that of the California gold rush of just ten years before. Well before the end of the Civil War, drilling derricks checkered western Pennsylvania, and refineries sprang up in Pittsburgh and Cleveland. Of the two cities, Cleveland had the edge in rail service, so Rockefeller focused his energies there.

Rockefeller recognized the potential profits in refining oil, and in 1870 he incorporated his various interests, naming the enterprise the **Standard Oil Company of Ohio**. Although Rockefeller was the largest refiner, he wanted to weed out the competition in order to raise prices. He bought out most of his Cleveland competitors; those who resisted were forced out. By 1879, Standard Oil controlled over 90 percent of the oil refining in the country.

Much of Rockefeller's success was based upon his determination to reduce expenses and eliminate waste as well as "pay nobody a profit." Instead of depending upon the products or services of other firms, known as middlemen, Standard Oil produced its own oil, barrels, and whatever else it needed—in economic terms, this is called vertical integration. The company also kept large amounts of cash reserves to make it independent of banks in case of a crisis. Furthermore, Rockefeller gained control of his transportation needs. With Standard Oil owning most of the pipelines leading to railroads, plus the railroad tank cars and the oil-storage facilities, it was able to dissuade the railroads from serving its eastern competitors. Those rivals that had insisted upon holding out rather than selling their enterprise to Rockefeller then faced a giant marketing organization capable of driving them to the wall with price wars.

To consolidate their scattered business interests under more efficient control, Rockefeller and his advisers resorted to a new legal device: in 1882 they organized the Standard Oil Trust. All thirty-seven stockholders in various Standard Oil enterprises conveyed their stock to nine trustees, receiving "trust certificates" in return, which paid them annual dividends from the company's earnings. The nine trustees thereby controlled all the varied Standard Oil companies.

But the trust device, widely copied by other companies in the 1880s, proved vulnerable to prosecution under state laws against monopoly or restraint of trade. In 1892, Ohio's supreme court ordered the Standard Oil Trust dissolved. Gradually, however, Rockefeller perfected the idea of the holding company: a company that controlled other companies by holding all or at least a majority of their stock. He was convinced that such big business was a natural result of capitalism at work. "It is too late," he declared in 1899, "to argue about the advantages of [huge] industrial combinations. They are a necessity." That year, Rockefeller brought his empire under the direction of the Standard Oil Company of New Jersey, a gigantic holding company. Though less vulnerable to prosecution under state law, some holding companies were broken up by the Sherman Anti-Trust Act of 1890.

The rise of oil

Wooden derricks crowd the farm of John Benninghoff in Oil Creek, Pennsylvania, in the 1860s.

Rockefeller not only made a colossal fortune, but he also gave much of it away, mostly to support education and medicine. A man of simple tastes who opposed the use of tobacco and alcohol and believed his fortune was a public trust awarded by God, he became the world's leading philanthropist. He donated more than $500 million during his ninety-eight-year lifetime. "I have always regarded it as a religious duty," Rockefeller said late in life, "to get all I could honorably and to give all I could."

CARNEGIE AND THE STEEL INDUSTRY   Like Rockefeller, **Andrew Carnegie** experienced an uncommon rise from poverty to riches. Born in Scotland, he migrated in 1848 with his family to Allegheny County, Pennsylvania. Then thirteen, he started work as a bobbin boy in a textile mill. In 1853 he became personal secretary and telegrapher to Thomas Scott, then district superintendent of the Pennsylvania Railroad and later its president. When Scott moved up, Carnegie took his place as superintendent. During the Civil War, when Scott became assistant secretary of war in charge of transportation, Carnegie went with him and developed a military telegraph system.

Carnegie kept on moving—from telegraphy to railroading to bridge building and then to steelmaking and investments. Intelligent, energetic, practical, and ferociously ambitious, he wanted not simply to compete in an industry; he wanted to dominate it. To do so he was willing to abuse his power and become a compulsive liar.

Until the mid–nineteenth century, steel could be made only from wrought iron—itself expensive—and only in small quantities. Then, in 1855, Briton Sir Henry Bessemer invented what became known as the Bessemer converter, a process by which steel could be produced directly and quickly from pig iron (crude iron made in a blast furnace). In 1873, Carnegie resolved to concentrate on steel. Steel was the miracle material of the post–Civil War era, not because it was new but because Bessemer's process had made it suddenly cheap. As more steel was produced, its price dropped and uses soared. In 1860 the United States had produced only 13,000 tons of steel. By 1880, production had reached 1.4 million tons.

Andrew Carnegie
Steel magnate and business icon.

Andrew Carnegie was never a technical expert on steel. He was a promoter, salesman, and organizer with a gift for hiring men of expert ability. He insisted upon up-to-date machinery and equipment and used times of recession to expand cheaply by purchasing struggling companies. He also preached to his employees a philosophy of continual innovation in order to reduce operating costs.

Carnegie believed that he and other captains of industry, however harsh their methods, were public benefactors. In his best-remembered essay, "The Gospel of Wealth" (1889), he argued that, "Not evil, but good, has come to the race from the accumulation of wealth by those who have the ability and energy that produces it." He applied Charles Darwin's concept of evolution to society, arguing that the law of human competition is "best for the trade, because it insures the survival of the fittest in every department."

Not only did Carnegie make an incredible amount of money; like Rockefeller, he also gave much of it away. After retiring from business at age sixty-five, he devoted himself to dispensing his fortune for the public good. He called himself a "distributor" of wealth (he disliked the term *philanthropy*). He gave money to many universities, built 1,700 public libraries, and helped fund numerous hospitals, parks, halls for meetings and concerts, swimming pools, and church buildings. He also donated eight hundred organs to churches around the world.

J. PIERPONT MORGAN, FINANCIER   Unlike Rockefeller and Carnegie, **J. Pierpont Morgan** was born to wealth. His father was a partner in a London bank. After attending boarding school in Switzerland and university in Germany, the younger Morgan was sent in 1857 to work in a New York firm representing his father's interests and in 1860 set himself up as its New York agent under the name J. Pierpont Morgan and Company. That firm, under various names, channeled European capital into the United States and grew into a financial power in its own right.

Morgan was an investment banker, which meant that he would buy corporate stocks and bonds wholesale and sell them at a profit. The growth of large corporations put investment firms such as Morgan's in an increasingly strategic position in the economy. Since the investment business depended upon the general good health of client companies, investment bankers became involved in the operation of their clients' firms, demanding seats on the boards of directors so as to influence company policies.

Like John D. Rockefeller, J. P. Morgan sought to consolidate rival firms into giant trusts. Morgan realized early on that railroads were the key modern industry, and he acquired and reorganized one line after another. By the

1890s, he alone controlled a sixth of the nation's railway system. To Morgan, an imperious, domineering man, the stability brought by his operations helped the economy and the public. His crowning triumph was consolidation of the steel industry. After a rapid series of mergers in the iron and steel industry, he bought out Andrew Carnegie's huge steel and iron holdings in 1901. In rapid succession, Morgan added other steel interests as well as the Rockefeller iron ore holdings in Minnesota's Mesabi Range and a Great Lakes shipping fleet. The new United States Steel Corporation, a holding company for these varied interests, was a marvel of the new century, the first billion-dollar corporation, the climactic event in the age of relentless business consolidation.

J. Pierpont Morgan

Morgan is shown here in a famous 1903 portrait by Edward Steichen.

THE WORKING CLASS

The captains of industry and finance dominated economic life during the so-called Gilded Age. Their innovations and their businesses provided a rapidly growing American population with jobs. But it was the laboring classes who actually produced the iron and steel, coal and oil, beef and pork, and the array of new consumer items filling city department stores and the shelves of "general" stores.

SOCIAL TRENDS Accompanying the spread of huge corporations after the Civil War was a rising standard of living for most people. If the rich were getting richer, a lot of other people were at least getting better off. But disparities in the distribution of wealth grew wider during the second half of the nineteenth century. In both 1860 and 1900, the richest 2 percent of American families owned more than a third of the nation's wealth, while the top 10 percent owned almost three fourths of it. The continuing demand for unskilled or semiskilled workers, meanwhile, attracted new groups entering the workforce at the bottom: immigrants above all, but also growing numbers of women and children. Because of a long-term decline in prices and the cost of living, real wages and earnings in manufacturing went up about 50 percent between 1860 and 1890 and another 37 percent from 1890 to 1914. By modern-day standards, however, working conditions were dreary and often dangerous. The average workweek was fifty-nine hours, or nearly six ten-hour days, but that was only an average. Most steelworkers put in a twelve-hour day, and as late as the 1920s a great many worked a seven-day, eighty-four-hour week.

Although wage levels were rising overall, working and living conditions remained precarious. In the crowded tenements of major cities, the death rate was much higher than that in the countryside. Factories often maintained poor health and safety conditions. American industry had the highest accident rate in the world. In 1913, for instance, there were some twenty-five thousand workplace fatalities and seven hundred thousand serious job-related injuries. The United States was the only industrial nation in the world that had no workmen's compensation program to provide financial support for workers injured on the job.

CHILD LABOR   A growing number of wage laborers after the Civil War were children—boys and girls who worked full-time for meager wages under unhealthy conditions. Young people had of course always worked in America: farms required everyone to pitch in. After the Civil War, however, millions of children took up work outside the home, operating machines, sorting coal, stitching clothes, shucking oysters, peeling shrimp, canning food, blowing glass, and tending looms. Parents desperate for income believed they had no choice but to put their children to work. By 1880, one out of every six children in the nation was working full-time; by 1900, there were almost 2 million child laborers in the United States. In southern cotton mills, where few African Americans were hired, a fourth of the employees were below the age of fifteen, with half of the children younger than twelve. Children as young as eight were laboring alongside adults twelve hours a day, six days a week. This meant they received little or no education and had little time for play or parental nurturance.

Factories, mills, mines, and canneries were dangerous places, especially for children. Few machines had safety devices, and few factories or mills had ventilating fans or fire escapes. Throughout Appalachia, soot-smeared boys worked deep in the coal mines. In New England and the South, thousands of young girls worked in dusty textile mills, brushing away lint from the clacking machines and retying broken threads. Children suffered three times as many accidents as adult workers, and respiratory diseases were common in the unventilated buildings. A child working in a textile mill was only half as likely to reach the age of twenty as a child outside a mill. Although some states passed laws limiting the number of hours children could work and establishing minimum-age requirements, they were rarely enforced and often ignored. By 1881 only seven states, mostly in New England, had laws requiring children to be at least twelve before they worked for wages. Yet the only proof required by employers in such states was a statement from a child's parents. Working-class and immigrant parents were often so desperate for income that they forged work permits for their children or taught them to lie about their age to keep a job.

DISORGANIZED PROTEST Under these circumstances it was very difficult for workers to organize unions. Most civic leaders respected property rights more than the rights of labor; they readily deferred to the wishes of business leaders. Many business executives believed that a "labor supply" was simply another commodity to be procured at the lowest possible price. Among factory workers and miners only recently removed from an agrarian world of independent farmers, the idea of labor unions was slow to take hold. And much of the workforce was made up of immigrant workers from a variety of cultures. They spoke different languages and harbored ethnic animosities. Nonetheless, with or without unions, workers staged impromptu strikes in response to wage cuts and other grievances. Such action often led to violence, however, and two incidents of the 1870s colored much of the public's view of labor unions thereafter.

THE GREAT RAILROAD STRIKE OF 1877 After the financial panic of 1873 and the ensuing depression, the major rail lines in the East had cut wages. In 1877, they announced another 10 percent wage cut, which led most of the railroad workers at Martinsburg, West Virginia, to walk off the job and block the tracks. Walkouts and sympathy demonstrations spread spontaneously from Maryland to California. The railroad strike soon engulfed hundreds of cities and towns, leaving in its wake over a hundred people dead and millions of dollars in property destroyed. In Pittsburgh thousands of striking workers burned thirty-nine buildings and destroyed over a thousand rail cars and locomotives. Nonstriking rail workers were harassed and assaulted. In San Francisco the strikers took out their wrath on Chinese immigrants. Such racist populism was commonplace across the Far West. Militiamen called in from Philadelphia managed to disperse one crowd at the cost of twenty-six lives but then found themselves besieged in the railroad's roundhouse, where they disbanded and shot their way out.

Federal troops finally quelled the widespread violence. Looting, rioting, and burning went on for another day until the frenzy wore itself out. A reporter described the scene as "the most horrible ever witnessed, except in the carnage of war. There were fifty miles of hot rails, ten tracks side by side, with as many miles of ties turned into glowing coals and tons on tons of iron car skeletons and wheels almost at white heat." Eventually the disgruntled workers, lacking organized bargaining power, had no choice but to drift back to work. The strike failed.

For many Americans, the railroad strike raised the specter of a worker-based social revolution. As a Pittsburgh newspaper warned, "This may be the beginning of a great civil war in this country between labor and capital." Equally disturbing to those in positions of corporate and political power was the presence of many women among the protesters. A Baltimore journalist noted that the "singular part of the disturbances is the very active part taken by the women, who are the wives and mothers of the [railroad] firemen." From the point of view of organized labor, however, the Great Railroad Strike demonstrated potential union strength and the need for tighter organization.

THE SAND-LOT INCIDENT   In California the railroad strike indirectly gave rise to a working-class political movement. In 1877, a meeting in a San Francisco sand lot intended to express sympathy for the railroad strikers ended with attacks on some passing Chinese. Within a few days, sporadic anti-Chinese riots had led to a mob attack on Chinatown. The depression of the 1870s had hit the West Coast especially hard, and the Chinese were handy scapegoats for frustrated white laborers who believed the Asians had taken their jobs. Soon an Irish immigrant, Denis Kearney, had organized the Workingmen's Party of California, whose platform called for the United States to stop Chinese immigration. A gifted agitator who had only recently become a naturalized American, Kearney harangued the "sand lotters" about the "foreign peril" and assaulted the rich railroad barons for exploiting the poor. The Workingmen's movement peaked in 1879, when it elected members to the state legislature and the mayor of San Francisco. Kearney lacked the gift for building a durable movement, but as his infant party fragmented, his anti-Chinese theme became a national issue—in 1882, Congress voted to prohibit Chinese immigration for ten years.

TOWARD PERMANENT UNIONS   As the size and power of railroad companies and corporations increased, workers felt the need to increase their leverage as well. Efforts to build a national labor union movement gained momentum during the second half of the nineteenth century. Earlier efforts, in the 1830s and 1840s, had largely been dominated by reformers with schemes that ranged from free homesteads to utopian socialism. But the 1850s had seen the beginning of "job-conscious" unions in selected skilled trades. By 1860 there were about twenty such craft unions. During the Civil War, because of the demand for skilled labor, those unions grew in strength and number.

Yet there was no overall federation of such groups until 1866, when the National Labor Union (NLU) convened in Baltimore. The NLU comprised delegates from labor and reform groups more interested in political and social reform than in bargaining with employers. The groups espoused ideas such as the eight-hour workday, workers' cooperatives, greenbackism (the printing of paper money to inflate the currency and thereby relieve debtors), and equal rights for women and African Americans. After the head of the union died suddenly, its support fell away quickly, and by 1872, the NLU had disbanded. The NLU was not a total failure, however. It was influential in persuading Congress to enact an eight-hour workday for federal employees and to repeal the 1864 Contract Labor Act, passed during the Civil War to encourage the importation of laborers by allowing employers to pay for their passage to America. Employers had taken advantage of the Contract Labor Act to recruit foreign laborers willing to work for lower wages than their American counterparts.

THE KNIGHTS OF LABOR   Before the NLU collapsed, another labor group of national standing had emerged: the Noble Order of the **Knights of Labor**, a name that evoked the aura of medieval guilds. The founder of the Knights of Labor, Uriah S. Stephens, a Philadelphia tailor, was a habitual joiner involved with several secret orders, including the Masons. His early training for the Baptist ministry also affected his outlook. Secrecy, he felt, along with a semireligious ritual, would protect members from retaliation by employers and create a sense of solidarity.

The Knights of Labor, started in 1869, grew slowly, but during the depression of the 1870s, as other unions collapsed, it spread more rapidly. In 1878 its first general assembly established it as a national organization. Its preamble and platform endorsed the reforms advanced by previous workingmen's groups, including the creation of bureaus of labor statistics and mechanics' lien laws (to ensure payment of salaries), elimination of convict-labor competition, establishment of the eight-hour day, and use of paper currency. One plank in the platform, far ahead of the times, called for equal pay for equal work by men and women. Throughout its existence the Knights of Labor emphasized reform measures and preferred boycotts to strikes as a way to put pressure on employers. The Knights of Labor also proposed to organize worker cooperatives that would enable members, collectively, to own their own large-scale manufacturing and mining operations. The Knights allowed as members all who had ever worked for wages, except lawyers, doctors, bankers, and those who sold liquor. Theoretically it was one big union of all workers, skilled and unskilled, regardless of race, color, creed, or sex.

In 1879, Terence V. Powderly, the thirty-year-old mayor of Scranton, Pennsylvania, succeeded Stephens as head of the Knights of Labor. Born of Irish immigrant parents, Powderly had started working for a railroad at age sixteen. In many ways he was unsuited to his new job as head of the Knights of Labor. He was frail, sensitive to criticism, and indecisive at critical moments. He was temperamentally opposed to strikes, and when they did occur, he did not always support the local groups involved. Yet the Knights owed their greatest growth to strikes that occurred under his leadership. In the 1880s the Knights increased their membership from about one hundred thousand to more than seven hundred thousand. In 1886, however, the organization peaked and went into rapid decline after the failure of a railroad strike.

ANARCHISM The increasingly violent tensions between labor and management during the late nineteenth century in the United States and Europe helped generate the doctrine of anarchism. Anarchists believed that government—any government—was in itself an abusive device used by the

Members of the Knights of Labor

This national union was more egalitarian than most of its contemporaries.

rich and powerful to oppress and exploit the working poor. Anarchists dreamed of the eventual disappearance of government altogether, and many of them believed that the transition to such a stateless society could be hurried along by promoting revolutionary action among the masses. One favored tactic was the use of dramatic acts of violence against representatives of the government. Many European anarchists emigrated to the United States during the last quarter of the nineteenth century, bringing with them their belief in the impact of "propaganda of the deed."

THE HAYMARKET AFFAIR Labor-related violence increased during the 1880s as the gap between the rich and working poor widened. Between 1880 and 1900, 6.6 million hourly workers participated in more than 23,000 strikes nationwide. Chicago, the fastest growing city in the nation, was a hotbed of labor unrest and a magnet for immigrants, especially German and Irish laborers, some of whom were socialists or anarchists who endorsed violence as a means of transforming the capitalist system. Their foremost demand was for an eight-hour working day.

What came to be called the Haymarket affair grew indirectly out of prolonged agitation for an eight-hour workday. In 1884, Knights of Labor organizers set May 1, 1886, as the deadline for adopting the eight-hour workday. When the deadline passed, forty thousand Chicago workers went on strike. On May 3, 1886, violence erupted at the McCormick Reaper Works plant, where farm equipment was made. Striking union workers and "scabs" (non-union workers who defied the strike) clashed outside the plant. The police arrived, shots rang out, and two strikers were killed.

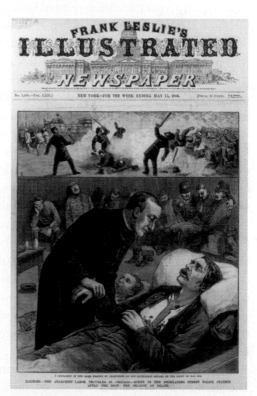

The Haymarket Affair

A priest gives last rites to policeman after anarchist-labor violence erupts in Haymarket Square, Chicago.

Evidence of police brutality infuriated the leaders of the minuscule anarchist movement in Chicago, which included many women. They printed leaflets demanding "Revenge!" and "Workingmen, to Arms!" Calls went out for a mass demonstration the following night at Haymarket Square to protest the killings. On the evening of May 4, after listening to long speeches complaining about low wages and long working hours and promoting anarchism, the crowd was beginning to break up when a group of policemen arrived and told the militants to disperse. At that point someone threw a bomb at the police; seven were killed and sixty wounded. People screamed and ran in every direction. Amid the chaos of America's first terrorist bombing, the police fired into the crowd, killing and wounding an unknown number of people, including other policemen. Throughout the night, rampaging police arbitrarily arrested scores of people without evidence and subjected them to harsh questioning. All labor meetings were banned across the city. Newspapers across the nation printed lurid headlines about anarchy erupting in Chicago. One New York newspaper demanded stern punishment for "the few long-haired, wild-eyed, bad-smelling, atheistic, reckless foreign wretches" who promoted such anarchistic labor unrest.

At trials during the summer of 1886, seven anarchist leaders were sentenced to death despite the lack of any evidence linking them to the bomb thrower, whose identity was never established. All but one of the convicted were German speaking, and that one held a membership card in the Knights of Labor. The facts of the case were lost amid the emotions of the moment. In a statement to the court after being sentenced to be hanged, Louis Lingg declared that he was innocent of the bombing but was proud to be an anarchist who was "in favor of using force" to attack the abuses of the capitalist system.

Lawyers for the anarchists appealed the convictions to the Illinois Supreme Court. Meanwhile, petitions from around the world arrived at the governor's office appealing for clemency for the seven convicted men. One of the petitioners was **Samuel Gompers**, the founding president of the American Federation of Labor (AFL), a new organization that would soon supplant the faltering Knights of Labor as the nation's leading union. "I abhor anarchy," Gompers stressed, "but I also abhor injustice when meted out even to the most despicable being on earth."

On September 14, 1887, the state supreme court upheld the convictions, and six weeks later the U.S. Supreme Court refused to consider the case. On November 10, 1887, Louis Lingg committed suicide in his cell. That same day, the Illinois governor commuted the sentences of two of the convicted conspirators to life imprisonment. The next day the four remaining condemned men were hanged. Two hundred thousand people lined the streets of Chicago as their caskets were taken for burial. To labor militants around the world, the executed anarchists were working-class martyrs; to the police and the economic elite in Chicago, they were demonic assassins.

The violent incident at Haymarket Square triggered widespread revulsion at the Knights of Labor and labor groups in general. Despite his best efforts, Terence Powderly could never dissociate in the public mind the Knights from the anarchists. He clung to leadership until 1893, but after that the union evaporated. By the turn of the century, it was but a memory. Besides fear of their supposed radicalism, several factors accounted for the Knights' decline: a leadership devoted more to reform than to the nuts and bolts of organization, the failure of the Knights' cooperative worker-owned enterprises, and a preoccupation with politics that led the Knights to sponsor labor candidates in hundreds of local elections.

The Knights nevertheless attained some lasting achievements, among them the creation of the federal Bureau of Labor Statistics in 1884 as well as several state labor bureaus; the Foran Act of 1885, which, though weakly enforced, penalized employers who imported contract labor (an arrangement similar to the indentured servitude of colonial times, in which workers were committed to a term of labor in exchange for transportation to America); and an 1880 federal law providing for the arbitration of labor disputes. The Knights by example also spread the idea of unionism and initiated a new type of union organization: the industrial union, an industry-wide union of skilled and unskilled workers.

GOMPERS AND THE AFL   The craft unions (skilled workers) generally opposed efforts to unite with industrial unionism. Leaders of the craft unions feared that joining with unskilled laborers would mean a loss of their craft's identity and a loss of the skilled workers' greater bargaining power. Thus in 1886, delegates from twenty-five craft unions organized the **American Federation of Labor** (AFL). Its structure differed from that of the Knights of Labor in that it was a federation of national organizations, each of which retained a large degree of autonomy and exercised greater leverage against management.

Samuel Gompers served as president of the AFL from its start until his death, in 1924, with only one year's interruption. Born in England of Dutch Jewish ancestry, Gompers came to the United States as a teenager, joined the Cigarmakers' Union in 1864, and became president of his New York City local union in 1877. Unlike Terence Powderly and the Knights of Labor, Gompers focused on concrete economic gains—higher wages, shorter hours, better working conditions—and avoided involvement with utopian ideas or politics.

The AFL at first grew slowly, but by 1890 it had surpassed the Knights of Labor in membership. By the turn of the century, it claimed 500,000 members in affiliated unions; in 1914, on the eve of World War I, it had 2 million; and in 1920 it reached a peak of 4 million. But even then the AFL embraced less than 15 percent of the nation's nonagricultural workers. All unions, including the unaffiliated railroad brotherhoods, accounted for little more than 18 percent of those workers. Organized labor's strongholds were in transportation and the building trades. Most of the larger manufacturing industries—including steel, textiles, tobacco, and packinghouses—remained almost untouched. Gompers never frowned upon industrial unions, and several became important affiliates of the AFL: the United Mine Workers, the International Ladies Garment Workers, and the Amalgamated Clothing Workers. But the AFL had its greatest success in organizing skilled workers.

THE HOMESTEAD STRIKE   Two violent incidents in the 1890s stalled the emerging industrial-union movement and set it back for the next forty years: the **Homestead steel strike** of 1892 and the **Pullman strike** of 1894. These two dramatic labor conflicts in several respects represented the culminating events of the Gilded Age, an era of riotous economic growth during which huge corporations came to exercise overweening influence over American life. Both events pitted organized labor in a bitter contest against two of the nation's largest and most influential corporations. In both cases the stakes were enormous. The two strikes not only represented a test of strength for the organized labor movement but also served to reshape the political landscape at the end of the nineteenth century.

The Amalgamated Association of Iron and Steel Workers, founded in 1876, was the largest craft union at the time. By 1891, it boasted 24,000 members. But it excluded unskilled steelworkers and had failed to organize the larger steel plants. The massive Homestead Works near Pittsburgh was an important exception. There the union, which included about a fourth of Homestead's 3,800 workers, had enjoyed friendly relations with Andrew Carnegie's company until Henry Clay Frick became its president in 1889. A showdown was delayed until 1892, however, when the union contract came up for renewal. Carnegie, who had expressed sympathy for unions in the past, had gone hunting in his native Scotland and left matters in Frick's hands. Yet Carnegie knew what was afoot: a cost-cutting reduction in the number of highly paid skilled workers through the use of labor-saving machinery and a deliberate attempt to smash the union. "Am with you to the end," he wrote to Frick.

As negotiations dragged on, the company announced on June 25 that it would treat workers as individuals unless an agreement with the union was reached by June 29. A strike—or, more properly, a lockout of unionists—began on that date. In no mood to negotiate, Frick built a twelve-foot-high fence around the entire plant, equipped it with watchtowers, searchlights, and barbed wire, and hired three hundred union-busting men from the Pinkerton Detective Agency to protect what was soon dubbed Fort Frick. On the morning of July 6, 1892, when the untrained Pinkertons floated up the Monongahela River on barges, unionists were waiting behind breastworks on shore. Who fired the first shot remains unknown, but a fourteen-hour battle broke out in which seven workers and three Pinkertons died. In the end the Pinkertons surrendered and were marched away, subjected to taunts and beatings from crowds in the street.

The strike dragged on until November, but by then the union was dead at Homestead, its leaders charged with murder and treason. Its cause was not helped when an anarchist, a Lithuanian immigrant named Alexander Berkman, tried to assassinate Frick on July 23, shooting him twice in the neck and stabbing him three times. Despite his wounds, Frick fought back fiercely and, with the help of staff members, subdued Berkman. Much of the local sympathy for the strikers evaporated. As a union leader explained, Berkman's bullets "went straight through the heart of the Homestead strike." Penniless and demoralized, the defeated workers ended their walkout on November 20 and accepted the company's terms. Only a fifth of the strikers were hired back. Carnegie and Frick, with the support of local, state, and national government officials, had eliminated the union. Across the nation in 1892, state militias intervened to quash twenty-three labor disputes. In the ongoing struggles between workers and owners, big business held sway—in the workplace and in state governments.

THE PULLMAN STRIKE   Even more than the confrontation at the Homestead steel plant, the Pullman strike of 1894 was a notable walkout in American history, for it paralyzed the economies of the twenty-seven states and territories making up the western half of the nation. It involved a dispute at Pullman, Illinois, a model industrial town built on four thousand acres outside Chicago, where workers of the Pullman Palace Car Company were housed. Employees who built rail cars were required to live in the company town, pay rents and utility costs that were higher than those in nearby towns, and buy goods from company stores. During the depression of 1893, George Pullman laid off 3,000 of his 5,800 employees and cut wages 25 to 40 percent, but not rents and other charges. After Pullman fired three members of a workers' grievance committee, a strike began on May 11, 1894.

During this tense period, Pullman workers had been joining the new American Railway Union, founded the previous year by **Eugene V. Debs**. The tall, gangly Debs was a man of towering influence and charismatic appeal. A child of working-class immigrants, he quit school at age fourteen and began working for an Indiana railroad. By the early 1890s Debs had become a tireless spokesman for labor radicalism, and he strove to organize *all* railway workers—skilled or unskilled—into the American Railway Union, which soon became a powerful new labor organization. Debs quickly turned his attention to the controversy in Pullman, Illinois.

In June 1894, after George Pullman refused Debs's plea for a negotiated settlement of the strike, the union workers stopped handling Pullman railcars. By the end of July they had shut down most of the railroads in the Midwest. Railroad executives then hired strikebreakers to connect mail cars to Pullman cars so that interference with Pullman cars would entail interference with the federal mail. The U.S. attorney general, a former attorney for railroad companies, swore in 3,400 special deputies to keep the trains running. When clashes occurred between those deputies and some of the strikers, angry workers ignored Debs's plea for an orderly boycott. They assaulted strikebreakers ("scabs") and destroyed property.

Finally, on July 3, 1894, President Grover Cleveland sent federal troops into the Chicago area, where the strike was centered. The Illinois governor insisted that the state could keep order, but President Cleveland claimed authority and stressed his duty to ensure delivery of the mail. Meanwhile, the attorney general won an injunction forbidding any interference with the mail or any effort to restrain interstate commerce. On July 13, the union called off the strike. A few days later, the district court cited Debs for violating the injunction, and he served six months in jail. The Supreme Court upheld the decree in the case of *In re Debs* (1895) on broad grounds of national sovereignty: "The strong arm of the national government may be put forth to brush away all obstructions to the freedom of interstate commerce or the transportation of the mails." Debs served his jail term, during which he read deeply in socialist literature, and emerged to devote the rest of his life to socialism.

SOCIALISM AND THE UNIONS   The major unions for the most part never allied themselves with socialists, as many European labor movements did. But socialist ideas had been circulating in the United States at least since the 1820s. Marxism, one strain of socialism, was imported mainly by German immigrants. Karl Marx's International Workingmen's Association, founded in 1864 and later called the First International, inspired only a few affiliates in the United States. In 1872, at Marx's urging, the headquarters was moved from London to New York. In 1877, Marxists in America organized the Socialist Labor party, a group so dominated by immigrants that German was initially its official language.

The movement gained little notice before the rise of Daniel De Leon in the 1890s. As editor of a Marxist newspaper, the *People,* he became the dominant figure in the Socialist Labor party. He proposed to organize socialist industrial unions and to build a political party that would abolish the government once it gained power, after which the unions of the Socialist Trade and Labor Alliance, formed under his supervision, would become the units of control. De Leon preached revolution at the ballot box, not by violence.

Eugene V. Debs was more successful than De Leon at building a socialist movement in America, however. In 1897, Debs announced that he was a socialist and organized the Social Democratic party from the remnants of the American Railway Union; he won over 96,000 votes as its candidate for president in 1900. The next year his followers joined a number of secessionists from De Leon's party to set up the Socialist Party of America. Debs polled over 400,000 votes as the party's candidate for president in 1904 and more than doubled that, to more than 900,000 votes, or 6 percent of the popular vote, in 1912. In 1910, Milwaukee elected a socialist mayor and congressman.

By 1912, the Socialist party seemed well on the way to becoming a permanent fixture in American politics. Thirty-three cities had socialist mayors. The party sponsored five English-language daily newspapers, eight foreign-language dailies, and a number of weeklies and monthlies. In the Southwest the party built a sizable grassroots following among farmers and tenants.

Eugene V. Debs

Founder of the American Railway Union and later candidate for president as head of the Socialist Party of America.

Oklahoma, for instance, had more paid-up party members in 1910 than any other state except New York and in 1912 gave 16.5 percent of its popular vote to Debs, a greater proportion than any other state ever gave him. But the Socialist party reached its peak in 1912. It would be racked by disagreements over America's participation in World War I and was split thereafter by desertions to the new Communist party.

THE WOBBLIES   During the years of Socialist party growth, a parallel effort to revive industrial unionism emerged, led by the **Industrial Workers of the World (IWW)**. The chief base for this group was the Western Federation of Miners, organized at Butte, Montana, in 1893. Over the next decade the Western Federation was the storm center of violent confrontations with unyielding mine operators who mobilized private armies against it in Colorado, Idaho, and elsewhere. In 1905 the founding convention of the IWW drew a variety of delegates who opposed the AFL's philosophy of organizing unions made up only of skilled workers. Eugene V. Debs participated, although many of his comrades preferred to work within the AFL. Daniel De Leon seized this chance to strike back at craft unionism. He argued that the IWW "must be founded on the class struggle" and "the irrepressible conflict between the capitalist class and the working class."

But the IWW waged class war better than it articulated class ideology. Like the Knights of Labor, it was designed to be "one big union," including all workers, skilled or unskilled. Its roots were in the mining and lumber camps of the West, where the unstable seasonal conditions of employment created a large number of nomadic workers, to whom neither the AFL's pragmatic approach nor the socialists' political appeal held much attraction. The revolutionary goal of the Wobblies, as they came to be called, was an idea labeled syndicalism by its French supporters: the ultimate destruction of the government and its replacement by one big union. But just how that union would govern remained vague.

Like other radical groups, the IWW was split by sectarian disputes. Because of policy disagreements all the major founders withdrew, first the Western Federation of Miners, then Debs, then De Leon. William D. "Big Bill" Haywood of the Western Federation remained, however, and as its leader he held the group together. Haywood was an imposing figure. Well over six feet tall, handsome and muscular, he commanded the attention and respect of his listeners. This hard-rock miner, union organizer, and socialist from Salt Lake City despised the AFL and its conservative labor philosophy. He called Samuel Gompers "a squat specimen of humanity" who was "conceited, petulant, and vindictive." Instead of following Gompers's advice to organize only skilled workers, Haywood promoted the concept of one all-inclusive union dedicated to a socialism "with its working clothes on."

Haywood and the Wobblies, however, were reaching out to the fringe elements of the labor force with the least power and influence, chiefly the migratory workers of the West and the ethnic groups of the East. Always ambivalent about diluting their revolutionary principles, Wobblies scorned the usual labor agreements even when they participated in them. As a consequence, they engaged in spectacular battles with employers but scored few victories. The largest was a textile strike at Lawrence, Massachusetts, in 1912 that garnered wage raises, overtime pay, and other benefits. But the next year a strike of silk workers at Paterson, New Jersey, ended in disaster, and the IWW entered a rapid decline.

The Wobblies' fading was accelerated by the hysterical opposition they aroused. Its members were branded anarchists, bums, and criminals. The IWW was effectively destroyed during World War I, when most of its leaders were jailed for conspiracy because of their militant opposition to American entry into the war. Big Bill Haywood fled to the Soviet Union, where he married a Russian woman, died in 1928, and was honored by burial in the Kremlin wall. The short-lived Wobblies left behind a rich folklore of nomadic workingmen and a gallery of heroic agitators, such as Elizabeth Gurley Flynn, a dark-haired Irishwoman who at age eighteen chained herself to a lamppost to impede her arrest during a strike. The movement also bequeathed martyrs such as the Swedish American singer and labor organizer Joe Hill, framed (so the faithful assumed) for murder and executed by a Utah firing squad. His last words were written to Haywood: "Goodbye, Bill. I die like a true blue rebel. Don't waste any time mourning. Organize." The intensity of conviction and devotion to a cause shown by Hill, Flynn, and others ensured that the IWW's ideal of a classless society did not die.

THE STRESSES OF SUCCESS The phenomenal industrial empires created by the Gilded Age captains of industry and finance generated enormous fortunes and marked improvements in the quality of everyday life. But the Industrial Revolution also created profound inequalities and fermenting social tensions. As often happens, unregulated capitalism led to excesses that bred instability and unrest. By the end of the nineteenth century, as the labor unions and farmers' organizations argued, an unregulated economy had become recklessly out of balance—and only state and federal government intervention could restore economic legitimacy and social stability.

End of Chapter Review

CHAPTER SUMMARY

- **Second Industrial Revolution** The postwar economy was characterized by large-scale industrial development and a burgeoning agriculture sector. The Second Industrial Revolution was fueled by the creation of national transportation and communications systems, the use of electric power, and the application of scientific research to industrial processes. The federal government encouraged growth by imposing high tariffs on imported products and granting the railroad companies public land.

- **Rising Big Business** The leading entrepreneurs were extraordinarily skilled at organizing and controlling industry. John D. Rockefeller eventually controlled nearly every facet of the oil industry, consolidating that control through trusts and holding companies. Andrew Carnegie, who believed that competition benefited both society and business, came to dominate the steel industry by buying struggling companies. J. Pierpont Morgan, an investment banker, not only controlled most of the nation's railroads but also bought Carnegie's steel interests in 1901, thereby creating the nation's first billion-dollar corporation.

- **Labor Conditions and Organizations** The labor force was largely composed of unskilled workers, including recent immigrants and growing numbers of women and children. Some children as young as eight years of age worked twelve hours a day in coal mines and southern mills. In hard times, business owners cut wages without discounting the rents they charged for company housing or the prices they charged in company stores.

- **Rising Labor Unions** It was difficult for unskilled workers to organize effectively. Strikebreakers were plentiful because new immigrants were desperate for work. Business owners often had recourse to state and local militias, which would be mobilized against strikers in the face of perceived anarchy. Craft unions made up of only skilled workers became more successful at organizing as the American Federation of Labor focused on concrete economic gains and better working conditions and avoided involvement in politics.

CHRONOLOGY

1855	Bessemer converter process allows steel to be made quickly and inexpensively
1859	First oil well is struck in Titusville, Pennsylvania
1869	First transcontinental railroad is completed at Promontory, Utah
1876	Alexander Graham Bell patents his telephone
1876	Thomas A. Edison makes the first successful incandescent lightbulb
1877	Great Railroad Strike
1882	John D. Rockefeller organizes the Standard Oil Trust
1886	In the Haymarket incident, a bomb set off at a Chicago labor rally kills and wounds police officers
1886	American Federation of Labor is organized
1892	Homestead Strike
1894	Pullman Strike
1901	J. Pierpont Morgan creates the U.S. Steel Corporation

KEY TERMS & NAMES

19

THE SOUTH AND THE WEST TRANSFORMED

FOCUS QUESTIONS wwnorton.com/studyspace

• How did life in the South change politically, economically, and socially after the Civil War?

• What happened to Native Americans as whites settled the West?

• What were the experiences of farmers, cowboys, and miners in the West?

• How did mining affect the development of the West?

• How important was the concept of the frontier to America's political and diplomatic development?

After the Civil War, the South and the West provided enticing opportunities for American inventiveness and entrepreneurship. The two distinctive regions were ripe for development, and each in its own way became like a colonial appendage of the more prosperous Midwest and Northeast. The war-devastated South had to be rebuilt; the sparsely settled trans-Mississippi West beckoned agricultural and commercial development. Entrepreneurs in the North eagerly sought to exploit both undeveloped regions by providing the capital for urbanization and industrialization. This was particularly true of the West, where before 1860 most Americans had viewed the region between the Mississippi River and California as a barren landscape unfit for human habitation or cultivation, an uninviting land suitable only for Indians and animals. Half the state of Texas, for instance, was still not settled at the end of the Civil War. After 1865, however, the federal government encouraged western settlement and economic development. The construction of transcontinental railroads, the military conquest of the Indians, and a generous policy of distributing government-owned lands combined to help lure thousands of pioneers and enterprising capitalists westward. Charles Goodnight, a Texas cattle rancher, recalled that "we were adventurers in a great land as fresh and full of the zest of darers." By 1900, the South and the West had been transformed in ways—for good and for ill—that few could have predicted, and twelve new states were created out of the western territories.

THE MYTH OF THE NEW SOUTH

A FRESH VISION   The major prophet of the so-called the **New South** during the 1880s was Henry W. Grady, editor of the Atlanta Constitution. "The Old South, " he said, "rested everything on slavery and agriculture, unconscious that these could neither give nor maintain healthy growth. " The New South, on the other hand, "presents a perfect democracy" of small farms and diversifying industries. The postwar South, Grady believed, held the promise of a real democracy, one no longer run by the planter aristocracy and no longer dependent upon slave labor.

Henry Grady's compelling vision of a New South, modeled after the North, attracted many supporters who fervently preached the gospel of industrial development. The Confederacy, they reasoned, had lost the war because it had relied too much upon King Cotton—and slavery. In the future, the South must follow the North's example and diversify its economy by developing an industrial sector to go along with its agricultural emphasis. From that central belief flowed certain corollaries: that a more efficient agriculture would be a foundation for economic growth, that more widespread education, especially vocational training, would promote regional prosperity, and that sectional peace and racial harmony would provide a stable social environment for economic growth.

ECONOMIC GROWTH   The New South vision of a more diversified economy made a lot of sense, but it was only partially fulfilled. The chief accomplishment of the New South movement was a dramatic expansion of the region's textile industry, which produced cotton-based bedding and clothing. From 1880 to 1900, the number of cotton mills in the South grew from 161 to 400, the number of mostly white mill workers (among whom women and children outnumbered men) increased fivefold, and the demand for cotton went up eightfold. By 1900, the South had surpassed New England as the largest producer of cotton fabric in the nation.

Tobacco growing and cigarette production also increased significantly. Essential to the rise of the tobacco industry was the Duke family of Durham,

North Carolina. At the end of the Civil War, the story goes, Washington Duke took a barnful of tobacco and, with the help of his two sons, beat it out with hickory sticks, stuffed it into bags, hitched two mules to his wagon, and set out across the state, selling tobacco in small pouches as he went. By 1872 the Dukes had a factory producing 125,000 pounds of tobacco annually, and Washington Duke prepared to settle down and enjoy success.

His son James Buchanan "Buck" Duke wanted even greater success, however. He recognized that the tobacco industry was "half smoke and half ballyhoo," so he poured large sums into advertising schemes and perfected the mechanized mass production of cigarettes. Duke also undersold competitors in their own markets and cornered the supply of ingredients needed to make cigarettes. Eventually his competitors agreed to join forces, and in 1890 Duke brought most of them into the American Tobacco Company, which controlled nine tenths of the nation's cigarette production and, by 1904, about three fourths of all tobacco production. In 1911 the Supreme Court ruled that the massive company was in violation of the Sherman Anti-Trust Act and ordered it broken up, but by then Duke had found new worlds to conquer, in hydroelectric power and aluminum.

Systematic use of other natural resources helped revitalize the region along the Appalachian Mountain chain from West Virginia to Alabama. Coal production in the South (including West Virginia) grew from 5 million tons in 1875 to 49 million tons by 1900. At the southern end of the mountains, Birmingham, Alabama, sprang up during the 1870s in the shadow of Red Mountain, so named for its iron ore, and boosters soon tagged the steelmaking city the Pittsburgh of the South.

Urban and industrial growth spawned a need for housing, and after 1870 lumbering became a thriving industry in the South. Northern investors bought up vast pine forests throughout the region. By the turn of the century, lumber had surpassed textiles in value. Tree cutting seemed to know no bounds, despite the resulting ecological devastation. In time the cutover southern forests would be saved only by the warm climate, which fostered quick growth of planted trees.

AGRICULTURE OLD AND NEW   By the end of the nineteenth century, however, the South fell far short of the diversified economy and racial harmony that Henry Grady and other proponents of the New South had envisioned in the mid-1880s. The South in 1900 remained the least urban, least industrial, least educated, and least prosperous region. The typical southerner was less apt to be tending a textile loom or iron forge than, as the saying went, facing the eastern end of a westbound mule or risking his life in an Appalachian coal mine. The traditional overplanting of cotton and tobacco fields continued after the Civil War and expanded over new acreage even as its export markets leveled off. The majority of southern farmers were not flourishing. A prolonged deflation in crop prices affected the entire economy during the last third of the nineteenth century. Sagging prices for farm crops made it more difficult than ever to own land. By 1890, low rates of farm ownership in the Deep South belied Henry Grady's dream of a southern democracy of small landowners: South Carolina, 39 percent; Georgia, 40 percent; Alabama, 42 percent; Mississippi, 38 percent; and Louisiana, 42 percent.

Poverty forced most southern farm workers to give up their hopes of owning land and become sharecroppers or tenants. **Sharecroppers**, who had

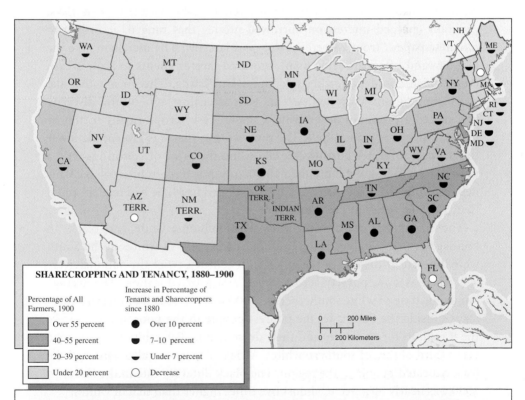

SHARECROPPING AND TENANCY, 1880–1900

Percentage of All Farmers, 1900
- ■ Over 55 percent
- ■ 40–55 percent
- ■ 20–39 percent
- □ Under 20 percent

Increase in Percentage of Tenants and Sharecroppers since 1880
- ● Over 10 percent
- ◗ 7–10 percent
- ◗ Under 7 percent
- ○ Decrease

Why was there a dramatic increase in sharecropping and tenancy in the late nineteenth century? Why did the South have more sharecroppers than other parts of the country? Why, in your opinion, was the rate of sharecropping low in the western territories of New Mexico and Arizona?

nothing to offer the landowner but their labor, worked the owner's land in return for seed, fertilizer, and supplies and a share of the crop, generally about half. Tenant farmers, hardly better off, might have their own mule, plow, and line of credit with the country store. They were entitled to claim a larger share of the crops. The sharecropper-tenant system was horribly inefficient and corrupting. It was in essence a post–Civil War version of land slavery. Tenants and landowners developed an intense suspicion of each other. Landlords often swindled the farm workers by not giving them their fair share of the crops.

The postwar South suffered from an acute, prolonged shortage of money; people in the former Confederacy had to devise ways to operate without cash. One innovation was the crop-lien system whereby rural merchants furnished supplies to small farm owners in return for liens (or mortgages) on their future crops. Over time the credit offered by the local store coupled with sagging prices for cotton and other crops created a hopeless cycle of perennial debt among farmers. The merchant, who assumed great risks, generally charged interest on borrowed money that ranged, according to one newspaper, "from 24 percent to grand larceny." The merchant, like the planter (and often the same man), required farmer clients to grow a cash crop, which could be readily sold upon harvesting. This meant that the sharecropping and crop-lien systems warred against agricultural diversity and placed a premium on growing a staple "cash" crop, usually cotton or tobacco. It was a vicious cycle. The more cotton that was grown, the lower the price. If a farmer borrowed $1000 when the price of cotton was 10¢ a pound, he had to grow more than 10,000 pounds of cotton to pay back his debt plus interest. If the price of cotton dropped to 5¢, he had to grow more than 20,000 pounds just to break even.

The stagnation of rural life thus held millions, white and black, in bondage to privation and ignorance. Eleven percent of whites in the South were illiterate at the end of the nineteenth century, twice the national average. Then as now, poverty accompanied a lack of education. The average annual income of white southerners in 1900 was about half of that of Americans outside the South. Yet the poorest people in the poorest region were the 9 million former slaves and their descendants. Per capita black income was a third of that of southern whites. African Americans also remained the least educated people in the region. The black illiteracy rate in the South in 1900 was nearly 50 percent, almost five times higher than that of whites.

THE REDEEMERS (BOURBONS)   In post–Civil War southern politics, centuries-old habits of social deference and political elitism still prevailed. "Every community," one U.S. Army officer noted in postwar South Carolina, "had its great man, or its little great man, around whom his fellow citizens gather when they want information, and to whose monologues they listen with a respect akin to humility." After Reconstruction, such "great" men dominated local southern politics, usually because of their ownership of land or their wealth. The supporters of these postwar Democratic leaders referred to them as "**redeemers**" because they supposedly saved the South from Yankee domination, as well as from the straitjacket of a purely rural economy. The redeemers included a rising class of lawyers, merchants, and entrepreneurs who were eager to promote a more diversified economy based upon industrial development and railroad expansion. The opponents of the redeemers labeled them "**Bourbons**" in an effort to depict them as reactionaries. Like the French royal family of the same name, which Napoléon had said forgot nothing and learned nothing in the ordeal of the French revolution, the ruling white Bourbons of the postwar South were said to have forgotten nothing and to have learned nothing in the ordeal of the Confederacy and the Civil War. During and after the late 1870s, the Bourbon governors and legislators of the New South slashed state expenditures, including those for the public-school systems started during the Reconstruction era immediately after the war.

Perhaps the ultimate paradox of the Bourbons' rule was that these champions of white supremacy tolerated a lingering black voice in politics and showed no haste to raise the barriers of racial segregation in public places. In the 1880s, southern politics remained surprisingly open and democratic, with 64 percent of eligible voters, blacks and whites, participating in elections. African Americans sat in the state legislature of South Carolina until 1900 and in the state legislature of Georgia until 1908; some of them were Democrats. The South sent African American congressmen to Washington, D.C., in every election except one until 1900, though they always represented gerrymandered districts in which most of the state's African American voters had been placed. Under the Bourbons the disenfranchisement of African American voters remained inconsistent, a local matter brought about mainly by fraud and intimidation, but it occurred often enough to ensure white control of the southern states.

A similar flexibility applied to other aspects of race relations. The color line was drawn less strictly immediately after the Civil War than it would be in the twentieth century. In some places, to be sure, racial segregation appeared before the end of Reconstruction, especially in schools, churches, hotels, and rooming houses and in private social relations. In places of public accommodation such as trains, depots, theaters, and diners, discrimination was more sporadic.

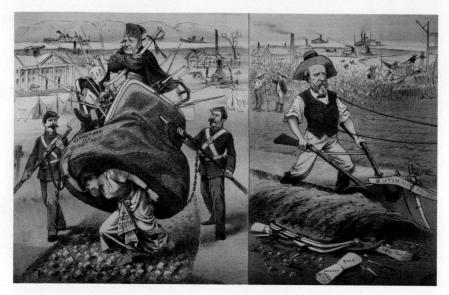

The effects of Radical and Bourbon rule in the South

This 1880 cartoon shows the South staggering under the oppressive weight of
military Reconstruction (left) and flourishing under the "Let 'Em Alone Policy"
of President Rutherford B. Hayes and the Bourbons (right).

The ultimate achievement of the New South promoters and their allies,
the Bourbons, was that they reconciled tradition with innovation. By promoting the growth of industry, the Bourbons led the South into a new economic era, but without sacrificing a mythic reverence for the Old South.
Bourbon rule left a permanent mark on the South's politics, economics, and
race relations.

THE NEW WEST

Like the South, the West is a region wrapped in myths and stereotypes.
The vast land west of the Mississippi River contains remarkable geographic
extremes: majestic mountains, roaring rivers, searing deserts, sprawling
grasslands, and dense forests. For vast reaches of western America, the
great epics of the Civil War and Reconstruction were remote events hardly
touching the lives of the Indians, Mexicans, Asians, trappers, miners, and
Mormons scattered through the plains and mountains. There the march of
settlement and exploitation continued, propelled by a lust for land and a
passion for profit. Between 1870 and 1900, Americans settled more land in

the West than had been occupied by all Americans up to 1870. On one level, western settlement beyond the Mississippi River constitutes a colorful drama of determined pioneers and two-fisted gunslingers overcoming all obstacles to secure their vision of freedom and opportunity amid the region's awesome vastness. The post–Civil War West offered the promise of democratic individualism, economic opportunity, and personal freedom that had long before come to define the American dream. On another level, however, the colonization of the Far West was a tragedy of shortsighted greed and irresponsible behavior, a story of reckless exploitation that scarred the land, decimated its wildlife, and nearly exterminated Native American culture.

In the second tier of trans-Mississippi states—Iowa, Kansas, Nebraska—and in western Minnesota, farmers began spreading across the Great Plains after midcentury. From California, miners moved east through the mountains, drawn by one new strike after another. From Texas, nomadic cowboys migrated northward onto the plains and across the Rocky Mountains, into the Great Basin of Utah. The settlers encountered climates and landscapes markedly different from those they had left behind. The Great Plains were arid, and the scarcity of water and timber rendered useless the familiar trappings of the pioneer: the ax, the log cabin, the rail fence, and the accustomed methods of tilling the soil. For a long time the region had been called the Great American Desert, unfit for human habitation and therefore, to white Americans, the perfect refuge for Indians. But that view changed in the last half of the nineteenth century as a result of newly discovered deposits of gold, silver, and other minerals, the completion of the transcontinental railroads, the destruction of the buffalo, the collapse of Indian resistance, the rise of the range-cattle industry, and the dawning realization that the arid region need not be a sterile desert. With the use of what water was available, new techniques of dry farming and irrigation could make the land fruitful after all.

THE MIGRATORY STREAM   During the second half of the nineteenth century, an unrelenting stream of migrants flowed into the largely Indian and Hispanic West. Millions of Anglo-Americans, African Americans, Mexicans, and European and Chinese immigrants transformed the patterns of western society and culture. Most of the settlers were relatively prosperous white, native-born farm folk. Because of the expense of transportation, land, and supplies, the very poor could not afford to relocate. Three quarters of the western migrants were men.

The largest number of foreign immigrants came from northern Europe and Canada. In the northern plains, Germans, Scandinavians, and Irish were especially numerous. In the new state of Nebraska in 1870, a quarter of the 123,000 residents were foreign-born. In North Dakota in 1890, 45 percent of the residents were immigrants. Compared with European immigrants, those from China and Mexico were much less numerous but nonetheless significant. More than 200,000 Chinese arrived in California between 1876 and 1890.

AFRICAN AMERICAN MIGRATION   In the aftermath of the collapse of Radical Republican rule in the South, thousands of African Americans began migrating west from Kentucky, Tennessee, Louisiana, Arkansas, Mississippi, and Texas. Some six thousand southern blacks arrived in Kansas in 1879, and as many as twenty thousand followed the next year. These African American migrants came to be known as Exodusters, because they were making their exodus from the South—in search of a haven from racism and poverty. The exodus of black southerners to the West died out by the early 1880s. Many of the settlers were unprepared for the living conditions on the plains. Their Kansas homesteads were not large enough to be self-sustaining, and most of the black farmers were forced to supplement their income by hiring themselves out to white ranchers. Drought, grasshoppers, prairie fires, and dust storms led to crop failures. The sudden influx of so many people taxed resources and patience. Many of the African American pioneers in Kansas soon abandoned their land and moved to the few cities in the state.

Nicodemus, Kansas

A colony founded by southern blacks in the 1860s.

Life on the frontier was not the "promised land" that settlers had been led to expect. Nonetheless, by 1890 some 520,000 African Americans lived west of the Mississippi River. As many as 25 percent of the cowboys who participated in the Texas cattle drives were African Americans.

MINING THE WEST   Valuable mineral deposits continued to lure people to the West after the Civil War. The California miners of 1849 (forty-niners) set the typical pattern, in which the sudden, disorderly rush of prospectors to a new find was quickly joined by camp followers—a motley crew of peddlers, saloon keepers, prostitutes, cardsharps, hustlers, and assorted desperadoes eager to mine the miners. If a new field panned out, the forces of respectability and more subtle forms of exploitation slowly worked their way in. Lawlessness gave way to vigilante rule and, finally, to a stable community.

The drama of the 1849 gold rush was reenacted time and again in the following three decades. Along the South Platte River, not far from Pikes Peak in Colorado, a prospecting party found gold in 1858, and stories of success brought perhaps one hundred thousand "fifty-niners" into the country by the next year. New discoveries in Colorado kept occurring: near Central City in 1859, at Leadville in the 1870s, and the last important strikes in the West, again gold and silver, at Cripple Creek in 1891 and 1894. During those years, farming and grazing had given the economy a stable base, and Colorado, the Centennial State, entered the union in 1876.

While the early miners were crowding around Pikes Peak, the Comstock Lode was discovered near Gold Hill, Nevada. H. T. P. Comstock, a Canadian-born fur trapper, had drifted to the Carson River diggings, which opened in 1856. He talked his way into a share in a new discovery made by two other prospectors in 1859 and gave it his own name. The lode produced gold and silver. Within twenty years, it had yielded more than $300 million from shafts that reached hundreds of feet into the mountainside. In 1861, largely on account of the settlers attracted to the Comstock Lode, Nevada became a territory, and in 1864 the state of Nevada was admitted to the Union in time to give two electoral votes to Abraham Lincoln (the new state's third electoral voter got caught in a snowstorm).

The growing demand for orderly government in the West led to the hasty creation of new territories and eventually the admission of a host of new states. After Colorado's admission in 1876, however, there was a long hiatus because of party divisions in Congress: Democrats were reluctant to create states out of territories that were heavily Republican. After the sweeping Republican victory in the 1888 legislative races, however, Congress admitted the Dakotas, Montana, and Washington in 1889 and Idaho and Wyoming in 1890. Utah entered the Union in 1896 (after the Mormons abandoned the practice of polygamy) and Oklahoma in 1907, and in 1912 Arizona and New Mexico rounded out the forty-eight contiguous states.

THE INDIAN WARS   As the frontier pressed in from east and west, some 250,000 Native Americans were forced into what was supposed to be their last refuge, the Great Plains and in the mountain regions of the Far West. The 1851 Fort Laramie Treaty, in which the chiefs of the Plains tribes agreed to accept definite tribal borders and allow white emigrants to travel on their trails unmolested, worked for a while, with wagon trains passing safely through Indian lands and the army building roads and forts without resistance. Fighting resumed, however, as the emigrants began to encroach upon Indian lands on the plains rather than merely pass through them.

From the early 1860s until the late 1870s, the frontier raged with Indian wars. In 1864, Colorado's governor persuaded most of the warring Indians in his territory to gather at Fort Lyon, on Sand Creek, where they were promised protection. Despite that promise, Colonel John M. Chivington's untrained militia attacked an Indian camp flying a white flag of truce, slaughtering two hundred peaceful Indians—men, women, and children—in what one general called the "foulest and most unjustifiable crime in the annals of America."

With other scattered battles erupting, a congressional committee in 1865 gathered evidence on the grisly Indian wars and massacres. Its 1867 "Report on the Condition of the Indian Tribes" led to the creation of an Indian Peace Commission charged with removing the causes of the Indian wars. Congress decided that this would be best accomplished at the expense of the Indians, by persuading them to take up life on out-of-the-way reservations. Yet the persistent encroachment of whites on Indian hunting grounds continued. In 1870, Indians outnumbered whites in the Dakota Territory by two to one; in 1880, whites outnumbered Indians by more than six to one.

In 1867, a conference at Medicine Lodge, Kansas, ended with the Kiowas, Comanches, Arapahos, and Cheyennes reluctantly accepting land in western Oklahoma. The following spring the Sioux agreed to settle within the Black Hills Reservation in Dakota Territory. But Indian resistance in the southern plains continued until the Red River War of 1874–1875, when General Philip Sheridan forced the Indians to disband in the spring of 1875. Seventy-two Indian chiefs were imprisoned for three years.

Meanwhile, trouble was brewing again in the north. In 1874, Lieutenant Colonel **George A. Custer**, a reckless, glory-seeking officer, led an exploratory expedition into the Black Hills. Miners were soon filtering onto the Sioux

The Battle of Little Bighorn, 1876

A painting by Amos Bad Heart Bull, an Oglala Sioux.

hunting grounds despite promises that the army would keep them out. The army had done little to protect Indian land, but when ordered to move against wandering bands of Sioux hunting on the range according to their treaty rights, it moved vigorously.

What became the **Great Sioux War** was the largest military event since the end of the Civil War and one of the largest campaigns against Indians in American history. The war lasted fifteen months and entailed fifteen battles in present-day Wyoming, Montana, South Dakota, and Nebraska. The heroic chief Sitting Bull ably led the Sioux. In 1876, after several indecisive encounters, Custer found the main encampment of Sioux and their Northern Cheyenne allies on the Little Bighorn River. Separated from the main body of soldiers and surrounded by 2,500 warriors, Custer's detachment of 210 men was annihilated.

Instead of following up their victory, the Indians celebrated and renewed their hunting. The army quickly regained the offensive and compelled the Sioux to give up their hunting grounds and goldfields in return for payments. Forced onto reservations situated on the least valuable land in the region, the Indians soon found themselves struggling to subsist under harsh conditions. Many of them died of starvation or disease. When a peace commission imposed a settlement, Chief Spotted Tail said: "Tell your people that since the Great Father promised that we should never be removed, we have been moved five times. . . . I think you had better put the Indians on wheels and you can run them about wherever you wish."

In the Rocky Mountains and to the west, the same story of hopeless resistance was repeated. Indians were the last obstacle to white western expansion, and they suffered as a result. The Blackfeet and Crows had to leave their homes in Montana. In a war along the California-Oregon boundary, the Modocs held out for six months in 1871–1872 before they were overwhelmed. In 1879 the Utes were forced to give up their vast territories in western Colorado. In Idaho the peaceful Nez Perce bands refused to surrender land along the Salmon River, and prolonged fighting erupted there and

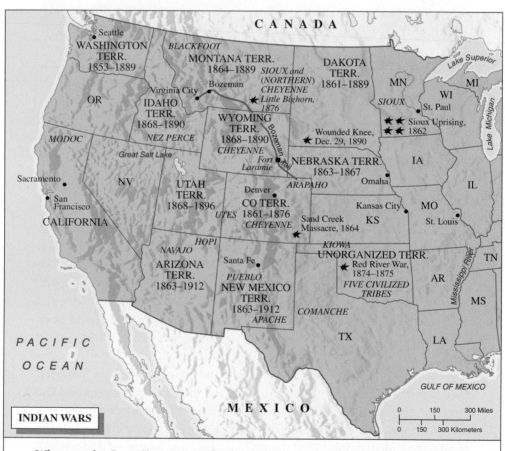

INDIAN WARS

What was the Great Sioux War? What happened at Little Bighorn, and what were the consequences? Why were hundreds of Indians killed at Wounded Knee?

in eastern Oregon. Joseph, one of several Nez Perce chiefs, delivered an eloquent speech of surrender that served as an epitaph to the Indians' efforts to withstand the march of American empire: "I am tired of fighting. Our chiefs are killed. . . . The old men are all dead. . . . I want to have time to look for my children, and see how many of them I can find. . . . Hear me, my chiefs! I am tired. My heart is sick and sad. From where the sun now stands I will fight no more forever."

A generation of Indian wars virtually ended in 1886 with the capture of Geronimo, a chief of the Chiricahua Apaches, who had fought white settlers in the Southwest for fifteen years. But there would be a tragic epilogue. Late in 1888, Wovoka (or Jack Wilson), a Paiute in western Nevada, fell ill and in a delirium imagined he had visited the spirit world, where he learned of a deliverer coming to rescue the Indians and restore their lands. To hasten their deliverance, he said, the Indians must take up a ceremonial dance at each new moon. The **Ghost Dance** craze fed upon old legends of a coming messiah and spread rapidly. In 1890 the Lakota Sioux adopted it with such fervor that it alarmed white authorities. They banned the Ghost Dance on Lakota reservations, but the Indians defied the order and a crisis erupted. On December 29, 1890, a bloodbath occurred at Wounded Knee, South Dakota. An accidental rifle discharge led nervous soldiers to fire into a group of Indians who had come to surrender. Nearly two hundred Indians and twenty-five soldiers died in the Battle of Wounded Knee. The Indian wars had ended with characteristic brutality and misunderstanding. General Philip Sheridan was acidly candid in summarizing how whites had treated the Indians: "We took away their country and their means of support, broke up their mode of living, their habits of life, introduced disease and decay and among them, and it was for this and against this that they made war. Could anyone expect less?"

INDIAN POLICY   The slaughter of buffalo and Indians ignited widespread criticism. Politicians and religious leaders castigated the persistent mistreatment of Indians. In his annual message of 1877, President Rutherford B. Hayes joined the protest: "Many, if not most, of our Indian wars have had their origin in broken promises and acts of injustice on our part." Helen Hunt Jackson, a novelist and poet, focused attention on the Indian cause in *A Century of Dishonor* (1881). Its impact on American attitudes toward the Indians was comparable to the effect that Harriet Beecher Stowe's *Uncle Tom's Cabin* (1852) had on the abolitionist movement before the Civil War. U.S. policies regarding Indians gradually became more benevolent, but this change did little to ease the plight of the Indians and actually helped destroy the remnants of their culture. The reservation policy inaugurated by the Peace Commission in 1867 did little more than extend a practice that dated from colonial Virginia. Partly humanitarian in motive, it also saved money: housing and feeding Indians on reservations cost less than fighting them.

Well-intentioned reformers sought to "Americanize" Indians by dealing with them as individuals rather than tribes. The fruition of such reform efforts came with the Dawes Severalty Act of 1887. Sponsored by Senator Henry L. Dawes of Massachusetts, the act divided tribal lands, granting 160 acres to each head of a family and lesser amounts to others. But the more it changed, the more Indian policy remained the same. Between 1887 and 1934, Indians lost an estimated 86 million of their 130 million acres. Most of what remained was unsuited for agriculture.

CATTLE AND COWBOYS While the West was being taken from the Indians, cattle entered the grasslands where the buffalo had roamed. For many years, wild cattle competed with the buffalo in the Spanish borderlands. Interbreeding with Anglo-American cattle produced the Texas longhorns: lean and rangy, they were noted more for speed and endurance than for yielding a choice steak. They had little value, moreover, because the largest markets for beef were too far away. New opportunities arose after the Civil War as railroads pushed farther west, where cattle could be driven through relatively vacant lands. Joseph G. McCoy, an Illinois livestock dealer, recognized the possibilities of moving the cattle trade west. In 1867 in Abilene, Kansas, he bought 250 acres for a stockyard; he then built a barn, an office building, livestock scales, a hotel, and a bank. He then sent an agent into Indian-owned areas to recruit owners of herds bound north to go through Abilene. Over the next few years, Abilene flourished as the first successful Kansas cowtown. The ability to ship huge numbers of western cattle by rail transformed ranching into a major industry.

The thriving cattle industry spurred rapid growth. The population of Kansas increased from 107,000 in 1860 to 365,000 ten years later and reached almost 1 million by 1880. Nebraska witnessed similar increases. The flush times of the cowtown soon passed, however, and the long cattle drives played out too, because they were economically unsound. The dangers of the trail, the wear and tear on men and cattle, the charges levied on drives across Indian territory, and the advance of farms across the trails combined to persuade cattlemen that they could function best near railroads. As railroads

The cowboy era

Cowboys herd cattle near Cimarron, Colorado, 1905.

spread out into Texas and across the plains, the cattle business spread with them over the High Plains as far as Montana and on into Canada.

In the absence of laws governing the open range, cattle ranchers at first worked out a code of behavior largely dictated by circumstances. As cattle often wandered onto other ranchers' claims, cowboys would "ride the line" to keep the animals off the adjoining ranches. In the spring they would "round up" the herds, which invariably got mixed up, and sort out owner-ship by identifying the distinctive ranch symbols "branded," or burned, into the cattle. All that changed in 1873, when Joseph Glidden, an Illinois farmer, invented the first effective barbed wire, which ranchers used to fence off their claims at relatively low cost. Ranchers rushed to buy the new wire fenc-ing, and soon the open range was no more. Cattle raising, like mining, evolved from a romantic adventure into a big business dominated by giant enterprises.

FARMERS AND THE LAND   Farming has always been a hard life, and it was made more so on the Great Plains by the region's unforgiving environment and mercurial weather. After 1865, on paper at least, the federal land laws offered farmers favorable terms. Under the Homestead Act of 1862, a settler ("homesteader") could gain title to federal land simply by staking out a claim and living on it for five years, or he could buy land at $1.25 an acre after six months. But such land legislation was predicated upon the tradition of farming the fertile lands east of the Mississippi River, and the laws were never adjusted to the fact that much of the prairie was suited only for cattle raising. Cattle ranchers were forced to obtain land by gradual acquisition from homesteaders or land-grant railroads.

The first arrivals on the sod-house frontier faced a grim struggle against danger, adversity, and monotony. Though land was relatively cheap, horses, livestock, wagons, wells, lumber, fencing, seed, and fertilizer were not. Freight rates and interest rates on loans seemed criminally high. As in the South, declining crop prices produced chronic indebtedness, leading strapped western farmers to embrace virtually any plan to inflate the money supply. The virgin land itself, although fertile, resisted planting; the heavy sod broke many a plow. Since wood was almost nonexistent on the prairie, pioneer families used buffalo chips (dried dung) for fuel.

Farmers and their families also fought a constant battle with the elements: tornadoes, hailstorms, droughts, prairie fires, blizzards, and pests. Swarms of locusts often clouded the horizon, occasionally covering the ground six inches deep. A Wichita newspaper reported in 1878 that the grasshoppers devoured "everything green, stripping the foliage off the bark and from the tender twigs of the fruit trees, destroying every plant that is good for food or pleasant to the eyes, that man has planted."

As the railroads brought piles of lumber from the East, farmers could leave their sod houses (homes built of sod) to build more comfortable frame dwellings. New machinery helped provide fresh opportunities. In 1868, James Oliver, a Scottish immigrant living in Indiana, made a successful chilled-iron plow. This "sodbuster" plow greatly eased the task of breaking the tough grass roots of the plains. Improvements and new inventions in threshing machines, hay mowers, planters, manure spreaders, cream separators, and other devices lightened the burden of farm labor but added to the farmers' capital outlay. In Minnesota, the Dakotas, and central California the gigantic "bonanza farms," with machinery for mass production, became the marvels of the age. On one farm in North Dakota, 13,000 acres of wheat made a single field. Another bonanza farm employed over 1,000 migrant workers to tend 34,000 acres.

While the overall value of farmland and farm products increased in the late nineteenth century, small farmers did not keep up with the march of progress. Their numbers grew in size but decreased in proportion to the population at large. Wheat in the Western states, like cotton in the antebellum South, was the great export crop that spurred economic growth. For a variety of reasons, however, few small farmers prospered. By the 1890s they were in open revolt against the "system" of corrupt processors (middlemen) and "greedy" bankers who they believed conspired against them.

PIONEER WOMEN   The West remained a largely male society throughout the nineteenth century. Women were not only a numerical minority; they also continued to face traditional legal barriers and social prejudice. A wife could not sell property without her husband's approval, for example. Texas women could not sue except for divorce, nor could they serve on juries, act as lawyers, or witness a will. But the fight for survival in the trans-Mississippi West made men and women more equal partners than in the East. Many women who lost their mates to the deadly toil of sod busting thereafter assumed complete responsibility for their farms. In general, women on the prairie became more independent than women leading domestic lives back East. A Kansas woman explained "that the environment was such as to bring out and develop the dominant qualities of individual

Women of the frontier

A woman and her family in front of their sod house. The difficult life on the prairie led to more egalitarian marriages than were found in other regions of the country.

character. Kansas women of that day learned at an early age to depend on themselves—to do whatever work there was to be done, and to face danger when it must be faced, as calmly as they were able."

THE END OF THE FRONTIER American life reached an important juncture at the end of the nineteenth century. The 1890 national census reported that the frontier era in American development was over; people by then had spread across the entire continent. This fact inspired the historian **Frederick Jackson Turner** to develop his influential frontier thesis, first outlined in "The Significance of the Frontier in American History," a paper delivered to the American Historical Association in 1893. "The existence of an area of free land," Turner wrote, "its continuous recession, and the advance of American settlement westward, explain American development." The frontier, he added, had shaped the national character in fundamental ways. It was

> to the frontier [that] the American intellect owes its striking characteristics. That coarseness and strength combined with acuteness and acquisitiveness; that practical, inventive turn of mind, quick to find expedients; that masterful grasp of material things, lacking in the artistic but powerful to effect great ends; that restless, nervous energy; that dominant individualism, working for good and for evil, and withal that buoyancy and exuberance which comes with freedom—these are traits of the frontier, or traits called out elsewhere because of the existence of the frontier.

In 1893, Turner concluded, "four centuries from the discovery of America, at the end of a hundred years under the Constitution, the frontier has gone and with its going has closed the first period of American history."

Turner's "frontier thesis" guided several generations of scholars and students in their understanding of the distinctive characteristics of American history. His view of the frontier as the westward-moving source of the nation's democratic politics, open society, unfettered economy, and rugged individualism, far removed from the corruptions of urban life, gripped the popular imagination as well. But it left out much of the story. The frontier experience Turner described exaggerated the homogenizing effect of the frontier environment and virtually ignored the role of women, African Americans, Native Americans, Mormons, Hispanics, and Asians in shaping the diverse human geography of the western United States. Turner also implied that the West would be fundamentally different after 1890 because the frontier experience was essentially over. But in many respects that region has retained the qualities associated with the rush for land, gold, timber, and water rights during the post–Civil War decades. The mining frontier, as one historian has recently written, "set a mood that has never disappeared from the West: the attitude of extractive industry—get in, get rich, get out."

End of Chapter Review

- **Indian Wars and Policies**   By 1900, Native Americans in the West were no longer free to roam the plains. Disease and the influx of farmers and miners reduced their numbers and curtailed their way of life. Instances of resistance, such as the Great Sioux War, were crushed. Initially, Indian tribes were forced to sign treaties and were confined to reservations. Beginning in 1887, the American government's Indian policy was aimed at forcing Indians to relinquish their traditional culture and adopt individual land ownership, settled agriculture, and Christianity.

- **Life in the West**   Life in the West was harsh and violent, but the promise of cheap land or wealth from mining drew settlers from the East. Most cowboys and miners did not acquire wealth, however, because raising cattle and mining became large-scale enterprises that enriched only a few. Although most westerners were white Protestant Americans or northern European immigrants, Mexicans, African Americans, and Chinese contributed to the West's diversity. As a consequence of the region's rugged isolation, women achieved greater equality in everyday life than did most women elsewhere in the country.

- **Growth of Mining**   Mining lured settlers to largely uninhabited regions, thereby hastening the creation of new territories and the admission of new states into the Union. By the 1880s, when mining became a big business employing large-scale equipment, its environmental impact could be seen in the blighted landscape.

- **The American Frontier**   The historian Frederick Jackson Turner believed that the enduring presence of the frontier was responsible for making Americans individualistic, materialistic, practical, democratic, and energetic. In 1893 he declared that the closing of the frontier had ended the first stage of America's history.

CHRONOLOGY

1859	Comstock Lode is discovered
1862	Congress passes the Homestead Act
1864	Sand Creek Massacre
1873	Joseph Glidden invents barbed wire
1876	Battle of Little Bighorn
1877	With the Compromise of 1877, Rutherford B. Hayes becomes president and Reconstruction comes to an end
1886	Surrender of Geronimo marks the end of the Indian wars
1887	Congress passes the Severalty Act
1890	Battle of Wounded Knee
1893	Frederick J. Turner's "frontier thesis"

KEY TERMS & NAMES

New South p. 607

sharecroppers p. 609

redeemers p. 611

Bourbons p. 611

George A. Custer p. 616

Great Sioux War p. 617

Ghost Dance movement p. 619

Frederick Jackson Turner p. 624

2 0

THE EMERGENCE
OF URBAN AMERICA

FOCUS QUESTIONS wwnorton.com/studyspace

- What accounted for the rise of cities in America?
- How did the "new immigration" change America at the end of the nineteenth century?
- What new forms of mass entertainment had emerged by 1900?
- What was the impact of Darwinian thought on social sciences?

Within three decades after the Civil War, a stunning transformation had occurred in American life. A society long rooted in the soil and focused on domestic issues became an urban-industrial nation inextricably involved in world markets and global politics. Cities are one of humanity's greatest creations, and in the United States during the second half of the nineteenth century, cities grew at a rate unparalleled in world history. The late nineteenth century, declared an economist in 1899, was "not only the age of cities, but the age of great cities." Between 1860 and 1910 the urban population mushroomed from 6 million to 44 million. By 1920, more than half the nation's population lived in urban areas. People from different ethnic and religious backgrounds and every walk of life poured into the high-rise apartment buildings and ramshackle tenements springing up in every major city. They came in search of jobs, wealth, and excitement.

Not surprisingly, the rise of metropolitan America created an array of new social problems. Rapid urban development produced widespread poverty and political corruption. How to feed, clothe, shelter, and educate the new arrivals taxed the imagination—and the patience—of urban leaders. Further complicating efforts to improve the quality of life in the nation's cities was increasing residential segregation according to racial and ethnic background and social class.

AMERICA'S MOVE TO TOWN

The prospect of good jobs and social excitement in the cities lured workers by the millions from the countryside and overseas. City people became distinctively urban in demeanor and outlook, and the contrasts between farm and city life grew more vivid with each passing year.

EXPLOSIVE URBAN GROWTH   The frontier was a societal safety valve, the historian Frederick Jackson Turner said in his influential thesis on American development. Its cheap lands afforded a release for the population pressures mounting in the cities. If there was such a thing as a safety valve in the nineteenth century, however, Turner had it exactly backward. The flow of population toward the cities was greater than the flow toward the West. Much of the westward movement, in fact, was itself an urban movement, spawning new towns near the mining digs or at the railheads. On the Pacific coast a greater portion of the population was urbanized than anywhere else; its major concentrations were around San Francisco Bay at first and then in Los Angeles, which became a boomtown after the arrival of the Southern Pacific and Santa Fe Railroads in the 1880s. In the Northwest, Seattle grew quickly, first as the terminus of three transcontinental railroad lines and, by the end of the century, as the staging area for the Yukon gold rush. Minneapolis, St. Paul, Omaha, Kansas City, and Denver experienced rapid growth as well. The South, too, produced new cities: Durham, North Carolina, and Birmingham, Alabama, which were centers of tobacco and iron production, and Houston, Texas, which handled cotton and cattle and, later, oil.

While the Far West had the greatest proportion of urban dwellers, the Northeast had far more people in its teeming cities. These city dwellers were increasingly landless and homeless: they had nothing but their labor to sell. By 1900, more than 90 percent of the residents in New York City's Manhattan lived in rented houses or congested multi-story apartment buildings, called tenements.

Several technological innovations allowed city buildings to expand vertically to accommodate their surging populations. In the 1870s, developments in heating, such as steam circulating through radiators, enabled the construction of large apartment buildings, since fireplaces were no longer needed. In 1889, the Otis Elevator Company installed the first electric elevator, which made possible the erection of taller buildings—before the 1860s few structures had risen beyond three or four stories. And during the 1880s, engineers developed cast-iron and steel-frame construction techniques. Because such materials were stronger than brick, they allowed developers to erect high-rise buildings, called skyscrapers.

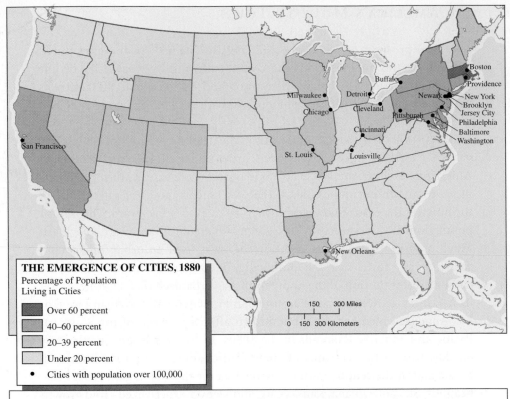

THE EMERGENCE OF CITIES, 1880

Percentage of Population Living in Cities

- Over 60 percent
- 40–60 percent
- 20–39 percent
- Under 20 percent
- Cities with population over 100,000

Which states had the largest urban population in 1880? What drove the growth of western cities? How were western cities different from eastern cities?

Cities also expanded horizontally after the introduction of important transportation innovations. Before the 1890s the chief power sources of urban transport were either animals or steam. Horse- and mule-drawn streetcars had appeared in antebellum cities, but they were slow and cumbersome, and cleaning up after the animals added to the cost. In 1873, San Francisco became the first city to use cable cars that clamped onto a moving underground cable driven by a central power source. Some cities used steam-powered trains on elevated tracks, but by the 1890s electric trolleys were preferred. Mass transit received an added boost when subways were built in Boston, New York City, and Philadelphia.

The spread of mass transit allowed large numbers of people to become commuters, and a growing middle class retreated from downtown to live in quieter tree-lined "streetcar suburbs," whence they could travel into the central city for business or entertainment (though working folk generally stayed

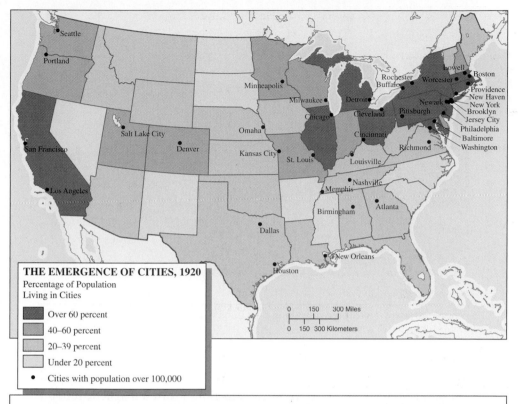

THE EMERGENCE OF CITIES, 1920

Percentage of Population
Living in Cities

- Over 60 percent
- 40–60 percent
- 20–39 percent
- Under 20 percent
- • Cities with population over 100,000

How did technology change urban life in the early twentieth century? What was the role of mass transit in expanding the urban population? How did the demographics of the new cities change between 1880 and 1920?

put, unable to afford even the nickel fare). Urban growth often became a sprawl, since it usually took place without plan, in the interest of a fast buck, and without thought to the need for parks and public services.

The use of horse-drawn railways, cable cars, and electric trolleys helped transform the social character of cities. After the Civil War, the emergence of suburbs began to segregate people according to their wealth. The more affluent moved outside the city, leaving behind the working folk, many of whom were immigrants or African Americans. The poorer districts of a city became more congested and crime ridden as the population grew, fueled by waves of newcomers from abroad.

THE ALLURE AND PROBLEMS OF THE CITIES The wonders of the cities—their glittering new electric lights, their streetcars, telephones,

Urban mass transit

A horse-drawn streetcar moving along rails in New York City.

department stores, vaudeville shows and other amusements, newspapers and magazines, and a thousand other attractions—cast a magnetic lure on rural youth. In times of rural depression, thousands left farms for the cities in search of opportunity and personal freedom. The exodus from the countryside was especially evident in the East, where the census documented the shift in population from country to city. Yet those who moved to the city often traded one set of problems for another. Workers in the big cities often had no choice but to live in crowded apartments, most of which were poorly designed. In 1900, Manhattan's 42,700 tenements housed almost 1.6 million people. Such unregulated urban growth created immense problems of sanitation, health, and morale.

During the last quarter of the nineteenth century, cities became so cramped and land so scarce that designers were forced to build upward. In New York City this resulted in tenement houses, shared buildings with multiple housing units. These structures were usually six to eight stories tall, lacked elevators, and were jammed tightly against one another. Twenty-four to thirty-two families would cram into each building. Some city blocks housed almost four thousand people. Shoehorned into their quarters, families living in tenements had no privacy, free space, or sunshine; children had few places to play except in the streets; infectious diseases and noxious odors were rampant. Not surprisingly, the mortality rate among the urban poor was much higher than that of the general population. In one poor Chicago district at the end of the century, three out of five babies died before their first birthday.

CITIES AND THE ENVIRONMENT   Nineteenth-century cities were filthy and disease ridden, noisy and smelly. They overflowed with garbage, contaminated water, horse urine and manure, roaming pigs, and untreated sewage. Providing clean water was a chronic problem, and raw sewage was dumped into streets and waterways. Epidemics of water-related diseases such as cholera, typhoid fever, and yellow fever ravaged urban populations. Animal waste was pervasive. In 1900, for example, there were over 3.5 million horses in American cities, each of which generated 20 pounds of manure and several gallons of urine daily. In Chicago alone, 82,000 horses produced 300,000 tons of manure each year. The life expectancy of urban draft horses was only two years, which meant that thousands of horse carcasses had to be disposed of each year. In New York City, 15,000 dead horses were removed annually.

During the late nineteenth century, municipal reformers organized to clean up the cities. The "sanitary reformers"—public health officials and municipal engineers—persuaded city governments to banish hogs and cattle within the city limits, mount cleanup campaigns, build water and sewage systems, institute trash collection, and replace horses with electric streetcars. By 1900, 94 percent of American cities had developed regular trash-collection services.

Yet such improvements in public health involved important social and ecological trade-offs and caused unanticipated problems. Waste that once had been put into the land was now dumped into waterways. Similarly, solving the horse-manure problem involved trade-offs. The manure dropped on city streets caused stench and bred countless flies, many of which carried diseases such as typhoid fever. But urban horse manure also had benefits. Farmers living on the outskirts of cities used it to fertilize hay and vegetable crops. City-generated manure was the agricultural lifeblood of the vegetable farms outside New York, Baltimore, Philadelphia, and Boston.

Ultimately, however, the development of public water and sewer systems and flush toilets separated urban dwellers and their waste from the agricultural cycle at the same time that the emergence of refrigerated railcars and massive meatpacking plants separated most people from their sources of food. While the advances provided great benefits, a flush-and-forget-it mentality emerged. Well into the twentieth century, people presumed that running water purified itself, so they dumped massive amounts of untreated

Urbanization and the environment

A garbage cart retrieves trash in New York City, ca. 1890.

waste into rivers and bays. What they failed to calculate was the carrying capacity of the waterways. The high phosphorous content of bodily waste dumped into streams led to algae blooms that sucked the oxygen out of the water and unleashed a string of environmental reactions that suffocated fish and affected marine ecology. In sum, city growth had unintended consequences.

THE NEW IMMIGRATION

The Industrial Revolution brought to American shores waves of new immigrants from every part of the globe. Between 1860 and 1920 about one in seven Americans was foreign-born. Immigrants were even more numerous in cities. By 1900 nearly 30 percent of the residents of major cities were foreign-born. These newcomers provided much-needed labor, but their arrival sparked ugly racial and ethnic tensions.

AMERICA'S PULL   The migration of foreigners to the United States has been one of the most powerful forces shaping American history, and this was especially true between 1860 and 1920. In steadily rising numbers, immigrants moved from the agricultural areas of eastern and southern Europe directly to the largest cities of America. Once in the United States, they wanted to live with others who shared their language, customs, and religion. Ethnic neighborhoods in American cities preserved familiar folkways and shielded newcomers from the shocks of a strange culture. In 1890, four out of five New Yorkers were foreign-born, a higher proportion than in any other city in the world. New York had twice as many Irish as Dublin, as many Germans as Hamburg, and half as many Italians as Naples. In 1893, Chicago claimed the largest Bohemian (Czech) community in the world, and by 1910 the size of its Polish population ranked behind only the populations of Warsaw and Lodz.

This nation of immigrants continued to draw new inhabitants for much the same reasons as before and from much the same segments of society. Immigrants took flight from famine or the dispiriting lack of opportunity in their native lands. They fled racial, religious, and political persecution and compulsory military service. Yet more immigrants were probably pulled by

Steerage deck of the S.S. *Pennland*, 1893

These immigrants are about to arrive at Ellis Island in New York Harbor. Many newcomers to America settled in cities because they lacked the means to take up farming.

America's promise than were pushed out by conditions at home. American industries, seeking cheap labor, sent recruiting agents abroad. Railroads, eager to sell land and build up the traffic on their lines, distributed tempting propaganda in Europe in a medley of languages. Under the Contract Labor Act of 1864, the federal government helped pay an immigrant's passage. The law was repealed in 1868, but not until 1885 did the government forbid companies to import contract labor, a practice that put immigrant workers under the control of their employers.

After the Civil War, the tide of immigration rose from just under 3 million in the 1870s to more than 5 million in the 1880s, then fell to a little over 3.5 million in the depression decade of the 1890s and rose to its high-water mark of nearly 9 million in the first decade of the twentieth century. The numbers declined to 6 million from 1910 to 1920 and to 4 million in the 1920s, after which official restrictions nearly cut the flow of immigrants.

Before 1880, immigrants were mainly from northern and western Europe. By the 1870s, however, that pattern had begun to change. The proportion of Slavs and Jews from southern and eastern Europe rose sharply. After 1890, these groups made up a majority of the newcomers, and by the first decade of the new century they formed 70 percent of the immigrants to this country. Among the new immigrants were Italians, Hungarians, Czechs, Slovaks, Poles, Serbs, Croats, Slovenes, Russians, Romanians, and Greeks—all people whose culture and language were markedly different from those of western Europe and whose religion for the most part was Judaism, Eastern Orthodox, or Roman Catholicism.

ELLIS ISLAND   Most immigrants arriving in America passed through a reception center on a tiny island off the New Jersey coast, a mile south of Manhattan, near the Statue of Liberty. In 1892, **Ellis Island** opened its doors to the "huddled masses" of the world. In 1907, the reception center's busiest year, more than 1 million new arrivals passed through the receiving center, an average of about 5,000 per day; in one day alone, immigration officials processed some 11,750. These were the immigrants who crammed into the steerage compartments deep in the ships' hulls. Those refugees who could afford first- and second-class cabins did not have to visit Ellis Island; they were examined on board, and most of them simply walked down the gangway onto the docks in lower Manhattan.

STRANGERS IN A NEW LAND   Once on American soil, immigrants felt exhilaration, exhaustion, and usually a desperate need for work. Many were

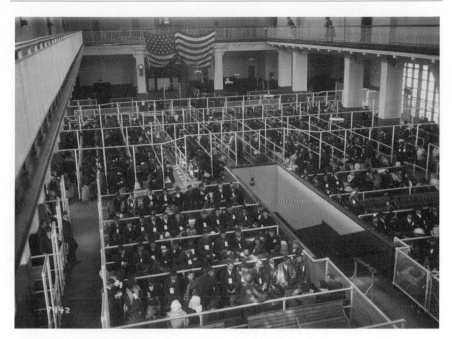

The Registry Room at Ellis Island

Inspectors asked arriving passengers twenty-nine probing questions, including "Are you a polygamist?"

greeted by family and friends who had come over before them, others by representatives of immigrant-aid societies or by hiring agents offering jobs in mines, mills, or sweatshops. Since most immigrants knew little if any English and nothing about American employment practices, they were easy subjects for exploitation. In exchange for a bit of whiskey and a job, obliging hiring agents claimed a healthy percentage of their wages. Other contractors provided train tickets to inland cities such as Buffalo, Pittsburgh, Cleveland, Chicago, Milwaukee, Cincinnati, and St. Louis.

As strangers in a new land, most of the immigrants naturally gravitated to neighborhoods populated by their own kind. The immigrant enclaves—nicknamed Little Italy, Little Hungary, Chinatown, and so on—served as crucial transitional communities between the newcomers' Old World past and their New World future. In such kinship communities, immigrants practiced their native religion, clung to their native customs, and conversed in their native tongue. But they paid a price for such community solidarity. When the "new immigrants" moved into an area, older residents typically moved out, taking with them whatever social prestige and political influence they had achieved. The quality of living conditions quickly deteriorated as housing and sanitation codes went unenforced.

THE NATIVIST RESPONSE   Then, as now, many native-born Americans saw the wave of new immigrants as a threat to their way of life and their jobs. These "**nativists**" felt that the newcomers threatened traditional American culture. A Stanford University professor called them "illiterate, docile, lacking in self-reliance and initiative, and not possessing the Anglo-Teutonic conceptions of law, order, and government." Cultural differences confirmed in the minds of nativists the assumption that the Nordic peoples of the old immigration were superior to the Slavic, Italian, Greek, and Jewish peoples of the new immigration. Many of the new immigrants were illiterate, and more appeared so because they could not speak English. Some resorted to crime, encouraging suspicions that criminals were being quietly helped out of Europe just as they had once been transported from England to the colonies.

IMMIGRATION RESTRICTION   Throughout American history, Congress has passed inconsistent laws regulating immigration, laws that frequently have been rooted in racial and ethnic prejudice. During the late nineteenth century such prejudice took an ugly turn. The Chinese were victims of every act of discrimination the European immigrants suffered and more. They were not white; they were not Christian; many were not literate. By 1880, there were some seventy-five thousand Chinese in California, about a ninth of the state's population. Many white workers resented the Chinese for accepting lower wages, but their greatest sin, the editor of the *New York Nation* opined with tongue-in-cheek irony, was perpetuating "those disgusting habits of thrift, industry, and self-denial."

In 1882, Congress overturned President Chester A. Arthur's veto of the **Chinese Exclusion Act**. It thus became the first federal law to restrict immigration on the basis of race and class, shutting the door to Chinese immigrants for ten years. The discriminatory legislation received overwhelming support. One congressman explained that because the "industrial army of Asiatic laborers" was increasing the tension between workers and management, "the gate must be closed." The Chinese Exclusion Act was periodically renewed before being extended indefinitely in 1902. Not until 1943 were barriers to Chinese immigration finally removed.

The 1882 Chinese Exclusion Act was the first federal law to restrict immigration explicitly on the basis of racial and class criteria. It was not the last. In 1891 the prominent politician Henry Cabot Lodge of Massachusetts took up the cause of excluding illiterate foreigners, a measure that would have affected much of the new wave of immigrants even though literacy in English was not required. Lodge and other prominent New Englanders organized the Immigrations Restriction League, an organization dedicated to saving the Anglo-Saxon "race" in America from being "contaminated" by alien immigrants. Three presidents vetoed bills embodying the restriction of illiterate immigrants on the grounds that they penalized people for lack of opportunity: Grover Cleveland in 1897, William H. Taft in 1913, and Woodrow Wilson in 1915 and 1917. The last time, however, Congress overrode the veto.

Although these legislative efforts sharply reduced the flow of Chinese immigrants, they did not stop the influx completely. In 1910 the West Coast counterpart of Ellis Island opened on rugged Angel Island, six miles off-shore from San Francisco, to process tens of thousands of Asian immigrants, most of them Chinese. Those arrivals from China who could claim a Chinese American parent were allowed to enter, as were certain officials, teachers, merchants, and students. The powerful prejudice that the Chinese immigrants encountered helps explain why over 30 percent of the arrivals at Angel Island were denied entry.

POPULAR CULTURE

The flood of people into large towns and cities created new patterns of recreation and leisure. Traditionally, people in rural areas were tied to the rituals of the harvest season and intimately connected to their neighbors and extended families. By contrast, most middle-class urban whites had enough money to be more mobile; they were primarily connected to the other members of their nuclear family (made up only of parents and children), and their affluence enabled them to enjoy greater leisure time and an increasing discretionary income. Middle- and upper-class urban families spent much of their leisure time together at home, usually in the parlor, singing around a piano, reading novels, or playing cards, dominoes, backgammon, chess, and checkers.

In the congested metropolitan areas, politics became as much a form of public entertainment as it was a means of providing civic representation and public services. People flocked to hear visiting candidates speak. Impassioned oratory, whether delivered by elected officials or ministers, was the primary medium of civic culture. In cities such as New York, Philadelphia, Boston, and Chicago, membership in a political party was akin to belonging to a social club. In addition, labor unions provided activities that were more social than economic in nature, and members often visited the union hall as

Vaudeville

For as little as one cent, vaudeville offered customers entertainment.

much to socialize as to discuss working conditions. The sheer number of city dwellers also helped generate new forms of mass entertainment, such as traveling Wild West shows, vaudeville shows, and spectator sports.

A READING PUBLIC In the half century after the Civil War, newspapers were the primary means of communication. They were not only the source of local and national news, but they also the primary medium for political life. Many of them also published poetry and fiction. Between 1870 and 1900, the number of daily newspapers—in English as well as numerous foreign languages—grew twice as fast as the population, and the number of subscribers grew even faster. Most of the newspapers were openly partisan, identifying with one of the major national political parties.

SALOON CULTURE The most popular destinations for the urban working class were saloons and dance halls. The saloon was the poor-man's social club during the late nineteenth century. By 1900, there were more saloons in the United States (over 325,000) than there were grocery stores and meat markets. Immigrants owned most saloons, many of which were financed by the huge, often German American–owned breweries such as Adolphus Busch's Budweiser. New York City alone had ten thousand saloons, or one for every five hundred residents. Often sponsored by beer brewers and frequented by local politicians, saloons offered a free lunch to encourage patrons to visit and buy 5¢ beer or 15¢ whiskey.

Saloons provided much more than food and drink, however; they were in effect public homes, offering haven and fellowship to people who often worked ten hours a day, six days a week. Saloons were especially popular among male immigrants seeking companionship in a new land. Saloons served as busy social hubs and were often aligned with local political machines. In New York City in the 1880s, most of the primary elections and local political caucuses were conducted in saloons.

Men went to saloons to learn about jobs, engage in labor union activities, cash paychecks, mail letters, read newspapers, and gossip about neighborhood affairs. Because saloons were heated and offered public restrooms, they also served as places of refuge for poor people whose own slum tenements or cramped lodging houses were not as accommodating. Many saloons included gymnasiums. Patrons could play handball, chess, billiards, darts, cards, or dice.

Saloons were defiantly male enclaves. Although women and children occasionally entered a saloon—through a side door—in order to carry home a pail of beer (called "rushing the growler") or to drink at a backroom party, the main bar at the front was for men only. Some saloons provided "snugs," small separate rooms for female patrons.

Saloons aroused intense criticism. Anti-liquor societies such as the Women's Christian Temperance Union and the Anti-Saloon League charged that saloons contributed to alcoholism, divorce, crime, and absenteeism from work. Reformers such as the colorful Carry Nation demanded that saloons be closed down. Yet drunkenness in saloons was the exception rather than the rule. To be sure, most patrons of working-class saloons had little money to waste, and recent studies have revealed that the average amount of money spent on liquor was no more than 5 percent of a man's annual income. Saloons were the primary locus of the workingman's leisure time and political activity. As a journalist observed, "The saloon is, in short, the social and intellectual center of the neighborhood."

OUTDOOR RECREATION   The congestion and disease associated with city life led many people to participate in forms of outdoor recreation to restore their vitality and improve their health. A movement to create urban parks flourished after the construction of New York's Central Park in 1858.

Its planner, **Frederick Law Olmsted**, went on to design parks for Boston, Brooklyn, Chicago, Philadelphia, San Francisco, and many other cities. Although originally intended as places where people could walk and commune with nature, parks soon offered more vigorous forms of exercise and recreation—for men and women.

Croquet and tennis courts were among the first additions to city parks because they took up little space and required little maintenance. Lawn tennis was invented by an Englishman in 1873 and arrived in the United States a year later. By 1885, New York's Central Park had thirty courts. Even more popular than croquet or tennis was cycling, or "wheeling." In the 1870s, bicycles began to be manufactured in the United States, and by the end of the century a bicycle craze had swept the country. Bicycles were especially popular with women who chafed at the restricting conventions of the Victorian era. The new vehicles offered exercise, freedom, and access to the countryside.

Tandem tricycle

In spite of the danger and discomfort of early bicycles, "wheeling" became a popular form of recreation and mode of transportation.

The urban working poor could not afford to acquire a bicycle or join a croquet club, however. Nor did they have as much free time as the affluent. At the end of their long days and on Sundays, they sought recreation and fellowship on street corners or on the front stoops of their apartment buildings. Organ grinders and other musicians would perform on the sidewalks among the food vendors. Many ethnic groups, especially the Germans and the Irish, formed male singing, drinking, or gymnastic clubs. Working folk also attended bare-knuckle boxing matches or baseball games and on Sundays would gather for picnics. By the end of the century, large-scale amusement parks such as the one at Brooklyn's Coney Island provided entertainment for the entire family. Yet many inner city youth could not afford the trolley fare, so the crowded streets and dangerous alleys remained their playgrounds.

WORKING WOMEN AND LEISURE   In contrast to the male public culture centered in saloons, the leisure activities of working-class women, many of them immigrants, were more limited at the end of the nineteenth century. Married women were so encumbered by housework and maternal responsibilities that they had little free time. As a social worker noted, "The men have the saloons, political clubs, trade-unions or [fraternal] lodges for their recreation . . . while the mothers have almost no recreation, only a dreary round of work, day after day, with occasionally doorstep gossip to vary the monotony of their lives." Married working-class women often used the streets as their public space. Washing clothes, supervising children, or shopping at the local market provided opportunities for fellowship with other women.

Single women had more time for leisure and recreation than did working mothers. They flocked to dance halls, theaters, amusement parks, and picnic grounds. On hot summer days many working-class folk went to public beaches. With the advent of movie theaters during the second decade of the twentieth century, the cinema became the most popular form of entertainment for women.

Young single women participated in urban amusements for a variety of reasons: escape, pleasure, adventure, companionship, and autonomy. As a promotional flyer for a movie theater promised, "If you are tired of life, go to the movies. If you are sick of troubles rife, go to the picture show. You will forget your unpaid bills, rheumatism and other ills, if you stow your pills and go to the picture show." Urban recreational and entertainment activities also allowed opportunities for romance and sexual relationships. Not surprisingly, young women eager for such recreation encountered far more

Steeplechase Park, Coney Island, Brooklyn, New York

Members of the working class could afford the inexpensive rides at this popular amusement park.

obstacles than did young men. Just as reformers sought to shut down saloons, parents and authorities tried to restrict the freedom of young women to engage in "cheap amusements." Yet many young women followed their own wishes and in so doing helped carve out their own social sphere.

SPECTATOR SPORTS   In the last quarter of the nineteenth century, new spectator sports such as college football and basketball and professional baseball gained mass appeal, reflecting the growing urbanization of life. People could gather easily for sporting events in the large cities. Spectator sports became urban extravaganzas, unifying the diverse ethnic groups in the large cities and attracting people with the leisure time and cash to spend on watching others perform—or bet on the outcome.

Football emerged as a modified form of soccer and rugby. The College of New Jersey (Princeton) and Rutgers played the first college football game in 1869. Basketball was invented in 1891, when Dr. James Naismith, a physical education instructor, nailed two peach baskets to the walls of the Young Men's Christian Association (YMCA) training school in Springfield, Massachusetts. Naismith wanted to create an indoor winter game that could be played between the fall football and spring baseball seasons. Basketball quickly grew in popularity among boys and girls. Vassar and Smith Colleges added the sport in 1892. In 1893, Vanderbilt University, in Nashville, became the first college to field a men's team.

Baseball laid claim to being America's national pastime at midcentury. Contrary to popular opinion, Abner Doubleday did not invent the game. Instead, Alexander Cartwright, a New York bank clerk and sportsman, is recognized as the father of organized baseball. In 1845 he gathered a group of merchants, stockbrokers, and physicians to form the Knickerbocker Base Ball Club of New York.

The first professional baseball team was the Cincinnati Red Stockings, which made its appearance in 1869. In 1900 the American League was organized, and two years later the first World Series was held. Baseball became the national pastime and the most democratic sport in America. People from all social classes (mostly men) attended the games, and recent immigrants were among the most faithful fans. The

WEIDMAN. P. Detroits

COPYRIGHTED BY GOODWIN & CO. 1887.

GOODWIN & CO. New York.

Baseball card, 1887

The excitement of rooting for the home team united all classes.

St. Louis Post-Dispatch reported in 1883 that "a glance at the audience on any fine day at the ball park will reveal . . . telegraph operators, printers who work at night, travelling [sales]men . . . men of leisure . . . men of capital, bank clerks who get away at 3 P.M., real estate men . . . barkeepers . . . hotel clerks, actors and employees of the theater, policemen and firemen on their day off . . . butchers and bakers." Cheering for a city baseball team gave rootless people a common loyalty and a sense of belonging.

Only white players were allowed in the major leagues. African Americans played on "minor league" teams or in all-black Negro leagues. In 1887, the Cuban Giants, an exhibition team made up of black players, traveled the country. A few major league white teams agreed to play them. An African American–owned newspaper announced in early 1888 that the Cuban

Giants "have defeated the New Yorks, 4 games out of 5, and are now virtually champions of the world." But, it added, "the St. Louis Browns, Detroits and Chicagos, afflicted by Negrophobia and unable to bear the odium of being beaten by colored men, refused to accept their challenge."

By the end of the nineteenth century, sports of all kinds had become a major cultural phenomenon in the United States. A writer for *Harper's Weekly* announced in 1895 that "ball matches, football games, tennis tournaments, bicycle races, [and] regattas, have become part of our national life." They "are watched with eagerness and discussed with enthusiasm and understanding by all manner of people, from the day-laborer to the millionaire." One reporter in the 1890s referred to the "athletic craze" that was sweeping the American imagination. Moreover, it was in 1892 that a Frenchman, Pierre de Coubertin, called for the revival of the ancient Olympic Games, and the first modern Olympiad was held four years later.

Education and Social Thought

Much as popular culture was transformed as a result of the urban-industrial revolution, intellectual life also adapted to new social realities. The new urban culture relished new knowledge and immediate experience. A growing number of writers, artists, and intellectuals were no longer interested in romantic themes and idealized life. They focused their attention on the emerging realities of scientific research and technology, factories and railroads, cities and immigrants, wage labor and social tensions.

INTELLECTUAL LIFE   The prestige and premises of modern science increased enormously during the second half of the nineteenth century. Researchers explored electromagnetic induction, the conservation of matter, the laws of thermodynamics, and the relationship between heat and energy. Breakthroughs in chemistry led to new understandings about the formation of compounds and the nature of chemical reactions. Discoveries of fossils opened up new horizons in geology and paleontology, and greatly improved microscopes enabled zoologists to decipher cell structures.

Virtually every field of thought in the post–Civil War years felt the impact of Charles Darwin's controversial book *On the Origin of Species* (1859). Darwin used extensive observations and cast-iron logic to argue that most organisms produce many more offspring than can survive. Those offspring with advantageous characteristics tend to live while others die—from disease or predators. This random process of "natural selection" over millions of years led to the evolution of species from less complex forms of life: those species that survived by reason of quickness, shrewdness, or other advantages reproduced their kind, while others fell by the wayside. As Darwin wrote, "the vigorous, the healthy, and the happy survive and multiply."

The idea of species evolution shocked people who embraced a literal interpretation of the biblical creation stories. Darwin's findings suggested that there was no providential God controlling the cosmos. Life was the result of the blind natural process of selection. And people were no different from plants and animals; like

Charles Darwin

Darwin's theories influenced more than a century of political debate.

everything else, they too evolved by trial and error rather than by God's purposeful hand. The fossil record revealed a natural history of conflict, pain, and species extinction. What kind of benevolent God would be so cruel as to create a world of such waste, strife, and sorrow? Darwin showed that there could be no proof for the existence of God.

Darwin's findings—as well as the implications that people drew from them—generated heated arguments between scientists and clergymen. Some Christians rejected Darwin's secular doctrine while others found their faith severely shaken not only by evolutionary theory but also by the urging of professional scientists to apply the critical standards of scholarship to the Bible itself. Most of the faithful, however, came to reconcile science and religion. They viewed evolution as the divine will, one of the secondary causes through which God worked.

SOCIAL DARWINISM   Although Charles Darwin's theory of evolution applied only to biological phenomena, others drew broader inferences from it. The temptation to apply evolutionary theory to the social (human) world proved irresistible. Darwin's fellow Englishman **Herbert Spencer**, a social philosopher, became the first major prophet of what came to be called **social Darwinism**, a cluster of ideas that exercised an important influence on American thought. Spencer argued that human society and institutions, like the organisms studied by Darwin, evolved through the same process of natural selection. The result, in Spencer's chilling phrase, was the "survival of the fittest." For Spencer, social evolution was the engine of progress, ending "only in the establishment of the greatest perfection and the most complete happiness." Darwin dismissed Spencer's theories as poppycock. Spencer's arguments, he said, "could never convince me." Darwin especially objected to Spencer's assumption that the evolutionary process in the natural world had any relevance to the human realm.

Others, however, eagerly endorsed Spencer's notion of social Darwinism. If, as Spencer believed, society naturally evolved for the better, then government interference with the process of social evolution was a serious mistake because it would keep unsound people from being weeded out. Social Darwinism implied a hands-off government policy; it decried the regulation of business, the graduated income tax, and sanitation and housing regulations. Such intervention, Spencer charged, would help the "unfit" survive and thereby impede progress. (Ironically, Spencer himself was notoriously frail and would not have been among the surviving "fittest.") The only acceptable charity to Spencer was voluntary, and even that was of dubious value. Spencer warned that "fostering the good-for-nothing [people] at the expense of the good, is an extreme cruelty."

For Spencer and his many American supporters, successful businessmen and corporations provided living proof of the concept of "survival of the fittest." If small businesses were crowded out by huge corporate trusts and monopolies, that too was part of the evolutionary process. The oil tycoon John D. Rockefeller told his Baptist Sunday-school class that the "growth of a large business is merely a survival of the fittest. . . . This is not an evil tendency in business. It is merely the working-out of a law of nature and a law of God."

The ideas of Charles Darwin and Herbert Spencer spread quickly. *Popular Science Monthly*, founded in 1872, became the chief medium for popularizing Darwinism. That year, Spencer's chief academic disciple, William Graham Sumner, began teaching at Yale University, where he preached the gospel of natural selection. Sumner's most lasting contribution, made in his book *Folkways* (1907), was to argue that it would be a mistake for government to interfere with established customs in the name of ideals of equality or natural rights.

REFORM DARWINISM   Sumner's efforts to use Darwinism to promote "rugged individualism" provoked strong criticism. **Reform Darwinism** found its major advocate in an obscure Washington civil servant, Lester Frank Ward, who fought his way up from poverty and never lost his empathy for the underdog. Ward's book *Dynamic Sociology* (1883) singled out one product of evolution that Darwin and Spencer had neglected: the human brain. People, like animals, compete, but they also collaborate; they have minds that shape social evolution. And humans also show compassion for others. Far from being the helpless pawn of evolution, Ward argued, humanity could control and shape the process. Ward's progressive reform Darwinism challenged Sumner's conservative social Darwinism, holding that cooperation, not competition, would better promote progress. According to Ward, Sumner's "irrational distrust of government" might have been justified in an earlier day of autocracy but was not applicable under a representative system. Government could become the agency of progress by pursuing two main goals: ameliorating poverty, which impeded the development of the mind, and promoting the education of the masses. "Intelligence, far more than necessity," Ward wrote, "is the mother of invention," and "the influence of knowledge as a social factor, like that of wealth, is proportional to the extent of its distribution." Intellect, rightly informed by science, could foster social improvement. The intellectual justification for social reform proved to be one of the pillars of the "progressive" movement that would transform urban America during the late nineteenth century and after.

CHAPTER SUMMARY

- **Rise of Cities** America's cities grew in all directions after the Civil War. Electric elevators and new steel-frame construction allowed architects to extend buildings upward. Mass transit enabled the middle class to retreat to suburbs. Crowded tenements bred disease and crime and created an opportunity for urban political bosses to accrue power, in part by distributing to the poor the only relief that existed.

- **New Immigration** By 1900, 30 percent of Americans were foreign-born, with many immigrants coming from eastern and southern Europe rather than western and northern Europe, like most immigrants of generations past. Thus their languages and culture were vastly different from those of native-born Americans. They tended to be Catholic, Eastern Orthodox, or Jewish rather than Protestant. Beginning in the 1880s, nativists advocated immigration laws to exclude the Chinese and the poor and demanded that immigrants pass a literacy test. A federal immigration station on Ellis Island, in New York Harbor, opened in 1892 to process immigrants arriving by ship from across the Atlantic.

- **Mass Entertainment** Cities began to create urban parks, like New York's Central Park, as places for all citizens to stroll, ride bicycles, or play games such as tennis. Vaudeville shows emerged as a popular form of entertainment. Saloons served as local social and political clubs for men. It was in this era that football, baseball, and basketball emerged as spectator sports.

- **Social Darwinism** Charles Darwin's *On the Origin of Species* shocked people who believed in a literal interpretation of the Bible's account of creation. Herbert Spencer and William Graham Sumner, who equated economic and social success with the "survival of the fittest" and advanced the idea that government should not interfere to promote equality, applied Darwin's scientific theory to human society and social institutions.

CHRONOLOGY

1858	Construction of New York's Central Park begins
1859	Darwin's *On the Origin of Species* is published
1882	Congress passes the Chinese Exclusion Act
1889	Otis Elevator Company installs the first electric elevator
1891	Basketball is invented
1892	Ellis Island, a federal center for processing immigrants, opens
1900	Baseball's National League is formed

KEY TERMS & NAMES

Ellis Island p. 636

nativist p. 638

Chinese Exclusion Act
p. 638

Frederick Law Olmsted
p. 642

Herbert Spencer p. 647

social Darwinism p. 647

reform Darwanism p. 648

21

GILDED AGE POLITICS
AND AGRARIAN REVOLT

FOCUS QUESTIONS wwnorton.com/studyspace

- What were the major features of American politics during the Gilded Age?
- What were the major issues in politics during this period?
- What were the main problems facing farmers in the South and the Midwest after the Civil War?
- How and why did farmers become politicized?
- What was significant about the election of 1896?
- How did African American leaders respond to the spread of segregation in the South?

In 1873, the writers Mark Twain and Charles Dudley Warner created an enduring label for the post–Civil War era when they collaborated on a novel titled *The Gilded Age*, a colorful depiction of the widespread political corruption and corporate greed that characterized the period. Generations of political scientists and historians have since reinforced the two novelists' judgment. As a young college graduate in 1879, future president Woodrow Wilson described the state of the political system after the Civil War: "No leaders, no principles; no principles, no parties." Indeed, the real movers and shakers of the Gilded Age were not the men who sat in the White House or Congress but the captains of industry who crisscrossed the continent with railroads and adorned its cities with plumed smokestacks and gaudy mansions.

PARADOXICAL POLITICS

Political life in the **Gilded Age**, the thirty-five years between the end of the Civil War and the end of the nineteenth century, had several distinctive elements. Perhaps the most important feature Gilded Age politics was its localism. Unlike today, the federal government in the nineteenth century was an insignificant force in the lives of Americans, in part because it was so small. In 1871 the entire federal workforce totaled 51,000 civilians (most of them postal workers), and only 6,000 of them actually worked in Washington, D.C. Not until the twentieth century did the federal government begin to overshadow the importance of local and state governments. By 1914, for example, there would be 401,000 federal civilian employees.

Most Americans were far more engaged in local politics. In cities crowded with waves of new immigrants, the political scene was usually controlled by "rings"—small groups of powerful political insiders who managed the nomination and election of candidates, conducted primaries, and influenced policy. Each ring typically had a powerful "boss" who ran things, using his "machine"—a network of neighborhood activists and officials—to govern the town or city. Bosses organized loyal neighborhood voters into wards or precincts, and staged torchlight election parades, fireworks displays, and free banquets—and alcoholic beverages—for voters. They also mediated disputes, helped the needy, and distributed patronage (municipal jobs and contracts) to loyal followers and corporate contributors. Throughout most of the nineteenth century, almost every governmental job—local, state, and federal—was subject to the latest election results. This meant that whichever political party was in power expected government employees to become campaign workers doing the bidding of the party bosses during important elections.

NATIONAL POLITICS   Several factors gave national politics during the Gilded Age its distinctive texture. First, like the urban political machines, the national political parties during the Gilded Age were much more dominant forces than they are today. Party loyalty was intense, often extending over several generations in Irish and Italian families in cities such as Boston, Providence, Rhode Island, New York City, Newark, New Jersey, and Philadelphia.

A second distinctive element of Gilded Age politics was the close division between Republicans and Democrats in Congress, which created the sense of a stalemated political system. Both parties avoided controversial issues or bold initiatives because neither gained dominant power. Voters of the time nonetheless thought politics was very important, making widespread political participation the third distinctive element of post–Civil War politics. Voter turnout during the Gilded Age was commonly about 70 to 80 percent, even in the South, where the disenfranchisement of African Americans was not yet complete. (By contrast, the turnout for the 2008 presidential election was almost 57 percent.)

The paradox of such a high rate of voter participation in the face of the inertia at the national political level raises an obvious question: How was it that elected officials who failed to address the "real issues" of the day presided over the most highly organized and politically active electorate in U.S. history? The answer is partly that the politicians and the voters believed that they *were* dealing with crucial issues: tariff rates, the regulation of corporations, monetary policy, Indian disputes, civil service reform, and immigration. But the answer also reflects the extreme partisanship of the times and the essentially local nature of political culture during the Gilded Age. Politics was then the most popular form of local entertainment.

PARTISAN POLITICS Americans after the Civil War were intensely loyal to one of the two major parties, Democratic or Republican. Most voters cast their ballots for the same party, year after year, generation after generation. Loyalty to a party was often an emotional choice. During the 1870s and 1880s, for example, people continued to fight the Civil War using highly charged political rhetoric as their weapon. Republicans regularly "waved the bloody shirt" in election campaigns, meaning that they reminded voters that the Democratic Party was the party of "secession and civil war" while their party, the party of Lincoln and Grant, had abolished slavery and saved the Union. Democrats, especially in the South, responded by reminding voters that they were the party of white supremacy and states' rights. Blacks in the South, by contrast, voted Republican (before they were disenfranchised) because it was the "party of Lincoln," the "Great Emancipator." Third parties, such as the Greenbackers, Populists, and Prohibitionists, appealed to particular interests and issues, such as currency inflation or temperance legislation.

Political parties also gave people an organizational anchor in an unstable world. Local party officials took care of those who voted their way and distributed appointive public offices and other favors to party loyalists. The city political machines used patronage and favoritism to keep the loyalty of business supporters while providing jobs or food or fuel to working-class voters who had fallen on hard times. Politics was also a form of popular entertainment. The party faithful eagerly took part in rallies and picnics and avidly read newspaper coverage of political issues. Members of political parties developed an intense camaraderie.

Party loyalties and voter turnout in the late nineteenth century reflected religious and ethnic divisions as well as geographic differences. The Republican party attracted mainly Protestants of British descent. The party was dominant in New England, New York, and the upper Midwest. The Republicans, the party of Abraham Lincoln, could also rely upon the votes of African Americans and Union veterans of the Civil War.

The Democrats, by contrast, tended to be a heterogeneous, often unruly coalition embracing southern whites, northern immigrants, Roman Catholics living in the northern states, Jews, freethinkers, and all those repelled by the "party of morality." As one Chicago Democrat explained, "A Republican is a man who wants you t' go t' church every Sunday. A Democrat says if a man wants to have a glass of beer on Sunday he can have it."

Republicans also promoted what were called nativist policies, which imposed restrictions on immigration and the employment of foreigners. Efforts to prohibit the sale of alcoholic beverages revived along with nativism in the 1880s. Among the immigrants who crowded into the growing cities were many Irish, Germans, and Italians, all of whom tended to enjoy wine and beer on a daily basis. The mostly rural Republican Protestant moralists increasingly saw saloons as the central social evil around which all others revolved, including vice, crime, political corruption, and neglect of families, and they associated these problems with the ethnic groups that frequented saloons. The feisty Carry Nation, a militant member of the Women's Christian Temperance Union (WCTU) who was known for attacking saloons with a hatchet, charged that saloons stripped women of everything by seducing working men: "Her husband is torn from her, she is robbed of her sons, her home, her food, and her virtue."

POLITICAL STALEMATE   Between 1869 and 1913, from the presidency of Ulysses S. Grant through that of William Howard Taft, Republicans monopolized the White House except for the two nonconsecutive terms of the conservative New York Democrat Grover Cleveland, but otherwise national politics was remarkably balanced between the two major parties. Between 1872 and 1896 no president won a majority of the popular vote. In each of those presidential elections, sixteen states invariably voted Republican and fourteen voted Democratic, leaving a pivotal six states whose results determined the outcome. The important swing-vote role played by two of those states, New York and Ohio, helps explain the election of eight presidents from those states from 1872 to 1908.

No chief executive between Abraham Lincoln and Theodore Roosevelt could be described as a "strong" president. None challenged the prevailing view that Congress, not the White House, should formulate policy. Senator John Sherman of Ohio expressed the widely held notion that the legislative branch should predominate in a republic: "The President should merely obey and enforce the law."

Republicans controlled the Senate and Democrats controlled the House during the Gilded Age. Only during 1881 to 1883 and 1889 to 1891 did a Republican president coincide with a Republican Congress, and only between 1893 and 1895 did a Democratic president enjoy a Democratic majority in Congress. On the important questions of the currency, regulation of big business, farm problems, civil service reform, and immigration, the parties differed very little. As a result, they primarily became vehicles for seeking office and dispensing "patronage" in the form of government jobs and contracts.

STATE AND LOCAL INITIATIVES   Americans during the Gilded Age expected little direct support from the federal government; most significant political activity occurred at the state and local levels. Only 40 percent of government spending and taxing occurred at the federal level. Then, unlike today, the large cities spent far more on local services than did the federal government, and three fourths of all public employees worked for state and local governments. Local issues generated far more excitement than complex national debates over tariffs and monetary policies. It was the state and local governments that first sought to curb the power and restrain the abuses of corporate interests.

CORRUPTION AND REFORM: HAYES TO HARRISON

After the Civil War, a close alliance developed between business and political leaders at every level. As a leading congressman, for example, James Gillespie Blaine of Maine saw nothing wrong in his accepting gifts of stock from an Arkansas railroad after helping it win a land grant from Congress. Free railroad tickets, free entertainment, and a host of other favors were regularly provided to politicians, newspaper editors, and other leaders in positions to influence public opinion or affect legislation.

Both Republican and Democratic leaders also squabbled over the "spoils" of office, the appointive political positions at the local and the national levels. After each election it was expected that the victorious party would replace the defeated party's government appointees with its own. The patronage system of awarding government jobs to supporters invited corruption. It also was so

"The Bosses of the Senate"

This 1889 cartoon bitingly portrays the period's corrupt alliance between big business and politics.

time-consuming that it distracted elected officials from more important issues. Yet George Washington Plunkitt, a Democratic boss in New York City, spoke for many Gilded Age politicians when he explained that "you can't keep an organization together without patronage. Men ain't in politics for nothin'. They want to get somethin' out of it." Each party had its share of corrupt officials willing to buy and sell government appointments or congressional votes, yet each also witnessed the emergence of factions promoting honesty in government. The struggle for "cleaner" government soon became one of the foremost issues of the day.

HAYES AND CIVIL SERVICE REFORM   President Rutherford B. Hayes brought to the White House in 1877 a new style of uprightness, in sharp contrast to the graft and corruption practiced by members of the Grant administration. The son of an Ohio farmer, Hayes was wounded four times in the Civil War and was promoted to the rank of major general. Elected governor of Ohio in 1867, he served three terms.

Hayes's own party, the Republicans, was split between so-called **Stalwarts** and Half-Breeds, led respectively by Senators Roscoe Conkling of New York and James Gillespie Blaine of Maine. The Stalwarts had been "stalwart" in their support of President Grant during the furor over the misbehavior of his cabinet members. They had also promoted Radical Reconstruction of the defeated South and benefited from the "spoils system" of distributing federal political jobs to party loyalists. The Half-Breeds acquired their name because they were only half-loyal to Grant and half-committed to reform of the spoils system. For the most part, the two Republican factions were loose alliances designed to advance the careers of Conkling and Blaine.

To his credit, Hayes aligned himself with the growing public discontent over political corruption. American leaders were just learning about the "merit system" for hiring government employees, which was long established in the bureaucracies of France and Germany, and the new British practice in which civil service jobs were filled by competitive written tests rather than awarded as political favors.

On the economic issues of the day, Hayes held to a conservative line that would guide his successors for the rest of the century. His solution to labor troubles, demonstrated in his response to the Great Railroad Strike of 1877, was to send in federal troops to break the strike. His answer to demands for an expansion of the currency was to veto the 1878 Bland-Allison Act, which provided for a limited increase in the supply of silver coins. The act passed anyway when Congress overrode Hayes's veto. A bruised president confided in his diary that he had lost the support of his own party. In 1879, with a year still left in his term, Hayes was ready to leave the White House. "I am now in my last year of the Presidency," he wrote a friend, "and look forward to its close as a schoolboy longs for the coming vacation."

THE 1880 ELECTION   With President Hayes out of the running for a second term, the Republicans nominated the dark-horse Ohio candidate, James A. Garfield. A native of Ohio and an early foe of slavery, Garfield, like Hayes and Grant, had distinguished himself during the Civil War and retired from the army as a major general before being elected to Congress in 1863, where he had become one of the outstanding leaders in the House. Now he was the Republican nominee for president. The convention named Chester A. Arthur, the deposed head of the New York Customhouse, as the candidate for vice president.

The Democrats in 1880 selected retired Union general Winfield Scott Hancock to counterbalance the Republicans' "bloody-shirt" attacks on Democrats as the party of secessionism and the Confederacy. Former Confederates nevertheless advised their constituents to "vote as you shot"—that is, against the Republicans. In an election characterized by widespread bribery, Garfield eked out a plurality of only 39,000 votes, or 48.5 percent of the vote, but with a comfortable margin of 214 to 155 in the Electoral College. In his inaugural address, President Garfield confirmed that the Republicans had ended efforts to reconstruct the former Confederacy and stamp out its racist heritage. He declared that southern blacks had been "surrendered to their own guardianship."

Garfield showed great potential as a new president, but never had a chance to prove it. On July 2, 1881, after only four months in office, he was walking through the Washington, D.C., railroad station when Charles Guiteau, a deranged man who had been turned down for a federal job, shot the president twice. As a policeman wrestled the assassin to the ground, Guiteau shouted: "Yes! I have killed Garfield! [Chester] Arthur is President of the United States. I am a Stalwart!"—a statement that would greatly embarrass the Stalwart Republicans. On September 19 Garfield died of complications resulting from his inept medical care. At his sensational ten-week-long trial, Charles Guiteau explained that God had ordered him to kill the president. The jury refused to believe that he was insane and pronounced him guilty of murder. On June 30, 1882, Guiteau was hanged; an autopsy revealed that his brain was diseased.

Chester Arthur proved to be a surprisingly competent president. He distanced himself from the Stalwarts and established a genuine independence, even becoming a civil service and tariff reformer. The assassin Guiteau had unwittingly stimulated widespread public support for reforming the distribution of government jobs. In 1883 a reform bill sponsored by "Gentleman George" H. Pendleton, a Democratic senator from Ohio, set up a three-member federal Civil Service Commission, the first federal regulatory agency established on a permanent basis. A growing percentage of all federal jobs would now be filled on the basis of competitive examinations rather than political favoritism. The Pendleton Civil Service Reform Act was thus the vital step in a new approach to government administration that valued merit over partisanship.

THE CAMPAIGN OF 1884   Chester Arthur's presidential record might have attracted voters, but it did not please leaders of his party. So in 1884 the Republicans dumped Arthur and turned to the glamorous senator **James Gillespie Blaine** of Maine, longtime leader of the Republican Half-Breeds. Blaine was the consummate politician. He inspired the party faithful with his oratory, and at the same time he knew how to wheel and deal in the backrooms, sometimes evading the law in the process. Newspapers turned up evidence of his corruption. Based on references in the "Mulligan letters," they

Senator James Gillespie Blaine of Maine

The Republican candidate in 1884.

revealed that Blaine was in the pocket of the railroad barons. While serving as Speaker of the House, he had sold his votes on measures favorable to their interests. Nobody ever proved that Blaine had committed any crimes, but the circumstantial evidence was powerful: his mansion in Washington, D.C., could not have been built on his senatorial salary alone, nor could his palatial home in Augusta, Maine (which has since become the state's governor's mansion).

During the campaign, more letters surfaced with disclosures embarrassing to Blaine. For the reform element of the Republican party, this was too much, and prominent leaders and supporters of the party refused to endorse Blaine's candidacy. Party regulars scorned them as "goo-goos"—the good-government crowd, who ignored partisan realities. The editor of the *New York Sun* jokingly called the anti-Blaine Republicans **Mugwumps**, after an Algonquian Indian word for a self-important chieftain. The Mugwumps were a self-conscious political elite dedicated to promoting the pulic welfare. They were centered in the large cities and major universities of the northeast. Mostly educators, writers, or editors, they included the most famous American of all, Mark Twain. The Mugwumps generally opposed tariffs and championed free trade. They opposed the regulation of railroads as well as efforts to inflate the money supply by coining more silver. Their foremost goal was to expand civil service reform by making all federal jobs non-partisan. Their break with the Republican party, the party of Lincoln, testified to the depth of their convictions.

The rise of the Mugwumps influenced the Democrats to nominate the New Yorker Grover Cleveland, a minister's son, as a reform candidate. He had first attracted national attention when, in 1881, he was elected as the anti-corruption mayor of Buffalo. In 1882 he was elected governor of New York, and he continued to build a reform record by fighting New York City's corrupt Tammany Hall ring. As mayor and as governor, he repeatedly vetoed bills serving selfish interests. He supported civil-service reform, opposed expanding the money supply, and preferred free trade rather than high tariffs.

A stocky 270-pound man, Cleveland provided a sharp contrast to the Republican Blaine. He possessed little charisma but impressed the public with his stubborn integrity. A juicy scandal erupted when the *Buffalo Evening Telegraph* revealed that as a bachelor, Cleveland had befriended an attractive Buffalo widow who later named him the father of a baby born to her in 1874. Cleveland had since provided financial support for the child. The respective escapades of Blaine and Cleveland provided some of the most colorful battle cries in political history: "Blaine, Blaine, James G. Blaine, the continental liar from the state of Maine," Democrats chanted; Republicans countered with "Ma, ma, where's my pa? Gone to the White House, ha, ha, ha!"

Grover Cleveland

As president, Cleveland made the issue of tariff reform central to the politics of the late 1880s.

Near the end of the toxic campaign, Blaine and his supporters committed two fateful blunders. The first occurred at New York City's fashionable Delmonico's restaurant, where Blaine went to a private dinner with several millionaire bigwigs to discuss campaign finances. Accounts of the event appeared in the opposition press for days. The second fiasco occurred when one member of a delegation of Protestant ministers visiting Republican headquarters in New York referred to the Democrats as the party of "rum, Romanism, and rebellion." Blaine, who was present, let pass the implied insult to Catholics—a fatal oversight, since he had always cultivated Irish American support with his anti-English talk and public reminders that his mother was Catholic. Democrats spread the word that Blaine was at heart anti-Irish and anti-Catholic. The two incidents may have tipped the 1884 presidential election. The electoral vote, in Cleveland's favor, stood at 219 to 182, but the popular vote ran far closer: Cleveland's plurality was fewer than 30,000 votes. Cleveland won the key state of New York by the razor-thin margin of 1,149 votes out of the 1,167,169 cast.

CLEVELAND AND THE SPECIAL INTERESTS President Cleveland was an unusual president in that he opposed any federal government favors to big business. "A public office is a public trust" was one of his favorite mottoes. He held to a strictly limited view of government's role in both economic and social matters, a rigid philosophy illustrated by his 1887 veto of a congressional effort to provide desperate Texas farmers with seeds in the aftermath of a devastating drought that had parched the western states, summer after summer, for five years between 1887 and 1892. "Though the people support the government, the government should not support the people," Cleveland asserted.

Cleveland urged Congress to adopt an important new policy: federal regulation of interstate railroads. Since the late 1860s, states had adopted laws regulating railroads, but in 1886 a Supreme Court decision in the case of *Wabash, St. Louis, and Pacific Railroad Company v. Illinois*, the justices denied the right of any state to regulate rates charged by railroads engaged in interstate traffic. Cleveland thereupon urged Congress to take the lead in regulating the rail industry.

Congress followed through, and in 1887 Cleveland signed into law an act creating the Interstate Commerce Commission (ICC). The law empowered the ICC's five members to ensure that freight rates had to be "reasonable and just." The commission's actual powers proved to be weak, however, when tested in the courts, in large part because of the vagueness of the phrase "reasonable and just."

TENSIONS OVER THE TARIFF   President Cleveland's most dramatic challenge to the power of Big Business focused on tariff reform. During the late nineteenth century, critics charged that government tariff policies had fostered big business at the expense of small producers and retailers by effectively shutting out foreign imports, thereby enabling U.S. corporations to dominate their American markets and charge higher prices for their products. Cleveland agreed that tariff rates were too high and often inequitable. Congress, Cleveland argued, should reduce the tariff rates. The stage was set for the election of 1888 to highlight a difference between the major parties on an issue of substance.

THE ELECTION OF 1888   Cleveland was the obvious nominee of his party for reelection. The Republicans, now calling themselves the GOP (Grand Old Party) to emphasize their party's longevity, turned to the obscure Benjamin Harrison, whose greatest attribute was his availability. The grandson of President William Henry Harrison, he resided in Indiana, a pivotal state, and had a good war record. There was little in his political record to offend any voter. He had lost a race for governor and served one term in the Senate (1881–1887). The Republican platform accepted Cleveland's challenge to make the tariff the chief issue. The Republicans enjoyed a huge advantage over the Democrats in funding and organization. To fend off

Cleveland's efforts to reduce the tariff, business executives contributed over $3 million to the Republican campaign. Still, the outcome was incredibly close. Cleveland won the popular vote by 5,538,000 to 5,447,000, but Harrison carried the Electoral College by 233 to 168.

REPUBLICAN REFORM UNDER HARRISON As president, Benjamin Harrison was a competent figurehead overshadowed by his flamboyant secretary of state, James Gillespie Blaine. Harrison owed a heavy debt to Union Civil War veterans, which he discharged by signing the Dependent Pension Act, substantially the same measure that Cleveland had vetoed. The number of veterans receiving federal pensions almost doubled between 1889 and 1893.

"King of the World"

Reformers targeted the growing power of monopolies, such as that of John D. Rockefeller's Standard Oil.

During the first two years of Harrison's term, the Republicans controlled the presidency and both houses of Congress for only the second time since 1875. In 1890, they passed a cluster of significant legislation. In addition to the Dependent Pension Act, Congress and the president approved the Sherman Anti-Trust Act, the Sherman Silver Purchase Act, the McKinley Tariff Act, and the admission of Idaho and Wyoming as new states, which followed the admission of the Dakotas, Montana, and Washington in 1889.

Both parties had pledged to do something about the growing power of big businesses to fix prices and control markets. The Sherman Anti-Trust Act, named for Ohio senator John Sherman, prohibited companies from conspiring to establish monopolies. Its passage turned out to be largely symbolic, however. During the next decade successive administrations rarely enforced the new law. From 1890 to 1901, only eighteen lawsuits were instituted, and four of those were against labor unions rather than corporations.

INADEQUATE CURRENCY Complex monetary issues dominated the political arena during the Gilded Age. The fact that several farm organizations organized the Greenback Party in 1876 illustrated the money issue's significance to voters. The nation's money supply in the late nineteenth century lacked the flexibility to grow along with the expanding economy. From 1865 to 1890, the amount of currency in circulation decreased about 10 percent. Such currency deflation raised the cost of borrowing money, as a shrinking money supply caused bankers to hike interest rates on loans.

In 1873, the Republican-controlled Congress declared that silver could no longer be used for coins, only gold. This gold-only decision occurred just when silver production in the western states had begun to increase. Debt-ridden farmers and laborers who advocated currency inflation through the coinage of silver denounced the "crime of '73," arguing that bankers and merchants had conspired to stop coining silver so as to ensure a nationwide scarcity of money. The Bland-Allison Act of 1878 and the Sherman Silver Purchase Act of 1890 provided for some silver coinage, but too little in each case to offset the overall contraction of the currency as the population and the economy grew.

Hard-pressed farmers in the West and South demanded increased coinage of silver to inflate the currency and raise commodity prices, making it easier for them to earn the money they needed to pay their debts. The farmers found allies among legislators representing the new western states. All six of the states admitted to the Union in 1889 and 1890 had substantial silver mines, and their new congressional delegations—largely Republican—wanted the federal government to mint more silver. The "silver delegates" shifted the balance in Congress enough to pass the Sherman Silver Purchase Act (1890), which required the Treasury to purchase 4.5 million ounces of silver each month with new paper money. Yet eastern business and financial groups viewed the inflationary act as a threat, setting the stage for the currency issue to eclipse all others during the financial panic that would sweep the country three years later.

Republicans viewed their victory over Grover Cleveland and the Democrats in 1888 as a mandate not just to maintain the high tariffs insulating American companies from foreign competition but to raise them even higher. Piloted through Congress by Ohio representative William McKinley, the McKinley Tariff Act of 1890 raised duties on manufactured goods to their highest level ever, so high that the threat of foreign competition diminished, encouraging many businesses to charge higher prices. Voters rebelled. In the 1890 midterm elections, citizens repudiated the McKinley Tariff with a landslide of Democratic votes. In the new House, Democrats outnumbered Republicans by almost three to one; in the Senate the Republican majority was reduced to eight. One of the election casualties was Congressman McKinley himself.

THE FARM PROBLEM AND AGRARIAN PROTEST MOVEMENTS

The 1890 congressional elections also revealed a deep-seated unrest in the farming communities of the South and on the plains of Kansas and Nebraska, as well as in the mining towns of the Rocky Mountain region. People used the term "revolution" to describe the swelling grassroots support for the Populists, a new third party focused on addressing the needs of small farmers, many of whom did not own the land they worked. In drought-devastated Kansas, Populists took over five Republican congressional seats. In Washington, D.C., the newly elected Populists and Democrats took control of Congress just as an acute economic crisis appeared on the horizon: farmers' debts were mounting as crop prices plummeted.

"I Feed You All!"

This 1875 poster shows the farmer at the center of society.

ECONOMIC CONDITIONS Since the end of the Civil War, farmers in the South and the plains states suffered from worsening economic and social conditions. The source of their problems was a long decline in commodity prices, from 1870 to 1898, caused by overproduction and growing international competition for world markets. The vast new land brought under cultivation in the West poured an ever-increasing supply of farm products into the market, driving prices down. Considerations of abstract economic forces puzzled many farmers, however. How could one speak of overproduction when so many remained in need? Instead, they reasoned, there must be a screw loose somewhere in the system.

Struggling farmers targeted the railroads and the food processors who handled the farmers' and ranchers' products as the prime villains. Farmers resented the high railroad freight rates that prevailed in farm regions with no alternative forms of transportation. High tariffs on imported goods also operated to farmers' disadvantage, because the tariffs deterred foreign competition, allowing U.S. companies to raise the prices of manufactured goods upon which farmers depended. Farmers, however, had to sell their wheat, cotton, and other staples in foreign markets, where competition lowered prices. Debt, too, had been a perennial problem of agriculture. After the Civil War, farmers had become ever more enmeshed in debts owed to local banks or merchants. As commodity prices dropped, the burden of debt grew because farmers had to cultivate more wheat or cotton to raise the same amount of money; and by growing more, they furthered the vicious cycle of commodity surpluses and price declines.

THE GRANGER MOVEMENT When the U. S. Department of Agriculture sent Oliver H. Kelley on a tour of the South in 1866, it was the isolation of people living on farms that most impressed him. To address the problem, Kelley and some government clerks in 1867 founded the National Grange of the Patrons of Husbandry, better known as the Grange (an old word for granary), as each chapter was called. In the next few years the Grange mushroomed, reaching a membership as high as 1.5 million by 1874. The Grange started as a social and educational response to the farmers' isolation, but as it grew, it began to promote farmer-owned cooperatives for the buying and selling of crops. The Grangers' long-range ideal was to free themselves from the high fees charged by grain-elevator operators and food processors.

The Grange soon became indirectly involved in politics, through independent third parties, especially in the Midwest during the early 1870s. The Grange's chief political goal was to regulate the rates charged by railroads and warehouses. In five states, Grangers brought about the passage of "Granger laws," which at first proved relatively ineffective but laid a foundation for stronger legislation. Owners subject to their regulation challenged the laws in the "Granger cases" that soon advanced to the Supreme Court, where they claimed to have been deprived of property without due process of law. In a key case involving warehouse regulation, *Munn v. Illinois* (1877), the Supreme Court ruled that the state, according to its "police powers," had the right to regulate property that was clothed in a public interest. If regulatory power were abused, the ruling said, "the people must resort to the polls, not the courts." Later, however, the courts would severely restrict state regulatory powers.

The **Granger movement** gradually declined as members directed their energies into both farm cooperatives, many of which failed, and political action. In 1875, out of the independent political movements, grew a third political party calling itself the Independent National party, more commonly known as the Greenback party because of its emphasis on the virtues of paper money. In the 1878 congressional elections the Greenbacks party polled over 1 million votes and elected fifteen congressmen. But in 1880, the party's fortunes declined, and it disintegrated after 1884.

FARMERS' ALLIANCES   As the Grange lost energy, other farm organizations, known as **Farmers' Alliances**, grew in size and significance. Like the Grange, the Farmers' Alliances (Northern and Southern) organized social and recreational activities, but they also emphasized political action. Struggling farmers throughout the South and Midwest, where tenancy rates were highest, rushed to join the Alliance movement as a means of addressing the hardships created by chronic indebtedness, declining crop prices, and devastating droughts. Yet unlike the Grange, which was a national organization that tended to attract more prosperous farmers, the Alliances were grassroots organizations that would become the largest and most dynamic farmers' movement in history.

The Alliance movement swept across the cotton belt in the South and established strong support in Kansas and the Dakotas. In 1886 a white minister in Texas responded to the appeals of African American farmers by organizing the Colored Farmers' National Alliance. The white leadership of the Alliance movement in Texas endorsed this development because the Colored Alliance stressed that its objective was economic justice, not social equality. By 1890, the Alliance movement had members from New York to California, numbering about 1.5 million, and the Colored Farmers' National Alliance claimed over 1 million members.

The Alliance movement sponsored some 1,000 rural newspapers to spread the word about the farm problem. It also recruited 40,000 lecturers, who fanned out across the countryside to help people understand the "tyrannical" forces arrayed against the farm sector: bankers and creditors, Wall Street financiers, railroads, and corporate giants who controlled both the markets and the political process. Unlike the Grange, however, the Alliance proposed an elaborate economic reform program. In 1890, Alliance agencies and exchanges in some eighteen states claimed a business of $10 million, but they soon went the way of the Granger cooperatives, victims of discrimination by wholesalers, manufacturers, railroads, and bankers—as well as their own inexperienced management and overextended credit.

FARM POLITICS   In the farm states west of the Mississippi River, hard times had descended after the blizzards of 1887, which killed most of the cattle and hogs across the northern plains. Two years later a prolonged drought destroyed millions of acres of corn, wheat, and oats. Distressed farmers lashed out against what they considered to be a powerful conspiracy of eastern financial and industrial interests, which they variously called "monopolies," "the money power," "Wall Street," or "organized wealth." Desperate for assistance, they agitated for third-party political action to address their economic concerns. In Colorado in 1890, farm radicals joined with miners and railroad workers to form the Independent party. That same year, Nebraska farmers formed the People's Independent party. Across the South, however, white Alliance members hesitated to bolt the Democratic party, seeking instead to influence or control it. Both approaches gained startling success. New third parties under various names upset the political balance in western states, almost electing a governor under the banner of the new **People's party** (also known as the **Populist** party) in Kansas (where a Populist was elected governor in 1892) and taking control of one house of the state legislature there and both houses in Nebraska. In South Dakota and Minnesota, Populists gained a balance of power in the state legislatures, and Kansas sent a Populist to the U.S. Senate. The Populist party claimed to represent small farmers and wage laborers, blacks and poor whites, in their fight against greedy banks and railroads, corporate monopolies, and corrupt politics. They called for more rather than less government intervention in the economy, for only government was capable of expanding the money supply, counterbalancing the power of big business, and providing efficient national transportation networks to support the needs of agribusiness.

The farm protest movement produced colorful leaders, especially in Kansas, where **Mary Elizabeth Lease** emerged as a fiery speaker. Born in Pennsylvania, Lease migrated to Kansas, taught school, raised a family, and failed at farming in the mid-1880s. She then studied law, "pinning sheets of notes above her wash tub," and became one of the state's first female attorneys. At the same time, she took up public speaking on behalf of various causes, including freedom for her ancestral Ireland, temperance, and women's suffrage. By the end of the 1880s, Lease had joined the Alliance as well as the Knights of Labor, and she soon applied her considerable oratorical gifts to the cause of currency inflation, arguing for the coining of massive amounts of silver. A tall, proud, and imposing woman, Lease drew attentive audiences. "The people are at bay," she warned in 1894; "let the bloodhounds of money beware." She urged angry

Mary Elizabeth Lease, 1890

A charismatic leader in the farm protest movement.

farmers to obtain their goals "with the ballot if possible, but if not that way then with the bayonet." Like so many of the Populists, Lease viewed the urban-industrial East as the enemy of the working classes. "The great common people of this country," she shouted, "are slaves, and monopoly is the master. The West and South are bound and prostrate before the manufacturing East."

In the South, the Alliance forced Democrats to nominate candidates pledged to their program. The southern states elected four pro-Alliance governors, seven pro-Alliance legislatures, forty-four pro-Alliance congressmen, and several senators. Among the most respected of the southern Alliance leaders was Thomas E. Watson of Georgia. The son of prosperous slaveholders who had lost everything after the Civil War, Watson became a successful lawyer and orator on behalf of the Alliance cause. He took the lead in urging African American tenant farmers and sharecroppers to join with their white counterparts in ousting the white political elite. "You are kept apart," he told black and white farmers, "that you may be separately fleeced of your earnings."

THE POPULIST PARTY AND THE ELECTION OF 1892 The success of the Alliances led to the formation of a third political party on the national level. In 1892, a gathering of Alliance leaders in St. Louis called for a national convention of the People's Party at Omaha, Nebraska, to adopt a platform and choose candidates. The Populist Convention opened on July 4, 1892. Delegates drafted a platform that included the subtreasury plan, unlimited coinage of silver, an income tax whose rates would rise with personal income levels, and federal control of the railroads. The Populists also called for the government to reclaim from railroads and other corporations lands "in excess of their actual needs" and to forbid land ownership by immigrants who had not gained citizenship. Finally, the platform endorsed the eight-hour workday (rather than ten or twelve hours) and restriction of immigration. The party took these last positions in an effort to win support from urban factory workers, whom Populists looked upon as fellow "producers." The party's platform turned out to be more exciting than its candidate. Iowa's James B. Weaver, an able, prudent man, carried the stigma of his defeat on the Greenback ticket twelve years before. To attract southern voters who might be distanced by Weaver's service as a Union general, the party named a former Confederate general for vice president.

The Populist party was the startling new feature of the 1892 campaign. The major parties renominated the same candidates who had run in 1888: Democrat Grover Cleveland and Republican Benjamin Harrison. The tariff issue monopolized their attention. Both major candidates polled over 5 million votes, but Cleveland carried a plurality of the popular votes and a majority of the Electoral College. The Populist Weaver polled over 1 million votes and carried Colorado, Kansas, Nevada, and Idaho, for a total of twenty-two electoral votes. Alabama was the banner Populist state of the South, with 37 percent of its vote going to Weaver.

The Economy and the Silver Solution

THE DEPRESSION OF 1893   While the farmers were funneling their discontent into politics during the fall of 1892, a fundamental weakness in the economy was about to cause a major collapse and a social rebellion. Just ten days before Grover Cleveland started his second term, in the winter of 1893, the Philadelphia and Reading Railroad declared bankruptcy, setting off a national financial panic that mushroomed into the worst depression the nation had ever experienced. Other overextended railroads collapsed, taking many banks with them. A quarter of unskilled urban workers lost their jobs, and by the fall of 1893 over six hundred banks had closed and fifteen thousand businesses had failed. Entire farm regions in the South and West were also devastated by the spreading depression that brought unprecedented suffering. Farm foreclosures soared. Between 1890 and 1894 more than eleven thousand farm mortgages were foreclosed in Kansas alone.

In fifteen rural Kansas counties, three quarters of the people lost their farms. Residents grimly said: "In God we trusted, in Kansas we busted." By 1900, a third of all farmers were tenants rather than owners.

By 1894, the nation's economy had reached bottom. The catastrophic depression lasted another four years, with unemployment hovering at 20 percent and hunger stalking the streets of many cities. In New York City some 35 percent were unemployed, and twenty thousand homeless people camped out at police stations and other makeshift shelters. President Cleveland's response to the economic catastrophe was to convince Congress to return the nation's money supply to a gold standard by repealing the Sherman Silver Purchase Act of 1890, a move that worsened rather than improved the financial situation. The

National panic

The New York Stock Exchange on the morning of Friday, May 5, 1893.

economy needed more money in circulation, not less. Unemployment and labor unrest only increased as investors rushed to exchange their silver for gold, thus further constricting the money supply. Violent labor strikes at Pullman, Illinois, and at the Homestead Works outside Pittsburgh symbolized the fracturing of the social order. In 1894 some 750,000 workers went on strike; railroad construction workers, laid off in the West, began tramping east and talked of marching on Washington, D.C. The devastating depression of the 1890s was reshaping America's economic and political landscape.

The 1894 congressional elections, taking place amid this climate of mushrooming anxiety, produced a severe setback for the Democrats, who paid politically for the economic downturn, and the Republicans were the chief beneficiaries. The Republicans gained 121 seats in the House, the largest increase ever. Only in the "Solid South" did the Democrats retain their advantage. The third-party Populists emerged with six senators and seven representatives. They polled 1.5 million votes for their congressional candidates and expected the festering discontent in rural areas to carry them to national power in 1896.

SILVERITES VERSUS GOLDBUGS   The course of events would dash that hope, however. In the mid-1890s, radical efforts to address the ravages of the depression focused on the currency issue. President Cleveland convinced Congress to repeal the Sherman Silver Purchase Act, and created an irreparable division in his own party. One embittered pro-silver Democrat labeled the president a traitor.

The western states with large silver deposits now escalated their demands for the "unlimited" coinage of silver, presenting a strategic dilemma for Populists: Should the party promote the long list of varied reforms it had originally advocated, or should it try to ride the silver issue into power? The latter seemed the practical choice. Although the coinage of silver would not have provided the economic panacea its advocates claimed, the "free silver" crusade took on powerful symbolic overtones. Just as Andrew Jackson mobilized a transformation of the Democratic party based on his moral outrage at the national bank, silverites also reshaped the political landscape. The Populist leaders decided, over the protests of more radical members, to hold their 1896 nominating convention after the two major party conventions, confident that the Republicans and Democrats would at best straddle the silver issue, enabling the Populists to lure away silverite Republicans and Democrats.

THE REMARKABLE ELECTION OF 1896   Contrary to those expectations, the major parties took opposite positions on the currency issue. The Republicans, as expected, nominated **William McKinley** on a gold standard–only platform. McKinley, a former congressman and governor of Ohio, symbolized the mainstream Republican values that had served the party well during the Gilded Age. After the convention, a friend told McKinley that the "money question" would determine the election. The Republican candidate dismissed that notion, insisting that the tariff would continue to govern national political campaigns. But one of McKinley's advisers disagreed. "In my opinion," said Judge William Day of Ohio, "in thirty days you won't hear of anything else" but the money question. He was right.

The Democratic nominating convention in the Chicago Coliseum, the largest building in the world, was one of the great turning points in American political history. The pro-silver, largely rural forces surprised the party leadership and the "Gold Democrats" by capturing the convention for their inflationary crusade. Thirty-six-year-old **William Jennings Bryan** from Nebraska gave the convention's final speech before the balloting began.

And what a speech it was. A fervent evangelical moralist, Bryan was a two-term congressman who had been defeated in the Senate race in 1894, when

Democrats were swept out of office by the dozens. In the months before the 1896 Democratic convention, he had traveled throughout the South and the West, speaking passionately for the unlimited coinage of silver and against President Cleveland's "do-nothing" response to the depression. Bryan was the first major candidate since Andrew Jackson to champion the poor, the discontented, and the oppressed against the financial and industrial titans. And he was the first leader of a major party to call for the expansion of the federal government to promote the welfare of the working and middle classes by providing subsidies for farmers, legalizing labor strikes, regulating railroads, taxing the rich, and breaking up "trusts" (financial and industrial monopolies).

William Jennings Bryan

His "cross of gold" speech at the 1896 Democratic Convention roused the delegates and secured him the party's presidential nomination.

Bryan was a magnetic public speaker with a booming voice, a crusading minister in the role of a politician, self-infatuated and self-dramatizing. At the 1896 Democratic Convention, Bryan was a "dark horse" candidate in a field of more prominent competitors for the presidential nomination. So he had to take a calculated risk: he would be intentionally provocative and disruptive. Bryan claimed to speak for the "producing masses of this nation" against the eastern "financial magnates" who enslaved them by constricting the money supply to ensure high interest rates for mortgages and loans. He reminded the delegates that the "man who is employed for wages is as much a business man as his employer." As his melodramatic twenty-minute speech reached a crescendo, Bryan fused Christian imagery with Populist anger:

> I come to speak to you in defense of a cause as holy as the cause of liberty—the cause of humanity. . . . . We have petitioned, and our petitions have been scorned. We have entreated, and our entreaties have been disregarded. We have begged, and they have mocked when our calamity came. We beg no longer; we entreat no more; we petition no more. We defy them!

The messianic Bryan then stretched his fingers across his forehead and reached his dramatic conclusion: "You shall not press down upon the brow of labor this crown of thorns. You shall not crucify mankind upon a cross of gold!" Bryan extended his arms straight out from his sides, posing as if being crucified. It was a riveting performance. As Bryan strode triumphantly off the stage, the delegates erupted in a frenzy of wild applause verging on adulation. "Everybody seemed to go mad at once," reported the *New York World*. It was pure theater, but it worked better than even Bryan had anticipated. Republicans were not amused. A partisan newspaper observed that no political movement had "ever before spawned such hideous and repulsive vipers."

The day after his riveting speech, the unlikely but righteous Bryan won the presidential nomination on the fifth ballot, but in the process the Democratic party was fractured. Disappointed pro-gold, pro-Cleveland Democrats dismissed Bryan as a fanatic and a socialist. They were so alienated by Bryan's inflationary crusade and populist rhetoric that they walked out of the convention and nominated their own candidate, Senator John M. Palmer of Illinois. "Fellow Democrats," Palmer announced, "I will not consider it any great fault if you decide to cast your vote for [the Republican] William McKinley."

When the Populists gathered in St. Louis for their own presidential nominating convention two weeks later, they faced an impossible choice. They could name their own candidate and divide the silver vote with the Democrats, or they could endorse Bryan and probably lose their identity as an independent party. In the end they backed Bryan, the "matchless champion of the people," but chose their own vice-presidential candidate, former congressman Thomas E. Watson of Georgia, and invited the Democrats to drop their vice-presidential nominee. Bryan refused the request.

The election of 1896 was one of the most dramatic in American history, in part because of the striking contrast between the candidates, and in part because the severity of the depression made the stakes so high. William Jennings Bryan, the nominee of both the Democrats and the Populists, tirelessly crisscrossed the country like a man on a mission, delivering impassioned speeches on behalf of "the struggling masses" of workers, farmers, and small-business owners. At every stop he promised that the unlimited coinage of silver would solve the nation's economic problems. In his self-appointed role as a champion of "the people," Bryan stressed that politics should be a moral enterprise. He was the first major-party leader, a "godly hero," to advocate the expansion of federal powers to promote the welfare of ordinary Americans. He said that strikes by labor unions should be legalized, farmers should be given federal subsidies, the rich should be taxed, corporate campaign contributions should be banned, and liquor should be outlawed. Bryan's populist crusade was for whites only, however. Like so many otherwise progressive Democratic leaders, he never challenged the pattern of racial segregation and violence against blacks in the solid Democratic South.

McKinley, meanwhile, stayed at home during the campaign. He knew he could not compete with Bryan as an orator, so he conducted a traditional "front-porch campaign," receiving select delegations of Republican supporters at his home in Canton, Ohio, and giving only prepared responses to the press. McKinley's brilliant campaign manager, Marcus "Mark" Hanna, a wealthy business executive, shrewdly portrayed Bryan as a "Popocrat," a radical whose "communistic spirit" would ruin the capitalist system and create a class war. Hanna convinced the Republican Party to proclaim that it was "unreservedly for sound money." Theodore Roosevelt, a rising star among the Republicans, was aghast at the thought of Bryan becoming president. "The silver craze surpasses belief," he wrote a friend. "Bryan's election would be a great calamity."

By preying upon such fears, the McKinley campaign raised vast sums of money from corporations and wealthy donors to finance an army of 1,400 Republican speakers who traveled the country in his support. It was the most sophisticated—and expensive—presidential campaign up to that point in history. McKinley promoted himself as the "advance agent of prosperity" who would provide workers with a "full dinner pail." In the end, Bryan and the Democratic-Populist-silverite candidates were overwhelmed by the better-organized Republican campaign. McKinley won the popular vote by 7.1 million to 6.5 million and the Electoral College vote by 271 to 176. Two million more voters cast their ballot than in 1892.

Bryan carried most of the West and the South but found little support in the metropolitan centers east of the Mississippi River and north of the Ohio and Potomac Rivers. In the critical Midwest, from Minnesota and Iowa eastward to Ohio, Bryan carried not a single state. Bryan's evangelical Protestantism repelled many Catholic voters, who were normally drawn to the Democrats. Farmers in the Northeast, moreover, were less attracted to agrarian radicalism than were farmers in the wheat and cotton belts of the West and South, where there were higher rates of tenancy. Among factory workers in the cities, Bryan aroused little support. Wage laborers found it easier to identify with McKinley's pledge to restore the industrial economy than with Bryan's free-silver evangelism. Although Bryan had lost, he had begun the process of transforming the Democratic party from being a bulwark of pro-business conservatism and fiscal restraint to the twentieth-century party of liberal reform. The Populist Party virtually disintegrated. Having garnered a million votes in 1896, it collected only fifty thousand votes in

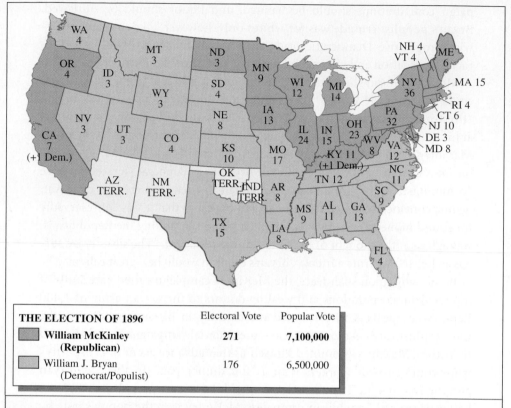

THE ELECTION OF 1896	Electoral Vote	Popular Vote
William McKinley (Republican)	271	7,100,000
William J. Bryan (Democrat/Populist)	176	6,500,000

How did Bryan's "cross of gold" speech divide the Democratic party? How did McKinley's strategy differ from Bryan's? Why was Bryan able to carry the West and the South but unable to win in cities and the Northeast?

1900. Conversely, McKinley's victory climaxed a generation-long struggle for the political control of industrializing America. The Republicans were dominant—for a while.

RACE RELATIONS DURING THE 1890s

The turbulence in American life during the 1890s also affected race relations—for the worse. Civil rights fell victim to the complex social, economic, political, and cultural forces unleashed by America's rapid growth. Even the supposedly radical William Jennings Bryan was not willing to support the human rights of African Americans.

DISENFRANCHISING AFRICAN AMERICANS Race relations were in part a victim of the terrible depression of the 1890s. At the end of the nineteenth century a violent "Negrophobia" swept across the South and much of the nation. In part, the new wave of racism was spurred by the revival in the United States and Europe of the old idea that the Anglo-Saxon "race" was genetically and culturally superior to the other races. Another reason for the intensification of racism was that many whites had come to resent any signs of African American economic success and political influence in the midst of the decade's economic downturn. An Alabama newspaper editor declared that "our blood boils when the educated Negro asserts himself politically." By the 1890s a new generation of African Americans born and educated since the end of the Civil War was determined to gain true equality. This younger generation was more assertive and less patient than their parents. "We are not the Negro from whom the chains of slavery fell a quarter century ago, most assuredly not," a black editor announced. A growing number of young white adults, however, were equally determined to keep "Negroes in their place."

Racial violence and repression escalated dramatically during the last decade of the nineteenth century and the first two decades of the twentieth. Ruling whites ruthlessly exercised their will over all areas of black life, imposing racial subjugation and segregation by preventing blacks from voting and by enacting **"Jim Crow" laws** mandating separation of the races in various public places. The phrase "Jim Crow" derived from "Jump Jim Crow," an old song-and-dance caricature of African Americans performed by white actor Thomas D. Rice in blackface during the 1830s. Thereafter, the term "Jim Crow" had become a pejorative expression meaning "Negro." The renewal of statutory racial segregation resulted from a calculated campaign by white elites and racist thugs to limit African American political, economic, and social participation at the end of the nineteenth century.

The political dynamics of the 1890s exacerbated the rise of racial tensions. The Populist revolt in the rural South divided the white vote (which had become all-Democratic) to such an extent that in some southern states the black vote determined election outcomes. Some white Populist leaders courted black votes and brought African Americans prominently into their leadership councils. In response, the traditional white economic and political elite—called Bourbons—began using the race issue to ensure continued white solidarity at the polls. In the 1890s, race-baiting white politicians argued that the black vote should be eliminated from southern elections. Because the Fifteenth Amendment made it impossible simply to deny African Americans the right to vote, white officials pursued disenfranchisement indirectly, through such "legal" devices as poll taxes (also called head taxes) and literacy tests designed to impede often-illiterate black voters—and many poor whites as well. And where such "legal" means were insufficient, insurgent white candidates were willing to use fraud and violence to overthrow the white ruling elite by eliminating the black vote.

Benjamin Tillman, the white supremacist governor of South Carolina (1890–1894), was a good example of the transformation in southern politics at the end of the nineteenth century. He and other political rebels ousted the Bourbon elite ("aristocrats") that had long governed in the former Confederate states. Tillman claimed that "I organized the majority [of voters] and put the old families out of business, and we became and are the rulers of the state." He also boasted about defeating the Bourbons by eliminating the black vote. "We have done our level best [to prevent blacks from voting] . . . we have scratched our heads to find out how we could eliminate the last one of them. We stuffed ballot boxes. We shot them. We are not ashamed of it."

Mississippi led the way to the near-total disenfranchisement of blacks and many poor whites as well. The state called a constitutional convention in 1890 to change the suffrage provisions included in the Radical Republican constitution of 1868. The so-called **Mississippi Plan** set the pattern that seven more states would follow over the next twenty years. First, a residence requirement—two years in the state, one year in an election district—struck at those African American tenant farmers who were in the habit of moving yearly in search of better economic opportunities. Second, voters were disqualified if convicted of certain crimes disproportionately involving blacks. Third, all taxes, including a poll tax, had to be paid before a person could vote. This proviso fell most heavily on poor whites and blacks. Fourth and finally, all voters had to be literate.

Other states added variations on the Mississippi Plan for eliminating black voting. In 1898, Louisiana invented the "grandfather clause," which allowed illiterate whites to vote if their fathers or grandfathers had been eligible to vote on January 1, 1867, when African Americans were still disenfranchised. By 1910, Georgia, North Carolina, Virginia, Alabama, and Oklahoma had adopted the grandfather clause. Every southern state, moreover, adopted a statewide Democratic primary between 1896 and 1915, which became the only meaningful election outside isolated areas of Republican strength. With minor exceptions, the Democratic primaries excluded African American voters altogether. The effectiveness of these measures can be seen in a few sample figures. Louisiana in 1896 had 130,000 registered black voters. By 1900 the number was only 5,320. In Alabama in 1900, 121,159 black men over twenty-one were literate, according to the census; only 3,742, however, were registered to vote.

THE SPREAD OF RACIAL SEGREGATION   At the same time that southern blacks were being shoved out of the political arena they were being segregated in the social sphere. The symbolic first target was the railroad passenger car. In 1885 the novelist George Washington Cable noted that in South Carolina, blacks "ride in first class [rail] cars as a right" and "their presence excites no comment." From 1875 to 1883, in fact, any local or state government-mandated racial segregation violated the federal Civil Rights Act (1875), which forbade racial discrimination in public places such as hotels, restaurants, and trains. By 1883, however, many northern whites endorsed the resegregation of southern life. In that year the U.S. Supreme Court ruled jointly on five separate civil rights cases involving discrimination against blacks by businesses or individuals. The Court held, with only one dissenting vote, that the Civil Rights Act of 1875 was unconstitutional. The judges explained that private *individuals* and *organizations* could engage in acts of racial discrimination because the Fourteenth Amendment specified only that "no State" could deny citizens equal protection of the law.

The Court's interpretation in what came to be called the *Civil Rights Cases* (1883) left as an open question the validity of various state laws *requiring* racially separate public facilities under the principle of "separate but equal," a slogan popular in the South in the late nineteenth century. In the 1880s, Tennessee and Mississippi required railroad passengers to occupy the car set aside for their race. When Louisiana followed suit in 1890, dissidents challenged the law in the case of *Plessy v. Ferguson,* which the Supreme Court decided in 1896.

The test case originated in New Orleans when Homer Plessy, an octoroon (a person having one-eighth African ancestry), refused to leave a whites-only railroad car when told to do so and was later convicted of violating the law. The Supreme Court ruled in 1896 that states had a right to create laws segregating public places such as schools, hotels, and restaurants. Justice John Marshall Harlan, a Kentuckian who had once owned slaves, was the only member of the Court to dissent from the ruling. He stressed that the Constitution is "color-blind, and neither knows nor tolerates classes among citizens. In respect of civil rights, all citizens are equal before the law." He feared that the Court's ruling would plant the "seeds of race hate" under "the sanction of law."

That is precisely what happened. The shameful ruling in the *Plessy* case legitimized the practice of racially **"separate but equal"** facilities in virtually

"Separate but equal"

Students exercising during the school day at an all-black elementary school in Washington, D.C.

every area of southern life, including streetcars, hotels, restaurants, hospitals, parks, sports stadiums, and places of employment. In 1900, the editor of the *Richmond Times* expressed the prevailing view throughout the South:

> It is necessary that this principle be applied in every relation of Southern life. God Almighty drew the color line and it cannot be obliterated. The negro must stay on his side of the line and the white man must stay on his side, and the sooner both races recognize this fact and accept it, the better it will be for both.

Widespread violence accompanied the creation of Jim Crow laws. From 1890 to 1899, lynchings in the United States averaged 188 per year, 82 percent of which occurred in the South; from 1900 to 1909, they averaged 93 per year, with 92 percent in the South. Whites were 32 percent of the victims during the former period but only 11 percent in the latter. Lynchings usually involved a black man (or men) accused of a crime, often rape. White mobs would seize the accused, torture, and kill him, often by hanging but always in ghastly ways. Lynchings became so common that participating whites viewed them as forms of outdoor recreation. Crowds, including women and children, would watch the grisly event amid a carnival-like atmosphere.

By the end of the nineteenth century, legalized racial discrimination—segregation of public facilities, political disenfranchisement, and vigilante justice—had elevated government-sanctioned bigotry to an official way of life in the South. South Carolina governor Benjamin Tillman murderously declared in 1892 that blacks "must remain subordinate or be exterminated."

MOB RULE IN NORTH CAROLINA White rule in the South at the end of the nineteenth century was violently imposed in the thriving coastal port of Wilmington, North Carolina, then the largest city in the state, with about twenty thousand residents. In 1894 and 1896, black voters, by then a majority in the city, elected a coalition of Republicans and Populists to various municipal offices. That blacks had come to control the electoral process infuriated the city's white elite. "We will never surrender to a ragged raffle of Negroes," warned a former congressman and Confederate colonel named Alfred Waddell, "even if we have to choke the Cape Fear River with [black] carcasses." It was not an idle threat.

On the morning of November 10, 1898, some two thousand well-armed white men and boys rampaged through the streets of Wilmington. They first destroyed the offices of *The Daily Record*, the city's black-owned newspaper. The vigilantes then moved into the black neighborhoods, indiscriminately shooting African Americans and destroying homes and businesses. Scores,

The Wilmington Insurrection

A mob of armed white supermacists destroyed the printing press of *The Daily Record*, a black-owned newspaper in Wilmington, North Carolina.

perhaps a hundred, all black, were killed. They then stormed the city hall, forced the white mayor and his board of black and white aldermen to resign, and declared that Colonel Waddell was the new mayor. The racist mob next forced the African American business leaders and elected officials to board northbound trains. The new self-appointed all-white city government issued their own "Declaration of White Independence" that stripped blacks of their voting rights and their jobs. Desperate black residents appealed for help to the governor as well as President William McKinley, but they did nothing.

The Wilmington Insurrection marked the first time in history that a lawfully elected municipal government had been overthrown in the United States. Two years later, in the 1900 statewide elections, white supremacist Democrats vowed to cement their control of the political process. The night before the election, Colonel Waddell urged supporters to use any means necessary to suppress black voting: "You are Anglo-Saxons. You are armed and prepared and you will do your duty. . . . Go to the polls tomorrow, and if you find the negro out voting, tell him to leave the polls and if he refuses, kill him, shoot him down in his tracks. We shall win tomorrow if we have to do it with guns." The Democratic party won by a landslide.

THE BLACK RESPONSE   African Americans responded to the resurgence of racism and statutory segregation in several ways. Some left the South in search of greater equality and opportunity, but the vast majority stayed in their native region. In the face of overwhelming force and prejudicial justice, most accommodated themselves to the realities of white supremacy and segregation. "Had to walk a quiet life," explained James Plunkett, a Virginia African American. "The least little thing you would do, they [whites] would kill ya."

Yet accommodation to the realities of white power did not mean submission. Excluded from the dominant white world and eager to avoid confrontations, black southerners after the 1890s adapted to the reality of segregation by nurturing their own culture and racial pride. A young white visitor to Mississippi in 1910 noticed that nearly every black person he met had "two distinct social selves, the one he reveals to his own people, the other he assumes among the whites."

African American churches continued to serve as the hub for black community life. Churches were used not only for worship but also for activities that had nothing to do with religion: social gatherings, club meetings, political rallies. For men especially, churches offered leadership roles and political status. Serving as a deacon was often one of the most prestigious positions an African American man could achieve. Churches enabled African Americans of all classes to interact and exercise roles denied them in the larger society.

One irony of mandated racial segregation was that it opened up economic opportunities for blacks. A new class of African American entrepreneurs emerged to provide services—insurance, banking, mortuaries, barbering— to the black community in the segregated South. At the same time, African Americans formed their own social and fraternal clubs and organizations, all of which helped bolster black pride and provided fellowship and opportunities for service.

Middle-class black women formed thousands of racial-uplift organizations across the South and around the nation. The women's clubs were engines of social service in their communities. Members cared for the aged and the infirm, the orphaned and the abandoned. They created homes for single mothers and provided nurseries for working mothers. They sponsored health clinics and classes in home economics for women. In 1896, the leaders of such women's clubs from around the country converged to form the National Association of Colored Women, an organization created to combat racism and segregation. Its first president, Mary Church Terrell, told members that they had an obligation to serve the "lowly, the illiterate, and even the vicious to whom we are bound by the ties of race and sex, and put forth every effort to uplift and reclaim them."

WASHINGTON AND DU BOIS   By the 1890s, **Booker T. Washington**, born in Virginia of a slave mother and a white father, had become the foremost black educator in the nation. He argued that blacks should not focus on fighting racial segregation. Instead, they should first establish an economic base for their advancement before striving for social equality. In a famous speech at the Cotton States and International Exposition in Atlanta in 1895, Washington advised fellow African Americans: "Cast down your bucket where you are—cast it down in making friends . . . of the people of all races by whom we are surrounded. Cast it down in agriculture, mechanics, in commerce, in domestic service, and in the professions." He conspicuously omitted politics from that list and offered an indirect endorsement of segregation: "In all things that are

Booker T. Washington

Founder of the Tuskegee Institute.

W.E.B. Du Bois

A fierce advocate for black education.

purely social we can be as separate as the five fingers, yet one as the hand in all things essential to mutual progress." In sum, Washington wanted first to build a prosperous black community; civil rights could wait.

By the turn of the century, Booker T. Washington had become the most influential African American leader in the nation. Some people, however, bitterly criticized him for making a bad bargain: the sacrifice of broad educational and civil rights for increased economic opportunities. **W.E.B. Du Bois** led this criticism. A native of Massachusetts, Du Bois first experienced southern racial prejudice as a student at Fisk University in Nashville, Tennessee. Later he was the first African American to earn degrees from Harvard (in history and sociology). In addition to an active career promoting civil rights, he left a distinguished record as a scholar, authoring over twenty books. Trim and dapper, sporting a goatee, carrying a cane, and often wearing gloves, Du Bois had a flamboyant personality and a combative spirit. Not long after he began his teaching career at Atlanta University in 1897, he began a very public assault on Booker T. Washington's strategy for improving the quality of life for African Americans.

Du Bois called Washington's 1895 speech "the Atlanta Compromise" and said that he would not "surrender the leadership of this race to cowards." Washington, Du Bois argued, preached "a gospel of Work and Money to such an extent as . . . to overshadow the higher aims of life." Washington was asking blacks to give up aspirations for political power, civil rights, and higher education so as to "concentrate all their energies on industrial education, the accumulation of wealth, and the conciliation of the South." Du Bois stressed that the priorities should be reversed. African American leaders should adopt a strategy of "ceaseless agitation" directed at ensuring the right to vote and winning civil equality. The education of blacks, Du Bois maintained, should not be merely vocational but should develop bold leaders willing to challenge segregation and discrimination through political action. He demanded that disenfranchisement and legalized segregation cease immediately and that the laws of the land be enforced. The dispute between Washington and Du Bois came to define the tensions that would divide the twentieth-century civil rights movement: militancy versus conciliation, separatism versus assimilation, social justice versus economic opportunities.

A NEW ERA   The dispute between W.E.B. Dubois and Booker T. Washington over the best strategy for blacks to regain their civil rights occurred at the same time that William Jennings Bryan and William McKinley were disputing the best way to end the terrible economic depression that had come to define the decade of the 1890s. The presidential election of 1896 was a climactic political struggle between the forces representing urban-industrial America and rural-agrarian America. Over 79 percent of eligible voters participated. McKinley's victory demonstrated that urban-industrial values had indeed taken firm hold of the political system. President McKinley's first important act was to call a special session of Congress to raise the tariff again. The Dingley Tariff of 1897 was the highest ever. By 1897 economic prosperity was returning, helped along by inflation of the currency, which bore out the arguments of the Greenbackers and silverites that the money supply was inadequate. But the inflation came, in one of history's many ironies, not from the federal government printing more greenbacks or coining more silver dollars but from a flood of new gold discovered in South Africa, northwest Canada, and Alaska that provided the inflation of the money supply long desired by ravaged farmers. Between 1897 and 1900 some $439 million worth of gold flowed into the U.S. Treasury. In 1900, Congress passed and President McKinley signed a bill affirming that the United States money supply would be based only on gold.

The decade of the 1890s marked the end of one era and the beginning of a new one. At the close of the nineteenth century, the longstanding issues of tariff and currency policy gave way to global concerns: the outbreak of the War of 1898 and the U.S. acquisition of territories outside the Western Hemisphere. At the same time, the advent of a new century brought new social and political developments. The most disturbing of those new developments was ever-deepening racial segregation and racial violence. The most positive was the emergence of progressivism, a diverse new national movement promoting social and political reform. Even though the Populist movement faded with William Jennings Bryan's defeat, most of the progressive agenda promoted by Bryan Democrats and Populists, dismissed as too radical and controversial in 1896, would be implemented by "progressive" political forces over the next two decades. Bryan's impassioned candidacy helped transform the Democratic party into a vigorous instrument of "progressive" reform during the early twentieth century. As the United States looked ahead to a new century, it began to place more emphasis on the role of the national government in society and the economy. Bigness in government began to counteract bigness in business.

CHAPTER SUMMARY

- **Gilded Age Politics**   Americans were intensely loyal to the two major parties, which operated on a local level by distributing favors. "City machines" also provided working-class men with jobs and gave relief (money or necessities) to the poor, thereby winning votes. The major political parties shared power nearly equally during the Gilded Age, and such parity made neither party willing to embrace bold initiatives.

- **National Politics**   Politicians focused on tariff reform, the regulation of corporations, Indian wars and Indian policy, civil service reform, and immigration. In the 1884 presidential election, Republicans favoring reform, dubbed Mugwumps, bolted their party to support the Democrat, Grover Cleveland, a reformer.

- **Farm Problems**   Farmers had serious grievances at the end of the nineteenth century. Commodity prices were falling because of domestic overproduction and international competition, and many farmers had gone into debt, buying new machinery on credit and paying the railroads exorbitant rates to ship their goods to market. In addition, high tariffs allowed manufacturers to raise the price of goods that farmers needed.

- **Farm Movements**   Despite farmers' traditional reluctance to organize, many reacted to their difficulties by joining the Granger movement, which promoted farmer-owned cooperatives and, subsequently, Farmers' Alliances, grassroots social organizations that also promoted political action. Influenced by their success, delegates from farm, labor, and reform organizations in 1892 established the People's party, also known as the Populist party. Populists sought greater regulation of business by the federal government and the free coinage of silver (because they hoped that the ensuing inflation of the money supply would make it easier for them to repay their debts).

- **Rise of Populism**   The Populists did well in 1892 and, with the depression of 1893, had high hopes for the next presidential election. But the Democrat, William Jennings Bryan, stole the silver issue from the Populists. The Populists thus fused with the Democrats, but Bryan lost the election to the Republicans. The People's party did not recover from the blow.

- **Southern Segregation**   By 1900 elite southern whites had regained control of state governments; prominent black Republicans had been squeezed out of political positions; and black men were being kept from exercising their right to vote. Segregation became the social norm. Some African American leaders, most prominently Booker T. Washington, believed that by showing deference to whites, blacks could avoid violence while quietly acquiring an education and property. Others, like W. E. B. Du Bois, wanted to fight segregation and lynching through the courts and the political system.

CHRONOLOGY

1877	Rutherford B. Hayes is inaugurated president
1877	Supreme Court issues *Munn v. Illinois* decision
1881	President James A. Garfield is assassinated
1883	Congress passes the Pendleton Civil Service Reform Act
1886	Supreme Court issues *Wabash, St. Louis, and Pacific Railroad Company v. Illinois* decision
1887	Interstate Commerce Commission is created
1890	Congress passes the Sherman Anti-Trust Act, the Sherman Silver Purchase Act, and the McKinley Tariff
1892	People's party drafts its Omaha platform
1893	Economic depression affects a substantial proportion of the population
1890	Mississippi Plan resegregates public facilities by race
1895	Booker T. Washington delivers his Atlanta Compromise speech
1896	Supreme Court issues *Plessy v. Ferguson* decision
1909	National Association for the Advancement of Colored People (NAACP) is created

KEY TERMS & NAMES

Part Six

MODERN
AMERICA

he United States entered the twentieth century on a wave of unrelenting change, not all of it beneficial. In 1800, the nation was a rural, agrarian society largely detached from the concerns of international affairs. By 1900, the United States had become a highly industrialized urban society with a growing involvement in world politics and international commerce. In other words, the nation was on the threshold of modernity.

The prospect of modernity both excited and scared Americans. Old truths and beliefs clashed with unsettling scientific discoveries and social practices. People debated the legitimacy of Darwinism, the existence of God, the dangers of jazz, and proposals to prohibit the sale of alcoholic beverages. The advent of automobiles and airplanes helped shrink distance, and such communications innovations as radio and film helped strengthen a sense of national consciousness. In the process, the United States began to emerge from its isolationist shell. Throughout most of the nineteenth century, policy makers had sought to isolate America from the intrigues and conflicts of the great European powers. As early as 1780, John Adams had warned Congress against involving the United States in the affairs of Europe. "Our business with them, and theirs with us," he wrote, "is commerce, not politics, much less war."

With only a few exceptions, statesmen during the nineteenth century followed such advice. Noninvolvement in foreign wars and nonintervention in the internal affairs of foreign governments formed the pillars of American foreign policy until the end of the century. During the 1890s, however, expanding commercial interests around the world led Americans to broaden the horizons of their concerns. Imperialism was the grand imperative among the great European powers, and a growing number of American expansionists demanded that the United States also adopt a global ambition and join in the hunt for new territories and markets. Such mixed motives helped spark the War of 1898 and helped to justify the resulting acquisition of colonies outside the continental United States. Entangling alliances with European powers soon followed.

The outbreak of the Great War in Europe in 1914 posed an even greater challenge to the tradition of isolation and nonintervention. The prospect of a German victory over the French and the British threatened the European balance of power, which had long ensured the security of the United States. By 1917 it appeared that Germany might emerge triumphant and begin to menace the Western Hemisphere. Woodrow Wilson's crusade to transform international affairs in accordance with his idealistic principles during the First World War severed American foreign policy from its isolationist moorings. It also spawned a prolonged debate about the role of the United States in world affairs, a debate that World War II would resolve for a time on the side of internationalism.

While the United States was entering the world stage as a formidable military power, it was also settling into its role as a great industrial power. Cities and factories sprouted across the landscape. An abundance of new jobs and affordable farmland served as a magnet attracting millions of immigrants from nearly every landmass on the globe. They were not always welcomed, nor were they readily assimilated. Ethnic and racial strife, as well as labor agitation, increased at the turn of the century. In the midst of such social turmoil and unparalleled economic development, reformers made their first sustained attempt to adapt political and social institutions to the realities of the industrial age. The worst excesses and injustices of urban-industrial development—corporate monopolies, child labor, political corruption, hazardous working conditions, urban ghettos—were finally addressed in a comprehensive way. During the Progressive Era (1890–1917), local, state, and federal governments sought to rein in the excesses of industrial capitalism and develop a more rational and efficient public policy.

A conservative Republican resurgence challenged the notion of the new regulatory state during the 1920s. Free enterprise and corporate capitalism witnessed a dramatic revival. But the stock market crash of 1929 helped propel the United States and the world into the worst economic downturn in history. The unprecedented severity of the Great Depression renewed public demands for federal programs to protect the general welfare. "This nation asks for action," declared President Franklin Delano Roosevelt in his 1933 inaugural address. The many New Deal initiatives and agencies instituted by Roosevelt and

his Democratic administration created the framework for a welfare state that has since served as the basis for public policy.

The New Deal helped revive public confidence and put people back to work, but it did not end the Great Depression. It took a world war to restore full employment. The necessity of mobilizing the nation in support of the Second World War also accelerated the growth of the federal government. And the unparalleled scope of the war helped catapult the United States into a leadership role in world politics. The use of atomic bombs to end the war against Japan ushered in a new era of nuclear diplomacy that held the fate of the world in the balance. For all of the new creature comforts associated with modern life, Americans in 1945 found themselves living amid an array of new anxieties.

22

SEIZING AN AMERICAN EMPIRE

FOCUS QUESTIONS wwnorton.com/studyspace

- What motivated America's "new imperialism"?
- What was the role of religion as a motive for American territorial expansion?
- What were the causes of the War of 1898?
- What did America gain from the War of 1898?
- What were the main achievements of President Roosevelt's foreign policy?

Throughout the nineteenth century, Americans displayed what one senator called "only a languid interest" in foreign affairs. The overriding priorities were at home: industrial development, western settlement, and domestic politics. Foreign relations simply were not important to the vast majority of Americans. After the Civil War an isolationist mood swept across the United States as the country basked in its geographic advantages: wide oceans as buffers, the powerful British navy situated between America and the powers of Europe, and militarily weak neighbors in the Western Hemisphere.

Yet the notion of the United States having been ordained by God to expand its territory and its democratic values remained alive in the decades after the Civil War. Several prominent political and business leaders argued that sustaining rapid industrial development required the acquisition—or conquest—of foreign territories in order to gain easier access to vital raw materials. In addition, as their exports grew, American manufacturers and commercial farmers became increasingly intertwined in the world economy. This growing involvement in international commerce, in turn, required an expanded naval force to protect the shipping lanes from hostile action. And a modern steam-powered navy needed bases where its ships could replenish their supplies of coal and water.

For these and other reasons, the United States during the last quarter of the nineteenth century expanded its military presence and territorial possessions beyond the Western Hemisphere. Its motives for doing so were a mixture of moral and religious idealism (spreading the benefits of democratic capitalism and Christianity to "backward peoples"), popular assumptions of racial superiority, and naked greed. Such confusion over ideals and purposes ensured that the results of America's imperialist adventures would be decidedly mixed. Within the span of a few months in 1898 the United States, which was born in a revolution against British colonial rule, would itself become an imperial ruler whose expanding overseas commitments would have unforeseen—and tragic—consequences.

TOWARD THE NEW IMPERIALISM

By the late nineteenth century, the major European nations had unleashed a new surge of imperialism in Africa and Asia, where they had seized territory, established colonies, and promoted economic exploitation, racial superiority, and Christian evangelism. Writing in 1902, the British economist J. A. Hobson declared that imperialism was "the most powerful factor in the current politics of the Western world."

IMPERIALISM IN A GLOBAL CONTEXT Western imperialism and industrial growth generated a quest for new markets, new sources of raw materials, and new opportunities for investment. The result was a widespread process of aggressive imperial expansion into Africa and Asia. Beginning in the 1880s, the British, French, Belgians, Italians, Dutch, Spanish, and Germans used military force and political guile to conquer those continents. Each of the imperial nations, including the United States, dispatched missionaries to convert conquered peoples to Christianity. By 1900, some 18,000 missionaries were scattered around the world.

AMERICAN IMPERIALISTS As the European nations expanded their control over much of the rest of the world, the United States also began to acquire new territories. A small yet vocal and influential group of public officials aggressively promoted the idea of acquiring overseas possessions. The expansionists included Senators Albert J. Beveridge of Indiana and

Henry Cabot Lodge of Massachusetts, as well as Theodore Roosevelt and naval captain Alfred Thayer Mahan.

During the 1880s, Captain Mahan had become a leading advocate of sea power and Western imperialism. In 1890 he published *The Influence of Sea Power upon History, 1660–1783*, in which he argued that national greatness flowed from maritime power. Mahan insisted that modern economic development required a powerful navy, a strong merchant marine, foreign commerce, colonies, and naval bases. A self-described imperialist, Mahan championed America's "destiny" to control the Caribbean, build an isthmian canal to connect the Pacific and the Caribbean, and spread Western civilization in the Pacific. His ideas were widely circulated in popular journals and within political and military circles. **Theodore Roosevelt**, the war-loving assistant secretary of the navy, ordered a copy of Mahan's book for every American warship. Yet even before Mahan's writings became influential, a gradual expansion of the navy had begun. In 1880 the nation had fewer than a hundred seagoing vessels, many of them rusting or rotting at the docks. By 1896, eleven powerful new steel battleships had been built or authorized.

IMPERIALIST THEORY   Claims of racial superiority bolstered the new imperialist spirit. Spokesmen in each industrial nation, including the United States, used the arguments of social Darwinism to justify economic exploitation and territorial conquest. Among nations as among individuals, expansionists claimed, the fittest survive and prevail. John Fiske, a historian and popular lecturer on Darwinism, stressed in 1885 the superior character of "Anglo-Saxon" institutions and peoples. The English-speaking "race," he argued, was destined to dominate the globe and transform the institutions, traditions, language—even the blood—of the world's peoples. Josiah Strong added the sanction of religion to theories of racial and national superiority. In his best-selling book *Our Country: Its Possible Future and Its Present Crisis* (1885), Strong asserted that the "Anglo-Saxon" embodied two great ideas: civil liberty and "a pure spiritual Christianity." The Anglo-Saxon was "divinely commissioned to be, in a peculiar sense, his brother's keeper."

EXPANSION IN THE PACIFIC

For Josiah Strong and other expansionists, Asia offered an especially alluring target for American imperialism. In 1866, the secretary of state, William H. Seward, had predicted that the United States must inevitably exercise commercial domination "on the Pacific Ocean, and its islands and continents." Eager for American manufacturers to exploit Asian markets, Seward believed the United States first had to remove all foreign interests from the northern Pacific coast and gain access to that region's valuable ports. To that end, he cast covetous eyes on the British colony of British Columbia, sandwiched between Russian America (Alaska) and the Washington Territory.

Late in 1866, while encouraging British Columbians to consider making their colony a U.S. territory, Seward learned of Russia's desire to sell Alaska. He leaped at the opportunity, in part because its acquisition might influence British Columbia to join the union. In 1867, the United States bought Alaska for $7.2 million, thus removing Russia, the most recent colonial power, from North America. Critics scoffed at "Seward's folly" of buying the Alaskan "icebox," but it proved to be the biggest bargain since the Louisiana Purchase.

HAWAII The Americans who were promoting expanded commercial relations with Asia coveted the Hawaiian islands. The islands, a united kingdom since 1795, had a sizable population of American missionaries and sugar. In 1875, the kingdom had signed a reciprocal trade agreement with the American government, according to which Hawaiian sugar would enter the United States duty-free and Hawaii promised that none of its territory would be leased or granted to a third power. This agreement resulted in a boom in sugar production, and American planters in Hawaii soon formed an economic elite that built its fortunes on cheap immigrant labor, mainly Chinese and Japanese. By the 1890s, the native Hawaiian population had been reduced to a minority by smallpox and other foreign diseases, and Asians quickly became the most numerous group.

In 1885, President Grover Cleveland called the Hawaiian Islands "the stepping-stone to the growing trade of the Pacific." Two years later, Americans in Hawaii forced the king to convert the monarchy to a constitutional government, which they dominated. In 1890, however, the McKinley Tariff destroyed Hawaii's favored position in the sugar trade by putting the sugar of all countries on the duty-free list and granting growers in the continental United States a 2¢ subsidy per pound of sugar. This change led to an economic crisis in Hawaii and brought political turmoil as well.

In 1891, when **Liliuokalani**, the king's sister, ascended the throne, she tried to eliminate the political power exercised by American planters. Two years later Hawaii's white population revolted and seized power. The U.S. ambassador brought in marines to support the coup. As he cheerfully reported to the secretary of state, "The Hawaiian pear is now fully ripe, and

Cutting sugar cane

Heightened demand for cheap labor in the sugar cane fields dramatically affected the demographic and political conditions of the Hawaiian islands.

this is the golden hour for the United States to pluck it." Within a month a committee of the new government in Hawaii turned up in Washington, D.C. with a treaty calling for the island nation to be annexed to the United States.

President Cleveland then sent a special commissioner to investigate the situation in Hawaii. The commissioner removed the marines and reported that the Americans in Hawaii had acted improperly. Most Hawaiians opposed annexation to the United States, the commissioner found. He concluded that the revolution had been engineered mainly by the American planters hoping to take advantage of the subsidy for sugar grown in the United States. Cleveland proposed to restore the queen to power in return for amnesty to the revolutionists. The provisional government controlled by the sugar planters refused to give up power, however, and on July 4, 1894, it created the Republic of Hawaii, which included in its constitution a provision for American annexation. In 1897, when William McKinley became president, he was looking for an excuse to annex the islands. "We need Hawaii," he claimed, "just as much and a good deal more than we did California. It is manifest destiny." When the Senate could not muster the two-thirds majority needed to approve an annexation treaty, McKinley used a joint resolution of the House and the Senate to achieve his aims. The resolution passed by simple majorities in both houses, and Hawaii was annexed by the United States in the summer of 1898.

The War of 1898

Until the 1890s, reservations about acquiring overseas possessions had checked America's drive to expand. Suddenly, in 1898 and 1899, such inhibitions collapsed, and the United States aggressively thrust its way to the far reaches of Asia. The spark for this explosion of imperialism lay not in Asia but in Cuba, a Spanish colony ninety miles southwest of the southern tip of Florida. Ironically, the chief motive was a sense of outrage at another country's imperialism. Americans wanted the Cubans to gain their independence from Spain.

"CUBA LIBRE"   Throughout the second half of the nineteenth century, Cubans had repeatedly revolted against centuries-old Spanish rule, only to be ruthlessly suppressed. As one of Spain's oldest colonies, Cuba was a major export market for the mother country. Yet American sugar and mining companies had also invested heavily in Cuba. The United States in fact traded more with Cuba than Spain did.

On February 24, 1895, insurrection again broke out as Cubans waged guerrilla warfare against Spanish troops. Events in Cuba supplied dramatic headlines for newspapers and magazines. **William Randolph Hearst's *New York Journal*** and **Joseph Pulitzer's *New York World*** were at the time locked in a monumental competition for readers, striving to outdo each other with sensational headlines about every Spanish atrocity in Cuba, real or invented. The newspapers' sensationalism as well as their intentional efforts to manipulate public opinion came to be called **yellow journalism**. Hearst wanted a war against Spain to catapult the United States into global significance. Once war was declared against Spain, Hearst took credit for it. One of his newspaper headlines blared: "HOW DO YOU LIKE THE JOURNAL'S WAR?"

PRESSURE FOR WAR   At the outset of the Cuban rebellion in 1895, President Grover Cleveland tried to protect U.S. business interests in Cuba while avoiding military involvement. Mounting public sympathy for the rebel cause prompted acute concern in Congress, however. By concurrent resolutions on April 6, 1896, the House and Senate endorsed the granting of official recognition to the Cuban rebels. After his inauguration in March 1897, President William McKinley continued the posture of sympathetic neutrality, but with each passing month Americans called for greater assistance to the Cuban insurgents. In 1897, Spain offered Cubans autonomy (self-government without formal independence) in return for ending the rebellion. The Cubans rejected the offer. Spain was impaled on the horns of a dilemma, unable to end the insurrection and unready to give up Cuba.

Early in 1898, events pushed the two nations into a war that neither government wanted. On January 25, the U.S. battleship *Maine* docked in Havana harbor, ostensibly on a courtesy call. On February 9, the *New York Journal* released the text of a letter from the Spanish ambassador Depuy de Lôme to a friend in Havana. In the so-called **de Lôme letter**, which had been stolen from the post office by a Cuban spy, de Lôme called President McKinley "weak and a bidder for the admiration of the crowd, besides being a would-be politician who tries to leave a door open behind himself while keeping on good terms with the jingoes of his party." De Lôme resigned to prevent further embarrassment to his government.

Six days later, during the night of February 15, 1898, the *Maine* exploded and sank in Havana harbor, with a horrible loss of 260 men. Although years later the sinking was ruled an accident resulting from a coal explosion, those eager for a war with Spain in 1898 saw no need to withhold judgment. Upon learning about the loss of the *Maine*, the 39-year-old assistant secretary of the navy, Theodore Roosevelt, told a friend that he "would give anything if President McKinley would order the fleet to Havana tomorrow." He called the sinking "an act of dirty treachery on the part of the Spaniards." The United States, he claimed, "needs a war." The outcry against Spain rose in a crescendo with the words "Remember the *Maine!*"

The weight of outraged public opinion and the influence of Republican militants such as Roosevelt and the president's closest friend, Senator Henry Cabot Lodge, eroded McKinley's neutrality. On April 11, McKinley asked Congress for authority to use armed forces in Cuba. On April 20, Congress declared Cuba independent and demanded the withdrawal of Spanish forces. The **Teller Amendment**, added on the Senate floor to the war resolution, disclaimed any U.S. designs on Cuban territory. McKinley signed the war resolution, and a copy went off to the Spanish government. McKinley called for 125,000 volunteers to supplement the 28,000 men in the U.S. Army. Among the first to enlist was the man who most lusted for war against Spain: Theodore Roosevelt. Never has an American war, so casually begun and so enthusiastically supported, generated such unexpected and far-reaching consequences.

The sinking of the *Maine* in Havana Harbor

The uproar created by the incident and its coverage in the "yellow press" helped to push President William McKinley to declare war.

MANILA   The war with Spain lasted only 114 days. The conflict was barely under way before the U.S. Navy produced a spectacular victory in an unexpected location in the Pacific Ocean: Manila Bay in the Philippines. Just before war had been declared, Theodore Roosevelt, still serving as the assistant secretary of the navy, had ordered (without getting the permission of his superiors) Commodore **George Dewey**, commander of the small U.S. fleet in Asia, to engage Spanish forces in the Philippines in case of war in Cuba. Commodore Dewey arrived late on April 30 with four cruisers and two gunboats, and they quickly destroyed or captured all the outdated Spanish warships in Manila Bay without suffering any major damage themselves. Dewey was now in awkward possession of the bay without any ground forces to go onshore. Promised reinforcements, he stayed while German and British warships cruised offshore like watchful vultures, ready to take control of the Philippines if the United States did not do so. In the meantime,

Turmoil in the Philippines

Emilio Aguinaldo (seated third from right) and other leaders of the Filipino insurgency.

Emilio Aguinaldo, the leader of the Filipino nationalist movement, declared the Philippines independent on June 12. With Aguinaldo's help, Dewey's forces entered Manila on August 13. The Spanish garrison preferred to surrender to the Americans rather than to the vengeful Filipinos. News of the American victory sent President McKinley scurrying to find a map of Asia to locate "these darned islands" now occupied by U.S. soldiers and sailors.

THE CUBAN CAMPAIGN   While these events transpired halfway around the world, the fighting in Cuba reached a surprisingly quick climax. The U.S. Navy blockaded the Spanish navy inside Santiago harbor while some 17,000 American troops hastily assembled at Tampa, Florida. One prominent unit was the First Volunteer Cavalry, better known as the **Rough Riders**, a regiment with "special qualifications" made up of former Ivy League athletes, ex-convicts, Cherokee, Choctaw, Chickasaw, Pawnee, and Creek Indians, and southwestern sharpshooters. Of course, the Rough Riders are best remembered because Lieutenant Colonel Theodore Roosevelt was second in command. One of the Rough Riders said that Lieutenant Colonel Roosevelt was "nervous, energetic, virile. He may wear out some day, but he will never rust out." When the 578 Rough Riders, accompanied by a gaggle of reporters and photographers, landed in oppressive heat on

June 22, 1898, at the undefended southeastern tip of Cuba, chaos ensued, as their horses and mules were mistakenly sent elsewhere, leaving the Rough Riders to become the "Weary Walkers." Only Roosevelt ended up with his horse, Little Texas.

Land and sea battles around Santiago quickly broke Spanish resistance. On July 1, about seven thousand U.S. soldiers took the fortified village of El Caney. While a much larger force attacked San Juan Hill, a smaller unit, including the dismounted Rough Riders together with African American soldiers from two cavalry units, with Roosevelt at their head yelling "Charge!", seized nearby Kettle Hill. A friend wrote to Roosevelt's wife that her husband was "reveling in victory and gore." Thanks to widespread media coverage, much of it exaggerated, Roosevelt had become a home-front legend, the most beloved hero of the brief war.

On July 26, 1898, the Spanish government in Madrid sued for peace. After discussions lasting two weeks, an armistice was signed on August 12, less than four months after the war's start and the day before Americans entered Manila. In Cuba, the Spanish forces formally surrendered to the U.S. commander, boarded ships, and sailed for Spain. Excluded from the ceremony were the Cubans, for whom the war had been fought. The peace treaty specified that Spain should give up Cuba and that the United States should annex Puerto Rico and occupy Manila pending the transfer of power in the Philippines.

In all, over 60,000 Spanish soldiers died of disease or wounds in the four-month war. Among the 274,000 Americans who served during the war, 5,462 died, but only 379 in battle. Most succumbed to malaria, typhoid, dysentery, or yellow fever. At such a cost the United States was launched onto the world scene as a great power, with all the benefits—and burdens—of a new colonial empire of its own.

America's role in the world was changed forever by the campaign, for the United States emerged as an imperial power. Halfway through the brief conflict in Cuba, John Hay, soon to be secretary of state, wrote a letter to his close friend, Theodore Roosevelt. In acknowledging Roosevelt's trial by fire, Hay called it "a splendid little war, begun with the highest motives, carried on with magnificent intelligence and spirit, favored by that fortune that loves the brave." Victory in the War of 1898 boosted American self-confidence and reinforced the self-serving American belief, tinged with racism, that the nation had a "manifest destiny" to reshape the world in its own image. As Josiah Strong had boasted in 1895, Americans "are a race of unequaled energy" who represent "the largest liberty, the purest Christianity, the highest civilization" in the world. "Can anyone

doubt that this race . . . is destined to dispossess many weaker races, assim-
ilate others, and mold the remainder until . . . it has Anglo-Saxonized
mankind?" The United States liberated Spain's remaining colonies, yet in
some cases it would substitute its own oppression for Spain's. If war with
Spain saved many lives by ending the insurrection in Cuba, it also led the
United States to suppress another anti-colonial insurrection, in the
Philippines, and the acquisition of its own imperial colonies created a
host of festering problems that persisted into the twentieth century.

THE DEBATE OVER ANNEXATION The United States and Spain
signed the Treaty of Paris on December 10, 1898, ending the war between the
two nations. It granted Cuba its independence, but the status of the Philippines remained unresolved. American business leaders wanted to keep the
Philippines so that they could more easily penetrate the vast markets of populous China. Missionary societies also wanted the United States to annex the
Philippines so that they could bring Christianity to "the little brown
brother." The Philippines promised to provide a useful base for all such
activities. President McKinley pondered the alternatives and later explained
his reasoning for annexing the Philippines to a group of fellow Methodists:

> And one night late it came to me this way—I don't know how it was, but it
> came: (1) that we could not give them back to Spain—that would be
> cowardly and dishonorable; (2) that we could not turn them over to France or
> Germany—our commercial rivals in the Orient—that would be bad business
> and discreditable; (3) that we could not leave them to themselves—they were
> unfit for self-government—and they would soon have anarchy and misrule
> over there worse than Spain's was; and (4) that there was nothing left for us
> to do but to take them all, and to educate the Filipinos, and uplift and civilize
> and Christianize them, and by God's grace do the very best we could by them,
> as our fellowmen for whom Christ also died. And then I went to bed, and
> went to sleep and slept soundly.

In one brief statement, McKinley had summarized the motivating ideas of
American imperialism: (1) national glory, (2) commerce, (3) racial superiority, and (4) evangelism. American negotiators in Paris finally offered the
Spanish $20 million for the Philippines, Puerto Rico, and Guam, a Spanish-
controlled island in the Pacific with a valuable harbor.

Meanwhile, Americans had taken other giant steps in the Pacific. Congress had annexed Hawaii in the midst of the War of 1898. In 1898, the
United States had also claimed Wake Island, located between Guam and the

Hawaiian Islands, which would become a vital link in a future transpacific telegraph cable. Then, in 1899, Germany and the United States agreed to partition the Samoa Islands. The United States annexed the easternmost islands; Germany took the rest.

By early 1899, the Treaty of Paris, ending the War of 1898, had yet to be ratified in the Senate, where most Democrats and Populists and some Republicans opposed it. Anti-imperialists argued that acquisition of the Philippines would corrupt the American principle dating back to the Revolution that people should be self-governing rather than colonial subjects. Opponents also noted the inconsistency of liberating Cuba and annexing the Philippines, as well as the danger that the Philippines would become impossible to defend if a foreign power such as Japan attacked. The opposition might have been strong enough to kill the treaty had not the Democrat William Jennings Bryan influenced the vote for approval. Ending the war, he argued, would open the way for the future independence of the Philippines. His support convinced enough Democrats to enable passage of the peace treaty in the Senate on February 6, 1899, by the narrowest of margins: only one vote more than the necessary two thirds.

President McKinley, however, had no intention of granting the Philippines independence. He insisted that the United States take control of the islands as an act of "benevolent assimilation." In February 1899, an American soldier outside Manila fired on soldiers in the Filipino Army of Liberation, and two of them were killed. Suddenly, the United States found itself in a new war, this time a crusade to suppress the Filipino independence movement. Since Aguinaldo's forces, called *insurrectos*, were more or less in control of the islands outside Manila, what followed was largely a brutal American war of conquest.

THE PHILIPPINE-AMERICAN WAR   The American effort to quash Filipino nationalism lasted three years, eventually involved some 126,000 U.S. troops, and took the lives of hundreds of thousands of Filipinos (most of them civilians) and 4,234 American soldiers. It was a sordid conflict, with grisly massacres committed by both sides. It did not help matters that many American soldiers referred to their Filipino opponents as "niggers." Within the first year of the war in the Philippines, American newspapers had begun to report an array of atrocities committed by U.S. troops—villages burned, prisoners tortured and executed. Thus did the United States alienate and destroy a Filipino independence movement modeled after America's own struggle for independence from Great Britain. Organized Filipino resistance had collapsed by the end of

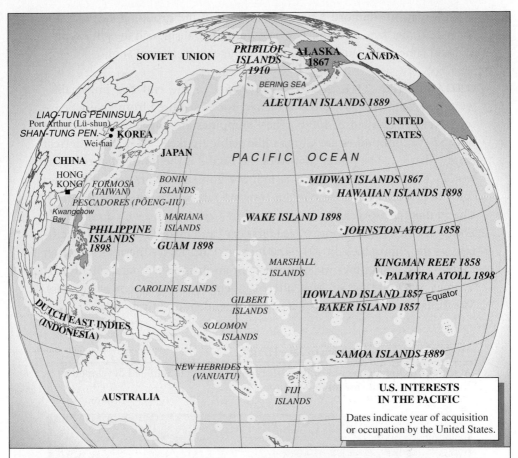

SOVIET UNION   PRIBILOF ISLANDS 1910   ALASKA 1867   CANADA

BERING SEA

ALEUTIAN ISLANDS 1889

LIAO-TUNG PENINSULA
Port Arthur (Lü-shun)
SHAN-TUNG PEN.   KOREA
Wei-hai

UNITED STATES

CHINA   JAPAN   PACIFIC OCEAN

HONG KONG   FORMOSA (TAIWAN)   BONIN ISLANDS   MIDWAY ISLANDS 1867
HAWAIIAN ISLANDS 1898

PESCADORES (PŌENG-IIU)
Kwangchow Bay   MARIANA ISLANDS   WAKE ISLAND 1898
PHILIPPINE ISLANDS 1898   GUAM 1898   JOHNSTON ATOLL 1858

MARSHALL ISLANDS   KINGMAN REEF 1858
PALMYRA ATOLL 1898

CAROLINE ISLANDS

GILBERT ISLANDS   HOWLAND ISLAND 1857   Equator
BAKER ISLAND 1857

DUTCH EAST INDIES (INDONESIA)   SOLOMON ISLANDS

SAMOA ISLANDS 1889

NEW HEBRIDES (VANUATU)

AUSTRALIA   FIJI ISLANDS

U.S. INTERESTS IN THE PACIFIC

Dates indicate year of acquisition or occupation by the United States.

Why was President McKinley eager to acquire territory in the Pacific and the Caribbean? What kind of political system did the U.S. government create in Hawaii and in the Philippines? How did Filipinos and Hawaiians resist the Americans?

1899, but even after the American capture of Aguinaldo in 1901, sporadic guerrilla action lasted until mid-1902.

Against the backdrop of this nasty guerrilla war, the great debate over imperialism continued in the United States. In 1899 several anti-imperialist groups combined to form the American Anti-Imperialist League. The league attracted members representing many shades of opinion. Former presidents Grover Cleveland and Benjamin Harrison urged President McKinley to withdraw U.S. forces from the Philippines. Andrew Carnegie footed the bills for the League; and on imperialism, at least, the union leader Samuel Gompers agreed with the steel king. Presidents Charles Eliot of Harvard and David

Starr Jordan of Stanford University supported the group, along with the social reformer Jane Addams. The drive for imperialism, said the philosopher William James, had caused the nation to "puke up its ancient soul."

ORGANIZING THE ACQUISITIONS In the end the imperialists won the debate over the status of the territories acquired from Spain. Senator Beveridge boasted in 1900: "The Philippines are ours forever. And just beyond the Philippines are China's illimitable markets. We will not retreat from either. . . . The power that rules the Pacific is the power that rules the world." On July 4, 1901, the U.S. military government in the Philippines came to an end, and Judge William Howard Taft became the civil governor. The Philippine Government Act, passed by Congress in 1902, declared the Philippine Islands an "unorganized territory" and made the inhabitants citizens of the Philippines. In 1917, the Jones Act affirmed America's intention to grant the Philippines independence on an unspecified date. Finally, the Tydings-McDuffie Act of 1934 offered independence after ten more years. The Philippines would finally become independent on July 4, 1946.

"Well, I Hardly Know Which to Take First!"

At the end of the nineteenth century, it seemed that Uncle Sam had developed a considerable appetite for foreign territory.

Closer to home, Puerto Rico had been acquired in part to serve as a U.S. outpost guarding the approach to the Caribbean Sea and any future isthmian canal in Central America. On April 12, 1900, the Foraker Act established a government on the island. The president appointed a governor and eleven members of an executive council, and an elected House of Delegates made up the lower house of the legislature. Residents of the island were declared citizens of Puerto Rico; they were not made citizens of the United States until 1917, when the Jones Act granted them U.S. citizenship and made both houses of the legislature elective. In 1947 the governor also became elective, and in 1952 Puerto Rico became a commonwealth with its own constitution and elected officials, a unique status. Like a state, Puerto Rico is free to change its constitution insofar as it does not conflict with the U.S. Constitution.

Finally, there was Cuba. Having liberated the Cubans from Spanish rule, the Americans found themselves propping up a shaky new government whose economy was in shambles. Technically, Cuba had not gained its independence in 1898. Instead, it remained a protectorate of the United States. American troops remained in control of Cuba for four years, after which they left, but on the condition that the United States could intervene again if the political conditions in Cuba did not satisfy American expectations. Clashes between U.S. soldiers and Cubans erupted almost immediately. When President McKinley set up a military government for the island late in 1898, it was at odds with rebel leaders from the start. The United States finally fulfilled the promise of independence after the military regime had restored order, organized schools, and improved sanitary conditions. The problem of disease in Cuba prompted the work of **Dr. Walter Reed**, who made an outstanding contribution to health in tropical regions around the world. Named head of the Army Yellow Fever Commission in 1900, he proved that mosquitoes carried yellow fever. The commission's experiments led the way to effective control of the disease worldwide.

In 1900, on President McKinley's order, Cubans drafted a constitution modeled on that of the United States. The Platt Amendment, added to an army appropriations bill passed by Congress in 1901, sharply restricted the new Cuban government's independence, however. The amendment required that Cuba never impair its independence by signing a treaty with a third power, that it keep its debt within the government's power to repay it out of ordinary revenues, and that it acknowledge the right of the United States to intervene in Cuba whenever it saw fit. Finally, Cuba had to sell or lease to the United States lands to be used for coaling or naval stations, a proviso that led to a U.S. naval base at Guantánamo Bay, which still exists today.

IMPERIAL RIVALRIES IN EAST ASIA

During the 1890s, the United States was not the only nation to emerge as a world power. Japan defeated China in the First Sino-Japanese War (1894–1895). China's weakness enabled European powers to exploit it. Russia, Germany, France, and Great Britain established spheres of influence in China by the end of the century. In early 1898 and again in 1899, the British asked the American government to join them in preserving the territorial integrity of China against further imperialist actions. Both times the Senate rejected the request because it risked an entangling alliance in a region—Asia—where the United States as yet had no strategic investment.

THE "OPEN DOOR"   The American outlook toward Asia changed with the defeat of Spain and the acquisition of the Philippines. Instead of acting jointly with Great Britain, however, the U.S. government decided to act alone. What came to be known as the **Open Door policy** was outlined in Secretary of State John Hay's Open Door Note, dispatched in 1899 to his European counterparts. It proposed to keep China open to trade with all countries on an equal basis. More specifically, it called upon foreign powers, within their spheres of influence, (1) to refrain from interfering with any treaty port (a port open to all by treaty) or any vested interest, (2) to permit Chinese authorities to collect tariffs on an equal basis, and (3) to show no favors to their own nationals in the matter of harbor dues or railroad charges. As it turned out, none of the European powers except Britain accepted Hay's principles, but none rejected them either. So Hay simply announced that all the major powers involved in China had accepted the policy.

"The Open Door"

Cartoon depicting Uncle Sam propping open a door for China with a brick labeled "U.S. Army and Navy Prestige," as colonial powers look on.

The Open Door policy was rooted in desire of American businesses to exploit Chinese markets. However, it also tapped the deep-seated sympathies of those who opposed imperialism, especially as the policy pledged to protect China's territorial integrity. But the much-trumpeted Open Door policy had little legal standing. When the Japanese, concerned about Russian pressure in Manchuria, asked how the United States intended to enforce the policy, Hay replied that America was "not prepared . . . to enforce these views." So it would remain for forty years, until continued Japanese expansion in China would bring America to war in 1941.

BIG-STICK DIPLOMACY

More than any other American of his time, Theodore Roosevelt transformed the role of the United States in world affairs. The nation had emerged from the War of 1898 a world power with major new responsibilities. To ensure that the United States accepted its international obligations, Roosevelt stretched both the Constitution and executive power to the limit. In the process he pushed a reluctant nation onto the center stage of world affairs.

ROOSEVELT'S RISE   Born in 1858, Roosevelt had grown up in Manhattan in cultured comfort, had visited Europe as a child, spoke German fluently, and had graduated from Harvard with honors in 1880. A sickly, scrawny boy with poor eyesight and chronic asthma, he built himself up into a physical and intellectual athlete, a man of almost superhuman energies who became a lifelong practitioner of the "strenuous life." Roosevelt loved rigorous exercise and outdoor activities. A boxer, wrestler, mountain climber, hunter, and outdoorsman, he also displayed extraordinary intellectual curiosity. He became a voracious reader, a learned natural scientist, dedicated bird-watcher, a renowned historian and essayist, and a zealous moralist. He wrote thirty-eight books on a wide variety of subjects. His boundless energy and fierce competitive spirit were infectious, and he was ever willing to express an opinion on any subject. Within two years of graduating from Harvard, Roosevelt won election to the New York legislature. "I rose like a rocket," he later observed.

But with the world seemingly at his feet, disaster struck. In 1884, Roosevelt's beloved mother Mittie, only forty-eight years old, died. Eleven hours later, in the same house, his twenty-two-year-old wife Alice died in his arms of kidney failure, having recently given birth to their only child. The double funeral was so wrenching that the officiating minister wept throughout his prayer. In an attempt to recover from this "strange and terrible fate," a distraught Roosevelt turned his baby daughter Alice over to his sister, quit his political career, sold the family house, and moved west to take up cattle ranching in the Dakota Territory. The blue-blooded New Yorker escaped his grief by plunging himself into virile western life: he relished hunting big game, leading cattle roundups, capturing outlaws, fighting Indians (whom he termed a "lesser race")—and reading novels by the campfire. Although his western career lasted only two years, he never got over being a cowboy.

Back in New York City, Roosevelt remarried and ran unsuccessfully for mayor in 1886; he later served six years as civil service commissioner and two years as New York City's police commissioner. In 1896, Roosevelt campaigned hard for William McKinley, and the new president was asked to reward him with the position of assistant secretary of the navy. McKinley initially balked, saying that young Roosevelt was too "hotheaded," but he eventually relented and appointed the war-loving aristocrat. Roosevelt took full advantage of his celebrity with the Rough Riders during the war in Cuba to win the governorship of New York in November 1898. By then he had become the most prominent Republican in the nation.

In the 1900 presidential contest, the Democrats turned once again to William Jennings Bryan, who sought to make American imperialism the "paramount issue" of the campaign. The Democratic platform condemned the Philippine conflict as "an unnecessary war" that had placed the United States "in the false and un-American position of crushing with military force the efforts of our former allies to achieve liberty and self-government."

The Republicans welcomed the chance to disagree. They renominated McKinley and named Theodore Roosevelt, now virtually Mr. Imperialism, his running mate. Roosevelt's much-publicized combat exploits in Cuba had made him a national celebrity. Colonel Roosevelt was named "Man of the Year" in 1898. Elected governor of New York that year, Roosevelt nevertheless leapt at the chance to be vice president in part because he despised Bryan as a dangerous "radical" who called for the federal government to take ownership of railroads. Roosevelt was more than a match for Bryan as a campaign speaker, and he crisscrossed the nation on behalf of McKinley, speaking in opposition to Bryan's "communistic and socialistic doctrines" promoting higher taxes and the free coinage of silver. McKinley outpolled Bryan by 7.2 million to 6.4 million popular votes and 292 to 155 electoral votes. Bryan even lost his own state of Nebraska.

Less than a year after McKinley's victory, however, his second term ended tragically. On September 6, 1901, at a reception at the Pan-American Exposition in Buffalo, an unemployed anarchist named Leon Czolgosz (pronounced chole-gosh) approached the fifty-eight-year-old president with a gun concealed in a bandaged hand and fired at point-blank range. McKinley died eight days later, and Theodore Roosevelt was elevated to the White House. "Now look," erupted Marcus "Mark" Hanna, the Ohio businessman and politico, "that damned cowboy is President of the United States!"

Six weeks short of his forty-third birthday, Roosevelt was the youngest man ever to reach the White House, but he had more experience in public affairs than most and perhaps more vitality than any. One observer compared him to Niagara Falls, "both great wonders of nature." Even Woodrow Wilson, Roosevelt's main political opponent, said that the former

Mr. Imperialism

This 1900 cartoon shows the Republican vice-presidential candidate, Theodore Roosevelt, overshadowing his running mate, President William McKinley.

"Rough Rider" was "a great big boy" at heart. "You can't resist the man." Roosevelt's glittering spectacles, glistening teeth, and overflowing gusto were a godsend to the cartoonists, who added another trademark when he pronounced the adage "Speak softly, and carry a big stick."

Along with Roosevelt's boundless energy went a sense of unshakable self-righteousness, which led him to cast nearly every issue in moral and patriotic terms. He was the first truly activist president. He considered the presidency his "bully pulpit," and he delivered fist-pumping speeches on the virtues of righteousness, honesty, civic duty, and strenuosity. Nowhere was President Roosevelt's forceful will more evident than in his conduct of foreign affairs.

THE PANAMA CANAL   After the War of 1898, the United States became more deeply involved in the Caribbean. One issue overshadowed every other in the region: the Panama Canal. The narrow isthmus of Panama had first become a major concern of Americans in the late 1840s, when it became an important overland route to the California goldfields. Two treaties dating from that period loomed years later as obstacles to the construction of a canal. The Bidlack Treaty (1846) with Colombia (then New Granada) guaranteed both Colombia's sovereignty over Panama and the neutrality of the isthmus. In the Clayton-Bulwer Treaty (1850) the British agreed to acquire no more Central American territory, and the United States joined them in agreeing to build or fortify a canal only by mutual consent.

After the War of 1898, Secretary of State John Hay asked the British ambassador for such consent. The outcome was the Hay-Pauncefote Treaty of 1901. Other obstacles remained, however. From 1881 to 1887, a French company under Ferdinand de Lesseps, who had engineered the Suez Canal in Egypt between 1859 and 1869, had spent nearly $300 million and some twenty thousand lives to dig less than a third of a canal across Panama, still under the control of Colombia. The company asked that the United States purchase its holdings, which it did. Meanwhile, Secretary Hay had opened negotiations with Ambassador Tomás Herrán of Colombia. In return for acquiring a canal zone six miles wide, the United States agreed to pay $10 million in cash and a rental fee of $250,000 a year. The U.S. Senate ratified the Hay-Herrán Treaty in 1903, but the Colombian senate held out for $25 million in cash. In response to this act by those "foolish and homicidal corruptionists in Bogotá," Theodore Roosevelt, by then president, flew into a rage. Meanwhile the Panamanians revolted against Colombian

Digging the canal

President Theodore Roosevelt operating a steam shovel during his 1906 visit to the Panama Canal.

rule. Philippe Bunau-Varilla, an employee of the French canal company, assisted them, and reported, after visiting Roosevelt and Hay in Washington, D.C., that American warships would arrive at Colón, Panama, on November 2.

The Panamanians revolted the next day. Colombian troops, who could not penetrate the overland jungle, found U.S. ships blocking the sea-lanes. On November 13, the Roosevelt administration received its first ambassador from Panama, who happened to be Philippe Bunau-Varilla; he eagerly signed a treaty that extended the Canal Zone from six to ten miles in width. For $10 million down and $250,000 a year, the United States received "in perpetuity the use, occupation and

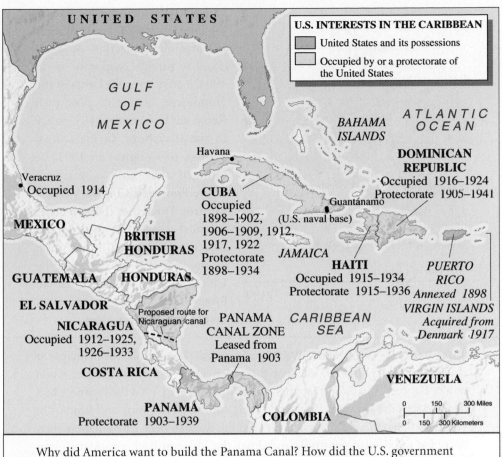

U.S. INTERESTS IN THE CARIBBEAN

☐ United States and its possessions

☐ Occupied by or a protectorate of the United States

UNITED STATES

GULF OF MEXICO

Havana

Veracruz
Occupied 1914

MEXICO

BRITISH HONDURAS

CUBA
Occupied 1898–1902,
1906–1909, 1912,
1917, 1922
Protectorate
1898–1934

Guantánamo
(U.S. naval base)

JAMAICA

GUATEMALA HONDURAS

EL SALVADOR

NICARAGUA
Occupied 1912–1925,
1926–1933

Proposed route for
Nicaraguan canal

PANAMA
CANAL ZONE
Leased from
Panama 1903

CARIBBEAN
SEA

COSTA RICA

PANAMÁ
Protectorate 1903–1939

COLOMBIA

BAHAMA
ISLANDS

ATLANTIC
OCEAN

DOMINICAN
REPUBLIC
Occupied 1916–1924
Protectorate 1905–1941

HAITI
Occupied 1915–1934
Protectorate 1915–1936

PUERTO
RICO
Annexed 1898

VIRGIN ISLANDS
Acquired from
Denmark 1917

VENEZUELA

0   150   300 Miles
0 150 300 Kilometers

Why did America want to build the Panama Canal? How did the U.S. government interfere with Colombian politics in an effort to gain control of the canal? What was the Roosevelt Corollary?

control" of the Canal Zone. The U.S. attorney general, asked to supply a legal opinion upholding Roosevelt's actions, responded wryly, "No, Mr. President, if I were you I would not have any taint of legality about it." Roosevelt later explained that "I took the Canal Zone and let Congress debate; and while the debate goes on the [construction of the] Canal does also." The strategic canal opened on August 15, 1914, two weeks after the outbreak of World War I in Europe.

THE ROOSEVELT COROLLARY   The behavior of the United States in gaining control of the Panama Canal created ill will throughout Latin America that would last for generations. Equally galling to Latin American sensibilities was the United States' constant meddling in the internal affairs of

The world's policeman

President Theodore Roosevelt wields "the big stick," symbolizing his aggressive diplomacy.

various nations. A prime excuse for intervention in those days was to force the collection of debts owed to foreign corporations. In 1904, a crisis over the debts of the Dominican Republic prompted Roosevelt to formulate U.S. policy in the Caribbean. In his annual address to Congress in 1904, he outlined what came to be known as the **Roosevelt Corollary to the Monroe Doctrine**: the principle, in short, that since the Monroe Doctrine prohibited intervention in the region by Europeans, the United States was justified in intervening first to forestall involvement by outsiders.

THE RUSSO-JAPANESE WAR   In east Asia, meanwhile, the principle of equal trading rights embodied in the Open Door policy was tested when rivalry between Russia and Japan flared into warfare. By 1904 the Japanese had decided that the Russians threatened their ambitions in China and Korea. On February 8, Japanese warships devastated the Russian fleet. The Japanese then occupied the Korean peninsula and drove the Russians back into Manchuria. When the Japanese signaled that they would welcome a negotiated settlement, Roosevelt sponsored a peace conference in Portsmouth, New Hampshire. With the Treaty of Portsmouth, signed on September 5, 1905, the concessions all went to the Japanese. Russia acknowledged Japan's "predominant political, military, and economic interests in Korea" (Japan would annex the kingdom in 1910), and both powers agreed to evacuate Manchuria.

Japan's show of strength against Russia raised doubts among American leaders about the security of the Philippines. During the Portsmouth talks, Roosevelt sent William Howard Taft to meet with the Japanese foreign minister in Tokyo. The two men negotiated the Taft-Katsura Agreement of July 29, 1905, in which the United States accepted Japanese control of Korea, and Japan disavowed any designs on the Philippines. Three years later the Root-Takahira Agreement, negotiated by Secretary of State Elihu Root and the Japanese ambassador, endorsed the status quo and reinforced the Open

Door policy by supporting "the independence and integrity of China" and "the principle of equal opportunity for commerce and industry in China."

Behind the diplomatic facade of goodwill, however, lay mutual distrust. For many Americans the Russian threat in east Asia now gave way to concerns about the "yellow peril" (a term apparently coined by Kaiser Wilhelm II of Germany). Racial animosities on the West Coast helped sour relations with Japan. In 1906, San Francisco's school board ordered students of Asian descent to attend a separate public school. The Japanese government sharply protested such prejudice, and President Roosevelt persuaded the school board to change its policy, but only after making sure that Japanese authorities would not issue "visas" to "laborers," except former residents of the United States; the parents, wives, or children of residents; or those who already possessed an interest in an American farming enterprise. This "Gentlemen's Agreement" of 1907, the precise terms of which have never been revealed, halted the influx of Japanese immigrants and brought some respite to racial agitation in California.

THE GREAT WHITE FLEET   Before Roosevelt left the White House in early 1909, he celebrated America's rise to the status of a world power with one great flourish. In 1907, he sent the entire U.S. Navy, by then second in strength only to the British fleet, on a grand tour around the world, announcing that he was ready for "a feast, a frolic, or a fight." He got mostly the first two and none of the last. At every port of call down the Atlantic coast of South America, up the west coast, out to Hawaii, and down to New Zealand and Australia, the "Great White Fleet" received rousing welcomes. The triumphal procession continued home by way of the Mediterranean and steamed back into American waters in early 1909, just in time to close out Roosevelt's presidency on a note of success.

Yet it was a success that would have mixed consequences. Roosevelt's effort to deploy American power abroad was accompanied by a racist ideology shared by many prominent political figures of the time. He once told the graduates of the Naval War College that all "the great masterful races have been fighting races, and the minute that a race loses the hard fighting virtues . . . it has lost the right to stand as equal to the best." On another occasion he called warfare the best way to promote "the clear instinct for race selfishness" and insisted that "the most ultimately righteous of all wars is a war with savages." Such a belligerent, self-righteous bigotry defied America's egalitarian ideals and would come back to haunt the United States in world affairs—and at home.

CHAPTER SUMMARY

- **New Imperialism** By the beginning of the twentieth century, the idea of a manifest destiny and American industrialists' need for new markets for their goods fueled America's "new imperialism." The ideology of social Darwinism was used to justify the colonization of less developed nations as white Americans held that their own industrial superiority proved their racial superiority and, therefore, the theory of the survival of the fittest. White Americans rationalized further that they had a duty to Christianize and uplift "backward" peoples.

- **Religion and Imperialism** Protestant missionaries felt impelled to take Christianity to native peoples throughout the world. An indigenous people's acceptance of Christianity was the first step toward the loss of their own culture.

- **War of 1898** Spain still had an extensive empire, and Cuba was one of its oldest colonies. When Cubans revolted against Spain in 1895, many Americans were sympathetic to their demand for independence. The insurrection was harshly suppressed, and sensational coverage in certain New York newspapers further aroused Americans' sympathy. Early in 1898, the publication of a letter by Spain's minister to the United States, Depuy de Lôme, which criticized President McKinley, and then the explosion of the U.S. battleship *Maine* in Havana Harbor propelled America into a war with Spain despite the reluctance of President McKinley and many business interests.

- **Results of the War of 1898** Although the Teller Amendment declared that the United States had no intention of annexing Cuba, America curtailed Cuba's freedom and annexed other territories taken from Spain in the War of 1898. Insurrection followed in the Philippines when insurgents saw that the islands would be administered by the United States. In the treaty that ended the war, the United States gained Puerto Rico as well as Guam and other islands in the Pacific. Meanwhile, Hawaii had been annexed during the war.

- **Big-Stick Diplomacy** As president, Theodore Roosevelt actively pursued an imperialist foreign policy, confirming the United States' new role as a world power. With his Big-Stick Diplomacy, he arbitrated the treaty that ended the Russo-Japanese War, proclaimed the Open Door policy with China, allowed his administration to engage in dealings that made possible American control over the Panama Canal, and sent the navy's entire fleet around the world as a symbol of American might. He articulated an extension of the Monroe Doctrine whereby the United States might intervene in disputes between North and South America and other world powers.

CHRONOLOGY

1894	Republic of Hawaii is proclaimed
1895	Cuban insurrection breaks out against Spanish rule
1898	U.S. battleship *Maine* explodes in Havana Harbor
1898	War of 1898
1898	United States annexes Hawaii
1899	U.S. Senate ratifies the Treaty of Paris, ending the War of 1898
1899–1902	Filipino insurgents resist U.S. domination
1900	Army Yellow Fever Commission confirms the cause of yellow fever
1900	International alliance quells the Boxer Rebellion
1903	Panamanians revolt against Colombia
1905	Russo-Japanese War
1907	Great White Fleet circumnavigates the globe in a demonstration of America's rise to world-power status
1914	Panama Canal opens

KEY TERMS & NAMES

23

"MAKING THE WORLD OVER": THE PROGRESSIVE ERA

FOCUS QUESTIONS wwnorton.com/studyspace

- Who were the progressives, and what were their major causes?
- Who were the muckrakers, and what impact did they have?
- What were Theodore Roosevelt's and William Howard Taft's progressive programs, and what were those programs' goals?
- Why was the election of 1912 significant?
- How was Woodrow Wilson's progressivism different from Roosevelt's?

Theodore Roosevelt's emergence as a national political leader coincided with the onset of what historians have labeled the Progressive Era (1890–1920), a period of dramatic political reform and social activism. During those thirty years, governments—local, state, and federal—grew in scope, power, and activism. Progressive reformers attacked corruption and inefficiency in government and used government authority to regulate businesses and workplaces through regular on-site inspections, regulatory commissions, and antitrust laws. The Progressive Era also witnessed the passage of a graduated ("progressive") federal income tax, the creation of a new national banking system, and the first governmental attempts to conserve natural resources and environmental treasures. In addition, the Progressive Era saw an explosion of grassroots reform efforts across the United States, including the prohibition of alcoholic beverages and the awarding of voting rights for women.

Progressivism was a wide-ranging impulse rather than a single organized movement, a multifaceted, often fragmented, and at times contradictory response to the urgent problems created by unregulated industrialization, unplanned urbanization, unrelenting immigration, and the unequal distribution of wealth and power. Progressives believed that America was in a serious crisis by the late nineteenth century, and the crisis would not resolve itself. It required action—by governments, by churches, by experts, and by volunteers. As Jane Addams, the nation's leading social reformer, who would become the first woman to win the Nobel Peace Prize, stressed, "Action is indeed the sole medium of expression for ethics."

Progressives came in all stripes: men and women; Democrats, Republicans, and Populists; labor unionists and business executives; teachers and professors; social workers and municipal workers; ardent religionists as well as atheists and agnostics. Whatever their motives and methods, they were earnest, well-intentioned, good-hearted people who greatly improved the quality of life and the effectiveness and integrity of government. By the 1920s, progressives had implemented significant changes at all levels of government and across all levels of society.

Yet progressivism had flaws too. The progressives were mostly middle-class urban reformers armed with Christian moralism as well as the latest research from the new social sciences, but their "do-good" perspective was often limited by class biases and racial prejudices. Progressivism had blind spots, especially concerning the volatile issues of race relations and immigration policy. Some reform efforts were in fact intended as middle-class tools to exercise paternalistic oversight of "common" people.

ELEMENTS OF REFORM

During the last quarter of the nineteenth century, political progressives at the local and state levels crusaded against the abuses of urban political bosses and corporate barons. Their goals were greater democracy, honest and efficient government, more effective regulation of business, and greater social justice for working people. Only by expanding the scope of local, state, and federal government involvement in society, they believed, could these goals be accomplished. The "real heart of the movement," declared one reformer, was "to use the government as an agency of human welfare."

Progressivism also contained an element of conservatism, however. In some cases the regulation of business was proposed *by* business leaders who preferred regulated stability in their marketplace to the chaos and uncertainty of unrestrained competition. In addition, many reformers were motivated by conservative religious beliefs that led them to focus their energies on moral regulations such as the prohibition of alcoholic beverages and Sunday closing laws, whereby businesses were not allowed to be open on the Christian Sabbath.

THE VARIED SOURCES OF PROGRESSIVISM The progressive impulse arose in response to many societal changes, the most powerful of which were the growing tensions between labor and management in the 1880s, the chronic corruption in political life, the abusive power of big business, the hazards of the industrial workplace, especially for women and children, and the social miseries created by the devastating depression of the 1890s. The depression brought hard times to the cities, worsened already dreadful working conditions in factories, mines, and mills, deepened distress in rural areas, and aroused both the fears and the conscience of the rapidly growing middle class. Although the United States boasted the highest per capita income in the world, it also harbored some of the poorest people. In 1900 an estimated 10 million of the 82 million Americans lived in desperate poverty. Most of the destitute were among the record number of arriving immigrants, many of whom lived in city slums.

Populism was one of the primary catalysts of progressivism. The Populist platform of 1892 outlined many political reforms that would be accomplished during the Progressive Era. After the collapse of the farmers' movement and the revival of the agricultural economy at the turn of the century, the reform spirit shifted to the cities, where middle-class activists had for years attacked the problems of political corruption and urban development.

The Mugwumps, those gentlemen reformers who had fought the spoils system and insisted that government jobs be awarded on the basis of merit, supplied progressivism with an important element of its thinking: the honest-government ideal. Over the years the honest-government movement had been broadened to include efforts to address festering urban problems such as crime, vice, and the efficient provision of gas, electricity, water, sewers, mass transit, and garbage collection.

Another significant force in fostering the most radical wing of progressivism was the influence of socialist doctrines. The small Socialist party served as the left wing of progressivism. Most progressives balked at the radicalism of socialist remedies and labor violence. In fact, the progressive impulse arose in part from a desire to counter the growing influence of militant socialism by promoting more mainstream reforms. The prominent role played by religious activists and women reformers was also an important source of progressive energy.

THE SOCIAL GOSPEL

During the late nineteenth century more and more people took action to address the complex social problems generated by rapid urban and industrial growth. Some reformers focused on legislative solutions to social problems; others stressed direct assistance to the laboring poor in their neighborhoods or organized charity. Whatever the method or approach, however, social reformers were on the march at the turn of the century, and their activities gave to American life a new urgency and energy.

CHRISTIAN CRUSADERS FOR REFORM Churches responded slowly to the mounting social concerns of urban America, for American Protestantism had become one of the main props of the established social order. The Reverend Henry Ward Beecher, pastor of the fashionable Plymouth Congregational Church in Brooklyn, preached the virtues of unregulated capitalism, social Darwinism, and the unworthiness of the poor. As the middle classes moved out to the new suburbs made possible by streetcar lines, their churches followed, leaving inner-city neighborhoods churchless. By the 1870s, however, a younger generation of Protestant and Catholic religious leaders had grown concerned that Christianity had turned its back on the poor and voiceless, the very people that Jesus had focused on. During the last quarter of the nineteenth century, a growing number of churches and synagogues began devoting their resources to community service and care of the unfortunate. The Young Men's Christian Association (YMCA) entered the United States from England in the 1850s and grew rapidly after 1870; the Salvation Army, founded in London in 1878, came to the United States a year later.

RELIGIOUS REFORMERS Church reformers who feared that Christianity was losing its relevance among the masses began to preach what came to be called the **social gospel**. In 1875, Washington Gladden, a widely respected Congregational pastor in Springfield, Massachusetts, invited striking workers at a shoe factory to attend his church. They refused because the factory owners and managers were members of the church. Gladden decided that there was something wrong when churches were divided along class lines, so he wrote a pathbreaking book titled *Working People and Their Employers* (1876). Gladden argued that true Christianity lies not in rituals, dogmas, or even the mystical experience of God but in the principle that "thou shalt love thy neighbor as thyself." He rejected the notion put forth by social Darwinists that the poor deserved their destitute fate and should not be helped. Christian values and virtues should govern the workplace, with worker and employer united in serving each other's interests. Gladden endorsed labor's right to organize unions and complained that class distinctions should not split congregations. Gladden's efforts helped launch a new era in the development of American religious life. He and other like-minded ministers during the 1870s and 1880s reached out to the working poor who worked long hours for low wages, had inadequate housing, lacked insurance coverage for on-the-job accidents, and had no legal right to form unions.

Early Efforts at Urban Reform

THE SETTLEMENT HOUSE MOVEMENT While preachers of the social gospel dispensed inspiration and promoted solidarity, other dedicated reformers attacked the problems of the slums from residential community centers called **settlement houses**. By 1900, perhaps a hundred settlement houses existed in the United States, some of the best known being Jane Addams and Ellen Gates Starr's Hull-House in Chicago (1889), Robert A. Woods's South End House in Boston (1891), and Lillian Wald's Henry Street Settlement (1893) in New York City.

Jane Addams

By the end of the century, religious groups were taking up the settlement house movement.

The settlement houses were designed to bring together prosperous men and women with the working poor, often immigrants. At Hull-House, for instance, **Jane Addams** focused on the practical needs of the working poor and newly arrived immigrants. She and her staff helped enroll neighborhood children in clubs and kindergartens and set up a nursery to care for the infant children of working mothers. The program gradually expanded as Hull-House sponsored health clinics, lectures, music and art studios, an employment bureau, men's clubs, training in skills such as bookbinding, a gymnasium, and a savings bank.

Settlement house leaders realized, however, that the spreading slums made their work as effective as bailing out the ocean with a teaspoon. They therefore organized political support for local and state laws that would ensure sanitary housing codes and create public playgrounds, juvenile courts, mothers' pensions, workers' compensation laws, and legislation prohibiting child labor and monitoring the working conditions in factory "sweatshops." Lillian Wald promoted the establishment of the federal Children's Bureau in 1912, and Jane Addams, for her work in the peace movement, received the Nobel Peace Prize for 1931. When Addams died, in 1935, she was the most venerated woman in America. The settlement houses provided portals of opportunity for women to participate and even lead many progressive efforts to improve living and working conditions for newly arrived immigrants as well as American citizens.

WOMEN'S EMPLOYMENT AND ACTIVISM Settlement house workers, insofar as they were paid, made up but a fraction of all gainfully employed women. With the rapid growth of the general population, the number of employed women steadily increased, as did the percentage of women in the labor force. The greatest leaps forward came in the 1880s and the first decade of the new century, which were also peak decades of immigration, a correlation that can be explained by the immigrants' need for income. The number of employed women went from over 2.6 million in 1880 to 4 million in 1890, then from 5.1 million in 1900 to 7.8 million in 1910. The employment of women in large numbers was the most significant event in women's history.

As women became more involved in the world of work and wages, the women's rights movement increasingly focused on gaining the right to vote. Immediately after the Civil War, Susan B. Anthony and Elizabeth Cady Stanton, seasoned leaders of the suffrage movement, demanded that the Fifteenth Amendment give the vote to women as well as black men. Such arguments, however, made little impression on the majority of men who insisted that women belonged in the domestic sphere. In 1869, a divisive issue broke the unity of the women's movement: whether the movement should concentrate on gaining the vote at the expense of promoting other women's issues. Susan B. Anthony and Elizabeth Cady Stanton founded the National Woman Suffrage Association (NWSA) to promote a women's suffrage amendment to the Constitution, but they considered gaining the right to vote as but one among many feminist causes to be promoted. Later that year, activists formed the American Woman Suffrage Association (AWSA), which focused single-mindedly on the suffrage as the first and basic reform.

It would be another half century before the battle for the vote would be won, and the long struggle focused the women's cause ever more on the primary

Elizabeth Cady Stanton

In this 1870s engraving, Stanton speaks at a meeting of the National Woman Suffrage Association.

objective of the vote. In 1890, after three years of negotiation, the rival groups united as the National American Woman Suffrage Association (NAWSA), with Elizabeth Cady Stanton as president for two years, to be followed by Susan B. Anthony until 1900. The work thereafter was carried on by a new generation of activists, led by Anna Howard Shaw and Carrie Chapman Catt. The suffrage movement remained in the doldrums until the cause of voting rights at the state level easily won a Washington state referendum in 1910 and then carried California by a close majority in 1911. The following year three more western states—Arizona, Kansas, and Oregon—joined in to make a total of nine western states with full suffrage. In 1913, Illinois granted women suffrage in presidential and municipal elections. Yet not until New York acted in 1917 did a state east of the Mississippi adopt universal suffrage.

THE MUCKRAKERS Chronic urban poverty, unsafe working conditions, and worrisome child labor in mills, mines, and factories were complex social issues; remedying them required raising public awareness and political action. The "**muckrakers**," investigative journalists who thrived on exposing social ills and corporate and political corruption, got their name from Theodore Roosevelt, who acknowledged that crusading journalists were "often indispensable to . . . society, but only if they know when to stop raking the muck." By writing exposés of social ills in newspapers and magazines, the muckrakers gave journalism a new social purpose, a political voice beyond simply endorsing one party or another.

The golden age of muckraking is sometimes dated from 1902, when Sam McClure, the owner of best-selling *McClure's Magazine*, decided to use the publication to expose the rampant corruption in politics and corporations. "Capitalists, workingmen, politicians, citizens—all breaking the law or letting it be broken. Who is left to uphold" American democracy, McClure asked. His answer was investigative journalism. *McClure's* and other "muckraking" magazines bravely took on corporate monopolies and crooked political machines while revealing the awful living and working conditions experienced by masses of Americans.

Without the muckrakers, the far-flung reform efforts of progressivism would never have achieved widespread popular support. In feeding the public's appetite for sordid social facts, the muckrakers demonstrated one of the salient features of the Progressive movement, and one of its central failures: the progressives were stronger on diagnosis than on remedy. They professed a naive faith in the power of democracy. Give the people the facts, expose corruption, and bring government close to the people, reformers believed, and the correction of evils would follow automatically. The cure for the ills of democracy, it seemed, was a more informed and a more active democracy. What they failed to acknowledge was that no reform would change the essentially flawed nature of human beings.

FEATURES OF PROGRESSIVISM

DEMOCRACY   Progressives at the state and local levels focused on cleaning up governments. Too many elected officials, they believed, did the bidding of corporations rather than served the interests of all the people. The most important reform that political progressives promoted to democratize government and encourage greater political participation was the direct primary, whereby all party members would participate in the election of candidates, rather than the traditional practice in which an inner circle of party activists chose the nominee. Under the traditional convention system, only a small proportion of voters attended the local caucuses or precinct meetings that sent delegates to party nominating conventions. After South Carolina adopted the first statewide primary in 1896, the movement spread within two decades to nearly every state.

The party primary was but one expression of a broad progressive movement for greater public participation in the political process. In 1898, South Dakota became the first state to adopt the initiative and referendum, procedures that allow voters to enact laws directly rather than having to wait for legislative action. If a designated number of voters petitioned to have a measure put on the ballot (the initiative), the electorate could then vote it up or down (the referendum). Oregon adopted a spectrum of reform measures, including a voter-registration law (1899), the initiative and referendum (1902), the direct primary (1904), a sweeping corrupt-practices act (1908), and the recall (1910), whereby corrupt or incompetent public officials could be removed by a public petition and vote. Within a decade, nearly twenty states had adopted the initiative and referendum, and nearly a dozen had accepted the recall.

Most states adopted the party primary even in the choice of U.S. senators, heretofore selected by state legislatures. Nevada was first, in 1899, to let voters express a choice that state legislators of their party were expected to follow in choosing senators. The popular election of U.S. senators required a constitutional amendment, and the House of Representatives, beginning in 1894, four times adopted such an amendment, only to see it defeated in the Senate, which came under increasing attack as a "millionaires' club." In 1912 the Senate finally accepted the inevitable and agreed to the Seventeenth Amendment, authorizing popular election of senators. The amendment was ratified in 1913.

EFFICIENCY   A second major theme of progressivism was the "gospel of efficiency." In the business world during the early twentieth century, Frederick W. Taylor, the original "efficiency expert," was developing the techniques he summed up in his book *The Principles of Scientific Management* (1911). **Taylorism**, as scientific industrial management came to be known, promised to reduce waste and inefficiency in the workplace through the scientific analysis of labor processes. By breaking down the production of goods into sequential steps and meticulously studying the time it took each worker to perform a task, Taylor prescribed the optimum technique for the average worker and established detailed performance standards for each job classification. The promise of higher wages for higher productivity, he believed, would motivate workers to exceed "average" expectations.

Instead, many workers resented Taylor's innovations. They saw in scientific management a tool for employers to make people work faster than was healthy, sustainable, or fair. Yet Taylor's controversial system brought concrete improvements in productivity, especially among those industries whose production processes were highly standardized and whose jobs were rigidly defined. "In the future," Taylor predicted in 1911, "the system [rather than the individual workers] will be first."

In government, the efficiency movement demanded the reorganization of agencies to eliminate redundancy, to establish clear lines of authority, and to assign responsibility and accountability to specific officials. Two progressive ideas for making municipal government more efficient gained headway in the first decade of the new century. One, the commission system, was first adopted by Galveston, Texas, in 1901, when local government there collapsed in the aftermath of a devastating hurricane and tidal wave. The system placed ultimate authority in a board composed of elected administrative heads of city departments—commissioners of sanitation, police, utilities, and so on. The more durable idea, however, was the city-manager plan, under which a professional administrator ran the municipal government in accordance with policies set by the elected council and mayor. Staunton, Virginia, first adopted the plan in 1908. By 1914 the National Association of City Managers had heralded the arrival of a new profession.

Robert M. La Follette

A progressive proponent of expertise in government.

By the early twentieth century, many complex functions of government and business had come to require specialists with technical expertise. As Woodrow Wilson wrote, progressive ideals could be achieved only if government at all levels—local, state, and national—was "informed and administered by experts." This principle of government by nonpartisan experts was promoted by progressive Governor Robert M. La Follette of Wisconsin, who established a Legislative Reference Bureau to provide elected officials with research, advice, and help in the drafting of legislation. The "Wisconsin idea" of efficient and more scientific government was widely publicized and copied. La Follette also pushed for such reforms as the direct primary, stronger railroad regulation, the conservation of natural resources, and workmen's compensation programs to support laborers injured on the job.

ANTI-TRUST REGULATION Of all the problems facing American society at the turn of the century, one engaged a greater diversity of progressive reformers and elicited more solutions than any other: the regulation of giant corporations, which became a third major theme of progressivism. Bipartisan concern over the concentration of economic power had brought passage of the Sherman Anti-Trust Act in 1890, but the act had turned out to be more symbolic than effective. The problem of concentrated economic power and its abuse offered a dilemma for progressives. Efforts to restore the competition of small firms proved unworkable partly because breaking up large corporations was a complicated process. More common were efforts to "regulate" big businesses, many of whose executives preferred regulation over cutthroat competition. As time passed, however, regulatory agencies often came under the influence or control of those they were supposed to regulate. Railroad executives, for instance, generally had more intimate knowledge of the intricate details involved in their business, giving them the advantage over the outsiders who might be appointed to the Interstate Commerce Commission (ICC).

SOCIAL JUSTICE A fourth important feature of the Progressive movement was the effort to promote greater social justice through the creation of nonprofit charitable service organizations; efforts by reformers to clean up cities through personal hygiene, municipal sewers, and public-awareness campaigns; and reforms aimed at regulating child labor and the consumption of alcohol.

Middle-class women were the driving force behind the grassroots **social justice** movement. In massive numbers they fanned out to address social ills. The Women's Christian Temperance Union (WCTU), founded in 1874, was the largest women's group in the nation at the end of the nineteenth century, boasting three hundred thousand members. Frances Willard, the dynamic president of the WCTU between 1879 and 1898, believed that all social problems were interconnected and that most of them resulted from alcohol abuse. Members of the WCTU strove to close saloons, improve prison conditions, shelter prostitutes and abused women and children, support female labor unions, and champion women's suffrage. The WCTU also lobbied for the eight-hour workday, the regulation of child labor, better nutrition, the federal inspection of food processors and drug manufacturers, free kindergartens and public playgrounds, and uniform marriage and divorce laws across the states.

With time it became apparent that social evils extended beyond the reach of private charities and grassroots organizations and demanded government intervention. In 1890, almost half of American workers toiled up to twelve hours a day—sometimes seven days a week—in unsafe, unsanitary, and unregulated conditions for bare subsistence wages. Labor legislation was perhaps the most significant reform to emerge from the drive for progressive social justice. It emerged first at the state level. The National Child Labor Committee, organized in 1904, led a movement for laws prohibiting the employment of young children. Within ten years, through the organization of state and local committees and a graphic documentation of the evils of child labor by the photographer Lewis W. Hine, the committee pushed through legislation in most states banning the labor of underage children (the minimum age varying from twelve to sixteen) and limiting the hours older children might work.

Child labor was commonplace

A young girl working as a spinner in a cotton mill in Vermont, 1910.

Closely linked to the child-labor reform movement was a concerted effort to regulate the hours of work for women. Spearheaded by **Florence Kelley**, the head of the National Consumers' League, this progressive crusade promoted state laws to regulate the long working hours imposed on women who were wives and mothers. Many states also outlawed night work and labor in dangerous occupations for both women and children. But numerous exemptions and inadequate enforcement often nullified the intent of those laws.

The Supreme Court pursued a curiously erratic course in ruling on state labor laws. In *Lochner v. New York* (1905), the Court voided a ten-hour-workday law because it violated workers' "liberty of contract" to accept any jobs they wanted, no matter how bad the working conditions or pay. But in *Muller v. Oregon* (1908), the high court upheld a ten-hour-workday law for women largely on the basis of sociological data regarding the effects of long hours on the health and morals of women. In *Bunting v. Oregon* (1917), the Court accepted a maximum ten-hour day for both men and women but for twenty more years held out against state minimum-wage laws.

Legislation to protect workers against avoidable accidents gained impetus from disasters such as the March 25, 1911, fire at the Triangle Shirtwaist factory (called a "sweatshop") in New York City, in which 146 of the

850 workers died, mostly foreign-born women in their teens, almost all of whom were Jewish and Italian immigrants. Escape routes were limited because the owner kept the stairway door locked to prevent theft. Workers trapped on the three upper floors of the ten-story building died in the fire or leaped to their death. The workers had wanted to form a union to negotiate safer working conditions, better pay, and shorter hours, but the owner had refused. The tragic fire served as the catalyst for progressive reforms. A state commission investigated the fire, and thirty-six new city and state laws and regulations were implemented, many of which were copied by other states around the nation.

PROGRESSIVISM AND RELIGION Religion was a crucial source of energy for progressive reformers. Many Christians and Jews embraced the social gospel, seeking to express their faith through aid to the less fortunate. Some of the reformers applied their crusade for social justice to organized religion itself. Frances Willard, who spent time as a traveling evangelist, lobbied church organizations to allow women to become ministers. As she said, "If women can organize missionary societies, temperance societies, and every kind of charitable organization . . . why not permit them to be ordained to preach the Gospel and administer the sacraments of the Church?"

PROHIBITION Opposition to alcohol abuse was an ideal cause in which to merge the older religious-based ethics with the new social ethics promoting reforms. Given the importance of saloons as arenas for often-corrupt local political machines, prohibitionists could equate the "liquor traffic" with progressive suspicion of bossism and "special interests." By eliminating booze and closing saloons, reformers hoped to remove one of the tools used by political bosses to win over converts. The battle against alcoholic beverages had begun in earnest during the nineteenth century. The WCTU had promoted the cause since 1874, and a Prohibition party had entered the national elections in 1876. But the most successful political action followed the formation in 1893 of the Anti-Saloon League, an organization that pioneered the strategy of the single-issue pressure group. Through its singleness of purpose, it forced the prohibition issue into the forefront of state and local elections. At its "Jubilee Convention" in 1913, the bipartisan Anti-Saloon League endorsed a prohibition amendment to the Constitution, adopted by Congress in 1917. By the time it was ratified, two years later, state and local action had already dried up areas occupied by nearly three fourths of the nation's population.

ROOSEVELT'S PROGRESSIVISM

While most progressive initiatives originated at the state and local levels during the late nineteenth century, federal reform efforts coalesced around 1900, with the emergence of Theodore Roosevelt as a national political leader. He brought to the White House in 1901 perhaps the most complex personality in American political history: he was a political reformer, an environmentalist, an obsessive hunter, a racist, and a militaristic liberal. Roosevelt developed an expansive vision of the presidency that well suited the cause of progressive reform. In one of his first addresses to Congress, he stressed the need for a new political approach. When the Constitution was drafted in 1787, he explained, the nation's social and economic conditions were quite unlike those at the dawn of the twentieth century. "The conditions are now wholly different and wholly different action is called for."

EXECUTIVE ACTION   Roosevelt accomplished more by vigorous executive action than by passing legislation. He argued that as president he might do anything not expressly forbidden by the Constitution. In 1902, Roosevelt endorsed a "Square Deal" for all, calling for more rigorous enforcement of existing anti-trust laws and stricter controls on big business. From the outset, however, Roosevelt avoided wholesale trust-busting. Effective regulation of corporate giants was better than a futile effort to dismantle large corporations. Because Congress balked at regulatory legislation, Roosevelt sought to force the issue by a more vigorous prosecution of the 1890 Sherman Anti-Trust Act. In 1902, Roosevelt ordered the U.S. attorney general to break up the Northern Securities Company, a giant conglomerate of interconnected railroads. In 1904 the Supreme Court ordered the railroad combination dissolved.

THE 1902 COAL STRIKE   Roosevelt also used the "big stick" against corporations in the coal strike of 1902. On May 12 some 150,000 members of the United Mine Workers (UMW) walked off the job in Pennsylvania and West Virginia. They were seeking a 20 percent wage increase, a reduction in daily working hours from ten to nine, and official recognition of the union by the mine owners. The mine operators refused to negotiate. Instead, they shut down the mines to starve out the miners, many of whom were immigrants from eastern Europe. One mine owner expressed the prejudices shared by many other owners when he proclaimed, "The miners don't suffer—why, they can't even speak English."

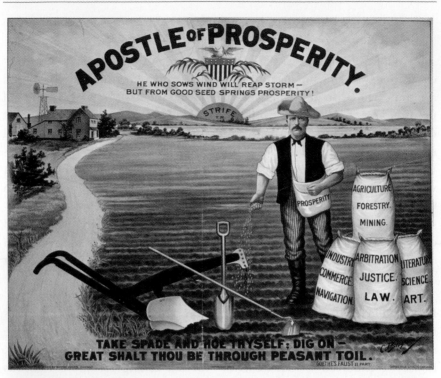

Roosevelt's duality

Theodore Roosevelt as an "apostle of prosperity" (top) and as a Roman tyrant (bottom). Roosevelt's energy, self-righteousness, and impulsiveness elicited sharp reactions.

By October 1902, the prolonged shutdown had caused the price of coal to soar, and hospitals and schools reported empty coal bins. President Roosevelt decided upon a bold move: he invited leaders of both sides to a conference in Washington, D.C., where he appealed to their "patriotism, to the spirit that sinks personal considerations and makes individual sacrifices for the public good." The mine owners attended the conference but arrogantly refused even to speak to the UMW leaders. The "extraordinary stupidity and temper" of the "wooden-headed" owners infuriated Roosevelt. The president wanted to grab the spokesman for the mine owners "by the seat of his breeches" and "chuck him out" a window. Roosevelt threatened to take over the mines and send in the army to run them. When a congressman questioned the constitutionality of such a move, an exasperated Roosevelt roared, "To hell with the Constitution when the people want coal!" The threat to militarize the mines worked. The coal strike ended on October 23. The miners won a reduction to a nine-hour workday but only a 10 percent wage increase and no union recognition by the owners. Roosevelt had become the first president to use his authority to arbitrate a dispute between management and labor.

EXPANDING FEDERAL POWER Roosevelt continued to use unprecedented executive powers to enforce the Sherman Anti-Trust Act (1890). Altogether, his administration initiated about twenty-five anti-trust suits against oversized corporations. In 1903, Congress passed the Elkins Act, which made it illegal for railroads to take, as well as to give, secret rebates on freight charges to their favorite customers. All shippers would pay the same price. That same year, Congress created a new Bureau of Corporations to monitor the activities of interstate corporations. When Standard Oil refused to turn over its records, the government brought an anti-trust suit that resulted in the breakup of the huge company in 1911. The Supreme Court also ordered the American Tobacco Company to divide its enterprises because it had come to monopolize the cigarette industry.

ROOSEVELT'S SECOND TERM

Roosevelt's aggressive leadership built a coalition of progressives and conservatives who assured his election in his own right in 1904. The Republican Convention chose him by acclamation. The Democrats, having lost with William Jennings Bryan twice, turned to the more conservative Alton B. Parker, chief justice of the New York Supreme Court. Roosevelt's invincible popularity plus the sheer force of his personality swept the president to an impressive victory by a popular vote of 7.6 million to 5.1 million. With 336 electoral votes for the president and 140 for Parker, Roosevelt savored his lopsided victory. The president told his wife that he was "no longer a political accident." He now had a popular mandate. On the eve of his inauguration in March 1905, Roosevelt announced: "Tomorrow I shall come into office in my own right. Then watch out for me!"

LEGISLATIVE LEADERSHIP   Elected in his own right, Roosevelt approached his second term with heightened confidence and an even stronger commitment to progressive reform. The independent-minded Roosevelt took aim at the railroads first. The Elkins Act of 1903, finally outlawing rebates, had been a minor step. Railroad executives themselves welcomed it as an escape from shippers clamoring for special favors. But a new proposal for railroad regulation endorsed by Roosevelt was something else again. Enacted in 1906, the Hepburn Act for the first time gave the ICC the power to set maximum freight rates for the railroad industry.

The meat industry

Pigs strung up along the hog-scraping rail at Armour's packing plant in Chicago, ca. 1909.

Regulating railroads was Roosevelt's first priority, but he also embraced the regulation of meat packers, food processors, and makers of drugs and patent medicines. Muckraking journalists revealed that companies were engaged in all sorts of unsanitary and dangerous activities in the preparation of food products. Perhaps the most telling blow against such abuses was struck by Upton Sinclair's novel *The Jungle* (1906). Sinclair wrote the book to promote socialism, but its main impact came from its portrayal of filthy conditions in Chicago's meat-packing industry:

It was too dark in these storage places to see well, but a man could run his hand over these piles of meat and sweep off handfuls of the dried dung of rats. These rats were nuisances, and the packers would put poisoned bread out for them, they would die, and then rats, bread, and meat would go into the hoppers together.

Roosevelt read *The Jungle*—and reacted quickly. He sent two agents to Chicago, and their report confirmed all that Sinclair had said about the unsanitary conditions in the packing plants. Congress and Roosevelt responded by creating the Meat Inspection Act of 1906. It required federal inspection of meats destined for interstate commerce and empowered officials in the Agriculture Department to impose sanitation standards in processing plants. The Pure Food and Drug Act, enacted the same day, placed restrictions on the makers of prepared foods and patent medicines and forbade the manufacture, sale, or transportation of adulterated, misbranded, or harmful foods, drugs, and liquors.

ENVIRONMENTAL CONSERVATION   One of the most enduring legacies of Roosevelt's leadership was his energetic support for the emerging environmental conservation movement. Roosevelt was the first president to challenge the long-standing myth of America's having inexhaustible natural resources. In fact, Roosevelt declared that conservation was the "great material

Nathaniel Pitt Langford

The first superintendent of Yellowstone National Park, on Jupiter Terrace at Mammoth Hot Springs, ca. 1875.

question of the day." Just as reformers promoted the regulation of business and industry for the public welfare, conservationists championed efforts to manage and preserve the natural environment for the benefit of future generations.

The first promoters of resource conservation were ardent sportsmen among the social elite (including Theodore Roosevelt), who worried that unregulated commercial hunters and trappers were wantonly killing game animals to the point of extermination. By 1900, most states had enacted laws regulating game hunting and had created game refuges and wardens to enforce the new rules, much to the chagrin of local hunters, including Native Americans, who now were forced to abide by state laws designed to protect the interests of wealthy recreational hunters.

Roosevelt and the sportsmen conservationists formed a powerful coalition promoting rational government management of natural resources: rivers and streams, forests, minerals, and natural wonders. Those concerns, as well as the desire of railroad companies to transport tourists to destinations featuring majestic scenery, led the federal government to displace Indians in order to establish the 2-million-acre Yellowstone National Park in 1872 at the junction of the Montana, Wyoming, and Idaho Territories (the National Park Service would be created in 1916 after other parks had been established). In 1881, Congress created a Division of Forestry (now the U.S. Forest Service) within the Department of the Interior. As president, Theodore Roosevelt created fifty federal wildlife refuges, approved five new national parks, fifty-one federal bird sanctuaries, and designated eighteen national monuments, including the Grand Canyon.

Gifford Pinchot

Pinchot is seen here with two children at the edge of a larch grove.

In 1898, while serving as vice president, Roosevelt had endorsed the appointment of **Gifford Pinchot**, a close friend and the nation's first professional forester, as the head of the U.S. Division of Forestry. Pinchot and Roosevelt were pragmatic conservationists; they believed in economic growth as well as environmental preservation. To them, conservation entailed the scientific ("progressive") management of natural resources to serve the public interest. Pinchot explained that the conservation movement sought to promote the "greatest good for the greatest number for the longest time." Roosevelt and Pinchot used the Forest Reserve Act (1891) to protect some 172 million acres of timberland. Lumber companies were furious, but Roosevelt held firm. As he bristled, "I hate a man who skins the land." Overall, Roosevelt's conservation efforts helped curb the unregulated exploitation of natural resources for private gain. He set aside over 234 million acres of federal land for conservation purposes, including the creation of 45 national forests in 11 western states. As Pinchot recalled late in life, "Launching the conservation movement was the most significant achievement of the T. R. Administration, as he himself believed."

FROM ROOSEVELT TO TAFT

Toward the end of his second term, Roosevelt declared, "I have had a great time as president." Although eligible to run again, he opted for retirement. He decided that his successor should be his secretary of war, William Howard Taft, and the Republican Convention ratified the choice on its first ballot in 1908. The Democrats gave William Jennings Bryan one more chance at the highest office. Still vigorous at forty-eight, Bryan retained a faithful following but struggled to attract national support. Roosevelt advised Taft: "Do not answer Bryan; *attack* him. Don't let him make the issues." Taft followed Roosevelt's advice, declaring that Bryan's election would result in a "paralysis of business."

The Republican platform endorsed Roosevelt's progressive policies. The Democratic platform hardly differed on the need for regulation of business, but it called for a lower tariff and opposed court injunctions against labor unions that organized strikes. In the end, voters opted for Roosevelt's chosen successor: Taft swept the Electoral College, 321 to 162. The real surprise of the election, however, was the strong showing of the Socialist party candidate, labor hero Eugene V. Debs. His 421,000 votes revealed again the depth of working-class resentment in the United States.

William Howard Taft had superb qualifications to be president. Born in Cincinnati in 1857, he had graduated second in his class at Yale and had become a preeminent legal scholar, serving on the Ohio Supreme Court and as U.S. solicitor general. In 1900, President William McKinley had appointed

William Howard Taft

Speaking at Manassas, Virginia, in 1911.

Taft as the first governor-general of the Philippines, and three years later Roosevelt named him secretary of war. Taft would become the only person to serve both as president and as chief justice of the Supreme Court. He was a progressive conservative who vowed to protect "the right of property" and the "right of liberty." In practice, this meant that the new president was even more determined than Roosevelt to preserve "the spirit of commercial freedom" against monopolistic trusts.

TARIFF REFORM   Taft's domestic policies generated a storm of controversy within his own party. Contrary to longstanding Republican tradition, Taft preferred a lower tariff, and he made this the first important issue of his presidency. But Taft proved less skillful than Roosevelt in dealing with Congress. The resulting tariff was a hodgepodge that on the whole changed very little. Temperamentally conservative, inhibited by scruples about interfering too much with the legislative process, Taft drifted into the orbit of the Republican Old Guard and quickly alienated the progressive wing of his party, whom he tagged "assistant Democrats."

BALLINGER AND PINCHOT   In 1910, President Taft's policies drove the wedge deeper between the conservative and progressive Republican factions. What came to be called the Ballinger-Pinchot controversy made Taft appear to be abandoning Roosevelt's conservation policies. The strongest conservation leaders, such as Roosevelt and Gifford Pinchot, a Pennsylvanian, were often easterners, and Taft's secretary of the interior, Richard A. Ballinger of Seattle, was well aware that many westerners opposed conservation programs on the grounds that they held back full economic development of the Far West. Ballinger therefore threw open to commercial use millions acres of federal lands that Roosevelt had ordered conserved. As chief of forestry, Pinchot reported to Taft his concerns about the land "giveaway," but the president refused to intervene. When Pinchot went public with the controversy early in 1910, Taft fired him. In doing so, he set in motion a feud with Roosevelt that would eventually cost him his reelection.

TAFT AND ROOSEVELT   Taft's dismissal of Pinchot infuriated Roosevelt, who eventually decided that Taft had fallen under the spell of the Republican Old Guard leadership. During the fall of 1910, Roosevelt made several speeches promoting "sane and progressive" Republican candidates in the congressional elections. In a speech at Osawatomie, a small town in eastern Kansas, he gave a catchy name to his latest progressive principles, the "**New Nationalism**," which greatly resembled the populist progressivism of William Jennings Bryan. Roosevelt issued a stirring call for more stringent federal regulation of huge corporations, a progressive income tax, laws limiting child labor, and a "Square Deal for the poor man." He also proposed the first efforts at campaign finance reform. His purpose was not to revolutionize the political system but to save it from the threat of revolution. "What I have advocated," he explained a few days later, "is not wild radicalism. It is the highest and wisest kind of conservatism."

On February 24, 1912 Roosevelt challenged Taft's leadership by entering the race for the presidency. He had decided that Taft had "sold the Square Deal down the river," and he now dismissed Taft as a "hopeless fathead." Roosevelt's rebuke of Taft was in many ways undeserved. Taft had at least attempted tariff reform, which Roosevelt had never dared. He replaced Roosevelt's friend Gifford Pinchot with men with impeccable credentials as conservationists. In the end his administration preserved more public land in four years than Roosevelt's had in nearly eight. Taft's administration also filed more anti-trust suits against big corporations, by a score of eighty to twenty-five.

In 1910, with Taft's support, Congress passed the Mann-Elkins Act, which for the first time empowered the ICC to initiate changes in railroad freight rates, extended its regulatory powers to telephone and telegraph companies, and set up the Commerce Court to expedite appeals of ICC rulings. Taft also established the Bureau of Mines and the federal Children's Bureau (1912),

Political giants

A cartoon showing Roosevelt charging through the air at Taft, who is seated on a mountain top.

and he called for statehood for Arizona and New Mexico and territorial government for Alaska (1912). The **Sixteenth Amendment** (1913), authorizing a federal income tax, was ratified with Taft's support before he left office, and the Seventeenth Amendment (1913), providing for the popular election of senators, was ratified soon after he left office.

But Taft's progressive record did not prevent Roosevelt from turning on him. Roosevelt won all but two of the thirteen states that held presidential primaries, even in Taft's home state of Ohio. Still, the groundswell of popular support for Roosevelt was no match for Taft's decisive position as sitting president and party leader. In state nominating conventions the Taft forces prevailed. So Roosevelt entered the Republican National Convention about a hundred votes short of victory. The Taft delegates proceeded to nominate their man by the same steamroller tactics that had nominated Roosevelt in 1904.

Roosevelt was outraged at what he called Taft's "successful fraud" in getting the nomination. The angry Roosevelt delegates—mostly social workers, reformers, intellectuals, and executives who favored Roosevelt's leadership—assembled in a rump convention in Chicago on August 5 to create a third political party. Roosevelt appeared before the delegates, feeling "fit as a bull moose." Many of the most prominent progressives endorsed Roosevelt's bid to be the first president representing a third party, the **"Bull Moose" progressive party**. But few professional politicians turned up, and progressive Republicans decided to preserve their party credentials and fight another day. The disruption of the Republican party caused by the rift between Taft and Roosevelt gave hope to the Democrats, whose leader, Virginia-born New Jersey governor **Woodrow Wilson**, had enjoyed remarkable success in his brief political career.

WOODROW WILSON'S PROGRESSIVISM

WILSON'S RISE   The emergence of Thomas Woodrow Wilson as the Democratic nominee in 1912 was surprisingly rapid. In 1910, before his nomination and election as governor of New Jersey, Wilson had been president of Princeton University, but he had never run for public office. Yet he had extraordinary abilities: a keen intellect and an analytical temperament, superb educational training, a fertile imagination, and a penchant for boldness. Born in Staunton, Virginia, in 1856, the son of a "noble-saintly mother" and a stern Presbyterian minister, Wilson had grown up in Georgia and the Carolinas during the Civil War and Reconstruction. Young Wilson, tall and slender with a lean, long face, inherited his father's unquestioning piety. Wilson also developed a consuming ambition to "serve" humankind. Driven by a sense of providential destiny, he nurtured an obstinate righteousness and habitual intransigence that would prove to be his undoing.

Wilson graduated from Princeton in 1879. After finishing "terribly boring" law school at the University of Virginia he had a brief, unfulfilling legal practice in Atlanta. From there he went to the new Johns Hopkins University in Baltimore, where he found his calling in the study of history and political science. After a seventeen-year stint as a popular college professor, he was unanimously elected president of Princeton University in 1902. Eight years later, in 1910, the Democratic party leaders in New Jersey offered Wilson their support for the 1910 gubernatorial nomination. Elected as a reform candidate, Governor Wilson turned the tables on the state's Democratic party bosses who had put him on the ticket by persuading the state legislature to adopt an array of progressive reforms: a workers' compensation law, a corrupt-practices law, measures to regulate public utilities, and ballot reforms. Such strong leadership brought Wilson to the attention of national Democratic party leaders. At the 1912 Democratic nominating convention Wilson faced stiff competition from several party regulars, but with the support of William Jennings Bryan, he prevailed on the forty-sixth ballot. Wilson justifiably called his nomination a "political miracle."

THE ELECTION OF 1912   The 1912 presidential campaign involved four candidates: Wilson and Taft represented the two major parties, while Eugene V. Debs ran as a Socialist, and Roosevelt headed the Progressive party ticket. They all shared a basic progressive assumption that modern living and working conditions required active governmental regulation, but they differed in the nature and extent of their activism.

As the campaign developed, Taft quickly lost ground. "There are so many people in the country who don't like me," he lamented. The contest settled down to a running debate over the competing programs touted by the two front-runners: Roosevelt's New Nationalism and Wilson's New Freedom. The New Nationalism would use government authority to promote social justice by enacting overdue reforms such as workers' compensation programs for on-the-job injuries, regulations to protect women and children in the workplace, and a stronger Bureau of Corporations. These ideas and more went into the platform of the Progressive party, which called for a federal trade commission with sweeping authority over business and a tariff commission to set rates on a "scientific basis."

Before the end of his administration, Woodrow Wilson would be swept into the current of the New Nationalism, too. But initially he adhered to the decentralizing anti-trust traditions of his party. At the start of the 1912 campaign, Wilson conferred with Louis D. Brandeis, a progressive lawyer from Boston who created the design for Wilson's **New Freedom** program. It differed from Roosevelt's New Nationalism in its insistence that the federal government should restore competition in the economy rather than focus on regulating huge monopolies. Whereas Roosevelt admired the power and efficiency of law-abiding corporations, even if they were virtual monopolies, Brandeis and Wilson were convinced that all huge industries needed to be broken up, not regulated. Wilson's approach to progressivism required a vigorous anti-trust policy, lower tariffs to allow more foreign goods to compete in American markets, and dissolution of the concentration of financial power in Wall Street.

On election day, the Republican schism between Taft and Roosevelt opened the way for Woodrow Wilson to win handily in the Electoral College, garnering 435 votes to 88 for Roosevelt and 8 for Taft. After learning of his election, Wilson told the chairman of the Democratic party that "God ordained that I should be the next president of the United States." Perhaps. But had the Republican party not been split in two, Wilson would have been trounced. His was the victory of a minority candidate over a divided opposition. A majority of voters had endorsed progressivism, but only a minority preferred Wilson's program of reform, the New Freedom.

The **election of 1912** was significant in several ways. First, it was a high-water mark for progressivism, with all the candidates claiming to be progressives of

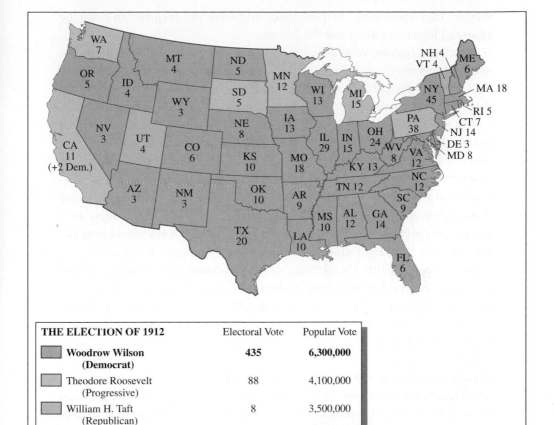

THE ELECTION OF 1912	Electoral Vote	Popular Vote
Woodrow Wilson (Democrat)	**435**	**6,300,000**
Theodore Roosevelt (Progressive)	88	4,100,000
William H. Taft (Republican)	8	3,500,000

Why was Taft so unpopular? How did the division between Roosevelt and Taft give Wilson the victory? Why was Wilson's victory in 1912 significant?

one sort or another. The election was also the first to feature party primaries. The two leading candidates debated the basic issues of progressivism in a campaign unique in its focus on vital alternatives and in its highly philosophical tone. This was an election with real choices. The Socialist party, the left wing of progressivism, polled over nine hundred thousand votes for Eugene V. Debs, its highest proportion ever. Debs, the son of immigrant shopkeepers, was a fabled union organizer who had run for president twice before, but had never garnered so many votes.

Second, the election gave Democrats effective national power for the first time since the Civil War. For two years during the second administration of Grover Cleveland, from 1893 to 1895, they had held the White House and majorities in both houses of Congress, but they had fallen quickly out of power during the severe economic depression of the 1890s. Now, under

Wilson, they again held the presidency and were the majority in both the House of Representatives and the Senate.

Third, the election of Wilson brought southerners back into the orbit of national and international affairs in a significant way for the first time since the Civil War. Five of Wilson's ten cabinet members were born in the South, three still resided there, and William Jennings Bryan, the secretary of state, was an idol of the southern masses. At the president's right hand, and one of the most influential members of the Wilson circle, at least until 1919, was "Colonel" Edward M. House of Texas. Wilson described House as "my second personality. He is my independent self." House was responsible for getting Wilson's proposals through Congress. Southern Congressmen, by virtue of their seniority, held the lion's share of committee chairmanships. As a result, much of the progressive legislation of the Wilson era would bear the names of the southern Democrats who guided it through Congress.

Fourth and finally, the election of 1912 altered the character of the Republican party. The defection of the Bull Moose Progressives had weakened the party's progressive wing. As a result, the leaders of the Republican party that would return to power in the 1920s would be more conservative in tone and temperament.

WILSONIAN REFORM   On March 4, 1913, a huge crowd surrounded the Capitol in Washington, D.C., to witness Woodrow Wilson's inauguration as the first Democratic president since Grover Cleveland. The president's eloquent speech championed the ideals of social justice that animated many progressives. "We have been proud of our industrial achievements," he said, "but we have not hitherto stopped thoughtfully enough to count the human cost . . . the fearful physical and spiritual cost to the men and women and children upon whom the dead weight and burden of it all has fallen pitilessly the years through." He promised specifically a lower tariff and a new nationally regulated banking system. If Roosevelt had been a strong president by force of personality, Wilson became a strong president by force of conviction. He was an expert on managing legislation through the Congress. During his first two years, Wilson pushed through more new bills than any previous president.

THE TARIFF   Wilson's leadership faced its first big test on the issue of tariff reform. He believed that corporations were misusing tariffs to suppress foreign competition and keep prices artificially high. Tariffs had thereby encouraged the growth of industrial monopolies and degraded the political process by producing armies of paid lobbyists who invaded Congress each year. In attacking high tariffs, Wilson sought to strike a blow for consumers and honest government. He acted quickly and boldly, summoning Congress to a special session (which lasted eighteen months—the longest in history) and addressing the legislators in person—the first president to do so since John Adams. Congress acted vigorously on tariff reductions; the new bill passed the House easily. The crunch came in the Senate, the traditional graveyard of tariff reform. Swarms of industry lobbyists got so thick in Washington, Wilson said, that "a brick couldn't be thrown without hitting one of them." The president turned the tables with a public statement that focused the spotlight on the "industrious and insidious" tariff lobby.

The Underwood-Simmons Tariff became law in 1913. It was the first time the tariff had been lowered since the Civil War. To compensate for the reduced tariff revenue, the bill created the first graduated income tax levied under the newly ratified Sixteenth Amendment: 1 percent on income over $3,000 ($4,000 for married couples) up to a top rate of 7 percent on annual income of $500,000 or more.

THE FEDERAL RESERVE ACT   Before the new tariff had cleared the Senate, the administration proposed the first major banking and currency reform since the Civil War. Ever since Andrew Jackson had killed the Second Bank of the United States in the 1830s, the nation had been without a central bank. Instead, the money supply was administered in a decentralized fashion by hundreds of private banks. Such a decentralized system fostered instability and inefficiency. By 1913 virtually everyone had agreed that the banking system needed restructuring. Wilson told Congress that a federal banking system was needed to ensure that "the banks may be the instruments, not the masters, of business and of individual enterprise and initiative."

The Federal Reserve Act of 1913 created a new national banking system, with regional reserve banks supervised by a central

"Reading the Death Warrant"

Woodrow Wilson's plan for banking and currency reform spells the death of the "money trust," according to this cartoon.

board of directors. There would be twelve Federal Reserve banks, each owned by member banks in its district, which could issue Federal Reserve notes (currency) to member banks. All national banks became members; state banks and trust companies could join if they wished. Each member bank had to transfer 6 percent of its capital to the Federal Reserve bank and deposit a portion of its reserves there. This arrangement made it possible to expand both the money supply and bank credit in times of high business activity or as the level of borrowing increased.

The new system corrected three great defects in the previous arrangement: now bank reserves could be pooled, affording greater security; both the nation's currency supply and bank credit became more elastic to respond to economic growth; and the concentration of the nation's monetary reserves in New York City was decreased. The new national banking system represented a dramatic new step in active government intervention and control in one of the most sensitive segments of the economy. It was the most significant domestic initiative of Wilson's presidency.

ANTI-TRUST LAWS   While promoting banking and tariff reforms, Wilson made trust-busting the central focus of the New Freedom. Giant corporations continued to grow despite the Sherman Anti-Trust Act and the federal watchdog agency, the Bureau of Corporations. Wilson's solution to the problem was a revision of the Sherman Act to define more explicitly what counted as restraint of trade. He decided to make a strong Federal Trade Commission (FTC) the cornerstone of his anti-trust program. Created in 1914, the five-member commission replaced Roosevelt's Bureau of Corporations and assumed new powers to define "unfair trade practices" and issue "cease-and-desist" orders when it found evidence of unfair competition.

Henry D. Clayton, a Democrat from Alabama on the House Judiciary Committee, drafted an anti-trust bill in 1914. Conservative southern Democrats and northern Republicans amended the Clayton Anti-Trust Act to allow for broad judicial review of the FTC's decisions, thus further weakening its freedom of action. In accordance with the president's recommendation, however, corporate officials were made individually responsible for any violations.

Agrarian activists in alliance with organized labor won a stipulation that declared farm-labor organizations were not unlawful combinations in restraint of trade. Injunctions in labor disputes, moreover, were not to be handed down by federal courts unless "necessary to prevent irreparable injury to property." Though hailed by union leaders as labor's Magna Carta, these provisions were later neutralized by court decisions. Wilson himself remarked that the act did little more than affirm the right of unions to exist by forbidding their dissolution for acting in restraint of trade.

SOCIAL JUSTICE   In November 1914 President Wilson announced that progressivism had accomplished its major goals. He had fulfilled his promises to lower the tariff, reorganize the banking system, and strengthen the anti-trust laws. The New Freedom was now complete, he wrote late in 1914; the future would be "a time of healing because [it would be] a time of just dealing." Wilson's announcement that the New Freedom was finished bewildered many progressives, especially those who had long advocated "social-justice" legislation. Although Wilson endorsed states allowing women to vote, he declined to support a federal suffrage amendment because his party platform had not done so. He also withheld support from federal child-labor legislation because he regarded it as a state matter. He opposed a bill providing low-interest loans to farmers on the grounds that it was "unwise and unjustifiable to extend the credit of the government to a single class of the community." Herbert Croly, the editor of *The New Republic*, who had written *The Promise of the American Life* and who was widely regarded as the leading progressive theorist, was dumbfounded by Wilson's conservative turn. He wondered how Wilson could assert "that the fundamental wrongs of a modern society can be easily and quickly righted as a consequence of [passing] a few laws." Wilson's about-face, he concluded, "casts suspicion upon his own sincerity or upon his grasp of the realities of modern social and industrial life."

PROGRESSIVISM FOR WHITES ONLY   African American leaders were also perplexed and disappointed by Wilson's resurgent conservatism. Like many other progressives, Woodrow Wilson showed little interest in the plight of African Americans. In fact, he shared many of the racist attitudes prevalent at the time. As a student at Princeton, Wilson had detested the enfranchisement of blacks, arguing that Americans of Anglo-Saxon origin would always resist domination by "an ignorant and inferior race." Later, as a politician, Wilson courted African American voters, but he rarely consulted black leaders and repeatedly avoided opportunities to associate with them in public or express support for African Americans. That he refused to create a National Race Commission was a great disappointment to the black community, as was Wilson's appointment to his cabinet of southerners who were uncompromising racists. Josephus Daniels, a North Carolina newspaper editor who became Wilson's secretary of the navy, wrote that "the subjection of the negro, politically, and the separation of the negro, socially, are paramount to all other considerations in the South." Daniels as well as other cabinet members set about racially segregating the employees in their agencies. Secretary of State William Jennings Bryan supported efforts to segregate federal employees by race—separate offices, dining facilities, restrooms, and water fountains.

The privileged elite

President Wilson and the First Lady ride in a carriage.

In November 1914 a delegation of national black leaders visited Wilson in the White House to complain about a self-proclaimed "progressive" president adopting such a "regressive" racial policy. Wilson initially claimed ignorance of the efforts to segregate federal offices, but he eventually argued that both races benefited from the new segregation policies because they eliminated "the possibility of friction." William Trotter, a Harvard-educated African-American newspaper editor who helped found the National Association for the Advancement of Colored People (NAACP) and the Equal Rights League, scolded the first-year president: "Have you a 'new freedom' for white Americans, and a new slavery for 'your Afro-American fellow citizens?' God forbid." A furious Wilson then told the black visitors to leave. The segregationist policies of the administration blatantly contradicted the "progressive" commitment of Bryan and Wilson to social equality. Their progressivism was for whites only.

THE WOMEN'S MOVEMENT The suffrage movement had garnered little support during Theodore Roosevelt's presidency. He explained that he personally supported voting rights for women but "I am not an enthusiastic advocate of it because I do not regard it as a very important matter." He believed that women should continue to focus their energies on motherhood, "which is more important than any man's work." By 1912, however, Roosevelt had changed his mind. During the presidential campaign, he admitted that "I am rather in favor of the suffrage, but very tepidly." For his part, Woodrow Wilson, despite having two daughters who were suffragists, insisted that the issue of women's voting rights should be left to the states. A Mississippi Democrat was more blunt in his opposition: "I would rather die and go to hell," he claimed, "than vote for woman's suffrage."

The lack of support from the progressive presidents led some leaders of the suffrage movement to revise their tactics in the second decade of the new century. In 1910, **Alice Paul**, a Quaker social worker who had earned a doctoral degree in political science from the University of Pennsylvania, returned from an apprenticeship with the militant suffragists of England, who had developed effective forms of civil disobedience as a way of generating attention and support. The courageously militant Paul became head of the National American Woman Suffrage Association (NAWSA). She instructed female activists to picket state legislatures, target and "punish" politicians who failed to endorse suffrage, chain themselves to public buildings, incite police to arrest them, and undertake hunger strikes. In 1913 Paul organized five thousand suffragists to march in protest at Woodrow Wilson's presidential inauguration. Four years later, Paul helped form the National Woman's Party. By 1917 she had decided that suffragists must do something even more dramatic to force President Wilson to support their cause: picket the White House. On January 11, 1917, Paul and her followers took up positions around the White House. They took turns carrying their signs on the sidewalks all day, five days a week, for six months, whereupon the president ordered their arrest. Some sixty suffragists were jailed. For her role, Alice Paul was sentenced to seven months in prison. She then went on a hunger strike, leading prison officials to force feed her through a tube inserted in her nose. Under an avalanche of press coverage and public criticism, President Wilson pardoned her and the other jailed activists.

The courageous proponents of women's suffrage put forth several arguments in favor of voting rights. Many assumed that the right to vote and hold office was a matter of simple justice: women were just as capable as men in exercising the rights and responsibilities of citizenship. Others insisted that women were morally superior to men and therefore would raise the quality of the political process by their participation in it. They also would be less prone to use warfare as a solution to international disputes and national differences. Women voters, advocates argued, would also promote the welfare of society rather than partisan or selfish gains. Allowing women to vote would create a great engine for progressive social change. One activist explicitly linked women's suffrage with the social gospel, declaring that women embraced Christ more readily than men; if they were elected to public office, they would "far more effectively guard the morals of society and the sanitary conditions of cities."

Yet the women's suffrage movement was not immune from the prevailing social, ethnic, and racial prejudices of the day. **Carrie Chapman Catt** echoed the fears of many middle- and upper-class women when she warned of the danger that "lies in the votes possessed by the males in the slums of the cities, and the ignorant foreign [immigrant] vote." She added that the nation, with "ill-advised haste" had enfranchised "the foreigner, the Negro and the Indian" but still balked at women voting. In the South, suffragists catered to generations of deeply embedded racism. One of them declared that giving white women the vote "would insure immediate and durable white supremacy." Most of the suffrage organizations excluded African American women.

Whatever the motives, a grudging President Wilson finally endorsed what journalists called the Susan B. Anthony Amendment in early 1918, explaining to the Senate that he saw it as a reward for the role women had played in supporting the war effort. After six months of delay, debate, and failed votes, the Congress passed the **Nineteenth Amendment** in the spring of 1919 and sent it to the states for ratification. Tennessee's legislature was the last of thirty-six state assemblies to approve the amendment, and it did so in dramatic fashion. The initial vote was deadlocked 48–48. Then a twenty-four-year-old legislator

Alice Paul

Alice Paul's strategies of civil disobedience became increasingly militant. Here she sews a suffrage flag, which she often brandished at strikes and protests.

named Harry Burn changed his vote to yes at the insistence of his mother. The Nineteenth Amendment was ratified on August 18, 1920, making the United States the twenty-second nation in the world to allow women's suffrage. It was the climactic achievement of the Progressive Era. Suddenly 9.5 million women were eligible to vote; in the 1920 presidential election they would make up 40 percent of the electorate.

MARGARET SANGER AND BIRTH CONTROL   Perhaps the most controversial women's issue of the Progressive Era involved birth control. In 1916 the first birth-control clinic in the nation opened in Brooklyn, New York. One of the staff members was a feisty woman named **Margaret Sanger**, a nurse and midwife. Sanger had grown up with ten siblings, one of whom she helped deliver when she was eight years old. While working in the working-class tenements of Manhattan, Sanger saw many poor, young mothers struggling to provide for their growing families. She also witnessed the consequences of unwanted pregnancies, tragic miscarriages, and amateur abortions. The young women she encountered were desperate for information about how to avoid pregnancy. Sanger insisted that women ("doomed people") could never "be on equal footing with men until they have complete control over their reproductive functions." So Sanger began to distribute birth-control information to working-class women in 1912 and resolved to spend the rest of her life helping women gain control of their bodies. Two years later she began publishing the *Woman Rebel*, a monthly feminist newspaper which authorities declared obscene. In 1921 Sanger organized the American Birth Control League, which later changed its name to Planned Parenthood. The Birth Control League distributed birth-control information to doctors, social workers, women's clubs, and the scientific community, as well as to thousands of women. Such efforts aroused intense opposition, but Sanger and others persisted in their efforts to enable women to control whether they became pregnant. Sanger was viewed as a hero by many progressive reformers. In the 1920s, however, she alienated supporters of birth control by endorsing what was called eugenics: the effort to reduce the number of genetically "unfit" people in society by sterilizing the mentally incompetent and other people with certain unwanted hereditary conditions. Birth control, she stressed in a chilling justification of eugenics, was "the most constructive and necessary of the means to racial health."

PROGRESSIVE RESURGENCE   The need to weld a winning political coalition in 1916 pushed Woodrow Wilson back onto the road of reform. Progressive Democrats were growing restless with his conservative stance, and after war broke out in Europe in August 1914, further divisions arose over defense preparedness and foreign policy issues. At the same time, the Republicans were repairing their own rift, as the "Bull Moose" Progressive party showed little staying power in the midterm elections and Theodore Roosevelt showed little will to preserve it. Wilson could gain reelection only by courting progressives of all parties. In 1916 the president scored points with them when he nominated Louis D. Brandeis to the Supreme Court. Conservatives waged a vigorous battle against Brandeis, but Senate progressives rallied to win confirmation of the social-justice champion, the first Jewish member of the Court.

Meanwhile, Wilson announced a broad new program of farm and labor reforms. The agricultural sector continued to suffer from a shortage of capital. To address the problem, Wilson supported a proposal to set up special rural banks to provide long-term farm loans. The Federal Farm Loan Act became law in 1916. Under the control of the Federal Farm Loan Board, twelve Federal Land banks paralleled the regional Federal Reserve banks and offered farmers loans of five to forty years' duration at low interest rates.

Thus the dream of federal loans to farmers, long advocated by Populists, finally came to fruition when Congress passed the Warehouse Act of 1916, which enabled farmers who stored their harvest in designated warehouses to receive federal receipts that could be used as collateral for short-term bank loans. Farmers were also pleased by the passage of the Smith-Lever Act of 1914 and the Smith-Hughes Act of 1917. The first provided federal financing for farm-demonstration agents who fanned out to educate farmers about new equipment and new ideas related to agricultural efficiency. The second measure extended agricultural and mechanical education to high schools. Farmers with the newfangled automobiles had more than a passing interest as well in the Federal Highways Act of 1916, which helped finance new highways. The progressive resurgence of 1916 broke the logjam on workplace reforms as well.

LABOR LEGISLATION   One of the longstanding goals of many progressive Democrats was a federal child labor law. When Congress passed the Keating-Owen Act, Wilson expressed doubts about its constitutionality, but he eventually signed the landmark legislation, which excluded from interstate commerce any goods manufactured by children under the age of fourteen. The Keating-Owen Act was later ruled unconstitutional by the Supreme Court on the grounds that regulating child labor was outside the bounds of regulating interstate commerce. Effective action against child labor abuses had to await the New Deal of the 1930s.

Another important accomplishment was the eight-hour workday for railroad workers, a measure that the Supreme Court upheld. The Adamson Act of 1916 resulted from a threatened strike of railroad unions demanding an eight-hour workday and other concessions. Wilson, who objected to some of the demands, nevertheless went before Congress to request action on the hours limitation. The Adamson Act required an eight-hour workday, with time and a half for overtime, and appointed a commission to study the problem of working conditions in the railroad industry.

LIMITS OF PROGRESSIVISM

During Wilson's two terms as president, progressivism reached its zenith. After two decades of political ferment (three if the Populist years are counted), the great contribution of progressive politics was the firm establishment and general acceptance of the public-service concept of government. The Progressive Era was an optimistic age in which all sorts of reformers assumed that no problem lay beyond solution. But like all great historic movements, progressivism displayed elements of paradox and irony. Despite all of the talk of greater democracy, progressivism had a blind spot when it came to racial equality. The Progressive Era was the age of disenfranchisement for southern blacks. The first two decades of the twentieth century also witnessed a new round of anti-immigrant prejudice. The initiative and referendum, supposedly democratic reforms, proved subject to manipulation by corporations and political machines that could mount well-financed publicity campaigns. And much of the public policy of the time came to be formulated by elites— technical experts and members of appointed boards—rather than by representative segments of the population. There is a fine irony in the fact that the drive to increase the political role of ordinary people paralleled efforts to strengthen executive leadership and exalt government technical expertise. This "progressive" age of efficiency and bureaucracy, in business as well as government, brought into being a society in which more and more of the decisions affecting people's lives were made by unelected bureaucrats.

Progressivism was largely a middle-class movement in which the destitute poor and unorganized had little influence. The supreme irony was that a movement so dedicated to the rhetoric of democracy should experience so steady a decline in voter participation. In 1912, the year of Roosevelt's Bull Moose campaign, with four presidential candidates, voting dropped off by between 6 and 7 percent. The new politics of issues and charismatic leaders proved to be less effective in turning out voters than traditional party organizations and party bosses had been. And by 1916, the optimism of an age that presumed social progress was already confronted by a vast slaughter. In 1914, Europe had stumbled into a horrific world war, and the United States would soon be drawn into its destruction. The twentieth century, which dawned with such bright hopes for social progress, held in store episodes of unparalleled brutality and holocaust.

CHAPTER SUMMARY

- **Progressivism** Progressives believed that industrialization and urbanization were negatively affecting American life. They were middle-class idealists in both political parties who sought reform and regulation in order to ensure social justice. Many progressives wished to curb the powers of local political machines and establish honest and efficient government. They also called for an end to child labor, laws promoting safety in the workplace, a ban on the sale of alcoholic beverages, legislation curbing trusts, and women's suffrage.

- **Muckrakers** Theodore Roosevelt named the journalists whose works exposed social ills "muckrakers." New, inexpensive popular magazines, such as *McClure's*, published articles about municipal corruption, horrendous conditions in meat-packing plants and urban slums, and predatory business practices. By raising public awareness of these issues, muckrakers contributed to major changes in the workplace and in governance.

- **Square Deal Program** President Roosevelt used his executive position to promote his progressive Square Deal program, which included regulating trusts, arbitrating the 1902 coal strike, regulating the railroads, and cleaning up the meat and drug industries. President Taft continued to bust trusts and reform the tariff, but Republican party bosses, reflecting their big business interests, ensured that the tariff reductions were too few to satisfy the progressives in the party. Roosevelt decided to seek the Republican presidential nomination in 1912 because of progressives' disillusionment with Taft.

- **Presidential Election of 1912** In 1912, after the Republicans renominated Taft, Roosevelt's supporters bolted the convention, formed the Progressive party, and nominated Roosevelt. Although some Democratic progressives supported Roosevelt, the split in the Republican party led to Woodrow Wilson's success. Having won a majority in both houses of Congress as well as the presidential election, the Democrats effectively held national power for the first time since the Civil War.

- **Wilsonian Progressivism** Although Woodrow Wilson was a progressive, his approach was different from Roosevelt's. His New Freedom program promised less federal intervention in business and a return to such traditional Democratic policies as a low tariff. Wilson began a rigorous anti-trust program and oversaw the establishment of the Federal Reserve System. He opposed federal programs promoting social justice and initially withheld support for federal regulation of child labor and a constitutional amendment guaranteeing women's suffrage. A southerner, he believed blacks were inferior and supported segregation.

CHRONOLOGY

1889	Hull-House, a settlement house, opens in Chicago
1902	Theodore Roosevelt attempts to arbitrate the coal strike
1902	Justice Department breaks up Northern Securities Company
1903	Congress passes the Elkins Act
1906	Upton Sinclair's *The Jungle* is published
1906	Congress passes the Meat Inspection Act and the Pure Food and Drug Act
1908	Supreme Court issues *Muller v. Oregon* decision
1909	William Taft is inaugurated president
1910	Congress passes the Mann-Elkins Act
1911	Triangle Shirtwaist Company fire
1913	Congress passes the Federal Reserve Act
1914	Congress passes the Clayton Anti-Trust Act
1916	Louis Brandeis is nominated to fill a seat on the Supreme Court
1920	Nineteenth Amendment, guaranteeing women's suffrage, is ratified

KEY TERMS & NAMES

24

AMERICA AND
THE GREAT WAR

FOCUS QUESTIONS wwnorton.com/studyspace

- Why did Woodrow Wilson involve the United States in Mexico's revolutionary turmoil?
- Why did the United States enter the Great War in Europe?
- How did Wilson promote his peace plan?
- Why did the Senate refuse to ratify the Treaty of Versailles?
- What were the consequences of the war at home and abroad?

Throughout the nineteenth century the United States reaped the benefits of its distance from the frequent wars that plagued Europe. The Atlantic Ocean provided a welcome buffer. During the early twentieth century, however, the nation's comfortable isolation ended. Ever-expanding world trade entwined American interests with the fate of Europe. In addition, the development of steam-powered ships and submarines meant that foreign navies could threaten American security. At the same time, the election of Woodrow Wilson in 1912 brought to the White House a self-righteous moralist determined to impose his standards for proper conduct on renegade nations. This combination of circumstances made the outbreak of the "Great War" in Europe in 1914 a profound crisis for the United States, a crisis that would transform the nation's role in international affairs.

WILSON AND FOREIGN AFFAIRS

Woodrow Wilson had no experience or expertise in international relations. The former college professor admitted before taking office that "it would be an irony of fate if my administration had to deal chiefly with foreign affairs." But events in Latin America and Europe were to make the irony all too real. From the summer of 1914, when a catastrophic world war erupted in Europe, foreign relations increasingly overshadowed all else, including Wilson's ambitious domestic program of progressive reforms. Wilson began his presidency as a pacifist, but by the end of his second term he had ordered more U.S. military interventions abroad than any president before or since.

IDEALISTIC DIPLOMACY   Although devoid of international experience, Wilson did not lack ideas or convictions about global issues. He saw himself as a man of providential destiny who would help create a new world order governed by morality and idealism rather than selfish national interests. Both Wilson and Secretary of State William Jennings Bryan believed that America had a religious duty to advance democracy and Christianity around the world. As Wilson had declared a few years before becoming president, "Every nation of the world needs to be drawn into the tutelage of America." Wilson and Bryan developed a diplomatic policy based on this pious idealism. During 1913 and 1914, the pacifist Bryan negotiated some thirty "cooling-off" treaties, under which participating nations pledged not to go to war over any disagreement for a period of twelve months pending mediation by an international arbitration panel. The treaties were of little consequence, however. They were soon forgotten in the revolutionary sweep of world events that would make the twentieth century the bloodiest in recorded history.

INTERVENTION IN MEXICO   Mexico, which had been in the throes of revolutions for nearly three years, presented a thorny problem for Woodrow Wilson soon after he took office early in 1913. In 1910, popular resentment against the long-standing Mexican dictatorship had boiled over into revolt. Revolutionary armies occupied Mexico City, and then the victorious rebels began squabbling among themselves. The leader of the rebellion, a progressive reformer named Francisco Madero, was himself overthrown by his chief of staff, General Victoriano Huerta, who assumed power in 1913 and had Madero murdered.

President Wilson refused to recognize any government that used force to gain power. Instead he stationed U.S. warships off Veracruz, on the Gulf of Mexico, to halt arms shipments to Huerta's regime. "I am going to teach the South American republics to elect good men," Wilson vowed to a British diplomat. On April 9, 1914, several American sailors gathering supplies in Tampico, Mexico, strayed into a restricted area and were arrested. Mexican officials quickly released them and apologized to the U.S. naval commander.

There the incident might have ended, but the pompous naval officer demanded that the Mexicans salute the American flag. Wilson backed him up by sending some six thousand U.S. marines and sailors ashore at Veracruz on April 21, 1914. They occupied the city at a cost of nineteen American lives; at least two hundred Mexicans were killed.

The use of U.S. military force in Mexico played out like many previous American interventions in the Caribbean and Central America. The public and the Congress readily endorsed the decision to send troops because American honor was presumed to be at stake, but the complex realities of U.S. troops fighting in a foreign country eventually led to prolonged involvement and public disillusionment. Wilson assumed the Mexican people would welcome the American troops as liberators. Instead, the U.S. occupation of Veracruz aroused the opposition of all factions against the "Yankee imperialists." The American troops finally left Veracruz in late 1914. A year later the United States and several Latin American governments recognized a new president of Mexico.

Still the troubles south of the border continued. Bickering among various Mexican factions erupted in chaotic civil war. The prolonged upheaval spawned rival revolutionary armies, the largest of which was led by **Francisco Pancho Villa**. Woodrow Wilson vowed to stay out of the turmoil. "The country is theirs," he concluded. "The government is theirs. Their liberty, if they can get it, is theirs, and so far as my influence goes while I am president, nobody shall interfere with them."

In 1916, the charismatic Villa and his men seized a train and murdered sixteen American mining engineers in a deliberate attempt to trigger U.S. intervention and to build up Villa as a popular opponent of the "gringos." That failing, he crossed the border on raids into Texas and New Mexico. On March 9, he and his men went on a rampage in Columbus, New Mexico, burned the town, and killed seventeen Americans, men and women. A furious Woodrow Wilson abandoned his policy of "watchful waiting." He sent General **John J. Pershing** across the Mexican border with a force of eleven thousand U.S. soldiers. For nearly a year, Pershing's troops chased Villa through northern Mexico. They had no luck and were ordered home in 1917.

OTHER PROBLEMS IN LATIN AMERICA In the Caribbean, Wilson found it as hard to act on his democratic ideals as it was in Mexico. The **"dollar diplomacy"** practiced by the Taft administration had encouraged U.S. bankers to aid debt-plagued governments in Haiti, Guatemala, Honduras, and Nicaragua. Despite Wilson's public stand against using military force to back up American investments, he kept U.S. marines in Nicaragua,

Pancho Villa

Villa (center) and his followers rebelled against the president of Mexico and antagonized the United States with attacks against "gringos."

where they had been sent by President Taft in 1912 to prevent renewed civil war. Then, in 1915, he dispatched more marines to Haiti after that country experienced two chaotic revolutions. The U.S. troops stayed in Nicaragua until 1933 and in Haiti until 1934. Disorders in the Dominican Republic brought U.S. Marines to that country in 1916; they remained until 1924. The repeated use of military force only exacerbated the hatred many Latin Americans felt toward the United States, then and since. As the *New York Times* charged, Wilson's frequent interventions made Taft's dollar diplomacy look like "ten cent diplomacy."

An Uneasy Neutrality

When the thunderbolt of war struck Europe in the summer of 1914, most Americans saw it "as lightning out of a clear sky," as one North Carolinian wrote. It seemed unreal that Europe could descend into an orgy of mutual destruction. At the beginning of the twentieth century, Europe had been peaceful and prosperous. No one imagined the scale of a new industrialized form of warfare; it would assume horrible proportions and involve such unprecedented ruthlessness. Between 1914 and 1921, the First World War was directly responsible for the deaths of over 9 million combatants and the horrible wounding of 15 million more; it would produce at least 3 million widows and 6 million orphans. The war's sheer horror and destructiveness, its obscene butchery and ravaged landscapes, defied belief.

The First World War resulted from festering imperial rivalries and ethnic conflicts in central Europe that set in motion a series of disastrous events and decisions. The Austro-Hungarian Empire had grown determined to suppress the aggressive expansionism of Serbia, a small, independent kingdom. Germany was equally eager to sustain its dominant standing in central Europe against a resurgent Russia and its ally France. War erupted when an Austrian citizen of Serbian descent assassinated the Austrian ruler, Archduke Franz Ferdinand, in the Bosnian town of Sarajevo. Austria-Hungary's furious determination to punish Serbia for the murder led Russia to mobilize its army in sympathy with its Slavic friends in Serbia. That in turn triggered reactions by a complex system of European alliances: the Triple Alliance, or Central Powers (Germany, Austria-Hungary, and Italy), and the Triple Entente, or Allied Powers (France, Great Britain, and Russia). When Russia refused to stop its army's mobilization, Germany, which backed Austria-Hungary, declared war on Russia on August 1, 1914, and on France two days later. Germany then activated a long-planned invasion plan of France that went through neutral Belgium, an action that brought Great Britain reluctantly into the rapidly widening war on August 4. Japan, eager to seize German colonies in the Pacific, declared war on August 23, and Turkey entered on the side of the Central Powers in October. Although allied with the Central Powers, Italy initially stayed out of the war and then struck a bargain under which it joined the Allied Powers in 1915. The early weeks of the war involved fast-moving assaults and enormous casualties. On one day, August 22, 1914, 27,000 French soldiers were killed. By 1915 almost twenty thousand square miles in Belgium and France were in German hands.

The real surprise in 1914 was not the outbreak of war but the nature of the war that unfolded. The First World War was unlike any previous conflict in its scale, scope, and carnage. Machine guns, high-velocity rifles, aerial bombing, poison gas delivered by wind and artillery shells, flame throwers, land mines, long-range artillery, and armored tanks changed the nature of warfare and produced horrific casualties and widespread destruction. Total war among industrialized nations meant that everyone was considered a combatant, including civilians. Each side tried to starve the other into submission by sealing off foreign trade, often by sinking commercial vessels and passenger liners.

What began as a war of quick movement in August 1914 bogged down after 1915 into a stalemated war of senseless attrition punctuated by massive battles that contributed little except more obscene slaughter. During the devastating Battle of Verdun, in northeast France, which lasted from February to December 1916, some 32 million artillery shells were fired—1,500 shells for every square meter of the battlefield. Such unprecedented massed firepower ravaged the landscape, shattering villages and turning farmland and forests into cratered wasteland. The casualties were staggering. Some 162,000 French soldiers died at Verdun; German losses were 143,000. Charles de Gaulle, a young French lieutenant who would become the nation's prime minister, said the conflict had become a "war of extermination."

Trench warfare gave the First World War its lasting character. Most battles were won not by skillful maneuvers or by superior generalship but by brute force. The object of what came to be called "**industrial war**" was not so much to gain ground but simply to decimate the other army in a prolonged war of attrition until their manpower and resources were exhausted. In one attack at Ypres in Belgium, the British lost thirteen thousand men in

Verdun

A landscape image from Verdun, taken immediately after the battle, shows how the firepower ravaged the land.

only three hours of fighting, which gained them only one hundred yards of meaningless acreage.

INITIAL REACTIONS   Shock in the United States over the bloodbath in Europe gave way to gratitude that a wide ocean stood between America and the killing fields. "Our isolated position and freedom from entangling alliances," said the *Literary Digest,* ensure that "we are in no peril of being drawn into the European quarrel." President Wilson repeatedly urged Americans to remain "neutral in thought as well as in action." That was more easily said than done. More than a third of the nation's citizens were "hyphenated Americans," first- or second-generation immigrants who retained strong ties to their native country. Among the 13 million immigrants from the countries at war living in the United States, German Americans were by far the largest group, numbering 8 million. And the 4 million Irish Americans harbored a deep-rooted enmity toward England, which over the centuries had conquered and subjugated the Irish. These groups instinctively leaned toward the Central Powers in the war. But old-line Americans, largely of British origin, supported the Allied Powers. American leaders were pro-British from the outset of the war. Robert Lansing, first counselor of the State Department; Walter Hines Page, ambassador to London; and "Colonel" Edward House, Wilson's closest adviser—all saw in German militarism a potential danger to the United States.

A STRAINED NEUTRALITY   At first, the war in Europe brought a slump in American exports and the threat of a depression, but by the spring of 1915 the Allies' demand for food and war supplies generated an incredible economic boom for American businesses, bankers, and farmers. To finance their purchases of American supplies, the Allies, especially Britain and France, needed loans. Early in the war, Secretary of State William Jennings Bryan, a strict pacifist, declared that loans to any warring nation were "inconsistent with the true spirit of neutrality." Yet Wilson quietly began approving short-term loans to sustain trade with the desperate Allies. By the fall of 1915, Wilson had removed all restrictions on loans. American investors would eventually advance over $2 billion to the Allies before the United States entered the war, and only $27 million to Germany.

The administration nevertheless clung to its official stance of neutrality through two and a half years of warfare in Europe. Wilson tried valiantly to uphold the "freedom of the seas," which had guided U.S. policy since the Napoleonic Wars of the early nineteenth century. On August 6, 1914, Secretary of State Bryan called upon the warring nations ("belligerents") to respect the rights of neutral nations like the United States to continue its commerce with them by shipping goods across the Atlantic. The Central Powers promptly accepted, but the British refused because they would lose some of their advantage in sea power. In November 1914 the British declared the whole North Sea a war zone, sowed it with mines, and ordered neutral ships to submit to searches. In March 1915 they announced that they would seize ships carrying goods to Germany. American protests were ignored.

WORLD WAR I IN EUROPE, 1914
- Central Powers (Triple Alliance)
- Allied Powers (Triple Entente)
- Neutral countries

How did the European system of alliances spread conflict across all of Europe? How was World War I different from previous wars? How did the war in Europe lead to ethnic tensions in the United States?

NEUTRAL RIGHTS AND SUBMARINES With the German fleet bottled up by the British blockade, the German government proclaimed a war zone around the British Isles. Enemy merchant ships in those waters would be attacked by submarines, the Germans declared, and "it may not always be possible to save crews and passengers." As the chief advantage of U-boat (*Unterseeboot*) warfare was in surprise, the German decision violated the long-established procedure of stopping an enemy vessel and providing for the safety of passengers and crew before sinking it. Since the British sometimes flew neutral flags as a ruse, neutral ships in this war zone would also be in danger.

The United States pronounced the new German submarine policy "an indefensible violation of neutral rights." Wilson warned that Germany would be held to "strict accountability" for any destruction of American lives and property. Then, on May 7, 1915, a German submarine sank a huge ocean liner moving slowly through the Irish Sea. Only as it tipped into the waves was the German commander able to make out the name *Lusitania* on the stern. Before the much-celebrated new British passenger liner had left New York City, bound for England, the German embassy had published warnings in American newspapers against travel to the war zone, but 128 Americans were nonetheless among the 1,198 persons lost.

Americans were outraged. The sinking of the *Lusitania* was an act of piracy, Theodore Roosevelt declared. To quiet the uproar, Wilson urged patience: "There is such a thing as a man being too proud to fight. There is such a thing as a nation being so right that it does not need to convince others by force that it is right." Critics lambasted his lame response to the deaths of 128 Americans. Roosevelt castigated Wilson's "unmanly" stance, calling him a "jackass" and threatening to "skin him alive if he doesn't go to war" over the *Lusitania* tragedy. Wilson acknowledged that he had misspoken. "I have a bad habit of thinking out loud," he confessed to a friend the day after his "too proud to fight" speech. The meek language, he admitted, had "occurred to me while I was speaking, and I let it out. I should have kept it in." His previous demand for "strict accountability" now forced him to make a stronger response. On May 13, Secretary of State Bryan reluctantly signed a note demanding that the Germans abandon unrestricted submarine warfare and pay reparations for the sinking of the *Lusitania*. The Germans responded that the ship was armed (which it was not) and secretly carried a cargo of rifles and ammunition (which it did). A second note, on June 9, repeated American demands in stronger terms. The United States, Wilson asserted, was "contending for nothing less high and sacred than the rights of humanity." Bryan, unwilling to risk war over the issue, resigned in protest.

Bryan's successor, Robert Lansing, signed the controversial "*Lusitania* Note" to the Germans.

In response to the uproar over the sinking of the *Lusitania,* the German government had secretly ordered U-boat captains to avoid sinking any more passenger vessels. When, despite the order, two American lives were lost in the sinking of the New York–bound British liner *Arabic,* the Germans paid a cash penalty to the families of the deceased and offered a public assurance on September 1, 1915: "Liners will not be sunk by our submarines without warning and without safety of the lives of non-combatants, provided that the liners do not try to escape or offer resistance." With this so-called *Arabic* Pledge, Wilson's resolute stand seemed to have resulted in a victory for his neutrality policy.

During early 1916, Wilson's trusted adviser Colonel House visited London, Paris, and Berlin in an effort to negotiate an end to the war but found neither side ready to begin serious negotiations. On March 24, 1916, a U-boat torpedoed the French steamer *Sussex,* injuring two Americans. When President Wilson threatened to break off relations, Germany renewed its pledge that U-boats would not torpedo merchant and passenger ships. This *Sussex* Pledge was far stronger than the earlier German promise after the *Arabic* sinking the year before. The *Sussex* Pledge implied the virtual abandonment of submarine warfare.

THE DEBATE OVER PREPAREDNESS   The *Lusitania* incident and, more generally, the quarrels over neutral commerce contributed to a growing demand in the United States for a stronger army and navy. On December 1, 1914, champions of "preparedness" organized the National Security League to promote their cause. After the *Lusitania* sinking, Wilson asked the War and Navy Departments to develop plans for military expansion.

Pacifists, however, as well as many isolationists in the rural South and West, were opposed to a defense buildup. During the fall of 1915, the administration's plan to enlarge the army and create a national reserve force of 400,000 ran into such stubborn opposition in Congress that Wilson was forced to accept a compromise between advocates of an expanded force under federal control and advocates of a traditional citizen army. The National Defense Act of 1916 expanded the regular federal army from 90,000 to 175,000 and permitted gradual enlargement to 223,000. It also increased the National Guard to 440,000. Former secretary of state Bryan complained in early 1916 that Wilson wanted to "drag this nation into war."

Opponents of the military buildup insisted that the financial burden should rest upon the wealthy people they held responsible for promoting the military expansion and profiting from trade with the Allies. The income tax became their weapon. Supported by a groundswell of popular support, legislators wrote into the Revenue Act of 1916 changes that doubled the basic income tax rate from 1 to 2 percent, lifted the surtax to a maximum of 13 percent (for a total of 15 percent) on income over $2 million, added an estate tax, levied a 12.5 percent tax on munitions makers, and added a new tax on excess corporate profits. The new taxes amounted to the most clearcut victory for radical progressives in the entire Progressive Era, a victory further consolidated and advanced after America entered the war. It was the capstone to the progressive legislation that Wilson supported in preparation for the upcoming presidential election.

THE ELECTION OF 1916 As the 1916 election approached, Republicans hoped to regain their normal electoral majority, and Theodore Roosevelt hoped to be their leader again. But he had committed the deadly political sin of bolting his party in 1912. His eagerness for the United States to enter the war also scared many voters. Needing a candidate who would draw Bull Moose Progressives back into the fold, the Republican leaders turned to Supreme Court Justice Charles Evans Hughes, who had a progressive record as governor of New York from 1907 to 1910.

The Democrats, as expected, chose Woodrow Wilson again. Their platform endorsed a program of social-welfare legislation and prudent military preparedness in case the nation was drawn into the European war. The party referred the idea of women's suffrage to the states and pledged support for a postwar league of nations to enforce peace. The Democrats' most popular issue, however, was an insistent pledge to keep the nation out of the war in Europe. The peace theme, refined in the slogan "He kept us out of war," became the rallying cry of the Wilson campaign.

The candidates in the 1916 presidential election were remarkably similar. Both Wilson and Hughes were the sons of preachers; both were attorneys and former professors; both had been progressive governors; both were known for their pristine integrity. Theodore Roosevelt highlighted the similarities between them when he called the bearded Hughes a "whiskered Wilson." Wilson, however, proved to be the better campaigner. In the end, his twin pledges to keep America out of war and to expand his progressive social agenda brought a narrow victory. The final vote showed a Democratic sweep of the Far West and the South, enough for narrow victories in the Electoral College, by 277 to 254, and in the popular vote, by 9 million to 8.5 million. Despite the victory, the closeness of the election did not bode well for the Democrats.

LAST EFFORTS FOR PEACE   Immediately after the election, Wilson again offered to mediate an end to the war in Europe, but neither side was willing to abandon its major war aims. In January 1917, impatient German military leaders decided to wage unrestricted submarine warfare on Allied shipping. They took the calculated risk of arousing American anger in the hope of scoring a quick knockout on the battlefields of Europe before U.S. troops could join the war. On January 31 the new policy was announced, effective the next day. All vessels would be sunk without warning. "Freedom of the seas," said the *Brooklyn Eagle*, "will now be enjoyed [only] by icebergs and fish."

On February 3, 1917, Wilson told a joint session of Congress that the United States had broken diplomatic relations with the German government. World events then took another unexpected turn—and another. On February 25, Wilson learned that the British had intercepted an important message from the German foreign minister, Arthur Zimmermann, to the Mexican government. The note urged the Mexicans to invade the United States. In exchange for their making war on America, Germany guaranteed that Mexico would recover its "lost territory in Texas, New Mexico, and Arizona." On March 1, news of the Zimmermann telegram broke in the American press, generating widespread anger at the Germans. Then, later in March 1917, on the other side of the world, a revolution overthrew Russia's czarist government and established the provisional government of a Russian republic. The fall of the czarist autocracy gave Americans the illusion that all the major Allied powers were now fighting for constitutional democracy—an illusion that was shattered in November 1917, when Vladimir Lenin and the Bolsheviks, a determined group of revolutionaries, seized power in war-weakened Russia and established a Communist dictatorship. The bookish Lenin transformed communism into an all-embracing ideology mercilessly imposed on an entire society, eliminating civil liberties, religious life, and the free press, and killing or imprisoning opposition leaders. Communism would become the most significant new political movement of the twentieth century.

America's Entry into the War

In March 1917, German submarines sank five U.S. merchant vessels in the North Atlantic. That was the last straw for a frustrated President Wilson, who on April 2 asked Congress to recognize that imperial Germany and the United States were at war. In his war message to Congress, Wilson transformed the war in Europe from being a conventional struggle for power among historic European rivals to a righteous conflict between democratic ideals and autocratic tyranny. America's effort to maintain a principled neutrality had become in Wilson's mind a "great crusade" to end wars forever. He insisted that "the world must be made safe for democracy." The war resolution passed the Senate by a vote of 82 to 6 on April 4. The House concurred, 373 to 50, and Wilson signed the measure on April 6, 1917.

How had matters come to this less than three years after Wilson's proclamation of neutrality? The most prominent causes for America's entrance into the war were the effects of British propaganda in the United States and America's deep involvement in trade with the Allies, which some observers credited to the intrigues of war profiteers and munitions makers. Some proponents of war thought an Allied defeat and German domination of Europe would threaten U.S. security, especially if it meant the destruction of the British navy. Such factors, however, would not have been decisive without the issue of Germany's unrestricted submarine warfare on the Atlantic. Once Wilson had taken a principled stand for the traditional rights of neutral nations and noncombatants on the high seas, he was to some extent at the mercy of ill-considered decisions by the German military leadership.

AMERICA'S EARLY ROLE War had been declared, but now it needed to be fought. Despite Congress's earlier military preparedness measures, the U.S. army remained small and untested. The navy also was largely undeveloped. Now the Wilson administration needed quickly to build and train an army of millions and transport them across an Atlantic Ocean infested with German submarines. The formidable challenge of mobilizing the entire nation for war led to an unprecedented expansion of federal government authority. Woodrow Wilson's administration did not invite Americans to support the war effort; it ordered them to do so. Power became increasingly centralized in Washington, as the government conscripted millions of men, directed the conversion of industries and farms to wartime needs, took over the railroads, mediated labor disputes, and in many other respects assumed control of national life. On June 26, 1917, just three months after the declaration of war, the first contingent of the American Expeditionary Force, about 14,500 soldiers commanded by General John J. Pershing, disembarked on the French coast.

MOBILIZING A NATION Complete economic mobilization on the home front was necessary to conduct the war efficiently. The Army Appropriation Act of 1916 had created a Council of National Defense, which in turn led to the creation of other wartime agencies. The **Food Administration**, headed by Herbert Hoover, a future president, sought to raise agricultural production while reducing civilian consumption of foodstuffs. "Food will win the war" was the slogan. Hoover directed a conservation campaign promoting "meatless Tuesdays," "wheatless Wednesdays," "porkless Saturdays," the planting of victory gardens, and the creative use of leftovers. The War Industries Board (WIB), established in 1917, soon became the most important of all the federal mobilization agencies. Bernard Baruch, a brilliant financier who exercised a virtual dictatorship over the economy, headed the WIB. Under Baruch's leadership, the WIB could allocate raw materials, order construction of new plants, and with the approval of the president, fix prices.

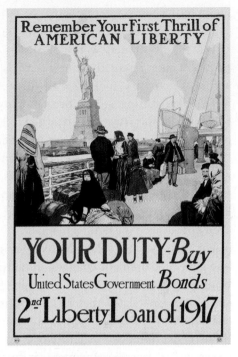

The thrill of American liberty

This Liberty Loan poster urges immigrants to do their duty for their new country by buying government bonds to help pay for the war.

A NEW LABOR FORCE The closing off of foreign immigration and the movement of 4 million men from the workforce into the armed services created an acute labor shortage across the United States. To meet it, women, African Americans, and other ethnic minorities were encouraged to enter industries and take on jobs heretofore dominated by white men. Northern businesses sent recruiting agents into the southern states to find workers for their factories and mills. Over four hundred southern blacks (and a significant number of whites) began a Great Migration northward during the war years, a mass movement that continued unabated through the 1920s and changed the political and social dynamics of northern cities. Recruiting agents and newspaper editors portrayed the North as the "land of promise" for southern blacks suffering from their region's depressed agricultural economy and rising racial intimidation and violence. The African American *Chicago Defender* exclaimed: "To die from the bite of frost is far more glorious than at the hands of a mob." By 1930 the number of African Americans living in the North was triple that of 1910. Mexican Americans followed the same migratory pattern in Texas and the Far West.

But the newcomers were not always welcomed. Many white workers in northern cities resented the new arrivals, and racial tensions sparked clashes across the country. In 1917 over forty African Americans and nine whites were killed during a riot over employment in a defense plant in East St. Louis, Illinois. Two years later the toll of a Chicago race riot was nearly as high, with twenty-three African Americans and fifteen whites left dead. In these and other incidents of racial violence, the pattern was the same: whites angered by the influx of southern blacks into their communities would seize upon an incident as an excuse to rampage through black neighborhoods, killing, burning, and looting while white policemen looked the other way or even encouraged the hooliganism.

For many women, black and white, intervention in the First World War also generated dramatic changes. Initially, women supported the war effort in traditional ways. They helped organize fundraising drives, conserved food-stuffs and war-related materials, supported the Red Cross, and joined the army nurse corps. But as the scope of the war widened, both government and industry recruited women to work on farms, loading docks, and railway crews, as well as in the armaments industry, machine shops, steel and lumber mills, and chemical plants. Many women leaders saw such opportunities as a breakthrough. "At last, after centuries of disabilities and discrimination," said a speaker at a Women's Trade Union League meeting in 1917, "women are coming into the labor [force] and festival of life on equal terms with men."

In fact, however, war-generated changes in female employment were limited and brief. About 1 million women participated in "war work," but most of them were young and single and already working outside the home. Most returned to their previous jobs once the war ended. In fact, male-dominated unions encouraged women to revert to their stereotypical domestic roles after the war ended. The Central Federated Union of New York insisted that "the same patriotism which induced women to enter industry during the war should induce them to vacate their positions after the war." The antici-pated gains of women in the workforce failed to materialize. In 1920 the 8.5 million working women made up a smaller percentage of the labor force than had working women in 1910. Still, one lasting result of women's contri-butions to the war effort was Woodrow Wilson's grudging decision to endorse women's suffrage. In the fall of 1918, he told the Senate that giving women the vote was "vital to the winning of the war."

WAR PROPAGANDA The war effort led the government to mobilize more than economic life: the progressive gospel of efficiency suggested

The Beast of Berlin

A scene from the movie *The Beast of Berlin*, which gave audiences a propagandistic view of World War I.

mobilizing public opinion as well. On April 14, 1917, eight days after the declaration of war, President Wilson established the **Committee on Public Information**, composed of the secretaries of state, war, and the navy. Its executive head, **George Creel**, a Denver newsman, sold Wilson on the idea that the best approach to influencing public opinion was propaganda instead of censorship. Creel organized a propaganda machine to explain the Allies' war aims to the people and, above all, to the enemy, where it might help sap their morale. To generate support for the war effort, Creel gathered a remarkable group of journalists, photographers, artists, entertainers, and others useful to his purpose.

CIVIL LIBERTIES By arousing public opinion to such a frenzy, the war effort spawned grotesque campaigns of "Americanism" and witch-hunting. Popular prejudice equated anything German with disloyalty. Symphonies refused to perform classical music written by Bach and Beethoven, schools dropped German language classes, and patriots translated *sauerkraut* into "liberty cabbage," *German measles* into "liberty measles," and *dachshunds* into "liberty pups." President Wilson had foreseen these consequences. "Once lead this people into war," he said, "and they'll forget there ever was such a thing as tolerance." What Wilson did not say was that he would lead the effort to suppress civil liberties during and after the war.

Under the Espionage and Sedition Acts, Congress suppressed criticism of government leaders and war policies. The Espionage Act of 1917 imposed penalties of up to $10,000 and twenty years in prison for anyone who gave aid to the enemy; who tried to incite insubordination, disloyalty, or refusal of duty in the armed services; or who sought to interfere with the war effort. President Wilson had also wanted the bill to allow the government to censor newspapers, but Congress refused. The Sedition Act of 1918 extended the penalties to those who did or said anything to obstruct the government sale of war bonds or to advocate cutbacks in production, and—just in case something had been overlooked—for saying, writing, or printing anything "disloyal, profane, scurrilous, or abusive" about the American form of government, the Constitution, or the army and navy.

In two important decisions just after the war, the Supreme Court upheld the Espionage and Sedition Acts. *Schenck v. United States* (1919) reaffirmed the conviction of a man for circulating anti-draft leaflets among members of the armed forces. In this case, Justice Oliver Wendell Holmes said, "Free speech would not protect a man in falsely shouting fire in a theater, and causing a panic." The government was allowed to suppress speech where there was "a clear and present danger." In *Abrams v. United States* (1919), the Court upheld the conviction of a man who circulated pamphlets opposing American intervention in Russia to oust the Bolsheviks. Here, Holmes and Louis Brandeis dissented from the majority view. The "surreptitious publishing of a silly leaflet by an unknown man," they argued, posed no danger to government policy.

AMERICA AT WAR

American troops played little more than a token role in the European fighting until early 1918. Before that they were parceled out in quiet sectors mainly for training purposes. All through 1917 the Allied armies remained on the defensive, and late in the year their situation turned desperate. In October the Italian lines collapsed and were overrun by Austrian forces. With the help of troops from France, the Italians finally held their ground. In November the Bolshevik Revolution overthrew the infant Russian republic, and the Communist leaders dropped out of the war. With the Central

The Meuse-Argonne offensive

U.S. soldiers fire an artillery gun in Argonne, France.

Powers victorious over Russia, they were free to concentrate their forces on the western front. The American war effort thus became a "race for the defense of France." The French premier Georges Clemenceau appealed to the Americans to accelerate their mobilization. "A terrible blow is imminent," he predicted to a journalist. "Tell your Americans to come quickly."

THE WESTERN FRONT On March 21, 1918, Clemenceau's prediction came true when the Germans began the first of several spring offensives in France and Belgium to try to end the war before the Americans arrived in force. By May 1918, there were 1 million fresh but untested and under-trained U.S. troops in Europe, and for the first time they made a difference. During the first week in June, a marine brigade blocked the Germans at Belleau Wood, and army troops took Vaux and opposed the Germans at Château-Thierry. Though these relatively modest actions had limited military significance, their effect on Allied morale was significant. The British and the French armies continued to bear the brunt of the fighting.

The climactic American role in the fighting occurred in the great Meuse-Argonne offensive, begun on September 26, 1918. American divisions joined British and French armies in a drive toward Sedan and its railroad, which supplied the entire German front. It was the largest American action of the war, involving 1.2 million U.S. troops and resulting in 117,000 American casualties, including 26,000 dead. But along the entire front from Sedan to Flanders, the Germans were in retreat. "America," wrote German general Erich Ludendorff, "thus became the decisive power in the war."

THE BOLSHEVIKS   When the war broke out in 1914, Russia was one of the Allied Powers. Over the next three years the Russians suffered some 6.6 million casualties. The czarist government fell into such disarray that it was forced to transfer power to a new provisional republican government that itself succumbed, in November 1917, to a revolution led by Vladimir Lenin and his Bolshevik party, who promised war-weary Russians "peace, land, and bread." The **Bolsheviks** were a small but determined sect of ruthless ideologues, convinced that they were in the irresistible vanguard of historical change as described by Karl Marx in the mid-nineteenth century. They found themselves in the right place at the right time—a backward country devastated by prolonged war, besieged by invading armies, and burdened by a mediocre government. As Lenin observed, power was lying in the streets, waiting to be picked up.

Once in control of the government, the Bolsheviks unilaterally stopped fighting in the First World War. With German troops deep in Russian territory and armies of "White" Russians (anti-Bolsheviks) organizing resistance to their power, the Bolsheviks concluded a separate peace with Germany, the Treaty of Brest-Litovsk, on March 3, 1918. To prevent military supplies from falling into German hands and encourage anti-Bolshevik forces in the developing Russian Civil War, President Wilson sent American forces into Russia's Arctic ports. Troops were also sent to eastern Siberia, where they remained until April 1920 in an effort to curb growing Japanese ambitions there. The Allied intervention in Russia failed because the Bolsheviks were able to consolidate their power. Russia took no further part in World War I and did not participate in the peace settlement. The failed Allied intervention largely served to generate among Soviets a long-lasting suspicion of the West.

THE FOURTEEN POINTS   As the conflict in Europe was ending, neither the Allies nor the Central Powers, despite Wilson's prodding, had stated openly what they hoped to gain from the fighting. Wilson repeated that the Americans had no selfish war aims: "We desire no conquest, no dominion," he stressed in his war message of 1917. "We are but one of the champions of the rights of mankind." But Wilson also believed that the United States had a special mission in the world. People everywhere, he assumed, "are looking to

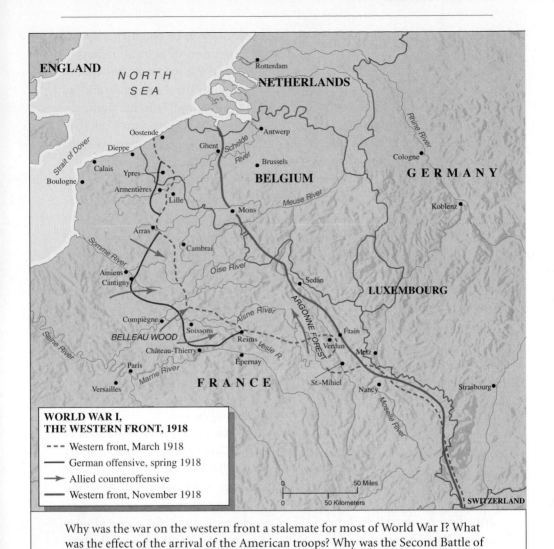

**WORLD WAR I,
THE WESTERN FRONT, 1918**

- - - Western front, March 1918

――― German offensive, spring 1918

⟶ Allied counteroffensive

――― Western front, November 1918

0   50 Miles

0   50 Kilometers

Why was the war on the western front a stalemate for most of World War I? What was the effect of the arrival of the American troops? Why was the Second Battle of the Marne the turning point of the war?

us for direction and leadership." Unfortunately for Wilson's idealistic purposes, America's European allies had different objectives, so Wilson began formulating his own plans to restructure postwar Europe and remake the world in the American image.

During 1917 a group of American experts, called the Inquiry, began drafting a peace plan. With advice from these experts, Wilson himself developed what would come to be called the **Fourteen Points**, which he presented to a joint session of Congress on January 8, 1918, "as the only possible program" for peace. The first five points called for diplomacy to be conducted openly rather than hidden in secret treaties, the recognition of neutral nations to continue oceangoing commerce in time of war ("freedom of the seas"), removal of international trade barriers, reduction of armaments, and an impartial reconfiguration of the victors' colonial empires based upon the desires of the populations involved. Most of the remaining points dealt with territorial claims: they called on the Central Powers to evacuate occupied lands and to allow the various overlapping nationalities and ethnic groups to develop their own new nation-states (the difficult principle of "self-determination"), a crucial principle for Wilson. Point 13 called for the creation of an independent nation for the Poles, a people long dominated by the Russians on the east and the Germans on the west. Point 14, the capstone of Wilson's postwar scheme, called for the creation of a "league" of nations to protect global peace. When the Fourteen Points were made public, African American leaders asked the president to add a fifteenth point: an end to racial discrimination. Wilson did not respond.

On October 3, 1918, a new German chancellor asked for an end to the fighting on the basis of the Fourteen Points. The Allies accepted the Fourteen Points as a basis of negotiations, but with two significant reservations: the British insisted on the right to discuss limiting freedom of the seas, and the French demanded reparations (payments by the vanquished to the victors) from Germany and Austria for war damages.

Meanwhile, the German home front was being torn apart by a loss of morale, culminating in a naval mutiny at Kiel. Germany's allies dropped out of the war: Bulgaria on September 29, 1918, Turkey on October 30, and Austria-Hungary on November 3. On November 9 the kaiser abdicated, and a German republic was proclaimed. Then, on November 11 at 5 A.M., an armistice was signed. Six hours later, at the eleventh hour of the eleventh day of the eleventh month, and after 1,563 days of warfare, the guns fell silent. Under the armistice agreement the Germans had to evacuate occupied territories, pull their troops back behind the Rhine River, and surrender their naval fleet and railroad equipment. The Germans were assured that Woodrow Wilson's Fourteen Points would be the basis for the peace conference.

During its nineteen months of participation in the Great War, the United States saw 126,000 of its servicemen killed. Germany's war dead totaled over 2 million, including civilians; France lost nearly 1.4 million combatants, Great Britain lost 703,000 soldiers, and Russia lost 1.7 million. The new Europe emerging from the carnage would be much different: much poorer, more violent, more polarized, more cynical, less sure of itself, and less capable of decisive action. The United States, for good or ill, would be sucked into the vacuum of power created by the destructiveness of the Great War. For the moment, however, the news of peace led to wild celebrations throughout the world. The madness was over, and fear and grief gave way to hope. "The nightmare is over," wrote the African American activist W.E.B. Du Bois. "The world awakes. The long, horrible years of dreadful night are passed. Behold the sun!"

THE FIGHT FOR THE PEACE

The gruesome combat and destruction had ended, but Europe's post-war future was a muddle. Woodrow Wilson had promised a "great crusade" that would "make the world safe for democracy." For a glorious moment, the American president was humanity's self-appointed prophet of peace. He felt guided "by the hand of God." His messianic vision of creating a universal "community of power," a peacekeeping "league of nations" to replace the old war-breeding power politics of Europe promised a bright future for the world. If the diplomats failed to follow his plans, he warned, "there will be another world war" within a generation.

DOMESTIC UNREST Woodrow Wilson made several fateful decisions at the war's end that would come back to haunt him. First, he decided to attend the peace conference that convened in Paris on January 18, 1919. Never before had an American president left the nation for such a prolonged period. Wilson's decision dramatized all the more his crusading vision for a lasting peace. From one viewpoint, it was shrewd, for his prestige and determination made a difference at the Paris peace talks. But during his prolonged trip abroad (six months) he lost touch with political developments at home. Second, in the midterm elections of 1918, Wilson defied his advisers and urged voters to elect a Democratic Congress to support his foreign policies. Republicans, who for the most part had supported Wilson's war measures, now took affront. In elections held on November 5, a week before the armistice, the Democrats lost control of both houses of Congress. With an opposition majority in the new Congress, Wilson further weakened his standing by making a third mistake: he failed to appoint a prominent Republican to the staff of peace commissioners. Former president Taft groused that Wilson's real intention in going to Paris was "to hog the whole show."

When Wilson reached Paris in December 1918, he was greeted as a hero, even a savior. The cheering millions saw in the American idealist a prophet of peace and a spokesman for humanity who had promised that the crusade

The Paris Peace Conference

Woodrow Wilson (second from left) with Georges Clemenceau of France (center) and Arthur Balfour of Great Britain (second from right) during the Paris Peace Conference in 1919.

in Europe would be the "war to end wars." Their heartfelt support no doubt strengthened his hand at the conference, but Wilson had to deal with some tough-minded statesmen who did not share his utopian zeal. They would force him to abandon many of his principles and ideals.

The Paris Peace Conference lasted from January to June 1919 and included delegates from all countries that had declared war or broken diplomatic relations with Germany. The conference was controlled by the Big Four: the prime ministers of Britain, France, and Italy and the president of the United States. Japan restricted its interests to Asia and the Pacific. French premier Georges Clemenceau was a stern realist who had little patience with Wilson's utopianism. "God gave us the Ten Commandments and we broke them," Clemenceau sneered. "Wilson gave us the Fourteen Points—we shall see." The French insisted on harsh provisions in the peace treaty to weaken Germany. So did the British prime minister David Lloyd George. Vittorio Orlando, prime minister of Italy, focused his efforts on getting territories from defeated Austria.

THE LEAGUE OF NATIONS   As the tense, complex negotiations began, Woodrow Wilson made another controversial decision: he insisted that his cherished **League of Nations** be the top priority in the treaty making. Whatever compromises he might have to make regarding territorial boundaries and financial claims, whatever mistakes might result, Wilson believed that a league of nations committed to collective security would ensure international stability. Wilson presided over the commission set up to draft its charter. Article X of the charter, which Wilson called "the heart of the League," pledged member nations to impose military and economic sanctions against aggressors. The use of armed force would be a last (and an improbable) resort. The League, it was assumed, would exercise enormous moral influence, making military action

"The League of Nations Argument in a Nutshell"

Jay N. "Ding" Darling's summation of the League controversy.

unnecessary. Its structure would allow each member an equal voice in the Assembly; the Big Five (Britain, France, Italy, Japan, and the United States) and four other nations would make up the executive Council; the administrative staff, with headquarters in Geneva, Switzerland, would make up the Secretariat; and a Permanent Court of International Justice (set up in 1921 and usually called the World Court) could "hear and determine any dispute of an international character."

On February 14, 1919, Wilson presented the finished draft of the League covenant to the Allies and departed Paris for a visit home. Already he faced opposition among Republicans. Wilson's proposed League of Nations, Theodore Roosevelt grumbled, would revive German militarism and undermine American morale. "To substitute internationalism for nationalism," the former president argued, "means to do away with patriotism." Roosevelt's close friend and fellow Republican, **Henry Cabot Lodge**, the powerful chairman of the Senate Foreign Relations Committee, also scorned Wilson's naive idealism. He announced that the League's structure was unacceptable because it would allow an international organization to usurp the Senate's constitutional authority to declare war. Lodge's statement bore the signatures of thirty-nine Republican senators or senators-elect, more than enough to block ratification.

TERRITORY AND REPARATIONS   Back in Paris in the spring of 1919, Wilson gave in to French demands for territorial concessions and **reparations** payments by Germany that would keep it dangerously weak, impoverished, and eager for revenge during the 1920s. Even after making major concessions, Wilson clashed sharply with the French premier Clemenceau over how to treat defeated Germany, but after the American president threatened to leave the conference, they decided that the Rhineland region along the border between France and Germany would be a "demilitarized" zone for fifteen years. France could also exploit Germany's Saar Valley coal mines for fifteen years, after which the region's residents would vote to determine their national allegiance.

In other territorial matters, Wilson had to abandon his lofty principle of national self-determination whereby every ethnic group would be allowed to form its own nation. Wonderful in theory, it proved disastrous in reality. As Robert Lansing, who succeeded William Jennings Bryan as Wilson's secretary of state, correctly predicted, trying to allow every ethnic group in Europe—Poles, Czechs, Slovaks, Slovenes, Serbs, Latvians, Lithuanians, Estonians, Hungarians, Romanians, Bulgarians, Italians, Turks, Armenians, and others—to determine its own fate "will raise hopes which can never be realized." In the end, Wilson's commitment to self-determination would be "discredited" as the "dream of an idealist who failed to realize the danger until it was too late." As a result of the Great War, four long-standing multinational empires had disintegrated: the Russian, Austro-Hungarian, German, and Ottoman (Turkish). Hundreds of millions of people had to be reorganized into new nations. There was in fact no way to make Europe's boundaries correspond to its tangled ethnic groupings. The folk wanderings of centuries had left ethnically mixed populations scattered throughout Central Europe. In some areas, moreover, national self-determination yielded to other interests: the Polish Corridor, for instance, gave newly independent Poland its much-needed outlet to the sea through German territory. One part of the Austro-Hungarian Empire became Czechoslovakia, which included the German-speaking Sudetenland, an area favored with good natural defenses. Another part united with Serbia to create the kingdom of Yugoslavia. Still other substantial parts of the former empire passed to Poland (Galicia), Romania (Transylvania), and Italy (Trentino–Alto Adige and Trieste). All in all, the new boundaries more nearly followed the ethnic divisions of Europe than had the prewar lines.

The discussion of reparations triggered bitter exchanges at the conference. The British and the French wanted Germany to pay for the entire financial cost of the war, including the payment of veterans' pensions. On this point, Wilson made perhaps his most fateful concessions. He accepted a clause in the treaty in which Germany confessed responsibility for the war and thus took responsibility for its entire expense. The "war guilt" clause offended Germans and made for persistent bitterness that Adolf Hitler would later seize upon to launch his Nazi party movement. Wilson himself privately admitted that if he were a German he would refuse to sign the treaty.

On May 7, 1919, the victorious powers presented the treaty to the German delegates, who returned three weeks later with 443 pages of criticism. A few changes were made, but when the Germans still refused to sign, the French threatened to move their army across the Rhine River. Finally, on June 28, 1919, the Germans gave up and signed the treaty in the glittering Hall of Mirrors at Versailles. When Adolph Hitler, a young German corporal, learned of the Versailles Treaty's provisions imposed upon Germany, he seethed with anger and vowed revenge. "It cannot be that two million Germans have fallen in vain," he screamed. ". . . we demand vengeance!"

WILSON'S LOSS AT HOME   On July 8, 1919, having been in Paris for most of the year, Woodrow Wilson returned home with the Versailles Treaty amid a great clamor of popular support. A third of the state legislatures had already endorsed the League of Nations, as had thirty-three of the nation's forty-eight governors. Two days later, on July 10, Wilson called upon the Senate to accept "this great duty" and ratify the treaty that had been guided "by the hand of God." "The stage is set, the destiny disclosed," he said. Wilson then grew needlessly confrontational. He dismissed critics of his beloved League of Nations as "blind and little provincial people." The whole world, Wilson claimed, was relying on the United States to sign the Versailles Treaty: "Dare we reject it and break the heart of the world?"

Congressional leaders were ready to break the world's heart. Senator Henry Cabot Lodge, a staunch Republican with an intense dislike for Wilson, sharpened his partisan knives. He denounced the Versailles Treaty's foolish "scheme of making mankind suddenly virtuous by a statute or a written constitution." Lodge and Wilson detested each other. Wilson, thought Lodge, was too filled with prophetic certitude, too prone to promise more than he could deliver when great principles entailed great sacrifices. Lodge was keenly aware of the undercurrents already stirring up opposition to the treaty in Congress: the resentment against the treaty felt by German American, Italian American, and Irish American ethnic groups within the United States, the disappointment of liberals with Wilson's compromises on reparations and territories, the distractions of demobilization and the resulting domestic problems of converting quickly to a peacetime economy, and the revival of isolationism. Some Republicans claimed that Wilson's preoccupation with his cherished League of Nations revealed that he really wanted to be president of the world.

In the Senate a group of "irreconcilables," fourteen Republicans and two Democrats, refused to support American membership in the League of Nations on any terms. They were mainly western and midwestern progressives who feared that such sweeping foreign commitments threatened domestic reforms. The irreconcilables would be useful to Lodge's purpose, but he

EUROPE AFTER THE TREATY OF VERSAILLES, 1918

- ········ 1914 boundaries
- New nations
- Plebiscite areas
- Occupied area

Why was self-determination difficult for states in Central Europe? How did territorial concessions weaken Germany? Why might territorial changes like the creation of the Polish Corridor or the concession of the Sudetenland to Czechoslovakia have created problems that would surface in the future?

belonged to a larger group called the "reservationists," men who insisted upon limiting American participation in the League. Lodge proposed a set of amendments that addressed his reservations. The only way to get Senate approval of the treaty was for Wilson to meet with Lodge and others and agree to revisions. Republican senator James Watson of Indiana told Wilson he had no choice: "Mr. President, you are licked. There is only one way you can take the United States into the League of Nations." The president lashed back: "Lodge reservations? Never!" Wilson was temperamentally incapable of compromising with Lodge and the Republicans. He especially opposed weakening Article X of the League covenant, which provided for collective action against aggression. Wilson would not retreat, nor would he compromise. He refused to negotiate with Lodge. As the months passed, he eventually sought to make the debate over the Versailles Treaty a partisan question by promising that the coming 1920 presidential election would become a "great solemn referendum" on the issue.

By September 1919, with momentum for ratification of the Versailles Treaty slackening, Wilson decided to outflank his Senate opponents by taking the treaty issue directly to the people. On the evening of September 2, 1919, Wilson, against his doctor's orders, set forth on a grueling railroad tour through the Midwest to the West Coast. In all he traveled ten thousand miles in twenty-two days, giving thirty-two major speeches. For a while, Wilson seemed to be regaining public support, but after delivering a speech on September 25, 1919, in Pueblo, Colorado, he experienced blinding headaches and numbness that forced his return to Washington. Then, on October 2, 1919, the president suffered a severe stroke (cerebral hemorrhage) that almost killed him. The episode left the president paralyzed on his left side and an invalid for the rest of his life. Even more devastating was the effect of the stroke on his personality. Wilson after 1919 became emotionally unstable and even delusional (he would die in 1924). For seventeen months his protective wife, Edith, along with aides and trusted Cabinet members, kept him isolated from all but the most essential business. Wilson's disability intensified his stubbornness. In the face of formidable opposition in the Senate to the League of Nations section in the Versailles Treaty, he refused to compromise and was needlessly confrontational. As he scoffed to an aide, "Let Lodge compromise." The president's hardened arteries hardened his political judgment as well.

For his part, Senator Lodge pushed through the Senate fourteen changes in the draft of the Versailles Treaty, most of them having to do with the League of Nations. Wilson scoffed at the proposed changes, arguing that Lodge's revisions did not "provide for ratification but, rather, for the nullification of the treaty." As a result, Wilson's supporters in the Senate found themselves thrown into an unlikely combination with the irreconcilables, who opposed the treaty under any circumstances. The Senate vote on Lodge's revised treaty was 39 for and 55 against. On the question of approving the original treaty without reservations, irreconcilables and the so-called reservationists, led by Lodge, combined to defeat ratification again, with 38 for and 53 against. Woodrow Wilson's grand effort at global peacemaking had failed.

LURCHING FROM WAR TO PEACE

The Versailles Treaty, for all the time it spent in the Senate, was but one issue clamoring for public attention in the turbulent period after the war. The year 1919 began with ecstatic victory parades that soon gave way to widespread labor unrest, race riots, domestic terror, and government tyranny. Demobilization of the armed forces and war industries proceeded in haphazard fashion. The end of the war brought the sudden cancellation of war-related contracts that left workers and business leaders to cope with the chaotic conversion to a peacetime economy on their own. Wilson's leadership was missing. Preoccupied by the war and the League, and then bedridden by the stroke, he became grim and peevish. His administration stumbled through its last two years.

THE SPANISH FLU Amid the confusion of postwar life, many Americans confronted a virulent menace that produced far more casualties than the war itself. It became known as the **Spanish flu** (although its origins were probably in a U.S. Army camp in Kansas), and its contagion spread around the globe, transformed modern medicine, and altered the course of world history. The pandemic erupted in the spring of 1918 and lasted a year, killing as many as 100 million people worldwide, twice as many as died in the First World War. In the United States alone it accounted for 675,000 deaths, nearly seven times the number of American combat deaths in France. No disease in human history had killed so many people. Mortuaries ran out of coffins; morgues ran out of space. By the spring of 1919, the pandemic had finally run its course. It ended as suddenly—and as inexplicably—as it had begun. Although another outbreak occurred in the winter of 1920, the population had grown more resistant to its assaults. No plague, war, famine, or natural catastrophe in world history killed so many people in such a short time.

THE ECONOMIC TRANSITION Disease was only one of many challenges confronting postwar America. Consumer prices continued to rise after the war, and discontented workers, released from wartime constraints, were more willing to go out on strike for their demands. In 1919 more than 4 million workers participated in 3,600 strikes against management. Most of the workers sought nothing more than higher wages and shorter workweeks, but their critics linked them with the worldwide Communist revolution being fomented in the Soviet Union. Some workers in the East won their demands early in the year, but after a general strike in Seattle, public opinion began to turn against labor's demands. Seattle's mayor denounced the walkout of sixty thousand workers as evidence of Bolshevik influence. The strike lasted only five days, but public alarm over the affair damaged the cause of unions across the country.

The most celebrated postwar labor dispute was the Boston police strike. Though less significant than the steel strike in the numbers involved, it inadvertently launched a presidential career. On September 9, 1919, most of Boston's police force went out on strike. Massachusetts governor Calvin Coolidge was furious. He mobilized the National Guard to keep order, and after four days the police strikers offered to return, but the commissioner refused to take them back. When labor leader Samuel Gompers appealed for their reinstatement, Coolidge responded in words that suddenly turned him into a national figure: "There is no right to strike against the public safety by anybody, anywhere, any time."

RACIAL FRICTION The summer of 1919 also sparked a season of deadly race riots across the nation. As more and more African Americans, 367,000 of whom were war veterans, moved to different parts of the nation, developed successful careers, and asserted their rights in the face of deeply embedded segregationist practices, resentful whites began to display an almost hysterical racism. What the African American leader James Weldon Johnson called the Red Summer (*red* here signifying blood) began in July, when a vengeful mob of whites invaded the black section of Longview, Texas, angry over rumors of interracial dating. They

Domestic unrest

A victim of racial rioting in Chicago, July 1919.

burned shops and houses and ran several African Americans out of town. A week later in Washington, D.C., often false or exaggerated reports of black assaults on white women aroused white mobs, and for four days gangs of white and black rioters waged a race war in the streets until soldiers and driving rains ended the fighting. These were but preliminaries to the Chicago riot of late July, in which 38 people were killed and 537 injured. The climactic disorders of the summer occurred in the rural area around Elaine, Arkansas, where African American tenant farmers tried to organize a union. According to official reports, 5 whites and 25 blacks died in the rioting, but the death toll may have actually included more than 100 blacks. Altogether, twenty-five race riots erupted in 1919, and there were eighty racial lynchings.

THE RED SCARE   Reactions to the wave of labor strikes and race riots reflected the impact of the Bolshevik Revolution in Russia. Some radicals thought America's domestic turbulence was the first scene in a drama of world revolution. Many Americans decided that they might be right. After all, a tiny faction in Russia, the Bolsheviks, had exploited confusion to impose its totalitarian will over a huge nation. In 1919, left-wing members of the Socialist party formed the Communist party (U.S.A.) and the short-lived Communist Labor party. Wartime hysteria against all things German was readily transformed into a postwar Red Scare against all Communists.

Fears of revolution in America were fueled by the actions of scattered militants. In April 1919 the post office intercepted nearly forty homemade mail bombs addressed to prominent citizens. One slipped through and blew off the hands of a Georgia senator's maid. In June another bomb destroyed the front of Attorney General **A. Mitchell Palmer**'s house in Washington, D.C. The explosion killed the terrorist and almost killed Palmer. Although the bombings were probably the work of a small group of Italian anarchists, the attorney general and many other Americans concluded that a Communist "blaze of revolution" was "sweeping over every American institution of law and order."

On November 7, 1919, while President Wilson lay incapacitated in the White House, federal agents rounded up 450 alien "radicals," most of whom were simply recent Russian immigrants looking for work. All were deported to Russia without a court hearing. On January 2, 1920, police raids in dozens of cities swept up 5,000 more suspects, many taken from their homes without arrest warrants. What came to be called the **First Red Scare** (followed by a similar outbreak of anti-communist hysteria during the 1950s) represented the largest violation of civil liberties in American history, but the panic subsided within a few months. By the summer of 1920, the Red Scare had begun to evaporate. Bombings in the United States tapered off; the wave of strikes and race riots receded. By September 1920, when a bomb explosion at the corner of Broad and Wall Streets in New York City killed thirty-eight people, Americans were ready to take it for what it was: the work of a crazed mind and not the start of a revolution. The Red Scare nonetheless left a lasting mark on American life. It bolstered the continuing crusade for "100 percent Americanism" and restrictions on immigration.

Despite the extraordinary turbulence in the immediate aftermath of the First World War, there was little doubt that the First World War had changed the trajectory of modern history. The Great War had destroyed old Europe, but peace did not bring stability. Most Germans and Austrians felt that they were the victims of a harsh, vindictive peace forced upon them by the victors. The Bolshevik Revolution caused Russia to abandon its western European allies and drop out of the war. Thereafter, Soviet communism would be one of the most powerful new forces shaping twentieth century. The new nations created at Versailles out of the defeated empires—Estonia, Latvia, Lithuania, Czechoslovakia, Finland, and Poland—were poor, unstable, insecure, and resentful of their neighbors. There was no real stability in Europe after the war, just an interlude born of exhaustion. The war wreaked havoc on trade relationships and bankrupted national treasuries. Such festering vengefulness among the vanquished would interact with widespread economic, social, and political instability throughout Europe to help spawn fascism in Italy, Austria, and Germany during the 1920s. America was a different story. For the first time in its history, the United States had decisively intervened in a major European war. And now, in the war's aftermath, the United States had emerged largely unscathed physically, and American capitalists were eager to fill the vacuum created by the wartime destruction of the European economies. What came to be called the "American Century" was at hand—for better or worse.

End of Chapter Review

CHAPTER SUMMARY

- **Wilson and Mexico** Woodrow Wilson wanted to foster democratic governments in Latin America; he got the United States involved in Mexican politics after Mexico experienced several military coups. The popular Francisco Pancho Villa tried to gain power in Mexico by promoting an anti-American program, even making raids across the border into New Mexico.

- **Causes of WWI** Europe had developed a system of alliances that divided the continent in two. Democratic Britain and France, along with the Russian Empire, had formed the Triple Entente. Central Powers were comprised of the new German Empire, Austria-Hungary, and Italy. The assassination of the heir to the Austro-Hungarian throne by a Serbian nationalist triggered the world war in August 1914.

- **U.S. Enters WWI** Most Americans supported the Triple Entente, or Allied Powers, at the outbreak of World War I. The Wilson administration declared the nation neutral but allowed businesses to extend credit to the Allies to purchase food and military supplies. Americans were outraged by the Germans' use of unlimited submarine warfare, especially after the 1915 sinking of the British liner *Lusitania*. In 1917 unrestricted submarine activity and the revelation of the Zimmermann telegram, in which the Germans sought to incite the Mexicans to wage war against the United States, led the United States to enter the Great War.

- **Wilson's Peace Plan** Wilson insisted that the United States wanted no selfish gains from the war, only a new, democratic Europe to emerge from the old empires. His famous Fourteen Points speech outlined his ideas for the establishment of continent-wide democratic nation-states and a league of nations.

- **Treaty of Versailles** The United States did not ratify the Treaty of Versailles because Wilson had alienated the Republican senators whose support he needed for ratification. A coalition of "irreconcilables" formed in the Senate: midwestern and western progressives who feared that involvement in a league of nations would stifle domestic reforms and that ratification would necessitate involvement in future wars. The irreconcilables were joined by "reservationists," who would accept the treaty with certain limitations on America's involvement in the League of Nations. Wilson's illness and his refusal to compromise ensured failure of ratification.

- **Consequences of WWI** As a result of the war, four European empires were dismantled, replaced by smaller nation-states. The reparations imposed on Germany and the "war guilt" clause laid the foundations for German bitterness. The presence of a Communist regime in the old Russian Empire had major consequences in America.

CHRONOLOGY

1914	United States intervenes in Mexico
1914	World War I begins in Europe
1915	British liner *Lusitania*, with Americans aboard, is torpedoed without warning by a German submarine
1916	Congress passes the National Defense Act
March 1917	Zimmermann telegram reveals that Germany is attempting to incite Mexico to enter the war against the United States
April 1917	United States enters the Great War
January 1918	Woodrow Wilson delivers his Fourteen Points speech
November 11, 1918	Representatives of warring nations sign armistice
1919	Supreme Court issues *Schenck v. United States* decision
May 1919	Treaty of Versailles is presented to the Germans
1919	Race riots break out in Chicago
1919	U.S. attorney general launches Red Scare
July 1921	Joint resolution of Congress officially ends the war among the United States, Germany, and Austria-Hungary

KEY TERMS & NAMES

25

THE MODERN TEMPER

FOCUS QUESTIONS wwnorton.com/studyspace

- What accounted for the nativism of the 1920s?
- What was meant by the Jazz Age?
- How did the new social trends of the 1920s challenge traditional attitudes?
- What was modernism, and how did it influence American culture?

All historical eras exhibit contradictions, but the 1920s were a decade of especially sharp extremes. The ten years between 1919 and the onset the Great Depression at the end of 1929 encompassed a period of unprecedented economic prosperity and cultural experimentation as well as political conservatism and religious fundamentalism. Having experienced the constraints of wartime, many Americans feverishly pursued personal pleasures. The new and unusual clashed openly with the conventional and the commonplace. Modernists and traditionalists waged cultural warfare with one another, one group looking to the future for inspiration and the other looking to the past for guidance. Terrorist attacks increased, as did labor and racial violence. Benton MacKaye, a leading environmentalist, said that America during the 1920s was the most "volcanic of any area on earth." The nation was roiling with change and conflict, and he predicted a period of "deep domestic strife."

The scope and pace of societal changes were bewildering. At long last, women were allowed to vote; meanwhile, beer and liquor were outlawed. Innovations such as national radio networks, talking motion pictures, mass ownership of automobiles, the emergence of national chain stores, the soaring popularity of spectator sports, and the rise of mass marketing and advertising transformed America into the world's leading consumer society. The culture of mass consumption fueled the explosive growth of middle-class urban life. The 1920 census revealed that for the first time more Americans lived in cities than in rural areas. The popularity of the consumer culture also assaulted traditional virtues such as frugality, prudence, and religiosity.

In the political arena reactionaries and rebels battled for control of a postwar society roiling in conflict. The brutal fight between Woodrow Wilson and the Republican-led Senate over the Versailles Treaty, coupled with the administration's savage crackdown on dissenters and socialists, had weakened an already fragmented and disillusioned progressive movement. As the tireless reformer Amos Pinchot bitterly observed, President Wilson had "put his enemies in office and his friends in jail." By 1920 many alienated progressives had grown skeptical of any politician claiming to be a reformer or an idealist. The prominent social reformer Jane Addams sighed that the 1920s were "a period of political and social sag."

At the same time, the postwar wave of strikes, bombings, anti-Communist hysteria, and race riots symbolized a frightening new era of turmoil that led many people to cling to old ideas and ways of life. Traditionalists, many of them from rural areas, were especially disturbed by urban political radicalism and carefree urbane ways of life. Those who believed in the "old-time religion" were dismayed by the inroads of secular materialism. It was just such a reversion to traditional values that led voters to elect Republican Warren G. Harding president in 1920. He promised to return America to "normalcy."

Mainstream Americans were also shocked by the new "modernist" forms of artistic expression and sexual liberation. Novelist F. Scott Fitzgerald wrote in *This Side of Paradise* (1920) that the younger generation of Americans, the "sad young men" who had fought in Europe to "make the world safe for democracy" had "grown up to find all Gods dead, all wars fought, all faiths in man shaken." Cynicism had displaced idealism for those alienated by the horrible war and the failed peace. As Fitzgerald asserted, "There's only one lesson to be learned from life anyway. . . . That there's no lesson to be learned from life." Fitzgerald and other self-conscious modernists were labeled a "lost generation" in the sense that many of them had lost faith in many of the values and institutions of Western civilization and were frantically looking for new gods. As Frederic Henry, a character in Ernest Hemingway's novel *A Farewell to Arms* (1929) declares, "Abstract words such as glory, honor, courage, or hallow were obscene" in the context of the colossal casualties caused by the war. Many of the modernists celebrated emotion over reason, change and "newness" over stability and tradition, youthful liberation and excesses over maturity, responsibility, and sobriety.

In sum, postwar life in America and Europe was fraught with turbulent changes, contradictory impulses, superficial frivolity, and seething tensions. As the French painter Paul Gauguin acknowledged, the upheavals of cultural modernism and the aftermath of the war produced "an epoch of confusion," a riotous clash of irreverent new ideas and enthusiasms with traditional manners and morals.

THE REACTIONARY TWENTIES

Many traditionalists were aghast at the social turmoil of 1919. They located the germs of dangerous radicalism in the multiethnic cities teeming with immigrants and foreign ideas such as socialism, communism, and anarchism. The reactionary conservatism of the 1920s fed on the growing popularity of nativism, Anglo-Saxon racism, and militant Protestantism.

NATIVISM   The Red Scare of 1919 helped generate a surge of anti-immigrant hysteria called **nativism**. The foreign connections of so many political radicals convinced many people that the troublemakers in the postwar era were foreign-born. The flow of immigrants, slowed by the war, rose again at its end. From June 1920 to June 1921, more than eight hundred thousand people emigrated to the United States, 65 percent of them from southern and eastern Europe. Many more were on the way. In the early 1920s over half of the white men and a third of the white women working in industry were immigrants, most of them from central or eastern Europe. That socialism and anarchism were popular in those regions made immigrant workers especially suspect in the eyes of many Americans concerned about the "foreign invasion."

SACCO AND VANZETTI   The most celebrated criminal case of the 1920s seemed to prove the connection between immigrants and radicalism. It involved two working-class Italian immigrants who described themselves as revolutionary anarchists: shoemaker **Nicola Sacco** and fish peddler **Bartolomeo Vanzetti**. On May 5, 1920, they were arrested outside Boston, Massachusetts, for stealing $16,000 from a shoe factory and killing the paymaster and a guard. Both were armed when arrested, both lied to police about their activities, and both were identified by eyewitnesses. But the stolen money was never found. The Sacco and Vanzetti case occurred at the height of Italian immigration to the United States and against the backdrop of numerous terror attacks by anarchists. It was amid such a charged atmosphere that the criminal case of Sacco and Vanzetti became a huge public spectacle. The judge who presided over the 1921 trial was openly prejudicial, referring to the defendants as "anarchist bastards." Sacco and Vanzetti were convicted and ordered executed, but appeals of the verdict lasted seven years. People then and since claimed that Sacco and Vanzetti were sentenced for their political ideas and ethnic origin rather than for any crime they had committed. But despite public demonstrations around the world on behalf of the two men, the evidence convicting them was compelling; after seven years of legal wrangling, political battles, and international protests, they were executed on August 23, 1927. After thanking the warden for his kindness, Vanzetti said, "I wish to forgive some people for what they are now doing to me."

IMMIGRATION RESTRICTION   Concerns about foreign radicals invading the United States generated new efforts to restrict immigration. An alarmed Congress passed the Emergency Immigration Act of 1921, which restricted European arrivals each year to 3 percent of the total number of each nationality represented in the 1910 census. The Immigration Act of 1924 reduced the number to 2 percent based on the 1890 census, which included fewer of the "new" immigrants from southern and eastern Europe. This law set a permanent limitation, which became effective in 1929, of slightly over 150,000 new arrivals per year based on the "national origins" of the U.S. population as of 1920. The purpose of the new quotas was clear: to tilt the balance in favor of immigrants from northern and western Europe, who were assigned about 85 percent of the total. The law completely excluded people from east Asia—a gratuitous insult to the Japanese, who were already kept out of the United States by their Gentlemen's Agreement with Theodore Roosevelt.

On the other hand, the Immigration Act of 1924 left the gate open to new arrivals from countries in the Western Hemisphere, so that an ironic consequence of the new law was a substantial increase in the Hispanic Catholic population of the United States. Legal arrivals from Mexico peaked at 89,000 in 1924. Lower figures after that date reflect the Mexican government's policies of clamping down on the outflow. Waves of illegal immigrants continued to flow across the border, however, in response to southwestern agriculture's demand for "stoop" labor. People of Latin American descent (chiefly Mexicans, Puerto Ricans, and Cubans) became the fastest-growing ethnic minority in the country.

THE KLAN   During the postwar years nativist prejudice against "foreigners" took on a new form: a revived, nationwide **Ku Klux Klan** modeled on

Klan rally

In 1925 the Ku Klux Klan staged a huge parade down Pennsylvania Avenue in Washington, D.C.

the white vigilante group founded to oppose Reconstruction in the post–Civil War South. The new Klan was devoted to "100 percent Americanism" and restricted its membership to militant white Protestants born in the United States. It was determined to protect its warped notion of the American way of life not only from African Americans but also from Roman Catholics, Jews, and immigrants. The United States was no melting pot, the twentieth-century Klan's founder, William J. Simmons, warned: "It is a garbage can! . . . When the hordes of aliens walk to the ballot box and their votes outnumber yours, then that alien horde has got you by the throat."

The revived Klan's appeal to bigotry extended well beyond the states of the former Confederacy: it thrived in small towns and cities in the North and especially in the Midwest, with major strongholds in Oregon and on Long Island, New York. The Klan was a vicious reaction to shifting moral standards and social status, the declining influence of churches, and the broad-mindedness of city dwellers and college students. As a prominent southern journalist observed, the new Klan attracted "respectable" members of communities. The South "swarmed with little businessmen . . . the rural clergy belonged to it [the Klan] or had traffic with it *en masse*." The Klan was "anti-Negro, anti-alien, anti-red, anti-Catholic, anti-Jew, anti-Darwin, anti-Modern, anti-Liberal, Fundamentalist, vastly Moral, militantly Protestant." In the mid-1920s the Klan's peak membership may have been as high as 4 million, but its influence evaporated after passage of the punitive 1924 immigration law. By 1930, Klan membership had dwindled to 100,000, mostly southerners. Yet the deep strain of bigotry and intolerance underlying the Klan lived on, fed by primal fears and hatreds that have yet to disappear.

FUNDAMENTALISM   While the Klan saw a threat mainly in the "alien menace," many adherents of the old-time religion saw secular threats emerging in many churches: new "liberal" ideas held that the Bible should be studied in the light of modern scholarship (the "higher criticism") or that it could be reconciled with biological theories of evolution. Such "modern" notions surfaced in schools and even pulpits. In resisting the inroads of secularism, orthodox Christians embraced a militant new **fundamentalism**, which was distinguished less by a faith that many others shared than by a posture of hostility toward any other belief.

Among rural fundamentalist leaders only former secretary of state and three-time presidential candidate William Jennings Bryan had the following, prestige, and eloquence to make the movement a popular crusade. The aging Bryan continued to espouse a colorful blend of progressive populism and religious fundamentalism. In 1921, he promoted state laws to prohibit the teaching of evolution in the public schools. He denounced the evolutionary theory of Charles Darwin with the same zeal he had once used in opposing Republican William McKinley. Anti-evolution bills emerged in legislatures, but the only victories came in the South—and there were few of those. Some officials took direct action without legislation. Governor Miriam "Ma" Ferguson of Texas outlawed textbooks upholding Darwinism. "I am a Christian mother," she declared, "and I am not going to let that kind of rot go into Texas schoolbooks."

DARWINISM ON TRIAL   The dramatic climax came in Tennessee, where in 1925 the state legislature passed a bill outlawing the teaching of evolution in public schools and colleges. In the tiny foothills town of Dayton, in eastern Tennessee, citizens eager to benefit from a burst of publicity persuaded a twenty-four-year-old high-school science teacher and part-time football coach, John T. Scopes, to accept an offer from the American Civil Liberties Union (ACLU) to defend a test case against the state's new "anti-evolution" law. They succeeded beyond their wildest hopes: the publicity was worldwide and enduring—but not all flattering.

Before the opening of the twelve-day "monkey trial" on July 10, 1925, the streets of Dayton swarmed with publicity hounds, curiosity seekers, evangelists, atheists, hot-dog and soda-pop hucksters, hundreds of reporters, and national radio coverage. The two stars of the show were both showmen who loved a big payday: William Jennings Bryan, who had offered his services to the prosecution, and Chicagoan Clarence Darrow, the nation's most famous trial lawyer. Darrow, who had supported Bryan's 1896 presidential candidacy, was a fierce defender of the rights of the working class and organized labor, leading one journalist to call him the "attorney for the damned." When Darrow learned that Bryan would be aiding the state attorneys, he volunteered his services—for free—to the ACLU attorneys defending John T. Scopes. Darrow had spent much of his career attacking religious intolerance. Bryan, however, was not intimidated by Darrow's arrival in Dayton. "Darrow is an atheist," he charged, while "I'm an upholder of Christianity. That's the difference between us." Bryan told the media that the trial was not about Scopes but about a state's right to determine what was taught in the public schools. He also raised the stakes when he announced that the "contest between evolution and Christianity is a duel to the death." Darrow countered: "Scopes is not on trial. Civilization is on trial. Nothing will satisfy us but broad victory." Darrow was determined to prove "that America is founded on liberty and not on narrow, mean, intolerable and brainless prejudice of soulless religio-maniacs."

On July 20, the defense called Bryan as an "expert" witness on biblical interpretation (Mencken described him as a "fundamentalist pope"). Darrow

Courtroom scene during the Scopes trial

The media, food vendors, and others flocked to Dayton, Tennessee, for the case against John T. Scopes, the teacher who taught evolution.

treated Bryan as a hostile witness, barraging him with sharp questions about inconsistencies and fables in the Bible. In a heated exchange with Darrow, Bryan repeatedly trapped himself in literal-minded interpretations (Jonah was swallowed by a whale, Joshua made the sun stand still, the earth was created in six days, etc.) and revealed his ignorance of biblical history and scholarship. Bryan gradually conceded that he had never thought through the possibility that many of the Bible's stories conflicted with common sense and basic scientific truths. At one point the agnostic Darrow, who had spent much of his career ridiculing religious fundamentalists, declared that Bryan was "not competent." Bryan lashed back, charging that Darrow was putting "revealed religion" on trial. "I am here to defend it." He claimed that Darrow was insulting Christians. Darrow, his thumbs clasping his colorful suspenders, shot back: "You insult every man of science and learning in the world because he does not believe in your fool religion." It was a bitter scene. At one point, Darrow and Bryan, their patience exhausted in the broiling summer heat, lunged at each other, shaking their fists, prompting the judge to adjourn court. Darrow claimed victory. His goal was to "show the country what an ignoramus Bryan was, and I succeeded."

The next day, as the trial ended, the judge ruled that the only issue before the jury was whether Scopes had taught evolution, and no one had denied that he had. He was found guilty, but the Tennessee Supreme Court, while upholding the state's anti-evolution statute, overruled the $100 fine on a technicality. Both sides were justified in claiming victory. With more accuracy than he intended, Bryan described the trial as a "duel to the death." Five days after it closed, he died of a heart condition aggravated by heat and fatigue. During the next two years, Mississippi, Texas, and other mostly southern states followed the lead of Tennessee in passing laws barring the teaching of evolution. The Scopes trial did not end the uncivil war between evolutionists and fundamentalists. It continues to this day.

PROHIBITION   William Jennings Bryan died knowing that one of his other crusades had succeeded: alcoholic beverages had been outlawed. The movement to prohibit beer, wine, and liquor offered another example of reforming zeal channeled into a drive for moral righteousness and social conformity. Around 1900, the nation's leading temperance organizations, the Women's Christian Temperance Union (WCTU) and the Anti-Saloon League, had launched a campaign for a national prohibition law. By the 1910s the Anti-Saloon League had become one of the most effective pressure groups in history, mobilizing Protestant churches behind its single-minded battle to elect "dry" candidates to local, state, and national offices.

At its Jubilee Convention in 1913, the league endorsed a prohibition amendment to the Constitution. The 1916 elections finally produced enough members in both houses of Congress to pass legislation outlawing alcoholic beverages. Soon the wartime spirit of sacrifice, the need to use grain for food rather than for booze, and wartime hostility to German-American brewers transformed the cause of prohibition into a virtual test of patriotism. On December 18, 1917, the wartime Congress sent to the states the Eighteenth Amendment, which on January 16, 1920, one year after ratification, banned the manufacture, sale, and transportation of intoxicating liquors.

Prohibition was the most ambitious social reform ever attempted in the United States. But it proved to be a colossal failure. The new amendment did not suddenly persuade people to stop drinking. Instead, it motivated millions of people to use ingenious—and illegal—ways to satisfy their thirst for alcohol. The Volstead Act (1919), which outlined the actual rules and regulations triggered by the Eighteenth Amendment, had so many loopholes that it virtually guaranteed failure. Individuals and organizations were allowed to keep and drink any liquor owned on January 16, 1919. Not surprisingly, people stocked up before then. The Yale Club in Manhattan, for example, stored enough liquor to subsist for the fourteen years that Prohibition was enforced. Farmers were still allowed to "preserve" their fruits through the process of fermenting them, which resulted in barns stockpiled with "hard cider" and homemade wine. So-called medicinal liquor was also still allowed, which meant that physicians (and even veterinarians) grew tired writing numerous prescriptions for "medicinal" brands such as Old Grand-Dad and Jim Beam whiskies.

An even greater weakness of the new Prohibition law was that Congress never supplied adequate funding to enforce it. In 1920 there were only 1,520 Prohibition agents spread across the United States. Given the perennial public thirst for booze, the spotty support for Prohibition among local officials, and the profits to be made in making illegal booze, called bootlegging, it would have taken armies of enforcement agents to police the nation. The mayor of New York City said that it would take 250,000 policemen to enforce the new amendment in his city alone. Nor did the Republican presidents during the 1920s embrace the "fanaticism" over temperance. Warren G. Harding, who regularly consumed bootleg liquor in the White House, said he was "unable to see this as a great moral issue." In working-class and ethnic-rich Detroit the bootleg liquor industry during the Prohibition era was second in size only to the auto industry. New York City's police commissioner estimated that there were 32,000 illegal bars ("speakeasies") in the

Prohibition

A 1926 police raid on a speakeasy, where illegal "bootleg" liquor was sold.

city during Prohibition. In Washington, D.C., the largest bootlegger reported that "a majority of both houses" of Congress were regular customers of his products. As the popular humorist Will Rogers quipped, "Prohibition is better than no liquor at all." What Congress did not count on was the staggering amount of liquor tax revenue that the federal treasury lost by outlawing alcohol.

It would be too much to say that Prohibition gave rise to organized crime, but it supplied criminals with a source of enormous new income while the automobile and the submachine gun provided criminals greater mobility and firepower. Organized crime leaders showed remarkable gifts for exploiting loopholes in the law when they did not simply bribe policemen and politicians. Well-organized crime syndicates behaved like giant corporations; they controlled the entire stream of liquor's production, pricing, and distribution. The result: Prohibition witnessed a fourteen-year-orgy of criminal activity unparalleled in history.

The most celebrated Prohibition-era gangster was **"Scarface" Al Capone.** Born in 1899 and raised in New York City, where he was connected to two murders before he reached the age of twenty, he left for Chicago in 1920. There he thuggishly seized control of the huge illegal liquor business in the city. In 1927 his Chicago-based bootlegging, prostitution, and gambling empire brought him an income of $60 million, which he flaunted with expensive suits and silk pajamas, a custom-upholstered bulletproof Cadillac, a platoon of bodyguards, and lavish support for city charities. Capone insisted that he was merely providing the public with the goods and services it demanded: "They say I violate the prohibition law. Who doesn't?" He neglected to say that he had also bludgeoned to death several police lieutenants and ordered the execution of dozens of rival criminals. Dedicated law-enforcement officials led by Federal Bureau of Investigation agent Eliot Ness began to smash his bootlegging operations in 1929, but they were unable to pin anything on Capone until a Treasury agent infiltrated his gang and uncovered evidence that nailed him for federal tax evasion. Tried in 1931, Capone was sentenced to eleven years in prison.

THE "JAZZ AGE" DURING THE "ROARING TWENTIES"

In many ways the reactionary temper of the 1920s and the repressive movements it spawned arose as reactions to a much publicized social and intellectual revolution that threatened to rip America from its old moorings. As described by various labels given to the times, most of them exaggerations, it was an era of excess, the Jazz Age, and the **Roaring Twenties**. During those years a cosmopolitan urban America confronted an insular, rural America, and cultural conflict reached new levels of tension. F. Scott Fitzgerald dubbed the postwar era the Jazz Age in 1922 not because he himself liked jazz music but because his circle of daring young people in the cities was, like a jazz musician, intoxicated with nervous energy. Unlike so many Americans of his age and wealth, Fitzgerald celebrated the era's spontaneity and sensual vitality.

THE NEW WOMAN AND THE NEW MORALITY Much of the shock to old-timers during the Jazz Age came from the revolution in manners and morals, evidenced first among young people, and especially on college campuses. In *This Side of Paradise* (1920), a novel of student life at Princeton University, F. Scott Fitzgerald wrote of "the great current American phenomenon, the 'petting party.'" Prudish mothers, he said, had no "idea how casually their daughters were accustomed to be kissed." From such novels and from scores of magazine articles, the heartland learned about the wild parties, bathtub gin, promiscuity, speakeasies, "shimmy dancers," and new uses to which automobiles were put on secluded lovers' lanes.

Sex came to be discussed with a new frankness during the 1920s. Much of the talk derived from a spreading awareness of Dr. **Sigmund Freud**, the Viennese father of psychoanalysis. When in 1909 Freud visited Clark University in Massachusetts, he was surprised to find himself so well known "even in prudish America." By the 1920s, his ideas had begun to percolate among the general public, and books and magazines discussed libido, inhibitions, Oedipus complexes, and repression. Some of the decade's most popular magazines were those that focused on romance and sex: *True Confessions, Telling Tales,* and *True Story.* Their story titles revealed their themes: "The Primitive Lover" ("She wanted a caveman husband"), "Indolent Kisses," and "Innocents Astray." Likewise, the most popular female movie stars—Madge Bellamy, Clara Bow, and Joan Crawford—projected an image of sensual freedom, energy, and independence. Advertisements for new movies reinforced the self-indulgent images of the Jazz Age: "brilliant men, beautiful jazz babies, champagne baths, midnight revels, petting parties in the purple dawn, all ending in one terrific climax that makes you gasp." Traditionalists were shocked at the behavior of rebellious young women. "One hears it said," lamented a Baptist magazine, "that the girls are actually tempting the boys more than the boys do the girls, by their dress and conversation."

Fashion also reflected the rebellion against prudishness and a loosening of inhibitions. The emancipated "new woman" in the 1920s was supposedly "independent, bright-eyed, alert, and alive," a young woman eager to gain new freedoms. This "new woman" eagerly discarded the constraining fashions of the nineteenth century—pinched-in corsets, confining petticoats, and floor-length dresses. In 1919 women's skirts were typically six inches above the ground; by 1927 they were at the knee, and the "flapper" was providing a shocking model of the new feminism. The name derived from the way fashionable young women allowed their unbuckled galoshes to "flap" around their ankles.

The "new woman" of the 1920s

Two flappers dance atop the Hotel Sherman in Chicago, 1926.

Flapper fashion featured bobbed hair, minimal undergarments, gauzy fabrics, and sheer stockings. Cigarettes, booze, makeup, and jazz dancing were necessary accessories.

F. Scott Fitzgerald said the ideal flapper was "lovely and expensive and about nineteen." Conservative moralists saw the flappers as just another sign of a degenerating society. A Catholic priest in Brooklyn lamented that the feminism emerging in the 1920s had provoked a "pandemonium of powder, a riot of rouge, and a moral anarchy of dress." Others saw in the "new women" an expression of American individualism. "By sheer force of violence," explained the *New York Times* in 1929, the flapper has "established the feminine right to equal representation in such hitherto masculine fields of endeavor as smoking and drinking, swearing, petting, and upsetting the community peace." For the most part, the college-educated "flappers" were indifferent to the legacy of progressive social reform or women's rights. Their priorities were courtship, marriage, and consumerism. Older social reformers regretted the changed priorities. Charlotte Perkins Gilman, a prominent writer and feminist, lamented in 1923 the "lowering in the standards in sex relations" among young Americans. Their cavalier use of birth control devices struck her as "selfish and fruitless indulgence." The emphasis on premarital sex, she said, illustrated the "lamentable behavior of our times." Jane Addams agreed, noting that the younger generation of Americans seemed self-absorbed. They lacked "reforming energy."

Most women in the 1920s were not flappers, however. Although many women were recruited during the war to take jobs vacated by men serving in the military, most of them were forced to give up those jobs once the war ended. True, more middle-class women attended college in the 1920s than ever before, but a higher percentage of them married after graduation than had been the case in the nineteenth century. Only 4 percent of working women in the 1920s were salaried professionals; the vast majority worked for wages. A student at all-female Smith College expressed frustration at the prevailing view that college-educated women were still expected to pursue marriage and motherhood: "We cannot believe that it is fixed in the nature of things that a woman must choose between a home and her work, when a man may have both. There must be a way out, and it is the problem of our generation to find the way."

Some women moved into new vocations created by the burgeoning consumer culture (two-thirds of purchases each year were made by women shoppers) such as accounting assistants and department store clerks. The sales of cosmetics and the number of beauty shops soared from five thousand in 1920 to forty thousand in 1930, thereby creating new jobs for hair stylists, manicurists, and cosmeticians. But the majority of women remained anchored in the domestic sphere, either as full-time wives and mothers or as household servants. African-American and Mexican-American women faced the greatest challenges. As a New York City newspaper observed, they were forced to do "work which white women will not do." Women of color usually worked as maids, laundresses, and seamstresses or on farms.

In addition to sexism, racism also continued to limit the freedom of women during the twenties. For example, in 1919, an interracial couple from Ayer, Massachusetts, Mabel Puffer, a wealthy college graduate, and Arthur Hazzard, a handyman and leader within the local black community, decided to get married in Concord, New Hampshire. They checked into separate rooms in a hotel, then met in the lobby and walked three blocks to the courthouse to apply for a marriage license, only to be told that there was a five-day waiting period. So they waited and made preparations for the wedding. The mayor of Concord agreed to perform the service, and Hazzard's siblings and mother made plans to attend. Others were not as supportive, however. News of the interracial couple strolling the streets of Concord reached the Boston newspapers. The first story's headline, in the *Boston Traveller*, read: "Will Marry Negro in 'Perfect Union': Rich Ayer Society Woman Determined to Wed Servant Although Hometown is Aflame with Protest." The news had outraged many residents of Ayer. The next day, the *Boston Evening Globe* ran the now-provocative story on its front page. The headline was sensational: "Hope to Prevent White Woman Wedding Negro: Two Friends of Mabel E. Puffer Have Gone to Concord, N.H." Puffer's friends and relatives rushed to Concord and began exerting pressure on her and the townspeople. Suddenly, the mayor reversed himself and announced he could not perform the wedding, claiming he was called out of town on important business. The betrothed couple, after being turned down several times, finally found a minister willing to marry them. The night before the wedding was to occur, however, the Ayer police chief arrived, arrested Hazzard on charge of "enticement," and took Puffer into custody because she had been deemed "insane" for having decided to marry a working-class African American. In reporting the dramatic story, the Concord newspaper concluded that the community "gazed after their departing dust with no regrets." The nation that Woodrow Wilson had led into World War I to "make the world safe for democracy" remained a very unsafe place for those crossing the color line.

THE "NEW NEGRO" The most significant development in African American life during the early twentieth century was the **Great Migration** northward from the South. The movement of blacks to the North began in

1915–1916, when rapidly expanding war industries and restrictions on immigration together created a labor shortage; legal restrictions on immigration continued the movement in the 1920s. Altogether between 1910 and 1920 the Southeast lost some 323,000 African Americans, or 5 percent of the native black population, and by 1930 it had lost another 615,000, or 8 percent of the native black population in 1920. With the migration, a slow but steady growth in black political influence in northern cities set in. African Americans were freer to speak and act in a northern setting; they also gained political leverage by settling in large cities in states with many electoral votes.

Along with political activity came a bristling spirit of protest, a spirit that received cultural expression in what came to be called the **Harlem Renaissance**, the nation's first self-conscious black literary and artistic movement. The Harlem Renaissance grew out of the fast-growing African-American community in New York City. In 1890, one in seventy people in Manhattan was African American; by 1930 it was one in nine. The "great, dark city" of Harlem, in poet Langston Hughes's phrase, contained more blacks per square mile than any other community in the nation. The dense concentration of urban blacks generated a sense of common identity, growing power, and cultural self-expression. Writer James Weldon Johnson described a "Black Manhattan" emerging in Harlem during the 1920s. Harlem, he wrote, was a "typically Negro" community of 175,000 in that it featured "movement, color, gaiety, singing, dancing, boisterous laughter, and loud talk."

The Harlem Renaissance was the self-conscious effort in the New York black community to cultivate racial equality by promoting African American cultural achievements. In 1924 blacks organized a banquet in Harlem to introduce the white-dominated publishing industry to African American writers. Howard University professor Alain Locke, a Harvard graduate and the nation's first black Rhodes Scholar, was the event's emcee, and he became the leader of the **New Negro** movement, an effort to promote racial equality by celebrating the cultural contributions of African Americans. In 1925, at Locke's behest, *Survey Graphic* magazine devoted its March issue ("Harlem: Mecca of the New Negro") to showcasing promising young black writers. In this sense, the writers of the Harlem Renaissance intentionally differentiated themselves from the alienated white writers making up what was called the "lost generation." They were the "found generation." James Weldon Johnson predicted that Harlem would become the "intellectual, cultural, and financial center for Negroes of the United States, and will exert a vital influence upon all Negro peoples." Johnson noted that "a people that has produced great art and literature has never been looked upon as inferior."

The writers associated with the Harlem Renaissance audaciously celebrated themselves, their black heritage, and their contemporary contributions to American culture, including jazz and the blues. As the poet Langston Hughes wrote, "I am a Negro—and beautiful. . . . The night is beautiful. So the faces of my people." Perhaps the greatest single literary creation of the time was Jean Toomer's novel *Cane* (1923), which pictured the lives both of simple rural folk in Georgia's black belt and the sophisticated African American middle class in Washington, D.C. Other writers making up the Harlem Renaissance included Zora Neale Hurston, Countee Cullen, Nella Larsen, and Claude McKay. The

"Into Bondage"

This painting by Aaron Douglas exemplifies how black artists in the Harlem Renaissance used their African roots and collective history as artistic inspiration.

Harlem group also promoted a racially integrated society. James Weldon Johnson coined the term "Aframerican" to combine "African American." He did so in order to emphasize that blacks were no longer divided by their heritage; they were Americans who happened to have an African ancestry. Blacks were not interlopers or "foundlings," in Locke's term, but "conscious collaborators" in the creation of American society and culture.

Alain Locke spoke for other leaders of the Harlem Renaissance by urging his literary and artistic friends to celebrate their African heritage and draw upon African art for their inspiration. Others disagreed. Langston Hughes stressed that he was an "American Negro." He "loved the surface of Africa and the rhythms of Africa—but I was not Africa. I was Chicago and Kansas City and Broadway and Harlem." The black sculptor Augusta Savage agreed. She explained that African Americans for three centuries had shared the "same cultural background, the same system, the same standard of beauty as white Americans. . . . It is impossible to go back to primitive [African] art for our models."

Frankie "Half Pint" Jackson and his band at the Sunset Cafe, Chicago, in the 1920s

Jazz emerged in the 1920s as an especially American expression of the modernist spirit. African American artists bent musical conventions to give fuller rein to improvisation and sensuality.

THE BIRTH OF JAZZ   F. Scott Fitzgerald fastened upon the "**Jazz Age**" as a label for the broad spirit of rebellion and spontaneity he saw welling up among young Americans during the 1920s. The new jazz music had first emerged in New Orleans as an ingenious synthesis of black rural folk traditions and urban dance entertainment. During the 1920s it spread to Kansas City, Memphis, the Harlem neighborhood of New York City, and Chicago's South Side. African American Louis Armstrong, an inspired trumpeter, was the Pied Piper of jazz. Born in a New Orleans shack in 1900, he grew up drenched in jazz music. In 1922 Armstrong moved to Chicago with King Oliver's Creole Jazz Band. Thereafter, he delighted audiences with his passionate performances. "The guys never heard anything like it," recalled the black composer and bandleader Duke Ellington. The syncopated rhythms of jazz were immensely popular among rebellious young adults—both black and white—and helped create carefree new dances such as the Charleston and the Black Bottom, whose sexual gyrations shocked guardians of morality. Through the vehicle of jazz, African American performers not only shaped American culture during the twenties but also European taste as well. The controversial European modernist painters Henri Matisse and Pablo Picasso were infatuated with the improvisational inventiveness of jazz music.

GARVEYISM   The spirit of jazz and the "New Negro" also found expression in what came to be called Negro nationalism, which exalted blackness, black cultural expression, and black separatism. The leading spokesman for such views was the flamboyant **Marcus Garvey**. In 1916, Garvey brought to the all-black Harlem neighborhood in New York City the headquarters of the Universal Negro Improvement Association (UNIA), which he had started in his native Jamaica two years before. Garvey had grown convinced that racial oppression and exploitation were prevalent in most societies around the world. Traditional efforts to use civil rights legislation and court rulings to end such oppression were not working. Garvey insisted that blacks had nothing in common with whites—and that was a good thing. He therefore called for the cultivation of black racial pride and promoted racial separation rather than integration. He was the first major black leader to champion what later came to be called "black power." In passionate speeches and in his newspaper, the *Negro World*, Garvey exhorted African Americans to liberate themselves from the surrounding white culture. He saw every white person as a "potential Klansman" and therefore endorsed the "social and political separation of all peoples to the extent that they promote their own ideals and civilization."

The UNIA grew rapidly amid the racial tensions of the postwar years. Garvey quickly enlisted half a million members in the UNIA and claimed as

Marcus Garvey

Garvey was the founder of the Universal Negro Improvement Association and a leading spokesman for "Negro nationalism" in the 1920s.

many as 6 million served by 800 offices by 1923. It became the largest black political organization in the twentieth century. In 1920 Garvey hosted in New York City UNIA's first international convention. Thousands of delegates from forty-eight states and more than twenty nations attended. In his keynote address to 25,000 delegates Garvey proclaimed that the long-suffering black peoples of the world would "suffer no longer. We shall now organize the 400,000,000 Negroes around the world into a vast organization to plant the banner of freedom on the great continent of Africa." In 1920, Garvey declared that the only lasting hope for blacks living in the United States was to flee America and build their own republic in Africa.

Garvey's simple message of black nationalism and racial solidarity appealed to many struggling African Americans living in slums in northern cities. Garvey and his aides created their own black version of Christianity, organized their own fraternal lodges and community cultural centers, started their own black businesses, and published their own newspaper. Such a separatist message appalled other black leaders, however. W. E. B. Du Bois, for example, labeled Garvey "the most dangerous enemy of the Negro race. . . . He is either a lunatic or a traitor." An African American newspaper pledged to help "drive Garvey and Garveyism in all its sinister viciousness from the American soil."

Garvey's black-only crusade came to a screeching halt in May 1923 when he and several associates were put on trial for fraud related to the sale of stock in one of his struggling for-profit enterprises, the Black Star Line, a steamship corporation intended to transport American blacks to Africa. The jury acquitted everyone but Garvey. The judge sentenced him to the maximum five-year prison term. In 1927 President Calvin Coolidge pardoned Garvey on the condition that he be deported to Jamaica. One of the largest crowds in Jamaican history greeted him upon his return to his native country. Garvey died in obscurity in 1940, but the memory of his movement kept alive an undercurrent of racial nationalism that would reemerge in the 1960s under the slogan "black power."

A more lasting force for racial equality was the National Association for the Advancement of Colored People (NAACP), founded in 1910 by white progressives and black activists. Black participants in the NAACP came mainly from the Niagara Movement, a group associated with W. E. B. Du Bois that had met each year since 1905 at places associated with the anti-slavery movement (Niagara Falls; Oberlin, Ohio; Boston; Harpers Ferry) and issued defiant statements against discrimination. Within a few years, the NAACP had become a broad-based national organization. The NAACP embraced the progressive idea that the solution to social problems begins with education, by informing the people of social ills. Du Bois became the new organization's director of publicity and research and editor of its journal, *Crisis,* from 1910 to 1934. The NAACP's main strategy focused on legal action to bring the Fourteenth and Fifteenth Amendments back to life. One early victory came with *Guinn v. United States* (1915), in which the Supreme Court struck down Oklahoma's grandfather clause, used to deprive African Americans of the vote. In *Buchanan v. Worley* (1917) the Court invalidated a residential segregation ordinance in Louisville, Kentucky.

In 1919, the NAACP launched a national campaign against lynching, then a still-common form of vigilante racism. An anti-lynching bill to make mob murder a federal offense passed the House in 1922 but lost to a filibuster by southerners in the Senate. NAACP field secretary James Weldon Johnson believed the continued agitation on the issue did more than the bill's passage would have to reduce lynchings, which decreased to a third of what they had been in the previous decade. But even one lynching was too many for a so-called progressive society.

The Crisis

This national journal of the NAACP carried the subtitle "A Record of the Darker Races."

MASS CULTURE

After 1920, changes in the economy, science, and social thought were more dramatic than those generated by Prohibition, the Klan, and fundamentalism. The large, growing middle class of Americans who had formed an important segment of the progressive political coalition were now absorbed instead into the prosperous "New Era" created by advances in communications, transportation, business organization, and the spread of mass consumerism.

THE GROWING CONSUMER CULTURE   Economic and social life was transformed during the 1920s. The nation's total wealth almost doubled between 1920 and 1930, while workers enjoyed a 26 percent increase in income, the sharpest increase in history to that point. More people than ever before had the money and time to indulge their consumer fancies, and a growing advertising industry fueled the appetites of the rapidly expanding middle and upper middle class. By the mid-1920s advertising had become a huge enterprise using sophisticated psychological research with powerful social significance. Old-time values of thrift and saving gave way to a new ethic of consumption that made spending a virtue. The innovation of installment buying enabled people to buy more by extending their payments over months rather than paying in cash. A newspaper editorial insisted that the American's "first importance to his country is no longer that of citizen but that of consumer. Consumption is a new necessity in response to dramatic increases in productivity."

Consumer-goods industries fueled much of the economic boom from 1922 to 1929. Perhaps no decade in American history witnessed such dramatic changes in everyday life. In 1920 only 35 percent of homes had electricity; by 1930 the number was 68 percent. At the same time, the number of homes with indoor plumbing doubled. Similar increases occurred in the number of households with washing machines and automobiles. Moderately priced creature comforts, including items such as flush toilets, handheld cameras, wristwatches, cigarette lighters, vacuum cleaners, washing machines, and linoleum floors, became more widely available. Inventions in communications and transportation, such as motion pictures, radio, telephones, airplanes, and automobiles, fueled the transformation in everyday life.

In 1896 a New York audience viewed the first moving-picture show. By 1908 there were nearly ten thousand movie theaters scattered across the nation; by 1924 there were twenty thousand theaters showing seven hundred new films a year. Hollywood, California, became the international center of movie production, grinding out cowboy Westerns and the timeless comedies of Mack Sennett's Keystone Company, where a raft of slapstick comedians, most notably Charlie Chaplin, perfected their art, transforming it into a form of social criticism. By the mid-1930s, every city and most small towns had movie theaters, and movies became the nation's chief form of mass entertainment. Movie attendance during the 1920s averaged 80 million people a week. Americans spent ten times as much on movies as they did on tickets to baseball and football games.

Radio broadcasting had an even more spectacular growth. Except for experimental broadcasts, radio served only for basic communication until 1920. In that year, station WWJ in Detroit began transmitting news bulletins from the *Detroit Daily News,* and KDKA in Pittsburgh, owned by the Westinghouse Electric and Manufacturing Company, began broadcasting regularly scheduled programs. The first radio commercial aired in New York in 1922. By the end of that year, there were 508 stations and some 3 million receivers in use. In 1926 the National Broadcasting Company (NBC), a subsidiary of the Radio Corporation of America (RCA), began linking stations into a national network; the Columbia Broadcasting System (CBS) entered the field the next year. In 1927 a Federal Radio Commission was established to regulate the industry; in 1934 it became the Federal Communications Commission (FCC), with authority over other forms of communication as well. Calvin Coolidge was the first president to address the nation by radio, and he did so monthly, paving the way for Franklin Delano Roosevelt's influential "fireside chats."

AIRPLANES, AUTOMOBILES, AND THE ECONOMY Advances in transportation were equally significant. Wilbur and Orville Wright, owners of a bicycle shop in Dayton, Ohio, built and flew the first airplane over the beach at Kitty Hawk, North Carolina, in 1903. But the use of planes advanced slowly until the outbreak of war in 1914, after which the Europeans rapidly developed the airplane as a military weapon. When the United States entered the war, it had no combat planes—American pilots flew British or French planes. An American aircraft industry developed during the war but foundered in the postwar demobilization. Under the Kelly Act of 1925, however, the federal government began to subsidize the industry through airmail contracts. The Air Commerce Act of 1926 provided federal funds to aid in the advancement of air transportation and navigation; among the projects it supported was the construction of airports.

The infant aviation industry received a huge psychological boost in 1927 when twenty-six-year-old Charles A. Lindbergh Jr., a St. Louis–based mail pilot, made the first *solo* transatlantic flight, traveling from New York to

Paris in thirty-three and a half hours. The heroic deed, which won him $25,000 and a Congressional Medal of Honor, was truly dramatic. The night before he took off, he could not sleep, so he was already exhausted when he began the grueling flight. He flew through severe storms as well as a dense fog for part of the way that forced him to descend to within ten feet of the ocean's surface before sighting the Irish coast and regaining his bearings. When he landed in France, there were one hundred thousand people greeting him with thunderous cheers. The New York City parade celebrating Lindbergh's accomplishment surpassed even the celebration of the armistice ending World War I. Flappers developed a new dance step in Lindbergh's honor, called the Lindy Hop.

Five years later, New York honored another pioneering aviator—Amelia Earhart, who in 1932 became the first woman to fly solo across the Atlantic Ocean. Born in Kansas in 1897, she made her first solo flight in 1921 and began working as a stunt pilot at air shows across the country. Earhart's popularity soared after her transatlantic solo flight. The fifteen-hour feat led Congress to award her the Distinguished Flying Cross, and she was named Outstanding American Woman of the Year in 1932. In 1937 Earhart and a navigator left Miami, Florida, heading east on a round-the-world flight. The voyage went smoothly until they attempted the most difficult leg: from New Guinea to a tiny Pacific island 2,556 miles away. The plane disappeared, and despite extensive searches, no trace of it or the aviators was ever found. It remains the most intriguing mystery in aviation history. The accomplishments of Lindbergh and Earhart helped catapult the aviation industry to prominence. By 1930 there were forty-three airline companies in operation in the United States.

Nonetheless, by far the most significant economic and social development of the early twentieth century was the automobile. The first motorcar had been manufactured for sale in 1895, but the founding of the Ford Motor Company in 1903 revolutionized the infant industry. Henry Ford vowed "to democratize the automobile. When I'm through everybody will be able to afford one, and about everyone will have one." Ford's reliable **Model T** (the celebrated Tin Lizzie) came out in 1908 at a price of $850 (in 1924 it would sell for $290). The Model T changed little from year to year, and it came in only one color: black.

In 1916, the total number of cars manufactured passed 1 million; by 1920 more than 8 million were registered, and in 1929 there were more than 23 million. The automobile revolution gave rise to a gigantic market for oil products just as the Spindletop gusher (drilled in 1901 in Texas) heralded the opening of vast southwestern oil fields. It quickened the movement for

Ford Motor Company's Highland Park plant, 1913

Gravity slides and chain conveyors contributed to the mass production of automobiles.

good roads, financed in large part from a gasoline tax; speeded transportation; encouraged suburban sprawl; and sparked real estate booms in California and Florida.

The automobile industry also became the leading example of modern mass-production techniques and efficiency. Ford's Highland Park plant outside Detroit was designed to increase output dramatically by creating a moving assembly line with conveyors pulling the parts along feeder lines and the chassis down an assembly line rather than making each car in place. Each worker performed a particular task, such as installing a fender or a wheel. The moving assembly line could produce a new car in ninety-three minutes. Such efficiency enabled Ford to lower the price of his cars, thereby increasing the number of people who could afford to buy them.

Just as the railroad helped transform the pace and scale of American life in the second half of the nineteenth century, the mass production of automobiles changed social life during the twentieth century. Cars enabled people to live farther away from their workplaces, thus fostering the suburban revolution. They also helped fuel the economic boom of the 1920s. Producing cars created tens of thousands of new jobs and provided "backward linkages" throughout the economy by generating a huge demand for steel, rubber, leather, oil, and gasoline. The burgeoning car culture spurred road construction, dotting the landscape with gasoline stations, traffic lights, billboards, and motor hotels ("motels"). By 1929, the federal government was constructing ten thousand miles of paved national highways each year.

SPECTATOR SPORTS   The widespread ownership of automobiles as well as rising incomes changed the way people spent their leisure time. People living in cities could drive into the countryside or visit friends and relatives in neighboring towns. On weekends they went to the ballparks, stadiums, or boxing rinks to see prizefights and baseball or football games. During the 1920s, the mania for spectator sports emerged as a primary form of mass entertainment—and big business. Baseball became the national pastime in the 1920s. Having been created in the 1870s in rural areas, by the 1920s baseball had gone urban. With larger-than-life heroes such as New York Yankee stars George Herman "Babe" Ruth Jr. and Henry Louis "Lou" Gehrig, professional baseball teams attracted intense loyalties and huge crowds. In 1920 more than a million spectators attended Ruth's games with the New York Yankees. Two years later, the Yankees built a new stadium, called the "house that Ruth built." The Yankees dominated baseball, winning world championships in 1923, 1927, and 1928. More than 20 million people attended professional baseball games in 1927, the year that Ruth, the "Sultan of Swat," set a record by hitting sixty home runs in a season. Because baseball remained a segregated sport in the 1920s, "Negro Leagues"—amateur, semiprofessional, and professional—were organized to provide opportunities for African Americans to play in and watch athletic contests.

Football, especially at the college level, also attracted huge crowds. Unlike baseball, football tended to attract more affluent spectators. It, too, benefited from outsized heroes such as Harold Edward "Red" Grange, the phenomenal running back for the University of Illinois. Grange, not Babe Ruth, was the first athlete to appear on the cover of *Time* magazine. Nicknamed the "Galloping Ghost," he was a phenomenal athlete. In a game against the University of Michigan, he scored a touchdown the first four times he carried the ball. After the victorious game, celebrating students carried Grange on their shoulders for two miles across the campus. When Grange signed a contract with the Chicago Bears in 1926, he single-handedly made professional football competitive with baseball as a spectator sport.

What Ruth and Grange were to their sports, William Harrison "Jack" Dempsey was to boxing. In 1919 he won the world heavyweight title from Jess Willard, a giant of a man weighing three hundred pounds and standing six and a half feet tall. Dempsey knocked him down seven times in the first round. By the fourth round, Willard, his face bruised and bloodied, threw in the towel. Dempsey thereafter became a dominant force in boxing, a national celebrity, and a wealthy man. Like Babe Ruth, the brawling Dempsey was especially popular with working-class men, for he too had been born poor, raised rough, and worked with his hands for wages. In 1927, when James Joseph "Gene" Tunney defeated Dempsey, over one hundred thousand people attended the dramatic fight, including a thousand reporters, ten state governors, and countless Hollywood celebrities. Some 60 million people listened to the fight over the radio. During the 1920s, spectator sports became a primary form of entertainment.

THE MODERNIST REVOLT

The dramatic changes in society and the economy during the 1920s were accompanied by continuing transformations in science and the arts that spurred the onset of a "modernist" sensibility. Modernists came to believe that the twentieth century marked a watershed in human development. Notions of reality and human nature were called into question by sophisticated scientific discoveries and radical new forms of artistic expression. As the prominent English writer and feminist Virginia Woolf declared, "On or about December 1910, human character changed. I am not saying that one went out, as one might into a garden, and there saw that a rose had flowered, or that a hen had laid an egg. The change was not sudden and definite like that. But a change there was, nevertheless; and, since one must be arbitrary, let us date it about the year 1910."

SCIENCE AND SOCIAL THOUGHT Physicists during the early twentieth century altered the image of the cosmos in bewildering ways. Since the eighteenth century, conventional wisdom had held that the universe was governed by laws that the scientific method could ultimately uncover. This rational world of order and certainty disintegrated at the beginning of the new century when Albert Einstein, a young German physicist with an irreverent attitude toward established truths, announced his theory of relativity, which maintained that space, time, and mass were not absolutes but instead were relative to the location and motion of the observer. Sir Isaac Newton's eighteenth-century laws of mechanics, according to Einstein's relativity theories, worked well enough at relatively slow speeds, but the more nearly one approached the velocity of light (about 186,000 miles per second), the more all measuring devices would change accordingly, so that yardsticks would become shorter, clocks and heartbeats would slow down, even the aging process would ebb.

The farther one reached out into the universe and the farther one reached inside the minute world of the atom, the more certainty dissolved. The discovery of radioactivity in the 1890s showed that atoms were not irreducible units of matter and that some of them emitted particles of energy. This meant, Einstein noted, that mass and energy were not separate phenomena but interchangeable. By 1921, when Einstein was awarded the Nobel Prize, his abstract concept of relativity had become internationally recognized—and popularized. Hundreds of books about relativity had been published. His theories also had consequences that Einstein had not foreseen. Younger physicists built upon Einstein's concepts to further transform notions of reality and the universe.

The pace of theoretical physics quickened as the twentieth century unfolded. The German physicist Max Planck suggested that electromagnetic emissions of energy, whether as electricity or light, come in little bundles that he called quanta. Einstein said much the same when he suggested that light was made up of particles, later called photons. The development of quantum theory suggested that atoms were far more complex than once believed and, as stated in 1927 in the "uncertainty principle" of the precocious twenty-five-year-old German physicist Werner Heisenberg, ultimately indescribable. One could never know both the position and the velocity of an electron, Heisenberg concluded, because the very process of observation would inevitably affect the behavior of the particle, altering its position or its velocity. The observer, in other words, changes what is being observed. Heisenberg's "uncertainty principle," which earned him a Nobel Prize, had profound philosophical and cultural implications. It posed a direct challenge to conventional notions of objectivity by declaring that observation is necessarily subjective—and therefore biased and imprecise.

Heisenberg's "uncertainty principle" constituted the most revolutionary scientific theory in 150 years, for it meant that there is no such thing as absolute truth; human knowledge has inherent limits (and biases). "The physicist thus finds himself in a world from which the bottom has dropped clean out," a Harvard mathematician wrote in 1929. The scientist had to "give up his most cherished convictions and faith. The world is not a world of reason. . . . "

MODERNIST ART AND LITERATURE The cluster of scientific ideas associated with Sigmund Freud and Albert Einstein helped to inspire a "modernist" revolution in the minds of a small but visible group of intellectuals and creative artists in Europe and America. **Modernism** is a slippery term, hard to grasp and even harder to define. At once a mood and a movement, full of contradictions, modernism asserted the sovereignty of art and the artist over other elements of society. Modernism emphasized the freedom of individual writers, artists, and musicians to be innovative rather than bound by traditions. At base, however, modernism trumpeted an unsettling premise: reality was no longer what it had seemed. The modernist world was one in which, as Karl Marx said, "all that is solid melts into air."

Until the twentieth century, most writers and artists took for granted an accessible "real" world that could be readily observed and accurately represented. On the contrary, the young generation of self-willed modernists viewed as a subjective realm, something to be created as much in their minds as copied from life, something to be imagined and expressed rather than observed and reproduced. They thus found the subconscious regions of the psyche more interesting and more potent than the traditional focus on reason, common sense, and logic. The American artist Marsden Hartley reported from Paris in 1912 that his reading of Sigmund Freud and the "new psychologists" had prompted him to abandon his emphasis on painting objects from "real life" in favor of expressing on canvas his "intuitive abstractions." He noted that he was now painting "very exceptional things of a most abstract psychic nature."

The horrors of World War I accelerated the insurgency of modernism in the arts by delivering a shattering blow to the widespread belief that Western civilization was progressing. The editors of *Presbyterian* magazine announced in 1919 that "every field of thought and action has been disturbed" by the terrible war and its aftermath. The war's colossal carnage disillusioned many young intellectuals and spurred a new "modernist" sensibility among some of the most talented artists and writers, many of whom had already been shorn of religious belief.

Modernism appeared first in Europe at the end of the nineteenth century and had become a pervasive international force by 1920. It arose out of a widespread recognition that Western civilization had entered an era of bewildering change and disorienting upheavals. New technologies, new modes of transportation and communication, and new scientific discoveries such as quantum mechanics, relativity theory, and Freudian psychology combined to rupture traditional perceptions of reality, herald new ways of understanding human behavior and consciousness, and generate new forms of artistic expression. "One must never forget," declared Gertrude Stein, the experimentalist poet, "that the reality of the twentieth century is not the reality of the nineteenth century, not at all." Modern artists were preoccupied with exploring the nature of consciousness and with experimenting with new artistic forms. The result was a bewildering array of avant-garde intellectual and artistic movements: impressionism, futurism, Dadaism, surrealism.

Gertrude Stein

Pablo Picasso's 1906 portrait of the writer.

THE "LOST GENERATION"

It was Gertrude Stein who in Paris in 1921 told young Ernest Hemingway that he and his friends who had served in the war "are a lost generation." Their anxieties outstripped their inexperience with life. When Hemingway objected, she held her ground. "You are [lost]. You have no respect for anything. You drink yourselves to death." When Hemingway published his first novel, *The Sun Also Rises* (1926), he used the phrase "lost generation" as the book's epigraph, drawing inspiration from both Stein and Ezra Pound. The bleak but captivating novel centers on Jake Barnes, a young American journalist castrated by a war injury. His despairing impotence leads him and his unhappy friends to wander the cafes and nightclubs of postwar Europe, acknowledging that they were all wounded and sterile in their own way: they had lost their innocence, their illusions, and their motivation. In Hemingway's next novel, *A Farewell to Arms* (1929), he adopted a similar focus, depicting the desperate search of the "lost generation" for "real" life punctuated by the doomed, war-tainted love affairs of young Americans. These novels feature the frenetic, hard-drinking lifestyle and the cult of robust masculinity that Hemingway himself epitomized. Hundreds of writers tried to imitate Hemingway's distinctively terse, tough but sensitive style of writing, but few had his exceptional gift, which lay less in what he had to say than in the way he said it.

The earliest chronicler of the "lost generation," F. Scott Fitzgerald, blazed up brilliantly and then quickly flickered out like all the tinseled, sad young characters who people his novels. Famous at age twenty-four, having published the spectacularly successful novel *This Side of Paradise* in 1920, Fitzgerald, along with his wife, Zelda, lived in and wrote about the "greatest, gaudiest spree in history." Fitzgerald's stories during the 1920s were painfully autobiographical. They centered on self-indulgent people during the Jazz Age—glamorous, brassy, and cynical young men and women who oscillate between parties and romances with carefree ease. What gave depth to the best of Fitzgerald's work was what a character in *The Great Gatsby* (1925), Fitzgerald's finest novel, called "a sense of the fundamental decencies" amid all the surface gaiety—and almost always a sense of impending doom in a world that had "lost" its meaning amid the revelations of modern science and the horrors of world war.

Societies do not readily surrender old values and attitudes for new. The great majority of Americans did not identify with the alienation and rebelliousness associated with Fitzgerald, Hemingway, and others claiming to represent the "lost generation." Most Americans—including most writers and artists—did not share their sense of rebellious despair or their disdain for the "booboisie" dominating middle-class life. Instead, most Americans were attracted to more traditional values and conventional forms of expression. They celebrated America's widespread prosperity and traditional pieties. Far more people read the uplifting poetry of Carl Sandburg than the despairing verse of T. S. Eliot. The best-selling novelist of the 1920s was not Ernest Hemingway or F. Scott Fitzgerald; it was Zane Grey, a former Ohio dentist who wrote dozens of popular western novels featuring violence and heroism on the frontier. "We turn to him," said one literary critic, "not for insight into human nature and human problems, nor for refinements of art, but simply for crude epic stories."

The sharp contrast between the fiction of Zane Grey and Ernest Hemingway—and their readers—showed yet again how conflicted and contradictory cultural life had become during the 1920s. For all of the attention given to modernism and cultural radicalism, then and since, the prevailing tone of life between the end of World War I and the onset of the Great Depression was not disillusionment or despair but optimism. During the 1920s, what one writer called the "ballyhoo years," political conservatism, economic growth, mass consumerism, and an often zany frivolity were the prevailing forces shaping the national mood—and anchoring a contradictory "epoch of confusion."

CHAPTER SUMMARY

- **Nativism** With the end of the Great War, race riots and the fear of communism ushered in a wave of virulent nativism. With many "old stock" Americans fearing that many immigrants were socialists, Communists, or anarchists, Congress passed laws to restrict immigration. The revived Ku Klux Klan was devoted to "100 percent Americanism" and regarded Catholics, Jews, immigrants, and African Americans as threats to America.

- **Jazz Age** The carefree fads and attitudes of the 1920s, perhaps best represented by the frantic rhythms of jazz music and the fast-paced, sexy movies from Hollywood, led F. Scott Fitzgerald to dub the decade the Jazz Age. The hemlines of women's dresses rose, and sex was openly discussed. The Harlem Renaissance gave voice to black literature and music, and African Americans in northern cities felt freer to speak out against racial injustice and express pride in their race.

- **Reactionary Mood** Many white Americans felt that their religion and way of life were under attack by modern trends. They feared that women's newly earned right to vote might destabilize the family and that scientific scholarship would undermine biblical truth. These modern and traditional forces openly clashed at the Scopes trial in Dayton, Tennessee, in 1925, where the right to teach evolution in public schools was tested in court.

- **Modernism** The carnage of the Great War shattered Americans' belief in the progress of Western civilization. In the movement known as modernism, young artists and intellectuals reflected this disillusionment. For modernists, the world could no longer be easily observed through reason, common sense, and logic; instead, reality was something to be created and expressed through new artistic and literary forms, like abstract painting, atonal music, free verse in poetry, and stream-of-conscious narrative and interior monologues in stories and novels.

CHRONOLOGY

1903	Wright Brothers fly the first airplane
1903	Ford Motor Company is founded
1905	First movie house opens
1910	National Association for the Advancement of Colored People is founded
1916	Marcus Garvey brings to New York the Universal Negro Improvement Association
1920	Prohibition begins
1920	F. Scott Fitzgerald's *This Side of Paradise* is published
1921	Albert Einstein receives the Nobel Prize in physics
1921	Congress passes the Emergency Immigration Act
1922	T. S. Eliot's *The Waste Land* is published
	First radio commercial is aired
1924	Congress passes the Immigration Act
1925	Scopes "monkey trial" tests the teaching of evolution in Tennessee public schools
1927	Charles Lindbergh Jr. makes first solo transatlantic flight

KEY TERMS & NAMES

26

REPUBLICAN
RESURGENCE AND
DECLINE

FOCUS QUESTIONS wwnorton.com/studyspace

- To what extent were the policies of the 1920s a rejection of progressivism?
- What was the effect of isolationism and the peace movement on American politics between the two world wars?
- Why were the 1920s an era of conservatism?
- What drove the growth of the American economy in the 1920s?
- What were the causes of the stock market crash and the Great Depression?

By 1920, the progressive political coalition that elected Theodore Roosevelt in 1904 and reelected Woodrow Wilson in 1916 had fragmented. It unraveled for several reasons. For one thing, its leaders were no more. Roosevelt died in 1919 at the age of sixty, just as he was beginning to campaign for the 1920 Republican presidential nomination. Wilson, too, had envisioned an unprecedented third term, but his stroke forced him to finish out his second term in office broken physically and mentally. Many Americans preferred other candidates anyway. Organized labor resented the Wilson administration's crackdown on striking workers in 1919–1920. Farmers in the Great Plains and the West thought that wartime price controls on commodities had discriminated against them. Liberal intellectuals became disillusioned with grassroots democracy because of popular support for Prohibition, the Ku Klux Klan, and religious fundamentalism. By 1920, the larger middle class had become preoccupied with restoring a "new era" of prosperity based on mass production and mass consumption. Finally, another reason for the public turning away from Progressivism was that it had accomplished its major goals: the Eighteenth Amendment, ratified in 1919, which outlawed alcoholic beverages, and the Nineteenth Amendment, ratified in 1920, which allowed women nationwide to vote.

Progressivism did not disappear in the 1920s, however. Progressive Republicans and Democrats dominated key leadership positions in Congress during much of the decade even while conservative Republicans occupied the White House. The progressive impulse for honest, efficient government and regulation of business remained strong, especially at the state and local levels, where movements for better roads, education, public health, and social-welfare programs gained momentum during the decade. At the national level, however, Republican conservatives returned to power.

"NORMALCY"

THE ELECTION OF 1920   After World War I most Americans had grown weary of Woodrow Wilson's crusading idealism and were suspicious of any leader who, like Wilson, promoted widespread reforms. Wilson himself recognized the shifting public mood. "It is only once in a generation," he remarked, "that a people can be lifted above material things. That is why conservative government is in the saddle two thirds of the time."

In 1920, Republican party leaders turned to a stunning mediocrity, the affable, dapper, silver-haired Ohio senator **Warren G. Harding.** He set the conservative tone of his presidential campaign when he told a Boston audience that it was time to end Wilsonian progressivism: "America's present need is not heroics, but healing; not nostrums, but normalcy; not revolution, but restoration; not agitation, but adjustment; not surgery, but serenity; not the dramatic, but the dispassionate." In contrast to Wilson's grandiose internationalism, Harding promised to "safeguard America first . . . to exalt America first, to live for and revere America first."

Harding's vanilla promise of a **"return to normalcy"** reflected both his own conservative values and the voters' desire for stability and order. The son of an Ohio farmer, he was neither a prophet nor a crusader. He described himself as "just a plain fellow" who was "old-fashioned and even reactionary in matters of faith and morals." But far from being an old-fashioned moralist in his personal life, Harding drank bootleg liquor in the midst of Prohibition, smoked and chewed tobacco, relished weekly poker games, and had numerous affairs and several children with women other than his austere wife, whom he called "the Duchess." The general public, however, remained unaware of Harding's escapades. Instead, voters saw him as a handsome, charming, lovable politician. Harding acknowledged his limitations in vision, leadership, and intellectual power, once admitting that "I cannot hope to be one of the great presidents, but perhaps I may be remembered as one of the best loved."

The Democrats in 1920 hoped that Harding would not be president at all. James Cox, a former newspaper publisher and former governor of Ohio, won the presidential nomination of an increasingly fragmented Democratic party on the forty-fourth ballot. For vice president the convention named New Yorker Franklin Delano Roosevelt, who as assistant secretary of the navy occupied the same position his Republican cousin Theodore Roosevelt had once held.

The Democrats suffered from the breakup of the Wilsonian coalition and the conservative postwar mood. In the words of the progressive journalist William Allen White, Americans in 1920 were "tired of issues, sick at heart of ideals, and weary of being noble." The country voted overwhelmingly for Harding's promised "return to normalcy." Harding polled 16 million votes to 9 million for Cox, who won no state outside the Democratic South. The Republican domination in both houses of Congress increased. As a disconsolate Wilson supporter said, "an age had ended."

EARLY APPOINTMENTS AND POLICY Harding in office had much in common with Ulysses S. Grant. His cabinet, like Grant's, mixed some of the "best minds" in the party, whom he had promised to seek out, with a few of the worst. Charles Evans Hughes, like Grant's Hamilton Fish, became a distinguished secretary of state. Herbert Hoover in the Commerce Department, **Andrew W. Mellon** in the Treasury Department, and Henry C. Wallace in the Agriculture Department functioned efficiently and made policy on their own. Other cabinet members and administrative appointees, however, were not so conscientious. The secretary of the interior landed in prison, and the attorney general narrowly escaped serving time. Many lesser offices went to members of the "Ohio gang," a group of Harding's drinking buddies who met in a house on K Street near the White House to help the president relieve the pressures of his high office.

Until he became president, Harding had loved politics. He was the party hack par excellence, "bloviating" (a favorite verb of his, which means "speaking with gaseous eloquence") at public events, jollying it up in the clubhouse and cloakroom, hobnobbing with the great and near great in Washington, D.C. As president, however, Harding was simply in over his head, and self-

The Ohio gang

President Warren Harding surrounded himself with a network of friends, often appointing them to public office despite inferior credentials.

doubt overwhelmed him. "I don't think I'm big enough for the Presidency," he confided to a friend. Harding much preferred to relax with the Ohio gang, who shared his taste for whiskey, poker, and women.

Still, Harding and his friends had a political agenda. They set about dismantling or neutralizing many of the social and economic components of progressivism. The president's four Supreme Court appointments were all conservatives, including Chief Justice William Howard Taft, the former president, who announced that he had been "appointed to reverse a few decisions." During the 1920s the Taft court struck down a federal child-labor law and a minimum-wage law for women, issued numerous injunctions against striking unions, and passed rulings limiting the powers of federal regulatory agencies.

The Harding administration inherited a slumping economy burdened by high wartime taxes and a national debt that had ballooned from $1 billion in 1914 to $24 billion in 1920. To address such challenges, the new president established a pro-business tone reminiscent of the McKinley White House in the 1890s. Harding vetoed a bill to provide war veterans with a cash bonus, arguing that it would increase the federal budget deficit. To deal with the postwar recession and generate economic growth, Secretary of the Treasury Mellon reduced government spending and lowered taxes. He persuaded Congress to pass the landmark Budget and Accounting Act of 1921, which created a new Bureau of the Budget to streamline the process of preparing an annual federal budget to be presented for approval by the Congress. The bill also created a General Accounting Office to audit spending by federal agencies. This act realized a long-held desire of progressives to bring greater efficiency and nonpartisanship to the budget preparation process. Mellon also initiated a series of general tax reductions from the wartime levels. Mellon insisted that the reductions should go mainly to the rich, on the "trickle down" principle that wealth in the hands of the few would spur economic growth through increased capital investment.

In Congress, a group of western Republicans and southern Democrats fought a dogged battle to preserve "progressive" approach to income taxes (a graduated scale of higher rates on higher income levels) built into wartime taxes, but Mellon, in office through the 1920s, eventually won out. At his behest, Congress in 1921 repealed the wartime excess-profits tax and lowered the maximum tax rate on personal income from 65 to 50 percent. Subsequent revenue acts lowered the maximum rate to 40 percent in 1924 and to 20 percent in 1926. The Revenue Act of 1926 extended further benefits to high-income groups by lowering estate taxes and repealing the gift tax. Unfortunately, much of the tax money released to the wealthy helped fuel the speculative excess of the late 1920s as much as it fostered gainful enterprise. Mellon, however, did balance the federal budget for a time. Government expenditures fell, as did the national debt. Mellon's admirers tagged him the greatest secretary of the Treasury since Alexander Hamilton in the late eighteenth century.

In addition to tax cuts, Mellon—the third-richest man in the United States, after John D. Rockefeller and Henry Ford—favored the time-honored Republican policy of high tariffs on imported goods. The Fordney-McCumber Tariff of 1922 increased rates on chemical and metal products to help prevent the revival of German corporations that had dominated those industries before the First World War. To please commercial farmers, who historically benefited little from tariffs, the new act further extended the duties on agricultural imports.

Rounding out the Republican economic program of the 1920s was a more lenient attitude toward government regulation of corporations. Neither Harding nor his successor, Calvin Coolidge, could dissolve the regulatory agencies created during the Progressive Era, but they named commissioners who promoted regulation "friendly" to business interests. Harding appointed conservatives to the Interstate Commerce Commission, the Federal Reserve Board, and the Federal Trade Commission. Progressive Republican senator George W. Norris characterized the new appointments as "the nullification of federal law by a process of boring from within." Senator Henry Cabot Lodge agreed, boasting that "we have torn up Wilsonism by the roots."

In one area, however, Warren G. Harding proved to be more progressive than Woodrow Wilson. He reversed the Wilson administration's segregationist policy of excluding African Americans from federal government jobs. He also spoke out against the vigilante racism that had flared up across the country during and after the war. In his first speech to a joint session of Congress in 1921, Harding insisted that the nation must deal with the festering "race question." The horrific racial incidents during and after World War I were a stain on American democratic ideals. The new president, unlike his Democratic predecessor, attacked the Ku Klux Klan for fomenting "hatred and prejudice and violence," and he urged Congress "to wipe the stain of barbaric lynching from the banners of a free and orderly, representative democracy." The Senate, however, failed to pass the bill Harding promoted.

ISOLATIONISM IN FOREIGN AFFAIRS

In 1920 the Americans who elected Warren G. Harding were weary of war and Woodrow Wilson's crusading internationalism. They wanted their new president to revive the tradition of isolationism, whereby the United States had sought to remain aloof from the squabbles among European nations. To that end, Harding said good riddance to Wilson's desire for America to play a leading role in the new League of Nations. As he said in his 1920 victory speech, "You just didn't want a surrender of the United States. That's why you didn't care for the League [of Nations], which is now deceased." The postwar spirit of isolation found other expressions as well: the higher tariff rates on foreign imports, the Red Scare, and the restrictive immigration laws with which the nation all but shut the door to newcomers.

Yet the desire to stay out of foreign wars did not mean that the United States could ignore its own expanding global interests. American businesses now had worldwide connections. The United States was the world's chief banker. American investments and loans abroad put in circulation the dollars that enabled foreigners to purchase U.S. exports. Moreover, America's overseas possessions, especially the Philippines, directly involved the country in world affairs.

WAR DEBTS AND REPARATIONS   Probably nothing did more to heighten American isolationism from foreign affairs—or anti-American feeling in Europe—than the complex issue of paying off huge war debts during the 1920s. In 1917, when France and Great Britain ran out of money to pay for military supplies, the U.S. government had advanced them massive loans, first for the war effort and then for postwar reconstruction projects. Most Americans, including Andrew W. Mellon, expected the war-related debts to be paid back, but Europeans had a different perception. The European Allies had held off the German army at great cost while the United States was raising an army in 1917. The British also noted that after the American Revolution, the newly independent United States had repudiated old debts to British investors; the French likewise pointed out that they had never been repaid for helping the Americans win the Revolution and gain their independence.

But the most difficult challenges in the 1920s were the practical problems of repayment. To get U.S. dollars to use to pay their war-related debts, European nations had to sell their goods to the United States. However, soaring American tariff rates during the 1920s made imported European goods more expensive and the war-related debts incurred by Britain and France harder to pay. The French and the British insisted that they could repay their debts to the United States only as they unrealistically sought to collect $33 billion in reparations from defeated Germany, whose economy was in a shambles during the 1920s, ravaged by runaway inflation. Twice during the 1920s the financial strain on Germany brought the structure of international payments to the verge of collapse, and both times the international Reparations Commission called in private American bankers to work out rescue plans. Loans provided by American banks thus propped up the German economy so that Germany could pay its reparations to Britain and France, thereby enabling them to pay their debts to the United States.

ATTEMPTS AT DISARMAMENT   After the First World War, many Americans decided that excessive armaments were responsible for causing the terrible conflict. The best way to keep the peace, they argued, was to limit the size of armies and navies. The United States had no intention of maintaining a large army after 1920, but under the shipbuilding program begun in 1916, it had constructed a powerful navy second only to that of Great Britain. Neither the British nor the Americans wanted a naval armaments race, but both were worried about the alarming growth of Japanese power.

To address the problem, President Harding in 1921 invited diplomats from eight nations to a naval-armaments conference in Washington, D.C. U.S. sec-

The Washington Conference, 1921

The Big Five at the conference were (from left) Iyesato Tokugawa (Japan), Arthur Balfour (Great Britain), Charles Evans Hughes (United States), Aristide Briand (France), and Carlo Schanzer (Italy).

retary of state Charles Evans Hughes welcomed the delegates by making a blockbuster proposal. The only way out of an expensive armaments race, he declared, "is to end it now" by eliminating scores of existing warships and prohibiting the construction of new battleships. It was one of the most dramatic moments in diplomatic history. In less than fifteen minutes, one journalist reported, Hughes had destroyed more warships "than all the admirals of the world have sunk in a cycle of centuries." His audacious proposal to end the naval arms race was greeted by a "tornado of cheering" among the delegates.

Following Hughes's lead, delegates from the United States, Britain, Japan, France, and Italy signed the Five-Power Treaty (1922), which limited the size of their navies. It was the first disarmament treaty in history. The five major powers also agreed to refrain from further fortification of their Pacific possessions. In particular, the United States and Great Britain promised not to build any new naval bases north of Singapore or west of Hawaii. The agreement in effect partitioned the world: U.S. naval power became supreme in the Western Hemisphere, Japanese power in the western Pacific, and British power dominated from the North Sea to Singapore.

With these agreements in hand, President Harding could boast of what seemed to be a brilliant diplomatic coup that relieved citizens of the need to pay for an enlarged navy and warded off potential conflicts in the Pacific. Yet the agreements were without obligation and without teeth. The naval-disarmament treaty set limits only on "capital" ships (battleships and aircraft carriers); the race to build cruisers, destroyers, submarines, and other smaller craft continued. Expansionist Japan withdrew from the agreement in 1934, and the Soviet Union and Germany had been excluded from the conference. Thus, twelve years after the Washington Conference, the dream of naval disarmament died.

THE KELLOGG-BRIAND PACT   During and after the First World War, many Americans embraced the fanciful ideal of simply abolishing war with a stroke of a pen. In 1921 a wealthy Chicagoan founded the American Committee for the Outlawry of War. "We can outlaw this war system just as we outlawed slavery and the saloon," said one of the more enthusiastic converts.

The seductive notion of simply abolishing war culminated in the signing of the Kellogg-Briand Pact. This unique treaty started with an initiative by the French foreign minister Aristide Briand, who in 1927 proposed to Secretary of State Frank B. Kellogg that the two countries agree never go to war against each other. This innocent-seeming proposal was actually a clever ploy to draw the United States into the French security system by the back door. In any future war, for instance, such a pact would inhibit the United States from seeking reprisals in response to any French intrusions on neutral rights. Kellogg was outraged to discover that Briand had urged leaders of the American peace movement to put pressure on the government to sign the accord.

Kellogg then turned the tables on Briand. He countered with a plan to have all nations sign the pact. Caught in a trap of his own making, the French foreign minister finally agreed. The Pact of Paris (its official name), signed on August 27, 1928, declared that the signatories "renounce it [war] as an instrument of national policy." Eventually sixty-two nations signed the pact, but all reserved the right of "self-defense" as an escape hatch. The U.S. Senate ratified the agreement by a vote of 85 to 1. One senator who voted for "this worthless, but perfectly harmless peace treaty" wrote a friend later that he feared it would "confuse the minds of many good people who think that peace may be secured by polite professions of neighborly and brotherly love."

IMPROVING RELATIONS IN LATIN AMERICA   Throughout the 1920s foreign relations were of much less concern than domestic affairs. But there were some important developments in international relations. Herbert Hoover and the other Republican presidents sought to improve America's relations with its Latin American neighbors. America's isolationist sentiments during the 1920s were welcomed in Latin America, where the spirit of non-involvement helped allay long-festering resentments against "Yankee imperialism." The Harding administration agreed in 1921 to pay the republic of Colombia the $25 million it had demanded for America's rights to the Panama Canal. In 1924, American troops left the Dominican Republic after eight years of intervention. U.S. Marines left Nicaragua in 1925 but returned a year later at the outbreak of disorder and civil war. There, in 1927, the Coolidge administration brought both parties into an agreement for U.S.-supervised elections, but one rebel leader, César Augusto Sandino, held out, and the marines stayed until 1933.

The troubles in Nicaragua increased strains between the United States and Mexico. Relations had already been soured by repeated Mexican threats to expropriate American oil properties in Mexico. In 1928, however, the U.S. ambassador negotiated an agreement protecting rights for American businesses acquired before 1917. Expropriation did in fact occur in 1938, but the Mexican government agreed to reimburse American owners.

THE HARDING SCANDALS

ADMINISTRATIVE CORRUPTION   Republican conservatives such as Henry Cabot Lodge, Andrew W. Mellon, Calvin Coolidge, and Herbert Hoover operated out of a philosophical conviction that was intended to benefit the nation. Members of President Harding's "**Ohio Gang**," however, used White House connections to line their own pockets. Early in 1923, for example, Harding learned that the head of the Veterans Bureau was systematically looting medical and hospital supplies. A few weeks later the legal adviser to the bureau committed suicide. Not long afterward a close friend of Attorney General Harry M. Daugherty, who had set up an office in the Justice Department from which he peddled influence for a fee, shot himself. Finally, the attorney general himself was implicated in the fraudulent handling of German assets seized after the war. When discovered, he refused to testify on the grounds that he might incriminate himself. These were but the most visible among the many scandals that touched the Justice Department, the Prohibition Bureau, and other federal agencies under Harding.

One major scandal rose above all the others, however. **Teapot Dome**, like the Watergate break-in fifty years later, became the catchphrase for the climate of corruption surrounding the Harding administration. The Teapot Dome was a government-owned oil field in Wyoming. It had been set aside as an oil reserve for ensuring fuel for warships. Harding decided to move administrative control of Teapot Dome from the Department of Navy to the Department of Interior. Thereafter, his secretary of interior, Albert B. Fall, a former Republican senator from New Mexico, began signing sweetheart contracts with close friends who were executives of petroleum companies that wanted access to the oil field. It turned out that he had taken bribes of about $400,000 (which came in "a little black bag") from an oil tycoon. Fall was convicted of conspiracy and bribery and sentenced to a year in prison, the first former cabinet official ever to serve time as a result of misconduct in office.

How much Harding himself knew of the scandals swirling about him is unclear, but he knew enough to be troubled. "My God, this is a hell of a job!" he confided to a journalist. "I have no trouble with my enemies; I can take care of my enemies all right. But my damn friends, my God-damn friends. . . . They're the ones that keep me walking the floor nights!" In 1923, Harding left on what would be his last journey, a speaking tour to the West Coast and a trip to the Alaska Territory. In Seattle he suffered an attack of food poisoning, recovered briefly, then died in a San Francisco hotel.

The nation was heartbroken. Not since the death of Abraham Lincoln had there been such an outpouring of grief for a "beloved president," for the kindly, ordinary man who found it in his heart (as Woodrow Wilson had

"Juggernaut" of corruption

This 1924 cartoon alludes to the dimensions of the Teapot Dome scandal.

not) to pardon Eugene V. Debs, the Socialist who had been jailed for opposing U.S. entry into World War I. As the funeral train carrying Harding's body crossed the continent to Washington, D.C., then back to Ohio, millions stood by the tracks to honor their lost leader. Eventually, however, grief yielded to scorn and contempt. For nearly a decade, the revelations of scandals within the Harding administration were paraded before investigating committees and then the courts. In 1927 an Ohio woman named Nan Britton published a sensational book that claimed that she had had numerous trysts with Harding in the White House and that he was the father of her daughter. Harding's love letters to another man's wife also surfaced.

As a result of Harding's amorous detours and corrupt associates, his foreshortened administration came to be viewed as one of the worst in history. More recent assessments suggest, however, that the scandals obscured accomplishments. Some historians credit Harding with leading the nation out of the turmoil of the postwar years and creating the foundation for the decade's remarkable economic boom. These revisionists also stress that Harding was a hardworking president who played a far more forceful role than previously assumed in shaping his administration's economic and foreign policies and in shepherding legislation through Congress. Harding also promoted diversity and civil rights. He appointed Jews to key federal positions, and he became the first president to criticize racial segregation in a speech before a white audience in the South. No previous president had promoted women's rights as forcefully as he did. But even Harding's foremost scholarly defender admits that he lacked good judgment and "probably should never have been president."

"SILENT CAL" The news of Harding's death found Vice President Calvin Coolidge visiting his father in the isolated mountain village of Plymouth, Vermont, his birthplace. There, at 2:47 A.M. on August 3, 1923, by the light of a kerosene lamp, Colonel John Coolidge administered the presidential oath of office to his son. The rustic simplicity of Plymouth, the very name itself, evoked just the image of traditional roots and solid integrity that the country would long for amid the coming disclosures of corruption and carousing in the Harding administration.

Coolidge brought to the White House a clear conviction that the presidency should revert to its Gilded Age stance of passive deference to Congress. "Four fifths of our troubles," Coolidge predicted, "would disappear if we would sit down and keep still." He abided by this rule, insisting on twelve hours of sleep and an afternoon nap. The satirist H. L. Mencken asserted that Coolidge "slept more than any other president, whether by day or by night."

Conservatives in the White House

Warren G. Harding (left) and Calvin Coolidge (right).

PRO-BUSINESS CONSERVATISM Americans embraced the unflappability and unstained integrity of **Silent Cal**. He was simple and direct, a self-righteous man of strong principles, intense patriotism, pinched frugality, and few words. After being reelected president of the Massachusetts State Senate, his four-sentence inaugural address was the shortest ever. It concluded with Coolidge urging that "above all things, be brief." President Coolidge, said a critic, "can be silent in five languages." Although a man of few words, he was not as bland or as dry as critics claimed. He promoted his regressive conservatism with a ruthless consistency. Even more than Harding, Coolidge identified the nation's welfare with the success of big business. "The chief business of the American people is business," he preached. "The man who builds a factory builds a temple. The man who works there worships there." Where Harding had sought to balance the interests of labor, agriculture, and industry, Coolidge focused on promoting industrial development. He strove to end federal regulation of business and industry and reduce taxes as well as the national debt. The nation had too many laws, Coolidge insisted, and "we would be better off if we did not have any more." His fiscal frugality and pro-business stance led the *Wall Street Journal* to exult: "Never before, here or anywhere else, has a government been so completely fused with business."

THE ELECTION OF 1924   In filling out Harding's unexpired term, Calvin Coolidge distanced himself from the scandals of the administration by putting in charge of the prosecutions two lawyers of undoubted integrity. A man of honesty and ability, a good administrator who delegated well and managed Republican factions adroitly, Coolidge quietly took control of the party machinery and seized the initiative in the 1924 campaign for the presidential nomination, which he won with only token opposition.

Meanwhile, the Democrats again fell victim to dissension, prompting the humorist Will Rogers's classic statement that "I am a member of no organized political party. I am a Democrat." The Democratic party's fractiousness illustrated the deep divisions between urban and rural America during the 1920s. It took the Democrats 103 ballots to decide on a presidential candidate: John W. Davis, a corporate lawyer from West Virginia who could nearly outdo Coolidge in his conservatism.

While the Democrats bickered, rural populists and urban progressives again decided to desert both national parties. Meeting in Cleveland, Ohio, on July 4, 1924, activists reorganized the old 1912 Progressive party and nominated Robert M. "Fighting Bob" La Follette for president. The sixty-nine-year-old Wisconsin progressive senator had voted against the 1917 war resolution against Germany. Now, he won the support of the Socialist party and the American Federation of Labor.

In the 1924 campaign, the voters preferred to "keep cool with Coolidge," who swept both the popular and the electoral votes by decisive majorities. Davis took only the solidly Democratic South, and La Follette carried only his native Wisconsin. The popular vote went 15.7 million for Coolidge, 8.4 million for Davis, and 4.8 million for La Follette—the largest popular vote ever polled by a third-party candidate.

THE NEW ERA

Coolidge's landslide victory represented the pinnacle of postwar conservatism. The Democratic party was in disarray, and the Republicans were triumphant. Business executives interpreted the Republican victory in 1924 as a vindication of their leadership, and Coolidge saw the economy's surging prosperity as a confirmation of his support of big business. In fact, the prosperity and technological achievements of the time known as the New Era had much to do with Coolidge's victory over the Democrats and Progressives.

STABILIZING THE ECONOMY   During the 1920s, the drive for efficiency, which had been a prominent feature of the progressive impulse, powered the tandem wheels of mass production and consumption and became a cardinal belief of Republican leaders. **Herbert Hoover**, who served as secretary of commerce in the Harding and Coolidge cabinets, was himself a remarkable success story. Born into an Iowa farm family in 1874, he had lost both of his parents by age ten. As an orphan he was raised by Quaker family members in Iowa and Oregon. The shy but industrious "loner" majored in geology at Stanford University and became a world-renowned mining engineer and multi-millionaire before the age of forty.

President Woodrow Wilson called upon Hoover to head up the Food Administration during World War I, and he served with Wilson among the U.S. delegation at the Versailles peace conference. Hoover idolized Wilson and supported American membership in the League of Nations. A young Franklin Delano Roosevelt, then serving as assistant secretary of the navy, was dazzled by Hoover, the man he would later defeat in the presidential election of 1932. He was "certainly a wonder, and I wish we could make him President of the United States." But Hoover later declared himself a Republican who promoted a progressive conservativism. In a book titled *American Individualism* (1922), he prescribed an "ideal of *service*" that went beyond "rugged individualism" to promote the greater good. He wanted government officials to encourage business leaders to forego "cutthroat competition" by engaging in "voluntary cooperation" through the formation of trade associations that would share information and promote standardization and efficiency.

As secretary of commerce during the 1920s, Hoover transformed the trifling Commerce Department into the government's most dynamic agency. He sought out new markets for business, promoted more efficient design, production, and distribution, created a Bureau of Aviation, and the next year established the Federal Radio Commission.

THE BUSINESS OF FARMING During the 1920s, agriculture remained the weakest sector in the economy. Briefly after the war, farmers' hopes soared on wings of prosperity. The wartime boom fed by sales abroad lasted into 1920, and then commodity prices collapsed as European agricultural production returned to prewar levels. Overproduction brought lower prices for crops. Wheat prices went in eighteen months from $2.50 a bushel to less than $1; cotton from 35¢ per pound to 13¢. Low crop prices persisted into 1923, especially in the wheat and corn belts, and after that improvement was spotty. A bumper cotton crop in 1926 resulted only in a price collapse and an early taste of depression in much of the South, where foreclosures and bankruptcies spread.

Yet the most successful farms, like the most successful corporations, were getting larger, more efficient, and more mechanized. By 1930 about 13 percent of all farmers had tractors, and the proportion was even higher on the western plains. Better plows, harvesters, combines, and other machines were part of the mechanization process that accompanied improved crop yields, fertilizers, and methods of animal breeding.

Most farmers in the 1920s were simply struggling to survive, however. And like their predecessors they sought political help for their plight. In 1924, Senator Charles L. McNary of Oregon and Representative Gilbert N. Haugen of Iowa introduced the first **McNary-Haugen bill**, which sought to secure "equality for agriculture in the benefits of the protective tariff." The proposed bill called for surplus American crops to be sold on the world market in order to raise prices in the home market. The goal was to achieve "parity"—that is, to raise domestic farm prices to a point where they would have the same purchasing power relative to other prices that they had enjoyed between 1909 and 1914, a time viewed in retrospect as a golden age of American agriculture.

The McNary-Haugen bill passed both houses of Congress in 1927, only to be vetoed by President Coolidge, who dismissed the bill as unsound. The process was repeated in 1928, when Coolidge criticized the measure as unconstitutional. In a broader sense, however, McNary-Haugenism did not fail. The debates over the bill made the "farm problem" a national policy issue and defined it as a problem of finding foreign markets for crop surpluses. Moreover, the evolution of the McNary-Haugen plan revived the idea of a political alliance between the rural South and the West, a coalition that in the next decade became a dominant influence on national farm policy.

SETBACKS FOR UNIONS Urban workers more than farmers shared in the affluence of the 1920s. "A workman is far better paid in America than anywhere else in the world," a French visitor wrote in 1927, "and his standard of living is enormously higher." Nonfarm workers gained about 20 percent in real wages between 1921 and 1928 while farm income rose only 10 percent.

Organized labor, however, did no better than organized agriculture in the 1920s. Although President Harding had endorsed collective bargaining and tried to reduce the twelve-hour workday and the six-day workweek so that the working class "may have time for leisure and family life," he ran into stiff opposition in Congress. Overall, unions suffered a setback after the growth years during the war. The Red Scare and strikes of 1919 created concerns that unions practiced subversion, an idea that the enemies of unions promoted. The brief postwar depression of 1921 further weakened the unions, and they felt the severe impact of open-shop associations designed to prevent unions that proliferated across the country after the war, led by chambers of commerce and other business groups. In 1921, business groups in Chicago designated the open shop the "American plan" of employment. Although the open shop in theory implied only an employer's right to hire anyone, in practice it meant discrimination against unionists and a refusal to recognize unions even in shops where most of the workers belonged to one.

To suppress unions, employers often required "yellow-dog" contracts, which forced workers to agree to stay out of a union. Owners also used labor spies, blacklists, intimidation, and coercion. Some employers tried to kill the unions with kindness. They introduced programs of "industrial democracy" guided by company unions or various schemes of "welfare capitalism," such

The Gastonia strike

These female textile workers pit their strength against that of a National Guardsman during a strike at the Loray Mill in Gastonia, North Carolina, in 1929.

as profit sharing, bonuses, pensions, health programs, recreational activities, and the like. The benefits of such programs were often considerable.

Prosperity, propaganda, and active hostility combined to cause union membership to drop from about 5 million in 1920 to 3.5 million in 1929. Samuel Gompers, founder and longtime president of the American Federation of Labor (AFL), died in 1924; William Green of the United Mine Workers (UMW), who took his place, embodied the conservative, even timid, attitude of unions during the period. The outstanding exception to the anti-union policies of the decade was the passage of the Railway Labor Act in 1926, which abolished the federal Railway Labor Board and substituted a new Board of Mediation. The act also provided for the formation of railroad unions "without interference, influence, or coercion," a statement of policy not extended to other workers until the 1930s.

PRESIDENT HOOVER, THE ENGINEER

HOOVER VERSUS SMITH   On August 2, 1927, while on vacation in the Black Hills of South Dakota, President Coolidge suddenly announced that "I do not choose to run for President in 1928." His retirement message surprised the nation and cleared the way for Herbert Hoover to win the Republican nomination in 1928. The Republican platform took credit for the nation's rampant prosperity, cost cutting, debt and tax reduction, and the protective tariff ("as vital to American agriculture as it is to manufacturing"). It rejected the McNary-Haugen farm program but promised to create a federal farm board to manage crop surpluses more efficiently.

The Democratic nomination went to four-term New York Governor **Alfred E. Smith**. The party's farm plank pledged "economic equality of agriculture with other industries." Like the Republicans, the Democrats promised to enforce the Volstead Act (1919), which had defined as "intoxicating" any drink having has much as 0.5 percent alcohol, even though Al Smith was himself a vocal opponent of Prohibition.

The two candidates' sharply different images obscured the essential similarities of their programs. Hoover was a child of a rural Quaker family, the successful engineer and businessman, the architect of Republican prosperity, while Smith was the prototype of those things that rural and small-town America distrusted: the son of Irish immigrants, Roman Catholic, and anti-Prohibition (in direct opposition to his party's platform). Outside the large cities those attributes were handicaps that Smith could scarcely surmount, for all his affability and wit. Militant Protestants launched a furious assault on

Herbert Hoover

"I have no fears for the future of our country," Hoover told the nation at his inauguration in 1929.

him, especially in the Democratic-controlled South. The Ku Klux Klan, for example, mailed thousands of postcards proclaiming that the Catholic New Yorker was the Antichrist.

In the election of 1928, more people voted than ever before. Hoover won in the third consecutive Republican landslide, with 21 million popular votes to Smith's 15 million and an even more top-heavy electoral-vote majority of 444 to 87. Hoover even cracked the Democrats' Solid South, leaving Smith only six Deep South states plus Massachusetts and Rhode Island. The election was above all a vindication of Republican prosperity, although Calvin Coolidge was skeptical that his successor could sustain the good times. He derisively called Hoover the Wonder Boy, and had quipped in 1928 that the new president had "offered me unsolicited advice for six years, all of it bad."

The shattering defeat of the Democrats concealed a major political realignment in the making. Al Smith had nearly doubled the vote for John W. Davis, the Democratic candidate of four years before. Smith's urban image, though a handicap in the hinterlands, swung big cities back into the Democratic column. In the farm states of the West, there were signs that some disgruntled farmers had switched over to the Democrats. A coalition of urban workers and unhappy farmers was in the making that would later rally behind Franklin D. Roosevelt.

HOOVER IN CONTROL   The milestone year 1929 dawned with high hopes. The economy seemed sound, per capita income was rising, and the chief architect of Republican prosperity was about to enter the White House. "I have no fears for the future of our country," Hoover told the audience at his inauguration. "It is bright with hope." No nation, he declared, was more secure in its accomplishments. Although four years later, Hoover would be savaged for such rosy pronouncements, at the time his upbeat pronouncements seemed justified. In 1929 more Americans were working than ever before, and they were earning record levels of income.

Hoover's programs to stabilize business growth carried over into his plans for agriculture, the weakest sector of the economy. To treat the malady of glutted commodities markets, he called Congress into special session and convinced the legislators to approve the Agricultural Marketing Act of 1929. It created a Federal Farm Board to help support voluntary farm "cooperatives"— an old idea first promoted by the Populists whereby farmers joined together to reduce their expenses and also moderate the sometimes dramatic fluctuations in commodities prices. Alas, before the new programs had a chance to prove themselves, the farm sector was devastated by the onset of the **Great Depression**.

Farmers gained even less from another prolonged Congressional debate over raising tariffs on imports. What Hoover won after fourteen months of struggle with lobbyists in Congress was in fact a disastrous hike in tariff duties on imported manufactured items as well as farm goods. The Tariff of 1930, authored by two leading Republican "protectionists," Willis C. Hawley and Reed Owen Smoot, was intended to help the farm sector by reducing imports of farm products into the United States. But the corporate lobbyists in Washington, D.C., convinced Congress to raise duties on hundreds of imported items to an all-time high. The result was a global disaster. Some 1,028 economists petitioned Hoover to veto the short-sighted bill because its logic was flawed: by trying to "protect" American farmers from foreign competition, the bill would actually raise prices on most raw materials and consumer products. The new Hawley-Smoot Tariff was a fiasco. It prompted other countries to retaliate, often by shipping their goods away from the United States and by passing tariffs of their own, thereby making it more difficult for American farms and businesses to ship their products abroad. As a result, U.S. exports plummeted after the passage of the infamous Hawley-Smoot Tariff.

THE ECONOMY OUT OF CONTROL   The new tariff did nothing to check a deepening economic crisis. After the postwar slump of 1921, the naïve idea grew that the economy had entered a new era of *perpetual* growth. Greed then propelled a growing contagion of get-rich-quick schemes. Such speculative mania fueled the Florida real estate boom. Thousands of people invested in Florida real estate, usually at long distance, eager for quick profits in the nation's fastest-growing state. In mid-1926, however, the Florida real estate bubble burst.

For the losers it was a sobering lesson, but it proved to be but an audition for the great bull market in stocks. Until 1927 stock values had gone up with corporate profits, but then they began to soar on wings of pure speculation.

Treasury Secretary Andrew W. Mellon's tax reductions had given affluent people more money to spend, much of which found its way to the stock market. Instead of speculating in real estate, one could **buy stock "on margin"**—that is, make a small down payment (the "margin") and borrow the rest from a broker, who held the stock as security in case the stock price plummeted. If the stock declined and the buyer failed to meet a "margin call" for more funds, the broker could sell the stock to cover his loan. Brokers' loans to stock purchasers more than doubled from 1927 to 1929.

Stock market investors ignored warning signs. By 1927, residential construction and automobile sales were slowing and the rate of consumer spending had also slowed. By mid-1929, production, employment, and other measures of economic activity were declining. Still the stock market rose. By 1929, the stock market had become a fantasy world, driven more by hope and greed than by actual business performance. The few financiers and brokers who counseled caution were ignored. President Hoover also voiced concern about the "orgy of mad speculation," and he tried to discourage the irrational faith in the stock markets, but to no avail. On October 22 a leading bank president assured reporters that there was "nothing fundamentally wrong with the stock market or with the underlying business and credit structure."

THE CRASH AND ITS CAUSES   The next day, stock values tumbled and triggered a wild scramble as panicking people tried to unload stocks. On Tuesday, October 29, the most devastating single day in the stock market's history to that point, widespread panic had set in. By the end of the month, stocks on the New York Stock Exchange had fallen in value by an average of 37 percent. Business and government leaders initially expressed confidence that the markets would rebound. According to President Hoover, "the fundamental business of the country" was sound. But the hysteria continued. The *New York Times* stock average, which stood at 452 in September 1929, bottomed at 52 in July 1932. The collapse of the stock market revealed that the much-trumpeted economic prosperity of the 1920s had been built on weak foundations. By 1932 the nation's economy had experienced a broad collapse that brought prolonged, record levels of unemployment and widespread human suffering. From 1929 to 1933, U.S. economic output (called gross domestic product or GDP) dropped almost 27 percent. The unemployment rate by 1932 was 23 percent.

The stock market crash did not cause the Great Depression, but it did shake public confidence in the nation's financial system and it revealed major reveal major structural flaws in the economy and in government policies. Too many businesses had maintained high retail prices and taken large profits while holding down wage increases. As a result, about a third of personal income went to only the top 5 percent of the population. By plowing most profits back into expansion rather than wage increases, the business sector brought on a growing imbalance between rising industrial productivity and declining consumer purchasing power. As consumer spending declined, the rate of investment in new factories and businesses also plummeted. For a time the erosion of consumer purchasing power was concealed by an increase in installment buying, and the volume of foreign loans and investments, which supported foreign demand for American goods, concealed the deflationary effects of the high tariffs. But the flow of American capital abroad began to dry up when the stock market began to look more attractive. Swollen corporate profits, together with Treasury Secretary Mellon's business-friendly tax policies, enticed the rich into more frenzied stock market speculation. When trouble came, the bloated corporate structure collapsed.

Government policies also contributed to the financial debacle. Andrew Mellon's tax reductions led to oversaving by the general public, which helped diminish the demand for consumer goods. Hostility toward labor unions impeded efforts to ensure that wage levels kept pace with corporate profits. High tariffs discouraged foreign trade. Lax enforcement of anti-trust laws also encouraged high retail prices.

Another culprit was the gold standard, whereby nations pegged the value of their paper currency to the size of their gold reserves so as to avoid hyperinflation. Gold had long been thought to be the foundation of a sound money supply. When gold drained out of a nation, the amount of paper money shrunk; when a nation accumulated gold, the money supply expanded. When economic output, prices, and savings began dropping in 1929, policy makers—certain that they had to keep their currencies tied to the gold supply at all costs—tightened access to money at the very moment that economies needed an expanding money supply to keep growing. The only way to restore economic stability within the constraints of the gold standard was to let prices and wages continue to fall, allowing the downturn, in Andrew Mellon's words, to "purge the rottenness out of the system." Instead, the lack of innovative engagement among government and financial leaders turned a recession into the world's worst depression as nations followed Mellon's contractionist philosophy. From 1929 to 1933, 40 percent of American banks disappeared, taking with them the savings accounts of millions of people. Unlike today, nothing was done by the Federal Reserve system to shore up the banking sector. As a result, defaults and bankruptcies fed deflation. The nation's money supply shrank by a third. Such a contraction of the money supply drove prices and production down. By 1936, the horrible effects of such a deflationary spiral would lead more than two dozen nations, including the United States, to abandon the gold standard, thereby enabling the expansion of the money supply which in turn led to economic growth.

THE HUMAN TOLL OF THE DEPRESSION   The devastating collapse of the economy caused immense social hardships. By 1933, 13 million people were out of work. Millions more who kept their jobs saw their hours and wages reduced. The contraction of the economy especially squeezed debtors, especially farmers and laborers who had made installment purchases or mortgages. By 1933, a thousand Americans per day were losing their homes to foreclosure. The home construction industry went dormant. Factories shut down, banks closed, farms went bankrupt, and millions of people found themselves not only jobless but also homeless and penniless. Hungry people lined up at soup kitchens; others rummaged through trash cans behind restaurants. Many slept on park benches or in alleys. Others congregated in makeshift shelters in vacant lots. Thousands of desperate men in search of jobs rode the rails. These hobos, or tramps, as they were derisively called, sneaked onto empty railway cars and rode from town to town, looking for work. During the winter, homeless people wrapped themselves in newspapers to keep warm, sarcastically referring to their coverings as Hoover blankets. Some died from exposure. Others grew so weary of their grim fate that they ended their lives. The suicide rate soared during the 1930s. Americans had never before, and have never since, experienced social distress on such a scale.

HOOVER'S EFFORTS AT RECOVERY   Although the policies of government officials helped to bring on the economic collapse, few politicians even acknowledged that there was an unprecedented crisis: all that was needed, they claimed, was a slight correction of the market. Those who held to the dogma of limited government thought the economy would cure itself. Nothing should be done; the depression should be allowed to run its course until the economy had purged itself of its excesses. The best policy, Treasury Secretary Mellon advised, would be to "liquidate labor, liquidate stocks, liquidate the farmers, liquidate real estate." Initially, this "liquidationist" philosophy prevailed in government. Wages, stock prices, and property values were allowed to keep falling on the assumption that eventually they would reach a point where people would start buying again. But it did not work. Falling wages and land values made it harder for farmers, businesses, and households to pay their debts. As people defaulted on loans and mortgages and more people lost jobs, wages and property values kept dropping, worsening the slump. With so many people losing jobs and income, consumers and businesses simply could not buy enough goods and services to get the economy growing again.

President Hoover was less willing than Mellon to sit by and let events take their course. He in fact did more than any president had ever done before in such dire economic circumstances. Still, his own political philosophy, now hardened into dogma, set firm limits on government action, and he was unwilling to set that philosophy aside even to meet an unprecedented national emergency. "You know," Hoover told a journalist, "the only trouble with capitalism is capitalists; they're too damn greedy."

As the economy floundered, Hoover believed that the nation's fundamental business structure was sound and that the people simply needed their confidence restored. So he invited business, financial, and labor leaders to the White House and urged them to keep their mills and shops open, maintain wage rates, and spread out the work to avoid layoffs—in short, to let the first shock of depression fall on corporate profits rather than on wage earners. In return, union leaders, who had little choice, agreed to refrain from demanding higher wages and going on strike. In speech after speech, Hoover exhorted people to keep up hope and reassured business leaders that the economy would rebound. To help steady the nation's nerves, the president intentionally described the economic downturn not as a "panic," or as a "crisis," but as a "depression," thinking that it was a less inflammatory word. By 1931 Hoover was calling the economic calamity "a great depression," an unfortunate choice of words that would come back to haunt him. In early May 1930 he told the U.S. Chamber of Commerce that he was "convinced we have passed the worst and with continued effort we shall rapidly recover." As it happened, however, uplifting words were not enough.

So Hoover did more than enlist the support of the business community and reassure the public. He accelerated the start of government construction projects in order to provide jobs, but cutbacks by state and local governments in their projects more than offset the new federal spending. At Hoover's demand, the Federal Reserve Board returned to an easier monetary policy, and Congress passed a modest tax reduction to put more cash into people's pockets. The Federal Farm Board stepped up its loans and its purchases of farm surpluses, only to face bumper crops in 1930 despite droughts in the Midwest and Southwest.

Hoover's efforts to address the burgeoning economic crisis were not enough, however. Because he never understood or acknowledged the seriousness of the economic problems, he and his administration never did enough to stop the Depression from worsening. Vice President Charles Curtis claimed that "prosperity was "just around the corner." Hoover shared the assumption that the nation was simply experiencing a short-term shock, not a prolonged malaise, so drastic action was not warranted. In June 1930 Hoover told a delegation of bankers that the "depression is over." But more and more people kept losing their jobs, and disappointment in the president deepened. By the fall of 1930, more than 25,000 businesses had failed, there were five million people unemployed, and many city governments were buckling under the strain of lost revenue and growing human distress. Hoover dismissed the concerns of "calamity mongers and weeping men." He balked at giving uplifting speeches, admitting that he was no Theodore Roosevelt.

STRESSES AND STRAINS   As always, a depressed economy hurt the party in power, and the Democrats shrewdly exploited Hoover's predicament. The squalid shantytowns that sprouted across the country to house the destitute and homeless became known as Hoovervilles; a Hoover flag was an

Impact of the Depression

Two children set up shop in a Hooverville in Washington, D.C.

empty pocket turned inside out. In November 1930 the Democrats gained their first national victory since 1916, winning a majority in the House and a near majority in the Senate. Hoover refused to see the elections as a warning signal. Instead he grew more resistant to calls for dramatic measures.

In the first half of 1931, economic indicators rose, renewing hope for an upswing. Then, as recovery beckoned, another shock occurred. In May 1931, the failure of Austria's largest bank triggered a financial panic in central Europe. To ease concerns, President Hoover negotiated in June a one-year moratorium on both payments of war reparations and war debts by the European nations. Hoover's moratorium was perhaps the most decisive, popular decision of his presidency, but it did little to stop the collapsing world economy. The global shortage of monetary exchange drove Europeans to withdraw their gold from American banks and dump their American securities (stocks and bonds). One European country after another abandoned the gold standard and devalued its currency. Even the Bank of England went off the gold standard.

At the end of 1932, after Hoover's debt moratorium ended, most European countries defaulted on their war debts to the United States. In retaliation, Congress passed the Johnson Debt Default Act of 1934, which prohibited even private loans to any government that had defaulted on its debts to the United States. Foreign withdrawals of money from U.S. banks helped spread a sense of panic. Using conventional wisdom, the Federal Reserve system sought to protect the value of the nation's gold reserves by raising interest rates. But what the American banks needed most was not tighter access to money but easier money to ease the *liquidity* crisis: banks desperately needed cash to meet the demands of panicky depositors who wanted to cash in their savings accounts. By the end of 1931 over six hundred U.S. banks had gone bankrupt. Almost 25 percent of the workforce—15 million people—were unemployed. The resulting societal misery was unprecedented. Some jobless, homeless people grew desperate. Men started forest fires in hopes of being hired to put them out. Others committed petty crimes in order to be arrested; at least jails provided them with food and shelter.

CONGRESSIONAL INITIATIVES   With a new Congress in session in 1932, demands for federal action impelled Hoover to stretch his individualistic philosophy to its limits. He was now ready to use government resources to shore up the financial institutions of the country. That year, the new Congress set up the **Reconstruction Finance Corporation** (RFC) with $500 million (and authority to borrow $2 billion more) for emergency loans to struggling banks, life-insurance companies, and railroads. Under Charles G. Dawes, Calvin Coolidge's vice president, the RFC had authorized $1.2 billion in loans within six months. It staved off several bankruptcies, but Hoover's critics called it favoritism to big businesses, the most damaging instance of which was a $90 million loan to Dawes's own Chicago bank, made soon after he left the RFC in 1932. The RFC nonetheless remained a key federal agency through the mid-1940s.

Hoover's critics said all these "unprecedented" measures reflected a dubious "trickle-down" theory. If government could help huge banks and railroads, asked New York Democratic senator Robert F. Wagner, "is there any reason why we should not likewise extend a helping hand to that forlorn American, in every village and every city of the United States, who has been without wages since 1929?" The contraction of the nation's money supply devastated debtors such as farmers and those who made purchases on the installment plan or held balloon-style mortgages, whose monthly payments increased over time.

By 1932, members of Congress, mostly Democrats, were filling the hoppers with bills for federal measures to provide relief to the people hit hardest by the economic collapse. At that point, Hoover might have pleaded "dire necessity" and taken the leadership of the relief movement and salvaged his political fortunes. Instead, he held back and only grudgingly edged toward addressing the widespread human distress. On July 21, 1932, he signed the Emergency Relief Act, which avoided a direct federal dole (cash payment) to individuals but gave the RFC $300 million for relief loans to the states, authorized loans of up to $1.5 billion for state and local construction projects, and appropriated $322 million for federal public works.

FARMERS AND VETERANS IN PROTEST Government expenditures to provide relief for farmers had long since dried up. In mid-1931 the federal government quit buying crop surpluses and helplessly watched prices for commodities slide. Faced with the loss of everything, desperate farmers defied the law. Angry mobs stopped foreclosures and threatened to lynch the judges sanctioning them. In Nebraska, farmers burned corn to keep warm. Iowans formed the militant Farmers' Holiday Association, which called a farmers' strike.

The economic crisis spawned desperate talk of revolution. "Folks are restless," Mississippi governor Theodore Bilbo told reporters in 1931. "Communism is gaining a foothold. . . . In fact, I'm getting a little pink myself." Across the country the once-obscure Communist party began to draw crowds to its rallies. Yet for all the sound and fury, few Americans embraced communism during the 1930s. Party membership in the United States never rose much above one hundred thousand.

Anger and frustration

Unemployed military veterans, members of the Bonus Expeditionary Force, clash with Washington, D.C., police at Anacostia Flats in July 1932.

Fears of organized revolt arose when unemployed veterans converged on the nation's capital in the spring of 1932. The "**Bonus Expeditionary Force**" grew quickly to more than twenty thousand. Their purpose was to get immediate payment of the cash bonus to nearly 4 million World War I veterans that Congress had approved in 1924. The House passed a bonus bill, but when the Senate voted it down, most of the veterans went home. The rest, along with their wives and children, having no place to go, camped in vacant federal buildings and in a shantytown at Anacostia Flats, within sight of the Capitol.

Eager to disperse the homeless veterans, Hoover persuaded Congress to pay for their tickets home. More left, but others stayed even after Congress adjourned, hoping at least to meet with the president. Late in July, the administration ordered the government buildings cleared. In the ensuing melee, a policeman panicked, fired into the crowd, and killed two veterans. The secretary of war then dispatched about seven hundred soldiers under overeager General Douglas MacArthur, who was aided by junior officers Dwight D. Eisenhower and George S. Patton. MacArthur, who dismissed the veterans as "communists," ordered his soldiers to use horses, tanks, tear gas, and bayonets to rout the unarmed veterans and their families and burn their makeshift camp. Dozens of protesters were injured in the melee, and an eleven-week-old boy born at Anacostia died from exposure to tear gas. Eisenhower, who had opposed the use of force, said it was "a pitiful scene." Franklin D. Roosevelt, then serving as governor of New York, concluded after learning of the army's action that General MacArthur was one of the most dangerous men in America.

The disheartened mood of the war veterans matched the mood of the country, as well as that of the beleaguered Hoover himself. He worked hard, seven days a week, but the stress had sapped his health and morale. "I am so tired," he said, "that every bone in my body aches." Presidential news conferences became more strained and less frequent. While traveling with a group of Cabinet officers, Hoover asked the secretary of the Treasury for a nickel to phone a friend; the secretary said, "Here are two nickels—call them both." When aides urged Hoover to seize the reins of leadership, he said "I have no Wilsonian qualities." The president's deepening sense of futility became increasingly evident to the country. In a mood more despairing than rebellious, Americans in 1932 eagerly anticipated what the next presidential campaign would produce.

GLOBAL CONCERNS

In 1928, with problems apparently clearing up in Mexico and Nicaragua, President Calvin Coolidge traveled to Havana, Cuba, to open the Pan-American Conference. It was an unusual gesture of friendship, and so was the choice of Charles Evans Hughes, the former secretary of state, to head the American delegation. Hughes announced the United States' intention to withdraw its marines from Nicaragua and Haiti as soon as possible, although he did block a resolution declaring that no nation "has the right to intervene in the affairs of another."

At the end of 1928, President-elect Herbert Hoover toured ten Latin American nations. Once in office, Hoover, reversed Woodrow Wilson's policy of refusing to recognize "bad" regimes and reverted to the older policy of recognizing governments in power regardless of their actions. In 1930, he generated more goodwill by permitting publication of a memorandum drawn up in 1928 by Undersecretary of State J. Reuben Clark. The Clark Memorandum denied that the Monroe Doctrine justified U.S. military intervention in Latin America. Although Hoover never endorsed the memorandum, he never intervened in the region. Before he left office, steps had been taken to withdraw American forces from Nicaragua and Haiti.

JAPAN INVADES CHINA   During the twentieth century, China had struggled amid a civil war to gain its own independence from European influence. Japan, however, had embraced Western imperialism as the model for its own expansionist ambitions on the Asian mainland. In 1931–1932, some ten thousand Japanese troops occupied Manchuria, a vast province in northeast China blessed with valuable deposits of iron ore and coal. The Japanese then renamed Manchuria "The Republic of Manchukuo" and proclaimed its independence from China. It was the first major step in the effort to control all of China.

The Japanese takeover of Manchuria challenged the will of the Western democracies to enforce world peace, and they failed the test. Hoover's secretary of state, Henry Stimson, wanted to use the threat of force to deter the Japanese advance in China but worried that the president "being a Quaker and an engineer did not understand the psychology of combat. . . . " Against the wishes of his secretary of state, President Hoover, who admired Japan's economic prowess, refused to join an international economic boycott of Japan. In January 1932 Hoover and Stimson announced that the United States would not recognize any territorial changes in China that violated previous treaties. In revealing that the United States was unwilling to use even the threat of force to stop Japanese aggression, the so-called Hoover-Stimson Doctrine foreshadowed the timid nature of American diplomacy during the 1930s and revealed the hollowness of the Kellogg-Briand Treaty outlawing war. But Hoover's stance also reflected American public opinion. "The American people don't give a hoot in a rain barrel who controls North China," said a Philadelphia newspaper. When the League of Nations condemned Japanese aggression in China, Japan simply withdrew from the League in 1933. An uneasy peace settled upon east Asia for four years, during which time aggressive Japanese military leaders increased their political sway in Tokyo.

FROM HOOVERISM TO THE NEW DEAL

THE ELECTION OF 1932   On June 14, 1932, while the ragtag Bonus Army was still encamped in Washington, D.C., glum Republicans gathered in Chicago to renominate Herbert Hoover. The delegates went through the motions in a mood of defeat. By contrast, the Democrats converged on Chicago later in June confident that they would nominate the next president. The fifty-year-old New York governor Franklin Delano Roosevelt was already the front-runner, with most of the delegates lined up, and he went over the top on the fourth ballot.

In a bold, unprecedented gesture, Roosevelt flew for nine hours to Chicago to accept the nomination instead of awaiting formal notification. He had intentionally broken with tradition, he told the delegates, because the stakes were so high. "Republican leaders not only have failed in material things, they have failed in national vision, because in disaster they have held out no hope. . . . I pledge you, I pledge myself to a new deal for the American people" that would "break foolish traditions." Roosevelt's acceptance speech was a bundle of contradictions, promising "to cut taxes and balance the budget" as well as to launch numerous innovations to provide the people with "work and security." What his New Deal "crusade" would be in practice Roosevelt had little idea as yet, but he was much more willing to experiment than Hoover. What was more, his upbeat personality communicated joy, energy, and hope. Roosevelt's campaign song was "Happy Days Are Here Again."

Born in 1882, the adored only child of wealthy parents, educated by tutors at Hyde Park, his father's Hudson River estate in New York, young Roosevelt led a cosmopolitan life. His parents arranged for a private railroad car to deliver him to Groton, an elite Massachusetts boarding school. He later attended Harvard College and Columbia University Law School. While a law student, he married his distant cousin, Anna Eleanor Roosevelt, a niece of his fifth cousin, Theodore Roosevelt, then president of the United States.

In 1910, Franklin Roosevelt won a Democratic seat in the New York State Senate. As a freshman legislator he displayed the contradictory qualities that would characterize his political career: he was an aristocrat with empathy for common folk, a traditionalist with a penchant for experimentation, an affable charmer with a buoyant smile and upturned chin who harbored enormous self-confidence and optimism as well as profound convictions, and a skilled political tactician with a shrewd sense of timing and a distinctive willingness to listen to and learn from others.

Tall, handsome, and athletic, Roosevelt seemed destined for greatness. In 1912 he backed Woodrow Wilson for president, and for both of Wilson's terms he served as assistant secretary of the navy. Then, in 1920, largely on the strength of his name, he became James Cox's running mate on the Democratic ticket. The following year, at age thirty-nine, his career was cut short by the onset of polio that left him permanently disabled, unable to stand or walk without braces. But the battle for recovery transformed the young aristocrat. He became less arrogant, less superficial, more focused, and more interesting. A friend recalled that Roosevelt emerged from his struggle with polio "completely warm-hearted, with a new humility of spirit" that led him to identify with the poor and the suffering. Justice Oliver

The "New Deal" candidate

Governor Franklin Delano Roosevelt, the Democratic nominee for president in 1932, campaigning in Topeka, Kansas. Roosevelt's confidence inspired voters.

Wendell Holmes later summed up his qualities this way: "a second-class intellect—but a first-class temperament."

For seven years, aided by his talented wife, Eleanor, Roosevelt strengthened his body to compensate for his disability, and in 1928 he won the governorship of New York. Reelected by a whopping majority of 700,000 in 1930, Roosevelt became the Democrats' favorite for president in 1932. Partly to dispel doubts about his health, the Democratic nominee set forth on a grueling campaign tour in 1932. He blamed the Depression on the Republicans, attacked Hoover for his "extravagant government spending," and he repeatedly promised Americans a New Deal. Like Hoover, Roosevelt pledged to balance the budget, but he was willing to incur short-term deficits to prevent starvation and revive the economy. On the tariff he was evasive. On farm policy he offered several options pleasing to farmers and ambiguous enough not to alarm city dwellers. He called for strict regulation of utilities and for at least some government development of electricity, and he consistently stood by his party's pledge to repeal the Prohibition amendment. Perhaps most important, he recognized that a revitalized economy would require national planning and new ideas. "The country needs, and, unless I mistake its temper, the country demands bold, persistent experimentation," he said. "Above all, try something."

What came across to voters, however, was less the content of Roosevelt's speeches than his uplifting confidence and his commitment to change. By contrast, Hoover lacked vitality and vision. Democrats, Hoover argued, ignored the international causes of the vision. They were also taking a reckless course. Roosevelt's proposals, he warned, "would destroy the very foundations of our American system." Pursue them, he warned, and "grass will grow in the streets of a hundred cities, a thousand towns." But few were listening. Mired in the persistent depression the country wanted a new course, a new leadership, a new deal.

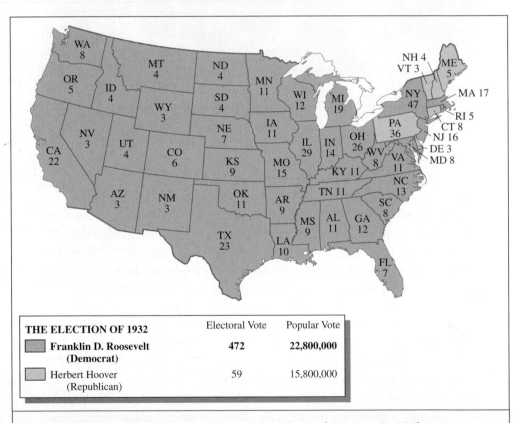

THE ELECTION OF 1932	Electoral Vote	Popular Vote
Franklin D. Roosevelt (Democrat)	472	22,800,000
Herbert Hoover (Republican)	59	15,800,000

Why did Roosevelt appeal to voters struggling during the Depression? What were Hoover's criticisms of Roosevelt's "New Deal"? What policies defined Roosevelt's New Deal during the presidential campaign?

Some disillusioned voters took a dim view of both major candidates. Those who believed that only a radical departure would suffice supported the Socialist party candidate, Norman Thomas, who polled 882,000 votes, and a few preferred the Communist party candidate, who won 103,000. The wonder is that a desperate people did not turn in greater numbers to radical candidates. Instead, they swept Roosevelt into office with 23 million votes to Hoover's 16 million. Hoover carried only four states in New England plus Pennsylvania and Delaware and lost decisively in the Electoral College by 472 to 59.

THE 1933 INAUGURATION   For the last time the nation waited four months, from early November until March 4, for a newly elected president and Congress to take office. The Twentieth Amendment, ratified on January 23, 1933, provided that presidents would thereafter take office on January 20 and the newly elected Congress on January 3. Just two weeks before his March inauguration, Roosevelt survived an attempted assassination while speaking in Miami, Florida. The gunman, an unemployed bricklayer and Italian-born anarchist, fired five shots at the president-elect. Roosevelt was not hit, but the mayor of Chicago was killed.

The bleak winter of 1932–1933 witnessed spreading destitution and misery. Unemployment increased, and panic struck the banking system. As bank after bank collapsed, people rushed to their own banks to remove their deposits. Many discovered that they, too, were caught short of cash. When the Hoover administration ended in early 1933, four fifths of the nation's banks were closed, and the country teetered on the brink of economic paralysis.

The profound crisis of confidence that greeted Roosevelt when he took the oath of office on March 4, 1933, soon gave way to a mood of expectancy and hope. The charismatic new president displayed monumental self-assurance when he declared "that the only thing we have to fear is fear itself—nameless, unreasoning, unjustified terror which paralyzes needed efforts to convert retreat into advance." If need be, he said, "I shall ask the Congress for . . . broad executive power to wage a war against the emergency as great as the power that would be given me if we were in fact invaded by a foreign foe." It was a measure of the country's mood that Roosevelt's call for unprecedented presidential power received the loudest applause.

CHAPTER SUMMARY

- **"Return to Normalcy"** Although progressivism lost its appeal after the Great War, the Eighteenth Amendment (paving the way for Prohibition) and the Nineteenth Amendment (guaranteeing women's suffrage) marked the culmination of that movement at the national level. Reformers still actively worked for good and efficient government at the local level, but overall the drive was for a "return to normalcy"—conformity and moral righteousness.

- **Isolationism** America distanced itself from global affairs—a stance reflected in the Red Scare, laws limiting immigration, and high tariffs. Yet America could not ignore international events because its business interests were becoming increasingly global. Although the United States never joined the League of Nations, it sent unofficial observers to Geneva. The widespread belief that arms limitations would reduce the chance of future wars led America to participate in the Washington Naval Conference of 1921 and the Kellogg-Briand Pact of 1928.

- **Era of Conservatism** Many Americans, particularly people in rural areas and members of the middle class, wanted a return to a quieter, more conservative way of life after World War I, and Warren G. Harding's landslide Republican victory allowed just that. The policies of Harding's pro-business cabinet were reminiscent of those of the McKinley White House more than two decades earlier. Union membership declined in the 1920s as workers' rights were rolled back by a conservative Supreme Court and in response to fears of Communist subversion. Workers, however, shared in the affluence of the 1920s, thereby contributing to the rise of a mass culture.

- **Growth of Economy** The budget was balanced through reductions in spending and taxes, while tariffs were raised to protect domestic industries, setting the tone for a prosperous decade. Harding's successor, Calvin Coolidge, actively promoted the interests of big business. The public responded enthusiastically to the mass marketing of new consumer goods such as radios and affordable automobiles. Agricultural production, however, lagged after the wartime boom evaporated.

- **The Great Depression** The stock market crash revealed the structural flaws in the economy, but it did not cause the Great Depression. Government policies throughout the twenties—high tariffs, lax enforcement of anti-trust laws, an absence of checks on speculation in real estate and the stock market, and adherence to the gold standard—contributed to the onset of the Depression. Hoover's attempts to remedy the problems were too few and too late. Banks failed, businesses closed, homes and jobs were lost.

CHRONOLOGY

1921	Representatives of the United States, Great Britain, France, Italy, and Japan attend the Washington Naval Conference
1922	United States begins sending observers to the League of Nations
	Benito Mussolini comes to power in Italy
1923	President Warren G. Harding dies in office
1928	Herbert Hoover is elected president
	More than sixty nations sign the Kellogg-Briand Pact pledging not to go to war with one another, except in matters of self-defense
October 29, 1929	Stock market crashes
1930	Congress passes the Hawley-Smoot Tariff
1932	Congress sets up the Reconstruction Finance Corporation
1932	Congress passes the Glass-Steagall Act
1933	Bonus Expeditionary Force converges on Washington to demand payment of bonuses promised to war veterans

KEY TERMS & NAMES

2 7

NEW DEAL AMERICA

FOCUS QUESTIONS   wwnorton.com/studyspace

- What were the immediate challenges facing Franklin Delano Roosevelt in March 1933?
- What were the lasting effects of the New Deal legislation?
- Why did the New Deal draw criticism from conservatives and liberals?
- How did the New Deal expand the federal government's authority?
- What were the major cultural changes of the 1930s?

Franklin Delano Roosevelt was elected in 1932 to lead an anxious nation mired in the third year of an unprecedented depression. No other business slump had been so deep, so long, or so painful. One out of every four Americans in 1932 was unemployed; in many large cities nearly half of the adults were out of work. Some five hundred thousand people had lost homes or farms because they could not pay their mortgages. Thousands of banks had failed; millions of depositors had lost their life savings. The suffering was global. The worldwide depression helped accelerate the rise of fascism and communism; totalitarianism was on the march in Europe and Asia. "The situation is critical," the prominent political analyst Walter Lippmann warned President-elect Roosevelt. "You may have to assume dictatorial powers." Roosevelt did not become a dictator, but he did take decisive action that transformed the scope and role of the federal government. He and a supportive Congress immediately adopted bold measures intended to relieve the human suffering and promote economic recovery. Although the New Deal initiatives produced mixed results, they halted the economic downturn and provided the foundation for a system of federal social welfare programs.

COMPETING PROPOSALS   In 1933, **President Roosevelt** confronted three major challenges: reviving the economy, relieving the widespread human misery, and rescuing the farm sector and its desperate families. To address these daunting challenges, Roosevelt assembled a "brain trust" of talented advisers who feverishly developed ideas to address the nation's compelling problems. Some promoted vigorous enforcement of the anti-trust laws as a means of restoring business competition; others argued for the opposite, saying that anti-trust laws should be suspended so as to enable the largest corporations to collaborate with the federal government and thereby better manage the overall economy. Still others called for a massive expansion of social welfare programs and a prolonged infusion of increased government spending to address the profound human crisis and revive the economy.

Roosevelt was willing to try some elements of each approach without ever embracing any one of them completely. In part his flexible outlook reflected a stern political reality: seasoned conservative southern Democrats controlled the Congress, and the new president could not risk alienating these powerful proponents of balanced budgets and limited government. Roosevelt's inconsistencies also reflected his own outlook. Roosevelt was a pragmatist rather than an ideologue, a tinkerer more than a dogmatist. As he once explained, "Take a method and try it. If it fails, admit it frankly and try another." Roosevelt's elastic New Deal would therefore take the form of a series of trial-and-error actions, some of which were well-intentioned failures.

Roosevelt and his advisers initially settled on a three-pronged strategy to revive the economy. First, they sought to remedy the immediate banking crisis and to provide short-term emergency relief for the jobless. Second, the New Dealers tried to jump start the economy by increasing federal spending and by facilitating cooperative agreements between management and organized labor. Third, they attempted to raise depressed commodity prices by paying farmers to reduce the size of their crops and herds. When the overall supply of agricultural products was reduced, prices for grain and meat would rise over time and thereby increase farm income. None of these initiatives worked perfectly, but their combined effect was to restore hope and energy to a nation paralyzed by fear and uncertainty.

STRENGTHENING THE MONETARY SYSTEM   Money is the lubricant of capitalism, and money was fast disappearing from circulation by 1933. Panicky depositors withdrew their savings from banks and hoarded their currency. By taking money out of circulation, however, people unwittingly exacerbated the Depression. On his second day in office, Roosevelt called upon Congress to meet in a special session on March 9 to pass the Emergency Banking Relief Act, which permitted sound banks to reopen and appointed managers for those that remained in trouble. On March 12, in the first of his radio-broadcast "fireside chats," the president assured the 60 million Americans listening that it was safer to "keep your money in a reopened bank than under the mattress." His reassurances soothed a nervous nation. The following day, deposits in reopened banks exceeded withdrawals. "Capitalism was saved in eight days," said one of Roosevelt's advisers. The banking crisis had ended, and the new administration was ready to get on with its broader program of economic recovery.

Roosevelt next followed through on two campaign pledges. At his behest, Congress passed an Economy Act, granting the executive branch the power to cut government workers' salaries, reduce payments to military veterans for non-service-connected disabilities, and reorganize federal agencies in the interest of reducing expenses. Second, Roosevelt ended Prohibition. The Beer-Wine Revenue Act amended the Volstead Act to permit the sale of beverages with an alcohol content of 3.2 percent or less. The **Twenty-first Amendment**, already submitted by Congress to the states, would be declared ratified on December 5, thus ending the "noble experiment" of Prohibition.

The measures of March were but the beginning of an avalanche of New Deal legislation. From March 9 to June 16, the so-called Hundred Days, a cooperative Congress endorsed fifteen major pieces of legislation proposed by the president that collectively transformed the role of the federal government in social and economic life.

Several of the programs comprising what came to be called the **First New Deal** addressed the acute debt problem faced by farmers and homeowners. During 1933, a thousand homes or farms were being foreclosed upon each day. By executive decree, Roosevelt reorganized all federal farm credit agencies into the Farm Credit Administration. By the Emergency Farm Mortgage Act and the Farm Credit Act, Congress authorized the extensive refinancing of

The galloping snail

A vigorous Roosevelt drives Congress to action in this *Detroit News* cartoon from March 1933.

farm mortgages at lower interest rates to stem the tide of foreclosures. The Home Owners' Loan Act provided a similar service to city dwellers through the Home Owners' Loan Corporation, which refinanced mortgage loans at lower monthly payments for strapped homeowners, again helping to slow the rate of foreclosures. In 1934, Roosevelt created the Federal Housing Administration (FHA), which offered Americans much longer home mortgages (twenty years) to reduce their monthly payments. The Banking Act further shored up confidence in the banking system. Its Federal Deposit Insurance Corporation (FDIC) guaranteed personal bank deposits up to $5,000.

RELIEF MEASURES   Another urgent priority in 1933 was relieving the widespread human distress caused by the Great Depression. Herbert Hoover had stubbornly refused to provide direct federal assistance to the unemployed and homeless. Roosevelt was more flexible. For example, he convinced Congress to create the Civilian Conservation Corps (CCC) to provide jobs to unemployed, unmarried young men aged eighteen to twenty-five. Nearly 3 million men were hired to work at a variety of CCC jobs in national forests, parks, and recreational areas and on soil-conservation projects. CCC workers built roads, bridges, campgrounds, and fish hatcheries; planted trees; taught farmers how to control soil erosion; and fought fires. The enrollees could also earn high-school diplomas.

The Federal Emergency Relief Administration (FERA) addressed the broader problems of human distress. The agency expanded federal assistance to the unemployed. Federal money flowed to the states in outright grants rather than "loans," and the states distributed the money as they saw fit.

The first large-scale experiment with *federal* work relief, which put people directly on the government payroll at competitive wages, came with the formation of the Civil Works Administration (CWA). Created in November 1933, after the state-sponsored programs funded by the FERA proved inadequate, the CWA provided federal jobs to those unable to find work that winter. It was hastily conceived and implemented but during its four-month existence the CWA put to work over 4 million people. The agency organized a variety of useful projects: making highway repairs and laying sewer lines, constructing or improving more than a thousand airports and forty thousand schools, and providing fifty thousand teaching jobs that helped keep rural schools open. As the number of people employed by the CWA soared, however, the program's costs skyrocketed to over $1 billion. Roosevelt balked at such expenditures and worried that people would become dependent upon federal jobs. So in the spring of 1934, he ordered the CWA dissolved. By April some 4 million workers were again unemployed.

REGULATORY EFFORTS

In addition to rescuing the banks and providing immediate relief to the unemployed, Roosevelt and his advisers promoted the long-term recovery of agriculture and industry during the Hundred Days in the spring of 1933. The languishing economy needed a boost—a big one. There were 13 million people without jobs.

AGRICULTURAL ASSISTANCE The sharp decline in commodity prices after 1929 meant that many farmers could not afford to plant or harvest their devalued crops. The **Agricultural Adjustment Act** of 1933 created a new federal agency, the Agricultural Adjustment Administration (AAA), which sought to raise prices for crops and herds by paying farmers to reduce production. The money for such payments came from a tax levied on the processors of certain basic commodities—cotton gins, for example, and flour mills.

By the time Congress acted, however, the spring growing season was already under way. The prospect of another bumper cotton crop forced the AAA to sponsor a plow-under program. To destroy a growing crop was a "shocking commentary on our civilization," Agriculture Secretary Henry A. Wallace lamented. "I could tolerate it only as a cleaning up of the wreckage from the old days of unbalanced production." Moreover, given the oversupply of hogs, some 6 million pigs were slaughtered and buried.

By the end of 1934, Wallace could report significant declines in wheat, cotton, and corn production and a simultaneous increase in commodity prices. Farm income increased by 58 percent between 1932 and 1935. The AAA was only partially responsible for the gains, however. A devastating drought that settled over the plains states between 1932 and 1935 played a major role in reducing production and creating the epic "**dust bowl**" migrations so poignantly evoked in John Steinbeck's famous novel, *The Grapes of Wrath* (1939). Many migrant families had actually been driven off the land by AAA benefit programs that encouraged large farmers to take land worked by tenants and sharecroppers out of cultivation.

Although it created unexpected problems, the AAA achieved successes in boosting the overall farm economy. Conservatives castigated its sweeping powers, however. On January 6, 1936, in *United States v. Butler*, the Supreme Court declared the AAA's tax on food processors unconstitutional. The administration hastily devised a new plan in the Soil Conservation and Domestic Allotment Act, which it pushed through Congress in six weeks.

The act was an almost unqualified success as an engineering and educational project because it helped heal the scars of erosion and the plague of dust storms. But soil conservation nevertheless failed as a device for limiting production. With their worst lands taken out of production, farmers cultivated their fertile acres more intensively. In response, Congress passed the Agricultural Adjustment Act of 1938, which reestablished the earlier crop-reduction programs but left out the processing taxes. Benefit payments would come from federal funds.

REVIVING INDUSTRIAL GROWTH   The industrial counterpart to the AAA was the **National Industrial Recovery Act** (NIRA), the two major parts of which dealt with economic recovery and public-works projects. The latter part created the Public Works Administration (PWA), granting $3.3 billion for new government buildings, highway construction, flood control projects, and other transportation improvements.

The more controversial part of the NIRA created the **National Recovery Administration** (NRA), headed by Hugh S. Johnson, a chain-smoking retired army general. Its purpose was twofold: (1) to stabilize the economy by reducing chaotic competition through the implementation of industry-wide codes that set wages and prices and (2) to generate more purchasing power for consumers by providing jobs, defining workplace standards, and raising wages. In each major industry, committees representing management, labor, and government drew up the fair practices codes. The labor standards featured in every code set a forty-hour workweek, minimum weekly wages of $13 ($12 in the South, where living costs were lower), and prohibited the employment of children under the age of sixteen.

Labor unions, already hard-pressed by the economic downturn and a loss of members, were understandably concerned about the NRA's efforts to reduce competition by allowing competing businesses to cooperate by fixing wages and prices. To gain union support, the NRA included a provision (Section 7a) that guaranteed the right of workers to organize unions. But while prohibiting employers from interfering with union-organizing efforts, the NRA did not create adequate enforcement measures, nor did it require employers to bargain in good faith with labor representatives.

For a time the NRA worked, and the downward spiral of wages and prices subsided. But as soon as economic recovery began, business owners complained that the larger corporations dominated the code-making activities and that price-fixing robbed small producers of the chance to compete. And because the NRA wage codes excluded agricultural and domestic workers,

three out of every four employed African Americans derived no direct benefit from the program. By 1935 the NRA had developed more critics than
friends. When it effectively died, in May 1935, struck down by the Supreme
Court as unconstitutional, few paused to mourn.

Yet the NRA experiment left an enduring mark. With dramatic suddenness
the industry-wide codes had set new workplace standards, such as the forty-
hour workweek, a minimum wage, and the abolition of child labor. The NRA's
endorsement of collective bargaining spurred the growth of unions. Moreover,
the codes advanced trends toward stabilization and rationalization that were
becoming the standard practice of business at large and that, despite misgivings about the concentration of power, would be further promoted by trade
associations. Yet as 1934 ended, economic recovery was nowhere in sight.

REGIONAL PLANNING One of the most innovative New Deal programs was the creation of the Tennessee Valley Authority (TVA), a bold venture designed to bring electrical power, flood control, and jobs to one of the
poorest regions in the nation. In May 1933, Congress created the TVA as a
multipurpose public corporation serving seven states: Alabama, Georgia, Illinois, Kentucky, Mississippi, North Carolina, and Tennessee. By 1936, it had six
dams completed or under way and a master plan to build nine high dams on
the Tennessee River, which would create the "Great Lakes of the South." The
agency, moreover, opened the rivers to boats and barges, fostered soil conservation and forestry, experimented with fertilizers, drew new industries to the
region, encouraged the formation of labor unions, improved schools and
libraries, and sent cheap electric power pulsating through the valley for the
first time. But the construction of dams and the creation of huge power-
generating lakes also meant the destruction of homes, farms, and communities. "I don't want to move," said an elderly East Tennessee woman. "I want to
sit here and look out over these hills where I was born." Inexpensive electricity
became more and more the TVA's reason for being—a purpose that would
become all the more important during World War II. The TVA transported
farm families from the age of kerosene to the age of electricity.

The Social Cost of the Depression

Although programs of the so-called First New Deal helped ease the devastation wrought by the Depression, they did not restore prosperity or end
the widespread human suffering. The Depression continued to take a toll on
Americans as the shattered economy slowly worked its way back to health.

CONTINUING HARDSHIPS   As late as 1939, some 9.5 million workers (17 percent of the labor force) remained unemployed. Prolonged economic hardship continued to create personal tragedies and tremendous social strains. Poverty led desperate people to do desperate things. Petty theft soared during the 1930s, as did street-corner begging, homelessness, and prostitution. Although the divorce rate dropped during the decade, in part because couples could not afford to live separately or pay the legal fees to obtain a divorce, all too often husbands down on their luck simply deserted their wives and children. A 1940 survey revealed that 1.5 million husbands had left home. With their future uncertain, married couples often decided not to have children; the birthrate plummeted. Parents sometimes could not support their children. In 1933 the Children's Bureau reported that one out of every five children was not getting enough to eat. Struggling parents sent their children to live with relatives or friends. Some nine hundred thousand children simply left home and joined the army of homeless "tramps."

DUST BOWL MIGRANTS   In the southern plains of the Midwest and the Mississippi Valley, a decade-long drought during the 1930s spawned an environmental and human catastrophe known as the dust bowl. Colorado,

Dust storm approaching, 1930s

When a dust storm blew in, it brought utter darkness, as well as the sand and grit that soon covered every surface, both indoors and out.

More Oklahomans reach Calif. via the cotton fields of Ariz.

"We got blowed out in Oklahoma"

Share-croppers family near Bakersfield Apr. 7- 1935

A sharecropper's family affected by the Oklahoma dust bowl

When the drought and dust storms showed no signs of relenting, many people headed west toward California.

New Mexico, Kansas, Nebraska, Texas, and Oklahoma were the states hardest hit. Crops withered and income plummeted. Relentless winds swept across the treeless plains, scooping up millions of tons of parched topsoil into billowing dark clouds that floated east across entire states, engulfing farms and towns in what were called black blizzards. By 1938, over 25 million acres of prairie land had lost most of its topsoil.

Human misery paralleled the environmental devastation. Parched farmers could not pay mortgages, and banks foreclosed on their property. Suicides soared. With each year, millions of people abandoned their farms. Uprooted farmers and their families formed a migratory stream of hardship flowing westward from the South and the Midwest toward California, buoyed by currents of hope and desperation. The West Coast was rumored to have plenty of jobs. So off they went on a cross-country trek in pursuit of new opportunities. Frequently lumped together as "Okies" or "Arkies," most of the dust bowl refugees were from cotton belt communities in Arkansas, Texas, and Missouri, as well as Oklahoma. During the 1930s and 1940s, some eight hundred thousand people left those four states and headed to the Far West. Not all were farmers; many were white-collar workers and retailers whose jobs had been tied to the health of the agriculture sector. Most of the dust bowl migrants were white. Some traveled on trains or buses; others hopped a freight train or hitched a ride; most rode in their own cars, the trip taking four to five days on average.

Most people uprooted by the dust bowl gravitated to California's urban areas—Los Angeles, San Diego, or San Francisco. Others moved into the San Joaquin Valley, the agricultural heartland of California. There they discovered that rural California was no paradise. Only a few of the Midwestern migrants, mostly whites, could afford to buy land. Most found themselves competing with local Hispanics and Asians for seasonal work as pickers in the cotton fields or orchards of large corporate farms. Living in tents or crude cabins and frequently on the move, they suffered from exposure and poor sanitation.

MINORITIES AND THE NEW DEAL The Great Depression was especially traumatic for the most disadvantaged groups. However progressive Franklin Delano Roosevelt was on social issues, he failed to assault long-standing patterns of racism and segregation for fear of alienating conservative southern Democrats in Congress. As a result, many of the New Deal programs discriminated against blacks. The FHA, for example, refused to guarantee mortgages on houses purchased by blacks in white neighborhoods. In addition, both the CCC and the TVA practiced racial segregation.

Mexican Americans suffered as well. Thousands of Mexicans had migrated to the United States during the 1920s, most of them settling in California, New Mexico, Arizona, Colorado, Texas, and the midwestern states. But because many of them were unable to prove their citizenship, either because they were ignorant of the regulations or because their migratory work hampered their ability to meet residency requirements, they were denied access to the new federal relief programs under the New Deal. As economic conditions worsened, government officials called for the deportation of Mexican-born Americans to avoid the cost of providing them with public services. By 1935, over 500,000 Mexican Americans and their American-born children had returned to Mexico. The state of Texas alone returned over 250,000 people.

The Great Depression also devastated Native Americans. They initially were encouraged by Roosevelt's appointment of John Collier as the commissioner of the Bureau of Indian Affairs (BIA). Collier steadily increased the

Migratory Mexican field worker at home

On the edge of a frozen pea field in Imperial Valley, California, this home to a migratory Mexican family reflects both poverty and impermanence.

number of Native Americans employed by the BIA and strove to ensure that Native Americans gained access to the various relief programs. Collier's primary objective, however, was passage of the Indian Reorganization Act. He wanted the new legislation to replace the provisions of the General Allotment Act (1887), known as the Dawes Act, which had sought to "Americanize" the indigenous peoples by breaking up their tribal land and allocating it to individuals. Collier insisted that the Dawes Act had produced only widespread poverty and demoralization. He hoped to reinvigorate Native American cultural traditions by restoring land to tribes, granting them the right to charter business enterprises and establish self-governing constitutions, and providing federal funds for vocational training and economic development. The act that Congress finally passed was a much-diluted version of Collier's original proposal, however, and the "Indian New Deal" brought only a partial improvement to the lives of Native Americans. But it did spur the various tribes to revise their constitutions so as to give women the right to vote and hold office.

The Scottsboro case

Heywood Patterson (center), one of the defendants in the case, is seen here with his attorney, Samuel Liebowitz (left) in Decatur, Alabama, in 1933.

COURT DECISIONS AND CIVIL RIGHTS   Although the National Association for the Advancement of Colored People (NAACP) waged a legal campaign against racial prejudice that gathered momentum during the 1930s, a major setback occurred in the Supreme Court decision *Grovey v. Townsend* (1935), which upheld the Texas Democrats' whites-only election primary. But the *Grovey* decision held for only nine years and marked the end of the major decisions that for half a century had narrowed application of the civil rights amendments ratified after the Civil War. A reversal had already set in.

Two important precedents arose from the celebrated Scottsboro case in Alabama in 1931, in which an all-white jury, on flimsy evidence, hastily convicted nine black youths, ranging in age from thirteen to twenty-one, of raping two white women while riding a freight train headed for Memphis. Eight of the youths were sentenced to death before cheering white audiences. The injustice of the Scottsboro case aroused protests throughout the nation and around the world. The two girls, it turned out, had been selling sex to white and black boys on the train. One of the girls eventually recanted the charges. Several groups, including the International Labor Defense (a Communist organization) and the NAACP, offered legal assistance in efforts to appeal the decision. No case in American legal history produced as many trials, appeals, reversals, and retrials. The Supreme Court in *Powell v. Alabama* (1932) overturned the original conviction because the judge had not ensured that the accused were provided adequate defense attorneys. It ordered new trials. In

Norris v. Alabama (1935), the Court ruled that the systematic exclusion of African Americans from Alabama juries had denied the Scottsboro defendants equal protection of the law—a principle that had widespread impact on state courts by opening up juries to blacks. Eventually, the state of Alabama dropped the charges against the four youngest of the "Scottsboro boys" and granted paroles to the others; the last one was released in 1950.

Like Woodrow Wilson, Franklin Delano Roosevelt did not give a high priority to racial issues, in part because of the power exerted by southern Democratic legislators. Nevertheless, Roosevelt included in his administration people who did care deeply about racial issues. As his first term drew to a close, Roosevelt found that there was a de facto "black cabinet" of some thirty to forty advisers in government departments and agencies, people who were very concerned about racial issues and the plight of African Americans. Moreover, by 1936 many black voters were fast transferring their political loyalty from the Republicans (the "party of Lincoln") to the Democrats and would vote accordingly in the coming presidential election. But few southern blacks were able to vote during the 1930s. The preponderant majority of African Americans still lived in the eleven southern states of the former Confederacy, the most rural region in the nation, where blacks remained disenfranchised, segregated, and largely limited to farm work. As late as 1940, fewer than 5 percent of eligible African Americans were registered to vote.

THE NEW DEAL MATURES

During Roosevelt's first year in office, his programs and his personal charm generated massive support. The president's travels and speeches, his twice-weekly press conferences, and his radio-broadcast fireside chats brought vitality and warmth in contrast to the aloofness of the Hoover White House. In the congressional elections of 1934, the Democrats increased their strength in both the House and the Senate, an almost unprecedented midterm victory for a party in power. Yet while Democrats remained dominant, critics of various aspects of the New Deal began to emerge in both parties as well as within the Supreme Court. Roosevelt's opponents stressed that the economy, while stabilized, remained mired in the Depression. In 1935 Roosevelt responded to the situation by launching a second wave of New Deal legislation.

ELEANOR ROOSEVELT One of the reasons for Roosevelt's unprecedented popularity was his wife, **Eleanor Roosevelt**, who had become an enormous political asset and would prove to be one of the most influential and revered leaders of the time. Born in 1884 in New York City, the niece of Theodore Roosevelt, Eleanor was barely eight years old when her mother died. Within two more years, her younger brother and her father, a chronic alcoholic, also died. Lonely and shy, she attended school in London before marrying Franklin, a distant cousin, in 1905. During the 1920s, Eleanor Roosevelt taught school, and began a lifelong crusade on behalf of women, blacks, and youth. Her compassion resulted in part from the loneliness she had experienced as she was growing up and in part from the sense of betrayal she felt upon

The First Lady

An intelligent, principled, and candid woman, Eleanor Roosevelt became a political figure in her own right. Here she is serving as guest host for a radio program, ca. 1935.

learning in 1918 that her husband was engaged in an extramarital affair with Lucy Mercer, her personal secretary. "The bottom dropped out of my own particular world," she recalled. Eleanor and Franklin resolved to maintain their marriage, but as their son James said, it became an "armed truce."

Eleanor Roosevelt redefined the role of the First Lady. She was an outspoken activist: the first woman to address a national political convention, to write a nationally syndicated column, and to hold regular press conferences. A tireless advocate and agitator, Eleanor crisscrossed the nation, representing the president and the New Deal, defying local segregation ordinances to meet with African American leaders, supporting women's causes and organized labor, highlighting the plight of unemployed youth, and imploring people to live up to their egalitarian and humanitarian ideals.

CRITICS   By the mid-1930s, the New Deal had stopped the economy's downward slide, but prosperity remained elusive. "We have been patient and long suffering," said a farm leader. "We were promised a New Deal. . . . Instead we have the same old stacked deck." Even more unsettling to conservatives was the dramatic growth of executive power and the emergence of welfare programs that led some people to develop a sense of entitlement to federal support programs. In 1934 a group of conservative businessmen and politicians, including Alfred E. Smith and John W. Davis, two former Democratic presidential candidates, formed the American Liberty League to oppose New Deal measures as violations of personal and property rights.

More potent threats to Roosevelt came from Louisiana's "Kingfish," Senator **Huey P. Long.** A short, strutting man, cunning and ruthless, Long grew up within the rural revivalism of central Louisiana and fashioned himself into a theatrical political preacher (demagogue). He sported pink suits and pastel shirts, red ties, and two-toned shoes. Long was a brilliant but unscrupulous reformer driven by a compulsive urge for power and attention. First as Louisiana's governor, then as Louisiana's political boss and senator, Long viewed the state as his political fiefdom. True, he delivered to his constituents tax favors, roads, schools, free textbooks, charity hospitals, and better public services. But in the process, he became a bullying dictator who used bribery, intimidation, and blackmail to achieve his goals.

In 1933, Long arrived in Washington as a Democratic senator. He initially supported Roosevelt and the New Deal but quickly grew suspicious of the NRA's collusion with big business. Having developed his own presidential aspirations, he had also grown jealous of "Prince Franklin" Roosevelt's mushrooming popularity. To facilitate his presidential candidacy, Long devised his own populist plan for dealing with the Great Depression, which he called the **Share-the-Wealth** Society.

Long proposed to confiscate large personal fortunes so as to guarantee every poor family a cash grant of $5,000 and every worker an annual income

"The Kingfish"

Huey Long, governor of Louisiana. Although he often led people to believe he was a country bumpkin, Long was a shrewd lawyer and consummate politician.

of $2,500, provide pensions to the aged, reduce working hours, pay veterans' bonuses, and ensure a college education for every qualified student. It did not matter to him that his projected budgets failed to add up or that his program offered little to stimulate an economic recovery. As he told a group of distressed Iowa farmers, "Maybe somebody says I don't understand it. Well, you don't have to. Just shut your damn eyes and believe it. That's all." By early 1935, the charismatic Long was claiming that there were twenty-seven thousand Share-the-Wealth clubs scattered across the nation with 8 million supporters. Long was convinced that he could unseat

Roosevelt. "I can take him," Long bragged. "He's a phony. . . . He's scared of me. I can outpromise him, and he knows it. People will believe me and they won't believe him."

Another popular social scheme critical of Roosevelt was hatched by a tall, gray-haired, mild-mannered California doctor, Francis E. Townsend. Outraged by the sight of three elderly women raking through garbage cans for scraps of food, Townsend called for government pensions for the aged. In 1934 he began promoting the Townsend Recovery Plan, which would pay $200 a month to every citizen over sixty who retired from employment and promised to spend the money within each month. The plan had the lure of providing financial security for the aged and stimulating economic growth by freeing up jobs for younger people. Critics noted that the cost of his program, which would serve 9 percent of the population, would be more than half the national income. Yet Townsend, like Long, was indifferent to details and balanced budgets. "I'm not in the least interested in the cost of the plan," he blandly told a House committee.

A third huckster of panaceas, Father Charles E. Coughlin, the Roman Catholic "radio priest," founded the National Union for Social Justice in 1935. In passionate broadcasts over the CBS radio network, he dismissed the New Deal as a Communist conspiracy and revived the old Populist scheme of coining vast amounts of silver to increase the money supply. His remarks grew more intemperate and anti-Semitic during 1936. Like Huey Long, Coughlin appealed to people who had lost the most during the Great Depression and were receiving the least benefits from the early New Deal programs.

Coughlin, Townsend, and Long were Roosevelt's most prominent critics. Of the three, Long had the widest following. A 1935 survey showed that he could draw over 5 million votes as a third-party candidate for president in 1936, perhaps enough to undermine Roosevelt's chances of reelection. Beset by pressures from both ends of the political spectrum, Roosevelt hesitated for months before deciding to "steal the thunder" from the left by instituting an array of new programs. "I'm fighting Communism, Huey Longism, Coughlinism, Townsendism," Roosevelt told a reporter in early 1935. He needed "to save our system, the capitalist system," from such "crackpot ideas."

OPPOSITION FROM THE COURT   A series of Supreme Court decisions finally galvanized the president to act. On May 27, 1935, the Court killed the National Industrial Recovery Act (NIRA) by a unanimous vote. In *Schechter Poultry Corporation v. United States*, the high court ruled that Congress had delegated too much power to the executive branch when it granted the code-making authority to the NRA. In a press conference soon

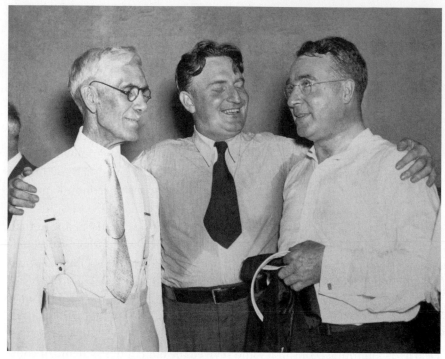

Promoters of welfare capitalism

Dr. Francis E. Townsend, Rev. Gerald L. K. Smith, and Rev. Charles E. Coughlin (left to right) attended the Townsend Recovery Plan convention in Cleveland, Ohio.

afterward, Roosevelt fumed: "We have been relegated to the horse-and-buggy definition of interstate commerce." The same line of conservative judicial reasoning, he warned, might endanger other New Deal programs—if he did not act swiftly.

THE SECOND NEW DEAL (1935–1936) To rescue his legislative program from such judicial and political challenges, Roosevelt in January 1935 launched the second phase of the New Deal, explaining that "social justice, no longer a distant ideal, has become a definite goal" of his administration. No longer was the New Deal to be focused on generating economic recovery. It would also provide stability and security for the most vulnerable Americans. The president called on Congress to pass "must" legislation that included a new public works program to employ the jobless, banking reform, increased taxes on high incomes and inheritances, and programs to protect workers against the hazards of unemployment, old age, and illness.

Over the next three months, dubbed the Second Hundred Days, Roosevelt used all of his considerable charm and skills to convince the Congress to pass most of the **Second New Deal**'s "must" legislation. The results changed the face of American life. The first major initiative, the $4.8-billion Emergency Relief Appropriation Act, sailed through the new Congress. Roosevelt called it the "Big Bill" because it was the largest peacetime spending bill in history. It included an array of new federal job programs managed by a new agency, the Works Progress Administration (WPA).

The WPA also employed a wide range of talented people in the Federal Theatre Project, the Federal Art Project, the Federal Music Project, and the **Federal Writers' Project**. Critics charged that these programs were frivolous, but Hopkins replied that writers and artists needed "to eat just like other people." The National Youth Administration (NYA), also under the WPA, provided part-time employment to students, set up technical training programs, and aided jobless youths. Twenty-seven-year-old Lyndon B. Johnson was director of an NYA program in Texas, and Richard M. Nixon, a penniless Duke University law student, found work through the NYA at 35¢ an hour. Although the WPA took care of only about 3 million out of some 10 million jobless at any one time, in all it helped some 9 million clients weather desperate times before it expired in 1943.

THE WAGNER ACT Another major element of the Second New Deal was the National Labor Relations Act, often called the Wagner Act in honor of the New York senator, Robert Wagner, who drafted it and convinced a reluctant Roosevelt to support it. The Wagner Act was one of the most important pieces of labor legislation in history, guaranteeing workers the right to organize unions and bargain with management. It also prohibited employers from interfering with union activities. The Wagner Act also created a National Labor Relations Board of five members to oversee labor activities across the nation. Emboldened by the Wagner Act, unions organized more workers across the nation during the late 1930s. More than 70 percent of Americans surveyed in a 1937 Gallup poll said they favored unions. Yet many companies continued to thwart union activities in defiance of the Wagner Act.

SOCIAL SECURITY As Francis E. Townsend stressed, the Great Depression hit older Americans and those with disabilities especially hard. To address the peculiar problems faced by the old, infirm, blind, and disabled, Roosevelt proposed the Social Security Act of 1935. It was, he announced, the Second New Deal's "cornerstone" and "supreme achievement." The basic concept was not new. Progressives during the early 1900s had proposed a federal

Social Security

A poster distributed by the government to educate the public about the new Social Security Act.

system of social security for the aged, indigent, disabled, and unemployed. Other nations had already enacted such programs, but the United States had remained steadfast in its tradition of individual self-reliance. The hardships caused by the Great Depression revived the idea of a social security program, however, and Roosevelt masterfully guided the legislation through Congress.

The Social Security Act, designed by Secretary of Labor Frances Perkins, included three major provisions. Its centerpiece was a self-financed pension fund for retired people over the age of sixty-five and their survivors. Beginning in 1937, workers and employers contributed payroll taxes to establish the fund. Roosevelt stressed that the pension program was not intended to guarantee a comfortable retirement; it was designed to supplement other sources of income and protect the elderly from some of the "hazards and vicissitudes of life." Only later did voters and politicians come to view Social Security as the *primary* source of retirement income for most of the aged.

The Social Security Act also set up a shared federal-state unemployment-insurance program, financed by a payroll tax on employers. In addition, the new legislation committed the national government to a broad range of social-welfare activities based upon the assumption that "unemployables"— people who were unable to work—would remain a state responsibility while the national government would provide work relief for the able-bodied. To that end the law inaugurated federal grants-in-aid for three state-administered public-assistance programs—old-age assistance, aid to dependent children, and aid for the blind—and further aid for maternal, child-welfare, and public health services.

When compared with similar programs in Europe, the new Social Security system was conservative. It was the only government pension program in the world financed by taxes on the earnings of workers: most other countries funded such programs out of general revenues. The Social Security payroll tax was also a regressive tax: it entailed a single fixed rate for all, regardless of income level. It thus pinched the poor more than the rich, and it also impeded Roosevelt's efforts to revive the economy because it removed from circulation a significant amount of money: the new Social Security tax took money out of workers' pockets and placed it into a retirement trust fund, exacerbating the shrinking money supply that was one of the main causes of the Depression. In addition, the Social Security system initially excluded 9.5 million workers who most needed the new program: farm laborers, domestic workers, and the self-employed, a disproportionate percentage of whom were African Americans.

Roosevelt regretted the limitations of the Social Security Act, but he knew that they were necessary compromises in order to see the legislation through Congress and enable it to withstand court challenges. As he replied to an aide who criticized funding the pension program out of employee contributions:

> I guess you're right on the economics, but those taxes were never a problem of economics. They are politics all the way through. We put those payroll contributions there so as to give the contributors a moral, legal, and political right to collect their pensions and their unemployment benefits. With those taxes in there, no damn politician can ever scrap my Social Security program.

Conservatives lambasted the Social Security Act as tyrannical. Herbert Hoover was among several Americans who initially refused to apply for a Social Security card because of his opposition to the federal government creating such a program. He was issued a number anyway.

SOAKING THE RICH Another major bill making up the second phase of the New Deal was the Revenue Act of 1935, sometimes called the Wealth-Tax Act but popularly known as the soak-the-rich tax. The Revenue Act raised tax rates on annual income above $50,000. Estate and gift taxes also rose, as did the corporate tax rate. Business leaders fumed over Roosevelt's tax and spending policies. They railed against the New Deal and Roosevelt, whom they called a traitor to his own class. Conservatives charged that Roosevelt had moved in a dangerously radical direction. The newspaper editor William Randolph Hearst growled that the wealth tax was "essentially communism." Roosevelt countered by stressing that he had no love for socialism: "I am fighting communism. . . . I want to save our system, the capitalistic system." Yet he added that to save it from revolutionary turmoil required a more equal "distribution of wealth."

ROOSEVELT'S SECOND TERM

THE ELECTION OF 1936   On June 27, 1936, Franklin Delano Roosevelt accepted the Democratic Party's nomination for a second term. The Republicans chose Governor Alfred M. Landon of Kansas, a progressive Republican who had endorsed many New Deal programs. He was probably more liberal than most of his backers and clearly more so than the party's platform, which lambasted the New Deal for overextending federal power. The Republicans hoped that the followers of Long, Coughlin, Townsend, and other dissidents would combine to draw enough Democratic votes away from Roosevelt to throw the election to them. But that possibility faded when an assassin, the son-in-law of a Louisiana judge whom Huey Long had sought to remove, shot and killed the forty-two-year-old senator in 1935. In the 1936 election, Coughlin, Townsend, and a remnant of the Long movement supported Representative William Lemke of North Dakota on a Union party ticket, but it was a forlorn effort, polling only 882,000 votes.

In the 1936 election, Roosevelt carried every state except Maine and Vermont, with a popular vote of 27.7 million to Landon's 16.7 million, the largest magin of victory in history. Democrats would also dominate Republicans in the new Congress, by 77 to 19 in the Senate and 328 to 107 in the House.

In winning another landslide election, Roosevelt forged a new electoral coalition that would affect national politics for years to come. While holding the support of most traditional Democrats, North and South, the president made strong gains in the West among beneficiaries of New Deal agricultural programs. In the northern cities he held on to the ethnic groups helped by New Deal welfare measures. Many middle-class voters whose property had been saved by New Deal measures flocked to support Roosevelt, as did intellectuals stirred by the ferment of new ideas coming from the government. The revived labor union movement threw its support to Roosevelt. And in the most profound departure of all, African American voters for the first time cast the majority of their ballots for a Democratic president. "My friends, go home and turn Lincoln's picture to the wall," a Pittsburgh journalist told black voters. "That debt has been paid in full." The final tally in the 1936 election revealed that 81 percent of those with an income under $1,000 a year opted for Roosevelt, as did 79 percent of those earning between $1,000 and $2,000. By contrast, only 46 percent of those earning over $5,000 voted for Roosevelt. He later claimed that never before had wealthy business leaders been "so united against one candidate." They were "unanimous in their hate for me—and I welcome their hatred."

THE COURT-PACKING PLAN   Roosevelt's second inaugural address, delivered on January 20, 1937, promised even greater reforms. The challenge to democracy, he maintained, was that millions of citizens "at this very moment are denied the greater part of what the very lowest standards of today call the necessities of life. . . . I see one-third of a nation ill-housed, ill-clad, ill-nourished." Roosevelt argued that the election of 1936 had been a mandate for even more extensive government action. The overwhelming three-to-one Democratic majorities in Congress ensured the passage of new legislation to buttress the Second New Deal. But one major roadblock stood in the way: the conservative Supreme Court.

By the end of its 1936 term, the Supreme Court had ruled against New Deal programs in seven of the nine major cases it reviewed. Suits challenging the constitutionality of the Social Security and Wagner acts were pending. Given the conservative tenor of the Court, the Second New Deal seemed in danger of being nullified, just as much of the original New Deal had been.

For that reason, Roosevelt devised an ill-conceived and impolitic plan to change the Court's conservative stance by enlarging it. Congress, not the Constitution, determines the size of the Supreme Court, which at different times has numbered six, seven, eight, nine, and ten justices. In 1937, the number was nine. On February 5, 1937, Roosevelt sent his controversial plan to Congress, without having consulted congressional leaders. He wanted to create up to six new Supreme Court justices.

But the "Court-packing" maneuver, as opponents quickly tagged the president's scheme, backfired. It was a shade too contrived, much too brazen, and far too political. A leading journalist said Roosevelt had become "drunk with power." Roosevelt's plan angered Republicans, but it also ran headlong into a deep-rooted public veneration of the courts and aroused fears among Democrats that a future president might use the precedent for quite different purposes.

As it turned out, unforeseen events blunted Roosevelt's clumsy effort to change the Court. A sequence of Court decisions during the spring of 1937 reversed previous judgments in order to uphold disputed provisions of the Wagner and Social Security acts. In addition, a conservative justice resigned,

Court packing

An editorial cartoon commenting on Roosevelt's grandiose plan to enlarge the
Supreme Court. He is speaking to Harold Ickes, director of the Public Works
Administration.

and Roosevelt named to the vacancy one of the most consistent New Dealers, Senator Hugo Black of Alabama. But Roosevelt insisted on forcing his
Court-packing bill through the Congress. On July 22, 1937, the Senate overwhelmingly voted it down. It was the biggest political blunder of Roosevelt's
career. He later claimed he had lost the battle but won the war. The Court
had reversed itself on important New Deal legislation, and the president was
able to appoint justices in harmony with the New Deal. But the episode fractured the Democratic Party and blighted Roosevelt's prestige. For the first
time, Democrats in large numbers, especially southerners, opposed the president, and the Republican opposition found a powerful new issue to use
against the administration. During the first eight months of 1937, the
momentum of Roosevelt's 1936 landslide victory evaporated. As Secretary of

Agriculture Henry A. Wallace later remarked, "The whole New Deal really went up in smoke as a result of the Supreme Court fight."

A NEW DIRECTION FOR UNIONS Rebellions erupted on other fronts even while the Court-packing bill pended. Under the impetus of the New Deal, the dormant labor union movement stirred anew. When the National Industrial Recovery Act (NIRA) demanded that every industry code affirm the workers' right to organize a union, alert unionists quickly translated it to mean "the president wants you to join the union." John L. Lewis, head of the United Mine Workers (UMW), was among the first to exploit the pro-union spirit of the NIRA. He rebuilt the UMW from 150,000 members to 500,000 within a year. Spurred by Lewis's success, Sidney Hillman of the Amalgamated Clothing Workers and David Dubinsky of the International Ladies Garment Workers organized workers in the clothing industry. As leaders of industrial unions (composed of all types of workers in a particular industry), which were in the minority by far, they found the smaller, more restrictive craft unions (composed of skilled male workers only, with each union serving just one trade) to be obstacles to organizing workers in the country's basic industries.

In 1935, with the passage of the Wagner Act, the industrial unionists formed a Committee for Industrial Organization (CIO), and craft unionists began to fear submergence by the mass unions made up of unskilled workers. Jurisdictional disputes divided them, and in 1936 the American Federation of Labor (AFL) expelled the CIO unions, which then formed a permanent structure, called after 1938 the Congress of Industrial Organizations (also known by the initials CIO). The rivalry spurred both groups to greater efforts.

The CIO's major organizing drives in the automobile and steel industries began in 1936, but until the Supreme Court upheld the Wagner Act in 1937, companies failed to cooperate with its pro-unionist provisions. Employers used various forms of intimidation to fight the infant unions. Early in 1937 automobile workers spontaneously adopted a new technique, the "sit-down strike," in which workers refused to leave a workplace until employers had granted collective-bargaining rights to their union.

Led by the fiery young autoworker and union organizer Walter Reuther, thousands of employees at the General Motors assembly plants in Flint, Michigan, occupied the factories and stopped all production. Female workers supported their male counterparts by picketing at the plant entrances. Company officials called in police to harass the strikers, sent spies to union meetings, and threatened to fire the workers. They also pleaded with President Roosevelt to dispatch federal troops. He refused, while expressing his displeasure with the sit-down strike, which the courts later declared illegal. The standoff lasted over a month. Then, on February 11, 1937, the company relented and signed a contract recognizing the fledgling United Automobile Workers (UAW) as a legitimate union. Other automobile manufacturers soon followed suit. And the following month, U.S. Steel capitulated to the Steel Workers Organizing Committee (later the United Steelworkers of America), granting the union recognition and its members a 10 percent wage hike and a forty-hour workweek. The unions made a difference in the lives of workers and in the political scene. Through their efforts, wages rose and working conditions improved, and Roosevelt and the Democratic party were the beneficiaries of the labor movement. But unions made little headway in the South, where conservative Democrats and mill owners stubbornly opposed efforts to organize workers.

A SLUMPING ECONOMY   During the years 1935 and 1936 the depressed economy finally showed signs of revival. By the spring of 1937, industrial output had moved above the 1929 level. The prosperity of early 1937 was achieved largely through federal spending. But in 1937, Roosevelt, worried about federal budget deficits and rising inflation, ordered sharp cuts in government spending. The result was that the economy suddenly stalled and then slid into a business slump deeper than that of 1929. When the spring of 1938 failed to bring economic recovery, Roosevelt asked Congress to adopt a new large-scale federal spending program, and Congress voted almost $3.3 billion in new expenditures. In a short time the increase in spending reversed the economy's decline, but only during World War II would employment reach pre-1929 levels.

The Court-packing fight, the sit-down strikes, and the 1937 recession all undercut Roosevelt's prestige and power. When the 1937 congressional session ended, the only major new bills were the Wagner-Steagall National Housing Act and the Bankhead-Jones Farm Tenant Act. The Housing Act, developed by Senator Robert F. Wagner, set up the Housing Authority which extended long-term loans to cities for public housing projects in blighted low-income neighborhoods. The agency also subsidized rents for poor people. Later, during World War II, it financed housing for workers in new defense plants.

The Farm Tenant Act addressed the epidemic of rural poverty. It created a new agency, the Farm Security Administration (FSA), that provided loans to keep farm owners from sinking into tenancy. It also made loans to tenant farmers to enable them to purchase their own farms. In the end, however, the FSA proved to be little more than another relief operation that tided a few farmers over during difficult times. A more effective answer to the problem eventually arrived in the form of national mobilization for war, which landed many struggling tenant farmers in military service or the defense industry, broadened their horizons, and taught them new skills.

In 1938, the Democratic Congress also enacted the Fair Labor Standards Act. It replaced many of the provisions that had been in the NIRA, which had been declared unconstitutional. The federal government established a minimum wage of 40¢ an hour and a maximum workweek of forty hours. The act, which applied only to businesses engaged in *interstate* commerce, also prohibited the employment of children under the age of sixteen.

THE LEGACY OF THE NEW DEAL

SETBACKS FOR THE PRESIDENT   During the late 1930s, the Democratic party fragmented. Many southern Democrats balked at the national party's growing dependence on the votes of northern labor unions and African Americans. Profane, tobacco-chewing Ellison "Cotton Ed" Smith of South Carolina, the powerful chair of the Committee on Agriculture, and several other southern delegates walked out of the 1936 Democratic party convention, with Smith declaring that he would not support any party that views "the Negro as a political and social equal." Other critics believed that Roosevelt was exercising too much power and spending too much money. Some disgruntled southern Democrats drifted toward a coalition with conservative Republicans. By the end of 1937, a bipartisan conservative bloc had coalesced against the New Deal.

The elections of November 1938 handed the administration another setback, partly a result of the friction among the Democrats. Roosevelt had failed in his efforts to liberalize the party by ousting southern conservatives. The Democrats lost seats in both the House and the Senate, and the president now headed a divided party. In his State of the Union message in 1939, Roosevelt for the first time proposed no new reforms but spoke of the need "to invigorate the process of [economic] recovery, in order to *preserve* our reforms." The conservative coalition of Republicans and southern Democrats had stalemated the Roosevelt juggernaut. As one observer noted, the New Deal "has been reduced to a movement with no program, with no effective political organization, with no vast popular party strength behind it."

A HALFWAY REVOLUTION   The New Deal had petered out in 1939 just as war was erupting in Europe and Asia, but it had wrought several enduring changes. By the end of the 1930s, the power of the national government was vastly larger than it had been in 1932, and hope had been restored to many people who had grown disconsolate. But the New Deal entailed more than just a bigger federal government and revived public confidence; it also constituted a significant change from the older liberalism embodied in the progressivism of Theodore Roosevelt and Woodrow Wilson. Those reformers, despite their sharp differences, had assumed that the function of progressive government was to use aggressive *regulation* of industry and business to ensure that people had an equal opportunity to pursue their notions of happiness.

Franklin Delano Roosevelt and the New Dealers went beyond this concept of regulated capitalism by insisting that the government not simply *respond* to social crises but also take positive steps to *avoid* them and their social effects. To this end the New Deal's various benefit programs sought to ensure a minimum level of well-being for all Americans. The New Deal had established basic qualitative standards for labor conditions and public welfare

Meeting of the anti–New Dealers

Senator Ellison D. "Cotton Ed" Smith of South Carolina cringes at the thought of a fourth term for Roosevelt, while meeting with fellow anti–New Dealers at the Mayflower Hotel in Washington.

and helped middle-class Americans hold on to their savings, their homes, and their farms. The protection afforded by bank-deposit insurance, unemployment pay, and Social Security pensions would come to be universally accepted as a safeguard against future depressions.

In implementing his domestic program, Roosevelt steered a zigzag course between the extremes of unregulated capitalism and socialism. The first New Deal experimented for a time with a managed economy under the NRA but abandoned that experiment for a turn toward enforcing competition and increasing government spending. The greatest failure of the New Deal was its inability to restore economic prosperity and end record levels of unemployment. In 1939 10 million Americans—nearly 17 percent of the workforce—remained jobless. Only the prolonged crisis of World War II would finally produce full employment.

Roosevelt's pragmatism was his greatest strength—and weakness. Impatient with political theory and at heart a fiscal conservative, he was flexible in developing policy: he kept what worked and discarded what did not. The result was, paradoxically, both profoundly revolutionary and profoundly conservative. Roosevelt sharply increased the regulatory powers of the federal government and laid the foundation for what would become an expanding welfare system. New Deal initiatives left a legacy of unprecedented social welfare innovations: a joint federal-state system of unemployment insurance; a compulsory, federally administered retirement system; financial support for families with dependent children, maternal and child-care programs, and several public health programs. The New Deal also improved working conditions and raised wage levels for millions of laborers. Despite what his critics charged, however, Roosevelt was no socialist; he sought to preserve the basic capitalist structure. In the process of such bold experimentation and dynamic preservation, the New Deal represented a "halfway revolution" that permanently altered the nation's social and political landscape.

CHAPTER SUMMARY

- **Stabilizing the Economy** In March 1933, the economy, including the farm sector, was shattered, and millions of Americans were without jobs and the most basic necessities of life. Franklin Delano Roosevelt and his "brain trust" of advisers set out to restore confidence in the economy by propping the banking industry and providing short-term emergency relief for the unemployed, promoting industrial recovery, and by raising commodity prices by encouraging farmers to cut back production.

- **The New Deal** Initially, most of the New Deal programs were conceived as temporary relief and recovery efforts. They eased hardships but did not restore prosperity. It was during the Second New Deal that major reform measures, such as Social Security and the Wagner Act, reshaped the nation's social structure.

- **New Deal Criticisms** Some conservatives criticized the New Deal for violating personal and property rights and for steering the nation toward socialism. Some liberals believed that the measures did not tax the wealthy enough to provide the aged and disadvantaged with adequate financial security.

- **Federal Expansion** The New Deal expanded the powers of the national government by establishing regulatory bodies and laying the foundation of a social welfare system. The federal government would in the future regulate business and provide social welfare programs to avoid social and economic problems.

CHRONOLOGY

March 1933	Congress passes the Emergency Banking Relief Act
March 1933	Congress passes the Beer-Wine Revenue Act
March 1933	Congress establishes the Civilian Conservation Corps
May 1933	Congress creates the Tennessee Valley Authority
June 1933	Congress establishes the Federal Deposit Insurance Corporation
November 1933	Congress creates the Civil Works Administration
1935	President Roosevelt creates the Works Progress Administration
1935	Congress passes the Wagner Act
1937	Social Security goes into effect
1939	John Steinbeck's *Grapes of Wrath* is published
1940	Richard Wright's *Native Son* is published

KEY TERMS & NAMES

Franklin Delano Roosevelt p. 859

Twenty-first Amendment p. 860

First New Deal p. 860

Agricultural Adjustment Act p. 862

dust bowl p. 862

National Industrial Recovery Act p. 863

National Recovery Administration p. 863

Eleanor Roosevelt p. 870

Huey P. Long p. 872

Share-the-Wealth program p. 872

Second New Deal p. 875

Federal Writers' Project p. 875

28

THE SECOND WORLD WAR

FOCUS QUESTIONS wwnorton.com/studyspace

- What were the major events leading up to the outbreak of war in Europe and in Asia?

- What effect did the Second World War have on American society?

- How did the Allied forces win the war in Europe?

- How did the United States gain the upper hand in the Pacific sphere?

- What efforts did the Allies make to shape the postwar world?

The unprecedented efforts of Franklin Delano Roosevelt and the New Dealers to end the Great Depression did not restore prosperity or return the economy to full employment. In 1940, over 14 percent of Americans remained jobless. That changed dramatically with American involvement in the Second World War. Within months after the surprise Japanese attack on Pearl Harbor in December 1941, Roosevelt mobilized all of the nation's resources to win the battle against fascism and imperialism. Of course, the horrible war did much more than revive the economy. It changed the direction and shape of world history and transformed America's role in international affairs.

FROM ISOLATIONISM TO INTERVENTION

Like Woodrow Wilson, Roosevelt had little experience or interest in international affairs when first elected president. The United States remained comfortable with its isolationism from international political turmoil.

However, an important initiative occurred in November 1933 when Roosevelt broke precedent with his Republican predecessors and officially recognized the Soviet Union in hopes of stimulating trade with the communist nation. That he did so in the face of a scolding from his mother testified to his courage. Overall, however, the prolonged Depression forced Roosevelt to adopt a low-profile foreign policy limited to the promotion of trade agreements. As had happened with Woodrow Wilson, the course of world events would eventually force him to shift from isolationism to intervention.

THE GOOD NEIGHBOR POLICY   Roosevelt announced in his 1933 inaugural address that he would continue the efforts of Herbert Hoover to promote what he called "the **policy of the good neighbor**" in the Western Hemisphere. That same year, at the Seventh Pan-American Conference, the United States supported a resolution declaring that no nation "has the right to intervene in the internal or external affairs of another." True to this noninterventionist commitment, the Roosevelt administration oversaw the final withdrawal of U.S. troops from Nicaragua and Haiti, and in 1934 the president negotiated with Cuba a treaty that dissolved the Platt Amendment and thus ended the last formal American claim to a right to intervene in Latin America.

FOREIGN CRISES

While the Roosevelt administration was grappling with the economic depression and its social effects, ominous foreign crises began to engage American attention and concern. Germany and Italy emerged during the 1930s as fascist nations bent on foreign conquest. At the same time, halfway around the world, in Asia, Japan increasingly fell under the control of militarists who were convinced that the entire continent should be governed by their "ruling race."

ITALY AND GERMANY   Despotism thrives during periods of economic distress and political unrest, and during the 1920s and 1930s mass movements led by demagogues appeared throughout Europe. In 1922, the bombastic journalist **Benito Mussolini** had seized power in Italy. Fascism, both in Italy and in Germany, was driven by a determined minority willing to use violence as a political tool. By 1925 Mussolini was wielding dictatorial power as "Il Duce" (the Leader). All opposition political parties were eliminated. "Mussolini is always right," screamed propaganda posters.

There was always something ludicrous about the strutting, chest-thumping Mussolini. Italy, after all, was a declining industrial power whose performance in World War I was a national embarrassment. Germany was another matter, however, and there was nothing amusing about Mussolini's German counterpart, **Adolf Hitler**. His strange transformation during the 1920s from failed artist and social misfit to head of the **National Socialist German Workers' (Nazi) party** startled the world. The global Depression offered Hitler the opportunity to portray himself as the nation's messianic savior. Made chancellor on January 30, 1933, five weeks before Franklin Roosevelt was first inaugurated, he banned all political parties except for the Nazis. A magnetic speaker, fanatical ideologue, and ruthless racist, Hitler assumed absolute power in 1934. There would be no more elections, no more political parties, no more labor unions. Throughout the 1930s Hitler's brutal Nazi police state cranked up the engines of tyranny and terrorism, propaganda and censorship. Brown-shirted "storm troopers" fanned out across the nation, burning books, sterilizing or euthanizing the disabled, and persecuting Communists and Jews, whom Hitler blamed for Germany's troubles.

Axis leaders

Mussolini and Hitler in Munich, June 1940.

THE EXPANDING AXIS As the 1930s unfolded, a catastrophic chain of events in Asia and Europe sent the world hurtling toward disaster. In 1934, Japan renounced the Five-Power Treaty and began an aggressive military build-up in anticipation of expanding its control in Asia. The next year, Mussolini launched Italy's conquest of Ethiopia in eastern Africa. In 1935 Hitler, in explicit violation of the Versailles Treaty, announced he was revitalizing Germany's armed forces. The next year, he again brazenly violated the Versailles Treaty by sending thirty-five thousand troops, with drums

AGGRESSION IN EUROPE, 1935–1939

← Aggressive moves

■ Axis powers

Keeping in mind the terms of the Treaty of Versailles, explain why Hitler began his campaign of expansion by invading the Rhineland and the Sudetenland. Why would Hitler have wanted to retake the Polish Corridor? Why did the attack on Poland begin World War II, whereas Hitler's previous invasions of his European neighbors did not?

beating and flags flying, into the Rhineland, the demilitarized buffer zone between France and Germany. The failure of France, Great Britain, and the United States to enforce the provisions of the Versailles Treaty convinced Hitler that the western democracies were unwilling to thwart his aggressive plans. Hitler admitted that his show of force was a theatrical bluff: "If the French had marched into the Rhineland, we would have had to withdraw with our tail between our legs."

The year 1936 also witnessed the outbreak of the Spanish Civil War, which began when Spanish troops loyal to General Francisco Franco and other right-wing officers, with the support of the Roman Catholic Church, revolted against the new democratically elected government. Hitler and Mussolini rushed troops ("volunteers"), warplanes, and massive amounts of military and financial aid to support Franco's fascist insurgency.

At the same time that fascism was on the march across Europe, Japanese imperialists were on the move again in China. On July 7, 1937, Japanese and Chinese troops clashed at the Marco Polo Bridge, west of Beijing. The incident quickly developed into a full-scale war. By December, the Imperial Japanese Army had captured the Nationalist Chinese capital of Nanjing, whereupon the undisciplined soldiers ran amok, looting the city and murdering and raping large numbers of Chinese. Tens of thousands (perhaps as many as three hundred thousand) civilians were murdered in what came to be called the Rape of Nanjing.

Meanwhile, the peace of Europe was unraveling. In 1937, Italy joined Germany and Japan in establishing the Rome-Berlin-Tokyo "Axis." Having rebuilt German military power, the Austrian-born Hitler forced the *Anschluss* (union) of Austria with Germany in March 1938. Paralyzed with fear of another world war, British and French leaders sought to "appease" Hitler by signing the notorious Munich Pact on September 30, 1938. Without the consent of the Czech government, the British and French transferred the Sudeten territory in Czechoslovakia to Germany. The mountainous Sudetenland along the German border hosted over 3 million ethnic Germans. However, it also contained seven hundred thousand Czechs and was vital to the defense of Czechoslovakia.

Having promised that the Sudetenland was his last territorial demand, Hitler violated his pledge on March 15, 1939, when he sent German tanks and soldiers to conquer the remainder of Czechoslovakia. Yet despite such provocative actions, the European democracies cowered in the face of Hitler's ruthless behavior. **Winston Churchill**, who would become the British prime minister in 1940, described the Munich Pact as "a defeat without a war." It marked the "culminating failure of British and French foreign policy and diplomacy over several years." The Munich Pact, he predicted, would not end Hitler's aggressions. "This is only the beginning of the reckoning."

DEGREES OF NEUTRALITY Most Americans during the 1930s, including both Republicans and Democrats, responded to the mounting global crises by deepening their commitment to isolationism. As a Minnesota senator declared in 1935, "To hell with Europe and the rest of those nations!" The isolationist mood was reinforced by a Senate inquiry into the role of bankers and munitions makers in the American decision to enter World War I. Chaired by Senator Gerald P. Nye of North Dakota, the committee concluded in 1937 that bankers and munitions makers had made scandalous profits from the war. The implication was that arms traders and bankers (the "merchants of death") had spurred American intervention in the European conflict and were still at work promoting wars for profit.

During the 1930s the United States moved toward complete isolation from the quarrels of Europe. In 1935 President Roosevelt signed the first of several neutrality laws intended to prevent the kind of entanglements that had drawn the United States into World War I. The Neutrality Act of 1935 prohibited Americans from traveling on ships owned by nations at war. It also forbade the sale of arms and munitions to any "belligerent" nation whenever the president proclaimed that a state of war existed abroad. A year later, in 1936, Congress revised the Neutrality Act by forbidding loans to nations at war. Although the Spanish Civil War involved a fascist military uprising against an elected government, Roosevelt accepted the French and British position that the western democracies should not intervene. That the conflict in Spain was technically not a "foreign war" led Roosevelt to ask Congress in January 1937 to revise the neutrality laws to apply to *civil* wars (he later called his action a "grave mistake"). The United States and the other western democracies then stood by as Hitler and Mussolini sent combat planes, tanks, and soldiers to Spain in support of General Franco's overthrow of democracy, which was completed in 1939.

In the spring of 1937, the Congress passed another neutrality law. The Neutrality Act of 1937 allowed the president to require that goods other than arms or munitions exported to warring nations be sold on a cash-and-carry basis (that is, a nation would have to pay cash and then carry the American-made goods away in its own ships). This was intended to preserve a profitable trade with combatants without running the risk of war.

The new law faced its first test in July 1937, when Japanese and Chinese forces clashed in China. Since neither Japan nor China officially declared war, Roosevelt was able to avoid invoking the neutrality law because its net effect would have favored the Japanese and penalized the supply-dependent Nationalist Chinese. Then, on December 12, 1937, Japanese planes sank the U.S. gunboat *Panay,* which had been lying at anchor in China, on the Yangtze River, prominently flying the American flag. The sinking of the *Panay* generated few calls for retaliation in the United States. In fact, a Texas Congressman said the incident should lead to the withdrawal of U.S. forces from Asia. "We should learn that it is about time to mind our own business."

Roosevelt, however, was not so sure that the United States could keep its back turned on an increasingly turbulent world. In October 1937 he delivered a speech in Chicago, the heartland of isolationism, in which he called for international cooperation to "quarantine the aggressors" disturbing world peace. But his appeal for a broader American role in world affairs fell flat in the Congress and across the nation. A survey revealed that 70 percent of Americans wanted all U.S. citizens to be removed from China in order to prevent a possible incident from triggering warfare.

Neutrality

A 1938 cartoon shows U.S. foreign policy entangled by the serpent of isolationism.

WAR CLOUDS

During the late 1930s, war clouds thickened over Asia and Europe. After Adolf Hitler's troops brazenly occupied Czechoslovakia in 1939, Franklin Delano Roosevelt abandoned his neutral stance. Hitler and Mussolini could no longer be ignored. They were "madmen" who "respect force and force alone." Throughout late 1938 and 1939, Roosevelt sought to educate Americans about the growing menace of fascism. He also convinced Congress to increase military spending in anticipation of a possible war.

THE CONQUEST OF POLAND   Meanwhile, the insatiable Hitler had set his sights on Poland, Germany's eastern neighbor. To ensure that the Soviet Union did not interfere with his plans to conquer Poland, Hitler, on August 23, 1939, contradicted his frequent denunciations of communism and signed a Nazi-Soviet Non-Aggression Pact with Soviet premier **Joseph Stalin** in which the two totalitarian tyrants secretly agreed to divide up northern and eastern Europe between them. At dawn on September 1, 1939, 1.5 million German troops with thousands of tanks and armored vehicles invaded Poland from the north, south, and west. Hitler ordered his armies "to kill without mercy men, women, and children of the Polish race or language."

This was the final straw. Having allowed Czechoslovakia to be gobbled up by Hitler's war machine, Britain and France now did an about-face and honored their commitment to go to war if Poland were invaded. On September 3, 1939, Europe, the world's smallest continent, again lapsed into widespread warfare. But it would take weeks for the British and French to mobilize large armies, in part because they were not eager for an offensive war, hoping against hope that the mere declaration of war would cause Hitler to pull back. They were wrong; the Germans massacred the Poles. Sixteen days after German troops moved across the Polish border, the Soviet Union invaded Poland from the east. Pressed from all sides, the large but poorly equipped Polish army (many of them fought on horseback) surrendered, having suffered seventy thousand deaths. On October 6, 1939, the Nazis and Soviets divided Poland between them. Thereafter, both the Nazis and the Soviets arrested, deported, enslaved, or murdered over 2 million Poles.

U.S. NEUTRALITY   President Roosevelt responded to the outbreak of war in Europe by proclaiming U. S. neutrality. However, the president would not, like Woodrow Wilson had done in 1914, ask Americans to remain neutral in thought because "even a neutral has a right to take account of the facts." In September, Roosevelt summoned Congress into special session to revise the Neutrality Act. "I regret the Congress passed the Act," the president said. "I regret equally that I signed the Act." Under the Neutrality Act of 1939, Britain and France were allowed to send their own freighters to the United States and buy military supplies. American public opinion supported such measures. "What the majority of the American people want," wrote the editors of the *Nation,* "is to be as un-neutral as possible without getting into war." After the quick German conquest of Poland, the war in Europe settled into a stalemate during early 1940 that began to be called "the phony war." What lay ahead, it seemed, was a long war of attrition in which Britain and France would have the resources to outlast Hitler. That illusion lasted through the winter before being shattered by new German assaults.

The Storm in Europe

BLITZKRIEG   In the spring of 1940, the winter's long *Sitzkrieg* (sitting war) suddenly erupted into ***Blitzkrieg*** (lightning war) featuring carefully coordinated columns of fast-moving German tanks, motorized artillery, and truck-borne infantry, all supported by warplanes. At dawn on April 9, without warning, Nazi armies occupied Denmark and landed along the Norwegian coast. Denmark fell in a day, Norway within a few weeks. On May 10, German forces invaded neutral Belgium, Luxembourg, and the Netherlands (Holland). A British army sent to help the Belgians and the French was forced to make a frantic retreat to the coast. The Germans then missed an opportunity to inflict a crushing defeat on the beleaguered Allies. On May 21, while the fast-moving German armored units paused to rest and refuel, Great Britain organized a desperate evacuation of British and French soldiers from the beaches at Dunkirk, on the northern French coast near the border with Belgium. Amid the chaos, some 338,000 desperate soldiers escaped to England on over a thousand ships and small boats, barges, and ferries, leaving behind vast stockpiles of vehicles, weaponry, and ammunition.

Meanwhile, German forces cut the French armies to pieces and spread panic throughout the civilian population. On June 14, 1940, the German swastika flag flew over Paris. Eight days later, French leaders surrendered to Hitler in the same railroad car in which Germans had been forced to surrender in 1918. The Germans established a puppet French government in Vichy to manage the vanquished nation and implement its own anti-Jewish policies. "The war is won," Hitler told Mussolini. "The rest [conquest of Great Britain and the Soviet Union] is only a matter of time."

THE DEBATE OVER AMERICA'S ROLE The rapid collapse of France stunned everyone, including the Germans. Great Britain now stood alone facing Hitler's triumphant war machine, but in Parliament the pugnacious new prime minister, Winston Churchill, breathed defiance. He vowed that the British people would confront Hitler's menace with "blood, toil, tears, and sweat." The British would "go on to the end," he said; "we shall never surrender." Instead, "we shall fight on and on forever and ever and ever." If the independence of Great Britain were to end, Churchill growled, "let it end only when each one of us lies choking in his own blood on the ground."

As Hitler prepared to unleash his air force against Britain, the United States seemed suddenly vulnerable, and it was in no condition to wage world war if attacked. After World War I, the U.S. Army had been reduced to a small force; by 1939 it numbered only 175,000 and ranked sixteenth in the world in size, just behind Romania. It would take time to create a viable military force to stop fascism. President Roosevelt called for a precautionary military build-up and the production of 50,000 combat planes a year. In response to Churchill's desperate appeal for military supplies, Roosevelt promised to provide all possible "aid to the Allies short of war."

The world crisis transformed Roosevelt. Having been stalemated for much of his second term by growing congressional opposition, he was revitalized by the urgent need to stop Nazism in Europe. In June 1940 the president set up the National Defense Research Committee to coordinate military research, including a top-secret effort to develop an atomic bomb. The famous physicist Albert Einstein, a Jewish Austrian refugee from Nazism, had alerted Roosevelt in the fall of 1939 that the Germans were trying to create atomic bombs, leading the president to take action. The Manhattan Project launched an alliance between scientific research and the U.S. military that would blossom into what Dwight D. Eisenhower would call the "military-industrial complex." The effort to develop an atomic bomb was so secretive that few members of Congress or the Roosevelt administration knew about it.

The fall of France in late June 1940 was a devastating blow that left Great Britain standing alone against the Nazi onslaught, just as the British had stood alone against the menace of Napoleon in 1805. The late summer of 1940 brought the desperate Battle of Britain. During August the Germans gained control of all of western Europe, and Hitler began preparations for an invasion of Britain. His first priority was to destroy the British air force, just as the Germans had done to the Polish, Dutch, Belgian, and French air forces. In July and August, the numerically superior German Air Force (*Luftwaffe*) launched daily bombing raids against military targets—ships and naval

The Blitz

In London, St. Paul's Cathedral looms above the destruction wrought by German bombs during the Blitz. Winston Churchill's response: "We shall never surrender."

bases, warplanes and airfields—across southeast England in preparation for an invasion across the English Channel from Nazi-controlled France.

The British Royal Air Force (RAF), with the benefit of radar, a new technology, surprised the world by fending off the German air assault. Hitler ordered the German bombers to change tactics and target factories, civilians, and cities (especially London) in massive nighttime raids designed to break British morale. His decision backfired. In what came to be called "the Blitz," during September and October of 1940, the Germans caused massive destruction in Britain's major cities. Waves of German bombers, escorted by hordes of fighter planes, crossed the English Channel. On some days a thousand German and British planes were locked in combat over British cities. The raids killed some 43,000 British civilians. But the Blitz enraged rather than deflated the British people at the same time that British warplanes were destroying large numbers of German fighters and bombers (1,300 between July and October). The British success in the air proved to be a decisive turning point in the war. In October 1940, Hitler was forced to postpone his planned invasion of the British Isles. If the Germans had destroyed the RAF, they could have invaded and conquered Great Britain. Instead, Great Britain, with growing assistance from the United States, became an increasingly powerful threat to Germany's western flank.

German submarine attacks on British ships, meanwhile, strained the resources of the battered Royal Navy. To address the challenge, Churchill and Roosevelt negotiated an executive agreement by which fifty "overaged" U.S. destroyers went to the British in return for allowing the U.S. to build naval and air bases on British islands in the Caribbean. Roosevelt explained the bold action as necessary for defense of the "American hemisphere." The stakes rose considerably when on September 16, Roosevelt signed the first peacetime conscription in American history, requiring the registration of all 16 million men aged twenty-one to thirty-five.

The rapidly shifting state of global affairs prompted vigorous debate between "internationalists," who believed America's security demanded aid to Britain, and isolationists, who charged that Roosevelt was drawing the United States into another European war. In 1940, internationalists organized the nonpartisan Committee to Defend America by Aiding the Allies. On the other hand, isolationists, mostly Republicans, formed the America First Committee. The isolationists argued that the war involved, in Idaho Senator William E. Borah's words, "nothing more than another chapter in the bloody volume of European power politics." Borah and others predicted that a Nazi victory over Great Britain, while distasteful, would pose no threat to America's security.

"The Only Way We Can Save Her [Democracy]"

Political cartoon suggesting the U.S. not intervene in European wars.

ROOSEVELT'S THIRD TERM In the midst of the terrible news from Europe, the 1940 presidential campaign dominated public attention. In June, just as France was falling to Germany, the Republicans nominated a dark-horse candidate, Wendell L. Willkie of Indiana, a plain-spoken corporate lawyer who as a former Democrat had voted for Roosevelt in 1932 and had remained registered as a Democrat until 1938. At the July Democratic convention in Chicago, Roosevelt easily won the nomination for a third term.

Willkie warned that Roosevelt was a "warmonger," predicting that "if you re-elect him you may expect war in April, 1941." To this Roosevelt responded, "I have said this before, but I shall say it again and again and again: Your boys are not going to be sent into any foreign wars." Neither man distinguished himself with such hollow statements, since both knew the risks of all-out military aid to Britain, which they both supported. In November Roosevelt, buoyed by near universal support among labor union members and northern blacks, won an unprecedented third term by a comfortable margin of 27 million votes to Willkie's 22 million and by a more decisive margin, of 449 to 82, in the Electoral College.

THE "ARSENAL OF DEMOCRACY" A reelected Roosevelt moved quickly to provide even more military aid to Britain, whose cash was running out. Since direct American loans to the British government were prohibited by the Johnson Debt Default Act of 1934, the president created an ingenious device to supply British needs: the lend-lease program. The **lend-lease bill**, introduced in Congress on January 10, 1941, authorized the president to lend or lease military equipment to "any country whose defense the President deems vital to the defense of the United States." Lend-lease became law in March, prompting Roosevelt to announce that it represented "the end of any attempts at appeasement. . . ." Most of the dissenting votes in Congress were Republicans from the staunchly isolationist Midwest.

While the nation debated neutrality, the European war expanded. Italy had officially entered the war in June 1940 as Germany's ally. In the spring of 1941, German troops joined Italian forces in Libya, forcing the British army in North Africa to withdraw to Egypt. In April 1941, Nazi forces overwhelmed Yugoslavia and Greece. With Hungary, Romania, and Bulgaria forced into the Axis fold, Hitler controlled nearly all of Europe. But his ambition was unbounded.

On June 22, 1941, without warning, massive German armies suddenly invaded the Soviet Union, their supposed ally. Hitler's objective was to destroy Communism, enslave the vast population of the Soviet Union, and exploit its considerable natural resources. Hitler's decision to attack the Soviet Union was the defining event of the European war. Joined by Romanian and Finnish allies, the Nazis massed 3.6 million troops and thousands of tanks and planes along the 1,800-mile front from the Arctic Ocean to the Black Sea. It was the largest invasion force in European history. Initially, the German armies raced across western Russia; entire Soviet armies were surrounded and destroyed. During 1941, 3 million Soviets were captured.

For four months the Soviets retreated in the face of the German blitzkrieg. Leningrad (formerly St. Petersburg) was besieged, and Moscow was threatened. The scale and brutality of the war on the Eastern Front were mind-boggling. When the Germans conquered the city of Kiev, some six hundred thousand Soviet troops surrendered. The siege of Leningrad lasted for nine hundred days and killed seven hundred and fifty thousand civilians, many of whom starved to death after the Germans surrounded the city. During the Battle of Moscow, Russian defenders executed eight thousand civilians because of "cowardice". Gradually, the Russians slowed the Nazi advance. Then, during the winter of 1941–1942, Hitler's legions began to learn the bitter lesson the Russians had taught Napoleon and the French army in 1812. Invading armies must contend with the brutal Russian winter and Russian tenacity.

Prime Minister Winston Churchill had already decided to offer British support to the Soviet Union in case of such an attack, for the Russians, so long as they held out against the Nazis, helped to ensure the survival of Britain. Roosevelt adopted the same pragmatic policy, offering U.S. aid to the Soviet Union. American supplies were now indispensable to Europe's defense. To deliver massive aid to Britain and the Soviet Union, convoys of supply ships had to maneuver through German submarine "wolf packs" in the North Atlantic. In April 1941, Roosevelt informed Churchill that the U.S. Navy would extend its patrols in the North Atlantic nearly all the way to Iceland in an effort to deter German submarine attacks.

In August 1941, Roosevelt and Churchill held a secret meeting off Newfoundland, where they drew up a joint statement of "common principles" known as the **Atlantic Charter**. It pledged that after the "final destruction of the Nazi tyranny" the victors would promote the self-determination of all peoples, economic cooperation, freedom of the seas, and a new system of international security. By September eleven anti-Axis nations, including the Soviet Union, had endorsed the charter.

Thus Roosevelt had led the United States into a joint statement of war aims with the anti-Axis powers. It was not long before shooting incidents involved American ships in the North Atlantic. On October 17, 1941, while the destroyer *Kearny* was attacking German submarines, a German torpedo hit it, and eleven lives were lost. Two weeks later a German submarine sank the destroyer *Reuben James,* with a loss of 115 seamen. The sinking spurred Congress to change the 1939 Neutrality Act by repealing the bans on arming merchant vessels and allowing them to enter combat zones and the ports of nations at war. Step by step, the United States had given up neutrality and embarked on naval warfare against Nazi Germany. Still, Americans hoped to avoid taking the final step into all-out war. The decision to go to war would be made in response to aggression in an unexpected quarter—Hawaii.

THE STORM IN THE PACIFIC

JAPANESE AGGRESSION   After the Nazi victories in Europe during the spring of 1940, U.S. relations with Japan took a turn for the worse. In 1940, Japan and the United States began a series of moves, each of which aggravated the other and pushed the two nations closer to war. During the summer, Japan forced the helpless Vichy French government, now under German control, to permit the construction of Japanese airfields in French-controlled northern Indochina and to cut off the railroad into south China.

The United States responded with the Export Control Act of July 2, 1940, which authorized the president to restrict the export of munitions and other strategic materials to Japan. Gradually, Roosevelt extended embargoes on aviation gas, scrap iron, and other supplies.

On September 27, 1940, the Tokyo government signed a Tripartite Pact with Nazi Germany and Fascist Italy, by which each pledged to declare war on any nation that attacked any of them. On April 13, 1941, Japan signed a non-aggression pact with the Soviet Union. When Germany invaded the Soviet Union in June, the Japanese were freed of any threat from the north—at least for a while. In July 1941, Japan announced that it was taking control of French Indochina. Roosevelt took three steps in response: he froze all Japanese assets

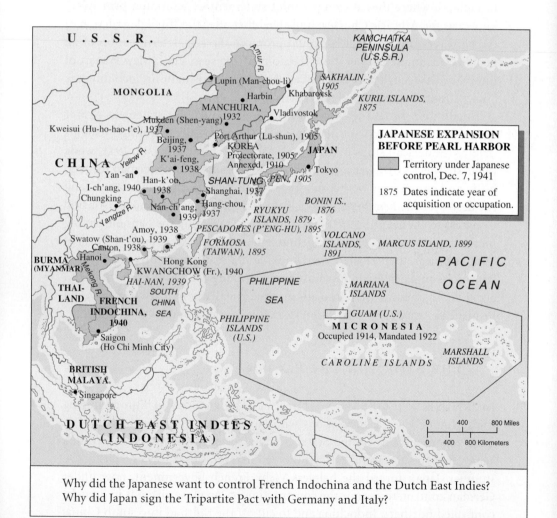

Why did the Japanese want to control French Indochina and the Dutch East Indies? Why did Japan sign the Tripartite Pact with Germany and Italy?

in the United States, he restricted oil exports to Japan (the United States was then producing half of the world's oil), and he merged the armed forces of the Philippines with the U.S. Army and put their commander, General Douglas MacArthur, in charge of all U.S. forces in east Asia. Forced by the American embargo to secure other oil supplies, the Japanese army and navy began planning attacks on the Dutch and British colonies in the South Pacific.

Actions by both sides put the United States and Japan on a collision course leading to a war that neither wanted. In his talks with the Japanese ambassador in Washington, Secretary of State Cordell Hull demanded that Japan withdraw from French Indochina and China as the price of renewed trade with the United States. Prime Minister Fumimaro Konoe, while known as a man of democratic principles who preferred peace, caved in to pressures from the militarists. Perhaps he had no choice. Whatever the case, the Japanese warlords seriously misjudged the United States when they decided that the U.S. Navy was a threat to their expansionist ambitions and must be destroyed.

THE ATTACK ON PEARL HARBOR   Late in August 1941, Japanese Prime Minister Konoe proposed a meeting with President Roosevelt. Soon afterward, on September 6, Japanese military leaders secretly approved a surprise attack on U.S. bases in Hawaii and gave Konoe six weeks in which to reach a settlement. In October, Konoe urged War Minister Hideki Tōjō to consider withdrawal of Japanese forces in China while saving face by keeping some troops in north China. General Tōjō refused. Konoe resigned on October 15; Tōjō became prime minister the next day. The war party had now assumed control of the Japanese government, and Tōjō viewed war with the United States as inevitable.

On November 20, a Japanese official presented Secretary of State Cordell Hull with Tōjō's final proposal: Japan promised to occupy no more territory in Asia if the United States would cut off aid to China and restore trade with Japan. On November 26, Hull insisted that Japan withdraw from China altogether. Tōjō, who had expected the United States to refuse the demands, ordered a powerful fleet of Japanese warships to begin steaming secretly toward Hawaii, crowded with U.S. military installations, including Pearl Harbor, the massive naval base. The naval commander, Admiral Isoroku Yamamoto, said his audacious plan was an all-or-nothing gamble "conceived in desperation" to destroy the U.S. Pacific fleet, while Japanese armies invaded British Malaya and the Dutch East Indies, both of which were rich in supplies of rubber and oil. He knew that the Japanese could not defeat the United States in a long war; their only hope was "to decide the fate of the war on the very first day."

The attack on Pearl Harbor

This view from an army airfield shows the destruction brought on by the surprise attack.

Officials in Washington, believing that war was imminent, sent warnings to U.S. commanders in the Pacific that the Japanese might attack somewhere in the southwest Pacific. But no one expected that Japan would launch a surprise attack five thousand miles away, at Hawaii's Pearl Harbor. In the early morning of December 7, 1941, Japanese planes began bombing the unsuspecting American fleet at Pearl Harbor. Of the eight American battleships, all were sunk or disabled, along with eleven other ships. At airfields on the island, the Japanese bombers destroyed 180 American planes. The raid, which lasted less than two hours, killed more than 2,400 American servicemen and civilians and wounded nearly 1,200 more.

The surprise attack fulfilled the dreams of its planners, but it fell short of success in two ways. The Japanese bombers ignored the onshore maintenance facilities and oil tanks in Hawaii that supported the U.S. fleet, without which the surviving ships might have been forced back to the West Coast, and they missed the American aircraft carriers that had left port a few days earlier. In the naval war to come, aircraft carriers would prove to be the decisive weapon. In a larger sense, the Japanese attack on Pearl Harbor was a spectacular miscalculation. It aroused the Americans to wage total war until a devastated Japan surrendered.

With one stroke at Pearl Harbor on December 7, the Japanese had silenced America's debate on neutrality. People boiled over in vengeful fury as the United States was yanked into the Second World War. The next day, President Roosevelt, calm, composed, and determined, delivered his war message to Congress: "Yesterday, December 7, 1941—a date which will live in infamy—the United States of America was suddenly and deliberately attacked by naval and air forces of the Empire of Japan." Congress voted for the war resolution with near unanimity, the sole exception being Representative Jeannette Rankin, a Montana pacifist who refused to vote for war in 1917 or 1941. On December 11, Germany and Italy declared war on what Hitler called the "half Judaized and the other half Negrified" United States, a nation that he insisted "was not dangerous to us." The separate wars that were being waged by armies in Asia, Europe, and Africa had become one global conflict, shattering American isolationism.

A WORLD WAR

The Japanese attack on Pearl Harbor embroiled the United States in a global conflict that would transform the nation's social and economic life, as well as its position in international affairs. The Second World War would become the most destructive conflict in history; over 50 million deaths resulted from the war, two thirds of them civilians. The fighting was so terrible in its intensity and obscene in its cruelties that it altered the nature of war itself. The warring nations developed powerful new weapons—plastic explosives, rockets, napalm, jet airplanes, and atomic bombs—and systematic genocide emerged as an explicit war aim of the Nazis. The scorching passions of such an all-out war encouraged horrific excesses. The Nazis murdered up to 6 million Jewish civilians and many others. Racist propaganda flourished on both sides, and seething hatred of the enemy led to the torture and execution of many military and civilian prisoners. The physical destruction was unprecedented, leveling whole cities, dismembering nations, and transforming societies. Many decades later, the world is still coping with the war's consequences.

SETBACKS IN THE PACIFIC   The United States had declared war on December 8, but the nation was woefully unprepared to wage a world war. The army and navy were understaffed and underequipped. And it would

Early defeats

U.S. prisoners of war, captured by the Japanese in the Philippines, 1942.

take months for the economy to make the transition to full-scale military production. Yet time was of the essence. Japanese and German forces were on the move. For months after the attack on Pearl Harbor, the news from the Pacific was "all bad," as President Roosevelt confessed. In quick sequence the Japanese captured numerous Allied outposts before the end of December 1941: Guam and Wake Islands, the Gilbert Islands, and Hong Kong. "Everywhere in the Pacific," said Winston Churchill, "we were weak and naked."

In the Philippines, U.S. forces and their Filipino allies, outmanned, outgunned, and malnourished, surrendered in the early spring of 1942. On April 10, the Japanese gathered some twelve thousand captured American troops along with sixty-six thousand Filipinos and forced them to march sixty-five miles in six days up the Bataan peninsula. Already underfed, ravaged by tropical diseases, and provided with little food and water, the prisoners of war were brutalized in what came to be known as the Bataan Death March. Those who fell out of line were bayoneted or shot. Others were beaten, stabbed, or shot for no reason. Over ten thousand of the prisoners of war died along the way. News of the Bataan Death March outraged Americans and helps explain the Pacific war's ferocious emotional intensity.

By the summer of 1942 Japan had seized control of a vast new Asian empire and was on the verge of assaulting Australia when Japanese naval leaders succumbed to what one admiral called "victory disease." Intoxicated with easy victories and lusting for more conquests, they pushed on into the South Pacific, intending to isolate Australia, and strike again at Hawaii. A Japanese mistake and a stroke of American luck enabled the U.S. Navy to frustrate the plan, however. The U.S. aircraft carriers that were luckily at sea during the Japanese attack on Pearl Harbor spent several months harassing Japanese outposts. Their most spectacular exploit, an air raid on Tokyo itself, was launched on April 18, 1942. B-25 bombers took off from the carrier *Hornet* and, unable to land on its deck, proceeded to China after dropping their bombs over Tokyo. The raid caused only token damage but did much to lift American morale amid a series of defeats elsewhere.

CORAL SEA AND MIDWAY   During the spring of 1942, U.S. forces finally halted the Japanese advance toward Australia in two key naval battles. The Battle of the Coral Sea (May 7–8, 1942) stopped a Japanese fleet convoying troops toward New Guinea. Planes from the *Lexington* and the *Yorktown* sank one Japanese carrier, damaged another, and destroyed smaller ships. American losses were greater, but the Japanese threat against Australia was repulsed.

Less than a month after the Coral Sea engagement, Admiral Yamamoto steered his armada for Midway, the westernmost of Hawaii's inhabited islands, from which he hoped to render Pearl Harbor helpless. This time it was the Japanese who were the victims of surprise. Working night and day deciphering some fifty thousand five-digit numerical groups, American cryptanalysts ("code breakers") had broken the Japanese military communications code. This breakthrough reshaped the balance of power in the Pacific war. Admiral Chester Nimitz, commander of the U.S. central Pacific fleet, now learned from intercepted Japanese messages where Yamamoto's fleet was heading. He reinforced the American base at tiny Midway Island with planes and aircraft carriers.

The first Japanese foray against Midway, on June 4, 1942, severely damaged the island's defenses, but at the cost of about a third of the Japanese planes. American bombers struck back. In the strategic Battle of Midway, U.S. planes sank three aircraft carriers and badly damaged a fourth that was later sunk by a torpedo; it was the first defeat for the Japanese navy in 350 years and the turning point of the Pacific war. It blunted Japan's military momentum, eliminated the threat to Hawaii, demonstrated that aircraft carriers, not battleships, were the decisive elements of modern naval warfare, and bought time for the United States to mobilize its massive industrial productivity for a wider war. Japanese hopes for a short, decisive war were dashed at the crucial naval battle.

MOBILIZATION AT HOME

A NATION AT WAR   Winning the war against Germany and Japan would require all of the nation's immense industrial capacity and full employment of the workforce. On December 18, 1941, Congress passed the

War Powers Act, which gave the president far-reaching authority to reorganize and create government agencies, regulate business and industry, and even censor mail and other forms of communication. With the declaration of war, men between the ages of eighteen and forty-five were drafted. At one time or another between 1941–1945, some 16 million men and several hundred thousand women were in the military. The average soldier or sailor who served in the war was 26 years old, stood five feet eight, and weighed 144 pounds, an inch taller and eight pounds heavier than the typical recruit in World War I.

ECONOMIC CONVERSION   The War Production Board, created in 1942, directed the conversion of industrial manufacturing to war production. In 1941, more than 3 million automobiles were manufactured in the United States; only 139 were built during the next four years. Instead of cars, the automobile plants began making tanks and airplanes. President Roosevelt wanted to confront the enemy with a "crushing superiority of equipment." To do so, he established staggering military production goals: sixty thousand warplanes in 1942 and twice as many the following year, fifty-five thousand anti-aircraft guns, and tens of thousands of tanks. Military-related production skyrocketed from 2 percent of the nation's economic production in 1939 to 40 percent in 1943. "Something is happening that Hitler doesn't understand," announced *Time* magazine in 1942. ". . . . It is the miracle of production."

FINANCING THE WAR   To cover the war's huge cost, Congress passed the Revenue Act of 1942 (also called the Victory Tax). It raised tax rates and increased the number of taxpayers. Whereas in 1939 only about 4 million people (about 5 percent of the workforce) filed tax returns, the new act made virtually everyone (75 percent) a taxpayer. By the end of war, 90 percent of workers were paying income tax. Tax revenues covered about 45 percent of military costs from 1939 to 1946; the government borrowed the rest. In all, by the end of the war the national debt was six times what it had been at the start of the war.

The size of the federal government soared along with its budget during the war. The number of federal workers grew from one million to four million. Throughout the economy, jobs were suddenly plentiful. The nation's unemployment rate plummeted from 14 percent in 1940 to 2 percent in 1943. Millions of people who had lived on the margins of the economic system, especially women, were now brought fully into the economy. Stubborn pockets of poverty did not disappear, but for most civilians, especially those who had earlier lost their jobs and homes to the Depression, the war spelled a better life than ever before, despite the rationing of various consumer items.

ECONOMIC CONTROLS   The war raised fears of inflation as consumer goods grew scarce. In 1942, Congress authorized the Office of Price Administration to set price ceilings. With prices frozen, basic goods had to be allocated through rationing, with coupons doled out for sugar, coffee, gasoline, automobile tires, and meat. The government promoted patriotic frugality with a massive public relations campaign that circulated posters with slogans such as "Use it up, wear it out, make it do, or do without." Businesses and workers chafed at the wage and price controls. On occasion the government seized industries threatened by strikes. Despite these problems the government effort to stabilize wages and prices succeeded. By the end of the war, consumer prices had risen about 31 percent, a record far better than the World War I rise of 62 percent.

USE IT UP – WEAR IT OUT – MAKE IT DO!

OUR LABOR AND OUR GOODS ARE FIGHTING

War-effort advertisement

The Office of War Information created the ad's slogan in 1943.

DOMESTIC CONSERVATISM   Despite government efforts to promote patriotic sacrifice among civilians, discontent with price controls, labor shortages, rationing, and other petty grievances spread. In the 1942 congressional elections, Republicans gained forty-six seats in the House and nine in the Senate. Democratic losses outside the "Solid South" strengthened the conservative southern delegation's position within the party. During the 1940s, a bipartisan coalition of conservatives dismantled "nonessential" New Deal agencies such as the as the Work Projects Administration (originally the Works Progress Administration), the National Youth Administration, the Civilian Conservation Corps, and the National Resources Planning Board.

Organized labor, despite substantial gains during the war, felt the impact of the conservative trend. In the spring of 1943, when John L. Lewis led the coal miners out on strike, Congress passed the Smith-Connally War Labor Disputes Act, which authorized the government to seize plants and mines useful to the war effort. In 1943 a dozen states adopted laws restricting picketing and other union activities, and in 1944 Arkansas and Florida set in motion a wave of "right-to-work" legislation that outlawed the closed shop (requiring that all employees be union members).

SOCIAL EFFECTS OF THE WAR

In making the United States the "great arsenal of democracy," the Roosevelt administration transformed the economy into the world's most efficient military machine. By 1945, the year the war ended, the United States would be manufacturing fully half of the goods produced in the world. Such an economic miracle transformed American society.

MOBILIZATION IN THE WEST AND SOUTH The dramatic expansion of military production after 1940 and the recruitment of millions of people into the armed forces and defense industries triggered rapid growth in the western states. The Far West experienced the fastest rate of urban growth in the country. Nearly 8 million people moved into the states west of the Mississippi River between 1940 and 1950. The migration of workers to new defense jobs in the West had significant demographic effects. Lured by news of job openings and higher wages, African Americans from Texas, Oklahoma, Arkansas, and Louisiana headed west. During the war years, Seattle's African American population jumped from four thousand to forty thousand, Portland's from two thousand to fifteen thousand.

The South also experienced dramatic social changes as a result of the war effort. Sixty of the one hundred new army camps created during the war were in southern states. The construction of military bases and the influx of new personnel transformed the local economies. The demand for military uniforms provided a boon to southern textile mills. Manufacturing jobs led tens of thousands of "dirt poor" sharecroppers and tenant farmers, many of them African Americans, to leave the land and gain a steady wage working in mills and factories. Throughout the United States during the Second World War, the rural population decreased by 20 percent.

CHANGING ROLES FOR WOMEN The war marked an important watershed in the status of women. With millions of men going into military service, the demand for civilian workers shook up old prejudices about sex roles in the workplace—and in the military. Nearly two hundred thousand women served in the **Women's Army Corps** (WAC) and the navy's equivalent, Women Accepted for Volunteer Emergency Service (WAVES). Others joined the Marine Corps, the Coast Guard, and the Army Air Force. Over 6 million women entered the workforce during the war, an increase of more than 50 percent overall and in manufacturing alone an increase of some 110 percent. One striking feature of the new labor scene was the proportion of older, married women in the workforce. In 1940 about 15 percent of married women were gainfully employed; by 1945 about 24 percent were. Many men opposed the trend. A disgruntled male legislator asked what would happen to traditional domestic tasks if women flocked to factories: "Who will do the cooking, the washing, the mending, the humble homey tasks to which every woman has devoted herself; who will rear and nurture the children?" Many women,

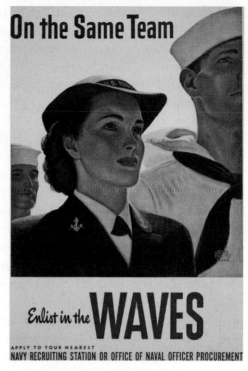

Women in the military

This navy-recruiting poster urged women to join the WAVES (Women Accepted for Volunteer Emergency Service).

however, were eager to get away from the grinding routine of domestic life. A female welder remembered that her wartime job "was the first time I had a chance to get out of the kitchen and work in industry and make a few bucks. This was something I had never dreamed would happen."

AFRICAN AMERICANS IN THE SECOND WORLD WAR Although Americans found themselves fighting against the explicit racial and ethnic bigotry promoted by fascism and Nazism, racism in the United States did not end during the war. The Red Cross, for example, initially refused to accept blood donated by blacks, and the president of North American Aviation announced that "we will not employ Negroes." Blacks who were hired often were limited to the lowest-paid, lowest-skilled jobs.

Some courageous black leaders refused to accept such racist practices. In 1941, A. Philip Randolph, the head of the Brotherhood of Sleeping Car Porters, planned a march on Washington, D.C., to demand an end to racial discrimination in defense industries. To fend off the march, the Roosevelt administration struck a bargain. The Randolph group called off its demonstration in return for a presidential order that forbade discrimination in defense industries. More than a half million African Americans left the South for better opportunities during the war years, and more than a million blacks nationwide joined the industrial workforce for the first time.

AFRICAN AMERICANS IN UNIFORM The most volatile social issue ignited by the war was African American participation in the military. In 1941 the armed forces were the most racially polarized institution in the nation. But African Americans rushed to enlist after the Japanese attack on Pearl Harbor. As African American Joe Louis, the world heavyweight boxing champion, stressed, "Lots of things [are] wrong with America, but Hitler ain't going to fix them." About a million African Americans—men and women— served in the armed forces during the war, but in racially segregated units. Black soldiers and sailors were initially excluded from combat units and relegated to menial tasks. Black officers also could not command white soldiers or sailors. Henry L. Stimson, the secretary of war, cavalierly claimed that "leadership is not embedded in the negro race." Every army camp and navy base had segregated facilities—and frequent and sometimes bloody racial "incidents." Among the most famous African American servicemen were some six hundred pilots trained in Tuskegee, Alabama. The so-called **Tuskegee Airmen** ended up flying more than fifteen thousand missions during the war. Their unquestionable excellence spurred military and civilian leaders to integrate the armed forces after the war.

THE DOUBLE V CAMPAIGN In 1942, the editors of the *Pittsburgh Courier*, the black newspaper with the largest national circulation, urged African Americans to promote civil rights while also supporting the war effort. It was called the Double V campaign because the newspaper published two interlocking Vs with the theme "Democracy: Victory at Home, Victory Abroad." The campaign encouraged blacks to support the war effort while fighting for civil rights and racial equality at home. The Double V campaign also demanded that African Americans who were risking their lives abroad receive full citizenship rights at home. As the newspaper explained, the Double V campaign represented a "two-pronged attack" against those who would enslave "us at home and those who abroad would enslave us. WE HAVE A STAKE IN THIS FIGHT. . . . WE ARE AMERICANS TOO!" The editors stressed that no one should interpret their "militant" efforts on behalf back civil rights "as a plot to impede the war effort. Negroes

Tuskegee Airmen, 1942

One of the last segregated military training schools, the flight school at Tuskegee trained African American men for air combat during the Second World War.

recognize that the first factor in the survival of this nation is the winning of the war. But they feel integration of Negroes into the whole scheme of things 'revitalizes' the U.S. war program." The response among the nation's black community to the *Courier*'s Double V campaign was "overwhelming." The *Courier* was swamped with telegrams and letters of support supporting the public relations campaign. Double V clubs sprouted across the nation. Other black newspapers across the nation joined the effort to promote the values at home that American forces were defending abroad.

Throughout the war, African Americans highlighted the irony of the United States fighting against racism abroad while tolerating racism at home. "The army is about to take me to fight for democracy," a Detroit draftee said, "but I would [rather] fight for democracy right here." During the summer of 1943 alone there were 274 race-related incidents in almost 50 cities. In Detroit, growing racial tensions on a hot afternoon sparked incidents at a park that escalated into a full-fledged riot. Fighting raged through June 20 and 21, until federal troops arrived on the second evening. By then, twenty-five blacks and nine whites had been killed, and more than seven hundred people had been injured.

MEXICANS AND MEXICAN AMERICANS   As rural dwellers moved to the western cities during the war, many farm counties experienced a labor shortage. In an ironic about-face, local and federal government authorities who before the war had forced undocumented Mexican laborers back across the border now recruited them to harvest crops on American farms. Before it would provide the needed workers, however, the Mexican government insisted that the United States ensure minimum working and living conditions for the migrant farm workers. The result was the creation of the *bracero* program in 1942, whereby Mexico agreed to provide seasonal farm workers to the southwestern states in exchange for a promise by the U.S. government: the bracero workers would not be used as strike breakers or as a pretext for lowering wages, and they would not be drafted into military service. The workers were hired on yearlong contracts, and American officials provided transportation from the border to their job sites. Under the bracero program some two hundred thousand Mexican farm workers entered the western United States. At least that many more crossed the border as undocumented workers.

The rising tide of Mexican Americans in Los Angeles prompted a growing stream of anti-Mexican editorials and ugly racial incidents. Even though some three hundred thousand Mexican Americans served in the war with great valor, earning a higher percentage of Congressional Medals of Honor than any other minority group, racial prejudices still prevailed. There was constant conflict between Anglo servicemen and Mexican American gang members and teenage "zoot-suiters" in southern California. (Zoot suits were the flamboyant attire popular in the 1940s and worn by some young Mexican American men.) In 1943 several thousand off-duty sailors and soldiers, joined by hundreds of local whites, rampaged through downtown Los Angeles streets, assaulting Hispanics, African Americans, and Filipinos. The weeklong violence came to be called the zoot-suit riots.

NATIVE AMERICANS Indians supported the war effort more fully than any other group in American society. Almost a third of eligible Native American men served in the armed forces. Many others worked in defense-related industries. Thousands of Indian women volunteered as nurses or joined the WAVES. As was the case with African Americans, Indians benefited from the experiences afforded by the war. Those who left reservations to work in defense plants or to join the military gained new vocational skills as well as a greater awareness of mainstream society and how to succeed within it.

Why did so many Native Americans fight for a nation that had stripped them of their land and decimated their heritage? Some felt that they had no choice. Mobilization for the war effort ended many New Deal programs that had provided Indians with jobs. Reservation Indians thus faced the necessity

Marine Navajo "code talkers"

The Japanese were never able to break the Native Americans' codes used by signal-men, such as those shown here during the Battle of Bougainville in 1943.

of finding new jobs elsewhere. Many viewed the Nazis and the Japanese warlords as threats to their own homeland. The most common sentiment, however, seems to have been a genuine sense of patriotism. Whatever the reasons, Indians distinguished themselves in the military. Unlike their African American counterparts, Indian servicemen were integrated into reg-ular units. Perhaps the most distinctive activity performed by Indians was their service as "code talkers": every military branch used Indians, especially Navajos, to quickly encode and decipher messages using ancient Indian lan-guages unknown to the Germans and Japanese.

DISCRIMINATION AGAINST JAPANESE AMERICANS The attack on Pearl Harbor ignited vengeful anger toward people of Japanese descent living in the United States, known as Nisei. As Idaho's governor declared, "A good solution to the Jap problem would be to send them all back to Japan, then sink the island." Such extreme hostility helps explain why the U.S. government sponsored the worst violation of civil liberties during the twentieth century when more than 112,000 Nisei were forcibly removed from their homes on the West Coast and transported to "war relocation camps" in the interior. President Roosevelt initiated the removal of Japanese Americans (he called them "Japs") when he issued Executive Order 9066 on February 19, 1942. More than 60 percent of the internees were U.S. citizens; a third were under the age of nineteen. Forced to sell their farms and businesses at great losses, the internees lost not only their property but also their liberty. Few if any were disloyal, but all were victims of fear and racial prejudice. Not until 1983 did the government acknowledge the injustice of the internment policy. Five years later it granted those Nisei still living $20,000 each in compensation, a tiny amount relative to what they had lost during four years of confinement.

The Allied Drive toward Berlin

By mid-1942, the "home front" was hearing good news from the war fronts. Japanese naval losses at the Battles of Coral Sea and Midway had secured Australia and Hawaii. U.S. naval forces had also been increasingly successful at destroying German U-boats off the Atlantic coast. This was all the more important because the Grand Alliance—Great Britain, the United States, and the Soviet Union—called for the defeat of Germany first.

WAR AIMS AND STRATEGY   A major factor affecting Allied strategy was the fighting on the vast Eastern Front in the Soviet Union, where, in fact, the outcome of the war against Hitler was largely decided. In eastern Europe during 1941–42 two totalitarian regimes—the Nazis and the Soviets—waged colossal battles while murdering millions of civilians in horrifying slave labor/extermination camps (Nazis) and forced labor concentration camps (Soviets). Among the combatant nations, the Soviets—by far—bore the brunt of the war against the Nazis, leading Joseph Stalin, the Soviet premier, to insist that the Americans and British relieve the pressure on them by attacking the Germans in western Europe.

Roosevelt and Churchill agreed that they needed to create a second front, but they could not agree on the location of their first attack against Hitler's armies. U.S. military planners were willing to take extraordinary, indeed foolhardy, risks by striking directly across the English Channel before the end of 1942. They wanted to secure a beachhead in German-occupied France, and then move briskly against Germany itself in 1943. "We've got to go to Europe and fight," General Dwight D. Eisenhower stressed. The British, however, were wary of moving too fast. An Allied defeat on the French coast, Churchill warned, was "the only way in which we could possibly lose this war." Roosevelt, concerned about upcoming Congressional elections, told the U.S. military planners to accept Churchill's compromise proposal for a joint Anglo-American invasion of French North Africa, which had been captured by German and Italian armies.

THE NORTH AFRICA CAMPAIGN On November 8, 1942, British and American forces commanded by U.S. general **Dwight D. Eisenhower** landed in Morocco and Algeria on the North African coast. Farther east, British armies were pushing the Germans back across Libya, and untested American forces were confronting seasoned German units pouring into Tunisia. Before spring, however, the British forces had taken Libya, and the Germans were caught in a gigantic pair of pincers. Hammered from all sides, unable to retreat across the Mediterranean, an army of some 250,000 Germans and Italians surrendered on May 12, 1943, leaving all of North Africa in Allied hands.

Five months earlier, in January 1943, Roosevelt, Churchill, and the Combined Chiefs of Staff met at Casablanca, the largest city in Morocco. It was a historic occasion. No U.S. president had ever flown abroad while in office, and none had ever visited Africa. Stalin declined to leave besieged Russia for the meeting, however, although he continued to press for a second front in western Europe to relieve the pressure on the Soviet Union. The British and American engagements with German forces in North Africa were minuscule in comparison with the scope and fury of the fighting in Russia. Throughout 1943, for example, while some sixty thousand British and American servicemen were killed by German forces, the Soviet Union lost *2 million* combatants.

At the Casablanca Conference, Churchill and Roosevelt spent eight days hammering out key strategic decisions. The British convinced the Americans that they should follow up a victory in North Africa with an assault on German and Italian forces on the Italian island of Sicily and in Italy itself. Roosevelt and Churchill also decided to step up the bombing of Germany and to increase shipments of military supplies to the Soviet Union and the Nationalist Chinese forces fighting the Japanese. American military-industrial productivity proved to be the most strategic asset in the war. Many of the Soviet troops who would advance west toward Berlin during the latter phase of the war rode in American trucks, ate American rations, and wore American boots. Yet, as Stalin often complained, the Americans were far more generous with supplies than they were committing large numbers of soldiers on the battlefield.

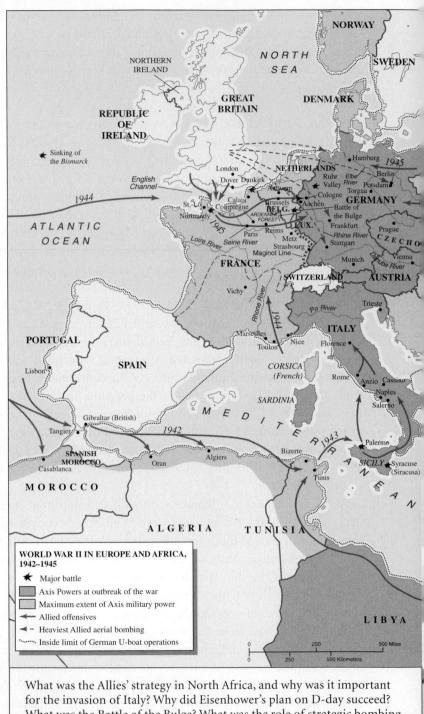

WORLD WAR II IN EUROPE AND AFRICA,
1942–1945

★ Major battle

Axis Powers at outbreak of the war

Maximum extent of Axis military power

◄— Allied offensives

◄- Heaviest Allied aerial bombing

········ Inside limit of German U-boat operations

What was the Allies' strategy in North Africa, and why was it important
for the invasion of Italy? Why did Eisenhower's plan on D-day succeed?
What was the Battle of the Bulge? What was the role of strategic bombing
in the war? Was it effective?

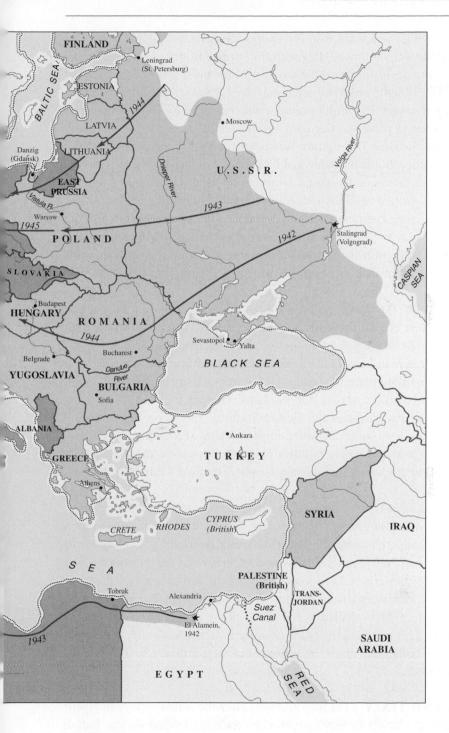

Before leaving Casablanca, Roosevelt announced, with Churchill's endorsement, that the war would end only with the "unconditional surrender" of all enemies. This decision was designed to quiet Soviet suspicions that the Western Allies might negotiate separately with the various enemy nations making up the Axis. The announcement also reflected Roosevelt's determination that "every person in Germany should realize that this time Germany is a defeated nation." This dictum was later criticized for having stiffened enemy resistance, but it probably had little effect; in fact, neither the Italian nor the Japanese surrender would be unconditional. But the decision did have one unexpected result: it opened an avenue for eventual Soviet control of eastern Europe because it required Russian armies to pursue Hitler's forces all the way to Germany. And as they liberated the nations of eastern Europe from Nazi control, the Soviets created new Communist governments under their own control.

THE BATTLE OF THE ATLANTIC   While fighting raged in North Africa, the more crucial Battle of the Atlantic reached its climax on the high seas. Isolated Britain desperately needed supplies from the United States. The fall of France in June 1940 allowed German submarines to use French ports, thus enabling them to venture all the way across the Atlantic to sink freighters and tankers headed for England. One of the U-boat captains referred to the east coast of the United States as the "American shooting gallery." By July 1942 some 230 Allied ships and almost 5 million tons of war supplies had been lost. Then, in July alone, 143 ships were sunk. "The only thing that ever frightened me during the war," recalled Churchill, "was the U-boat peril."

By the end of 1942 the Allies had discovered ways to thwart the U-boats. A key breakthrough occurred when British experts deciphered the German naval radio codes, enabling Allied convoys to steer clear of U-boats or to hunt them down. New technology also helped. Sonar and radar enabled Allied ships to track submarines. The most effective tactic was to organize the ships into convoys with protective warships surrounding them. After May 1943, the U-boats were on the defensive, and Allied shipping losses fell significantly. The U-boats kept up the Battle of the Atlantic until the war's end; when Germany finally collapsed, almost 50 submarines were still at sea, but 783 had been destroyed.

SICILY AND ITALY   On July 10, 1943, after the Allied victory in North Africa, about 250,000 British and American troops landed on the Italian island of Sicily in the first effort to reclaim European territory since the war began. The entire island was in Allied hands by August 17. Allied success in Sicily ended Mussolini's twenty years of Fascist rule. On July 25, 1943, Italy's king dismissed Mussolini as prime minister and had him arrested. The new Italian government startled the Allies when it offered not only to surrender but also to switch sides in the war. Unfortunately, mutual suspicions prolonged talks until September 3, during which time the Germans poured reinforcements into Italy. Mussolini, plucked from imprisonment by a daring German airborne raid, became head of a puppet Fascist government in northern Italy. On June 4, 1944, the U.S. Fifth Army entered Rome. The capture of Rome received only a brief moment of glory, however, for the long-awaited cross-Channel Allied landing in German-occupied France came two days later. Italy, always a secondary front, faded from the world's attention.

THE TEHRAN MEETING   Late in the fall of 1943, Churchill and Roosevelt had their first joint meeting with Joseph Stalin, in Tehran, Iran. Although as much competitors as collaborators, they were able to forge several key agreements. Their chief subject was the planned invasion of France and a Russian offensive across eastern Europe timed to coincide with it. Stalin repeated his promise to enter the war against Japan, and the three leaders agreed to create an international organization (the United Nations) to maintain peace after the war. Upon arriving back in the United States, Roosevelt confided to Churchill his distrust of Stalin, stressing that it was a "ticklish" business keeping the "Russians cozy with us." Indeed it was.

THE STRATEGIC BOMBING OF EUROPE   Behind the long-postponed Allied invasion of German-controlled France lay months of preparation. While waiting for D-day, the U.S. Army Air Force and the British Royal Air Force (RAF) had sought to pound Germany into submission. The Allied air campaign killed perhaps six hundred thousand German civilians. Yet while causing widespread damage, the strategic air offensive failed to devastate German morale or industrial production. But with air supremacy over Europe assured by 1944, the Allies were free to provide cover for the much-anticipated invasion of Hitler's "Fortress Europa." On April 14, 1944, General Eisenhower assumed control of the strategic air forces for the invasion of German-controlled France. On D-day, June 6, 1944, he told the troops, "If you see fighting aircraft over you, they will be ours."

D-DAY AND AFTER   In early 1944, General Dwight D. Eisenhower arrived in London to take command of the Allied forces. Battle-tested in North Africa and the Mediterranean, he now faced the daunting task of planning **Operation Overlord**, the daring assault on Hitler's "Atlantic Wall," a formidable series of fortifications and mines along the French coastline.

The prospect of an amphibious assault against such defenses unnerved some Allied planners. As D-day approached in June, Eisenhower's chief of staff predicted only a fifty-fifty chance of success. Operation Overlord succeeded largely because it was meticulously planned and because it surprised the Germans. The Allies fooled the Nazis into believing that the invasion would come at Pas-de-Calais, on the French-Belgian border, where the English Channel was narrowest. Instead, the landings occurred in Normandy, almost two hundred miles south. In April and May 1944, while the vast invasion forces made final preparations, the Allied air forces disrupted the transportation network of northern France, smashing railroads and bridges. By early June all was ready, and D-day fell on June 6, 1944.

On the evening of June 5, Eisenhower visited some of the sixteen thousand American paratroopers preparing to land at night behind the German lines in France to seize key bridges and roads. The men noticed his look of grave concern and tried to lift his spirits. "Now quit worrying, General," one of them

Operation Overlord

General Dwight D. Eisenhower instructing paratroopers before they boarded their airplanes to launch the D-day assault.

said, "we'll take care of this thing for you." After the planes took off, Eisenhower returned to his car with tears in his eyes. "Well," he said quietly to his driver, "it's on." He knew that many of his troops would die within a few hours.

At dawn on June 6, the invasion fleet of some 5,300 Allied vessels carrying 370,000 soldiers and sailors filled the horizon off the Normandy coast. Sleepy German soldiers awoke to see the vast armada arrayed before them. For several hours the local German commanders misinterpreted the Normandy landings as merely a diversion for the "real" attack at Pas-de-Calais. When Hitler learned of the Allied landings, he boasted that "the news couldn't be better. As long as they were in Britain, we couldn't get at them. Now we have them where we can destroy them." In the United States, word that the long-anticipated Allied invasion of Nazi Europe had begun captured the attention of the nation. Businesses closed, church bells tolled, and traffic was stopped so that people could pray in the streets.

Despite Eisenhower's intensive planning and the imposing array of Allied troops and firepower, the D-day invasion almost failed. Thick clouds and

The landing at Normandy

D-day, June 6, 1944. Before they could huddle under a seawall and begin to root out the region's Nazi defenders, soldiers on Omaha Beach had to cross a fifty-yard stretch that exposed them to bullets fired from machine guns housed in concrete bunkers.

German anti-aircraft fire caused many of the paratroopers and glider pilots to miss their landing zones. Oceangoing landing craft delivered their troops to the wrong locations. Low clouds led the Allied planes to drop their bombs too far inland—and often on Allied troops. The naval bombardment was equally ineffective. Rough seas caused injuries and nausea and capsized dozens of troop-filled landing craft. Radios were waterlogged. Over a thousand men drowned. The first units ashore lost over 90 percent of their troops to German machine guns. In one company, 197 of the 205 men were killed or wounded within ten minutes. By nightfall the bodies of some five thousand killed or wounded Allied soldiers were strewn across the sand and surf of Normandy.

German losses were much higher; entire units were decimated or captured. Operation Overlord was the greatest amphibious invasion in the annals of warfare, but it was small when compared with the offensive launched by the Russians a few weeks after D-day. Between June and August 1944, the Soviet Army killed, wounded, or captured more German soldiers (350,000) than were stationed in all of western Europe. Still, the Normandy invasion was a turning point in the war—and a pivotal point in America's rise to global power. With the beachhead secured, the Allied leaders knew that victory was in their grasp. "What a plan!" Churchill exclaimed to the British Parliament. Within two weeks of the Normandy assault, the Allies had landed 1 million troops, 556,000 tons of supplies, and 170,000 vehicles in France. On July 25, 1944, American armies in Normandy broke out westward into Brittany and eastward toward Paris. On August 15, a joint American-French invasion force landed on the French Mediterranean coast and raced up the Rhone Valley in central France. German resistance in France collapsed. A division of the Free French Resistance, aided by American forces, had the honor of liberating Paris on August 25. By mid-September, most of France and Belgium had been cleared of German troops.

LEAPFROGGING TO TOKYO

MACARTHUR IN NEW GUINEA   Meanwhile, in Asia, the Allies began to strike back against the Japanese after the crucial Battle of Midway in June 1942. American and Australian forces under General Douglas MacArthur's command had begun to dislodge the Japanese from islands they had conquered in the southwest Pacific. In the summer American and British troops pushed the Japanese back in New Guinea. Then, on August 7, 1942, U.S. Marines landed on Guadalcanal Island and seized the Japanese airstrip. The savage fighting on Guadalcanal lasted through February 1943, but the result was the first defeat of the Japanese army in the war.

ISLAND HOPPING   The Japanese were skilled defensive fighters. It was their suicidal fanaticism in New Guinea and on Guadalcanal that led American military strategists to adopt a "leapfrogging" strategy whereby they used airpower and seapower to neutralize Japanese strongholds on Pacific islands rather than assault them with ground troops. U.S. warplanes, for example, destroyed the Japanese airfield at Rabaul in eastern New Guinea, leaving 135,000 Japanese troops stranded on the island to sit out the war, cut off from resupply by air and sea. What the Allies did to the Japanese garrison on Rabaul set the pattern for the remainder of the war in the Pacific.

BATTLES IN THE CENTRAL PACIFIC   On June 15, 1944, just days after the D-day invasion, U.S. forces liberated Tinian, Guam, and Saipan, three Japanese-controlled islands in the Mariana Islands. Saipan was strategically important because it allowed the new American B-29 "Superfortress" bombers to strike Japan itself. With New Guinea and the Mariana Islands all but liberated, General MacArthur's forces invaded the Japanese-held Philippines on October 20, landing first on the island of Leyte. The Japanese, knowing that the loss of the Philippines would cut them off from the essential raw materials of the East Indies, brought in warships from three directions. The three encounters that resulted on October 25, 1944, came to be known collectively as the Battle of Leyte Gulf, the largest naval engagement in history. It was a strategic victory for the Allies. The Japanese lost most of their remaining warships as well as their ability to defend the Philippines. The battle also brought the first Japanese kamikaze attacks as pilots deliberately crash-dived their bomb-laden planes into American warships. The "kamikaze" suicide units, named for the "divine wind" that centuries before was believed to have saved Japan from a Mongol invasion, inflicted considerable damage.

A NEW AGE IS BORN

ROOSEVELT'S FOURTH TERM   In 1944, war or no war, the calendar dictated another presidential election. This time the Republicans turned to former crime fighting district attorney and New York governor Thomas E. Dewey as their candidate. Dewey ran under the same handicap as Landon and Willkie had before him. He did not propose to dismantle Roosevelt's

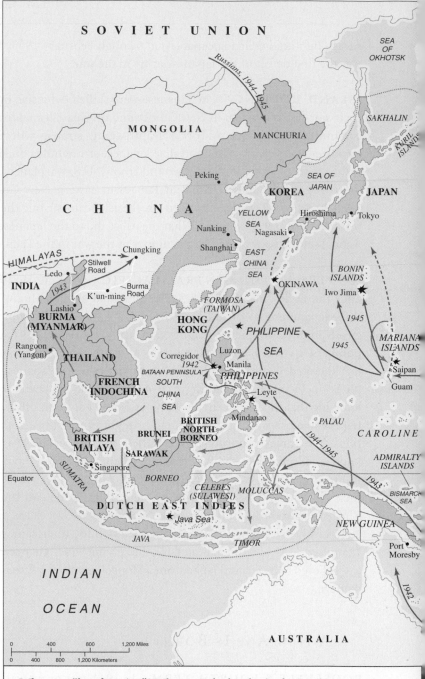

SOVIET UNION

SEA OF OKHOTSK

MONGOLIA

MANCHURIA

Russians, 1944–1945

SAKHALIN

KURIL ISLANDS

Peking

KOREA

SEA OF JAPAN

JAPAN

C H I N A

YELLOW SEA

Hiroshima

Tokyo

Nanking

Nagasaki

Shanghai

Chungking

EAST CHINA SEA

HIMALAYAS

Stilwell Road

Ledo

Burma Road

INDIA

1943

K'un-ming

OKINAWA

BONIN ISLANDS

Iwo Jima

Lashio

BURMA (MYANMAR)

FORMOSA (TAIWAN)

HONG KONG

1945

MARIANA ISLANDS

Rangoon (Yangon)

THAILAND

Corregidor

1942

Luzon

PHILIPPINE SEA

1945

Saipan

BATAAN PENINSULA

Manila

FRENCH INDOCHINA

SOUTH CHINA SEA

PHILIPPINES

Guam

Leyte

BRITISH NORTH BORNEO

Mindanao

PALAU

CAROLINE

BRITISH MALAYA

BRUNEI

SARAWAK

1944–1945

ADMIRALTY ISLANDS

Singapore

BORNEO

1943

Equator

SUMATRA

CELEBES (SULAWESI)

MOLUCCAS

BISMARCK SEA

DUTCH EAST INDIES

Java Sea

NEW GUINEA

JAVA

TIMOR

Port Moresby

INDIAN

1942

OCEAN

AUSTRALIA

0   400   800   1,200 Miles

0   400   800   1,200 Kilometers

What was "leapfrogging"? Why were the battles in the Marianas a major turning point in the war? What was the significance of the Battle of Leyte Gulf? How did the battle at Okinawa affect the way both sides proceeded in the war? Why did President Truman decide to drop atomic bombs on Hiroshima and Nagasaki?

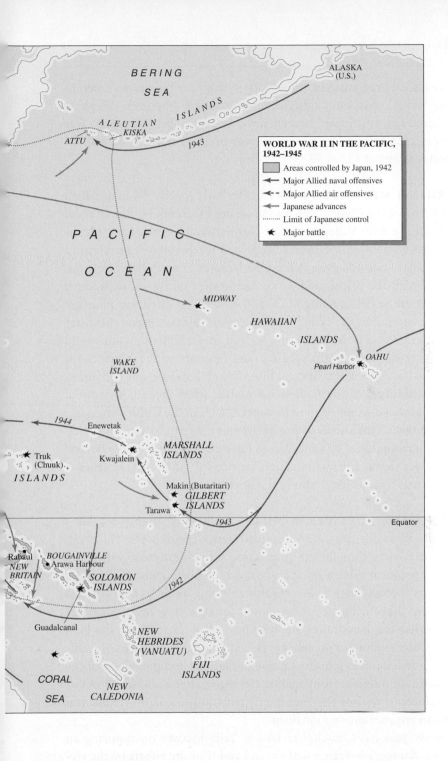

WORLD WAR II IN THE PACIFIC,
1942–1945

- Areas controlled by Japan, 1942
- Major Allied naval offensives
- Major Allied air offensives
- Japanese advances
- Limit of Japanese control
- ★ Major battle

BERING SEA

ALASKA (U.S.)

ALEUTIAN ISLANDS

KISKA

ATTU

1943

PACIFIC

OCEAN

MIDWAY

HAWAIIAN

ISLANDS

WAKE ISLAND

OAHU

Pearl Harbor

1944

Enewetak

Truk (Chuuk)

ISLANDS

Kwajalein

MARSHALL ISLANDS

Makin (Butaritari)

GILBERT ISLANDS

Tarawa

1943

Equator

Rabaul

NEW BRITAIN

BOUGAINVILLE

Arawa Harbour

SOLOMON ISLANDS

1942

Guadalcanal

NEW HEBRIDES (VANUATU)

FIJI ISLANDS

CORAL SEA

NEW CALEDONIA

popular New Deal programs but argued that it was time for younger men to replace the "tired" old Democratic leaders. An aging Roosevelt did show signs of illness and exhaustion; nevertheless, on November 7, 1944, he was once again elected, this time by a popular vote of 25.6 million to 22 million and an electoral vote of 432 to 99.

CONVERGING MILITARY FRONTS By early March 1944, the Allied armies had crossed the Rhine River, on the western German border. In April they encircled the Ruhr Valley, center of Germany's heavy industry. Meanwhile, the Soviet offensive in eastern Europe had reached the eastern border of Germany, after taking Warsaw, Poland, on January 17 and Vienna, Austria, on April 13. With the British and American armies racing across western Germany and the Soviets moving in from the east, the Allied war planners turned their attention to Berlin, the German capital. Prime Minister Churchill worried that if the Red Army arrived in Berlin first, Stalin would control the postwar map of Europe. He urged Eisenhower to get his troops to Berlin ahead of the Soviets. General Eisenhower, however, was convinced the Soviets would get to Berlin first no matter what the Allies decided. Churchill disagreed and appealed to Roosevelt, who in the end left the decision to Eisenhower. When analysts predicted that it would cost one hundred thousand Americans killed or wounded to liberate Berlin before the Soviets did, Eisenhower decided it was too high a price for what an aide called a "prestige objective," so he left Berlin to the Soviets.

YALTA AND THE POSTWAR WORLD As the final offensives against Nazi Germany got under way, the **Yalta Conference** (February 4–11, 1945), hosted by the Soviets, brought the "Big Three" Allied leaders together in a czar's former palace at Yalta, a seaside resort on the north coast of the Black Sea. Two aims loomed large in Roosevelt's thinking at Yalta. One was the need to ensure that the Soviet Union would join the ongoing war against Japan. The other was based upon the lessons he had drawn from the First World War. Chief among the mistakes to be remedied this time were the failure of the United States to join the League of Nations and the failure of the Allies to maintain a united front against Germany after the war. Roosevelt was determined to replace the "outdated" isolationism of the 1920s and 1930s with an engaged internationalism.

The seventy-year-old Churchill arrived at Yalta focused on restoring an independent, democratic France and Poland and limiting efforts by the victors to extract punitive reparations on defeated Germany, lest Europe recreate the problems caused by the Versailles Treaty ending World War I. Stalin's

The Yalta Conference

Churchill, Roosevelt, and Stalin confer on the shape of the postwar world in February 1945.

goals were defensive and imperialistic: he wanted to retrieve former Russian territory given to Poland after World War I and to impose Soviet control over the newly liberated countries of eastern Europe. At Yalta, Stalin was confident he would have his way. That the Soviet Army already controlled key areas in eastern Europe would ensure that his demands were met. As he confided to a Communist leader, "whoever occupies a territory also imposes his own social system."

The Yalta meeting began with the U.S. delegation calling for a conference to create a new world security organization, which Roosevelt termed the United Nations, to be held in the United States beginning on April 25, 1945. The next major topic was how a defeated Germany would be governed. The war map dictated the basic pattern of occupation zones: the Soviets would control eastern Germany, and the Americans and British would control the rich industrial areas of the west. Berlin, the German capital isolated within the Soviet zone, would be subject to joint occupation.

With respect to eastern Europe, Poland became the main focus of Allied concern at Yalta. Britain and France had gone to war in 1939 to defend Poland, and now, six years later, the course of the war had left Poland's fate in the hands of the Soviets. When Soviet forces reentered Poland in 1944, they had created a puppet Communist regime in Lublin. As Soviet troops reached the gates of Warsaw, the historic Polish capital, courageous Poles rose up against the Nazi occupiers. Instead of working with the Polish resistance, however, Stalin cynically ordered the Soviet army to stop its offensive for two months so as to enable the besieged Germans to kill thousands of poorly armed Poles. Stalin viewed the members of the Polish Home Army as potential rivals of the Soviets' Lublin puppet government.

Having suffered almost 30 million deaths during the war, the Soviets were determined to dictate the postwar situation in eastern Europe. At Yalta the Big Three promised to sponsor free elections, democratic governments, and constitutional safeguards of freedom throughout liberated Europe. The Yalta Declaration of Liberated Europe reaffirmed the principles of the Atlantic Charter, but in the end it made little difference. The Yalta Accords only postponed Soviet takeovers in eastern Europe for a few years. Russia, twice invaded by Germany in the twentieth century, was determined to create compliant buffer states between it and the Germans. Seven weeks after the Yalta meetings, Roosevelt could only lamely protest to Stalin the "discouraging lack of progress made in carrying out" his promises to organize free elections in Poland.

YALTA'S LEGACY   Critics, mostly Republicans, later attacked Roosevelt for "giving" Eastern Europe over to Soviet domination at Yalta. But the course of the war shaped the actions at Yalta, not Roosevelt's diplomacy. The United States had no real leverage to exert in the region. As a U.S. diplomat admitted, "Stalin held all the cards" at Yalta. The Americans and British could not have done anything to alter these facts. Allied forces in Europe would have been hopelessly outmanned and outgunned by the Red Army.

Perhaps the most bitterly criticized of the Yalta accords was a secret agreement about the Far East, not made public until after the war. As the Big Three met at Yalta, fighting still raged against the Japanese in Asia. Military analysts estimated that Japan could hold out for eighteen months after the defeat of Germany. Roosevelt, eager to gain Soviet participation in the war against Japan, therefore accepted Stalin's demands on postwar arrangements in the Far East. Stalin demanded continued Soviet control of Outer Mongolia through its puppet People's Republic, acquisition of the Kuril Islands from Japan, and recovery of territory lost after the Russo-Japanese War of 1905. Stalin in return promised to enter the war against Japan two or three months after the German defeat, recognize Chinese sovereignty over

Manchuria, and conclude a treaty of friendship and alliance with the Chinese Nationalists.

THE COLLAPSE OF NAZI GERMANY   By 1945, the collapse of Nazi Germany was imminent, but President Roosevelt did not live to join the victory celebrations. In the spring of 1945, he went to his second home, in Warm Springs, Georgia, to rest up for the conference creating the United Nations. On April 12, 1945, he died from a cerebral hemorrhage. A desperate Adolf Hitler saw in Roosevelt's death a "great miracle" for the besieged Germans. "The war is not lost," he told an aide. "Read it. Roosevelt is dead!"

Hitler's Nazi empire collapsed less than a month later. The Allied armies met advance detachments of Soviet soldiers on April 25. Three days later Italian partisans killed Mussolini as he tried to flee. In Berlin, which was under siege by the Soviets, Hitler married his mistress, Eva Braun, in an underground bunker on the last day of April. He then killed her and himself. On May 2, Berlin fell to the Soviets. Finally, on May 7, in the Allied headquarters at Reims, France, the chief of staff of the German armed forces

May 8, 1945

The celebration in New York City's Times Square on V-E day.

signed a treaty agreeing to an unconditional surrender. So ended Nazi domination of Europe, little more than twelve years after the monomaniacal Hitler had come to power.

Allied victory in Europe generated massive celebrations on V-E day, May 8, 1945, but the elation was tempered by the tragedies that had engulfed the world: the death of Franklin Roosevelt and the deaths of untold millions over the course of the war. The Allied armies, chiefly the Americans, British, and Soviets, were unprepared for the challenges of reconstructing defeated Germany. The German economy had to be revived, a new democratic government had to be formed, and many of the German people had to be clothed, housed, and fed. There were also some 11 million foreigners left stranded in Germany, people from all over Europe who had been captured and put to work in labor camps, concentration camps, or death camps. Now the Allies were responsible for feeding, housing, and repatriating those "displaced persons."

Most shocking was the extent of the Holocaust, scarcely believable until the Allied armies liberated the Nazi death camps in eastern Europe where the Germans had enacted their **"final solution"** to what Hitler called the "Jewish problem": the wholesale extermination of some 6 million Jews along with more than 1 million other captured peoples. Reports of the Nazis' systematic genocide against the Jews had appeared as early as 1942, but such ghastly stories seemed beyond belief. The Allied troops were horrified at what they discovered in the concentration camps. Bodies were piled as high as buildings; survivors were virtually skeletons. General Eisenhower reported from one of the camps that the evidence of "starvation, cruelty, and bestiality were so overpowering as to leave me a bit sick." At Dachau, the first Nazi concentration camp in Germany, the American troops were so enraged by the sight of murdered civilians that they (and some inmates), in horrific violation of the Geneva Convention, executed the 550 Nazi guards who had surrendered.

American officials, even some Jewish leaders, had dragged their feet in acknowledging the Holocaust for fear that relief efforts for Jewish refugees might stir up latent anti-Semitism at home. Under pressure, President Roosevelt had set up a War Refugee Board early in 1944. It managed to rescue about two hundred thousand European Jews and some twenty thousand others. More might have been done by broadcasts warning people in Europe that Nazi "labor camps" were in fact death traps. The Allies rejected a plan to bomb the rail lines into Auschwitz, the largest concentration camp, in Poland, although bombers hit industries five miles away. And few refugees were accepted by the United States. The Allied handling of the Holocaust was inept at best and disgraceful at worst. In 1944, Churchill called the Nazi extermination of the Jews the "most horrible crime ever committed in the history of the world."

A GRINDING WAR AGAINST JAPAN   Victory in Europe enabled Allied war planners to focus their attention on the pressing need to defeat Japan. Yet the closer the Allies got to Japan, the fiercer the resistance they encountered and the higher the casualties. While fighting continued in the Philippines, U.S. Marines landed on Japanese-controlled Iwo Jima Island on February 19, 1945, a speck of volcanic rock 760 miles from Tokyo that was needed as a base for fighter planes escorting bombers over Japan. It took nearly six weeks to secure the tiny island at a cost of nearly seven thousand American lives. The Japanese defenders on Iwo Jima and other islands fought to the death rather than surrender, often attacking in mass suicide assaults.

The fight for Okinawa Island, beginning on Easter Sunday, April 1, was even bloodier. Okinawa was strategically important because it would serve as the staging area for the planned invasion of Japan. The conquest of Japanese-controlled Okinawa was the largest amphibious operation of the Pacific war, involving some 300,000 troops, and it took almost three months to secure the island.

The Allied commanders then began planning for an invasion of Japan. To soften up the Japanese defenses, degrade their industrial capacity, and erode the morale of the civilian populace, the Allied command launched massive bombing raids over Japan in the summer of 1944. In early 1945 General Curtis Lemay, head of the U.S. Bomber Command, ordered devastating "firebomb" raids over Japanese cities. On March 9, for example, some three hundred B-29 bombers dropped napalm bombs on Tokyo, incinerating sixteen square miles of the city and killing eighty-five thousand people in the process.

THE ATOMIC BOMB   In early 1945, new president Harry S. Truman learned of the first successful test explosion of an atomic bomb in New Mexico. Now that the bomb had been shown to work, military planners selected two Japanese cities as targets. The first was Hiroshima, a port city of four hundred thousand people in southern Japan that was a major assembly point for Japanese naval convoys, a center of war-related industries, and headquarters of a Japanese army. On July 25, 1945, President Truman ordered that the atomic bomb be used if Japan did not surrender before August 3. Although an intense debate has emerged over the decision to drop the atomic bomb, Truman said that he "never had any doubt that it should be used." He was convinced that the new weapon would save lives by avoiding a costly invasion of Japan against its "ruthless, merciless, and fanatic" defenders.

Military planners had estimated that an invasion of Japan could cost as many as 250,000 Allied casualties and even more Japanese losses. Moreover, some 100,000 Allied prisoners of war being held in Japan would probably be executed when an invasion began. By that time, the firebombing of cities and the widespread killing of civilians had become accepted military practice. The use of atomic bombs on Japanese cities was thus seen as a logical next step to end the war. As it turned out, scientists greatly underestimated the physical effects of the atomic bomb. They predicted that 20,000 people would be killed, an estimate was much too low.

In mid-July the Allied leaders met in Potsdam, Germany, near Berlin, to discuss the fate of defeated Germany and the ongoing war against Japan. While there, they issued the Potsdam Declaration, demanding that Japan surrender or face "prompt and utter destruction." The deadline passed, and on August 6, 1945, a B-29 bomber named the *Enola Gay* took off at 2 A.M. from the island of Tinian and headed for Hiroshima. At 8:15 A.M., flying at 31,600 feet, the *Enola Gay* released the five-ton, ten-foot-long uranium bomb nicknamed Little Boy. Forty-three seconds later, as the *Enola Gay* turned sharply to avoid the blast, the bomb tumbled to an altitude of 1,900 feet, where it exploded, creating a blinding flash of light followed by a fireball towering to 40,000 feet. The tail gunner on the *Enola Gay* described the scene: "It's like bubbling molasses down there . . . the mushroom is spreading out . . . fires are springing up everywhere . . . it's like a peep into hell."

The bomb's shock wave and firestorm killed some seventy-eight thousand people, including thousands of Japanese soldiers and twenty-three American prisoners of war housed in the city. By the end of the year, the death toll had reached one hundred and forty thousand as the effects of radiation burns and infection took their toll. In addition, seventy thousand buildings were destroyed, and four square miles of the city turned to rubble.

President Harry Truman was aboard the battleship *Augusta* returning from the Potsdam Conference when news arrived that the bomb had been dropped. "This is the greatest thing in history!" he exclaimed. In the United States, Americans greeted the news with similar elation. To them, the atomic bomb promised a quick end to the long nightmare of war. "No tears of sympathy will be shed in America for the Japanese people," the *Omaha World-Herald* predicted. "Had they possessed a comparable weapon at Pearl Harbor, would they have hesitated to use it?" Others were more sobering about the implications of atomic warfare. "Yesterday," the journalist Hanson

The American Chemical Society exhibit on atomic energy

Physicist J. Robert Oppenheimer points to a photograph of the huge column of smoke and flame caused by the bomb upon Hiroshima.

Baldwin wrote in the *New York Times,* "we clinched victory in the Pacific, but we sowed the whirlwind."

Two days after the Hiroshima bombing an opportunistic Soviet Union hastened to enter the war against Japan in order to share in the spoils of victory. Truman and his aides, frustrated by the stubborn refusal of Japanese leaders to surrender and fearful that the Soviet Union's entry into the war would complicate negotiations, ordered the second atomic bomb ("Fat Man") dropped. On August 9, the city of Nagasaki, a shipbuilding center, experienced the same nuclear devastation that had destroyed Hiroshima. That night the Japanese emperor urged his cabinet to surrender. Frantic exchanges between leaders in Washington, D.C., and Tokyo ended with Japanese acceptance of the surrender terms on August 14, 1945.

The aftermath of Little Boy

This image shows the wasteland that remained after the atomic bomb Little Boy decimated Hiroshima in 1945.

THE FINAL LEDGER

Thus ended the largest and costliest military event in human history. Between 50 and 60 million people were killed in the war between 1939 and 1945—perhaps 60 percent of them civilians, including Jews and other ethnic minorities murdered in Nazi death camps and Soviet concentration camps. An average of 27,000 people died each day during the six years of warfare. The Second World War was more costly for the United States than any other foreign war: 292,000 battle deaths and 114,000 other deaths. A million Americans were wounded; half of them were seriously disabled. But in proportion to its population, the United States suffered a far smaller loss than that of any of the other major Allies or their enemies, and American territory escaped the devastation visited on so many other parts of the world. The Soviet Union, for example, suffered 20 million deaths, China 10 million, Germany 5.6 million, and Japan 2.3 million.

The Second World War was the pivotal event of the twentieth century; it reshaped the world order. Until 1941, European colonial empires still dominated the globe, and world affairs were still determined by decisions made in European capitals. In 1941, when Japan, the Soviet Union, and the United States entered the war, the old imperial world order led by France, Germany, and the United Kingdom, dating back to the eighteenth century, came to an end. German and Italian fascism as well as Japanese militarism were destroyed. And the United States had emerged by 1945 as the acknowledged "leader of the free world." With the dropping of the atomic bombs on Japan, Winston Churchill told the House of Commons, "America stands at this moment at the summit of the world."

Of course, the Second World War also transformed American life. The war finally brought an end to the Great Depression and laid the foundation for an era of unprecedented prosperity. Big businesses were transformed into gigantic corporations as a result of huge government contracts for military production, and the size of the federal government bureaucracy mushroomed. The number of government employees increased four-fold during the war. New technologies and products developed for military purposes—radar, computers, electronics, plastics and synthetics, jet engines, rockets, atomic energy— began to transform the private sector as well. And new opportunities for women as well as for African Americans, Mexican Americans, and other minorities set in motion major social changes that would culminate in the civil rights movement of the 1960s and the feminist movement of the 1970s.

The dramatic war-related expansion of the federal government continued after 1945. Presidential authority increased enormously at the expense of congressional and state power. At the same time, the isolationist sentiment in foreign relations that had been so powerful in the 1920s and 1930s evaporated as the United States emerged from the war with new global political and military responsibilities and expanded economic interests.

The war opened a new era for the United States in the world arena. It accelerated the growth of American power and prestige while devastating all other world powers. As President Truman told the nation in a radio address in August 1945, the United States had "emerged from this war the most powerful nation in this world—the most powerful nation, perhaps, in all history." But the Soviet Union, despite its profound human and material losses during the war, emerged with much new territory and enhanced influence, making it the greatest power in Europe and Asia. Just a little over a century after the Frenchman Alexis de Tocqueville had predicted that western Europe would be overshadowed by the power of the United States and Russia, his prophecy had come to pass.

CHAPTER SUMMARY

- **Totalitarianism** In Italy, Benito Mussolini assumed control by promising law and order. Adolf Hitler rearmed Germany in defiance of the Treaty of Versailles and aimed to unite all German speakers. Civil war in Spain and the growth of the Soviet Union under Joseph Stalin contributed to a precarious balance of power in Europe.

- **American Neutrality** By March 1939, Hitler had annexed austria and seized Czechoslovakia. He sent troops to invade Poland in September of 1939, after signing a nonaggression pact with the Soviet Union. At last, the British and French governments declared war. The United States issued declarations of neutrality, but with the fall of France, accelerated aid to France and Britain.

- **Japanese Threat** After Japan allied with Germany and Italy and announced its intention to take control of French Indochina, President Roosevelt froze Japanese assets in the United States and restricted oil exports to Japan. The Japanese bombed the Pacific Fleet in a surprise attack at Pearl Harbor, Hawaii.

- **World War II and American Society** White and black Americans migrated west to take jobs in defense factories; unemployment was soon a thing of the past. Farmers, too, recovered from hard times. Many women took nontraditional jobs, some in the military. About 1 million African Americans served in the military, in segregated units. Japanese Americans, however, were interned in "war relocation camps."

- **Road to Allied Victory** By 1943, the Allies controlled all of North Africa. From there they launched attacks on Sicily and then Italy. Joseph Stalin, meanwhile, demanded a full-scale Allied attack on the Atlantic coast to ease pressure on the Eastern Front, but D-day was delayed until June 6, 1944.

- **The Pacific War** The Japanese advance was halted as early as June 1942 with the Battle of Midway. The Americans fought slow, costly battles in New Guinea, then, in 1943, headed toward the Philippines. Fierce resistance at Iwo Jima and Okinawa and Japan's refusal to surrender after the firebombing of Tokyo led the new president, Harry S. Truman, to order the use of the atomic bomb.

- **Postwar World** In January 1942, the Allied nations signed the Declaration of the United Nations. The Big Three—Roosevelt, Churchill, and Stalin—meeting in Yalta in February 1945, decided that Europe would be divided into occupation zones.

CHRONOLOGY

1933	Adolf Hitler becomes chancellor of Germany
1937	*Panay* incident
1938	Hitler forces the *Anschluss* (union) of Austria and Germany
1939	Soviet Union agrees to a nonaggression pact with Germany
September 1939	German troops invade Poland
1940	Battle of Britain
September 1940	Germany, Italy, and Japan sign the Tripartite Pact
December 7, 1941	Japanese launch surprise attack at Pearl Harbor, Hawaii
June 1942	Battle of Midway
January 1943	Roosevelt, Churchill, and the Combined Chiefs of Staff meet at Casablanca
July 1943	Allied forces land on Sicily
1943	Roosevelt and Churchill meet Stalin in Tehran
June 6, 1944	D-day
February 1945	Yalta Conference
April 1945	Franklin Delano Roosevelt dies; Hitler commits suicide
May 8, 1945	V-E day
August 1945	Atomic bombs dropped on Hiroshima and Nagasaki
September 2, 1945	Japanese surrender

KEY TERMS & NAMES

Part Seven

THE
AMERICAN
AGE

he United States emerged from the Second World War as the world's pre-eminent military and economic power. America exercised a commanding role in international trade and was the only nation in possession of atomic bombs. While much of Europe and Asia struggled to recover from the horrific physical devastation of the war, the United States was virtually unscathed, its economic infrastructure intact and operating at peak efficiency. In 1945, the United States produced half of the world's manufactured goods. Jobs that had been scarce in the 1930s were now available for the taking. American capitalism not only demonstrated its economic strength but became a dominant cultural force around the world as well. In Europe, Japan, and elsewhere, American products, forms of entertainment, and styles of fashion attracted excited attention. Henry Luce, the publisher of *Life* magazine, proclaimed that the twentieth century had become the "American century."

Yet the specter of a deepening "cold war" cast a pall over the buoyant revival of the economy. The tense ideological contest with the Soviet Union and Communist China produced numerous foreign crises and sparked a domestic witch hunt for Communists in the United States that far surpassed earlier episodes of political and social repression.

Both major political parties accepted the geopolitical assumptions embedded in the ideological cold war with international communism. Both Republican and Democratic presidents affirmed the need to "contain" the spread of Communist influence around the world. This bedrock assumption eventually embroiled the United States in a costly war in Southeast Asia, which destroyed Lyndon B. Johnson's presidency and revived isolationist sentiments. The Vietnam War was also a catalyst for a countercultural movement in which young idealists of the "baby boom" generation provided energy for many overdue social reforms, including the reforms that were the focus of the civil rights, gay rights, feminist, and environmental movements. But the youth revolt also contributed to an array of social ills, from street riots to drug abuse to sexual license. The social upheavals of the 1960s and early 1970s provoked a conservative backlash as well. Richard M. Nixon's paranoid reaction to his critics led to the Watergate affair and the destruction of his presidency.

Through all of this turmoil, however, the basic premises of welfare-state capitalism that Franklin Delano Roosevelt had instituted with his

New Deal programs remained essentially intact. With only a few exceptions, Republicans and Democrats after 1945 accepted the notion that the federal government must assume greater responsibility for the welfare of individuals. Even Ronald Reagan, a sharp critic of federal social-welfare programs, recognized the need for the government to provide a "safety net" for those who could not help themselves.

Yet this fragile consensus on public policy began to disintegrate in the late 1980s amid stunning international developments and less visible domestic events. The surprising collapse of the Soviet Union and the disintegration of European communism sent policy makers scurrying to respond to a post–cold war world in which the United States remained the only legitimate superpower. After forty-five years, U.S. foreign policy was no longer keyed to a single adversary, and world politics lost its bipolar quality. During the early 1990s East and West Germany reunited, apartheid in South Africa ended, and Israel and the Palestinians signed a previously unimaginable treaty ending hostilities—for a while.

At the same time, U.S. foreign policy began to focus less on military power and more on economic competition and technological development. In those arenas, Japan, a reunited Germany, and China challenged the United States for preeminence. By reducing the public's fear of nuclear annihilation, the end of the cold war also reduced public interest in foreign affairs. The presidential election of 1992 was the first since 1936 in which foreign-policy issues played virtually no role. This was an unfortunate development, for post–cold war world affairs remained volatile and dangerous. The implosion of Soviet communism after 1989 unleashed a series of ethnic, nationalist, and separatist

conflicts. In the face of inertia among other governments and pleas for assistance, the United States found itself being drawn into crises in far-away lands such as Bosnia, Somalia, Afghanistan, and Iraq.

As the new multipolar world careened toward the end of the twentieth century and the start of a new millennium, fault lines began to appear in the social and economic landscape. A gargantuan federal debt and rising annual deficits threatened to bankrupt a nation that was becoming top-heavy with retirees. Without fully realizing it, much less appreciating its cascading consequences, the American population was becoming dis-proportionately old. The number of people aged ninety-five to ninety-nine doubled between 1980 and 1990, and the number of centenarians increased 77 percent. The proportion of the population aged sixty-five and older rose steadily during the 1990s. By the year 2010, over half of the elderly population was over seventy-five. This positive demographic fact had profound social and political implications. It made the tone of political debate more conservative and exerted increasing stress on health-care costs, nursing-home facilities, and the very survival of the Social Security system.

At the same time that the gap between young and old was increasing, so, too, was the disparity between rich and poor. This trend threatened to stratify a society already experiencing rising levels of racial and ethnic tension. Between 1960 and 2010 the gap between the richest 20 percent of the population and the poorest 20 percent more than doubled. Over 20 percent of all American children in 2012 lived in poverty compared to 15 percent in 2000, and the infant-mortality rate rose. Despite the much-ballyhooed "war-on-poverty" programs initiated by Lyndon B. Johnson and continued in one form or another by his successors, the chronically poor at the start of the twenty-first century were more numerous than in 1964.

29

THE FAIR DEAL AND CONTAINMENT

FOCUS QUESTIONS   wwnorton.com/studyspace

- How did the cold war emerge?
- How did Harry Truman respond to the Soviet occupation of eastern Europe?
- What was Truman's Fair Deal?
- What was the background of the Korean War, and how did the United States become involved?
- What were the roots of McCarthyism?

o sooner did the Second World War end than a "cold war" began. The awkward wartime alliance between the United States and the Soviet Union had collapsed by the fall of 1945. The two strongest nations to emerge from the war's carnage could not bridge their ideological differences over basic issues such as human rights, individual liberties, economic freedom, and religious belief. Mutual suspicion and a race to gain influence and control over the so-called non-aligned or third world countries further polarized the two nations. The defeat of Japan and Germany had created power vacuums that sucked the Soviet Union and the United States into an unrelenting war of words fed by clashing strategic interests. At the same time, the devastation wrought by the war in western Europe and the exhaustion of its peoples led to anti-colonial uprisings in Asia and Africa that would strip Britain, France, and Holland of their empires. The emergence of Communist China (the People's Republic) after 1949 further complicated global politics. The postwar world was thus an unstable one in which international tensions shaped the contours of domestic politics and culture as well as foreign relations.

DEMOBILIZATION UNDER TRUMAN

TRUMAN'S UNEASY START "Who the hell is Harry Truman?" Roosevelt's chief of staff asked the president in the summer of 1944. The question was on more lips when, after less than twelve weeks as vice president, Harry S. Truman took the presidential oath on April 12, 1945. Clearly he was not Franklin Delano Roosevelt, and that was one of the burdens he would bear. Roosevelt and Truman came from starkly different backgrounds. For Truman there had been no inherited wealth, no European travel, no Harvard—indeed, no college at all. Born in 1884 in western Missouri, Truman grew up in Independence, near Kansas City. Bookish and withdrawn, he moved to his grandmother's farm after high school, spent a few years working in Kansas City banks, and grew into an outgoing young man.

During the First World War, Truman served in France as captain of an artillery battery. Afterward he and a partner started a clothing business; then he became a professional politician under the tutelage of Kansas City's Democratic machine. In 1934, Missouri sent him to the U.S. Senate, where he remained obscure until he chaired a committee investigating fraud in the war mobilization effort.

Truman was a plain, decent man who lacked Roosevelt's dash and charm, his brilliance and creativity. He was terribly nearsighted and a clumsy public speaker. Yet he had virtues of his own. Some aspects of Truman's personality evoked the spirit of Andrew Jackson: his decisiveness, bluntness, feistiness, loyalty, and folksy manner. Despite his lack of executive experience, he was confident and self-assured—and he needed to be. Managing the transition from war to peace was a monumental task fraught with dangers. For instance, the wartime economy had ended the Great Depression and brought about full employment, but what would happen as the federal government cut back on military spending and industries transitioned from building tanks and warplanes to automobiles and washing machines? Would the peacetime economy be able to absorb the millions of men and women who had served in the armed forces? These and related issues greatly complicated Truman's efforts to lead America out of combat and into a postwar era complicated by a cold war against Communism and the need to rebuild a devastated Europe and Asia.

On September 6, 1945, Truman sent Congress a comprehensive proposal that included the expansion of unemployment insurance to cover more workers, a higher minimum wage, the construction of low-cost public housing, regional hydroelectric development of the nation's river valleys, and a public-works program. "Not even President Roosevelt asked for so much at one sitting," said the House Republican leader. "It's just a plain case of out-dealing the New Deal." But Truman soon saw his new domestic proposals mired in disputes over the transition to a peacetime economy.

CONVERTING TO PEACE   The raucous celebrations that greeted the news of Japan's surrender in the summer of 1945 signaled what would become the most rapid military demobilization in world history. By 1947, the total armed forces had shrunk from 12 million to 1.5 million. After the Second World War ended, military veterans eagerly returned to schools, jobs, wives, and babies. Population growth, which had dropped off sharply in the 1930s, now soared. Americans born during this postwar period (roughly 1946–1964) composed what came to be known as the baby boom generation, a disproportionately large generation of Americans that would become a dominant force shaping the nation's social and cultural life throughout the second half of the twentieth century and after.

The end of the war, with its sudden demobilization and conversion to a peacetime economy, did not generate the postwar depression that many had feared. Several shock absorbers cushioned the economic impact of demobilization: federal unemployment insurance and other Social Security benefits; the

The Eldridge General Store, Fayette County, Illinois

Postwar America quickly demobilized, turning its attention to the pursuit of abundance.

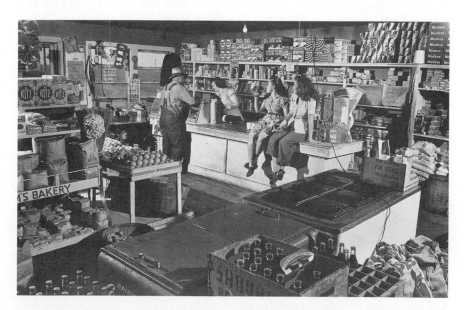

Servicemen's Readjustment Act of 1944, known as the GI Bill of Rights, under which the federal government spent $13 billion on military veterans for education, vocational training, medical treatment, unemployment insurance, and loans for building houses and going into business; and most important, the pent-up postwar demand for consumer goods caused by wartime deprivation.

CONTROLLING INFLATION The most acute economic problem Truman faced was not depression but inflation. During the war, America was essentially fully employed. The government also froze wages and prices—and prohibited labor union strikes. When wartime economic controls on the economy were removed, prices for consumer items shot up. Prices of farm commodities soared 14 percent in one month and by the end of 1945 were 30 percent higher than they had been in August. As prices rose, so, too, did corporate profits. The gap between soaring consumer prices and stagnant hourly wages prompted growing demands by labor unions for pay increases. When such raises were not forthcoming, a series of strikes erupted. By January 1946 more workers were on strike than ever before.

Major disputes developed in the coal and railroad industries. Like Theodore Roosevelt before him, Truman grew frustrated with the stubbornness of both management and labor. He took control of the coal mines, whereupon the mine owners agreed to union demands. Truman also seized control of the railroads and won a five-day postponement of a strike. But when the union leaders refused to make further concessions, the president lashed out against their "obstinate arrogance" and threatened to draft striking workers into the armed forces. The strike ended a few weeks later.

PARTISAN COOPERATION AND CONFLICT As congressional elections approached in the fall of 1946, public discontent ran high, with most of it focusing on the Truman administration. Both sides held the president responsible for the prolonged labor turbulence. A speaker at the national convention of the Congress of Industrial Organizations (CIO) had tagged Truman "the No. 1 strikebreaker," while much of the public, angry at the striking unions, also blamed the strikes on the White House. Republicans won majorities in both houses of Congress for the first time since 1928. "The New Deal is kaput," one newspaper editor crowed—prematurely, as it turned out, for the feisty Truman launched a ferocious defense of his administration and its policies.

The new Republican Congress, in an effort to curb the power of the unions, passed the Taft-Hartley Labor Act of 1947, which prohibited what was called a closed shop (in which nonunion workers could not be hired) but permitted a "union shop" (in which workers newly hired were required to join the union) unless banned by state law. It included provisions forbidding "unfair" union practices such as staging secondary boycotts or jurisdictional strikes (by one union to exclude another from a given company or field), "featherbedding" (paying for work not done), refusing to bargain in good faith, and contributing to political campaigns. Furthermore, union leaders had to take oaths declaring that they were not members of the Communist party. The act also forbade strikes by federal employees and imposed a "cooling-off" period of eighty days on any strike that the president found to be dangerous to the national health or safety.

Taft-Hartley Act cartoon

Taft and Hartley look for John Lewis, the head of the Mine Workers Union.

Truman's veto of the "shocking" Taft-Hartley bill, which unions called "the slave-labor act," restored his credit with working-class Democrats. Many blue-collar unionists who had gone over to the Republicans in 1946 returned to the Democrats. The Taft-Hartley bill passed over Truman's veto, however. By 1954 fifteen states, mainly in the South, had used the Taft-Hartley Act's authority to enact "right-to-work" laws forbidding union shops.

The conflicts between Truman and the Republican-controlled Congress obscured the high degree of bipartisan cooperation in matters of government reorganization and foreign policy. In 1947, Congress passed the National Security Act, which created a National Military Establishment, headed by the secretary of defense with subcabinet Departments of the Army, the Navy, and the Air Force, and the National Security Council. The act made permanent the Joint Chiefs of Staff, a wartime innovation, and established the Central Intelligence Agency (CIA) to coordinate global intelligence-gathering activities in the cold war against communism.

THE COLD WAR

BUILDING THE UNITED NATIONS The wartime military alliance against Nazism disintegrated after 1945. Like Woodrow Wilson before him, Franklin Delano Roosevelt had focused his efforts on creating a collective security organization, the United Nations. On April 25, 1945, two weeks after Roosevelt's death and two weeks before the German surrender, delegates from fifty nations at war with Germany and Japan met in San Francisco to draw up the Charter of the United Nations. The General Assembly, one of the two major entities created by the charter, included delegates from all member nations and was to meet annually. The **Security Council**, the other major agency called for in the charter, would remain in permanent session and would have "primary responsibility for the maintenance of international peace and security." Its eleven members (fifteen after 1965) included six (later ten) members elected for two-year terms and five permanent members: the United States, the Soviet Union (replaced by the Russian Federation in 1991), Great Britain, France, and the Republic of China (replaced by the People's Republic of China in 1971). Each permanent member has a veto on any question of substance.

DIFFERENCES WITH THE SOVIETS   Since the end of the Second World War, historians have debated the tempting but unanswerable question: Was the United States or the Soviet Union more responsible for the onset of the cold war. The conventional view argues that the Soviets, led by Joseph Stalin, a paranoid Communist dictator ruling a traditionally insecure nation, set out to dominate the globe after 1945. The United States had no choice but to stand firm in defense of democratic capitalist values. By contrast, "revisionist" scholars insist that Truman was the culprit. Instead of continuing Roosevelt's efforts to collaborate with Stalin and the Soviets, revisionists assert, Truman adopted an aggressive, confrontational foreign policy that sought to create American spheres of influence around the world. In this view, Truman's provocative policies aggravated the tensions between the two countries. Yet such an interpretation fails to recognize that both sides engaged in a military arms race and superheated rhetoric. East and West in the postwar world were captives of a nuclear nightmare of fear, suspicion, and posturing. Scholars eager to choose sides also at times fail to acknowledge that President Truman inherited a deteriorating relationship with the Soviets. Events during 1945 made compromise and conciliation more difficult, whether for Roosevelt or for Truman.

There were signs of trouble in the Grand Alliance of Britain, the Soviet Union, and the United States as early as the spring of 1945 as the Soviet Union installed compliant governments in eastern Europe, violating the promises of democratic elections made at the Yalta Conference. On February 1, the Polish Committee of National Liberation, a puppet group already claiming the status of provisional government, moved from Lublin to Warsaw.

In March the Soviets appointed a puppet prime minister in Romania. Protests against such actions led to Soviet counter protests that the British and Americans were negotiating a German surrender in Italy "behind the back of the Soviet Union" and that German forces were being concentrated against the Soviet Union.

Such was the charged atmosphere when Truman entered the White House. A few days before the San Francisco conference to organize the United Nations, Truman gave Soviet foreign minister Vyacheslav Molotov a tongue-lashing in Washington on the Polish situation. "I have never been talked to like that in my life," Molotov said. "Carry out your agreements," Truman snapped, "and you won't get talked to like that."

On May 12, 1945, four days after victory in Europe, Winston Churchill sent a telegram to Truman: "What is to happen about Europe? An **iron curtain** is drawn down upon [the Russian] front. We do not know what is going on behind [it]." Churchill wanted to lift the iron curtain created by Soviet military occupation and install democratic governments in eastern Europe. Instead, as a gesture of goodwill, and over Churchill's protest, U.S. forces withdrew from the German occupation zone that had been assigned to the Soviet Union at the Yalta Conference. American diplomats still hoped that the Yalta agreements would be carried out and that the Soviet Union would help defeat Japan. There was little the Western powers could have done to prevent Soviet control of the region even if they had not let their military forces dwindle. The presence of Soviet armed forces frustrated the efforts of non-Communists to gain political influence in eastern European countries. The leaders of those opposed to Soviet influence were exiled, silenced, executed, or imprisoned.

Secretary of State James F. Byrnes, who took office in 1945, struggled through 1946 with the problems of postwar treaties. In early 1947 the Council of Foreign Ministers finally produced treaties for Italy, Hungary, Romania, Bulgaria, and Finland. In effect these treaties confirmed Soviet control over eastern Europe, which in Russian eyes seemed but a parallel to American control over Japan and Western control over most of Germany and all of Italy. The Yalta guarantees of democracy in eastern Europe had turned out much like the Open Door policy in China: little more than pious rhetoric sugar coating the realities of raw power and national interest. The Soviets controlled eastern Europe and refused to budge.

Byrnes's impulse to pressure Soviet diplomats by brandishing the atomic bomb only added to the irritations, intimidating no one. As early as April 1945, he had suggested to Truman that possession of the new weapon "might well put us in position to dictate our own terms at the end of the war." After becoming secretary of state, he had threatened Soviet diplomats with America's growing arsenal of nuclear weapons. But they paid little notice, in part because they were developing their own atomic bombs.

CONTAINMENT By the beginning of 1947, relations with the Soviet Union had become even more troubled. A year before, in February 1946, Stalin had pronounced international peace impossible "under the present capitalist development of the world economy." His provocative statement impelled the State Department to send an urgent request for an interpretation of Stalin's speech to forty-two-year-old **George F. Kennan**, a brilliant diplomat and political analyst stationed at the U.S. embassy in Moscow. Kennan responded on February 22, 1946, with a "Long Telegram" in which he sketched the roots of Russian history and Soviet policy. In his extensive analysis, Kennan insisted that Roosevelt's assumptions that the Soviets would cooperate with the United States and the United Nations after the war ("peaceful coexistence") were dangerously naive. Stalin would not be swayed by good-will gestures or democratic ideals. The Soviet Union was founded on an ideology (Leninism) that presumed a fundamental conflict between the communist and capitalist worlds. The best way to deal with such an ideological foe was to employ patient, persistent, and prolonged efforts ("resolve") to "contain" Soviet expansionism over the long term.

Secretary of State George C. Marshall was so impressed by Kennan's analysis that he appointed him to a new position in the State Department in charge of policy planning. No other American diplomat at the time forecast so accurately what would in fact happen to the Soviet Union some forty years later. In its broadest dimensions, Kennan's "**containment**" concept dovetailed with the outlook of Truman and his advisers. But Kennan's analysis remained vague on several key issues: How exactly were the United States and its allies to "contain" the Soviet Union? How should the United States respond to specific acts of Soviet aggression around the world?

Kennan was an analyst, not a policymaker. He left the task of converting the concept of "containment" into action to President Truman and his inner circle of advisers, most of whom viewed containment as a military doctrine. They harbored a growing fear that the Soviet lust for power reached beyond eastern Europe, posing dangers in the eastern Mediterranean, the Middle East, and western Europe itself. Indeed, the Soviet Union sought to gain access to the Mediterranean Sea, long important to Russia for purposes of trade and defense. After the war the Soviet Union pressed Turkey for territorial concessions and the right to build naval bases on the Bosporus, an important gateway between the Black Sea and the Mediterranean. In 1946, civil war broke out in Greece between a government backed by the British and a Communist-led faction that held the northern part of the country and drew supplies from Soviet-dominated Yugoslavia, Bulgaria, and Albania. On February 21, 1947, the British ambassador informed the U.S. government that the British could no longer bear the economic and military burden of aiding Greece; they would withdraw in five weeks. The American reaction was immediate. Within days, Truman conferred with congressional leaders, whereupon the chairman of the Senate Foreign Relations Committee recommended a strong presidential appeal to the nation. The president needed to "scare the hell out of the American people" about the menace of communism.

THE TRUMAN DOCTRINE On March 12, 1947, President Truman gave a speech broadcast over national radio, in which he asked Congress for $400 million in economic aid to Greece and Turkey. In his speech, the president enunciated what quickly came to be known as the **Truman Doctrine**. "I believe," Truman declared, "that it must be the policy of the United States to support free peoples who are resisting attempted subjugation by armed minorities or by outside pressures." Otherwise, the Soviet Union would come to dominate Europe, the Middle East, and Asia. George F. Kennan cringed at Truman's open-ended, indiscriminate commitment to "contain" communism everywhere; he insisted that American counter-pressure needed to be exercised selectively. All crises were not equally significant; American power was limited. The United States could not intervene in every "hot spot" around the world. But other presidential advisers had come to see the world as being in a permanent crisis because of the Communist menace, and they were determined to create a militarized containment policy.

In 1947, Congress passed a Greek-Turkish aid bill that helped Turkey achieve economic stability and enabled Greece to defeat a Communist insurrection in 1949. But the principles embedded in the Truman Doctrine committed the United States to intervene throughout the world in order to "contain" the spread of communism, a global commitment that would produce failures as well as successes in the years to come.

The Truman Doctrine marked the beginning, or at least the open acknowledgment, of a contest that the former government official Bernard Baruch named in a 1947 speech to the legislature of South Carolina: "Let us not be deceived—today we are in the midst of a *cold war*." Greece and Turkey were but the front lines in an ideological struggle that was spreading to western Europe, where wartime damage and dislocation had devastated cities, factories, mines, bridges, railroads, and farms. Inflation soared. Amid the chaos the Communist parties of France and Italy garnered growing support for their promised solutions to the difficulties.

THE MARSHALL PLAN   In the spring of 1947, former general **George C. Marshall**, who had replaced James F. Byrnes as secretary of state in January, called for massive American aid to rescue Europe from disaster. A retired U.S. Army chief of staff, who had been the highest-ranking general during the Second World War. Marshall used the occasion of the 1947 Harvard graduation ceremonies to outline his ingenious plan for the reconstruction of Europe, which came to be known as the **Marshall Plan**. "Our policy," he said, "is directed not against country or doctrine, but against hunger, poverty, desperation, and chaos." Marshall offered U.S. aid to all European countries, including the Soviet Union, and called upon them to take the lead in judging their own needs.

In December 1947, Truman submitted Marshall's proposal for the European Recovery Program to a special session of Congress. Two months later, a Communist-led coup in Czechoslovakia ensured congressional passage of the Marshall Plan. It seemed to confirm the threat to western Europe. From 1948 until 1951, the newly created Economic Cooperation Administration, which managed the Marshall Plan, poured $13 billion into economic recovery efforts in Europe. Most of the aid went to Great Britain, France, Italy, and West Germany.

"It's the Same Thing"

The Marshall Plan, which distributed aid throughout Europe, is represented in this 1949 cartoon as a modern tractor driven by a prosperous farmer. In the foreground a poor, overworked man is yoked to an old-fashioned "Soviet" plow, forced to go over the ground of the "Marshal Stalin Plan," while Stalin himself tries to persuade others that "it's the same thing without mechanical problems."

DIVIDING GERMANY   The Marshall Plan drew the nations of western Europe closer together, but it increased tensions with the

Soviet Union, for Stalin correctly viewed the massive American effort to rebuild the European economy as a way to diminish Soviet influence in the region. The breakdown of the wartime alliance between the United States and the Soviet Union also left the problem of postwar Germany unsettled. Berlin had been divided into four sectors or zones, each governed by one of the four allied nations, including the Soviet Union. The war-devastated German economy languished, requiring the U.S. Army to provide food and basic necessities to civilians. Slowly, the Allied occupation zones evolved into functioning governments. In 1948, the British, French, and Americans united their three zones into one and developed a common currency to be used in West Germany as well as West Berlin. The West Germans set about organizing state governments and elected delegates to a federal constitutional convention.

The political unification of West Germany infuriated Stalin, and the status of Berlin, sitting deep inside the Soviet occupation zone (East Germany), had become an explosive powder keg. In March 1948, Stalin decided to force the issue of Berlin's future by trying to prevent the new West German currency from being delivered into the city. On June 23, the Soviets stopped all traffic into the beleaguered city, hoping the blockade of Berlin would force the Allies to give up the city. This warfare by starvation and intimidation placed the United States on the horns of a dilemma: risk a third world war by using force to break the blockade or begin a humiliating retreat from West Berlin, leaving the residents to be swallowed up by the Soviet bloc.

General Lucius D. Clay, the iron-willed U.S. army commander in Germany, proposed to stand firm and even use force to break the blockade. Truman agreed, saying, "We [are going to] stay in Berlin—period." The United States then organized a massive, sustained airlift to provide needed food and supplies to West Berliners. By October 1948, the U.S. and British air forces were flying in thirteen thousand tons of food, medicine, coal, and equipment a day. The massive Berlin airlift went on for eleven months. Finally, on May 12, 1949, after extended talks, the Soviets lifted the blockade, in part because bad Russian harvests made them desperate for food grown in West Germany. Before the end of the year, the Federal Republic of Germany had a government functioning under Chancellor Konrad Adenauer. At the end of May 1949, an independent German Democratic Republic arose in the Soviet-controlled eastern zone, formalizing the division of Germany. West Germany gradually acquired more authority, until the Western powers recognized its full sovereignty in 1955. The Berlin airlift was the first explicit "victory" for the West in the Cold War. Its success transformed West Berliners from defeated and surly adversaries to ardent American allies.

THE OCCUPATION OF GERMANY AND AUSTRIA

	French zone		U.S. zone
	British zone		Soviet zone

How did the Allies divide Germany and Austria at the Yalta Conference? What was the "iron curtain"? Why did the Allies airlift supplies to Berlin?

BUILDING ALLIANCES   The Soviet blockade of Berlin convinced the allied nations that they needed to act collectively to thwart Soviet efforts at expansion into western Europe. On April 4, 1949, the North Atlantic Treaty was signed by representatives of twelve nations: the United States, Britain, France, Belgium, the Netherlands, Luxembourg, Canada, Denmark, Iceland, Italy, Norway, and Portugal. Greece and Turkey joined the alliance in 1952, West Germany in 1955, and Spain in 1982. The treaty pledged that an attack against any one of the members would be considered an attack against all and provided for a council of the **North Atlantic Treaty Organization (NATO)**.

The eventful year of 1948 produced another foreign-policy decision with long-term consequences. Palestine, as the biblical Holy Land had come to be known, had been under Turkish rule until the League of Nations made it a British protectorate after the First World War. During the early years of the twentieth century, many Zionists, who advocated a Jewish nation in the region, had migrated there. More arrived after the British gained control, and many more arrived during the Nazi persecution of European Jews and just after the Second World War ended. Having been promised a national homeland by the British, the Jews of Palestine demanded their own nation after the war, and they received energetic support from American Jews and worldwide Jewish organizations.

Late in 1947, the United Nations voted to partition Palestine into Jewish and Arab states, but this plan met fierce Arab opposition. No action was taken until the British control of Palestine expired on May 14, 1948, at which time Jewish leaders in Palestine, most of them immigrants from wartime Europe, proclaimed the independence of Israel. President Truman, who had been in close touch with American Jewish leaders, officially recognized the new Israeli state within minutes. The creation of a Jewish state in Palestine prompted the neighboring Arab nations to attack Israel. UN mediators gradually worked out a truce agreement, restoring an uneasy peace by May 11, 1949, when Israel joined the United Nations. But the hard feelings and intermittent warfare between Israel and the Arab states have festered ever since, complicating U.S. foreign policy, which has tried to maintain friendship with both sides but has tilted toward Israel.

CIVIL RIGHTS DURING THE 1940s

The social tremors triggered by the Second World War and the onset of the cold war transformed America's racial landscape. The government-sponsored racism of the German Nazis, the Italian Fascists, and the Japanese imperialists focused attention on the need for the United States to improve its own race relations and to provide for equal rights under the law. As a *New York Times* editorial explained in early 1946, "This is a particularly good time to campaign against the evils of bigotry, prejudice, and race hatred because we have witnessed the defeat of enemies who tried to found a mastery of the world upon such cruel and fallacious policy." The postwar confrontation with the Soviet Union gave American leaders an added incentive to improve race relations at home. Soviet Communists were eager to gain influence in the emerging nations of Africa. But in the ideological contest with communism for influence in post-colonial Africa, U.S. diplomats were at a disadvantage as long as racial segregation continued in the United States; the Soviets often compared racism in the South to the Nazis' treatment of the Jews.

Another factor in postwar efforts to improve race relations was the unwillingness of many black military veterans to put up with traditional racial abuse. In the postwar South, however, many white racist groups such the Ku Klux Klan and the all-white Citizens' Councils were not eager to improve race relations. One black veteran arrived home in a uniform festooned with combat medals, only to be welcomed by a white neighbor who said: "Don't you forget . . . that you're still a nigger." Those black veterans who spoke out against such racial bigotry risked their lives—literally. In 1946, two African American couples in rural Georgia were gunned down by a white mob. One of the murderers explained that George Dorsey, one of the victims, was "a good nigger" until he went in the army. "But when he came out, he thought he was as good as any white people."

Harry S. Truman was horrified by such incidents and grew ever more determined to promote civil rights. For most of his political career, Truman had shown little concern for the plight of African Americans. As president, however, he began to reassess his convictions. In the fall of 1946, a delegation of civil rights activists urged Truman to issue a public statement condemning the resurgence of the Ku Klux Klan and the lynching of African Americans. The delegation graphically described incidents of torture and intimidation against blacks in the South. Truman was aghast. He soon appointed a Committee on Civil Rights to investigate violence against African Americans and to recommend preventive measures.

On July 26, 1948, Truman banned racial discrimination in the hiring of federal employees. Four days later he issued an executive order ending racial segregation in the armed forces. The air force and navy quickly complied, but the army dragged its feet until the early 1950s. By 1960, the armed forces were the most racially integrated of all national organizations. Desegregating the military was, Truman claimed, "the greatest thing that ever happened to America."

JACKIE ROBINSON Meanwhile, racial segregation was being confronted in a much more public field of endeavor: professional baseball. In April 1947, as the baseball season opened, the National League's Brooklyn

Dodgers included on its roster the first African American player to cross the color line in major league baseball: **Jackie Robinson**. During his first season with the Dodgers, teammates and opposing players viciously baited Robinson, pitchers threw at him, base runners spiked him, and spectators booed him in every city. Hotels refused him rooms, and restaurants denied him service. Hate mail arrived by the bucket load. On the other hand, black spectators were electrified by Robinson's courageous example; they turned out in droves to watch him play. As time passed, Robinson won over many fans and players with his quiet courage, self-deprecating wit, and determined performance. Soon other teams signed black players.

Jackie Robinson

Racial discrimination remained widespread throughout the postwar period. In 1947, Jackie Robinson of the Brooklyn Dodgers became the first black player in major league baseball.

SHAPING THE FAIR DEAL   The determination Truman projected in foreign affairs did not alter his weak image on the domestic front. By early 1948, after three years in the White House, he had yet to shake the impression that he was not up to the job. The Democratic party seemed about to fragment: southern conservatives resented Truman's outspoken support of civil rights, while the left had flared up in 1946 over his firing of Secretary of Commerce Henry A. Wallace after a speech critical of the administration's policy. "Getting tough [with the Soviet Union]," Wallace had argued, "never brought anything real and lasting—whether for schoolyard bullies or world powers. The tougher we get, the tougher the Russians will get." The left itself was splitting between the Progressive Citizens of America, formed in 1946, which supported Wallace, and the Americans for Democratic Action, formed in 1947, which also criticized Truman but endorsed his firm anti-Communist stance.

By 1948, most political analysts assumed that Truman would lose the November election. Such gloomy predictions did not faze the combative president, however. He mounted a furious reelection campaign. His first step was to shore up the major elements of the New Deal coalition: farmers, labor unionists, and African Americans. In his 1948 State of the Union message, Truman offered something to nearly every group the Democrats hoped to attract. The first goal, Truman said, was to ensure civil rights. He added proposals to increase federal aid to education, expand unemployment and retirement benefits, create a comprehensive system of health insurance, enhance federal support for public housing projects, enable more rural people to connect to electricity, and increase the minimum wage.

THE ELECTION OF 1948 The Republican-controlled Congress spurned the Truman program, an action it would later regret. At the Republican Convention, New York governor Thomas E. Dewey won the presidential nomination on the third ballot. The platform endorsed most of the New Deal reforms and approved the administration's bipartisan foreign policy; Dewey promised to run things more efficiently, however. In July, a glum Democratic Convention gathered in Philadelphia. But delegates who expected to do little more than go through the motions were doubly surprised: first by the battle over the civil rights plank and then by Truman's acceptance speech. To keep from stirring southern hostility, the administration sought a platform plank that opposed racial discrimination only in general terms. Liberal Democrats, however, sponsored a plank that called on Congress to take specific action and commended Truman "for his courageous stand on the issue of civil rights." White segregationist delegates from Alabama and Mississippi walked out of the convention in protest. The solidly Democratic South had fractured for the first time since Reconstruction.

"I Stand Pat!"

Truman's support of civil rights for African Americans had its political costs, as this 1948 cartoon suggests.

On July 17, a group of rebellious southern Democrats met in Birmingham, Alabama. While waving Confederate flags and singing "Dixie," the dissident Democrats nominated South Carolina governor Strom Thurmond on a States' Rights Democratic ticket, quickly dubbed the Dixiecrat party. The **Dixiecrats** denounced Truman's "infamous" civil rights initiatives and championed states' rights. They hoped to draw enough electoral votes to preclude a majority for either major party, throwing the election into the House of Representatives, where they might strike a sectional bargain. A few days later, on July 23, the left wing of the Democratic party gathered in Philadelphia to form a new Progressive party and nominate for president Henry A. Wallace, Roosevelt's former secretary of agriculture and vice president. These splits in the Democratic ranks seemed to spell the final blow to Truman, but the feisty president was undaunted. He pledged to "win this election and make the Republicans like it!" He then set out on a 31,000-mile "whistle-stop" train tour, during which he castigated the "do-nothing" Eightieth Congress. Friendly audiences shouted, "Pour it on, Harry!" and "Give 'em hell, Harry." Truman responded: "I don't give 'em hell. I just tell the truth and they think

"Dewey Defeats Truman"

Truman's victory in 1948 was a huge upset, so much so that even the early edition of the *Chicago Daily Tribune* was caught off guard, running this presumptuous headline.

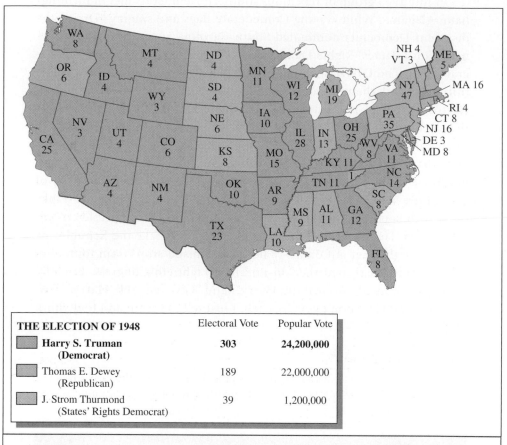

THE ELECTION OF 1948	Electoral Vote	Popular Vote
Harry S. Truman **(Democrat)**	**303**	**24,200,000**
Thomas E. Dewey (Republican)	189	22,000,000
J. Strom Thurmond (States' Rights Democrat)	39	1,200,000

Why did the political pundits predict a Dewey victory? Why was civil rights a divisive issue at the Democratic Convention? How did the candidacies of Thurmond and Wallace help Truman?

it's hell." Dewey, in contrast, ran a restrained campaign designed to avoid rocking the boat.

The polls and the pundits predicted a sure win for Dewey, but on election day Truman won the biggest upset in history, taking 24.2 million votes (49.5 percent) to Dewey's 22 million (45.1 percent) and winning a thumping margin of 303 to 189 in the Electoral College. Thurmond and Wallace each got more than 1 million votes, but the revolt of right and left had worked to Truman's advantage. The Dixiecrat rebellion backfired by angering black voters, who turned out in droves to support Truman, while the Progressive party's radicalism made it hard to tag Truman as soft on communism. Thurmond carried four Deep South states (South Carolina, Mississippi, Alabama, and Louisiana) with 39 electoral votes, including one from a Tennessee elector who repudiated his state's decision for Truman. Thurmond's success hastened a momentous disruption of the Democratic Solid South that would begin a long transition in the region to Republicanism.

Truman viewed his victory as a vindication for the New Deal and a mandate for liberalism. "We have rejected the discredited theory that the fortunes of the nation should be in the hands of a privileged few," he said. His State of the Union message repeated the agenda he had set forth the year before. "Every segment of our population and every individual," he declared, "has a right to expect from his government a fair deal." Whether deliberately or not, he had invented a tag, the Fair Deal, to distinguish his program from the New Deal.

Most of Truman's Fair Deal proposals were extensions or enlargements of New Deal programs already in place: a higher minimum wage, expansion of Social Security coverage to workers not included in the original bill, increased farm subsidies, and a sizable slum-clearance and public-housing program. Despite Democratic majorities, however, the conservative coalition of southern Democrats and Republicans thwarted any drastic new departures in domestic policy. Congress rejected civil rights bills, national health insurance, federal aid to education, and a plan to provide subsidies that would have raised farm income rather than farm prices. Congress also turned down Truman's demand for repeal of the Taft-Hartley Act.

The Cold War Heats Up

As was true during Truman's first term, global concerns repeatedly distracted the president's attention from domestic issues. In his 1949 inaugural address, Truman called for a vigilant anti-Communist foreign policy resting on four pillars: the United Nations, the Marshall Plan, NATO, and a "bold new plan" for providing financial and technical assistance to underdeveloped parts of the world, which came to be known simply as Point Four. But other issues kept the Point Four program from ever reaching its potential as a means of increasing American influence abroad at the expense of communism.

"LOSING" CHINA AND THE BOMB One of the most intractable postwar problems, the China tangle, was fast unraveling in 1949. The Chinese Nationalists, led by Chiang Kai-shek, had been fighting Mao Zedong and the Communists since the 1920s. After the Second World War, the Nationalists were put on the defensive as the Communists won over the land-hungry peasantry. By the end of 1949, the Nationalist government had fled to the island of Formosa, which it renamed Taiwan. Truman's critics—mostly Republicans—now asked bitterly, "Who lost China?" But it is hard to imagine how the U.S. government could have prevented a Communist victory short of getting involved in a massive military intervention, which would have been risky, unpopular, and expensive. The United States continued to recognize the Nationalist government on Taiwan as the rightful government of China, delaying formal relations with Communist China (the People's Republic of China) for thirty years.

As the Communists were gaining control of China, the Soviets were successfully testing an atomic bomb. The American nuclear monopoly had lasted just four years. The discovery of the Soviet bomb in 1949 triggered an intense reappraisal of the strategic balance of power in the world, causing Truman in 1950 to order the construction of a hydrogen bomb, a weapon far more powerful than the atomic bombs dropped on Japan, lest the Soviets make one first. That the Soviets now possessed atomic weapons heightened every confrontation between East and West, including an unexpected war in Korea.

WAR IN KOREA   The Japanese had occupied the Korean Peninsula since 1910, and after their defeat and withdrawal in 1945 the victorious Allies faced the difficult task of creating a new Korean nation. Complicating that task was the fact that Soviet troops had advanced into northern Korea and accepted the surrender of Japanese forces above the 38th parallel, while U.S. forces had done the same south of that line. The opportunistic Soviets quickly organized a Korean government in the North along Stalinist lines, while the Americans set up a western-style regime in the South.

The division of Korea at the end of the Second World War, like the division of Germany, was a temporary necessity that became permanent. In the hectic days of August 1945, the Soviets accepted an American proposal to divide desperately poor Korea at the 38th parallel until steps could be taken to unify the war-torn country. With the onset of the cold war, however, the two sides could not agree on unification. By the end of 1948, separate regimes had appeared in the two sectors and occupation forces had withdrawn. The weakened state of the U.S. military contributed to the impression that South Korea was vulnerable to a Communist assault. Evidence later gleaned from Soviet archives reveals that Stalin as well as Mao encouraged the North Koreans to unify their country and oust the Americans from the peninsula. The Soviet-designed war plan called for North Korean forces to seize South Korea within a week. Stalin apparently assumed that the United States would not intervene.

On June 25, 1950, over eighty thousand North Korean soldiers crossed the boundary into South Korea and drove the South Korean army down the peninsula in a headlong retreat. Seoul, the South Korean capital, was captured in three days. President Truman responded decisively. He and his advisers assumed that the North Korean attack was directed by Moscow and was a brazen indication of the aggressive designs of Soviet communism. Truman then made a critical decision: he decided to wage war under the auspices of the United Nations rather than seeking a declaration of war from Congress.

An emergency meeting of the UN Security Council quickly censured the North Korean "breach of peace." The Soviet delegate, who held a veto power, was at the time boycotting the council because it would not seat Communist China in place of Nationalist China. On June 27, the Security Council took advantage of his absence to call on UN members to "furnish such assistance to the Republic of Korea as may be necessary to repel the armed attack and to restore international peace and security in the area." Truman ordered American air, naval, and ground forces into action, and **General Douglas MacArthur** was put in command. The American defense of South Korea set a precedent of profound consequence: war by order of a president rather than by vote of Congress.

Truman's assumption that Stalin and the Soviets were behind the invasion of South Korea prompted two other decisions that had far-reaching consequences. First, Truman mistakenly viewed the Korean conflict as actually a diversion for a Soviet invasion of western Europe, so he ordered a major expansion of U.S. military forces in Europe. Second, he increased assistance to French troops fighting a Communist independence movement in Indochina (Vietnam), starting America's deepening military involvement in Southeast Asia.

For three months the fighting in Korea went badly for the Republic of Korea and the UN forces. By September they were barely hanging on to the southeast corner of Korea. Then, in a brilliant maneuver on September 15, 1950, MacArthur staged a surprise amphibious landing behind the North Korean lines at Inch'ŏn, the port city for Seoul. The sudden blow stampeded the North Korean forces back across the border. At that point, MacArthur persuaded Truman to allow him to push north across the North Korean border and seek to reunify Korea. Containment of communism was not enough; MacArthur was determined to rid North Korea of the "red menace." President Truman, concerned about military intervention by Communist China, flew seven thousand miles to Wake Island for a conference with General

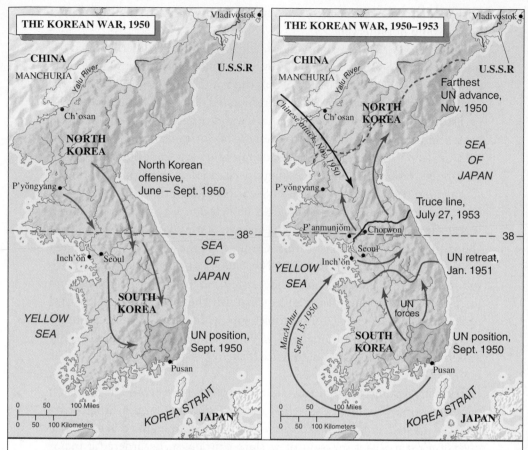

THE KOREAN WAR, 1950

CHINA
MANCHURIA
Yalu River
U.S.S.R
Vladivostok
Ch'osan
NORTH KOREA
P'yŏngyang
North Korean offensive, June – Sept. 1950
38°
Inch'ŏn Seoul
SEA OF JAPAN
SOUTH KOREA
YELLOW SEA
UN position, Sept. 1950
Pusan
KOREA STRAIT JAPAN
0 50 100 Miles
0 50 100 Kilometers

THE KOREAN WAR, 1950–1953

CHINA
MANCHURIA
Yalu River
U.S.S.R
Vladivostok
Farthest UN advance, Nov. 1950
Chinese attack, Nov. 1950
NORTH KOREA
Ch'osan
SEA OF JAPAN
P'yŏngyang
Truce line, July 27, 1953
P'anmunjŏm Chorwon
Seoul
38
YELLOW SEA
Inch'ŏn
UN retreat, Jan. 1951
UN forces
MacArthur Sept. 15, 1950
SOUTH KOREA
UN position, Sept. 1950
Pusan
KOREA STRAIT JAPAN
0 50 100 Miles
0 50 100 Kilometers

How did the surrender of the Japanese in Korea set up the conflict between Soviet-influenced North Korea and U.S.-influenced South Korea? What was General MacArthur's strategy for retaking Korea? Why did President Truman remove MacArthur from command?

MacArthur on October 15. There the general discounted chances that the Chinese Red Army would act, but if it did, he predicted, "there would be the greatest slaughter."

That same day, the Communist government in Peking announced that China "cannot stand idly by." On October 20, UN forces had entered P'yŏngyang, the North Korean capital, and on October 26, advance units had reached Ch'osan, on the Yalu River, Korea's northern border with China. MacArthur predicted total victory by Christmas. On the night of November 25, however, some 260,000 Chinese "volunteers" counterattacked, sending the U.S. forces into a desperate retreat just at the onset of winter. It had become "an entirely new war," MacArthur said. He asked for thirty-four atomic bombs and proposed air raids on China's "privileged sanctuary" in Manchuria, a naval blockade of China, and an invasion of the Chinese mainland by the Taiwan Nationalists.

Truman opposed leading the United States into the "gigantic booby trap" of war with China, and the UN forces soon rallied. By January 1951 over nine hundred thousand UN troops under General Matthew B. Ridgway finally secured their lines below Seoul and then launched a counterattack that in some places carried them back across the 38th parallel. When Truman offered to begin negotiations with the North Koreans to restore the prewar boundary, General MacArthur undermined the move by issuing an ultimatum for China to make peace or suffer an attack on their own country. On April 5, on the floor of Congress, the Republican minority leader read a letter in which General MacArthur criticized the president and said that "there is no substitute for victory." Such an act of open insubordination left the commander in chief no choice but to accept MacArthur's aggressive demands or fire him. Civilian control of the military was at stake, Truman later said, and he acted swiftly. On April 11, 1951, the president removed the popular MacArthur (Truman called him "Mr. Prima Donna") from his command and replaced him with Ridgway.

September 1950

American soldiers engaged in the recapture of Seoul from the North Koreans.

On June 24, 1951, the Soviet representative at the United Nations proposed a cease-fire in Korea along the 38th parallel, the original dividing line between North and South; Secretary of State Dean Acheson accepted the cease-fire a few days later with the consent of the United Nations. China and North Korea responded favorably—at the time, General Ridgway's "meatgrinder" offensive was inflicting severe losses—and truce talks started on July 10, 1951, at P'anmunjŏm, only to drag on for two years while the fighting continued. The chief snags were exchanges of prisoners and the South Korean president's insistence on unification. By the time a truce was reached, on July 27, 1953, Truman had relinquished the White House to Dwight D. Eisenhower. The truce line followed the war front at that time, mostly a little north of the 38th parallel, with a demilitarized zone of two and a half miles separating the forces; repatriation of military prisoners would be voluntary, supervised by a neutral commission. No peace conference ever took place, and Korea, like Germany, remained divided. The war had cost the United States more than 33,000 battle deaths and 103,000 wounded or missing. South Korean casualties, all told, were about 1 million, and North Korean and Chinese casualties an estimated 1.5 million.

ANOTHER RED SCARE   The Korean War excited a second Red Scare as people grew fearful that Communists were infiltrating American society. Since 1938 the **House Committee on Un-American Activities** (known as **HUAC**) had kept up a drumbeat of accusations about supposed Communist subversives in the federal government. On March 21, 1947, just nine days after he announced the Truman Doctrine, the president signed an executive order creating a loyalty program in the federal government. Every person entering federal service would be subject to a background investigation. By early 1951, the Civil Service Commission had cleared over 3 million people, while over 2,000 had resigned and 212 had been dismissed for doubtful loyalty.

Perhaps the case most damaging to the administration involved **Alger Hiss**, president of the Carnegie Endowment for International Peace, who had earlier served in several government agencies, including the State Department. Whittaker Chambers, a former Soviet agent and later an editor of *Time* magazine, told the HUAC in 1948 that Hiss had given him secret documents ten years earlier, when Chambers was spying for the Soviets and Hiss was working in the State Department. Hiss sued for libel, and Chambers produced microfilms of the State Department documents that he said Hiss had passed to him. Hiss denied the accusation, whereupon he was indicted and, after one mistrial, convicted in 1950. The charge was perjury, but he was convicted of lying about espionage, for which he could not be tried because the statute of limitations on that crime had expired.

More cases of Communist infiltration surfaced. In 1949 eleven top leaders of the Communist party in the United States were convicted under the Smith Act of 1940, which outlawed any conspiracy to advocate the overthrow of the government. The Supreme Court upheld the law under the doctrine of a "clear and present danger," which overrode the right to free speech. What was more, in 1950 the government unearthed the existence of a British-American spy network that had fed information about the development of the atomic bomb to the Soviet Union. These disclosures led to the arrest of, among others, Klaus Fuchs in Britain and Julius and Ethel Rosenberg in the United States.

MCCARTHY'S WITCH HUNT   Revelations of Soviet spying in the United States encouraged politicians to exploit the public's fears of the Communist menace at home. Early in 1950 a little-known Republican senator, **Joseph R. McCarthy** of Wisconsin, suddenly surfaced as the most ruthless exploiter of the nation's anxieties. He took up the cause of anti-communism with an incendiary speech at Wheeling, West Virginia, on February 9, 1950, in which he charged that the State Department was infested with Communists—and he claimed to have their names, although he never provided them. In the summer of 1951, McCarthy outrageously accused General George Marshall of making "common cause with Stalin." Concerns about the truth or fair play did not faze him. He refused to answer critics or provide evidence; his focus was on fearmongering. Despite his outlandish claims and boorish bullying, McCarthy never uncovered a single Communist agent in the government. His smear campaign went unchallenged until the end of the Korean War.

Fears of Communist espionage led Congress in 1950 to pass the McCarran Internal Security Act over President Truman's veto, making it unlawful "to combine, conspire, or agree with any other person to perform any act which would substantially contribute to . . . the establishment of a totalitarian dictatorship." Communist and Communist-front organizations had to register with the attorney general. Aliens who had belonged to totalitarian parties were barred from admission to the United States. The McCarran Internal Security Act, Truman said in his veto message, would "put the Government into the business of thought control." He might in fact have said as much about the Smith Act of 1940 or even his own program of loyalty investigations. Yet documents recently uncovered in Russian archives and U.S. security agencies reveal that the Soviets did indeed operate an extensive

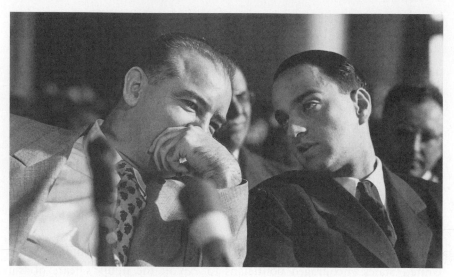

Joseph McCarthy

Senator McCarthy (left) and his aide Roy Cohn (right) exchange comments during testimony.

espionage ring in the United States. The United States did the same in Eastern Europe and the Soviet Union.

ASSESSING THE COLD WAR   In retrospect the onset of the cold war after the end of the Second World War takes on an appearance of terrible inevitability. America's traditional commitment to democratic capitalism, political self-determination, and religious freedom conflicted with the Soviet Union's preference for spheres of influence on its periphery, totalitarianism at home, and state-mandated atheism. Insecurity, more than ideology, drove much of Soviet behavior during and after the Second World War. Russia, after all, had been invaded by Germany twice in the first half of the twentieth century, and Soviet leaders wanted tame buffer states on their borders for protection. The people of eastern Europe were again caught in the middle.

If international conditions set the stage for the cold war, the actions of political leaders and thinkers set events in motion. Hindsight is always clearer than foresight, and President Truman may have erred in 1947 when he pledged to "contain" communism everywhere. The government loyalty program he launched may also have helped aggravate the anti-Communist hysteria. Containment itself proved hard to contain amid the ideological posturing. Its theorist, George F. Kennan, later confessed that he was to blame in part because he failed at the outset to spell out its limits and to stress that the United States needed to prioritize its responses to Soviet adventurism.

The years after the Second World War were unlike any other postwar period in American history. Having taken on global burdens, the nation had become committed to a permanent national military establishment, along with the attendant creation of shadowy new bureaucracies such as the National Security Council (NSC), the National Security Agency (NSA), and the Central Intelligence Agency (CIA). The federal government—and the presidency—continued to grow during the Cold War, fueled by the actions of both major political parties as well as by the intense lobbying efforts of what Dwight D. Eisenhower would call the "military-industrial complex."

CHAPTER SUMMARY

- **The Cold War** The cold war was an ideological contest between the Western democracies (especially the United States) and the Communist countries that emerged after the Second World War. Immediately after the war, the Soviet Union established satellite governments in eastern Europe, violating promises made at the Yalta Conference. The United States and the Soviet Union, former allies, differed on issues of human rights, individual liberties, and self-determination.

- **Containment** President Truman responded to the Soviet occupation of eastern Europe with the policy of containment, the aim of which was to halt the spread of communism. Truman proposed giving economic aid to countries in danger of Communist control, such as Greece and Turkey; and, with the Marshall Plan, he offered such aid to all European nations. In a defensive move, the United States in 1949 became a founding member of the North Atlantic Treaty Organization (NATO), a military alliance of Western democracies.

- **Truman's Fair Deal** Truman proposed not only to preserve the New Deal but also to expand it. He vetoed a Republican attempt to curb labor unions. He oversaw the expansion of Social Security and through executive orders ended segregation in the military and banned racial discrimination in the hiring of federal employees.

- **The Korean War** After a Communist government came to power in China in 1949, Korea became a "hot spot." The peninsula had been divided at the 38th parallel after the Second World War, with a Communist regime in the North and a Western-style regime in the South. After North Korean troops crossed the dividing line in June 1950, Truman decided to go to war under the auspices of the United Nations and without asking Congress to declare war. The war was thus waged by the United States with the participation of more than a dozen member nations of the United Nations. A truce, concluded in July 1953, established a demilitarized zone on either side of the 38th parallel.

- **McCarthyism** The onset of the cold war inflamed another Red Scare. During the Korean War, investigations by the House Committee on Un-American Activities (known as HUAC) sought to find "subversives" within the federal government. Senator Joseph R. McCarthy of Wisconsin exploited Americans' fears of Soviet spies' infiltrating the highest levels of the U.S. government. McCarthy was successful in the short term because, with most eastern European nations being held as buffer states by the Soviet Union and the war in Korea being indirectly fought against Communist China, the threat of a world dominated by Communist governments seemed real to many Americans.

CHRONOLOGY

1944	Congress passes the Servicemen's Readjustment Act (GI Bill of Rights)
April 1945	Fifty nations at war with the Axis Powers sign the United Nations Charter
1947	Congress passes the Taft-Hartley Labor Act
1947	National Security Council (NSC) is established
May 1948	Israel is proclaimed an independent nation
July 1948	Truman issues an executive order ending segregation in the U.S. armed forces
October 1948	Allied forces begin airlifting supplies to West Berlin
November 1948	Truman defeats Dewey in the presidential election
1949	North Atlantic Treaty Organization (NATO) is created
1949	China "falls" to communism
1950	United States and other UN members go to war in Korea

KEY TERMS & NAMES

30

THE 1950s: AFFLUENCE AND ANXIETY IN AN ATOMIC AGE

FOCUS QUESTIONS wwnorton.com/studyspace

- Why did the U.S. economy grow rapidly in the period after the Second World War?

- To what extent was conformity the main characteristic of society in the 1950s?

- What was the image of the family in this period, and what was the reality?

- What were the main characteristics of Dwight D. Eisenhower's "dynamic conservatism"?

- How did the civil rights movement come to emerge in the 1950s?

- What shaped American foreign policy in the 1950s?

In the summer of 1959, a newlywed couple spent their honeymoon in an underground bomb shelter in the backyard of their home. *Life* magazine showed the couple in their twenty-two-ton steel and concrete bunker stocked with enough food and water to survive an atomic attack. The image of the newlyweds seeking sheltered security in a new nuclear age symbolized how America in the 1950s was awash in contrasting emotions.

A fog of fear and worry shrouded the 1950s. For all of the decade's prosperity and pleasures, the deepening cold war spawned what commentators called "an age of anxiety." The confrontation between two global superpowers—the United States and the Soviet Union—generated chronic international tensions and provoked daily anxieties about the terrible possibility of nuclear warfare. In 1959, two out of three Americans listed the possibility of atomic war as the nation's most urgent problem.

However, a very different social outlook accompanied the terrifying expectation of nuclear holocaust in the aftermath of the Allied victory in the Second World War. The nation had emerged from the war elated, proud of its military strength, international stature, and industrial might. Having experienced years of deprivation during the Depression and the war, Americans were eager to indulge themselves in peacetime prosperity. As the editors of *Fortune* magazine proclaimed in 1946, "This is a dream era, this is what everyone was waiting through the blackouts for. The Great American Boom is on."

So it was, at least for the growing number of middle-class Americans. During the late 1940s and throughout the 1950s, the United States generated unprecedented economic growth that created a dazzling array of new consumer products. Amid the insecurities spawned by the cold war, most Americans were remarkably content in the 1950s. Marriage rates set an all-time high, divorce and homicide rates fell, the birth rate soared, and people lived longer on average, thanks in part to medical breakthroughs such as new antibiotics and the "miraculous" polio vaccine. In 1957, the editors of *U.S. News and World Report* proclaimed that "never have so many people anywhere, been so well off."

A People of Plenty

POSTWAR PROSPERITY   After a surprisingly brief postwar recession in 1945–1946, the economy shifted from wartime production to the peacetime manufacture of an array of consumer goods. The economy soared to record heights. By 1970, the gap between the living standard in the United States and that in the rest of the world had become a chasm: with 6 percent of the world's population, America produced and consumed two thirds of its goods. During the 1950s, government officials assured the citizenry that they should not fear another economic collapse. "Never again shall we allow a depression in the United States," President Dwight D. Eisenhower promised.

African Americans and other minority groups did not share equally in America's bounty, however. True, by 1950, blacks were earning on average more than four times their 1940 wages. And over the two decades after 1940, life expectancy for nonwhites rose ten years and black wage earnings increased fourfold. But African Americans and members of other minority groups lagged well behind whites in their *rate* of improvement. The gap between the average yearly income of whites and minorities such as African Americans and Hispanics widened during the decade of the 1950s. At least

40 million people remained "poor" during the 1950s, but their plight was largely ignored amid the wave of middle-class consumerism.

Several factors fueled the nation's unprecedented economic strength. First, the huge federal expenditures during the Second World War and the Korean War had catapulted the economy out of the Great Depression. The massive government assistance to the economy continued after 1945. No sooner was the war over than the federal government turned over to civilian owners many of its war-related plants, thus giving them a boost as they retooled for peacetime manufacturing. High government spending at all levels—federal, state, and local—continued in the 1950s, thanks to the arms race generated by the cold war as well as the massive construction of new highways, bridges, airports, and ports. The military budget after 1945 represented the single most important stimulant to the economy. Military-related research also helped spawn the new glamour industries of the 1950s: chemicals (including plastics), electronics, and aviation. By 1957, the aircraft industry was the nation's largest employer.

A second major factor stimulating economic growth was the extraordinary increase in productivity stimulated by new technologies, including computers. Factories and industries became increasingly "automated." Still another reason for the surge in economic growth was the lack of foreign competition in the aftermath of the Second World War. Most of the other major industrial nations of the world—England, France, Germany, Japan, the Soviet Union—had been physically devastated during the war, leaving American manufacturers with a virtual monopoly on international trade.

The major catalyst in promoting economic expansion after 1945 was the unleashing of pent-up consumer demand. Postwar America witnessed a new phase of economic development centered on carefree consumption. The new shopping malls dotting the suburban landscape epitomized the emphasis on spending as a new form of leisure recreation. In 1955, a marketing consultant stressed that America's "enormously productive economy demands that we make consumption a way of life, that we convert the buying and use of goods into rituals, that we seek our spiritual satisfaction, our ego satisfaction, in consumption." The consumer culture, he explained, demands that things be "consumed, burned up, worn out, replaced, and discarded at an ever-increasing rate."

Americans after the Second World War engaged in a prolonged buying spree, in part because of demand from the war years and in part because of new ways to buy things. In 1949 the first credit card was issued; by the end of the decade there were tens of millions of them. "Buying with plastic" became the new form of currency, enabling people to spend more than they had in cash. The new "consumer culture" reshaped the contours of American life: the nature of work, where people lived, how they interacted with others, and what they valued. It also affected the class structure, race relations, and gender dynamics. In 1956, *BusinessWeek* magazine trumpeted that "all of our business forces are bent on getting everyone to Borrow. Spend. Buy. Waste. Want." Such uncritical praise for the "throwaway" culture of consumption during the 1950s masked the chronic poverty amid America's mythic plenty. In 1959, a quarter of the population had no assets; over half the population had no savings accounts. Poverty afflicted nearly half of the African American population compared to a quarter of whites.

A CONSUMER CULTURE   What most Americans wanted to buy after the Second World War was a new house. In 1945 only 40 percent of Americans owned homes; by 1960 the proportion increased to 60 percent. And those new homes featured the latest electrical appliances—refrigerators, washing machines, vacuum cleaners, electric mixers, carving knives, shoe polishers. During the 1950s, consumer use of electricity tripled.

By far the most popular new household product was the television set. Watching television quickly displaced listening to the radio or going to the movies as an essential daily activity for millions of people. In 1954, grocery stores began selling "TV dinners," heated and consumed while the family watched popular shows such as *Father Knows Best*, *I Love Lucy*, *Leave It to Beaver*, and *The General Electric Theater*, hosted by Ronald Reagan.

What differentiated the affluence of the post–World War II era from earlier periods of prosperity was its ever-widening dispersion among workers as well as executives. Between 1947 and 1960, the average real income for the working class increased by as much as it had in the previous fifty years. When George Meany was sworn in as head of the American Federation of Labor–Congress of Industrial Organizations (AFL-CIO) in 1955, he proclaimed that "American labor never had it so good."

THE GI BILL OF RIGHTS   Fears that a sharp drop in military spending and the sudden influx of veterans into the workforce would disrupt the economy and produce widespread unemployment led Congress to pass the Servicemen's Readjustment Act of 1944. Popularly known as the GI Bill of Rights (GI meaning "government issue," a phrase that was stamped on military uniforms and became slang for "serviceman"), it created a new government agency, the Veterans Administration (VA), and included provisions for unemployment pay for veterans for one year, preference for veterans applying for government jobs, loans for home construction, access to government

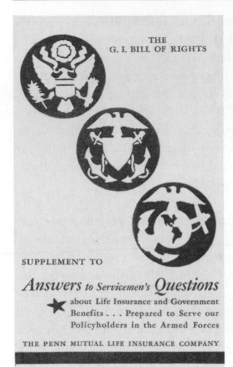

THE
G. I. BILL OF RIGHTS

SUPPLEMENT TO

Answers to Servicemen's *Questions*

★ about Life Insurance and Government
Benefits . . . Prepared to Serve our
Policyholders in the Armed Forces

THE PENN MUTUAL LIFE INSURANCE COMPANY

GI Bill of Rights supplement

This booklet informed servicemen about the new legislation.

hospitals, and generous subsidies for postsecondary education.

Between 1944 and 1956, almost 8 million veterans took advantage of $14.5 billion in GI Bill subsidies to attend college or job-training programs. Some 5 million veterans bought new homes with VA-backed mortgage loans, which required no down payment and provided up to twenty years for repayment. Before the Second World War, approximately 160,000 Americans graduated from college each year. By 1950 the figure had risen to 500,000. In 1949, veterans accounted for 40 percent of all college enrollments, and the United States could boast the world's best-educated workforce.

Many African American veterans, however, could not take equal advantage of the education benefits. Most colleges and universities after the war remained racially segregated, either by regulation or by practice. Of the nine thousand students enrolled at the University of Pennsylvania in 1946, for example, only forty-six were African Americans. Those blacks who were admitted to white colleges or universities were barred from playing on athletic teams, attending dances and other social events, and joining fraternities or sororities. In 1946 only a fifth of the one hundred thousand African Americans who had applied for education benefits had enrolled in a program.

THE BABY BOOM   The return of some 16 million veterans to private life also helped generate the postwar "**baby boom**." Many young married couples who had delayed having children during the Depression or the Second World War were intent on making up for lost time. Between 1946 and 1964, 76 million Americans were born, reversing a century-long decline in the nation's birth rate and creating a demographic upheaval whose repercussions are still being felt. The baby boom peaked in 1957, when a record 4.3 million births occurred, one every seven seconds. The unusually large

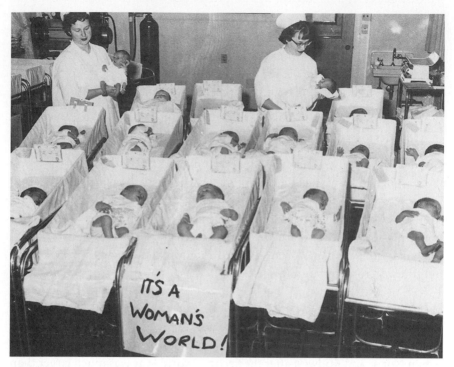

IT'S A
WOMAN'S
WORLD!

The baby boom

Much of America's social history since the 1940s has been the story of the baby boom generation.

baby boom generation has shaped much of America's social history and economic development since the 1940s. The postwar baby boom created a surge in demand for diapers, baby food, toys, medicine, schools, automobiles, books, teachers, furniture, and housing.

THE SUBURBAN FRONTIER   The second half of the twentieth century witnessed a mass migration to a new frontier—the suburbs. The acute housing shortage in the late 1940s (98 percent of cities reported shortages of houses and apartments in 1945) spurred the suburban revolution. Almost the entire population increase of the 1950s and 1960s (97 percent) was an urban or suburban phenomenon. Rural America continued to lose population as many among the exploding middle-class white population during the 1950s—and after—moved to what were called the Sunbelt states— California, Arizona, Florida, Texas, and the southeast region. Air conditioning became a common household fixture in the 1950s and enhanced the appeal of living in warmer climates.

Suburbia met an acute need—affordable housing—and fulfilled a conventional dream—personal freedom and familial security within commuting distance of cities. During the 1950s, suburbs grew six times as fast as cities did. By 1970, more people lived in suburbs than in central cities. Governments encouraged and even subsidized the suburban revolution. Federal and state tax codes favored homeowners over renters, and local governments paid for the infrastructure required by new subdivisions: roads, water and sewer lines, fire and police protection.

During the half century after the Second World War, the suburban good life was presumed to include a big home with a big yard on a big lot accessed by a big car—or two. Cars were the ultimate status symbol. Nine out of ten suburban families in the 1950s owned a car, as compared to six of ten urban households. The "car culture" soon transformed social behavior and spawned "convenience stores," drive-in movies, and a new form of dining out: the fast-food restaurant.

MINORITIES ON THE MOVE African Americans were not part of the initial wave of suburban development, but they began moving in large numbers after 1945. The mass migration of rural southern blacks to the urban North and Midwest after the Second World War was much larger than that after the First World War, and its social consequences were more dramatic. After 1945, more than 5 million African Americans formed a new "great migration" northward in search of better jobs, higher wages, decent housing, and greater social equality. By 1960, for the first time in history, more blacks were living in urban areas than in rural areas. As African Americans moved into northern cities, many white residents moved to the suburbs, leaving behind proliferating racial ghettos. Nine of the nation's ten largest cities lost population to the suburbs during the 1950s.

The "promised land" in the North sought by African Americans was not perfect, however. Because they were undereducated, poor, and black, the migrants were regularly denied access to good jobs, good schools, and good housing. Although states in the North, Midwest, and the Far West did not have the most blatant forms of statutory racial discrimination common in the South, African Americans still found themselves subject to racial prejudice in the every aspect of life: discrimination in hiring, in treatment in the workplace, in housing, in schools, and in social life. In cities outside the South, blacks and whites typically lived in separate neighborhoods and led unequal lives. When a black family tried to move into Levittown, Pennsylvania, the white residents greeted them by throwing rocks. Between 1945 and 1954, Chicago witnessed nine large race riots.

Family on relief

Many black families who migrated from the South became a part of a marginalized population in Chicago, dependent on public housing.

Such deeply entrenched racial attitudes forced blacks outside the South to organize their own efforts to assault the hostility and complacency they confronted. Through organizations such as the NAACP, the Congress of Racial Equality, and the National Urban League, they sought to change the hearts and minds of their white neighbors. Animated by anger, hope, and solidarity, local black leaders by the late 1950s had convinced most northern states to adopt some form of anti-discrimination legislation. Segregation of schools on the basis of race ended.

For all of the forms of racism that black migrants to the North and West encountered, however, most of them found their new lives preferable to the official segregation and often violent racism that they had left behind in the South. Southern blacks still faced voting discrimination and segregation in theaters, parks, schools, colleges, hospitals, buses, cinemas, libraries, restrooms, beaches, bars, prisons, and drinking fountains.

Just as African Americans were on the move, so, too, were Mexicans and Puerto Ricans. Congress renewed the bracero program, begun during the Second World War, that enabled Mexicans to work as contract laborers in the United States. Mexicans streamed across the southwest border of the United States in growing numbers. By 1960 Los Angeles had the largest concentration of Mexican Americans in the nation. Like African Americans who served in the military during the war, Mexican Americans, Puerto Ricans, and other Latino minorities benefited from the GI Bill, expanding economic opportunities, and prolonged national prosperity to join the growing middle class. Between 1940 and 1960, nearly a million Puerto Ricans, mostly small farmers and agricultural workers, moved into mainland American cities, mostly New York City. By the late 1960s, more Puerto Ricans lived in New York City than in the capital of Puerto Rico, San Juan. The popular Broadway musical drama *West Side Story* highlights the tensions generated by the influx of Puerto Ricans into traditionally white neighborhoods.

A CONFORMIST CULTURE

As evidenced in many of the new look-alike suburbs sprouting up across the land, much of white middle-class social life during the 1950s exhibited an increasingly homogenized character. Suburban life encouraged uniformity. "There is no need to rub elbows with fellow Americans who are of a different class," explained one analyst of the suburban revolution. Changes in corporate life as well as the influence of the consumer culture and the cold war also played an important socializing role. "Conformity," predicted a journalist in 1954, "may very well become the central social problem of this age."

CORPORATE LIFE The composition of the workforce and the very nature of work itself changed dramatically during the 1950s. Fewer people were self-employed, and manual labor was rapidly giving way to mental labor. The high-performing American economy began shifting from its traditional emphasis on manufacturing to service industries: telecommunications (including the newfangled computer), sales, financial services, advertising, marketing, public relations, entertainment, clerical, and government. By the mid-1950s, white-collar (salaried) employees outnumbered blue-collar (hourly wage) workers for the first time in history. During the Second World War, big business had grown bigger—and the process continued during the 1950s. The government relaxed its anti-trust activity, and huge defense contracts promoted corporate concentration and consolidation. After the war, a wave of mergers occurred, and dominant corporate giants— General Motors, IBM, General Electric, Westinghouse, AT&T, Xerox, DuPont, and Boeing—appeared in every major industry, providing the primary source of new jobs. Most people in the 1950s worked for giant corporations. In such huge companies, as well as similarly large government agencies and universities, the working atmosphere promoted conformity rather than individualism.

WOMEN'S "PLACE"   Increasing conformity in the workplace was mirrored in middle-class homes. The soaring birth rate reinforced the deeply embedded notion that a woman's place was in the home. "Of all the accomplishments of the American woman," *Life* magazine proclaimed, "the one she brings off with the most spectacular success is having babies."

During the Second World War, millions of women had responded to patriotic appeals and joined the traditionally male workforce. After the war ended, however, most middle-class women turned their wartime jobs over to the returning male veterans and resumed their full-time commitment to home and family. *Newsweek* magazine discouraged women from even attending college when it proclaimed that "books and babies don't mix." In 1956, one fourth of all white women in college married while still a student, and most of them dropped out before receiving a degree.

The new household

A Tupperware party in a middle-class suburban home.

CRACKS IN THE PICTURE WINDOW

Amid the surging affluence of the supposed "happy days" decade, there was also growing anxiety, dissent, and diversity. Many social critics, writers, and artists expressed a growing sense of unease with the much-celebrated consumer culture. One of the most striking aspects of the decade was the sharp contrast between the buoyant public mood and the increasingly bitter social criticism coming from intellectuals, theologians, novelists, playwrights, poets, and artists. Writer Norman Mailer, for instance, said the 1950s was "one of the worst decades in the history of man."

Norman Mailer was one of many social critics who challenged what they viewed as the postwar era's moral complacency and bland conformity. In *The Affluent Society* (1958), for example, the economist John Kenneth Galbraith attacked the prevailing notion that sustained economic growth was solving chronic social problems. He reminded readers that for all of America's vaunted prosperity, the nation had yet to eradicate poverty, especially among minorities in inner cities, female-headed households, Mexican American migrant farm workers in the Southwest, Native Americans, and rural southerners, both black and white.

ALIENATION AND LIBERATION

Ralph Ellison

Ellison is best remembered for his 1952 novel *Invisible Man*.

LITERATURE During the 1950s, a growing number of writers and artists called into question the prevailing complacency about the goodness and superiority of the American way of life. As novelist John Updike observed, he and other writers felt estranged "from a government that extolled business and mediocrity." The most enduring novels of the postwar period featured the individual's struggle for survival amid the smothering forces of mass society. The characters in novels such as James Jones's *From Here to Eternity* (1951), Saul Bellow's *Seize the Day* (1956), J. D. Salinger's *Catcher in the Rye* (1951), William Styron's *Lie*

Down in Darkness (1951), and Updike's *Rabbit, Run* (1961), among many others, are restless, tormented souls who can find neither contentment nor respect in an overpowering or uninterested world.

The immensely talented African American writer Ralph Ellison explored the theme of the lonely individual imprisoned in privacy in his kaleidoscopic novel *Invisible Man* (1952). By using a black narrator struggling to find and liberate himself in the midst of an oppressive white society, Ellison forcefully exposed the problem of alienation amid affluence. The narrator opens by confessing: "All my life I had been looking for something, and everywhere I turned someone tried to tell me what it was. I accepted their answers too, though they were often in contradiction and even self-contradictory. I was naive. I was looking for myself and asking everyone except myself questions which I, and only I, could answer."

PAINTING   After the Second World War, a group of young painters in New York City decided that the modern atomic era demanded something different from literal representation of recognizable scenes. During the late 1940s and 1950s, abstract painters dominated the international art scene. Jackson Pollock explained that "the modern painter cannot express this age—the airplane, the atomic bomb, the radio—in the old form of the Renaissance or of any past culture. Each age finds its own technique." The spontaneous artistic technique that Pollock mastered came to be called abstract expressionism. For Pollock and others engaged in what was called "action painting," a canvas was not simply a flat surface on which to paint a recognizable scene; it was instead a dynamic arena for expressing the artist's subjective inner world. The gestural *act* of painting was more important than the painting itself. Pollock, nicknamed "Jack the Dripper," put his canvases on the floor and walked around attacking them, throwing, pouring, splashing, flicking, and dribbling paint in random patterns. Such anarchic spontaneity created mystifying canvases adorned only with splashes, drips, swaths, lines, bands, and slashes. The idiosyncratic intensity of abstract expressionism perplexed the general public but intrigued the art world.

THE BEATS   The desire expressed by the abstract expressionists to liberate self-expression and discard traditional artistic conventions was also the central concern of a small but highly visible and controversial group of young writers, poets, painters, and musicians known as the **Beats**, a term with multiple meanings: "upbeat," "beatific," and the concept of being "on the beat" in "real cool" jazz music. Jack Kerouac, Allen Ginsberg, and other Beats rebelled against middle-class life and conventional literary expression.

"Jack the Dripper"

Artist Jackson Pollock became famous for his unique painting style; here he dribbles house paint and sand on a canvas in his studio barn in Springs, NY.

The self-described Beat hipsters grew out of the bohemian underground in New York City's Greenwich Village. Undisciplined and unkempt, they were essentially apolitical throughout the 1950s, more interested in transforming themselves than in reforming the world. They sought personal rather than social solutions to their anxieties; they wanted their art and literature to change consciousness rather than reform social ills. As Kerouac insisted, his friends were not beat in the sense of beaten down; they were "mad to live, mad to talk, mad to be saved." They nursed an ecstatic urge to "go, go, go" and not stop until they get there, wherever "there" might be. Their road to salvation lay in hallucinogenic drugs and alcohol, casual sex, a penchant for jazz, fast cars, the street life of urban ghettos, an affinity for Buddhism, and a restless, vagabond spirit that took them speeding back and forth across the country between San Francisco and New York during the 1950s. The rebellious gaiety of the Beats played an important role in preparing for the more widespread youth revolt of the 1960s.

ROCK AND ROLL Many concerned observers blamed teen delin-
quency on a new form of music that emerged during the 1950s: rock and
roll. Alan Freed, a Cleveland disc jockey, coined the term *rock and roll* in
1951. He had noticed white teenagers buying rhythm and blues (R&B)
records that had heretofore been purchased only by African Americans and
Hispanic Americans. Freed began playing R&B records on his radio show
but labeled the music "rock and roll" (a phrase used in African American
communities to refer to dancing and sex). Freed's popular radio program
helped bridge the gap between "white" and "black" music. African American singers such as Chuck Berry, Little Richard, and Ray Charles as well as
Hispanic American performers such as Ritchie Valens (Richard Valenzuela)
captivated young white middle-class audiences eager to claim their own
cultural style.

At the same time, Elvis Presley, the lanky son of a poor Mississippi farm
family who moved to a public housing project in Memphis, Tennessee, when
he was fourteen, began experimenting with "rockabilly" music, a unique
blend of gospel, country-and-western, and R&B rhythms and lyrics. In 1956,
the twenty-one-year-old Presley released his smash hit "Heartbreak Hotel."
Over the next two years, he emerged as the most popular musician in American history. Presley's gyrating, sensual stage performances and his incom-
parably rich and raw baritone voice drove teenagers wild and garnered him
fans across the social spectrum and around the world.

Cultural conservatives were outraged. Critics urged parents to destroy
Presley's records because they promoted "a pagan concept of life." A Catholic
cardinal denounced Presley as a vile symptom of a teenage "creed of dishon-
esty, violence, lust and degeneration." Patriotic groups claimed that rock-
and-roll music was a tool of Communist insurgents designed to corrupt
youth. Yet rock and roll survived amid the criticism, and in the process it gave
adolescents a self-conscious sense of belonging to a unique social group with
distinctive characteristics. More important, the rock music phenomenon
brought together on equal terms musicians (and their audiences) of varied
races and backgrounds. In doing so, it helped dispel the long-prevailing racial
prejudices that conflicted with the American egalitarian ideal.

MODERATE REPUBLICANISM—
THE EISENHOWER YEARS

The carefree prosperity of the 1950s was encouraged by the decade's
political culture. Dwight David Eisenhower dominated the political landscape during the 1950s. The authentic military hero with an infectious grin

was a model of moderation, stability, and optimism. Eisenhower's commitment to a "moderate Republicanism" promised to restore the authority of state and local governments and restrain the federal government from political and social "engineering." In the process, the former general sought to renew traditional virtues and inspire Americans with a vision of a brighter future amid a continuing cold war.

"TIME FOR A CHANGE" By 1952, the Truman administration had piled up a heavy burden of political liabilities. Its bold stand in Korea had brought a bloody stalemate in the war, renewed wage and price controls at home, and the embarrassing exposure of corrupt lobbyists and influence peddlers who rigged defense-related federal contracts. The disclosure of corruption led Truman to fire nearly 250 employees of the Internal Revenue Service, but doubts lingered that the president would ever finish the housecleaning.

It was, Republicans claimed, "time for a change," and they saw public sentiment turning their way as the 1952 election approached. Beginning in the late 1940s, both Republican and Democratic leaders, including President Truman, recruited the nonpartisan General Eisenhower to be their presidential candidate. The affable Eisenhower, whose friends called him "Ike," had displayed remarkable organizational and diplomatic abilities in coordinating the Allied invasion of Nazi-controlled Europe. In 1952, after serving as the president of Columbia University, he had moved to Paris to become the supreme commander of NATO forces in Europe, only to be recruited as a presidential candidate. Eisenhower's decision to seek the Republican presidential nomination was wildly popular. Bumper stickers announced simply, "I Like Ike."

Eisenhower won the Republican nomination on the first ballot. He then tried to reassure the conservative wing of the party by balancing the ticket with a youthful Californian, the thirty-nine-year-old senator Richard M. Nixon, who had built a career by exposing supposed left-wing "subversives" holding government posts in the Truman administration. The Republican party platform declared that the Democratic emphasis on "containing" communism was a "negative, futile, and misguided" form of appeasement. The Eisenhower administration, if elected, would roll back the communist menace by bringing "genuine independence" to the "captive peoples" of Eastern Europe.

THE ELECTION OF 1952 The 1952 presidential campaign matched two contrasting personalities. Eisenhower, though a political novice, had been in the public eye for a decade. Illinois governor Adlai Stevenson, the Democratic candidate, was hardly known outside Illinois. Eisenhower's campaign pledged to clean up "the mess in Washington." To this he added a promise, late in the campaign, that he would secure "an early and honorable" peace in Korea. Stevenson was outmatched. Although a brilliant man who gave witty speeches that charmed liberals, he came across to most voters as a tad too aloof, a shade too intellectual. The Republicans labeled him an "egghead" (a recently coined term describing balding professors who had more intellect than common sense).

On election night, the war hero triumphed in a landslide, gathering nearly 34 million votes to Stevenson's 27 million. The electoral vote was much more lopsided: 442 to Stevenson's 89. The hapless Stevenson failed to win his home state of Illinois. More important, the election marked a turning point in Republican fortunes in the South: for the first time in over a century, the

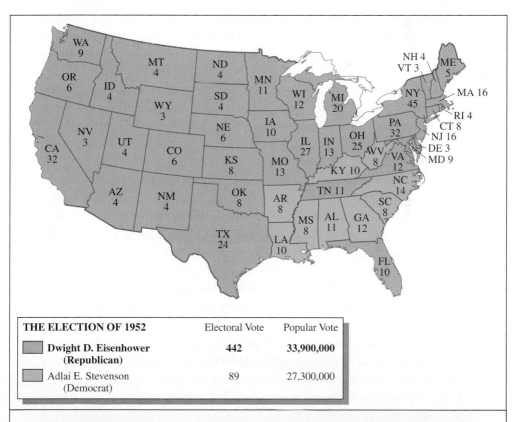

THE ELECTION OF 1952	Electoral Vote	Popular Vote
Dwight D. Eisenhower (Republican)	442	33,900,000
Adlai E. Stevenson (Democrat)	89	27,300,000

Why was the contest between Adlai Stevenson and Dwight D. Eisenhower lopsided? Why was Eisenhower's victory in the South remarkable? Did Eisenhower's broad appeal help congressional Republicans win more seats?

Democratic "Solid South" was moving toward a two-party system. Stevenson carried only eight southern states plus West Virginia. Eisenhower had made it respectable, even fashionable, to vote for a Republican presidential candidate in the South.

The voters liked Eisenhower's folksy charm and battle-tested poise better than they liked his political party. In the 1952 election, Democrats retained most of the governorships, lost control of the House by only eight seats, and broke even in the Senate, where only the vote of the vice president ensured Republican control. The congressional elections two years later would weaken the Republican grip on Congress, and Eisenhower would have to work with a Democratic Congress throughout his second term.

A "MIDDLE WAY" PRESIDENCY   Eisenhower was the first professional soldier elected president since Ulysses S. Grant in 1868, and the last president born in the nineteenth century. His goal was to pursue a "middle way between untrammelled freedom of the individual and the demands of the welfare of the whole nation." He did not intend to dismantle all of the New Deal and Fair Deal programs. Instead, he wanted to rectify the "excesses" resulting from the Democratic control of the White House for the previous twenty years. He pledged to reduce the federal government bureaucracy and restore the balance between the executive and congressional branches. Eisenhower's cautious personality and genial leadership style aligned perfectly with the prevailing mood of most voters. He was a conciliator rather than an ideologue; he sought consensus and compromise; he avoided confrontation. Eisenhower reverted to the nineteenth-century view that Congress should make policy and the president should carry it out. A journalist noted in 1959 that "the public loves Ike. The less he does, the more they love him."

"DYNAMIC CONSERVATISM" AT HOME   Eisenhower called his domestic program dynamic conservatism, by which he meant being "conservative when it comes to money and liberal when it comes to human beings." The new administration set out to reduce defense spending after the Korean War, lower tax rates, weaken government regulation of business, and restore power to the states and corporate interests. Eisenhower warned repeatedly against the dangers of "creeping socialism," "huge bureaucracies," and perennial budget deficits.

In the end, however, Eisenhower kept intact the basic structure and premises of the New Deal, much to the chagrin of conservative Republicans. A self-described pragmatist, Eisenhower told his more conservative brother

Edgar in 1954 that if the "stupid" right-wing of the Republican party tried "to abolish Social Security and eliminate labor laws and farm programs, you would not hear of that party again in our political history." In some ways, the Eisenhower administration actually expanded New Deal programs, especially after 1954, when it had the help of Democratic majorities in Congress. Amendments to the Social Security Act in 1954 and 1956 expanded coverage to millions of workers formerly excluded: white-collar professionals, domestic and clerical workers, farm workers, and members of the armed forces. Eisenhower also approved increases in the minimum wage and additional public housing projects for low-income occupants.

President Eisenhower launched two massive federal construction projects that served national needs: the St. Lawrence Seaway and the interstate highway system. The St. Lawrence Seaway project (in partnership with Canada) opened the Great Lakes to oceangoing freighters and tankers. Even more important, the Federal-Aid Highway Act (1956) created a national network of interstate highways to serve the needs of commerce and defense, as well as the convenience of citizens. The interstate highway system, funded by gasoline taxes, took twenty-five years to construct and was the largest federal construction project in history. It stretches for 47,000 miles, and contains 55,512 bridges and 14,800 interchanges. The vast project created jobs, stimulated the economy, spurred the tourism, motor hotel ("motel"), and long-haul trucking industries, and transformed the way people traveled and lived by reinforcing America's car-centered culture. At the same time, the interstate highways also hastened the decay of the passenger railroad system, deflected attention from the need for mass transit systems, and helped foster the automobile culture that over time created a national dependency on imported oil.

THE RED SCARE　The Republicans thought their presidential victory in 1952 would curb the often-unscrupulous efforts of Wisconsin senator Joseph R. McCarthy to find Communist spies in the federal government. But the paranoid, publicity-seeking senator grew more outlandish in his charges. Eisenhower despised the unprincipled McCarthy, but refused to criticize him in public.

The cynical, bullying McCarthy finally overreached himself when he made the absurd charge that the U.S. Army itself was "soft" on communism. On December 2, 1954, the Senate voted 67 to 22 to "condemn" McCarthy for his reckless tactics. Soon thereafter, McCarthy's political influence collapsed. In 1957, at the age of forty-eight, he died of a liver inflammation brought on by years of alcohol abuse (he frequently bragged about drinking a fifth of whiskey a day). His savage crusade against communists in government had catapulted him into the limelight and captured the nation's attention for several years, but the former marine trampled upon civil liberties. McCarthy's political demise played a role in the fall elections in 1954, helping the Democrats capture control of both houses of Congress.

THE EARLY YEARS OF THE CIVIL RIGHTS MOVEMENT

Soon after the cold war began, Soviet diplomats began to use America's continuing racial discrimination against African Americans as a propaganda tool. During the mid-1950s, race relations in the United States threatened to explode the domestic tranquility masking years of social injustice. The volatile issue of ending racial segregation in the South offered Eisenhower an opportunity to exercise transformational leadership. That he balked at remedying the nation's gravest injustice constituted his greatest failure as president.

EISENHOWER AND RACE Eisenhower had entered the White House committed to civil rights in principle, and he pushed the issue in some areas of federal authority. During his first three years as president, for example, public facilities in Washington, D.C., were desegregated. Eisenhower also

Chief Justice Earl Warren

One of the most influential Supreme Court justices of the twentieth century.

intervened to end discrimination at several military bases in Virginia and South Carolina. The president also appointed the first African American to an executive office: E. Frederic Morrow, who was named Administrative Officer for Special Projects. Beyond that, however, Eisenhower refused to push the issue of civil rights.

Two aspects of Eisenhower's philosophy limited his commitment to racial equality: his preference for state or local action over federal involvement and his doubt that laws could change racist attitudes. "I don't believe you can change the hearts of men with laws or decisions," he said. Eisenhower's tepid stance meant that governmental leadership in the civil rights field would come from the judiciary more than from the executive or legislative branch.

In 1953, Eisenhower appointed former three-term Republican governor Earl Warren of California as chief justice of the Supreme Court, a decision he later pronounced the "biggest damn fool mistake I ever made." Warren, who had seemed safely conservative while active in elected politics, displayed a social conscience and a streak of libertarianism that was shared by another Eisenhower appointee to the Supreme Court, William J. Brennan Jr. The Warren Court (1953–1969), under the chief justice's influence, became a powerful force for social and political change through the 1960s.

WE SHALL OVERCOME However, the most important leadership related to the civil rights movement came not from government officials but from the long-suffering people whose rights were most suppressed: African Americans, Hispanic Americans, Asian Americans, and other minorities. Rural and urban, young and old, male and female, courageous blacks formed the vanguard of what would become the most important social movement in American history. With brilliance, bravery, and dignity, they fought on all fronts—in the courts, at the ballot box, and in the streets—

Civil rights stirrings

In the late 1930s the NAACP began to test the constitutionality of racial segregation.

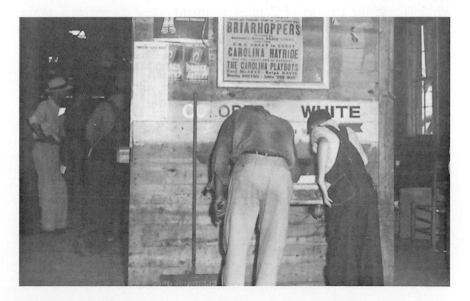

against deeply entrenched patterns of racial segregation and discrimination. Although many African Americans moved to the North and West during and after the Second World War, a majority remained in the eleven former Confederate states. There they were forced to attend segregated public schools, accept the least desirable jobs, and operate within an explicitly segregated society that systematically restricted their civil rights. In the 1952 presidential election, for example, only 20 percent of eligible African Americans were registered to vote.

In the mid-1930s the National Association for the Advancement of Colored People (NAACP) had resolved to test the separate-but-equal judicial doctrine that had upheld racial segregation since the *Plessy* decision in 1896. Charles H. Houston, a dean at the Howard University Law School, laid the plans, and his former student Thurgood Marshall served as the NAACP's chief attorney. They focused first on higher education. But it would take almost fifteen years to convince the courts that racial segregation must end. In *Sweatt v. Painter* (1950), the Supreme Court ruled that a separate black law school in Texas was not equal in quality to the state's whites-only schools. The Court ordered the state to remedy the situation. It was the first step of many that would be required to dismantle America's segregated tradition.

THE *BROWN* DECISION   By the early 1950s, challenges to state laws mandating racial segregation in the public schools were rising through the appellate courts. Five such cases, from Kansas, Delaware, South Carolina, Virginia, and the District of Columbia—usually cited by reference to the first, ***Brown v. Board of Education of Topeka, Kansas***—came to the Supreme Court for joint argument by NAACP attorneys in 1952. The landmark case provided an opportunity for courageous presidential leadership. President Eisenhower, however, let the opportunity slip through his fingers. He told the attorney general that he hoped the justices would defer dealing with the case "until the next Administration took over." When it became obvious that the Court was moving forward, Eisenhower invited Earl Warren to a White House dinner where he urged the chief justice to side with segregationists. Warren responded: "You mind your business and I'll mind mine."

On May 17, 1954, Chief Justice Warren wrote the opinion, handed down on May 17, 1954, in which a unanimous Court declared that "in the field of public education the doctrine of 'separate but equal' has no place." In support of its opinion, the Court cited sociological and psychological findings demonstrating that even if racially separate facilities were equal in quality, the mere fact of separating students by race engendered feelings of inferiority. A year later, after further argument, the Court directed that the process of racial integration should move "with all deliberate speed."

In the greatest mistake of his presidency, Eisenhower refused to endorse or enforce the Court's ruling. Privately, he maintained "that the Supreme Court decision set back progress in the South at least fifteen years. The fellow who tries to tell me you can do these things by force is just plain nuts." While token integration began as early as 1954 in the border states of Kentucky and Missouri, hostility mounted in the Deep South and Virginia. The Alabama senate passed a resolution "nullifying" the Supreme Court's decision; Virginia's legislature asserted the state's right to "interpose its sovereignty" against the Court's ruling.

The grassroots opposition among southern whites to the Brown case was led by the newly formed Citizens' Councils, middle-class versions of the Ku Klux Klan that spread quickly across the South and eventually enrolled 250,000 members. Instead of physical violence, the Councils used economic coercion against blacks who crossed racial boundaries. The Citizens' Councils grew so powerful in many communities that membership became almost a prerequisite for an aspiring white politician. Opponents of court-ordered integration shouted defiance. Virginia senator Harry F. Byrd supplied a rallying cry: "**Massive Resistance**." In 1956, 101 members of Congress signed a "Southern Manifesto" denouncing the Supreme Court's decision in the *Brown* case as "a clear abuse of judicial power." In six southern states at the end of 1956, not a single black child attended school with whites.

THE MONTGOMERY BUS BOYCOTT The essential role played by the NAACP and the courts in providing a legal lever for the civil rights movement often overshadows the courageous contributions of individual African Americans who took great personal risks to challenge segregation. For example, in Montgomery, Alabama, on December 1, 1955, Mrs. **Rosa Parks**, a forty-two-year-old black seamstress and department store worker who was a long-time critic of segregation and secretary of the local NAACP chapter, boldly refused to give up her seat on a city bus to a white man. Like many southern communities, Montgomery, the "Cradle of the Confederacy," required blacks to give up their bus or train seat to a white when asked. Parks, however, was "tired of giving in" to the system of white racism. When the bus driver told her that "niggers must move back" and that he would have her arrested if she did not move, she replied with quiet courage and gentle dignity, saying, "You may do that." Police then arrested her. The next night, black community leaders, including the Women's Political Council, a group of middle-class black women, met in the Dexter Avenue Baptist Church, near the State Capitol, to organize a long-planned boycott of the city's bus system, seventy-five percent of whose riders were black. Student and faculty volunteers from Alabama State University stayed up all night to distribute thirty-five thousand flyers denouncing the arrest of Rosa Parks and urging support for the boycott.

In the Dexter Avenue church's twenty-six-year-old pastor, **Martin Luther King Jr.**, the boycott movement found a brave and charismatic leader. Born in Atlanta, the grandson of a slave and the son of a prominent minister, King was intelligent and courageous. He also was a speaker of celestial eloquence and passion. "We must use the weapon of love," King told his supporters. "We must realize so many people are taught to hate us that they are not totally responsible for their hate." To his antagonists, the self-controlled King said, "We will soon wear you down by our capacity to suffer, and in winning our freedom we will so appeal to your heart and conscience that we will win you in the process."

Montgomery, Alabama

Martin Luther King Jr., here facing arrest for leading a civil rights march, advocated nonviolent resistance to racial segregation.

The Montgomery bus boycott achieved remarkable solidarity. For 381 days, African Americans, women and men, used car pools, black-owned taxis, hitchhiked, or simply walked. White supporters provided rides. A few boycotters rode horses or mules to work. Such an unprecedented mass protest infuriated many whites. Civic leaders staunchly opposed the boycott. Police harassed and ticketed black carpools, and white thugs attacked walkers. Ku Klux Klan members bombed houses owned by King and other boycott leaders; they also burned black churches. King was arrested twice. In trying to calm an angry crowd of blacks eager for revenge against their white tormentors, King urged restraint: "Don't get panicky. Don't get your weapons. We want to love our enemies."

On December 20, 1956, the Montgomery boycotters finally won a federal case they had initiated against racial segregation on public buses. The Supreme Court affirmed that "the separate but equal doctrine can no longer be safely followed as a correct statement of the law." The next day, King and other African Americans boarded the buses. The success of the staunchly pacifist bus boycott revealed that well-coordinated, nonviolent black activism could trigger major changes in public policy. The successful bus boycott led thousands of African Americans to replace resignation with hope; action supplanted passivity. The boycott also catapulted King into the national spotlight.

THE CIVIL RIGHTS ACTS OF 1957 AND 1960 President Eisenhower's timidity in the field of race relations appeared again when he was asked to protect the right of African Americans to vote. In 1956, hoping to exploit divisions between northern and southern Democrats and to reclaim some of the black vote for the Republicans, congressional leaders agreed to support what became the Civil Rights Act of 1957. The first civil rights law passed since 1875, it finally got through the Senate, after a year's delay, with the help of majority leader Lyndon B. Johnson, a Texas Democrat who won southern acceptance by watering down the proposed legislation. Eisenhower reassured Johnson that the final version represented "the mildest civil rights bill possible." The Civil Rights Act established the Civil Rights Commission and a new Civil Rights Division in the Justice Department intended to prevent interference with the right to vote. Yet by 1959 the Civil Rights Act had not added a single southern black to the voting rolls. Neither did the Civil Rights Act of 1960, which provided for federal courts to register African Americans to vote in districts where there was a "pattern and practice" of discrimination. This bill, too, lacked teeth and depended upon vigorous presidential enforcement to achieve any tangible results.

DESEGREGATION IN LITTLE ROCK A few weeks after the Civil Rights Act of 1957 was passed, Arkansas governor Orval Faubus called out the National Guard to prevent nine black students (six females and three males) from entering Little Rock's Central High School under a federal court order. The National Guard commander's orders were explicit: "No niggers in the building." A federal judge ordered Governor Faubus to withdraw the National Guard. When Elizabeth Eckford, a fifteen-year-old African American student, tried to enter the school, just a few blocks from the state capitol, jeering white students shrieked, "Lynch her! Lynch her!" Local authorities removed the students from the school in an effort to protect them from harm. The mayor frantically called the White House asking for federal troops to quell the violence. At that point, President Eisenhower reluctantly dispatched a thousand paratroopers to Little Rock to protect the black students as they entered the school. The soldiers stayed through the school year. Diehard southern segregationists lashed out at the president's actions. Senator Richard Russell of Georgia said the paratroopers were behaving like "Hitler's storm troops." Eisenhower was quick to explain that his use of federal troops had little to do with "the integration or segregation question" and everything to do with maintaining law and order. It was the first time since the 1870s that federal troops were sent to the South to protect the rights of African Americans. Martin Luther King, Jr., who had earlier criticized Eisenhower's tepid support of civil rights, now told the president that the "overwhelming majority of southerners, Negro and white, stand behind your resolute action to restore law and order in Little Rock."

In the summer of 1958, Govenor Faubus decided to close the Little Rock high schools rather than allow racial integration, and court proceedings dragged on into 1959 before the schools could be reopened. In that year, resistance to integration in Virginia collapsed when both state and federal courts struck down state laws that had cut off funds to integrated public schools. Thereafter, massive resistance to racial integration was confined mostly to the Deep South, where five states—from South Carolina west through Louisiana—still opposed even token integration. The demagogic Faubus went on to serve six terms as governor of Arkansas.

FOREIGN POLICY IN THE 1950s

The commitment of the Truman administration to "contain" communism was focused on the Soviet threat to western Europe. During the 1950s, the Eisenhower administration expanded America's objective from protecting a divided Europe to combating Communist tyranny around the globe. To the Eisenhower administration, merely "containing" communism was no longer enough: the explicit objective became a "policy of boldness" designed to "roll back" communism around the world. Unfortunately, the confrontational rhetoric about "rolling back" communism forced U.S. policy into an ever-widening global commitment to resist all Soviet initiatives, no matter how localized, in regions where the communists enjoyed geopolitical advantages. Privately, Eisenhower acknowledged that world communism was not a monolithic force always directed by the Soviets, but in public he talked tough, in part because of the expectations of right-wing Republicans whose support he needed. The result was often an incoherent diplomacy made up of bellicose rhetoric and cautious action. The Eisenhower administration discovered that the complexities of world affairs and the realities of Soviet and Communist Chinese power made the commitment to manage the destiny of the world unrealistic—and costly.

CONCLUDING AN ARMISTICE   To break the stalemate in the Korean peace talks, Eisenhower took the bold step in mid-May 1953 of intensifying the aerial bombardment of North Korea. Then the president let it be known that he would use nuclear weapons if a truce were not forthcoming. Whether for that reason or others, negotiations moved quickly toward an armistice agreement on July 26, 1953, affirming the established border between the two Koreas just above the 38th parallel. Other factors in bringing about the Korean armistice were China's rising military losses in the conflict and the spirit of uncertainty and caution felt by the Soviet Communists after the death of Joseph Stalin on March 5, 1953, six weeks after Eisenhower's inauguration.

DULLES AND MASSIVE RETALIATION   The architect of the Eisenhower administration's efforts to "roll back" communism was Secretary of State **John Foster Dulles**. Like Woodrow Wilson before him, Dulles was a minister's son, a pompous, self-righteous, confrontational, and humorless statesman, a man of immense energy and intelligence who believed that the United States was "born with a sense of destiny and mission" to lead the world. His British counterparts, however, were not impressed with Dulles's sermonizing speeches. They liked to say, "Dull, duller, Dulles."

The Democratic policy of "containing" communism was both "immoral" and passive, Dulles insisted. Americans should instead work toward the "liberation" of the "captive peoples" of Eastern Europe and China from atheistic communism. George F. Kennan, the leading Soviet analyst in the State Department, dismissed such rhetoric as lunacy, whereupon Dulles fired him. Eisenhower was quick to explain that the new "liberation" doctrine would not involve military force. He would promote the removal of Communist control "by every peaceful means, but only by peaceful means."

Dulles and Eisenhower knew that the United States could not win a ground war against the Soviet Union or Communist China, both of whose "Red" armies had millions more soldiers than did the United States. Nor could the administration afford—politically or financially—to sustain military expenditures at the levels required by the Korean War. So in an effort to get "more bang for the buck," as the secretary of defense bluntly admitted, Dulles and Eisenhower crafted a new diplomatic/military strategy that would enable them to reduce military spending. It came to be called "**massive retaliation**," using the threat of nuclear warfare ("massive retaliatory power") to prevent Communist aggression. As Dulles told an army general, why have an atomic bomb if you don't plan "to use it." The massive retaliation strategy, Eisenhower, Dulles, and the military chiefs argued, would provide a "maximum deterrent at bearable cost." Soon thereafter, the Department of Defense announced significant troop cuts coupled with increased expenditures on nuclear weapon delivery systems—long-range bombers and missiles.

"Don't Be Afraid—I Can Always Pull You Back."

Secretary of State John Foster Dulles pushes a reluctant America to the brink of war.

Dulles's pledge to liberate the nations of eastern Europe under Soviet control had unfortunate consequences—for the "captive peoples." In 1953, when East Germans rebelled against Soviet control, and in 1956, when Hungarians rose up against Soviet occupation troops, they painfully discovered that the United States would do nothing to assist them. Soviet troops and tanks crushed the brave but outgunned rebels.

The notion of "massive retaliation" also had ominous weaknesses. By the mid-1950s, both the United States and the Soviet Union had developed hydrogen bombs, which were 750 times as powerful as the two atomic bombs dropped on Japan in 1945. A single hydrogen bomb would have a devastating global ecological impact, yet war planners envisioned using hundreds of them. "The necessary art," Dulles explained, was "the ability to get to the verge without getting into war. . . . If you are scared to go to the brink, you are lost."

FOREIGN INTERVENTIONS

At the same time that Eisenhower and Dulles were promoting "liberation" and "massive retaliation" in their public statements, they were using covert operations orchestrated by the Central Intelligence Agency (CIA), created in 1947 and headed by Dulles's younger brother Allen Welsh Dulles, to influence the political dynamics of countries around the world.

THE CIA AND THE COLD WAR The anti-colonial movements unleashed by the Second World War placed the United States in the awkward position of watching independence movements around the globe rebel against British and French rule. In Iran in 1951, a newly elected prime minister, European-educated Mohammed Mossadegh, organized a nationalist movement that won overwhelming control of the Iranian parliament and then, in October 1952, severed all diplomatic relations with Great Britain. The British, concerned about the loss of their oil-related investments in a nation that then possessed the world's largest known oil reserves, asked the Eisenhower administration to help undermine the Mossadegh regime. The CIA then launched Operation Ajax, designed, in the words of Allen Dulles, to "bring about the fall of Mossadegh." The CIA bribed Iranian army officers and hired mercenaries to arrest Mossadegh, who was then convicted of high treason, imprisoned for three years, and then put under house arrest until his death in 1967. In return for access to Iranian oil, the American government thereafter provided massive support for the Shah of Iran's authoritarian regime, thereby creating a legacy of hatred among Iranians that would cause major problems later.

The success of the CIA-engineered coup in Iran emboldened Eisenhower to authorize other covert operations designed to undermine "unfriendly" government regimes in other parts of the world. In 1954 the target was Guatemala, a desperately poor Central American country led by Colonel Jacobo Arbenz Guzman, the former defense minister. Arbenz's decision to take over U.S.-owned property and industries in Guatemala convinced Secretary of

State John Foster Dulles that Guatemala was falling victim to "international communism." Dulles persuaded Eisenhower to approve a covert CIA operation to organize a ragtag Guatemalan army in Honduras. On June 18, 1954, aided by CIA-piloted warplanes, the 150 paid "liberators" crossed the border into Guatemala and forced Arbenz Guzman into exile in Mexico. The United States then installed a new ruler in Guatemala who created a police state and eliminated all political opposition.

The CIA operations in Iran and Guatemala revealed that the United States had become so enmeshed in cold war ideological warfare that it was secretly overthrowing elected governments around the world to ensure that they did not join the Soviet bloc. A classified report assessing the CIA's covert operations concluded in 1954 that "There are no rules" in the cold war. "Hitherto acceptable norms of human conduct do not apply." The illegal CIA operations in Iran and Guatemala succeeded in toppling rulers, but in doing so they destabilized the two countries, creating long-term problems in the Middle East and Central America.

INDOCHINA: THE BACKGROUND TO WAR It was during the Eisenhower administration that the United States became enmeshed in the complex geopolitics of Southeast Asia. Indochina, created by French imperialists in the nineteenth century out of the old kingdoms of Cambodia, Laos, and Vietnam, offered a distinctive case of anti-colonial nationalism. During the Second World War, after Japanese troops occupied the region, they continued to use French bureaucrats and opposed the Vietnamese nationalists. Chief among the nationalists were members of the Viet Minh (League for the Independence of Vietnam), the resistance movement which fell under the influence of Communists led by wispy **Ho Chi Minh**, a seasoned revolutionary and passionate nationalist. Mild-mannered and soft-spoken, Ho was obsessed by a single goal: independence for his country. At the end of the war against Japan, the Viet Minh controlled part of northern Vietnam, and, on September 2, 1945, Ho Chi Minh proclaimed a Democratic Republic of Vietnam, with its capital in Hanoi.

The French, like the Americans later, grossly underestimated the determination of Vietnamese nationalists to gain their independence. In 1946 the First Indochina War began when Ho's fifty thousand forces forcibly resisted French efforts to restore their colonial regime. French forces quickly regained control of the cities while the Viet Minh controlled the countryside. In 1949, having set up puppet rulers in Laos and Cambodia, the French reinstated former emperor Bao Dai as the head of quasi-independent Vietnam. The Viet Minh movement thereafter became more dependent upon Communist China and the Soviet Union for financial support and military supplies. In 1950, with the outbreak of fighting in Korea, the struggle in Vietnam became a major battleground in the cold war. When the Korean War ended, the United States continued its efforts to bolster French control of Vietnam. By the end of 1953, the Eisenhower administration was paying nearly 80 percent of the cost of the French military effort in Indochina, and the United States had found itself at the "brink" of military intervention. In December 1953, some twelve thousand French soldiers parachuted into **Dien Bien Phu**, a cluster of villages in a valley ringed by mountains in northern Vietnam near the Laotian border. The French plan, which Eisenhower deemed foolish, was to use the well-fortified base to lure Viet Minh guerrillas into the open and overwhelm them with superior fire-

Ho Chi Minh

A seasoned revolutionary, Ho Chi Minh cultivated a humble, proletarian image of himself as Uncle Ho, a man of the people.

power. But the plan backfired in March 1954 when the French found themselves surrounded by fifty thousand Viet Minh fighters equipped with Chinese Communist weapons.

As the weeks passed, the French government pleaded with the United States to launch an air strike to relieve the pressure on Dien Bien Phu, which a French journalist called "Hell in a very small place." The National Security Council—Dulles, Nixon, and the chairman of the Joint Chiefs of Staff—urged Eisenhower to use atomic bombs to aid the trapped French force. Eisenhower snapped back: "You boys must be crazy. We can't use those awful things against Asians for the second time in less than ten years. My God!" The president opposed U.S. intervention unless the British joined the effort. When they refused, Eisenhower told the French that U.S. military action in Vietnam was "politically impossible." As Eisenhower stressed, "No one could be more bitterly opposed to ever getting the U.S. involved in a hot war in that region than I am." On May 7, 1954, the Viet Minh fighters overwhelmed the last French resistance at Dien Bien Phu. The catastrophic defeat at Dien Bien Phu signaled the end of French colonial rule in Asia.

Dien Bien Phu

Captured French soldiers march through the battlefield after their surrender.

Six weeks later, a new French government promised to negotiate a complete withdrawal from Indochina after nearly a hundred years of interrupted colonial control. On July 20, representatives of France, Britain, the Soviet Union, the People's Republic of China, and the Viet Minh signed the Geneva Accords. The complex agreement gave Laos and Cambodia their independence and divided Vietnam in two at the 17th parallel. The accords gave the Viet Minh Communists control in the North; the French would remain South of the line until nationwide elections in 1956 would reunify all of Vietnam. American and South Vietnamese representatives refused to sign the Geneva Accords, arguing that the treaties legitimized the Communist victory.

In South Vietnam, power gravitated to a new premier imposed by the French at American urging: Ngo Dinh Diem, a Catholic nationalist who had opposed both the French and the Viet Minh. In 1954, Eisenhower offered to assist Diem "in developing and maintaining a strong, viable state, capable of resisting attempted subversion or aggression through military means." In return the United States expected Diem to enact democratic reforms and distribute land to peasants. American aid took the form of training the

South Vietnamese armed forces and police. Eisenhower remained opposed to the use of U.S. combat troops, believing that military intervention would bog down into a costly stalemate—as it eventually did.

Instead of instituting the promised political and economic reforms, however, the authoritarian Diem suppressed his political opponents, offering little or no land distribution and permitting widespread corruption. In 1956 he refused to join in the elections to reunify Vietnam. Diem's autocratic efforts to eliminate all opposition played into the hands of the communists, who found eager recruits among the discontented South Vietnamese. By 1957, guerrilla forces known as the **Viet Cong** were launching attacks on the Diem government, and in 1960 the resistance groups coalesced as the National Liberation Front. As guerrilla warfare intensified in South Vietnam, the Eisenhower administration viewed its only option was to "sink or swim with Diem."

By the mid-1950s, cold war ideology had led American officials to presume that the United States must thwart every act of Communist insurgency or aggression around the world. In 1954, Eisenhower used what he called the "falling domino" theory to explain why the United States needed to repulse Vietnamese communism: "You have a row of dominos set up, you knock over the first one, and what will happen to the last one is the certainty that it will go over very quickly." If South Vietnam were to succumb to Communist insurgency, he predicted, the rest of Southeast Asia would soon follow.

However, the domino analogy, used later by presidents Kennedy, Johnson, and Nixon, was too simplistic, because it assumed that communism was a monolithic global movement directed from Moscow that operated with the chain-reaction properties of chemical reactions. Yet anti-colonial insurgencies such as those in Southeast Asia might be animated by nationalist rather than ideological motives. The domino analogy also meant that the United States was coming to assume that it must police the world to ensure that the dominoes, no matter how small, did not begin falling. As a consequence, every worldwide insurgency mushroomed into strategic crises.

REELECTION AND FOREIGN CRISES

As Secretary of State John Foster Dulles tried to intimidate Communist governments by practicing nuclear brinkmanship, a new presidential campaign unfolded. Eisenhower retained widespread public support although the Democrats controlled Congress. Meanwhile, new crises in foreign and domestic affairs required him to take more decisive action than he initially deemed prudent in order to "wage peace."

A TURBULENT ELECTION YEAR In 1956 the Republicans eagerly renominated Eisenhower and Nixon. The party platform endorsed what Eisenhower called "modern Republicanism," meaning balanced budgets, reduced government intervention in the economy, and an internationalist rather than an isolationist foreign policy. The Republicans promised "peace, progress, and prosperity," crowing that "everything's booming but the guns." The Democrats turned again to Adlai Stevenson. During the last week of the campaign, fighting erupted along the Suez Canal in Egypt and in the streets of Budapest, Hungary. These two unrelated but simultaneous world events caused a profound international crisis.

REPRESSION IN HUNGARY During the 1950s, eastern Europeans tried to take advantage of changes in Soviet leadership to seek greater independence from Moscow. On October 23, 1956, Hungarian nationalists revolted against Communist troops in Budapest. The Soviets responded by sending two hundred thousand Soviet troops and four thousand tanks into Hungary. The Soviets killed some forty thousand Hungarian "freedom fighters" before installing a more compliant leader in Hungary. It was a tragic ending to an independence movement that pleaded for the United States to back up its promise of "liberation" with force.

THE SUEZ WAR The most fateful developments in the Middle East turned on the rise of the Egyptian army officer Gamal Abdel Nasser after the overthrow of King Farouk in 1952. Once in power, Nasser set out to become the acknowledged leader of the entire Arab world. To do so, he promised to destroy the new Israeli nation. Nasser, with Soviet support, sought control of the Suez Canal, the crucial international waterway in Egypt connecting the Mediterranean and Red Seas. The canal had opened in 1869 as a joint French-Egyptian venture, and from 1882 on, British troops posted along the canal protected the British Empire's maritime "lifeline" to India and other colonies. When Nasser's nationalist regime pressed for the withdrawal of British forces from the Canal Zone, Eisenhower and Dulles supported the demand; in 1954 an Anglo-Egyptian treaty provided for British withdrawal within twenty months.

In 1955, Nasser, adept at playing both sides in the cold war, announced a huge arms deal with the Soviet Union. The United States countered by offering to help Egypt finance a massive hydroelectric dam at Aswān on the

Nile River. In 1956, when Nasser increased trade with the Soviet bloc and recognized the People's Republic of China, Dulles abruptly cancelled the offer to fund the Aswān Dam. Unable to retaliate against the United States, Nasser seized control of the Suez Canal Company and denied access to Israeli-bound ships. The British and the French were furious. On October 29, 1956, Israeli, British, and French forces invaded Egypt. Nasser responded by sinking all of the forty international ships then in the Suez Canal. A few days later, Anglo-French commandos and paratroopers took control of the canal.

The attack on Egypt by Britain, France, and Israel almost destroyed the NATO alliance. Eisenhower saw the military action by the three American

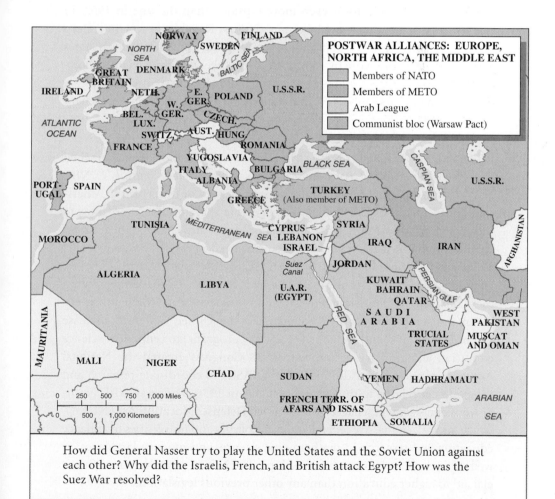

How did General Nasser try to play the United States and the Soviet Union against each other? Why did the Israelis, French, and British attack Egypt? How was the Suez War resolved?

allies as a revival of the "old-fashioned gunboat diplomacy" associated with colonial imperialism: "How could we possibly support Britain and France," he demanded, "if in doing so we lose the whole Arab world." Eisenhower adopted a bold stance. He demanded that the British and French forces withdraw from the Suez Canal and that the Israelis evacuate the Sinai Peninsula—or face severe economic sanctions. That the three aggressor nations grudgingly complied with a cease-fire agreement on November 7 testified to Eisenhower's strength, influence, and savvy.

The two international crises in the fall of 1956—the Hungarian revolt and the Suez War—led Adlai Stevenson to declare the administration's foreign policy "bankrupt." Most voters, however, reasoned that the foreign turmoil spelled a poor time to switch leaders, and they handed Eisenhower a landslide victory over Stevenson even more lopsided than the one in 1952. In carrying Louisiana, Eisenhower became the first Republican to win a Deep South state since Reconstruction; nationally, he carried all but seven states and won the electoral vote by 457 to 73. Eisenhower's decisive victory, however, failed to swing a congressional majority for his party in either house, the first time events had transpired that way since the election of Zachary Taylor in 1848.

REACTIONS TO SPUTNIK   On October 4, 1957, the Soviets launched the first earth-orbiting communications satellite, called *Sputnik 1*. NBC News reported that it was "the most important story of the century." Americans panicked at the news. The Soviet success in space dealt a severe blow to the prestige of American science and technology. It also changed the military balance of power. If the Soviets were so advanced in rocketry, many people reasoned, then perhaps they could hit U.S. cities with armed missiles. Democrats charged that the Soviet feat had "humiliated" the United States; they launched a congressional investigation to assess the new Soviet threat to the nation's security. "*Sputnik* mania" led the United States to increase defense spending and establish a crash program to enhance science education and military research. In 1958 Congress created the National Aeronautics and Space Administration (NASA) to coordinate research and development related to outer space. Finally, in 1958, Congress, with Eisenhower's endorsement, enacted the National Defense Education Act (NDEA), which authorized massive federal grants to colleges and universities to enhance education and research in mathematics, science, and modern languages, as well as for student loans and fellowships. The NDEA provided more financial aid to higher education than any other previous legislation.

FESTERING PROBLEMS ABROAD

THE EISENHOWER DOCTRINE   In the aftermath of the Suez Crisis, Eisenhower decided that the United States must replace Great Britain and France as the guarantor of Western interests in the Middle East. In 1958, Congress approved what came to be called the Eisenhower Doctrine, a resolution that promised to extend economic and military aid to Arab nations and to use armed force if necessary to assist any such nation against Communist aggression. When Lebanon's government appealed to the United States to help fend off an insurgency, Eisenhower ordered five thousand marines into Lebanon. In October 1958, once the situation had stabilized, U.S. forces (up to fifteen thousand at one point) withdrew.

CRISIS IN BERLIN   The unique problem of West Berlin, an island of Western capitalism deep in Soviet-controlled East Germany, boiled over in the late 1950s. After the Second World War, West Berlin served as a "show-place" of Western democracy and prosperity, a listening post for Western intelligence gathering, and a funnel through which news and propaganda from the West penetrated what British leader Winston Churchill had labeled the iron curtain. Although East Germany had sealed its western frontiers, refugees could still pass from East to West Berlin. On November 10, 1958, however, the unpredictable Khrushchev, who called West Berlin "a bone in his throat," threatened to give East Germany control of East Berlin and the air lanes into West Berlin. After the deadline he set, May 27, 1959, Western occupation authorities would have to deal with the Soviet-controlled East German government, in effect recognizing it, or face the possibility of another blockade. Eisenhower refused to budge from his position on Berlin but sought a settlement. There was little hope of resolving the conflicting views on Berlin and German reunification, but the negotiations distracted attention from Khrushchev's deadline of May 27: it passed almost unnoticed. In September 1959, Khrushchev and Eisenhower agreed that the time was ripe for a summit meeting.

Nikita Khrushchev

The Soviet premier speaks on the problem of Berlin, 1959.

THE U-2 SUMMIT   The planned summit meeting blew up in Eisenhower's face, however. On Sunday morning, May 1, 1960, he learned that a Soviet rocket had brought down a U.S. spy plane (called the U-2) flying at 70,000 feet some 1,200 miles inside the Soviet border. Khrushchev, embarrassed by the ability of American spy planes to traverse the Soviet Union, sprang a trap on Eisenhower. At first the Soviets announced only that the plane had been shot down. The U.S. government, not realizing that the Soviets had captured the downed pilot, issued a fabricated story that it was missing a weather plane over Turkey. Khrushchev then disclosed that the Soviets had veteran American pilot Francis Gary Powers "alive and kicking" and also had the photographs he had taken of Soviet military installations. On May 11, Eisenhower abandoned efforts to cover up the incident, acknowledging that "we will now just have to endure the storm." Rather than blame others, Eisenhower took personal responsibility for the aerial spying, explaining that such illegally obtained intelligence information was crucial to national security. At a testy summit meeting in Paris five days later, Khrushchev lambasted Eisenhower for forty-five minutes before walking out. The incident set back efforts between the two superpowers to reduce cold war tensions in Berlin and worldwide. Later, in 1962, Francis Gary Powers was exchanged for a captured Soviet spy.

CASTRO'S CUBA   Amid all of Eisenhower's crises in foreign affairs, the greatest embarrassment was **Fidel Castro**'s new Communist regime in Cuba, which came to power on January 1, 1959, after two years of guerrilla warfare against the U.S.-supported dictator. Castro readily embraced Soviet support, leading a CIA agent to predict that "We're going to take care of Castro just like we took care of Arbenz [in Guatemala]." The Soviets warned in response that any American intervention in Cuba would trigger a military response. One of Eisenhower's last acts as president, on January 3, 1961, was to suspend diplomatic relations with Castro's Cuba. The president also authorized the CIA to begin secretly training a force of Cuban refugees to oust Castro. But the final decision on the use of that anti-Castro invasion force would rest with the next president, John F. Kennedy.

ASSESSING THE EISENHOWER PRESIDENCY

During President Eisenhower's second term, Congress added Alaska and Hawaii as the forty-ninth and fiftieth states (1959), while the nation experienced in 1958 the worst economic slump since the Great Depression.

Volatile issues such as civil rights, defense policy, and corrupt aides, including White House Chief of Staff Sherman Adams, Eisenhower's most trusted and influential adviser, compounded the administration's troubles. The president's desire to avoid contentious issues and maintain the public goodwill at times led him to value harmony and public popularity over justice. By avoiding or postponing critical issues such as civil rights for all Americans, he unwittingly bequeathed even more explosive issues for his successors. One observer called the Eisenhower years "the time of the great postponement," during which the president left domestic and foreign policies "about where he found them in 1953."

Opinion of Eisenhower's presidency has improved with time, however. After all, the former general had ended the war in Korea, refused to intervene militarily in Indochina, and maintained the peace in the face of combustible global tensions. If Eisenhower failed to end the cold war and in fact institutionalized global confrontation, he also recognized the limits of America's power and applied it only to low-risk situations. For the most part, he acted with poise, restraint, and intelligence in managing an increasingly complex cold war that he predicted would last for decades. If Eisenhower took few initiatives in addressing social and racial problems, he did sustain the major reforms of the New Deal. If he tolerated unemployment of as much as 7 percent, he saw to it that inflation remained minimal during his two terms. Even Adlai Stevenson, defeated twice by Eisenhower, admitted that Ike's victory in 1952 had been good for the nation. Eisenhower presided over a nation content with a leader whose essential virtue was prudence.

Eisenhower's January 17, 1961, televised farewell address to the American people focused on a topic never before addressed by a public official: the threat posed to government integrity by "an immense military establishment and a large arms industry." As a much-celebrated former general, Eisenhower highlighted—better than anyone else could have—the dangers of a large "military-industrial complex" exerting "unwarranted influence" in the halls of Congress and the White House. "The potential for the disastrous rise of misplaced power exists and will persist," he warned. Eisenhower confessed that his greatest disappointment as he prepared to leave the White House was that he could affirm only that "war has been avoided," not that "a lasting peace is in sight." His successors were not as successful.

CHAPTER SUMMARY

- **Growth of U.S. Economy** High levels of government spending, begun before the war, continued during the postwar period. The GI Bill of Rights gave a boost to home buying and helped many veterans attend college and thereby enter the middle class. Unemployment was virtually nonexistent, and consumer demand for homes, cars, and household goods that had been unavailable during the war fueled the economy, as did buying on credit.

- **Conformity in American Society** After the Second World War, with the growth of suburbs, corporations, and advertising, society appeared highly uniform, yet pockets of poverty persisted, and minorities did not prosper to the extent that white Americans did. Although popular culture reflected the affluence of the white middle class, the art and literature of the period revealed an underlying alienation.

- **Eisenhower's Dynamic Conservatism** As president, Eisenhower expanded Social Security coverage and launched ambitious public works programs, such as the construction of the interstate highway system. He opposed large budget deficits, however, so he cut spending on an array of domestic programs and on national defense.

- **Civil Rights Movement** By the early 1950s, the NAACP was targeting state-mandated segregation in public schools. In the most significant case, *Brown v. Board of Education*, the Court nullified the "separate but equal" doctrine. Whereas white southerners defended their old way of life, rallying to a call for "Massive Resistance," proponents of desegregation sought to achieve integration through nonviolent means, as demonstrated in the Montgomery, Alabama, bus boycott and the desegregation of a public high school in Little Rock, Arkansas.

- **American Foreign Policy in the 1950s** Eisenhower continued the policy of containment to stem the spread of communism. His first major foreign-policy accomplishment in this respect was to end the fighting in Korea. To confront Soviet aggression, Eisenhower relied on nuclear deterrence, which allowed for reductions in conventional military forces and thus led to budgetary savings.

- **Communism in Southeast Asia** In Southeasts Asia, Eisenhower believed that the French should regain control of Indochina so it could slow the spread of communism. But by 1957, after the defeat of the French and the division of the country in half, the Eisenhower administration had no option but to "sink or swim with the government of Ngo Dinh Diem" and the South Vietnamese.

CHRONOLOGY

1944	Congress passes the Servicemen's Readjustment Act (GI Bill of Rights)
1952	Ralph Ellison's *Invisible Man* is published
June 1953	Ethel and Julius Rosenberg are executed
July 1953	Armistice is reached in Korea
1954	Supreme Court issues ruling in *Brown v. Board of Education of Topeka, Kansas*
July 1954	Geneva Accords adopted
December 1955	Montgomery, Alabama, bus boycott begins
1956	In Suez War, Israel, Britain, and France attack Egypt
1956	Hungarian revolt against the Warsaw Pact suppressed
1956	Allen Ginsberg's *Howl* is published
1957	Federal troops ordered to protect students attempting to integrate Central High School in Little Rock, Arkansas
1957	Soviet Union launches *Sputnik 1*
1957	Jack Kerouac's *On the Road* is published
1957	Baby boom peaks
1960	U-2 incident reveals that the United States is flying spy planes over the Soviet Union

KEY TERMS & NAMES

31

NEW FRONTIERS: POLITICS AND SOCIAL CHANGE IN THE 1960s

FOCUS QUESTIONS wwnorton.com/studyspace

- What were the goals of John F. Kennedy's New Frontier program, and how successful was it?
- What was the aim of Lyndon B. Johnson's Great Society program, and how successful was it?
- What were the achievements of the civil rights movement by 1968?
- Why did the United States become increasingly involved in Vietnam?
- Why and how did Kennedy attempt to combat communism in Cuba?

For those pundits who considered the social and political climate of the fifties dull, the following decade would provide a striking contrast. The sixties were years of extraordinary social turbulence and insurgent liberalism in public affairs—as well as sudden tragedy and prolonged trauma. Many social ills that had been festering for decades suddenly forced their way onto the national agenda. At the same time, the deeply entrenched assumptions of the cold war directed against communism led the nation into the longest, most controversial, and least successful war in its history.

THE NEW FRONTIER

KENNEDY VERSUS NIXON In 1960, there was little awareness of such dramatic change on the horizon. The presidential election of that year pitted against each other two candidates—Richard M. Nixon and

Kennedy-Nixon debates

John Kennedy's poise and precision in the debates with Richard Nixon impressed viewers and voters.

John F. Kennedy—with very different personalities and backgrounds. Although better known than Kennedy because of his eight years as Eisenhower's vice president, Nixon had developed the reputation of a cunning chameleon, the "Tricky Dick" who concealed his duplicity behind a series of masks. "Nixon doesn't know who he is," Kennedy told an aide, "and so each time he makes a speech he has to decide which Nixon he is, and that will be very exhausting."

But Nixon could not be so easily dismissed. He possessed a shrewd intelligence and a compulsive love for combative politics. In 1946, having completed law school and a wartime stint in the navy, Nixon jumped into the political arena as a Republican and won election to Congress. Four years later he became the junior senator from California. Nixon emerged as both a respected and an effective member of Congress, and by 1950 he was the most requested Republican speaker in the country. The reward for his rapid rise to political stardom was the vice-presidential nomination in 1952, which led to successive terms as the partner of the popular Eisenhower and ensured his nomination for president in 1960.

John F. Kennedy lacked Nixon's political experience but boasted an abundance of assets, including a record of heroism in the Second World War, a glamorous wife and two adorable children, a bright, agile mind and a

Harvard education, a rich, powerful Roman Catholic family, a handsome face, movie-star charisma, and a robust outlook. Yet the forty-three-year-old candidate had not distinguished himself in the House or the Senate. His political rise owed not so much to his abilities or his accomplishments as to the effective public relations campaign engineered by his ambitious father, Joseph Kennedy, a self-made tycoon.

In his speech accepting the Democratic nomination for the presidency, the youthful Kennedy featured the stirring, muscular rhetoric that would stamp the rest of his campaign and his presidency: "We stand today on the edge of a **New Frontier**—the frontier of unknown opportunities and perils—a frontier of unfulfilled hopes and threats." Kennedy and his staff fastened upon the frontier metaphor as the label for their domestic program because Americans had always been adventurers, eager to conquer and exploit new frontiers. Kennedy promised to use his administration to get the country "moving again."

Three events shaped the presidential campaign that fall. First, as the only Catholic to run for the presidency since Alfred E. Smith in 1928, Kennedy strove to dispel the impression that his religion was a major political liability, especially among southern Protestants. In a speech before the Greater Houston Ministerial Association in 1960, he stressed that "the separation of church and state is absolute" and that the pope would never "tell the President—should he be a Catholic—how to act and no Protestant minister should tell his parishioners for whom to vote." The religious question thereafter drew little public attention; Kennedy's candor had neutralized it.

Second, the 1960 election elevated the role of images over substance. During the first-ever televised debate, some 70 million people saw an obviously uncomfortable Nixon, still weak from a recent illness, perspiring heavily and looking haggard, uneasy, and even sinister before the camera. Kennedy, on the other hand, appeared tanned and calm, projected a cool poise and offered crisp answers that made him seem equal, if not superior, in his fitness for the nation's highest office. Kennedy's popularity immediately shot up in the polls. In the words of a bemused southern senator, Kennedy combined "the best qualities of Elvis Presley and Franklin D. Roosevelt."

When the votes were counted, Kennedy and his running mate, Lyndon B. Johnson of Texas, had won the closest presidential election since 1888. The winning margin was only 118,574 votes out of more than 68 million cast. Kennedy's wide lead in the electoral vote, 303 to 219, belied the close vote in several key states. Nixon had in fact carried more states than Kennedy, sweeping most of the West and holding four of the six southern states that Eisenhower had carried in 1956.

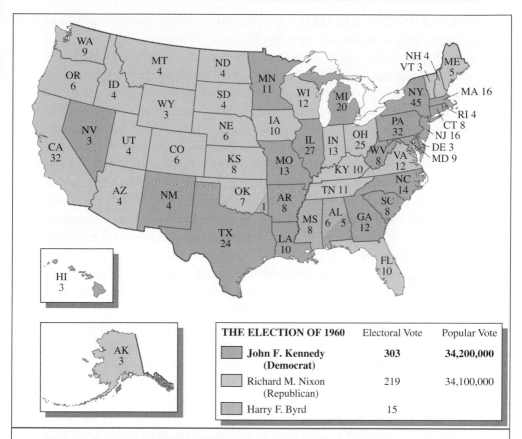

THE ELECTION OF 1960	Electoral Vote	Popular Vote
John F. Kennedy (Democrat)	303	34,200,000
Richard M. Nixon (Republican)	219	34,100,000
Harry F. Byrd	15	

How did the election of 1960 represent a sea change in American presidential politics? What three events shaped the campaign? How did John F. Kennedy win the election in spite of winning fewer states than Richard M. Nixon?

A VIGOROUS NEW ADMINISTRATION John F. Kennedy was the youngest person ever elected president, and his inaugural ceremonies set the tone of elegance and youthful vigor that would come to be called the Kennedy style. President Kennedy dazzled listeners with uplifting rhetoric provided by talented speechwriters. "Let the word go forth from this time and place," he proclaimed. "Let every nation know, whether it wishes us well or ill, that we shall pay any price, bear any burden, meet any hardship, support any friend, oppose any foe, to assure the survival and success of liberty. And so, my fellow Americans: ask not what your country can do for you—ask what you can do for your country." Spines tingled at the time; the glittering atmosphere and inspiring language of the inauguration seemed to herald an era of fresh promise and youthful energy.

THE KENNEDY RECORD Despite his idealistic rhetoric, Kennedy called himself a realist or "an idealist without illusions," and he had a difficult time launching his New Frontier domestic program. Elected by a razor-thin margin, he did not enjoy a popular mandate. The new president preferred dealing with foreign policy rather than domestic issues. He struggled to shepherd legislation through a Congress controlled by conservative southern Democrats, who blocked his efforts to increase federal aid to education, provide health insurance for the aged, and create a department of urban affairs. When Kennedy finally followed the advice of his advisers in 1963 and submitted a drastic tax cut, Congress blocked that as well. During 1962 Kennedy admitted that his first year had been a "disaster": the social, political, and international "problems are more difficult than I imagined them to be. . . . It is much easier to make the speeches than it is to finally make the judgments."

Administration proposals did nevertheless win some notable victories in Congress. Legislators readily approved broad Alliance for Progress programs to help Latin America and they endorsed the celebrated Peace Corps, created in 1961 to supply volunteers who would provide educational and technical services abroad. Kennedy's greatest legislative accomplishment, however, may have been the Trade Expansion Act of 1962, which eventually led to tariff cuts averaging 35 percent on goods traded between the United States and the European Economic Community (the Common Market).

In the field of domestic social legislation, the Kennedy administration persuaded Congress to pass a Housing Act that earmarked nearly $5 billion for urban renewal over four years; an increase in the minimum wage and its application to more than 3 million additional workers; the Area Redevelopment Act of 1961, which provided nearly $400 million in loans and grants to "distressed areas"; an increase in Social Security benefits; and additional funds for sewage-treatment plants. Kennedy also won support for an accelerated outer-space exploration program with the goal of landing astronauts on the moon before the end of the decade.

THE WARREN COURT Under Chief Justice Earl Warren the Supreme Court continued to be a decisive influence on domestic life during the sixties. In 1962 the Court ruled that a school prayer adopted by the New York State Board of Regents violated the constitutional prohibition against an established religion. In *Gideon v. Wainwright* (1963), the Court required that every felony defendant be provided a lawyer regardless of the defendant's ability to pay. In 1964 the Court ruled in *Escobedo v. Illinois* that a person accused of a crime must also be allowed to consult a lawyer before being interrogated by police. Two years later, in **Miranda v. Arizona,** the Court issued its most bitterly criticized ruling when it ordered that an accused person in police custody be informed of certain basic rights: the right to remain silent; the right to know that anything said can be used against the individual in court; and the right to have a defense attorney present during interrogation. In addition, the Court established rules for police to follow in informing suspects of their legal rights before questioning could begin.

EXPANSION OF THE CIVIL RIGHTS MOVEMENT

The most important development in domestic life during the sixties occurred in civil rights. John F. Kennedy entered the White House reluctant to challenge conservative southern Democrats on the race issue. While committed to racial equality in theory, he balked at making civil rights a priority of his presidency because it was such an explosive issue, especially in the South. Neither he nor his brother Robert ("Bobby"), the president's closest adviser, embraced civil rights as a compelling cause that transcended political considerations. Both had to be dragged unwillingly into active support for the civil rights movement. Despite a few dramatic gestures of support toward African American leaders, President Kennedy only belatedly grasped the moral and emotional significance of the most widespread reform movement of the decade. Like Franklin D. Roosevelt, he celebrated racial equality but did little to promote it. For the most part, he viewed the grassroots civil rights movement led by Martin Luther King Jr. as an irritant.

SIT-INS AND FREEDOM RIDES After the Montgomery bus boycott of 1955–1956, King's philosophy of "militant nonviolence" inspired others to challenge the deeply entrenched patterns of racial segregation in the South. At the same time, lawsuits to desegregate the public schools got thousands of parents and young people involved. The momentum generated the first genuine mass movement in African American history when four well-dressed, polite black students enrolled at North Carolina A&T College sat down and ordered coffee and doughnuts at Woolworth's lunch counter in Greensboro, North Carolina, on February 1, 1960. The clerk refused to serve them because only whites could sit at the counter; blacks had to eat standing up or take their food outside. The Greensboro Four, waited for forty-five minutes and then returned the next day with two dozen more students. They returned every day thereafter for a week, patiently tolerating being jeered, cuffed, and spat upon by hooligans. By then hundreds of rival protesters rallied outside. Meanwhile, the "sit-in" movement had spread to six more towns in the state, and within two months similar sit-in demonstrations—involving blacks and whites, men and women, young and old—had occurred in fifty-four cities in thirteen states. By the end of July, 1960, officials in Greensboro lifted the whites-only policy at the Woolworth's lunch counter. And the civil rights movement had found a new voice among courageous young activists and an effective new tactic: nonviolent direct action against segregation.

A few weeks later, in April 1960, some two hundred student activists, black and white, converged in Raleigh, North Carolina, to form the Student Nonviolent Coordinating Committee (SNCC). Their goal was to ratchet up the effort to dismantle segregation. The sit-ins, which began at restaurants, broadened to include "kneel-ins" at all-white churches and "wade-ins" at segregated public swimming pools. Most of the activists practiced King's concept of nonviolent interracial protest. They refused to retaliate, even when struck with clubs, poked with cattle prods, or subjected to vicious verbal abuse. During the year after the Greensboro sit-ins, over 3,600 black and white activists spent time in jail. In many communities they were pelted with rocks, burned with cigarettes, and subjected to unending verbal abuse.

In 1961 leaders of the civil rights movement adopted a powerful new tactic directed at segregation in public transportation: buses and trains. Their larger goal was to force the Kennedy administration to engage the cause of civil rights in the Democratic South. On May 4, the New York–based Congress of Racial Equality (CORE), led by James Farmer, sent a courageous group of eighteen black and white **freedom riders**, as they were called, including three women, on two buses from Washington, D.C., through the Deep South. They wanted to test a federal court ruling that had banned segregation on buses and trains and in terminals. Farmer warned Attorney General Robert F. Kennedy of the strong possibility that the bus riders would encounter violence as they headed south.

The warning was needed, for on May 14, a mob of white racists in rural Alabama surrounded the Greyhound bus carrying white and black "freedom riders." After throwing a firebomb into the bus, angry whites barricaded the bus's door. "Burn them alive," one of them yelled. "Fry the damned niggers." After the gas tank exploded, the riders were able to escape the burning bus, only to be attacked with fists, pipes, and bats. A few hours later, freedom riders on other buses, many of them SNCC members, were beaten after they entered whites-only waiting rooms at bus terminals in Birmingham, and were firebombed in Anniston, Alabama.

President Kennedy and his brother Bobby were not inspired by the courageous freedom riders. They viewed the civil rights bus rides as unnecessarily provocative publicity stunts. The Kennedy brothers were "fed up with the Freedom Riders." Preoccupied with a crisis in Berlin, they ordered an aide to tell the civil rights leaders to "call it off." The freedom riders, whom the Kennedys dismissed as "publicity seekers" and whom white critics disparaged as "outside agitators," were in fact the vanguard of a civil rights movement determined to win

Freedom Riders

Two activists are escorted by armed National Guardsmen on a bus to Jackson, Mississippi.

over the hearts and minds of the American public. Finally, under pressure from Bobby Kennedy, the federal Interstate Commerce Commission (ICC) ordered in September 1961 that all whites-only waiting areas in interstate transportation facilities be integrated. The freedom rides had worked. Widespread media coverage showed the nation that the nonviolent protesters were prepared to die for their rights rather than continue to submit to the assault on their dignity.

FEDERAL INTERVENTION The Freedom Rides were a turning point in the civil rights movement. They revealed that African Americans— especially young African Americans—were tired of waiting for the segregationist South to abide by federal laws and to align with American values. With each passing month, more southern blacks were willing to confront the deeply embedded racist political and social structure. In 1962, **James Meredith,**

an African American student whose grandfather had been a slave, tried to enroll at the all-white University of Mississippi in Oxford. Ross Barnett, the governor of Mississippi, who believed that God made "the Negro different to punish him," ignored a court order by refusing to allow Meredith to register for classes. Attorney General Robert F. Kennedy then dispatched federal marshals to enforce the law. When the marshals were assaulted by a white mob, federal troops (all white) intervened. The presence of soldiers ignited a night of rioting that left two deaths and dozens of injuries. But once the violence subsided, James Meredith was registered at Ole Miss a few days later.

In 1963, Martin Luther King Jr. defied the wishes of the Kennedy brothers by launching a series of demonstrations in Birmingham, Alabama, a state presided over by a governor—George Wallace—whose inauguration vow had been a pledge of "segregation now, segregation tomorrow, segregation forever!" King knew that a peaceful demonstration in Birmingham would likely provoke violence, but victory there would "break the back of segregation all over the nation." As King and other activists demonstrated against

Birmingham, Alabama, May 1963

Eugene "Bull" Connor's police unleash dogs on civil rights demonstrators.

the city's continuing segregationist practices, the all-white police used dogs, tear gas, electric cattle prods, and fire hoses on the protesters while millions of outraged Americans watched the confrontations on television.

King was arrested and jailed. While incarcerated, he wrote his now-famous "Letter from Birmingham City Jail," a stirring defense of the nonviolent strategy that became a classic document of the civil rights movement. "One who breaks an unjust law," he stressed, "must do so openly, lovingly, and with a willingness to accept the penalty." In his letter, King signaled a shift in his strategy for social change. Heretofore he had emphasized the need to educate southern whites about the injustice of segregation and other patterns of discrimination. Now he focused more on gaining federal enforcement of the law by provoking racists to display their violent hatred in public.

King's actions and sacrifices prevailed when Birmingham officials finally agreed to end their segregationist practices. The sublime courage that King and many other grassroots protesters displayed helped mobilize national support for their integrationist objectives. (In 1964, King would be awarded the Nobel Peace Prize.) Nudged by his brother Robert, President Kennedy finally decided that enforcement of existing statutes was not enough; new legislation was needed to deal with the race question. In 1963, he told the nation that racial discrimination "has no place in American life or law." He then endorsed an ambitious federal civil rights bill intended to end discrimination in public facilities, desegregate public schools, and protect African American voters. But southern Democrats quickly blocked the bill in Congress.

Throughout the Deep South, white traditionalists defied efforts at racial integration. In the fall of 1963, Alabama governor George Wallace dramatically stood in the doorway of a building at the University of Alabama to block the enrollment of African American students, but he stepped aside in the face of insistent federal marshals. That night, an African American civil rights activist, Medgar Evers, was shot to death as he returned to his home in Jackson, Mississippi. Civil rights had become the nation's most acute social issue.

The high point of the integrationist phase of the civil rights movement occurred on August 28, 1963, when over two hundred thousand blacks and whites marched down the Mall in Washington, D.C., toward the Lincoln Memorial, singing "We Shall Overcome." The **March on Washington** for Jobs and Freedom was the largest civil rights demonstration in history. Standing in front of Lincoln's famous statue, Martin Luther King Jr. delivered one of the century's most memorable speeches:

I say to you today, my friends, that in spite of the difficulties and frustrations of the moment I still have a dream. It is a dream deeply rooted in the American dream.

I have a dream that one day this nation will rise up and live out the true meaning of its creed: "We hold these truths to be self-evident; that all men are created equal."

I have a dream that one day . . . the sons of former slaves and the sons of former slaveowners will be able to sit together at the table of brotherhood.

Such racial harmony had not yet arrived, however. Two weeks later a bomb exploded in a Birmingham church, killing four black girls. Yet King's dream—shared and promoted by thousands of other activists—survived. The intransigence and violence that civil rights workers encountered won converts to their cause all across the country. Moreover, corporate and civic leaders in large southern cities promoted civil rights advances in large part because the continuing protests threatened economic development. Atlanta, for example, described itself as "the city too busy to hate."

"I Have a Dream," August 28, 1963

Protesters in the March on Washington make their way to the Lincoln Memorial, where Martin Luther King Jr. delivered his now-famous speech.

FOREIGN FRONTIERS

At the same time that the Kennedy administration was becoming increasingly embroiled in the civil rights movement, it was also wrestling with significant international issues. Kennedy had assumed the presidency at the peak of the cold war, and he was determined to take the offensive against Soviet communism by accelerating the arms race. He and his aides believed that Dwight D. Eisenhower had not been aggressive enough with the Soviets. Where Eisenhower had been cautious and conciliatory, Kennedy was determined to be bold and confrontational.

EARLY SETBACKS John F. Kennedy's record in foreign relations, like that in domestic affairs, was mixed, but more spectacularly so. As a senator, he had blasted Eisenhower for allowing Fidel Castro and his communist supporters to take over Cuba. Upon taking office, Kennedy learned that a secret CIA operation approved by President Eisenhower was training 1,500 anti-Castro Cubans in Guatemala for an invasion of their homeland at the same time that the CIA was working with Mafia crime bosses in the United States to arrange for the assassination of Castro. Based on their assumption that the president would authorize the use of U.S. military forces if the Cuban exiles ran into trouble, the Joint Chiefs of Staff assured the inexperienced Kennedy that the invasion plan (Operation Trinidad) was theoretically feasible; CIA analysts predicted that the invasion would inspire Cubans to rebel against Castro and his Communist regime.

In reality, the covert operation had little chance of succeeding. Secretary of State Dean Rusk urged the president to cancel the operation, but Kennedy willfully ignored such advice and approved the ill-fated invasion. When the ragtag force, transported on American ships, landed at the Bay of Pigs on the southern shore of Cuba on April 17, 1961, it was brutally subdued in two days; more than 1,100 men were captured. Kennedy called the bungled Bay of Pigs invasion a "colossal mistake." It was, he added, "the worst experience of my life. How could I have been so stupid?"

Two months after the Bay of Pigs debacle, Kennedy met Soviet premier Nikita Khrushchev at a summit conference in Vienna, Austria. Khrushchev had decided after the Bay of Pigs disaster that young Kennedy was incompetent and could be intimidated, so he bullied and browbeat Kennedy and threatened to limit American access to Berlin, the divided city located one hundred miles within Communist East Germany. Kennedy was stunned by the Soviet leader's verbal assault; he told a journalist that Khrushchev "just beat the hell out of me."

Kennedy had long had an abiding fear of appearing weak, so upon returning home, he demonstrated his resolve to protect West Berlin by calling up Army Reserve and National Guard units. The Soviets responded on August 13, 1961, by erecting what would become the twenty-seven-mile-long Berlin Wall, which was made of concrete and topped with barbed wire. The wall isolated U.S.-supported West Berlin and prevented all movement between the two parts of the city. Never before had a wall been built around a city to keep people from leaving. The Berlin Wall demonstrated the Soviets' willingness to challenge American resolve in Europe, and it became another intractable barrier to improved relations between East and West. Kennedy and Secretary of Defense McNamara thereupon embarked upon the most intense arms race in world history, increasing the number of nuclear missiles fivefold, growing the armed forces by three hundred thousand men, and creating the U.S. Special Forces (Green Berets), an elite group of commandos specializing in guerrilla warfare.

THE CUBAN MISSILE CRISIS A year later, in the fall of 1962, Khrushchev and the Soviets posed another challenge, this time only ninety miles off the coast of Florida. Khrushchev had interpreted Kennedy's unwillingness to commit the forces necessary to overthrow Fidel Castro at the Bay of Pigs as a failure of will. So the Soviet leader decided to install missiles with nuclear warheads in Cuba, assuming that Kennedy would not act if the Americans discovered what was going on. Khrushchev wanted to protect Cuba from another American-backed invasion, which Castro believed to be imminent, and to redress the strategic imbalance caused by the presence of U.S. missiles in Turkey aimed at the Soviet Union. Khrushchev relished the idea of throwing "a hedgehog at Uncle Sam's pants."

On October 14, 1962, U.S. intelligence analysts discovered evidence in photos taken by U-2 spy planes that Soviet missile sites were being constructed in Cuba. A furious Kennedy decided that the forty or so missiles had to be removed, even though the Soviet actions violated no law or treaty; the only question was how. As the air force chief of staff told Kennedy, "You're in a pretty bad fix, Mr. President." In a grueling series of secret meetings, the Executive Committee of the National Security Council narrowed the options to a choice between a "surgical" air strike and a naval blockade of Cuba. President Kennedy wisely opted for a blockade, which was carefully disguised by the euphemism *quarantine,* since a blockade was technically an act of war. A blockade offered the advantage of forcing the Soviets to shoot first, if matters came to that, and left open the options of stronger action. Thus, Monday, October 22, began one of the most perilous weeks in world history. That evening the president delivered a speech of extraordinary gravity to the American people, revealing that the Soviets were constructing missile sites in Cuba and that the U.S. Navy was establishing a quarantine of the island nation. He urged the Soviets to "move the world back from the abyss of destruction." The United States and the Soviet Union now headed toward their closest encounter with nuclear war.

Tensions grew as Khrushchev announced that Soviet ships would ignore the quarantine. But on Wednesday, October 24, five Soviet ships, presumably with more missiles aboard, stopped short of the quarantine line. Two days later the Soviets offered to withdraw the missiles in return for a public pledge by the United States not to invade Cuba. Secretary of State Dean Rusk replied that the administration was interested in such a solution but stressed to a newscaster, "Remember, when you report this, [to say] that eyeball to eyeball, they [the Soviets] blinked first."

On Sunday, October 28, Khrushchev agreed to remove the Soviet missiles from Cuba In the aftermath of the crisis, tensions between the United States and the Soviet Union subsided, relaxed in part by several symbolic steps: an agreement to sell the Soviet Union surplus American wheat, the installation of a "hot-line" telephone between Washington and Moscow to provide instant contact between the heads of government, and the removal of obsolete American missiles from Turkey, Italy, and Britain. On June 10, 1963, President Kennedy revealed that direct discussions with the Soviets would soon begin, and he called upon Americans to reexamine their attitudes toward peace, the Soviet Union, and the cold war. Those discussions resulted in a treaty with the Soviet Union and Britain to end nuclear weapons tests in the atmosphere, oceans, and outer space. The treaty, ratified in September 1963, was an important symbolic and substantive move toward détente (warmer relations). As Kennedy put it, "A journey of a thousand miles begins with one step."

KENNEDY AND VIETNAM   As tensions with the Soviet Union eased, a crisis was growing in Southeast Asia. Events there were moving toward what would become the greatest American foreign-policy calamity of the century. The situation in South Vietnam had worsened under the leadership of Premier Ngo Dinh Diem. He reneged on promised social and economic reforms. His repressive tactics, directed not only against Communists but also against the Buddhist majority and other critics, played into the hands of his enemies. Kennedy continued to dispatch more military "advisers" in the hope of stabilizing the situation: when he took office, there had been two thousand U.S. troops in Vietnam; by the end of 1963, there were sixteen thousand, all of whom were classified as advisers.

By 1963, Kennedy was receiving sharply divergent reports from South Vietnam. U.S. military analysts expressed confidence in the Army of the Republic of Vietnam. On-site journalists, however, predicted civil turmoil as long as Diem remained in power. By midyear, growing Buddhist demonstrations against Diem ignited widespread discontent. The spectacle of Buddhist monks setting themselves on fire in protest against government tyranny stunned Americans. By the fall of 1963, the Kennedy administration had decided that the autocratic Diem had to go. On November 1 dissident generals seized the South Vietnamese government and murdered Diem. But the rebel generals provided no more political stability than had earlier regimes, and successive coups set the fragile country spinning from one military leader to another.

KENNEDY'S ASSASSINATION   By the fall of 1963, President Kennedy had grown perplexed by the instability in Vietnam. In September he declared of the South Vietnamese: "In the final analysis it's their war. They're the ones who have to win it or lose it. We can help them as advisers but they have to win it." The following month he announced the administration's intention to withdraw U.S. forces from South Vietnam by the end of 1965. What Kennedy would have done thereafter has remained a matter of endless controversy, endless because it is unanswerable, and unanswerable because on November 22, 1963, while riding in an open car through Dallas, Texas Kennedy was shot in the neck and head by Lee Harvey Oswald. A twenty-four-year-old ex-marine drifter, Oswald worked in the Texas School Book Depository, from which the shots were fired at Kennedy.

Oswald's motives remain unknown. Although a federal commission appointed by President Lyndon B. Johnson and headed by Chief Justice Earl Warren concluded that Oswald acted alone, debate still swirls around various conspiracy theories. Two days after the assassination, Jack Ruby, a Dallas nightclub owner dying of cancer, shot and killed Oswald as he was being transported to a court hearing in handcuffs. Kennedy's assassination enshrined the young president in the public imagination as a martyred leader cut down in the prime of his life. His short-lived but drama-filled presidency had flamed up and out like a comet hitting the earth's atmosphere.

LYNDON B. JOHNSON AND THE GREAT SOCIETY

Texan **Lyndon B. Johnson** took the presidential oath of office on board the plane that brought John F. Kennedy's body back to Washington from Dallas. Fifty-five years old, he had spent twenty-six years on the Washington

Presidential assassination

John F. Kennedy's vice president, Lyndon B. Johnson, takes the presidential oath aboard Air Force One before its return from Dallas with Jacqueline Kennedy (right), the presidential party, and the body of the assassinated president.

scene and had served nearly a decade as Democratic leader in the Senate, where he had displayed the greatest gift for compromise since Henry Clay.

Johnson brought to the White House a marked change of style from Kennedy. A self-made, self-centered man who had worked his way out of a hardscrabble rural Texas environment to become one of Washington's most powerful figures, Johnson had none of the Kennedy elegance. He was a bundle of conflicting elements: earthy, idealistic, domineering, insecure, gregarious, suspicious, affectionate, manipulative, ruthless, and compassionate. Johnson's ego was as huge as his ambition; he insisted on being the center of attention wherever he went. Like another southern president, Andrew Johnson, he harbored a sense of being the perpetual outsider despite his long experience with legislative power. And indeed he was so regarded by Kennedy insiders. He, in turn, "detested" the way Kennedy and his aides had ignored him as vice president.

Those who viewed Johnson as a stereotypical southern conservative failed to appreciate his long-standing admiration for Franklin D. Roosevelt, the depth of his concern for the poor, and his commitment to the cause of civil rights. "I'm going to be the best friend the Negro ever had," he told a member of the White House staff. In foreign affairs, however, he was, like Woodrow Wilson, a novice. Johnson wanted to be the greatest American president, the one who did the most good for the most people. And he would let nothing stand in his way. In the end, however, the grandiose Johnson promised far more than he could accomplish, raising false hopes and stoking fiery resentments.

POLITICS AND POVERTY Johnson was a chain smoker addicted to hard work. Impatient and demanding, he required his staff to work day and night. He even conducted business with aides or visitors while using the bathroom. Unlike Kennedy, domestic policy was Johnson's first priority. Amid the national grief after the assassination, he knew that he would never again have such popular support. He needed to act quickly to take advantage of the honeymoon period provided by the assassination. The logjam in Congress that had blocked Kennedy's legislative efforts broke under Johnson's forceful leadership, and a torrent of legislation poured through.

Johnson put at the top of his agenda Kennedy's stalled measures for tax reductions and civil rights. In 1962, Kennedy had announced a then-unusual plan to jump-start the sluggish economy: a tax cut to stimulate consumer spending. Congressional Republicans opposed the idea because it would increase the federal budget deficit, and polls showed that public opinion was also skeptical. So Kennedy had postponed the proposed tax cut for a year. It was still bogged down in Congress when the president was assassinated, but Johnson was able to break the logjam. The Revenue Act of 1964 did provide a needed boost to the economy.

Likewise, the Civil Rights Act that Kennedy had presented to Congress in 1963 became law in 1964 through Johnson's aggressive leadership and legislative savvy. It outlawed racial segregation in public facilities such as bus terminals, restaurants, theaters, and hotels. It also gave new powers to the federal government to bring lawsuits against organizations or businesses that violated constitutional rights, and it established the Equal Employment Opportunities Commission to ensure equal opportunities for people applying for jobs, regardless of race or gender. The civil rights bill passed the House in February 1964. In the Senate, however, southern legislators launched a filibuster that lasted two months. Johnson finally prevailed, and the bill became law on July 2. But the new president knew that it had come at a political price. On the night after signing the bill, Johnson told an aide that "we have just delivered the South to the Republican Party for a long time to come."

In addition to fulfilling Kennedy's major promises, Johnson launched an ambitious legislative program of his own. In his 1964 State of the Union address, he added to his must-do list a bold new idea that bore the Johnson brand as he declared "unconditional war on poverty in America."

The Civil Rights Act of 1964

President Johnson reaches to shake hands with Dr. Martin Luther King Jr. after presenting the civil rights leader with one of the pens used to sign the Civil Rights Act of 1964.

The particulars of this "war on poverty" were to come later, the product of a task force that was at work before Johnson took office.

Americans had "rediscovered" poverty in 1962 when the social critic Michael Harrington published a powerful exposé titled *The Other America*. Harrington argued that more than 40 million people were mired in an invisible "culture of poverty" with a standard of livng and a way of life quite different from the American Dream. In such a culture of poverty, being poor was not simply a matter of low income; rather, prolonged poverty created a subculture whose residents were unlikely to escape from it. Poverty led to poor housing conditions, which in turn led to poor health, poor attendance at school or work, alcohol and drug abuse, unwanted pregnancies, single-parent families, and so on. Unlike the upwardly mobile immigrant poor at the beginning of the century, the modern poor lacked hope. Harrington added that poverty was much more extensive and more tenacious in the United States than people realized because much of it was hidden from view: in isolated rural areas or inner-city slums often unseen by more prosperous Americans. He urged the United States to launch a "comprehensive assault on poverty."

President Kennedy had read Harrington's book and had asked his advisers in the fall of 1963, just before his assassination, to investigate the poverty problem and suggest solutions. Upon taking office as president, President Johnson announced that he wanted an anti-poverty package that was "big and bold, that would hit the nation with real impact." Money for the program would come from the tax revenues generated by corporate profits made possible by the tax reduction of 1964, which had led to one of the longest sustained economic booms in history.

The Johnson administration's war on poverty was embodied in an economic-opportunity bill passed in August 1964 that incorporated a wide range of programs designed to help the poor help themselves by providing a "hand up, not a hand out": a Job Corps for inner-city youths aged sixteen to twenty-one, a Head Start program for disadvantaged preschoolers, work-study programs for college students, grants to farmers and rural businesses, loans to employers willing to hire the chronically unemployed, the Volunteers in Service to America (a domestic Peace Corps), and the Community Action Program, which would allow the poor "maximum feasible participation" in directing neighborhood programs designed for their benefit. Speaking at Ann Arbor, Michigan, in 1964, Johnson called for a "Great Society" resting on "abundance and liberty for all. The Great Society demands an end to poverty and racial injustice, to which we are fully committed in our time."

THE ELECTION OF 1964 Johnson's well-intentioned but hastily conceived "war on poverty" and Great Society social programs provoked a Republican counterattack. Arizona senator Barry Goldwater, a millionaire department-store magnate, emerged as the straight-talking leader of the Republican right. In his book *The Conscience of a Conservative* (1960), Goldwater proposed the abolition of the income tax and a drastic reduction in federal entitlement programs.. Almost from the time of Kennedy's victory in 1960, a movement to draft Goldwater had begun, mobilizing right-wing activists to capture party caucuses and contest primaries. In 1964 they swept the all-important California primary, thereby enabling them to control the Republican Convention when it gathered in San Francisco. "I would remind you," Goldwater told the delegates, "that extremism in the defense of liberty is no vice." He later explained that his objective was "to reduce the size of government. Not to pass laws but repeal them."

Barry Goldwater later claimed in his memoirs that he had no chance to win the presidency: "I just wanted the conservatives to have a real voice in the country." His campaign certainly confirmed that prediction, for candidate Goldwater displayed a gift for frightening voters. He urged wholesale bombing of North Vietnam and left the impression of being trigger-happy. He savaged Johnson's war on poverty and the entire New Deal tradition. In Tennessee he proposed the sale of the Tennessee Valley Authority, a series of hydroelectric dams and recreational lakes; in St. Petersburg, Florida, a major retirement community, he questioned the value of Social Security. He also opposed the nuclear test ban and the 1964 Civil Rights Act. To Republican campaign buttons that claimed "In your heart, you know he's right," Democrats responded, "In your guts, you know he's nuts."

Johnson, on the other hand, portrayed himself as a responsible centrist. He chose as his running mate Hubert H. Humphrey of Minnesota, a prominent liberal senator who had long promoted civil rights. In contrast to Goldwater's bellicose rhetoric on Vietnam, Johnson pledged, "We are not about to send American boys nine or ten thousand miles from home to do what Asian boys ought to be doing for themselves."

The result was a landslide. Johnson polled 61 percent of the total vote; Goldwater carried only Arizona and five states in the Deep South, where race remained the salient issue. Vermont went Democratic for the first time ever in a presidential election. Johnson won the electoral vote by a whopping 486 to 52. In the Senate the Democrats increased their majority by two (68 to 32) and in the House by thirty-seven (295 to 140), but Goldwater's success in the Deep South continued that traditionally Democratic region's shift to the Republican party, whose conservative wing was riding a wave of grassroots momentum that would transform the landscape of American politics over the next half century. Goldwater's quixotic campaign failed to win the election but it proved to be a turning point in the development of the national conservative movement. The Goldwater campaign inspired a young generation of conservative activists and the formation of conservative organizations such as Young Americans for Freedom that would eventually transform the dynamics of American politics.

LANDMARK LEGISLATION Lyndon Johnson knew that the mandate provided by his lopsided victory could quickly erode; he shrewdly told his aides, "Every day I'm in office, I'm going to lose votes. I'm going to alienate somebody. . . . We've got to get this legislation fast. You've got to get it during my honeymoon." In 1965, Johnson flooded the new Congress with **Great Society** legislation that, he promised, would end poverty, revitalize decaying central cities, provide every young American with the chance to attend college, protect the health of the elderly, enhance the nation's cultural life, clean up the air and water, and make the highways safer and prettier.

The scope of Johnson's legislative program was unparalleled since Franklin D. Roosevelt's Hundred Days, in part because of the nation's humming prosperity. "This country," Johnson proclaimed, "is rich enough to do anything it has the guts to do and the vision to do and the will to do." Priority went to federal health insurance and aid to education, proposals that had languished since President Truman had proposed them in 1945. For twenty years the steadfast opposition of the physicians making up the American Medical Association (AMA) had stalled a comprehensive medical-insurance program. But now that Johnson had the votes, the AMA joined Republicans in supporting a bill serving those over age sixty-five. The act that finally emerged went well beyond the original proposal. It created not just a Medicare program for the aged but also a program of federal grants to states to help cover medical payments for the indigent. President Johnson signed the bill on July 30, 1965, in Independence, Missouri, with eighty-one-year-old Harry Truman looking on.

Five days after he submitted his Medicare program, Johnson sent to Congress a massive program of federal aid to elementary and secondary schools. Such proposals had been ignored since the forties, blocked alternately by issues of segregation and issues of separation of church and state. The **Civil Rights Act of 1964** had laid the first issue to rest, legally at least. Now Congress devised a means of extending aid to "poverty-impacted" school districts regardless of their public or religious character.

The momentum generated by these measures had already begun to carry others along, and that process continued through the following year. Before the Eighty-ninth Congress adjourned, it had established a record in the passage of landmark legislation unequalled since the time of the New Deal. Altogether, the tide of Great Society legislation had carried 435 bills through the Congress. Among them was the Appalachian Regional Development Act of 1966, which allocated $1 billion for programs in remote mountain areas that had long been pockets of desperate poverty. The Housing and Urban Development Act of 1965 provided for construction of 240,000 public-housing units and $3 billion for urban renewal. Funds for rent supplements for low-income families followed in 1966, and in that year a new Department of Housing and Urban Development appeared, headed by Robert C. Weaver, the first African American cabinet member. Lyndon Johnson had, in the words of one Washington reporter, "brought to harvest a generation's backlog of ideas and social legislation."

THE IMMIGRATION ACT Little noticed in the stream of legislation flowing from Congress was a major new immigration bill that had origi-nated in the Kennedy White House. President Johnson signed the Immigra-tion and Nationality Services Act of 1965 in a ceremony held on Liberty Island in New York Harbor. In his speech he stressed that the new law would redress the wrong done to those "from southern and eastern Europe" and the "developing continents" of Asia, Africa, and Latin America. It would do so by abolishing the discriminatory quotas based upon national origin that had governed immigration policy since the twenties. The new law treated all nationalities and races equally. In place of national quotas, it created hemi-spheric ceilings on visas issued: 170,000 for persons from outside the Western Hemisphere, 120,000 for persons from within. It also stipulated that no more than 20,000 people could come from any one country each year. The new act allowed the entry of immediate family members of American residents without limit. During the sixties, Asians and Latin Americans became the largest contingent of new Americans.

ASSESSING THE GREAT SOCIETY The Great Society programs cost too much and did too little, but included several successes. The guarantee of civil rights and voting rights remains protected. Medicare and Medicaid have become two of the most appreciated government programs. Consumer rights now have federal advocates and protections. The Highway Safety Act and the National Traffic and Motor Vehicle Safety Act (both 1966) established safety standards for highway design and automobile manufacturers, and the schol-arships provided for college students under the Higher Education Act (1965) were quite popular. Many of the Great Society initiatives aimed at improving the health, nutrition, and education of poor Americans, young and old, made some headway. So, too, did federal efforts to clean up air and water pollution. Several of Johnson's most ambitious programs, however, were ill conceived, others were vastly underfunded, and many were mismanaged. As Joseph Cal-ifano, one of Johnson's senior aides, confessed: "Did we legislate too much? Were mistakes made? Plenty of them." Medicare, for example, removed incentives for hospitals to control costs, so medical bills skyrocketed. The Great Society helped reduce the number of people living in poverty, but it did so largely by providing federal welfare payments, not by finding people pro-ductive jobs. The war on poverty ended up being as disappointing as the war in Vietnam. Often funds appropriated for a program never made it through the tangled bureaucracy to the needy. Widely publicized cases of welfare fraud became a powerful weapon in the hands of those who were opposed to liberal social programs. By 1966 middle-class resentment over the cost and waste of the Great Society programs had generated a conservative backlash that fueled a Republican resurgence at the polls. By then, however, the Great Society had transformed public expectations of the power and role of the federal government—for good and for ill.

FROM CIVIL RIGHTS TO BLACK POWER

During late 1963 and throughout 1964 the civil rights movement grew in scope, visibility, and power. But government-sanctioned racism remained entrenched in the Deep South. Blacks continued to be excluded from the political process. For example, in 1963 only 6.7 percent of Mississippi blacks were registered to vote, the lowest percentage in the nation. White officials in the South systematically kept African Americans from voting through a variety of means: charging them expensive poll taxes, forcing them to take difficult literacy tests, making the application process inconvenient, and intimidating blacks through the use of arson, beatings, and lynchings.

FREEDOM SUMMER   In early 1964 Harvard-educated Robert "Bob" Moses, a black New Yorker who served as field secretary of the Student Non-violent Coordinating Committee (SNCC) office in Mississippi, the nation's most rural and poorest state, decided it would take "an army" to penetrate the state's longstanding effort to deny voting rights to blacks. So he set about recruiting such an army of idealistic volunteers who would live with rural blacks, teach them in "freedom schools," and help people register to vote. Moses recruited a thousand volunteers, most of them white college students, many of whom were Jewish, to participate in what came to be called "Freedom Summer." Mississippi's white leaders resented Moses's efforts. They prepared for "the nigger-communist invasion" by doubling the state police force and stockpiling tear gas, electric cattle prods, and shotguns. The prominent writer Eudora Welty reported from her hometown of Jackson that she had heard that "this summer all hell is going to break loose."

In mid-June the volunteer activists converged at an Ohio college to learn about southern racial history, nonviolence, and the likely abuses they would suffer from the white community. On the final evening of the training session, Robert Moses pleaded with anyone who felt uncertain about their undertaking to go home; several of them did. The next day the volunteers boarded buses and headed south, fanning across the rural state to hamlets named Harmony and Holly Springs as well as cities such as Hattiesburg and Jackson.

They lived with rural blacks (many of whom had never had a white person enter their home) and fanned out to teach children math, writing, and history and tutor blacks about the complicated process of voter registration.

In response to the activities of freedom summer, the Ku Klux Klan, local police, and other white racists assaulted and arrested the volunteers and murdered several of them. Yet Freedom Summer was successful in refocusing the civil rights movement on political rights. The number of blacks registered to vote inched up.

CIVIL RIGHTS LEGISLATION   Early in 1965, Martin Luther King Jr. organized an effort to enroll the 3 million African Americans in the South who had not registered to vote. In Selma, Alabama, civil rights protesters began a march to Montgomery, the state capital, about forty miles away, only to be dispersed by five hundred state troopers. A federal judge agreed to allow the march to continue, and President Johnson provided troops for protection. By March 25, when the demonstrators reached Montgomery, some twenty-five thousand people were with them, and King delivered a rousing address from the steps of the state capitol. Several days earlier, President Johnson had urged Congress to "overcome the crippling legacy of big otry and intolerance." He then concluded by slowly intoning the words of the civil rights movement's hymn: "And we shall overcome." The resulting Voting Rights Act of 1965 ensured all citizens the right to vote. It authorized the attorney general to dispatch federal examiners to register voters. In states or counties where fewer than half the adults had voted in 1964, the act suspended literacy tests and other devices commonly used to defraud citizens of the vote. By the end of the year, some 250,000 African Americans were newly registered.

BLACK POWER Amid this success, however, the civil rights movement began to fragment. On August 11, 1965, less than a week after the passage of the Voting Rights Act, Watts, a predominantly black and poor community in Los Angeles, exploded in a frenzy of rioting and looting. When the uprising ended, thirty-four were dead, almost four thousand rioters were in jail, and property damage exceeded $35 million. Chicago and Cleveland, along with forty other American cities, experienced similar race riots in the summer of 1966. The following summer, Newark and Detroit burst into flames. Between 1965 and 1968 there were nearly three hundred racial uprisings that shattered the peace of urban America and undermined Johnson's much-vaunted war on poverty.

In retrospect, it was predictable that the civil rights movement would shift its focus from the rural South to the plight of urban blacks nationwide. By the mid-sixties about 70 percent of the nation's African Americans were living in metropolitan areas, most in central-city ghettos that the postwar prosperity had bypassed. At the same time, a disproportionate number of blacks were serving in an increasingly unpopular war in Vietnam. As those military veterans returned, they often grew disgruntled at what they came back to. "I had left one war and came back and got into another one," said a black soldier.

By 1966, "black power" had become a riveting rallying cry for young militants. When Stokely Carmichael, a twenty-five-year-old graduate of Howard University, became head of the SNCC in 1966, he made the separatist philosophy of black power the official objective of the organization and ousted whites from the organization. "When you talk of black power," Carmichael shouted, "you talk of bringing this country to its knees, of building a movement that will smash everything Western civilization has created." H. Rap Brown, who succeeded Carmichael as head of SNCC in 1967, was even more outspoken and incendiary. He urged blacks to "get you some guns" and "kill the honkies." Carmichael, meanwhile, had moved on to the Black Panther party, a group of urban revolutionaries founded in Oakland, California, in 1966. Headed by Huey P. Newton, Bobby Seale, and Eldridge Cleaver, the provocative, armed Black Panthers initially terrified the public but eventually fragmented in spasms of violence.

MALCOLM X The most articulate spokesman for black power was **Malcolm X** (formerly Malcolm Little, the X denoting his lost African surname). Born in 1925, tall and austere Malcolm had spent his childhood in Lansing, Michigan, where his family home was burned to the ground by white racists. His parents were courageous supporters of Marcus Garvey's crusade for black nationalism. His abusive father died violently when he was six, and his mother was confined to a mental hospital when he was fourteen. He then moved to Boston to live with his half-sister, who was repeatedly arrested for minor crimes. Malcolm quit school during ninth grade and began to display what would become a lifelong ability to reinvent himself. By age nineteen, known as Detroit Red, he had become a thief, drug dealer, and pimp. Between the ages of twenty and twenty-seven he was incarcerated in Massachusetts prisons, during which time he joined a small Chicago-based sect called the Nation of Islam (NOI), whose members were often called Black Muslims. The organization had little to do with Islam and everything to do with its domineering leader, Elijah Muhammad, and the cult-like devotion he required. Muhammad, a Georgian, characterized whites as "devils" and espoused black nationalism, racial pride, self-respect, and self-discipline. By 1953, a year after leaving prison, Malcolm X was a full-time NOI minister famous for his angry but electrifying speeches decrying white racism and black passivity, as well as his abilities as a grassroots community organizer. "We have a common oppressor, a common exploiter," he told black audiences. ". . . He's an enemy to all of us."

Malcolm X dismissed the mainstream civil rights leaders such as Martin Luther King as being "nothing but modern Uncle Toms" who "keep you and me in check, keep us under control, keep us passive and peaceful and nonviolent." His militant candor inspired thousands of blacks to join NOI. "Yes, I'm an extremist," Malcolm acknowledged in 1964. "The black race in the United States is in extremely bad shape. You show me a black man who isn't an extremist and I'll show you one who needs psychiatric attention." By 1964, Malcolm had broken with Elijah Muhammad, toured Africa and the Middle East, embraced the Muslim faith, and founded an organization committed to the establishment of alliances between African Americans and the people of color around the world. More than most black leaders, Malcolm X experienced and expressed the turbulent emotions and frustrations of the African American poor and working class. After the publication of his acclaimed *Autobiography* in 1964, Malcolm became a symbol of the international human-rights movement. But his conflict with Elijah Muhammad proved fatal; assassins representing a rival faction of Black Muslims shot Malcolm X in Manhattan on February 21, 1965. With him went the most effective voice for urban black militancy since Marcus Garvey in the twenties. What made the assassination of Malcolm X especially tragic was that he had just months before begun to abandon his strident anti-white rhetoric and preach a biracial message of social change.

Malcolm X

Malcolm X was the black power movement's most influential spokesman.

Although widely publicized and highly visible, the **black power movement** never attracted more than a small minority of mostly young African Americans. Only about 15 percent of American blacks labeled themselves separatists. The preponderant majority continued to identify with the philosophy of nonviolent, Christian-centered integration promoted by Martin Luther King Jr. and with organizations such as the NAACP. King dismissed black separatism and the promotion of violent social change. He reminded his followers that "we can't win violently."

Despite its hyperbole, violence, and few adherents, the black power philosophy had two positive effects upon the civil rights movement. First, it motivated African Americans to take greater pride in their racial heritage. As Malcolm X often pointed out, prolonged slavery and institutionalized racism had eroded the self-esteem of many blacks. "The worst crime the white man has committed," he declared, "has been to teach us to hate ourselves." He and others helped blacks appreciate their African roots and their American accomplishments. In fact, it was Malcolm X who insisted that blacks call themselves African Americans as a symbol of pride in their roots and as a spur to learn more about their history as a people. As the popular singer James Brown urged, "Say it loud—I'm black and I'm proud."

Second, the assertiveness of black power advocates forced King and other mainstream black leaders and organizations to focus attention on the plight of poor inner-city blacks. Legal access to restaurants, schools, and other public accommodations, King pointed out, meant little to people mired in a culture of urban poverty. They needed jobs and decent housing as much as they needed legal rights. To this end, King began to emphasize the economic plight of the black urban underclass. The time had come for radical measures "to provide jobs and income for the poor." Yet as King and others sought to heighten the war on poverty at home, the escalating war in Vietnam was consuming more and more of America's resources and energies.

The Tragedy of Vietnam

As racial violence erupted in America's cities, the war in Vietnam reached new levels of intensity and destruction. In November 1963, when President Kennedy was assassinated, there were sixteen thousand U.S. military "advisers" in South Vietnam. Lyndon B. Johnson inherited from Kennedy and Eisenhower a long-standing commitment to prevent a Communist takeover in Indochina as well as a reluctance on the part of American presidents to assume primary responsibility for fighting the Viet Cong (the Communist-led guerrillas in South Vietnam) and their North Vietnamese allies. Beginning with Harry S. Truman, one president after another had done just enough to avoid being charged with having "lost" Vietnam to communism. Johnson initially sought to do the same, fearing that any other course of action would undermine his political influence and jeopardize his Great Society programs in Congress. But this path took the United States deeper into an expanding military commitment in Southeast Asia. Early on, Johnson doubted that the poverty-stricken, peasant-based Vietnam was worth military involvement. In May 1964 he told his national security adviser, McGeorge Bundy, that he had spent a sleepless night worrying about Vietnam: "It looks to me like we are getting into another Korea. . . . I don't think we can fight them 10,000 miles away from home. . . . I don't think it's worth fighting for. And I don't think we can get out. It's just the biggest damned mess that I ever saw."

Yet Johnson's fear of appearing weak abroad was stronger than his misgivings and forebodings. By the end of 1965, there were 184,000 U.S. troops in Vietnam; in 1966 there were 385,000; and by 1969, at the height of the American presence, 542,000. By the time the last troops left, in March 1973, some 58,000 Americans had died and another 300,000 had been wounded. The massive, prolonged war had cost taxpayers $150 billion and siphoned funding from many Great Society programs; it had produced 570,000 draft offenders and 563,000 less-than-honorable military discharges, toppled Johnson's administration, and divided the country as no event in history had since the Civil War.

ESCALATION   The official sanction for military "escalation" in Southeast Asia—a Defense Department term favored in the Vietnam era—was the **Tonkin Gulf resolution**, voted by Congress on August 7, 1964, after merely thirty minutes of discussion. On that day, Johnson told a national television audience that on August 2 and 4, North Vietnamese vessels had attacked two destroyers, the U.S.S. *Maddox* and the U.S.S. *C. Turner Joy*, in the Gulf of Tonkin, off the coast of North Vietnam. Johnson described the attack, called the Gulf of Tonkin incident, as unprovoked. In truth the destroyers had been monitoring South Vietnamese attacks against two North Vietnamese islands—attacks planned by American advisers. The Tonkin Gulf resolution authorized the president to "take all necessary measures to repel any armed attack against the forces of the United States and to prevent further aggression." Only Senator Wayne Morse of Oregon and Senator Ernest Gruening of Alaska voted against the resolution, which Johnson thereafter interpreted as equivalent to a congressional declaration of war.

Soon after his landslide victory over Goldwater in November 1964, Johnson, while still plagued by private doubts, made the crucial decisions that committed the United States to a full-scale war in Vietnam for the next four years. On February 5, 1965, Viet Cong guerrillas killed 8 and wounded

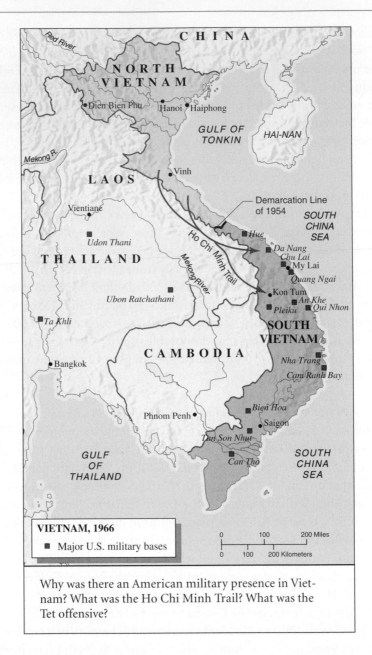

VIETNAM, 1966

■ Major U.S. military bases

0   100   200 Miles

0   100   200 Kilometers

Why was there an American military presence in Vietnam? What was the Ho Chi Minh Trail? What was the Tet offensive?

126 Americans at Pleiku, in South Vietnam. More attacks later that week led Johnson to order Operation Rolling Thunder, the first sustained bombing of North Vietnam, which was intended to stop the flow of soldiers and supplies into the south. Six months later an extensive study concluded that the bombing had not slowed the supplies pouring down the Ho Chi Minh Trail from North Vietnam through Laos and into South Vietnam.

In March 1965 the new U.S. commander in Vietnam, General William C. Westmoreland, greeted the first installment of combat troops. By the summer, American forces were engaged in "search-and-destroy" operations throughout South Vietnam. As combat operations increased, so did casualties, announced each week on the nightly television news, along with the "body count" of alleged Viet Cong dead. "Westy's war," although fought with helicopter gunships, chemical defoliants, and napalm, became like the trench warfare of World War I—a war of attrition. "We will not be defeated," Johnson told the nation in April. "We will not grow tired. We will not withdraw."

THE CONTEXT FOR POLICY President Johnson's decision to "Americanize" the Vietnam War, so ill-starred in retrospect, was consistent with the foreign-policy principles pursued by all presidents after the Second World War. The version of the theory intended to "contain" communism articulated in the Truman Doctrine, endorsed by Eisenhower throughout the fifties, and reaffirmed by Kennedy, pledged U.S. opposition to the advance of communism anywhere in the world. "Why are we in Vietnam?" Johnson asked rhetorically at Johns Hopkins University in 1965. "We are there because we have a promise to keep. . . . To leave Vietnam to its fate would shake the confidence of all these people in the value of American commitment." Secretary of State Dean Rusk frequently repeated this rationale, warning that the rest of Southeast Asia would fall "like dominoes" to communism if American forces withdrew from Vietnam. Military intervention was thus a logical culmination of the assumptions that were widely shared by the foreign-policy establishment and the leaders of both political parties since the early days of the cold war.

At the same time, Johnson and his advisers presumed that military involvement in Vietnam must not reach levels that would cause the Chinese or Soviets to intervene directly. And that meant, in effect, that a complete military victory was never possible. The goal of the United States was not to win the war in any traditional sense but to prevent the North Vietnamese and the Viet Cong from winning and, eventually, to force a negotiated settlement with the North Vietnamese. This meant that the United States would have to maintain a military presence as long as the enemy retained the will to fight.

As it turned out, American support for the war eroded faster than the will of the North Vietnamese leaders to tolerate devastating casualties and destruction. Systematic opposition to the war on college campuses began in 1965 with "teach-ins" at the University of Michigan. The following year, Senator J. William Fulbright of Arkansas, chairman of the Senate Foreign Relations Committee, began congressional investigations into American policy in Vietnam. George F. Kennan, the author of the containment doctrine, told

"How Deep Do You Figure We'll Get Involved, Sir?"

Although U.S. soldiers were first sent to Vietnam as noncombatant advisers, they soon found themselves involved in a quagmire of fighting.

Senator Fulbright's committee that the doctrine was appropriate for Europe but not for Southeast Asia. And a respected general testified that General Westmoreland's military strategy had no chance of achieving victory. By 1967 anti-war demonstrations were attracting massive support. Nightly television accounts of the fighting—Vietnam was the first war to receive extended television coverage and hence was dubbed the living-room war—called into question the official optimism. By May 1967 even Secretary of Defense Robert McNamara was wavering: "The picture of the world's greatest superpower killing or injuring 1,000 non-combatants a week, while trying to pound a tiny backward nation into submission on an issue whose merits are hotly disputed, is not a pretty one."

In a war of political will, North Vietnam had the advantage. Johnson and his advisers grievously underestimated the tenacity of the North Vietnamese commitment to unify Vietnam and expel American forces. While the United States fought a limited war for limited objectives, the Vietnamese Communists fought an all-out war for their very survival. Just as General Westmoreland was assuring Johnson and the public that the war effort in early 1968 was on the verge of gaining the upper hand, the Communists organized widespread assaults that jolted American confidence and resolve.

THE TURNING POINT On January 31, 1968, the first day of the Vietnamese New Year (Tet), the Viet Cong defied a holiday truce to launch ferocious assaults on American and South Vietnamese forces throughout South Vietnam. The old capital city of Hue fell to the Communists, and Viet Cong (VC) units temporarily occupied the grounds of the U.S. embassy in Saigon, the capital of South Vietnam. General Westmoreland proclaimed the **Tet offensive** a major defeat for the Viet Cong, and most students of military strategy later agreed with him. While Viet Cong casualties were enormous, however, the impact of the surprise attacks on the American public was more telling. The scope and intensity of the offensive contradicted upbeat claims by U.S. commanders that the war was going well. *Time* and *Newsweek* magazines soon ran anti-war editorials urging withdrawal. Polls showed that Johnson's popularity had declined to 35 percent. Civil rights leaders and social activists felt betrayed as they saw federal funds earmarked for the war on poverty gobbled up by the expanding war. In 1968 the United States was spending $322,000 on every Communist killed in Vietnam; the poverty programs at home received only $53 per person. As Martin Luther King Jr. pointed out, "the bombs in Vietnam explode at home—they destroy the hopes and possibilities for a decent America." He repeatedly pointed out that the amount being spent to kill each Vietnamese communist was greater than the amount spent by the federal government on assisting an American living in poverty.

During 1968, a despondent President Johnson grew increasingly embittered and isolated. He suffered from depression and bouts of paranoia. It had at last become painfully evident to him that the Vietnam War was a

The Tet offensive

Many Vietnamese were driven from their homes during the bloody street battles of the 1968 Tet offensive. Here, following a lull in the fighting, civilians carrying a white flag approach U.S. Marines.

never-ending stalemate that was fragmenting the nation and undermining the Great Society programs. Clark Clifford, Johnson's new secretary of defense, reported to the president that a task force of prominent soldiers and civilians saw no prospect for a military victory. Robert F. Kennedy, now a senator from New York, was considering a run for the presidency in order to challenge Johnson's Vietnam policy. Senator Eugene McCarthy of Minnesota, a devout Catholic and a poet, had already decided to oppose Johnson in the Democratic primaries. With anti-war students rallying to his "Dump Johnson" candidacy, McCarthy polled a stunning 42 percent of the vote to Johnson's 48 percent in New Hampshire's March primary. It was a remarkable showing for a little-known senator. Each presidential primary now promised to become a referendum on Johnson's Vietnam policy. The war in Vietnam had become President Johnson's war; as more and more voters soured on the fighting, he saw his public support evaporate. In Wisconsin, scene of the next Democratic primary, the president's political advisers forecast a humiliating defeat.

On March 31, Johnson made a dramatic decision. He appeared on national television to announce a limited halt to the bombing of North Vietnam and fresh initiatives for a negotiated cease-fire. Then he added a stunning postscript: "I shall not seek, and I will not accept, the nomination of my party for another term as your President." Although U.S. troops would remain in Vietnam for five more years and the casualties would continue, the quest for military victory had ended. Now the question was how the most powerful nation in the world could extricate itself from Vietnam with a minimum of damage to its prestige and its South Vietnamese allies.

SIXTIES CRESCENDO

A TRAUMATIC YEAR Change moved at a fearful pace throughout the sixties, but 1968 was the most turbulent and the most traumatic year of all. On April 4, only four days after Johnson's withdrawal from the presidential race, a white racist named James Earl Ray assassinated Martin Luther King Jr. in Memphis, Tennessee. King's death set off an outpouring of grief among whites and blacks and ignited riots in over sixty cities.

Two months later, on June 5, a young Jordanian named Sirhan Sirhan, who resented Senator Robert F. Kennedy's strong support of Israel, shot forty-two-year-old Kennedy in the head. Kennedy's death occurred at the end of the day on which he had convincingly defeated Eugene McCarthy in the California Democratic primary, thereby momentarily assuming leadership of the anti-war forces in the race for the presidential nomination. Political reporter David Halberstam of the *New York Times* thought back to the assassinations of John Kennedy and Malcolm X, then to the violent end of King, the most influential African American leader of the twentieth century, and then to Robert Kennedy, the heir to leadership of the Kennedy clan. "We could make a calendar of the decade," Halberstam wrote, "by marking where we were at the hours of those violent deaths."

CHICAGO AND MIAMI In the summer of 1968, the social unrest roiling the nation morphed into political melodrama at the disruptive, divisive, and often brutal Democratic National Convention. In August, delegates gathered inside a Chicago convention hall to nominate Lyndon B. Johnson's faithful vice president, Hubert H. Humphrey. Outside, almost twenty thousand police officers and national guardsmen and a mob of television reporters stood watch over a gathering of eclectic protesters herded together miles away in a public park. Chicago's gruff Democratic mayor Richard J. Daley warned that he would not tolerate disruptions in his city. Nonetheless, riots broke out and were televised nationwide. As police used tear gas and billy clubs to pummel anti-war demonstrators, others chanted, "The whole world is watching." (See pages 1056–57 for further details.)

The Democratic party's liberal tradition was clearly in disarray, a fact that gave heart to the Republicans, who gathered in Miami Beach to nominate Richard Nixon. Only six years earlier, after he had lost the California gubernatorial race, Nixon had vowed never again to run for public office. But by 1968 he had changed his mind and had become a spokesman for the values of "middle America." Nixon and the Republicans offered a vision of stability and order that appealed to a majority of Americans—soon to be called the silent majority.

George Wallace, the Democratic governor of Alabama who had made his reputation as an outspoken defender of segregation, ran on the American Independent party ticket. Wallace moderated his position on the race issue but appealed even more candidly than Nixon to voters' concerns about rioting anti-war protesters, the mushrooming welfare system, and the growth of the federal government. Wallace's reactionary candidacy generated considerable appeal outside his native South, especially among white working-class communities, where resentment of Johnson's Great Society liberalism flourished. Although never a possible winner, Wallace hoped to deny Humphrey or Nixon an electoral majority and thereby throw the choice into the House of Representatives, which would have provided an appropriate climax to a chaotic year.

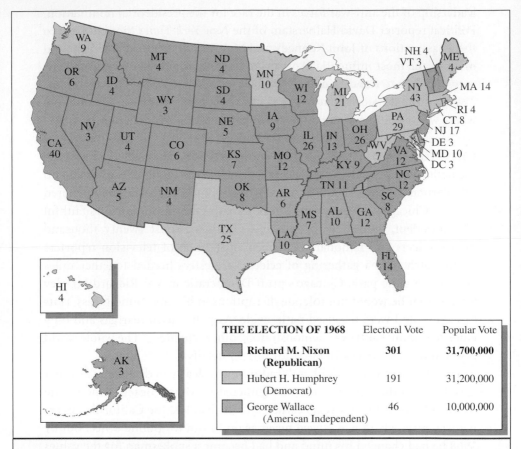

THE ELECTION OF 1968	Electoral Vote	Popular Vote
Richard M. Nixon (Republican)	**301**	**31,700,000**
Hubert H. Humphrey (Democrat)	191	31,200,000
George Wallace (American Independent)	46	10,000,000

How did the riots at the Chicago Democratic Convention affect the 1968 presidential campaign? What does the electoral map reveal about the support base for each of the three major candidates? How was Nixon able to win enough electoral votes in such a close, three-way presidential race? What was Wallace's appeal to 10 million voters?

NIXON AGAIN It did not happen that way. Richard Nixon enjoyed an enormous lead in the polls, which narrowed as the election approached. Wallace's campaign was hurt by his outspoken running mate, retired air force general Curtis LeMay, who favored expanding the war in Vietnam and using nuclear weapons. In October 1968, Hubert Humphrey infuriated Johnson when he announced that, if elected, he would stop bombing North Vietnam "as an acceptable risk for peace."

Nixon and Governor Spiro Agnew of Maryland, his acid-tongued running mate, eked out a narrow victory of about 500,000 votes, a margin of about 1 percentage point. The electoral vote was more decisive, 301 to 191. George Wallace received 10 million votes, 13.5 percent of the total. It was the best showing by a third-party candidate since Robert M. La Follette ran on the Progressive party ticket in 1924. All but one of Wallace's 46 electoral votes were from the Deep South. Nixon swept all but four of the states west of the Mississippi. Humphrey's support came almost exclusively from the Northeast.

So at the end of a turbulent year, near the end of a traumatic decade, a nation on the verge of violent chaos looked to Richard Nixon to provide what he had promised in the campaign: "peace with honor" in Vietnam and a middle ground on which a majority of Americans, silent or otherwise, could come together.

End of Chapter Review

- **Kennedy's New Frontier** President Kennedy promised "new frontiers" in domestic policy, but without a clear Democratic majority in Congress he was unable to increase federal aid to education, provide health insurance for the aged, create a cabinet-level department of urban affairs, or expand civil rights. He championed tariff cuts, however, and an expanded space program.

- **Johnson's Great Society** President Johnson was committed to social reform, including civil rights. He forced the Civil Rights Act through Congress in 1964 and declared a "war" on poverty. Under the Great Society, welfare was expanded, Medicare and Medicaid were created, more grants for college students were established, and racial quotas for immigration were abolished. These programs were expensive and, coupled with the soaring costs of the war in Vietnam, necessitated tax increases, which were unpopular.

- **Civil Rights' Achievements** By the sixties, significant numbers of African Americans and whites were staging nonviolent sit-ins. In 1961, "freedom riders" attempted to integrate buses, trains, and bus and train stations in the South. The high point of the early phase of the civil rights movement was the 1963 March on Washington for Jobs and Freedom, at which Martin Luther King Jr. delivered his famous "I Have a Dream" speech. In 1964, President Johnson signed the far-reaching Civil Rights Act. In 1965, King set in motion a massive drive to enroll the 3 million southern African Americans who were not registered to vote. Later that year, Johnson persuaded Congress to pass the Voting Rights Act. The legislation did little to ameliorate the poverty of inner-city blacks or stem the violence that swept northern cities in the hot summers of the late sixties. By 1968, nonviolent resistance had given way to the more militant black power movement.

- **Escalation in Vietnam** The United States supported the government of South Vietnam even though it failed to deliver promised reforms, win the support of its citizens, or defeat the Communist insurgents, the Viet Cong. Kennedy increased America's commitment by sending 16,000 advisers, and Johnson went further, deploying combat troops. A turning point in the war was the Viet Cong's Tet offensive, which served to rally anti-war sentiment.

- **Communist Cuba** In early 1961, Kennedy inherited a CIA plot to topple the regime of Fidel Castro, the premier of Cuba. Kennedy naïvely agreed to the plot, whereby some 1,500 anti-Castro Cubans landed at Cuba's Bay of Pigs. The plotters failed to inspire a revolution, and most were quickly captured. Kennedy's seeming weakness in the face of Soviet aggression led the Russian premier, Nikita Khrushchev, to believe that the Soviets could install ballistic missiles in Cuba without American opposition. In October 1962 in a tense standoff, Kennedy ordered a blockade of Cuba and succeeded in forcing Khrushchev to withdraw the missiles.

CHRONOLOGY

1960	Students in Greensboro, North Carolina, stage a sit-in to demand service at a "whites-only" lunch counter
1961	Bay of Pigs fiasco
1961	Soviets erect the Berlin Wall
October 1962	Cuban missile crisis
August 1963	March on Washington for Jobs and Freedom
November 1963	John F. Kennedy is assassinated in Dallas, Texas
1964	Congress passes the Civil Rights Act
August 1964	Congress passes the Tonkin Gulf resolution
1965	Malcolm X is assassinated by a rival group of black Muslims
1965	Riots break out in the African American community of Watts, California
January 1968	Viet Cong stages the Tet offensive
April 1968	Martin Luther King Jr. is assassinated
June 1968	Robert Kennedy is assassinated

KEY TERMS & NAMES

John F. Kennedy p. 1015

New Frontier p. 1016

Miranda v. Arizona p. 1019

freedom riders p. 1020

James Meredith p. 1021

March on Washington p. 1023

Cuban missile crisis p. 1026

Lyndon B. Johnson p. 1028

Great Society p. 1033

Civil Rights Act of 1964 p. 1034

Malcolm X p. 1038

black power movement p. 1039

Tonkin Gulf resolution p. 1041

Tet offensive p. 1044

32

REBELLION AND REACTION: THE 1960s AND 1970s

FOCUS QUESTIONS

 wwnorton.com/studyspace

- What characterized the social rebellion and struggles for civil rights in the sixties and seventies?
- How did the war in Vietnam end?
- Why did President Ford issue a pardon to Richard M. Nixon?
- What was "stagflation"?

As Richard M. Nixon entered the White House in early 1969, he took charge of a nation whose social fabric was in tatters. Everywhere, it seemed, conventional institutions and notions of authority were under attack. The traumatic events of 1968 were like a knife blade splitting past and future, then and now. They revealed how deeply divided society had become and how difficult a task Nixon faced in carrying out his pledge to restore social harmony. In the end, the stability he promised proved elusive. His controversial policies and his combative temperament heightened rather than reduced societal tensions. Ironically, many of the same forces that had enabled the complacent prosperity of the fifties—the baby boom, the cold war, and the burgeoning consumer culture—helped generate the social upheaval of the sixties and seventies. It was one of the most turbulent periods in American history— exciting, threatening, explosive, and transforming.

THE ROOTS OF REBELLION

YOUTH REVOLT   By the early sixties, the baby boomers were maturing. Now young adults, they differed from their parents in that they had experienced neither economic depression nor a major war during their lifetimes. In record numbers they were attending colleges and universities: enrollment quadrupled between 1945 and 1970. Many universities had become gigantic institutions dependent upon huge research contracts from corporations and the federal government. As these "multiversities" grew larger and more bureaucratic, they unwittingly invited resistance from a generation of students wary of involvement in what President Dwight D. Eisenhower had labeled the military-industrial complex.

The Greensboro sit-ins in 1960 not only precipitated a decade of civil rights activism but also signaled an end to the complacency that had enveloped many college campuses and much of social life during the fifties. The sit-ins, marches, protests, ideals, and sacrifices associated with the civil rights movement inspired other groups—women, Native Americans, Hispanics, and gays—to demand justice, freedom, and equality as well.

During 1960–1961, a significant number of white students joined African Americans in the sit-in movement. They and many others were also inspired by President Kennedy's direct appeals to their youthful idealism. Thousands enrolled as volunteers in the Peace Corps and VISTA (Volunteers in Service to America), while others continued to participate in civil rights demonstrations. But as criticism of escalating military involvement in Vietnam mounted, more and more young people grew disillusioned with the government. During the mid-sixties, a full-fledged youth revolt erupted across the nation. The youth revolt grew out of several impulses: to challenge authority; to change the world; and, to indulge in pleasures of all sorts. As a popular song by Steppenwolf declared in 1968, "Like a true nature child/We were born, born to be wild/We have climbed so high/Never want to die." During the sixties and seventies, rebellious and often idealistic young people flowed into two distinct yet frequently overlapping movements: the New Left and the counterculture.

THE NEW LEFT   The explicitly political strain of the youth revolt originated when Tom Hayden and Al Haber, two University of Michigan students, formed Students for a Democratic Society (SDS) in 1960, an organization very much influenced by the tactics and successes of the civil rights movement. In 1962, Hayden and Haber convened a meeting of sixty upstart activists at Port Huron, Michigan, all of whom shared a desire to remake the

United States into a more democratic society. Hayden drafted an impassioned manifesto that became known as the Port Huron Statement. It begins: "We are the people of this generation, bred in at least moderate comfort, housed in universities, looking uncomfortably to the world we inherit." Hayden then called for political reforms, racial equality, and workers' rights. Inspired by the example of African American activism in the South, Hayden declared that college students had the power to restore "participatory democracy" by wresting "control of the educational process from the administrative bureaucracy." He and others adopted the term New Left to distinguish their efforts at grassroots democracy from those of the Old Left of the thirties, which had espoused an orthodox Marxism.

In the fall of 1964, students at the University of California at Berkeley took Hayden's program to heart. Several of them had returned to the campus after spending the summer working with the Student Nonviolent Coordinating Committee (SNCC) voter-registration project in Mississippi, where three volunteers had been killed and nearly a thousand arrested. Their idealism and activism had been pricked by their participation in Freedom Summer, and they were eager to bring changes to campus life. When the UC Berkeley chancellor announced that political demonstrations would no longer be allowed on campus, several hundred students staged a sit-in. Thousands more joined in. After a tense thirty-two-hour standoff the administration relented. Student groups then formed the free-speech movement (FSM).

Led by Mario Savio, a philosophy major who had participated in Freedom Summer in Mississippi, the FSM initially protested on behalf of students' rights. But it quickly mounted a more general criticism of the university and what Savio called the "depersonalized, unresponsive bureaucracy" smothering American life. In 1964, Savio led hundreds of students into UC Berkeley's administration building and organized a sit-in. In the early-morning hours, six hundred policemen, dispatched by the governor, arrested the protesters. But their example lived on.

The goals and tactics of the FSM and SDS spread to colleges across the country. Escalating U.S. military involvement in Vietnam soon changed the students' agenda. With the dramatic expansion of the war after 1965, millions of young men faced the grim prospect of being drafted to fight in an increasingly unpopular conflict. In fact, however, the Vietnam War, like virtually every other, was primarily a poor man's fight. Deferments enabled college students to postpone military service until they received their degree or reached the age of twenty-four; in 1965–1966, college students made up only 2 percent of all military inductees. In 1966, however, the Selective Service

The free-speech movement

Mario Savio, a founder of the free-speech movement, speaks at a rally at the University of California at Berkeley.

System modified the provisions so that even undergraduates were eligible for the draft.

As the war dragged on and opposition mounted, 200,000 young men ignored their draft notices, and some 4,000 of them served prison sentences. Another 56,000 men qualified for conscientious objector status during the Vietnam War, compared with only 7,600 during the Korean conflict. Still others left the country altogether—several thousand fled to Canada or Sweden—to avoid military service. The most popular way to escape the draft was to flunk the physical examination. Whatever the preferred method, many students succeeded in avoiding military service. Of the 1,200 men in the Harvard senior class of 1970, only 56 served in the military, and just 2 of those went to Vietnam.

Throughout 1967 and 1968, the anti-war movement grew more volatile as inner-city ghettos were exploding in flames fanned by racial injustice. Frustration over patterns of discrimination in employment and housing and staggering rates of joblessness among inner-city African American youths provoked chaotic violence in scores of urban ghettos. "There was a sense everywhere, in 1968," the journalist Garry Wills wrote, "that things were giving way. That man had not only lost control of his history, but might never regain it."

During the eventful spring of 1968—when Lyndon B. Johnson announced that he would not run for re-election and Martin Luther King Jr. was assassinated—campus unrest exploded across the country. The turmoil reached a climax with the disruption of Columbia University, where Mark Rudd, an SDS leader, joined other student radicals in occupying the president's office and classroom buildings. The administration was forced to cancel classes and call in the New York City police. The riotous events at Columbia inspired similar clashes among students, administrators, and police at Harvard, Cornell, and San Francisco State.

At the 1968 Democratic National Convention in Chicago, the polarization of society reached a bizarre climax. Inside the tightly guarded convention hall, Democrats nominated Hubert H. Humphrey while on Chicago's streets the whole spectrum of antiwar dissenters gathered, from the earnest supporters of Senator Eugene McCarthy to the nihilistic Yippies, members of the new Youth International party. Abbie Hoffman, one of the Yippie leaders, explained that their "conception of revolution is that it's fun."

The outlandish behavior of the Yippies and the other demonstrators provoked an equally outlandish response by Mayor Richard J. Daley and his army of city police. As a horrified television audience watched, many police officers went berserk, clubbing and gassing demonstrators as well as

Upheaval in Chicago

The violence that accompanied the 1968 Democratic National Convention in Chicago seared the nation.

bystanders caught up in the melee. The chaotic spectacle lasted three days and seriously damaged Humphrey's candidacy. The televised Chicago riots also angered middle-class Americans, many of whom wondered: "Is America coming apart?" At the same time, the riots fragmented the anti-war movement. Those groups committed to nonviolent protest, while castigating the reactionary policies of Mayor Daley and the police, felt betrayed by the actions of the Yippies and other anarchists. By 1971, the New Left was dead as a political movement. In large measure it had committed suicide by abandoning the pacifist principles that had originally inspired participants and given the movement moral legitimacy. The larger anti-war movement also began to fade. There would be a wave of student protests against the Nixon administration in 1970–1971, but thereafter campus unrest virtually disappeared as Nixon launched initiatives to end the military draft, which defused the resistance movement.

THE COUNTERCULTURE   The numbing events of 1968 led other disaffected young activists to abandon political action in favor of **the counterculture**. Long hair on men and women, blue jeans, tie-dyed shirts, sandals, mind-altering drugs, rock music, and experimental living arrangements were more important than revolutionary ideology to the "hippies." The countercultural hippies were primarily middle-class whites alienated by the Vietnam War, racism, political corruption, parental demands, runaway technology, and a crass corporate mentality that equated the good life with material goods. In their view a complacent materialism had settled over urban and suburban life. But they were not attracted to organized political action or militant protests. Instead, they embraced the tactics promoted by the zany Harvard professor Timothy Leary: "Tune in, turn on, drop out."

For some, the counterculture entailed the embrace of Asian mysticism. For many it meant the daily use of hallucinogenic drugs. Collective living in urban enclaves such as San Francisco's Haight-Ashbury district was the rage for a time; rural communes also attracted bourgeois rebels. During the sixties and early seventies, thousands of inexperienced romantics flocked to the countryside, eager to liberate themselves from parental and institutional restraints, live in harmony with nature, and coexist in an atmosphere of love and openness. The participants in the back-to-the-land movement, as it became known, were seeking a path to more authentic living that would deepen their sense of self and life. They equated the good life with living close to nature and in conformity with its ecological imperatives and limits.

Huge outdoor concerts were a popular source of community among the counterculture. The largest of these was the sprawling **Woodstock** Music and Art Fair ("Aquarian Exposition"). In mid-August 1969 some four hundred thousand young people converged on a six-hundred-acre farm near the tiny rural town of Bethel, New York. For three days the assembled flower children reveled in good music, rivers of mud, cheap marijuana, and casual sex. Drug use was rampant, but there was little crime and virtually no violence. The carefree spirit of the Woodstock festival was short-lived, however. It did not produce the peaceful revolution its sponsors had promised. Just four months later, when other concert promoters tried to replicate the

Woodstock

The Woodstock music festival drew nearly half a million people to a farm in Bethel, New York. The concert was billed as three days of "peace, music, . . . and love."

"Woodstock Nation" experience at Altamont Speedway, forty miles east of San Francisco, the counterculture encountered the criminal culture. The Rolling Stones hired the Hells Angels motorcycle gang to provide "security" for their show. During the band's performance of "Under My Thumb," drunken white motorcyclists beat to death an eighteen-year-old African American man wielding a gun in front of the stage. Three other spectators were accidentally killed that night; much of the vitality and innocence of the counterculture died with them. After 1969 the hippie phenomenon began to wane as the counterculture had become counterproductive.

FEMINISM   The ideal of liberation spawned during the sixties helped accelerate a powerful women's rights crusade. Like the New Left, the new feminism drew much of its inspiration and many of its tactics from the civil rights movement. Its aim was to challenge the conventional cult of female domesticity that had prevailed since the fifties.

Betty Friedan, a forty-two-year-old mother of three from Peoria, Illinois, led the mainstream of the women's movement. Her influential book, *The*

Feminine Mystique (1963), helped launch the new phase of female protest on a national level. Women, Friedan wrote, had actually lost ground during the years after the Second World War, when many left wartime employment and settled down in suburbia. A propaganda campaign engineered by advertisers and women's magazines encouraged them to do so by creating the "feminine mystique" of blissful domesticity. Women, Friedan claimed, "were being duped into believing homemaking was their natural destiny."

The Feminine Mystique, an immediate best seller, inspired many affluent, well-educated women who felt trapped in their domestic doldrums. Friedan helped to transform the feminist movement from the clear-cut demands of suffrage and equal pay to the less-defined but more fulfilling realm of empowerment—in the home, in schools, in offices, on college campuses, and in politics. In 1966, Friedan and other activists founded the National Organization for Women (NOW). NOW initially sought to end discrimination in the workplace on the basis of gender and went on to spearhead efforts to legalize abortion and obtain federal and state support for child-care centers. The membership of NOW soared from one thousand in 1967 to forty thousand in 1974.

In the early seventies, members of Congress, the Supreme Court, and NOW advanced the cause of gender equality politically. Under Title IX of the Educational Amendments of 1972, colleges were required to institute "affirmative-action" programs to ensure equal opportunities for women in admissions and athletics. Also in 1972, Congress overwhelmingly approved an equal-rights amendment (ERA) to the federal constitution, which had been bottled up in a House committee since the twenties. In 1973 the Supreme Court, in *Roe v. Wade,* made history by striking down state laws forbidding abortions during the first three months of pregnancy. Meanwhile, the all-male educational bastions, including Yale and Princeton, led a movement for coeducation that swept the country. "If the 1960s belonged to blacks," said one feminist, "the next ten years are ours."

During the late sixties, a new wave of younger feminists emerged who challenged everything from women's economic, political, and legal status to the sexual double standards for men and women. The new generation of feminists was more militant than the older, more moderate generation that had established NOW. The goals of the women's liberation movement, said Susan Brownmiller, a self-described "radical feminist" who was also a veteran of the civil rights struggles, were to "go beyond a simple concept of equality. NOW's emphasis on legislative change left the radicals cold." She dismissed Friedan as "hopelessly bourgeois." Overthrowing the embedded structures and premises of centuries-old patriarchy, Brownmiller and others believed, required transforming every aspect of society: sexual relations, child rearing, entertainment, domestic duties, business, and the arts. Radical liberationists took direct action, such as picketing the 1968 Miss America Pageant, burning copies of *Playboy* and other men's magazines, tossing their bras into "freedom cans," and assaulting gender-based discrimination in all of its forms.

Whether young or old, conventional or radical, the women's movement focused on several basic issues: gender discrimination in the workplace, equal pay for equal work, the availability of high-quality day care for children, and easier access to abortions. Women in growing numbers also began winning elected offices at the local, state, and national levels. In 1960, some 38 percent of women were working outside the home; by 1980, 52 percent were doing so.

By the end of the seventies, however, sharp disputes between moderate and radical feminists had fractured the women's movement in ways similar to the fragmentation experienced by civil rights organizations. The movement's failure to broaden its appeal much beyond the confines of the middle class also caused reform efforts to stagnate. The ERA, which had once seemed a straightforward assertion of equal opportunity ("Equality of rights under the law shall not be denied or abridged by the United States or by any State on account of sex"), was stymied in several state legislatures. By 1982 it had died, several states short of passage. And the very success of NOW's efforts to liberalize local and state abortion laws generated a powerful backlash, especially among Catholics and fundamentalist Protestants, who mounted a potent "right-to-life" crusade against abortion that helped fuel the conservative political resurgence in the seventies and thereafter.

Yet the success of the women's movement endured long after the militant rhetoric had evaporated. A growing presence in the labor force brought women a greater share of economic and political influence. By 1976, over half the married women and nine out of ten female college graduates were employed outside the home, a development that one economist called "the single most outstanding phenomenon of this century." Women also enrolled in graduate and professional schools in record numbers. Whatever their motives, women were changing traditional gender roles and childbearing practices to accommodate the two-career family and the sexual revolution.

THE SEXUAL REVOLUTION AND THE PILL   The feminist movement coincided with the so-called sexual revolution, a much-discussed loosening of traditional restrictions on social behavior. Americans became more tolerant of premarital sex, and women became more sexually active. Between 1960 and 1975 the number of college women engaging in sexual intercourse doubled, from 27 percent to 50 percent. Facilitating this change was a scientific breakthrough in contraception: the birth-control pill, first approved by the Food and Drug Administration in 1960.

Widespread access to the pill, as it came to be known, gave women a greater sense of sexual freedom than had any previous contraceptive device. Although it also contributed to a rise in sexually transmitted diseases, many women viewed the birth-control pill as a godsend. "When the pill came out, it was a savior," recalled Eleanor Smeal, president of the Feminist Majority Foundation. "The whole country was waiting for it. I can't even describe to you how excited people were."

HISPANIC RIGHTS   The activism that animated the student revolt, the civil rights movement, and the crusade for women's rights soon spread to various ethnic minority groups. *Hispanic*, a term used in the United States to refer to people who trace their ancestry to Spanish-speaking Latin America or Spain, came into increasing use after 1945 in conjunction with growing efforts to promote economic and social justice. (Although frequently used as a synonym for Hispanic, the term *Latino* technically refers only to people of Latin American descent.) The labor shortages during the Second World War had led defense industries to offer Hispanic Americans their first significant access to skilled-labor jobs. And as was the case with African Americans, service in the military during the war years helped to heighten an American identity among Hispanic Americans and excite their desire for equal rights and social opportunities.

But social equality was elusive. After the Second World War, Hispanic Americans still faced widespread discrimination in hiring, housing, and education. Poverty was widespread. In 1960, for example, the median income of a Mexican American family was only 62 percent of the median income of a family in the general population. Hispanic American activists during the fifties and sixties mirrored the efforts of black civil rights leaders. They, too, denounced segregation, promoted efforts to improve the quality of public education, and struggled to increase Hispanic American political influence and economic opportunities.

The chief strength of the Hispanic rights movement lay less in the duplication of civil rights strategies than in the rapid growth of the Hispanic population. In 1960, Hispanics in the United States numbered slightly more than 3 million; by 1970 their numbers had increased to 9 million; and by 2012 they numbered well over 52 million, making them the nation's largest minority group. By 1980, aspiring presidential candidates were openly courting the Hispanic vote. The voting power of

Hispanics and their concentration in states with key electoral votes has helped give the Hispanic point of view significant political clout.

NATIVE AMERICAN RIGHTS   American Indians—many of whom had begun calling themselves Native Americans—also emerged as a political force in the late sixties. Two conditions combined to make Indian rights a priority: first, many whites felt a persistent sense of guilt for the destructive policies of their ancestors toward a people who had, after all, been here first; second, the plight of the Native American minority was more desperate than that of any other group in the country. Indian unemployment was ten times the national rate, life expectancy was twenty years lower than the national average, and the suicide rate was a whopping hundred times higher than the rate for whites.

Although President Lyndon B. Johnson recognized the poverty of the Native Americans and attempted to funnel federal anti-poverty-program funds into reservations, militants within the Indian community grew impatient with the pace of change. They organized protests and demonstrations against local, state, and federal agencies. In 1963 two Chippewas (or Ojibwas) living in Minneapolis, George Mitchell and Dennis Banks, founded the **American Indian Movement (AIM)** to promote "red power." In 1973, AIM led two hundred Sioux in the occupation of the tiny village of Wounded Knee, South Dakota, where the Seventh Cavalry massacred a Sioux village in 1890. Outraged by the light sentences given a group of local whites who had killed a Sioux in 1972, the organizers also sought to draw attention to the plight of the Indians living on the reservation there. After the militants took eleven hostages, federal marshals and FBI agents surrounded the encampment. For ten weeks the two sides engaged in a tense standoff. When AIM leaders tried to bring in food and supplies, a shoot-out resulted, with one Indian killed and another wounded. Soon thereafter the tense confrontation ended with a government promise to re-examine Indian treaty rights.

Indian protesters subsequently discovered a more effective tactic than direct action and sit-ins: they went into federal courts armed with copies of old treaties and demanded that those documents become the basis for restitution. In Alaska, Maine, South Carolina, and Massachusetts they won significant settlements that provided legal recognition of their tribal rights and financial compensation at levels that upgraded the standard of living on several reservations.

GAY RIGHTS   The liberationist impulses of the sixties also encouraged gays to assert their right to equal treatment. Throughout the sixties, gay men and lesbians continued to be treated with disgust, cruelty, and violence. On

Wounded Knee

Instigating a standoff with the FBI, members of AIM and local Oglala Sioux occupied the town of Wounded Knee, South Dakota, in March 1973 in an effort to focus attention on poverty and rampant alcoholism among Indians on reservations.

Saturday night, June 28, 1969, New York City vice police raided the Stonewall Inn, a popular gay bar in the heart of Greenwich Village. The patrons bravely fought back, and the chaotic struggle spilled into the streets. Hundreds of other gays and their supporters joined the fracas against the police. Raucous rioting lasted throughout the weekend. When it ended, gays had forged a new sense of solidarity and a new organization, the Gay Liberation Front. "Gay is good for all of us," proclaimed one of its members. "The artificial categories 'heterosexual' and 'homosexual' have been laid on us by a sexist society."

As news of the Stonewall riots spread across the country, the gay rights movement assumed national proportions. By 1973, almost eight hundred gay organizations had been formed across the country, and every major city had a visible gay community and cultural life. As was the case with the civil rights crusade and the women's movement, however, the campaign for gay rights soon suffered from internal divisions and a conservative backlash. Gay activists engaged in fractious disputes over tactics and objectives, and conservative moralists and Christian fundamentalists launched a nationwide counterattack. By the end of the seventies, the gay movement had lost its initial momentum and was struggling to salvage many of its hard-won gains.

NIXON AND MIDDLE AMERICA

The turmoil of the sixties—anti-war protesters, counter-cultural rebellions, liberationist movements, street violence—spawned a cultural backlash that propelled **Richard M. Nixon**'s narrow election victory in 1968. On many levels he was an unlikely president with a peculiar personality. The hardworking son of poor, unloving parents, he grew up under difficult circumstances in southern California during the Great Depression. Nixon was a loner all of his life who displayed violent mood swings punctuated by raging temper tantrums and anti-Semitic outbursts. Nixon nursed bitter grudges and took politics personally. He was a good hater who could be ruthless and vindictive in attacking his opponents. A leading Republican, Senator Robert A. Taft of Ohio, characterized young Congressman Nixon in the early fifties as a "little man in a big hurry" with "a mean and vindictive streak."

But Nixon also had extraordinary gifts: he was smart, shrewd, cunning, conniving, and doggedly determined to succeed in politics. He knew how to get things done, although he did not worry much about the ethics of his methods. He was nicknamed "Tricky Dick" for good reason. One of his presidential aides admitted that "we did often lie, mislead, deceive, try to use [the media], and to con them." Throughout his long public career, Nixon displayed remarkable grit and resilience. As Henry Kissinger, Nixon's national security adviser, who later became secretary of state, acknowledged, "Can you imagine what this man would have been like if somebody had loved him?"

The new president selected men for his cabinet and White House staff who would carry out his orders with blind obedience. John Mitchell, the gruff attorney general who had been a senior partner in Nixon's New York law firm, was the new president's closest confidant. H. R. (Bob) Haldeman, an imperious former advertising executive, served as Nixon's chief of staff. As Haldeman explained, "Every President needs a son of a bitch, and I'm Nixon's. I'm his buffer, I'm his bastard." He was succeeded in 1973 by Colonel (later General) Alexander Haig, whom Nixon described as "the meanest, toughest, most ambitious son of a bitch I ever knew." John Ehrlichman, a Seattle attorney and college schoolmate of Haldeman's, served as chief domestic-policy adviser.

Nixon tapped as secretary of state his old friend William Rogers, who had served as attorney general under Dwight D. Eisenhower, but the president had no intention of making Rogers the nation's chief diplomat. Rogers's control over foreign policy was quickly preempted by **Henry Kissinger**, a distinguished German-born Harvard political scientist who served as national security adviser before becoming secretary of state in 1973. Kissinger came to dominate the Nixon administration's diplomatic planning and emerged as one of the most respected and internationally famous members of the staff. Nixon often had to mediate the tensions between Rogers and Kissinger, noting that Rogers considered Kissinger "Machiavellian, deceitful, egotistical, arrogant, and insulting," while Kissinger viewed Rogers as "vain, emotional, unable to keep a secret, and hopelessly dominated by the State Department bureaucracy."

NIXON'S SOUTHERN STRATEGY   Nixon was no friend of the civil rights movement, the youth revolt or the counterculture. He had been elected in 1968 as the representative of middle America, those middle-class citizens fed up with the liberal politics and radical culture of the sixties. Nixon explicitly appealed to the "silent majority" of predominantly white working-class and middle-class citizens determined to regain control of a society they feared was in permissiveness, anarchy, and tyranny by the minority. He promised voters that he would return "law and order" to a nation in turmoil.

A major reason for Nixon's election victories in 1968 and 1972 was the effective "southern strategy" fashioned by his campaign staffers. Of all the nation's regions, the South had long been the most conservative. The majority of southern white voters were pious and patriotic, fervently anti-Communist, and skeptical of social welfare programs. For a century, the "Solid South" had steadfastly voted for Democrats in national elections. During the late sixties and seventies, however, a surging economy and wave of population growth transformed the so-called Sunbelt states in the South and the Southwest. The southern states had long been the nation's poorest and most backward-looking region, but that changed dramatically, in part because of the rapid expansion of air conditioning. By 1980, over 70 percent of southern homes were air-conditioned. The Sunbelt's warm climate, low cost of living, low taxes, and promotion of economic development convinced waves of businesses and workers to relocate to the region.

Between 1970 and 1990 the South's population grew by 40 percent, more than twice the national average. The New South promoted by Henry Grady in the 1880s had finally arrived. The "Sunbelt" states were attractive to migrants not only because of their mild climate and abundant natural resources; they also had the lowest rates of taxation and labor union participation as well as the highest rates of economic growth. In the seventies, southern "redneck" culture suddenly became all the rage, as people across the nation embraced

NASCAR racing, cowboy boots, pickup trucks, and barbecue. As singer Charlie Daniels sang in 1974, "The South's Gonna Do It Again."

Nixon and his aides forged a new conservative coalition that included two traditionally Democratic voting blocs: blue-collar ethnic voters in the North and white southerners. In the South, Nixon shrewdly played the race card: he assured southern conservatives that he would appoint justices to the Supreme Court who would undermine federal enforcement of civil rights laws, including mandatory school busing to achieve racial integration and affirmative-action programs designed to give minorities priority in hiring decisions. Nixon also appealed to the economic concerns of middle-class southern whites by promising lower tax rates and less government regulation. Finally, Nixon specialized in hard-hitting, polarizing rhetoric, drawing vivid contrasts between the turmoil in the streets of Chicago during the Democratic nominating convention and the "law-and-order" theme of his own campaign.

Once in the White House, Nixon followed through on his campaign pledges to southern conservatives. In the 1972 election Nixon carried every southern state by whopping majorities. The transformation of the once "solid" Democratic South into the predominantly Republican South was the greatest realignment in American politics since Franklin D. Roosevelt's election in 1932.

President Nixon expressed contempt for the civil rights movement, set out to dismantle the war on poverty, appointed no African Americans to his cabinet, and refused to meet with the Congressional Black Caucus. "We've had enough social programs: forced integration, education, housing," he told his chief of staff. "People don't want more [people] on welfare. They don't want to help the working poor, and our mood needs to be harder on this, not softer."

In 1970, Nixon launched a concerted effort to block congressional renewal of the Voting Rights Act of 1965 and delay implementation of court orders requiring the desegregation of school districts in Mississippi. Sixty-five lawyers in the Justice Department signed a letter of protest against the administration's stance. The Democratic Congress then extended the Voting Rights Act over Nixon's veto. The Supreme Court, in the first decision made under the new chief justice, Warren Burger—a Nixon appointee—mandated the integration of the Mississippi public schools. In *Alexander v. Holmes County Board of Education* (1969), a unanimous Court ordered a quick end to segregation. During Nixon's first term and despite his wishes, more schools were desegregated than in all the Kennedy-Johnson years combined.

Nixon also failed in his attempts to block desegregation efforts in urban areas. The Burger Court ruled unanimously in *Swann v. Charlotte-Mecklenburg*

Board of Education (1971) that school systems must bus students out of their neighborhoods if necessary to achieve racially integrated schools. Protest over desegregation now began to erupt more in the North, the Midwest, and the Southwest than in the South as white families in Boston, Denver, and other cities denounced the destruction of "the neighborhood school." Angry parents in Pontiac, Michigan, firebombed school buses. Racial violence was no longer a southern issue.

To transfer greater responsibility from the federal government to the states, President Nixon in 1972 pushed through Congress a five-year revenue-sharing plan that would distribute $30 billion of federal revenues to the states for use as they saw fit. But Nixon was less an ideologue than a shrewd pragmatist. His domestic program was a hodgepodge of reactionary and progressive initiatives. Nixon juggled opposing positions in an effort to maintain public support. He was, said the journalist Tom Wicker, "at once liberal and conservative, generous and begrudging, cynical and idealistic, choleric and calm, resentful and forgiving." Nixon also had to deal with a stern political fact: the Democrats controlled both houses of Congress during his first term. Congress moved forward with significant new legislation which Nixon signed: the right of eighteen-year-olds to vote in national elections (1970) and in all elections under the Twenty-sixth Amendment (1971); increases in Social Security benefits indexed to the inflation rate and a rise in food-stamp funding; the Occupational Safety and Health Act (1970) to ensure safe workplaces; and the Federal Election Campaign Act (1971), which modified the rules of campaign finance to reduce the role of corporate financial donations.

ENVIRONMENTAL PROTECTION   Dramatic increases in the price of oil and gasoline during the seventies fueled a major energy crisis in the United States. People began to realize that natural resources were limited— and increasingly expensive. The widespread recognition that America faced limits to economic growth spurred broad support for environmental protection in the 1970s. Bowing to pressure from both parties, as well as polls showing that 75 percent of voters supported stronger environmental protections, President Nixon told an aide to "keep me out of trouble on environmental issues." Ever the pragmatic politician, the president recognized that the public mood had shifted toward greater environmental protections. Nixon feared that if he vetoed legislative efforts to improve environmental quality, the Congress would overrule him, so he would not stand in the way. In late 1969, he reluctantly signed the amended Endangered Species Preservation Act and the National Environmental Policy Act. The latter became effective on

January 1, 1970, the year that environmental groups established an annual Earth Day celebration. In 1970, Nixon by executive order created two new federal environmental agencies, the Environmental Protection Agency (EPA) and the National Oceanic and Atmospheric Administration (NOAA). That same year, he also signed the Clean Air Act to reduce air pollution on a national level. Two years, later, however, Nixon vetoed a new clean water act, only to see Congress override his effort.

ECONOMIC MALAISE   The major domestic development during the Nixon years was a floundering economy. Overheated by the accumulated expense of the Vietnam War, the annual inflation rate began to rise in 1967, when it was at 3 percent. By 1973, it was at 9 percent; a year later it was at 12 percent, and it remained in double digits for most of the seventies. Meanwhile unemployment, at a low of 3.3 percent when Nixon took office, climbed to 6 percent by the end of 1970 and threatened to keep rising. Somehow the economy was undergoing a recession and inflation at the same time. Economists coined the term *stagflation* to describe the unprecedented syndrome that defied the orthodox laws of economics. The unusual combination of a stagnant economy with inflationary prices befuddled experts. There were no easy answers, no certain solutions.

The economic malaise had at least three deep-rooted causes. First, the Johnson administration had financed both the far-flung Great Society social-welfare programs and the Vietnam War without a major tax increase, thereby generating larger federal deficits, a major expansion of the money supply, and price inflation. Second and more important, by the late sixties U.S. companies faced stiff competition in international markets from West Germany, Japan, and other emerging industrial powers. American technological and economic superiority was no longer unchallenged. Third, the post–World War II economy had depended heavily upon cheap sources of energy; no other nation was more dependent than the United States upon the automobile and the automobile industry, and no other nation was more wasteful in its use of fossil fuels in factories and homes.

Just as domestic petroleum reserves began to dwindle and dependence upon foreign sources increased, the Organization of Petroleum Exporting Countries (OPEC) resolved to use its huge oil supplies as a political and economic weapon. In 1973, the United States sent massive aid to Israel after a devastating Syrian-Egyptian attack on Yom Kippur, the holiest day on the Jewish calendar. OPEC responded by announcing announced that it would not sell oil to nations supporting Israel and that it was raising its prices by 400 percent. Gasoline grew scarce, and prices soared. American motorists thereafter faced long lines at gas stations, and factories cut production.

Oil crisis, 1973

The scarcity of oil was dealt with by the rationing of gasoline. Gas stations, such as this one in Colorado, closed on Sundays to conserve supplies.

Another condition leading to stagflation was the flood of new workers—mainly baby boomers and women—entering the labor market. From 1965 to 1980, the workforce grew by 40 percent, almost 30 million workers, a number greater than the total labor force of France or West Germany. The number of new jobs could not keep up with the size of the workforce, leaving many unemployed. At the same time, worker productivity declined, further increasing inflation in the face of rising demand for goods and services.

Nixon responded erratically and ineffectively to stagflation, trying old remedies for a new problem. First he sought to reduce the federal deficit by raising taxes and cutting the budget. When the Democratic Congress refused to cooperate with that approach, he encouraged the Federal Reserve Board to reduce the nation's money supply by raising interest rates. The stock market immediately collapsed, and the economy plunged into the "Nixon recession."

A sense of desperation seized the White House as economic advisers struggled to respond to stagflation. In 1969, when asked about the possibility of imposing government restrictions on wages and prices, Nixon had been unequivocal: "Controls. Oh, my God, no! . . . We'll never go to controls." But in 1971 he reversed himself. He froze all wages and prices for ninety days. Still the economy floundered. By 1973 the wage and price guidelines were made voluntary and therefore ineffective.

Nixon and Vietnam

During the early 1970s the Vietnam War remained the dominant event of the time. Until the war ended and all troops had returned home, the nation would find it difficult to achieve the equilibrium that President Nixon had promised.

GRADUAL WITHDRAWAL   When Nixon was inaugurated as president in January 1969, there were 530,000 U.S. troops in Vietnam. Nixon believed that "there's no way to win the war. But we can't say that of course," because the United States needed to "keep some bargaining leverage" at the Paris negotiations with the North Vietnamese. During the 1968 presidential campaign, he had claimed to have a secret plan that would bring "peace with honor" in Vietnam. Peace, however, was long in coming and not very honorable. Nixon and Kissinger misread their ability to coerce the South Vietnamese government to sign an agreement. By the time a settlement was reached, in 1973, another twenty thousand Americans had died, the morale of the U.S. military had been shattered, millions of Asians had been killed or wounded, and fighting continued in Southeast Asia. In the end, Nixon's policy gained nothing the president could not have accomplished in 1969.

The new Vietnam policy implemented by Nixon and Kissinger moved along three fronts. First, U.S. negotiators in Paris demanded the withdrawal of Communist forces from South Vietnam and the preservation of the U.S.-backed regime of President Nguyen Van Thieu. The North Vietnamese and Viet Cong negotiators insisted on retaining a Communist military presence in the south and reunifying the Vietnamese people under a government dominated by the Communists. There was no common ground on which to come together. Hidden from public awareness and from America's South Vietnamese allies were secret meetings between Henry Kissinger, then Nixon's national security adviser, and the North Vietnamese.

On the second front, Nixon tried to quell domestic unrest stemming from the war. He labeled the anti-war movement a "brotherhood of the misguided, the mistaken, the well-meaning, and the malevolent." He sought to defuse the anti-war movement by reducing the number of U.S. troops in Vietnam, justifying the reduction as the natural result of "**Vietnamization**"—the equipping and training of South Vietnamese soldiers and pilots to assume the burden of combat in place of Americans. From a peak of 560,000 in 1969, U.S. combat forces were withdrawn at a steady pace. By 1973 only 50,000 troops remained in Vietnam. In 1969, Nixon also established a draft lottery system that eliminated many inequities and clarified the likelihood of being drafted: only nineteen-year-olds with low lottery numbers would have to go—and in 1973 the president did away with the draft altogether by creating an all-volunteer military. Nixon was more successful in reducing anti-war activity than in forcing concessions from the North Vietnamese negotiators in Paris.

On the third front, while reducing the number of U.S. combat troops, Nixon and Kissinger expanded the air war over Vietnam in hopes of persuading the North Vietnamese to come to terms. In March 1969 the United States began a fourteen-month-long bombing campaign aimed at Communist forces that were using Cambodia as a sanctuary for raids into South Vietnam. Congress did not learn of those secret raids until 1970, although the total tonnage of bombs dropped was four times that dropped on Japan during the Second World War. Still, Hanoi's leaders did not flinch. Then, on April 30, 1970, Nixon announced what he called an "incursion" into "neutral" Cambodia by U.S. troops to "clean out" North Vietnamese military bases. Nixon knew that sending troops into Cambodia would ignite ferocious criticism. Secretary of State William Rogers predicted that "this will make the [anti-war] students puke." Nixon told Kissinger, who strongly endorsed the decision to extend the fighting into Cambodia, "If this doesn't work, it'll be your ass, Henry."

News of the Cambodian "incursion" prompted explosive demonstrations on college campuses in the spring of 1970. Student protests led to the closing of hundreds of colleges and universities. At Kent State University, the Ohio National Guard was called in to quell rioting. The poorly trained guardsmen panicked and opened fire on the rock-throwing demonstrators, killing four student bystanders. Eleven days after the **Kent State** tragedy, on May 15, Mississippi highway patrolmen riddled a dormitory at Jackson State College with bullets, killing two students. In New York City, anti-war demonstrators who gathered to protest the deaths at Kent State and the invasion of Cambodia were attacked by "hard-hat" construction workers, who forced the protesters to disperse and then marched on City Hall to raise the U.S. flag, which had been lowered to half staff in mourning for the Kent State victims.

The following year, in June, the *New York Times* began publishing excerpts from *The History of the U.S. Decision-Making Process of Vietnam Policy*, a secret Defense Department study commissioned by Robert McNamara before his resignation as Lyndon Johnson's secretary of defense in 1968. The so-called **Pentagon Papers**, leaked to the press by a former Defense Department official,

Kent State University

National guardsmen shot and killed four student bystanders during anti-war demonstrations on the campus of Kent State University in Ohio.

Daniel Ellsberg, confirmed what many critics of the war had long suspected: Congress and the public had not received the full story on the Gulf of Tonkin incident of 1964, and contingency plans for American entry into the war were being drawn up while President Johnson was promising that combat troops would never be sent to Vietnam. Moreover, there was no plan for bringing the war to an end so long as the North Vietnamese persisted. Although the Pentagon Papers dealt with events only up to 1965, the Nixon administration blocked their publication, arguing that they endangered national security and that their publication would prolong the war. By a vote of 6 to 3, the Supreme Court ruled against the government. Newspapers throughout the country began publication of the controversial documents the next day.

NIXON TRIUMPHANT

Amid the ongoing controversies about the Vietnam War, Nixon, in tandem with Henry Kissinger, achieved several major breakthroughs in foreign policy. Nixon displayed his savvy and flexibility by making dramatic changes in U.S. relations with the major powers of the Communist world—China and the Soviet Union—changes that transformed the dynamics of the cold war.

By 1969, Nixon and Kissinger had come to envision a new multipolar world order replacing the conventional bipolar confrontation between the United States and the Soviet Union. Since 1945 the United States had lost its monopoly on nuclear weapons and its overwhelming economic dominance and geopolitical influence. The rapid rise of competing power centers in Europe, China, and Japan complicated international relations—the People's Republic of China (Communist China) had replaced the United States as the Soviet Union's most threatening competitor—but the competition between the two largest communist nations also provided strategic opportunities for the United States, which Nixon and Kissinger seized. Their grand vision of the future world order entailed cultivating a partnership with Communist China, slowing the perennial arms race with the Soviet Union, and ending the war in Vietnam.

In early 1970, Nixon announced a significant alteration in U.S. foreign policy. The United States could no longer be the world's policeman containing the expansion of communism: "America cannot—and will not—conceive *all* the plans, design *all* the programs, execute *all* the decisions, and undertake *all* the defense of the free nations of the world." In explaining what became known as the Nixon Doctrine, the president declared that "our *interests* must shape our *commitments*, rather than the other way around." The United States, he and Kissinger stressed, must become more selective in its commitments abroad, and it would begin to establish selected partnerships with Communist countries in areas of mutual interest. That Nixon, a Republican with a history of rabid anti-communism, would pursue such a policy of détente shocked many observers and demonstrated yet again his innovative flexibility.

CHINA   In 1971, Nixon sent Henry Kissinger on a secret trip to Beijing to explore the possibility of U.S. recognition of Communist China. Since 1949, when Mao Zedong's revolutionary movement established control in China, the United States had refused to recognize Communist China, preferring to regard Chiang Kai-shek's exiled regime on the island of Taiwan as the legitimate Chinese government. But now the time seemed ripe for a bold renewal of ties. Both the United States and Communist China were exhausted from prolonged wars (in Vietnam and clashes along the Sino-Soviet border) and intense domestic strife (antiwar protests in America, the Cultural Revolution in China). Both nations were eager to resist Soviet expansionism around the world.

The United States and China

With President Richard M. Nixon's visit to China in 1972, the United States formally recognized China's Communist government. Here Nixon and Chinese premier Zhou Enlai drink a toast.

During their secret discussions, Kissinger and Chinese leaders agreed that continuing confrontation made no sense for either nation. Seven months later, on February 21, 1972, stunned Americans watched on television as President Nixon drank toasts in Beijing with prime minister Zhou Enlai and Chairman Mao Zedong. In one simple but astonishing stroke, Nixon and Kissinger had ended two decades of diplomatic isolation of the People's Republic of China. They had seen a geopolitical opportunity and seized it. The United States and China agreed to scientific and cultural exchanges, steps toward the resumption of trade, and the eventual reunification of Taiwan with the mainland. A year after the Nixon visit, "liaison offices" were established in Washington and Beijing that served as unofficial embassies, and in 1979 diplomatic recognition was formalized. Richard Nixon had accomplished a diplomatic feat that his Democratic predecessors could not.

DÉTENTE   In truth, China welcomed the breakthrough in relations with the United States because its festering rivalry with the Soviet Union, with which it shares a long border, had become more threatening than its rivalry with the West. The Soviet leaders, troubled by the Sino-American agreements, were also eager to ease tensions with the United States. This was especially true now that they had, as a result of a huge arms build-up following the Cuban missile crisis, achieved virtual parity with the United States in nuclear weapons. Once again President Nixon surprised the world, announcing that he would visit Moscow in 1972 for discussions with Leonid Brezhnev, the Soviet premier. The high drama of the China visit was repeated in Moscow, with toasts and elegant dinners attended by world leaders who had previously regarded each other as incarnations of evil.

What became known as **détente** with the Soviets offered the promise of a more restrained competition between the two superpowers. Nixon and

Brezhnev signed pathbreaking agreements reached at the Strategic Arms Limitation Talks (SALT), which negotiators had been working on since 1969. The SALT agreement did not end the arms race, but it did limit the number of missiles with nuclear warheads each nation could possess and prohibited the construction of antiballistic missile systems. The Moscow summit also produced new trade agreements, including an arrangement whereby the United States sold almost a quarter of its wheat crop to the Soviets at a favorable price. In sum, the Moscow summit revealed the dramatic easing of tensions between the two cold war superpowers. For Nixon and Kissinger the agreements with China and the Soviet Union represented monumental changes in the global order that would have lasting consequences. Over time, the détente policy with the Soviet Union would help end the cold war by lowering Soviet hostility to Western influences penetrating their closed society, which slowly eroded Communist rule from the inside.

SHUTTLE DIPLOMACY   The Nixon-Kissinger initiatives in the Middle East were less dramatic and less conclusive than the agreements with China and the Soviet Union, but they did show that the United States at long last recognized the legitimacy of Arab interests in the region and its own dependence upon Middle Eastern oil, even though the Arab nations were adamantly opposed to the existence of Israel. In the Six-Day War of 1967, Israeli forces routed the armies of Egypt, Syria, and Jordan and seized territory from all three nations. Moreover, the number of Palestinian refugees, many of them homeless since the creation of Israel in 1948, increased after the 1967 Israeli victory.

The Middle East remained a tinderbox of tensions. On October 6, 1973, the Jewish holy day of Yom Kippur, Syria and Egypt, backed by Soviet weapons, attacked Israel, igniting what became the Yom Kippur War. It created the most dangerous confrontation between the United States and the Soviet Union since the Cuban missile crisis. President Nixon asked Henry Kissinger, now secretary of state, to keep the Soviets out of the Middle Eastern war. On October 20, Kissinger flew to Moscow to meet directly with Leonid Brezhnev just as "all hell had broken loose" in the White House with Nixon's firing of the attorney general and his staff for their unwillingness to cover up the Watergate mess. Kissinger deftly negotiated a cease-fire and exerted pressure to prevent Israel from taking additional Arab territory. In an attempt to broker a lasting settlement, Kissinger made numerous flights among the capitals of the Middle East. His "shuttle diplomacy" won acclaim from all sides, but Kissinger failed to find a comprehensive formula for peace in the troubled region and ignored the

Henry Kissinger's "shuttle diplomacy"

President Anwar el-Sadat of Egypt and Secretary of State Henry Kissinger, during one of Kissinger's many visits to the Middle East, talk with reporters in an effort to bring peace.

Palestinian problem. He did, however, lay groundwork for the accord between Israel and Egypt in 1977.

WAR WITHOUT END   During 1972, the mounting social divisions at home and the approach of the presidential election influenced the negotiations in Paris between the United States and representatives of North Vietnam. In the summer of 1972, Henry Kissinger again began meeting privately with the North Vietnamese negotiators, and he now dropped his insistence upon the removal of all North Vietnamese troops from the South before the withdrawal of the remaining U.S. troops. On October 26, only a week before the U.S. presidential election, Kissinger announced, "Peace is at hand." But this was a cynical ploy to win votes. Several days earlier the Thieu regime in South Vietnam had rejected the Kissinger plan for a cease-fire, fearful that allowing North Vietnamese troops to remain in the south would virtually guarantee a Communist victory. The Paris peace talks broke off on December 16, and two days later the newly reelected Nixon ordered massive bombing of Hanoi and Haiphong, the two largest cities in North Vietnam. These so-called Christmas bombings and the simultaneous mining of North Vietnamese harbors aroused worldwide protest.

But the bombings also made the North Vietnamese more flexible at the negotiating table. The Christmas bombings stopped on December 29, and the talks in Paris soon resumed. On January 27, 1973, the United States, North and South Vietnam, and the Viet Cong signed an "agreement on ending the war and restoring peace in Vietnam." While Nixon and Kissinger claimed that the bombing had brought North Vietnam to its senses, in truth the North Vietnamese never altered their basic stance; they kept 150,000 troops in the South and remained committed to the reunification of Vietnam under one government. What had changed since the previous fall was the willingness of the South Vietnamese, who were never allowed to participate in the negotiations, to accept the agreement, albeit reluctantly, on the basis of Nixon's promise that the United States would respond "with full force" to any Communist violation of the agreement. Kissinger had little confidence that the treaty provisions would enable South Vietnam to survive on its own. He told a White House staffer, "If they're lucky, they can hold out for a year and a half."

THE ELECTION OF 1972   Nixon's foreign-policy achievements allowed him to stage the presidential campaign of 1972 as a triumphal procession. The main threat to his re-election came from Alabama's Democratic governor George Wallace, a populist segregationist who had the potential as a third-party candidate to deprive the Republicans of conservative southern votes and thereby throw the election to the Democrats or to the Democratic-controlled Congress. That threat ended, however, on May 15, 1972, when Wallace was shot by a man eager to achieve a grisly brand of notoriety. Wallace survived but was left paralyzed below the waist, forcing him to withdraw from the campaign.

Meanwhile, the Democrats were further ensuring Nixon's victory by nominating Senator McGovern of South Dakota, a steadfast anti-war liberal. In the 1972 election Nixon won the greatest victory of any Republican presidential candidate in history, capturing 520 electoral votes to only 17 for McGovern. The popular vote was equally decisive: 46 million to 28 million, a proportion of the total vote (60.8 percent) that was second only to Lyndon B. Johnson's victory over Barry Goldwater in 1964. After his landslide victory, Nixon promised to complete his efforts at a conservative revolution. He planned to promote the "more conservative values and beliefs of the New Majority throughout the country and use my power to put some teeth in my new American Revolution."

But Nixon's easy victory and triumphant outlook would be short-lived. During the course of the presidential campaign, McGovern had complained about the numerous "dirty tricks" orchestrated by members of the Nixon administration during the campaign. The insecure Nixon, it turned out, had ordered aides to harass Democratic party leaders—by any means necessary. Nixon, for example, ordered illegal wiretaps on his opponents (as well as his aides), tried to coerce the Internal Revenue Service to intimidate Democrats, and told his chief of staff to break into the safe at the Brookings Institution, a Washington think tank with liberal ties. "Goddamnit," he told Bob Haldeman, "get in and get those files. Blow the safe and get it."

McGovern was especially disturbed by a curious incident on June 17, 1972, when five burglars were caught breaking into the Democratic National Committee headquarters in the Watergate apartment and office complex in Washington, D.C. The burglars were former CIA agents, one of whom, James W. McCord, worked for the Nixon campaign. At the time, McGovern's shrill Watergate accusations seemed like sour grapes from a candidate running far behind in the polls. Nixon and his staff ignored the news of the burglary. The president said that no one cares "when somebody bugs somebody else." Privately, however, he and his senior aides Bob Haldeman, John Dean, and John Ehrlichman began feverish efforts to cover up the Watergate break-in. The White House secretly provided legal assistance ("hush money") to the burglars to buy their silence and tried to keep the FBI out of the investigation. Nixon and his closest aides also discussed using the CIA to derail the Justice Department investigation of the Watergate burglary.

WATERGATE

During the trial of the accused Watergate burglars in January 1973, the relentless prodding of federal Judge John J. Sirica led one of the accused to tell the full story of the Nixon administration's complicity in the **Watergate** episode. James W. McCord, security chief of the Committee to Re-Elect the President (CREEP), was the first in a long line of informers in a political melodrama that unfolded over two years, revealing the systematic efforts of Nixon and his aides to create an "imperial presidency" above the law. The scandal ended in the first presidential resignation in history, the conviction and imprisonment of twenty-five administration officials, including four cabinet members, and the most serious constitutional crisis since the impeachment trial of President Andrew Johnson in 1868.

UNCOVERING THE COVER-UP   The trail of evidence pursued first by Judge Sirica, then by a grand jury, and then by a Senate committee headed by Democrat Samuel J. Ervin Jr. of North Carolina led directly to the White House. Nixon was personally involved in the cover-up of the Watergate incident, using his presidential powers to discredit and block the investigation. And most alarming, as it turned out, the Watergate burglary was merely one small part of a larger pattern of corruption and criminality sanctioned by the Nixon White House.

For all of his abilities and accomplishments, Nixon was a chronically insecure person with a thirst for vengeance and a hair trigger temper. The vicious partisanship of the Sixties fed his paranoia. As president, he began keeping lists of enemies and launched secret efforts to embarrass and punish them. In 1970, after the *New York Times* had disclosed that secret American bombings in Cambodia had been going on for years, a furious Nixon ordered illegal telephone taps on several journalists and government employees suspected of leaking the story. The covert activity against the press and critics of Nixon's Vietnam policies increased in 1971, during the crisis generated by the publication of the Pentagon Papers, when a team of burglars under the direction of White House adviser John Ehrlichman broke into Daniel Ellsberg's psychiatrist's office in an effort to obtain damaging information on Ellsberg, the man who had given the Pentagon Papers to the press. By the spring of 1972, Ehrlichman was overseeing a team of "dirty tricksters" who performed various acts of sabotage against Democrats—for example, falsely accusing Senators Hubert H. Humphrey and Henry Jackson of sexual improprieties, forging press releases, setting off stink bombs at Democratic campaign events, and planting spies on the McGovern campaign plane. By the time of the Watergate break-in, the money to finance these pranks was being illegally collected through CREEP and had been placed under the control of the White House staff.

The Watergate cover-up unraveled as various people, including John Dean, legal counsel to the president, began to cooperate with prosecutors. At the same time, two reporters for the *Washington Post*, Carl Bernstein and Bob Woodward, relentlessly pursued the story and its money trail. It unraveled further in 1973 when L. Patrick Gray, acting director of the FBI, resigned after confessing that he had confiscated and destroyed several incriminating documents. On April 30, Ehrlichman and Haldeman resigned (they would later serve time in prison), together with Attorney General Richard Kleindienst. A few days later the president nervously assured the public in a television address, "I am not a crook." Then John Dean, whom Nixon had dismissed because of his cooperation with prosecutors, testified to the Ervin committee in the Senate that there had been a White House-orchestrated cover-up approved by the president. Nixon, meanwhile, refused to provide Senator Ervin's committee with documents it requested, citing "executive privilege" to protect national security. In another shocking disclosure, a White House aide told the Ervin committee that Nixon had installed a taping system in the White House and that many of the conversations about the Watergate burglary and cover-up had been recorded.

That bombshell revelation set off a yearlong legal battle for the "Nixon tapes." Harvard law professor Archibald Cox, whom Nixon's new attorney general, Elliot Richardson, had appointed as special prosecutor to investigate the Watergate case, took the president to court in October 1973 to obtain the tapes. Nixon refused to release the recordings and ordered Cox fired. In what became known as the Saturday Night Massacre, on October 20 Attorney General Elliot Richardson and Deputy Attorney General William Ruckelshaus resigned rather than fire the special prosecutor. Solicitor General Robert Bork finally fired Cox. Nixon's dismissal of Cox ("that fucking Harvard professor") produced a firestorm of public indignation. Numerous newspaper and magazine editorials, as well as a growing chorus of legislators, called for the president to be impeached for obstructing justice. A Gallup poll revealed that Nixon's approval rating had plunged to 17 percent, its lowest level the lowest level any president had ever experienced.

The firing of Cox failed to end Nixon's legal troubles. Cox's replacement as special prosecutor, Leon Jaworski, also took the president to court. In March 1974 the Watergate grand jury indicted John Ehrlichman, Bob Haldeman, and John Mitchell for obstruction of justice and named Nixon as an "unindicted co-conspirator." On April 30, Nixon, still refusing to turn over the actual Oval Office tapes, released 1,254 pages of transcribed recordings that he had edited himself, often substituting the phrase "expletive deleted" for the vulgar language and anti-Semitic rants he had frequently unleashed. At one point in the transcripts the president told his aides that they should have frequent memory lapses when testifying about the cover-up. The transcripts provoked widespread shock and revulsion as well as renewed demands for the president to resign. By the summer of 1974, Nixon was in full retreat, besieged on all fronts. He became alternately combative, melancholy, or petty. During White House visits, Kissinger found him increasingly unstable and drinking heavily. Alcohol made Nixon even more surly and combative, and he drank a lot. After a meeting with Nixon, Senator Barry Goldwater reported that the president "jabbered incessantly, often incoherently." He seemed "to be cracking."

For months, the drama of Watergate transfixed Americans. Each day they watched the Ervin committee hearings as if they were daytime soap operas. On July 24, 1974, the Supreme Court ruled unanimously, in *United States v. Richard M. Nixon,* that the president must surrender *all* of the tape recordings. A few days later the House Judiciary Committee voted to recommend three articles of impeachment: obstruction of justice through the payment of "hush money" to witnesses and the withholding of evidence, abuse of power through the use of federal agencies to deprive citizens of their constitutional rights, and defiance of Congress by withholding the tapes. But before the House of Representatives could meet to vote on impeachment, Nixon grudgingly handed over the complete set of White House tapes. Investigators then learned that sections of certain recordings were missing, including eighteen minutes of a key conversation in June 1972 during which Nixon first mentioned the Watergate burglary. The president's loyal secretary tried to accept blame for the erasure, claiming that she had accidentally pushed the wrong button, but technical experts later concluded that the missing segments had been intentionally deleted. The other transcripts, however, provided more than enough evidence of Nixon's involvement in the cover-up. At one point, the same president who had been the architect of détente with the Soviet Union and the recognition of Communist China had

yelled at aides asking what they and others should say to Watergate investigators, "I don't give a shit what happens. I want you all to stonewall it, let them plead the Fifth Amendment, cover-up or anything else, if it'll save it, save the plan."

On August 9, 1974, Richard Nixon resigned from office, the only president ever to do so. In 1969, he had begun his presidency hoping to heal America, to "bring people together." He left the presidency having deeply wounded the nation. The credibility gap between the presidency and the public that had developed under Lyndon B. Johnson had become a chasm

Nixon's resignation

Having resigned his office, Richard M. Nixon waves farewell outside the White House on August 9, 1974.

under Nixon, as the Watergate revelations fueled a widespread cynicism about the integrity of politics and politicians. Nixon claimed that "virtue is not what lifts great leaders above others" and insisted that a president's actions could not be "illegal." He was wrong. The Watergate affair's clearest lesson was that not even a president is above the law.

THE EFFECTS OF WATERGATE   Vice President Spiro Agnew did not succeed Nixon because he had been forced to resign in October 1973 for having accepted bribes from contractors before and during his term as vice president. The vice president at the time of Nixon's resignation was **Gerald Ford**, the congenial former Michigan congressman and House minority leader whom Nixon had appointed, with the approval of Congress, under the provisions of the Twenty-fifth Amendment. Ratified in 1967, the amendment provided for the appointment of a vice president when the office became vacant. On August 9, 1974, Gerald Ford was sworn in as the nation's first politically appointed chief executive.

Ford assumed the presidency by reassuring the nation that "our long nightmare is over." But restoring national harmony was not so easy. Tensions over racial and gender issues spawned ongoing battles in a variety of "culture wars" that erupted over incendiary issues such as gay rights, religious beliefs, and abortion. Only a month after taking office, Ford reopened the wounds of Watergate by issuing a "full, free, and absolute pardon" to a despondent and distraught Richard Nixon. Many Americans, however, were not in a forgiving mood when it came to Nixon's devious scheming. The announcement of Ford's pardon of Nixon ignited a storm of controversy. The new president was grilled by a House subcommittee wanting to know if he and Nixon had made a deal whereby Nixon would resign and Ford would become president if Ford granted the pardon. Ford steadfastly denied such charges and said that nothing was to be gained by putting Nixon in prison, but the Nixon pardon hobbled Ford's presidency. His approval rating plummeted from 71 percent to 49 percent in one day, the steepest drop ever recorded. Even the president's press secretary resigned in protest. Ford was devastated by the "hostile reaction" to the pardon; he never recovered the public's confidence.

If there was a silver lining in the dark cloud of Watergate, it was the vigor and resilience of the institutions that had brought a rogue president to justice—the press, Congress, the courts, and an aroused public opinion. Congress responded to the Watergate revelations with several pieces of legislation designed to curb executive power. Already nervous about possible efforts to renew American military assistance to South Vietnam, the Democratic-led Congress passed the War Powers Act (1973), which requires a president to inform Congress within forty-eight hours if U.S. troops are deployed in combat abroad and to withdraw troops after sixty days unless Congress specifically approves their stay. In an effort to correct abuses in the use of campaign funds, Congress enacted legislation in 1974 that set new ceilings on political contributions and expenditures. And in reaction to the Nixon claim of "executive privilege" as a means of withholding evidence, Congress strengthened the 1966 Freedom of Information Act to require prompt responses to requests for information from government files and to place on government agencies the burden of proof for classifying information as secret.

An Unelected President

During Richard Nixon's last year in office, the Watergate crisis so dominated national politics that major domestic and foreign problems received little executive attention. The perplexing combination of inflation and recession worsened, as did the oil crisis. At the same time, Secretary of State Henry Kissinger, who assumed control of foreign policy, watched helplessly as the South Vietnamese forces crumbled before North Vietnamese attacks, attempted with limited success to establish a framework for peace in the Middle East, and supported a CIA role in the overthrow of Salvador Allende Gossens, the popularly elected Marxist president of Chile, although neither Nixon nor Kissinger ever explained why a leftist government in Chile constituted a threat to the United States. Allende was subsequently murdered and replaced by General Augusto Pinochet Ugarte, a ruthless military dictator supposedly friendly to the United States.

THE FORD YEARS   As president, Gerald Ford soon adopted the posture he had developed as the minority leader in the House of Representatives: naysaying leader of the opposition who believed that the federal government exercised too much power. In his first fifteen months as president, Ford vetoed thirty-nine bills passed by the Democratic-controlled Congress, thereby outstripping Herbert Hoover's veto record in less than half the time. By resisting congressional pressure to reduce taxes and increase federal spending, he helped steer the struggling economy into the deepest recession since the Great Depression. Unemployment jumped to 9 percent in 1975, the annual rate of inflation had reached double digits, and the federal deficit hit a record the next year. Ford announced that inflation had become "Public Enemy No. 1," but he rejected bold actions such as implementing wage and

Gerald Ford

Ford listens apprehensively to the rising rates of unemployment and inflation at an economic conference in 1974.

price controls to curb inflation, preferring instead a timid public relations campaign, created by an advertising agency, featuring lapel buttons that simply read WIN, symbolizing the administration's publicity campaign to "Whip Inflation Now." The WIN buttons instead became a national joke and a popular symbol of Ford's ineffectiveness in the fight against stagflation. He himself admitted that it was a failed "gimmick." By 1975, when Ford delivered his State of the Union address, the president lamely admitted that "the state of the union is not good."

In foreign policy, Ford retained Henry Kissinger as secretary of state (while stripping him of his dual role of national security advisor) and attempted to continue Nixon's goals of stability in the Middle East, rapprochement with China, and détente with the Soviet Union. In addition, Kissinger's tireless Middle East diplomacy produced an important agreement: Israel promised to return to Egypt most of the Sinai territory captured in the 1967 War, and the two nations agreed to rely upon negotiations rather than force to settle future disagreements. These limited but significant achievements should have enhanced Ford's image, but they were drowned in the sea of criticism and carping that followed the collapse of South Vietnam to the Communists in May 1975.

THE COLLAPSE OF SOUTH VIETNAM On March 29, 1973, the last U.S. combat troops left Vietnam. On that same day almost six hundred American prisoners of war, most of them downed pilots, were released from Hanoi. Henry Kissinger was awarded the Nobel Peace Prize. Within months of the U.S. withdrawal, however, the cease-fire in Vietnam collapsed, the war between North and South resumed, and the Communist forces gained the upper hand. In Cambodia (renamed the Khmer Republic after it fell to the Communists and now called Kampuchea) and Laos, where fighting had been more sporadic, a Communist victory also seemed inevitable. In 1975, the North Vietnamese launched a full-scale invasion, and South Vietnamese president Thieu appealed to Washington for the promised U.S. assistance. Congress refused. The much-mentioned "peace with honor" had proved to be, in the words of one CIA official, only a "decent interval"—enough time for the United States to extricate itself from Vietnam before the collapse of the South Vietnamese government. On April 30, 1975, Americans watched on television as North Vietnamese tanks rolled into Saigon, soon to be renamed Ho Chi Minh City, and helicopters lifted the U.S. embassy officials to ships waiting offshore.

The longest, most controversial, and least successful war in American history was finally over, leaving in its wake a bitter legacy. During the period of U.S. involvement in the fighting, almost 2 million combatants and civilians were killed on both sides. North Vietnam absorbed incredible losses—some 600,000 soldiers and countless civilians killed. More than 58,000 Americans died in Vietnam, 300,000 were wounded, 2,500 were declared missing, and almost 100,000 returned missing one or more limbs.

The "loss" of the war and revelations of American atrocities such as those at My Lai eroded respect for the military so thoroughly that many young people came to regard military service as corrupting and ignoble. The Vietnam War, initially described as a crusade on behalf of democratic ideals, instead suggested that democracy was not easily transferable to third world regions that lacked any historical experience with representative government. Fought to show the world that the United States would be steadfast in containing the spread of communism, the war instead sapped the national will and fragmented the national consensus that had governed foreign affairs since 1947. It also changed the balance of power in domestic politics. Not only did the war undermine Lyndon B. Johnson's presidency; it also created enduring fissures in the Democratic party. As anti-war senator and 1972 Democratic presidential candidate George S. McGovern said, "The Vietnam tragedy is at the root of the confusion and division of the Democratic party. It tore up our souls."

Not only had a decade of American effort in Vietnam proved futile, but the Khmer Rouge, the Cambodian Communist movement, had also won a resounding victory, plunging that country into a colossal bloodbath. The maniacal Khmer Rouge leaders organized a genocidal campaign to destroy their opponents, killing almost a third of the total population. Meanwhile, the OPEC oil cartel was threatening another worldwide boycott, and various third world nations denounced the United States as a depraved and declining imperialist power. Ford lost his patience when he sent marines to rescue the crew of the American merchant ship *Mayaguez,* which had been captured by the Cambodian Communists. This vigorous move won popular acclaim until it was disclosed that the Cambodians had already agreed to release the captured Americans: the forty-one Americans killed in the operation had died for no purpose.

THE ELECTION OF 1976   Amid years of turmoil both national parties were in disarray as they prepared for the 1976 presidential election. At the Republican Convention, Gerald Ford had to fend off a powerful challenge for the nomination from the darling of the conservative wing of the party, Ronald Reagan, a former two-term California governor and Hollywood actor. Nixon mistakenly told Ford that Reagan was "a lightweight and not someone to be considered seriously or feared." But Reagan's candidacy was hurt when Barry Goldwater endorsed Ford's candidacy. The fractured Democrats chose an obscure former naval officer and engineer turned peanut farmer who had served one term as governor of Georgia. James Earl (Jimmy) Carter Jr. represented the new moderate wing of the Democratic party. He was one of several Democratic southern governors who self-consciously sought to reorient their party away from runaway liberalism. Carter insisted that he was neither a liberal nor a conservative but a pragmatist who would be adept at getting the "right thing" done in the "right ways." He capitalized on the post-Watergate cynicism by promising that he would "never tell a lie to the American people." Carter also trumpeted the advantages of his being a political "outsider" whose inexperience in Washington politics would be an asset to a nation still reeling from the Watergate debacle. Carter was certainly different from conventional candidates. Jaded political reporters covering the presidential campaign marveled at a Southern Baptist candidate who claimed to be "born again."

To the surprise of many pundits, the little-known Carter revived the New Deal coalition of southern whites, blacks, urban labor unionists, and ethnic groups to eke out a narrow win over Ford. Carter had 41 million votes to Ford's 39 million. A heavy turnout of African Americans in the South enabled Carter to sweep every state in the region except Virginia. Carter also benefited from the appeal of Walter F. Mondale, his liberal running mate and a favorite among blue-collar workers and the urban poor. Carter lost most of the trans-Mississippi West, but no Democratic candidate had made much headway there since Harry S. Truman in 1948. The significant story of the election was the low voter turnout. "Neither Ford nor Carter won as many votes as Mr. Nobody," said one reporter, commenting on the fact that almost half the eligible voters, apparently alienated by Watergate, the stagnant economy, and the two lackluster candidates, chose to sit out the election.

End of Chapter Review

CHAPTER SUMMARY

- **Rebellion and Reaction** Civil rights activism was the catalyst for a heightened interest in social causes during the sixties, especially among the young. Students for a Democratic Society (SDS) launched the New Left. Other prominent causes of the era included the anti-war movement, the women's liberation movement, Native American rights, Hispanic rights, and gay rights. By 1970 a counterculture had emerged, featuring young people who used mind-altering drugs, lived on rural communes, and in other ways "dropped out" of the conventional world, which they viewed as corrupt.

- **End of the Vietnam War** In 1968, Richard Nixon campaigned for the presidency pledging to secure a "peace with honor" in Vietnam, but years would pass before the war ended. His delays prompted an acceleration of anti-war protests. After the Kent State University shootings, the divisions between supporters and opponents of the war became especially contentious. The publication of the Pentagon Papers in 1971 and the heavy bombing of North Vietnam by the United States in December 1972 aroused intense worldwide protests. A month later North and South Vietnam agreed to end the war. The last U.S. troops left Vietnam in March 1973; two years later the government of South Vietnam collapsed, and the country was reunited under a Communist government.

- **Watergate** In an incident in 1972, burglars were caught breaking into the Democratic campaign headquarters at the Watergate complex in Washington, D.C. Eventually the Committee to Re-Elect the President (CREEP) was implicated, and investigators began to probe the question of President Nixon's involvement. Nixon tried to block the judicial process, which led the public to call for the president to be impeached for obstruction of justice. In 1974, in *United States v. Richard M. Nixon,* the Supreme Court ruled that the president had to surrender the so-called Watergate tapes. Nixon resigned to avoid being impeached.

- **Middle East Crisis** After the 1973 Yom Kippur War in the Middle East, the Organization of Petroleum Exporting Countries (OPEC) declined to sell oil to nations supporting Israel. President Carter brokered the Camp David Accords of 1978, which laid the groundwork for a peace treaty between Israel and Egypt.

CHRONOLOGY

1960	U.S. Food and Drug Administration approves the birth-control pill
1963	Betty Friedan's *The Feminine Mystique* is published
March 1969	U.S. planes begin a fourteen-month-long bombing campaign aimed at Communist sanctuaries in Cambodia
1971	Ratification of the Twenty-sixth Amendment gives eighteen-year-olds the right to vote in all elections
1972–74	The Watergate scandal unfolds
January 1973	In Paris, the United States, North and South Vietnam, and the Viet Cong agree to restore peace in Vietnam
1973	Congress passes the War Powers Act
April 1975	Saigon falls to the North Vietnamese

KEY TERMS & NAMES

33

A CONSERVATIVE
REALIGNMENT: 1977–1990

FOCUS QUESTIONS wwnorton.com/studyspace

- What explains the rise of Ronald Reagan and Republican conservatism?

- What was the Iran-Contra affair, and what did it show about the nature of the executive branch of government, even after Watergate?

- What factors led to the end of the cold war?

- What characterized the economy and society in the eighties?

- What were the causes of the First Gulf War?

During the seventies, America began to lose its self-confidence. The failed Vietnam War, the sordid revelations of Watergate, and the explosion in oil prices, interest/mortgage rates, and inflation revealed the limits of American power, prosperity, and virtue. For a nation long accustomed to economic growth and spreading affluence, the frustrating persistence of stagflation and gasoline shortages undermined national optimism. At the same time, the growing environmental movement highlighted the damages imposed by runaway pollution and unregulated development on the nation's air, water, and other natural resources. In short, many people during the seventies began downsizing their expectations of the American Dream. Out with global interventionism required by the efforts to "contain" and "roll back" communism, in with the isolationism spawned by what became known as the Vietnam Syndrome. Out with gas-guzzling U.S.-produced Cadillacs, in with economical Toyotas made in Japan. Out with the "imperial presidency," in with honesty, transparency, humility, and hesitancy abroad.

THE CARTER PRESIDENCY

James (Jimmy) Earl Carter Jr. won the very close election of 1976 for two primary reasons: he convinced voters that he was an incorruptible "outsider" who would restore integrity and honesty to the presidency in the aftermath of the Watergate scandal (his campaign slogan was "I'll never tell a lie"), and he represented a new generation of "moderate" southern Democratic leaders who were committed to fiscal responsibility rather than "big government." As he stressed in his 1977 inaugural address, "We have learned that 'more' is not necessarily 'better,' that even our great nation has limits." He did not heed his own remarks, however. Instead of focusing on a few top priorities, Carter tried to do too much too fast. In the end, his crusading comprehensiveness would be his undoing. Carter's inexperience in Washington politics often translated into incompetence, and his relentless moralizing depressed rather than excited the public mood. By the end of the decade, Carter's painful failure of leadership and his gloomy sermonizing would give way to Ronald Reagan's uplifting conservative crusade to restore American greatness.

Like Gerald Ford before him, **Jimmy Carter** faced vexing domestic problems and formidable international challenges. He was expected to cure the recession and reduce inflation at a time when all industrial economies were shaken by a shortage of oil and confidence. American industrial productivity was declining, as were the opportunities for upward economic mobility. If those harsh economic realities were not challenging enough, Carter was expected to restore American stature abroad and lift the national spirit through a set of political institutions in which many people had lost faith. Meeting such expectations would be miraculous, but Carter, for all of his "almost arrogant self-confidence," was no miracle worker.

Still, during the first two years of his presidency, Carter enjoyed several successes. His administration included more African Americans and women than ever before. Carter fulfilled a controversial campaign pledge by offering amnesty to the thousands of young men who had fled the country rather than serve in Vietnam. He reorganized the executive branch and reduced government red tape by slowing the issuance of burdensome new regulations and creating two new cabinet-level agencies, the departments of Energy and Education. He also pushed through Congress several significant environmental initiatives, including new controls over strip coal mining, the creation of a $1.6 billion "Superfund" to clean up toxic chemical waste sites, and a proposal to protect over 100 million acres of Alaskan land from development.

But success was short-lived. As president, the bright, energetic Carter was his own worst enemy. By nature, he was a bureaucrat rather than a leader, a compulsive micro-manager unable to establish a compelling vision for the nation's future. As a self-defined "Washington outsider," Carter recruited most of his staff and many of his cabinet members from people he had worked with in Georgia while serving as govenor. The eccentric White House staffers and cabinet members who constituted what journalists called the "Georgia mafia," like the president, lacked experience and expertise at a national level. And it showed. Only too late did Carter acknowledge that he needed the wisdom of Washington insiders.

Carter's political naïveté surfaced in the protracted debate over energy policy. He insisted that managing the energy crisis was the nation's (and his) greatest challenge. It constituted what he called the "moral equivalent of war," borrowing the phrase from the nineteenth-century philosopher William James. But Carter chose to keep Congress in the dark as he and a few close advisers developed his national energy program. Carter disliked stroking legislators or wheeling and dealing to get legislation passed. When he presented his energy bill to the Congress, it contained 113 separate initiatives. It was a miscellany, not a program, providing a little of everything and much of nothing. Carter's energy package was not well received in the Senate. As a result, the energy bill that the president signed in 1978 was a gutted version of the original, reflecting the power of special-interest lobbyists representing the oil, gas, and automotive industries. One Carter aide said that the bill looked like it had been "nibbled to death by ducks."

Several of Carter's early foreign-policy initiatives also got caught in political crossfires. Soon after his inauguration, Carter revived the idealistic spirit of Woodrow Wilson's internationalism when he vowed that "the soul of our foreign policy" should be the defense of human rights abroad. He and his judicious secretary of state decided to cut off U.S. aid to nations that chronically violated basic human rights. This human rights campaign aroused opposition from two sides, however: those who feared it sacrificed a detached appraisal of national interest for high-level moralizing, and those who believed that human rights were important but that the administration was applying the standard inconsistently.

Similarly, Carter's heroic negotiation of treaties to turn over control of the Panama Canal to the Panamanian government generated intense criticism. Although former Republican presidents Ford and Nixon, as well as Henry Kissinger, endorsed Carter's efforts, Republican Ronald Reagan claimed that the Canal Zone was sovereign American soil purchased "fair and square" during Theodore Roosevelt's administration. (In the congressional debate one senator quipped, "We stole it fair and square, so why can't we keep it?") Carter argued that the limitations on U.S. influence in Latin America and the deep resentment of American colonialism in Panama left the United States with no other choice but to transfer the canal to Panama. The Canal Zone would revert to Panama in stages, with completion of the process in 1999. The Senate ratified the treaties by a paper-thin margin (68 to 32, two votes more than the required two thirds), but conservatives lambasted Carter for surrendering American authority in a critical part of the world.

THE CAMP DAVID ACCORDS Carter's crowning foreign-policy achievement, which even his most bitter critics applauded, was his brokering of a peace agreement between Israel and Egypt. In 1977, Egyptian president Anwar el-Sadat flew to Tel Aviv at the invitation of Israeli prime minister Menachem Begin. Sadat's bold act, and his accompanying announcement that Egypt was willing to recognize the legitimacy of the Israeli state, opened

The Camp David Accords

Egyptian president Anwar el-Sadat (left), Jimmy Carter (center), and Israeli prime minister Menachem Begin (right) at the announcement of the Camp David Accords, September 1978.

up diplomatic opportunities that Carter and Secretary of State Cyrus Vance quickly pursued.

In 1978, Carter invited Sadat and Begin to the presidential retreat at Camp David, in Maryland, for two weeks of difficult negotiations. The first part of the eventual agreement called for Israel to return all land in the Sinai in exchange for Egyptian recognition of Israel's sovereignty. This agreement, dubbed the **Camp David Accords**, was implemented in 1982, when the last Israeli settler vacated the peninsula. But the second part of the agreement, calling for Israel to negotiate with Sadat to resolve the Palestinian refugee dilemma, began to unravel soon after the Camp David summit.

By March 26, 1979, when Begin and Sadat returned to Washington to sign the formal treaty, Begin had already refused to block new Israeli settlements on the West Bank of the Jordan River, which Sadat had regarded as a prospective homeland for the Palestinians. In the wake of the Camp David Accords, most of the Arab nations condemned Sadat as a traitor. Islamic extremists assassinated him in 1981. Still, Carter and Vance's high-level diplomacy made an all-out war between Israel and the Arab world less likely.

MOUNTING TROUBLES Carter's crowning failure, which even his most avid supporters acknowledged, was his mismanagement of the economy. In effect, he inherited a bad situation from President Ford and made it worse. Carter employed the same economic policies as Nixon and Ford to fight the mystery of stagflation, but he reversed the order of the federal "cure," preferring first to fight unemployment with a tax cut and increased public spending. Unemployment declined slightly, from 8 to 7 percent in 1977, but the annual inflation rate soared; at 5 percent when he took office, it reached 10 percent in 1978 and kept rising. During one month in 1980, it measured 18 percent. Stopping the runaway inflation preoccupied Carter's attention, but his efforts made little headway. Like previous presidents, Carter then reversed himself to fight the other side of the economic malaise: mushrooming federal budget deficits caused by the sagging economy. By midterm, he was delaying tax reductions and vetoing government spending programs that he had proposed in his first year. The result was the worst of both possible worlds: a deepened recession and inflation averaging between 12 and 13 percent per year.

The signing of a controversial new Strategic Arms Limitation Talks treaty with the Soviets (SALT II) put Carter's leadership to the test just as the mounting economic problems made him the subject of biting editorial cartoons nationwide. The new agreement placed a ceiling of 2,250 bombers and missiles on each side and set limits on the number of warheads and new weapons systems each power could assemble. But the proposed SALT II treaty became moot in 1979 when the Soviet army invaded Afghanistan to prop up the faltering Communist government there, which was being challenged by Muslim rebels. To protest the Soviet action, Carter immediately shelved SALT II, suspended grain shipments to the Soviet Union, and called for an international boycott of the 1980 Olympics, which were to be held that summer in Moscow.

IRAN   Then came the Iranian crisis, a yearlong cascade of unwelcome events that epitomized the inability of the United States to control world affairs and heightened public perceptions of Carter's weak leadership. On November 4, 1979, a frenzied mob of Iranian youths stormed the U.S. embassy in Tehran and seized the diplomats and staff. The Iranian Islamist leader, Ayatollah Ruhollah Khomeini, endorsed the mob action and demanded the return of the hated shah of Iran from the United States along with all his wealth in exchange for the release of the fifty-two hostages still held captive.

Indignant Americans demanded a military response, but Carter's range of options was limited. He appealed to the United Nations, but Khomeini scoffed at UN requests for the release of the hostages. Carter then froze all Iranian assets in the United States and appealed to American allies to join in a trade embargo of Iran. The trade restrictions were only partially effective—even America's most loyal European allies did not want to lose their access to Iranian oil—so a frustrated and besieged Carter authorized a risky rescue attempt by U.S. commandos in 1980. Secretary of State Cyrus Vance resigned in protest against the secret mission and Carter's sharp turn toward a more hawkish foreign policy. The commando raid was aborted because of helicopter failures and ended on April 25, 1980, with eight fatalities when a helicopter collided with a transport plane in the desert. Nightly television coverage of the taunting Iranian rebels generated a near obsession with the falling fortunes of the United States and the fate of the hostages. The end came after 444 days, on January 20, 1981, when a feckless Carter released several billion dollars of Iranian assets to ransom the kidnapped hostages. By then however, Ronald Reagan had been elected president, and Carter was headed into retirement.

While the lackluster Carter administration was foundering, conservative Republicans were forging an aggressive plan to win the White House in 1980 and assault runaway "liberalism" in Washington. Those plans centered on the popularity of plain-speaking **Ronald Reagan**, the Hollywood actor turned two-term California governor and prominent political commentator. Reagan was not a deep thinker, but he was a superb reader of the public mood, an unabashed patriot, and a committed champion of conservative principles. He was also charming and cheerful, a genial politician renowned for his folksy anecdotes and upbeat outlook. Where the self-righteous Carter denounced the evils of free-enterprise capitalism and scolded Americans to revive long-forgotten virtues of frugality and simplicity, a sunny Reagan promised a "revolution of ideas" that would reverse the tide of Democratic "New Deal liberalism" by unleashing free-enterprise capitalism, restoring national pride, and regaining international respect.

In contrast to Carter, Reagan insisted that there were "simple answers" to the complex problems facing the United States, but they were not easy answers. He pledged to increase military spending, dismantle the "bloated" federal bureaucracy, respect states' rights, reduce taxes and government regulation of business, and in general shrink the role of the federal government. He also wanted to affirm old-time religious values by banning abortions and reinstituting prayer in public schools (he ended up doing neither). Reagan's appeal derived from his remarkable skill as a public speaker and his steadfast commitment to a few overarching ideas and simple themes. As a true believer and an able compromiser, he combined the fervor of a revolutionary with the pragmatism of a diplomat.

THE ELECTION OF 1980   Voters, including many long-time Democrats, applauded Reagan's cheery promises to shrink the federal government and restore prosperity. His "trickle-down," "supply-side" economic proposals, soon dubbed "**Reaganomics**" by supporters and "voodoo economics" by critics, argued that the stagflation of the seventies had resulted from excessive income taxes, which weakened incentives for individuals and businesses to increase productivity, save, and reinvest. The solution was to slash tax rates so as to boost economic growth by allowing affluent Americans to pay less taxes and thereby spend more money on consumer goods. For a long-suffering nation, it was an alluring economic panacea. Voters loved Reagan's simple solutions and upbeat personality. "Our optimism," he said during the campaign, "has once again been turned loose. And all of us recognize that these people [Jimmy Carter] who kept talking about the age of limits are really talking about their own limitations, not America's."

For his part, Carter portrayed Reagan as dangerously conservative, implying that his Republican opponent would roll back civil rights legislation and risk nuclear war against the Soviet Union. Voters, however, were more concerned with the stagnant economy. On election day, Reagan swept to a decisive victory, with 489 electoral votes to 49 for Carter, who carried only six states. The popular vote was 44 million (51 percent) for Reagan to Carter's 35 million (41 percent), with 7 percent going to John Anderson, a moderate Republican who bolted the party after the conservative Reagan's nomination and ran on an independent ticket. Flush with a sense of power and destiny, President-elect Reagan, the oldest president ever elected, headed toward Washington with an energetic blueprint for reorienting America.

But however optimistic Ronald Reagan was about America's future, the turbulent and often tragic events of the seventies—the Communist conquest of South Vietnam, the Watergate scandal and Nixon's resignation, the energy shortage and stagflation, the Iranian hostage episode—generated what Carter labeled a "crisis of confidence" that had sapped America's energy. By 1980, U.S. power and prestige seemed to be on the decline, the economy remained in a shambles, and the social revolution launched in the sixties had sparked a backlash of resentment among middle America. With theatrical timing, Ronald Reagan emerged to tap the growing reservoir of public frustration and transform his political career into a crusade to make

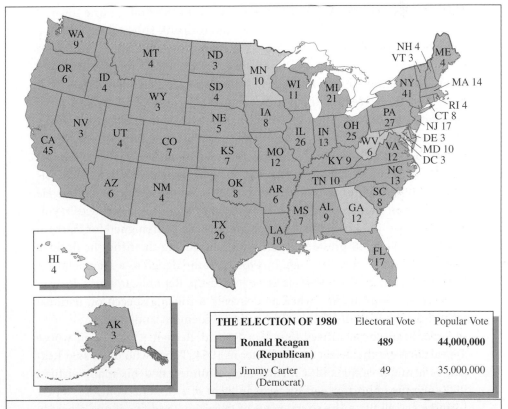

THE ELECTION OF 1980	Electoral Vote	Popular Vote
Ronald Reagan (Republican)	489	44,000,000
Jimmy Carter (Democrat)	49	35,000,000

Why was Ronald Reagan an appealing candidate in 1980? What was the impact of "nonvoting"? Why was there so much voter apathy?

America "stand tall again." He told his supporters that there was "a hunger in this land for a spiritual revival, a return to a belief in moral absolutes." The United States, he declared, remained the "greatest country in the world. We have the talent, we have the drive, we have the imagination. Now all we need is the leadership."

Reagan's ability to make the American people again believe in the greatness of their country won him two presidential elections, in 1980 and 1984, and ensured the victory of his anointed successor, Vice President George H. W. Bush, in 1988. Just how revolutionary the Reagan era was remains a subject of intense debate. What cannot be denied, however, is that Ronald Reagan's actions and beliefs set the tone for the decade's political and economic life.

THE REAGAN REVOLUTION

THE MAKING OF A PRESIDENT Born in the drab prairie town of Tampico, Illinois, in 1911, the son of an often-drunk shoe salesman and a devout, Bible-quoting mother, Ronald Reagan graduated from tiny Eureka College in 1932 during the depths of the Great Depression. He first worked as a radio sportscaster before starting a movie career in Hollywood in 1937. He served three years in the army during the Second World War, making training films. At that time, as he recalled, he was a Democrat, "a New Dealer to the core" who voted for Franklin D. Roosevelt four times. After the war, Reagan became president of the acting profession's union, the Screen Actors Guild (SAG). His leadership of SAG honed his negotiating skills and intensified his anti-communism as he fended off efforts to infiltrate the union. He learned "from firsthand experience how Communists used lies, deceit, violence, or any other tactic that suited them." Reagan campaigned for Harry S. Truman in the 1948 presidential election, but during the fifties he decided that federal taxes were too high. In 1960 he campaigned as a Democrat for Richard Nixon, and two years later he joined the Republican party. Reagan achieved stardom in 1964 when he delivered a rousing speech on national television on behalf of Barry Goldwater's presidential candidacy.

Republican conservatives found in Ronald Reagan a new idol, whose appeal survived the defeat of Goldwater in 1964. Those who dismissed Reagan as a minor actor and a mental midget underrated his many virtues, including the importance of his years in front of a camera. Politics is a performing art, all the more so in an age of television, and few if any others in public life had Reagan's stage presence. Blessed with a baritone voice and a wealth of entertaining stories, he was a superb speaker who charmed audiences. Wealthy admirers convinced Reagan to run for governor of California in 1966, and he won by a landslide. As a two-term governor, Reagan displayed flexible practicality in working with Democrats in the state legislature.

THE RISE OF THE "NEW RIGHT" By the eve of the 1980 election, Reagan had benefited from demographic developments that made his conservative vision a major asset. The 1980 census revealed that the proportion of the population over age sixty-five was soaring and moving from the Midwest and the Northeast to the Sunbelt states of the South and the West. Fully 90 percent of the nation's total population growth during the eighties occurred in southern or western states. These population shifts forced a massive redistricting of the House of Representatives, with Florida, California, and Texas gaining seats and northern states such as New York losing them. The sunbelt states were attractive not only because of their mild climate; they also had the lowest tax rates in the nation, the highest rates of economic growth, and growing numbers of evangelical Christians and retirees. Such attributes also made the sunbelt states fertile ground for the Republican party. This dual development—an increase in the number of senior citizens and the steady relocation of a significant portion of the population to conservative regions of the country, where hostility to "big government" was deeply rooted—meant that demographics were carrying the United States toward Reagan's conservative political philosophy.

A related development during the seventies was a burgeoning tax revolt that swept across the nation as a result of the prolonged inflationary spiral. Inflation increased home values, which in turn brought a dramatic spike in property taxes. In California, Reagan's home state, voters organized a massive grassroots taxpayer revolt. Skyrocketing property taxes threatened to force many working-class people from their homes. The solution? Cut back on the size and cost of government to enable reductions in property taxes. In June 1978, tax rebels

"The Great Communicator"

Ronald Reagan in 1980, shortly before his election.

in California, with Reagan's support, succeeded in getting Proposition 13 on the state ballot. An overwhelming majority of voters—both Republicans and Democrats—approved the measure, which slashed property taxes by 57 percent and amended the state constitution to make raising taxes much more difficult. The tax revolt in California soon spread across the nation as other states passed measures similar to those in California. The *New York Times* compared the phenomenon to a "modern Boston Tea Party."

THE MORAL MAJORITY   The tax revolt fed into a national conservative resurgence that benefited from a massive revival of evangelical religion aggressively working to influence social and political change at the local and national levels. By the eighties, religious conservatism was no longer a local or provincial phenomenon. Catholic conservatives and Protestant evangelicals now owned television and radio stations, operated numerous schools and universities, and organized "mega churches" that sprung up in the sprawling suburbs, where they served as animating centers of social activity and spiritual life. A survey in 1977 revealed that more than 70 million Americans described themselves as "born-again Christians." And religious conservatives formed the strongest grassroots movement of the late twentieth century. During the seventies and eighties, they launched a cultural crusade against the forces of secularism and liberalism.

The Reverend Jerry Falwell's **Moral Majority** (later renamed the Liberty Alliance), formed in 1979, expressed the major political and social goals of the religious right wing: the economy should operate without "interference" by the government, which should be reduced in size; the Supreme Court decision in *Roe v. Wade* (1973) legalizing abortion should be reversed; Darwinian evolution should be replaced in school textbooks by the biblical story of creation; prayer should be allowed back in public schools; women should submit to their husbands; and Soviet communism should be opposed as a form of pagan totalitarianism. Falwell, the "televangelist" minister of a huge Baptist church in Lynchburg, Virginia, stressed that the Moral Majority was not a religious fellowship; it was a purely political organization open to conservatives of all faiths. "If you would like to know where I am politically," Falwell told reporters, "I am to the right of wherever you are. I thought [Barry] Goldwater was too liberal." The moralistic zeal and financial resources of the religious right made its adherents formidable opponents of liberal political candidates and programs. Falwell's Moral Majority recruited over 4 million members in eighteen states. Its base of support was in the South and was strongest among Baptists, but its appeal extended across the country.

That Ronald Reagan became the messiah of the religious right was a tribute both to the force of social issues and to the candidate's political skills. Although famous for his personal piety, Carter lost the support of religious conservatives because he failed to promote their key social issues. He was not willing to ban abortions or restore daily prayers in public schools. His support for state ratification of the equal-rights constitutional amendment (ERA), passed by the Congress in 1972, also lost him votes from the religious conservatives.

ANTI-FEMINIST BACKLASH Another factor contributing to the conservative resurgence was a well-organized and well-financed backlash against the feminist movement. During the seventies, women who opposed the social goals of feminism formed counter organizations with names like Women Who Want to Be Women and Females Opposed to Equality. Spearheading those efforts was **Phyllis Schlafly**, a conservative Catholic attorney and Republican activist from Alton, Illinois. Schlafly led the successful campaign to keep the ERA amendment from being ratified by the required thirty-eight states. In the process, she became the galvanizing force behind a growing anti-feminist movement. Schlafly dismissed feminists as a "bunch of bitter women seeking a constitutional cure for their personal problems." Feminists, she claimed, were "anti-family, anti-children, and pro-abortion" fanatics who viewed the "home as a prison and the wife and mother as a slave." They were determined to "replace the image of woman as virtue and mother with the image of prostitute, swinger, and lesbian."

Schlafly's STOP (Stop Taking Our Privileges) ERA organization, founded in 1972, warned that the ERA would allow husbands to abandon wives without any financial support, force women into military service, and give gay "perverts" the right to marry. She and others also stressed that the sexual equality provided by the proposed amendment violated biblical teachings about women's God-given roles as nurturer and helpmate. By the late seventies, the effort to gain ratification of the ERA, although endorsed by First Lady Betty Ford, had failed, largely because no states in the conservative South and West ("Sunbelt") voted in favor of the amendment.

Many of Schlafly's supporters in the anti-ERA campaign also participated in the mushrooming anti-abortion, or "pro-life," movement. By 1980 more than a million legal abortions were occurring each year. To many religious conservatives, this constituted infanticide. The National Right to Life Committee, supported by the National Conference of Catholic Bishops, boasted 11 million members representing most religious denominations. The intensity of the anti-abortion movement made it a powerful political force in its own right, and the Reagan campaign was quick to highlight its own support

Anti-abortion movement

Anti-abortion demonstrators pass the Washington Monument on their way to the Capitol.

for traditional "family values," gender roles, and the "rights" of the unborn. Such charged cultural issues helped persuade many northern Democrats— mostly working-class Catholics—to switch parties and support Reagan. White evangelicals alienated by the increasingly liberal social agenda of the Democratic party became a crucial element in Reagan's electoral strategy.

PROMOTING CONSERVATIVE IDEAS   Throughout the seventies, the business community also had become a source of conservative activism. In 1972, the leaders of the nation's largest corporations formed the Business Roundtable to promote business interests in Congress. Within a few years, many of those same corporations had formed political action committees (PACs) to distribute campaign contributions to pro-business political candidates. Corporate donations also helped spawn an array of conservative think tanks, such as the Heritage Foundation, founded in 1973 by the conservative business titan Joseph Coors. By 1980, the national conservative insurgency had coalesced into a powerful political force with substantial financial resources, carefully articulated ideas, and grassroots energy, all of which helped to fuel Ronald Reagan's presidential victory.

REAGAN'S FIRST TERM

Ronald Reagan was neither brilliant nor sophisticated, but he was blessed with keen insight, reliable intuition, and far more energy than his critics admitted. And most of all he was sincere and easy to understand. Reagan succeeded where Carter failed because of three main reasons. First, he fastened with stubborn certitude on a few essential priorities (lower tax rates, a reduced federal government, increased military spending, and an aggressive anti-Soviet foreign policy); he knew what he wanted to accomplish and steadfastly pursued his primary goals with dogged consistency. Second, unlike Carter, Reagan was adept at tactical compromises and legislative maneuvering with congressional leaders as well as foreign heads of state. As a former union leader, Reagan was a masterful negotiator willing to modify his positions on some issues while sustaining his overarching goals. Third, Reagan had the gift of inspiration. His infectious optimism inspired Americans with a sense of common purpose and a revived faith in the American spirit.

REAGANOMICS Reagan inherited an America suffering from what Jimmy Carter had called a "crisis of confidence." The economy was in a shambles: the annual rate of inflation had reached 13 percent and unemployment hovered at 7.5 percent. At the same time, the cold war was heating up. The Soviet Union had just invaded Afghanistan. None of this fazed Reagan, however. He brought to Washington a cheerful conservative philosophy embodied in a simple message: "Government is not the solution to our problem," he insisted, "government is the problem." He credited President Calvin Coolidge's Treasury secretary, Andrew W. Mellon, with demonstrating in the twenties that by reducing taxes and easing government regulation of business, free-market capitalism would spur economic growth that would produce *more* government revenues, which in turn would help reduce the budget deficit. On August 1, 1981, the president signed the Economic Recovery Tax Act, which cut personal income taxes by 25 percent, lowered the maximum rate from 70 to 50 percent for 1982, cut the capital gains tax by a third, and offered a broad array of other tax concessions.

BUDGET CUTS David Stockman, Reagan's budget director, assumed responsibility for the president's efforts to dampen federal spending on various domestic programs. Liberal Democrats howled at efforts to dismantle welfare programs. Reagan responded that he remained committed to maintaining the "safety net" of government services for the "truly needy." Reagan was true to his word. Government subsidies to help poor people buy groceries ("food stamps") were cut only 4 percent from what the Carter administration had planned to spend, about $100 million out of a total budget of $11.4 billion.

Within a year David Stockman realized that the cuts in domestic spending had fallen far short of what would be needed to balance the budget in four years, as Reagan had promised. The president, he said, was "too kind, gentle, and sentimental" to make the necessary cuts. Massive increases in military spending complicated the situation. In the summer of 1981, Stockman warned Reagan and his top aides that "we're heading for a crash landing on the budget. We're facing potential deficit numbers so big that they could wreck the president's entire economic program." Stockman was right. The soaring, fast-growing budget deficit, which triggered the worst economic recession since the 1930s, was Reagan's greatest failure. Aides finally convinced the president that the government needed "revenue enhancements," a euphemism for tax increases. With Reagan's support, Congress passed a new tax bill in 1982 that would raise almost $100 billion, but the economic slump persisted through 1982, with unemployment standing at 10.4 percent. By the summer of 1983, a major economic recovery was under way, in part because of increased government spending and lower interest rates and in part because of lower tax rates. But the federal deficits had grown ever larger, so much so that the president, who in 1980 had pledged to balance the federal budget by 1983, had in fact run up debts larger than those of all his predecessors combined. Reagan was willing to tolerate growing budget deficits in part because he believed that they would force more responsible spending behavior in Congress and in part because he was so committed to increased military spending.

REAGAN'S ANTI-LIBERALISM   During Reagan's presidency, organized labor suffered severe setbacks, despite the fact that Reagan himself had been a union leader. In 1981 Reagan fired members of the Professional Air Traffic Controllers Organization who had participated in an illegal strike intended to shut down air travel. Even more important, Reagan's smashing electoral victories in 1980 and 1984 broke the political power of the American Federation of Labor–Congress of Industrial Organizations (AFL-CIO), the powerful national confederation of labor unions that traditionally supported Democratic candidates. His criticism of unions reflected a general trend in public opinion. Although record numbers of new jobs were created during the eighties, union membership steadily dropped. By 1987, unions represented only 17 percent of the nation's full-time workers, down from 24 percent in 1979.

Reagan also went on the offensive against feminism. Echoing Phyllis Schlafly, he opposed the ERA, abortion, and proposals to require equal pay for jobs of comparable worth. He did name Sandra Day O'Connor as the first woman Supreme Court justice, but critics labeled it a token gesture rather than a reflection of any genuine commitment to gender equality. Reagan also cut funds for civil rights enforcement and the Equal Employment Opportunity Commission, and he opposed renewal of the Voting Rights Act of 1965 before being overruled by Congress.

A MASSIVE DEFENSE BUILDUP   Reagan's conduct of foreign policy reflected his belief that trouble in the world stemmed mainly from Moscow, the capital of what he called the "evil empire." Reagan had long believed that former Republican presidents Nixon and Ford—following the advice of Henry Kissinger—had been too soft on the Soviets. Kissinger's emphasis on détente, he said, had been a "one-way street" favoring the Soviets. Reagan first wanted to reduce the risk of nuclear war by convincing the Soviets they

Strategic Defense Initiative

President Reagan addresses the nation on March 23, 1983, about the development of a space-age shield to intercept Soviet missiles.

could not win such a conflict. To do so, he and Secretary of Defense Caspar Weinberger embarked upon a major buildup of nuclear and conventional weapons. Reagan also hoped to bankrupt the Soviets by forcing them to spend much more on their own military budgets. To critics who complained about the enormous sums of money being spent on U.S. weapons systems, Reagan replied that "It will break the Soviets first." It did.

In 1983, Reagan escalated the nuclear arms race by authorizing the Defense Department to develop a controversial Strategic Defense Initiative (SDI) to construct a complex anti-missile defense system in outer space intended to "intercept and destroy" Soviet missiles in flight. Despite skepticism among the media, many scientists, and the secretaries of defense and state that such a "Star Wars" defense system could be built, the new program forced the Soviets to launch an expensive research and development effort of their own to keep pace.

Reagan's anti-Soviet strategy involved more than accelerated defense spending. He borrowed the rhetoric of Harry S. Truman, John Foster Dulles, and John F. Kennedy to express American resolve in the face of "Communist aggression anywhere in the world." When the Soviets imposed martial law in Poland during the winter of 1981, Reagan forcefully protested and imposed economic sanctions against Poland's Communist government. He also worked behind the scenes to support the Solidarity movement promoting Polish independence from Soviet control.

THE AMERICAS   Reagan's foremost international concern, however, was in Central America, where he detected the most serious Communist threat. The tiny nation of El Salvador, caught up since 1980 in a brutal struggle between Communist-supported revolutionaries and right-wing militants, received U.S. economic and military assistance. Critics argued that U.S. involvement ensured that the revolutionary forces would gain public support by capitalizing on "anti-Yankee" sentiment. Supporters countered that allowing a Communist victory in El Salvador would lead all of Central America to enter the Communist camp (a new "domino" theory). By 1984, however, the U.S.-backed government of President José Napoleón Duarte had brought a modicum of stability to El Salvador.

Even more troubling to Reagan was the situation in Nicaragua. The State Department claimed that the Cuban-sponsored Sandinista socialist government, which had seized power in 1979 after ousting a corrupt dictator, was sending Soviet and Cuban arms to leftist Salvadoran rebels. In response, the Reagan administration ordered the CIA to train anti-Communist Nicaraguans, tagged **Contras** (short for counterrevolutionaries), who staged attacks on Sandinista bases from sanctuaries in Honduras. In supporting these "freedom

"Shhhh. It's Top Secret."

A comment on the Reagan administration's covert operations in Nicaragua.

fighters," Reagan sought not only to impede the traffic in arms to Salvadoran rebels but also to replace the Sandinistas with a democratic government in Nicaragua. Critics of Reagan's anti-Sandinista policy accused the Contras of being mostly right-wing fanatics who indiscriminately killed civilians as well as Sandinista soldiers. They also feared that the United States might eventually commit its own combat forces, thereby precipitating a Vietnam-like intervention. Reagan warned that if the Communists prevailed in Central America, "our credibility would collapse, our alliances would crumble, and the safety of our homeland would be jeopardized."

GRENADA   Fortune, as it happened, presented Reagan the chance for an easy triumph closer to home. On the tiny Caribbean island of Grenada, the smallest independent country in the Western Hemisphere, a leftist government had welcomed Cuban workers to build a new airfield and signed military agreements with Communist countries. In 1983, an even more radical military council seized power. Appeals from the governments of nearby island nations led Reagan to order 1,900 marines to invade Grenada, depose the new government, and evacuate a small group of American students enrolled in medical school. The UN General Assembly condemned the action, but it was popular among Grenadans and in the United States. Although a lopsided affair, the decisive action served notice to Latin American revolutionaries that Reagan might use military force elsewhere in the region.

REAGAN'S SECOND TERM

By 1983, prosperity had returned, and Reagan's "supply-side" economic program was at last working as touted—except for growing budget deficits. Reagan's decision to remove government price controls on oil and natural gas as well as his efforts to pressure Saudi Arabia to increase oil production produced a decline in energy prices that helped to stimulate economic growth.

THE ELECTION OF 1984 By 1984, Reagan had restored strength and vitality to the White House and the nation. Reporters began to speak of the "Reagan Revolution." The economy surged with new energy. The slogan at the Republican National Convention was "America is back and standing tall." By contrast, the presidential nominee of the Democrats, former vice president Walter Mondale, struggled to mold a competing vision. Endorsed by the AFL-CIO, the National Organization for Women (NOW), and many prominent African Americans, Mondale was viewed as the candidate of liberal special interest groups. He set a precedent by choosing as his running mate New York representative Geraldine Ferraro, who was quickly placed on the defensive by the need to explain her spouse's complicated business dealings.

A fit of frankness in Mondale's acceptance speech further complicated his campaign. "Mr. Reagan will raise taxes, and so will I," he told the convention. "He won't tell you. I just did." Reagan responded by vowing never to approve a tax increase and by chiding Mondale for his commitment to tax increases. Reagan also repeated a theme he had used in his campaign against Jimmy Carter: the future according to Mondale and the Democrats was "dark and getting darker." His vision of America's future, however, was bright, buoyed by optimism and hope. Mondale never caught up. In the end, Reagan took 59 percent of the popular vote and lost only Minnesota and the District of Columbia.

DOMESTIC CHALLENGES Buoyed by his overwhelming victory, Reagan called for "a Second American Revolution of hope and opportunity." He dared Democrats in Congress to raise taxes; his veto pen was ready: "Go ahead and make my day," he said in an echo of a popular line from a Clint

Eastwood movie. Through much of 1985, the president drummed up support for a tax-simplification plan. After vigorous debate that ran nearly two years, Congress passed, and in 1986 the president signed, a comprehensive Tax Reform Act. The new measure reduced the number of federal tax brackets from fourteen to two and reduced rates from the maximum of 50 percent to 15 and 28 percent—the lowest since Calvin Coolidge was president.

THE IRAN-CONTRA AFFAIR   But Reagan's second term was not the triumph he and his supporters expected. During the fall of 1986, Democrats regained control of the Senate by 55 to 45. The Democrats picked up only 6 seats in the House, but they increased their already comfortable margin to 259 to 176. For his last two years as president, Reagan would face an opposition Congress.

What was worse, reports surfaced in late 1986 that the United States had been secretly selling arms to Iran in the hope of securing the release of American hostages held in Lebanon by extremist groups sympathetic to Iran. Such action contradicted Reagan's repeated insistence that his administration would never negotiate with terrorists. The disclosures angered America's allies as well as many Americans who vividly remembered the 1979 Iranian takeover of their country's embassy in Tehran. Over the next several months, revelations reminiscent of the Watergate affair disclosed a complicated series of covert activities carried out by administration officials. At the center of what came to be called the **Iran-Contra affair** was marine lieutenant colonel Oliver North. A swashbuckling aide to the National Security Council who specialized in counterterrorism, North, from the basement of the White House, had been secretly selling military supplies to Iran and using the money to subsidize the Contra rebels fighting in Nicaragua at a time when Congress had voted to ban such aid.

Oliver North's illegal activities, it turned out, had been approved by national security adviser Robert McFarlane; McFarlane's successor, Admiral John Poindexter; and CIA director William Casey. Both Secretary of State George Shultz and Secretary of Defense Caspar Weinberger criticized the arms sale to Iran, but their objections were ignored, and they were thereafter kept in the dark about what was going on. Later, on three occasions, Shultz threatened to resign over the continuing operation of the "pathetic" scheme. After information about the secret (and illegal) dealings surfaced in the press, McFarlane attempted suicide, Poindexter resigned, and North was fired. Casey, who denied any connection, left the CIA for health reasons and died shortly thereafter from a brain tumor.

The Iran-Contra affair

National security adviser Robert McFarlane (left) tells reporters about his resignation. Vice Admiral John Poindexter (far right) succeeds him in the post.

Under increasing criticism, Reagan appointed both an independent counsel and a three-man commission, led by former Republican senator John Tower, to investigate the scandal. The Tower Commission issued a devastating report early in 1987 that placed much of the responsibility for the bungled Iran-Contra affair on Reagan's loose management style. During the spring and summer of 1987, a joint House-Senate investigating committee began holding hearings into the Iran-Contra affair. The televised sessions revealed a tangled web of inept financial and diplomatic transactions, the shredding of incriminating government documents, crass profiteering, and misguided patriotism.

The investigations of the independent counsel led to six indictments in 1988. A Washington jury found Oliver North guilty of three relatively minor charges but innocent of nine more serious counts, apparently reflecting the jury's reasoning that he acted as an agent of higher-ups. His conviction was later overturned on appeal. Of those involved in the affair, only John Poindexter got a jail sentence—six months for his conviction on five felony counts of obstructing justice and lying to Congress.

THE CHANGING SOCIAL LANDSCAPE

During the eighties, profound changes transformed the tone and texture of American life. The economy went through a wrenching transformation in an effort to adapt to the shifting dynamics of an increasingly interconnected global marketplace. The nations that had been devastated by the Second World War—France, Germany, the Soviet Union, Japan, and China—by the eighties had developed formidable economies with higher levels of productivity than the United States. More and more American manufacturing companies shifted their production overseas, thereby accelerating the transition of the economy from its once-dominant industrial base to a more services-oriented economy. Driving all of these changes was the phenomenal impact of the computer revolution and the development of the Internet.

THE COMPUTER REVOLUTION   The idea of a programmable machine that would rapidly perform mental tasks had been around since the eighteenth century, but it took the crisis of the Second World War to gather the intellectual and financial resources needed to create such a "computer." In 1946 a team of engineers at the University of Pennsylvania created ENIAC (electronic numerical integrator and computer), the first all-purpose, all-electronic digital computer.

The next major breakthrough was the invention in 1971 of the microprocessor—a tiny computer on a silicon chip. The functions that had once been performed by huge computers taking up an entire room could now be performed by a microchip circuit the size of a postage stamp. The microchip made possible the personal computer. In 1975 an engineer named Ed Roberts developed the prototype of the so-called personal computer. The Altair 8800 was imperfect and cumbersome, with no display, no keyboard, and not enough memory to do anything useful. But its potential excited a Harvard sophomore named Bill Gates. He improved the software of the Altair 8800, dropped out of college, and formed a company called Microsoft to sell the new system. By 1977, Gates and others had helped transform the personal computer from a machine for hobbyists into a mass consumer product. The development of the Internet, electronic mail (e-mail), and cell-phone technology during the eighties and nineties allowed for instantaneous communication, thereby accelerating the globalization of the economy and dramatically increasing productivity in the workplace.

The computer age

Beginning with the cumbersome electronic numerical integrator and computer (ENIAC), pictured here in 1946, computer technology flourished, leading to the development of personal computers in the 1980s and the popularization of the Internet in the 1990s.

DEBT AND THE STOCK MARKET PLUNGE   In the late seventies, Jimmy Carter had urged Americans to lead simpler lives, cut back on conspicuous consumption, reduce energy use, and invest more time in faith and family. During the eighties, Ronald Reagan promoted very different behavior: he reduced tax rates so people would have more money to spend. Americans preferred Reagan's emphasis on prosperity rather than frugality, for it endorsed entrepreneurship as well as an increasingly consumption-oriented culture. But Reagan succeeded too well in shifting the public mood back to the "more is more," "bigger is better" tradition of heedless consumerism. During the "Age of Reagan," marketers and advertisers celebrated instant gratification at the expense of the future. Michelob beer commercials began assuring Americans that "you can have it all," and many Americans went on a self-indulgent spending spree. The more they bought the more they wanted. The money fever was contagious. Compulsive shoppers donned T-shirts proclaiming: "Born to Shop." By 1988, 110 million Americans had an average of seven credit cards each. Money—lots of it—came to define the

American Dream. In the hit movie *Wall Street* (1987), the high-flying land developer and corporate raider Gordon Gekko, played by actor Michael Douglas, announces that "greed . . . is good. Greed is right."

During the eighties, many Americans caught up in the materialism of the times began spending more money than they made. All kinds of debt—personal, corporate, and government—increased dramatically. Americans in the sixties had saved on average 10 percent of their income; in 1987 the figure was less than 4 percent. The federal debt more than tripled, from $908 billion in 1980 to $2.9 trillion at the end of the 1989 fiscal year. Then, on October 19, 1987, the bill collector suddenly arrived at the nation's doorstep. On that "Black Monday," the stock market experienced a tidal wave of selling reminiscent of the 1929 crash. The market plunge of 22.6 percent nearly doubled the record 12.8 percent fall on October 28, 1929. Wall Street's selling frenzy reverberated throughout the capitalist world, sending stock prices plummeting in Tokyo, London, Paris, and Toronto.

In the aftermath of the calamitous selling spree on Black Monday, fears of an impending recession led business leaders and economists to attack President Reagan for allowing such huge budget deficits. Within a few weeks, Reagan had agreed to work with Congress to develop a deficit-reduction package and for the first time indicated a willingness to include increased taxes in such a package. But the eventual compromise plan was so modest that it did little to restore investor confidence. As one Republican senator lamented, "There is a total lack of courage among those of us in the Congress to do what we all know has to be done."

THE POOR, THE HOMELESS, AND THE VICTIMS OF AIDS
The eighties were years of vivid contrast. Despite unprecedented prosperity among the wealthiest Americans, there were growing numbers of underclass Americans bereft of hope: beggars in the streets and homeless people sleeping in doorways, in cardboard boxes, and on ventilation grates. Homelessness was the most acute social issue of the eighties. A variety of causes had led to a shortage of low-cost housing: the government had given up on building public housing; urban-renewal programs had demolished blighted areas but provided no housing for those they displaced; and owners had abandoned unprofitable buildings in poor neighborhoods or converted them into expensive condominiums, a process called gentrification. In addition, after new medications allowed for the deinstitutionalization of certain mentally ill patients, many of them ended up on the streets because the promised community mental-health services failed to materialize. Drug and alcohol abuse were rampant among the homeless, mostly unemployed single adults, a quarter

of whom had spent time in mental institutions; some 40 percent had spent time in jail; a third were delusional.

Still another group of outcasts was composed of people suffering from a newly identified malady named AIDS (acquired immunodeficiency syndrome). At the beginning of the eighties, public health officials had reported that gay men and intravenous drug users were especially at risk for developing AIDS. People contracted the virus, HIV, by coming into contact with the blood or body fluids of an infected person. Those infected with the virus that causes AIDS showed signs of extreme fatigue, developed a strange combination of infections, and soon died.

The Reagan administration showed little interest in AIDS in part because it was initially viewed as a "gay" disease. Patrick Buchanan, the conservative spokesman who served as Reagan's director of communications, said that homosexuals had "declared war on nature, and now nature is extracting an awful retribution." Buchanan and others convinced Reagan not to engage the **HIV/AIDS** issue. By 2000, AIDS had claimed almost three hundred thousand American lives and was spreading among a larger segment of the population. Nearly 1 million Americans were carrying the deadly virus, and it had become the leading cause of death among men aged twenty-five to forty-four.

A HISTORIC TREATY   The most positive achievement at the end of Reagan's second term was a surprising arms-reduction agreement with the Soviet government. Under **Mikhail Gorbachev**, who came to power in 1985, the Soviets pursued renewed détente so that they could focus their energies and financial resources on pressing domestic problems. The logjam that had impeded arms negotiations suddenly broke in 1987, when Gorbachev announced that he was willing to consider mutually reducing nuclear weaponry. After nine months of strenuous negotiations, Reagan and Gorbachev met amid much fanfare in Washington, D.C., on December 9, 1987, and signed a treaty to eliminate intermediate-range (300- to 3,000-mile) nuclear missiles.

The treaty marked the first time that the two nations had agreed to destroy a whole class of weapons systems. Under the terms of the treaty, the United States would destroy 859 missiles, and the Soviets would eliminate 1,752. Still, the reductions represented only 4 percent of the total nuclear-missile count on both sides. Arms-control advocates thus looked toward a second and more comprehensive treaty dealing with long-range strategic missiles.

Gorbachev's successful efforts to liberalize Soviet domestic life and improve East-West foreign relations cheered Americans. The Soviets suddenly began stressing cooperation with the West in dealing with hot spots

Foreign relations

A light moment at a meeting between U.S. president Ronald Reagan (left) and Soviet premier Mikhail Gorbachev (right).

around the world. In the Middle East they urged the PLO to recognize Israel's right to exist and advocated a greater role for the United Nations in the volatile Persian Gulf. Perhaps the most dramatic symbol of a thawing cold war was the phased withdrawal of 115,000 Soviet troops from Afghanistan, which began in 1988.

REAGAN'S LEGACY   Ronald Reagan was a transformational president. He restored the stature of the presidency and in the process transformed the tone and tenor of American political life. Politically, Reagan played the central role in accelerating the nation's shift toward conservatism and the Republican party. But he did not dismantle the federal welfare state; he fine-tuned it, in part because the Democrats controlled the House of Representatives throughout his presidency. Although Reagan had declared in 1981 his intention to "curb the size and influence of the federal establishment," the federal welfare state remained intact when he left office in early 1989. Neither the Social Security system nor Medicare had been dismantled or overhauled, nor had any other major welfare programs. And the federal agencies that Reagan had threatened to abolish, such as the Department of Education, not only survived but had seen their budgets grow. The federal budget as a percentage of economic output was higher when Reagan left office than when he had entered; the budget deficit when he retired was an all-time record. Moreover, he backed off his campaign promises directed at the religious right, such as reinstituting daily prayer in public schools and a ban on abortions.

What Ronald Reagan the genial conservative did accomplish was to end the prolonged period of economic "stagflation" and set in motion what economists called "The Great Expansion," an unprecedented twenty-year-long burst of productivity and prosperity. True, Reagan's presidency left the nation with a massive debt burden that would eventually cause major structural problems, and the prolonged prosperity served to widen inequality, but the "Great Communicator" also renewed America's self-confidence and soaring sense of possibilities.

Reagan also helped end the cold war by negotiating the nuclear disarmament treaty and lighting the fuse of democratic freedom in Eastern Europe. In June 1987, Reagan visited the Berlin Wall and in a dramatic speech called upon the Soviet Union to allow greater freedom within the Warsaw Pact countries under its control. "General Secretary Gorbachev, if you seek peace, if you seek prosperity for the Soviet Union and Eastern Europe, if you seek liberalization: Come here to this gate! Mr. Gorbachev, open this gate! Mr. Gorbachev, tear down this wall!" It was great theatre and good politics. Through his policies and persistence, Reagan helped light the fuse of freedom in East Germany, Hungary, Poland, and Czechoslovakia. By redirecting the thrust of both domestic and foreign policy during the eighties, Reagan put the fragmented Democratic party on the defensive and forced conventional New Deal "liberalism" into a panicked retreat. Reagan would cast a long shadow. He had fashioned the most consequential presidency since Franklin D. Roosevelt, the man he had voted for on four occasions.

THE ELECTION OF 1988 In 1988, eight Democratic presidential candidates engaged in a wild scramble for their party's nomination. As the primary season progressed, however, it soon became a two-man race between Massachusetts governor Michael Dukakis and Jesse Jackson, a charismatic African American civil rights activist who had been one of Martin Luther King Jr.'s chief lieutenants. Dukakis eventually won out and managed a difficult reconciliation with the Jackson forces that left the Democrats unified and confident as the fall campaign began.

The Republicans nominated Reagan's two-term vice president, Texan **George H. W. Bush**, who after a bumpy start had easily cast aside his rivals in the primaries. A veteran government official, having served as a Texas congressman, an envoy to China, an ambassador to the UN, and head of the

CIA, Bush projected none of Reagan's charisma or rhetorical skills. One Democrat described him as a man born "with a silver foot in his mouth." Early polls showed Dukakis with a wide lead.

Yet Bush delivered a forceful address at the nominating convention that sharply enhanced his stature. While pledging to continue the Reagan agenda, he also recognized that "things aren't perfect" in America. Bush was a centrist Republican who had never embraced the dogmatic assumptions of right-wing conservatism. He promised to use the White House to fight bigotry, illiteracy, and homelessness. Humane sympathies, he insisted, would guide his conservatism. "I want a kinder, gentler nation," Bush said in his acceptance speech. But the most memorable line in the speech was a defiant statement ruling out any tax increases as a means of dealing with the massive budget deficits created during the Reagan years "The Congress will push me

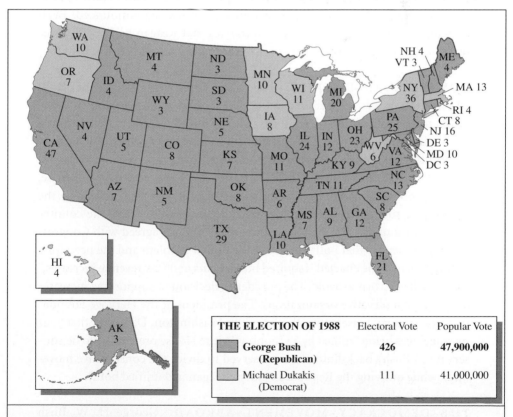

THE ELECTION OF 1988	Electoral Vote	Popular Vote
George Bush (Republican)	426	47,900,000
Michael Dukakis (Democrat)	111	41,000,000

How did George H. W. Bush overtake Michael Dukakis's lead in the polls? What was the role of race and class in the election results?

to raise taxes, and I'll say no, and they'll push, and I'll say no, and they'll push again. And I'll say to them: Read my lips. No new taxes."

In a not-so-gentle campaign given over to mudslinging, Bush and his aides attacked Dukakis as a camouflaged liberal in the mold of George McGovern, Jimmy Carter, and Walter Mondale. In the end, Dukakis took only ten states plus the District of Columbia, with clusters of support in the Northeast, Midwest, and Northwest. Bush carried the rest, with a margin of about 54 percent to 46 percent in the popular vote and 426 to 111 in the Electoral College.

THE BUSH ADMINISTRATION

George H. W. Bush viewed himself as a guardian president rather than an activist. He lacked Reagan's visionary outlook. Bush was eager to avoid "stupid mistakes" and to find a way to get along with the Democratic majority in Congress. "We don't need to remake society," he announced. Bush therefore sought to consolidate the initiatives that Reagan had put in place rather than launch his own array of programs and policies.

DOMESTIC INITIATIVES   The biggest problem facing the Bush administration was the national debt, which stood at $2.6 trillion in 1989, nearly three times its 1980 level. Bush's pledge not to increase taxes (meaning mainly income taxes) and his insistence upon lowering capital-gains taxes—on profits from the sale of corporate stock and other property—made it more difficult to reduce the annual deficit or trim the long-term debt. Likewise, Bush was not willing to make substantial cutbacks in spending on defense, the federal bureaucracy, and welfare programs. As a result, by 1990 the country faced "a fiscal mess." During the summer of 1990 Bush agreed with Congressional Democrats "that both the size of the deficit problem and the need for a package that can be enacted" required budget cuts and "tax revenue increases," which he had sworn to avoid. The president's decision to support tax increases infuriated conservative organizations. The president of the Heritage Foundation, the leading conservative think tank in Washington, D.C., said that "our message" was being "sullied by a visionless White House pretending to be conservative." Bush's backsliding on taxes served to divide the conservative movement while unifying the Republican party (Reagan had unified both).

THE DEMOCRACY MOVEMENT ABROAD   George H. W. Bush entered the White House with more foreign-policy experience than most presidents, and he found the spotlight of the world stage more congenial than wrestling with the intractable problems of the inner cities, drug abuse, and the deficit. Within two years of his inauguration, Bush would lead the United States into two wars. Throughout most of 1989, however, he merely had to sit back and observe the dissolution of one totalitarian or authoritarian regime after another. For the first time in years, democracy was on the march in a sequence of mostly bloodless revolutions that surprised the world.

Although a grassroots democracy movement in communist China came to a tragic end in 1989 when government forces mounted a deadly assault on demonstrators in Beijing's Tiananmen Square, eastern Europe had an entirely different experience. With a rigid economic system failing to deliver the goods to the Soviet people, Mikhail Gorbachev responded with policies of *perestroika* (restructuring) and *glasnost* (openness), a loosening of centralized economic planning and censorship. His foreign policy sought rapprochement and trade with the West, and he aimed to relieve the Soviet economy of burdensome military costs.

Gorbachev also backed off from Soviet imperial ambitions. Early in 1989, Soviet troops left Afghanistan after spending nine years bogged down in civil war there. Gorbachev then repudiated the Brezhnev Doctrine, which asserted the right of the Soviet Union to intervene in the internal affairs of other Communist countries. The days when Soviet tanks rolled through Warsaw and Prague were over, and hard-line leaders in the Eastern-bloc countries found themselves beset by demands for reform from their own people. With opposition strength building, the old regimes fell with surprisingly little bloodshed. Communist party rule ended first in Poland and Hungary, then in Czechoslovakia and Bulgaria. In Romania the year of peaceful revolution ended in a bloodbath when the people joined the army in a bloody uprising against the brutal dictator Nicolae Ceauşescu. He and his wife were captured, tried, and then executed on Christmas Day.

The most spectacular event in the collapse of the Soviet Empire came on November 9, 1989, when Germans—using small tools and even their hands— tore down the chief symbol of the cold war, the Berlin Wall. The massive wall had long seemed impregnable and permanent, like the Cold War itself. With the barrier down, East Germans streamed across the border. As people celebrated in the streets, they were amazed, delighted, and moved to tears. With the borders to the West now fully open, the Communist government of East Germany collapsed, a freely elected government came to power, and on October 3, 1990, the five states of East Germany were united with West Germany. The unified German nation remained in NATO, and the Communist Warsaw Pact alliance was dissolved.

Dissolution of the Soviet Empire

West Germans hacking away at the Berlin Wall on November 11, 1989, two days after all crossings between East Germany and West Germany were opened.

The reform impulse that Gorbachev helped unleash in the Eastern-bloc countries careened out of control within the Soviet Union, however. Gorbachev proved unusually adept at political restructuring, yielding the Communist monopoly of government but building a new presidential system that gave him, if anything, increased powers. His skills in the Byzantine politics of the Kremlin, though, did not extend to an antiquated economy that resisted change. The revival of ethnic allegiances added to the instability. Although Russia proper included slightly more than half the Soviet Union's population, it was only one of fifteen constituent republics, most of which began to seek autonomy, if not independence, from Russia.

Gorbachev's popularity shrank in the Soviet Union as it grew abroad. It especially eroded among the Communist hard-liners, who saw in his reforms the unraveling of their bureaucratic and political empire. Once the genie of freedom was released from the Communist lamp, however, it took on a momentum of its own. On August 18, 1991, a cabal of political and military leaders tried to seize the reins of power in Russia. They accosted Gorbachev at his vacation retreat in the Crimea and demanded that he sign a decree proclaiming a state of emergency and transferring his powers to them. He replied, "Go to hell," whereupon he was placed under house arrest.

The coup was doomed from the start, however. Poorly planned and clumsily implemented, it lacked effective coordination. The plotters failed to arrest popular leaders such as Boris Yeltsin, the president of the Russian republic; they neglected to close the airports or cut off telephone and television communications; and they were opposed by key elements of the military and KGB (the secret police). But most important, the plotters failed to recognize the strength of the democratic idealism unleashed by Gorbachev's reforms.

As the political drama unfolded in the Soviet Union, foreign leaders denounced the coup. On August 20, President Bush responded favorably to Yeltsin's request for support and persuaded other leaders to join him in refusing to recognize the legitimacy of the new Soviet government. The next day, word began to seep out that the plotters had given up and were fleeing. Several committed suicide, and a newly released Gorbachev ordered the others arrested. Yet things did not go back to the way they had been. Although Gorbachev reclaimed the title of president of the Soviet Union, he was forced to resign as head of the Communist party and admit that he had made a grave mistake in appointing the men who had turned against him. Boris Yeltsin emerged as the most popular political figure in the country.

Action against Gorbachev

In August 1991, one day after Mikhail Gorbachev was placed under house arrest by Communists planning a coup, Russian president Boris Yeltsin (holding papers) makes a speech criticizing the plotters.

So what had begun as a reactionary coup turned into a powerful accelerant for stunning changes in the Soviet Union, or the "Soviet Disunion," as one wag termed it. Most of the fifteen republics proclaimed their independence from Russia, with the Baltic republics of Latvia, Lithuania, and Estonia regaining the status of independent nations. The Communist party apparatus was dismantled, prompting celebrating crowds to topple statues of Lenin and other Communist heroes.

A chastened Gorbachev could only acquiesce in the breakup of the Soviet Empire, whereas the systemic problems burdening the Soviet Union before the coup remained intractable. The economy was stagnant, food and coal shortages loomed on the horizon, and consumer goods remained scarce. The reformers had won, but they had yet to establish deep roots in a country with no democratic tradition. Leaping into the unknown, they faced years of hardship and uncertainty.

The aborted coup also accelerated Soviet and American efforts to reduce their stockpiles of nuclear weapons. In late 1991, President Bush stunned the world by announcing that the United States would destroy all its tactical nuclear weapons on land and at sea in Europe and Asia, take its long-range bombers off twenty-four-hour-alert status, and initiate discussions with the Soviet Union for the purpose of instituting sharp cuts in missiles with multiple warheads. Bush explained that the prospect of a Soviet invasion of western Europe was "no longer a realistic threat," and this transformation provided an unprecedented opportunity for reducing the threat of nuclear holocaust. President Gorbachev responded by announcing reciprocal Soviet cutbacks.

PANAMA   The end of the cold war did not spell the end of international tensions and conflict, however. Indeed, before the end of 1989, U.S. troops were engaged in battle in Panama, where a petty tyrant provoked the first of America's military engagements under George H. W. Bush. In 1983, General Manuel Noriega had maneuvered himself into the position of leader of the Panamanian Defense Forces, which made him the de facto head of the government in fact if not in title. Earlier, when Bush headed the CIA, Noriega, as chief of military intelligence, had developed a profitable business of supplying information on the region to the CIA. At the same time, he developed avenues in the region for drug smuggling and gunrunning, laundering the money from those activities through Panamanian banks. For a time, American intelligence analysts looked the other way, regarding Noriega as a useful contact, but eventually he became an embarrassment. In 1987 a rejected associate published charges of Noriega's drug activities and accused him further of rigged elections and political assassination.

In 1988, federal grand juries in Miami and Tampa indicted Noriega and fifteen others on drug charges. The next year the Panamanian president tried to fire Noriega, but the National Assembly ousted the president and named Noriega "maximum leader." The legislators then declared Panama "in a state of war" with the United States. The next day, December 16, 1989, a U.S. marine in Panama was killed. President Bush thereupon ordered an invasion of Panama with the purpose of capturing Noriega so that he might stand trial in the United States and installing a government headed by President Guillermo Endara.

The twelve thousand U.S. military personnel already in Panama were quickly joined by twelve thousand more, and in the early morning of December 20 five military task forces struck at strategic targets in the country. Within hours, Noriega had surrendered. Twenty-three U.S. servicemen were killed in the action, and estimates of Panamanian casualties, including many civilians, were as high as four thousand. In April 1992, Noriega was convicted in the United States on eight counts of racketeering and drug distribution.

THE GULF WAR Months after Panama had moved to the background of public attention, **Saddam Hussein**, dictator of Iraq, focused attention on the Middle East when his army suddenly invaded tiny Kuwait on August 2, 1990. Kuwait had raised its production of oil, contrary to agreements with the Organization of the Petroleum Exporting Countries (OPEC). The resulting drop in global oil prices offended the Iraqi regime, deep in debt and heavily dependent upon oil revenues. Saddam Hussein was surprised by the backlash his invasion of Kuwait caused. The UN Security Council unanimously condemned the invasion and demanded withdrawal. U.S. Secretary of State James A. Baker III and the Soviet foreign minister issued a joint statement of condemnation. On August 6 the Security Council endorsed Resolution 661, an embargo on trade with Iraq.

Bush condemned Iraq's "naked aggression" and dispatched planes and troops to Saudi Arabia on a "wholly defensive" mission: to protect Saudi Arabia. British forces soon joined in, as did Arab units from Egypt, Morocco, Syria, Oman, the United Arab Emirates, and Qatar. On August 22, Bush ordered the mobilization of American reserve forces for the operation, now dubbed **Operation Desert Shield.**

A flurry of peace efforts sent diplomats scurrying, but without result. Iraq refused to yield. On January 12, Congress authorized the use of U.S. armed forces. By January 1991, over thirty nations were committed to Operation Desert Shield. Some nations sent only planes, ships, or support forces, but sixteen, including ten Islamic countries, committed ground forces. Desert

The Gulf War

U.S. soldiers adapt to desert conditions during Operation Desert Shield, December 1990.

Shield became **Operation Desert Storm** when the first allied cruise missiles began to hit Iraq on January 16.

Saddam Hussein, expecting a landing on the Kuwaiti coast and an allied attack northward into Kuwait, concentrated his forces in that country. The Iraqis were outflanked when two hundred thousand allied troops, largely American, British, and French, turned up on the undefended Iraqi border with Saudi Arabia one hundred to two hundred miles to the west. The swift-moving allied ground assault began on February 24 and lasted only four days. Iraqi soldiers surrendered by the thousands.

On February 28, six weeks after the fighting began, President Bush called for a cease-fire, the Iraqis accepted, and the shooting ended. There were 137 American fatalities. The lowest estimate of Iraqi deaths, civilian and military, was 100,000. The coalition forces occupied about a fifth of Iraq, but Hussein's tyrannical regime was intact. What came to be called the First Gulf War was thus a triumph without victory. Hussein had been defeated, but he was allowed to escape to foster greater mischief. The consequences of the brief but intense First Gulf War, the "mother of all battles" in Saddam Hussein's words, would be played out in the future in ways that no one had predicted. Arabs humiliated by the American triumph over the Iraqis began plotting revenge that would spiral into a new war of terrorism.

CULTURAL CONSERVATISM

Cultural conservatives helped elect Ronald Reagan and George Bush in the eighties, but they were disappointed with the results. Once in office, neither president had adequately addressed the moral agenda of the religious right, including a complete ban on abortions and the restoration of prayer in public schools. By the nineties, a new generation of young conservative activists, mostly political independents or Republicans and largely from the sunbelt states, had emerged as a major force in national affairs. They were more ideological, more libertarian, more partisan, more dogmatic, and more impatient than their predecessors. The new breed of cultural conservatives abhorred the excesses of social liberalism. They lamented the disappearance of basic forms of decency and propriety, and they attacked affirmative-action programs designed to redress historic injustices committed against women and minorities. During the nineties, powerful groups inside and outside the Republican party mobilized to roll back government programs that gave preference to certain social groups. Prominent African American conservatives supported such efforts, arguing that racially based preferences were demeaning and condescending remedies for historical injustices.

THE RELIGIOUS RIGHT   Although quite diverse, cultural conservatives tended to be evangelical Christians or orthodox Catholics, and they joined together to exert increasing religious pressure on the political process. In 1989 the Virginia-based television evangelist Pat Robertson organized the Christian Coalition to replace Jerry Falwell's Moral Majority as the flagship organization of the resurgent religious right. The Christian Coalition chose the Republican party as the best vehicle for promoting its pro–school prayer, anti-abortion, and anti–gay rights positions. In addition to celebrating "traditional family values," it urged politicians to "radically downsize and delimit government." In many respects, the religious right took control of the political and social agendas in the nineties. As one journalist acknowledged in 1995, "the religious right is moving toward center stage in American secular life."

CHAPTER SUMMARY

- **Rise of Conservatism** Ronald Reagan's charm, coupled with disillusionment over Jimmy Carter's presidency and the Republicans' call for a return to traditional values, won Reagan the presidency in 1980. The Republican insurgency, characterized by a cultural backlash against the feminist movement, was dominated by Christian evangelicals and people who wanted lower taxes and a smaller, less intrusive federal government.

- **Iran-Contra Scandal** During an Islamic revolution in Iran, enraged militants stormed the U.S. embassy in Tehran and seized American diplomats and staff members. In retaliation, President Carter froze all Iranian assets in the United States. Carter at last released several billion dollars in Iranian assets to ransom the hostages. The Iranians released the hostages—but not until Ronald Reagan was in office. Members of Reagan's administration secretly sold arms to Iran in the hopes of securing the release of American hostages held in Lebanon by extremists sympathetic to Iran. The deal contradicted the president's public claims that he would never deal with terrorists. Furthermore, profits from the arms sales were used to fund right-wing rebels in Nicaragua, known as Contras, despite Congress's having voted to ban any aid to the Contras. An independent commission appointed by the president determined that Reagan's loose management style was responsible for the illegal activities, and Reagan admitted that he had lied to the American people.

- **End of the Cold War** Toward the end of the century, democratic movements exploded in communist China, where they failed, and in Eastern Europe, where they largely succeeded. In the Soviet Union, Mikhail Gorbachev's steps to restructure the economy and promote more open policies led to demands for further reform. Communist party rule collapsed in the Soviet satellite states. In November 1989, the Berlin Wall was torn down, and a year later Germany was reunified. Russia itself survived a coup by hard-liners, and by 1991 the cold war had ended.

- **Reaganomics** Americans in the eighties experienced unprecedented prosperity, yet beggars and homeless people were visible in most cities. The prevailing mood was conservative, and AIDS was condemned as a "gay" disease. "Reaganomics" failed to reduce public spending, but the president nevertheless championed tax cuts for the rich. The result was massive public debt and the stock market collapse of 1987.

- **The Gulf War** Saddam Hussein of Iraq invaded Kuwait in 1990. The United Nations condemned Hussein's action and authorized the use of force to dislodge Iraq from Kuwait. Over thirty nations committed themselves to Operation Desert Shield. When Hussein did not withdraw, the allied forces launched Operation Desert Storm, and the Iraqis surrendered within six weeks.

CHRONOLOGY

1978	President Carter brokers the Camp David Accords
1978	Supreme Court issues the *Bakke* decision
November 1979	Islamic militants storm the U.S. embassy in Tehran and take more than fifty Americans hostage
1981	President Reagan fires members of PATCO for illegaly striking
1982	Israeli troops invade Lebanon
1987	Tower Commission issues report on Iran-Contra affair
1987	Reagan delivers his famous Berlin Wall speech
October 1987	Stock market experiences Black Monday
1989	Tiananmen Square protests in China
Pat Robertson forms the Christian Coalition
November 1989	Berlin Wall is torn down
December 1989	U.S. troops invade Panama and capture Manuel Noriega
August 1990	Saddam Hussein invades Kuwait

KEY TERMS & NAMES

34

AMERICA IN A NEW MILLENNIUM

FOCUS QUESTIONS

 wwnorton.com/studyspace

- How did the demographics of the United States change between 1980 and 2010?
- What led to the Democratic resurgence of the early nineties and the surprising Republican landslide of 1994?
- What caused the surge and decline of the financial markets in the nineties and the early twenty-first century?
- What were the consequences of the rise of global terrorism in the early twenty-first century?
- In what ways was the 2008 presidential election historic?

The United States entered the final decade of the twentieth century triumphant. American vigilance in the cold war had contributed to the shocking collapse of the Soviet Union and the birth of democratic capitalism in eastern Europe. The United States was now the world's only superpower. Not since ancient Rome had one nation exercised such widespread influence, for good and for ill. By the mid-nineties the American economy would become the marvel of the world as remarkable gains in productivity afforded by new technologies created the greatest period of prosperity in modern history. Yet no sooner did the century come to an end than America's sense of physical and material comfort was shattered by a horrifying terrorist assault that killed thousands, exacerbated the economic recession, and called into question conventional notions of national security and personal safety.

AMERICA'S CHANGING MOSAIC

DEMOGRAPHIC SHIFTS The nation's population had grown to over 309 million by 2010, and its racial and ethnic composition was rapidly changing. During the nineties, the foreign-born population increased by 57 percent, to 31 million, the largest ever, and far more than predicted. By 2010, the United States had more foreign-born and first-generation residents than ever before, and each year 1 million more immigrants arrived. Over 36 percent of Americans claimed African, Asian, Hispanic, or American Indian ancestry. Hispanics represented 16 percent of the total population, African Americans 11 percent, Asians about 4 percent, and American Indians almost 1 percent. The rate of increase among those four groups was twice as fast as it had been during the seventies. In 2005, Hispanics became the nation's largest minority group.

The primary cause of this dramatic change in the nation's ethnic mix was a surge of immigration. In 2000, the United States welcomed more than twice as many immigrants as all other countries in the world combined. For the first time in the nation's history, the majority of immigrants came not from Europe but from other parts of the world: Asia, Latin America, and Africa. Among the legal immigrants, Mexicans made up the largest share, averaging over one hundred thousand a year. Many new immigrants compiled an astonishing record of achievement, yet their very success contributed to the resentment they encountered from other groups.

Other aspects of American life were also changing. The decline of the traditional family unit continued. In 2005, less than 65 percent of children lived with two parents, down from 85 percent in 1970. And more people were living alone than ever before, largely as a result of high divorce rates or a growing practice among young people of delaying marriage until well into their twenties. The number of single mothers increased 35 percent during the decade. The rate was much higher for African Americans: in 2000 fewer than 32 percent of black children lived with both parents, down from 67 percent in 1960.

Young African Americans in particular faced shrinking economic opportunities at the start of the twenty-first century. The urban poor more than others were victimized by high rates of crime and violence, with young black men suffering the most. In 2000, the leading cause of death among African American men between the ages of fifteen and twenty-four was homicide. Over 25 percent of African American men aged twenty to twenty-nine were in prison, on parole, or on probation, while only 4 percent were enrolled in college. And nearly 40 percent of African American men were functionally illiterate.

BUSH TO CLINTON

The changing demographic of American society would have a profound impact on politics. But during the last decade of the twentieth century, changing global dynamics held sway. For months after the First Gulf War in 1991, George H. W. Bush seemed unbeatable; his public approval rating soared to 91 percent. But the aftermath of Desert Storm was mixed, with Saddam Hussein's despotic grip on Iraq still intact. The Soviet Union meanwhile stumbled on to its surprising end. On December 25, 1991, the Soviet flag over the Kremlin was replaced by the flag of the Russian Federation. The cold war had ended with the dismemberment of the Soviet Union and its fifteen constituent republics. As a result, the United States had become the world's only dominant military power.

"Containment" of the Soviet Union, the bedrock of U.S. foreign policy for more than four decades, had become irrelevant. Bush struggled to interpret the fluid new international scene. He spoke of a "new world order" but never defined it. By his own admission he had trouble with "the vision thing." By the end of 1991, a listless Bush faced a challenge in the Republican primary from the feisty conservative commentator and former White House aide Patrick Buchanan, who adopted the slogan "America First" and called on Bush to "bring home the boys." As the euphoria of the Gulf War victory wore off, a popular bumper sticker reflected the growing public frustration with the economic policies of the Bush administration: "Saddam Hussein still has his job. What about you?"

RECESSION AND DOWNSIZING For the Bush administration and for the nation, the most devastating development in the early nineties was a prolonged economic recession as the roller coaster dynamic at the center of the capitalist system, continually counterbalancing periods of prosperity with periods of recession or depression, sent the economy plunging into the longest recession since the Great Depression. During 1991, 25 million workers—about 20 percent of the labor force—were unemployed at some point. The economy barely grew at all during the first three years of the Bush administration—the worst record since the end of the Second World War. Meanwhile, the federal budget deficit mushroomed by 57 percent, to $4.1 trillion. The euphoria over the allied victory in the Gulf War quickly gave way to surly anxiety generated by the depressed economy. In addressing the recession, Bush tried a clumsy balancing act, on the one hand acknowledging that "people are hurting" while on the other telling Americans that "this is a good time to buy a car." By 1991, the public approval rating of his economic policy had plummeted to 18 percent.

REPUBLICAN TURMOIL   President Bush had already set a political trap for himself when he declared at the 1988 Republican Convention: "Read my lips. No new taxes." Fourteen months into his presidency, he decided that the federal budget deficit was a greater risk than violation of his no-new-taxes pledge. His backsliding set off a revolt among House Republicans, but a bipartisan majority (with most Republicans still opposed) finally approved a tax increase, raising the top tax rate on personal income from 28 to 31 percent, disallowing certain deductions in the upper brackets, and raising various special taxes. Such actions increased federal revenue but eroded Bush's political support among conservative Republicans.

At the 1992 Republican Convention, Patrick Buchanan, who had won about a third of the votes in the party's primaries, lambasted Bush for breaking his pledge not to raise taxes and for becoming the "biggest spender in American history." Buchanan claimed to be a crusader "for a Middle American revolution" that would halt illegal immigration and the gay rights movement. As the 1992 election unfolded, Bush's real problem was not Pat Buchanan and the conservative wing of the Republican party, however. What threatened his reelection was his own failed effort to jump-start the economy.

DEMOCRATIC RESURGENCE   In contrast to divisions among Republicans, the Democrats at their 1992 convention presented an image of centrist forces in control. For several years the Democratic Leadership Council, in which Arkansas governor **William Jefferson Clinton** figured prominently, had been pushing the party from the liberal left to the center of the political spectrum. Clinton called for a "third way" positioned in between conservatism and liberalism, something he labeled "progressive centrism."

Born in Hope, Arkansas, Bill Clinton grew to be a bright, ambitious young man who yearned to be a political leader on a national scale. To that end, he attended Georgetown University in Washington, D.C., won a Rhodes Scholarship to Oxford University, and then earned a law degree from Yale University, where he met his future wife, Hillary Rodham. Clinton returned to Arkansas and won election as the state's attorney general. By 1979, at age thirty-two, Bill Clinton was the youngest governor in the country. He served three more terms as Arkansas governor and in the process emerged as a dynamic young leader of the "New Democrats" committed to winning back the middle-class whites ("Reagan Democrats") who had voted Republican during the 1980s.

A self-described moderate seeking the Democratic presidential nomination, Clinton promised to cut the defense budget, provide tax relief for the middle class, and create a massive economic aid package for the former republics of the Soviet Union to help them forge democratic societies. Witty, intelligent, and charismatic, with an in-depth knowledge of public policy, Clinton was adept at campaigning; he projected energy, youth, and optimism, reminding many political observers of John F. Kennedy.

But beneath the veneer of Clinton's charisma and his deep knowledge of public policy issues were several flaws. Self-absorbed and self-indulgent, he yearned to be loved. The *New York Times* explained that Clinton was "emotionally needy, indecisive, and undisciplined." He was a political opportunist who had earned a well-deserved reputation for half-truths, exaggerations, and talking out of both sides of his mouth. Clinton was a policy "wonk" who relished the details and nuances of complex legislation. He was also very much a political animal. He made extensive use of polls to shape his stance on issues, pandered to special-interest groups, and flip-flopped on controversial subjects, leading critics to label him "Slick Willie." Even more enticing to the media were charges that Clinton was a chronic adulterer and that he had manipulated the Reserve Officers' Training Corps (ROTC) program during the Vietnam War to avoid military service. Clinton's evasive denials of both allegations could not dispel a lingering distrust of his character.

Yet after a series of bruising party primaries, Clinton won the Democratic nomination in the summer of 1992. He chose Senator Albert "Al" Gore Jr. of

The 1992 presidential campaign

Presidential candidate Bill Clinton and his running mate, Al Gore, brought youthful enthusiasm to the campaign trail.

Tennessee as his running mate. Gore described himself as a "raging moderate." So the Democratic candidates were two Southern Baptists from adjoining states. Flushed with their convention victory and sporting a ten-point lead over Bush in the polls, the Clinton-Gore team stressed economic issues to win over working-class voters. Clinton won the election with 370 electoral votes and about 43 percent of the vote; Bush received 168 electoral votes and 39 percent of the vote; and off-and-on independent candidate H. Ross Perot of Texas garnered 19 percent of the popular vote, more than any other third-party candidate since Theodore Roosevelt in 1912. A puckish billionaire, Perot found a large audience for his simplified explanations of national problems and his criticism of Reaganomics as "voodoo economics."

DOMESTIC POLICY IN CLINTON'S FIRST TERM

Clinton's inexperience in international affairs and congressional maneuvering led to several missteps in his first year as president. Like George H. W. Bush before him, he reneged on several campaign promises. He abandoned his proposed middle-class tax cut in order to keep down the federal deficit. Then he dropped his promise to allow gays to serve in the armed forces after military commanders expressed strong opposition. Instead, he later announced an ambiguous new policy concerning gays in the military that came to be known as "don't ask, don't tell." In Clinton's first two weeks in office, his approval rating dropped 20 percent. But the true test for presidents is not how they begin but how fast they learn, how resilient they are, and where they end up.

THE ECONOMY   As a candidate, Clinton had pledged to reduce the federal deficit without damaging the economy or hurting the nation's most vulnerable people. To this end, on February 17 he proposed higher taxes for corporations and for individuals in higher tax brackets. He also called for an economic stimulus package for "investment" in public works (transportation, utilities, and the like) and "human capital" (education, skills, health, and welfare). The hotly contested bill finally passed by 218 to 216 in the House and 51 to 50 in the Senate, with Vice President Gore breaking the tie.

Equally contested was congressional approval of the **North American Free Trade Agreement (NAFTA)**, which the Bush administration had negotiated with Canada and Mexico. The debate revived old arguments on the tariff. Clinton stuck with his party's tradition of low tariffs and urged

NAFTA protesters

Protesters going to a rally opposing NAFTA.

approval of NAFTA, which would make North America the largest free-trade area in the world, enabling the three nations to trade with each other on an equal footing. Opponents of the bill, such as gadfly Ross Perot and organized labor, favored tariff barriers that would discourage the importation of cheaper foreign products. Perot predicted that NAFTA would result in the "giant sucking sound" of American jobs being drawn to Mexico. Yet Clinton prevailed with solid Republican support while losing a sizable minority of Democrats, mostly from the South, where people feared that many textile mills would lose business to "cheap-labor" countries, as they did.

HEALTH-CARE REFORM   Clinton's major public-policy initiative was a federal health-care plan. "If I don't get health care," he declared, "I'll wish I didn't run for President" Government-subsidized health insurance was not a new idea. Medicare, initiated in 1965, provided health insurance for people sixty-five and older, and Medicaid supported state medical assistance for the poor. Sentiment for health-care reform spread as annual medical costs skyrocketed and some 39 million Americans went without medical insurance, most of them poor or unemployed. The Clinton administration argued that universal medical insurance would reduce the costs of health care to the nation as a whole.

President Clinton made a tactical error when he appointed his spouse, Hillary, to head up the task force created to design a federal health-care plan. She chose not to work with Congressional leaders in drafting the proposal. Instead, the final version, essentially designed by the Clintons, was presented to Congress with little consultation. The maddeningly complicated plan, dubbed "Hillarycare" by journalists, proposed to give access to health insurance to every citizen and legal immigrant. Under the proposal, people would no longer purchase health insurance through their employers. Instead, workers would be pooled into "regional health alliances" run by the states that would offer private insurance options. Employers would pay most of the premiums. Government would subsidize all or part of the payments for small businesses and the poor, the latter from funds that formerly went to Medicaid, and would collect a new "sin tax" on tobacco products and perhaps alcoholic beverages to pay for the program. The bill aroused opposition from Republicans and even moderate Democrats, as well as the pharmaceutical and insurance industries. By the summer of 1994, the Clinton health-insurance plan was doomed. Lacking the votes to stop a filibuster by Senate Republicans, the Democrats acknowledged defeat and gave up the fight for universal medical insurance.

REPUBLICAN INSURGENCY

During 1994, Bill Clinton began to see his coveted presidency unravel. Unable to get either health-care reform or welfare-reform bills through the Democratic Congress and having failed to carry out his campaign pledge for middle-class tax relief, he and his party found themselves on the defensive. In the midterm elections of 1994, the Democrats suffered a humbling defeat. It was the first election since 1952 in which Republicans captured both houses of Congress at the same time.

THE CONTRACT WITH AMERICA   The Republican insurgency in Congress during the mid-nineties was led by a feisty, self-infatuated Georgian named Newton Leroy Gingrich. In early 1995 he became the first Republican Speaker of the House in forty-two years. Gingrich, a former history professor with a lust for controversy and an unruly ego, was a superb tactician who had helped mobilize religious and social conservatives associated with the Christian Coalition. In 1995, he announced that "we are at the end of an era." Liberalism, he claimed, was dead, and the Democratic party itself was dying. The imperious Gingrich pledged to start a new reign of congressional Republican dominance that would dismantle the "corrupt liberal welfare state." He was aided in his efforts by newly elected Republican House members who promoted what Gingrich called with great fanfare the **Contract with America**. The ten-point contract outlined an anti-big-government program featuring less regulation of businesses, less environmental conservation, term limits for members of Congress, welfare reform, and a balanced-budget amendment. As one of the congressional Republicans explained, "We are ideologues. We have an agenda" to change America. Gingrich was blunter. He said that Republicans had not been "nasty" enough. That was about to change, as Gingrich launched an unrelenting assault on the Clinton administration and the Democratic party.

Yet the much-ballyhooed Contract with America quickly fizzled out. Triumph often undermines judgment, and the Republican revolution touted by Gingrich could not be sustained by the slim Republican majority in Congress. What is more, many of the seventy-three new Republican House, members were dogmatists scornful of compromise. As legislative amateurs they limited Gingrich's ability to maneuver. The Senate rejected many of the bills that had been passed in the House. Most of all, the Contract with America disintegrated because Newt Gingrich himself became such an unpopular figure, both in Congress and among the electorate. He was too ambitious, too slick, too abrasive, too rambunctious, too polarizing. Republican senator Bob Dole said Gingrich was "a one-man band who rarely took advice."

Gingrich's clumsy bravado backfired. "No political figure in modern time," a journalist declared in 1996, "has done more to undermine the power of his message with the defects of his personality than the disastrously voluble Speaker of the House." In 1997, the House of Representatives censured Gingrich for an array of ethics violations, the first time in history that a Speaker of the House was disciplined for ethical wrongdoing. The following year, Republicans ousted Gingrich as Speaker of the House. The emerging lesson of politics in the 1990s was that Americans wanted elected federal officials to govern from the center rather than the extremes. As *Time* magazine noted in 1995, "Clinton and Gingrich—powerful yet indefinably immature—give off a bright, undisciplined energy, a vibration of adolescent recklessness."

LEGISLATIVE BREAKTHROUGH   In the late summer of 1996, the Congress broke through its partisan gridlock and passed a flurry of legislation that President Clinton quickly signed, including bills increasing the minimum wage and broadening public access to health insurance. Most significant was a comprehensive welfare-reform measure that ended the federal government's open-ended guarantee of aid to the poor, a guarantee that had been in place since 1935. The Personal Responsibility and Work Opportunity Act of 1996 (PRWOA) was a centrist measure that illustrated Clinton's efforts to move the Democratic party away from the tired liberalism it had promoted since the 1930s. "The era of big government is over," Clinton proclaimed.

PRWOA abolished the Aid to Families with Dependent Children (AFDC) program and replaced it with the Temporary Assistance for Needy Families, which limited the duration of welfare payments to the unemployed to two years. Equally significant was that the PRWOA transferred administrative responsibility to the states, which were free to design their own aid programs funded by federal grants. PRWOA also required that at least half of a state's welfare recipients have jobs or be enrolled in job-training programs by 2002. States failing to meet the deadline would have their federal funds cut.

The welfare-reform bill represented a turning point in modern politics. The war on poverty launched by Lyndon B. Johnson in 1964 and broadened by Richard M. Nixon's expansion of the federal food-stamp program, had ended in defeat. Despite the massive amount of federal funds spent on various anti-poverty and social welfare programs, poverty was growing. Now, the federal government was turning over responsibility for several welfare programs to the states. And, despite criticism, the new approach seemed to work. Welfare recipients and poverty rates both declined during the late nineties, leading the editors of the left-leaning *The New Republic* to report that welfare reform had "worked much as its designers had hoped."

THE 1996 CAMPAIGN After clinching the Republican presidential nomination in 1996, Senate majority leader Bob Dole resigned his seat in order to devote his attention to defeating Bill Clinton. As the 1996 presidential campaign unfolded, however, Clinton maintained a large lead in the polls. With an improving economy and no major foreign-policy crises to confront, cultural and personal issues again surged into prominence. Concern about Dole's age (seventy-three) and his acerbic personality, as well as rifts in the Republican party between economic conservatives and social conservatives over volatile issues such as abortion and gun control, hampered Dole's efforts to generate widespread support, especially among the growing number of independent voters.

On November 5, 1996, Clinton won again, with an electoral vote of 379 to 159 and 49 percent of the popular vote. Clinton was the first Democratic presidential candidate to win an election while the Republicans controlled Congress. And he was the first Democratic president to win a second term since Franklin D. Roosevelt in 1936. Dole received only 41 percent of the popular vote, and third-party candidate Ross Perot got

Bob Dole

The Republican presidential candidate and former Senate majority leader on the campaign trail.

8 percent. The Republicans lost eight seats in the House but retained an edge, 227 to 207, over the Democrats in the House; in the Senate, Republicans gained two seats for a 55–45 majority.

THE CLINTON YEARS AT HOME

As the twentieth century came to a close, the United States benefited from a prolonged period of unprecedented prosperity. Buoyed by low inflation, high employment, declining federal budget deficits, dramatic improvements in industrial productivity and the sweeping globalization of economic life, business and industry witnessed record profits.

THE "NEW ECONOMY" By the end of the twentieth century, the "new economy" was centered on high-flying computer, software, telecommunications, and Internet firms. These "dot-com" enterprises had come to represent almost a third of stock-market values even though many of them were hollow-shelled companies fueled by the speculative mania. The result was a high-tech financial bubble that soon burst, but during the run-up in the 1990s investors gave little thought to a possible collapse. The robust economy set records in every area: low inflation, low unemployment, federal budget surpluses for the first time in modern history, and dizzying corporate profits and personal fortunes. People began to claim that the new economy defied the boom-and-bust cycles of the previous hundred years. Alan Greenspan, the Federal Reserve Board chairman, foolishly suggested "that we have moved 'beyond history'"—into an economy that seemed only to grow. Only too late would people remember that human greed always breeds recklessness leading to what Greenspan later called "irrational exuberance."

One major factor producing the economic boom of the nineties was the so-called "peace dividend." The end of the cold war had enabled the U.S. government to reduce the proportion of the federal budget devoted to defense spending. Another major factor was the Clinton administration's 1993 initiative cutting taxes and reducing overall federal spending. But perhaps the single most important reason for the surge in prosperity was dramatic growth in per-worker productivity. New information technologies and high-tech production processes allowed for greater efficiency.

GLOBALIZATION Another major feature of the "new economy" was globalization. Globe-spanning technologies shrank time and distance, enabling U.S.-based multinational companies to conduct a growing proportion of their business abroad as more and more nations lowered trade barriers such as tariffs and import fees. By 2000, over a third of the production of American multinational companies was occurring abroad, compared with only 9 percent in 1980. Many U.S. manufacturing companies moved their production "offshore" to take advantage of lower labor costs and lax workplace regulations abroad, a controversial phenomenon often labeled "outsourcing." At the same time, many foreign manufacturers, such as Toyota, Honda, and BMW, built production facilities in the United States. The U.S. economy had become internationalized to such a profound extent that global concerns exercised an ever-increasing influence on domestic and foreign policies.

RACE INITIATIVES   After the triumphs of the civil rights movement in the sixties, the momentum for minority advancement had run out by the nineties—except for gains in college admissions and employment under the rubric of affirmative action. The conservative mood during the mid-nineties manifested itself in the Supreme Court. In 1995 the Court ruled against election districts redrawn to create African American or Latino majorities and narrowed federal affirmative-action programs intended to benefit minorities underrepresented in the workplace.

In one of those cases, *Adarand Constructors v. Peña* (1995), the Court assessed a program that gave some advantages to businesses owned by "disadvantaged" minorities. A Hispanic-owned firm had won a highway guardrail contract over a lower bid by a white-owned company that sued on the grounds of "reverse discrimination." Writing for the majority, Justice Sandra Day O'Connor said that such affirmative-action programs had to be "narrowly tailored" to serve a "compelling national interest." O'Connor did not define what the Court meant by a "compelling national interest," but the implication of her language was clear: the Court had come to share the growing public suspicion of the value and legality of such race-based benefit programs.

In 1996, two major steps were taken against affirmative action in college admissions. In *Hopwood v. Texas,* the U.S. Court of Appeals for the Fifth Circuit ruled that considering race to achieve a diverse student body at the University of Texas was "not a compelling interest under the Fourteenth Amendment." Later that year, the state of California passed Proposition 209, an initiative that ruled out race, sex, ethnicity, and national origin as criteria for preferring any group. These rulings gutted affirmative-action programs and reduced African American college enrollments, prompting second thoughts. In addition, the nation still had not addressed intractable problems that lay beyond civil rights—that is, chronic problems of adult illiteracy, poverty, unemployment, urban decay, and slums.

THE SCANDAL MACHINE   During his first term, President Clinton was dogged by allegations of improper involvement in the Whitewater Development Corporation. In 1978, while serving as governor of Arkansas, he had invested in a resort to be built in northern Arkansas. The project turned out to be a fraud and a failure, and the Clintons took a loss on their investment. In 1994, Kenneth Starr, a Republican, was appointed as independent counsel in an investigation of the Whitewater case. Starr did not uncover evidence that the Clintons were directly involved in the fraud, although several of their close associates had been caught in the web and convicted of various charges, some related to Whitewater and some not.

In the course of another investigation, a salacious scandal erupted when it was revealed that President Clinton had engaged in a prolonged sexual affair with a White House intern, Monica Lewinsky, a recent college graduate. Even more disturbing, he had pressed her to lie about their relationship under oath. Like Richard M. Nixon's handling of the Watergate incident, Clinton initially denied the charges, but the scandal would not disappear. For the next thirteen months, "Monicagate" captured public attention and enlivened partisan debate about Clinton's presidency. In August 1998 Clinton agreed to appear before a grand jury convened to investigate the sexual allegations, thus becoming the first president in history to testify before a grand jury. On August 17, Clinton, a dogged fighter, self-pitying and defiant, recanted his earlier denials and acknowledged having had "inappropriate intimate physical contact" with Lewinsky. That evening the president delivered a four-minute nationally televised address in which he admitted an improper relationship with Lewinsky, but insisted that he had done nothing illegal.

Public reaction to Clinton's remarkable about-face was mixed. A majority of Americans expressed sympathy for the president because of his public humiliation; they wanted the entire matter dropped. But Clinton's credibility had suffered a serious blow on account of his reckless lack of self-discipline and his efforts first to deny and then to cover up the scandal. Then, on September 9, 1998, the special prosecutor submitted to Congress a 445-page, sexually graphic report. The Starr Report found "substantial and creditable" evidence of presidential wrongdoing, prompting the House of Representatives on October 8 to begin a wide-ranging impeachment inquiry of the president. Thirty-one Democrats joined the Republicans in supporting the investigation. On December 19, 1998, William Jefferson Clinton became

Impeachment

Representative Edward Pease, a member of the House Judiciary Committee, covers his face during the vote on the third of four articles of impeachment charging President Clinton with "high crimes and misdemeanors," December 1998.

the second president to be impeached by the House of Representatives. The House officially approved two articles of impeachment, charging Clinton with lying under oath to a federal grand jury and obstructing justice. House Speaker Newt Gingrich led the effort to impeach the president over the Lewinsky scandal—even though he himself was secretly engaged in an adulterous affair with a congressional staffer.

The Senate trial of President Clinton began on January 7, 1999. Five weeks later, on February 12, Clinton was acquitted. Rejecting the first charge of perjury, 10 Republicans and all 45 Democrats voted "not guilty." On the charge of obstruction of justice, the Senate split 50–50 (which meant acquittal, since 67 votes were needed for conviction). In both instances, senators had a hard time interpreting Clinton's adultery and lies as constituting "high crimes and misdemeanors," the constitutional requirement for removal of a president from office. Politically astute and well informed, Clinton had as much ability and potential as any president. Yet he was also shamelessly self-indulgent. The result was a scandalous presidency punctuated by dramatic achievements in welfare reform, economic growth, and foreign policy.

FOREIGN-POLICY CHALLENGES

Like Woodrow Wilson, Lyndon Johnson, and Jimmy Carter before him, Bill Clinton was a Democratic president who came into office determined to focus on the nation's domestic problems only to find himself mired in foreign entanglements. Clinton continued the Bush administration's military intervention in Somalia, on the northeastern horn of Africa, where collapse of the government early in 1991 had left the country in anarchy, prey to tribal marauders. President Bush in 1992 had gained UN sanction for a military force led by American troops to relieve hunger and restore peace. The Somalian operation proved successful at its primary mission, but it never resolved the political anarchy that lay at the root of the population's starvation.

HAITI During its first term, the Clinton administration's most rewarding foreign-policy endeavor came in Haiti. The Caribbean island nation had emerged suddenly from a cycle of coups with a democratic election in 1990, which brought to the presidency a popular priest, Jean-Bertrand Aristide. When a Haitian army general ousted Aristide, the United States announced its intention to bring him back with the aid of the United Nations. With drawn-out negotiations leading nowhere, Clinton moved in July 1994 to get a UN resolution authorizing force as a last resort. At that juncture, former president Jimmy Carter asked permission to negotiate. He convinced the military leaders to quit by October 15. Aristide returned to Haiti and on March 31, 1995, the occupation was turned over to a UN force commanded by an American general.

THE MIDDLE EAST President Clinton also continued George H. W. Bush's policy of sponsoring patient negotiations between the Arabs and the Israelis. A new development was the inclusion of the Palestinian Liberation Organization (PLO) in the negotiations. In 1993, secret talks between Israeli and Palestinian representatives in Oslo, Norway, resulted in a draft agreement between Israel and the PLO. This agreement provided for the restoration of Palestinian self-rule in the occupied Gaza Strip and in Jericho, on the West Bank, in an exchange of land for peace as provided in UN Security Council resolutions. A formal signing occurred at the White House on September 13, 1993. With President Clinton presiding, Israeli prime minister Yitzhak Rabin and PLO leader Yasir Arafat exchanged handshakes, and their foreign ministers signed the agreement.

The Middle East peace process suffered a terrible blow in early November 1995, however, when Prime Minister Rabin was assassinated by an Israeli zealot who resented Rabin's efforts to negotiate with the Palestinians. Some observers feared that the assassin had killed the peace process as well when seven months later conservative hard-liner Benjamin Netanyahu narrowly defeated the U.S.-backed Shimon Peres in the Israeli national elections. Yet in October 1998, Clinton brought Arafat, Netanyahu, and King Hussein of Jordan together at a conference in Maryland, where they reached an agreement. Under the Wye River Accord, Israel agreed to surrender land in return for security guarantees by the Palestinians.

THE BALKANS　Clinton's foreign policy also addressed the chaotic transition in eastern Europe from Soviet domination to independence. When combustible Yugoslavia imploded in 1991, fanatics and tyrants triggered ethnic conflict as four of its six republics seceded. Serb minorities, backed by the new republic of Serbia, stirred up civil wars in Croatia and Bosnia. In Bosnia especially, the war involved "**ethnic cleansing**"—driving Muslims from their homes and towns. Clinton sent food and medical supplies to besieged Bosnians and dispatched warplanes to retaliate for attacks on places designated "safe havens" by the United Nations.

In 1995, U.S. negotiators finally persuaded the foreign ministers of Croatia, Bosnia, and the Federal Republic of Yugoslavia to agree to a comprehensive peace plan. Bosnia would remain a single nation but would be divided into two states: a Muslim-Croat federation controlling 51 percent of the territory and a Bosnian-Serb republic controlling the remaining 49 percent. Basic human rights would be restored and free elections would be held to appoint a parliament and joint president. To enforce the agreement, sixty thousand NATO peacekeeping troops would be dispatched to Bosnia. A cease-fire went into effect in October 1995.

In 1998, the Balkan tinderbox flared up again, this time in the Yugoslav province of Kosovo, which had long been considered sacred ground by Christian Serbs. By 1989, however, over 90 percent of the 2 million Kosovars were ethnic Albanian Muslims. In that year, Yugoslav president Slobodan Milošević decided to reassert Serbian control over the province. He stripped Kosovo of its autonomy and established de facto martial law. When the Albanian Kosovars resisted and large numbers of Muslim men began to join the Kosovo Liberation Army, Serbian soldiers and state police ruthlessly burned Albanian villages, murdering men, raping women, and displacing hundreds of thousands of Muslim Kosovars.

On March 24, 1999, NATO, relying heavily upon U.S. military resources and leadership, launched air strikes against Yugoslavia. "Ending this tragedy is a moral imperative," explained President Clinton. After seventy-two days of unrelenting bombardment, Milošević sued for peace on NATO's terms, in part because his Russian allies had finally abandoned him. An agreement was reached on June 3, 1999. President Clinton pledged extensive U.S. aid in helping the Yugoslavs rebuild their war-torn economy.

THE CLINTON PRESIDENCY Personality matters in presidential politics. Bill Clinton was a man of driving ambition and considerable talent. His charisma charmed people, and his rhetoric inspired them. His two terms included many successes. He presided over an unprecedented period of prolonged prosperity (115 consecutive months of economic growth and the lowest unemployment rate in thirty years), generated unheard-of federal budget surpluses, and passed a welfare-reform measure with support from both parties. In the process he salvaged liberalism from the dustbin and re-centered the Democratic party. Clinton also helped bring peace and stability to the Balkans, one of the most fractious and violent regions in all of Europe. Although less successful, his tireless efforts to mediate a lasting peace between Israel and the Palestinians displayed his courage and persistence.

Throughout his presidency, Clinton displayed a remarkable ability to manage crises and rebound from adversity. His resilience was extraordinary, in part because he was a master at spinning events and circumstances to his benefit. At times, however, his loyalty seemed focused on his ambition. His inflated self-confidence occasionally led to arrogant recklessness. He may have balanced the budget, but he also debased the presidency. He may have pushed through a dramatic reform of the welfare system, but his effort to bring health insurance to the uninsured was a clumsy failure. Clinton was less a great statesman than he was a great escape artist. He even survived his awful handling of the Monica Lewinsky scandal and his intensely partisan impeachment trial. In 2000, his last year in office, the smooth-talking Clinton enjoyed a public approval rating of 65 percent, the highest end-of-term rating since President Dwight D. Eisenhower. Yet Clinton's popularity was not deep enough to ensure the election of his vice president, Al Gore, as his successor.

THE ELECTION OF 2000

The election of 2000 proved to be one of the closest and most controversial in history. The two major-party candidates for president, Vice President **Albert Gore Jr.**, the Democrat, and Texas governor **George W. Bush**, the son of the former Republican president, presented contrasting views on the role of the federal government, tax cuts, environmental policies, and the best way to preserve Social Security and Medicare. Gore, a Tennessee native and Harvard graduate whose father had been a senator, favored an active federal government that would subsidize prescription-medicine expenses for the elderly, and protect the environment.

Bush, on the other hand, proposed a transfer of power from the federal government to the states, particularly in regard to environmental and educational policies. In international affairs, Bush questioned the need to maintain U.S. peacekeeping forces in Bosnia and the continuing expense of other global military commitments. He urged a more "humble" foreign policy, one that would end U.S. efforts to install democratic governments in undemocratic countries ("nation building") around the world.

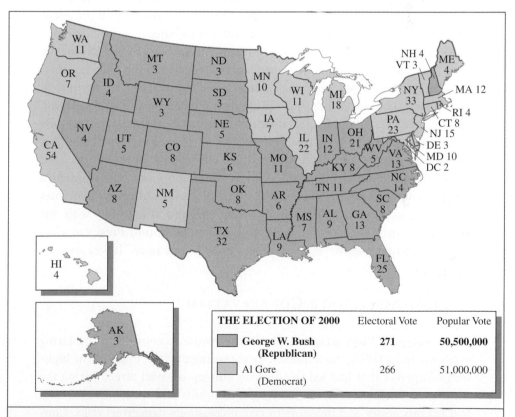

THE ELECTION OF 2000	Electoral Vote	Popular Vote
George W. Bush (Republican)	271	50,500,000
Al Gore (Democrat)	266	51,000,000

Why was the 2000 presidential election so close? How was the conflict over the election results resolved? How were differences between urban and rural voters key to the outcome of the election?

The polarization of politics at the start of the twentieth century continued to spawn various third-party candidates at the extremes. Two independent candidates added zest to the 2000 presidential campaign: conservative columnist Patrick Buchanan and liberal activist Ralph Nader. Buchanan focused his campaign on criticism of NAFTA, while Nader lamented the corrupting effects of large corporate donations on the political process and the need for more robust efforts to protect the environment.

In the end, the election created high drama. The television networks initially reported that Gore had narrowly won the state of Florida and its decisive twenty-five electoral votes. Later in the evening, however, the networks reversed themselves, saying that Florida was too close to call. In the chaotic early-morning hours, the networks declared that Bush had been elected president. Gore called Bush to concede, only to issue a retraction a short time later when it appeared that the results in Florida remained a toss-up. The final tally in Florida showed Bush with a razor-thin lead, and state law required a recount. For the first time in 125 years, the results of a presidential election remained in doubt for weeks after the voting.

As a painstaking hand count of presidential ballots proceeded in Florida, supporters of Bush and Gore pursued legal maneuvers in the Florida courts and the U.S. Supreme Court; each side accused the other of trying to steal the election. The political drama remained stalemated for five weeks. At last, on December 12, 2000, a harshly divided Supreme Court halted the recounts in Florida. In the case known as *Bush v. Gore,* a bare 5–4 majority ruled that any new recount would clash with existing Florida law. Bush was declared the winner in Florida by only 537 votes. Although Gore had amassed a 540,000-vote lead nationwide, he lost in the Electoral College by two votes when he lost Florida. Although Al Gore "strongly disagreed" with the Supreme Court's decision, he asked voters to rally around President-elect Bush and move forward: "Partisan rancor must be put aside." It was not.

COMPASSIONATE CONSERVATISM

George W. Bush arrived in the White House to confront a sputtering economy and a falling stock market. By the spring of 2000, many of the high-tech companies that had led the dizzying run-up on Wall Street during the nineties had collapsed. Greed fed by record profits and speculative excesses had led businesses and investors to take increasingly dangerous risks. Consumer confidence and capital investment plummeted with the falling stock market. By March 2001 the economy was in recession for the first time in over a decade. Yet neither the floundering economy nor the close political balance in Congress prevented President Bush from launching an ambitious legislative agenda. Confident that he could win over conservative Democrats, he promised to provide "an explosion of legislation" promoting his goal of "compassionate conservatism." The top item on Bush's wish list was a tax cut intended to stimulate the sagging economy. Bush signed it into law on June 7, 2001. By cutting taxes, however, federal revenue diminished, thus increasing the budget deficit. It also shifted more of the tax burden from the rich to the middle and working classes, and increased already high levels of income inequality.

NO CHILD LEFT BEHIND In addition to tax reduction, one of President Bush's top priorities was to reform primary and secondary education. In late 2001, Congress passed a comprehensive education-improvement plan called **No Child Left Behind** that sought to improve educational quality by requiring states to set new learning standards and to develop standardized tests to ensure that all students were "proficient" at reading and math by 2014. It also mandated that all teachers be "highly qualified" in their subject area by 2005, allowed children in low-performing schools to transfer to other schools, and required states to submit annual standardized student test scores. A growing number of states criticized the program, claiming that it provided insufficient funds for remedial programs and that poor school districts, many of them in blighted inner cities or rural areas, would be especially hard-pressed to meet the new guidelines. The most common criticism, however, was that the federal program created a culture whereby teachers, feeling pressured to increase student performance, focused their classroom teaching on preparing students for the tests rather than fostering learning.

GLOBAL TERRORISM

As had happened so often with presidents during the twentieth century, President Bush soon found himself distracted by global issues and foreign crises. With the implosion of the Soviet Union and the end of the cold war, world politics had grown less potent but more unstable during the nineties. Whereas competing ideologies such as capitalism and communism had earlier provided the fulcrum of foreign relations, issues of religion, ethnicity, and clashing cultural values now divided peoples. Islamic militants around the world especially resented what they viewed as the "imperial" globalization of

U.S. culture and power. Multinational groups inspired by religious fanaticism and anti-American rage used high-tech terrorism to gain notoriety and exact vengeance. Well-financed and well-armed terrorists flourished in the cracks of fractured nations such as Sudan, Somalia, Pakistan, Yemen, and Afghanistan. Throughout the nineties the United States fought a losing secret war against organized terrorism. The ineffectiveness of Western intelligence agencies in tracking the movements and intentions of militant extremists became tragically evident in the late summer of 2001.

9/11: A DAY OF INFAMY At 8:45 A.M. on September 11, 2001, a commercial airliner hijacked by Islamic terrorists slammed into the north tower of the majestic World Trade Center in New York City. A second hijacked jumbo jet crashed into the south tower eighteen minutes later. The fuel-laden planes turned the majestic buildings into infernos, forcing desperate

9/11

Smoke pours out of the north tower of the World Trade Center as the south tower bursts into flames after being struck by a second hijacked airplane. Both towers collapsed about an hour later.

people who worked in the skyscrapers to jump to their deaths. The iconic twin towers, both 110 stories tall and occupied by thousands of employees, imploded from the intense heat. Surrounding buildings also collapsed. The southern end of Manhattan—ground zero—became a hellish scene of twisted steel, suffocating smoke, and wailing sirens.

While the catastrophic drama in New York City was unfolding, a third hijacked plane crashed into the Pentagon in Washington, D.C. A fourth airliner, probably headed for the White House, missed its mark when passengers—who had heard reports of the earlier hijackings via cell phones—assaulted the hijackers to prevent the plane from being used as a weapon. During the struggle in the cockpit, the plane went out of control and plummeted into the Pennsylvania countryside, killing all aboard.

Within hours of the hijackings, officials had identified the nineteen dead terrorists as members of al Qaeda (the Base), a well-financed worldwide network of Islamic extremists led by a wealthy Saudi renegade, **Osama bin Laden**. Years before, bin Laden had declared jihad (holy war) on the United States, Israel, and the Saudi monarchy. He believed that the United States, like the Soviet Union, was on the verge of collapse; all it needed was a spark to ignite its self-destruction. To that end, for several years he had been using remote bases in war-torn Afghanistan as terrorist training centers. Collaborating with bin Laden's terrorist network was Afghanistan's ruling Taliban, a coalition of ultraconservative Islamists that had emerged in the mid-nineties following the forced withdrawal of Soviet troops from Afghanistan. Taliban leaders provided bin Laden with a safe haven, enabling him to recruit Muslim militants and mobilize them into a global strike force. As many as twenty thousand recruits from twenty different countries circulated through Afghan training camps before joining secret jihadist cells around the world. Their goal was to engage in urban warfare, assassination, demolition, and sabotage, with the United States and Europe as the primary targets.

WAR ON TERRORISM   The **9/11** assault on the United States changed the course of modern life. The economy, already in decline, went into free fall. President Bush, who had never professed to know much about international relations or world affairs, was thrust onto center stage as commander in chief of a wounded nation eager for vengeance. The new president told the nation that the "deliberate and deadly attacks . . . were more than acts of terror. They were acts of war."

The Bush administration mobilized America's allies to assault terrorism worldwide. The coalition demanded that Afghanistan's Taliban government surrender the al Qaeda terrorists or risk military attack. On October 7,

2001, after the Taliban refused to turn over bin Laden, the United States and its allies launched a ferocious military campaign—Operation Enduring Freedom—to punish terrorists or "those harboring terrorists." American and British cruise missiles and bombers destroyed Afghan military installations and al Qaeda training camps. On December 9, only two months after the U.S.-led military campaign in Afghanistan had begun, the Taliban regime collapsed. The war in Afghanistan then devolved into a high-stakes manhunt for the elusive Osama bin Laden and his international network of terrorists.

TERRORISM AT HOME While the military campaign continued in Afghanistan, officials in Washington worried that terrorists might launch additional attacks in the United States with biological, chemical, or even nuclear weapons. To address the threat and to help restore public confidence, President Bush created a new federal agency, the Office of Homeland Security. Another new federal agency, the Transportation Security Administration, assumed responsibility for screening airline passengers for weapons and bombs. At the same time, President Bush and a supportive Congress created the USA Patriot Act, which gave government agencies the right to eavesdrop on confidential conversations between prison inmates and their lawyers and permitted suspected terrorists to be tried in secret military courts. Civil liberties groups voiced grave concerns that the measures jeopardized constitutional rights and protections. But the crisis atmosphere after 9/11 led most people to support these extraordinary steps.

THE BUSH DOCTRINE In the fall of 2002, President Bush unveiled a new national security doctrine that marked a distinct shift from that of previous administrations. Containment and deterrence of communism had been the guiding strategic concepts of the cold war years. In the new unconventional war against terrorism, however, the cold war policies were outdated. Fanatics willing to act as suicide bombers would not be deterred or contained. The growing menace posed by "shadowy networks" of terrorist groups and unstable rogue nations with "weapons of mass destruction," President Bush declared, required a new doctrine of preemptive military action. "If we wait for threats to fully materialize," he explained, "we will have waited too long. In the world we have entered, the only path to safety is the path of action. And this nation will act."

A SECOND PERSIAN GULF WAR During 2002 and 2003, Iraq emerged as the focus of the Bush administration's aggressive new policy of "preemptive" military action. In September 2002, President Bush urged the

Bush's defense policy

President George W. Bush addresses soldiers in July 2002 as part of an appeal to Congress to speed approval of increased defense spending after the 9/11 terrorist attacks.

United Nations to confront the "grave and gathering danger" posed by Saddam Hussein's dictatorial regime and its supposed possession of biological and chemical weapons of mass destruction (WMDs). In November the UN Security Council passed Resolution 1441 ordering Iraq to disarm immediately or face "serious consequences."

On March 17, 2003, President Bush issued an ultimatum to Saddam Hussein: he and his sons must leave Iraq within forty-eight hours or face a U.S.-led invasion. Hussein refused. Two days later, on March 19, American and British forces, supported by other allies making up what Bush called the "coalition of the willing," attacked Iraq. Operation Iraqi Freedom involved a massive bombing campaign followed by a fast-moving invasion across the Iraqi desert from bases in Kuwait. Some 250,000 American soldiers, sailors, and marines were joined by 50,000 British troops as well as small contingents from other countries. On April 9, after three weeks of intense fighting amid sweltering heat and blinding sandstorms, allied forces occupied Baghdad, the capital of Iraq. Hussein's regime and his inept army collapsed and fled a week later.

The six-week war came at a cost of fewer than two hundred combat deaths among the three hundred thousand coalition troops. Over two thousand Iraqi soldiers were killed; civilian casualties numbered in the tens of thousands. The one glaring disappointment amid the Allied victory was that no weapons of mass destruction were found. Bush later said that the absence of WMDs in Iraq left him with a "sickening feeling," for he knew that his primary justification for the assault on Iraq had been undermined.

REBUILDING IRAQ   It proved far easier to win the brief war than to rebuild Iraq in America's image. The allies faced the daunting task of restoring order and installing a democratic government in a chaotic Iraq fractured by age-old religious feuds and ethnic tensions. Violence engulfed the war-torn country. Vengeful Islamic jihadists from around the world streamed in to wage a merciless campaign of terror and sabotage against the U.S.-led coalition forces and their Iraqi allies.

Defense Department analysts had greatly underestimated the difficulty and expense of occupying, pacifying, and reconstructing postwar Iraq. By the fall of 2003, President Bush admitted that substantial numbers of American troops (around 150,000) would remain in Iraq much longer than origi-

A continued presence in Iraq

U.S. military police patrol the market in Abu Ghraib, on the outskirts of Baghdad.

nally anticipated and that rebuilding the splintered nation would take years and cost almost a trillion dollars. Victory on the battlefields of Iraq did not bring peace to the Middle East. Militant Islamic groups seething with hatred for the United States remained a constant global threat. In addition, the destruction of Saddam Hussein's regime in Iraq made for a stronger, tyrannical Iran and the accelerating descent of Pakistan into sectarian violence. The dispute over the legitimacy of the allied war on Iraq also strained relations between the Anglo-American alliance and France, Germany, and Russia, all of which had opposed the Iraq War.

Throughout 2003 and 2004, the Iraqi insurgency and its campaign of terror grew in scope and savagery. Suicide car bombings and roadside ambushes of U.S. military convoys wreaked havoc among Iraqi civilians and allied troops. Terrorists kidnapped foreign civilians and beheaded several of them in grisly rituals videotaped for the world to see. In the United States the euphoria of battlefield victory turned to dismay as the number of casualties and the expense of the occupation soared. In the face of mounting criticism, President Bush urged Americans to "stay the course," insisting that a democratic Iraq would bring stability to the volatile Middle East and thereby blunt the momentum of Islamic terrorism.

By September 2004, U.S. military deaths in Iraq had reached one thousand, and by the end of 2006 the number was nearly three thousand. Although Saddam Hussein had been captured in December 2003 and a new Iraqi government would hold its first democratic elections in January 2005, Iraq seemed less secure than ever to an anxious American public worried about the rising cost of an unending commitment in Iraq. The continuing guerrilla wars in Iraq and Afghanistan strained U.S. military resources and the federal budget.

THE ELECTION OF 2004 Growing public concern about the turmoil in Iraq complicated George W. Bush's campaign for a second presidential term in 2004. The Democratic nominee, Senator John Kerry of Massachusetts, lambasted the Bush administration for misleading the nation about weapons of mass destruction in Iraq and for its inept handling of the reconstruction of postwar Iraq. Kerry also highlighted the record budget deficits occurring under the Republican administration. Bush countered that the tortuous efforts to create a democratic government in Iraq would enhance America's long-term security.

On election day, November 2, 2004, the exit polls suggested a Kerry victory, but in the end the election hinged on the crucial swing state of Ohio.

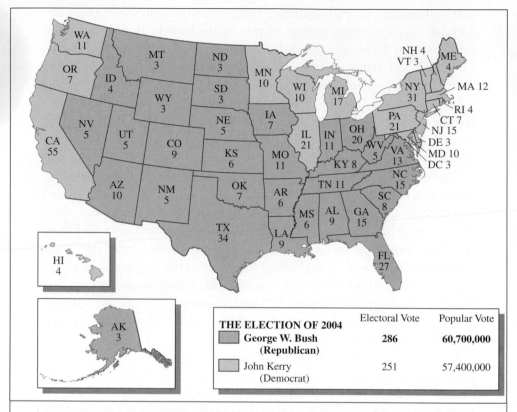

THE ELECTION OF 2004	Electoral Vote	Popular Vote
George W. Bush (Republican)	286	60,700,000
John Kerry (Democrat)	251	57,400,000

How did the war in Iraq polarize the electorate? In what ways did the election of 2004 give Republicans a mandate?

No Republican had ever lost Ohio and still won the presidency. After an anxious night viewing returns from Ohio, Kerry conceded the election. "The outcome," he stressed, "should be decided by voters, not a protracted legal battle." By narrowly winning Ohio, Bush garnered 286 electoral votes to Kerry's 251. Yet in some respects the close election was not so close. Bush received 3.5 million more votes nationwide than Kerry, and Republicans increased their control of both the House and the Senate. Trumpeting "the will of the people at my back," Bush pledged after his reelection to bring democracy and stability to Iraq, overhaul the tax code and eliminate the estate tax, revamp Social Security, trim the federal budget deficit, pass a major energy bill, and create many more jobs. "I earned capital in the campaign, political capital, and now I intend to spend it," he told reporters.

SECOND-TERM BLUES

Yet like many modern presidents, George Bush stumbled in his second term. In 2005 he pushed through Congress an energy bill and a Central American Free Trade Act. But his effort to privatize Social Security retirement accounts, enabling individuals to invest their accumulated pension dollars themselves, went nowhere, and soaring budget deficits made many fiscal conservatives feel betrayed.

HURRICANE KATRINA   In 2005, President Bush's eroding public support suffered another blow, this time when a natural disaster turned into a political crisis. In late August a killer hurricane named Katrina slammed into the Gulf coast, devastating large areas of Alabama, Mississippi, and Louisiana. In New Orleans, whole neighborhoods were under water, often up to the roofline. Nearly five hundred thousand city residents were displaced, most of them poor and many of them African American. Looting was so widespread that officials declared martial law; the streets were awash with soldiers and police. Katrina's awful wake left

Katrina's aftermath

Two men paddle through high water with wooden planks in a devastated New Orleans.

over a thousand people dead in three states and millions homeless and hopeless.

Local political officials and the Federal Emergency Management Agency (FEMA) were caught unprepared as the catastrophe unfolded. Disaster plans were incomplete; confusion and incompetence abounded. A wave of public outrage crashed against the Bush administration. In the face of blistering criticism, President Bush accepted responsibility for the balky federal response to the disaster and accepted the resignation of the FEMA director. Rebuilding the Gulf coast would take a long time and a lot of money.

A STALLED PRESIDENCY George W. Bush bore the brunt of public indignation over the bungled federal response to the Katrina disaster. Thereafter, his second presidential term was beset by political problems, a sputtering economy, and growing public dissatisfaction with his performance and the continuing war in Iraq. Even his support among Republicans crumbled, and many social conservatives felt betrayed by his handling of their concerns. The editors of the *Economist*, an influential conservative newsmagazine, declared that Bush had become "the least popular re-elected president since Richard Nixon became embroiled in the Watergate fiasco." Soaring gasoline prices and the federal budget deficit fueled public frustration with the Bush administration. The president's efforts to reform the tax code, Social Security, and immigration laws languished during his second term, and the turmoil and violence in Iraq showed no signs of abating. Senator Chuck Hagel, a Nebraska Republican, declared in 2005 that "we're losing in Iraq."

VOTER REBELLION In the November 2006 congressional elections, the Democrats capitalized on the public disapproval of the Bush administration to win control of the House of Representatives, the Senate, and a majority of governorships and state legislatures. The election results were so lopsided that for the first time in history the victorious party (the Democrats) did not lose a single incumbent or open congressional seat or governorship. Former Texas Republican congressman Dick Armey said that "the Republican Revolution of 1994 officially ended" with the 2006 election. "It was a rout." The transformational election also included a significant milestone: Californian Nancy Pelosi, the leader of the Democrats in the House of Representatives, became the highest-ranking woman in the history of the U.S. Congress upon her election as House Speaker in January 2007.

ECONOMIC SHOCK After the intense but brief 2001 recession, the economy had begun another period of prolonged expansion. Prosperity was fueled primarily by a prolonged housing boom, ultra-low interest and mortgage rates, easy credit, and reckless consumer spending. Between 1997 and 2006, home prices in the United States, especially in the sunbelt states, rose 85 percent, leading to a frenzy of irresponsible mortgage lending for new homes—and a debt-fueled consumer spending spree. Tens of millions of people bought houses that were more expensive than they could afford, refinanced their mortgages, or tapped home-equity loans to make discretionary purchases. The irrational confidence in soaring housing prices also led government regulatory agencies and mortgage lenders to ease credit restrictions so that more people could buy homes.

House Speaker Nancy Pelosi

At a news conference on Capitol Hill.

Financial collapses typically follow real-estate bubbles, rising indebtedness, and prolonged budget deficits. The housing bubble burst in 2007, when home values and housing sales began a precipitous decline. During 2008, the loss of trillions of dollars in home-equity value set off a seismic shock across the economy. Record numbers of mortgage borrowers defaulted on their payments. Foreclosures soared, adding to the glut of homes for sale and further reducing home prices. Banks lost billions, first on shaky mortgages, then on most other categories of debt: credit cards, car loans, student loans, and an array of commercial mortgage-backed securities.

The sudden contraction of consumer credit, corporate spending, and consumer purchases pushed the economy into a deepening recession in 2008. The scale and suddenness of the slump caught economic experts and business leaders by surprise. Some of the nation's most prestigious banks, investment firms, and insurance companies went belly-up. The price of food and gasoline spiked. Unemployment soared.

What had begun as a sharp decline in home prices had become a global economic meltdown—fed by the paralyzing fright of insecurity. No investment seemed safe. As people saw their home values plummet and their retirement savings accounts gutted, they were left confused, anxious, and angry. Even Alan Greenspan, the former chairman of the Federal Reserve Board, found himself in a state of "shocked disbelief" at the onset of what began to be called the Great Recession, which officially lasted from December 2007 to January 2009.

But its effects would linger long thereafter. "The Age of Prosperity is over," announced the prominent Republican economist Arthur Laffer in 2008.

The economic crisis demanded decisive action. On October 3, 2008, after two weeks of contentious and often emotional congressional debate, President Bush signed into law a far-reaching historic bank bailout fund called the **Troubled Asset Relief Program (TARP)**. The TARP called for the Treasury Department to spend $700 billion to keep banks and other financial institutions from collapsing. Despite such unprecedented government investment in the private financial sector, the economy still sputtered. In early October, stock markets around the world began to crash. Economists warned that the world was at risk of careening into a depression.

A HISTORIC ELECTION

The economic crisis had potent political effects. Budget deficits, trade deficits, and consumer debt had reached record levels, and the total expense of the American war in Iraq was projected to top $3 trillion. During President Bush's last year in office, just 29 percent of the voters "approved" of his leadership. And more than 80 percent said that the nation was headed in the "wrong direction." Even a prominent Republican strategist, Kevin Phillips, deemed Bush "perhaps the least competent president in modern history."

Bush's vulnerability excited Democrats about the possibility of regaining the White House in the 2008 election. The early front-runner for the Democratic nomination was New York senator **Hillary Rodham Clinton**, the highly visible spouse of ex-president Bill Clinton. Like her husband, she displayed an impressive command of policy issues and mobilized a well-funded campaign team. And as the first woman with a serious chance of gaining the presidency, she garnered widespread support among voters eager for female leadership. In the end, however, an overconfident Clinton was upset in the Democratic primaries and caucuses by little-known first-term senator **Barack Obama** of Illinois, an inspiring speaker who attracted huge crowds by promising a "politics of hope" and bolstering their desire for "change." While the Clinton campaign courted the powerful members of the party establishment, Obama mounted an innovative Internet-based campaign directed at grassroots voters, donors, and volunteers. In early June 2008, he gained enough delegates to secure the Democratic nomination.

Obama was the first African American presidential nominee of either party, the gifted biracial son of a white mother from Kansas and a black Kenyan father who left the household and returned to Africa when Barack was a

The 2008 presidential debates

Republican presidential candidate John McCain (left) and Democratic presidential candidate Barack Obama (right) focused on foreign policy, national security, and the financial crisis at the first of three presidential debates.

toddler. The forty-seven-year-old Harvard Law School graduate and former professor, community organizer, and state legislator presented himself as a conciliator who could inspire and unite a diverse people and forge bipartisan collaborations. Obama exuded poise, confidence, and energy. By contrast, his Republican opponent, seventy-two-year-old Arizona senator John McCain, was the oldest presidential candidate in history. As a twenty-five-year veteran of Congress, a leading Republican senator, and a 2000 candidate for the Republican presidential nomination, he had developed a reputation as a bipartisan maverick willing to work with Democrats to achieve key legislative goals.

THE 2008 ELECTION   On November 4, 2008, Barack Obama made history by becoming the nation's first person of color elected president. The inspirational Obama won the popular vote by seven points: 53 percent to 46 percent. His margin in the electoral vote was even more impressive: 365 to 173. Obama also helped the Democrats win solid majorities in the House and Senate races. Within days of his electoral

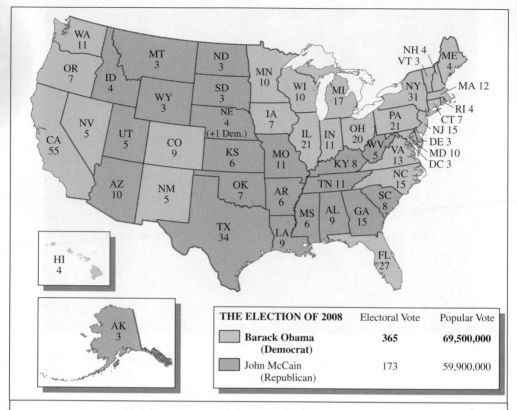

THE ELECTION OF 2008	Electoral Vote	Popular Vote
Barack Obama (Democrat)	**365**	**69,500,000**
John McCain (Republican)	173	59,900,000

How did the economic crisis affect the outcome of the election? What are the similarities and differences between the map of the 2004 election and the map of the 2008 election?

victory, Barack Obama adopted a bipartisan approach in selecting his new cabinet members. He appointed Hillary Clinton secretary of state, renewed Republican Robert Gates as secretary of defense, selected retired general James Jones, who had campaigned for McCain, as his national security adviser, and appointed Eric Holder as the nation's first African American attorney general.

OBAMA'S FIRST TERM

THE SLUGGISH ECONOMY The new Obama administration's main challenge was to keep the deepening global recession from becoming a prolonged depression. Unemployment in early 2009 had passed 8 percent and was still rising. More than 5 million people had lost their jobs since 2007. The financial sector remained paralyzed. When Obama promised to act "boldly and wisely" to fulfill his campaign pledges and stimulate the stagnant economy, many progressive Democrats expected him to mimic Franklin D. Roosevelt in 1933 and launch an array of New Deal-like programs to help the needy and restore public confidence. That did not happen. Most of Obama's financial advisers, as it turned out, came from the gigantic Wall Street investment banks like Goldman Sachs and Citigroup that were in part responsible for the greatest financial crisis since the Great Depression. In responding to that crisis, the new administration focused most of its efforts on helping shore up Wall Street—the very financial interests that had provoked the crisis. The big banks and brokerage houses received lavish government bailouts, while the working class and hard-pressed homeowners received much less help in the form of spending to provide debt relief or to stimulate the flagging economy. Yes, the massive infusion of federal money shored up the largest banks, but in a way that required taxpayers to assume all the risk for the reckless speculation the banks had engaged in that had triggered the crisis.

In mid-February, after a prolonged and often strident debate, Congress passed, and Obama signed, a $787-billion economic stimulus bill called the **American Recovery and Reinvestment Act**. It was the largest in history, but in the end not large enough to serve its purpose of jumpstarting economic growth. The bill included cash distributions to the states, additional funds for food stamps, unemployment benefits, construction projects to renew the nation's infrastructure (roads, bridges, levees, government buildings, and the electricity grid), money for renewable-energy systems, and $212 billion in tax reductions for individuals and businesses. Yet the stimulus package was not robust enough to reverse the deepening recession. Moreover, the congressional passage of the stimulus bill showed no evidence that Obama was successful in implementing a "bipartisan" presidency. Only three Senate Republicans voted for the bill. Not a single House Republican voted for it, and eleven House Democrats opposed it as well.

HEALTH CARE REFORM   Obama compounded his error in underestimating the depth and complexity of the recession by choosing to emphasize comprehensive health-care reform rather than concentrate on creating jobs and restoring prosperity. Obama explained to the nation that the health-care system in the United States was so broken that it was "bankrupting families, bankrupting businesses, and bankrupting our government at the state and federal level." The president's goal in creating the Patient

Protection and Affordable Care Act (PPACA) was to streamline the nation's health care system, make health insurance more affordable, and make health care accessible for everyone.

The ten-year-long, $940 billion proposal (a thousand pages long!), modeled after a Massachusetts health-care program enacted in 2006 under then–Republican governor, Mitt Romney, centered on the so-called individual mandate, which required the uninsured must purchase an approved private insurance policy made available through state agencies or pay a tax penalty. Employers who did not offer health insurance would also have to pay higher taxes, and drug companies as well as manufacturers of medical devices would have to pay annual government fees. Everyone would pay higher Medicare payroll taxes to help fund the changes. The individual mandate was designed to ensure that all Americans had health insurance so as to reduce the skyrocketing costs of hospitals providing "charity care" for the 32 million uninsured Americans. But the idea of forcing people to buy health insurance flew in the face of the principle of individual freedom and personal responsibility. As a result, the health-care reform legislation became a highly partisan issue. Critics questioned not only the individual mandate but also the administration's projections that the new program would reduce federal expenditures over the long haul. Despite strident Republican opposition, Obama signed the PPACA into law on March 23, 2010. Its major provisions would be implemented over a four-year transition period.

REGULATING WALL STREET The unprecedented meltdown of the nation's financial system beginning in 2008 prompted calls for overhauling the nation's financial regulatory system. On July 21, 2010, Obama signed the Wall Street Reform and Consumer Protection Act, also called Dodd–Frank after its two congressional sponsors. It was the most comprehensive overhaul of the financial system since the New Deal in the thirties. The 2,319-page law acknowledged the need for government agencies to exercise greater oversight over complex new financial instruments and protected consumers from unfair practices in loans and credit cards by establishing a new consumer financial-protection agency.

WARS IN IRAQ AND AFGHANISTAN President Obama had more success in dealing with foreign affairs than in reviving the economy. His foremost concern was to rein in what he believed was the overextension of American power and prestige abroad. What journalists came to call the

Obama Doctrine stressed that the United States could not afford to be the world's only policeman.

The Obama Doctrine grew out of the fact that the president inherited two enormously expensive wars, one in Iraq and the other in Afghanistan. On February 27, 2009, Obama announced that all U.S. combat troops would be withdrawn from Iraq by the end of 2011. Until then, a "transitional force" of thirty-five thousand to fifty thousand troops would assist Iraqi security forces, protect Americans, and fight terrorism. True to his word, the last U.S. combat troops left Iraq in December 2011. Their exit marked the end of a bitterly divisive war that had raged for nearly nine years and left Iraq shattered, with troubling questions lingering over whether the newly democratic Arab nation would be self-sustaining as well as a steadfast U.S. ally amid chronic sectarian clashes in a turbulent region. The U.S. intervention in Iraq had cost over four thousand American lives, over one hundred thousand

Home from Iraq

American troops returned from Iraq to more somber, humbler homecomings than the great fanfare that rounded off previous wars.

Iraqi lives, and $800 billion. Whether it was worth such an investment remained to be seen.

At the same time that President Obama was reducing U.S. military involvement in Iraq, he dispatched twenty-one thousand additional troops to Afghanistan, which he called "ground zero" in the continuing battle against global terrorism. By the summer of 2011, it appeared that the American strategy was working. President Obama announced that the "tide of war was receding" and that the United States had largely achieved its goals in Afghanistan, setting in motion a substantial withdrawal of U.S. forces beginning in 2011 and lasting until 2014. As was true in Iraq, Obama stressed that the Afghans must determine the future stability of Afghanistan. "We will not try to make Afghanistan a perfect place," he said. "We will not police its streets or patrol its mountains indefinitely. That is the responsibility of the Afghan government."

THE DEATH OF OSAMA BIN LADEN   The crowning achievement of Obama's anti-terrorism efforts was the discovery, at long last, of Osama bin Laden's hideout. Ever since the attacks of 9/11, bin Laden had eluded an intense manhunt after crossing the Afghan border into Pakistan. His luck ran out in August 2011, however, when U.S. intelligence officials discovered bin Laden's sanctuary in a walled residential compound outside of Abbottabad, Pakistan. On May 1, 2011, President Obama authorized a daring night raid by a U.S. Navy SEAL team of two dozen specially trained commandos transported by helicopters from Afghanistan. After a brief firefight, caught on videotape and fed live by a satellite link to the White House situation room, the Navy SEAL team killed bin Laden. Ten years earlier, bin Laden had told a reporter that he "loves death. The Americans love life. I will engage them and fight. If I am to die, I would like to be killed by the bullet." The U.S. Special Forces assault team granted his wish.

THE "ARAB AWAKENING"   In late 2010 and early 2011, something remarkable and unexpected occurred: spontaneous democratic uprisings emerged throughout much of the Arab world, as long-oppressed peoples rose up against generations-old authoritarian regimes. One by one, corrupt Arab tyrants were forced out of power by a new generation of young idealists inspired by democratic ideals and connected by social media on the Internet. They did not simply demand change; they embodied it, putting their lives on the line.

The **Arab Awakening** began in mid-December 2010 in Tunisia, on the coast of North Africa. On December 17, Mohamed Bouazizi, a twenty-six-year-old street vendor distraught over rough police treatment, set himself on fire in a public square. His suicidal act was like a stone thrown into a pond whose ripples quickly spread outward. It sparked waves of pro-democracy demonstrations across Tunisia that forced the president, who had been in power for twenty-three years, to step down when his own security forces refused orders to shoot protesters. An interim government thereafter allowed democratic elections.

Rippling waves of unrest sparked by the Tunisian "Burning Man"" soon rolled across Algeria, Bahrain, Jordan, Morocco, Egypt, Oman, Yemen, Libya, Saudi Arabia, and Syria. The people's insistence on exercising their basic rights as citizens, the marches and rallies in the streets and parks, and the sudden coming to voice of the voiceless were tangible signs of an old order crumbling. In Egypt, the Arab world's most populous country, several thousand protesters led by university students converged in the streets of teeming Cairo in late January, 2011. They demanded the end of the long rule of strongman President Hosni Moubarak, a staunch American ally who had treated his own people with contempt. The boldness of the youthful rebels was contagious. Within a few days, hundreds of thousands of demonstrators representing all walks of life converged on Tahrir Square, where many of them encamped for eighteen days, singing songs, holding candlelight vigils, and waving flags in the face of a brutal crackdown by security forces. Violence erupted when Moubarak's supporters attacked the protesters. The government tried to cut off access to social communications—mobile telephones, text-messaging, and the Internet—but its success was

Arab Awakening

Thousands of protestors converge in Cairo's Tahrir Square to call for an end to Moubarak's rule.

limited. Desperate to stay in power, Moubarak replaced his entire cabinet, but it was not enough to quell the anti-government movement. On February 11, 2011, Moubarak resigned, ceding control to the military leadership. On March 4, a civilian was appointed prime minister, and elections were promised within a year.

As the so-called Arab Awakening flared up in other parts of the region, some of the rebellions grew violent, some were brutally smashed (Syria), and some achieved substantial political changes. The remarkable uprisings heralded a new era in the history of the Middle East struggling to be born. Arabs had suddenly lost their fear, not just their fear of violent rulers but also their fear that they were not capable of democratic government. By the millions, they demonstrated with their actions that they would no longer passively accept the old way of being governed.

LIBYA OUSTS GADDAFI   The pro-democracy turmoil in North Africa quickly spread to oil-rich Libya, long governed by the zany dictator Colonel Muammar Gaddafi, the Arab world's most violent despot. Anti-government demonstrations began on February 15, prompting Gaddafi to order Libyan soldiers and foreign mercenaries to suppress the rebellious "rats." By the end of February, what began as a peaceful pro-democratic uprising had turned into a full-scale civil war. On March 17, the United Nations Security Council authorized a no-fly zone over Libya designed to prevent Gaddafi's use of warplanes against the civilian rebels.

President Obama handled the Libyan uprising with patience and ingenuity. Eager to avoid the mistakes made in the Iraq War, he insisted on several conditions being met before involving U.S. forces in Libya. First, the pro-democratic rebel force needed to request American assistance. Second, any UN coalition must include Arab nations as well as the United States and its European allies. Third, the United States would commit warplanes and cruise missiles but not ground forces; it could not afford a third major war in the region. On March 19, those conditions were met. With the Arab League's support, France, the United States, and the United Kingdom intervened in Libya with a bombing campaign against pro-Gaddafi forces. In late August, anti-Gaddafi forces, accompanied by television crews, captured the capital of Tripoli, scattering Gaddafi's government and marking the end of his forty-two-year dictatorship. On October 20, rebel fighters captured and killed Gaddafi in his hometown of Sirt.

THE TEA PARTY   At the same time that Arabs were rebelling against entrenched political elites, grassroots rebellions were occurring in the

United States as well. No sooner was Obama sworn in than limited-government conservatives frustrated by his election began mobilizing to thwart any renewal of "tax-and-spend" liberalism. In January 2009, a New York stock trader named Graham Makohoniuk sent out an e-mail message urging people to send tea bags to the Senate and House of Representatives. He fastened on tea bags to symbolize the famous Boston Tea Party of 1773 during which outraged American colonists protested against British tax policies. Within weeks the efforts of angry activists coalesced into a decentralized nationwide protest movement soon labeled "the **Tea Party**."

Within a year or so, there were about a thousand Tea Party groups spread across the fifty states. The Tea Party is at once a mood, an attitude, and an ideology, an eruption of libertarians, mostly white, male, middle-class Republicans over the age of forty-five, boiling mad at a political system that they believe has grown dependent on spending their taxes. The overarching aim of the Tea Party is to transform the Republican party into a vehicle of conservative ideology and eliminate all those who resist the true faith. More immediately the "tea parties" rallied against President Obama's health-care initiative and economic stimulus package, arguing that they verged on

The Tea Party Movement

Tea Party supporters gather outside the New Hampshire Statehouse for a tax day rally.

socialism in their efforts to bail out corporate America and distressed homeowners. On April 15, 2009, the Internal Revenue Service tax-filing deadline,
Tea Party demonstrations occurred in 750 cities.

As candidates began to campaign for the 2010 congressional elections, the
Tea Party mobilized to influence the results, not by forming a third political
party but by trying to take over the leadership of the Republican party.
Members of the Tea Party were as frustrated by the old-line Republican
establishment (RINOs—Republicans in Name Only) as they were disgusted
by liberal Democrats. The Tea Party members were not seeking simply to
rebuild the Republican party; they wanted to take over a "decaying" Republican party and restore its anti-tax focus. Democrats, including President
Obama, initially dismissed the Tea Party as a fringe group of extremists, but
the 2010 election results proved them wrong.

CONSERVATIVE RESURGENCE   Barack Obama had campaigned in
2008 on the promise of bringing dramatic change to the federal government.
"Yes, we can" was his echoing campaign slogan. In the fall of 2010, however,
many of the same voters who had embraced Obama's promises in 2008 now
answered, "Oh, no you don't!" Democratic House and Senate candidates (as well
a moderate Republicans), including many long-serving leaders, were defeated in
droves as insurgent conservatives recaptured control of the House of Representatives (gaining sixty-three seats) and won a near majority in the Senate. Republicans also took control of both the governorships and the legislatures in twelve
states; ten states were already Republican-controlled. It was the most lopsided
midterm election since 1938. A humbled Obama called it a "shellacking" reminiscent of what congressional Republicans had experienced in 2006.

Exit polls on election day showed widespread frustration about Obama's
handling of the slumping economy. Recovery and jobs growth remained elusive. Voters said that Obama and the Democrats had tried to do too much too
fast—bailing out huge banks and automobile companies, spending nearly a
trillion dollars on various pet projects designed to stimulate the flaccid economy, and reorganizing the national health-care system. Republican candidates
were carried into office on a wave of discontent fomented by the Tea Party
movement that demanded ideological purity from its candidates. "We've come
to take our government back," declared one Republican congressional winner.
Thereafter, Obama and the Republican-dominated Congress engaged in a strident sparring match, each side refusing to accommodate the other as the
incessant partisan bickering postponed meaningful action on the languishing
economy and the runaway federal budget deficit.

OCCUPY WALL STREET   The emergence of the Tea Party illustrated the growing ideological extremism of twenty-first-century politics. On the left wing of the political spectrum, the **Occupy Wall Street** (OWS) movement, founded in the fall of 2011, represented the radical alternative to the Tea Party. In the spring of 2011 Kalle Lasn, the founding editor of *Adbusters*, an anti-consumerism magazine published in Vancouver, Canada, decided to promote a grassroots uprising against a capitalist system that was promoting mindless materialism and growing economic and social inequality.

Lasn began circulating through his magazine and on-line networks a poster showing a ballerina perched atop the famous "Charging Bull" sculpture on Wall Street. The caption read: "What Is Our Demand? Occupy Wall Street. Bring tent." The call to arms quickly circulated over the Internet, and another decentralized grassroots movement was born. Within a few days OWS moved the headquarters for the anti-capitalist uprising from Vancouver to New York City. Dozens, then hundreds, then thousands of people, mostly young adults, many of them unemployed, converged on Zuccotti Park in southern Manhattan in a kind of spontaneous democracy. They formed tent villages and gathered in groups to "occupy" Wall Street to protest corrupt banks and brokerage houses whose "fraudsters," they claimed, had caused the 2008 economic crash and forced the severe government cutbacks in social welfare programs.

The protesting "occupiers" drafted a "Declaration of the Occupation" that served as the manifesto of a decentralized movement dedicated to undermining the disproportionate political and economic power exercised by the Wall Street power brokers. Economic data showed that for decades the super-rich had been garnering a growing percentage of national wealth at the expense of the working and middle classes. Throughout the first decade of the twenty-first century, poverty was growing. By 2010, there were 46.2 million Americans living below the U.S. poverty line, an all-time record. In 1980 the richest 1 percent of Americans controlled 10 percent of the nation's wealth; by 2012, 1 percent controlled over twice that much. The protesters were determined to reverse such economic and social trends. They described themselves as the voice of the 99 percent of Americans who were being victimized by the 1 percent of the wealthiest and most politically connected Americans.

The OWS protesters excelled at creative disruption. A "horizontal" movement with organizers and facilitators but no leaders morphed into a chaotic mob punctuated by antic good cheer and zaniness (organizers dressed up as

Occupy Wall Street

The grassroots movement expanded rapidly from rallies in Zuccotti Park, Manhattan, (left) into massive marches on financial districts nationwide. Right, thousands of protesters storm downtown Los Angeles.

Wall Street executives, stuffed Monopoly "play" money in their mouths, etc.). At the same time, however, the anarchic energies of OWS began to spread like a virus across the nation. Similar efforts calling for a "government accountable to the people, freed up from corporate influence" emerged in cities around the globe; encampments of alienated activists sprang up in over a thousand towns and cities. On December 6, 2011, President Obama echoed the OWS movement when he said that the effort to restore economic "fairness" was the "defining issue of our time." Although the OWS demonstrations receded after many cities ordered police to arrest the protesters and dismantle the ramshackle encampments, by the end of 2011 the OWS effort to spark a national conversation about growing income inequality had succeeded. As the *New York Times* announced, "The new progressive age has begun."

POLARIZED POLITICS   American politics has always been chaotic, combative, and fractious; its raucous energy is one of its strengths. But the 2010 election campaigns were spirited to the point of violence; polarizing partisan rhetoric had never been fiercer. Obama's pledge to be a bipartisan president fell victim to toxic battles between the two political parties. As a House Republican predicted in the aftermath of the 2010 elections, there would be "no compromise on stopping runaway spending, deficits, and debt. There will be no compromise on repealing Obamacare." The strident refusal to compromise became a point of honor for both parties—and created a nightmarish stalemate for the nation, as the dysfunctional political system harmed an already sick economy. The gulf between the two parties had become a chasm. "American politicians are intent," said the editors of *The Economist*, "not on improving the country's competitiveness, but on gouging each other's eyes out."

The politics of impasse stalemated American government during 2011 and 2012. Rather than work responsibly together to close the nation's gaping budget deficit, the two warring parties proved incapable of reaching a compromise; they instead opted for the easy way out by applying temporary patches that would expire after the November 2012 elections. Those patches created a fiscal "cliff" at the end of 2012, whereby the tax cuts created by George W. Bush would expire, as would a cut in payroll taxes. At the same time, a string of across-the-board federal budget cuts (called "sequesters") would also automatically occur unless Congress acted. Rather than bridge their differences during 2011–2012, both sides preferred to fight it out during the presidential election campaign in hopes that the voters would signal a clear message.

BOLD DECISIONS   In May 2012 President Obama jumped headfirst into the simmering cultural wars by courageously changing his longstanding position and announcing his support for the rights of gay couples to marry. That his statement came a day after the state of North Carolina legislature voted to ban all rights for gay couples illustrated how incendiary the issue was around the country. While asserting it was the "right" thing to do, Obama also knew that endorsing gay marriage had political ramifications. The gay community would play an energetic role in the 2012 presidential election, and the youth vote, the under-30 electorate who of all the voting-age cohorts supported gay marriage, would be equally crucial to Obama's reelection chances. No sooner had Obama made his pathbreaking announcement than polls showed that American voters split half and half on the charged issue, with Democrats and independent voters constituting the majority of such support.

The following month, in June 2012, Obama again stunned the nation by issuing an executive order (soon labeled the DREAM Act) allowing undocumented immigrants who were brought to the United States as children to remain in the country as citizens. His unanticipated decision thrilled Latino supporters who had lost heart over his failure to convince

Congress to support a more comprehensive reform of immigration laws. The nation's changing demographics bolstered Obama's immigration initiatives. In 2005 Hispanics had become the largest minority group in the nation, surpassing African Americans. By 2012 the United States had more foreign-born and first-generation residents than ever before, and each year 1 million more immigrants arrived.

THE COURT RULES   No sooner had Obama pushed his controversial health care plan through Congress in 2010 than opponents—state governors, conservative organizations, businesses, and individual citizens, largely divided along party lines—began challenging the constitutionality of the Patient Protection and Affordable Care Act (PPACA), which Republicans labeled Obamacare. During the spring and summer of 2012, as the Supreme Court deliberated over the merits of the PPACA, most observers expected the conservative justices to declare Obama's most significant presidential achievement unconstitutional. But that did not happen. On June 28, 2012, the Court issued its much-awaited decision in a case titled *National Federation of Independent Business v. Sebelius*. The landmark 5-to-4 ruling surprised Court observers by declaring most of the new federal law constitutional. Even more surprising was that the deciding vote was cast by the chief justice, John G. Roberts, a philosophical conservative who had never before voted with the four "liberal" justices on the Court. Roberts upheld the PPACA's "individual mandate," requiring virtually every adult to buy private health insurance or else pay a tax, arguing that it was within the Congress's power to impose taxes as outlined in Article 1 of the Constitution. Because Congress had such authority, Justice Roberts declared, "it is not our role to forbid it, or to pass upon its wisdom or fairness." That would be up to the voters who elect the members of Congress. Many conservatives, including the four dissenting justices, felt betrayed by Roberts's unexpected ruling. The Court decision sent ripples through the 2012 presidential election campaign. The surprising verdict boosted Obama's reelection chances, leading the *New York Times* to predict that the ruling "may secure Obama's place in history." Republican candidate Mitt Romney, who as governor of Massachusetts had signed a similar health care bill only to repudiate it once he decided to run for president, promised to repeal the PPACA if elected.

As the November 2012 presidential election approached, it remained to be seen whether President Obama could shift the focus of voters from the sluggish economy to cultural politics and social issues. Mitt Romney won the Republican presidential nomination because he promised, as a former corporate executive, to accelerate economic growth. Romney sought to downplay volatile social issues, in part because of his inconsistent stances on volatile topics such as abortion, gay marriage, and immigration reform. His shifting stances reflected a shift in the Republican strategy. Over the past forty years, their conservative positions on social issues were vote-getters; now they feared that too much moralizing by the religious right ran the risk of alienating the independent voters who continue to be the decisive factor in presidential elections. The question for Romney was whether the still-powerful religious right would allow him to sidestep tough social issues; the question for Obama was whether he could sidestep his failure to restore prosperity to an economy experiencing the slowest recession recovery since the 1930s.

End of Chapter Review

CHAPTER SUMMARY

- **Changing Demographics** From 1980 to 2010, the population of the United States grew by 25 percent to 306 million. The number of traditional family units continued to decline; the poverty rate was especially high among African Americans. A wave of immigrants caused Latinos to surpass African Americans as the nation's largest minority.

- **Divided Government** The popularity of President George H. W. Bush waned after the Gulf War, an economic recession, and his decision to raise taxes. The election of William Jefferson Clinton in 1992 aroused Republican Newton Leroy Gingrich to craft his Contract with America to achieve the Republican landslide of 1994.

- **Economic Prosperity and Crises** The United States benefited from a period of unprecedented prosperity during the 1990s, fueled by the dramatic effect of the new computer-based industries on the economy. The collapse of high-tech companies in 2000 betrayed the underlying insecurity of the market. Economic growth soon surged again primarily because of consumers' ability to borrow against the skyrocketing value of their home mortgages. In 2007, the country experienced an unparalleled crisis when the global financial markets collapsed under the weight of "toxic" financial securities.

- **Global Terrorism** The 9/11 attacks led President George W. Bush to declare a war on terrorism and enunciate the Bush Doctrine. In 2002 the Bush administration shifted its focus to Saddam Hussein. The American-led Operation Iraqi Freedom succeeded in removing Hussein from power but was fully unprepared to establish order in a country that was soon wracked by sectarian violence. The American public became bitterly divided over the Iraq War.

- **2008 Presidential Election** The 2008 presidential campaigns, included the first major female candidate, Senator Hillary Clinton; an African American, Senator Barack Obama; and Senator John McCain, the oldest candidate in history. Obama won the popular vote and a landslide victory in the Electoral College, becoming the nation's first African American president. His victory was facilitated by the collapse of the economy, an unprecedented Internet- and grassroots-based campaign, and voters' weariness with President Bush and the Republican policies of the preceding eight years.

CHRONOLOGY

1991	Ethnic conflict explodes in Yugoslavia
1995	Republicans promote the Contract with America
1996	Congress passes the Personal Responsibility and Work Opportunity Act
1998	Kenneth Starr issues his report on the Whitewater investigation
1998	Bill Clinton brokers the Wye Mills Accord with Israel, the Palestine Liberation Organization, and Jordan
2000	Supreme Court issues *Bush v. Gore* decision
September 11, 2001	Terrorists hijack four commercial jets to carry out the deadliest terrorist attacks in the nation's history
March 2003	Iraq War begins with Operation Iraqi Freedom
August 2005	Hurricane Katrina
2007	Nancy Pelosi becomes the first female Speaker of the House of Representatives
2008	Global financial markets collapse
2009	Barack Obama becomes the nation's first African American president
2011	Occupy Wall Street movement begins
2011	U.S. troops return from Iraq

KEY TERMS & NAMES

William Jefferson Clinton p. 1131

North American Free Trade Agreement (NAFTA) p. 1133

Contract with America p.1135

ethnic cleansing p. 1143

Albert Gore Jr. p. 1144

George W. Bush p. 1144

No Child Left Behind p. 1147

Osama bin Laden p. 1149

9/11 p. 1149

Troubled Asset Relief Program (TARP) p. 1158

Hillary Rodham Clinton p. 1158

Barack Obama p. 1158

American Recovery and Reinvestment Act p. 1161

Arab Awakening p. 1165

Tea Party p. 1167

Occupy Wall Street p. 1169

GLOSSARY

36°30′ According to the Missouri Compromise, any part of the Louisiana Purchase north of this line (Missouri's southern border) was to be excluded from slavery.

54th Massachusetts Regiment After President Abraham Lincoln's Emancipation Proclamation, the Union army organized all black military units, which white officers led. The 54th Massachusetts Regiment was one of the first of such units to be organized.

Abigail Adams (1744–1818) As the wife of John Adams, she endured long periods of separation from him while he served in many political roles. During these times apart, she wrote often to her husband; and their correspondence has provided a detailed portrait of life during the Revolutionary War.

abolition In the early 1830s, the anti-slavery movement shifted its goal from the gradual end of slavery to the immediate end or abolition of slavery.

John Adams (1735–1826) He was a signer of the Declaration of Independence and a delegate to the First and Second Continental Congress. During the Revolutionary War, he worked as a diplomat in France and Holland and negotiated the peace treaty with Britain. After the Revolutionary War, he served as the minister to Britain as well as the vice president and the second president of the United States. As president, he passed the Alien and Sedition Acts and endured a stormy relationship with France, which included the XYZ affair.

John Quincy Adams (1767–1848) As secretary of state under President Monroe, he negotiated agreements to define the boundaries of the Oregon country and the Transcontinental Treaty. He urged President Monroe to issue the Monroe Doctrine, which incorporated Adams's views. As president, Adams envisioned an expanded federal government and a broader use of federal powers. Adams's nationalism and praise of European leaders caused a split in his party. Some Republicans suspected him of being a closet monarchist and left to form the Democrat party. In the presidential election of 1828, Andrew Jackson claimed that Adams had gained the presidency through a "corrupt bargain" with Henry Clay, which helped Jackson win the election.

Samuel Adams (1722–1803) A genius of revolutionary agitation, he believed that English Parliament had no right to legislate for the colonies. He organized the Sons of Liberty as well as protests in Boston against the British.

Jane Addams (1860–1935) As the leader of one of the best known settlement houses, she rejected the "do-goodism" spirit of religious reformers. Instead, she focused on solving the practical problems of the poor and tried to avoid the assumption that she and other social workers knew what was best for poor immigrants. She established child care for working mothers, health clinics, job training, and other social programs. She was also active in the peace movement and was awarded the Noble Peace Prize in 1931 for her work on its behalf.

Agricultural Adjustment Act (1933) New Deal legislation that established the Agricultural Adjustment Administration (AAA) to improve agricultural prices by limiting market supplies; declared unconstitutional in *United States v. Butler* (1936).

Emilio Aguinaldo (1869?–1964) He was a leader in Filipino struggle for independence. During the war of 1898, Commodore George Dewey brought Aguinaldo back to the Philippines from exile to help fight the Spanish. However, after the Spanish surrendered to Americans, America annexed the Philippines and Aguinaldo fought against the American military until he was captured in 1901.

Alamo, Battle of the Siege in the Texas War for Independence of 1836, in which the San Antonio mission fell to the Mexicans. Davy Crockett and Jim Bowie were among the courageous defenders.

Alien and Sedition Acts (1798) Four measures passed during the undeclared war with France that limited the freedoms of speech and press and restricted the liberty of noncitizens.

American Colonization Society An organization created in 1816 to address slavery and racial issues in the Old South. Proposed that slaves and freed blacks would be shipped to Africa.

American Federation of Labor Founded in 1881 as a federation of trade unions made up of skilled workers, the AFL under president Samuel Gompers successfully pushed for the eight-hour workday.

American Indian Movement (AIM) Fed up with the poor conditions on Indian reservations and the federal government's unwillingness to help, Native Americans founded the American Indian Movement (AIM) in 1963. In 1973, AIM led 200 Sioux in the occupation of Wounded Knee. After a ten-week standoff with the federal authorities, the government agreed to reexamine Indian treaty rights and the occupation ended.

American Recovery and Reinvestment Act Hoping to restart the weak economy, President Obama signed this $787-billion economic stimulus bill in February of 2009. The bill included cash distributions to states, funds for food stamps, unemployment benefits, construction projects to renew the nation's infrastructure, funds for renewable-energy systems, and tax reductions.

American System Program of internal improvements and protective tariffs promoted by Speaker of the House Henry Clay in his presidential campaign of 1824; his proposals formed the core of Whig ideology in the 1830s and 1840s.

anaconda strategy Union General Winfield Scott developed this three-pronged strategy to defeat the Confederacy. Like a snake strangling its prey, the Union army would crush its enemy through exerting pressure on Richmond, blockading Confederate ports, and dividing the South by invading its major waterways.

Annapolis Convention In 1786, all thirteen colonies were invited to a convention in Annapolis to discuss commercial problems, but only representatives from five states attended. However, the convention was not a complete failure because the delegates decided to have another convention in order to write the constitution.

anti-Federalists Forerunners of Thomas Jefferson's Democratic-Republican party; opposed the Constitution as a limitation on individual and states' rights, which led to the addition of a Bill of Rights to the document.

Anti-Masonic party This party grew out of popular hostility toward the Masonic fraternal order and entered the presidential election of 1832 as a third party. It was the first party to run as a third party in a presidential election as well as the first to hold a nomination convention and announce a party platform.

Arab Awakening A wave of spontaneous democratic uprisings that spread throughout the Arab world beginning in 2011, in which long-oppressed peoples demanded basic liberties from generations-old authoritarian regimes.

Benedict Arnold (1741–1801) A traitorous American commander who planned to sell out the American garrison at West Point to the British, but his plot was discovered before it could be executed and he joined the British army.

Atlanta Compromise Speech to the Cotton States and International Exposition in 1895 by educator Booker T. Washington, the leading black spokesman of the day; black scholar W. E. B. Du Bois gave the speech its derisive name and criticized Washington for encouraging blacks to accommodate segregation and disenfranchisement.

Atlantic Charter Issued August 12, 1941, following meetings in Newfoundland between President Franklin D. Roosevelt and British Prime Minister Winston Churchill, the charter signaled the allies' cooperation and stated their war aims.

Crispus Attucks (1723–1770) During the Boston Massacre, he was supposedly at the head of the crowd of hecklers who baited the British troops. He was killed when the British troops fired on the crowd.

Stephen F. Austin (1793–1836) He established the first colony of Americans in Texas, which eventually attracted 2,000 people.

Axis powers In the Second World War, the nations of Germany, Italy, and Japan.

Aztec Empire Mesoamerican people who were conquered by the Spanish under Hernando Cortés, 1519–1528.

baby boom Markedly higher birth rate in the years following the Second World War; led to the biggest demographic "bubble" in American history.

Bacon's Rebellion Unsuccessful 1676 revolt led by planter Nathaniel Bacon against Virginia governor William Berkeley's administration, because it had failed to protect settlers from Indian raids.

Bank of the United States Proposed by the first Secretary of the Treasury Alexander Hamilton, the bank opened in 1791 and operated until 1811 to issue a uniform currency, make business loans, and collect tax monies. The second Bank of the United States was chartered in 1816 but was not renewed by President Andrew Jackson twenty years later.

barbary pirates Plundering pirates off the Mediterranean coast of Africa; President Thomas Jefferson's refusal to pay them tribute to protect American ships sparked an undeclared naval war with North African nations, 1801–1805.

Battle of the Bulge On December 16, 1944, the German army launched a counter attack against the Allied forces, which pushed them back. However, the Allies were eventually able to recover and breakthrough the German lines. This defeat was a great blow to the Nazi's morale and their army's strength. The battle used up the last of Hitler's reserve units and opened a route into Germany's heartland.

Bear Flag Republic On June 14, 1846, a group of Americans in California captured Sonoma from the Mexican army and declared it the Republic of California whose flag featured a grizzly bear. In July, the commodore of the U.S. Pacific Fleet landed troops on California's shores and declared it part of the United States.

Beats A group of writers, artists, and musicians whose central concern was the discarding of organizational constraints and traditional conventions in favor of liberated forms of self expression. They came out of the bohemian underground in New York's Greenwich Village in the 1950s and included the writers Jack Kerouac, Allen Ginsberg, and William Burroughs. Their attitudes and lifestyles had a major influence on the youth of the 1960s.

beatnik A name referring to almost any young rebel who openly dissented from the middle-class life. The name itself stems from the Beats.

Nicholas Biddle (1786–1844) He was the president of the second Bank of the United States. In response to President Andrew Jackson's attacks on the bank, Biddle curtailed the bank's loans and exchanged its paper currency for gold and silver. He was hoping to provoke an economic crisis to prove the bank's importance. In response, state banks began printing paper without restraint and lent it to speculators, causing a binge in speculating and an enormous increase in debt.

Bill of Rights First ten amendments to the U.S. Constitution, adopted in 1791 to guarantee individual rights and to help secure ratification of the Constitution by the states.

Osama bin Laden (1957–2011) The Saudi-born leader of al Qaeda, whose members attacked America on September 11, 2001. Years before the attack, he had declared jihad (holy war) on the United States, Israel, and the Saudi monarchy. In Afghanistan, the Taliban leaders gave bin Laden a safe haven in exchange for aid in fighting the Northern Alliance, who were rebels opposed to the Taliban. After the 9/11 terrorist attacks, the United States asked the Taliban to turn over bin Laden. Following their refusal, America and a multinational coalition invaded Afghanistan and overthrew the Taliban. In May 2011, bin Laden was shot and killed by American special forces during a covert operation in Pakistan.

black codes Laws passed in southern states to restrict the rights of former slaves; to combat the codes, Congress passed the Civil Rights Act of 1866 and the Fourteenth Amendment and set up military governments in southern states that refused to ratify the amendment.

black power movement A more militant form of protest for civil rights that originated in urban communities, where nonviolent tactics were less effective than in the South. Black power encouraged African Americans to take pride in their racial heritage and forced black leaders and organizations to focus attention on the plight of poor inner-city blacks.

James Gillepsie Blaine (1830–1893) As a Republican congressman from Maine, he developed close ties with business leaders, which contributed to him losing the presidential election of 1884. He later opposed President Cleveland's efforts to reduce tariffs, which became a significant issue in the 1888 presidential election. Blaine served as secretary of state under President Benjamin Harrison and his flamboyant style often overshadowed the president.

"bleeding" Kansas Violence between pro- and antislavery settlers in the Kansas Territory, 1856.

blitzkrieg The German "lightening war" strategy used during the Second World War; the Germans invaded Poland, France, Russia, and other countries with fast-moving, well-coordinated attacks using aircraft, tanks, and other armored vehicles, followed by infantry.

Bolsheviks Under the leadership of Vladimir Lenin, this Marxist party led the November 1917 revolution against the newly formed provisional government in Russia. After seizing control, the Bolsheviks negotiated a peace treaty with Germany, the Treaty of Brest-Litovsk, and ended their participation in World War I.

Bonus Expeditionary Force Thousands of World War I veterans, who insisted on immediate payment of their bonus certificates, marched on Washington in 1932; violence ensued when President Herbert Hoover ordered their tent villages cleared.

Daniel Boone (1734–1820) He found and expanded a trail into Kentucky, which pioneers used to reach and settle the area.

John Wilkes Booth (1838?–1865) He assassinated President Abraham Lincoln at the Ford's Theater on April 14, 1865. He was pursued to Virginia and killed.

Bourbons In post–Civil War southern politics, the opponents of the Redeemers were called Bourbons. They were known for having forgotten nothing and learned nothing from the ordeal of the Civil War.

Joseph Brant (1742?–1807) He was the Mohawk leader who led the Iroquois against the Americans in the Revolutionary War.

brinksmanship Secretary of State John Foster Dulles believed that communism could be contained by bringing America to the brink of war with an aggressive communist nation. He believed that the aggressor would back down when confronted with the prospect of receiving a mass retaliation from a country with nuclear weapons.

John Brown (1800–1859) He was willing to use violence to further his antislavery beliefs. In 1856, a pro-slavery mob sacked the free-state town of Lawrence, Kansas. In response, John Brown went to the pro-slavery settlement of Pottawatomie, Kansas and hacked to death several people, which led to a guerrilla war in the Kansas territory. In 1859, he attempted to raid the federal arsenal at Harpers Ferry. He had hoped to use the stolen weapons to arm slaves, but he was captured and executed. His failed raid instilled panic throughout the South, and his execution turned him into a martyr for his cause.

***Brown v. Board of Education of Topeka, Kansas* (1954)** U.S. Supreme Court decision that struck down racial segregation in public education and declared "separate but equal" unconstitutional.

William Jennings Bryan (1860–1925) He delivered the pro-silver "cross of gold" speech at the 1896 Democratic Convention and won his party's nomination for president. Disappointed pro-gold Democrats chose to walk out of the convention and nominate their own candidate, which split the Democratic party and cost them the White House. Bryan's loss also crippled the Populist movement that had endorsed him.

"Bull Moose" Progressive party In the 1912 election, Theodore Roosevelt was unable to secure the Republican nomination for president. He left the Republican party and formed his own party of progressive Republicans, called the "Bull Moose" party. Roosevelt and Taft split the Republican vote, which allowed Democrat Woodrow Wilson to win.

Bull Run, Battles of (First and Second Manassas) First land engagement of the Civil War took place on July 21, 1861, at Manassas Junction, Virginia, at which surprised Union troops quickly retreated; one year later, on August 29–30, Confederates captured the federal supply depot and forced Union troops back to Washington.

Martin Van Buren (1782–1862) During President Jackson's first term, he served as secretary of state and minister to London. He often politically fought Vice President John C. Calhoun for the position of Jackson's successor. A rift between Jackson and Calhoun led to Van Buren becoming vice president during Jackson's second term. In 1836, Van Buren was elected president, and he inherited a financial crisis. He believed that the government should not continue to keep its deposits in state banks and set up an independent Treasury, which was approved by Congress after several years of political maneuvering.

General John Burgoyne (1722–1792) He was the commander of Britain's northern forces during the Revolutionary War. He and most of his troops surrendered to the Americans at the Battle of Saratoga.

burned-over district Area of western New York strongly influenced by the revivalist fervor of the Second Great Awakening; Disciples of Christ and Mormons are among the many sects that trace their roots to the phenomenon.

Aaron Burr (1756–1836) Even though he was Thomas Jefferson's vice president, he lost favor with Jefferson's supporters who were Republicans. He sought to work with the Federalists and run as their candidate for the governor of New York. Alexander Hamilton opposed Burr's candidacy and his stinging remarks on the subject led to Burr challenging him to duel in which Hamilton was killed.

George H. W. Bush (1924–) He had served as vice president during the Reagan administration and then won the presidential election of 1988. During his presidential campaign, Bush promised not to raise taxes. However, the federal deficit had become so big that he had to raise taxes. Bush chose to make fighting illegal drugs a priority. He created the Office of National Drug Control Policy, but it was only moderately successful in stopping drug use. In 1989, Bush ordered the invasion of Panama and the capture of Panamanian leader Manuel Noriega, who was wanted in America on drug charges. He was captured, tried, and convicted. In 1990, Saddam Hussein invaded Kuwait; and Bush sent the American military to Saudi Arabia on a defensive mission. He assembled a multinational force and launched Operation Desert Storm, which took Kuwait back from Saddam in 1991. The euphoria over the victory in Kuwait was short lived as the country slid into a recession. He lost the 1992 presidential election to Bill Clinton.

George W. Bush (1946–) In the 2000 presidential election, Texas governor George W. Bush ran as the Republican nominee against Democratic nominee Vice President Al Gore. The election ended in controversy over the final vote tally in Florida. Bush had slightly more votes, but a recount was required by state law. However, it was stopped by Supreme Court and Bush was declared president. After the September 11 terrorist attacks, he launched his "war on terrorism." President George W. Bush adapted the Bush Doctrine, which claimed the right to launch preemptive military attacks against enemies. The United States invaded Afghanistan and Iraq with unclear outcomes leaving the countries divided. In the summer of 2006, Hurricane Katrina struck the Gulf Coast and left destruction across several states and three-quarters of New Orleans flooded. Bush was attacked for the unpreparedness of the federal government to handle the disaster as well as his own slowness to react. In September 2008, the nation's economy nosedived as a credit crunch spiraled into a global economic meltdown. Bush signed into law the bank bailout fund called Troubled Asset Relief Program (TARP), but the economy did not improve.

***Bush v. Gore* (2000)** The close 2000 presidential election came down to Florida's decisive twenty-five electoral votes. The final tally in Florida gave Bush a slight lead, but it was so small that a recount was required by state law. While the votes were being recounted, a legal battle was being waged to stop the recount. Finally, the case, *Bush v. Gore*, was present to the Supreme Court who ruled 5–4 to stop the recount and Bush was declared the winner.

Bush Doctrine Believing that America's enemies were now terrorist groups and unstable rogue nations, President George W. Bush adapted a foreign policy that claimed the right to launch preemptive military attacks against enemies.

buying (stock) on margin The investment practice of making a small down payment (the "margin") on a stock and borrowing the rest of money need for the purchase from a broker who held the stock as security against a down market. If the stock's value declined and the buyer failed to meet a margin call for more funds, the broker could sell the stock to cover his loan.

John C. Calhoun (1782–1850) He served in both the House of Representatives and the Senate for South Carolina before becoming secretary of war under President Monroe and then John Quincy Adams's vice president. He introduced the bill for the second national bank to Congress and led the minority of southerners who voted for the Tariff of 1816. However, he later chose to oppose tariffs. During his time as secretary of war under President Monroe, he authorized the use of federal troops against the Seminoles who were attacking settlers. As John Quincy Adams's vice president, he supported a new tariffs bill to win presidential candidate Andrew Jackson additional support. Jackson won the election, but the new tariffs bill passed and Calhoun had to explain why he had changed his opinion on tariffs.

Camp David Accords Peace agreement between Israeli Prime Minister Menachem Begin and Egyptian President Anwar Sadat, brokered by President Jimmy Carter in 1978.

"Scarface" Al Capone (1899–1947) He was the most successful gangster of the Prohibition era whose Chicago-based criminal empire included bootlegging, prostitution, and gambling.

Andrew Carnegie (1835–1919) He was a steel magnate who believed that the general public benefited from big business even if these companies employed harsh business practices. This philosophy became deeply ingrained in the conventional wisdom of some Americans. After retiring, he devoted himself to philanthropy in hopes of promoting social welfare and world peace.

carpetbaggers Northern emigrants who participated in the Republican governments of the reconstructed South.

Jimmy Carter (1924–) Jimmy Carter, an outsider to Washington, capitalized on the post-Watergate cynicism and won the 1976 presidential election. He created departments of Energy and Education and signed into law several environmental initiatives. However, his efforts to support the Panama Canal Treaties and his unwillingness to make deals with legislators caused other bills to be either gutted or stalled in Congress. Despite his efforts to improve the economy, the recession continued and inflation increased. In 1978, he successfully brokered a peace agreement between Israel and Egypt called the Camp David Accords. Then his administration was plagued with a series of crises. Fighting in the Middle East produced a fuel shortage in the United States. The Soviets invaded Afghanistan and Carter responded with the suspension of an arms-control treaty with the Soviets, the halting of grain shipments to the Soviet Union, and a call for a boycott of the Olympic Games in Moscow. In Iran, revolutionaries toppled the shah's government and seized the American embassy, taking hostage those inside. Carter struggled to get the hostages released and was unable to do so until after he lost the 1980 election to Ronald Reagan. He was awarded the Nobel Peace Prize in 2002 for his efforts to further peace and democratic elections around the world.

Jacques Cartier (1491–1557) He led the first French effort to colonize North America and explored the Gulf of St. Lawrence and reached as far as present day Montreal on the St. Lawrence River.

Bartolomé de Las Casas (1484–1566) A Catholic missionary who renounced the Spanish practice of coercively converting Indians and advocated the better treatment for them. In 1552, he wrote *A Brief Relation of the Destruction of the Indies*, which described the Spanish's cruel treatment of the Indians.

Fidel Castro (1926–) In 1959, his Communist regime came to power in Cuba after two years of guerrilla warfare against the dictator Fulgenico Batista. He enacted land redistribution programs and nationalized all foreign-owned property. The latter action as well as his political trials and summary executions damaged relations between Cuba and America. Castro was turned down when he asked for loans from the United States. However, he did receive aid from the Soviet Union.

Carrie Chapman Catt (1859–1947) She was a leader of a new generation of activists in the women's suffrage movement who carried on the work started by Elizabeth Cady Stanton and Susan B. Anthony.

Cesar Chavez (1927–1993) He founded the United Farm Workers (UFW) in 1962 and worked to organize migrant farm workers. In 1965, the UFW joined Filipino farm workers striking against corporate grape farmers in California's San Joaquin Valley. In 1970, the strike and a consumer boycott on grapes compelled the farmers to formally recognize the UFW. As the result of Chavez's efforts, wages and working conditions improved for migrant workers. In 1975, the California state legislature passed a bill that required growers to bargain collectively with representatives of the farm workers.

Chinese Exclusion Act (1882) The first federal law to restrict immigration on the basis of race and class. Passed in 1882, the act halted Chinese immigration for ten years, but it was periodically renewed and then indefinitely extended in 1902. Not until 1943 were the barriers to Chinese immigration finally removed.

Church of Jesus Christ of Latter-day Saints / Mormons Founded in 1830 by Joseph Smith, the sect was a product of the intense revivalism of the burned-over district of New York; Smith's successor Brigham Young led 15,000 followers to Utah in 1847 to escape persecution.

Winston Churchill (1874–1965) The British prime minister who led the country during the Second World War. Along with Roosevelt and Stalin, he helped shape the post-war world at the Yalta Conference. He also coined the term "iron curtain," which he used in his famous "The Sinews of Peace" speech.

"city machines" Local political party officials used these organizations to dispense patronage and favoritism amongst voters and businesses to ensure their loyal support to the political party.

Civil Rights Act of 1957 First federal civil rights law since Reconstruction; established the Civil Rights Commission and the Civil Rights Division of the Department of Justice.

Civil Rights Act of 1964 Outlawed discrimination in public accommodations and employment.

Henry Clay (1777–1852) In the first half of the nineteenth century, he was the foremost spokesman for the American system. As speaker of the House in the 1820s, he promoted economic nationalism, "market revolution," and the rapid development of western states and territories. He formulated the "second" Missouri Compromise, which denied the Missouri state legislature the power to exclude the rights of free blacks and mulattos. In the deadlocked presidential election of 1824, the House of Representatives decided the election. Clay supported John Quincy Adams, who won the presidency and appointed Clay to secretary of state. Andrew Jackson claimed that Clay had entered into a "corrupt bargain" with Adams for his own selfish gains.

Hillary Rodham Clinton (1947–) In the 2008 presidential election, Senator Hillary Clinton, the spouse of former President Bill Clinton, initially was the front-runner for the Democratic nomination, which made her the first woman with a serious chance to win the presidency. However, Senator Barack Obama's Internet-based and grassroots-orientated campaign garnered him enough delegates to win the nomination. After Obama became president, she was appointed secretary of state.

William Jefferson Clinton (1946–) The governor of Arkansas won the 1992 presidential election against President George H. W. Bush. In his first term, he pushed through Congress a tax increase, an economic stimulus package, the adoption of the North America Free Trade Agreement, welfare reform, a raise in the minimum wage, and improved public access to health insurance. However, he failed to institute major health-care reform, which had been one of his major goals. In 1996, Clinton defeated Republican presidential candidate

Bob Dole. Clinton was scrutinized for his investment in the fraudulent Whitewater Development Corporation, but no evidence was found of him being involved in any wrongdoing. In 1998, he was revealed to have had a sexual affair with a White House intern. Clinton had initially lied about the affair and tried to cover up it, which led to a vote in Congress on whether or not to begin an impeachment inquiry. The House of Representatives voted to impeach Clinton, but the Senate found him not guilty. Clinton's presidency faced several foreign policy challenges. In 1994, he used U.S. forces to restore Haiti's democratically elected president to power after he had been ousted during a coup. In 1995, the Clinton Administration negotiated the Dayton Accords, which stopped the ethnic strife in the former Yugoslavia and the Balkan region. Clinton sponsored peace talks between Arabs and Israelis, which culminated in Israeli Prime Minister Yitzhak Rabin and the Palestine Liberation Organization leader Yasir Arafat signing the Oslo Accords in 1993. This agreement provided for the restoration of Palestinian self-rule in specific areas in exchange for peace as provided in UN Security Council resolutions.

Coercive Acts / Intolerable Acts (1774) Four parliamentary measures in reaction to the Boston Tea Party that forced payment for the tea, disallowed colonial trials of British soldiers, forced their quartering in private homes, and set up a military government.

coffin ships Irish immigrants fleeing the potato famine had to endure a six-week journey across the Atlantic to reach America. During these voyages, thousands of passengers died of disease and starvation, which led to the ships being called "coffin ships."

Christopher Columbus (1451–1506) The Italian sailor who persuaded King Ferdinand and Queen Isabella of Spain to fund his expedition across the Atlantic to discover a new trade route to Asia. Instead of arriving at China or Japan, he reached the Bahamas in 1492.

Committee on Public Information During the First World War, this committee produced war propaganda that conveyed the Allies' war aims to Americans as well as attempted to weaken the enemy's morale.

Committee to Re-elect the President (CREEP) During Nixon's presidency, his administration engaged in a number of immoral acts, such as attempting to steal information and falsely accusing political appointments of sexual improprieties. These acts were funded by money illegally collected through CREEP.

Thomas Paine's *Common Sense* This pamphlet refocused the blame for the colonies' problems on King George III rather than on Parliament and advocated a declaration of independence, which few colonialists had considered prior to its appearance.

Compromise of 1850 Complex compromise mediated by Senator Henry Clay that headed off southern secession over California statehood; to appease the South it included a stronger fugitive slave law and delayed determination of the slave status of the New Mexico and Utah territories.

Compromise of 1877 Deal made by a special congressional commission on March 2, 1877, to resolve the disputed presidential election of 1876; Republican Rutherford B. Hayes, who had lost the popular vote, was declared the winner in exchange for the withdrawal of federal troops from the South, marking the end of Reconstruction.

Conestoga wagons These large horse-drawn wagons were used to carry people or heavy freight long distances, including from the East to the western frontier settlements.

conquistadores Spanish term for "conqueror," applied to European leaders of campaigns against indigenous peoples in central and southern America.

consumer culture In the post-World War II era, affluence seemed to be forever increasing in America. At the same time, there was a boom in construction as well as products and appliances for Americans to buy. As a result, shopping became a major recreational activity. Americans started spending more, saving less, and building more shopping centers.

containment U.S. strategy in the cold war that called for containing Soviet expansion; originally devised in 1947 by U.S. diplomat George F. Kennan.

Continental army Army authorized by the Continental Congress, 1775–1784, to fight the British; commanded by General George Washington.

Contract with America A ten-point document released by the Republican party during the 1994 Congressional election campaigns, which outlined a small-government program featuring less regulation of business, diminished environmental regulations, and other core values of the Republican revolution.

Contras The Reagan administration ordered the CIA to train and supply guerrilla bands of anti-Communist Nicaraguans called Contras. They were fighting the Sandinista government that had recently come to power in Nicaragua. The State Department believed that the Sandinista government was supplying the leftist Salvadoran rebels with Soviet and Cuban arms. A cease-fire agreement between the Contras and Sandinistas was signed in 1988.

Calvin "Silent Cal" Coolidge (1872–1933) After President Harding's death, his vice president, Calvin Coolidge, assumed the presidency. Coolidge believed that the nation's welfare was tied to the success of big business, and he worked to end government regulation of business and industry as well as reduce taxes. In particular, he focused on the nation's industrial development.

Hernán Cortés (1485–1547) The Spanish conquistador who conquered the Aztec Empire and set the precedent for other plundering conquistadores.

General Charles Cornwallis (1738–1805) He was in charge of British troops in the South during the Revolutionary War. His surrendering to George Washington at the Battle of Yorktown ended the Revolutionary War.

Corps of Discovery Meriwether Lewis and William Clark led this group of men on an expedition of the newly purchased Louisiana territory, which took them from Missouri to Oregon. As they traveled, they kept detailed journals and drew maps of the previously unexplored territory. Their reports attracted traders and trappers to the region and gave the United States a claim to the Oregon country by right of discovery and exploration.

"corrupt bargain" A vote in the House of Representatives decided the deadlocked presidential election of 1824 in favor of John Quincy Adams, who Speaker of the House Henry Clay had supported. Afterward, Adams appointed Clay secretary of state. Andrew Jackson charged Clay with having made a "corrupt bargain" with Adams that gave Adams the presidency and Clay a place in his administration. There was no evidence of such a deal, but it was widely believed.

the counterculture "Hippie" youth culture of the 1960s, which rejected the values of the dominant culture in favor of illicit drugs, communes, free sex, and rock music.

court-packing plan President Franklin D. Roosevelt's failed 1937 attempt to increase the number of U.S. Supreme Court justices from nine to fifteen in order to save his Second New Deal programs from constitutional challenges.

covenant theory A Puritan concept that believed true Christians could enter a voluntary union for the common worship of God. Taking the idea one step further, the union could also be used for the purposes of establishing governments.

Coxey's Army Jacob S. Coxey, a Populist, led this protest group that demanded the federal government provide the unemployed with meaningful employment. In 1894, Coxey's Army joined other protests groups in a march on Washington D.C. The combination of the march and the growing support of Populism scared many Americans.

Crédit Mobilier scandal Construction company guilt of massive overcharges for building the Union Pacific Railroad were exposed; high officials of the Ulysses S. Grant administration were implicated but never charged.

George Creel (1876–1953) He convinced President Woodrow Wilson that the best approach to influencing public opinion was through propaganda rather than censorship. As the executive head of the Committee on Public Information, he produced propaganda that conveyed the Allies' war aims.

"Cross of Gold" Speech In the 1896 election, the Democratic party split over the issue of whether to use gold or silver to back American currency. Significant to this division was the "Cross of Gold" speech that William Jennings Bryan delivered at the Democratic convention. This pro-silver speech was so well received that Bryan won the nomination to be their presidential candidate. Disappointed pro-gold Democrats chose to walk out of the convention and nominate their own candidate.

Cuban missile crisis Caused when the United States discovered Soviet offensive missile sites in Cuba in October 1962; the U.S.–Soviet confrontation was the cold war's closest brush with nuclear war.

cult of domesticity The belief that women should stay at home to manage the household, educate their children with strong moral values, and please their husbands.

George A. Custer (1839–1876) He was a reckless and glory-seeking Lieutenant Colonel of the U.S. Army who fought the Sioux Indians in the Great Sioux War. In 1876, he and his detachment of soldiers were entirely wiped out in the Battle of Little Bighorn.

D-day June 6, 1944, when an Allied amphibious assault landed on the Normandy coast and established a foothold in Europe from which Hitler's defenses could not recover.

Jefferson Davis (1808–1889) He was the president of the Confederacy during the Civil War. When the Confederacy's defeat seemed invitable in early 1865, he refused to surrender. Union forces captured him in May of that year.

Eugene V. Debs (1855–1926) He founded the American Railway Union, which he organized against the Pullman Palace Car Company during the Pullman strike. Later he organized the Social Democratic party, which eventually became the Socialist Party of America. In the 1912 presidential election, he ran as the Socialist party's candidate and received more than 900,000 votes.

Declaratory Act Following the repeal of the Stamp Act in 1766, Parliament passed this act which asserted Parliament's full power to make laws binding the colonies "in all cases whatsoever."

deism Enlightenment thought applied to religion; emphasized reason, morality, and natural law.

détente In the 1970s, the United States and Soviet Union began working together to achieve a more orderly and restrained competition between each other. Both countries signed an agreement to limit the number of Intercontinental Long Range Ballistic Missiles (ICBMs) that each country could possess and to not construct antiballistic missiles systems. They also signed new trade agreements.

George Dewey (1837–1917) On April 30, 1898, Commodore George Dewey's small U.S. naval squadron defeated the Spanish warships in Manila Bay in the Philippines. This quick victory aroused expansionist fever in the United States.

John Dewey (1859–1952) He is an important philosopher of pragmatism. However, he preferred to use the term *instrumentalism*, because he saw ideas as instruments of action.

Ngo Dinh Diem (1901–1963) Following the Geneva Accords, the French, with the support of America, forced the Vietnamese emperor to accept Dinh Diem as the new premier of South Vietnam. President Eisenhower sent advisors to train Diem's police and army. In return, the United States expected Diem to enact democratic reforms and distribute land to the peasants. Instead, he suppressed his political opponents, did little or no land distribution, and let corruption grow. In 1956, he refused to participate in elections to reunify Vietnam. Eventually, he ousted the emperor and declared himself president.

Dorothea Lynde Dix (1802–1887) She was an important figure in increasing the public's awareness of the plight of the mentally ill. After a two-year investigation of the treatment of the mentally ill in Massachusetts, she presented her findings and won the support of leading reformers. She eventually convinced twenty states to reform their treatment of the mentally ill.

Dixiecrats Deep South delegates who walked out of the 1948 Democratic National Convention in protest of the party's support for civil rights legislation and later formed the States' Rights (Dixiecrat) party, which nominated Strom Thurmond of South Carolina for president.

dollar diplomacy The Taft administration's policy of encouraging American bankers to aid debt-plagued governments in Haiti, Guatemala, Honduras, and Nicaragua.

Donner party Forty-seven surviving members of a group of migrants to California were forced to resort to cannibalism to survive a brutal winter trapped in the Sierra Nevadas, 1846–1847; highest death toll of any group traveling the Overland Trail.

Stephen A. Douglas (1812–1861) As a senator from Illinois, he authored the Kansas-Nebraska Act. Once passed, the act led to violence in Kansas between pro- and antislavery factions and damaged the Whig party. These damages prevented Senator Douglas from being chosen as the presidential candidate of his party. Running for senatorial reelection in 1858, he engaged Abraham Lincoln in a series of public debates about slavery in the territories. Even though Douglas won the election, the debates gave Lincoln a national reputation.

Frederick Douglass (1818–1895) He escaped from slavery and become an eloquent speaker and writer against slavery. In 1845, he published his autobiography entitled *Narrative of the Life of Frederick Douglass* and two years later he founded an abolitionist newspaper for blacks called the *North Star*.

dot-coms In the late 1990s, the stock market soared to new heights and defied the predictions of experts that the economy could not sustain such a performance. Much of the economic success was based on dot-com enterprises, which were firms specializing in computers, software, telecommunications, and the internet. However, many of the companies' stock market values were driven higher and higher by speculation instead of financial success. Eventually the stock market bubble burst.

***Dred Scott v. Sandford* (1857)** U.S. Supreme Court decision in which Chief Justice Roger B. Taney ruled that slaves could not sue for freedom and that Congress could not prohibit slavery in the territories, on the grounds that such a prohibition would violate the Fifth Amendment rights of slaveholders.

W. E. B. Du Bois (1868–1963) He criticized Booker T. Washington's views on civil rights as being accommodationist. He advocated "ceaseless agitation" for civil rights and the immediate end to segregation and an enforcement of laws to protect civil rights and equality. He promoted an education for African Americans that would nurture bold leaders who were willing to challenge discrimination in politics.

John Foster Dulles (1888–1959) As President Eisenhower's secretary of state, he institutionalized the policy of containment and introduced the strategy of deterrence. He believed in using brinkmanship to halt the spread of communism. He attempted to employ it in Indochina, which led to the United States' involvement in Vietnam.

Dust Bowl Great Plains counties where millions of tons of topsoil were blown away from parched farmland in the 1930s; massive migration of farm families followed.

Peggy Eaton (1796–1879) The wife of John Eaton, President Jackson's secretary of war, was the daughter of a tavern owner with an unsavory past. Supposedly her first husband had committed suicide after learning that she was having an affair with John Eaton. The wives of members of Jackson's cabinet snubbed her because of her lowly origins and past. The scandal that resulted was called the Eaton Affair.

Jonathan Edwards (1703–1758) New England Congregationalist minister, who began a religious revival in his Northampton church and was an important figure in the Great Awakening.

election of 1912 The presidential election of 1912 featured four candidates: Wilson, Taft, Roosevelt, and Debs. Each candidate believed in the basic assumptions of progressive politics, but each had a different view on how progressive ideals should be implemented through policy. In the end, Taft and Roosevelt split the Republican party votes and Wilson emerged as the winner.

Queen Elizabeth I of England (1533–1603) The protestant daughter of Henry VIII, she was Queen of England from 1558–1603 and played a major role in the Protestant Reformation. During her long reign, the doctrines and services of the Church of England were defined and the Spanish Armada was defeated.

General Dwight D. Eisenhower (1890–1969) During the Second World War, he commanded the Allied Forces landing in Africa and was the supreme Allied commander as well as planner for Operation Overlord. In 1952, he was elected president on his popularity as a war hero and his promises to clean up Washington and find an honorable peace in the Korean War. His administration sought to cut the nation's domestic programs and budget, but he left the basic structure of the New Deal intact. In July of 1953, he announced the end of fighting in Korea. He appointed Earl Warren to the Supreme Court whose influence helped the court become an important force for social and political change. His secretary of state, John Foster Dulles, institutionalized the policies of containment and deterrence. Eisenhower supported the withdrawal of British forces from the Suez Canal and established the Eisenhower doctrine, which promised to aid any nation against aggression by a communist nation. Eisenhower preferred that state and local institutions to handle civil rights issues, and he refused to force states to comply with the Supreme Court's civil rights decisions. However, he did propose the legislation that became the Civil Rights Act of 1957.

Ellis Island Reception center in New York Harbor through which most European immigrants to America were processed from 1892 to 1954.

Emancipation Proclamation (1863) President Abraham Lincoln issued a preliminary proclamation on September 22, 1862, freeing the slaves in the Confederate states as of January 1, 1863, the date of the final proclamation.

Ralph Waldo Emerson (1803–1882) As a leader of the transcendentalist movement, he wrote poems, essays, and speeches that discussed the sacredness of nature, optimism, self-reliance, and the unlimited potential of the individual. He wanted to transcend the limitations of inherited conventions and rationalism to reach the inner recesses of the self.

encomienda System under which officers of the Spanish conquistadores gained ownership of Indian land.

Enlightenment Revolution in thought begun in the seventeenth century that emphasized reason and science over the authority of traditional religion.

enumerated goods According to the Navigation Act, these particular goods, like tobacco or cotton, could only be shipped to England or other English colonies.

Erie Canal Most important and profitable of the barge canals of the 1820s and 1830s; stretched from Buffalo to Albany, New York, connecting the Great Lakes to the East Coast and making New York City the nation's largest port.

ethnic cleansing The act of killing an entire group of people in a region or country because of its ethnic background. After the collapse of the former Yugoslavia in 1991, Serbs in Bosnia attacked communities of Muslims, which led to intervention by the United Nations. In 1998, fighting broke out again in the Balkans between Serbia and Kosovo. Serbian police and military attacked, killed, raped, or forced Muslim Albanian Kosovars to leave their homes.

Fair Employment Practices Commission Created in 1941 by executive order, the FEPC sought to eliminate racial discrimination in jobs; it possessed little power but represented a step toward civil rights for African Americans.

Farmers' Alliance Two separate organizations (Northwestern and Southern) of the 1880s and 1890s that took the place of the Grange, worked for similar causes, and attracted landless, as well as landed, farmers to their membership.

Federal Writers' Project During the Great Depression, this project provided writers, such as Ralph Ellison, Richard Wright, and Saul Bellow, with work, which gave them a chance to develop as artists and be employed.

The Federalist Collection of eighty-five essays that appeared in the New York press in 1787–1788 in support of the Constitution; written by Alexander Hamilton, James Madison, and John Jay but published under the pseudonym "Publius."

Federalists Proponents of a centralized federal system and the ratification of the Constitution. Most Federalists were relatively young, educated men who supported a broad interpretation of the Constitution whenever national interest dictated such flexibility. Notable Federalists included Alexander Hamilton and John Jay.

Geraldine Ferraro (1935–) In the 1984 presidential election, Democratic nominee, Walter Mondale, chose her as his running mate. As a member of the U.S. House of Representatives from New York, she was the first woman to be a vice-presidential nominee for a major political party. However, she was placed on the defensive because of her husband's complicated business dealings.

Fifteenth Amendment This amendment forbids states to deny any person the right to vote on grounds of "race, color or pervious condition of servitude." Former Confederate states were required to ratify this amendment before they could be readmitted to the Union.

"final solution" The Nazi party's systematic murder of some 6 million Jews along with more than a million other people including, but not limited to, gypsies, homosexuals, and handicap individuals.

Food Administration After America's entry into World War I, the economy of the home front needed to be reorganized to provide the most efficient means of conducting the war. The Food Administration was a part of this effort. Under the leadership of Herbert Hoover, the organization sought to increase agricultural production while reducing civilian consumption of foodstuffs.

force bill During the nullification crisis between President Andrew Jackson and South Carolina, Jackson asked Congress to pass this bill, which authorized him to use the army to force South Carolina to comply with federal law.

Gerald Ford (1913–2006) He was President Nixon's vice president and assumed the presidency after Nixon resigned. President Ford issued Nixon a pardon for any crimes related to the Watergate scandal. The American public's reaction was largely negative; and Ford never regained the public's confidence. He resisted congressional pressure to both reduce taxes and increase federal spending, which sent the American economy into the deepest recession since the Great Depression. Ford retained Kissinger as his secretary of state and continued Nixon's foreign policy goals, which included the signing of another arms-control agreement with the Soviet Union. He was heavily criticized following the collapse of South Vietnam.

Fort Laramie Treaty (1851) Restricted the Plains Indians from using the Overland Trail and permitted the building of government forts.

Fort Necessity After attacking a group of French soldiers, George Washington constructed and took shelter in this fort from vengeful French troops. Washington eventually surrendered to them after a day-long battle. This conflict was a significant event in igniting the French and Indian War.

Fort Sumter First battle of the Civil War, in which the federal fort in Charleston (South Carolina) Harbor was captured by the Confederates on April 14, 1861, after two days of shelling.

"forty-niners" Speculators who went to northern California following the discovery of gold in 1848; the first of several years of large-scale migration was 1849.

Fourteen Points President Woodrow Wilson's 1918 plan for peace after World War I; at the Versailles peace conference, however, he failed to incorporate all of the points into the treaty.

Fourteenth Amendment (1868) Guaranteed rights of citizenship to former slaves, in words similar to those of the Civil Rights Act of 1866.

Franciscan Missions In 1769, Franciscan missioners accompanied Spanish soldiers to California and over the next fifty years established a chain of missions from San Diego to San Francisco. At these missions, friars sought to convert Indians to Catholicism and make them members of the Spanish empire. The friars stripped the Indians of their native heritage and used soldiers to enforce their will.

Benjamin Franklin (1706–1790) A Boston-born American, who epitomized the Enlightenment for many Americans and Europeans, Franklin's wide range of interests led him to become a publisher, inventor, and statesman. As the latter, he contributed to the writing of the Declaration of Independence, served as the minister to France during the Revolutionary War, and was a delegate to the Constitutional Convention.

Free-Soil party Formed in 1848 to oppose slavery in the territory acquired in the Mexican War; nominated Martin Van Buren for president in 1848, but by 1854, most of the party's members had joined the Republican party.

Freedmen's Bureau Reconstruction agency established in 1865 to protect the legal rights of former slaves and to assist with their education, jobs, health care, and landowning.

freedom riders In 1961, the Congress of Racial Equality had this group of black and white demonstrators ride buses to test the federal court ruling that had banned segregation on buses and trains and in terminals. Despite being attacked, they never gave up. Their actions drew national attention and generated respect and support for their cause.

Freeport Doctrine Senator Stephen Douglas' method to reconcile the Dred Scott court ruling of 1857 with "popular sovereignty," of which he was a champion. Douglas believed that so long as residents of a given territory had the right to pass and uphold local laws, any Supreme Court ruling on slavery would be unenforceable and irrelevant.

John C. Frémont "the Pathfinder" (1813–1890) He was an explorer and surveyor who helped inspire Americans living in California to rebel against the Mexican government and declare independence.

French and Indian War Known in Europe as the Seven Years' War, the last (1755–1763) of four colonial wars fought between England and France for control of North America east of the Mississippi River.

Sigmund Freud (1865–1939) He was the founder of psychoanalysis, which suggested that human behavior was motivated by unconscious and irrational forces. By the 1920s, his ideas were being discussed more openly in America.

Fugitive Slave Act of 1850 Gave federal government authority in cases involving runaway slaves; so much more punitive and prejudiced in favor of slaveholders than the 1793 Fugitive Slave Act had been that Harriet Beecher Stowe was inspired to write *Uncle Tom's Cabin* in protest; the new law was part of the Compromise of 1850, included to appease the South over the admission of California as a free state.

fundamentalism Anti-modernist Protestant movement started in the early twentieth century that proclaimed the literal truth of the Bible; the name came from *The Fundamentals*, published by conservative leaders.

"gag rule" In 1831, the House of Representatives adopted this rule, which prevented the discussion and presentation of any petitions for the abolition of slavery to the House. John Quincy Adams, who was elected to the House after his presidency ended, fought the rule on the grounds that it violated the First Amendment. In 1844, he succeeded in having it repealed.

William Lloyd Garrison (1805–1879) In 1831, he started the anti-slavery newspaper *Liberator* and helped start the New England Anti-Slavery Society. Two years later, he assisted Arthur and Lewis Tappan in the founding of the American Anti-Slavery Society. He and his followers believed that America had been thoroughly corrupted and needed a wide range of reforms. He embraced every major reform movement of the day: abolition, temperance, pacifism, and women's rights. He wanted to go beyond just freeing slaves and grant them equal social and legal rights.

Marcus Garvey (1887–1940) He was the leading spokesman for Negro Nationalism, which exalted blackness, black cultural expression, and black exclusiveness. He called upon African Americans to liberate themselves from the surrounding white culture and create their own businesses, cultural centers, and newspapers. He was also the founder of the Universal Negro Improvement Association.

Citizen Genet (1763–1834) As the ambassador to the United States from the new French Republic, he engaged American privateers to attack British ships and conspired with frontiersmen and land speculators to organize an attack on Spanish Florida and Louisiana. His actions and the French radicals excessive actions against their enemies in the new French Republic caused the French Revolution to lose support among Americans.

Geneva Accords In 1954, the Geneva Accords were signed, which ended French colonial rule in Indochina. The agreement created the independent nations of Laos and Cambodia and divided Vietnam along the 17th parallel until an election in 1956 would reunify the country.

Gettysburg, Battle of Fought in southern Pennsylvania, July 1–3, 1863; the Confederate defeat and the simultaneous loss at Vicksburg spelled the end of the South's chances in the Civil War.

Ghost Dance movement This spiritual and political movement came from a Paiute Indian named Wovoka (or Jack Wilson). He believed that a messiah would come and rescue the Indians and restore their lands. To hasten the arrival of the messiah, the Indians needed to take up a ceremonial dance at each new moon.

Newt Gingrich (1943–) He led the Republican insurgency in Congress in the mid 1990s through mobilizing religious and social conservatives. Along with other Republican congressmen, he created the Contract with America, which was a ten-point anti-big government program. However, the program fizzled out after many of its bills were not passed by Congress.

Gilded Age (1860–1896) An era of dramatic industrial and urban growth characterized by loose government oversight over corporations, which fostered unfettered capitalism and widespread political corruption.

The Gilded Age Mark Twain and Charles Dudley Warner's 1873 novel, the title of which became the popular name for the period from the end of the Civil War to the turn of the century.

glasnost Soviet leader Mikhail Gorbachev instituted this reform, which brought about a loosening of censorship.

Glorious Revolution In 1688, the Protestant Queen Mary and her husband, William of Orange, took the British throne from King James II in a bloodless coup. Afterward, Parliament greatly expanded its power and passed the Bill of Rights and the Act of Toleration, both of which would influence attitudes and events in the colonies.

Barry Goldwater (1909–1998) He was a leader of the Republican right whose book, *The Conscience of a Conservative*, was highly influential to that segment of the party. He proposed eliminating the income tax and overhauling Social Security. In 1964, he ran as the Republican presidential candidate and lost to President Johnson. He campaigned against Johnson's war on poverty, the tradition of New Deal, the nuclear test ban and the Civil Rights Act of 1964. He advocated the wholesale bombing of North Vietnam.

Samuel Gompers (1850–1924) He served as the president of the American Federation of Labor from its inception until his death. He focused on achieving concrete economic gains such as higher wages, shorter hours, and better working conditions.

"good neighbor" policy Proclaimed by President Franklin D. Roosevelt in his first inaugural address in 1933, it sought improved diplomatic relations between the United States and its Latin American neighbors.

Mikhail Gorbachev (1931–) In the late 1980s, Soviet leader Mikhail Gorbachev attempted to reform the Soviet Union through his programs of *perestroika* and *glasnost*. He pursued a renewal of détente with America and signed new arms-control agreements with President Reagan. Gorbachev chose not to involve the Soviet Union in the internal affairs of other Communist countries, which removed the threat of armed Soviet crackdowns on reformers and protesters in Eastern Europe. Gorbachev's decision allowed the velvet revolutions of Eastern Europe to occur without outside interference. Eventually the political, social, and economic upheaval he had unleashed would lead to the break-up of the Soviet Union.

Albert Gore Jr. (1948–) He served as a senator of Tennessee and then as President Clinton's vice president. In the 2000 presidential election, he was the Democratic candidate and campaigned on preserving Social Security, subsidizing prescription-medicine expenses for the elderly, and protecting the environment. His opponent was Governor George W. Bush, who promoted compassionate conservatism and the transferring of power from the federal government to the states. The election ended in controversy. The close election came down to Florida's electoral votes. The final tally in Florida gave Bush a slight lead, but it was so small that a recount was required by state law. While the votes were being recounted, a legal battle was being waged to stop the recount. Finally, the case, *Bush v. Gore*, was presented to the Supreme Court who ruled 5–4 to stop the recount and Bush was declared the winner.

Jay Gould (1836–1892) As one of the biggest railroad robber barons, he was infamous for buying rundown railroads, making cosmetic improvements and then reselling them for a profit. He used corporate funds for personal investments and to bribe politicians and judges.

gradualism This strategy for ending slavery involved promoting the banning of slavery in the new western territories and encouraging the release of slaves from slavery. Supporters of this method believed that it would bring about the gradual end of slavery.

Granger movement Political movement that grew out of the Patrons of Husbandry, an educational and social organization for farmers founded in 1867; the Grange had its greatest success in the Midwest of the 1870s, lobbying for government control of railroad and grain elevator rates and establishing farmers' cooperatives.

Ulysses S. Grant (1822–1885) After distinguishing himself in the western theater of the Civil War, he was appointed general in chief of the Union army in 1864. Afterward, he defeated General Robert E. Lee through a policy of aggressive attrition. He constantly attacked Lee's army until it was grind down. Lee surrendered to Grant on April 9th, 1865 at the Appomattox Court House. In 1868, he was elected President and his tenure suffered from scandals and fiscal problems including the debate on whether or not greenbacks, paper money, should be removed from circulation.

Great Awakening Fervent religious revival movement in the 1720s through the 1740s that was spread throughout the colonies by ministers like New England Congregationalist Jonathan Edwards and English revivalist George Whitefield.

great migration After World War II, rural southern blacks began moving to the urban North and Midwest in large numbers in search of better jobs, housing, and greater social equality. The massive influx of African American migrants overwhelmed the resources of urban governments and sparked racial conflicts. In order to cope with the new migrants and alleviate racial tension, cities constructed massive public-housing projects that segregated African Americans into overcrowded and poor neighborhoods.

Great Compromise (Connecticut Compromise) Mediated the differences between the New Jersey and Virginia delegations to the Constitutional Convention by providing for a bicameral legislature, the upper house of which would have equal representation and the lower house of which would be apportioned by population.

Great Depression Worst economic depression in American history; it was spurred by the stock market crash of 1929 and lasted until the Second World War.

Great Sioux War In 1874, Lieutenant Colonel Custard led an exploratory expedition into the Black Hills, which the United States government had promised to the Sioux Indians. Miners soon followed and the army did nothing to keep them out. Eventually, the army attacked the Sioux Indians and the fight against them lasted for fifteen months before the Sioux Indians were forced to give up their land and move onto a reservation.

Great Society Term coined by President Lyndon B. Johnson in his 1965 State of the Union address, in which he proposed legislation to address problems of voting rights, poverty, diseases, education, immigration, and the environment.

Horace Greeley (1811–1872) In reaction to Radical Reconstruction and corruption in President Ulysses S. Grant's administration, a group of Republicans broke from the party to form the Liberal Republicans. In 1872, the Liberal Republicans chose Horace Greeley as their presidential candidate who ran on a platform of favoring civil service reform and condemning the Republican's Reconstruction policy.

greenbacks Paper money issued during the Civil War. After the war ended, a debate emerged on whether or not to remove the paper currency from circulation and revert back to hard-money currency (gold coins). Opponents of hard-money feared that eliminating the greenbacks would shrink the money supply, which would lower crop prices and make it more difficult to repay long-term debts. President Ulysses S. Grant, as well as hard-currency advocates, believed that gold coins were morally preferable to paper currency.

Greenback party Formed in 1876 in reaction to economic depression, the party favored issuance of unsecured paper money to help farmers repay debts; the movement for free coinage of silver took the place of the greenback movement by the 1880s.

General Nathanael Greene (1742–1786) He was appointed by Congress to command the American army fighting in the South during the Revolutionary War. Using his patience and his skills of managing men, saving supplies, and avoiding needless risks, he waged a successful war of attrition against the British.

Sarah Grimké (1792–1873) and **Angelina Grimké (1805–1879)** These two sisters gave anti-slavery speeches to crowds of mixed gender that caused some people to condemn them for engaging in unfeminine activities. The sisters rejected this opinion and made the role of women in the anti-slavery movement a prominent issue. In 1840, William Lloyd Garrison convinced the Anti-Slavery Society to allow women equal participation in the organization. A group of members that did not agree with this decision left the Anti-Slavery Society to form the American and Foreign Anti-Slavery Society.

Half-Way Covenant Allowed baptized children of church members to be admitted to a "halfway" membership in the church and secure baptism for their own children in turn, but allowed them neither a vote in the church, nor communion.

Alexander Hamilton (1755–1804) His belief in a strong federal government led him to become a contributor to *The Federalist* and leader of the Federalists. As the first secretary of the Treasury, he laid the foundation for American capitalism through his creation of a federal budget, funded debt, a federal tax system, a national bank, a customs service, and a coast guard. His "Reports on Public Credit" and "Reports on Manufactures" outlined his vision for economic development and government finances in America. He died in a duel against Aaron Burr.

Warren G. Harding (1865–1923) In the 1920 presidential election, he was the Republican nominee who promised Americans a "return to normalcy," which would mean a return to conservative values and a turning away from President Wilson's internationalism. His message resonated with voters' conservative postwar mood; and he won the election. Once in office, Harding's administration dismantled many of the social and economic components of progressivism and pursued a pro-business agenda. Harding appointed four pro-business Supreme Court Justices and his administration cut taxes, increased tariffs and promoted a lenient attitude towards government regulation of corporations. However, he did speak out against racism and ended the exclusion of African Americans from federal positions. His administration did suffer from a series of scandals as the result of him appointing members of the Ohio gang to government positions.

Harlem Renaissance African American literary and artistic movement of the 1920s and 1930s centered in New York City's Harlem district; writers Langston Hughes, Jean Toomer, Zora Neale Hurston, and Countee Cullen were among those active in the movement.

Hartford Convention Meeting of New England Federalists on December 15, 1814, to protest the War of 1812; proposed seven constitutional amendments (limiting embargoes and changing requirements for officeholding, declaration of war, and admission of new states), but the war ended before Congress could respond.

Patrick Henry (1736–1799) He inspired the Virginia Resolves, which declared that Englishmen could only be taxed by their elected representatives. In March of 1775, he met with other colonial leaders to discuss the goals of the upcoming Continental Congress and famously declared "Give me liberty or give me death." During the ratification process of the U.S. Constitution, he became one of the leaders of the anti-federalists.

Alger Hiss (1904–1996) During the second Red Scare, Alger Hiss, who had served in several government departments, was accused of being a spy for the Soviet Union and was convicted of lying about espionage. The case was politically damaging to the Truman administration because the president called the charges against Hiss a "red herring." Richard Nixon, then a California congressman, used his persistent pursuit of the case and his anti-Communist rhetoric to raise his national profile and to win election to the Senate.

Adolph Hitler "*Führer***" (1889–1945)** The leader of the Nazis who advocated a violent anti-Semitic, anti-Marxist, pan-German ideology. He started World War II in Europe and orchestrated the systematic murder of some 6 million Jews along with more than a million others.

HIV/AIDS Human Immunodeficiency Virus (HIV) is a virus that attacks the body's T-cells, which are necessary to help the immune system fight off infection and disease. Acquired Immunodeficiency Syndrome (AIDS) occurs after the HIV virus has destroyed the body's immune system. HIV is transferred when body fluids, such as blood or semen, which carry the virus, enter the body of an uninfected person. The virus appeared in America in the early 1980s. The Reagan administration was slow to respond to the "AIDS Epidemic," because effects of the virus were not fully understood and they deemed the spread of the disease as the result of immoral behavior.

Homestead Act (1862) Authorized Congress to grant 160 acres of public land to a western settler, who had only to live on the land for five years to establish title.

Homestead steel strike A violent labor conflict at the Homestead Steel Works near Pittsburgh, Pennsylvania, that occurred when its president, Henry Clay Frick, refused to renew the union contract with Amalgamated Association of Iron and Steel Workers. The strike, which began on June 29, 1892, culminated in an attempt on Frick's life and was swiftly put down by state militias. The strike marks one of the great setbacks in the emerging industrial-union movement.

Herbert Hoover (1874–1964) Prior to becoming president, Hoover served as the secretary of commerce in both the Harding and Coolidge administrations. During his tenure at the Commerce Department, he pursued new markets for business and encouraged business leaders to share information as part of the trade-association movement. The Great Depression hit while he was president. Hoover believed that the nation's business structure was sound and sought to revive the economy through boosting the nation's confidence. He also tried to restart the economy with government constructions projects, lower taxes and new federal loan programs, but nothing worked.

House Un-American Activities Committee (HUAC) Formed in 1938 to investigate subversives in the government; best-known investigations were of Hollywood notables and of former State Department official Alger Hiss, who was accused in 1948 of espionage and Communist party membership.

Sam Houston (1793–1863) During Texas's fight for independence from Mexico, Sam Houston was the commander in chief of the Texas forces, and he led the attack that captured General Antonio López de Santa Anna. After Texas gained its independence, he was name its first president.

Jacob Riis' *How the Other Half Lives* Jacob Riis was an early muckraking journalist who exposed the slum conditions in New York City in his book *How the Other Half Lives*.

General William Howe (1729–1814) As the commander of the British army in the Revolutionary War, he seized New York City from Washington's army, but failed to capture it. He missed several more opportunities to quickly end the rebellion, and he resigned his command after the British defeat at Saratoga.

Saddam Hussein (1937–2006) The former dictator of Iraq who became the head of state in 1979. In 1980, he invaded Iran and started the eight-year-long Iran-Iraq War. In 1990, he invaded Kuwait, which caused the Gulf War of 1991. In 2003, he was overthrown and captured when the United States invaded. He was sentenced to death by hanging in 2006.

Anne Hutchinson (1591–1643) The articulate, strong-willed, and intelligent wife of a prominent Boston merchant, who espoused her belief in direct divine revelation. She quarreled with Puritan leaders over her beliefs; and they banished her from the colony.

impressment The British navy used press-gangs to kidnap men in British and colonial ports who were then forced to serve in the British navy.

"Indian New Deal" This phrase refers to the reforms implemented for Native Americans during the New Deal era. John Collier, the commissioner of the Bureau of Indian Affairs (BIA), increased the access Native Americans had to relief programs and employed more Native Americans at the BIA. He worked to pass the Indian Reorganization Act. However, the version of the act passed by Congress was a much-diluted version of Collier's original proposal and did not greatly improve the lives of Native Americans.

indentured servant Settler who signed on for a temporary period of servitude to a master in exchange for passage to the New World; Virginia and Pennsylvania were largely peopled in the seventeenth and eighteenth centuries by English indentured servants.

Indian Removal Act (1830) Signed by President Andrew Jackson, the law permitted the negotiation of treaties to obtain the Indians' lands in exchange for their relocation to what became Oklahoma.

Indochina This area of Southeast Asian consists of Laos, Cambodia, and Vietnam and was once controlled by France as a colony. After the Viet Minh defeated the French, the Geneva Accords were signed, which ended French colonial rule. The agreement created the independent nations of Laos and Cambodia and divided Vietnam along the 17th parallel until an election would reunify the country. Fearing a communist take over, the United States government began intervening in the region during the Truman administration, which led to President Johnson's full-scale military involvement in Vietnam.

industrial war A new concept of war enabled by industrialization that developed from the early 1800s through the Atomic Age. New technologies, including automatic weaponry, forms of transportation like the railroad and airplane, and communication technologies such as the telegraph and telephone, enabled nations to equip large, mass-conscripted armies with chemical and automatic weapons to decimate opposing armies in a "total war."

Industrial Workers of the World (IWW) A radical union organized in Chicago in 1905, nick-named the Wobblies; its opposition to World War I led to its destruction by the federal government under the Espionage Act.

internationalists Prior to the United States' entry in World War II, internationalists believed that America's national security depended on aiding Britain in its struggle against Germany.

interstate highway system In the late 1950s, construction began on a national network of interstate superhighways for the purpose of commerce and defense. The interstate highways would enable the rapid movement of military convoys and the evacuation of cities after a nuclear attack.

Iranian Hostage Crisis In 1979, a revolution in Iran placed the Ayatollah Ruhollah Khomeini, a fundamental religious leader, in power. In November 1979, revolutionaries seized the American embassy in Tehran and held those inside hostage. President Carter struggled to get the hostages. He tried pressuring Iran through appeals to the United Nations, freezing Iranian assets in the United States and imposing a trade embargo. During an aborted rescue operation, a helicopter collided with a transport plane and killed eight U.S. soldiers. Finally, Carter unfroze several billion dollars in Iranian assets, and the hostages were released after being held for 444 days; but not until Ronald Reagan had become president of the United States.

Iran-Contra affair Scandal of the second Reagan administration involving sale of arms to Iran in partial exchange for release of hostages in Lebanon and use of the arms money to aid the Contras in Nicaragua, which had been expressly forbidden by Congress.

Irish Potato Famine In 1845, an epidemic of potato rot brought a famine to rural Ireland that killed over 1 million peasants and instigated a huge increase in the number or Irish immigrating to America. By 1850, the Irish made up 43 percent of the foreign-born population in the United States; and in the 1850s, they made up over half the population of New York City and Boston.

iron curtain Term coined by Winston Churchill to describe the cold war divide between western Europe and the Soviet Union's Eastern European satellites.

Iroquois League An alliance of the Iroquois tribes that used their strength to force Europeans to work with them in the fur trade and to wage war across what is today eastern North America.

Andrew Jackson (1767–1837) As a major general in the Tennessee militia, he defeated the Creek Indians, invaded the panhandle of Spanish Florida and won the Battle of New Orleans. In 1818, his successful campaign against Spanish forces in Florida gave the

United States the upper hand in negotiating for Florida with Spain. As president, he vetoed bills for the federal funding of internal improvements and the re-chartering of the Second National Bank. When South Carolina nullified the Tariffs of 1828 and 1832, Jackson requested that Congress pass a "force bill" that would authorize him to use the army to compel the state to comply with the tariffs. He forced eastern Indians to move west of the Mississippi River so their lands could be used by white settlers. Groups of those who opposed Jackson come together to form a new political part called the Whigs.

Jesse Jackson (1941–) An African American civil rights activist who had been one of Martin Luther King Jr.'s chief lieutenants. He is most famous for founding the social justice organization the Rainbow Coalition. In 1988, he ran for the Democratic presidential nomination, which became a race primarily between him and Michael Dukakis. Dukakis won the nomination, but lost the election to Republican nominee Vice President George H. W. Bush.

Thomas "Stonewall" Jackson (1824–1863) He was a Confederate general who was known for his fearlessness in leading rapid marches, bold flanking movements, and furious assaults. He earned his nickname at the Battle of the First Bull Run for standing courageously against Union fire. During the battle of Chancellorsville, his own men accidently mortally wounded him.

William James (1842–1910) He was the founder of Pragmatism and one of the fathers of modern psychology. He believed that ideas gained their validity not from their inherent truth, but from their social consequences and practical application.

Jay's Treaty Treaty with Britain negotiated in 1794 by Chief Justice John Jay; Britain agreed to vacate forts in the Northwest Territories, and festering disagreements (border with Canada, prewar debts, shipping claims) would be settled by commission.

Jazz Age A term coined by F. Scott Fitzgerald to characterize the spirit of rebellion and spontaneity that spread among young Americans during the 1920s, epitomized by the emergence of jazz music and the popularity of carefree, improvisational dances, such as the Charleston and the Black Bottom.

Thomas Jefferson (1743–1826) He was a plantation owner, author, the drafter of the Declaration Independence, ambassador to France, leader of the Republican party, secretary of state, and the third president of the United States. As president, he purchased the Louisiana territory from France, withheld appointments made by President Adams leading to *Marybury v. Madison*, outlawed foreign slave trade, and was committed to a "wise and frugal" government.

Jesuits A religious order founded in 1540 by Ignatius Loyola. They sought to counter the spread of Protestantism during the Protestant Reformation and spread the Catholic faith through work as missionaries. Roughly 3,500 served in New Spain and New France.

"Jim Crow" laws In the New South, these laws mandated the separation of races in various public places that served as a way for the ruling whites to impose their will on all areas of black life.

Andrew Johnson (1808–1875) As President Abraham Lincoln's vice president, he was elevated to the presidency after Lincoln's assassination. In order to restore the Union after the

Civil War, he issued an amnesty proclamation and required former Confederate states to ratify the Thirteenth Amendment. He fought Radical Republicans in Congress over whether he or Congress had the authority to restore states rights to the former Confederate states. This fight weakened both his political and public support. In 1868, the Radical Republicans attempted to impeach Johnson but fell short on the required number of votes needed to remove him from office.

Lyndon B. Johnson (1908–1973) Former member of the United States House of Representatives and the former Majority Leader of the United States Senate, Vice President Lyndon Johnson, assumed the presidency after President Kennedy's assassination. He was able to push through Congress several pieces of Kennedy's legislation that had been stalled including the Civil Rights Act of 1964. He declared "war on poverty" and promoted his own social program called the Great Society, which sought to end poverty and racial injustice. In 1965, he signed the Immigration and Nationality Service Act, which abolished the discriminatory quotas system that had been the immigration policy since the 1920s. Johnson greatly increased America's role in Vietnam. By 1969, there were 542,000 U.S. troops fighting in Vietnam and a massive anti-war movement had developed in America. In 1968, Johnson announced that he would not run for re-election.

Kansas-Nebraska Act (1854) Law sponsored by Illinois senator Stephen A. Douglas to allow settlers in newly organized territories north of the Missouri border to decide the slavery issue for themselves; fury over the resulting nullification of the Missouri Compromise of 1820 led to violence in Kansas and to the formation of the Republican party.

Florence Kelley (1859–1932) As the head of the National Consumer's League, she led the crusade to promote state laws to regulate the number of working hours imposed on women who were wives and mothers.

George F. Kennan (1904–2005) While working as an American diplomat, he devised the strategy of containment, which called for the halting of Soviet expansion. It became America's choice strategy throughout the cold war.

John F. Kennedy (1917–1963) Elected president in 1960, he was interested in bringing new ideas to the White House. Despite the difficulties he had in getting his legislation through Congress, he did establish the Alliance for Progress programs to help Latin America, the Peace Corps, the Trade Expansion Act of 1962, and funding for urban renewal projects and the space program. He mistakenly proceeded with the Bay of Pigs invasion, but he successfully handled the Cuban missile crisis. In Indochina, his administration became increasingly involved in supporting local governments through aid, advisors, and covert operations. In 1963, he was assassinated by Lee Harvey Oswald in Dallas, Texas.

Kent State During the spring of 1970, students on college campuses across the country protested the expansion of the Vietnam War into Cambodia. At Kent State University, the National Guard attempted to quell the rioting students. The guardsmen panicked and shot at rock-throwing demonstrators. Four student bystanders were killed.

Kentucky and Virginia Resolutions (1798–1799) Passed in response to the Alien and Sedition Acts, the resolutions advanced the state-compact theory that held states could nullify an act of Congress if they deemed it unconstitutional.

Francis Scott Key (1779–1843) During the War of 1812, he watched British forces bombard Fort McHenry, but fail to take it. Seeing the American flag still flying over the fort at dawn inspired him to write "The Star-Spangled Banner," which became the American national anthem.

Keynesian economics A theory of economics developed by John Maynard Keynes. He argued that increased government spending, even if it increased the nation's deficit, during an economic downturn was necessary to reinvigorate a nation's economy. This view was held by Harry Hopkins and Harold Ickes who advised President Franklin Roosevelt during the Great Depression.

Martin Luther King Jr. (1929–1968) As an important leader of the civil rights movement, he urged people to use nonviolent civil disobedience to demand their rights and bring about change. He successfully led the Montgomery bus boycott. While in jail for his role in demonstrations, he wrote his famous "Letter from Birmingham City Jail," in which he defended his strategy of nonviolent protest. In 1963, he delivered his famous "I Have a Dream Speech" from the steps of the Lincoln Memorial as a part of the March on Washington. A year later, he was awarded the Nobel Peace Prize. In 1968, he was assassinated.

King William's War (War of the League of Augsburg) First (1689–1697) of four colonial wars between England and France.

King Philip (?–1676) or **Metacomet** The chief of the Wampanoages, who the colonists called King Philip. He resented English efforts to convert Indians to Christianity and waged a war against the English colonists in which he was killed.

Henry Kissinger (1923–) He served as the secretary of state and national security advisor in the Nixon administration. He negotiated with North Vietnam for an end to the Vietnam War. In 1973, an agreement was signed between America, North and South Vietnam, and the Viet Cong to end the war. The cease-fire did not last; and South Vietnam fell to North Vietnam. He helped organize Nixon's historic trips to China and the Soviet Union. In the Middle East, he negotiated a cease-fire between Israel and its neighbors following the Yom Kippur War and solidified Israel's promise to return to Egypt most of the land it had taken during the 1967 war.

Knights of Labor Founded in 1869, the first national union picked up many members after the disastrous 1877 railroad strike, but lasted under the leadership of Terence V. Powderly, only into the 1890s; supplanted by the American Federation of Labor.

Know-Nothing party Nativist, anti-Catholic third party organized in 1854 in reaction to large-scale German and Irish immigration; the party's only presidential candidate was Millard Fillmore in 1856.

Ku Klux Klan Organized in Pulaski, Tennessee, in 1866 to terrorize former slaves who voted and held political offices during Reconstruction; a revived organization in the 1910s and 1920s stressed white, Anglo-Saxon, fundamentalist Protestant supremacy; the Klan revived a third time to fight the civil rights movement of the 1950s and 1960s in the South.

Marquis de Lafayette (1757–1834) A wealthy French idealist excited by the American cause, he offered to serve in Washington's army for free in exchange for being named a major general. He overcame Washington's initial skepticism to become one of his most trusted aides.

Land Ordinance of 1785 Directed surveying of the Northwest Territory into townships of thirty-six sections (square miles) each, the sale of the sixteenth section of which was to be used to finance public education.

Bartolomé de Las Casas (1484–1566) A Catholic missionary who renounced the Spanish practice of coercively converting Indians and advocated the better treatment for them. In 1552, he wrote *A Brief Relation of the Destruction of the Indies*, which described the Spanish's cruel treatment of the Indians.

League of Nations Organization of nations to mediate disputes and avoid war established after the First World War as part of the Treaty of Versailles; President Woodrow Wilson's "Fourteen Points" speech to Congress in 1918 proposed the formation of the league.

Mary Elizabeth Lease (1850–1933) She was a leader of the farm protest movement who advocated violence if change could not be obtained at the ballot box. She believed that the urban-industrial East was the enemy of the working class.

Robert E. Lee (1807–1870) Even though he had served in the United States Army for thirty years, he chose to fight on the side of the Confederacy and took command of the Army of North Virginia. Lee was excellent at using his field commanders; and his soldiers respected him. However, General Ulysses S. Grant eventually wore down his army, and Lee surrendered to Grant at the Appomattox Court House on April 9, 1865.

Lend-Lease Act (1941) Permitted the United States to lend or lease arms and other supplies to the Allies, signifying increasing likelihood of American involvement in the Second World War.

Levittown First low-cost, mass-produced development of suburban tract housing built by William Levitt on Long Island, New York, in 1947.

Lexington and Concord, Battle of The first shots fired in the Revolutionary War, on April 19, 1775, near Boston; approximately 100 Minutemen and 250 British soldiers were killed.

Liberator William Lloyd Garrison started this anti-slavery newspaper in 1831 in which he renounced gradualism and called for abolition.

Queen Liliuokalani (1838–1917) In 1891, she ascended to the throne of the Hawaiian royal family and tried to eliminate white control of the Hawaiian government. Two years later, Hawaii's white population revolted and seized power with the support of American marines.

Abraham Lincoln (1809–1865) His participation in the Lincoln-Douglas debates gave him a national reputation and he was nominated as the Republican party candidate for president in 1860. Shortly after he was elected president, southern states began succeeding from the Union and in April of 1861 he declared war on the succeeding states. On January 1, 1863, Lincoln signed the Emancipation Proclamation, which freed all slaves. At the end of the war, he favored a reconstruction strategy for the former Confederate states that did not radically alter southern social and economic life. However, before his plans could be finalized, John Wilkes Booth assassinated Lincoln at Ford's Theater on April 14, 1865.

Lincoln-Douglas debates Series of senatorial campaign debates in 1858 focusing on the issue of slavery in the territories; held in Illinois between Republican Abraham Lincoln, who made a national reputation for himself, and incumbent Democratic senator Stephen A. Douglas, who managed to hold onto his seat.

John Locke (1632–1704) An English philosopher whose ideas were influential during the Enlightenment. He argued in his *Essay on Human Understanding* (1690) that humanity is largely the product of the environment, the mind being a blank tablet, *tabula rasa*, on which experience is written.

Henry Cabot Lodge (1850–1924) He was the chairman of the Senate Foreign Relations Committee who favored limiting America's involvement in the League of Nations' covenant and sought to amend the Treaty of Versailles.

de Lôme letter Spanish ambassador Depuy de Lôme wrote a letter to a friend in Havana in which he described President McKinley as "weak" and a seeker of public admiration. This letter was stolen and published in the *New York Journal*, which increased the American public's dislike of Spain and moved the two countries closer to war.

Lone Star Republic After winning independence from Mexico, Texas became its own nation that was called the Lone Star Republic. In 1836, Texans drafted themselves a constitution, legalized slavery, banned free blacks, named Sam Houston president, and voted for the annexation to the United States. However, quarrels over adding a slave state and fears of instigating a war with Mexico delayed Texas's entrance into the Union until December 29, 1845.

Huey P. Long (1893–1935) He began his political career in Louisiana where he developed a reputation for being an unscrupulous reformer. As a U.S. senator, he became a critic of President Roosevelt's New Deal Plan and offered his alternative called the Share-the-Wealth program. He was assassinated in 1935.

Lords Commissioners of Trade and Plantations (the Board of Trade) William III created this organization in 1696 to investigate the enforcement of the Navigations Act, recommend ways to limit colonial manufactures, and encourage the production of raw materials in the colonies that were needed in Britain.

Louisiana Purchase President Thomas Jefferson's 1803 purchase from France of the important port of New Orleans and 828,000 square miles west of the Mississippi River to the Rocky Mountains; it more than doubled the territory of the United States at a cost of only $15 million.

Lowell "girls" Young female factory workers at the textile mills in Lowell, Massachusetts, which in the early 1820s provided its employees with prepared meals, dormitories, moral discipline, and educational opportunities.

Lowell System Lowell mills were the first to bring all the processes of spinning and weaving cloth together under one roof and have every aspect of the production mechanized. In addition, the Lowell mills were designed to be model factory communities that provided the young women employees with meals, a boardinghouse, moral discipline, and educational and cultural opportunities.

Martin Luther (1483–1546) A German monk who founded the Lutheran church. He protested abuses in the Catholic Church by posting his Ninety-five Theses, which began the Protestant Reformation.

General Douglas MacArthur (1880–1964) During World War II, he and Admiral Chester Nimitz dislodged the Japanese military from the Pacific Islands they had occupied. Following the war, he was in charge of the occupation of Japan. After North Korea invaded South Korea, Truman sent the U.S. military to defend South Korea under the command of MacArthur. Later in the war, Truman expressed his willingness to negotiate the restoration of prewar boundaries which MacArthur attempted to undermine. Truman fired MacArthur for his open insubordination.

James Madison (1751–1836) He participated in the Constitutional Convention during which he proposed the Virginia Plan. He believed in a strong federal government and was a leader of the Federalists and a contributor to *The Federalist*. However, he also presented to Congress the Bill of Rights and drafted the Virginia Resolutions. As the secretary of state, he withheld a commission for William Marbury, which led to the landmark *Marbury v. Madison* decision. During his presidency, he declared war on Britain in response to violations of American shipping rights, which started the War of 1812.

Alfred Thayer Mahan's *The Influence of Sea Power Upon History, 1660–1783* Alfred Thayer Mahan was an advocate for sea power and Western imperialism. In 1890, he published *The Influence of Sea Power Upon History, 1660–1783* in which he argued that a nation's greatness and prosperity comes from maritime power. He believed that America's "destiny" was to control the Caribbean, build the Panama Canal, and spread Western civilization across the Pacific.

Malcolm X (1925–1964) The most articulate spokesman for black power. Originally, the chief disciple of Elijah Muhammad, the black Muslim leader in the United States, Malcolm X broke away from him and founded his own organization committed to establishing relations between African Americans and the nonwhite peoples of the world. Near the end of his life, he began to preach a biracial message of social change. In 1964, he was assassinated by members of a rival group of black Muslims.

Manchuria incident The northeast region of Manchuria was an area contested between China and Russia. In 1931, the Japanese claimed that they needed to protect their extensive investments in the area and moved their army into Manchuria. They quickly conquered the region and set up their own puppet empire. China asked both the United States and the League of Nations for help and neither responded.

Manifest Destiny Imperialist phrase first used in 1845 to urge annexation of Texas; used thereafter to encourage American settlement of European colonial and Indian lands in the Great Plains and Far West.

Horace Mann (1796–1859) He believed the public school system was the best way to achieve social stability and equal opportunity. As a reformer of education, he sponsored a state board of education, the first state-supported "normal" school for training teachers, a state association for teachers, the minimum school year of six months, and led the drive for a statewide school system.

Marbury v. Madison **(1803)** First U.S. Supreme Court decision to declare a federal law—the Judiciary Act of 1801—unconstitutional; President John Adams's "midnight appointment" of Federalist judges prompted the suit.

March on Washington Civil rights demonstration on August 28, 1963, where the Reverend Martin Luther King Jr. gave his "I Have a Dream" speech on the steps of the Lincoln Memorial.

George C. Marshall (1880–1959) As the chairman of the Joint Chiefs of Staff, he orchestrated the Allied victories over Germany and Japan in the Second World War. In 1947, he became President Truman's secretary of state and proposed the massive reconstruction program for western Europe called the Marshall Plan.

Chief Justice John Marshall (1755–1835) During his long tenure as chief justice of the supreme court (1801–1835), he established the foundations for American jurisprudence, the authority of the Supreme Court, and the constitutional supremacy of the national government over states.

Marshall Plan U.S. program for the reconstruction of post–Second World War Europe through massive aid to former enemy nations as well as allies; proposed by General George C. Marshall in 1947.

massive resistance In reaction to the *Brown v. Board of Education* decision of 1954, U.S. Senator Harry Byrd encouraged southern states to defy federally mandated school integration.

massive retaliation A doctrine of nuclear strategy in which the United States committed itself to retaliate with "massive retaliatory power" (nuclear weapons) in the event of an attack. Developed by Secretary of State John Foster Dulles during the Eisenhower administration to prevent communist aggression from the Soviet Union and China.

Senator Joseph R. McCarthy (1908–1957) In 1950, this senator became the shrewdest and most ruthless exploiter of America's anxiety of communism. He claimed that the United States government was full of Communists and led a witch hunt to find them, but he was never able to uncover a single communist agent.

George B. McClellan (1826–1885) In 1861, President Abraham Lincoln appointed him head of the Army of the Potomac and, later, general in chief of the U.S. Army. He built his army into well trained and powerful force. However, he often delayed taking action against the enemy even though Lincoln wanted him to attack. After failing to achieve a decisive victory against the Confederacy, Lincoln removed McClellan from command in 1862.

Cyrus Hall McCormick (1809–1884) In 1831, he invented a mechanical reaper to harvest wheat, which transformed the scale of agriculture. By hand a farmer could only harvest a half an acre a day, while the McCormick reaper allowed two people to harvest twelve acres of wheat a day.

William McKinley (1843–1901) As a congressman, he was responsible for the McKinley Tariff of 1890, which raised the duties on manufactured products to their highest level ever. Voters disliked the tariff and McKinley, as well as other Republicans, lost their seats in Congress the next election. However, he won the presidential election of 1896 and raised the tariffs again. In 1898, he annexed Hawaii and declared war on Spain. The war concluded with the Treaty of Paris, which gave America control over Puerto Rico, Guam, and the Philippines. Soon America was fighting Filipinos, who were seeking independence for their country. In 1901, McKinley was assassinated.

Robert McNamara (1916–) He was the secretary of defense for both President Kennedy and President Johnson and a supporter of America's involvement in Vietnam.

McNary-Haugen Bill Vetoed by President Calvin Coolidge in 1927 and 1928, the bill to aid farmers would have artificially raised agricultural prices by selling surpluses overseas for low prices and selling the reduced supply in the United States for higher prices.

Andrew W. Mellon (1855–1937) As President Harding's secretary of the Treasury, he sought to generate economic growth through reducing government spending and lowering taxes. However, he insisted that the tax reductions mainly go to the rich because he believed the wealthy would reinvest their money and spur economic growth. In order to bring greater efficiency and nonpartisanship to the government's budget process, he persuaded Congress to pass the Budget and Accounting Act of 1921, which created a new Bureau of the Budget and a General Accounting Office.

mercantile system A nationalistic program that assumed that the total amount of the world's gold and silver remained essentially fixed with only a nation's share of that wealth subject to change.

James Meredith (1933–) In 1962, the governor of Mississippi defied a Supreme Court ruling and refused to allow James Meredith, an African American, to enroll at the University of Mississippi. Federal marshals were sent to enforce the law which led to clashes between a white mob and the marshals. Federal troops intervened and two people were killed and many others were injured. A few days later, Meredith was able to register at the university.

Merrimack* (ship renamed the *Virginia*) and the *Monitor First engagement between ironclad ships; fought at Hampton Roads, Virginia, on March 9, 1862.

Metacomet (?–1676) or King Philip The chief of the Wampanoages, who the colonists called King Philip. He resented English efforts to convert Indians to Christianity and waged a war against the English colonists in which he was killed.

militant nonviolence After the success of the Montgomery bus boycott, people were inspired by Martin Luther King Jr.'s use of this nonviolent form of protest. Throughout the civil rights movement, demonstrators used this method of protest to challenge racial segregation in the South.

Ho Chi Minh (1890–1969) He was the Vietnamese communist resistance leader who drove the French and the United States out of Vietnam. After the Geneva Accords divided the region into four countries, he controlled North Vietnam, and ultimately became the leader of all of Vietnam at the conclusion of the Vietnam War.

minstrelsy A form of entertainment that was popular from the 1830s to the 1870s. The performances featured white performers who were made up as African Americans or blackface. They performed banjo and fiddle music, "shuffle" dances and lowbrow humor that reinforced racial stereotypes.

Minutemen Special units organized by the militia to be ready for quick mobilization.

Miranda v. Arizona (1966) U.S. Supreme Court decision required police to advise persons in custody of their rights to legal counsel and against self-incrimination.

Mississippi Plan In 1890, Mississippi instituted policies that led to a near-total loss of voting rights for blacks and many poor whites. In order to vote, the state required that citizens pay all their taxes first, be literate, and have been residents of the state for two years and one year in an electoral district. Convicts were banned from voting. Seven other states followed this strategy of disenfranchisement.

Missouri Compromise Deal proposed by Kentucky senator Henry Clay to resolve the slave/free imbalance in Congress that would result from Missouri's admission as a slave state; in the compromise of March 20, 1820, Maine's admission as a free state offset Missouri, and slavery was prohibited in the remainder of the Louisiana Territory north of the southern border of Missouri.

Model T Ford Henry Ford developed this model of car so that it was affordable for everyone. Its success led to an increase in the production of automobiles which stimulated other related industries such steel, oil, and rubber. The mass use of automobiles increased the speed goods could be transported, encouraged urban sprawl, and sparked real estate booms in California and Florida.

modernism As both a mood and movement, modernism recognized that Western civilization had entered an era of change. Traditional ways of thinking and creating art were being rejected and replaced with new understandings and forms of expression.

Molly Maguires Secret organization of Irish coal miners that used violence to intimidate mine officials in the 1870s.

Monroe Doctrine President James Monroe's declaration to Congress on December 2, 1823, that the American continents would be thenceforth closed to colonization but that the United States would honor existing colonies of European nations.

Montgomery bus boycott Sparked by Rosa Parks's arrest on December 1, 1955, a successful year-long boycott protesting segregation on city buses; led by the Reverend Martin Luther King Jr.

Moral Majority Televangelist Jerry Falwell's political lobbying organization, the name of which became synonymous with the religious right—conservative evangelical Protestants who helped ensure President Ronald Reagan's 1980 victory.

J. Pierpont Morgan (1837–1913) As a powerful investment banker, he would acquire, reorganize, and consolidate companies into giant trusts. His biggest achievement was the consolidation of the steel industry into the United States Steel Corporation, which was the first billion-dollar corporation.

James Monroe (1758–1831) He served as secretary of state and war under President Madison and was elected president. As the latter, he signed the Transcontinental Treaty with

Spain which gave the United States Florida and expanded the Louisiana territory's western border to the Pacific coast. In 1823, he established the Monroe Doctrine. This foreign policy proclaimed the American continents were no longer open to colonization and America would be neutral in European affairs.

Robert Morris (1734–1806) He was the superintendent of finance for the Congress of the Confederation during the final years of the Revolutionary War. He envisioned a national finance plan of taxation and debt management, but the states did not approve the necessary amendments to the Articles of Confederation need to implement the plan.

Samuel F. B. Morse (1791–1872) In 1832, he invented the telegraph and revolutionized the speed of communication.

mountain men Inspired by the fur trade, these men left civilization to work as trappers and reverted to a primitive existence in the wilderness. They were the first whites to find routes through the Rocky Mountains, and they pioneered trails that settlers later used to reach the Oregon country and California in the 1840s.

muckrakers Writers who exposed corruption and abuses in politics, business, meat-packing, child labor, and more, primarily in the first decade of the twentieth century; their popular books and magazine articles spurred public interest in progressive reform.

Mugwumps Reform wing of the Republican party that supported Democrat Grover Cleveland for president in 1884 over Republican James G. Blaine, whose influence peddling had been revealed in the Mulligan letters of 1876.

mulattoes People of mixed racial ancestry, whose status in the Old South was somewhere between that of blacks and whites.

Benito Mussolini "*Il Duce*" (1883–1945) The Italian founder of the Fascist party who came to power in Italy in 1922 and allied himself with Adolf Hitler and the Axis powers during the Second World War.

My Lai Massacre In 1968, Lieutenant William Calley and his soldiers massacred 347 Vietnamese civilians in the village of My Lai. Twenty-five army officers were charged with complicity in the massacre and its cover-up but only Calley was convicted. Later, President Nixon granted him parole.

North American Free Trade Agreement (NAFTA) Approved in 1993, the North American Free Trade Agreement with Canada and Mexico allowed goods to travel across their borders free of tariffs; critics argued that American workers would lose their jobs to cheaper Mexican labor.

National Industrial Recovery Act (1933) Passed on the last of the Hundred Days; it created public-works jobs through the Federal Emergency Relief Administration and established a system of self-regulation for industry through the National Recovery Administration, which was ruled unconstitutional in 1935.

National Recovery Administration This organization's two goals were to stabilize business and generate purchasing power for consumers. The first goal was to be achieved through the implementation industry-wide codes that set wages and prices, which would reduce the chaotic competition. To provide consumers with purchasing power, the administration would provide jobs, define workplace standards, and raise wages.

National Socialist German Workers' Party (Nazi) Founded in the 1920s, this party gained control over Germany under the leadership of Adolf Hitler in 1933 and continued in power until Germany's defeat at the end of the Second World War. It advocated a violent anti-Semitic, anti-Marxist, pan-German ideology. The Nazi party systematically murdered some 6 million Jews along with more than a million others.

nativism Anti-immigrant and anti-Catholic feeling in the 1830s through the 1850s; the largest group was New York's Order of the Star-Spangled Banner, which expanded into the American, or Know-Nothing, party in 1854. In the 1920, there was a surge in nativism as Americans grew to fear immigrants who might be political radicals. In response, new strict immigration regulations were established.

nativist A native-born American who saw immigrants as a threat to his way of life and employment. During the 1880s, nativist groups worked to stop the flow of immigrates into the United States. Of these groups, the most successful was the American Protective Association who promoted government restrictions on immigration, tougher naturalization requirements, the teaching of English in schools and workplaces that refused to employ foreigners or Catholics.

Navigation Acts Passed by the English Parliament to control colonial trade and bolster the mercantile system, 1650–1775; enforcement of the acts led to growing resentment by colonists.

new conservatism The political philosophy of those who led the conservative insurgency of the early 1980s. This brand of conservatism was personified in Ronald Reagan who believed in less government, supply-side economics, and "family values."

First New Deal Franklin D. Roosevelt's campaign promise, in his speech to the Democratic National Convention of 1932, to combat the Great Depression with a "new deal for the American people;" the phrase became a catchword for his ambitious plan of economic programs.

New France The name used for the area of North America that was colonized by the French. Unlike Spanish or English colonies, New France had a small number of colonists, which forced them to initially seek good relations with the indigenous people they encountered.

New Freedom Democrat Woodrow Wilson's political slogan in the presidential campaign of 1912; Wilson wanted to improve the banking system, lower tariffs, and, by breaking up monopolies, give small businesses freedom to compete.

New Frontier John F. Kennedy's program, stymied by a Republican Congress and his abbreviated term; his successor Lyndon B. Johnson had greater success with many of the same concepts.

New Jersey Plan The delegations to the Constitutional Convention were divided between two plans on how to structure the government: New Jersey wanted one legislative body with equal representation for each state.

New Nationalism Platform of the Progressive party and slogan of former President Theodore Roosevelt in the presidential campaign of 1912; stressed government activism, including regulation of trusts, conservation, and recall of state court decisions that had nulli-fied progressive programs.

"New Negro" In the 1920s, a slow and steady growth of black political influence occurred in northern cities where African Americans were freer to speak and act. This political activity created a spirit of protest that expressed itself culturally in the Harlem Renais-sance and politically in "new Negro" nationalism.

New Netherland Dutch colony conquered by the English to become four new colonies New York, New Jersey, Pennsylvania, and Delaware.

New South *Atlanta Constitution* editor Henry W. Grady's 1886 term for the prosperous post–Civil War South: democratic, industrial, urban, and free of nostalgia for the defeated plan-tation South.

William Randolph Hearst's *New York Journal* In the late 1890s, the *New York Journal* and its rival, the *New York World*, printed sensationalism on the Cuban revolution as part of their heated competition for readership. The *New York Journal* printed a negative letter from the Spanish ambassador about President McKinley and inflammatory coverage of the sinking of the *Maine* in Havana Harbor. These two events roused the American public's outcry against Spain.

Joseph Pulitzer's *New York World* In the late 1890s, the *New York World* and its rival, *New York Journal*, printed sensationalism on the Cuban revolution as part of their heated compe-tition for readership.

Admiral Chester Nimitz (1885–1966) During the Second World War, he was the commander of central Pacific. Along with General Douglas MacArthur, he dislodged the Japanese military from the Pacific Islands they had occupied.

Nineteenth Amendment (1920) Granted women the right to vote.

Richard M. Nixon (1913–1994) He first came to national prominence as a congressman involved in the investigation of Alger Hiss. Later he served as vice president during the Eisenhower administration. In 1960, he ran as the Republican nominee for president and lost to John Kennedy. In 1968, he ran and won the presidency against Democratic nominee Hubert Humphrey. During his campaign, he promised to bring about "peace with honor" in Viet-nam. He told southern conservatives that he would slow the federal enforcement of civil rights laws and appoint pro-southern justices to the Supreme Court. After being elected, he fulfilled the latter promise attempted to keep the former. He opened talks with the North Vietnamese and began a program of Vietnamization of the war. He also bombed Cambo-dia. In 1973, America, North and South Vietnam, and the Viet Cong agreed to end the war and the United States withdrew. However, the cease-fire was broken, and the South Viet-nam fell to North Vietnam. In 1970, Nixon changed U.S. foreign policy. He declared that the America was no longer the world's policemen and he would seek some partnerships with Communist countries. With his historic visit to China, he ended twenty years of diplomatically isolating China and he began taking steps towards cultural exchanges and trade. In 1972, Nixon travelled to Moscow and signed agreements with the Soviet Union on arms control and trade. That same year, Nixon was reelected, but the Watergate scandal erupted shortly after his victory. When his knowledge of the break-in and subsequent cover-up was revealed, Nixon resigned the presidency under threat of impeachment.

No Child Left Behind President George W. Bush's education reform plan that required states to set and meet learning standards for students and make sure that all students were "proficient" in reading and writing by 2014. States had to submit annual reports of students' standardized test scores. Teachers were required to be "proficient" in their subject area. Schools who failed to show progress would face sanctions. States criticized the lack of funding for remedial programs and noted that poor school districts would find it very difficult to meet the new guidelines.

Lord North (1732–1792) The first minister of King George III's cabinet whose efforts to subdue the colonies only brought them closer to revolution. He helped bring about the Tea Act of 1773, which led to the Boston Tea Party. In an effort to discipline Boston, he wrote, and Parliament passed, four acts that galvanized colonial resistance.

North Atlantic Treaty Organization (NATO) Defensive alliance founded in 1949 by ten western European nations, the United States, and Canada to deter Soviet expansion in Europe.

Northwest Ordinance Created the Northwest Territory (area north of the Ohio River and west of Pennsylvania), established conditions for self-government and statehood, included a Bill of Rights, and permanently prohibited slavery.

nullification Concept of invalidation of a federal law within the borders of a state; first expounded in the Kentucky and Virginia Resolutions (1798), cited by South Carolina in its Ordinance of Nullification (1832) of the Tariff of Abominations, used by southern states to explain their secession from the Union (1861), and cited again by southern states to oppose the *Brown v. Board of Education* decision (1954).

Nuremberg trials At the site of the annual Nazi party rallies, twenty-one major German offenders faced an international military tribunal for Nazi atrocities. After a ten-month trial, the court acquitted three and sentenced eleven to death, three to life imprisonment, and four to shorter terms.

Barack Obama (1961–) In the 2008 presidential election, Senator Barack Obama mounted an innovative Internet based and grassroots orientated campaign that garnered him enough delegates to win the Democratic nomination. As the nation's economy nosedived in the fall of 2008, Obama linked the Republican economic philosophy with the country's dismal financial state and promoted a message of "change" and "politics of hope," which resonated with voters. He decisively won the presidency and became America's first person of colored to be elected president.

Occupy Wall Street A grassroots movement protesting a capitalist system that fostered social and economic inequality. Begun in Zuccotti Park, New York City, during 2011, the movement spread rapidly across the nation, triggering a national conversation about income inequality and protests of the government's "bailouts" of the banks and corporations allegedly responsible for the Great Recession.

Sandra Day O'Connor (1930–) She was the first woman to serve on the Supreme Court of the United States and was appointed by President Reagan. Reagan's critics charged that her appointment was a token gesture and not a sign of any real commitment to gender equality.

Ohio gang In order to escape the pressures of the White House, President Harding met with a group of people, called the "Ohio gang," in a house on K Street in Washington D.C. Members of this gang were given low-level positions in the American government and they used their White House connection to "line their pockets" by granting government contracts without bidding, which led to a series of scandals, most notably the Teapot Dome Scandal.

Frederick Law Olmsted (1822–1903) In 1858, he constructed New York's Central Park, which led to a growth in the movement to create urban parks. He went on to design parks for Boston, Brooklyn, Chicago, Philadelphia, San Francisco, and many other cities.

Opechancanough (?–1644) The brother and successor of Powhatan who led his tribe in an attempt to repel the English settlers in Virginia in 1622.

Open Door Policy In hopes of protecting the Chinese market for U.S. exports, Secretary of State John Hay unilaterally announced in 1899 that Chinese trade would be open to all nations.

Operation Desert Shield After Saddam Hussein invaded Kuwait in 1990, President George H. W. Bush sent American military forces to Saudi Arabia on a strictly defensive mission. They were soon joined by a multinational coalition. When the coalition's mission changed to the retaking of Kuwait, the operation was renamed Desert Storm.

Operation Desert Storm Multinational allied force that defeated Iraq in the Gulf War of January 1991.

Operation Overlord The Allies' assault on Hitler's "Atlantic Wall," a seemingly impregnable series of fortifications and minefields along the French coastline that German forces had created using captive Europeans for laborers.

J. Robert Oppenheimer (1904–1967) He led the group of physicists at the laboratory in Los Alamos, New Mexico, who constructed the first atomic bomb.

Oregon Country The Convention of 1818 between Britain and the United States established the Oregon Country as being west of the crest of the Rocky Mountains and the two countries were to jointly occupy it. In 1824, the United States and Russia signed a treaty that established the line of 54°40′ as the southern boundary of Russia's territorial claim in North America. A similar agreement between Britain and Russia finally gave the Oregon Country clearly defined boarders, but it remained under joint British and American control.

Oregon fever Enthusiasm for emigration to the Oregon Country in the late 1830s and early 1840s.

Osceola (1804?–1838) He was the leader of the Seminole nation who resisted the federal Indian removal policy through a protracted guerilla war. In 1837, he was treacherously seized under a flag of truce and imprisoned at Fort Moultrie, where he was left to die.

Overland (Oregon) Trails Trail Route of wagon trains bearing settlers from Independence, Missouri, to the Oregon Country in the 1840s to 1860s.

A. Mitchell Palmer (1872–1936) As the attorney general, he played an active role in government's response to the Red Scare. After several bombings across America, including one at Palmer's home, he and other Americans became convinced that there was a well-organized Communist terror campaign at work. The federal government launched a campaign of raids, deportations, and collecting files on radical individuals.

Panic of 1819 Financial collapse brought on by sharply falling cotton prices, declining demand for American exports, and reckless western land speculation.

panning A method of mining that used a large metal pan to sift gold dust and nuggets from riverbeds during the California gold rush of 1849.

Rosa Parks (1913–2005) In 1955, she refused to give up her seat to a white man on a city bus in Montgomery, Alabama, which a local ordinance required of blacks. She was arrested for disobeying the ordinance. In response, black community leaders organized the Montgomery bus boycott.

paternalism A moral position developed during the first half of the nineteenth century which claimed that slaves were deprived of liberty for their own "good." Such a rationalization was adopted by some slave owners to justify slavery.

Alice Paul (1885–1977) She was a leader of the women's suffrage movement and head of the Congressional Committee of National Women Suffrage Association. She instructed female suffrage activists to use more militant tactics, such as picketing state legislatures, chaining themselves to public buildings, inciting police to arrest them, and undertaking hunger strikes.

Norman Vincent Peale (1898–1993) He was a champion of the upbeat and feel-good theology that was popular in the 1950s religious revival. He advocated getting rid of any depressing or negative thoughts and replacing them with "faith, enthusiasm and joy," which would make an individual popular and well liked.

"peculiar institution" This term was used to describe slavery in America because slavery so fragrantly violated the principle of individual freedom that served as the basis for the Declaration of Independence.

Pentagon Papers Informal name for the Defense Department's secret history of the Vietnam conflict; leaked to the press by former official Daniel Ellsberg and published in the *New York Times* in 1971.

Pequot War Massacre in 1637 and subsequent dissolution of the Pequot Nation by Puritan settlers, who seized the Indians' lands.

perestroika Soviet leader Mikhail Gorbachev introduced these political and economic reforms, which included reconstructing the state bureaucracy, reducing the privileges of the political elite, and shifting from a centrally planned economy to a mixed economy.

Commodore Matthew Perry (1794–1858) In 1854, he negotiated the Treaty of Kanagawa, which was the first step in starting a political and commercial relationship between the United States and Japan.

John J. Pershing (1860–1948) After Pancho Villa had conducted several raids into Texas and New Mexico, President Woodrow Wilson sent troops under the command of General

John J. Pershing into Mexico to stop Villa. However, after a year of chasing Villa and not being able to catch him, they returned to the United States. During the First World War, Pershing commanded the first contingent of U.S. soldiers sent to Europe and advised the War Department to send additional American forces.

"pet banks" During President Andrew Jackson's fight with the national bank, Jackson resolved to remove all federal deposits from it. To comply with Jackson's demands, Secretary of Treasury Taney continued to draw on government's accounts in the national bank, but deposit all new federal receipts in state banks. The state banks that received these deposits were called "pet banks."

Pilgrims Puritan Separatists who broke completely with the Church of England and sailed to the New World aboard the *Mayflower*, founding Plymouth Colony on Cape Cod in 1620.

Dien Bien Phu The defining battle in the war between French colonialists and the Viet Minh. The Viet Minh's victory secured North Vietnam for Ho Chi Minh and was crucial in compelling the French to give up Indochina as a colony.

Gifford Pinchot (1865–1946) As the head of the Division of Forestry, he implemented a conservation policy that entailed the scientific management of natural resources to serve the public interest. His work helped start the conservation movement. In 1910, he exposed to the public the decision of Richard A. Ballinger's, President Taft's secretary of the interior, to open up previously protected land for commercial use. Pinchot was fired, but the damage to Taft's public image resulted in the loss of many pro-Taft candidates in 1910 congressional election.

Elizabeth Lucas Pinckney (1722? –1793) One of the most enterprising horticulturists in colonial America, she began managing her family's three plantations in South Carolina at the age of sixteen. She had tremendous success growing indigo, which led to many other plantations growing the crop as well.

Pinckney's Treaty Treaty with Spain negotiated by Thomas Pinckney in 1795; established United States boundaries at the Mississippi River and the 31st parallel and allowed open transportation on the Mississippi.

Francisco Pizarro (1478?–1541) In 1531, he lead his Spanish soldiers to Peru and conquered the Inca Empire.

planters In the antebellum South, the owner of a large farm worked by twenty or more slaves.

political "machine" A network of political activists and elected officials, usually controlled by a powerful "boss," that attempts to manipulate local politics

James Knox Polk "Young Hickory" (1795–1849) As president, his chief concern was the expansion of the United States. In 1846, his administration resolved the dispute with Britain over the Oregon Country border. Shortly, after taking office, Mexico broke off relations with the United States over the annexation of Texas. Polk declared war on Mexico and sought to subvert Mexican authority in California. The United States defeated Mexico; and the two nations signed the Treaty of Guadalupe Hidalgo in which Mexico gave up any claims on Texas north of the Rio Grande River and ceded New Mexico and California to the United States.

Pontiac's Rebellion The Peace Treaty of 1763 gave the British all French land east of the Mississippi River. This area included the territory of France's Indian allies who were not consulted about the transfer of their lands to British control. In an effort to recover their autonomy, Indians captured British forts around the Great Lakes and in the Ohio Valley as well as attacked settlements in Pennsylvania, Maryland, and Virginia.

popular sovereignty Allowed settlers in a disputed territory to decide the slavery issue for themselves.

Populist/People's party Political success of Farmers' Alliance candidates encouraged the formation in 1892 of the People's party (later renamed the Populist party); active until 1912, it advocated a variety of reform issues, including free coinage of silver, income tax, postal savings, regulation of railroads, and direct election of U.S. senators.

Pottawatomie Massacre In retaliation for the "sack of Lawrence," John Brown and his abolitionist cohorts hacked five men to death in the pro-slavery settlement of Pottawatomie, Kansas, on May 24, 1856, triggering a guerrilla war in the Kansas Territory that cost 200 settler lives.

Chief Powhatan Wahunsonacock He was called Powhatan by the English after the name of his tribe, and was the powerful, charismatic chief of numerous Algonquian-speaking towns in eastern Virginia representing over 10,000 Indians.

pragmatism William James founded this philosophy in the early 1900s. Pragmatists believed that ideas gained their validity not from their inherent truth, but from their social consequences and practical application.

Proclamation of 1763 Royal directive issued after the French and Indian War prohibiting settlement, surveys, and land grants west of the Appalachian Mountains; although it was soon over-ridden by treaties, colonists continued to harbor resentment.

proprietary colonies A colony owned by an individual, rather than a joint-stock company.

pueblos The Spanish term for the adobe cliff dwellings of the indigenous people of the southwestern United States.

Pullman strike Strike against the Pullman Palace Car Company in the company town of Pullman, Illinois, on May 11, 1894, by the American Railway Union under Eugene V. Debs; the strike was crushed by court injunctions and federal troops two months later.

Puritans English religious group that sought to purify the Church of England; founded the Massachusetts Bay Colony under John Winthrop in 1630.

Quakers George Fox founded the Quaker religion in 1647. They rejected the use of formal sacraments and ministry, refused to take oaths and embraced pacifism. Fleeing persecution, they settled and established the colony of Pennsylvania.

Radical Republicans Senators and congressmen who, strictly identifying the Civil War with the abolitionist cause, sought swift emancipation of the slaves, punishment of the rebels, and tight controls over the former Confederate states after the war.

Raleigh's Roanoke Island Colony English expedition of 117 settlers, including Virginia Dare, the first English child born in the New World; colony disappeared from Roanoke Island in the Outer Banks sometime between 1587 and 1590.

A. Philip Randolph (1889–1979) He was the head of the Brotherhood of Sleeping Car Porters who planned a march on Washington D.C. to demand an end to racial discrimination in the defense industries. To stop the march, Roosevelt administration negotiated an agreement with the Randolph group. The demonstration would be called off and an executive order would be issued that forbid discrimination in defense work and training programs and set up the Fair Employment Practices Committee.

range wars In the late 1800s, conflicting claims over land and water rights triggered violent disputes between farmers and ranchers in parts of the western United States.

Ronald Reagan (1911–2004) In 1980, the former actor and governor of California was elected president. In office, he reduced social spending, cut taxes, and increased defense spending. He was criticized for cutting important programs, such as housing and school lunches and increasing the federal deficit. By 1983, prosperity had returned to America and Reagan's economic reforms appeared to be working, but in October of 1987 the stock market crashed. Some blamed the federal debt, which had tripled in size since Reagan had taken office. In the early 1980s, HIV/AIDS cases were beginning to be reported in America, but the Reagan administration chose to do little about the growing epidemic. Reagan believed that most of the world's problems came from the Soviet Union, which he called the "evil empire." In response, he conducted a major arms build up. Then in 1987, he signed an arms-control treaty with the Soviet Union. He authorized covert CIA operations in Central America. In 1986, the Iran-Contra scandal came to light which revealed arms sales were being conducted with Iran in a partial exchange for the release of hostages in Lebanon. The arms money was being used to aid the Contras.

Reaganomics Popular name for President Ronald Reagan's philosophy of "supply side" economics, which combined tax cuts, less government spending, and a balanced budget with an unregulated marketplace.

Reconstruction Finance Corporation (RFC) Federal program established in 1932 under President Herbert Hoover to loan money to banks and other institutions to help them avert bankruptcy.

First Red Scare Fear among many Americans after the First World War of Communists in particular and noncitizens in general, a reaction to the Russian Revolution, mail bombs, strikes, and riots.

redeemers In post–Civil War southern politics, redeemers were supporters of postwar Democratic leaders who supposedly saved the South from Yankee domination and the constraints of a purely rural economy.

Dr. Walter Reed (1851–1902) His work on yellow fever in Cuba led to the discovery that the fever was carried by mosquitoes. This understanding helped develop more effective controls of the worldwide disease.

Reform Darwinism A social philosophy that challenged the ruthlessness of Social Darwinism by asserting that humans could actively shape the process of evolutionary social development through cooperation and innovation.

Reformation European religious movement that challenged the Catholic Church and resulted in the beginnings of Protestant Christianity. During this period, Catholics and Protestants persecuted, imprisoned, tortured, and killed each other in large numbers.

reparations As a part of the Treaty of Versailles, Germany was required to confess its responsibility for the First World War and make payments to the victors for the entire expense of the war. These two requirements created a deep bitterness among Germans.

Alexander Hamilton's Report on Manufactures First Secretary of the Treasury Alexander Hamilton's 1791 analysis that accurately foretold the future of American industry and proposed tariffs and subsidies to promote it.

Republicans First used during the early nineteenth century to describe supporters of a strict interpretation of the Constitution, which they believed would safeguard individual freedoms and states' rights from the threats posed by a strong central government. The idealist Republican vision of sustaing an agrarian-oriented union was developed largely by Thomas Jefferson.

"return to normalcy" In the 1920 presidential election, Republican nominee Warren G. Harding campaigned on the promise of a "return to normalcy," which would mean a return to conservative values and a turning away from President Wilson's internationalism.

Paul Revere (1735–1818) On the night of April 18, 1775, British soldiers marched towards Concord to arrest American Revolutionary leaders and seize their depot of supplies. Paul Revere famously rode through the night and raised the alarm about the approaching British troops.

Roaring Twenties In 1920s, urban America experienced an era of social and intellectual revolution. Young people experimented with new forms of recreation and sexuality as well as embraced jazz music. Leading young urban intellectuals expressed a disdain for old-fashioned rural and small-town values. The Eastern, urban cultural shift clashed with conservative and insular midwestern America, which increased the tensions between the two regions.

Jackie Robinson (1919–1972) In 1947, he became the first African American to play major league baseball. He won over fans and players and stimulated the integration of other professional sports.

rock-and-roll music Alan Freed, a disc jockey, noticed white teenagers were buying rhythm and blues records that had been only purchased by African Americans and Hispanic Americans. Freed began playing these records, but called them rock-and-roll records as a way to overcome the racial barrier. As the popularity of the music genre increased, it helped bridge the gap between "white" and "black" music.

John D. Rockefeller (1839–1937) In 1870, he founded the Standard Oil Company of Ohio, which was his first step in creating his vast oil empire. Eventually, he perfected the idea of a holding company: a company that controlled other companies by holding all or at least a majority of their stock. During his lifetime, he donated over $500 million in charitable contributions.

Romanticism Philosophical, literary, and artistic movement of the nineteenth century that was largely a reaction to the rationalism of the previous century; Romantics valued emotion, mysticism, and individualism.

Eleanor Roosevelt (1884–1962) She redefined the role of the presidential spouse and was the first woman to address a national political convention, write a nationally syndicated column and hold regular press conferences. She travelled throughout the nation to promote the New Deal, women's causes, organized labor, and meet with African American leaders. She was her husband's liaison to liberal groups and brought women activists and African American and labor leaders to the White House.

Franklin Delano Roosevelt (1882–1945) Elected during the Great Depression, Roosevelt sought to help struggling Americans through his New Deal programs that created employment and social programs, such as Social Security. Prior to American's entry into the Second World War, he supported Britain's fight against Germany through the lend-lease program. After the bombing of Pearl Harbor, he declared war on Japan and Germany and led the country through most of the Second World War before dying of cerebral hemorrhage. In 1945, he met with Winston Churchill and Joseph Stalin at the Yalta Conference to determine the shape of the post-war world.

Theodore Roosevelt (1858–1919) As the assistant secretary of the navy, he supported expansionism, American imperialism and war with Spain. He led the First Volunteer Cavalry, or Rough Riders, in Cuba during the war of 1898 and used the notoriety of this military campaign for political gain. As President McKinley's vice president, he succeeded McKinley after his assassination. His forceful foreign policy became known as "big stick diplomacy." Domestically, his policies on natural resources helped start the conversation movement. Unable to win the Republican nomination for president in 1912, he formed his own party of progressive Republicans called the "Bull Moose" party.

Roosevelt Corollary to the Monroe Doctrine (1904) President Theodore Roosevelt announced in what was essentially a corollary to the Monroe Doctrine that the United States could intervene militarily to prevent interference from European powers in the Western Hemisphere.

Rough Riders The First U.S. Volunteer Cavalry, led in battle in the Spanish-American War by Theodore Roosevelt; they were victorious in their only battle near Santiago, Cuba; and Roosevelt used the notoriety to aid his political career.

Nicola Sacco (1891–1927) In 1920, he and Bartolomeo Vanzetti were Italian immigrants who were arrested for stealing $16,000 and killing a paymaster and his guard. Their trial took place during a time of numerous bombings by anarchists and their judge was openly prejudicial. Many liberals and radicals believe that the conviction of Sacco and Vanzetti was based on their political ideas and ethnic origin rather than the evidence against them.

"salutary neglect" Edward Burke's description of Robert Walpole's relaxed policy towards the American colonies, which gave them greater independence in pursuing both their economic and political interests.

Sandinista Cuban-sponsored government that came to power in Nicaragua after toppling a corrupt dictator. The State Department believed that the Sandinistas were supplying the leftist Salvadoran rebels with Cuban and Soviet arms. In response, the Reagan administration ordered the CIA to train and supply guerrilla bands of anti-Communist Nicaraguans called Contras. A cease-fire agreement between the Contras and Sandinistas was signed in 1988.

Margaret Sanger (1883–1966) As a birth-control activist, she worked to distribute birth control information to working-class women and opened the nation's first family-planning clinic in 1916. She organized the American Birth Control League, which eventually changed its name to Planned Parenthood.

General Antonio López de Santa Anna (1794–1876) In 1834, he seized political power in Mexico and became a dictator. In 1835, Texans rebelled against him and he led his army to Texas to crush their rebellion. He captured the missionary called the Alamo and killed all of its defenders, which inspired Texans to continue to resistance and Americans to volunteer to fight for Texas. The Texans captured Santa Anna during a surprise attack and he bought his freedom by signing a treaty recognizing Texas's independence.

Saratoga, Battle of Major defeat of British general John Burgoyne and more than 5,000 British troops at Saratoga, New York, on October 17, 1777.

scalawags White southern Republicans—some former Unionists—who served in Reconstruction governments.

Phyllis Schlafly (1924–) A right-wing Republican activist who spearheaded the anti-feminism movement. She believed feminist were "anti-family, anti-children, and pro-abortion." She worked against the equal-rights amendment for women and civil rights protection for gays.

Winfield Scott (1786–1866) During the Mexican War, he was the American general who captured Mexico City, which ended the war. Using his popularity from his military success, he ran as a Whig party candidate for President.

Sears, Roebuck and Company By the end of the nineteenth century, this company dominated the mail-order industry and helped create a truly national market. Its mail-order catalog and low prices allowed people living in rural areas and small towns to buy products that were previously too expensive or available only to city dwellers.

secession Shortly after President Abraham Lincoln was elected, southern states began dissolving their ties with the United States because they believed Lincoln and the Republican party were a threat to slavery.

second Bank of the United States In 1816, the second Bank of the United States was established in order to bring stability to the national economy, serve as the depository for national funds, and provide the government with the means of floating loans and transferring money across the country.

Second Great Awakening Religious revival movement of the early decades of the nineteenth century, in reaction to the growth of secularism and rationalist religion; began the predominance of the Baptist and Methodist churches.

Second New Deal To rescue his New Deal program form judicial and political challenges, President Roosevelt launched a second phase of the New Deal in 1935. He was able to convince Congress to pass key pieces of legislation including the National Labor Relations act and Social Security Act. Roosevelt called the latter the New Deal's "supreme achievement" and pensioners started receiving monthly checks in 1940.

Seneca Falls Convention First women's rights meeting and the genesis of the women's suffrage movement; held in July 1848 in a church in Seneca Falls, New York, by Elizabeth Cady Stanton and Lucretia Coffin Mott.

"separate but equal" Principle underlying legal racial segregation, which was upheld in *Plessy v. Ferguson* (1896) and struck down in *Brown v. Board of Education* (1954).

separation of powers The powers of government are split between three separate branches (executive, legislative, and judicial) who check and balance each other.

September 11 On September 11, 2001, Islamic terrorists, who were members of al Qaeda terrorist organization, hijacked four commercial airliners. Two were flown into the World Trade Center and a third into the Pentagon. A fourth plane was brought down in Shanksville, Pennsylvania, when its passengers attacked the cockpit. In response, President George W. Bush launched his "war on terrorism." His administration assembled an international coalition to fight terrorism, and they invaded Afghanistan after the country's government would not turn over al Qaeda's leader, Osama bin Laden. However, bin Laden evaded capture. Fearful of new attacks, Bush created the Office of Homeland Security and the Transportation Security Administration. Bush and Congress passed the U.S.A. Patriot Act, which allowed government agencies to try suspected terrorists in secret military courts and eavesdrop on confidential conversations.

settlement houses Product of the late nineteenth-century movement to offer a broad array of social services in urban immigrant neighborhoods; Chicago's Hull House was one of hundreds of settlement houses that operated by the early twentieth century.

Shakers Founded by Mother Ann Lee Stanley in England, the United Society of Believers in Christ's Second Appearing settled in Watervliet, New York, in 1774 and subsequently established eighteen additional communes in the Northeast, Indiana, and Kentucky.

sharecropping Type of farm tenancy that developed after the Civil War in which landless workers—often former slaves—farmed land in exchange for farm supplies and a share of the crop; differed from tenancy in that the terms were generally less favorable.

Share-the-Wealth program Huey Long, a critic of President Roosevelt, offered this program as an alternative to the New Deal. The program proposed to confiscate large personal fortunes, which would be used to guarantee every poor family a cash grant of $5,000 and every worker an annual income of $2,500. Under this program, Long promised to provide pensions, reduce working hours, pay veterans' bonuses, and ensures a college education to every qualified student.

Shays's Rebellion Massachusetts farmer Daniel Shays and 1,200 compatriots, seeking debt relief through issuance of paper currency and lower taxes, stormed the federal arsenal at Springfield in the winter of 1787 but were quickly repulsed.

William T. Sherman's "March to the Sea" Union General William T. Sherman believed that there was a connection between the South's economy, morale, and ability to wage war. During his March through Georgia, he wanted to demoralize the civilian populace and destroy the resources they needed to fight. His army seized food and livestock that the Confederate Army might have used as well as wrecked railroads and mills and burned plantations.

Sixteenth Amendment (1913) Legalized the federal income tax.

Alfred E. Smith (1873–1944) In the 1928 presidential election, he won the Democratic nomination, but failed to win the presidency. Rural voters distrusted him for being Catholic and the son of Irish immigrants as well as his anti-Prohibition stance.

Captain John Smith (1580–1631) A swashbuckling soldier of fortune with rare powers of leadership and self-promotion, he was appointed to the resident council to manage Jamestown.

Joseph Smith (1805–1844) In 1823, he claimed that the Angel Moroni showed him the location of several gold tablets on which the Book of Mormon was written. Using the Book of Mormon as his gospel, he founded the Church of Jesus Christ of Latter-day Saints, or Mormons. Joseph and his followers upset non-Mormons living near them so they began looking for a refuge from persecution. In 1839, they settled in Commerce, Illinois, which they renamed Nauvoo. In 1844, Joseph and his brother were arrested and jailed for ordering the destruction of a newspaper that opposed them. While in jail, an anti-Mormon mob stormed the jail and killed both of them.

social Darwinism Application of Charles Darwin's theory of natural selection to society; used the concept of the "survival of the fittest" to justify class distinctions and to explain poverty.

social gospel Preached by liberal Protestant clergymen in the late nineteenth and early twentieth centuries; advocated the application of Christian principles to social problems generated by industrialization.

social justice An important part of the Progressive's agenda, social justice sought to solve social problems through reform and regulation. Methods used to bring about social justice ranged from the founding of charities to the legislation of a ban on child labor.

Sons of Liberty Organized by Samuel Adams, they were colonialists with a militant view against the British government's control of the colonies.

Hernando de Soto (1500?–1542) A conquistador who explored the west coast of Florida, western North Carolina, and along the Arkansas river from 1539 till his death in 1542.

Southern Christian Leadership Conference (SCLC) Civil rights organization founded in 1957 by the Reverend Martin Luther King Jr. and other civil rights leaders.

"southern strategy" This strategy was a major reason for Richard Nixon's victory in the 1968 presidential election. To gain support in the South, Nixon assured southern conservatives that he would slow the federal enforcement of civil rights laws and appoint pro-southern justices to the Supreme Court. As president, Nixon fulfilled these promises.

Spanish flu Unprecedentedly lethal influenza epidemic of 1918 that killed more than 22 million people worldwide.

Herbert Spencer (1820–1903) As the first major proponent of social Darwinism, he argued that human society and institutions are subject to the process of natural selection and that society naturally evolves for the better. Therefore, he was against any form of government interference with the evolution of society, like business regulations, because it would help the "unfit" to survive.

spirituals Songs, often encoded, which enslaved peoples used to express their frustration at being kept in bondage and forged their own sense of hope and community.

spoils system The term—meaning the filling of federal government jobs with persons loyal to the party of the president—originated in Andrew Jackson's first term; the system was replaced in the Progressive Era by civil service.

stagflation During the Nixon administration, the economy experienced inflation and a recession at the same time, which is syndrome that defies the orthodox laws of economics. Economists named this phenomenon "stagflation."

Joseph Stalin (1879–1953) The Bolshevik leader who succeeded Lenin as the leader of the Soviet Union in 1924 and ruled the country until his death. During his totalitarian rule of the Soviet Union, he used purges and a system of forced labor camps to maintain control over the country. During the Yalta Conference, he claimed vast areas of Eastern Europe for Soviet domination. After the end of the Second World War, the alliance between the Soviet Union and the Western powers altered into the tension of the cold war and Stalin erected the "iron curtain" between Eastern and Western Europe.

Stalwarts Conservative Republican party faction during the presidency of Rutherford B. Hayes, 1877–1881; led by Senator Roscoe B. Conkling of New York, Stalwarts opposed civil service reform and favored a third term for President Ulysses S. Grant.

Stamp Act Congress Twenty-seven delegates from nine of the colonies met from October 7 to 25, 1765 and wrote a Declaration of the Rights and Grievances of the Colonies, a petition to the King and a petition to Parliament for the repeal of the Stamp Act.

Standard Oil Company of Ohio John D. Rockefeller found this company in 1870, which grew to monopolize 90 to 95 percent of all the oil refineries in the country. It was also a "vertical monopoly" in that the company controlled all aspects of production and the services it needed to conduct business. For example, Standard Oil produced their own oil barrels and cans as well as owned their own pipelines, railroad tank cars, and oil-storage facilities.

Elizabeth Cady Stanton (1815–1902) She was a prominent reformer and advocate for the rights of women, and she helped organize the Seneca Falls Convention to discuss women's rights. The convention was the first of its kind and produced the Declaration of Sentiments, which proclaimed the equality of men and women.

staple crop, or cash crop A profitable market crop, such as cotton or tobacco.

Thaddeus Stevens (1792–1868) As one of the leaders of the Radical Republicans, he argued that the former Confederate states should be viewed as conquered provinces, which were subject to the demands of the conquerors. He believed that all of southern society needed to be changed, and he supported the abolition of slavery and racial equality.

Adlai E. Stevenson (1900–1965) In the 1952 and 1956 presidential elections, he was the Democratic nominee who lost to Dwight Eisenhower. He was also the U.S. Ambassador to the United Nations and is remembered for his famous speech in 1962 before the UN Security Council that unequivocally demonstrated that the Soviet Union had built nuclear missile bases in Cuba.

Strategic Defense Initiative ("Star Wars") Defense Department's plan during the Reagan administration to build a system to destroy incoming missiles in space.

Levi Strauss (1829–1902) A Jewish tailor who followed miners to California during the gold rush and began making durable work pants that were later dubbed blue jeans or Levi's.

Students for a Democratic Society (SDS) Major organization of the New Left, founded at the University of Michigan in 1960 by Tom Hayden and Al Haber.

suburbia The postwar era witnessed a mass migration to the suburbs. As the population in cities areas grew, people began to spread further out within the urban areas, which created new suburban communities. By 1970 more people lived in the suburbs (76 million) than in central cities (64 million).

Sunbelt The label for an arc that stretched from the Carolinas to California. During the postwar era, much of the urban population growth occurred in this area.

the "surge" In early 2007, President Bush decided he would send a "surge" of new troops to Iraq and implement a new strategy. U.S. forces would shift their focus from offensive operations to the protection of Iraqi civilians from attacks by terrorist insurgents and sectarian militias. While the "surge" reduced the violence in Iraq, Iraqi leaders were still unable to develop a self-sustaining democracy.

Taliban A coalition of ultraconservative Islamists who rose to power in Afghanistan after the Soviets withdrew. The Taliban leaders gave Osama bin Laden a safe haven in their country in exchange for aid in fighting the Northern Alliance, who were rebels opposed to the Taliban. After September 11 terrorist attacks, the United States asked the Taliban to turn over bin Laden. After they refused, America invaded Afghanistan, but bin Laden evaded capture.

Tammany Hall The "city machine" used by "Boss" Tweed to dominate politics in New York City until his arrest in 1871.

Tariff of 1816 First true protective tariff, intended strictly to protect American goods against foreign competition.

Tariff of 1832 This tariff act reduced the duties on many items, but the tariffs on cloth and iron remained high. South Carolina nullified it along with the tariff of 1828. President Andrew Jackson sent federal troops to the state and asked Congress to grant him the authority to enforce the tariffs. Henry Clay presented a plan of gradually reducing the tariffs until 1842, which Congress passed and ended the crisis.

Troubled Asset Relief Program (TARP) In 2008 President George W. Bush signed into law the bank bailout fund called Troubled Asset Relief Program (TARP), which required the Treasury Department to spend $700 billion to keep banks and other financial institutions from collapsing.

Zachary Taylor (1784–1850) During the Mexican War, he scored two quick victories against Mexico, which made him very popular in America. President Polk chose him as the commander in charge of the war. However, after he was not put in charge of the campaign to capture Mexico City, he chose to return home. Later he used his popularity from his military victories to be elected the president as a member of the Whig party.

Taylorism In his book *The Principles of Scientific Management*, Frederick W. Taylor explained a management system that claimed to be able to reduce waste through the scientific analysis of the labor process. This system called Taylorism, promised to find the optimum technique for the average worker and establish detailed performance standards for each job classification.

Tea Party A decentralized, nationwide movement of limited-government conservatives that emerged during the early twenty-first century. Its members sent thousands of tea bags into congressional offices to draw a parallel between President Obama's "tax-and-spend" liberalism and the British tax policies that led to the famous Boston Tea Party of 1773.

Teapot Dome Harding administration scandal in which Secretary of the Interior Albert B. Fall profited from secret leasing to private oil companies of government oil reserves at Teapot Dome, Wyoming, and Elk Hills, California.

Tecumseh (1768–1813) He was a leader of the Shawnee tribe who tried to unite all Indians into a confederation that could defend their hunting grounds. He believed that no land cessions could be made without the consent of all the tribes since they held the land in common. His beliefs and leadership made him seem dangerous to the American government and they waged war on him and his tribe. He was killed at the Battle of the Thames.

Tejanos Texas settlers of Spanish or Mexican descent.

Teller Amendment On April 20, 1898, a joint resolution of Congress declared Cuba independent and demanded the withdrawal of Spanish forces. The Teller amendment was added to this resolution, and it declaimed any designs the United States had on Cuban territory.

Tenochtitlán The capital city of the Aztec Empire. The city was built on marshy islands on the western side of Lake Tetzcoco, which is the site of present-day Mexico City.

Tet offensive Surprise attack by the Viet Cong and North Vietnamese during the Vietnamese New Year of 1968; turned American public opinion strongly against the war in Vietnam.

Thirteenth Amendment This amendment to the U.S. Constitution freed all slaves in the United States. After the Civil War ended, the former confederate states were required to ratify this amendment before they could be readmitted to the Union.

Gulf of Tonkin incident On August 2 and 4 of 1964, North Vietnamese vessels attacked two American destroyers in Gulf of Tonkin off the coast of North Vietnam. President Johnson described the attacks as unprovoked. In reality, the U.S. ships were monitoring South Vietnamese attacks on North Vietnamese islands that America advisors had planned. The incident spurred the Tonkin Gulf resolution.

Tonkin Gulf resolution (1964) Passed by Congress in reaction to supposedly unprovoked attacks on American warships off the coast of North Vietnam; it gave the president unlimited authority to defend U.S. forces and members of SEATO.

Tories Term used by Patriots to refer to Loyalists, or colonists who supported the Crown after the Declaration of Independence.

Trail of Tears Cherokees' own term for their forced march, 1838–1839, from the southern Appalachians to Indian lands (later Oklahoma); of 15,000 forced to march, 4,000 died on the way.

Transcendentalism Philosophy of a small group of mid-nineteenth-century New England writers and thinkers, including Ralph Waldo Emerson, Henry David Thoreau, and Margaret Fuller; they stressed "plain living and high thinking."

Transcontinental railroad First line across the continent from Omaha, Nebraska, to Sacramento, California, established in 1869 with the linkage of the Union Pacific and Central Pacific railroads at Promontory, Utah.

triangular trade Means by which exports to one country or colony provided the means for imports from another country or colony. For example, merchants from colonial New England shipped rum to West Africa and used it to barter for slaves who were then taken to the West Indies. The slaves were sold or traded for materials that the ships brought back to New England including molasses which is need to make rum.

Treaty of Ghent The signing of this treaty in 1814 ended the War of 1812 without solving any of the disputes between Britain and the United States.

Harry S. Truman (1884–1972) As President Roosevelt's vice president, he succeeded him after his death near the end of the Second World War. After the war, Truman wrestled with the inflation of both prices and wages, and his attempts to bring them both under control led to clashes with organized labor and Republicans. He did work with Congress to pass the National Security Act, which made the Joint Chiefs of Staff a permanent position and created the National Military Establishment and the Central Intelligence Agency. He banned racial discrimination in the hiring of federal employees and ended racial segregation in the armed forces. In foreign affairs, he established the Truman Doctrine to contain communism and the Marshall Plan to rebuild Europe. After North Korea invaded South Korea, Truman sent the U.S. military to defend South Korea under the command of General Douglas MacArthur. Later in the war, Truman expressed his willingness to negotiate the restoration of prewar boundaries which MacArthur attempted to undermine. Truman fired MacArthur for his open insubordination.

Truman Doctrine President Harry S. Truman's program of post–Second World War aid to European countries—particularly Greece and Turkey—in danger of being undermined by communism.

Sojourner Truth (1797?–1883) She was born into slavery, but New York State freed her in 1827. She spent the 1840s and 1850s travelling across the country and speaking to audiences about her experiences as slave and asking them to support abolition and women's rights.

Harriet Tubman (1820–1913) She was born a slave, but escaped to the North. Then she returned to the South nineteen times and guided 300 slaves to freedom.

Frederick Jackson Turner An influential historian who authored the "Frontier Thesis" in 1893, arguing that the existence of an alluring frontier and the experience of persistent westward expansion informed the nation's democratic politics, unfettered economy, and rugged individualism.

Nat Turner (1800–1831) He was the leader of the only slave revolt to get past the planning stages. In August of 1831, the revolt began with the slaves killing the members of Turner's master's household. Then they attacked other neighboring farmhouses and recruited more slaves until the militia crushed the revolt. At least fifty-five whites were killed during the uprising and seventeen slaves were hanged afterwards.

Tuskegee Airmen During the Second World War, African Americans in the armed forces usually served in segregated units. African American pilots were trained at a separate flight school in Tuskegee, Alabama, and were known as Tuskegee Airmen.

Mark Twain (1835–1910) Born Samuel Langhorne Clemens in Missouri, he became a popular humorous writer and lecturer and established himself as one of the great American authors. Like other authors of the local-color movement, his stories expressed the nostalgia people had for rural culture and old folkways as America became increasingly urban. His two greatest books, *The Adventures of Tom Sawyer* and *The Adventures of Huckleberry Finn*, drew heavily on his childhood in Missouri.

"Boss" Tweed (1823–1878) An infamous political boss in New York City, Tweed used his "city machine," the Tammany Hall ring, to rule, plunder and sometimes improve the city's government. His political domination of New York City ended with his arrest in 1871 and conviction in 1873.

Twenty-first Amendment (1933) Repealed prohibition on the manufacture, sale, and transportation of alcoholic beverages, effectively nullifying the Eighteenth Amendment.

Underground Railroad Operating in the decades before the Civil War, the "railroad" was a clandestine system of routes and safehouses through which slaves were led to freedom in the North.

Unitarianism Late eighteenth-century liberal offshoot of the New England Congregationalist church; Unitarianism professed the oneness of God and the goodness of rational man.

United Nations Security Council A major agency within the United Nations which remains in permanent session and has the responsibility of maintaining international peace and security. Originally, it consisted of five permanent members, (United States, Soviet Union, Britain, France, and the Republic of China), and six members elected to two-year terms. After 1965, the number of rotating members was increased to ten. In 1971, the Republic of China was replaced with the People's Republic of China and the Soviet Union was replaced by the Russian Federation in 1991.

Unterseeboot (or U-boat) A military submarine operated by the German government in the First World War, used to attack enemy merchant ships in war zone waters. The sinking of the ocean liner *Lusitania* by a German submarine caused a public outcry in America, which contributed to the demands to expand the United States' military.

Utopian communities These communities flourished during the Jacksonian era and were attempts to create the ideal community. They were social experiments conducted in relative isolation, so they had little impact on the world outside of their communities. In most cases, the communities quickly ran out of steam and ended.

Cornelius Vanderbilt (1794–1877) In the 1860s, he consolidated several separate railroad companies into one vast entity, New York Central Railroad.

Bartolomeo Vanzetti (1888–1927) In 1920, he and Nicola Sacco were Italian immigrants who were arrested for stealing $16,000 and killing a paymaster and his guard. Their trial took place during a time of numerous bombings by anarchists and their judge was openly prejudicial. Many liberals and radicals believe that the conviction of Sacco and Vanzetti was based on their political ideas and ethnic origin rather than the evidence against them.

Amerigo Vespucci (1455–1512) Italian explorer who reached the New World in 1499 and was the first to suggest that South America was a new continent. Afterward, European map-makers used a variant of his first name, America, to label the New World.

Viet Cong In 1956, these guerrilla forces began attacking South Vietnam's government and in 1960 the resistance groups coalesced as the National Liberation Front.

Vietnamization President Nixon's policy of equipping and training the South Vietnamese so that they could assume ground combat operations in the place of American soldiers. Nixon hoped that a reduction in U.S. forces in Vietnam would defuse the anti-war movement.

Vikings Norse people from Scandinavia who sailed to Newfoundland about A.D. 1001.

Francisco Pancho Villa (1877–1923) While the leader of one of the competing factions in the Mexican civil war, he provoked the United States into intervening. He hoped attacking the United States would help him build a reputation as an opponent of the United States, which would increase his popularity and discredit Mexican President Carranza.

Virginia Company A joint stock enterprise that King James I chartered in 1606. The company was to spread Christianity in the New World as well as find ways to make a profit in it.

Virginia Plan The delegations to the Constitutional Convention were divided between two plans on how to structure the government: Virginia called for a strong central govern-ment and a two-house legislature apportioned by population.

George Wallace (1919–1998) An outspoken defender of segregation. As the governor of Alabama, he once attempted to block African American students from enrolling at the University of Alabama. He ran as the presidential candidate for the American Indepen-dent party in 1968. He appealed to voters who were concerned about rioting anti-war protestors, the welfare system, and the growth of the federal government.

war hawks In 1811, congressional members from the southern and western districts who clamored for a war to seize Canada and Florida were dubbed "war hawks."

Warren Court The U.S. Supreme Court under Chief Justice Earl Warren, 1953–1969, decided such landmark cases as *Brown v. Board of Education* (school desegregation), *Baker v. Carr* (legislative redistricting), and *Gideon v. Wainwright* and *Miranda v. Arizona* (rights of criminal defendants).

Booker T. Washington (1856–1915) He founded a leading college for African Americans in Tuskegee, Alabama, and become the foremost black educator in America by the 1890s. He believed that the African American community should establish an economic base for its advancement before striving for social equality. His critics charged that his phi-losophy sacrificed educational and civil rights for dubious social acceptance and eco-nomic opportunities.

George Washington (1732–1799) In 1775, the Continental Congress named him the commander in chief of the Continental Army. He had previously served as an officer in the French and Indian War, but had never commanded a large unit. Initially, his army was poorly supplied and inexperienced, which led to repeated defeats. Washington realized that he could only defeat the British through wearing them down, and he implemented a strategy of evasion and selective confrontations. Gradually, the army developed into an effective force and, with the aid of the French, defeated the British. In 1787, he was the presiding officer over the Constitutional Convention, but participated little in the debates. In 1789, the Electoral College chose Washington to be the nation's first president. He assembled a cabinet of brilliant minds, which included Thomas Jefferson, James Madison, and Alexander Hamilton. Together, they would lay the foundations of American government and capitalism. Washington faced the nation's first foreign and domestic crises. In 1793, the British and French were at war. Washington chose to keep America neutral in the conflict even though France and the United States had signed a treaty of alliance. A year later, the Whiskey Rebellion erupted in Pennsylvania, and Washington sent militiamen to suppress the rebels. After two terms in office, Washington chose to step down; and the power of the presidency was peacefully passed to John Adams.

Watergate Washington office and apartment complex that lent its name to the 1972–1974 scandal of the Nixon administration; when his knowledge of the break-in at the Watergate and subsequent cover-up was revealed, Nixon resigned the presidency under threat of impeachment.

Daniel Webster (1782–1852) As a representative from New Hampshire, he led the New Federalists in opposition to the moving of the second national bank from Boston to Philadelphia. Later, he served as representative and a senator for Massachusetts and emerged as a champion of a stronger national government. He also switched from opposing to supporting tariffs because New England had built up its manufactures with the understanding tariffs would protect them from foreign competitors.

Webster-Ashburton Treaty Settlement in 1842 of U.S.–Canadian border disputes in Maine, New York, Vermont, and in the Wisconsin Territory (now northern Minnesota).

Webster-Hayne debate U.S. Senate debate of January 1830 between Daniel Webster of Massachusetts and Robert Hayne of South Carolina over nullification and states' rights.

Ida B. Wells (1862–1931) After being denied a seat on a railroad car because she was black, she became the first African American to file a suit against such discrimination. As a journalist, she criticized Jim Crow laws, demanded that blacks have their voting rights restored and crusaded against lynching. In 1909, she helped found the National Association for the Advancement of Colored People (NAACP).

western front The military front that stretched from the English Channel through Belgium and France to the Alps during the First World War.

Whig party Founded in 1834 to unite factions opposed to President Andrew Jackson, the party favored federal responsibility for internal improvements; the party ceased to exist by the late 1850s, when party members divided over the slavery issue.

Whigs Another name for revolutionary Patriots.

Whiskey Rebellion Violent protest by western Pennsylvania farmers against the federal excise tax on corn whiskey, 1794.

Eli Whitney (1765–1825) He invented the cotton gin which could separate cotton from its seeds. One machine operator could separate fifty times more cotton than worker could by hand, which led to an increase in cotton production and prices. These increases gave planters a new profitable use for slavery and a lucrative slave trade emerged from the coastal South to the Southwest.

George Whitefield (1714–1770) A true catalyst of the Great Awakening, he sought to reignite religious fervor in the American congregations. During his tour of the American Colonies in 1739, he gave spellbinding sermons and preached the notion of "new birth"—a sudden, emotional moment of conversion and salvation.

Wilderness Road Originally an Indian path through the Cumberland Gap, it was used by over 300,000 settlers who migrated westward to Kentucky in the last quarter of the eighteenth century.

Roger Williams (1603–1683) Puritan who believed that the purity of the church required a complete separation between church and state and freedom from coercion in matters of faith. In 1636, he established the town of Providence, the first permanent settlement in Rhode Island and the first to allow religious freedom in America.

Wendell L. Willkie (1892–1944) In the 1940 presidential election, he was the Republican nominee who ran against President Roosevelt. He supported aid to the Allies and criticized the New Deal programs. Voters looked at the increasingly dangerous world situation and chose to keep President Roosevelt in office for a third term.

Wilmot Proviso Proposal to prohibit slavery in any land acquired in the Mexican War, but southern senators, led by John C. Calhoun of South Carolina, defeated the measure in 1846 and 1847.

Woodrow Wilson (1856–1924) In the 1912 presidential election, Woodrow Wilson ran under the slogan of New Freedom, which promised to improve of the banking system, lower tariffs, and break up monopolies. He sought to deliver on these promises through passage of the Underwood-Simmons Tariff, the Federal Reserve Act of 1913, and new antitrust laws. Though he was weak on implementing social change and showed a little interest in the plight of African Americans, he did eventually support some labor reform. At the beginning of the First World War, Wilson kept America neutral, but provided the Allies with credit for purchases of supplies. However, the sinking of U.S. merchant ships and the news of Germany encouraging Mexico to attack America caused Wilson to ask Congress to declare war on Germany. Following the war, Wilson supported the entry of America into the League of Nations and the ratification of the Treaty of Versailles; but Congress would not approve the entry or ratification.

John Winthrop Puritan leader and Governor of the Massachusetts Bay Colony who resolved to use the colony as a refuge for persecuted Puritans and as an instrument of building a "wilderness Zion" in America.

Women Accepted for Voluntary Emergency Services (WAVES) During the Second World War, the increased demand for labor shook up old prejudices about gender roles in workplace and in the military. Nearly 200,000 women served in the Women's Army Corps or its naval equivalent, Women Accepted for Volunteer Emergency Service (WAVES).

Women's Army Corps (WAC) During the Second World War, the increased demand for labor shook up old prejudices about gender roles in workplace and in the military. Nearly 200,000 women served in the Women's Army Corps or its naval equivalent, Women Accepted for Volunteer Emergency Service (WAVES).

Woodstock In 1969, roughly a half a million young people converged on a farm near Bethel, New York, for a three-day music festival that was an expression of the flower children's free spirit.

Wounded Knee, Battle of Last incident of the Indians Wars took place in 1890 in the Dakota Territory, where the U.S. Cavalry killed over 200 Sioux men, women, and children who were in the process of surrender.

XYZ affair French foreign minister Tallyrand's three anonymous agents demanded payments to stop French plundering of American ships in 1797; refusal to pay the bribe led to two years of sea war with France (1798–1800).

Yalta Conference Meeting of Franklin D. Roosevelt, Winston Churchill, and Joseph Stalin at a Crimean resort to discuss the postwar world on February 4–11, 1945; Soviet leader Joseph Stalin claimed large areas in eastern Europe for Soviet domination.

yellow journalism A type of journalism, epitomized in the 1890s by the newspaper empires of William Randolph Hearst and Joseph Pulitzer, that intentionally manipulates public opinion through sensational headlines about both real and invented events.

yeomen Small landowners (the majority of white families in the South) who farmed their own land and usually did not own slaves.

surrender at Yorktown Last battle of the Revolutionary War; General Lord Charles Cornwallis along with over 7,000 British troops surrendered at Yorktown, Virginia, on October 17, 1781.

Brigham Young (1801–1877) Following Joseph Smith's death, he became the leader of the Mormons and promised Illinois officials that the Mormons would leave the state. In 1846, he led the Mormons to Utah and settled near the Salt Lake. After the United States gained Utah as part of the Treaty of Guadalupe Hidalgo, he became the governor of the territory and kept the Mormons virtually independent of federal authority.

youth culture The youth of the 1950s had more money and free time than any previous generation which allowed a distinct youth culture to emerge. A market emerged for products and activities that were specifically for young people such as transistor radios, rock records, *Seventeen* magazine, and Pat Boone movies.

APPENDIX

THE DECLARATION OF INDEPENDENCE (1776)

WHEN IN THE COURSE OF HUMAN EVENTS, it becomes necessary for one people to dissolve the political bands which have connected them with another, and to assume the Powers of the earth, the separate and equal station to which the Laws of Nature and of Nature's God entitle them, a decent respect to the opinions of mankind requires that they should declare the causes which impel them to the separation.

We hold these truths to be self-evident, that all men are created equal, that they are endowed by their Creator with certain unalienable rights, that among these are Life, Liberty, and the pursuit of Happiness. That to secure these rights, Governments are instituted among Men, deriving their just powers from the consent of the governed. That whenever any Form of Government becomes destructive of these ends, it is the Right of the People to alter or to abolish it, and to institute new Government, laying its foundation on such principles and organizing its powers in such form, as to them shall seem most likely to effect their Safety and Happiness. Prudence, indeed, will dictate that Governments long established should not be changed for light and transient causes; and accordingly all experience hath shown, that mankind are more disposed to suffer, while evils are sufferable, than to right themselves by abolishing the forms to which they are accustomed. But when a long train of abuses and usurpations, pursuing invariably the same Object evinces a design to reduce them under absolute Despotism, it is their right, it is their duty, to throw off such Government, and to provide new Guards for their future security.—Such has been the patient sufferance of these Colonies; and such is now the necessity which constrains them to alter their former Systems of Government. The history of the present King of Great Britain is a history of repeated injuries and usurpations, all having in direct object the establishment of an absolute Tyranny over these States. To prove this, let Facts be submitted to a candid world.

He has refused his Assent to Laws, the most wholesome and necessary for the public good.

He has forbidden his Governors to pass Laws of immediate and pressing importance, unless suspended in their operation till his Assent should be obtained; and when so suspended, he has utterly neglected to attend to them.

He has refused to pass other Laws for the accommodation of large districts of people, unless those people would relinquish the right of Representation in the Legislature, a right inestimable to them and formidable to tyrants only.

He has called together legislative bodies at places unusual, uncomfortable, and distant from the depository of their public Records, for the sole purpose of fatiguing them into compliance with his measures.

He has dissolved Representative Houses repeatedly, for opposing with manly firmness his invasions on the rights of the people.

He has refused for a long time, after such dissolutions, to cause others to be elected; whereby the Legislative powers, incapable of Annihilation, have returned to the People at large for their exercise; the State remaining in the mean time exposed to all dangers of invasion from without, and convulsions within.

He has endeavoured to prevent the population of these States; for that purpose obstructing the Laws of Naturalization of Foreigners; refusing to pass others to encourage their migrations hither, and raising the conditions of new Appropriations of Lands.

He has obstructed the Administration of Justice, by refusing his Assent to Laws for establishing Judiciary powers.

He has made Judges dependent on his Will alone, for the tenure of their offices, and the amount and payment of their salaries.

He has erected a multitude of New Offices, and sent hither swarms of Officers to harass our People, and eat out their substance.

He has kept among us, in times of peace, Standing Armies without the Consent of our legislatures.

He has affected to render the Military independent of and superior to the Civil Power.

He has combined with others to subject us to a jurisdiction foreign to our constitution, and unacknowledged by our laws; giving his Assent to their Acts of pretended Legislation:

For quartering large bodies of armed troops among us:

For protecting them, by a mock Trial, from Punishment for any Murders which they should commit on the Inhabitants of these States:

For cutting off our Trade with all parts of the world:

For imposing taxes on us without our Consent:

For depriving us of many cases, of the benefits of Trial by jury:

For transporting us beyond Seas to be tried for pretended offences:

For abolishing the free System of English Laws in a neighbouring Province, establishing therein an Arbitrary government, and enlarging its

Boundaries so as to render it at once an example and fit instrument for introducing the same absolute rule into these Colonies:

For taking away our Charters, abolishing our most valuable Laws, and altering fundamentally the Forms of our Governments:

For suspending our own Legislatures, and declaring themselves in vested with Power to legislate for us in all cases whatsoever.

He has abdicated Government here, by declaring us out of his Protection and waging War against us.

He has plundered our seas, ravaged our Coasts, burnt our towns, and destroyed the lives of our people.

He is at this time transporting large armies of foreign mercenaries to compleat the works of death, desolation, and tyranny, already begun with circumstances of Cruelty & perfidy scarcely paralleled in the most barbarous ages, and totally unworthy the Head of a civilized nation.

He has constrained our fellow Citizens taken Captive on the high Seas to bear Arms against their Country, to become the executioners of their friends and Brethren, or to fall themselves by their Hands.

He has excited domestic insurrections amongst us, and has endeavoured to bring on the inhabitants of our frontiers, the merciless Indian Savages, whose known rule of warfare, is an undistinguished destruction of all ages, sexes, and conditions.

In every stage of these Oppressions We have Petitioned for Redress in the most humble terms: Our repeated Petitions have been answered only by repeated injury. A Prince, whose character is thus marked by every act which may define a Tyrant, is unfit to be the ruler of a free people.

Nor have We been wanting in attention to our British brethren. We have warned them from time to time of attempts by their legislature to extend an unwarrantable jurisdiction over us. We have reminded them of the circumstances of our emigration and settlement here. We have appealed to their native justice and magnanimity, and we have conjured them by the ties of our common kindred to disavow these usurpations, which, would inevitably interrupt our connections and correspondence. They too must have been deaf to the voice of justice and of consanguinity. We must, therefore, acquiesce in the necessity, which denounces our Separation, and hold them, as we hold the rest of mankind, Enemies in War, in Peace Friends.

WE, THEREFORE, the Representatives of the UNITED STATES OF AMERICA, in General Congress, Assembled, appealing to the Supreme Judge of the world for the rectitude of our intentions, do, in the Name, and by Authority of the good People of these Colonies, solemnly publish and declare, That these United Colonies are, and of Right ought to be FREE AND INDEPENDENT STATES; that they are Absolved from all Allegiance to the

British Crown, and that all political connection between them and the State of Great Britain, is and ought to be totally dissolved; and that as Free and Independent States, they have full Power to levy War, conclude Peace, contract Alliances, establish Commerce, and to do all other Acts and Things which Independent States may of right do. And for the support of this Declaration, with a firm reliance on the Protection of Divine Providence, we mutually pledge to each other our Lives, our Fortunes, and our sacred Honor.

The foregoing Declaration was, by order of Congress, engrossed, and signed by the following members:

John Hancock

NEW HAMPSHIRE
Josiah Bartlett
William Whipple
Matthew Thornton

MASSACHUSETTS BAY
Samuel Adams
John Adams
Robert Treat Paine
Elbridge Gerry

RHODE ISLAND
Stephen Hopkins
William Ellery

CONNECTICUT
Roger Sherman
Samuel Huntington
William Williams
Oliver Wolcott

NEW YORK
William Floyd
Philip Livingston
Francis Lewis
Lewis Morris

NEW JERSEY
Richard Stockton
John Witherspoon
Francis Hopkinson
John Hart
Abraham Clark

PENNSYLVANIA
Robert Morris
Benjamin Rush
Benjamin Franklin
John Morton
George Clymer
James Smith
George Taylor
James Wilson
George Ross

DELAWARE
Caesar Rodney
George Read
Thomas M'Kean

MARYLAND
Samuel Chase
William Paca
Thomas Stone
Charles Carroll, of Carrollton

VIRGINIA
George Wythe
Richard Henry Lee
Thomas Jefferson
Benjamin Harrison
Thomas Nelson, Jr.
Francis Lightfoot Lee
Carter Braxton

NORTH CAROLINA
William Hooper
Joseph Hewes
John Penn

SOUTH CAROLINA
Edward Rutledge
Thomas Heyward, Jr.
Thomas Lynch, Jr.
Arthur Middleton

GEORGIA
Button Gwinnett
Lyman Hall
George Walton

Resolved, that copies of the declaration be sent to the several assemblies, conventions, and committees, or councils of safety, and to the several commanding officers of the continental troops; that it be proclaimed in each of the united states, at the head of the army.

ARTICLES OF
CONFEDERATION (1778)

To all to whom these Presents shall come, we the undersigned Delegates of the States affixed to our Names send greeting.

Whereas the Delegates of the United States of America in Congress assembled did on the fifteenth day of November in the Year of our Lord One Thousand Seven Hundred and Seventy-seven, and in the Second Year of the Independence of America agree to certain articles of Confederation and perpetual Union between the States of Newhampshire, Massachusetts-bay, Rhodeisland and Providence Plantations, Connecticut, New York, New Jersey, Pennsylvania, Delaware, Maryland, Virginia, North-Carolina, South-Carolina and Georgia in the Words following, viz.

Articles of Confederation and perpetual Union between the States of Newhampshire, Massachusetts-bay, Rhodeisland and Providence Plantations, Connecticut, New-York, New-Jersey, Pennsylvania, Delaware, Maryland, Virginia, North-Carolina, South-Carolina and Georgia.

Article I. The stile of this confederacy shall be "The United States of America."

Article II. Each State retains its sovereignty, freedom and independence, and every power, jurisdiction and right, which is not by this confederation expressly delegated to the United States, in Congress assembled.

Article III. The said States hereby severally enter into a firm league of friendship with each other, for their common defence, the security of their liberties, and their mutual and general welfare, binding themselves to assist each other, against all force offered to, or attacks made upon them, or any of them, on account of religion, sovereignty, trade or any other pretence whatever.

ARTICLE IV. The better to secure and perpetuate mutual friendship and inter-course among the people of the different States in this Union, the free inhab-itants of each of these States, paupers, vagabonds and fugitives from justice excepted, shall be entitled to all privileges and immunities of free citizens in the several States; and the people of each State shall have free ingress and regress to and from any other State, and shall enjoy therein all the privileges of trade and commerce, subject to the same duties, impositions and restric-tions as the inhabitants thereof respectively, provided that such restrictions shall not extend so far as to prevent the removal of property imported into any State, to any other State of which the owner is an inhabitant; provided also that no imposition, duties or restriction shall be laid by any State, on the property of the United States, or either of them.

If any person guilty of, or charged with treason, felony, or other high mis-demeanor in any State, shall flee from justice, and be found in any of the United States, he shall upon demand of the Governor or Executive power, of the State from which he fled, be delivered up and removed to the State having jurisdiction of his offence.

Full faith and credit shall be given in each of these States to the records, acts and judicial proceedings of the courts and magistrates of every other State.

ARTICLE V. For the more convenient management of the general interests of the United States, delegates shall be annually appointed in such manner as the legislature of each State shall direct, to meet in Congress on the first Monday in November, in every year, with a power reserved to each State, to recall its delegates, or any of them, at any time within the year, and to send others in their stead, for the remainder of the year.

No State shall be represented in Congress by less than two, nor by more than seven members; and no person shall be capable of being a delegate for more than three years in any term of six years; nor shall any person, being a delegate, be capable of holding any office under the United States, for which he, or another for his benefit receives any salary, fees or emolument of any kind.

Each State shall maintain its own delegates in a meeting of the States, and while they act as members of the committee of the States.

In determining questions in the United States, in Congress assembled, each State shall have one vote.

Freedom of speech and debate in Congress shall not be impeached or questioned in any court, or place out of Congress, and the members of Con-gress shall be protected in their persons from arrests and imprisonments, during the time of their going to and from, and attendance on Congress, except for treason, felony, or breach of the peace.

ARTICLE VI. No State without the consent of the United States in Congress assembled, shall send any embassy to, or receive any embassy from, or enter into any conference, agreement, alliance or treaty with any king, prince or state; nor shall any person holding any office of profit or trust under the United States, or any of them, accept of any present, emolument, office or title of any kind whatever from any king, prince or foreign state; nor shall the United States in Congress assembled, or any of them, grant any title of nobility.

No two or more States shall enter into any treaty, confederation or alliance whatever between them, without the consent of the United States in Congress assembled, specifying accurately the purposes for which the same is to be entered into, and how long it shall continue.

No State shall lay any imposts or duties, which may interfere with any stipulations in treaties, entered into by the United States in Congress assembled, with any king, prince or state, in pursuance of any treaties already proposed by Congress, to the courts of France and Spain.

No vessels of war shall be kept up in time of peace by any State, except such number only, as shall be deemed necessary by the United States in Congress assembled, for the defence of such State, or its trade; nor shall any body of forces be kept up by any State, in time of peace, except such number only, as in the judgment of the United States, in Congress assembled, shall be deemed requisite to garrison the forts necessary for the defence of such State; but every State shall always keep up a well regulated and disciplined militia, sufficiently armed and accoutred, and shall provide and constantly have ready for use, in public stores, a due number of field pieces and tents, and a proper quantity of arms, ammunition and camp equipage.

No State shall engage in any war without the consent of the United States in Congress assembled, unless such State be actually invaded by enemies, or shall have received certain advice of a resolution being formed by some nation of Indians to invade such State, and the danger is so imminent as not to admit of a delay, till the United States in Congress assembled can be consulted: nor shall any State grant commissions to any ships or vessels of war, nor letters of marque or reprisal, except it be after a declaration of war by the United States in Congress assembled, and then only against the kingdom or state and the subjects thereof, against which war has been so declared, and under such regulations as shall be established by the United States in Congress assembled, unless such State be infested by pirates, in which case vessels of war may be fitted out for that occasion, and kept so long as the danger shall continue, or until the United States in Congress assembled shall determine otherwise.

ARTICLE VII. When land-forces are raised by any State of the common defence, all officers of or under the rank of colonel, shall be appointed by the Legislature of each State respectively by whom such forces shall be raised, or in such manner as such State shall direct, and all vacancies shall be filled up by the State which first made the appointment.

ARTICLE VIII. All charges of war, and all other expenses that shall be incurred for the common defence or general welfare, and allowed by the United States in Congress assembled, shall be defrayed out of a common treasury, which shall be supplied by the several States, in proportion to the value of all land within each State, granted to or surveyed for any person, as such land and the buildings and improvements thereon shall be estimated according to such mode as the United States in Congress assembled, shall from time to time direct and appoint.

The taxes for paying that proportion shall be laid and levied by the authority and direction of the Legislatures of the several States within the time agreed upon by the United States in Congress assembled.

ARTICLE IX. The United States in Congress assembled, shall have the sole and exclusive right and power of determining on peace and war, except in the cases mentioned in the sixth article—of sending and receiving ambassadors—entering into treaties and alliances, provided that no treaty of commerce shall be made whereby the legislative power of the respective States shall be restrained from imposing such imposts and duties on foreigners, as their own people are subjected to, or from prohibiting the exportation or importation of and species of goods or commodities whatsoever—of establishing rules for deciding in all cases, what captures on land or water shall be legal, and in what manner prizes taken by land or naval forces in the service of the United States shall be divided or appropriated—of granting letters of marque and reprisal in times of peace—appointing courts for the trial of piracies and felonies committed on the high seas and establishing courts for receiving and determining finally appeals in all cases of captures, provided that no member of Congress shall be appointed a judge of any of the said courts.

The United States in Congress assembled shall also be the last resort on appeal in all disputes and differences now subsisting or that hereafter may arise between two or more States concerning boundary, jurisdiction or any other cause whatever; which authority shall always be exercised in the manner following. Whenever the legislative or executive authority or lawful agent of any State in controversy with another shall present a petition to Congress, stating the matter in question and praying for a hearing, notice thereof shall be given by order of Congress to the legislative or executive authority of the other State in controversy, and a day assigned for the appearance of the parties by their lawful agents, who shall then be directed to appoint by joint consent, commissioners or judges to constitute a court for hearing and determining the matter in question: but if they cannot agree, Congress shall name three persons out of each of the United States, and from the list of such persons each party shall alternately strike out one, the petitioners beginning, until the number shall be reduced to thirteen; and from that number not less than seven, nor more than nine names as Congress shall direct, shall in the presence of Congress be drawn out by lot, and the persons whose names shall be so drawn or any five of them, shall be commissioners or judges, to hear and finally determine the controversy, so always as a major part of the judges who shall hear the cause shall agree in the determination: and if either party shall neglect to attend at the day appointed, without reasons, which Congress shall judge sufficient, or being present shall refuse to strike, the Congress shall proceed to nominate three persons out of each State, and the Secretary of Congress shall strike in behalf of such party absent or refusing; and the judgment and sentence of the court to be appointed, in the manner before prescribed, shall be final and conclusive; and if any of the parties shall refuse to submit to the authority of such court, or to appear or defend their claim or cause, the court shall nevertheless proceed to pronounce sentence, or judgment, which shall in like manner be final and decisive, the judgment or sentence and other proceedings being in either case transmitted to Congress, and lodged among the acts of Congress for the security of the parties concerned: provided that every commissioner, before he sits in judgment, shall take an oath to be administered by one of the judges of the supreme or superior court of the State where the case shall be tried, "well and truly to hear and determine the matter in question, according to the best of his judgment, without favour, affection or hope of reward:" provided also that no State shall be deprived of territory for the benefit of the United States.

All controversies concerning the private right of soil claimed under different grants of two or more States, whose jurisdiction as they may respect such lands, and the states which passed such grants are adjusted, the said grants or either of them being at the same time claimed to have originated antecedent to such settlement of jurisdiction, shall on the petition of either party to the Congress of the United States, be finally determined as near as may be in the same manner as is before prescribed for deciding disputes respecting territorial jurisdiction between different States.

The United States in Congress assembled shall also have the sole and exclusive right and power of regulating the alloy and value of coin struck by their own authority, or by that of the respective States—fixing the standard of weights and measures throughout the United States—regulating the trade and managing all affairs with the Indians, not members of any of the States, provided that the legislative right of any State within its own limits be not infringed or violated—establishing and regulating post-offices from one State to another, throughout all of the United States, and exacting such postage on the papers passing thro' the same as may be requisite to defray the expenses of the said office—appointing all officers of the land forces, in the service of the United States, excepting regimental officers—appointing all the officers of the naval forces, and commissioning all officers whatever in the service of the United States—making rules for the government and regulation of the said land and naval forces, and directing their operations.

The United States in Congress assembled shall have authority to appoint a committee, to sit in the recess of Congress, to be denominated "a Committee of the States," and to consist of one delegate from each State; and to appoint such other committees and civil officers as may be necessary for managing the general affairs of the United States under their direction—to appoint one of their number to preside, provided that no person be allowed to serve in the office of president more than one year in any term of three years; to ascertain the necessary sums of money to be raised for the service of the United States, and to appropriate and apply the same for defraying the public expenses—to borrow money, or emit bills on the credit of the United States, transmitting every half year to the respective States an account of the sums of money so borrowed or emitted,—to build and equip a navy—to agree upon the number of land forces, and to make requisitions from each State for its quota, in proportion to the number of white inhabitants in such State; which requisition shall be binding, and thereupon the Legislature of each State shall appoint the regimental officers, raise the men and cloath, arm and equip them in a soldier like manner, at the expense of the United States; and the officers and men so cloathed, armed and equipped shall march to the place appointed, and within the time agreed on by the United States in Congress assembled: but if the United States in Congress assembled shall, on consideration of circumstances judge proper that any State should not raise men, or should raise a smaller number of men than the quota thereof, such extra number shall be raised, officered, cloathed, armed and equipped in the same manner as the quota of such State, unless the legislature of such State shall judge that such extra number cannot be safely spared out of the same, in which case they shall raise officer, cloath, arm and equip as many of such extra number as they judge can be safely spared. And the officers and men so cloathed, armed and equipped, shall march to the place appointed, and within the time agreed on by the United States in Congress assembled.

The United States in Congress assembled shall never engage in a war, nor grant letters of marque and reprisal in time of peace, nor enter into any treaties or alliances, nor coin money, nor regulate the value thereof, nor ascertain the sums and expenses necessary for the defence and welfare of the United States, or any of them, nor emit bills, nor borrow money on the credit of the United States, nor appropriate money, nor agree upon the number of vessels to be built or purchased, or the number of land or sea forces to be raised, nor appoint a commander in chief of the army or navy, unless nine States assent to the same: nor shall a question on any other point, except for adjourning from day to day be determined, unless by the votes of a majority of the United States in Congress assembled.

The Congress of the United States shall have power to adjourn to any time within the year, and to any place within the United States, so that no period of adjournment be for a longer duration than the space of six months, and shall publish the journal of their proceedings monthly, except such parts thereof relating to treaties, alliances or military operations, as in their judgment require secresy; and the yeas and nays of the delegates of each State on any question shall be entered on the Journal, when it is desired by any delegate; and the delegates of a State, or any of them, at his or their request shall be furnished with a transcript of the said journal, except such parts as are above excepted, to lay before the Legislatures of the several States.

ARTICLE X. The committee of the States, or any nine of them, shall be authorized to execute, in the recess of Congress, such of the powers of Congress as the United States in Congress assembled, by the consent of nine States, shall from time to time think expedient to vest them with; provided that no power be delegated to the said committee, for the exercise of which, by the articles of confederation, the voice of nine States in the Congress of the United States assembled is requisite.

ARTICLE XI. Canada acceding to this confederation, and joining in the measures of the United States, shall be admitted into, and entitled to all the advantages of this Union: but no other colony shall be admitted into the same, unless such admission be agreed to by nine States.

ARTICLE XII. All bills of credit emitted, monies borrowed and debts contracted by, or under the authority of Congress, before the assembling of the United States, in pursuance of the present confederation, shall be deemed and considered as a charge against the United States, for payment and satisfaction whereof the said United States, and the public faith are hereby solemnly pledged.

ARTICLE XIII. Every State shall abide by the determinations of the United States in Congress assembled, on all questions which by this confederation are submitted to them. And the articles of this confederation shall be inviolably observed by every State, and the Union shall be perpetual; nor shall any alteration at any time hereafter be made in any of them; unless such alteration be agreed to in a Congress of the United States, and be afterwards confirmed by the Legislatures of every State.

And whereas it has pleased the Great Governor of the world to incline the hearts of the Legislatures we respectively represent in Congress, to approve of, and to authorize us to ratify the said articles of confederation and perpetual union. Know ye that we the undersigned delegates, by virtue of the power and authority to us given for that purpose, do by these presents, in the name and in behalf of our respective constituents, fully and entirely ratify and confirm each and every of the said articles of confederation and perpetual union, and all and singular the matters and things therein contained: and we do further solemnly plight and engage the faith of our respective constituents, that they shall abide by the determinations of the United States in Congress assembled, on all questions, which by the said confederation are submitted to them. And that the articles thereof shall be inviolably observed by the States we respectively represent, and that the Union shall be perpetual.

In witness thereof we have hereunto set our hands in Congress. Done at Philadelphia in the State of Pennsylvania the ninth day of July in the year of our Lord one thousand seven hundred and seventy-eight, and in the third year of the independence of America.

THE CONSTITUTION OF THE UNITED STATES (1787)

WE THE PEOPLE OF THE UNITED STATES, in order to form a more perfect Union, establish Justice, insure domestic Tranquility, provide for the common defence, promote the general Welfare, and secure the Blessings of Liberty to ourselves and our Posterity, do ordain and establish this Constitution for the United States of America.

ARTICLE. I.

Section. 1. All legislative Powers herein granted shall be vested in a Congress of the United States, which shall consist of a Senate and House of Representatives.

Section. 2. The House of Representatives shall be composed of Members chosen every second Year by the People of the several States, and the Electors in each State shall have the Qualifications requisite for Electors of the most numerous Branch of the State Legislature.

No Person shall be a Representative who shall not have attained to the Age of twenty five Years, and been seven Years a Citizen of the United States, and who shall not, when elected, be an Inhabitant of that State in which he shall be chosen.

Representatives and direct Taxes shall be apportioned among the several States which may be included within this Union, according to their respective Numbers, which shall be determined by adding to the whole Number of free Persons, including those bound to Service for a Term of Years, and excluding Indians not taxed, three fifths of all other Persons. The actual Enumeration shall be made within three Years after the first Meeting of the Congress of the United States, and within every subsequent Term of ten Years, in such

Manner as they shall by Law direct. The Number of Representatives shall not exceed one for every thirty Thousand, but each State shall have at Least one Representative; and until such enumeration shall be made, the State of New Hampshire shall be entitled to chuse three, Massachusetts eight, Rhode-Island and Providence Plantations one, Connecticut five, New-York six, New Jersey four, Pennsylvania eight, Delaware one, Maryland six, Virginia ten, North Carolina five, South Carolina five, and Georgia three.

When vacancies happen in the Representation from any state, the Executive Authority thereof shall issue Writs of Election to fill such Vacancies.

The House of Representatives shall chuse their Speaker and other Officers; and shall have the sole Power of Impeachment.

Section. 3. The Senate of the United States shall be composed of two Senators from each State, chosen by the legislature thereof, for six Years; and each Senator shall have one Vote.

Immediately after they shall be assembled in Consequence of the first Election, they shall be divided as equally as may be into three Classes. The Seats of the Senators of the first Class shall be vacated at the Expiration of the second Year, of the second Class at the Expiration of the fourth Year, and of the third Class at the Expiration of the sixth Year, so that one third maybe chosen every second Year; and if Vacancies happen by Resignation, or otherwise, during the Recess of the Legislature of any State, the Executive thereof may make temporary Appointments until the next Meeting of the Legislature, which shall then fill such Vacancies.

No Person shall be a Senator who shall not have attained to the Age of thirty Years, and been nine Years a Citizen of the United States, and who shall not, when elected, be an Inhabitant of that State for which he shall be chosen.

The Vice President of the United States shall be President of the Senate, but shall have no Vote, unless they be equally divided.

The Senate shall chuse their other Officers, and also a President pro tempore, in the Absence of the Vice President, or when he shall exercise the Office of President of the United States.

The Senate shall have the sole Power to try all Impeachments. When sitting for that Purpose, they shall be on Oath or Affirmation. When the President of the United States is tried, the Chief Justice shall preside: And no Person shall be convicted without the Concurrence of two thirds of the Members present.

Judgment in Cases of Impeachment shall not extend further than to removal from Office, and disqualification to hold and enjoy any Office of honor, Trust or Profit under the United States: but the Party convicted shall nevertheless be liable and subject to Indictment, Trial, Judgment and Punishment, according to Law.

Section. 4. The Times, Places and Manner of holding Elections for Senators and Representatives, shall be prescribed in each State by the Legislature thereof; but the Congress may at any time by Law make or alter such Regulations, except as to the Places of chusing Senators.

The Congress shall assemble at least once in every Year, and such Meeting shall be on the first Monday in December, unless they shall by Law appoint a different Day.

Section. 5. Each House shall be the Judge of the Elections, Returns and Qualifications of its own Members, and a Majority of each shall constitute a Quorum to do Business; but a smaller Number may adjourn from day to day, and may be authorized to compel the Attendance of absent Members, in such Manner, and under such Penalties as each House may provide.

Each House may determine the Rules of its Proceedings, punish its Members for disorderly Behaviour, and, with the Concurrence of two thirds, expel a Member.

Each House shall keep a Journal of its Proceedings, and from time to time publish the same, excepting such Parts as may in their Judgment require Secrecy; and the Yeas and Nays of the Members of either House on any question shall, at the Desire of one fifth of those Present, be entered on the Journal.

Neither House, during the Session of Congress, shall, without the Consent of the other, adjourn for more than three days, not to any other Place than that in which the two Houses shall be sitting.

Section. 6. The Senators and Representatives shall receive a Compensation for their Services, to be ascertained by Law, and paid out of the Treasury of the United States. They shall in all Cases, except Treason, Felony and Breach of the Peace, be privileged from Arrest during their Attendance at the Session of their respective Houses, and in going to and returning from the same; and for any Speech or Debate in either House, they shall not be questioned in any other Place.

No Senator or Representative shall, during the Time for which he was elected, be appointed to any civil Office under the Authority of the United States, which shall have been created, or the Emoluments whereof shall have been encreased during such time; and no Person holding any Office under the United States, shall be a Member of either House during his Continuance in Office.

Section. 7. All Bills for raising Revenue shall originate in the House of Representatives; but the Senate may propose or concur with Amendments as on other Bills.

Every Bill which shall have passed the House of Representatives and the Senate shall, before it become a Law, be presented to the President of the United States; If he approve he shall sign it, but if not he shall return it, with his Objections to that House in which it shall have originated, who shall enter the Objections at large on their Journal, and proceed to reconsider it. If after such Reconsideration two thirds of that House shall agree to pass the Bill, it shall be sent, together with the Objections, to the other House, by which it shall likewise be reconsidered, and if approved by two thirds of that House, it shall become a Law. But in all such Cases the Votes of both Houses shall be determined by yeas and Nays, and the Names of the Persons voting for and against the Bill shall be entered on the Journal of each House respectively. If any Bill shall not be returned by the President within ten Days (Sundays excepted) after it shall have been presented to him, the Same shall be a Law, in like Manner as if he had signed it, unless the Congress by their Adjournment prevent its Return, in which Case it shall not be a Law.

Every Order, Resolution, or Vote to which the Concurrence of the Senate and House of Representatives may be necessary (except on a question of Adjournment) shall be presented to the President of the United States; and before the Same shall take Effect, shall be approved by him, or being disapproved by him, shall be repassed by two thirds of the Senate and House of Representatives, according to the Rules and Limitations prescribed in the Case of a Bill.

Section. 8. The Congress shall have Power To lay and collect Taxes, Duties, Imposts and Excises, to pay the Debts and provide for the common Defence and general Welfare of the United States; but all Duties, Imposts and Excises shall be uniform throughout the United States;

To borrow Money on the credit of the United States;

To regulate Commerce with foreign Nations, and among the several States, and with the Indian Tribes;

To establish an uniform Rule of Naturalization, and uniform Laws on the subject of Bankruptcies throughout the United States;

To coin Money, regulate the Value thereof, and of foreign Coin, and fix the Standard of Weights and Measures;

To provide for the Punishment of counterfeiting the Securities and current Coin of the United States;

To establish Post Offices and Post Roads;

To promote the Progress of Science and useful Arts, by securing for limited Times to Authors and Inventors the exclusive Right to their respective Writings and Discoveries;

To constitute Tribunals inferior to the supreme Court;

To define and punish Piracies and Felonies committed on the high Seas, and Offences against the Law of Nations;

To declare War, grant Letters of Marque and Reprisal, and make Rules concerning Captures on land and Water;

To raise and support Armies, but no Appropriation of Money to that Use shall be for a longer Term than two Years;

To provide and maintain a Navy;

To make Rules for the Government and Regulation of the land and naval Forces;

To provide for calling forth the Militia to execute the Laws of the Union, suppress Insurrections and repel Invasions;

To provide for organizing, arming, and disciplining, the Militia, and for governing such Part of them as may be employed in the Service of the United States, reserving to the States respectively, the Appointment of the Officers, and the Authority of training the Militia according to the discipline prescribed by Congress.

To exercise exclusive Legislation in all Cases whatsoever, over such District (not exceeding ten Miles square) as may, by Cession of Particular States, and the Acceptance of Congress, become the Seat of the Government of the United States, and to exercise like Authority over all Places purchased by the Consent of the Legislature of the State in which the Same shall be, for the Erection of Forts, Magazines, Arsenals, dock-Yards, and other needful Buildings;—And

To make all Laws which shall be necessary and proper for carrying into Execution the foregoing Powers, and all other Powers vested by this Constitution in the Government of the United States, or in any Department or Officer thereof.

Section. 9. The Migration or Importation of such Persons as any of the States now existing shall think proper to admit, shall not be prohibited by the Congress prior to the Year one thousand eight hundred and eight, but a Tax or duty may be imposed on such Importation, not exceeding ten dollars for each Person.

The Privilege of the Writ of Habeas Corpus shall not be suspended, unless when in Cases of Rebellion or Invasion the public Safety may require it.

No Bill of Attainder or ex post facto Law shall be passed.

No Capitation, or other direct, Tax shall be laid, unless in Proportion to the Census or Enumeration herein before directed to be taken.

No Tax or Duty shall be laid on Articles exported from any State.

No Preference shall be given by any Regulation of Commerce or Revenue to the Ports of one State over those of another: nor shall Vessels bound to, or from, one State, be obliged to enter, clear, or pay Duties in another.

No Money shall be drawn from the Treasury, but in Consequence of Appropriations made by Law; and a regular Statement and Account of the Receipts and Expenditures of all public Money shall be published from time to time.

No Title of Nobility shall be granted by the United States: And no Person holding any Office of Profit or trust under them, shall, without the Consent of the Congress, accept of any present, Emolument, Office, or Title, of any kind whatever, from any King, Prince, or foreign State.

Section 10. No State shall enter into any Treaty, Alliance, or Confederation; grant Letters of Marque and Reprisal; coin Money; emit Bills of Credit; make any Thing but gold and silver Coin a Tender in Payment of Debts; pass any Bill of Attainder, ex post facto Law, or Law impairing the Obligation of Contracts, or grant any Title of Nobility.

No State shall, without the Consent of the Congress, lay any Imposts or Duties on Imports or Exports, except what may be absolutely necessary for executing its inspection Laws: and the net Produce of all Duties and Imposts, laid by any State on Imports or Exports, shall be for the Use of the Treasury of the United States; and all such Laws shall be subject to the Revision and Controul of the Congress.

No State shall, without the Consent of Congress, lay any Duty of Tonnage, keep Troops, or Ships of War in time of Peace, enter into any Agreement or Compact with another State, or with a foreign Power, or engage in War, unless actually invaded, or in such imminent Danger as will not admit of delay.

Article. II.

Section. 1. The executive Power shall be vested in a President of the United States of America. He shall hold his Office during the term of four Years, and, together with the Vice President, chosen for the same Term, be elected, as follows:

Each State shall appoint, in such Manner as the Legislature thereof may direct, a Number of Electors, equal to the whole Number of Senators and Representatives to which the State may be entitled in the Congress: but no Senator or Representative, or Person holding an Office of Trust or Profit under the United States, shall be appointed an Elector.

The Electors shall meet in their respective States, and vote by Ballot for two Persons, of whom one at least shall not be an Inhabitant of the same State with themselves. And they shall make a List of all the Persons voted for, and of the Number of Votes for each; which List they shall sign and certify, and transmit sealed to the Seat of the Government of the United States, directed to the President of the Senate. The President of the Senate shall, in the Presence of the Senate and House of Representatives, open all the Certificates, and the Votes shall then be counted. The Person having the greatest Number of Votes shall be the President, if such Number be a Majority of the whole Number of Electors appointed; and if there be more than one who have such Majority, and have an equal Number of Votes, then the House of Representatives shall immediately chuse by Ballot one of them for President; and if no Person have a Majority, then from the five highest on the List the said House shall in like Manner chuse the President. But in chusing the President, the Votes shall be taken by States, the Representation from each State having one Vote; A quorum for this Purpose shall consist of a Member or Members from two thirds of the States, and a Majority of all the States shall be necessary to a Choice. In every Case, after the Choice of the President, the Person having the greatest Number of Votes of the Electors shall be the Vice President. But if there should remain two or more who have equal Votes, the Senate shall chuse from them by Ballot the Vice President.

The Congress may determine the Time of chusing the Electors, and the Day on which they shall give their Votes; which Day shall be the same throughout the United States.

No Person except a natural born Citizen, or a Citizen of the United States, at the time of the Adoption of this Constitution, shall be eligible to the Office of President; neither shall any Person be eligible to that Office who shall not have attained to the Age of thirty five Years, and been fourteen Years a Resident within the United States.

In Case of the Removal of the President from Office, or of his Death, Resignation, or Inability to discharge the Powers and Duties of the said Office, the Same shall devolve on the Vice President, and the Congress may by Law provide for the Case of Removal, Death, Resignation or Inability, both of the President and Vice President, declaring what Officer shall then act as President, and such Officer shall act accordingly, until the Disability be removed, or a President shall be elected.

The President shall, at stated Times, receive for his Services, a Compensation, which shall neither be encreased or diminished during the Period for which he shall have been elected, and he shall not receive within that Period any other Emolument from the United States, or any of them.

Before he enters on the Execution of his Office, he shall take the following Oath or Affirmation:—"I do solemnly swear (or affirm) that I will faithfully execute the Office of President of the United States, and will to the best of my Ability, preserve, protect and defend the Constitution of the United States."

Section. 2. The President shall be Commander in Chief of the Army and Navy of the United States, and of the Militia of the several States, when called into the actual Service of the United States; he may require the Opinion, in writing, of the principal Officer in each of the executive Departments, upon any Subject relating to the Duties of their respective Offices, and he shall have Power to grant Reprieves and Pardons for Offences against the United States, except in Cases of Impeachment.

He shall have Power, by and with the Advice and Consent of the Senate, to make Treaties, provided two thirds of the Senators present concur; and he shall nominate, and by and with the Advice and Consent of the Senate, shall appoint Ambassadors, other public Ministers and Consuls, Judges of the supreme Court, and all other Officers of the United States, whose Appointments are not herein otherwise provided for, and which shall be established by Law; but the Congress may by Law vest the Appointment of such inferior Officers, as they think proper, in the President alone, in the Courts of Law, or in the Heads of Departments.

The President shall have Power to fill up all Vacancies that may happen during the Recess of the Senate, by granting Commissions which shall expire at the End of their next Session.

Section. 3. He shall from time to time give to the Congress Information of the State of the Union, and recommend to their Consideration such Measures as he shall judge necessary and expedient; he may, on extraordinary Occasions, convene both Houses, or either of them, and in Case of Disagreement between them, with Respect to the Time of Adjournment, he may adjourn them to such Time as he shall think proper; he shall receive Ambassadors and other public Ministers; he shall take Care that the Laws be faithfully executed, and shall Commission all the Officers of the United States.

Section. 4. The President, Vice President and all civil Officers of the United States, shall be removed from Office on Impeachment for, and Conviction of, Treason, Bribery, or other high Crimes and Misdemeanors.

ARTICLE. III.

Section. 1. The judicial Power of the United States, shall be vested in one supreme Court, and in such inferior Courts as the Congress may from time to time ordain and establish. The Judges, both of the supreme and inferior Courts, shall hold their Offices during good Behavior, and shall, at stated Times, receive for their Services, a Compensation, which shall not be diminished during their Continuance in Office.

Section. 2. The judicial Power shall extend to all Cases, in Law and Equity, arising under this Constitution, the Laws of the United States, and Treaties made, or which shall be made, under their Authority;—to all Cases affecting Ambassadors, other public Ministers and Consuls;—to all Cases of admiralty and maritime Jurisdiction;—the Controversies to which the United States shall be a Party;—to Controversies between two or more States;—between a State and Citizens of another State;—between Citizens of different States;—between Citizens of the same State claiming Lands under Grants of different States, and between a State, or the Citizens thereof, and foreign States, Citizens or Subjects.

In all cases affecting Ambassadors, other public Ministers and Consuls, and those in which a State shall be Party, the supreme Court shall have original Jurisdiction. In all the other Cases before mentioned, the supreme Court shall have appellate Jurisdiction, both as to Law and Fact, with such Exceptions, and under such Regulations as the Congress shall make.

The Trial of all Crimes, except in Cases of Impeachment, shall be by Jury; and such Trial shall be held in the State where the said Crimes shall have been committed; but when not committed within any State, the Trial shall be at such Place or Places as the Congress may by Law have directed.

Section. 3. Treason against the United States, shall consist only in levying War against them, or in adhering to their Enemies, giving them Aid and Comfort. No Person shall be convicted of Treason unless on the Testimony of two Witnesses to the same overt Act, or on Confession in open Court.

The Congress shall have Power to declare the Punishment of Treason, but no Attainder of Treason shall work Corruption of Blood, or Forfeiture except during the Life of the Person attainted.

ARTICLE. IV.

Section. 1. Full Faith and Credit shall be given in each State to the public Acts, Records, and judicial Proceedings of every other State. And the Congress may by general Laws prescribe the Manner in which such Acts, Records and Proceedings shall be proved, and the Effect thereof.

Section. 2. The Citizens of each State shall be entitled to all Privileges and Immunities of Citizens in the several States.

A Person charged in any State with Treason, Felony, or other Crime, who shall flee from Justice, and be found in another State, shall on Demand of the executive Authority of the State from which he fled, be delivered up, to be removed to the State having Jurisdiction of the Crime.

No Person held to Service or Labour in one State, under the Laws thereof, escaping into another, shall, in Consequence of any Law or Regulation therein, be discharged from such Service or Labour, but shall be delivered up on Claim of the Party to whom such Service or Labour may be due.

Section. 3. New States may be admitted by the Congress into this Union; but no new State shall be formed or erected within the Jurisdiction of any other State; nor any State be formed by the Junction of two or more States, or Parts of States, without the consent of the Legislatures of the States concerned as well as of the Congress.

The Congress shall have Power to dispose of and make all needful Rules and Regulations respecting the Territory or other Property belonging to the United States; and nothing in this Constitution shall be so construed as to Prejudice any Claims of the United States, or of any particular States.

Section. 4. The United States shall guarantee to every State in this Union a Republican Form of Government, and shall protect each of them against Invasion; and on Application of the Legislature, or of the Executive (when the Legislature cannot be convened) against domestic Violence.

ARTICLE. V.

The Congress, whenever two thirds of both Houses shall deem it necessary, shall propose Amendments to this Constitution, or, on the Application of the

Legislatures of two thirds of the several States, shall call a Convention for proposing Amendments, which, in either Case, shall be valid to all Intents and Purposes, as Part of this Constitution, when ratified by the Legislatures of three fourths of the several States, or by Conventions in three fourths thereof, as the one or the other Mode of Ratification may be proposed by the Congress; Provided that no Amendment which may be made prior to the Year One thousand eight hundred and eight shall in any Manner affect the first and fourth Clauses in the Ninth Section of the first Article; and that no State, without its Consent, shall be deprived of its equal Suffrage in the Senate.

ARTICLE. VI.

All Debts contracted and Engagements entered into, before the Adoption of this Constitution, shall be as valid against the United States under this Constitution, as under the Confederation.

This Constitution, and the Laws of the United States which shall be made in Pursuance thereof; and all Treaties made, or which shall be made, under the Authority of the United States, shall be the supreme Law of the Land; and the Judges in every State shall be bound thereby, any Thing in the Constitution or Laws of any State to the Contrary notwithstanding.

The Senators and Representatives before mentioned, and the Members of the several State Legislatures, and all executive and judicial Officers, both of the United States and of the several States, shall be bound by Oath or Affirmation, to support this Constitution; but no religious Test shall ever be required as a Qualification to any Office or public Trust under the United States.

ARTICLE. VII.

The Ratification of the Conventions of nine States, shall be sufficient for the Establishment of this Constitution between the States so ratifying the Same.

Done in Convention by the Unanimous Consent of the States present the Seventeenth Day of September in the Year of our Lord one thousand seven hundred and Eighty seven and of the Independence of the United States of America the Twelfth. In witness thereof We have hereunto subscribed our Names,

Go. WASHINGTON—Presdt.
and deputy from Virginia.

New Hampshire	{ John Langdon Nicholas Gilman		
		Delaware	{ Geo: Read Gunning Bedford jun John Dickinson Richard Bassett Jaco: Broom
Massachusetts	{ Nathaniel Gorham Rufus King		
Connecticut	{ Wm Saml Johnson Roger Sherman	Maryland	{ James McHenry Dan of St Thos Jenifer Danl Carroll
New York: ...	Alexander Hamilton		
		Virginia	{ John Blair— James Madison Jr.
New Jersey	{ Wil: Livingston David A. Brearley. Wm Paterson. Jona: Dayton		
		North Carolina	{ Wm Blount Richd Dobbs Spaight. Hu Williamson
Pennsylvania	{ B Franklin Thomas Mifflin Robt Morris Geo. Clymer Thos FitzSimons Jared Ingersoll James Wilson Gouv Morris	South Carolina	{ J. Rutledge Charles Cotesworth Pinckney Charles Pinckney Pierce Butler.
		Georgia	{ William Few Abr Baldwin

AMENDMENTS TO THE CONSTITUTION

ARTICLES IN ADDITION TO, and Amendment of the Constitution of the United States of America, proposed by Congress, and ratified by the Legislatures of the several States, pursuant to the fifth Article of the original Constitution.

AMENDMENT I.

Congress shall make no law respecting an establishment of religion, or prohibiting the free exercise thereof; or abridging the freedom of speech, or of the press; or the right of the people peaceably to assemble, and to petition the Government for a redress of grievances.

AMENDMENT II.

A well regulated Militia, being necessary to the security of a free State, the right of the people to keep and bear Arms, shall not be infringed.

AMENDMENT III.

No Soldier shall, in time of peace be quartered in any house, without the consent of the Owner, nor in time of war, but in a manner to be prescribed by law.

AMENDMENT IV.

The right of the people to be secure in their persons, houses, papers, and effects, against unreasonable searches and seizures, shall not be violated, and no Warrants shall issue, but upon probable cause, supported by Oath or affirmation, and particularly describing the place to be searched, and the persons or things to be seized.

AMENDMENT V.

No person shall be held to answer for a capital, or otherwise infamous crime, unless on a presentment or indictment of a Grand Jury, except in cases arising in the land or naval forces, or in the Militia, when in actual service in time of War or public danger; nor shall any person be subject for the same offence to be twice put in jeopardy of life or limb; nor shall be compelled in any criminal case to be a witness against himself, nor be deprived of life, liberty, or property, without due process of law; nor shall private property be taken for public use, without just compensation.

AMENDMENT VI.

In all criminal prosecutions, the accused shall enjoy the right to a speedy and public trial, by an impartial jury of the State and district wherein the crime shall have been committed, which district shall have been previously ascertained by law, and to be informed of the nature and cause of the accusation; to be confronted with the witnesses against him; to have compulsory process for obtaining witnesses in his favor, and to have the Assistance of Counsel for his defence.

AMENDMENT VII.

In Suits at common law, where the value in controversy shall exceed twenty dollars, the right of trial by jury shall be preserved, and no fact tried by a jury, shall be otherwise re-examined in any Court of the United States, than according to the rules of the common law.

AMENDMENT VIII.

Excessive bail shall not be required, nor excessive fines imposed, nor cruel and unusual punishments inflicted.

AMENDMENT IX.

The enumeration in the Constitution, of certain rights, shall not be construed to deny or disparage others retained by the people.

AMENDMENT X.

The powers not delegated to the United States by the Constitution, nor prohibited by it to the States, are reserved to the States respectively, or to the people. [The first ten amendments went into effect December 15, 1791.]

AMENDMENT XI.

The Judicial power of the United States shall not be construed to extend to any suit in law or equity, commenced or prosecuted against one of the United States by Citizens of another State, or by Citizens or Subjects of any Foreign State. [January 8, 1798.]

AMENDMENT XII.

The Electors shall meet in their respective states, and vote by ballot for President and Vice-President, one of whom, at least, shall not be an inhabitant of the same state with themselves; they shall name in their ballots the person voted for as President, and in distinct ballots the person voted for as Vice-President, and they shall make distinct lists of all persons voted for as President, and of all persons voted for as Vice President, and of the number of votes for each, which lists they shall sign and certify, and transmit sealed to the seat of the government of the United States, directed to the President of the Senate;—The President of the Senate shall, in the presence of the Senate and House of Representatives, open all the certificates and the votes shall then be counted;—The person having the greatest number of votes for President, shall be the President, if such number be a majority of the whole number of Electors appointed; and if no person have such majority, then from the persons having the highest numbers not exceeding three on the list of those voted for as President, the House of Representatives shall choose immediately, by ballot, the President. But in choosing the President, the votes shall be taken by states, the representation from each state having one vote; a quorum for this purpose shall consist of a member or members from two-thirds of the states, and a majority of all the states shall be necessary to a choice. And if the House of Representatives shall not choose a President whenever the right of choice shall devolve upon them, before the fourth day of March next following, then the Vice-President shall act as President, as in the case of the death or other constitutional disability of the President.— The person having the greatest number of votes as Vice-President, shall be the Vice-President, if such number be a majority of the whole number of Electors appointed, and if no person have a majority, then from the two highest numbers on the list, the Senate shall choose the Vice-President; a quorum for the purpose shall consist of two-thirds of the whole number of Senators, and a majority of the whole number shall be necessary to a choice. But no person constitutionally ineligible to the office of President shall be eligible to that of Vice-President of the United States. [September 25, 1804.]

AMENDMENT XIII.

Section 1. Neither slavery nor involuntary servitude, except as a punishment for crime whereof the party shall have been duly convicted, shall exist within the United States, or any place subject to their jurisdiction.

   Section 2. Congress shall have power to enforce this article by appropriate legislation. [December 18, 1865.]

AMENDMENT XIV.

Section 1. All persons born or naturalized in the United States, and subject to the jurisdiction thereof, are citizens of the United States and of the State wherein they reside. No State shall make or enforce any law which shall abridge the privileges or immunities of citizens of the United States; nor shall any State deprive any person of life, liberty, or property, without due process of law; nor deny to any person within its jurisdiction the equal protection of the laws.

Section 2. Representatives shall be apportioned among the several States according to their respective numbers, counting the whole number of persons in each State, excluding Indians not taxed. But when the right to vote at any election for the choice of electors for President and Vice President of the United States, Representatives in Congress, the Executive and Judicial officers of a State, or the members of the Legislature thereof, is denied to any of the male inhabitants of such State, being twenty-one years of age, and citizens of the United States, or in any way abridged, except for participation in rebellion, or other crime, the basis of representation therein shall be reduced in the proportion which the number of such male citizens shall bear to the whole number of male citizens twenty-one years of age in such State.

Section 3. No person shall be a Senator or Representative in Congress, or elector of President and Vice President, or hold any office, civil or military, under the United States, or under any State, who, having previously taken an oath, as a member of Congress, or as an officer of the United States, or as a member of any State legislature, or as an executive or judicial officer of any State, to support the Constitution of the United States, shall have engaged in insurrection or rebellion against the same, or given aid or comfort to the enemies thereof. But Congress may by a vote of two-thirds of each House, remove such disability.

Section 4. The validity of the public debt of the United States, authorized by law, including debts incurred for payment of pensions and bounties for services in suppressing insurrection or rebellion, shall not be questioned. But neither the United States nor any State shall assume or pay any debt or obligation incurred in aid of insurrection or rebellion against the United States, or any claim for the loss or emancipation of any slave; but all such debts, obligations and claims shall be held illegal and void.

Section 5. The Congress shall have power to enforce, by appropriate legislation, the provisions of this article. [July 28, 1868.]

AMENDMENT XV.

Section 1. The right of citizens of the United States to vote shall not be denied or abridged by the United States or by any State on account of race, color, or previous condition of servitude—

Section 2. The Congress shall have power to enforce this article by appropriate legislation.—[March 30, 1870.]

AMENDMENT XVI.

The Congress shall have power to lay and collect taxes on incomes, from whatever source derived, without apportionment among the several

States, and without regard to any census or enumeration. [February 25, 1913.]

AMENDMENT XVII.

The Senate of the United States shall be composed of two senators from each State, elected by the people thereof, for six years; and each Senator shall have one vote. The electors in each State shall have the qualifications requisite for electors of the most numerous branch of the State legislature.

When vacancies happen in the representation of any State in the Senate, the executive authority of such State shall issue writs of election to fill such vacancies: *Provided,* That the legislature of any State may empower the executive thereof to make temporary appointments until the people fill the vacancies by election as the legislature may direct.

This amendment shall not be so construed as to affect the election or term of any senator chosen before it becomes valid as part of the Constitution. [May 31, 1913.]

AMENDMENT XVIII.

After one year from the ratification of this article, the manufacture, sale, or transportation of intoxicating liquors within, the importation thereof into, or the exportation thereof from the United States and all territory subject to the jurisdiction thereof for beverage purposes is hereby prohibited.

The Congress and the several States shall have concurrent power to enforce this article by appropriate legislation.

This article shall be inoperative unless it shall have been ratified as an amendment to the Constitution by the legislatures of the several States, as provided in the Constitution, within seven years from the date of the submission thereof to the States by Congress. [January 29, 1919.]

AMENDMENT XIX.

The right of citizens of the United States to vote shall not be denied or abridged by the United States or by any State on account of sex.

The Congress shall have power by appropriate legislation to enforce the provisions of this article. [August 26, 1920.]

AMENDMENT XX.

Section 1. The terms of the President and Vice-President shall end at noon on the twentieth day of January, and the terms of Senators and Representatives at noon on the third day of January, of the years in which such terms would have ended if this article had not been ratified; and the terms of their successors shall then begin.

Section 2. The Congress shall assemble at least once in every year, and such meeting shall begin at noon on the third day of January, unless they shall by law appoint a different day.

Section 3. If, at the time fixed for the beginning of the term of the President, the President-elect shall have died, the Vice-President-elect shall become President. If a President shall not have been chosen before the time fixed for the beginning of his term, or if the President-elect shall have failed to qualify, then the Vice-President-elect shall act as President until a President shall have qualified; and the Congress may by law provide for the case wherein neither a President-elect nor a Vice-President-elect shall have qualified, declaring who shall then act as President, or the manner in which one who is to act shall be selected, and such person shall act accordingly until a President or Vice-President shall have qualified.

Section 4. The Congress may by law provide for the case of the death of any of the persons from whom the House of Representatives may choose a President whenever the right of choice shall have devolved upon them, and for the case of the death of any of the persons from whom the Senate may choose a Vice-President whenever the right of choice shall have devolved upon them.

Section 5. Sections 1 and 2 shall take effect on the 15th day of October following the ratification of this article.

Section 6. This article shall be inoperative unless it shall have been ratified as an amendment to the Constitution by the legislatures of three-fourths of the several States within seven years from the date of its submission. [February 6, 1933.]

Amendment XXI.

Section 1. The eighteenth article of amendment to the Constitution of the United States is hereby repealed.

Section 2. The transportation or importation into any State, Territory or possession of the United States for delivery or use therein of intoxicating liquors, in violation of the laws thereof, is hereby prohibited.

Section 3. This article shall be inoperative unless it shall have been ratified as an amendment to the Constitution by convention in the several States, as provided in the Constitution, within seven years from the date of the submission thereof to the States by the Congress. [December 5, 1933.]

Amendment XXII.

Section 1. No person shall be elected to the office of the President more than twice, and no person who has held the office of President, or acted as President, for more than two years of a term to which some other person was elected President shall be elected to the office of the President more than once. But this Article shall not apply to any person holding the office of President when this Article was proposed by the Congress, and shall not prevent any person who may be holding the office of President, or acting as President, during the term within which this Article becomes operative from holding the office of President or acting as President during the remainder of such term.

Section 2. This article shall be inoperative unless it shall have been ratified as an amendment to the Constitution by the legislatures of three-fourths of the several states within seven years from the date of its submission to the States by the Congress. [February 27, 1951.]

Amendment XXIII.

Section 1. The District constituting the seat of government of the United States shall appoint in such manner as the Congress may direct:
A number of electors of President and Vice-President equal to the whole number of Senators and Representatives in Congress to which the District would be entitled if it were a State, but in no event more than the least

populous State; they shall be in addition to those appointed by the States, but they shall be considered, for the purposes of the election of President and Vice-President, to be electors appointed by a State; and they shall meet in the District and perform such duties as provided by the twelfth article of amendment.

Section 2. The Congress shall have the power to enforce this article by appropriate legislation. [March 29, 1961.]

AMENDMENT XXIV.

Section 1. The right of citizens of the United States to vote in any primary or other election for President or Vice President, for electors for President or Vice President, or for Senator or Representative in Congress, shall not be denied or abridged by the United States or any State by reason of failure to pay any poll tax or other tax.

Section 2. The Congress shall have power to enforce this article by appropriate legislation. [January 23, 1964.]

AMENDMENT XXV.

Section 1. In case of the removal of the President from office or of his death or resignation, the Vice President shall become President.

Section 2. Whenever there is a vacancy in the office of Vice President, the President shall nominate a Vice President who shall take office upon confirmation by a majority vote of both Houses of Congress.

Section 3. Whenever the President transmits to the President pro tempore of the Senate and the Speaker of the House of Representatives his written declaration that he is unable to discharge the powers and duties of his office, and until he transmits to them a written declaration to the contrary, such powers and duties shall be discharged by the Vice President as Acting President.

Section 4. Whenever the Vice President and a majority of either the principal officers of the executive departments or of such other body as Congress may by law provide, transmit to the President pro tempore of the Senate and the Speaker of the House of Representatives their written declaration that the President is unable to discharge the powers and duties of his office, the Vice President shall immediately assume the powers and duties of the office as Acting President.

Thereafter, when the President transmits to the President pro tempore of the Senate and the Speaker of the House of Representatives his written declaration that no inability exists, he shall resume the powers and duties of his office unless the Vice President and a majority of either the principal officers of the executive departments or of such other body as Congress may by law provide, transmit within four days to the President pro tempore of the Senate and the Speaker of the House of Representatives their written declaration that the President is unable to discharge the powers and duties of his office. Thereupon Congress shall decide the issue, assembling within forty-eight hours for that purpose if not in session. If the Congress, within twenty-one days after receipt of the latter written declaration, or, if Congress is not in session, within twenty-one days after Congress is required to assemble, determines by two-thirds vote of both Houses that the President is unable to discharge the powers and duties of his office, the Vice President shall continue to discharge the same as Acting President; otherwise, the President shall resume the powers and duties of his office. [February 10, 1967.]

AMENDMENT XXVI.

Section 1. The right of citizens of the United States, who are eighteen years of age or older, to vote shall not be denied or abridged by the United States or by any State on account of age.

Section 2. The Congress shall have power to enforce this article by appropriate legislation [June 30, 1971.]

AMENDMENT XXVII.

No law, varying the compensation for the services of the Senators and Representatives shall take effect, until an election of Representatives shall have intervened. [May 8, 1992.]

PRESIDENTIAL ELECTIONS

Year	Number of States	Candidates	Parties	Popular Vote	% of Popular Vote	Electoral Vote	% Voter Participation
1789	11	**GEORGE WASHINGTON**	No party designations			69	
		John Adams				34	
		Other candidates				35	
1792	15	**GEORGE WASHINGTON**	No party designations			132	
		John Adams				77	
		George Clinton				50	
		Other candidates				5	
1796	16	**JOHN ADAMS**	Federalist			71	
		Thomas Jefferson	Democratic-Republican			68	
		Thomas Pinckney	Federalist			59	
		Aaron Burr	Democratic-Republican			30	
		Other candidates				48	
1800	16	**THOMAS JEFFERSON**	Democratic-Republican			73	
		Aaron Burr	Democratic-Republican			73	
		John Adams	Federalist			65	
		Charles C. Pinckney	Federalist			64	
		John Jay	Federalist			1	
1804	17	**THOMAS JEFFERSON**	Democratic-Republican			162	
		Charles C. Pinckney	Federalist			14	

Year	Number of States	Candidates	Parties	Popular Vote	% of Popular Vote	Electoral Vote	% Voter Participation
1808	17	**JAMES MADISON**	Democratic-Republican			122	
		Charles C. Pinckney	Federalist			47	
		George Clinton	Democratic-Republican			6	
1812	18	**JAMES MADISON**	Democratic-Republican			128	
		DeWitt Clinton	Federalist			89	
1816	19	**JAMES MONROE**	Democratic-Republican			183	
		Rufus King	Federalist			34	
1820	24	**JAMES MONROE**	Democratic-Republican			231	
		John Quincy Adams	Independent			1	
1824	24	**JOHN QUINCY ADAMS**	Democratic-Republican	108,740	30.5	84	26.9
		Andrew Jackson	Democratic-Republican	153,544	43.1	99	
		Henry Clay	Democratic-Republican	47,136	13.2	37	
		William H. Crawford	Democratic-Republican	46,618	13.1	41	
1828	24	**ANDREW JACKSON**	Democratic	647,286	56.0	178	57.6
		John Quincy Adams	National-Republican	508,064	44.0	83	

Year	Number of States	Candidates	Parties	Popular Vote	% of Popular Vote	Electoral Vote	% Voter Participation
1832	24	**ANDREW JACKSON**	Democratic	688,242	54.5	219	55.4
		Henry Clay	National-Republican	473,462	37.5	49	
		William Wirt	Anti-Masonic	101,051	8.0	7	
		John Floyd	Democratic			11	
1836	26	**MARTIN VAN BUREN**	Democratic	765,483	50.9	170	57.8
		William H. Harrison	Whig	739,795	49.1	73	
		Hugh L. White	Whig			26	
		Daniel Webster	Whig			14	
		W. P. Mangum	Whig			11	
1840	26	**WILLIAM H. HARRISON**	Whig	1,274,624	53.1	234	80.2
		Martin Van Buren	Democratic	1,127,781	46.9	60	
1844	26	**JAMES K. POLK**	Democratic	1,338,464	49.6	170	78.9
		Henry Clay	Whig	1,300,097	48.1	105	
		James G. Birney	Liberty	62,300	2.3		
1848	30	**ZACHARY TAYLOR**	Whig	1,360,967	47.4	163	72.7
		Lewis Cass	Democratic	1,222,342	42.5	127	
		Martin Van Buren	Free Soil	291,263	10.1		
1852	31	**FRANKLIN PIERCE**	Democratic	1,601,117	50.9	254	69.6
		Winfield Scott	Whig	1,385,453	44.1	42	
		John P. Hale	Free Soil	155,825	5.0		
1856	31	**JAMES BUCHANAN**	Democratic	1,832,955	45.3	174	78.9
		John C. Frémont	Republican	1,339,932	33.1	114	
		Millard Fillmore	American	871,731	21.6	8	

Year	Number of States	Candidates	Parties	Popular Vote	% of Popular Vote	Electoral Vote	% Voter Participation
1860	33	**ABRAHAM LINCOLN**	Republican	1,865,593	39.8	180	81.2
		Stephen A. Douglas	Democratic	1,382,713	29.5	12	
		John C. Breckinridge	Democratic	848,356	18.1	72	
		John Bell	Constitutional Union	592,906	12.6	39	
1864	36	**ABRAHAM LINCOLN**	Republican	2,206,938	55.0	212	73.8
		George B. McClellan	Democratic	1,803,787	45.0	21	
1868	37	**ULYSSES S. GRANT**	Republican	3,013,421	52.7	214	78.1
		Horatio Seymour	Democratic	2,706,829	47.3	80	
1872	37	**ULYSSES S. GRANT**	Republican	3,596,745	55.6	286	71.3
		Horace Greeley	Democratic	2,843,446	43.9	66	
1876	38	Rutherford B. Hayes	Republican	4,036,572	48.0	185	81.8
		Samuel J. Tilden	Democratic	4,284,020	51.0	184	
1880	38	**JAMES A. GARFIELD**	Republican	4,453,295	48.5	214	79.4
		Winfield S. Hancock	Democratic	4,414,082	48.1	155	
		James B. Weaver	Greenback-Labor	308,578	3.4		
1884	38	**GROVER CLEVELAND**	Democratic	4,879,507	48.5	219	77.5
		James G. Blaine	Republican	4,850,293	48.2	182	
		Benjamin F. Butler	Greenback-Labor	175,370	1.8		
		John P. St. John	Prohibition	150,369	1.5		
1888	38	**BENJAMIN HARRISON**	Republican	5,477,129	47.9	233	79.3
		Grover Cleveland	Democratic	5,537,857	48.6	168	
		Clinton B. Fisk	Prohibition	249,506	2.2		
		Anson J. Streeter	Union Labor	146,935	1.3		

Year	Number of States	Candidates	Parties	Popular Vote	% of Popular Vote	Electoral Vote	% Voter Participation
1892	44	GROVER CLEVELAND	Democratic	5,555,426	46.1	277	74.7
		Benjamin Harrison	Republican	5,182,690	43.0	145	
		James B. Weaver	People's	1,029,846	8.5	22	
		John Bidwell	Prohibition	264,133	2.2		
1896	45	WILLIAM McKINLEY	Republican	7,102,246	51.1	271	79.3
		William J. Bryan	Democratic	6,492,559	47.7	176	
1900	45	WILLIAM McKINLEY	Republican	7,218,491	51.7	292	73.2
		William J. Bryan	Democratic; Populist	6,356,734	45.5	155	
		John C. Wooley	Prohibition	208,914	1.5		
1904	45	THEODORE ROOSEVELT	Republican	7,628,461	57.4	336	65.2
		Alton B. Parker	Democratic	5,084,223	37.6	140	
		Eugene V. Debs	Socialist	402,283	3.0		
		Silas C. Swallow	Prohibition	258,536	1.9		
1908	46	WILLIAM H. TAFT	Republican	7,675,320	51.6	321	65.4
		William J. Bryan	Democratic	6,412,294	43.1	162	
		Eugene V. Debs	Socialist	420,793	2.8		
		Eugene W. Chafin	Prohibition	253,840	1.7		
1912	48	WOODROW WILSON	Democratic	6,296,547	41.9	435	58.8
		Theodore Roosevelt	Progressive	4,118,571	27.4	88	
		William H. Taft	Republican	3,486,720	23.2	8	
		Eugene V. Debs	Socialist	900,672	6.0		
		Eugene W. Chafin	Prohibition	206,275	1.4		

Year	States	Candidates	Parties	Popular Vote	% of Popular Vote	Electoral Vote	% Participation
1916	48	**WOODROW WILSON**	Democratic	9,127,695	49.4	277	61.6
		Charles E. Hughes	Republican	8,533,507	46.2	254	
		A. L. Benson	Socialist	585,113	3.2		
		J. Frank Hanly	Prohibition	220,506	1.2		
1920	48	**WARREN G. HARDING**	Republican	16,143,407	60.4	404	49.2
		James M. Cox	Democratic	9,130,328	34.2	127	
		Eugene V. Debs	Socialist	919,799	3.4		
		P. P. Christensen	Farmer-Labor	265,411	1.0		
1924	48	**CALVIN COOLIDGE**	Republican	15,718,211	54.0	382	48.9
		John W. Davis	Democratic	8,385,283	28.8	136	
		Robert M. La Follette	Progressive	4,831,289	16.6	13	
1928	48	**HERBERT C. HOOVER**	Republican	21,391,993	58.2	444	56.9
		Alfred E. Smith	Democratic	15,016,169	40.9	87	
1932	48	**FRANKLIN D. ROOSEVELT**	Democratic	22,809,638	57.4	472	56.9
		Herbert C. Hoover	Republican	15,758,901	39.7	59	
		Norman Thomas	Socialist	881,951	2.2		
1936	48	**FRANKLIN D. ROOSEVELT**	Democratic	27,752,869	60.8	523	61.0
		Alfred M. Landon	Republican	16,674,665	36.5	8	
		William Lemke	Union	882,479	1.9		
1940	48	**FRANKLIN D. ROOSEVELT**	Democratic	27,307,819	54.8	449	62.5
		Wendell L. Willkie	Republican	22,321,018	44.8	82	
1944	48	**FRANKLIN D. ROOSEVELT**	Democratic	25,606,585	53.5	432	55.9
		Thomas E. Dewey	Republican	22,014,745	46.0	99	

Year	Number of States	Candidates	Parties	Popular Vote	% of Popular Vote	Electoral Vote	% Voter Participation
1948	48	**HARRY S. TRUMAN**	Democratic	24,179,345	49.6	303	53.0
		Thomas E. Dewey	Republican	21,991,291	45.1	189	
		J. Strom Thurmond	States' Rights	1,176,125	2.4	39	
		Henry A. Wallace	Progressive	1,157,326	2.4		
1952	48	**DWIGHT D. EISENHOWER**	Republican	33,936,234	55.1	442	63.3
		Adlai E. Stevenson	Democratic	27,314,992	44.4	89	
1956	48	**DWIGHT D. EISENHOWER**	Republican	35,590,472	57.6	457	60.6
		Adlai E. Stevenson	Democratic	26,022,752	42.1	73	
1960	50	**JOHN F. KENNEDY**	Democratic	34,226,731	49.7	303	62.8
		Richard M. Nixon	Republican	34,108,157	49.5	219	
1964	50	**LYNDON B. JOHNSON**	Democratic	43,129,566	61.1	486	61.9
		Barry M. Goldwater	Republican	27,178,188	38.5	52	
1968	50	**RICHARD M. NIXON**	Republican	31,785,480	43.4	301	60.9
		Hubert H. Humphrey	Democratic	31,275,166	42.7	191	
		George C. Wallace	American Independent	9,906,473	13.5	46	
1972	50	**RICHARD M. NIXON**	Republican	47,169,911	60.7	520	55.2
		George S. McGovern	Democratic	29,170,383	37.5	17	
		John G. Schmitz	American	1,099,482	1.4		

Year	States	Candidates	Parties	Popular Vote	% Popular Vote	Electoral Vote	% Voter Participation
1976	50	**JIMMY CARTER**	Democratic	40,830,763	50.1	297	53.5
		Gerald R. Ford	Republican	39,147,793	48.0	240	
1980	50	**RONALD REAGAN**	Republican	43,901,812	50.7	489	52.6
		Jimmy Carter	Democratic	35,483,820	41.0	49	
		John B. Anderson	Independent	5,719,437	6.6		
		Ed Clark	Libertarian	921,188	1.1		
1984	50	**RONALD REAGAN**	Republican	54,451,521	58.8	525	53.1
		Walter F. Mondale	Democratic	37,565,334	40.6	13	
1988	50	**GEORGE H. W. BUSH**	Republican	47,917,341	53.4	426	50.1
		Michael Dukakis	Democratic	41,013,030	45.6	111	
1992	50	**BILL CLINTON**	Democratic	44,908,254	43.0	370	55.0
		George H. W. Bush	Republican	39,102,343	37.4	168	
		H. Ross Perot	Independent	19,741,065	18.9		
1996	50	**BILL CLINTON**	Democratic	47,401,185	49.0	379	49.0
		Bob Dole	Republican	39,197,469	41.0	159	
		H. Ross Perot	Independent	8,085,295	8.0		
2000	50	**GEORGE W. BUSH**	Republican	50,455,156	47.9	271	50.4
		Al Gore	Democrat	50,997,335	48.4	266	
		Ralph Nader	Green	2,882,897	2.7		
2004	50	**GEORGE W. BUSH**	Republican	62,040,610	50.7	286	60.7
		John F. Kerry	Democrat	59,028,444	48.3	251	
2008	50	**BARACK OBAMA**	Democrat	69,456,897	52.92%	365	63.0
		John McCain	Republican	59,934,814	45.66%	173	

Candidates receiving less than 1 percent of the popular vote have been omitted. Thus the percentage of popular vote given for any election year may not total 100 percent.

Before the passage of the Twelfth Amendment in 1804, the electoral college voted for two presidential candidates; the runner-up became vice president.

ADMISSION OF STATES

Order of Admission	State	Date of Admission	Order of Admission	State	Date of Admission
1	Delaware	December 7, 1787	26	Michigan	January 26, 1837
2	Pennsylvania	December 12, 1787	27	Florida	March 3, 1845
3	New Jersey	December 18, 1787	28	Texas	December 29, 1845
4	Georgia	January 2, 1788	29	Iowa	December 28, 1846
5	Connecticut	January 9, 1788	30	Wisconsin	May 29, 1848
6	Massachusetts	February 7, 1788	31	California	September 9, 1850
7	Maryland	April 28, 1788	32	Minnesota	May 11, 1858
8	South Carolina	May 23, 1788	33	Oregon	February 14, 1859
9	New Hampshire	June 21, 1788	34	Kansas	January 29, 1861
10	Virginia	June 25, 1788	35	West Virginia	June 30, 1863
11	New York	July 26, 1788	36	Nevada	October 31, 1864
12	North Carolina	November 21, 1789	37	Nebraska	March 1, 1867
13	Rhode Island	May 29, 1790	38	Colorado	August 1, 1876
14	Vermont	March 4, 1791	39	North Dakota	November 2, 1889
15	Kentucky	June 1, 1792	40	South Dakota	November 2, 1889
16	Tennessee	June 1, 1796	41	Montana	November 8, 1889
17	Ohio	March 1, 1803	42	Washington	November 11, 1889
18	Louisiana	April 30, 1812	43	Idaho	July 3, 1890
19	Indiana	December 11, 1816	44	Wyoming	July 10, 1890
20	Mississippi	December 10, 1817	45	Utah	January 4, 1896
21	Illinois	December 3, 1818	46	Oklahoma	November 16, 1907
22	Alabama	December 14, 1819	47	New Mexico	January 6, 1912
23	Maine	March 15, 1820	48	Arizona	February 14, 1912
24	Missouri	August 10, 1821	49	Alaska	January 3, 1959
25	Arkansas	June 15, 1836	50	Hawaii	August 21, 1959

POPULATION OF THE UNITED STATES

Year	Number of States	Population	% Increase	Population per Square Mile
1790	13	3,929,214		4.5
1800	16	5,308,483	35.1	6.1
1810	17	7,239,881	36.4	4.3
1820	23	9,638,453	33.1	5.5
1830	24	12,866,020	33.5	7.4
1840	26	17,069,453	32.7	9.8
1850	31	23,191,876	35.9	7.9
1860	33	31,443,321	35.6	10.6
1870	37	39,818,449	26.6	13.4
1880	38	50,155,783	26.0	16.9
1890	44	62,947,714	25.5	21.1
1900	45	75,994,575	20.7	25.6
1910	46	91,972,266	21.0	31.0
1920	48	105,710,620	14.9	35.6
1930	48	122,775,046	16.1	41.2
1940	48	131,669,275	7.2	44.2
1950	48	150,697,361	14.5	50.7
1960	50	179,323,175	19.0	50.6
1970	50	203,235,298	13.3	57.5
1980	50	226,504,825	11.4	64.0
1985	50	237,839,000	5.0	67.2
1990	50	250,122,000	5.2	70.6
1995	50	263,411,707	5.3	74.4
2000	50	281,421,906	6.8	77.0
2005	50	296,410,404	5.3	77.9
2010	50	308,745,538	9.7	87.4

IMMIGRATION TO THE UNITED STATES, FISCAL YEARS 1820–2011

Year	Number	Year	Number	Year	Number	Year	Number
1820–1989	55,457,531	1871–80	2,812,191	1921–30	4,107,209	1971–80	4,493,314
1820	8,385	1871	321,350	1921	805,228	1971	370,478
1821–30	143,439	1872	404,806	1922	309,556	1972	384,685
1821	9,127	1873	459,803	1923	522,919	1973	400,063
1822	6,911	1874	313,339	1924	706,896	1974	394,861
1823	6,354	1875	227,498	1925	294,314	1975	386,914
1824	7,912	1876	169,986	1926	304,488	1976	398,613
1825	10,199	1877	141,857	1927	335,175		103,676
1826	10,837	1878	138,469	1928	307,255	1977	462,315
1827	18,875	1879	177,826	1929	279,678	1978	601,442
1828	27,382	1880	457,257	1930	241,700	1979	460,348
1829	22,520	1881–90	5,246,613	1931–40	528,431	1980	530,639
1830	23,322	1881	669,431	1931	97,139	1981–90	7,338,062
1831–40	599,125	1882	788,992	1932	35,576	1981	596,600
1831	22,633	1883	603,322	1933	23,068	1982	594,131
1832	60,482	1884	518,592	1934	29,470	1983	559,763
1833	58,640	1885	395,346	1935	34,956	1984	543,903
1834	65,365	1886	334,203	1936	36,329	1985	570,009
1835	45,374	1887	490,109	1937	50,244	1986	601,708
1836	76,242	1888	546,889	1938	67,895	1987	601,516
1837	79,340	1889	444,427	1939	82,998	1988	643,025
1838	38,914	1890	455,302	1940	70,756	1989	1,090,924
1839	68,069	1891–1900	3,687,564	1941–50	1,035,039	1990	1,536,483
1840	84,066	1891	560,319	1941	51,776	1991–2000	9,090,857
1841–50	1,713,251	1892	579,663	1942	28,781	1991	1,827,167
1841	80,289	1893	439,730	1943	23,725	1992	973,977
1842	104,565	1894	285,631	1944	28,551	1993	904,292
		1895	258,536	1945	38,119	1994	804,416
		1896	343,267	1946	108,721		

Year	Number	Year	Number	Year	Number	Year	Number
1843	52,496	1897	230,832	1947	147,292	1995	720,461
1844	78,615	1898	229,299	1948	170,570	1996	915,900
1845	114,371	1899	311,715	1949	188,317	1997	798,378
1846	154,416	1900	448,572	1950	249,187	1998	660,477
1847	234,968					1999	644,787
1848	226,527	**1901–10**	**8,795,386**	**1951–60**	**2,515,479**	2000	841,002
1849	297,024	1901	487,918	1951	205,717	**2001–10**	**10,501,053**
1850	369,980	1902	648,743	1952	265,520	2001	1,058,902
		1903	857,046	1953	170,434	2002	1,059,356
1851–60	**2,598,214**	1904	812,870	1954	208,177	2003	705,827
1851	379,466	1905	1,026,499	1955	237,790	2004	957,883
1852	371,603	1906	1,100,735	1956	321,625	2005	1,122,373
1853	368,645	1907	1,285,349	1957	326,867	2006	1,266,129
1854	427,833	1908	782,870	1958	253,265	2007	1,052,415
1855	200,877	1909	751,786	1959	260,686	2008	1,107,126
1856	200,436	1910	1,041,570	1960	265,398	2009	1,130,818
1857	251,306					2010	1,042,625
1858	123,126	**1911–20**	**5,735,811**	**1961–70**	**3,321,677**	2011	1,062,040
1859	121,282	1911	878,587	1961	271,344		
1860	153,640	1912	838,172	1962	283,763		
		1913	1,197,892	1963	306,260		
1861–70	**2,314,824**	1914	1,218,480	1964	292,248		
1861	91,918	1915	326,700	1965	296,697		
1862	91,985	1916	298,826	1966	323,040		
1863	176,282	1917	295,403	1967	361,972		
1864	193,418	1918	110,618	1968	454,448		
1865	248,120	1919	141,132	1969	358,579		
1866	318,568	1920	430,001	1970	373,326		
1867	315,722						
1868	138,840						
1869	352,768						
1870	387,203						

Source: U.S. Department of Homeland Security.

IMMIGRATION BY REGION AND SELECTED COUNTRY OF LAST RESIDENCE, FISCAL YEARS 1820–2011

Region and country of last residence	1820 to 1829	1830 to 1839	1840 to 1849	1850 to 1859	1860 to 1869	1870 to 1879	1880 to 1889	1890 to 1899
Total	128,502	538,381	1,427,337	2,814,554	2,081,261	2,742,137	5,248,568	3,694,294
Europe	99,272	422,771	1,369,259	2,619,680	1,877,726	2,251,878	4,638,677	3,576,411
Austria-Hungary	—	—	—	—	3,375	60,127	314,787	534,059
Austria	—	—	—	—	2,700	54,529	204,805	268,218
Hungary	—	—	—	—	483	5,598	109,982	203,350
Belgium	28	20	3,996	5,765	5,785	6,991	18,738	19,642
Bulgaria	—	—	—	—	—	—	—	52
Czechoslovakia	—	—	—	—	—	—	—	—
Denmark	173	927	671	3,227	13,553	29,278	85,342	56,671
Finland	—	—	—	—	—	—	—	—
France	7,694	39,330	75,300	81,778	35,938	71,901	48,193	35,616
Germany	5,753	124,726	385,434	976,072	723,734	751,769	1,445,181	579,072
Greece	17	49	17	32	51	209	1,807	12,732
Ireland	51,617	170,672	656,145	1,029,486	427,419	422,264	674,061	405,710
Italy	430	2,225	1,476	8,643	9,853	46,296	267,660	603,761
Netherlands	1,105	1,377	7,624	11,122	8,387	14,267	52,715	29,349
Norway-Sweden	91	1,149	12,389	22,202	82,937	178,823	586,441	334,058
Norway	—	—	—	—	16,068	88,644	185,111	96,810
Sweden	—	—	—	—	24,224	90,179	401,330	237,248
Poland	19	366	105	1,087	1,886	11,016	42,910	107,793
Portugal	177	820	196	1,299	2,083	13,971	15,186	25,874
Romania	—	—	—	—	—	—	5,842	6,808
Russia	86	280	520	423	1,670	35,177	182,698	450,101
Spain	2,595	2,010	1,916	8,795	6,966	5,540	3,995	9,189
Switzerland	3,148	4,430	4,819	24,423	21,124	25,212	81,151	37,020
United Kingdom	26,336	74,350	218,572	445,322	532,956	578,447	810,900	328,759
Yugoslavia	—	—	—	—	—	—	—	—
Other Europe	3	40	79	4	9	590	1,070	145

Asia	34	55	121	36,080	54,408	134,128	71,151	61,285
China	3	8	32	35,933	54,028	133,139	65,797	15,268
Hong Kong	9	38	33	42	50	166	247	102
India	—	—	—	—	—	—	—	102
Iran	—	—	—	—	—	—	—	—
Israel	—	—	—	—	—	—	—	—
Japan	—	—	—	—	138	193	1,583	13,998
Jordan	—	—	—	—	—	—	—	—
Korea	—	—	—	—	—	—	—	—
Philippines	—	—	—	—	—	—	—	—
Syria	—	—	—	—	—	—	—	—
Taiwan	—	—	—	—	—	—	—	—
Turkey	19	8	45	94	129	382	2,478	27,510
Vietnam	—	—	—	—	—	—	—	—
Other Asia	3	1	11	11	63	248	1,046	4,407
America	9,655	31,905	50,516	84,145	130,292	345,010	524,826	37,350
Canada and Newfoundland	2,297	11,875	34,285	64,171	117,978	324,310	492,865	3,098
Mexico	3,835	7,187	3,069	3,446	1,957	5,133	2,405	734
Caribbean	3,061	11,792	11,803	12,447	8,751	14,285	27,323	31,480
Cuba	—	—	—	—	—	—	—	—
Dominican Republic	—	—	—	—	—	—	—	—
Haiti	—	—	—	—	—	—	—	—
Jamaica	—	—	—	—	—	—	—	—
Other Caribbean	3,061	11,792	11,803	12,447	8,751	14,285	27,323	31,480
Central America	57	94	297	512	70	173	279	649
Belize	—	—	—	—	—	—	—	—
Costa Rica	—	—	—	—	—	—	—	—
El Salvador	—	—	—	—	—	—	—	—
Guatemala	—	—	—	—	—	—	—	—
Honduras	—	—	—	—	—	—	—	—
Nicaragua	—	—	—	—	—	—	—	—
Panama	—	—	—	—	—	—	—	—
Other Central America	57	94	297	512	70	173	279	649
South America	405	957	1,062	3,569	1,536	1,109	1,954	1,389
Argentina	—	—	—	—	—	—	—	—
Bolivia	—	—	—	—	—	—	—	—

Region and country of last residence	1820 to 1829	1830 to 1839	1840 to 1849	1850 to 1859	1860 to 1869	1870 to 1879	1880 to 1889	1890 to 1899
Brazil	—	—	—	—	—	—	—	—
Chile	—	—	—	—	—	—	—	—
Colombia	—	—	—	—	—	—	—	—
Ecuador	—	—	—	—	—	—	—	—
Guyana	—	—	—	—	—	—	—	—
Paraguay	—	—	—	—	—	—	—	—
Peru	—	—	—	—	—	—	—	—
Suriname	—	—	—	—	—	—	—	—
Uruguay	—	—	—	—	—	—	—	—
Venezuela	—	—	—	—	—	—	—	—
Other South America	405	957	1,062	3,569	1,536	1,109	1,954	1,389
Other America	—	—	—	—	—	—	—	—
Africa	15	50	61	84	407	371	763	432
Egypt	—	—	—	—	4	29	145	51
Ethiopia	—	—	—	—	—	—	—	—
Liberia	1	8	5	7	43	52	21	9
Morocco	—	—	—	—	—	—	—	—
South Africa	—	—	—	—	35	48	23	9
Other Africa	14	42	56	77	325	242	574	363
Oceania	3	7	14	166	187	9,996	12,361	4,704
Australia	2	1	2	15	—	8,930	7,250	3,098
New Zealand	—	—	—	—	—	39	21	12
Other Oceania	1	6	12	151	187	1,027	5,090	1,594
Not Specified	19,523	83,593	7,366	74,399	18,241	754	790	14,112

Total	8,202,388	6,347,380	4,295,510	699,375	856,608	2,499,268	3,213,749	6,244,379
Europe	7,572,569	4,985,411	2,560,340	444,399	472,524	1,404,973	1,133,443	668,866
Austria-Hungary	2,001,376	1,154,727	60,891	12,531	13,574	113,015	27,590	20,437
Austria	532,416	589,174	31,392	5,307	8,393	81,354	17,571	15,374
Hungary	685,567	565,553	29,499	7,224	5,181	31,661	10,019	5,063
Belgium	37,429	32,574	21,511	4,013	12,473	18,885	9,647	7,028
Bulgaria	34,651	27,180	2,824	1,062	449	97	598	1,124
Czechoslovakia	—	—	101,182	17,757	8,475	1,624	2,758	5,678
Denmark	61,227	45,830	34,406	3,470	4,549	10,918	9,797	4,847
Finland	—	—	16,922	2,438	2,230	4,923	4,310	2,569
France	67,735	60,335	54,842	13,761	36,954	50,113	46,975	32,066
Germany	328,722	174,227	386,634	119,107	119,506	576,905	209,616	85,752
Greece	145,402	198,108	60,774	10,599	8,605	45,153	74,173	37,729
Ireland	344,940	166,445	202,854	28,195	15,701	47,189	37,788	22,210
Italy	1,930,475	1,229,916	528,133	85,053	50,509	184,576	200,111	55,562
Netherlands	42,463	46,065	29,397	7,791	13,877	46,703	37,918	11,234
Norway-Sweden	426,981	192,445	170,329	13,452	17,326	44,224	36,150	13,941
Norway	182,542	79,488	70,327	6,901	8,326	22,806	17,371	3,835
Sweden	244,439	112,957	100,002	6,551	9,000	21,418	18,779	10,106
Poland	—	—	223,316	25,555	7,577	6,465	55,742	63,483
Portugal	65,154	82,489	44,829	3,518	6,765	13,928	70,568	42,685
Romania	57,322	13,566	67,810	5,264	1,254	914	2,339	24,753
Russia	1,501,301	1,106,998	61,604	2,463	605	453	2,329	33,311
Spain	24,818	53,262	47,109	3,669	2,774	6,880	40,793	22,783
Switzerland	32,541	22,839	31,772	5,990	9,904	17,577	19,193	8,316
United Kingdom	469,518	371,878	341,552	61,813	131,794	195,709	220,213	153,644
Yugoslavia	—	—	49,215	6,920	2,039	6,966	17,990	16,267
Other Europe	514	6,527	22,434	9,978	5,584	11,756	6,845	3,447
Asia	299,836	269,736	126,740	19,231	34,532	135,844	358,605	2,391,356
China	19,884	20,916	30,648	5,874	16,072	8,836	14,060	170,897
Hong Kong	—	—	—	—	—	13,781	67,047	112,132
India	3,026	3,478	2,076	554	1,692	1,850	18,638	231,649
Iran	—	—	208	198	1,144	3,195	9,059	98,141
Israel	—	—	—	—	98	21,376	30,911	43,669

Region and country of last residence	1900 to 1909	1910 to 1919	1920 to 1929	1930 to 1939	1940 to 1949	1950 to 1959	1960 to 1969	1980 to 1989
Japan	139,712	77,125	42,057	2,683	1,557	40,651	40,956	44,150
Jordan	—	—	—	—	—	4,899	9,230	28,928
Korea	—	—	—	—	83	4,845	27,048	322,708
Philippines	—	—	5,307	391	4,099	17,245	70,660	502,056
Syria	—	—		2,188	1,179	1,091	2,432	14,534
Taiwan	—	—	—	—	—	721	15,657	119,051
Turkey	127,999	160,717	40,450	1,327	754	2,980	9,464	19,208
Vietnam	—	—	—	—	—	290	2,949	200,632
Other Asia	9,215	7,500	5,994	6,016	7,854	14,084	40,494	483,601
America	277,809	1,070,539	1,591,278	230,319	328,435	921,610	1,674,172	2,695,329
Canada and Newfoundland	123,067	708,715	949,286	162,703	160,911	353,169	433,128	156,313
Mexico	31,188	185,334	498,945	32,709	56,158	273,847	441,824	1,009,586
Caribbean	100,960	120,860	83,482	18,052	46,194	115,661	427,235	790,109
Cuba	—	—	12,769	10,641	25,976	73,221	202,030	132,552
Dominican Republic	—	—	—	1,026	4,802	10,219	83,552	221,552
Haiti	—	—	—	156	823	3,787	28,992	121,406
Jamaica	—	—	—	—	—	7,397	62,218	193,874
Other Caribbean	100,960	120,860	70,713	6,229	14,593	21,037	50,443	120,725
Central America	7,341	15,692	16,511	6,840	20,135	40,201	98,560	339,376
Belize	77	40	285	193	433	1,133	4,185	14,964
Costa Rica	—	—	—	431	1,965	4,044	17,975	25,017
El Salvador	—	—	—	597	4,885	5,094	14,405	137,418
Guatemala	—	—	—	423	1,303	4,197	14,357	58,847
Honduras	—	—	—	679	1,874	5,320	15,078	39,071
Nicaragua	—	—	—	405	4,393	7,812	10,383	31,102
Panama	—	—	—	1,452	5,282	12,601	22,177	32,957
Other Central America	7,264	15,652	16,226	2,660	—	—	—	—

South America	15,253	39,938	43,025	9,990	19,662	78,418	250,754	399,862
Argentina	—	—	—	1,067	3,108	16,346	49,384	23,442
Bolivia	—	—	—	50	893	2,759	6,205	9,798
Brazil	—	—	4,627	1,468	3,653	11,547	29,238	22,944
Chile	—	—	—	347	1,320	4,669	12,384	19,749
Colombia	—	—	—	1,027	3,454	15,567	68,371	105,494
Ecuador	—	—	—	244	2,207	8,574	34,107	48,015
Guyana	—	—	—	131	596	1,131	4,546	85,886
Paraguay	—	—	—	33	85	576	1,249	3,518
Peru	—	—	—	321	1,273	5,980	19,783	49,958
Suriname	—	—	—	25	130	299	612	1,357
Uruguay	—	—	—	112	754	1,026	4,089	7,235
Venezuela	—	—	—	1,155	2,182	9,927	20,758	22,405
Other South America	15,253	39,938	38,398	4,010	7	17	28	61
	—	—	29	25	25,375	60,314	22,671	83
Africa	6,326	8,867	6,362	2,120	6,720	13,016	23,780	141,990
Egypt	—	—	1,063	781	1,613	1,996	5,581	26,744
Ethiopia	—	—	—	10	28	302	804	12,927
Liberia	—	—	—	35	37	289	841	6,420
Morocco	—	—	—	73	879	2,703	2,880	3,471
South Africa	6,326	8,867	5,299	312	1,022	2,278	4,360	15,505
Other Africa	—	—	—	909	3,141	5,448	9,314	76,923
Oceania	12,355	12,339	9,860	3,306	14,262	11,353	23,630	41,432
Australia	11,191	11,280	8,404	2,260	11,201	8,275	14,986	16,901
New Zealand	—	—	935	790	2,351	1,799	3,775	6,129
Other Oceania	1,164	1,059	521	256	710	1,279	4,869	18,402
Not Specified	33,493	488	930	—	135	12,472	119	305,406

Region and country of last residence	1990 to 1999	2000 to 2009	2010	2011
Total	9,775,398	10,299,430	1,042,625	1,062,040
Europe	1,348,612	1,349,609	95,429	90,712
Austria-Hungary	27,529	33,929	4,325	4,703
Austria	18,234	21,151	3,319	3,654
Hungary	9,295	12,778	1,006	1,049
Belgium	7,077	8,157	732	700
Bulgaria	16,948	40,003	2,465	2,549
Czechoslovakia	8,970	18,691	1,510	1,374
Denmark	6,189	6,049	545	473
Finland	3,970	3,970	414	398
France	35,945	45,637	4,339	3,967
Germany	92,207	122,373	7,929	7,072
Greece	25,403	16,841	966	1,196
Ireland	65,384	15,642	1,610	1,533
Italy	75,992	28,329	2,956	2,670
Netherlands	13,345	17,351	1,520	1,258
Norway-Sweden	17,825	19,382	1,662	1,530
Norway	5,211	4,599	363	405
Sweden	12,614	14,783	1,299	1,125
Poland	172,249	117,921	7,391	6,634
Portugal	25,497	11,479	759	878
Romania	48,136	52,154	3,735	3,679
Russia	433,427	167,152	7,502	8,548
Spain	18,443	17,695	2,040	2,319
Switzerland	11,768	12,173	868	861
United Kingdom	156,182	171,979	14,781	13,443
Yugoslavia	57,039	131,831	4,772	4,611
Other Europe	29,087	290,871	22,608	20,316

Asia	2,859,899	3,470,835	410,209	438,580
China	342,058	591,711	67,634	83,603
Hong Kong	116,894	57,583	3,263	3,149
India	352,528	590,464	66,185	66,331
Iran	76,899	76,755	9,078	9,015
Israel	41,340	54,081	5,172	4,389
Japan	66,582	84,552	7,100	6,751
Jordan	42,755	53,350	9,327	8,211
Korea	179,770	209,758	22,022	22,748
Philippines	534,338	545,463	56,399	55,251
Syria	22,906	30,807	7,424	7,983
Taiwan	132,647	92,657	6,785	6,206
Turkey	38,687	48,394	7,435	9,040
Vietnam	275,379	289,616	30,065	33,486
Other Asia	637,116	745,444	112,320	122,417
America	5,137,743	4,441,529	426,981	423,277
Canada and Newfoundland	194,788	236,349	19,491	19,506
Mexico	2,757,418	1,704,166	138,717	142,823
Caribbean	1,004,687	1,053,357	139,389	133,012
Cuba	159,037	271,742	33,372	36,261
Dominican Republic	359,818	291,492	53,890	46,036
Haiti	177,446	203,827	22,336	21,802
Jamaica	177,143	172,523	19,439	19,298
Other Caribbean	181,243	113,773	10,352	9,615
Central America	610,189	591,130	43,597	43,249
Belize	12,600	9,682	997	933
Costa Rica	17,054	21,571	2,306	2,230
El Salvador	273,017	251,237	18,547	18,477
Guatemala	126,043	156,992	10,263	10,795
Honduras	72,880	63,513	6,381	6,053

Region and country of last residence	1990 to 1999	2000 to 2009	2010	2011
Nicaragua	80,446	70,015	3,476	3,314
Panama	28,149	18,120	1,627	1,447
Other Central America	—			—
South America	570,624	856,508	85,783	84,687
Argentina	30,065	47,955	4,312	4,335
Bolivia	18,111	21,921	2,211	2,113
Brazil	50,744	115,404	12,057	11,643
Chile	18,200	19,792	1,940	1,854
Colombia	137,985	236,570	21,861	22,130
Ecuador	81,358	107,977	11,463	11,068
Guyana	74,407	70,373	6,441	6,288
Paraguay	6,082	4,623	449	501
Peru	110,117	137,614	14,063	13,836
Suriname	2,285	2,363	202	167
Uruguay	6,062	9,827	1,286	1,521
Venezuela	35,180	82,087	9,497	9,229
Other South America	28	2	1	2
Other America	37	19	4	—
Africa	346,416	759,734	98,246	97,429
Egypt	44,604	81,564	9,822	9,096
Ethiopia	40,097	87,207	13,853	13,985
Liberia	13,587	23,316	2,924	3,117
Morocco	15,768	40,844	4,847	4,249
South Africa	21,964	32,221	2,705	2,754
Other Africa	210,396	494,582	64,095	64,228
Oceania	56,800	65,793	5,946	5,825
Australia	24,288	32,728	3,077	3,062
New Zealand	8,600	12,495	1,046	1,006
Other Oceania	23,912	20,570	1,823	1,757
Not Specified	25,928	211,930	5,814	6,217

— Represents zero or not available.

PRESIDENTS, VICE PRESIDENTS, AND SECRETARIES OF STATE

President	Vice President	Secretary of State
1. George Washington, Federalist 1789	John Adams, Federalist 1789	Thomas Jefferson 1789 Edmund Randolph 1794 Timothy Pickering 1795
2. John Adams, Federalist 1797	Thomas Jefferson, Dem.-Rep. 1797	Timothy Pickering 1797 John Marshall 1800
3. Thomas Jefferson, Dem.-Rep. 1801	Aaron Burr, Dem.-Rep. 1801 George Clinton, Dem.-Rep. 1805	James Madison 1801
4. James Madison, Dem.-Rep. 1809	George Clinton, Dem.-Rep. 1809 Elbridge Gerry, Dem.-Rep. 1813	Robert Smith 1809 James Monroe 1811
5. James Monroe, Dem.-Rep. 1817	Daniel D. Tompkins, Dem.-Rep. 1817	John Q. Adams 1817
6. John Quincy Adams, Dem.-Rep. 1825	John C. Calhoun, Dem.-Rep. 1825	Henry Clay 1825
7. Andrew Jackson, Democratic 1829	John C. Calhoun, Democratic 1829 Martin Van Buren, Democratic 1833	Martin Van Buren 1829 Edward Livingston 1831 Louis McLane 1833 John Forsyth 1834
8. Martin Van Buren, Democratic 1837	Richard M. Johnson, Democratic 1837	John Forsyth 1837
9. William H. Harrison, Whig 1841	John Tyler, Whig 1841	Daniel Webster 1841

President	Vice President	Secretary of State
10. John Tyler, Whig and Democratic 1841	None	Daniel Webster 1841 Hugh S. Legaré 1843 Abel P. Upshur 1843 John C. Calhoun 1844
11. James K. Polk, Democratic 1845	George M. Dallas, Democratic 1845	James Buchanan 1845
12. Zachary Taylor, Whig 1849	Millard Fillmore, Whig 1848	John M. Clayton 1849
13. Millard Fillmore, Whig 1850	None	Daniel Webster 1850 Edward Everett 1852
14. Franklin Pierce, Democratic 1853	William R. King, Democratic 1853	William L. Marcy 1853
15. James Buchanan, Democratic 1857	John C. Breckinridge, Democratic 1857	Lewis Cass 1857 Jeremiah S. Black 1860
16. Abraham Lincoln, Republican 1861	Hannibal Hamlin, Republican 1861 Andrew Johnson, Unionist 1865	William H. Seward 1861
17. Andrew Johnson, Unionist 1865	None	William H. Seward 1865
18. Ulysses S. Grant, Republican 1869	Schuyler Colfax, Republican 1869 Henry Wilson, Republican 1873	Elihu B. Washburne 1869 Hamilton Fish 1869
19. Rutherford B. Hayes, Republican 1877	William A. Wheeler, Republican 1877	William M. Evarts 1877

	President	Vice President	Secretary of State
20.	James A. Garfield, Republican 1881	Chester A. Arthur, Republican 1881	James G. Blaine 1881
21.	Chester A. Arthur, Republican 1881	None	Frederick T. Frelinghuysen 1881
22.	Grover Cleveland, Democratic 1885	Thomas A. Hendricks, Democratic 1885	Thomas F. Bayard 1885
23.	Benjamin Harrison, Republican 1889	Levi P. Morton, Republican 1889	James G. Blaine 1889 John W. Foster 1892
24.	Grover Cleveland, Democratic 1893	Adlai E. Stevenson, Democratic 1893	Walter Q. Gresham 1893 Richard Olney 1895
25.	William McKinley, Republican 1897	Garret A. Hobart, Republican 1897 Theodore Roosevelt, Republican 1901	John Sherman 1897 William R. Day 1898 John Hay 1898
26.	Theodore Roosevelt, Republican 1901	Charles Fairbanks, Republican 1905	John Hay 1901 Elihu Root 1905 Robert Bacon 1909
27.	William H. Taft, Republican 1909	James S. Sherman, Republican 1909	Philander C. Knox 1909
28.	Woodrow Wilson, Democratic 1913	Thomas R. Marshall, Democratic 1913	William J. Bryan 1913 Robert Lansing 1915 Bainbridge Colby 1920
29.	Warren G. Harding, Republican 1921	Calvin Coolidge, Republican 1921	Charles E. Hughes 1921
30.	Calvin Coolidge, Republican 1923	Charles G. Dawes, Republican 1925	Charles E. Hughes 1923 Frank B. Kellogg 1925

	President	Vice President	Secretary of State
31.	Herbert Hoover, Republican 1929	Charles Curtis, Republican 1929	Henry L. Stimson 1929
32.	Franklin D. Roosevelt, Democratic 1933	John Nance Garner, Democratic 1933 Henry A. Wallace, Democratic 1941 Harry S. Truman, Democratic 1945	Cordell Hull 1933 Edward R. Stettinius, Jr. 1944
33.	Harry S. Truman, Democratic 1945	Alben W. Barkley, Democratic 1949	Edward R. Stettinius, Jr. 1945 James F. Byrnes 1945 George C. Marshall 1947 Dean G. Acheson 1949
34.	Dwight D. Eisenhower, Republican 1953	Richard M. Nixon, Republican 1953	John F. Dulles 1953 Christian A. Herter 1959
35.	John F. Kennedy, Democratic 1961	Lyndon B. Johnson, Democratic 1961	Dean Rusk 1961
36.	Lyndon B. Johnson, Democratic 1963	Hubert H. Humphrey, Democratic 1965	Dean Rusk 1963
37.	Richard M. Nixon, Republican 1969	Spiro T. Agnew, Republican 1969 Gerald R. Ford, Republican 1973	William P. Rogers 1969 Henry Kissinger 1973
38.	Gerald R. Ford, Republican 1974	Nelson Rockefeller, Republican 1974	Henry Kissinger 1974
39.	Jimmy Carter, Democratic 1977	Walter Mondale, Democratic 1977	Cyrus Vance 1977 Edmund Muskie 1980

	President	Vice President	Secretary of State
40.	Ronald Reagan, Republican 1981	George H. W. Bush, Republican 1981	Alexander Haig 1981 George Schultz 1982
41.	George H. W. Bush, Republican 1989	J. Danforth Quayle, Republican 1989	James A. Baker 1989 Lawrence Eagleburger 1992
42.	William J. Clinton, Democratic 1993	Albert Gore, Jr., Democratic 1993	Warren Christopher 1993 Madeleine Albright 1997
43.	George W. Bush, Republican 2001	Richard B. Cheney, Republican 2001	Colin L. Powell 2001 Condoleezza Rice 2005
44.	Barack Obama, Democratic 2009	Joseph R. Biden, Democratic 2009	Hillary Rodham Clinton 2009

FURTHER READINGS

CHAPTER 1

A fascinating study of pre-Columbian migration is Brian M. Fagan's *The Great Journey: The Peopling of Ancient America*, rev. ed. (2004). Alice B. Kehoe's *North American Indians: A Comprehensive Account*, 2nd ed. (1992), provides an encyclopedic treatment of Native Americans. See also Charles Mann's *1491: New Revelations of the Americas before Columbus* (2005) and *1493: Uncovering the New World that Columbus Created* (2011), and Daniel K. Richter, *Before the Revolution: America's Ancient Pasts* (2011). On North America's largest Native American city, see Timothy R. Pauketat, *Cahokia* (2010).

The conflict between Native Americans and Europeans is treated well in James Axtell's *The Invasion Within: The Contest of Cultures in Colonial North America* (1986) and *Beyond 1492: Encounters in Colonial North America* (1992). Colin G. Calloway's *New Worlds for All: Indians, Europeans, and the Remaking of Early America* (1997) explores the ecological effects of European settlement.

The voyages of Columbus are surveyed in William D. Phillips Jr. and Carla Rahn Phillips's *The Worlds of Christopher Columbus* (1992). For sweeping overviews of Spain's creation of a global empire, see Henry Kamen's *Empire: How Spain Became a World Power, 1492–1763* (2003) and Hugh Thomas's *Rivers of Gold: The Rise of the Spanish Empire, from Columbus to Magellan* (2004). David J. Weber examines Spanish colonization in *The Spanish Frontier in North America* (1992). For the French experience, see William J. Eccles's *France in America*, rev. ed. (1990). For an insightful comparison of Spanish and English modes of settlement, see J. H. Elliott, *Empires of the Atlantic World: Britain and Spain in America, 1492–1830* (2006).

CHAPTER 2

Two excellent surveys of early American history are Peter C. Hoffer's *The Brave New World: A History of Early America*, 2nd ed. (2006), and William R. Polk's *The Birth of America: From before Columbus to the Revolution* (2006).

Bernard Bailyn's *Voyagers to the West: A Passage in the Peopling of America on the Eve of the Revolution* (1986) provides a comprehensive view of migration to the New World. Jack P. Greene offers a brilliant synthesis of British colonization in *Pursuits of Happiness: The Social Development of Early Modern British Colonies and the Formation of American Culture* (1988). The best overview of the colonization of North America is Alan Taylor's *American Colonies: The Settling of North America* (2001). On the interactions among Indian, European, and

African cultures, see Gary B. Nash's *Red, White, and Black: The Peoples of Early North America*, 5th ed. (2005). See Daniel K. Richter's *The Ordeal of the Longhouse: The Peoples of the Iroquois League in the Era of European Colonization* (1992) and Daniel P. Barr's *Unconquered: The Iroquois League at War in Colonial America* (2006) for a history of the Iroquois Confederacy. A splendid overview of Indian infighting is Peter Silver, *Our Savage Neighbors: How Indian War Transformed* (2008).

Andrew Delbanco's *The Puritan Ordeal* (1989) is a powerful study of the tensions inherent in the Puritan outlook. For information regarding the Puritan settlement of New England, see Virginia DeJohn Anderson's *New England's Generation: The Great Migration and the Formation of Society and Culture in the Seventeenth Century* (1991). The best biography of John Winthrop is Francis J. Bremer's *John Winthrop: America's Forgotten Founding Father* (2003).

The pattern of settlement in the middle colonies is illuminated in Barry Levy's *Quakers and the American Family: British Settlement in the Delaware Valley* (1988). On the early history of New York, see Russell Shorto's *The Island at the Center of the World: The Epic Story of Dutch Manhattan and the Forgotten Colony That Shaped America* (2004). Settlement of the areas along the Atlantic in the South is traced in James Horn's *Adapting to a New World: English Society in the Seventeenth-Century Chesapeake* (1994). On shifting political life in England, see Steve Pincus, *1688: The First Modern Revolution* (2009). For a study of race and the settlement of South Carolina, see Peter H. Wood's *Black Majority: Negroes in Colonial South Carolina from 1670 through the Stono Rebellion* (1974). A brilliant book on relations between the Catawba Indians and their black and white neighbors is James H. Merrell's *The Indians' New World: Catawbas and Their Neighbors from European Contact through the Era of Removal* (1989). On the flourishing trade in captive Indians, see Alan Gallay's *The Indian Slave Trade: The Rise of the English Empire in the American South, 1670–1717* (2002). On the Yamasee War, see Steven J. Oatis's *A Colonial Complex: South Carolina's Frontiers in the Era of the Yamasee War, 1680–1730* (2004).

CHAPTER 3

The diversity of colonial societies may be seen in David Hackett Fischer's *Albion's Seed: Four British Folkways in America* (1989). On the economic development of New England, see Christine Leigh Heyrman's *Commerce and Culture: The Maritime Communities of Colonial Massachusetts, 1690–1750* (1984) and Stephen Innes's *Creating the Commonwealth: The Economic Culture of Puritan New England* (1995). John Frederick Martin's *Profits in the Wilderness: Entrepreneurship and the Founding of New England Towns in the Seventeenth Century* (1991) indicates that economic concerns rather than spiritual motives were driving forces in many New England towns. For a fascinating account of the impact of livestock on colonial history, see Virginia DeJohn Anderson's *Creatures of Empire: How Domestic Animals Transformed Early America* (2004).

Paul Boyer and Stephen Nissenbaum's *Salem Possessed: The Social Origins of Witchcraft* (1974) connects the notorious witch trials to changes in community structure. Bernard Rosenthal challenges many myths concerning the Salem witch trials in *Salem Story: Reading the Witch Trials of 1692* (1993). Mary Beth Norton's *In the Devil's Snare: The Salem Witchcraft Crisis of 1692* (2002) emphasizes the role of Indian violence.

Discussions of women in the New England colonies can be found in Laurel Thatcher Ulrich's *Good Wives: Image and Reality in the Lives of Women in Northern New England, 1650–1750* (1980), Joy Day Buel and Richard Buel Jr.'s *The Way of Duty: A Woman and Her Family in Revolutionary America* (1984), and Mary Beth Norton's *Separated by Their Sex: Women in Public and Private in the Colonial Atlantic World* (2011). On women and religion, see Susan Juster's *Disorderly Women: Sexual Politics and Evangelicalism in Revolutionary New England* (1994). John Demos describes family life in *A Little Commonwealth: Family Life in Plymouth Colony*, new ed. (2000).

For an excellent overview of Indian relations with Europeans, see Colin G. Calloway's *New Worlds for All: Indians, Europeans, and the Remaking of Early America* (1997). On New England Indians, see Kathleen J. Bragdon's *Native People of Southern New England, 1500–1650* (1996). For analyses of Indian wars, see Alfred A. Cave's *The Pequot War* (1996) and Jill Lepore's *The Name of War: King Philip's War and the Origins of American Identity* (1998). The story of the Iroquois is told well in Daniel K. Richter's *The Ordeal of the Longhouse: The Peoples of the Iroquois League in the Era of European Colonization* (1992). Indians in the southern colonies are the focus of James Axtell's *The Indians' New South: Cultural Change in the Colonial Southeast* (1997). On the fur trade, see Eric Jay Dolan, *Fur, Fortune, and Empire: The Epic Story of the Fur Trade in America* (2010).

For the social history of the southern colonies, see Allan Kulikoff's *Tobacco and Slaves: The Development of Southern Cultures in the Chesapeake, 1680–1800* (1986) and Kathleen M. Brown's *Good Wives, Nasty Wenches, and Anxious Patriarchs: Gender, Race, and Power in Colonial Virginia* (1996). Family life along the Chesapeake Bay is described in Gloria L. Main's *Tobacco Colony: Life in Early Maryland, 1650–1720* (1982) and Daniel Blake Smith's *Inside the Great House: Planter Family Life in Eighteenth-Century Chesapeake Society* (1980).

Edmund S. Morgan's *American Slavery, American Freedom: The Ordeal of Colonial Virginia* (1975) examines Virginia's social structure, environment, and labor patterns in a biracial context. On the interaction of the cultures of blacks and whites, see Mechal Sobel's *The World They Made Together: Black and White Values in Eighteenth-Century Virginia* (1987). African American viewpoints are presented in Timothy H. Breen and Stephen Innes's *"Myne Owne Ground": Race and Freedom on Virginia's Eastern Shore, 1640–1676*, new ed. (2004). David W. Galenson's *White Servitude in Colonial America: An Economic Analysis* (1981) looks at the indentured labor force.

Henry F. May's *The Enlightenment in America* (1976) and Donald H. Meyer's *The Democratic Enlightenment* (1976) examine intellectual trends in eighteenth-century America. Lawrence A. Cremin's *American Education: The Colonial Experience, 1607–1783* (1970) surveys educational developments.

On the Great Awakening, see Patricia U. Bonomi's *Under the Cope of Heaven: Religion, Society, and Politics in Colonial America*, updated ed. (2003), Timothy D. Hall's *Contested Boundaries: Itinerancy and the Reshaping of the Colonial American Religious World* (1994), Frank Lambert's *Inventing the "Great Awakening"* (1999), and Thomas S. Kidd's *The Great Awakening: The Roots of Evangelical Christianity in Colonial America* (2007). The best biography of Edwards is Phillip F. Gura's *Jonathan Edwards: A Life* (2003). For evangelism in the South, see Christine Leigh Heyrman's *Southern Cross: The Beginnings of the Bible Belt* (1997).

CHAPTER 4

The economics motivating colonial policies is covered in John J. McCusker and Russell R. Menard's *The Economy of British America, 1607–1789,* rev. ed. (1991). The problems of colonial customs administration are explored in Michael Kammen's *Empire and Interest: The American Colonies and the Politics of Mercantilism* (1970).

The Andros crisis and related topics are treated in Jack M. Sosin's *English America and the Revolution of 1688: Royal Administration and the Structure of Provincial Government* (1982).

Stephen Saunders Webb's *The Governors-General: The English Army and the Definition of the Empire, 1569–1681* (1979) argues that the Crown was more concerned with military administration than with commercial regulation, and Webb's *1676: The End of American Independence* (1984) shows how the Indian wars undermined the autonomy of the colonial governments.

On the Jesuits, see Nicholas P. Cushner's *Why Have You Come Here? The Jesuits and the First Evangelization of Native America* (2006). The early Indian wars are treated in Jill Lepore's *The Name of War: King Philip's War and the Origins of American Identity* (1998). Gregory Evans Dowd describes the unification efforts of Indians east of the Mississippi in *A Spirited Resistance: The North American Indian Struggle for Unity, 1745–1815* (1992). See also James H. Merrell's *Into the American Woods: Negotiators on the Pennsylvania Frontier* (1999).

A good introduction to the imperial phase of the colonial conflicts is Douglas Edward Leach's *Arms for Empire: A Military History of the British Colonies in North America, 1607–1763* (1973). Also useful is Brendan Simms's *Three Victories and a Defeat: The Rise and Fall of the Fiurst British Empire* (2008). Fred Anderson's *Crucible of War: The Seven Years' War and the Fate of Empire in British North America, 1754–1766* (2000) is the best history of the Seven Years' War. For the implications of the British victory in 1763, see Colin G. Calloway's *The Scratch of a Pen: 1763 and the Transformation of North America* (2006). On the French colonies in North America, see Allan Greer's *The People of New France* (1997).

For a narrative survey of the events leading to the Revolution, see Edward Countryman's *The American Revolution,* rev. ed. (2003). For Great Britain's perspective on the imperial conflict, see Ian R. Christie's *Crisis of Empire: Great Britain and the American Colonies, 1754–1783* (1966). Also see Jeremy Black's *George III: America's Last King* (2007).

The intellectual foundations of revolt are traced in Bernard Bailyn's *The Ideological Origins of the American Revolution,* enlarged ed. (1992). To understand how these views were connected to organized protest, see Pauline Maier's *From Resistance to Revolution: Colonial Radicals and the Development of American Opposition to Britain, 1765–1776* (1972) and Jon Butler's *Becoming America: The Revolution before 1776* (2000).

On the efforts of colonists to boycott the purchase of British goods, see T. H. Breen's *The Marketplace of Revolution: How Consumer Politics Shaped American Independence* (2004). An excellent overview of the political turmoil leading to war is John Ferling's *A Leap in the Dark: The Struggle to Create the American Republic* (2003). See also Timoth Breen's *American Insurgents, American Patriots* (2010). A fascinating account of the smallpox epidemic during the Revolutionary War is Elizabeth A. Fenn's *Pox Americana: The Great Smallpox Epidemic of 1775–1782* (2001).

Pauline Maier's *American Scripture: Making the Declaration of Independence* (1997) is the best analysis of the framing of that document. Jack M. Sosin chronicles events west of the Appalachians concisely in *The Revolutionary Frontier, 1763–1783* (1967). Military affairs in the early phases of the war are handled in John W. Shy's *Toward Lexington: The Role of the British Army in the Coming of the American Revolution* (1965).

CHAPTER 5

The Revolutionary War is the subject of Colin Bonwick's *The American Revolution,* 2nd ed. (2005), Gordon S. Wood's *The Radicalism of the American Revolution* (1991), and Jeremy Black's *War for America: The Fight for Independence, 1775–1783* (1991). John Ferling's *Setting the World Ablaze: Washington, Adams, Jefferson, and the American Revolution* (2000) highlights the roles played by key leaders.

On the social history of the Revolutionary War, see John W. Shy's *A People Numerous and Armed: Reflections on the Military Struggle for American Independence*, rev. ed. (1990). Colin G. Calloway tells the neglected story of the Indian experiences in the Revolution in *The American Revolution in Indian Country: Crisis and Diversity in Native American Communities* (1995). The imperial, aristocratic, and racist aspects of the Revolution are detailed in Francis Jennings's *The Creation of America: Through Revolution to Empire* (2000).

Why some Americans remained loyal to the Crown is the subject of Thomas B. Allen's *Tories: Fighting for the King in America's First Civil War* (2010) and Maya Jasanoff's *Liberty's Exiles: American Loyalists in the Revolutionary War* (2011). A superb study of African Americans during the Revolutionary era is Douglas R. Egerton's *Death or Liberty: African Americans and Revolutionary America* (2009). Mary Beth Norton's *Liberty's Daughters: The Revolutionary Experience of American Women, 1750–1800*, new ed. (1996), Linda K. Kerber's *Women of the Republic: Intellect and Ideology in Revolutionary America* (1980), and Carol Berkin's *Revolutionary Mothers: Women in the Struggle for America's Independence* (2005) document the role that women played in securing independence. A superb biography of Revolutionary America's most prominent woman is Woody Holton's *Abigail Adams* (2010). A fine new biography of America's commander in chief is Ron Chernow's *Washington: A Life* (2010).

CHAPTER 6

A good overview of the Confederation period is Richard B. Morris's *The Forging of the Union, 1781–1789* (1987). Another useful analysis of this period is Richard Buel Jr.'s *Securing the Revolution: Ideology in American Politics, 1789–1815* (1972). David P. Szatmary's *Shays's Rebellion: The Making of an Agrarian Insurrection* (1980) covers that fateful incident. For a fine account of cultural change during the period, see Joseph J. Ellis's *After the Revolution: Profiles of Early American Culture* (1979).

Excellent treatments of the post-Revolutionary era include Edmund S. Morgan's *Inventing the People: The Rise of Popular Sovereignty in England and America* (1988), Michael Kammen's *Sovereignty and Liberty: Constitutional Discourse in American Culture* (1988), and Joyce Appleby's *Inheriting the Revolution: The First Generation of Americans* (2000). On the political philosophies contributing to the drafting of the Constitution, see Ralph Lerner's *The Thinking Revolutionary: Principle and Practice in the New Republic* (1987). For the dramatic story of the framers of the Constitution, see Richard Beeman's *Plain, Honest Men: The Making of the American Constitution* (2009). Woody Holton's *Unruly Americans and the Origins of the Constitution* (2007) emphasizes the role of taxes and monetary policies in the crafting of the Constitution. The complex story of ratification is well told in Pauline Maier's *Ratification: The People Debate the Constitution, 1787–1788* (2010).

CHAPTER 7

The best introduction to the early Federalists remains John C. Miller's *The Federalist Era, 1789–1801*, rev. ed. (2011). Other works analyze the ideological debates among the nation's first leaders. Richard Buel Jr.'s *Securing the Revolution: Ideology in American Politics, 1789–1815* (1972), Joyce Appleby's *Capitalism and a New Social Order: The Republican Vision of the 1790s* (1984), and Stanley Elkins and Eric McKitrick's *The Age of Federalism: The Early American Republic, 1788–1800* (1993) trace the persistence and transformation of ideas first fostered during the

Revolutionary crisis. On the first ten constitutional amendments, see Leonard W. Levy's *Origins of the Bill of Rights* (1999). The best study of Washington's political career is John Ferling's *The Ascent of George Washington: The Hidden Political Genius of an American Icon* (2009).

The 1790s may also be understood through the views and behavior of national leaders. Joseph J. Ellis's *Founding Brothers: The Revolutionary Generation* (2000) is a superb group study. See also the following biographies: Richard Brookhiser's *Founding Father: Rediscovering George Washington* (1996) and *Alexander Hamilton, American* (1999) and Joseph J. Ellis's *Passionate Sage: The Character and Legacy of John Adams* (1993). For a female perspective, see Phyllis Lee Levin's *Abigail Adams: A Biography* (1987). The Republican viewpoint is the subject of Lance Banning's *The Jeffersonian Persuasion: Evolution of a Party Ideology* (1978).

Federalist foreign policy is explored in Jerald A. Comb's *The Jay Treaty: Political Battleground of the Founding Fathers* (1970) and William Stinchcombe's *The XYZ Affair* (1980). For specific domestic issues, see Thomas P. Slaughter's *The Whiskey Rebellion: Frontier Epilogue to the American Revolution* (1986) and Harry Ammon's *The Genet Mission* (1973). The treatment of Indians in the Old Northwest is explored in Richard H. Kohn's *Eagle and Sword: The Federalists and the Creation of the Military Establishment in America, 1783–1802* (1975). For the Alien and Sedition Acts, consult James Morton Smith's *Freedom's Fetters: The Alien and Sedition Laws and American Civil Liberties* (1956).

Several books focus on social issues of the post-Revolutionary period, including *Keepers of the Revolution: New Yorkers at Work in the Early Republic* (1992), edited by Paul A. Gilje and Howard B. Rock; Ronald Schultz's *The Republic of Labor: Philadelphia Artisans and the Politics of Class, 1720–1830* (1993); and Peter Way's *Common Labour: Workers and the Digging of North American Canals, 1780–1860* (1993).

CHAPTER 8

Marshall Smelser's *The Democratic Republic, 1801–1815* (1968) presents an overview of the Republican administrations. Even more comprehensive is Gordon S. Wood's *Empire of Liberty: A History of the Early Republic, 1789–1815* (2010). The best treatment of the election of 1800 is Edward J. Larson's *A Magnificent Catastrophe: The Tumultuous Election of 1800* (2008). The standard biography of Jefferson is Joseph J. Ellis's *American Sphinx: The Character of Thomas Jefferson* (1996). On the life of Jefferson's friend and successor, see Drew R. McCoy's *The Last of the Fathers: James Madison and the Republican Legacy* (1989). Joyce Appleby's *Capitalism and a New Social Order: The Republican Vision of the 1790s* (1984) minimizes the impact of Republican ideology.

Linda K. Kerber's *Federalists in Dissent: Imagery and Ideology in Jeffersonian American* (1970) explores the Federalists while they were out of power. The concept of judicial review and the courts can be studied in Cliff Sloan and David McKean's *The Great Decision: Jefferson, Adams, Marshall, and the Battle for the Supreme Court* (2009). On John Marshall, see G. Edward White's *The Marshall Court and Cultural Change, 1815–1835* (1988) and James F. Simon's *What Kind of Nation: Thomas Jefferson, John Marshall, and the Epic Struggle to Create a United States* (2002). Milton Lomask's two volumes, *Aaron Burr: The Years from Princeton to Vice President, 1756–1805* (1979) and *The Conspiracy and the Years of Exile, 1805–1836* (1982) trace the career of that remarkable American.

For the Louisiana Purchase, consult Jon Kukla's *A Wilderness So Immense: The Louisiana Purchase and the Destiny of America* (2003). For a captivating account of the Lewis and Clark expedition, see Stephen Ambrose's *Undaunted Courage: Meriwether Lewis, Thomas Jefferson, and the*

Opening of the American West (1996). Bernard W. Sheehan's *Seeds of Extinction: Jeffersonian Philanthropy and the American Indian* (1973) is more analytical in its treatment of the Jeffersonians' Indian policy and the opening of the West. Burton Spivak's *Jefferson's English Crisis: Commerce, Embargo, and the Republican Revolution* (1979) discusses Anglo-American relations during Jefferson's administration; Clifford L. Egan's *Neither Peace Nor War: Franco-American Relations, 1803–1812* (1983) covers America's relations with France. An excellent revisionist treatment of the events that brought on war in 1812 is J. C. A. Stagg's *Mr. Madison's War: Politics, Diplomacy, and Warfare in the Early American Republic, 1783–1830* (1983). The war itself is the focus of Donald R. Hickey's *The War of 1812: A Forgotten Conflict* (1989). See also Alan Taylor's *The Civil War of 1812: American Citizens, British Subjects, Irish Rebels, and Indian Allies* (2011).

CHAPTER 9

The best overview of the second quarter of the nineteenth century is Daniel Walker Howe, *What Hath God Wrought: The Transformation of America, 1815–1845* (2007). On economic development in the nation's early decades, see Stuart Bruchey's *Enterprise: The Dynamic Economy of a Free People* (1990). The classic study of transportation and economic growth is George Rogers Taylor's *The Transportation Revolution, 1815–1860* (1951). A fresh view is provided in Sarah H. Gordon's *Passage to Union: How the Railroads Transformed American Life, 1829–1929* (1996). On the Erie Canal, see Carol Sheriff's *The Artificial River: The Erie Canal and the Paradox of Progress, 1817–1862* (1996).

The impact of technology is traced in David J. Jeremy's *Transatlantic Industrial Revolution: The Diffusion of Textile Technologies between Britain and America, 1790–1830s* (1981). On the invention of the telegraph, see Kenneth Silverman's *Lightning Man: The Accursed Life of Samuel F. B. Morse* (2003). For the story of steamboats, see Andrea Sutcliffe's *Steam: The Untold Story of America's First Great Invention* (2004). The best treatment of public works, such as the Erie Canal in the development of nineteenth-century America, is John Lauritz Larson's *Internal Improvement: National Public Works and the Promise of Popular Government in the Early United States* (2001).

Paul E. Johnson's *A Shopkeeper's Millenium: Society and Revivals in Rochester, New York, 1815–1837* (1978) studies the role religion played in the emerging industrial order. The attitude of the worker during this time of transition is surveyed in Edward E. Pessen's *Most Uncommon Jacksonians: The Radical Leaders of the Early Labor Movement* (1967). Detailed case studies of working communities include Anthony F. C. Wallace's *Rockdale: The Growth of an American Village in the Early Industrial Revolution* (1978), Thomas Dublin's *Women at Work: The Transformation of Work and Community in Lowell, Massachusetts, 1826–1860* (1979), and Sean Wilentz's *Chants Democratic: New York and the Rise of the American Working Class, 1788–1850* (1984). Walter Licht's *Working for the Railroad: The Organization of Work in the Nineteenth Century* (1983) is rich in detail.

For a fine treatment of urbanization, see Charles N. Glaab and A. Theodore Brown's *A History of Urban America* (1967). On immigration, see Jay P. Dolan's *The Irish Americans* (2008).

CHAPTER 10

The standard overview of the Era of Good Feelings remains George Dangerfield's *The Awakening of American Nationalism, 1815–1828* (1965). A classic summary of the economic trends of the period is Douglass C. North's *The Economic Growth of the United States, 1790–1860*

(1961). An excellent synthesis of the era is Charles Sellers's *The Market Revolution: Jacksonian America, 1815–1846* (1991). On diplomatic relations during James Monroe's presidency, see William Earl Weeks's *John Quincy Adams and American Global Empire* (1992). For relations after 1812, see Ernest R. May's *The Making of the Monroe Doctrine* (1975). For background on Andrew Jackson, see the readings cited in Chapter 11. The campaign that brought Jackson to the White House is analyzed in Robert Vincent Remini's *The Election of Andrew Jackson* (1963).

CHAPTER 11

An excellent survey of events covered in this chapter is Daniel Feller's *The Jacksonian Promise: America, 1815–1840* (1995). Even more comprehensive surveys of politics and culture during the Jacksonian era are Daniel Walker Howe's *What Hath God Wrought: The Transformation of America, 1815–1848* (2007) and David S. Reynolds's *Waking Giant: America in the Age of Jackson* (2008). A more political focus can be found in Harry L. Watson's *Liberty and Power: The Politics of Jacksonian America* (1990).

For an outstanding analysis of women in New York City during the Jacksonian period, see Christine Stansell's *City of Women: Sex and Class in New York, 1789–1860* (1986). In *Chants Democratic: New York City and the Rise of the American Working-Class, 1788–1850* (1984), Sean Wilentz analyzes the social basis of working-class politics. More recently, Wilentz has traced the democratization of politics in *The Rise of American Democracy: Jefferson to Lincoln*, abridged college ed. (2009).

The best biography of Jackson remains Robert Vincent Remini's three-volume work: *Andrew Jackson: The Course of American Empire, 1767–1821* (1977), *Andrew Jackson: The Course of American Freedom, 1822–1832* (1981), and *Andrew Jackson: The Course of American Democracy, 1833–1845* (1984). A more critical study of the seventh president is Andrew Burstein's *The Passions of Andrew Jackson* (2003). On Jackson's successor, consult John Niven's *Martin Van Buren: The Romantic Age of American Politics* (1983) and Ted Widmer's *Martin Van Buren* (2005). Studies of other major figures of the period include John Niven's *John C. Calhoun and the Price of Union: A Biography* (1988), Merrill D. Peterson's *The Great Triumvirate: Webster, Clay, and Calhoun* (1987), and Robert Vincent Remini's *Henry Clay: Statesman for the Union* (1991) and *Daniel Webster: The Man and His Time* (1997).

The political philosophies of Jackson's opponents are treated in Michael F. Holt's *The Rise and Fall of the American Whig Party: Jacksonian Politics and the Onset of the Civil War* (1999) and Harry L. Watson's *Andrew Jackson vs. Henry Clay: Democracy and Development in Antebellum America* (1998). On a crucial election, see Lynn Hudson Parsons's *The Birth of Modern Politics: Andrew Jackson, John Quincy Adams, and the Election of 1828* (2009).

On the Eaton affair, see John F. Marszalek's *The Petticoat Affair: Manners, Mutiny, and Sex in Andrew Jackson's White House* (1998). Two studies of the impact of the bank controversy are William G. Shade's *Banks or No Banks: The Money Issue in Western Politics, 1832–1865* (1972) and James Roger Sharp's *The Jacksonians versus the Banks: Politics in the States after the Panic of 1837* (1970).

The outstanding book on the nullification issue remains William W. Freehling's *Prelude to Civil War: The Nullification Controversy in South Carolina, 1816–1836* (1965). John M. Belohlavek's *"Let the Eagle Soar!": The Foreign Policy of Andrew Jackson* (1985) is a thorough study of Jacksonian diplomacy. A. J. Langguth's *Driven West: Andrew Jackson and the Trail of Tears to the Civil War* (2010) analyzes the controversial relocation policy.

CHAPTER 12

Those interested in the problem of discerning myth and reality in the southern experience should consult William R. Taylor's *Cavalier and Yankee: The Old South and American National Character* (1961). Three recent efforts to understand the mind of the Old South and its defense of slavery are Eugene D. Genovese's *The Slaveholders' Dilemma: Freedom and Progress in Southern Conservative Thought, 1820–1860* (1992), Eric H. Walther's *The Fire-Eaters* (1992), and William W. Freehling's *The Road to Disunion: Secessionists Triumphant, 1854–1861* (2007).

Contrasting analyses of the plantation system are Eugene D. Genovese's *The World the Slaveholders Made: Two Essays in Interpretation,* with a new introduction (1988), and Gavin Wright's *The Political Economy of the Cotton South: Households, Markets, and Wealth in the Nineteenth Century* (1978). Stephanie McCurry's *Masters of Small Worlds: Yeoman Households, Gender Relations, and the Political Culture of the Antebellum South Carolina Low Country* (1995) greatly enriches our understanding of southern households, religion, and political culture.

Other essential works on southern culture and society include Bertram Wyatt-Brown's *Honor and Violence in the Old South* (1986), Elizabeth Fox-Genovese's *Within the Plantation Household: Black and White Women of the Old South* (1988), Catherine Clinton's *The Plantation Mistress: Woman's World in the Old South* (1982), Joan E. Cashin's *A Family Venture: Men and Women on the Southern Frontier* (1991), and Theodore Rosengarten's *Tombee: Portrait of a Cotton Planter* (1986).

A provocative discussion of the psychology of African American slavery can be found in Stanley M. Elkins's *Slavery: A Problem in American Institutional and Intellectual Life,* 3rd ed. (1976). John W. Blassingame's *The Slave Community: Plantation Life in the Antebellum South,* rev. and enlarged ed. (1979), Eugene D. Genovese's *Roll, Jordan, Roll: The World the Slaves Made* (1974), and Herbert G. Gutman's *The Black Family in Slavery and Freedom, 1750–1925* (1976) all stress the theme of a persisting and identifiable slave culture. On the question of slavery's profitability, see Robert William Fogel and Stanley L. Engerman's *Time on the Cross: The Economics of American Negro Slavery* (1974).

The best study of the political dimensions of slavery in the South is Lacy K. Ford's *Deliver Us from Evil: The Slavery Question in the Old South* (2009). On the Louisiana slave revolt in 1811, see Daniel Rasmussen's *American Uprising: The Untold Story of America's Largest Slave Revolt* (2011). Other works on slavery include Lawrence W. Levine's *Black Culture and Black Consciousness: Afro-American Folk Thought from Slavery to Freedom* (1977); Albert J. Raboteau's *Slave Religion: The "Invisible Institution" in the Antebellum South* (1978); *We Are Your Sisters: Black Women in the Nineteenth Century,* edited by Dorothy Sterling (1984); Deborah Gray White's *Ar'n't I a Woman? Female Slaves in the Plantation South,* rev. ed. (1999); and Joel Williamson's *The Crucible of Race: Black-White Relations in the American South since Emancipation* (1984). Charles Joyner's *Down by the Riverside: A South Carolina Slave Community* (1984) offers a vivid reconstruction of one community.

CHAPTER 13

Russel Blaine Nye's *Society and Culture in America, 1830–1860* (1974) provides a wide-ranging survey of the Romantic movement. On the reform impulse, consult Ronald G. Walter's *American Reformers, 1815–1860,* rev. ed. (1997). Revivalist religion is treated in Nathan O.

Hatch's *The Democratization of American Christianity* (1989), Christine Leigh Heyrman's *Southern Cross: The Beginnings of the Bible Belt* (1997), and Ellen Eslinger's *Citizens of Zion: The Social Origins of Camp Meeting Revivalism* (1999). On the Mormons, see Leonard Arrington's *Brigham Young: American Moses* (1985).

The best treatments of transcendentalist thought are Paul F. Boller's *American Transcendentalism, 1830–1860: An Intellectual Inquiry* (1974) and Philip F. Gura's *American Transcendentalism: A History* (2007). Several good works describe various aspects of the antebellum reform movement. For temperance, see W. J. Rorabaugh's *The Alcoholic Republic: An American Tradition* (1979) and Barbara Leslie Epstein's *The Politics of Domesticity: Women, Evangelism, and Temperance in Nineteenth-Century America* (1981). Stephen Nissenbaum's *Sex, Diet, and Debility in Jacksonian America: Sylvester Graham and Health Reform* (1980) looks at a pioneering reformer concerned with diet and lifestyle. On prison reform and other humanitarian projects, see David J. Rothman's *The Discovery of the Asylum: Social Order and Disorder in the New Republic*, rev. ed. (2002), and Thomas J. Brown's biography *Dorothea Dix: New England Reformer* (1998). Lawrence A. Cremin's *American Education: The National Experience, 1783–1876* (1980) traces early school reform.

On women during the antebellum period, see Nancy F. Cott's *The Bonds of Womanhood: "Woman's Sphere" in New England, 1780–1835*, rev. ed. (1997), and Ellen C. DuBois's *Feminism and Suffrage: The Emergence of an Independent Women's Movement in America, 1848–1869* (1978). Michael Fellman's *The Unbounded Frame: Freedom and Community in Nineteenth-Century American Utopianism* (1973) surveys the utopian movements.

Useful surveys of abolitionism include Seymour Drescher's *Abolition: A History of Slavery and Antislavery* (2009), James Brewer Stewart's *Holy Warriors: The Abolitionists and American Slavery*, rev. ed. (1997), and Julie Roy Jeffrey's *The Great Silent Army of Abolitionism: Ordinary Women in the Antislavery Movement* (1998). On William Lloyd Garrison, see Henry Mayer's *All on Fire: William Lloyd Garrison and the Abolition of Slavery* (1998) and Bruce Laurie's *Beyond Garrison: Antislavery and Social Reform* (2005). For the pro-slavery argument as it developed in the South, see Larry E. Tise's *Proslavery: A History of the Defense of Slavery in America, 1701–1840* (1987) and James Oakes's *The Ruling Race: A History of American Slaveholders* (1982). The problems southerners had in justifying slavery are explored in Kenneth S. Greenberg's *Masters and Statesmen: The Political Culture of American Slavery* (1985).

CHAPTER 14

For background on Whig programs and ideas, see Michael F. Holt's *The Rise and Fall of the American Whig Party: Jacksonian Politics and the Onset of the Civil War* (1999). On John Tyler, see Edward P. Crapol's *John Tyler: The Accidental President* (2006). Several works help interpret the expansionist impulse. Frederick Merk's *Manifest Destiny and Mission in American History: A Reinterpretation* (1963) remains a classic. A more recent treatment of expansionist ideology is Thomas R. Hietala's *Manifest Design: Anxious Aggrandizement in Late Jacksonian America* (1985).

The best surveys of western expansion are Bruce Cumings's *Dominion from Sea to Sea: Pacific Ascendancy and American Power* (2009), Walter Nugent's *Habits of Empire: A History of American Expansionism* (2008), and Richard White's *"It's Your Misfortune and None of My Own": A New History of the American West* (1991). For the expansionism of the 1840s, see Steven E. Woodworth's *Manifest Destinies: America's Westward Expansion and the Road to the Civil War* (2010). Robert M.

Utley's *A Life Wild and Perilous: Mountain Men and the Paths to the Pacific* (1997) tells the dramatic story of the rugged pathfinders who discovered corridors over the Rocky Mountains. The movement of settlers to the West is ably documented in John Mack Faragher's *Women and Men on the Overland Trail*, 2nd ed. (2001), and David Dary's *The Santa Fe Trail: Its History, Legends, and Lore* (2000). On the tragic Donner party, see Ethan Rarick's *Desperate Passage: The Donner Party's Perilous Journey West* (2008).

Gene M. Brack's *Mexico Views Manifest Destiny, 1821–1846: An Essay on the Origins of the Mexican War* (1975) takes Mexico's viewpoint on U.S. designs on the West. For the American perspective on Texas, see Joel H. Silbey's *Storm over Texas: The Annexation Controversy and the Road to Civil War* (2005). On the siege of the Alamo, see William C. Davis's *Three Roads to the Alamo: The Lives and Fortunes of David Crockett, James Bowie, and William Barret Travis* (1998). An excellent biography related to the emergence of Texas is Gregg Cantrell's *Stephen F. Austin: Empresario of Texas* (1999). On James K. Polk, see Robert W. Merry's *A Country of Vast Designs: James K. Polk, the Mexican War, and the Conquest of the American Continent* (2009). The best survey of the military conflict is John S. D. Eisenhower's *So Far from God: The U.S. War with Mexico, 1846–1848* (1989). The Mexican War as viewed from the perspective of the soldiers is ably described in Richard Bruce Winders's *Mr. Polk's Army: American Military Experience in the Mexican War* (1997). On the diplomatic aspects of Mexican-American relations, see David M. Pletcher's *The Diplomacy of Annexation: Texas, Oregon, and the Mexican War* (1973).

CHAPTER 15

The best surveys of the forces and events leading to the Civil War include James M. McPherson's *Battle Cry of Freedom: The Civil War Era* (1988), Stephen B. Oates's *The Approaching Fury: Voices of the Storm, 1820–1861* (1997), and Bruce Levine's *Half Slave and Half Free: The Roots of Civil War* (1992). The most recent narrative of the political debate leading to secession is Michael A. Morrison's *Slavery and the American West: The Eclipse of Manifest Destiny and the Coming of the Civil War* (1997).

Mark J. Stegmaier's *Texas, New Mexico, and the Compromise of 1850: Boundary Dispute and Sectional Crisis* (1996) probes that crucial dispute, while Michael F. Holt's *The Political Crisis of the 1850s* (1978) traces the demise of the Whigs. Eric Foner, in *Free Soil, Free Labor, Free Men: The Ideology of the Republican Party before the Civil War* (1970), shows how events and ideas combined in the formation of a new political party. A more straightforward study of the rise of the Republicans is William E. Gienapp's *The Origins of the Republican Party, 1852–1856* (1987). The economic, social, and political crises of 1857 are examined in Kenneth M. Stampp's *America in 1857: A Nation on the Brink* (1990). Another perspective on the economic causes of the Civil War is Marc Egnal's *Clash of Extremes: The Economic Origins of the Civil War* (2009). On the Anthony Burns case, see Albert J. von Frank's *The Trials of Anthony Burns: Freedom and Slavery in Emerson's Boston* (1998). The *Dred Scott* case is ably assessed in Earl M. Maltz's *Dred Scott and the Politics of Slavery* (2007). For an assessment of the Revival of 1857–1858, see Kathryn Teresa Long, *The Revival of 1857–1858: Interpreting an American Religious Awakening* (1998).

Robert W. Johannsen's *Stephen A. Douglas* (1973) analyzes the issue of popular sovereignty. A more national perspective is provided in James A. Rawley's *Race and Politics: "Bleeding Kansas" and the Coming of the Civil War* (1969). On the role of John Brown in the sectional crisis, see Robert E. McGlone's *John Brown's War Against Slavery* (2009) and David S. Reynolds's *John Brown, Abolitionist: The Man Who Killed Slavery, Sparked the Civil War, and Seeded Civil*

Rights (2005). An excellent study of the South's journey to secession is William W. Freehling's *The Road to Disunion*, vol. 1, *Secessionists at Bay, 1776–1854* (1990), and *The Road to Disunion*, vol. 2, *Secessionists Triumphant, 1854–1861* (2007). Robert E. Bonner traces the emergence of southern nationalism in *Mastering America: Southern Slaveholders and the Crisis of American Nationhood* (2009).

On the Buchanan presidency, see Jean H. Baker's *James Buchanan* (2004). On Lincoln's role in the coming crisis of war, see Don E. Fehrenbacher's *Prelude to Greatness: Lincoln in the 1850s* (1962). Harry V. Jaffa's *Crisis of the House Divided: An Interpretation of the Issues in the Lincoln-Douglas Debate*, 50th anniversary ed. (2009), details the debates, and Maury Klein's *Days of Defiance: Sumter, Secession, and the Coming of the Civil War* (1997) treats the Fort Sumter controversy. An excellent collection of interpretive essays is *Why the Civil War Came* (1996), edited by Gabor S. Boritt.

CHAPTER 16

On the start of the Civil War, see Adam Goodheart's *1861: The Civil War Awakening* (2011). The best one-volume overview of the Civil War period is James M. McPherson's *Battle Cry of Freedom: The Civil War Era* (1988). A good introduction to the military events is Herman Hattaway's *Shades of Blue and Gray: An Introductory Military History of the Civil War* (1997). The outlook and experiences of the common soldier are explored in James M. McPherson's *For Cause and Comrades: Why Men Fought in the Civil War* (1997) and Earl J. Hess's *The Union Soldier in Battle: Enduring the Ordeal of Combat* (1997).

The northern war effort is ably assessed in Gary W. Gallagher's *The Union War* (2011). For emphasis on the South, see Gallagher's *The Confederate War* (1997). A sparkling account of the birth of the Rebel nation is William C. Davis's *"A Government of Our Own": The Making of the Confederacy* (1994). The same author provides a fine biography of the Confederate president in *Jefferson Davis: The Man and His Hour* (1991). On the best Confederate commander, see John M. Taylor's *Duty Faithfully Performed: Robert E. Lee and His Critics* (1999). On the key Union generals, see Lee Kennett's *Sherman: A Soldier's Life* (2001) and Josiah Bunting III's *Ulysses S. Grant* (2004).

Analytical scholarship on the military conflict includes Joseph L. Harsh's *Confederate Tide Rising: Robert E. Lee and the Making of Southern Strategy, 1861–1862* (1998), Steven E. Woodworth's *Jefferson Davis and His Generals: The Failure of Confederate Command in the West* (1990), and Paul D. Casdorph's *Lee and Jackson: Confederate Chieftains* (1992). Lonnie R. Speer's *Portals to Hell: Military Prisons of the Civil War* (1997) details the ghastly experience of prisoners of war.

The history of the North during the war is surveyed in Philip Shaw Paludan's *A People's Contest: The Union and Civil War, 1861–1865*, 2nd ed. (1996), and J. Matthew Gallman's *The North Fights the Civil War: The Home Front* (1994). See also Jennifer L. Weber's *Copperheads: The Rise and Fall of Lincoln's Opponents in the North* (2006). A good synthesis of the war and its effects is David Goldfield's *America Aflame: How the Civil War Created a Nation* (2011).

The central northern political figure, Abraham Lincoln, is the subject of many books. See James McPherson's *Abraham Lincoln* (2009) and Ronald C. White Jr.'s *A. Lincoln: A Biography* (2009). On Lincoln's great speeches, see Ronald C. White Jr.'s *The Eloquent President: A Portrait of Lincoln through His Words* (2005). The election of 1864 is treated in John C. Waugh's *Reelecting Lincoln: The Battle for the 1864 Presidency* (1997). On Lincoln's assassination, see William Hanchett's *The Lincoln Murder Conspiracies* (1983). For the religious implication of the war, see George C. Rable's *God's Almost Chosen Peoples: A Religious History of the Civil War* (2011).

Concerning specific military campaigns, see Larry J. Daniel's *Shiloh: The Battle That Changed the Civil War* (1997), Thomas Goodrich's *Black Flag: Guerrilla Warfare on the Western Border, 1861–1865* (1995), Stephen W. Sears's *To the Gates of Richmond: The Peninsula Campaign* (1992), James M. McPherson's *Crossroads of Freedom: Antietam* (2002), James Lee McDonough and James Pickett Jones's *"War So Terrible": Sherman and Atlanta* (1987), Robert Garth Scott's *Into the Wilderness with the Army of the Potomac*, rev. and enl. ed. (1992), Marc Wortman's *The Bonfire: The Siege and Burning of Atlanta* (2008), Richard Slotkin's *No Quarter: The Battle of the Crater, 1864* (2009), and Noah Andre Trudeau's *Southern Storm: Sherman's March to the Sea* (2008). On the final weeks of the war, see William C. Davis's *An Honorable Defeat: The Last Days of the Confederate Government* (2001).

The experience of the African American soldier is surveyed in Joseph T. Glatthaar's *Forged in Battle: The Civil War Alliance of Black Soldiers and White Officers* (1990) and Ira Berlin, Joseph P. Reidy, and Leslie S. Rowland's *Freedom's Soldiers: The Black Military Experience in the Civil War* (1998). For the African American woman's experience, see Jacqueline Jones's *Labor of Love, Labor of Sorrow: Black Women, Work and the Family, from Slavery to the Present* (1985). On Lincoln's evolving racial views, see Eric Foner's *The Fiery Trial: Abraham Lincoln and American Slavery* (2010).

Recent gender and ethnic studies include Nina Silber's *Gender and the Sectional Conflict* (2008), Drew Gilpin Faust's *Mothers of Invention: Women of the Slaveholding South in the American Civil War* (1996), George C. Rable's *Civil Wars: Women and the Crisis of Southern Nationalism* (1989), and William L. Burton's *Melting Pot Soldiers: The Union's Ethnic Regiments*, 2nd ed. (1998).

CHAPTER 17

The most comprehensive treatment of Reconstruction is Eric Foner's *Reconstruction: America's Unfinished Revolution, 1863–1877* (1988). On Andrew Johnson, see Hans L. Trefousse's *Andrew Johnson: A Biography* (1989) and David D. Stewart's *Impeached: The Trial of Andrew Johnson and the Fight for Lincoln's Legacy* (2009). An excellent brief biography of Grant is Josiah Bunting III's *Ulysses S. Grant* (2004).

Scholars have been sympathetic to the aims and motives of the Radical Republicans. See, for instance, Herman Belz's *Reconstructing the Union: Theory and Policy during the Civil War* (1969) and Richard Nelson Current's *Those Terrible Carpetbaggers: A Reinterpretation* (1988). The ideology of the Radicals is explored in Michael Les Benedict's *A Compromise of Principle: Congressional Republicans and Reconstruction, 1863–1869* (1974). On the black political leaders, see Phillip Dray's *Capitol Men: The Epic Story of Reconstruction through the Lives of the First Black Congressmen* (2008).

The intransigence of southern white attitudes is examined in Michael Perman's *Reunion without Compromise: The South and Reconstruction, 1865–1868* (1973) and Dan T. Carter's *When the War Was Over: The Failure of Self-Reconstruction in the South, 1865–1867* (1985). Allen W. Trelease's *White Terror: The Ku Klux Klan Conspiracy and Southern Reconstruction* (1971) covers the various organizations that practiced vigilante tactics. On the massacre of African Americans, see Charles Lane's *The Day Freedom Died: The Colfax Massacre, the Supreme Court, and the Betrayal of Reconstruction* (2008). The difficulties former slaves had in adjusting to the new labor system are documented in James L. Roark's *Masters without Slaves: Southern Planters in the Civil War and Reconstruction* (1977). Books on southern politics during Reconstruction include Michael Perman's *The Road to Redemption: Southern Politics,*

1869–1879 (1984), Terry L. Seip's *The South Returns to Congress: Men, Economic Measures, and Intersectional Relationships, 1868–1879* (1983), and Mark W. Summers's *Railroads, Reconstruction, and the Gospel of Prosperity: Aid under the Radical Republicans, 1865–1877* (1984).

Numerous works study the freed blacks' experience in the South. Start with Leon F. Litwack's *Been in the Storm So Long: The Aftermath of Slavery* (1979). Joel Williamson's *After Slavery: The Negro in South Carolina during Reconstruction, 1861–1877* (1965) argues that South Carolina blacks took an active role in pursuing their political and economic rights. The Freedmen's Bureau is explored in William S. McFeely's *Yankee Stepfather: General O. O. Howard and the Freedmen* (1968). The situation of freed slave women is discussed in Jacqueline Jones's *Labor of Love, Labor of Sorrow: Black Women, Work and the Family, from Slavery to the Present* (1985).

The politics of corruption outside the South is depicted in William S. McFeely's *Grant: A Biography* (1981). The political maneuvers of the election of 1876 and the resultant crisis and compromise are explained in Michael Holt's *By One Vote: The Disputed Presidential Election of 1876* (2008).

CHAPTER 18

For masterly syntheses of post–Civil War industrial development, see Walter Licht's *Industrializing America: The Nineteenth Century* (1995) and Maury Klein's *The Genesis of Industrial America, 1870–1920* (2007). On the growth of railroads, see Richard White's *Railroaded: The Transcontinentals and the Making of Modern America* (2011) and Albro Martin's *Railroad Triumphant: The Growth, Rejection, and Rebirth of a Vital American Force* (1992).

On entrepreneurship in the iron and steel sector, see Thomas J. Misa's *A Nation of Steel: The Making of Modern America, 1865–1925* (1995). The best biographies of the leading business tycoons are Ron Chernow's *Titan: The Life of John D. Rockefeller, Sr.* (1998), David Nasaw's *Andrew Carnegie* (2006), and Jean Strouse's *Morgan: American Financier* (1999). Nathan Rosenberg's *Technology and American Economic Growth* (1972) documents the growth of invention during the period.

For an overview of the struggle of workers to organize unions, see Philip Bray's *There Is Power in a Union: The Epic Story of Labor in America* (2010). On the 1877 railroad strike, see David O. Stowell's *Streets, Railroad, and the Great Strike of 1877* (1999). For the role of women in the changing workplace, see Alice Kessler-Harris's *Out to Work: A History of Wage-Earning Women in the United States* (1982) and Susan E. Kennedy's *If All We Did Was to Weep at Home: A History of White Working-Class Women in American* (1979). On Mother Jones, see Elliott J. Gorn's *Mother Jones: The Most Dangerous Woman in America* (2001). To trace the rise of socialism among organized workers, see Nick Salvatore's *Eugene V. Debs: Citizen and Socialist* (1982). The key strikes are discussed in Paul Arvich's *The Haymarket Tragedy* (1984) and Paul Krause's *The Battle for Homestead, 1880–1892: Politics, Culture, and Steel* (1992).

CHAPTER 19

The classic study of the emergence of the New South remains C. Vann Woodward's *Origins of the New South, 1877–1913* (1951). A more recent treatment of southern society after the end of Reconstruction is Edward L. Ayers's *Southern Crossing: A History of the American South,*

1877–1906 (1995). A thorough survey of industrialization in the South is James C. Cobb's *Industrialization and Southern Society, 1877–1984* (1984).

C. Vann Woodward's *The Strange Career of Jim Crow,* commemorative ed. (2002), remains the standard on southern race relations. Some of Woodward's points are challenged in Howard N. Rabinowitz's *Race Relations in the Urban South, 1865–1890* (1978). Leon F. Litwack's *Trouble in Mind: Black Southerners in the Age of Jim Crow* (1998) treats the rise of legal segregation, while Michael Perman's *Struggle for Mastery: Disfranchisement in the South, 1888–1908* (2001) surveys efforts to keep African Americans from voting. An award-winning study of white women and the race issue is Glenda Elizabeth Gilmore's *Gender and Jim Crow: Women and the Politics of White Supremacy in North Carolina, 1896–1920* (1996). On W. E. B. Du Bois, see David Levering Lewis's *W. E. B. Du Bois: Biography of a Race, 1868–1919* (1993). On Booker T. Washington, see Robert J. Norrell's *Up from History: The Life of Booker T. Washington* (2009).

For stimulating reinterpretations of the frontier and the development of the West, see William Cronon's *Nature's Metropolis: Chicago and the Great West* (1991), Patricia Nelson Limerick's *The Legacy of Conquest: The Unbroken Past of the American West* (1987), Richard White's *"It's Your Misfortune and None of My Own": A New History of the American West* (1991), and Walter Nugent's *Into the West: The Story of Its People* (1999). An excellent overview is James M. McPherson's *Into the West: From Reconstruction to the Final Days of the American Frontier* (2006).

The role of African Americans in western settlement is the focus of William Loren Katz's *The Black West: A Documentary and Pictorial History of the African American Role in the Westward Expansion of the United States,* rev. ed. (2005), and Nell Irvin Painter's *Exodusters: Black Migration to Kansas after Reconstruction* (1977). The best account of the conflicts between Indians and whites is Robert M. Utley's *The Indian Frontier of the American West, 1846–1890* (1984). On the Battle of the Little Bighorn, see Nathaniel Philbrick's *The Last Stand: Custer, Sitting Bull, and the Battle of the Little Bighorn* (2010). On Crazy Horse, see Thomas Powers's *The Killing of Crazy Horse* (2010). For a presentation of the Native American side of the story, see Peter Nabokov's *Native American Testimony: A Chronicle of Indian-White Relations from Prophecy to the Present, 1492–2000,* rev. ed. (1999). On the demise of the buffalo herds, see Andrew C. Isenberg's *The Destruction of the Bison: An Environmental History, 1750–1920* (2000).

CHAPTER 20

For a survey of urbanization, see David R. Goldfield's *Urban America: A History,* 2nd ed. (1989). Gunther Barth discusses the emergence of a new urban culture in *City People: The Rise of Modern City Culture in Nineteenth-Century America* (1980). John Bodnar offers a synthesis of the urban immigrant experience in *The Transplanted: A History of Immigrants in Urban America* (1985). See also Roger Daniels's *Guarding the Golden Door: American Immigration Policy and Immigrants since 1882* (2004). Walter Nugent's *Crossings: The Great Transatlantic Migrations, 1870–1914* (1992) provides a wealth of demographic information and insight. Efforts to stop Chinese immigration are described in Erika Lee's *At America's Gates: Chinese Immigration during the Exclusion Era* (2003).

On urban environments and sanitary reforms, see Martin V. Melosi's *The Sanitary City: Urban Infrastructure in America from Colonial Times to the Present* (2000), Joel A. Tarr's *The Search for the Ultimate Sink: Urban Pollution in Historical Perspective* (1996), and Suellen Hoy's *Chasing Dirt: The American Pursuit of Cleanliness* (1995).

For the growth of urban leisure and sports, see Roy Rosenzweig's *Eight Hours for What We Will: Workers and Leisure in an Industrial City, 1870–1920* (1983) and Steven A. Riess's *City Games: The Evolution of American Urban Society and the Rise of Sports* (1989). Saloon culture is examined in Madelon Powers's *Faces along the Bar: Lore and Order in the Workingman's Saloon, 1870–1920* (1998).

On the impact of the theory of evolution, see Barry Werth's *Banquet at Delmonico's: Great Minds, the Gilded Age, and the Triumph of Evolution in America* (2009). On the rise of realism in thought and the arts during the second half of the nineteenth century, see David E. Shi's *Facing Facts: Realism in American Thought and Culture, 1850–1920* (1995). Pragmatism is the focus of Louis Menand's *The Metaphysical Club: A Story of Ideas in America* (2001).

CHAPTER 21

Two good overviews of the Gilded Age are Sean Cashman's *America in the Gilded Age: From the Death of Lincoln to the Rise of Theodore Roosevelt* (1984) and Mark Summers's *The Gilded Age or, The Hazard of New Functions* (1996). Nell Irvin Painter's *Standing at Armageddon: The United States, 1877–1919* (1987) focuses on the experience of the working class. For a stimulating overview of the political, social, and economic trends during the Gilded Age, see Jack Beatty's *Age of Betrayal: The Triumph of Money in America, 1865–1900* (2007). On the development of city rings and bosses, see Kenneth D. Ackerman's *Boss Tweed: The Rise and Fall of the Corrupt Pol Who Conceived the Soul of Modern New York* (2005). Excellent presidential biographies include Hans L. Trefousse's *Rutherford B. Hayes* (2002), Zachary Karabell's *Chester Alan Arthur* (2004), Henry F. Graff's *Grover Cleveland* (2002), and Kevin Phillips's *William McKinley* (2003). On the political culture of the Gilded Age, see Charles Calhoun's *Minority Victory: Gilded Age Politics and the Front Porch Campaign of 1888* (2008).

Scholars have also examined various Gilded Age issues and interest groups. Gerald W. McFarland's *Mugwumps, Morals, and Politics, 1884–1920* (1975) examines the issue of reforming government service. Tom E. Terrill's *The Tariff, Politics, and American Foreign Policy, 1874–1901* (1973) lends clarity to that complex issue. The finances of the Gilded Age are covered in Walter T. K. Nugent's *Money and American Society, 1865–1880* (1968).

A balanced account of Populism is Charles Postel's *The Populist Vision* (2007). The election of 1896 is the focus of R. Hal Williams's *Realigning America: McKinley, Bryan, and the Remarkable Election of 1896* (2010). On the role of religion in the agrarian protest movements, see Joe Creech's *Righteous Indignation: Religion and the Populist Revolution* (2006). The best biography of Bryan is Michael Kazin's *A Godly Hero: The Life of William Jennings Bryan* (2006). For an innovative of the politics and culture of the Gilded Age, see Jackson Lears, *Rebirth of a Nation: The Making of Modern America, 1877–1920* (2009).

CHAPTER 22

An excellent survey of the diplomacy of the era is Charles S. Campbell's *The Transformation of American Foreign Relations, 1865–1900* (1976). For background on the events of the 1890s, see David Healy's *U.S. Expansionism: The Imperialist Urge in the 1890s* (1970). The dispute over American policy in Hawaii is covered in Thomas J. Osborne's *"Empire Can Wait": American Opposition to Hawaiian Annexation, 1893–1898* (1981).

Ivan Musicant's *Empire by Default: The Spanish-American War and the Dawn of the American Century* (1998) is the most comprehensive volume on the conflict. A colorful treatment of the powerful men promoting war is Evan Thomas's *The War Lovers: Roosevelt, Lodge, Mahan, and the Rush to Empire, 1898* (2010). For the war's aftermath in the Philippines, see Stuart Creighton Miller's *"Benevolent Assimilation": The American Conquest of the Philippines, 1899–1903* (1982). Robert L. Beisner's *Twelve against Empire: The Anti-Imperialists, 1898–1900* (1968) handles the debate over annexation. On the Philippine-American War, see David J. Silbey's *A War of Frontier and Empire: The Philippine-American War, 1899–1902* (2007).

A good introduction to American interest in China is Michael H. Hunt's *The Making of a Special Relationship: The United States and China to 1914* (1983). Kenton J. Clymer's *John Hay: The Gentleman as Diplomat* (1975) examines the role of this key secretary of state in forming policy.

For U.S. policy in the Caribbean and Central America, see Walter LaFeber's *Inevitable Revolutions: The United States in Central America*, 2nd ed. (1993). David McCullough's *The Path between the Seas: The Creation of the Panama Canal, 1870–1914* (1977) presents an admiring account of how the United States secured the Panama Canal. A more sober assessment is Julie Greene's *The Canal Builders: Making America's Empire at the Panama Canal* (2009).

CHAPTER 23

Splendid analyses of progressivism can be found in John Whiteclay Chambers II's *The Tyranny of Change: America in the Progressive Era, 1890–1920*, rev. ed. (2000), John M. Cooper's *Pivotal Decades: The United States, 1900–1920* (1990), Steven J. Diner's *A Very Different Age: Americans of the Progressive Era* (1997), Maureen A. Flanagan's *America Reformed: Progressives and Progressivisms, 1890–1920* (2006), Michael McGerr's *A Fierce Discontent: The Rise and Fall of the Progressive Movement in America* (2003), and David Traxel's *Crusader Nation: The United States in Peace and the Great War, 1898–1920* (2006). On Ida Tarbell and the muckrakers, see Steve Weinberg's *Taking on the Trust: The Epic Battle of Ida Tarbell and John D. Rockefeller* (2008). The evolution of government policy toward business is examined in Martin J. Sklar's *The Corporate Reconstruction of American Capitalism, 1890–1916: The Market, the Law, and Politics* (1988). Mina Carson's *Settlement Folk: Social Thought and the American Settlement Movement, 1885–1930* (1990) and Jack M. Holl's *Juvenile Reform in the Progressive Era: William R. George and the Junior Republic Movement* (1971) examine the social problems in the cities. Robert Kanigel's *The One Best Way: Frederick Winslow Taylor and the Enigma of Efficiency* (1997) highlights the role of efficiency in the Progressive Era.

An excellent study of the role of women in progressivism's emphasis on social justice is Kathryn Kish Sklar's *Florence Kelley and the Nation's Work: The Rise of Women's Political Culture, 1830–1900* (1995). On the tragic fire at the Triangle Shirtwaist Company, see David Von Drehle's *Triangle: The Fire That Changed America* (2003). Eleanor Flexner and Ellen Fitzpatrick's *Century of Struggle: The Woman's Rights Movement in the United States*, enl. ed. (1996), surveys the condition of women in the late nineteenth century. The best study of the settlement house movement is Jean Bethke Elshtain's *Jane Addams and the Dream of American Democracy: A Life* (2002).

On Theodore Roosevelt and the conservation movement, see Douglas Brinkley's *The Wilderness Warrior: Theodore Roosevelt and the Crusade for America* (2009). The pivotal election of 1912 is covered in James Chace's *1912: Wilson, Roosevelt, Taft, and Debs—The Election That*

Changed the Country (2004) and Sidney M. Milkis's *TR, the Progressive Party, and the Transformation of Democracy* (2009). Excellent biographies include Kathleen Dalton's *Theodore Roosevelt: A Strenuous Life* (2002) and H. W. Brands's *Woodrow Wilson* (2003). For banking developments, see Allan H. Meltzer's *A History of the Federal Reserve*, vol. 1, *1913–1951* (2003). The racial blind spot of Progressivism is assessed in David W. Southern's *The Progressive Era and Race: Reform and Reaction, 1900–1917* (2006).

CHAPTER 24

A lucid overview of international events in the early twentieth century is Robert H. Ferrell's *Woodrow Wilson and World War I, 1917–1921* (1985). For a vivid account of U.S. intervention in Mexico, see Frederick Katz's *The Life and Times of Pancho Villa* (1999). On Wilson's stance toward war, see Robert W. Tucker's *Woodrow Wilson and the Great War: Reconsidering America's Neutrality, 1914–1917* (2007). An excellent biography is John Milton Cooper Jr.'s *Woodrow Wilson: A Biography* (2010).

For the European experience in the First World War, see Adam Hochschild's *To End All Wars: A Story of Loyalty and Rebellion, 1914–1918* (2011). Edward M. Coffman's *The War to End All Wars: The American Military Experience in World War I* (1968) is a detailed presentation of America's military involvement. See also Gary Mead's *The Doughboys: America and the First World War* (2000). For a survey of the impact of the war on the home front, see Meirion Harries and Susie Harries's *The Last Days of Innocence: America at War, 1917–1918* (1997). Maurine Weiner Greenwald's *Women, War, and Work: The Impact of World War I on Women Workers in the United States* (1980) discusses the role of women. Ronald Schaffer's *America in the Great War: The Rise of the War Welfare State* (1991) shows the effect of war mobilization on business organization. Richard Polenberg's *Fighting Faiths: The Abrams Case, the Supreme Court, and Free Speech* (1987) examines the prosecution of a case under the 1918 Sedition Act. See also Ernest Freeberg's *Democracy's Prisoner: Eugene V. Debs, the Great War, and the Right to Dissent* (2009).

How American diplomacy fared in the making of peace has received considerable attention. Thomas J. Knock interrelates domestic affairs and foreign relations in his explanation of Wilson's peacemaking in *To End All Wars: Woodrow Wilson and the Quest for a New World Order* (1992). See also John Milton Cooper Jr.'s *Breaking the Heart of the World: Woodrow Wilson and the Fight for the League of Nations* (2002).

The problems of the immediate postwar years are chronicled by a number of historians. The best overview is Ann Hagedorn's *Savage Peace: Hope and Fear in America, 1919* (2007). On the Spanish flu, see John M. Barry's *The Great Influenza: The Epic Story of the Deadliest Plague in History* (2004). Labor tensions are examined in David E. Brody's *Labor in Crisis: The Steel Strike of 1919* (1965) and Francis Russell's *A City in Terror: Calvin Coolidge and the 1919 Boston Police Strike* (1975). On racial strife, see Jan Voogd's *Race Riots and Resistance: The Red Summer of 1919* (2008). The fear of Communists is analyzed in Robert K. Murray's *Red Scare: A Study in National Hysteria, 1919–1920* (1955).

CHAPTER 25

For a lively survey of the social and cultural changes during the interwar period, start with William E. Leuchtenburg's *The Perils of Prosperity, 1914–32*, 2nd ed. (1993). Even more comprehensive s Michael E. Parrish's *Anxious Decades: America in Prosperity and Depression,*

1920–1941 (1992). The best introduction to the culture of the twenties remains Roderick Nash's *The Nervous Generation: American Thought, 1917–1930* (1990). See also Lynn Dumenil's *The Modern Temper: American Culture and Society in the 1920s* (1995).

John Higham's *Strangers in the Land: Patterns of American Nativism, 1860–1925*, 2nd ed. (2002) details the story of immigration restriction. The controversial Sacco and Vanzetti case is the focus of Moshik Temkin's *The Sacco-Vanzetti Affair: America on Trial* (2009). For analysis of the revival of Klan activity, see Thomas R. Pegram's *One Hundred Percent American: The Rebirth and Decline of the Ku Klux Klan in the 1920s* (2011). The best analysis of the Scopes trial is Edward J. Larson's *Summer for the Gods: The Scopes Trial and America's Continuing Debate over Science and Religion* (1997). On Prohibition, see Daniel Okrent's *Last Call: The Rise and Fall of Prohibition* (2011).

Woman suffrage is treated in Sara Hunter Graham's *Woman Suffrage and the New Democracy* (1996) and Kristi Anderson's *After Suffrage: Women in Partisan and Electoral Politics before the New Deal* (1996). The best study of the birth-control movement is Ellen Chesler's *Woman of Valor: Margaret Sanger and the Birth Control Movement in America* (1992). See Charles Flint Kellogg's *NAACP: A History of the National Association for the Advancement of Colored People* (1967) for his analysis of the pioneering court cases against racial discrimination. Nathan Irvin Huggins's *Harlem Renaissance* (1971) assesses the cultural impact of the Great Migration on New York City. The emergence of jazz is ably documented in Burton W. Peretti's *The Creation of Jazz: Music, Race, and Culture in Urban America* (1992). On the African American migration from the South, see James N. Gregory's *The Southern Diaspora: How the Great Migrations of Black and White Southerners Transformed America* (2005).

Scientific breakthroughs are analyzed in Manjit Kumar's *Quantum: Einstein, Bohr, and the Great Debate about the Nature of Reality* (2010). The best overview of cultural modernism in Europe is Peter Gay's *Modernism: The Lure of Heresy from Baudelaire to Beckett and Beyond* (2009). See also Stephen Kern's *The Culture of Time and Space, 1880–1918* (2003). A compelling biography the champion of modernist verse is David Moody's *Ezra Pount: Poet* (2007). On southern modernism, see Daniel Joseph Singal's *The War Within: From Victorian to Modernist Thought in the South, 1919–1945* (1982). Stanley Coben's *Rebellion against Victorianism: The Impetus for Cultural Change in 1920s America* (1991) surveys the appeal of modernism among writers, artists, and intellectuals.

CHAPTER 26

A fine synthesis of events immediately following the First World War is Ellis W. Hawley's *The Great War and the Search for a Modern Order: A History of the American People and Their Institutions, 1917–1933*, 2nd ed. (1992). On the election of 1920, see David Pietrusza, *1920: The Year of the Six Presidents* (2006).

On Harding, see Robert K. Murray's *The Harding Era: Warren G. Harding and His Administration* (1969). On Coolidge, see Robert H. Ferrell's *The Presidency of Calvin Coolidge* (1998). On Hoover, see Martin L. Fausold's *The Presidency of Herbert C. Hoover* (1985). The Democratic candidate for president in 1928 is explored in Robert A. Slayton's *Empire Statesman: The Rise and Redemption of Al Smith* (2001). The influential secretary of the Treasury during the twenties is ably analyzed in David Cannadine's *Mellon: An American Life* (2006).

On the stock-market crash in 1929 see Maury Klein's *Rainbow's End: The Crash of 1929* (2000). Overviews of the depressed economy are found in Charles P. Kindleberger's *The World in Depression, 1929–1939*, rev. and enlarged ed. (1986) and Peter Fearon's *War, Prosperity, and Depression: The U.S. Economy, 1917–1945* (1987). John A. Garraty's *The Great Depression: An*

Inquiry into the Causes, Course, and Consequences of the Worldwide Depression of the Nineteen-Thirties (1986) describes how people survived the Depression. On the removal of the Bonus Army, see Paul Dickson and Thomas B. Allen's *The Bonus Army: An American Epic* (2004).

CHAPTER 27

A comprehensive overview of the New Deal is David M. Kennedy's *Freedom from Fear: The American People in Depression and War, 1929–1945* (1999). A lively biography of Franklin D. Roosevelt is H. W. Brands's *Traitor to His Class: The Privileged Life and Radical Presidency of Franklin Delano Roosevelt* (2009). The Roosevelt marriage is well described in Hazel Rowley's *Franklin and Eleanor: An Extraordinary Marriage* (2011). On the first woman cabinet member, see Kirstin Downey's *The Woman behind the New Deal: The Life of Frances Perkins* (2009). The busy first year of the New Deal is ably detailed in Anthony J. Badger's *FDR: The First Hundred Days* (2008). Perhaps the most successful of the early New Deal programs is the focus of Neil M. Maher's *Nature's New Deal: The Civilian Conservation Corps and the Roots of the American Environmental Movement* (2008). On the political opponents of the New Deal, see Alan Brinkley's *Voices of Protest: Huey Long, Father Coughlin, and the Great Depression* (1982). Roosevelt's battle with the Supreme Court is detailed in Jeff Shesol's *Supreme Power: Franklin Roosevelt vs. The Supreme Court* (2010). The actual effects of the New Deal on the economy are detailed in Elliot A. Rosen's *Roosevelt, the Great Depression, and the Economics of Recovery* (2005).

A critical assessment of Roosevelt and the New Deal is Amity Schlaes's *The Forgotten Man* (2007). James N. Gregory's *American Exodus: The Dust Bowl Migration and Okie Culture in California* (1989) describes the migratory movement. On the environmental and human causes of the dust bowl, see Donald Worster, *Dust Bowl: The Southern Plains in the 1930s* (1979). On cultural life during the thirties, see Morris Dickstein's *Dancing in the Dark: A Cultural History of the Great Depression* (2009).

The best overview of diplomacy between the world wars remains Selig Adler's *The Uncertain Giant, 1921–1941: American Foreign Policy between the Wars* (1965). Robert Dallek's *Franklin D. Roosevelt and American Foreign Policy, 1932–1945* (1979) provides a judicious assessment of Roosevelt's foreign-policy initiatives during the thirties.

A noteworthy study is Waldo Heinrichs's *Threshold of War: Franklin D. Roosevelt and American Entry into World War II* (1988). See also David Reynolds's *From Munich to Pearl Harbor: Roosevelt's America and the Origins of the Second World War* (2001). On the surprise attack on Pearl Harbor, see Gordon W. Prange's *Pearl Harbor: The Verdict of History* (1986). Japan's perspective is described in Akira Iriye's *The Origins of the Second World War in Asia and the Pacific* (1987).

CHAPTER 28

For sweeping surveys of the Second World War, consult Anthony Roberts's *The Storm of War: A New History of the Second World War* (2011) and Max Hastings's *The World at War, 1939–1945* (2011), while Charles B. MacDonald's *The Mighty Endeavor: The American War in Europe* (1986) concentrates on U.S. involvement. Roosevelt's wartime leadership is analyzed in Eric Larrabee's *Commander in Chief: Franklin Delano Roosevelt, His Lieutenants, and Their War* (1987).

Books on specific European campaigns include Anthony Beevor's *D-Day: The Battle for Normandy* (2010) and Charles B. MacDonald's *A Time for Trumpets: The Untold Story of the Battle of the Bulge* (1985). On the Allied commander, see Carlo D'Este's *Eisenhower: A Soldier's Life* (2002).

For the war in the Far East, see John Costello's *The Pacific War, 1941–1945* (1981), Ronald H. Spector's *Eagle against the Sun: The American War with Japan* (1985), John W. Dower's award-winning *War without Mercy: Race and Power in the Pacific War* (1986), and Dan van der Vat's *The Pacific Campaign: The U.S.-Japanese Naval War, 1941–1945* (1991).

An excellent overview of the war's effects on the home front is Michael C. C. Adams's *The Best War Ever: America and World War II* (1994). On economic effects, see Harold G. Vatter's *The U.S. Economy in World War II* (1985). Susan M. Hartmann's *The Home Front and Beyond: American Women in the 1940s* (1982) treats the new working environment for women. Kenneth D. Rose tells the story of problems on the home front in *Myth and the Greatest Generation: A Social History of Americans in World War II* (2008). Neil A. Wynn looks at the participation of blacks in *The Afro-American and the Second World War* (1976). A more focused study of black airmen is J. Todd Moye's *Freedom Flyers: The Tuskeegee Airmen of World War II* (2010). The story of the oppression of Japanese Americans is told in Greg Robinson's *A Tragedy for Democracy: Japanese Confinement in North America* (2009). On the development of the atomic bomb, see Jim Baggott's *The First War of Physics: The Secret History of the Atomic Bomb* (2010).

A sound introduction to U.S. diplomacy during the conflict can be found in Gaddis Smith's *American Diplomacy during the Second World War, 1941–1945* (1965). To understand the role that Roosevelt played in policy making, consult Warren F. Kimball's *The Juggler: Franklin Roosevelt as Wartime Statesman* (1991). The most important wartime summit is assessed in S. M. Plokhy's *Yalta: The Price of Peace* (2010). The issues and events that led to the deployment of atomic weapons are addressed in Martin J. Sherwin's *A World Destroyed: The Atomic Bomb and the Grand Alliance* (1975).

CHAPTER 29

The cold war remains a hotly debated topic. The traditional interpretation is best reflected in John Lewis Gaddis's *The Cold War: A New History* (2005). Both superpowers, Gaddis argues, were responsible for causing the cold war, but the Soviet Union was more culpable. The revisionist perspective is represented by Gar Alperovitz's *Atomic Diplomacy: Hiroshima and Potsdam: The Use of the Atomic Bomb and the American Confrontation with Soviet Power,* 2nd ed. (1994). Alperovitz places primary responsibility for the conflict on the United States. Also see H. W. Brands's *The Devil We Knew: Americans and the Cold War* (1993) and Melvyn P. Leffler's *For the Soul of Mankind: The United States, the Soviet Union, and the Cold War* (2007). On the architect of the containment strategy, see John L. Gaddis, *George F. Kennan: An American Life* (2011).

Arnold A. Offner indicts Truman for clumsy statesmanship in *Another Such Victory: President Truman and the Cold War, 1945–1953* (2002). For a positive assessment of Truman's leadership, see Alonzo L. Hamby's *Beyond the New Deal: Harry S. Truman and American Liberalism* (1973) and Robert Dallek's *The Lost Peace: Leadership in a Time of Horror and Hope, 1945–1953* (2010). The domestic policies of the Fair Deal are treated in William C. Berm00000000000000000000000000000000000an's *The Politics of Civil Rights in the Truman*

Administration (1970), Richard M. Dalfiume's *Desegregation of the U.S. Armed Forces: Fighting on Two Fronts, 1939–1953* (1969), and Maeva Marcus's *Truman and the Steel Seizure Case: The Limits of Presidential Power* (1977). The most comprehensive biography of Truman is David McCullough's *Truman* (1992).

For an introduction to the tensions in Asia, see Akira Iriye's *The Cold War in Asia: A Historical Introduction* (1974). For the Korean conflict, see Callum A. MacDonald's *Korea: The War before Vietnam* (1986) and Max Hasting's *The Korean War* (1987).

The anti-Communist syndrome is surveyed in David Caute's *The Great Fear: The Anti-Communist Purge under Truman and Eisenhower* (1978). Arthur Herman's *Joseph McCarthy: Reexamining the Life and Legacy of America's Most Hated Senator* (2000) covers McCarthy himself. For a well-documented account of how the cold war was sustained by superpatriotism, intolerance, and suspicion, see Stephen J. Whitfield's *The Culture of the Cold War,* 2nd ed. (1996).

CHAPTER 30

Two excellent overviews of social and cultural trends in the postwar era are William H. Chafe's *The Unfinished Journey: America since World War II,* 6th ed. (2006) and William E. Leuchtenburg's *A Troubled Feast: America since 1945,* rev. ed. (1979). For insights into the cultural life of the fifties, see Jeffrey Hart's *When the Going Was Good! American Life in the Fifties* (1982) and David Halberstam's *The Fifties* (1993).

The baby boom generation and its impact are vividly described in Paul C. Light's *Baby Boomers* (1988). The emergence of the television industry is discussed in Erik Barnouw's *Tube of Plenty: The Evolution of American Television,* 2nd rev. ed. (1990), and Ella Taylor's *Prime-Time Families: Television Culture in Postwar America* (1989).

A comprehensive account of the process of suburban development is Kenneth T. Jackson's *Crabgrass Frontier: The Suburbanization of the United States* (1985). Equally good is Tom Martinson's *American Dreamscape: The Pursuit of Happiness in Postwar Suburbia* (2000).

The middle-class ideal of family life in the fifties is examined in Elaine Tyler May's *Homeward Bound: American Families in the Cold War Era,* rev. ed. (2008). Thorough accounts of women's issues are found in Wini Breines's *Young, White, and Miserable: Growing Up Female in the Fifties* (1992). For an overview of the resurgence of religion in the fifties, see George M. Marsden's *Religion and American Culture,* 2nd ed. (2000).

A lively discussion of movies of the fifties can be found in Peter Biskind's *Seeing Is Believing: How Hollywood Taught Us to Stop Worrying and Love the Fifties* (1983). The origins and growth of rock and roll are surveyed in Carl Belz's *The Story of Rock,* 2nd ed. (1972). Thoughtful interpretive surveys of postwar literature include Josephine Hendin's *Vulnerable People: A View of American Fiction since 1945* (1978) and Malcolm Bradbury's *The Modern American Novel* (1983). The colorful Beats are brought to life in Steven Watson's *The Birth of the Beat Generation: Visionaries, Rebels, and Hipsters, 1944–1960* (1995).

Scholarship on the Eisenhower years is extensive. A carefully balanced overview of the period is Chester J. Pach Jr. and Elmo Richardson's *The Presidency of Dwight D. Eisenhower,* rev. ed. (1991). For the manner in which Eisenhower conducted foreign policy, see Robert A. Divine's *Eisenhower and the Cold War* (1981). Tom Wicker deems Eisenhower a better person than a president in *Dwight D. Eisenhower* (2002).

The best overview of American foreign policy since 1945 is Stephen E. Ambrose and Douglas G. Brinkley's *Rise to Globalism: American Foreign Policy since 1938,* 9th ed. (2011). For the buildup of U.S. involvement in Indochina, consult Lloyd C. Gardner's *Approaching Vietnam: From World War II through Dienbienphu, 1941–1954* (1988) and David L. Anderson's *Trapped by Success: The Eisenhower Administration and Vietnam, 1953–61* (1991). How the Eisenhower Doctrine came to be implemented is traced in Stephen E. Ambrose and Douglas G. Brinkley's *Rise to Globalism: American Foreign Policy since 1938*, 8th ed. (1997). The cold war strategy of the Eisenhower administration is the focus of Chris Tudda's *The Truth Is Our Weapon: The Rhetorical Diplomacy of Dwight D. Eisenhower and John Foster Dulles* (2006).

The impact of the Supreme Court during the fifties is the focus of Archibald Cox's *The Warren Court: Constitutional Decision as an Instrument of Reform* (1968). A masterly study of the important Warren Court decision on school desegregation is James T. Patterson's *Brown v. Board of Education: A Civil Rights Milestone and Its Troubled Legacy* (2001).

For the story of the early years of the civil rights movement, see Taylor Branch's *Parting the Waters: America in the King Years, 1954–1963* (1988), Robert Weisbrot's *Freedom Bound: A History of America's Civil Rights Movement* (1990), and David A. Nicholas's *A Matter of Justice: Eisenhower and the Beginning of the Civil Rights Revolution* (2007).

CHAPTER 31

A dispassionate analysis of John F. Kennedy's life is Thomas C. Reeves's *A Question of Character: A Life of John F. Kennedy* (1991). The 1960 campaign is detailed in Gary A. Donaldson's *The First Modern Campaign: Kennedy, Nixon, and the Election of 1960* (2007). The best study of the Kennedy administration's domestic policies is Irving Bernstein's *Promises Kept: John F. Kennedy's New Frontier* (1991). For details on the still swirling conspiracy theories about the assassination, see David W. Belin's *Final Disclosure: The Full Truth about the Assassination of President Kennedy* (1988).

The most comprehensive biography of Lyndon B. Johnson is Robert Dallek's two-volume work, *Lone Star Rising: Lyndon Johnson and His Times, 1908–1960* (1991) and *Flawed Giant: Lyndon Johnson and His Times, 1961–1973* (1998). On the Johnson administration, see Vaughn Davis Bornet's *The Presidency of Lyndon B. Johnson* (1984).

Among the works that interpret liberal social policy during the sixties, John E. Schwarz's *America's Hidden Success: A Reassessment of Twenty Years of Public Policy* (1983) offers a glowing endorsement of Democratic programs. For a contrasting perspective, see Charles Murray's *Losing Ground: American Social Policy, 1950–1980*, rev. ed. (1994).

On foreign policy, see *Kennedy's Quest for Victory: American Foreign Policy, 1961–1963* (1989), edited by Thomas G. Paterson. To learn more about Kennedy's problems in Cuba, see Mark J. White's *Missiles in Cuba: Kennedy, Khrushchev, Castro and the 1962 Crisis* (1997). See also Aleksandr Fursenko and Timothy Naftali's *"One Hell of a Gamble": Khrushchev, Castro and Kennedy, 1958–1964* (1997).

American involvement in Vietnam has received voluminous treatment from all political perspectives. For an excellent overview, see Larry Berman's *Planning a Tragedy: The Americanization of the War in Vietnam* (1983) and *Lyndon Johnson's War: The Road to Stalemate in Vietnam* (1989), as well as Stanley Karnow's *Vietnam: A History*, 2nd rev. ed. (1997). An analysis of policy making concerning the Vietnam War is David M. Barrett's *Uncertain Warriors: Lyndon Johnson and His Vietnam Advisors* (1993). A fine account of the military involvement is Robert D. Schulzinger's *A Time for War: The United States and Vietnam, 1941–1975* (1997). On the legacy of the Vietnam

War, see Arnold R. Isaacs's *Vietnam Shadows: The War, Its Ghosts, and Its Legacy* (1997).

Many scholars have dealt with various aspects of the civil rights movement and race relations in the sixties. See especially Carl M. Brauer's *John F. Kennedy and the Second Reconstruction* (1977), David J. Garrow's *Bearing the Cross: Martin Luther King, Jr., and the Southern Christian Leadership Conference* (1986), and Adam Fairclough's *To Redeem the Soul of America: The Southern Christian Leadership Conference and Martin Luther King, Jr.* (1987). William H. Chafe's *Civilities and Civil Rights: Greensboro, North Carolina, and the Black Struggle for Freedom* (1980) details the original sit-ins. An award-winning study of racial and economic inequality in a representative American city is Thomas J. Sugrue's *The Origins of the Urban Crisis: Race and Inequality in Postwar Detroit* (1996).

CHAPTER 32

An engaging overview of the cultural trends of the sixties is Maurice Isserman and Michael Kazin's *America Divided: The Civil War of the 1960s*, 3rd ed. (2007). The New Left is assessed in Irwin Unger's *The Movement: A History of the American New Left, 1959–1972* (1974). On the Students for a Democratic Society, see Kirkpatrick Sale's *SDS* (1973) and Allen J. Matusow's *The Unraveling of America: A History of Liberalism in the 1960s* (1984). Also useful is Todd Gitlin's *The Sixties: Years of Hope, Days of Rage*, rev. ed. (1993).

Two influential assessments of the counterculture by sympathetic commentators are Theodore Roszak's *The Making of a Counter-culture: Reflections on the Technocratic Society and Its Youthful Opposition* (1969) and Charles A. Reich's *The Greening of America: How the Youth Revolution Is Trying to Make America Livable* (1970). A good scholarly analysis that takes the hippies seriously is Timothy Miller's *The Hippies and American Values* (1991).

The best study of the women's liberation movement is Ruth Rosen's *The World Split Open: How the Modern Women's Movement Changed America*, rev. ed. (2006). The organizing efforts of Cesar Chavez are detailed in Ronald B. Taylor's *Chavez and the Farm Workers* (1975). The struggles of Native Americans for recognition and power are sympathetically described in Stan Steiner's *The New Indians* (1968).

The best overview of the seventies and eighties is James T. Patterson's *Restless Giant: The United States from Watergate to Bush v. Gore* (2005). On Nixon, see Melvin Small's thorough analysis in *The Presidency of Richard Nixon* (1999). A good slim biography is Elizabeth Drew's *Richard M. Nixon* (2007). For an overview of the Watergate scandal, see Stanley I. Kutler's *The Wars of Watergate: The Last Crisis of Richard Nixon* (1990). For the way the Republicans handled foreign affairs, consult Tad Szulc's *The Illusion of Peace: Foreign Policy in the Nixon Years* (1978).

The Communist takeover of Vietnam and the end of American involvement there are traced in Larry Berman's *No Peace, No Honor: Nixon, Kissinger, and Betrayal in Vietnam* (2001). William Shawcross's *Sideshow: Kissinger, Nixon and the Destruction of Cambodia*, rev. ed. (2002), deals with the broadening of the war, while Larry Berman's *Planning a Tragedy: The Americanization of the War in Vietnam* (1982) assesses the final impact of U.S. involvement. The most comprehensive treatment of the anti-war movement is Tom Wells's *The War Within: America's Battle over Vietnam* (1994).

A comprehensive treatment of the Ford administration is contained in John Robert Greene's *The Presidency of Gerald R. Ford* (1995). The best overview of the Carter administration is Burton I. Kaufman's *The Presidency of James Earl Carter, Jr.*, 2nd rev. ed. (2006). A work more sympathetic to the Carter administration is John Dumbrell's *The Carter Presidency: A Re-evaluation*, 2nd ed. (1995). Gaddis Smith's *Morality, Reason, and Power: American Diplo-*

macy in the Carter Years (1986) provides an overview. Background on how the Middle East came to dominate much of American policy is found in William B. Quandt's *Decade of Decisions: American Policy toward the Arab-Israeli Conflict, 1967–1976* (1977).

CHAPTER 33

Two brief accounts of Reagan's presidency are David Mervin's *Ronald Reagan and the American Presidency* (1990) and Michael Schaller's *Reckoning with Reagan: America and Its President in the 1980s* (1992). More substantial biographies are John Patrick Diggins's *Ronald Reagan: Fate, Freedom, and the Making of History* (2007) and Richard Reeves's *President Reagan: The Triumph of Imagination* (2005). The best political analysis is Robert M. Collins's *Transforming America: Politics and Culture during the Reagan Years* (2007). An excellent analysis of the 1980 election is Andrew E. Busch's *Reagan's Victory: The Presidential Election of 1980 and the Rise of the Right* (2005). A more comprehensive summary of the Reagan years is Sean Wilentz's *The Age of Reagan: A History, 1974–2008* (2008).

The story of the rise of modern conservatism is well told in Patrick Allitt's *The Conservatives: Ideas and Personalities throughout American History* (2009) and Michael Schaller's *Right Turn: American Life in the Reagan-Bush Era, 1980–1992* (2007).

On Reaganomics, see David A. Stockman's *The Triumph of Politics: Why the Reagan Revolution Failed* (1986) and Robert Lekachman's *Greed Is Not Enough: Reaganomics* (1982). On the issue of arms control, see Strobe Talbott's *Deadly Gambits: The Reagan Administration and the Stalemate in Nuclear Arms Control* (1984).

For Reagan's foreign policy in Central America, see James Chace's *Endless War: How We Got Involved in Central America—and What Can Be Done* (1984) and Walter LaFeber's *Inevitable Revolutions: The United States in Central America,* 2nd ed. (1993). Insider views of Reagan's foreign policy are offered in Alexander M. Haig Jr.'s *Caveat: Realism, Reagan, and Foreign Policy* (1984) and Caspar W. Weinberger's *Fighting for Peace: Seven Critical Years in the Pentagon* (1990).

On Reagan's second term, see Jane Mayer and Doyle McManus's *Landslide: The Unmaking of the President, 1984–1988* (1988). For a masterly work on the Iran-Contra affair, see Theodore Draper's *A Very Thin Line: The Iran Contra Affairs* (1991). Several collections of essays include varying assessments of the Reagan years. Among these are *The Reagan Revolution?* (1988), edited by B. B. Kymlicka and Jean V. Matthews; *The Reagan Presidency: An Incomplete Revolution?* (1990), edited by Dilys M. Hill, Raymond A. Moore, and Phil Williams, and *Looking Back on the Reagan Presidency* (1990), edited by Larry Berman.

On the 1988 campaign, see Jack W. Germond and Jules Witcover's *Whose Broad Stripes and Bright Stars? The Trivial Pursuit of the Presidency, 1988* (1989) and Sidney Blumenthal's *Pledging Allegiance: The Last Campaign of the Cold War* (1990). For a social history of the decade, see John Ehrman's *The Eighties: America in the Age of Reagan* (2005).

CHAPTER 34

Analysis of the Clinton years can be found in Joe Klein's *The Natural: The Misunderstood Presidency of Bill Clinton* (2002). Clinton's impeachment is assessed in Richard A. Posner's *An Affair of State: The Investigation, Impeachment, and Trial of President Clinton* (1999).

On changing demographic trends, see Sam Roberts's *Who We Are Now: The Changing Face of America in the Twenty-First Century* (2004). On social and cultural life in the nineties, see Haynes Johnson's *The Best of Times: America in the Clinton Years* (2001). Economic and technological changes are assessed in Daniel T. Rogers's *Age of Fracture* (2011). The onset and growth of the AIDS epidemic are traced in *And the Band Played On: Politics, People, and the AIDS Epidemic,* 20th anniversary ed. (2007), by Randy Shilts.

Aspects of fundamentalist and apocalyptic movements are the subject of Paul Boyer's *When Time Shall Be No More: Prophecy Belief in Modern American Culture* (1992), George M. Marsden's *Understanding Fundamentalism and Evangelicalism,* new ed. (2006), and Ralph E. Reed's *Politically Incorrect: The Emerging Faith Factor in American Politics* (1994).

On the invention of the computer and the Internet, see Paul E. Ceruzzi's *A History of Modern Computing,* 2nd ed. (2003), and Janet Abbate's *Inventing the Internet* (1999). The booming economy of the nineties is well analyzed in Joseph E. Stiglitz's *The Roaring Nineties: A New History of the World's Most Prosperous Decade* (2003). On the rising stress within the workplace, see Jill Andresky Fraser's *White-Collar Sweatshop: The Deterioration of Work and Its Rewards in Corporate America* (2001). Aspects of corporate restructuring and downsizing are the subjects of Bennett Harrison's *Lean and Mean: The Changing Landscape of Corporate Power in the Age of Flexibility* (1994).

For further treatment of the end of the cold war, see Michael R. Beschloss and Strobe Talbott's *At the Highest Levels: The Inside Story of the End of the Cold War* (1993) and Richard Crockatt's *The Fifty Years War: The United States and the Soviet Union in World Politics, 1941–1991* (1995). On the Persian Gulf conflict, see Lester H. Brune's *America and the Iraqi Crisis, 1990–1992: Origins and Aftermath* (1993). On the transformation of American foreign policy, see James Mann's *Rise of the Vulcans: The History of Bush's War Cabinet* (2004), Claes G. Ryn's *America the Virtuous: The Crisis of Democracy and the Quest for Empire* (2003), and Stephen M. Walt's *Taming American Power: The Global Response to U.S. Primacy* (2005).

The disputed 2000 presidential election is the focus of Jeffrey Toobin's *Too Close to Call: The Thirty-Six-Day Battle to Decide the 2000 Election* (2001). On the Bush presidency, see *The Presidency of George W. Bush: A First Historical Assessment,* edited by Julian E. Zelizer (2010). On the 9/11 attacks and their aftermath, see *The Age of Terror: America and the World after September 11,* edited by Strobe Talbott and Nayan Chanda (2001).

For a devastating account of the Bush administration by a White House insider, see Scott McClellan's *What Happened: Inside the Bush White House and Washington's Culture of Deception* (2008). On the historic 2008 election, see Michael Nelson's *The Elections of 2008* (2009). An excellent early interpretation of the nation's first African American president is Pete Souza's *The Rise of Barack Obama* (2010).

The Tea Party movement is assessed in Theda Skocpol and Vanessa Williamson's *The Tea Party and the Remaking of Republican Conservatism* (2012) and Elizabeth Price Foley's *The Tea Party: Three Principles* (2012).

CREDITS

CHAPTER 1: **p. 1**: The New York Public Library/Art Resource, NY; **p. 3**: Granger Collection; **p. 5**: Bettmann/Corbis; **p. 14**: MPI/Getty Images; **p. 17**: The Benson Latin American Collection, University of Texas; **p. 19**: Atlantide Phototravel/Corbis; **p. 24**: Werner Forman/Art Resource, NY; **p. 29**: Bettmann/Corbis.

CHAPTER 2: **p. 32**: Granger Collection; **p. 36**: Bridgeman Art Library; **p. 39**: Granger Collection; **p. 45**: Granger Collection; **p. 47**: Granger Collection; **p. 49**: Library of Congress; **p. 54**: The Mariners' Museum/Corbis; **p. 60**: Stapleton Collection/Corbis.

CHAPTER 3: **p. 68**: Granger Collection; **p. 69**: Granger Collection; **p. 72**: Connecticut Historical Society Museum; **p. 74**: Granger Collection; **p. 76**: Granger Collection; **p. 79**: Abby Aldrich Rockefeller Folk Art Center Colonial Williamsburg; **p. 81**: Granger Collection; **p. 91**: Library Company of Philadelphia; **p. 94**: Stock Montage/Getty Images; **p. 96**: Granger Collection; **p. 97**: National Portrait Gallery, London.

CHAPTER 4: **p. 102**: Library of Congress; **p. 105**: I.N. Phelps Stokes Collection Miriam and Ira D. Wallach Division of Art, Prints and Photographs, New York Public Library, Astor, Lenox and Tilden Foundations; **p. 110**: Snark/Art Resource, NY; **p. 114**: Library of Congress; **p. 115**: Granger Collection; **p. 123**: Library of Congress; **p. 126**: Library of Congress; **p. 132**: Granger Collection; **p. 135**: American Antiquarian Society; **p. 137**: National Archives; **p. 138**: North Wind Picture Archives/Alamy.

CHAPTER 5: **p. 143**: Art Resource, NY; **p. 144**: Library of Congress; **p. 147**: Giraudon/Art Resource NY; **p. 149**: Library of Congress; **p. 150**: U.S. Senate Collection; **p. 153**: Anne S.K. Brown Military Collection, Brown University Library; **p. 157**: Granger Collection; **p. 176**: Granger Collection.

CHAPTER 6: **p. 180**: Bettmann/Corbis; **p. 187**: Historical Society of Pennsylvania; **p. 189**: Granger Collection; **p. 191**: Library of Congress; **p. 197**: Independence National Historical Park; **p. 202**: MPI/Getty Images.

CHAPTER 7: **p. 206**: Art Resource, NY; **p. 207**: Library of Congress; **p. 211**: Independence National Historical Park; **p. 216**: Granger Collection; **p. 222**: Granger Collection; **p. 226**: Granger Collection; **p. 227**: Granger Collection.

CHAPTER 8: **p. 236**: Giraudon/Art Resource NY; **p. 240**: NYPL Digital Gallery; **p. 243**: Collection of the New-York Historical Society/ Bridgeman Art Library; **p. 245**: Copyright American Philosophical Society; **p. 249**: Library of Congress; **p. 253**: Library of Congress; **p. 264**: Collection of Davenport West, Jr.

CHAPTER 9: **p. 269**: Library of Congress; **p. 271**: Library of Congress; **p. 273**: Granger Collection; **p. 275**: Granger Collection; **p. 282**: Granger Collection; **p. 287**: Maryland Historical Society

1934.2.1; **p. 288**: Granger Collection; **p. 289**: Library of Congress; **p. 290**: Board of Trustees, National Gallery of Art, Washington 1980.62.9. (2794) PA; **p. 291**: Library of Congress; **p. 295**: Library of Congress; **p. 298**: John W. Bennett Labor Collection, Special Collections and University Archives, W. E. B. Du Bois Library, University of Massachusetts Amherst.

CHAPTER 10: **p. 304**: Library of Congress; **p. 309**: Granger Collection; **p. 312**: Library of Congress; **p. 316**: Henry Clay Memorial Foundation; **p. 318**: Corbis; **p. 323**: Corbis.

CHAPTER 11: **p. 330**: Library of Congress; **p. 333**: Library of Congress; **p. 335**: Library of Congress; **p. 336**: National Portrait Gallery, Smithsonian Institution/Art Resource, NY; **p. 337**: Library of Congress; p. 339: Library of Congress; **p. 344**: Granger Collection; **p. 347**: Collection of the New-York Historical Society; **p. 352**: Library of Congress.

CHAPTER 12: **p. 360**: Bettmann/Corbis; **p. 363**: Private Collection/Peter Newark American Pictures/Bridgeman Art Library; **p. 367**: Bettmann/Corbis; **p. 368**: Used with Permission of Documenting the American South, The University of North Carolina at Chapel Hill Libraries; **p. 370**: The Charleston Museum; **p. 377**: Library of Congress; **p. 380**: Library of Congress.

CHAPTER 13: **p. 384**: Bettmann/Corbis; **p. 387**: Alamy: **p. 389**: Library of Congress; **p. 393**: Lordprice Collection/Alamy; **p. 396**: Bettmann/Corbis; **p. 397**: Bettmann/Corbis; **p. 399**: The Walters Art Museum, Baltimore; **p. 400**: Granger Collection; **p. 404**: Warder Collection; **p. 408**: Granger Collection; **p. 410 (both)**: Library of Congress; **p. 412 (left)**: Granger Collection; **(right)**: Library of Congress.

CHAPTER 14: **p. 419**: Granger Collection; **p. 420**: Library of Congress; **p. 423**: Granger Collection; **p. 429**: Library of Congress; **p. 431**: Image copyright © The Metropolitan Museum of Art/Art Resource, NY; **p. 436**: Richard Collier, Wyoming Dept. of State Parks and Cultural Resources; **p. 435**: Macduff Everton/Corbis; **p. 439**: National Archives; **p. 444**: Library of Congress.

CHAPTER 15: **p. 454**: Granger Collection; **p. 459**: Library of Congress; **p. 460**: Granger Collection; **p. 463**: Granger Collection; **p. 464**: Granger Collection; **p. 466**: Granger Collection; **p. 468**: Granger Collection; **p. 473**: akg-images/The Image Works; **p. 480**: Granger Collection; **p. 482**: Library of Congress; **p. 485**: Library of Congress; **p. 486**: Granger Collection.

CHAPTER 16: **p. 494**: Library of Congress; **p. 496**: Library of Congress; **p. 503**: Bettmann/Corbis; **p. 504**: Granger Collection; **p. 514 (both)**: Library of Congress; **p. 517**: Library of Congress; **p. 520**: Granger Collection; **p. 521**: Library of Congress; **p. 523**: National Archives; **p. 524**: Library of Congress; **p. 526**: Library of Congress; **p. 528**: Bettmann/Corbis; **p. 531**: Bettmann/Corbis; **p. 533**: Library of Congress; **p. 534**: Library of Congress.

CHAPTER 17: **p. 538**: Library of Congress; **p. 540**: Library of Congress; **p. 545**: Library of Congress; **p. 547**: Library of Congress; **p. 555**: Bettmann/Corbis; **p. 559**: Library of Congress; **p. 565**: Library of Congress; **p. 568**: Library of Congress.

CHAPTER 18: **p. 573**: Granger Collection; **p. 574**: Granger Collection; **p. 577**: Library of Congress; **p. 581**: Bettmann/Corbis; **p. 583**: Union Pacific Museum; **p. 585**: Warder Collection; **p. 586**: American Petroleum Institute Historical Photo Collection; **p. 587**: Carnegie Library of Pittsburgh; **p. 589**: National Portrait Gallery, Smithsonian Institution/Art Resource, NY; **p. 594**: T.V. Powderly Photographic Collection, The American Catholic History Research Center University Archives, The Catholic University of America, Washington, D.C; **p. 601**: Walter P. Reuther Library, Wayne State University.

CHAPTER 19: **p. 606**: Library of Congress; **p. 612**: Granger Collection; **p. 614**: Kansas State Historical Society; **p. 617**: Warder Collection: **p. 621**: Bettmann/Corbis; **p. 623**: Western Historical Collections University of Oklahoma Library.

CHAPTER 20: p. 628: Library of Congress; p. 632: The Art Archive/Culver Pictures/Art Resource; p. 634: Bettmann/Corbis; p. 635: The Bryon Collection, Museum of the City of New York; p. 637: William Williams Papers, Manuscripts and Archives Division, The New York Public Library, Astor, Lenox and Tilden Foundations; p. 640: Bettmann/Corbis; p. 642: Brown Brothers; p. 644: Old York Library/Avery Library, Columbia University; p. 645: Library of Congress; p. 647: Bettmann/Corbis.

CHAPTER 21: p. 652: Library of Congress; p. 657: Library of Congress; p. 660: Warder Collection; p. 661: Bettmann/Corbis; p. 663: Bettmann/Corbis; p. 665: Library of Congress; p. 669: Kansas State Historical Society; p. 671: Library of Congress; p. 673: Library of Congress; p. 680: Granger Collection; p. 682: Photograph courtesy of the New Hanover County Public Library; p. 683: Library of Congress; p. 684: Warder Collection.

CHAPTER 22: p. 689: Library of Congress; p. 691: Library of Congress; p. 693: Bettmann/Corbis; p. 697: Adoc-photos/Art Resource, NY; p. 700: Library of Congress; p. 701: National Archives; p. 706: Library of Congress; p. 708: Granger Collection; p. 711: Granger Collection; p. 712: Bettmann/Corbis; p. 714: Bettmann/Corbis.

CHAPTER 23: p. 718: Library of Congress; p. 722: University of Illinois at Chicago; p. 724: Granger Collection; p. 727: Library of Congress; p. 729: Bettmann/Corbis; p. 732 (top): Collection of the New-York Historical Society; (bottom): Library of Congress; p. 734: Library of Congress; p. 735: Bettmann/Corbis; p. 736: Bettmann/Corbis; p. 738: Library of Congress; p. 740: Library of Congress; p. 745: Warder Collection; p. 748: Corbis; p. 750: Granger Collection.

CHAPTER 24: p. 756: Library of Congress; p. 759: Bettmann/Corbis; p. 761: Alamy; p. 769: Bettmann/Corbis; p. 771: Everett Collection; p. 773: Bettmann/Corbis; p. 778: Mary Evans Picture Library; p. 779: Courtesy of the "Ding" Darling Wildlife Society; p. 785: Chicago History Museum.

CHAPTER 25: p. 790: Bettmann/Corbis; p. 794: Bettmann/Corbis; p. 796: Bettmann/Corbis; p. 799: Bettmann/Corbis; p. 801: Bettmann/Corbis; p. 805: Art © Heirs of Aaron Douglas/Licensed by VAGA, New York, NY *Into Bondage*, 1936 (oil on canvas), Douglas, Aaron (1899–1979) / Corcoran Gallery of Art, Washington D.C., USA / Museum Purchase and partial gift of Thurlow Evans Tibbs, Jr. The Evans-Tibbs Collection/Bridgeman Art Library; p. 806: Ramsey Archive; p. 808: AP Photo; p. 809: Library of Congress; p. 813: From the Collections of The Henry Ford Museum; p. 818: Image copyright © The Metropolitan Museum of Art / Art Resource, NY. ©2012 Estate of Pablo Picasso / Artists Rights Society (ARS), New York.

CHAPTER 26: p. 822: Bettmann/Corbis; p. 825: Corbis; p. 829: AP Photo; p. 832: *The Washington Post*. Reprinted with permission; p. 834: Hulton Archive/Getty Images; p. 838: Bettmann/Corbis; p. 840: Herbert Hoover Presidential Library; p. 846: Bettmann/Corbis; p. 849: *New York Daily News*; p. 853: AP Photo.

CHAPTER 27: p. 858: Bettmann/Corbis; p. 860: National Archives; p. 865: National Archives; p. 866: Library of Congress; p. 868: Library of Congress; p. 869: Bettmann/Corbis; p. 871: Hulton Archives/Getty Images; p. 872: Bettmann/Corbis; p. 874: Bettmann/Corbis; p. 876: Library of Congress; p. 880: 1936, *The Washington Post*; p. 884: Bettmann/Corbis.

CHAPTER 28: p. 888: Bettmann/Corbis; p. 890: National Archives; p. 894: 1938, *The Washington Post*; p. 898: British Information Services; p. 899: Granger Collection; p. 904: Library of Congress; p. 906: Warder Collection; p. 909: Image by Swim Ink 2, LLC/Corbis; p. 911: Library of Congress; p. 913: AP Photo; p. 915: Bettmann/Corbis; p. 922: Eisenhower Presidential Library; p. 923: National Archives; p. 929: National Archives; p. 931: National Archives; p. 935: Bettmann/Corbis; p. 936: Hulton Archives/Getty Images.

CHAPTER 29: p. 941: Bill Eppridge/Getty Images; **p. 943:** Peter Turnley/Corbis; **p. 945:** Bettmann/Corbis; **p. 947:** University of Louisville; **p. 949:** Granger Collection; **p. 955:** Library of Congress; **p. 959:** Hy Peskin/Getty Images; **p. 960:** 1948, *The Washington Post*; **p. 961:** Bettmann/Corbis; **p. 967:** Bettmann/Corbis; **p. 970:** Yale Joel/Getty Images.

CHAPTER 30: p. 974: Hulton Archives/Getty Images; **p. 978:** William Joseph O'Keefe Collection, Veterans History Project, Library of Congress; **p. 979:** AP Photo; **p. 981:** Library of Congress; **p. 983:** Fogg Art Museum, Harvard University; **p. 985:** Bernard Gotfryd/Getty Images; **p. 986:** Time & Life Pictures/Getty Images; **p. 992:** AP Photo; **p. 993:** University of Louisville; **p. 996:** Charles Moore/Black Star; **p. 1000:** Herb Block Foundation; **p. 1003:** AP Photo; **p. 1004:** AP Photo; **p. 1009:** AP Photo.

CHAPTER 31: p. 1014: Bettmann/Corbis; **p. 1015:** Time & Life Pictures/Getty Images; **p. 1021:** Time & Life Pictures/Getty Images; **p. 1022:** AP Photo; **p. 1024:** Hulton Archives/Getty Images; **p. 1029:** National Archives; **p. 1031:** AP Photo; **p. 1039:** Bettmann/Corbis; **p. 1044:** © 1963, *The Star-Ledger*, All rights reserved, Reprinted with permission; **p. 1045:** Bettmann/Corbis.

CHAPTER 32: p. 1052: Bettmann/Corbis; **p. 1055:** Ted Streshinsky/Corbis; **p. 1056:** © Roger Malloch/Magnum Photos; **p. 1058:** John Dominis/Getty Images; **p. 1062:** Bettmann/Corbis; **p. 1069:** Bettmann/Corbis; **p. 1072:** Howard Ruffner/Time & Life Pictures/Getty Images; **p. 1074:** John Dominis/Getty Images; **p. 1076:** AP Photo; **p. 1081:** AP Photo; **p. 1084:** Dirck Halstead/Time Life Pictures/Getty Images.

CHAPTER 33: p. 1090: Robert Maass/Corbis; **p. 1094:** AP Photo; **p. 1099:** Bettmann/Corbis; **p. 1102:** Bettmann/Corbis; **p. 1106:** Bettmann/Corbis; **p. 1107:** Los Angeles Times Syndicate; **p. 1110:** Bettmann/Corbis; **p. 1112:** Library of Congress; **p. 1115:** AP Photo; **p. 1120:** Woodfin Camp; **p. 1121:** AP Photo; **p. 1124:** Bettmann/Corbis.

CHAPTER 34: p. 1128: Smiley N. Pool/Dallas Morning News/Corbis; **p. 1132:** Chris Wilkins/Getty Images; **p. 1134:** AP Photo; **p. 1137:** AP Photo; **p. 1141:** AP Photo; **p. 1148:** Sean Adair/Reuters/Corbis; **p. 1151:** Reuters/Corbis; **p. 1152:** Ed Kashi/Corbis; **p. 1155:** Mario Tama/Getty Images; **p. 1157:** AP Photo; **p. 1159:** Shawn Thew/epa/Corbis; **p. 1163:** AP Photo; **p. 1165:** Jeff J Mitchell/Getty Images; **p. 1167:** Darren McCollester/Getty Images; **p. 1170 (left):** Mario Tama/Getty Images; **(right):** AP Photo.

Page numbers in *italics* refer to illustrations.

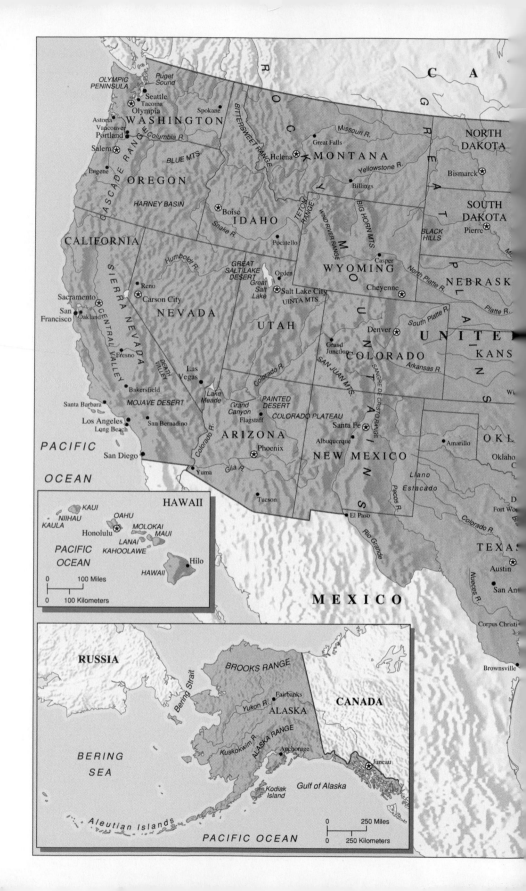

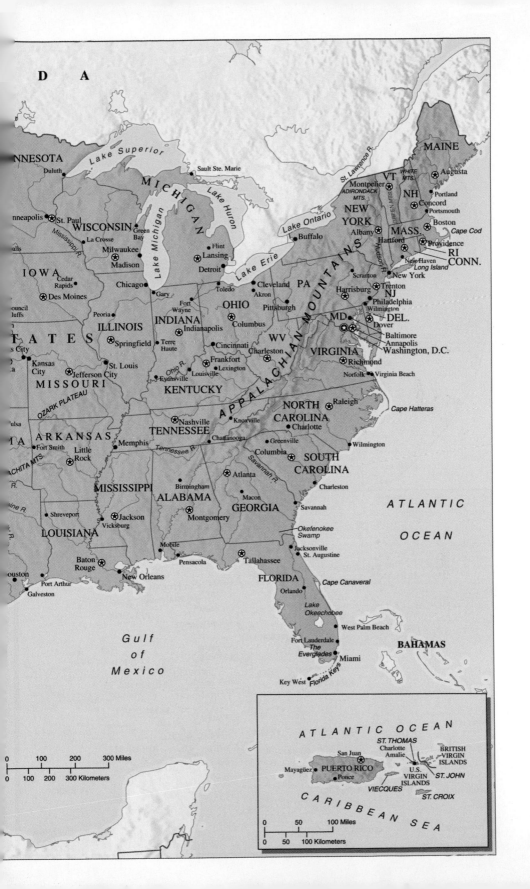